PENGUIN REFERENCE

The *Puzzler* Crossword Companion

The name *Puzzler* is synonymous with enjoyable puzzles. *Puzzler* is the oldest and best known of all puzzle magazines, and the company is renowned for its puzzle expertise. As the largest puzzle publisher in the UK, and probably the world, *Puzzler* Media now publishes sixty titles in more than twenty countries.

The *Puzzler* Crossword Companion

Puzzler

PENGUIN BOOKS

PENGUIN BOOKS

Published by the Penguin Group
Penguin Books Ltd, 80 Strand, London WC2R 0RL, England
Penguin Group (USA) Inc., 375 Hudson Street, New York, New York 10014, USA
Penguin Group (Canada), 90 Eglinton Avenue East, Suite 700, Toronto, Ontario,
Canada M4P 2Y3 (a division of Pearson Penguin Canada Inc.)
Penguin Ireland, 25 St Stephen's Green, Dublin 2, Ireland
(a division of Penguin Books Ltd)
Penguin Group (Australia), 250 Camberwell Road, Camberwell,
Victoria 3124, Australia (a division of Pearson Australia Group Pty Ltd)
Penguin Books India Pvt Ltd, 11 Community Centre,
Panchsheel Park, New Delhi – 110 017, India
Penguin Group (NZ), 67 Apollo Drive, Rosedale, North Shore 0632,
New Zealand (a division of Pearson New Zealand Ltd)
Penguin Books (South Africa) (Pty) Ltd, 24 Sturdee Avenue,
Rosebank, Johannesburg 2196, South Africa

Penguin Books Ltd, Registered Offices: 80 Strand, London WC2R 0RL, England

www.penguin.com

First published 2007
1

Copyright © Puzzler, 2007
All rights reserved

ISBN: 978–0–141–02744–9

Contents

Introduction

This book's exhaustive word coverage, together with its direct accessibility, will be both a delight and an end to frustration for crossword fans everywhere.

The Puzzler Crossword Companion covers over 260 subjects, each with entries in word-length order. As well as a main contents list, there is a comprehensive index at the back. So, if you're looking for a specific 7-letter bird, a 9-letter film director or an 11-letter town in France, all will be revealed – in double-quick time.

As well as crossword addicts, both quiz buffs and that army of people who just love browsing will find this book an invaluable reference library addition.

The *Puzzler* Crossword Companion

BICHON FRISE
BLACK AND TAN
BULL MASTIFF
BULL TERRIER
GIANT POODLE
IBIZAN HOUND
IRISH SETTER
JACK RUSSELL
ROUGH COLLIE
SKYE TERRIER
SLEUTH-HOUND

12
BORDER COLLIE
CAIRN TERRIER
FINNISH SPITZ
GORDON SETTER
IRISH TERRIER
NEWFOUNDLAND
PHARAOH HOUND
SILKY TERRIER
WATER SPANIEL

WELSH TERRIER

13
AFFENPINSCHER
BEARDED COLLIE
BORDER TERRIER
BOSTON TERRIER
COCKER SPANIEL
DANDIE DINMONT
ENGLISH SETTER
HUNGARIAN PULI
SIBERIAN HUSKY
SUSSEX SPANIEL
WELSH SPRINGER

14
CLUMBER SPANIEL
GERMAN SHEPHERD
IRISH WOLFHOUND
NORFOLK TERRIER
PIT BULL TERRIER
TIBETAN SPANIEL

15
ABERDEEN TERRIER
AIREDALE TERRIER
BLENHEIM SPANIEL
BRITTANY SPANIEL
BRUSSELS GRIFFON
ENGLISH SPRINGER
GOLDEN RETRIEVER
LAKELAND TERRIER
SCOTTISH TERRIER
SEALYHAM TERRIER
SPINONE ITALIANO
SPRINGER SPANIEL

16
KERRY BLUE TERRIER
YORKSHIRE TERRIER

17
BEDLINGTON TERRIER
DOBERMANN PINSCHER
LABRADOR RETRIEVER

Animals – Animal Breeds – FARM ANIMALS

3
GIR cattle

4
BOND sheep
DALL sheep
GLAN cattle
JAVA chicken
KELE pig
LONK sheep
SOAY sheep

5
ALTAI sheep
ASEEL chicken
BAGOT goat
BORAN cattle
CHIOS sheep
DEVON cattle
DUMPY chicken
DUROC pig
IRISH goat
JACOB sheep

KERRY cattle
KHAKI duck
LLEYN sheep
LUING cattle
MARAN chicken
PEARL guinea fowl
PEKIN duck
ROUEN duck
SLATE turkey
TEXEL sheep
WELSH pig

The *Puzzler* Crossword Companion

Animals

Animals – Animal Breeds – CATS

4
MANX

5
ASIAN
KORAT

6
ANGORA
BENGAL
BIRMAN
BOMBAY
CYMRIC
EXOTIC
HAVANA
LAPERM
OCICAT
SOKOKE
SOMALI

SPHYNX
USSURI

7
BURMESE
CHAUSIE
PERSIAN
RAGDOLL
SIAMESE

8
BALINESE
BURMILLA
DEVON REX
JAVANESE
MUNCHKIN
NEBELUNG
ORIENTAL
PIXIE-BOB

SAVANNAH
SIBERIAN
SNOWSHOE
TIFFANIE

9
ANATOLIAN
CHARTREUX
GERMAN REX
HIMALAYAN
MAINE COON
PETERBALD
SINGAPURA
TONKINESE

10
ABYSSINIAN
CORNISH REX
RAGAMUFFIN

SELKIRK REX
TURKISH VAN
VICHIEN MAS

11
EGYPTIAN MAU
LIMAU KOHLUM
RUSSIAN BLUE

12
AMERICAN CURL
SCOTTISH FOLD

13
TORTOISESHELL
TURKISH ANGORA

14
AUSTRALIAN MIST

SIBERIAN FOREST

15
AMERICAN BOBTAIL
EUROPEAN BURMESE

EXOTIC SHORTHAIR
JAPANESE BOBTAIL
NORWEGIAN FOREST
PERSIAN LONGHAIR

16
AMERICAN WIREHAIR
BRITISH SHORTHAIR
RUSSIAN SHORTHAIR

Animals – Animal Breeds – DOGS

3
POM
PUG

4
CHOW
PEKE
PULI
SKYE

5
AKITA
BOXER
CAIRN
CORGI
DHOLE
HOUND
HUSKY
LAIKA
SPITZ

6
AFGHAN
AKBASH
BASSET
BEAGLE
BORZOI
BRIARD

COCKER
COLLIE
GUN DOG
KELPIE
KUVASZ
LAPDOG
POODLE
PUG DOG
RATTER
RED DOG
SALUKI
SETTER
TECKEL
TOY DOG
VIZSLA

7
BASENJI
BOBTAIL
BULLDOG
GRIFFON
HARRIER
KLEE KAI
LOWCHEN
LURCHER
MALTESE
MAREMMA
MASTIFF

PIT BULL
POINTER
SAMOYED
SCOTTIE
SHAR PEI
SHELTIE
SHIH-TZU
SPANIEL
TERRIER
VOLPINO
WHIPPET
WILD DOG

8
AIREDALE
ALSATIAN
BLENHEIM
CHOW CHOW
ELKHOUND
FOXHOUND
GUARD DOG
GUIDE DOG
HOUSE DOG
KEESHOND
KOMONDOR
LABRADOR
MALEMUTE
PAPILLON

PEKINESE
SEALYHAM
SHEEPDOG
SHIBA-INU
SPRINGER
WARRIGAL
WATCHDOG

9
BADGER DOG
BEAUCERON
BOARHOUND
BUCKHOUND
CHIHUAHUA
DACHSHUND
DALMATIAN
DEERHOUND
DOBERMANN
DRAG HOUND
GREAT DANE
GREYHOUND
HARLEQUIN
KERRY BLUE
LHASA APSO
PEKINGESE
POLICE DOG
RED SETTER
RETRIEVER

RIDGEBACK
SCHNAUZER
STAGHOUND
ST BERNARD
TOY POODLE
WOLFHOUND

10
BEDLINGTON
BLOODHOUND
FOX TERRIER
MALTESE DOG
OTTER HOUND
POMERANIAN
RACCOON DOG
RAT TERRIER
ROTTWEILER
SCHIPPERKE
SCOTTIE DOG
SPOTTED DOG
TRACKER DOG
WEIMARANER
WELSH CORGI
WORKING DOG

11
AFGHAN HOUND
BASSET HOUND

BICHON FRISE
BLACK AND TAN
BULL MASTIFF
BULL TERRIER
GIANT POODLE
IBIZAN HOUND
IRISH SETTER
JACK RUSSELL
ROUGH COLLIE
SKYE TERRIER
SLEUTH-HOUND

12
BORDER COLLIE
CAIRN TERRIER
FINNISH SPITZ
GORDON SETTER
IRISH TERRIER
NEWFOUNDLAND
PHARAOH HOUND
SILKY TERRIER
WATER SPANIEL

WELSH TERRIER

13
AFFENPINSCHER
BEARDED COLLIE
BORDER TERRIER
BOSTON TERRIER
COCKER SPANIEL
DANDIE DINMONT
ENGLISH SETTER
HUNGARIAN PULI
SIBERIAN HUSKY
SUSSEX SPANIEL
WELSH SPRINGER

14
CLUMBER SPANIEL
GERMAN SHEPHERD
IRISH WOLFHOUND
NORFOLK TERRIER
PIT BULL TERRIER
TIBETAN SPANIEL

15
ABERDEEN TERRIER
AIREDALE TERRIER
BLENHEIM SPANIEL
BRITTANY SPANIEL
BRUSSELS GRIFFON
ENGLISH SPRINGER
GOLDEN RETRIEVER
LAKELAND TERRIER
SCOTTISH TERRIER
SEALYHAM TERRIER
SPINONE ITALIANO
SPRINGER SPANIEL

16
KERRY BLUE TERRIER
YORKSHIRE TERRIER

17
BEDLINGTON TERRIER
DOBERMANN PINSCHER
LABRADOR RETRIEVER

Animals – Animal Breeds – FARM ANIMALS

3
GIR cattle

4
BOND sheep
DALL sheep
GLAN cattle
JAVA chicken
KELE pig
LONK sheep
SOAY sheep

5
ALTAI sheep
ASEEL chicken
BAGOT goat
BORAN cattle
CHIOS sheep
DEVON cattle
DUMPY chicken
DUROC pig
IRISH goat
JACOB sheep

KERRY cattle
KHAKI duck
LLEYN sheep
LUING cattle
MARAN chicken
PEARL guinea fowl
PEKIN duck
ROUEN duck
SLATE turkey
TEXEL sheep
WELSH pig

6
ANCONA chicken
ANGORA goat
AWASSI sheep
BANTAM chicken
BRAHMA chicken
BRONZE turkey
CANADA goose
CAYUGA duck
COCHIN chicken
DEXTER cattle
DORSET sheep
EMBDEN goose
GHEZEL sheep
HOUDAN chicken
JERSEY cattle
LAMONA chicken
MERINO sheep
ORKNEY sheep
OXFORD sheep
POLISH chicken
ROMNEY sheep
SALERS cattle
SULTAN chicken
SUSSEX cattle, chicken

7
BALUCHI sheep
BANDARA chicken
BEEFALO cattle
BOURBON turkey
BRAFORD cattle
BRAHMAN cattle
BRANGUS cattle
BUCKEYE chicken
CAMPINE chicken
CHEVIOT sheep
CORNISH chicken

DORKING chicken
HAMBURG chicken
IBERIAN pig
KARAKUL sheep
LACOMBE pig
LEGHORN chicken
LINCOLN sheep
MINORCA chicken
MORUCHA cattle
MUSCOVY duck
PILGRIM goose
STYRIAN chicken
SUFFOLK sheep

8
AYRSHIRE cattle
CATALANA chicken
DELAWARE chicken
DRYSDALE sheep
FRIESIAN cattle
GALLOWAY cattle
GIMMIZAH chicken
GUERNSEY cattle
HERDWICK sheep
HEREFORD cattle
HIGHLAND cattle
HOLSTEIN cattle
LANDRACE pig
LANGSHAN chicken
LAVENDER guinea fowl
LIMOUSIN cattle
LOURDAIS cattle
PIETRAIN pig
POLWARTH sheep
PORTLAND sheep
PYRENEAN goat
TAMWORTH pig
TOULOUSE goose

9
APPENZELL chicken
AYLESBURY duck
BERKSHIRE pig
CHAROLAIS cattle
HAMPSHIRE pig, sheep
HEBRIDEAN sheep
KERRY HILL sheep
OLDENBURG sheep
ORPINGTON chicken,
              duck
RAZORBACK pig
ROUGH FELL sheep
ROYAL PALM turkey
SHORTHORN cattle
SIMMENTAL cattle
SWALEDALE sheep
TEESWATER sheep
WELSUMMER chicken
WYANDOTTE chicken

10
ANDALUSIAN chicken
AUSTRALORP chicken
BELTSVILLE turkey
BRITISH LOP pig
CHITTAGONG chicken
CORRIEDALE sheep
FAVEROLLES chicken
LINCOLN RED cattle
MURRAY GREY cattle
ROSS RANGER chicken
SADDLEBACK pig
SEBASTOPOL goose
WELSH BLACK cattle

11
BARNEVELDER chicken
JAMAICA HOPE cattle
MARCHIGIANA cattle
ROMNEY MARSH sheep
SPANISH FOWL chicken
SWABIAN HALL pig
WENSLEYDALE sheep

12
BLACK NORFOLK turkey
CHESTER WHITE pig
NARRAGANSETT turkey
SILKIE BANTAM chicken
WHITE HOLLAND turkey

13
ABERDEEN ANGUS cattle
BRITISH ALPINE goat
BUFF ORPINGTON chicken, duck
DROUGHTMASTER cattle
KHAKI CAMPBELL duck
TEXAS LONGHORN cattle
WELSH MOUNTAIN sheep

14
BELTED GALLOWAY cattle
RHODE ISLAND RED chicken
WELSH HARLEQUIN duck

Animals – Animal Breeds – HORSES AND PONIES

3
BAY
COB
DUN

4
ARAB
BARB
GREY
ROAN

5
ALTAI
HUCUL
LOKAI
PINTO
PUNCH
SHIRE

TERSK
TORIK
WALER

6
BRETON
CANUCK
CAYUSE
GARRON
GIDRAN
HUNTER
JENNET
MORGAN
NONIUS
SORREL
TANGUN
TATTOO
VYATKA

7
BALUCHI
BASHKIR
BUDENNY
CASPIAN
COMTOIS
CRIOLLO
HACKNEY
JUTLAND
KABARDA
MUSTANG
NORIKER
PIEBALD
SHELTIE
SORRAIA

8
ARDENNES

CAMARGUE
CHESTNUT
FELL PONY
GALICEÑO
KARABAIR
KARABAKH
LUSITANO
PALOMINO
SCHIMMEL
SKEWBALD

9
AKHAL TEKE
APPALOOSA
CARTHORSE
CONNEMARA
DALES PONY
FALABELLA

HAFLINGER
KNABSTRUP
OLDENBURG
PERCHERON
WELSH PONY

10
ANDALUSIAN
CARTHUSIAN
CLYDESDALE
EXMOOR PONY
HANOVERIAN
HOLSTEINER
LIPIZZANER
MÉRENS PONY
PRZEWALSKI
RUSSIAN DON
SHIRE HORSE

11
BASOTHO PONY
ERISKAY PONY
POLISH KONIK

12
CLEVELAND BAY
DARTMOOR PONY

GELDERLANDER
HIGHLAND PONY
IRISH DRAUGHT
ORLOV TROTTER
SHETLAND PONY
STANDARDBRED
SUFFOLK PUNCH
THOROUGHBRED

13
CONNEMARA PONY
LIVER CHESTNUT
NEW FOREST PONY

14
STRAWBERRY ROAN

Animals – ANIMAL FAMILIES

cr = cross *f* = female *m* = male *y* = young

3
COB *m* swan
COW *f* cattle, camel etc
CUB *y* bear, lion etc
CUR *cr* dog
DAM *f* parent
DOE *f* deer, rabbit etc
DZO *cr* cow/yak
EWE *f* sheep
FRY *y* fish
HEN *f* bird
HOB *m* ferret
KID *y* goat
KIT *y* ferret, skunk etc
PEN *f* swan
PUP *y* dog, seal etc
RAM *m* sheep
REE *f* ruff (sandpiper)
  or reeve
SOW *f* pig, badger etc
TOM *m* cat
TUP *m* sheep

4
BOAR *m* pig, badger etc

BRIT *y* herring
BUCK *m* antelope, rabbit etc
BULL *m* cattle, camel etc
CALF *y* cattle, hippo etc
COCK *m* bird
COLT *y* stallion
EYAS *y* hawk
FAWN *y* deer
FOAL *y* horse
GILT *y* sow
HART *m* deer
HIND *f* deer
JACK *m* merlin, opossum etc
JILL *f* ferret
JOEY *y* kangaroo, wallaby etc
KELT *y* salmon, trout
LAMB *y* sheep
MAID *y* skate
MARE *f* horse
MULE *cr* canary/finch
  cr m donkey/*f* horse
PARR *y* salmon, trout
PEAL *y* sea trout
SILD *y* herring
STAG *m* deer

5

BILLY *m* goat
BITCH *f* dog
BUNNY *y* rabbit
CHICK *y* fowl
DRAKE *m* duck
DRONE *m* bee
ELVER *y* eel
FILLY *y* mare
HENNY *f* fowl
HINNY *cr f* donkey/*m* horse
LIGER *cr m* lion/tigress
NANNY *f* goat
NURSE *f* bee, ant etc
OWLET *y* owl
PIPER *y* bird
POULT *y* fowl
PUPPY *y* dog
QUEEN *f* cat, bee etc
REEVE *f* ruff (sandpiper) or ree
SHOAT *y* pig
SMOLT *y* salmon, trout
SQUAB *y* pigeon
STEER *m* cattle
STIRK *y* heifer
TIGON *cr m* tiger/lioness
VIXEN *f* fox
WHELP *y* dog

6

BANDOG *cr* dog
BOOMER *m* kangaroo
CYGNET *y* swan
EAGLET *y* eagle
FARROW *y* pigs
GANDER *m* goose
GENTLE trained falcon
GRILSE *y* salmon

HEIFER *f* cattle
HOPPER *y* locust
INFANT *y* monkey, ape etc
KITTEN *y* cat
LITTER *y* cats, dogs etc
MUSKET *m* sparrow-hawk
PEAHEN *f* peafowl
PEEPER *y* bird
PIGLET *y* pig
PUGGLE *y* echidna
PYE-DOG *cr* dog
SAMLET *y* salmon
TERCEL *m* falcon hawk
WORKER *f* bee

7

BULLOCK *m* cattle
BULL-PUP *y* bulldog
CATTABU *cr* cattle/zebu
CODLING *y* cod
FINNOCK *y* sea trout
FLAPPER *y* wild duck, partridge
GOBBLER *m* turkey
GORCOCK *m* red grouse
GOSLING *y* goose
GREYHEN *f* black grouse
HATCHER *y* bird
HERLING *y* sea trout
JACKASS *m* ass donkey
LEVERET *y* hare
LIONESS *f* lion
MONGREL *cr* dog
PEACOCK *m* peafowl
PIGLING *y* pig
ROOSTER *m* fowl
SAKERET *m* saker (falcon)
SARDINE *y* pilchard
SHEDDER *y/f* salmon

SKEGGER *y* salmon
SPAWNER *y* fish
TIGRESS *f* tiger
ZEBRASS *cr m* zebra/f ass
ZEBRULE *cr m* zebra/f horse

8
BRANCHER *y* hawk
COCKEREL *y* rooster
DANDY-HEN *f* bantam chicken
DUCKLING *y* duck
HEATH-HEN *f* black grouse
LANNERET *m* lanner (falcon)
MOORCOCK *m* red grouse
NESTLING *y* bird
PEACHICK *y* peafowl
QUEEN BEE *f* bee
SALMONET *y* salmon
SEECATCH *m* fur seal
STALLION *m* horse
TROUTLET *y* trout
WHITECAP *m* redstart
WHITLING *ym* trout
YEARLING *y* horse
ZEBRINNY *cr m* horse/f zebra

9
BLACKCOCK *m* black grouse
CHICKLING *y* fowl

COCK ROBIN *m* robin
DANDY-COCK *m* bantam chicken
DICKY BIRD *y* bird
ERGATANER *m* ant
FLEDGLING *y* bird
GUINEA HEN *f* guinea fowl
HATCHLING *y* bird, turtle etc
HEATHCOCK *m* black grouse
HERONSHAW *y* heron
SHELDRAKE *m* shelduck
TURKEY-HEN *f* turkey
WORKER BEE *f* bee

10
ERGATOGYNE *f* ant
FINGERLING *y* salmon
HEATH-POULT *y* black grouse
LEOPARDESS *f* leopard
PANTHERESS *f* panther
SPIDERLING *y* spider
TURKEYCOCK *m* turkey
WEASEL-COOT *y/f* smew

11
COCK SPARROW *m* sparrow

12
TERCEL-JERKIN *m* gyrfalcon
THROSTLE-COCK *m* song thrush

Animals – ANIMAL HOMES & SHELTERS

3
DEN lion
PEN pig, sheep
RUN chicken
STY pig
WEB spider

4
BYRE cattle
CAVE bats, bear
COOP chicken
DREY squirrel
FOLD sheep
FORM hare
HILL ants

HIVE bees
HOLE fox, mole
HOLT otter
LAIR tiger, wolf
NEST birds, insects,
    snakes
SETT badger

5
EARTH fox
EYRIE eagle
HUTCH rabbit

LODGE beaver
MOUND termites
ROOST bats

6
BURROW mole, rabbit
CORRAL cattle, horses
KENNEL dog
STABLE horse
WARREN rabbits

7
CATTERY cats
COWSHED cattle
KENNELS dogs
PADDOCK horses
SHIPPON cattle

8
VESPIARY wasps

9
FORMICARY ants

Animals – BIRDS

3	CROW	LORY	TODY	GREBE
AUK	DOVE	MONK	WEKA	HERON
DAW	DUCK	MYNA	WREN	HOBBY
EMU	ERNE	NENE		JUNCO
HEN	FOWL	PERN	**5**	MACAW
JAY	GUAN	RAIL	ARGUS	MADGE
KEA	GULL	RHEA	ARIEL	MAVIS
MEW	HAWK	ROOK	BOOBY	MURRE
NUN	IBIS	RUFF	COLIN	MYNAH
OWL	JYNX	RYPE	CRAKE	NANDU
PIE	KAGU	SHAG	CRANE	NODDY
TIT	KAKA	SKUA	DIVER	OUSEL
TUI	KITE	SMEW	EAGLE	OUZEL
	KIWI	SORA	EGRET	PEGGY
4	KNOT	SWAN	EIDER	PIPIT
CHAT	KORA	TAHA	FINCH	POAKA
COLY	LARK	TEAL	GALAH	PRION
COOT	LOON	TERN	GOOSE	QUAIL

RAVEN
ROBIN
SAKER
SCAUP
SCRAY
SERIN
SHAMA
SNIPE
SOLAN
STILT
STINT
STORK
SWIFT
TEREK
TWITE
URUBU
VEERY
WADER

6
AMAZON
ARGALA
AUKLET
AVOCET
BARBET
BISHOP
BONXIE
BUDGIE
BULBUL
CANARY
CHOUGH
CHUKOR
CONDOR
CORBIE
COUCAL
CUCKOO
CULVER
CURLEW

DARTER
DIPPER
DRONGO
DUIKER
DUNLIN
ELANET
FALCON
FULMAR
GANNET
GARROT
GENTOO
GODWIT
GOSLET
GROUSE
HARELD
HERMIT
HOOPOE
JABIRU
JACANA
KAKAPO
KERERU
LANNER
LINNET
LORIOT
MAGPIE
MARTIN
MERLIN
MONAUL
MOPOKE
MOTMOT
ORIOLE
OSPREY
PARROT
PASTOR
PEEWIT
PETREL
PIGEON
PLOVER

PUFFIN
QUELEA
RATITE
REDCAP
SCOTER
SHRIKE
SISKIN
TAKAHE
THRUSH
TOMTIT
TOUCAN
TOWHEE
TROGON
TURACO
TURKEY
WEAVER
WHYDAH
WILLET
YAFFLE
YNAMBU
YUCKER

7
ANT-BIRD
APTERYX
BABBLER
BARN OWL
BEE-KITE
BITTERN
BLUECAP
BLUE-EYE
BLUE JAY
BLUE TIT
BOOBOOK
BUNTING
BUSH TIT
BUSTARD
BUZZARD

CAT-BIRD
CHEWINK
CHICKEN
COAL TIT
COLIBRI
CORELLA
COTINGA
COURLAN
COURSER
COWBIRD
CREEPER
DOVEKIE
DUNNOCK
EMU-WREN
FANTAIL
FINFOOT
FLICKER
GADWALL
GOSHAWK
GRACKLE
GREY JAY
GREYLAG
GREY OWL
HACKLET
HALCYON
HARRIER
HAWK OWL
HOATZIN
JACAMAR
JACKDAW
KAMICHI
KESTREL
LAPWING
MALLARD
MANAKIN
MARABOU
MARTLET
MINIVET

MOORHEN
MUDLARK
OILBIRD
ORTOLAN
OSTRICH
PEAFOWL
PELICAN
PENGUIN
PINNOCK
PINTADO
PINTAIL
POCHARD
QUETZAL
RAINBOW
RED KITE
REDPOLL
REDWING
ROSELLA
RUDDOCK
SAWBILL
SCOOPER
SEABIRD
SEAGULL
SERIEMA
SIRGANG
SKIMMER
SKYLARK
SPARROW
SQUACCO
SUNBIRD
SWALLOW
TANAGER
TATTLER
TINAMOU
TITLARK
TITLING
TOURACO
TUMBLER

VULTURE
VULTURN
WAGTAIL
WARBLER
WAXBILL
WAXWING
WHOOPER
WIDGEON
WOOD OWL
WREN-TIT
WRYBILL
WRYNECK

8
AASVOGEL
ACCENTOR
ADJUTANT
ALCATRAS
ARAPUNGA
AVADAVAT
BALD CROW
BATELEUR
BEE-EATER
BELLBIRD
BLACKCAP
BLUEBIRD
BLUEWING
BOATBILL
BOBOLINK
BOBWHITE
BROWN OWL
CAGE-BIRD
CALL-BIRD
CARACARA
CARDINAL
CARGOOSE
COCKATOO
CURASSOW

DABCHICK
DIDAPPER
DOTTEREL
EAGLE OWL
FALCONET
FIREBACK
FIREBIRD
FISH HAWK
FLAMINGO
FORKTAIL
GAME BIRD
GARGANEY
GREAT TIT
GREENLET
GROSBEAK
GUACHARO
HACKBOLT
HANGBIRD
HARDHEAD
HAWFINCH
HICKWALL
HORNBILL
KILLDEER
KINGBIRD
KING-CROW
LANDRAIL
LORIKEET
LOVEBIRD
LYREBIRD
MAORI HEN
MEGAPODE
MIRE-DRUM
MOORFOWL
MURRELET
MUSK DUCK
MUTE SWAN
NIGHTJAR
NUTHATCH

OXPECKER
PARAKEET
PERCOLIN
PETCHARY
PHEASANT
POORWILL
PUFFBIRD
PYGMY OWL
RAINBIRD
REDSHANK
REDSTART
REEDBIRD
REEDLING
REED WREN
RICEBIRD
RIFLEMAN
RING-DOVE
RINGTAIL
ROCK-BIRD
ROCK DOVE
ROCKETER
SAPPHIRE
SCOPS OWL
SCREAMER
SEA EAGLE
SEA SNIPE
SHELDUCK
SHOEBILL
SILKTAIL
SNOWBIRD
SNOWY OWL
SONGBIRD
STARLING
SURFBIRD
SWAMP-HEN
SWIFTLET
TAPACULO
TAWNY OWL

TERU-TERO
THRASHER
THROSTLE
TITMOUSE
TOUCANET
TRAGOPAN
TREMBLER
TROUPIAL
UMBRETTE
WATER-HEN
WHEATEAR
WHIMBREL
WHINCHAT
WHIPBIRD
WHISTLER
WHITE-EYE
WILD DUCK
WILDFOWL
WOODCHAT
WOODCOCK
WOOD IBIS
WOODLARK
WOOD WREN
ZOPILOTE

9
ALBATROSS
ANT-THRUSH
BALD EAGLE
BALDICOOT
BECCAFICO
BLACKBIRD
BLACK SWAN
BLOODBIRD
BOWERBIRD
BRAMBLING
BROADBILL
BULLFINCH

CAMPANERO
CASSOWARY
CHAFFINCH
CHICKADEE
COCKATIEL
CORMORANT
CORNCRAKE
CROSSBILL
CURRAWONG
EAGLE HAWK
EIDER DUCK
FAIRY TERN
FAIRY WREN
FIELDFARE
FIG PARROT
FIGPECKER
FIRECREST
FLUTEBIRD
FRANCOLIN
FRIARBIRD
FROGMOUTH
GALLINAZO
GALLINULE
GOLDCREST
GOLDEN-EYE
GOLDFINCH
GOOSANDER
GREY GOOSE
GUILLEMOT
GYRFALCON
HARLEQUIN
HONEYBIRD
HORNED OWL
JACK SNIPE
KITTIWAKE
LITTLE AUK
MALLEMUCK
MERGANSER

MEROPIDAN
MIRE SNIPE
MOUSEBIRD
NIGHT-BIRD
NIGHT-HAWK
NUTPECKER
OSSIFRAGE
OWL PARROT
PARTRIDGE
PEREGRINE
PHALAROPE
PINEFINCH
PTARMIGAN
RAZORBILL
REDBREAST
RED GROUSE
RIFLE BIRD
RING OUSEL
RING OUZEL
ROCK PIPIT
ROSEFINCH
SABREWING
SALANGANE
SANDPIPER
SATIN BIRD
SCRUB BIRD
SEA PARROT
SHOVELLER
SNAKEBIRD
SNOWFINCH
SNOW GOOSE
SPOONBILL
STOCK DOVE
STONECHAT
STORMCOCK
SWARTBACK
SWORDBILL
TALEGELLA

THICKHEAD
THICK-KNEE
THORNBILL
TROCHILUS
TRUMPETER
TURNSTONE
WATER-BIRD
WATERCOCK
WATERFOWL
WHALEHEAD
WHITEHEAD
WHITEWING
WIDOWBIRD
WILD GOOSE
WILLOW TIT
WINDHOVER
WOODSPITE

10
ABERDEVINE
ARCTIC TERN
BANANAQUIT
BEARDED TIT
BISHOP BIRD
BLUETHROAT
BRENT GOOSE
BRONZEWING
BUDGERIGAR
BUFFLEHEAD
BUSH SHRIKE
BUTTERBIRD
CANVASBACK
CAPE PIGEON
CHIFFCHAFF
CHINA GOOSE
CRESTED TIT
DEMOISELLE
DICKCISSEL

EMBER GOOSE
FLYCATCHER
FOUR O'CLOCK
GOATSUCKER
GOONEY BIRD
GREENFINCH
GREENSHANK
GREY PARROT
GROUND DOVE
GUINEA FOWL
HARPY EAGLE
HEN HARRIER
HONEY-EATER
HONEY-GUIDE
HOODED CROW
INDIGO BIRD
JUNGLE FOWL
KINGFISHER
KOOKABURRA
MALLEE BIRD
MALLEE FOWL
MEADOWLARK
MUTTON-BIRD
NIGHT HERON
NUTCRACKER
ORANGEQUIT
PARSON-BIRD
PETTICHAPS
PICK-CHEESE
PIPING CROW
PRAIRIE HEN
PRATINCOLE
QUAKER-BIRD
RACKET-TAIL
RAFTER-BIRD
RAIN PLOVER
REED-THRUSH
RING PLOVER

ROADRUNNER
ROCK-HOPPER
ROCK PIGEON
ROCK THRUSH
RUBYTHROAT
SACRED IBIS
SADDLEBACK
SAGE GROUSE
SANDERLING
SAND GROUSE
SAND MARTIN
SARUS CRANE
SCREECH OWL
SEA SWALLOW
SHEARWATER
SHEATHBILL
SICKLEBILL
SOLAN GOOSE
SONG THRUSH
STITCHBIRD
STONEHATCH
SUN BITTERN
TAILORBIRD
TROPIC-BIRD
TURTLE DOVE
WATER OUSEL
WATER OUZEL
WATTLE-BIRD
WEAVERBIRD
WHISKY JACK
WILLOW WREN
WONGA-WONGA
WOODGROUSE
WOODPECKER
WOOD PIGEON
WOOD THRUSH
ZEBRA FINCH

11
BEWICK'S SWAN
BLACK GROUSE
BRUSH-TURKEY
BUFFALO-BIRD
BUTCHER-BIRD
BUTTON QUAIL
CALLING BIRD
CARRION CROW
CIRL BUNTING
DIAMOND-BIRD
DRAGOON-BIRD
FALLOW-FINCH
FRIGATE BIRD
GNATCATCHER
GOLDEN EAGLE
GREEN LINNET
GREEN PIGEON
GROUND-ROBIN
HAZEL GROUSE
HERRING GULL
HONEYSUCKER
HOUSE MARTIN
HUMMINGBIRD
JAVA SPARROW
KING PENGUIN
KING VULTURE
LAMMERGEIER
LAMMERGEYER
MOCKINGBIRD
MOOR-BUZZARD
NIGHTINGALE
PURPLE FINCH
REED BUNTING
REED WARBLER
ROCK SPARROW
ROYSTON CROW
SCISSORBILL

SCISSORTAIL
SCREECH-HAWK
SCRUB-TURKEY
SEA DOTTEREL
SHELL PARROT
SNOW BUNTING
SONG SPARROW
SPARROW-HAWK
STILT PLOVER
STONE CURLEW
STONE FALCON
STORM PETREL
SWALLOWTAIL
TREECREEPER
WALLCREEPER
WATER-THRUSH
WHITETHROAT
WOOD SWALLOW
WOOD WARBLER

12
ADJUTANT BIRD
BURROWING OWL
CAPERCAILLIE
CARDINAL-BIRD
CHIMNEY SWIFT
CUCKOO-SHRIKE
DABBLING DUCK
DRONGO-CUCKOO
DRONGO-SHRIKE
ELEPHANT BIRD
FLOWERPECKER
GOLDEN ORIOLE
GOLDEN PLOVER
GREYLAG GOOSE
GROUND PIGEON
HEDGE-SPARROW
HERMIT THRUSH

HONEY BUZZARD
HONEY-CREEPER
HOUSE SPARROW
INDIAN RUNNER
LANNER FALCON
MAN-OF-WAR BIRD
MANDARIN DUCK
MARSH HARRIER
MISSEL THRUSH
MISTLE THRUSH
MOUND-BUILDER
MOURNING DOVE
PAINTED SNIPE
REED PHEASANT
RING DOTTEREL
RINGED PLOVER
SAGE-THRASHER
SEDGE WARBLER
SERPENT-EATER
STANDARD-WING
UMBRELLA-BIRD
WATER-WAGTAIL
WHIPPOORWILL
WILLOW GROUSE
YELLOWHAMMER
YELLOWTHROAT

13
ADJUTANT STORK
ARGUS PHEASANT

BARNACLE GOOSE
CHAPARRAL COCK
COACHWHIP BIRD
COCK-OF-THE-ROCK
CROCODILE BIRD
CUTHBERT'S DUCK
FAIRY BLUEBIRD
FANTAIL PIGEON
HARLEQUIN DUCK
HAWAIIAN GOOSE
HEDGE-ACCENTOR
ICELAND FALCON
LONG-TAILED TIT
OYSTERCATCHER
PLANTAIN-EATER
SCREECH-MARTIN
SCREECH-THRUSH
SECRETARY BIRD
SHELL PARAKEET
TRUMPETER SWAN
TURKEY BUZZARD
TURKEY VULTURE
WHISTLING DUCK
WHISTLING SWAN
WHOOPING CRANE
WILLOW WARBLER
WOOD SANDPIPER
YELLOW BUNTING
ZEBRA PARAKEET

14
BABBLING THRUSH
BEARDED VULTURE
BIRD OF PARADISE
BRAIN-FEVER BIRD
CHIMNEY SWALLOW
EMPEROR PENGUIN
GOLDEN PHEASANT
GREAT HORNED OWL
GRIFFON VULTURE
MANX SHEARWATER
PLAINS WANDERER
PRAIRIE CHICKEN
RHINOCEROS BIRD
SILVER PHEASANT
SKUNK BLACKBIRD
SOOTY ALBATROSS

15
BALTIMORE ORIOLE
DARTFORD WARBLER
FIRE-CRESTED WREN
GOLD-CRESTED WREN
GREEN WOODPECKER
LAUGHING JACKASS
MACARONI PENGUIN
PEREGRINE FALCON
PURPLE GALLINULE
REGENT BOWERBIRD

Animals – EXTINCT ANIMALS

3
MOA

4
DODO
HUIA

URUS
(or aurochs)

6
PIKAIA
QUAGGA
TARPAN

7
AUROCHS
(or urus)
MAMMOTH

RED RAIL

8
ASTRODON
BLUEBUCK
CAPE LION
CERATOPS
DEINODON
DINOSAUR
EOHIPPUS
 (or hyracotherium)
EORAPTOR
GAREFOWL
 (or great auk)
GREAT AUK
 (or garefowl)
IRISH ELK
MASTODON
PTILODUS
SAUROPOD

9
AMMONITE
CARNOSAUR
DACENTRUS
ECHINODON
IGUANODON
OVIRAPTOR
PTEROSAUR
SOLITAIRE

THYLACINE
TRILOBITE

10
ALLOSAURUS
DICERATOPS
DIPLODOCUS
GALLIMIMUS
LYCORHINUS
NODOSAURUS
PLESIOSAUR
PTERANODON
RED GAZELLE

11
APATOSAURUS
BARBARY LION
GROUND SLOTH
ICHTHYOSAUR
PTERODACTYL
RHYNCHOSAUR
SPINOSAURUS
STEGOSAURUS
TRICERATOPS

12
ANKYLOSAURUS
BRONTOSAURUS
ELEPHANT BIRD
LABRADOR DUCK

MEGALOSAURUS
PISANOSAURUS
PYRENEAN IBEX
VELOCIRAPTOR

13
ARCHAEOPTERYX
BRACHIOSAURUS
CORYTHOSAURUS
HYRACOTHERIUM
 (or eohippus)
TASMANIAN WOLF
TYRANNOSAURUS
WOOLLY MAMMOTH

14
STELLER'S SEA COW
TASMANIAN TIGER

15
BUBAL HARTEBEEST
PASSENGER PIGEON
RODRIGUES PIGEON
SABRE-TOOTHED CAT

16
TYRANNOSAURUS REX
WOOLLY RHINOCEROS

Animals – FISH & SEA CREATURES
st = development stage

3	DAB	HAG	RAY	**4**	CARP
BIB	EEL	IDE	ROE *st*	BASS	CHAR
COD	GAR	KOI	TAI	BLAY	CHUB

CHUM	TUNA	POGGE	BLENNY	NATIVE
CLAM	WELS	POLYP	BONITO	NERITE
COHO		PORGY	BOUNCE	OYSTER
CRAB	**5**	POULP	BOWFIN	PLAICE
CUSK	ABLET	POWAN	BRAISE	POLLAN
DACE	BLAIN	PRAWN	BRASSY	PUFFER
DORY	BLEAK	ROACH	BURBOT	QUAHOG
GOBY	BREAM	ROKER	CARIBE	RED-EYE
GRIG	BRILL	SAURY	CHEVEN	REMORA
HAKE	CHARR	SEWIN	COCKLE	ROBALO
HUSO	CISCO	SHARK	COMBER	SAITHE
HUSS	COBIA	SKATE	CONGER	SALMON
JACK	COLEY	SMELT	CONNER	SAUGER
KETA	CONCH	SNOEK	COTTUS	SAUREL
LANT	CORAL	SNOOK	COWRIE	SCAMPI
LING	DANIO	SPAWN *st*	CUTTLE	SCAMPO
LUCE	DORSE	SPRAT	CYPRIS	SEA BUN
MASU	FLUKE	SQUID	DARTER	SEA CAT
OPAH	GAPER	TENCH	DOCTOR	SEA COW
ORCA	GIBEL	TETRA	DORADO	SEA DOG
ORFE	GRUNT	TOGUE	DUGONG	SEA EAR
PAUA	GUPPY	TORSK	ELLOPS	SEA EGG
PIKE	HYDRA	TROUT	EPHYRA	SEA FOX
POPE	LAKER	TUNNY	*st* jellyfish	SEA OWL
POUT	LOACH	WHALE	FOGASH	SEA PIG
RUDD	LYTHE	WHELK	GANOID	SEPHEN
RUFF	MANTA	WHIFF	GUNNEL	SHANNY
SALP	MOLLY	WITCH	LAUNCE	SHINER
SCAD	MORAY	YAPOK	LIMPET	SHRIMP
SCAR	MORSE		LUCINE	SPONGE
SCUP	NERKA	**6**	MARLIN	SQUILL
SHAD	NURSE	ALEVIN *st*	MEDUSA	STROMB
SOLE	OLIVE	salmon,	MEGRIM	SUCKER
SPAT *st*	ORMER	trout	MINNOW	TARPON
oyster	OSCAR	ALLICE	MORGAY	TAUTOG
TANG	OTARY	BALLAN	MULLET	TEREDO
TOBY	PERCH	BARBEL	MURENA	TURBOT
TOPE	PIPER	BELUGA	MUSSEL	TWAITE

URCHIN
VOLUTE
WALRUS
WEEVER
WINKLE
WRASSE
ZANDER
ZINGEL

7

ABALONE
ACALEPH
ALEWIFE
ANCHOVY
AZURINE
BATFISH
BERGYLT
BLUEFIN
BOXFISH
BUMMALO
CAPELIN
CATFISH
CAVALLA
CHIMERA
CICHLID
CODFISH
COWFISH
CROAKER
CRUCIAN
CUSK EEL
DAPHNIA
DOGFISH
DOLPHIN
ECHINUS
EELPOUT
ESCOLAR
FANTAIL
FINBACK

FUR SEAL
GARFISH
GARPIKE
GOLDEYE
GOURAMI
GRAMPUS
GRIBBLE
GROUPER
GROWLER
GRUNTER
GUDGEON
GURNARD
GWYNIAD
HADDOCK
HAGFISH
HALIBUT
HERRING
HOGFISH
HOMELYN
HYDROID
ICEFISH
JEWFISH
KOI CARP
LAMPERN
LAMPREY
LOBSTER
LUBFISH
MAHSEER
MANATEE
MONODON
MOON-EYE
MUDFISH
NARWHAL
OARFISH
OCTOPUS
OSSETER
PANDORA
PIDDOCK

PIGFISH
PINFISH
PIRANHA
POLLACK
POMFRET
POMPANO
PORIFER
POUTING
QUINNAT
RATFISH
ROCK COD
RONQUIL
RORQUAL
ROTIFER
SAND DAB
SAND EEL
SARDINE
SAWFISH
SCALLOP
SCULPIN
SEA BASS
SEA CALF
SEA HARE
SEA LION
SEA PIKE
SEA SLUG
SEA STAR
SEA WOLF
SKIPPER
SNAPPER
SOCKEYE
STARLET
STERLET
SUNFISH
TELEOST
TIDDLER
TOHEROA
TORGOCH

TORPEDO
TREPANG
TUBFISH
VENDACE
WALL-EYE
WHITING

8

ALBACORE
AMPHIPOD
ARAPAIMA
ARK SHELL
ASCIDIAN
ASTEROID
ATHERINE
BANDFISH
BARNACLE
BILLFISH
BLUEBACK
BLUEFISH
BOARFISH
BONY PIKE
BRISLING
BULLHEAD
CACHALOT
CAVEFISH
CETACEAN
CHARACIN
CLUPEOID
CRAWFISH
CRAYFISH
DEALFISH
DEVIL RAY
DOG WHELK
DRAGONET
DRUMFISH
EAGLE RAY
EAR SHELL

ECHINOID
ESCALLOP
EULACHON
FILEFISH
FIN WHALE
FLATFISH
FLATHEAD
FLOUNDER
FOUR-EYES
FOX SHARK
FROGFISH
GILLAROO
GOATFISH
GOLDFISH
GRAYLING
HAIR SEAL
HAIRTAIL
HALF-BEAK
HALICORE
HARP SEAL
HUMPBACK
JOHN DORY
KABELJOU
KING CRAB
KINGFISH
KLIPFISH
LAMANTIN
LANCELET
LAND CRAB
LEMON DAB
LUMPFISH
LUNGFISH
MACKEREL
MANTA RAY
MEDUSOID
MENHADEN
MILLIONS
MONKFISH

MONK SEAL
MOONFISH
MORAY EEL
NAUTILUS
NINE-EYES
OPHIURID
OSTRACOD
PEARL-EYE
PICKEREL
PILCHARD
PIPEFISH
PIRARUCU
PORPOISE
REDBELLY
ROCKFISH
ROCKLING
RONCADOR
ROSEFISH
SAIBLING
SAILFISH
SAND CRAB
SANDFISH
SCARFISH
SEA BREAM
SEA HORSE
SEA LEMON
SEA MOUSE
SEA OTTER
SEA PERCH
SEA ROBIN
SEA SNAIL
SEA TROUT
SERRANID
SHIPWORM
SILUROID
SKIPJACK
STARFISH
STINGRAY

STURGEON
TARAKIHI
TARWHINE
THRESHER
TILEFISH
TOADFISH
TOP SHELL
TREVALLY
TRIDACNA
TUBE WORM
WOLF FISH

9

AMBERFISH
AMPHIOXUS
ANGELFISH
BARRACUDA
BLACK BASS
BLACKFISH
BLINDFISH
BLUE SHARK
BLUE WHALE
BULL TROUT
CHAVENDER
CIRRIPEDE
CLINGFISH
CLOWNFISH
CONE SHELL
CONGER EEL
CORALFISH
CORYPHENE
CRABEATER
CRAMPFISH
CROSSFISH
DATE SHELL
DEVILFISH
DOG COCKLE
FIRE CORAL

FISH LOUSE
GASPEREAU
GHOST CRAB
GLASSFISH
GLOBEFISH
GOLDFINNY
GOLOMYNKA
GOOSEFISH
GREEN-BONE
GRENADIER
HARP SHELL
HOTTENTOT
HOUNDFISH
JACULATOR
JELLYFISH
KILLIFISH
KING PRAWN
LAKE TROUT
LAMP SHELL
LANGOUSTE
LEMON SOLE
MENOMINEE
MIDAS'S EAR
MILLEPORE
MUD-MINNOW
MUMMICHOG
NOCTILUCA
OPHIUROID
PEARLFISH
PIKE-PERCH
PILOTFISH
PORBEAGLE
RAZOR CLAM
RAZORFISH
RED MULLET
RED SALMON
REEF SHARK
ROCK BORER

ROCK PERCH
ROUNDFISH
SAIL-FLUKE
SAND PRIDE
SAND SHARK
SCALDFISH
SEA DRAGON
SEA NETTLE
SEA SPIDER
SEA SQUIRT
SEA URCHIN
SHEATFISH
SHORE CRAB
SHUBUNKIN
SNAILFISH
SNAKEFISH
SNIPEFISH
SOLENETTE
SPEARFISH
STARGAZER
STINGAREE
STINGFISH
STONE CRAB
STONEFISH
SURMULLET
SWORDFISH
SWORDTAIL
THORNBACK
THREADFIN
TIGER FISH
TOP MINNOW
TRUMPETER
TRUNKFISH
TUSK SHELL
WATER FLEA
WHITEBAIT
WHITE BASS
WHITEFISH

WHORE'S EGG
WING SHELL
WRECKFISH
YELLOWFIN

10
ACORN SHELL
ANGLER-FISH
ARCHER-FISH
BARRAMUNDI
BÊCHE-DE-MER
BITTERLING
BOMBAY DUCK
BONNETHEAD
BOTTLEFISH
BRISTLE WORM
BROWN TROUT
BUTTERFISH
CAMEO SHELL
CANDLEFISH
COELACANTH
CORNETFISH
CTENOPHORE
CUTTLEFISH
CYCLOSTOME
DAMSELFISH
DEMOISELLE
DRAGONFISH
ECHINODERM
FLUTEMOUTH
FLYING FISH
GROUNDLING
GUITAR-FISH
HAMMERHEAD
HEART SHELL
HERMIT CRAB
HORSELEECH
LANCET-FISH

LUMPSUCKER
MIDSHIPMAN
MITRE SHELL
MITTEN CRAB
MOSSBUNKER
MUD-SKIPPER
NEEDLEFISH
NETTLEFISH
NURSE HOUND
NURSE SHARK
OLIVE SHELL
PADDLEFISH
PARROT-FISH
PERIWINKLE
PILOT WHALE
PINK SALMON
RABBIT-FISH
RAZOR SHELL
RED SNAPPER
RIBBONFISH
RIBBON WORM
RIGHT WHALE
ROBBER CRAB
ROCK SALMON
ROCK TURBOT
ROUGH HOUND
RUDDERFISH
SAND DOLLAR
SANDHOPPER
SCRAG WHALE
SEA ANEMONE
SEA LEOPARD
SEA SURGEON
SHEEP'S-HEAD
SHOVELHEAD
SILVERFISH
SLEEVE FISH
SPERM WHALE

SPIDER CRAB
SQUETEAGUE
SUCKERFISH
SWAN MUSSEL
TIGER PRAWN
TIGER SHARK
TOOTH SHELL
TORPEDO RAY
TWAITE SHAD
VELVET CRAB
VENUS SHELL
WENTLETRAP
WHALE SHARK
WHITE SHARK
WHITE WHALE

11
BELLOWS FISH
BRINE SHRIMP
BRITTLESTAR
BUBBLE SHELL
CALLING CRAB
CUSHION STAR
DISCOPHORAN
DOLLY VARDEN
DRACUNCULUS
ELECTRIC EEL
ELECTRIC RAY
FIDDLER CRAB
FLYING SQUID
HATCHET-FISH
HEART COCKLE
HEART URCHIN
HELMET SHELL
HIPPOCAMPUS
HOLOTHURIAN
HORSE MUSSEL
KILLER WHALE

LANGOUSTINE
LANTERN-FISH
LEPIDOSIREN
MOORISH IDOL
NEMATOPHORE
PEARL MUSSEL
PEARL OYSTER
PELICAN-FISH
PRICKLEBACK
REEF-BUILDER
ROCK LOBSTER
SALMON TROUT
SAND-SKIPPER
SEA CUCUMBER
SEA ELEPHANT
SEA SCORPION
SOLDIER CRAB
STICKLEBACK
SURGEON-FISH
TRIGGERFISH
TROUGH SHELL
TRUMPET-FISH
UNICORN FISH
WHISTLE-FISH

12
BALLAN WRASSE
BASKING SHARK
BRAMBLE SHARK
COELENTERATE
ELEPHANT SEAL
FIGHTING FISH
FOUR-EYED FISH
GOLDEN SALMON
MANTIS SHRIMP
MILLER'S THUMB
MOUTHBROODER
PARADISE FISH

PARROT WRASSE
RAINBOW TROUT
REQUIEM SHARK
RIVER DOLPHIN
SCABBARD-FISH
SCORPION-FISH
SEA BUTTERFLY
SEA PORCUPINE
SENTINEL CRAB
SERGEANT FISH
SILVER SALMON
SKIPJACK TUNA
SPINDLE SHELL
SPINY LOBSTER
TRUMPET SHELL
UNICORN SHELL
VENUS'S GIRDLE

13
ACORN BARNACLE
BUTTERFLY FISH
CLIMBING PERCH
CRABEATER SEAL
FLYING GURNARD
HORSE MACKEREL
HORSESHOE CRAB
HUMPBACK WHALE
KEYHOLE LIMPET
LABYRINTH FISH
LEATHERJACKET
MACKEREL GUIDE
MACKEREL SHARK
NORWAY LOBSTER
PORCELAIN CRAB
PORCUPINE FISH
SEA GOOSEBERRY

SLIPPER LIMPET
SOCKEYE SALMON
THRESHER SHARK
YELLOWFIN TUNA

14
DUBLIN BAY PRAWN
GREENLAND WHALE
SKELETON SHRIMP

15
BONNETHEAD SHARK
BOTTLENOSE WHALE
CROSSOPTERYGIAN
GREAT WHITE SHARK
HAMMERHEAD SHARK
SHOVELHEAD SHARK

Animals – INSECTS & TINY CREATURES
st = development stage

3
ANT
BEE
BOT
BUG
DOR
FLY
KED
LOB
LUG
NIT

4
BLUE
CLEG
FLEA
FRIT
GNAT
GRIG
GRUB *st*
HAWK
MITE
MOTH
NUNU
PIUM

PUPA *st*
SLUG
TICK
WASP
WORM
ZIMB

5
APHID
APHIS
ARGUS
COMMA
DRAKE
EGGAR

EMMET
FLUKE
IMAGO *st*
LARVA *st*
LEECH
LOUSE
MIDGE
MIRID
NURSE
NYMPH *st*
OWLET
OX-BOT *st*
    warble fly
PIPER

SAUBA
SNAIL
SWIFT
Y-MOTH

6
ACARID
BAT FLY
BEDBUG
BEETLE
BOGONG
BOTFLY
BREEZE
BURNET

CADDIS
CAPSID
CHAFER
CHIGOE
CHINCH
CICADA
COCCID
DOR-FLY
EARWIG
ELATER
GADFLY
GRU-GRU
  st weevil
HOPDOG *st*
  tussock moth
HOP-FLY
HORNET
IO MOTH
JIGGER
LACKEY
LAPPET
LOCUST
LOOPER
  st moth
MAGGOT *st* fly
MANTID
MANTIS
MAY BUG
MAYFLY
MEASLE *st*
  tapeworm
MOTUCA
MUSCID
MYGALE
PIERID
PINKIE *st* fly
PSOCID
RED ANT

SAWFLY
SCARAB
SOW BUG
SPIDER
TETTIX
THRIPS
TSETSE
WEEVIL
WOUBIT *st*
  tiger moth

7
ANNELID
ANT LION
ARANEID
ARMY ANT
ASCARID
BEE MOTH
BEET-FLY
BLOWFLY
BOAT-FLY
BROMMER
CESTODE
CHIGGER
CORNFLY
CRICKET
CUTWORM
  st moth
DEW WORM
DUCK ANT
EELWORM
ERGATES *st* ant
FIRE ANT
FIREFLY
FOX MOTH
FRIT FLY
GALL-FLY
GOLDBUG

GOUT-FLY
HORNBUG
JUNE BUG
KATYDID
LADYBUG
LOBWORM
LUGWORM
MEAT ANT
MEAT FLY
MONARCH
NOCTUID
OWL MOTH
PHASMID
PINWORM
PYRALID
RAGWORM
RINGLET
SANDFLY
SATYRID
SCIARID
SKEETER
SKIPPER
STYLOPS
SYRPHID
TERMITE
TORTRIX
WAX MOTH
WOOD ANT

8
ALDERFLY
ARACHNID
ARMY WORM
BEE LOUSE
BLACKFLY
BOLLWORM
  st moth
BOMBYCID

BOOKWORM
  st beetle
CECROPIA
CINNABAR
CORN-MOTH
CRANE FLY
CURCULIO
DART-MOTH
DIPTERAN
DYTISCID
ESCARGOT
FIREBRAT
FIREWORM
FLATWORM
FLESH FLY
FROTH-FLY
FRUIT FLY
GALL WASP
GAPEWORM
GEOMETER
GLOW-WORM
GOAT-MOTH
GOLD WASP
GREENFLY
HAIR WORM
HAWK-MOTH
HELMINTH
HESPERID
HONEY ANT
HONEY BEE
HOOKWORM
HORNTAIL
HORNWORM
  st hawk-moth
HORSEFLY
HOUSEFLY
HOVERFLY
ITCH MITE

LACEWING
LADYBIRD
LONGHORN
LUNA MOTH
MASON BEE
MEALWORM
   st meal beetle
MEALY BUG
MILKWEED
MOON MOTH
MOSQUITO
NEMATODE
OAK EGGAR
OX-WARBLE
PUSS MOTH
RUBYTAIL
SAND FLEA
SAUBA ANT
SCORPION
SEDGE FLY
SHEEP KED
SILK MOTH
SILKWORM
   st silk moth
SKIPJACK
SNAKE FLY
SNOW FLEA
SPHINGID
STINK BUG
STONEFLY
TAPEWORM
TOXOCARA
TRICHINA
VAPOURER
WHEAT FLY
WHIPWORM
WHITE ANT
WHITEFLY

WIREWORM *st*
   click beetle
WOOD TICK
WOODWASP
WOODWORM *st*
   furniture beetle

9

AMAZON ANT
ANOPHELES
ARTHROPOD
BOOKLOUSE
BRANDLING
BRIMSTONE
BUMBLE-BEE
BUTTERFLY
CADDIS FLY
CARROT FLY
CENTIPEDE
CHEESE FLY
CHINCH BUG
CHRYSALIS *st*
CLAVICORN
CLEARWING
COCHINEAL
COCKROACH
COFFEE BUG
CORN BORER
DAMSEL BUG
DAMSELFLY
DOBSON FLY
DOODLEBUG
   st ant lion
DOR BEETLE
DRAGONFLY
DRIVER ANT
DUSKY WING
EARTHWORM

FOREST FLY
GALL MIDGE
GEOMETRID
GHOST MOTH
GYPSY MOTH
HARVESTER
HODMANDOD
HUMBLE-BEE
ICHNEUMON
LONGICORN
MILLIPEDE
NEMERTINE
NUT WEEVIL
NYMPHALID
OIL BEETLE
ORANGE TIP
OWLET MOTH
PLANARIAN
PLUME MOTH
RED SPIDER
ROBBER FLY
ROUNDWORM
SATURNIID
SHEEP TICK
SHIELD BUG
STRONGYLE
SUGAR MITE
SWIFT MOTH
TARANTULA
TIGER MOTH
TIGERTAIL
TORTRICID
TREMATODE
TSETSE FLY
TUMBLEBUG
UNDERWING
VELVET ANT
VERMICULE

WARBLE FLY
WATER FLEA
WHEAT MOTH
WHIRLIGIG
WOODLOUSE

10

ANOPHELINE
ANTLER MOTH
BARK BEETLE
BLACK WIDOW
BLISTER FLY
BLUEBOTTLE
BOLL WEEVIL
BURNET MOTH
CADDIS WORM
   st caddis fly
CANKERWORM
CARPET MOTH
CHEESE MITE
CHIRONOMID
COCKCHAFER
CODLIN MOTH
CORN THRIPS
CORN WEEVIL
DEMOISELLE
DIGGER WASP
DROSOPHILA
DUNG BEETLE
FEN CRICKET
FRITILLARY
FROGHOPPER
GATEKEEPER
GOLD BEETLE
GREEN DRAKE
   st mayfly
GUINEA WORM
HAIRSTREAK

HARVESTMAN
HEMIPTERAN
HESSIAN FLY
KITTEN MOTH
LACKEY MOTH
LANTERN FLY
LAPPET MOTH
LEAF BEETLE
LEAFHOPPER
LEAF INSECT
MAGPIE MOTH
MEAL BEETLE
MUSK BEETLE
PAPILIONID
PHYLLOXERA
PILL BEETLE
PINE BEAUTY
PINE BEETLE
PINECHAFER
PLANT LOUSE
POND SKATER
POTTER WASP
RED ADMIRAL
ROSECHAFER
ROVE BEETLE
SCARABAEID
SHEEP LOUSE
SILVERFISH
SOLDIER ANT
SPANISH FLY
SPHINX MOTH
SPITTLEBUG
SPRINGTAIL
STAG BEETLE
THREADWORM
TREEHOPPER
TURNIP MOTH
VINEGAR FLY

WHEAT MIDGE
WOLF SPIDER
WOOLLY BEAR
   st tiger moth,
   carpet beetle

11

ASSASSIN BUG
BAGWORM MOTH
BITING LOUSE
BLACK BEETLE
BLOODSUCKER
BRISTLETAIL
BUFFALO GNAT
BUSH CRICKET
CABBAGE MOTH
CATERPILLAR
   st butterfly, moth
CLICK BEETLE
CLOTHES MOTH
CODLING MOTH
COLEOPTERAN
CYSTICERCUS
   st tapeworm
EMPEROR MOTH
FROTH-HOPPER
GRASSHOPPER
GREENBOTTLE
HARVEST MITE
LAMELLICORN
LEOPARD MOTH
MEADOW BROWN
MOLE CRICKET
MONEY SPIDER
MYGALOMORPH
NOCTUID MOTH
OLIGOCHAETE
PAINTED LADY

PLANT-HOPPER
PYRALID MOTH
SCALE INSECT
SCHISTOSOME
SCORPION FLY
SCOTCH ARGUS
STICK INSECT
SWALLOWTAIL
TIGER BEETLE
TORTRIX MOTH
TUSSOCK MOTH
UMBRELLA ANT
WATER BEETLE

12

CABBAGE WHITE
CARPENTER ANT
CARPENTER BEE
CARPET BEETLE
CECROPIA MOTH
CINNABAR MOTH
DIADEM SPIDER
DIVING BEETLE
GARDEN CHAFER
GEOMETER MOTH
GROUND BEETLE
HARVESTER ANT
ICHNEUMON FLY
MARBLED WHITE
PEPPERED MOTH
RUBYTAIL WASP
SCARAB BEETLE
SCREW-WORM FLY
SEXTON BEETLE
SPRING BEETLE
WALKING-STICK
WATER BOATMAN
WATER STRIDER

WHIP SCORPION
WHITE ADMIRAL

13
BLISTER BEETLE
BURYING BEETLE
CHEESE-SKIPPER
CLEARWING MOTH
COTTON STAINER
DADDY-LONG-LEGS
ELM BARK BEETLE
GEOMETRID MOTH
GOLIATH BEETLE
HARVEST SPIDER
LEAFCUTTER ANT
LEAFCUTTER BEE
LEATHERJACKET
   st crane fly
PRAYING MANTIS

PURPLE EMPEROR
SATURNIID MOTH
SOLDIER BEETLE
TORTOISESHELL
UNDERWING MOTH
WATER SCORPION

14
AMBROSIA BEETLE
CABBAGE ROOT FLY
COLORADO BEETLE
DARKLING BEETLE
DEATH'S HEAD MOTH
EPHEMEROPTERAN
HERCULES BEETLE
LONGHORN BEETLE
SCORPION SPIDER
SKIPJACK BEETLE
SLAVE-MAKING ANT

TORTOISE BEETLE
TRAPDOOR SPIDER

15
DIAMONDBACK MOTH
FURNITURE BEETLE
PEACOCK BUTTERFLY
WHIRLIGIG BEETLE

16
BOMBARDIER BEETLE
CAMBERWELL BEAUTY
DEATH-WATCH BEETLE
DEVIL'S COACH-HORSE
EMPEROR DRAGONFLY
MONARCH BUTTERFLY
STINKING DUNGWORM

Animals – LAND ANIMALS

3	ROE	DOUC	MOLE	TAHR
APE	SAI	EURO	MONA	TANA
ASS	YAK	EYRA	MULE	TITI
BAT		GAUR	OONT	UNAU
BOK	**4**	GOAT	ORYX	URVA
CAT	ANOA	HARE	PACA	VOLE
DOG	ATOK	IBEX	PACO	WOLF
ELK	AXIS	KUDU	PEBA	ZATI
FOX	BEAR	LION	PIKA	ZEBU
GNU	CAVY	LOBO	PONY	
HOG	CONY	LYNX	PUMA	**5**
KOB	COON	MARA	RUSA	ADDAX
PIG	DEER	MICO	SAKI	BISON
RAT	DIEB	MINK	SIKA	BONGO

BURRO	OTTER	BADGER	MARGAY	BIGHORN
CAMEL	OUNCE	BEAVER	MARMOT	BLESBOK
CHIMP	PANDA	BHARAL	MARTEN	BLUE FOX
CHIRU	PEKAN	BOBCAT	MONKEY	BUFFALO
CIVET	POTTO	BONOBO	MUSANG	CANE RAT
COATI	QUOLL	CABRIE	MUSK OX	CARACAL
CONEY	RASSE	CHITAL	NILGAI	CARIBOU
COYPU	RATEL	COAITA	NUMBAT	CHAMOIS
DHOLE	RHINO	COLUGO	OCELOT	CHEETAH
DINGO	SABLE	COUGAR	OLINGO	CHIKARA
DRILL	SAIGA	COYOTE	ONAGER	COLOBUS
ELAND	SASIN	CUSCUS	PONGID	DASYURE
FOSSA	SEROW	DASSIE	POSSUM	ECHIDNA
GAYAL	SHEEP	DESMAN	RABBIT	GAZELLE
GENET	SHREW	DIK-DIK	RACOON	GEMSBOK
GORAL	SKUNK	DONKEY	RED FOX	GERENUK
HIPPO	SLOTH	DUIKER	REEBOK	GIRAFFE
HORSE	STOAT	ERMINE	RHEBOK	GLUTTON
HUTIA	SWINE	FENNEC	SAGUIN	GORILLA
HYENA	TAKIN	FERRET	SAMBAR	GRIZZLY
HYRAX	TAPIR	FISHER	SERVAL	GRYSBOK
INDRI	TATOU	FOX BAT	SIFAKA	GUANACO
IZARD	TAYRA	GALAGO	SIMPAI	GUEREZA
KIANG	TIGER	GELADA	TAGUAN	GYMNURE
KOALA	URIAL	GERBIL	TELEDU	HAMSTER
KULAN	URSON	GIBBON	TENREC	HANUMAN
LEMUR	VISON	GOPHER	VERVET	HEMIONE
LLAMA	ZEBRA	GRISON	VICUÑA	HOG DEER
LORIS	ZERDA	GRIVET	WAPITI	HOOLOCK
MAGOT	ZORRO	GUENON	WEASEL	JACCHUS
MANIS		HOWLER	WISENT	KEITLOA
MANUL	**6**	IMPALA	WOMBAT	KLIPDAS
MHORR	AGOUTI	JACKAL		LEMMING
MOOSE	ALPACA	JAGUAR	**7**	LEOPARD
MOUSE	AOUDAD	JERBOA	ACOUCHI	LINSANG
NYALA	ARGALI	KALONG	ANT-BEAR	MACAQUE
OKAPI	AYE-AYE	LANGUR	BANTENG	MADOQUA
ORIBI	BABOON	MALMAG	BEARCAT	MARKHOR

MEERKAT
MOLE RAT
MOONRAT
MOUFLON
MUNTJAC
MUSKRAT
NANDINE
ONDATRA
OPOSSUM
PANTHER
PECCARY
POLECAT
POTOROO
RACCOON
RED DEER
ROE DEER
SAIMIRI
SAPAJOU
SIAMANG
SOUSLIK
SUN BEAR
TAMARIN
TARSIER
TRAGULE
WALLABY
WARTHOG
WILDCAT
WISTITI
ZAMOUSE
ZORILLA

8
AARDVARK
AARDWOLF
ANTEATER
ANTELOPE
AXIS DEER
BABIRUSA

BANXRING
BLACK RAT
BLUEBUCK
BLUE HARE
BONTEBOK
BROWN RAT
BUSHBABY
BUSHBUCK
CAPYBARA
CARCAJOU
CARIACOU
CHIPMUNK
DORMOUSE
DUCKBILL
ELEPHANT
ENTELLUS
FRUIT BAT
GREY WOLF
HEDGEHOG
KANGAROO
KINKAJOU
MANDRILL
MANGABEY
MARMOSET
MONGOOSE
MULE DEER
MUSK CAVY
MUSK DEER
MUSQUASH
PANGOLIN
PLATYPUS
RED PANDA
REEDBUCK
REINDEER
RINGTAIL
SAPI-UTAN
SELADANG
SEROTINE

SEWELLEL
SEWER RAT
SQUIRREL
STEENBOK
STEINBOK
SURICATE
TALAPOIN
TAMANDUA
TIGER CAT
TODDY CAT
TUCU-TUCO
VISCACHA
WALLAROO
WANDEROO
WATER RAT
WHISTLER
WILD BOAR

9
AMUR TIGER
ARCTIC FOX
ARMADILLO
BABACOOTE
BANDICOOT
BINTURONG
BLACKBUCK
BROWN BEAR
CAPE HYRAX
CATAMOUNT
CHICKAREE
CORSAC FOX
DEER MOUSE
DESERT RAT
DROMEDARY
DZIGGETAI
FLYING FOX
GOLDEN CAT
GROUNDHOG

GUINEA PIG
HAMADRYAS
HONEY BEAR
ICHNEUMON
KOALA BEAR
MONOTREME
MOUSE DEER
MUSK SHREW
NORWAY RAT
ORANG-UTAN
PADEMELON
PALM CIVET
PETAURIST
PHALANGER
POLAR BEAR
PORCUPINE
PRONGHORN
SHREW-MOLE
SILVER FOX
SITATUNGA
SLOTH BEAR
SOLENODON
SPRINGBOK
TIGER WOLF
TIMOR DEER
TREE SHREW
WATERBUCK
WATER DEER
WATER VOLE
WOLVERINE
WOODCHUCK
WOODSHOCK

10
ANGWANTIBO
ARCTIC HARE
BARBARY APE
CACOMISTLE

CHEVROTAIN
CHIMPANZEE
CHINCHILLA
COATIMUNDI
COTTONTAIL
DOLICHOTIS
FALLOW DEER
FIELDMOUSE
GIANT PANDA
GOLDEN MOLE
HARTEBEEST
HONEY MOUSE
JACK-RABBIT
JAGUARUNDI
KODIAK BEAR
LEOPARD CAT
MALABAR RAT
MEXICAN HOG
MONA MONKEY
NOTORYCTES
OTTER SHREW
PALLAS'S CAT
PARADOXURE
PICHICIEGO
PINE MARTEN
PIPING HARE
POUCHED RAT
PRAIRIE DOG
RACCOON DOG
RHINOCEROS
ROCK RABBIT
SPECTRE BAT
SPRINGBUCK
SPRINGHAAS
SPRING-HARE
TIMBER WOLF
VAMPIRE BAT
WATER SHREW

WILDEBEEST

11
BARBASTELLE
BARKING DEER
BEECH MARTEN
BELGIAN HARE
DIANA MONKEY
DOUROUCOULI
FLYING LEMUR
GRIZZLY BEAR
HOARY MARMOT
HONEY BADGER
HONEY POSSUM
KANGAROO RAT
LEISLER'S BAT
PATAS MONKEY
PIPISTRELLE
PRAIRIE WOLF
RED SQUIRREL
SNOW LEOPARD
STONE MARTEN

12
BONNET MONKEY
CATAMOUNTAIN
CHACMA BABOON
CINNAMON BEAR
GOAT-ANTELOPE
GREY SQUIRREL
HARVEST MOUSE
HIPPOPOTAMUS
HORSESHOE BAT
HOWLER MONKEY
JUMPING MOUSE
KLIPSPRINGER
MARSUPIAL CAT
MOUNTAIN GOAT

MOUNTAIN HARE
MOUNTAIN LION
POCKET GOPHER
RHESUS MONKEY
ROAN ANTELOPE
SNOWSHOE HARE
SPECTRE LEMUR
SPIDER MONKEY
TREE KANGAROO
WATER BUFFALO

13
BACTRIAN CAMEL
BRUSH KANGAROO
COLOBUS MONKEY
DORCAS GAZELLE
GOLDEN HAMSTER
MARSUPIAL MOLE
MOUNTAIN SHEEP
SABLE ANTELOPE
SOOTY MANGABEY
STAR-NOSED MOLE
WALTZING MOUSE

14
CAPUCHIN MONKEY
CLOUDED LEOPARD
FAIRY ARMADILLO
FLYING SQUIRREL
GROUND SQUIRREL
HUNTING LEOPARD
INDIAN ELEPHANT
MARSUPIAL MOUSE
MOUNTAIN BEAVER
PATAGONIAN HARE
PÈRE DAVID'S DEER
SNOWSHOE RABBIT
SPECTACLED BEAR

SQUIRREL MONKEY
TASMANIAN DEVIL

15
AFRICAN ELEPHANT

BLACK RHINOCEROS
FLYING PHALANGER
PROBOSCIS MONKEY
WHITE RHINOCEROS

16
CHINESE WATER DEER
GRASSHOPPER MOUSE

Animals – REPTILES AND AMPHIBIANS
st = stage

3
ASP
BOA
EFT
OLM

4
BOMA
EMYS
FROG
GILA
NAGA
NEWT
SEPS
TEGU
TOAD

5
ADDER
AGAMA
ANOLE
COBRA
CRIBO
  (or indigo
  snake)
DRACO
GECKO

KRAIT
MAMBA
SIREN
SKINK
SNAKE
SPAWN *st* frog
TOKAY
VARAN
VIPER

6
AGAMID
CAIMAN
CAYMAN
DRAGON
GAVIAL
GOANNA
IGUANA
LIZARD
MOLOCH
MUGGER
PYTHON
SLIDER
TAIPAN
TURTLE
WORRAL

7
AXOLOTL
FROGLET
GHARIAL
HOGNOSE
LANGAHA
MONITOR
RATTLER
SERPENT
TADPOLE *st* frog
TUATARA

8
ANACONDA
BASILISK
BULLFROG
CERASTES
HICCATEE
JARARACA
MAPEPIRE
MATAMATA
MENOPOME
MOCCASIN
MUD PUPPY
PIT VIPER
PLATANNA
POLLIWOG *st* frog

REDBELLY
RINKHALS
SEA SNAKE
SLOW-WORM
STELLION
SUCURUJÚ
SURUCUCU
TEGUEXIN
TERRAPIN
TORTOISE
TREE FROG
WATER BOA

9
ALLIGATOR
BERG ADDER
BLINDWORM
BOOMSLANG
BOX TURTLE
CAECILIAN
CHAMELEON
COACHWHIP
CROCODILE
GALLIWASP
HAMADRYAD
HAWKSBILL
HOOP-SNAKE

KING COBRA
MUD TURTLE
PORWIGGLE *st* frog
POUCH-TOAD
PUFF ADDER
RING-SNAKE
RIVER-JACK
ROCK SNAKE
SAND SNAKE
SEA TURTLE
SPADEFOOT
TREE SNAKE
WART SNAKE
WHIP SNAKE
WORM SNAKE

10
BANDY-BANDY
BATRACHIAN
BLACK MAMBA
BUSHMASTER
CHUCKWALLA
CLAWED TOAD
COPPERHEAD
CORAL SNAKE
FER-DE-LANCE
FLYING FROG
GLASS SNAKE
GRASS SNAKE
HELLBENDER
HORNED TOAD
LOGGERHEAD
NATTERJACK
POND TURTLE
SALAMANDER

SAND LIZARD
SIDEWINDER
SMOOTH NEWT
TIGER SNAKE
WALL LIZARD
WATER SNAKE
WORM LIZARD

11
ANOLE LIZARD
CARPET SNAKE
CONSTRICTOR
COTTONMOUTH
DIAMONDBACK
DRACO LIZARD
FENCE LIZARD
FLYING SNAKE
GABOON VIPER
GARTER SNAKE
GILA MONSTER
GLASS LIZARD
GOLIATH FROG
GREEN TURTLE
HORNED VIPER
INDIGO SNAKE
  (or cribo)
LEATHERBACK
LEOPARD FROG
MIDWIFE TOAD
RATTLESNAKE
SMOOTH SNAKE
THORNY DEVIL

12
CARPET PYTHON

FALSE GHARIAL
FLYING DRAGON
FLYING LIZARD
HOGNOSE SNAKE
HORNED LIZARD
KOMODO DRAGON
POND TERRAPIN
SPRING-KEEPER
SURINAME TOAD

13
BEARDED LIZARD
FRILLED LIZARD
GIANT TORTOISE
MONITOR LIZARD
RUSSELL'S VIPER
SPADEFOOT TOAD
STELLIO LIZARD
WATER MOCCASIN

14
BOA CONSTRICTOR
COACHWHIP SNAKE
FIRE SALAMANDER
NATTERJACK TOAD
RIVER-JACK VIPER
SNAPPING TURTLE

15
HAWKSBILL TURTLE
SPECTACLED COBRA

16
LOGGERHEAD TURTLE

Arts

Arts – Cinema – ACTORS & ACTRESSES
Also see TV & Radio Personalities

3
ASH Leslie
BOW Clara
COX Courteney
DAY Doris, Jill
DEE Sandra
EGE Julie
EVE Trevor
FOX Edward,
  Emilia, James,
  Michael J
FRY Stephen
HAY Will
LAW Jude
LEE Belinda,
  Bernard, Bruce,
  Christopher
LOE Judy

LOM Herbert
LOY Myrna
MIX Tom
RAY Aldo
RIX Lord Brian
ROC Patricia
SIM Alastair,
  Sheila
YIP David

4
ABEL Walter
ADAM Ronald
AIRD Holly
ALDA Alan
AMES Leon
AUER Mischa
BACH Barbara

BALL Lucille,
  Nicholas,
  Vincent
BARA Theda
BARI Lynn
BARR Patrick
BASS Alfie
BELL Ann, Tom
BOHT Jean
BOND Derek,
  Ward
BOYD Stephen,
  William
BRON Eleanor
BURR Raymond
CAAN James
CAGE Nicolas
CHER

COBB Lee J
COLE George
COPE Kenneth
CULP Robert
DAHL Arlene
DALE Jim
DALY Tyne
DEAN James, Letitia
DEPP Johnny
DORS Diana
DOWN Lesley-Anne
DUNN Clive
EDDY Nelson
EGAN Peter,
  Richard
EHLE Jennifer
ELAM Jack
FALK Peter

FARR Derek
FAYE Alice
FORD Glenn, Harrison
GENN Leo
GERE Richard
GISH Lillian
GRAY Donald, Dulcie, Linda
GREY Jennifer
GYNT Greta
HALE Alan, Barbara, Georgina, Sonnie
HALL Huntz, Porter
HARE Doris, Robertson
HAWN Goldie
HIRD Dame Thora
HOLM Sir Ian
HOPE Bob
HUDD Roy
HUNT Gareth, Helen
HURT John
IDLE Eric
IVES Burl
JEAN Gloria
KAHN Madeline
KAYE Danny, Gorden
KEEL Howard
KEEN Diane
KEMP Ross, Martin
KENT Jean
KERR Deborah
KNOX Alexander, Barbara
KWAN Nancy
KYDD Sam
LADD Alan, Cheryl
LAHR Bert
LAKE Veronica

LANE Lupino
LANG Belinda, Robert
LAYE Evelyn
LEON Valerie
LISI Virna
LORD Jack
LOTT Barbara
LOWE Arthur, Rob
LYNN Ralph
LYON Ben, Sue
MAIN Marjorie
MARX Chico, Groucho, Gummo, Harpo, Zeppo
MAYO Virginia
MORE Kenneth
MUIR Jean
MUNI Paul
NAIL Jimmy
NEAL Patricia
NEFF Hildegard
NEIL Hildegarde
NERO Franco
OWEN Bill, Clive, Reginald
PAGE Geraldine
PECK Bob, Gregory
PENN Sean
RAFT George
REED Donna, Oliver
REES Angharad
REID Anne, Beryl
RIGG Dame Diana
ROSS Katharine
ROTH Lillian, Tim
RUSH Barbara, Geoffrey
RYAN John P, Meg, Robert
SABU

SHAW Martin, Robert
SHER Sir Antony
SIMS Joan
SOUL David
SWIT Loretta
SYMS Sylvia
TATE Sharon
TATI Jacques
TEAL Ray
THAW John
TODD Ann, Bob, Richard
TONE Franchot
TORN Rip
TOTO
TREE Sir Herbert
WARD Burt, Rachel, Robert, Simon
WEBB Clifton, Jack
WELD Tuesday
WEST Adam, Mae, Timothy
WILD Jack
WOOD Natalie
WRAY Fay
YORK Michael, Susannah

5

ADAMS Edie, Julie
ADLER Luther
AIMÉE Anouk
AKINS Claude
ALLEN Gracie, Patrick, Woody
ANNIS Francesca
ARDEN Eve
ARKIN Alan
ARLEN Richard
ARNAZ Desi

ASHER Jane
ASNER Ed
ASTOR Mary
AUTRY Gene
AYRES Lew
BAKER Carroll, Colin, George, Sir Stanley, Tom
BANKS Leslie
BARON Lynda
BARRY Gene
BATES Sir Alan, Florence, Ralph
BEENY Christopher
BEERY Noah, Wallace
BERLE Milton
BERRY Halle, Nick
BEWES Rodney
BIXBY Bill
BLACK Karen
BLAIR Isla
BLAKE Amanda
BLOOM Claire
BLORE Eric
BLYTH Ann
BOLAM James
BONDI Beulah
BOONE Richard
BOOTH Anthony, Connie
BOWIE David
BOYER Charles
BRENT George
BRETT Jeremy
BROOK Clive
BROWN Joe E, June
BRUCE Brenda, Nigel
BRYAN Dora
BUONO Victor

BURKE Alfred, Kathy
BURNS George
BYRNE Peter
CAINE Sir Michael
CAREY Joyce
CARON Leslie
CARTY Todd
CHASE Chevy, Lorraine
CLARK Fred, Petula
CLIFT Montgomery
CLIVE EE
CLOSE Glenn
CONTE Richard
CONTI Tom
CORRI Adrienne
COSBY Bill
COURT Hazel
CRAIG Daniel, Michael, Wendy
CROSS Ben
CROWE Russell
DALIO Marcel
DANCE Charles
DARIN Bobby
DAVIS Bette, Joan, Judy, Sammy
DELON Alain
DENCH Dame Judi
DEREK Bo, John
DOBIE Alan
DONAT Robert
DOYLE Tony
DRAKE Gabrielle
DUFFY Patrick
DUNNE Irene
DYALL Valentine
EATON Shirley

EBSEN Buddy
EGGAR Samantha
ELVEY Maurice
ESSEX David
EVANS Barry, Dale, Dame Edith, Linda
EWELL Tom
FAITH Adam
FIELD Betty, Sally, Shirley Ann, Sid
FINCH Peter
FIRTH Colin
FLYNN Barbara, Errol, Jerome
FONDA Henry, Jane, Peter
FROBE Gert
GABIN Jean
GABLE Clark
GABOR Eva, Zsa Zsa
GARBO Greta
GAUGE Alexander
GAUNT William
GLESS Sharon
GOUGH Michael
GOULD Elliott
GRANT Cary, Hugh, Lee, Richard E
GREEN Robson
GROOM Sam
GROUT James
GWENN Edmund
HAGEN Jean
HAIGH Kenneth
HANDL Irene
HANKS Tom
HARDY Oliver, Robert
HAUER Rutger

HAYES Helen, Melvyn, Patricia
HEALY Tim
HENIE Sonja
HINES Gregory
HODGE Patricia
HOGAN Paul
HOWES Bobby, Sally Ann
HULCE Tom
IMRIE Celia
INMAN John
IRONS Jeremy
JAFFE Sam
JAMES Geraldine, Sid
JANUS Samantha
JASON Sir David
JAYNE Jennifer
JEWEL Jimmy
JOHNS Glynis, Mervyn, Stratford
JOLIE Angelina
JONES Allan, James Earl, Jennifer, Peter, Shirley, Tommy Lee
JOYCE Yootha
KEACH Stacy
KEITH Penelope
KELLY Gene, Grace, Paul, Sam
KLINE Kevin
KWOUK Burt
LACEY Ronald
LAINE Frankie
LANGE Hope, Jessica
LANZA Mario
LEACH Rosemary
LEIGH Janet, Vivien

LENYA Lotte
LE ROY Mervyn
LEWIS Jerry
LLOYD Harold, Jeremy, Sue
LODGE David
LOGAN Phyllis
LOREN Sophia
LORRE Peter
LUCAN Arthur
LUCAS William
LUKAS Paul
MADOC Philip, Ruth
MAGEE Patrick
MALIK Art
MARCH Fredric
MARKS Alfred
MARSH Jean, Reginald
MASON James
MAYNE Ferdy
MCCOY Sylvester
MCKEE Gina
MILES Sir Bernard, Sarah
MILLS Hayley, Sir John, Juliet
MOODY Ron
MOORE Clayton, Dudley, Mary Tyler, Sir Roger
MORSE Barry, David, Helen
MOUNT Peggy
MOWER Patrick
MUNRO Janet
NAISH J Carrol
NARES Owen
NEILL Sam
NIMMO Derek

NIMOY Leonard
NIVEN David
NOLAN Lloyd
NOLTE Nick
NOVAK Kim
OAKIE Jack
OATES Warren
O'HARA Maureen
OLAND Warner
OLSEN Gary
O'MARA Kate
O'NEAL Patrick, Ryan, Tatum
O'SHEA Milo, Tessie
PALIN Michael
PAPAS Irene
PARKS Larry
PAYNE Laurence
PERRY Matthew
PITTS ZaSu
POSTA Adrienne
POWER Tyrone
PRAED Michael
PRICE Dennis, Vincent
PRIOR Maureen
PRYCE Jonathan
PRYOR Richard
QUICK Diana
QUINN Anthony
RAINS Claude
RALPH Jessie
REEVE Christopher
RIGBY Terence
ROMAN Ruth
RYDER Winona
SACHS Andrew
SAINT Eva Marie
SAXON John

SCOTT George C,
  Janette, Randolph,
  Terry, Zachary
SEARS Heather
SEGAL George
SELBY Tony
SETON Sir Bruce
SHANE Paul
SHARP Lesley
SHEEN Charlie, Martin
SILVA Henry
SIMON Simone
SMITH Sir C Aubrey, Liz,
  Dame Maggie, Ray, Will
SOLON Ewen
SPALL Timothy
STACK Robert
STAFF Kathy
STAMP Terence
STARK Graham
STEEL Anthony
STING
STOCK Nigel
STONE Lewis, Milburn,
  Sharon
STORM Gale
STOTT Ken
SWANK Hilary
SYKES Eric
TANDY Jessica
TERRY Dame Ellen
TILLY Meg
TOLER Sidney
TOPOL
TORMÉ Mel
TRACY Lee, Spencer
TUTIN Dame Dorothy
URICH Robert

VANCE Vivian
VEIDT Conrad
WAITE Ralph
WALSH Bradley, Kay
WAYNE John
WEISZ Rachel
WELCH Raquel
WHITE Carol
WILDE Cornel, Brian
WYATT Jane
WYMAN Jane
YATES Pauline
YOUNG Alan, Gig,
  Loretta, Robert, Roland
ZUCCO George

6

ABBOTT Bud
ADDAMS Dawn
AHERNE Brian
AITKEN Maria
ALBERT Eddie
AMECHE Don
ANGELI Pier
ANGERS Avril
ANHOLT Tony
ANSARA Michael
ARLISS George
ARNATT John
ARNAUD Yvonne
ARNESS James
ARNOLD Edward
ARNOUL Françoise
ARTHUR Jean
ATKINS Coral,
  Dame Eileen
ATWILL Lionel
AUDRAN Stéphane

AVALON Frankie
AYLMER Sir Felix
BACALL Lauren
BACKUS Jim
BAILEY Pearl, Robin
BALSAM Martin
BANNEN Ian
BARDOT Brigitte
BARBER Glynis
BARKER Eric, Lex
BARNES Binnie
BARRIE Amanda
BARRON John, Keith
BARTOK Eva
BAXTER Anne,
  Sir Stanley, Warner
BEATTY Ned, Robert,
  Warren
BENDIX William
BENING Annette
BENSON Sir Frank
BERGEN Candice
BIRKIN Jane
BISSET Jacqueline
BOGART Humphrey
BOLGER Ray
BOSLEY Tom
BOWLES Peter
BRANDO Marlon
BRAZZI Rossano
BRIERS Richard
BRIGGS Johnny
BROLIN James
BROOKS Ray
BROWNE Coral, Jill
BRYANT Michael
BURTON Amanda,
  Richard

BYRNES Edd
CADELL Simon
CAGNEY James
CALLOW Simon
CANNON Dyan, Esma
CANTOR Eddie
CARNEY Art
CARREY Jim
CARSON Jack, Jeannie, Violet
CARTER Lynda
CASSON Sir Lewis
CHANEY Lon
CHASEN Heather
CHERRY Helen
CHITTY Erik
CLARKE Warren
CLEESE John
CLUNES Martin
COBURN Charles, James
COLMAN Ronald
CONNOR Kenneth
COOGAN Jackie, Steve
COOMBS Pat
COOPER Gary, Dame Gladys
COTTEN Joseph
COWARD Sir Noël
CRABBE Buster
CRAVEN Gemma
CROSBY Bing
CRUISE Tom
CULVER Roland
CURRIE Finlay
CURTIS Jamie Lee, Tony
CUSACK Cyril, Niamh, Sinead
DAILEY Dan

DALTON Timothy
DAMONE Vic
DANSON Ted
DARREN James
DAVIES Alan, Rupert, Windsor
DAWSON Anna
DECKER Diana
DEL RIO Dolores
DENHAM Maurice
DE NIRO Robert
DENNIS Stefan
DE SICA Vittorio
DEVANE William
DEVINE Andy
DEVITO Danny
DEXTER Brad
DIBLEY Janet
DILLER Phyllis
DILLON Matt
DOBSON Anita
DRIVER Betty
DUMONT Margaret
DUNCAN Archie
DURBIN Deanna
EKBERG Anita
EKLAND Britt
ESMOND Carl
FARGAS Antonio
FARROW Mia
FERRER José, Mel
FERRIS Pam
FIELDS Dame Gracie, WC
FINLAY Frank
FINNEY Albert
FISHER Carrie, Gregor
FORBES Bryan
FORMBY George

FOSTER Barry, Jodie, Julia
FOWLDS Derek
FOWLER Harry
FRASER Bill, Liz, Ronald
FRENCH Dawn
FULLER Leslie
GAMBON Sir Michael
GARNER James
GARSON Greer
GAYNOR Janet, Mitzi
GEESON Judy, Sally
GEORGE Susan
GIBSON Henry, Mel
GLASER Paul Michael
GLOVER Brian, Julian
GORCEY Leo
GORDON Gale, Hannah, Mary, Noele
GORING Marius
GRABLE Betty
GRAVES Peter
GREENE Lorne, Richard
GUYLER Deryck
GWYNNE Fred, Haydn
HAGMAN Larry
HAMILL Mark
HANLEY Jenny, Jimmy
HANNAH Daryl, John
HARDIN Ty
HARKER Susannah
HARLOW Jean
HARPER Gerald, Jessica, Valerie
HARRIS Julie, Richard
HARVEY Jan, Laurence
HAVERS Nigel
HAYDEN Sterling
HAYTER James

HEDLEY Jack
HEDREN Tippi
HEFLIN Van
HEMPEL Anouska
HENDRY Ian
HENSON Gladys, Nicky
HEPTON Bernard
HESTON Charlton
HILLER Dame Wendy
HOBSON Valerie
HOLDEN Amanda, Fay,
    William
HOWARD Arthur, Leslie,
    Ron, Trevor
HOWERD Frankie
HUDSON Rock
HUGHES Geoffrey,
    Nerys, Wendy
HUNTER Holly, Ian,
    Russell, Tab
HUSSEY Olivia, Ruth
HUSTON Walter
HUTTON Betty
INGRAM Rex
IRVING Sir Henry
JACOBI Sir Derek
JARVIS Martin
JESSEL George
JOLSON Al
JOSEPH Lesley
KARLIN Miriam
KEATON Buster, Diane
KEELER Ruby
KENDAL Felicity
KIDMAN Nicole
KIRWAN Dervla
KRUGER Hardy
KUDROW Lisa

LAMARR Hedy
LAMOUR Dorothy
LANDAU Martin
LANDEN Dinsdale
LANDON Michael
LATHAM Philip
LAUREL Stan
LAURIE Hugh, John, Piper
LAWSON Denis, Wilfrid
LAYTON George
LEMMON Jack
LENSKA Rula
LESLIE Joan
LESSER Anton
LESTER Mark
LEVANT Oscar
LILLIE Beatrice
LINDEN Jennie
LIPMAN Maureen
LISTER Moira
LUGOSI Béla
LUMLEY Joanna
LUNGHI Cherie
LUPINO Ida
MACKAY Fulton
MACNEE Patrick
MACRAE Duncan
MAJORS Lee
MALDEN Karl
MALONE Dorothy
MARTIN Dean, Mary
    Millicent, Pamela Sue,
    Steve
MARVIN Lee
MASSEY Anna, Raymond
MATURE Victor
MAYALL Rik
MCCREA Joel

MCEWAN Geraldine
MCKERN Leo
MEDWIN Michael
MENJOU Adolphe
MERMAN Ethel
MERVYN William
MIDLER Bette
MIRREN Dame Helen
MONROE Marilyn
MOREAU Jeanne
MORELL André
MORGAN Dermot,
    Frank, Garfield
MORLEY Robert
MORRIS Chester, Lana
MORROW Vic
MOSTEL Zero
MULLEN Barbara
MURPHY Audie, Brian,
    Eddie, George
MURRAY Barbara, Bill,
    Don
MURTON Lionel
NAPIER Alan
NEAGLE Dame Anna
NEESON Liam
NELSON Ed, Gene
NEWLEY Anthony
NEWMAN Barry,
    Nanette, Paul
NEWTON Robert
NOIRET Philippe
NORTON Alex
OBERON Merle
O'BRIAN Hugh
O'BRIEN Edmond,
    Margaret, Pat, Richard
OGILVY Ian

O'KEEFE Dennis
O'TOOLE Peter
PACINO Al
PAGETT Nicola
PALMER Geoffrey, Lilli
PARISH Sarah
PARKER Cecil
PARTON Dolly
PICKUP Ronald
PIERCE David Hyde
PITHEY Wensley
PLANER Nigel
PORTER Eric, Nyree
  Dawn
POWELL Dick, Jane,
  Robert
POWERS Stefanie
PROWSE Juliet
PURDOM Edmund
QUALEN John
QUAYLE Anna,
  Sir Anthony
QUIRKE Pauline
RAINER Luise
REAGAN Ronald
REDMAN Amanda,
  Joyce
REEVES Keanu, Kynaston
REINER Carl
REMICK Lee
RENNIE Michael
RHODES Erik, Marjorie
RIDGES Stanley
RIDLEY Arnold
RIPLEY Fay
RITTER Tex, Thelma
ROACHE Linus,
  William

ROBSON Dame Flora,
  Linda, Mark, May
ROGERS Ginger, Roy,
  Will
ROLAND Gilbert
ROMAIN Yvonne
ROMERO Cesar
ROONEY Mickey
ROURKE Mickey
SALLIS Peter
SCALES Prunella
SCHELL Maria,
  Maximilian
SEAGAL Steven
SEWELL George
SHARIF Omar
SHINER Ronald
SIDNEY Sylvia
SINDEN Sir Donald
SINGER Campbell
SLATER John
SLOANE Everett
SOMMER Elke
SPACEK Sissy
SPACEY Kevin
STEELE Tommy
ST JOHN Jill
STREEP Meryl
STRIDE John
STRONG Gwyneth
STUBBS Una
SUCHET David
SUGDEN Mollie
SUZMAN Janet
SWAYZE Patrick
TAFLER Sidney
TAYLOR Elizabeth, Robert
TEARLE Sir Godfrey

TEMPLE Shirley
TEWSON Josephine
THORNE Angela
TOBIAS George, Oliver
TOMLIN Lily
TOM MIX
TREVOR Claire
TUCKER Forrest, Sophie
TURNER Kathleen, Lana
TURPIN Ben
TWIGGY
TYZACK Margaret
ULLMAN Tracey
URECAL Minerva
VALLEE Rudy
VARNEY Reg
VAUGHN Robert
VERNON Richard
VOIGHT Jon
WAGNER Lindsay, Robert
WALKER Clint
WALTER Harriet
WARNER David, HB, Jack
WATSON Jack, Wylie
WATTIS Richard
WAXMAN Al
WEAVER Dennis,
  Sigourney
WELLES Orson
WERNER Oskar
WHITTY Dame May
WILCOX Paula
WILDER Gene
WILLIS Bruce
WILSON Richard
WILTON Penelope
WINGER Debra
WISDOM Sir Norman

WOLFIT Sir Donald
WRIGHT Teresa
WYMARK Patrick
WYNTER Dana
YUN-FAT Chow
ZADORA Pia

7
ABRAHAM F Murray
ACKLAND Joss
AGUTTER Jenny
ALDO RAY
ALLGOOD Sara
ALLYSON June
ANDRESS Ursula
ANDREWS Anthony,
   Dana, Harry, Dame Julie
ANISTON Jennifer
ANN BELL
ANN TODD
ARLETTY
ASKWITH Robin
ASTAIRE Fred
AYKROYD Dan
BABCOCK Barbara
BAINTER Fay
BALFOUR Michael
BASTEDO Alexandra
BAYLDON Geoffrey
BEACHAM Stephanie
BELLAMY Ralph
BENIGNI Roberto
BEN LYON
BENNETT Hywel, Jill,
   Joan
BERGMAN Ingrid
BINOCHE Juliette
BLAKELY Colin

BLESSED Brian
BLETHYN Brenda
BLOCKER Dan
BOB HOPE
BOB PECK
BOB TODD
BO DEREK
BOGARDE Sir Dirk
BOTTOMS Timothy
BOUCHET Barbara
BRACKEN Eddie
BRANAGH Kenneth
BRENNAN Walter
BRIDGES Beau, Jeff,
   Lloyd
BRITTON Tony
BRONSON Charles
BROSNAN Pierce
BRYNNER Yul
BUTTONS Red
CALHERN Louis
CALHOUN Rory
CALLARD Beverley
CALVERT Phyllis
CAMERON Rod
CARGILL Patrick
CARLYLE Robert
CARROLL Diahann, Leo
CHAPLIN Sir Charles
   (Charlie), Syd
CILENTO Diane
CLOONEY George
COLBERT Claudette
COLLINS Joan, Lewis,
   Michelle, Pauline, Ray
COLONNA Jerry
COMPTON Fay
CONKLIN Chester

CONNERY Jason,
   Sir Sean
CONNORS Chuck
CORBETT Harry H
CRANHAM Kenneth
CROSBIE Annette
CUSHING Peter
DALTREY Roger
DANEMAN Paul
DANIELL Henry
DANIELS Bebe
DARNELL Linda
DAVISON Peter
DE HAVEN Gloria
DENEUVE Catherine
DENISON Michael
DONOVAN Jason
DOTRICE Karen,
   Michele, Roy
DOUGLAS Angela, Jack,
   Kirk, Melvyn, Michael
DRESDEL Sonia
DUNAWAY Faye
DURANTE Jimmy
DUTTINE John
ED ASNER
EDWARDS Glynn,
   Jimmy, Vince
EE CLIVE
ELLIOTT Denholm
ELPHICK Michael
ESTRADA Erik
FANTONI Sergio
FARRELL Glenda
FAWCETT Farrah
FAY WRAY
FELDMAN Marty
FIENNES Joseph, Ralph

FIRBANK Ann
FLEMING Rhonda
FORREST Steve
FORSYTH Brigit
FRANCIS Anne, Clive,
  Jan, Kay, Raymond
FRAWLEY William
FREEMAN Morgan
FRICKER Brenda
GARDNER Ava
GARLAND Judy
GAZZARA Ben
GIELGUD Sir John
GILBERT John
GINGOLD Hermione
GLEASON Jackie
GODDARD Liza, Paulette
GODSELL Vanda
GRAHAME Gloria
GRAMMER Kelsey
GRANGER Stewart
GRAYSON Kathryn
GREGORY James
GREGSON John
GRIFFIN Angela
GUTHRIE Arlo
HACKMAN Gene
HAMMOND Kay
HANCOCK Sheila
HARDING Ann
HAWKINS Jack
HAWTREY Charles
HAYWARD Susan
HELMOND Katherine
HENREID Paul
HEPBURN Audrey,
  Katharine
HEYWOOD Anne

HICKSON Joan
HOFFMAN Dustin
HOMOLKA Oscar
HOPKINS Sir Anthony,
  Bo
HORDERN Sir Michael
HOSKINS Bob
HOUSTON Donald,
  Glyn, Renée
HOWELLS Ursula
HOWLETT Noël
HULBERT Jack
HUNTLEY Raymond
IAN HOLM Sir
IRELAND Jill, John
JACKSON Glenda
  Gordon, Samuel L
JACQUES Hattie
JAMESON Louise
JANSSEN David
JAYSTON Michael
JENKINS Megs
JILL DAY
JIM DALE
JOHNSON Dame Celia,
  Don, Van
JOURDAN Louis
JUDE LAW
JUDY LOE
JURGENS Curt
JUSTICE James Robertson
KARLOFF Boris
KENDALL Kay, Suzy
KENNEDY Arthur,
  George
KINNEAR Roy
KITCHEN Michael
KOSSOFF David

KRISTEL Sylvia
LANGDON Harry
LAZENBY George
LEBLANC Matt
LEO GENN
LINDSAY Robert
LIVESEY Roger
LOMBARD Carole
MACGRAW Ali
MADDERN Victor
MADONNA
MAE WEST
MAGNANI Anna
MAHARIS George
MARSDEN Roy
MATTHAU Walter
MAXWELL Lois
MAYNARD Bill
MCCOWEN Alec
MCGUIRE Dorothy
MCKENNA Virginia
MCMANUS Mark
MCQUEEN Steve
MCSHANE Ian
MEG RYAN
MERCIER Sheila
MICHELL Keith
MILLAND Ray
MINOGUE Kylie
MIRANDA Carmen
MITCHUM Robert
MONTAND Yves
MULLARD Arthur
NEDWELL Robin
NESBITT Derren, James
NETTLES John
NEVILLE John
NICHOLS Dandy

NOVARRO Ramon
O'CONNOR Donald, Una
O'HANLON Ardal
OLIVIER Lord Laurence
ORCHARD Julian
PALANCE Jack
PALTROW Gwyneth
PARKINS Barbara
PATRICK Nigel
PEARSON Neil
PEPPARD George
PERKINS Anthony
PERREAU Gigi
PERTWEE Bill, Jon
PHOENIX Pat
PICKLES Wilfred
PIDGEON Walter
PLUMMER Christopher
POITIER Sidney
POLLARD Su
PORTMAN Eric
PRESLEY Elvis
PRESTON Robert
PRINGLE Bryan
PROVINE Dorothy
QUENTIN Caroline
QUILLEY Denis
RANDALL Joan, Leslie, Tony
RANDELL Ron
RAY TEAL
REDFORD Robert
RENALDO Duncan
RICHARD Sir Cliff, Wendy
RICKMAN Alan
RINGHAM John
RIP TORN

RITCHIE June
ROBARDS Jason
ROBERTS Julia, Rachel
ROBESON Paul
ROB LOWE
RODGERS Anton
ROY HUDD
RUGGLES Charles
RUSSELL Jane, Rosalind
SAM KYDD
SANDERS George
SARGENT Dick
SAVALAS Telly
SAWALHA Julia
SELLARS Elizabeth
SELLECK Tom
SELLERS Peter
SEYMOUR Jane
SHATNER William
SHEARER Moira, Norma
SHELLEY Barbara
SHIELDS Arthur, Brooke
SILVERA Carmen
SILVERS Phil
SIMMONS Jean
SIMPSON Bill
SINATRA Frank
SKELTON Red
SOTHERN Ann
STEIGER Rod
STEVENS Connie, Ronnie, Stella
STEWART James, Patrick
STRITCH Elaine
SUE LYON
SWANSON Gloria
TAMBLYN Russ
TARBUCK Liza

TEMPEST Dame Marie
THORSON Linda
TIERNEY Gene
TIMOTHY Christopher
TIM ROTH
TOM BELL
TRAVERS Bill
ULLMANN Liv
USTINOV Sir Peter
VALLONE Raf
VAN DYKE Dick
VAUGHAN Peter
VENTHAM Wanda
WALLACE Julie T
WALLACH Eli
WALTERS Julie, Thorley
WARRICK Ruth
WATFORD Gwen
WATLING Jack
WELLAND Colin
WHATELY Kevin
WHITING Leonard
WHITMAN Stuart
WIDMARK Richard
WILDING Michael
WILL HAY
WINDSOR Barbara, Frank
WINKLER Henry
WINSLET Kate
WINTERS Shelley
WITHERS Googie
WOOLLEY Monty
YARDLEY Stephen

8
ADAM WEST
ALAN ALDA
ALAN HALE

ALAN LADD
ALBRIGHT Hardie
ALDERTON John
AL JOLSON
AL PACINO
ALVARADO Don, Trini
AL WAXMAN
ANDERSON Barbara,
  Eddie, Jean,
  Dame Judith, Warner
ANN BLYTH
ANNE REID
ARBUCKLE Fatty
ART MALIK
ASHCROFT Dame Peggy
BADDELEY Angela
BANCROFT Anne
BANDERAS Antonio
BANERJEE Victor
BANKHEAD Tallulah
BASEHART Richard
BASINGER Kim
BEN CROSS
BENEDICT Billy, Dirk
BERT LAHR
BICKFORD Charles
BILL OWEN
BLACKMAN Honor
BLONDELL Joan
BORGNINE Ernest
BRAMBELL Wilfrid
BRESSLAW Bernard
BRIAN RIX Lord
BROMBERG J Edward
BRUCE LEE
BUCHANAN Colin,
  Edgar, Jack
BURL IVES

BURT WARD
CALDICOT Richard
CAMPBELL Cheryl
CAPUCINE
CARRILLO Leo
CAVANAGH Paul
CAZENOVE Christopher
CHAKIRIS George
CHANDLER Helen, Jeff
CHANNING Carol
CHARISSE Cyd
CHRISTIE Julie
CLARA BOW
CLEMENTS Sir John
COLLEANO Bonar
COLTRANE Robbie
CONNELLY Jennifer
CONNOLLY Walter
COSTELLO Lou
CRANITCH Lorcan
CRAWFORD Broderick,
  Joan, Michael
CRIBBINS Bernard
CUMMINGS Robert
DANIELLE Suzanne
DAVID YIP
DAY-LEWIS Daniel
DE LA TOUR Frances
DESMONDE Jerry
DIETRICH Marlene
DIFFRING Anton
DONNELLY Ruth
DORIS DAY
DRESSLER Marie
DREYFUSS Richard
DUCHOVNY David
EASTWOOD Clint
ED NELSON

ERIC IDLE
ERICKSON Leif
EVA GABOR
EVE ARDEN
FIELDING Fenella
FLANNERY Susan
FONTAINE Joan
FORSYTHE John
FRANKLYN William
GASCOINE Jill
GIG YOUNG
GOLDBERG Whoopi
GOODYEAR Julie
GRANTHAM Leslie
GRENFELL Joyce
GRIFFITH Hugh
GUARDINO Harry
GUINNESS Sir Alec
HAGGERTY Dan
HALLIDAY John
HAMILTON George
HARRISON Kathleen,
  Sir Rex
HARTNELL William
HAYWORTH Rita
HB WARNER
HELPMANN Sir Robert
HEMMINGS David
HOLLIDAY Judy
HOLLOWAY Stanley
HOUSEMAN John
JACK ELAM
JACK LORD
JACK WEBB
JACK WILD
JAMES FOX
JEAN BOHT
JEAN KENT

JEAN MUIR
JEFFRIES Lionel
JOAN SIMS
JOHN HURT
JOHN RYAN
JOHNSTON Sue
JOHN THAW
JULIE EGE
KAY WALSH
KELLAWAY Cecil
KEN STOTT
KIM NOVAK
KINGSLEY Sir Ben
LANGFORD Bonnie
LANSBURY Angela
LAUGHTON Charles
LAVENDER Ian
LAVERICK June
LAWRENCE Gertrude
LEE GRANT
LEE J COBB
LEE TRACY
LEIGHTON Margaret
LEON AMES
LEW AYRES
LIZ SMITH
LOCKHART Gene, June
LOCKWOOD Julia,
  Margaret
LYNN BARI
MACLAINE Shirley
MACREADY George
MALAHIDE Patrick
MATTHEWS AE, Francis,
  Jessie
MCCALLUM David
MCDOWALL Betty,
  Roddy

MCFADDEN Steve
MCGOOHAN Patrick
MCGREGOR Ewan
MCKELLEN Sir Ian
MCKENZIE Julia
MCLAGLEN Victor
MEG TILLY
MEL TORMÉ
MERCOURI Melina
MEREDITH Burgess
MINNELLI Liza
MITCHELL Warren
MYRNA LOY
NELLIGAN Kate
NICHOLAS Paul
NICHOLLS Sue
O'FARRELL Bernadette
PAUL MUNI
PERCIVAL Lance
PHILLIPS Conrad,
  Leslie, Sian
PICKFORD Mary
PRENTISS Paula
RAFFERTY Chips
RAMPLING Charlotte
RATHBONE Basil
RAY SMITH
REDGRAVE Corin,
  Jemma, Lynn,
  Sir Michael, Vanessa
REYNOLDS Burt, Debbie
ROBINSON Edward G,
  Tony
RON MOODY
ROSSITER Leonard
ROSS KEMP
ROWLANDS Patsy
SAM GROOM

SAM JAFFE
SAM KELLY
SAM NEILL
SARANDON Susan
SARRAZIN Michael
SAUNDERS Jennifer
SCHEIDER Roy
SCHRODER Rick
SCOFIELD Paul
SEAGROVE Jenny
SEAN PENN
SEINFELD Jerry
SESSIONS John
SHEPHERD Cybill, Jack
SHERIDAN Ann, Dinah
SID FIELD
SID JAMES
SIGNORET Simone
SPINETTI Victor
STALLONE Sylvester
STANDING Sir Guy, John
STANWYCK Barbara
STEADMAN Alison
STERLING Jan
SUE LLOYD
TALMADGE Norma
THOMPSON Emma, Jack
THOMSETT Sally
THORBURN June
THORNTON Frank
TIM HEALY
TINGWELL Charles
TOM BAKER
TOM CONTI
TOM EWELL
TOM HANKS
TOM HULCE
TRAVOLTA John

TY HARDIN
TYNE DALY
URQUHART Robert
VAN CLEEF Lee
VAN DOREN Mamie
VILLIERS James
WARD BOND
WATERMAN Dennis
WC FIELDS
WHEATLEY Alan
WHITELAW Billie
WILLIAMS Esther,
  Kenneth, Michael,
  Robin, Simon
WINFIELD Paul
WINSTONE Ray
WOODWARD Edward,
  Joanne
WYNGARDE Peter

9

ADAM FAITH
ALAN ARKIN
ALAN BATES Sir
ALAN DOBIE
ALAN YOUNG
ALEXANDER Jean,
  Terence
ALFIE BASS
ALICE FAYE
ANDERSSON Bibi
ARMSTRONG Alun,
  Robert
ART CARNEY
BARKWORTH Peter
BARRYMORE Drew,
  Ethel, John, Lionel
BAXENDALE Helen

BEL GEDDES Barbara
BEN TURPIN
BERNHARDT Sarah
BERYL REID
BILL BIXBY
BILL COSBY
BLANCHETT Cate
BO HOPKINS
BROADBENT Jim
BUD ABBOTT
BURT KWOUK
CARDINALE Claudia
CARRADINE David, John,
  Keith
CARY GRANT
CHEVALIER Maurice
CHICO MARX
CHURCHILL Diana, Sarah
CLIVE DUNN
CLIVE OWEN
COLBOURNE Maurice
COURTENAY Tom
CRUTCHLEY Rosalie
DALE EVANS
DAN DAILEY
DANNY KAYE
DAVENPORT Harry, Jack,
  Nigel
DAVID SOUL
DEREK BOND
DEREK FARR
DESI ARNAZ
DIANA DORS
DIANA RIGG Dame
DIANE KEEN
DICKINSON Angie,
  Sandra
DON AMECHE

DON MURRAY
DONNA REED
DORA BRYAN
DORIS HARE
ECCLESTON Christopher
EDD BYRNES
EDDINGTON Paul
EDIE ADAMS
EDMONDSON Adrian
EDWARD FOX
EMILIA FOX
ERIC BLORE
ERIC SYKES
EVA BARTOK
EWEN SOLON
FAIRBANKS Douglas
FAIRCHILD Morgan
FAY HOLDEN
FAY RIPLEY
FERNANDEL
FLOCKHART Calista
FRED CLARK
FREDERICK Lynne
FULLERTON Fiona
GALE STORM
GARY OLSEN
GENE AUTRY
GENE BARRY
GENE KELLY
GEORGESON Tom
GERT FROBE
GINA MCKEE
GLENN FORD
GREENWOOD Joan
GRETA GYNT
GRIFFITHS Richard
GUILLAUME Robert
GUMMO MARX

HAMPSHIRE Susan
HARDWICKE Sir Cedric
HARPO MARX
HAWTHORNE Sir Nigel
HELEN HUNT
HENDERSON Don
HOLLY AIRD
HOPE LANGE
HUGH GRANT
HUNNICUTT Gayle
HUNTZ HALL
HYDE-WHITE Wilfrid
IAN BANNEN
IAN HENDRY
IAN HUNTER
IAN OGILVY
IDA LUPINO
ISLA BLAIR
JACK OAKIE
JAMES CAAN
JAMES DEAN
JANE ASHER
JANE FONDA
JANE WYATT
JANE WYMAN
JAN HARVEY
JEAN GABIN
JEAN HAGEN
JEAN MARSH
JIM BACKUS
JIM CARREY
JIMMY NAIL
JOAN DAVIS
JOE E BROWN
JOHANSSON Scarlett
JOHN DEREK
JOHN INMAN
JOHN MILLS Sir

JOHN P RYAN
JOHN SAXON
JOHN WAYNE
JON VOIGHT
JUDI DENCH Dame
JUDY DAVIS
JUNE BROWN
KATE O'MARA
KELLERMAN Sally
KERCHEVAL Ken
KNIGHTLEY Keira
LANCASTER Burt
LAPOTAIRE Jane
LEE MAJORS
LEE MARVIN
LEE REMICK
LEO GORCEY
LEO MCKERN
LESLIE ASH
LEX BARKER
LINDA GRAY
LIZ FRASER
LLOYD-PACK Roger
LON CHANEY
LYNDHURST Nicholas
MACARTHUR Charles,
   James
MACDOWELL Andie
MACMURRAY Fred
MANSFIELD Jayne
MARGOLYES Miriam
MARY ASTOR
MAY ROBSON
MAY WHITTY Dame
MCINNERNY Tim
MEL FERRER
MEL GIBSON
MIA FARROW

MILO O'SHEA
MOOREHEAD Agnes
MORRISSEY Neil
NANCY KWAN
NED BEATTY
NETTLETON Lois
NICHOLSON Jack
NICK BERRY
NICK NOLTE
NOAH BEERY
O'SULLIVAN Richard
OUTHWAITE Tamzin
OWEN NARES
PAM FERRIS
PAT COOMBS
PAT O'BRIEN
PAUL HOGAN
PAUL KELLY
PAUL LUKAS
PAUL SHANE
PETER EGAN
PETER FALK
PIA ZADORA
PLEASENCE Donald
PLOWRIGHT Joan
PRINCIPAL Victoria
RALPH LYNN
RAY BOLGER
RAY BROOKS
REG VARNEY
REX INGRAM
RIK MAYALL
ROBERTSON Cliff, Dale
RON HOWARD
ROUTLEDGE Patricia
ROY ROGERS
RUTH MADOC
RUTH ROMAN

RYAN O'NEAL
SANDERSON Joan
SANDRA DEE
SCHNEIDER Romy
SCHWIMMER David
SHEILA SIM
SIMON WARD
SLAUGHTER Tod
ST CLEMENT Pam
STOCKWELL Dean
STREISAND Barbra
STRUTHERS Sally
SU POLLARD
TAB HUNTER
TAYLFORTH Gillian
TED DANSON
TEX RITTER
THEDA BARA
THORA HIRD Dame
THORNDIKE Dame
    Sybil
THRELFALL David
TODD CARTY
TOM BOSLEY
TOM CRUISE
TOMLINSON David,
    Ricky
TONY DOYLE
TONY SELBY
TREVOR EVE
TROUGHTON Patrick
UNA STUBBS
VALENTINE Anthony,
    Karen
VALENTINO Rudolph
VAN HEFLIN
VAN PATTEN Dick,
    Joyce

VIC DAMONE
VIC MORROW
VIRNA LISI
WANAMAKER Zoë
WATERSTON Sam
WHITFIELD June
WILKINSON Tom
WILL SMITH
ZASU PITTS
ZEPPO MARX
ZETA-JONES Catherine
ZIMBALIST Efrem

10
AE MATTHEWS
ALAIN DELON
ALAN DAVIES
ALAN NAPIER
ALEX NORTON
ALI MACGRAW
ALLAN JONES
ANDY DEVINE
ANNA DAWSON
ANNA MASSEY
ANNA NEAGLE Dame
ANNA QUAYLE
ANNE BAXTER
ANN FIRBANK
ANN HARDING
ANN-MARGRET
ANN SOTHERN
ANOUK AIMÉE
ANTONY SHER Sir
ARLENE DAHL
ARTHUR LOWE
AVA GARDNER
BARRY EVANS
BARRY MORSE

BECKINSALE Kate,
    Richard
BÉLA LUGOSI
BELINDA LEE
BELLINGHAM Lynda
BEN GAZZARA
BERNARD LEE
BETTE DAVIS
BETTY FIELD
BILL FRASER
BILL MURRAY
BING CROSBY
BOBBY DARIN
BOBBY HOWES
BOB HOSKINS
BRAD DEXTER
BRIAN WILDE
BRUCE SETON Sir
BUDDY EBSEN
CARL ESMOND
CARL REINER
CARMICHAEL Ian
CAROL WHITE
CASSAVETES John
CELIA IMRIE
CHERYL LADD
CHEVY CHASE
CHOW YUN-FAT
CLARK GABLE
CLIVE BROOK
COLIN BAKER
COLIN FIRTH
DANA WYNTER
DAN AYKROYD
DAN BLOCKER
DAVID BOWIE
DAVID ESSEX
DAVID JASON Sir

DAVID LODGE
DAVID MORSE
DAVID NIVEN
DAWN ADDAMS
DAWN FRENCH
DEAN MARTIN
DEREK NIMMO
DIANA QUICK
DICK POWELL
DONALD GRAY
DON JOHNSON
DRINKWATER Carol
DULCIE GRAY
DYAN CANNON
EDITH EVANS Dame
ELI WALLACH
ELKE SOMMER
ELLEN TERRY Dame
ERIC BARKER
ERIC PORTER
ERIK CHITTY
ERIK RHODES
ERROL FLYNN
ESMA CANNON
EVELYN LAYE
FAY BAINTER
FAY COMPTON
FERDY MAYNE
FITZGERALD Barry
FRANCO NERO
FRED GWYNNE
GALE GORDON
GARETH HUNT
GARY COOPER
GENE NELSON
GENE WILDER
GEORGE COLE
GEORGE RAFT

GLENN CLOSE
GLORIA JEAN
GOLDIE HAWN
GORDEN KAYE
GRACE KELLY
GRETA GARBO
HALLE BERRY
HASSELHOFF David
HAZEL COURT
HEDY LAMARR
HELEN HAYES
HELEN MORSE
HENRY FONDA
HENRY SILVA
HERBERT LOM
HOWARD KEEL
HUGH LAURIE
HUGH O'BRIAN
IAN MCSHANE
IRENE DUNNE
IRENE HANDL
IRENE PAPAS
JACK CARSON
JACK HEDLEY
JACK LEMMON
JACK WARNER
JACK WATSON
JAMES BOLAM
JAMES GROUT
JAMES MASON
JANE BIRKIN
JANE POWELL
JANET LEIGH
JANET MUNRO
JAN FRANCIS
JEAN ARTHUR
JEAN HARLOW
JERRY LEWIS

JILL BROWNE
JILL ST JOHN
JIMMY JEWEL
JOAN LESLIE
JOEL MCCREA
JOHN ARNATT
JOHN BARRON
JOHN CLEESE
JOHN HANNAH
JOHN LAURIE
JOHNNY DEPP
JOHN QUALEN
JOHN SLATER
JOHN STRIDE
JON PERTWEE
JOSÉ FERRER
JOYCE CAREY
JUDY GEESON
JULIE ADAMS
KAREN BLACK
KARL MALDEN
KATHY BURKE
KATHY STAFF
KAY FRANCIS
KAY HAMMOND
KAY KENDALL
KEVIN KLINE
LANA MORRIS
LANA TURNER
LANCASHIRE Sarah
LANCHESTER Elsa
LARRY PARKS
LE MESURIER John
LEO CARROLL
LE VAILLANT Nigel
LEWIS STONE
LIAM NEESON
LILY TOMLIN

LINDA EVANS
LISA KUDROW
LIV ULLMANN
LLOYD NOLAN
LOTTE LENYA
LUPINO LANE
LYNDA BARON
MARIO LANZA
MARK HAMILL
MARK LESTER
MARK ROBSON
MARTIN KEMP
MARTIN SHAW
MARY GORDON
MARY MARTIN
MATT DILLON
MIDDLEMASS Frank
MISCHA AUER
MONTGOMERY Elizabeth
NELSON EDDY
NIGEL BRUCE
NIGEL STOCK
NOËL COWARD Sir
OLIVER REED
OMAR SHARIF
PAT PHOENIX
PAUL NEWMAN
PEGGY MOUNT
PENHALIGON Susan
PETER BYRNE
PETER FINCH
PETER FONDA
PETER JONES
PETER LORRE
PIER ANGELI
PORTER HALL
RACHEL WARD
RAF VALLONE

RALPH BATES
RALPH WAITE
RAY COLLINS
RAY MILLAND
RED BUTTONS
RED SKELTON
RICHARDSON Ian, Joely,
    Miranda, Natasha,
    Sir Ralph
ROBERT CULP
ROBERT LANG
ROBERT RYAN
ROBERT SHAW
ROBERT WARD
ROCK HUDSON
ROD CAMERON
ROD STEIGER
ROGER MOORE Sir
RONALD ADAM
RON RANDELL
ROSSINGTON Jane
ROY DOTRICE
ROY KINNEAR
ROY MARSDEN
RUBY KEELER
RUDY VALLEE
RULA LENSKA
RUTHERFORD
    Dame Margaret
RUTH HUSSEY
SALLY FIELD
SAMMY DAVIS
SARAH MILES
SHARON TATE
SONJA HENIE
SONNIE HALE
STACY KEACH
STAN LAUREL

STEPHEN FRY
STEPHENSON Henry,
    Pamela
SUTHERLAND Donald,
    Kiefer
SYD CHAPLIN
SYLVIA SIMS
TATUM O'NEAL
TERRY SCOTT
TOMPKINSON Stephen
TOM SELLECK
TONY ANHOLT
TONY CURTIS
TUSHINGHAM Rita
UNA O'CONNOR
VAN JOHNSON
WALTER ABEL
WASHINGTON Denzel
WENDY CRAIG
WILLIAMSON Nicol
WILL ROGERS
WOODY ALLEN
YUL BRYNNER
ZERO MOSTEL
ZETTERLING Mai

11
ALAN RICKMAN
ALASTAIR SIM
ALEC MCCOWEN
ALFRED BURKE
ALFRED MARKS
AMANDA BLAKE
ANDRÉ MORELL
ANDREW SACHS
ANITA DOBSON
ANITA EKBERG
ANNA MAGNANI

ANNE FRANCIS
ANNE HEYWOOD
ANN SHERIDAN
ANTON LESSER
ARLO GUTHRIE
ARTHUR LUCAN
AUDIE MURPHY
AVRIL ANGERS
BARBARA BACH
BARBARA HALE
BARBARA KNOX
BARBARA LOTT
BARBARA RUSH
BARRACLOUGH Roy
BARRY FOSTER
BARRY NEWMAN
BARTHOLOMEW
  Freddie
BEAU BRIDGES
BEBE DANIELS
BELINDA LANG
BEN KINGSLEY Sir
BETTE MIDLER
BETTY DRIVER
BETTY GRABLE
BETTY HUTTON
BEULAH BONDI
BILL MAYNARD
BILL PERTWEE
BILL SIMPSON
BILL TRAVERS
BRENDA BRUCE
BRIAN AHERNE
BRIAN GLOVER
BRIAN MURPHY
BRITT EKLAND
BRUCE WILLIS
BRYAN FORBES

BUTTERWORTH Peter
CECIL PARKER
CESAR ROMERO
CHAMBERLAIN Richard
CLAIRE BLOOM
CLAUDE AKINS
CLAUDE RAINS
CLIFTON WEBB
CLINT WALKER
CONNIE BOOTH
CONRAD VEIDT
CORAL ATKINS
CORAL BROWNE
CORNEL WILDE
COURTNEIDGE
  Dame Cicely
CRUICKSHANK Andrew
CURT JURGENS
CUTHBERTSON Iain
CYD CHARISSE
CYRIL CUSACK
DANA ANDREWS
DAN HAGGERTY
DANIEL CRAIG
DANNY DEVITO
DARYL HANNAH
DAVID SUCHET
DAVID WARNER
DEBORAH KERR
DEBRA WINGER
DE HAVILLAND Olivia
DENIS LAWSON
DENNIS PRICE
DEREK FOWLDS
DEREK JACOBI Sir
DIANA DECKER
DIANE KEATON
DICK SARGENT

DICK VAN DYKE
DIRK BOGARDE Sir
DOLLY PARTON
DON ALVARADO
DUDLEY MOORE
EDDIE ALBERT
EDDIE CANTOR
EDDIE MURPHY
EDMUND GWENN
ELEANOR BRON
ERIC PORTMAN
ERIK ESTRADA
ETHEL MERMAN
FAYE DUNAWAY
FELIX AYLMER Sir
FLORA ROBSON Dame
FRANK BENSON Sir
FRANK FINLAY
FRANK MORGAN
FRED ASTAIRE
GEMMA CRAVEN
GENE HACKMAN
GENE TIERNEY
GEORGE BAKER
GEORGE BRENT
GEORGE BURNS
GEORGE SEGAL
GEORGE ZUCCO
GIGI PERREAU
GLYN HOUSTON
GLYNIS JOHNS
GRACIE ALLEN
GRAHAM STARK
GREENSTREET Sydney
GREER GARSON
GREGORY PECK
GROUCHO MARX
GWEN WATFORD

GUY STANDING Sir
HARDY KRUGER
HAROLD LLOYD
HARRY FOWLER
HAYDN GWYNNE
HAYLEY MILLS
HELEN CHERRY
HELEN MIRREN Dame
HENRY GIBSON
HENRY IRVING Sir
HERBERT TREE Sir
HILARY SWANK
HOLLY HUNTER
IAN LAVENDER
IAN MCKELLEN Sir
JACK DOUGLAS
JACK HAWKINS
JACK HULBERT
JACK PALANCE
JACK WATLING
JACQUES TATI
JAMES ARNESS
JAMES BROLIN
JAMES CAGNEY
JAMES COBURN
JAMES DARREN
JAMES GARNER
JAMES HAYTER
JANE RUSSELL
JANE SEYMOUR
JANET DIBLEY
JANET GAYNOR
JANET SUZMAN
JAN STERLING
JEAN SIMMONS
JEFF BRIDGES
JENNY HANLEY
JEREMY BRETT

JEREMY IRONS
JEREMY LLOYD
JEROME FLYNN
JESSIE RALPH
JILL BENNETT
JILL IRELAND
JIMMY HANLEY
JOAN BENNETT
JOAN COLLINS
JOAN HICKSON
JOAN RANDALL
JODIE FOSTER
JOHN DUTTINE
JOHN GIELGUD Sir
JOHN GILBERT
JOHN GREGSON
JOHN IRELAND
JOHN NETTLES
JOHN NEVILLE
JOHN RINGHAM
JOSS ACKLAND
JOYCE REDMAN
JUDY GARLAND
JULIA FOSTER
JULIE HARRIS
JULIET MILLS
JUNE ALLYSON
JUNE RITCHIE
KATE WINSLET
KEANU REEVES
KEITH BARRON
KENNETH COPE
KENNETH MORE
KEVIN SPACEY
KIM BASINGER
KIRK DOUGLAS
LARRY HAGMAN
LEE VAN CLEEF

LEO CARRILLO
LESLEY SHARP
LESLIE BANKS
LESLIE CARON
LETITIA DEAN
LEWIS CASSON Sir
LILLIAN GISH
LILLIAN ROTH
LILLI PALMER
LINDA ROBSON
LINUS ROACHE
LIZA GODDARD
LIZA TARBUCK
LOIS MAXWELL
LORETTA SWIT
LORNE GREENE
LOU COSTELLO
LUCILLE BALL
LUISE RAINER
LUTHER ADLER
LYNDA CARTER
MAGGIE SMITH Dame
MARCEL DALIO
MARIA AITKEN
MARIA SCHELL
MARK MCMANUS
MARTIN SHEEN
MASTROIANNI
   Marcello
MATT LEBLANC
MEGS JENKINS
MELVYN HAYES
MERLE OBERON
MERVYN JOHNS
MERVYN LE ROY
MERYL STREEP
MICHAEL J FOX
MICHAEL YORK

MILTON BERLE
MITZI GAYNOR
MOIRA LISTER
NATALIE WOOD
NEIL PEARSON
NERYS HUGHES
NIAMH CUSACK
NICKY HENSON
NICOLAS CAGE
NIGEL HAVERS
NIGEL PLANER
NOELE GORDON
NOËL HOWLETT
OLIVER HARDY
ORSON WELLES
OSCAR LEVANT
OSKAR WERNER
PATRICIA ROC
PATRICK BARR
PAULA WILCOX
PAUL DANEMAN
PAUL HENREID
PAUL ROBESON
PEARL BAILEY
PETER BOWLES
PETER GRAVES
PETER O'TOOLE
PETER SALLIS
PETULA CLARK
PHILIP MADOC
PHIL SILVERS
PIGOTT-SMITH Tim
PIPER LAURIE
RACHEL WEISZ
RAQUEL WELCH
RAYMOND BURR
RAY WINSTONE
REX HARRISON Sir

RICHARD EGAN
RICHARD GERE
RICHARD TODD
ROBERT DONAT
ROBERT HARDY
ROBERT STACK
ROBERT URICH
ROBERT YOUNG
ROBIN BAILEY
ROBSON GREEN
RODNEY BEWES
ROLAND YOUNG
RONALD LACEY
RORY CALHOUN
ROY SCHEIDER
RUSS TAMBLYN
RUTGER HAUER
RUTH WARRICK
SALLY GEESON
SARA ALLGOOD
SARAH PARISH
SCHILDKRAUT Joseph
SCOTT THOMAS Kristin
SEAN CONNERY Sir
SHARON GLESS
SHARON STONE
SIDNEY TOLER
SILVERHEELS Jay
SIMON CADELL
SIMON CALLOW
SIMONE SIMON
SISSY SPACEK
SONDERGAARD Gale
SOPHIA LOREN
STEPHEN BOYD
STEVE COOGAN
STEVE MARTIN
SUE JOHNSTON

SUE NICHOLLS
SUMMERFIELD Eleanor
SUSAN GEORGE
SUZY KENDALL
TERRY-THOMAS
TESSIE O'SHEA
TIMOTHY WEST
TIPPI HEDREN
TOMMY STEELE
TONY BRITTON
TONY RANDALL
TUESDAY WELD
TYRONE POWER
VALERIE LEON
VICTOR BUONO
VINCENT BALL
VIVIAN VANCE
VIVIEN LEIGH
VON STROHEIM Erich
WARNER OLAND
WARREN OATES
WEISSMULLER Johnny
WENDY HILLER Dame
WENDY HUGHES
WILLIAM BOYD
WINONA RYDER
WITHERSPOON Reese
WYLIE WATSON
YOOTHA JOYCE
YVES MONTAND
ZSA ZSA GABOR

12
ALAN WHEATLEY
ALBERT FINNEY
ALEC GUINNESS Sir
AMANDA BARRIE
AMANDA BURTON

AMANDA HOLDEN
AMANDA REDMAN
ANGELA THORNE
ANGHARAD REES
ANNE BANCROFT
ANTHONY BOOTH
ANTHONY QUINN
ANTHONY STEEL
ANTON RODGERS
ARCHIE DUNCAN
ARDAL O'HANLON
ARNOLD RIDLEY
ARTHUR HOWARD
ATTENBOROUGH
  Lord Richard
BARBARA FLYNN
BERNARD MILES Sir
BINNIE BARNES
BORIS KARLOFF
BRADLEY WALSH
BRIAN BLESSED
BRYAN PRINGLE
BURT REYNOLDS
BUSTER CRABBE
BUSTER KEATON
CARRIE FISHER
CARROLL BAKER
C AUBREY SMITH Sir
CELIA JOHNSON Dame
CHARLES BOYER
CHARLES DANCE
CHARLIE SHEEN
CHERIE LUNGHI
CHUCK CONNORS
CLAIRE TREVOR
CLAYTON MOORE
CLIFF RICHARD Sir
CLIVE FRANCIS

COLIN BLAKELY
COLIN WELLAND
COURTENEY COX
DANDY NICHOLS
DAVID JANSSEN
DAVID KOSSOFF
DEANNA DURBIN
DENIS QUILLEY
DENNIS O'KEEFE
DENNIS WEAVER
DERMOT MORGAN
DERVLA KIRWAN
DERYCK GUYLER
DIANE CILENTO
DIRK BENEDICT
DONALD SINDEN Sir
DONALD WOLFIT Sir
DON HENDERSON
DOROTHY TUTIN Dame
DUNCAN MACRAE
EDDIE BRACKEN
EDMOND O'BRIEN
EDMUND PURDOM
EDWARD ARNOLD
EILEEN ATKINS Dame
ELLIOTT GOULD
ELVIS PRESLEY
EMMA THOMPSON
EWAN MCGREGOR
FINLAY CURRIE
FRANCHOT TONE
FRANKIE LAINE
FRANK SINATRA
FRANK WINDSOR
FREDRIC MARCH
FULTON MACKAY
GENE LOCKHART
GEOFFREY RUSH

GEORGE ARLISS
GEORGE C SCOTT
GEORGE FORMBY
GEORGE JESSEL
GEORGE LAYTON
GEORGE MURPHY
GEORGE SEWELL
GEORGE TOBIAS
GEORGINA HALE
GERALD HARPER
GINGER ROGERS
GLADYS COOPER Dame
GLADYS HENSON
GLYNIS BARBER
GLYNN EDWARDS
GRACIE FIELDS Dame
GREGOR FISHER
GREGORY HINES
HANNAH GORDON
HARRISON FORD
HARRY ANDREWS
HARRY LANGDON
HEATHER SEARS
HENRY DANIELL
HENRY WINKLER
HUGH GRIFFITH
HYWEL BENNETT
JACK BUCHANAN
JACKIE COOGAN
JACK SHEPHERD
JACK THOMPSON
JAMES GREGORY
JAMES NESBITT
JAMES STEWART
JANETTE SCOTT
JASON CONNERY
JASON DONOVAN
JASON ROBARDS

J CARROL NAISH	JUNE THORBURN	MAUREEN O'HARA
JEAN ANDERSON	KAREN DOTRICE	MAUREEN PRIOR
JEANNE MOREAU	KATE NELLIGAN	MAURICE ELVEY
JEFF CHANDLER	KEITH MICHELL	MICHAEL CAINE Sir
JENNIE LINDEN	KEN KERCHEVAL	MICHAEL CRAIG
JENNIFER EHLE	KENNETH HAIGH	MICHAEL GOUGH
JENNIFER GREY	KEVIN WHATELY	MICHAEL PALIN
JENNY AGUTTER	KYLIE MINOGUE	MICHAEL PRAED
JERRY COLONNA	LAUREN BACALL	MICKEY ROONEY
JESSICA LANGE	LEIF ERICKSON	MICKEY ROURKE
JESSICA TANDY	LEONARD NIMOY	MILBURN STONE
JILL GASCOINE	LESLEY JOSEPH	MIRIAM KARLIN
JIM BROADBENT	LESLIE FULLER	MOIRA SHEARER
JIMMY DURANTE	LESLIE HOWARD	MOLLIE SUGDEN
JIMMY EDWARDS	LEWIS COLLINS	MONTY WOOLLEY
JOAN BLONDELL	LINDA DARNELL	NICHOLAS BALL
JOAN CRAWFORD	LINDA THORSON	NICOLA PAGETT
JOAN FONTAINE	LIONEL ATWILL	NICOLE KIDMAN
JOANNA LUMLEY	LIONEL MURTON	NIGEL PATRICK
JOHN ALDERTON	LIZA MINNELLI	NORMAN WISDOM Sir
JOHN CLEMENTS Sir	LLOYD BRIDGES	NORMA SHEARER
JOHN FORSYTHE	LOLLOBRIGIDA Gina	OLIVER TOBIAS
JOHN HALLIDAY	LORETTA YOUNG	OLIVIA HUSSEY
JOHN HOUSEMAN	LOUIS CALHERN	OSCAR HOMOLKA
JOHNNY BRIGGS	LOUIS JOURDAN	PAM ST CLEMENT
JOHN SESSIONS	LYNN REDGRAVE	PATRICIA NEAL
JOHN STANDING	MADELINE KAHN	PATRICK ALLEN
JOHN TRAVOLTA	MARIE TEMPEST Dame	PATRICK DUFFY
JOSEPH COTTEN	MARIUS GORING	PATRICK MAGEE
JUDY HOLLIDAY	MARJORIE MAIN	PATRICK MOWER
JULIAN GLOVER	MARLON BRANDO	PATRICK O'NEAL
JULIA ROBERTS	MARTIN BALSAM	PAUL CAVANAGH
JULIA SAWALHA	MARTIN CLUNES	PAULINE YATES
JULIE ANDREWS Dame	MARTIN JARVIS	PAUL NICHOLAS
JULIET PROWSE	MARTIN LANDAU	PAUL SCOFIELD
JULIE WALTERS	MARTY FELDMAN	PAUL WINFIELD
JUNE LAVERICK	MARY PICKFORD	PETER CUSHING
JUNE LOCKHART	MATTHEW PERRY	PETER DAVISON

PETER SELLERS
PETER USTINOV Sir
PETER VAUGHAN
PHILIP LATHAM
PHYLLIS LOGAN
RALPH BELLAMY
RALPH FIENNES
RAMON NOVARRO
REGINALD OWEN
RENÉE HOUSTON
RICHARD ARLEN
RICHARD BOONE
RICHARD CONTE
RICHARD PRYOR
RICK SCHRODER
RITA HAYWORTH
ROBERT BEATTY
ROBERT DE NIRO
ROBERT MORLEY
ROBERT NEWTON
ROBERT POWELL
ROBERT TAYLOR
ROBERT VAUGHN
ROBERT WAGNER
ROBIN ASKWITH
ROBIN NEDWELL
ROGER DALTREY
ROGER LIVESEY
ROLAND CULVER
RONALD COLMAN
RONALD FRASER
RONALD PICKUP
RONALD REAGAN
RONALD SHINER
RUPERT DAVIES
RUSSELL CROWE
RUTH DONNELLY
SAM WATERSTON

SHIRLEY EATON
SHIRLEY JONES
SIAN PHILLIPS
SIDNEY TAFLER
SINEAD CUSACK
SONIA DRESDEL
SOPHIE TUCKER
SPENCER TRACY
STANLEY BAKER Sir
STEFAN DENNIS
STEVE FORREST
STEVE MCQUEEN
STEVEN SEAGAL
SUSAN HAYWARD
SUSANNAH YORK
SYLVIA SIDNEY
TELLY SAVALAS
TERENCE RIGBY
TERENCE STAMP
TERESA WRIGHT
THELMA RITTER
TIM MCINNERNY
TIMOTHY SPALL
TOD SLAUGHTER
TOM COURTENAY
TOM GEORGESON
TOM WILKINSON
TONY ROBINSON
TRACEY ULLMAN
TREVOR HOWARD
VANDA GODSELL
VERONICA LAKE
VICTOR MATURE
VINCE EDWARDS
VINCENT PRICE
VIOLET CARSON
VIRGINIA MAYO
WALLACE BEERY

WALTER HUSTON
WANDA VENTHAM
WARNER BAXTER
WARREN BEATTY
WARREN CLARKE
WENDY RICHARD
WHITSUN-JONES Paul
WILLIAM GAUNT
WILLIAM LUCAS
YVONNE ARNAUD
YVONNE ROMAIN
ZACHARY SCOTT
ZOË WANAMAKER

13
ADOLPHE MENJOU
ADRIENNE CORRI
ADRIENNE POSTA
ALEXANDER KNOX
ALUN ARMSTRONG
ANGELA DOUGLAS
ANGELA GRIFFIN
ANGELINA JOLIE
ANNETTE BENING
ANOUSKA HEMPEL
ANTHONY NEWLEY
ANTHONY QUAYLE Sir
ANTON DIFFRING
ANTONIO FARGAS
ARTHUR KENNEDY
ARTHUR MULLARD
ARTHUR SHIELDS
AUDREY HEPBURN
BARBARA MULLEN
BARBARA MURRAY
BASIL RATHBONE
BERNARD HEPTON
BETTY MCDOWALL

BIBI ANDERSSON	EDDIE ANDERSON	IAN CARMICHAEL
BILLY BENEDICT	EDGAR BUCHANAN	IAN RICHARDSON
BONAR COLLEANO	ELAINE STRITCH	INGRID BERGMAN
BRENDA BLETHYN	EVA MARIE SAINT	JACK DAVENPORT
BRENDA FRICKER	EVERETT SLOANE	JACKIE GLEASON
BRIGIT FORSYTH	FARRAH FAWCETT	JACK NICHOLSON
BROOKE SHIELDS	FATTY ARBUCKLE	JAMES VILLIERS
BURT LANCASTER	FLORENCE BATES	JANE LAPOTAIRE
CANDICE BERGEN	FORREST TUCKER	JEAN ALEXANDER
CARMEN MIRANDA	FRANKIE AVALON	JEANNIE CARSON
CARMEN SILVERA	FRANKIE HOWERD	JEMMA REDGRAVE
CAROL CHANNING	FRANK THORNTON	JENNIFER JAYNE
CAROLE LOMBARD	FRED MCMURRAY	JENNIFER JONES
CATE BLANCHETT	GEORGE CLOONEY	JENNY SEAGROVE
CECIL KELLAWAY	GEORGE KENNEDY	JERRY DESMONDE
CHARLES COBURN	GEORGE LAZENBY	JERRY SEINFELD
CHESTER MORRIS	GEORGE MAHARIS	JESSICA HARPER
CHIPS RAFFERTY	GEORGE PEPPARD	JOAN GREENWOOD
CLINT EASTWOOD	GEORGE SANDERS	JOAN PLOWRIGHT
COLIN BUCHANAN	GERALDINE PAGE	JOAN SANDERSON
CONNIE STEVENS	GILBERT ROLAND	JOHN BARRYMORE
CORIN REDGRAVE	GLENDA FARRELL	JOHN CARRADINE
DALE ROBERTSON	GLENDA JACKSON	JONATHAN PRYCE
DAVID DUCHOVNY	GLORIA DE HAVEN	JOSEPH FIENNES
DAVID HEMMINGS	GLORIA GRAHAME	JOYCE GRENFELL
DAVID MCCALLUM	GLORIA SWANSON	JULIA LOCKWOOD
DEAN STOCKWELL	GODFREY TEARLE Sir	JULIA MCKENZIE
DERREN NESBITT	GOOGIE WITHERS	JULIAN ORCHARD
DICK VAN PATTEN	GORDON JACKSON	JULIE CHRISTIE
DINAH SHERIDAN	GWYNETH STRONG	JULIE GOODYEAR
DOLORES DEL RIO	HARRIET WALTER	JULIE T WALLACE
DONALD HOUSTON	HARRY GUARDINO	JUNE WHITFIELD
DONALD O'CONNOR	HARRY H CORBETT	KATHARINE ROSS
DOROTHY LAMOUR	HATTIE JACQUES	KELSEY GRAMMER
DOROTHY MALONE	HEATHER CHASEN	KENNETH CONNOR
DREW BARRYMORE	HELEN CHANDLER	KRISTOFFERSON Kris
DUNCAN RENALDO	HILDEGARD NEFF	LANCE PERCIVAL
DUSTIN HOFFMAN	HONOR BLACKMAN	LAURENCE PAYNE

LESLIE RANDALL
LINDSAY WAGNER
LOIS NETTLETON
LORRAINE CHASE
LOUISE JAMESON
MACCORKINDALE Simon
MAI ZETTERLING
MAMIE VAN DOREN
MARIE DRESSLER
MARILYN MONROE
MAUREEN LIPMAN
MAURICE DENHAM
MELVYN DOUGLAS
MICHAEL ANSARA
MICHAEL BRYANT
MICHAEL GAMBON Sir
MICHAEL LANDON
MICHAEL MEDWIN
MICHAEL RENNIE
MINERVA URECAL
MORGAN FREEMAN
NANETTE NEWMAN
NEIL MORRISSEY
NORMA TALMADGE
PATRICIA HAYES
PATRICIA HODGE
PATRICK MACNEE
PATRICK SWAYZE
PATRICK WYMARK
PATSY ROWLANDS
PAULA PRENTISS
PAUL EDDINGTON
PAULINE QUIRKE
PEGGY ASHCROFT Dame
PENELOPE KEITH
PETER WYNGARDE
PHYLLIS DILLER
PIERCE BROSNAN

POSTLETHWAITE Pete
RACHEL ROBERTS
RANDOLPH SCOTT
RAYMOND MASSEY
REGINALD MARSH
RHONDA FLEMING
RICHARD BRIERS
RICHARD BURTON
RICHARD E GRANT
RICHARD GREENE
RICHARD HARRIS
RICHARD O'BRIEN
RICHARD VERNON
RICHARD WATTIS
RICHARD WILSON
ROBERT CARLYLE
ROBERT LINDSAY
ROBERT MITCHUM
ROBERT PRESTON
ROBERT REDFORD
ROBERTSON HARE
ROBIN WILLIAMS
RODDY MCDOWALL
ROMY SCHNEIDER
RONNIE STEVENS
ROSEMARY LEACH
ROSSANO BRAZZI
RUSSELL HUNTER
SALLY ANN HOWES
SALLY THOMSETT
SAMANTHA EGGAR
SAMANTHA JANUS
SERGIO FANTONI
SHEILA HANCOCK
SHEILA MERCIER
SHIRLEY TEMPLE
SIDNEY POITIER
SIMON WILLIAMS

STANLEY BAXTER Sir
STANLEY RIDGES
STELLA STEVENS
STEVE MCFADDEN
STUART WHITMAN
SUSAN FLANNERY
SUSAN SARANDON
SYLVIA KRISTEL
TIMOTHY DALTON
TOMMY LEE JONES
TRINI ALVARADO
URSULA ANDRESS
URSULA HOWELLS
VALERIE HARPER
VALERIE HOBSON
VICTOR MADDERN
WALTER BRENNAN
WALTER MATTHAU
WALTER PIDGEON
WENSLEY PITHEY
WILFRID LAWSON
WILLIAM BENDIX
WILLIAM DEVANE
WILLIAM HOLDEN
WILLIAM MERVYN
WILLIAM ROACHE
WINDSOR DAVIES

14

AGNES MOOREHEAD
ALEXANDER GAUGE
ALISON STEADMAN
ANDIE MACDOWELL
ANGELA BADDELEY
ANGELA LANSBURY
ANGIE DICKINSON
ANNETTE CROSBIE
ANTHONY ANDREWS

ANTHONY HOPKINS Sir
ANTHONY PERKINS
BARBARA BABCOCK
BARBARA BOUCHET
BARBARA PARKINS
BARBARA SHELLEY
BARBARA WINDSOR
BEATRICE LILLIE
BILLIE WHITELAW
BONNIE LANGFORD
BRIGITTE BARDOT
CAMPBELL SINGER
CHARLES BRONSON
CHARLES CHAPLIN Sir
  (Charlie)
CHARLES HAWTREY
CHARLES RUGGLES
CHARLTON HESTON
CHERYL CAMPBELL
CHESTER CONKLIN
CHRISTOPHER LEE
CLIFF ROBERTSON
CONRAD PHILLIPS
CYBILL SHEPHERD
DANIEL DAY-LEWIS
DAVID CARRADINE
DAVID SCHWIMMER
DAVID THRELFALL
DAVID TOMLINSON
DEBBIE REYNOLDS
DENHOLM ELLIOTT
DENNIS WATERMAN
DIAHANN CARROLL
DIANA CHURCHILL
DINSDALE LANDEN
DOROTHY MCGUIRE
DOROTHY PROVINE
EDWARD WOODWARD

EFREM ZIMBALIST
ELSA LANCHESTER
ERNEST BORGNINE
ESTHER WILLIAMS
ETHEL BARRYMORE
FELICITY KENDAL
FIONA FULLERTON
F MURRAY ABRAHAM
FRANCESCA ANNIS
GABRIELLE DRAKE
GARFIELD MORGAN
GAYLE HUNNICUTT
GEOFFREY HUGHES
GEOFFREY PALMER
GEORGE CHAKIRIS
GEORGE HAMILTON
GEORGE MACREADY
GERALDINE JAMES
GWYNETH PALTROW
HARDIE ALBRIGHT
HELEN BAXENDALE
HILDEGARDE NEIL
HUMPHREY BOGART
JAMES EARL JONES
JAMES MACARTHUR
JAMIE LEE CURTIS
JANE ROSSINGTON
JAYNE MANSFIELD
JAY SILVERHEELS
JESSIE MATTHEWS
JOANNE WOODWARD
JOHN CASSAVETES
JOHN LE MESURIER
JOYCE VAN PATTEN
JUDITH ANDERSON
  Dame
KAREN VALENTINE
KATE BECKINSALE

KATHLEEN TURNER
KATHRYN GRAYSON
KEIRA KNIGHTLEY
KEITH CARRADINE
KENNETH BRANAGH
KENNETH CRANHAM
KYNASTON REEVES
LAURENCE HARVEY
LEONARD WHITING
LESLEY-ANNE DOWN
LESLIE GRANTHAM
LESLIE PHILLIPS
LIONEL JEFFRIES
LORCAN CRANITCH
LYNNE FREDERICK
MARGARET DUMONT
MARGARET O'BRIEN
MARGARET TYZACK
MARJORIE RHODES
MARY TYLER MOORE
MELINA MERCOURI
MICHAEL BALFOUR
MICHAEL DENISON
MICHAEL DOUGLAS
MICHAEL ELPHICK
MICHAEL HORDERN Sir
MICHAEL JAYSTON
MICHAEL KITCHEN
MICHAEL WILDING
MICHELE DOTRICE
NIGEL DAVENPORT
NIGEL HAWTHORNE Sir
PATRICK CARGILL
PATRICK STEWART
PAULINE COLLINS
PENELOPE WILTON
PETER BARKWORTH
PHILIPPE NOIRET

PHYLLIS CALVERT
PRUNELLA SCALES
RAYMOND FRANCIS
RAYMOND HUNTLEY
RICHARD WIDMARK
RICKY TOMLINSON
RITA TUSHINGHAM
ROBBIE COLTRANE
ROBERT CUMMINGS
ROBERT HELPMANN Sir
ROBERTO BENIGNI
ROBERT URQUHART
ROGER LLOYD-PACK
ROY BARRACLOUGH
SALLY KELLERMAN
SALLY STRUTHERS
SAMUEL L JACKSON
SARAH BERNHARDT
SARAH CHURCHILL
SCHWARZENEGGER
  Arnold
SHELLEY WINTERS
SIMONE SIGNORET
STEFANIE POWERS
STÉPHANE AUDRAN
STEPHEN YARDLEY
STERLING HAYDEN
STEWART GRANGER
STRATFORD JOHNS
SUSAN HAMPSHIRE
SUSANNAH HARKER
SYBIL THORNDIKE Dame
SYLVESTER MCCOY
THORLEY WALTERS
TIMOTHY BOTTOMS
TIM PIGOTT-SMITH
VALENTINE DYALL
VICTOR BANERJEE

VICTOR MCLAGLEN
VICTOR SPINETTI
VITTORIO DE SICA
WALTER CONNOLLY
WARNER ANDERSON
WARREN MITCHELL
WHOOPI GOLDBERG
WILFRED PICKLES
WILLIAM FRAWLEY
WILLIAM SHATNER

15
ADRIAN EDMONDSON
ANTONIO BANDERAS
BARBARA ANDERSON
BARBARA STANWYCK
BARBRA STREISAND
BARRY FITZGERALD
BERNARD BRESSLAW
BERNARD CRIBBINS
BEVERLEY CALLARD
BURGESS MEREDITH
CAROL DRINKWATER
CAROLINE QUENTIN
CEDRIC HARDWICKE Sir
CHARLES BICKFORD
CHARLES LAUGHTON
CHARLES TINGWELL
DAVID HASSELHOFF
DAVID HYDE PIERCE
DONALD PLEASENCE
EDWARD G ROBINSON
ELIZABETH TAYLOR
FENELLA FIELDING
FRANCES DE LA TOUR
FRANCIS MATTHEWS
FRANÇOISE ARNOUL
FRANK MIDDLEMASS

GALE SONDERGAARD
GEOFFREY BAYLDON
GERALDINE MCEWAN
HENRY STEPHENSON
HERMIONE GINGOLD
IAIN CUTHBERTSON
J EDWARD BROMBERG
JENNIFER ANISTON
JOELY RICHARDSON
JOSEPHINE TEWSON
JULIETTE BINOCHE
KENNETH WILLIAMS
LAURENCE OLIVIER Lord
LEONARD ROSSITER
LIONEL BARRYMORE
LYNDA BELLINGHAM
MARLENE DIETRICH
MICHAEL CRAWFORD
MICHAEL REDGRAVE Sir
MICHAEL SARRAZIN
MICHAEL WILLIAMS
MICHELLE COLLINS
MILLICENT MARTIN
MIRIAM MARGOLYES
MONTGOMERY CLIFT
MORGAN FAIRCHILD
NICOL WILLIAMSON
NIGEL LE VAILLANT
NYREE DAWN PORTER
PAMELA SUE MARTIN
PATRICK MALAHIDE
PATRICK MCGOOHAN
PAULETTE GODDARD
RALPH RICHARDSON Sir
RICHARD BASEHART
RICHARD CALDICOT
RICHARD DREYFUSS
ROBERT ARMSTRONG

ROBERT GUILLAUME
ROSALIND RUSSELL
SANDRA DICKINSON
SARAH LANCASHIRE
SHIRLEY ANN FIELD
SHIRLEY MACLAINE
SIGOURNEY WEAVER
STANLEY HOLLOWAY
SUSAN PENHALIGON
SUZANNE DANIELLE
TAMZIN OUTHWAITE
VANESSA REDGRAVE
VIRGINIA MCKENNA
WILFRED BRAMBELL
WILLIAM FRANKLYN
WILLIAM HARTNELL

16
ALEXANDRA BASTEDO
ANTHONY VALENTINE
BARBARA BEL GEDDES
CALISTA FLOCKHART
CATHERINE DENEUVE
CHARLES MACARTHUR
CHRISTOPHER BEENY
CHRISTOPHER REEVE
CLAUDETTE COLBERT
CLAUDIA CARDINALE
DENZEL WASHINGTON
DONALD SUTHERLAND
DOUGLAS FAIRBANKS
ELIZABETH SELLARS
ERICH VON STROHEIM
GERTRUDE LAWRENCE
GILLIAN TAYLFORTH
GINA LOLLOBRIGIDA
JACQUELINE BISSET
JENNIFER CONNELLY

JENNIFER SAUNDERS
KATHARINE HEPBURN
KATHERINE HELMOND
KATHLEEN HARRISON
KIEFER SUTHERLAND
MARGARET LEIGHTON
MARGARET LOCKWOOD
MAURICE CHEVALIER
MAURICE COLBOURNE
MAXIMILIAN SCHELL
PAMELA STEPHENSON
PATRICK TROUGHTON
PAUL WHITSUN-JONES
PETER BUTTERWORTH
REESE WITHERSPOON
RICHARD GRIFFITHS
RICHARD O'SULLIVAN
ROSALIE CRUTCHLEY
RUDOLPH VALENTINO
STEPHANIE BEACHAM
TALLULAH BANKHEAD
TERENCE ALEXANDER
WILFRID HYDE-WHITE

17
ANDREW CRUICKSHANK
BRODERICK CRAWFORD
CHARLOTTE RAMPLING
CICELY COURTNEIDGE
  Dame
JOHNNY WEISSMULLER
JOSEPH SCHILDKRAUT
KRIS KRISTOFFERSON
MIRANDA RICHARDSON
NATASHA RICHARDSON
NICHOLAS LYNDHURST
OLIVIA DE HAVILLAND
PATRICIA ROUTLEDGE

PAUL MICHAEL GLASER
PETE POSTLETHWAITE
RICHARD BECKINSALE
SCARLETT JOHANSSON
STEPHEN TOMPKINSON
SYDNEY GREENSTREET
SYLVESTER STALLONE
VICTORIA PRINCIPAL

18
BERNADETTE O'FARRELL
CATHERINE ZETA-JONES
CHRISTOPHER PLUMMER
CHRISTOPHER TIMOTHY
ELEANOR SUMMERFIELD
FREDDIE BARTHOLOMEW
KRISTIN SCOTT THOMAS
MARGARET RUTHERFORD
  Dame
RICHARD CHAMBERLAIN
SIMON MACCORKINDALE

19
CHRISTOPHER CAZENOVE
ELIZABETH MONTGOMERY
MARCELLO MASTROIANNI
RICHARD ATTENBOROUGH
  Lord

20
ARNOLD SCHWARZENEGGER
CHRISTOPHER ECCLESTON

Arts – Cinema – CINEMA TERMS

3
CAN
CUT
DUB
PAN
SET

4
BOOM
CAST
CLIP
EPIC
FILM
GATE
IMAX
PART
REEL
ROLE
RUSH
SHOT
TAKE
WRAP

5
BAFTA
CAMEO
DOLLY
DRAMA
FOYER
FRAME
GENRE
KLIEG
MOVIE
OSCAR
PITCH
PRINT

SCENE
SHOOT
SHORT
SPOOL
STUNT

6
BIOPIC
B MOVIE
CAMERA
CINEMA
COMEDY
FADE-IN
FLICKS
REMAKE
RETAKE
SCREEN
SCRIPT
SEQUEL
SERIAL
STUDIO
TALKIE
VIEWER
WEEPIE

7
ART FILM
BALCONY
BIT-PART
CARTOON
CASTING
CLASSIC
CLOSE-UP
CREDITS
CUTTING
DUBBING

EDITING
EFFECTS
EPISODE
EXCERPT
FADE-OUT
FILMDOM
FLEAPIT
MATINÉE
MONTAGE
MUSICAL
PANNING
PICTURE
PREQUEL
PREVIEW
RELEASE
STARDOM
STUDIOS
TRAILER
WESTERN

8
BIOGRAPH
BIOSCOPE
BLOCKING
CINEPLEX
CINERAMA
CRITIQUE
DIALOGUE
EPISCOPE
FILMLAND
FILM NOIR
LIGHTING
LOCATION
LONG SHOT
NEWSREEL
PICTURES

PREMIERE
SCENARIO
SEQUENCE
SHOOTING
SUBTITLE
THRILLER
VIGNETTE
ZOETROPE

9
ANIMATION
BOX OFFICE
BURLESQUE
CAMEO ROLE
CELLULOID
DIRECTION
DOCUDRAMA
FLASHBACK
MULTIPLEX
MUTOSCOPE
NARRATION
PROGRAMME
PROJECTOR
RECORDING
SCREENING
SKINFLICK
SLAPSTICK
SUBTITLES
VITAPHONE
VITASCOPE
VOICE-OVER

10
ACTION FILM
CINÉ CAMERA
DOUBLE-TAKE

HORROR FILM
KLIEG LIGHT
PRE-RELEASE
PRODUCTION
PROJECTION
SCREENPLAY
SCREEN TEST
SILENT FILM
SOUNDTRACK
TEAR-JERKER
WALK-ON PART
WIDESCREEN

11
BLOCKBUSTER
CINEMASCOPE
CLIFFHANGER
DEVELOPMENT
DOCUMENTARY
DOLLY CAMERA
EPIDIASCOPE
FEATURE FILM
KINETOSCOPE
PERFORMANCE
STEP OUTLINE
TECHNICOLOR
THAUMATROPE

12
ACADEMY AWARD
CINÉMATHEQUE
CINÉMA VÉRITÉ
CLAPPERBOARD
CREDIT TITLES
DIRECTOR'S CUT
DISTRIBUTION

DRIVE-IN MOVIE
FILM FESTIVAL
FILM PREMIERE
GANGSTER FILM
INTERMISSION
LANTERN SLIDE
MAGIC LANTERN
PICTURE HOUSE
PRAXINOSCOPE
SILVER SCREEN
SOUND EFFECTS
STEREOPTICON

13
CAMERA OBSCURA
CHARACTER PART
CINEMATOGRAPH
CINÉ PROJECTOR
DISASTER MOVIE
MOTION PICTURE
NOUVELLE VAGUE
PICTURE PALACE
PRE-PRODUCTION

14
CINEMATOGRAPHY
MOVING PICTURES
POST-PRODUCTION
ROMANTIC COMEDY
SPECIAL EFFECTS
SUPPORTING ROLE

16
SPAGHETTI WESTERN

Arts – Cinema – DIRECTORS & PRODUCERS

3
BOX Betty E, Muriel
DAY Robert
LEE Ang, Jack, Norman
RAY Fred Olen,
   Nicholas, Satyajit
WOO John

4
AUER John H
BAVA Marlo, Lamberto
COEN Joel
FORD John
GLEN John
GOLD Jack
HALL Alexander
HILL George Roy,
   Walter
KING Henry, Louis
LANG Fritz, Otto,
   Walter

LEAN Sir David
MANN Anthony,
   Daniel, Delbert,
   Michael
PENN Arthur
RANK Lord J Arthur
REED Sir Carol
RICH David Lowell,
   Roy
RITT Martin
ROEG Nicolas
ROSS Benjamin,
   Herbert
TATI Jacques
TODD Mike
TORS Ivan
WEIR Peter
WISE Robert
WOOD Edward D,
   Sam
YANG Edward

5
ALLEN Irwin, Woody
AMATO Giuseppe
APTED Michael
ASHBY Hal
BACON Lloyd
CAPRA Frank
CARNÉ Marcel
CLAIR René
CLINE Edward F
CUKOR George
DEMME Jonathan
DONEN Stanley
ELVEY Maurice
FORDE Walter
FOSSE Bob
FREED Arthur
GOLAN Menahem
GREEN Alfred E
GUEST Val
HAWKS Howard

IVORY James
JOFFÉ Roland
JURAN Nathan
KARNO Fred
KAZAN Elia, Nicholas
KORDA Sir Alexander
LEIGH Mike
LEVIN Henry
LLOYD Frank
LOACH Ken
LOSEY Joseph
LUBIN Arthur
LUCAS George
LUMET Sidney
MALLE Louis
MAMET David
MARIN Edwin L
MAYER Louis B
MEYER Russ
MOXEY John
NEAME Ronald
NOYCE Phillip
PABST GW
PONTI Carlo
RELPH Michael
ROACH Hal
SCOTT Ridley
SEITZ George B
SHARP Don, Ian
STARK Ray
STONE Andrew L, Oliver
VADIM Roger
VIDOR Charles, King
WALSH Raoul
WHALE James
WYLER William
YATES Peter
YOUNG Harold, Terence

ZUKOR Adolph

6
ALTMAN Robert
ARNOLD Jack
BALCON Sir Michael
BARTON Charles
BEATTY Warren
BENTON Robert
BERMAN Monty,
  Pandro S
BROOKS James L, Mel
BUÑUEL Luis
BUTLER David, Robert
CASTLE William
CIMINO Michael
CONWAY Jack
CORMAN Roger
CURTIZ Michael
DALDRY Stephen
DASSIN Jules
DE SICA Vittorio
DISNEY Walt
DONNER Clive, Richard
FISHER Terence
FLOREY Robert
FORBES Bryan
FORMAN Milos
GIBSON Mel
GODARD Jean-Luc
HANSON Curtis
HARVEY Anthony
HERZOG Werner
HILLER Arthur
HOWARD Ron
HUGHES Howard, John,
  Ken
HUSTON John

KOSTER Henry
KRAMER Stanley
LAMONT Charles
LANDIS John
LEISEN Mitchell
LESTER Dick, Mark L
LEVINE Joseph E
LITVAK Anatole
MENDES Sam
MILLER Claude, David,
  George, Sir Jonathan
NEWELL Mike
NORMAN Leslie
OPHULS Max
PARKER Sir Alan
PICHEL Irving
POTTER HC
POWELL Michael, Nik
RENOIR Jean
ROBSON Mark
ROGERS Maclean, Peter
ROSSEN Robert
RYDELL Mark
SIEGEL Don, Sol C
TAUROG Norman
THOMAS Gerald,
  Jeremy, Ralph
THORPE Richard
TROTTI Lamar
TUTTLE Frank
VARNEL Marcel
WALLIS Hal B
WANGER Walter
WARHOL Andy
WELLES Orson
WHELAN Tim
WILCOX Herbert
WILDER Billy

WINNER Michael
WITNEY William
ZANUCK Darryl F
ZELNIK Fred

7

AHLBERG Mac
ALDRICH Robert
ANNAKIN Ken
ASQUITH Anthony
BERGMAN Ingmar
BORZAGE Frank
BRANAGH Kenneth
CAMERON James
CAMPION Jane
CHABROL Claude
CHOMSKY Marvin
CLAYTON Jack
CLÉMENT René
COCTEAU Jean
COMFORT Lance
COPPOLA Francis Ford
COSTNER Kevin
DEARDEN Basil
DE MILLE Cecil B
DMYTRYK Edward
DOUGLAS Gordon
EDWARDS Blake
ENRIGHT Ray
FELLINI Federico
FLEMING Victor
FORSYTH Bill
GARNETT Tay
GILBERT Lewis
GOLDWYN Sam
JACKSON Peter
JEWISON Norman
KARLSON Phil

KUBRICK Stanley
LANDERS Lew
LEACOCK Philip
LEONARD Robert Z
MCCAREY Leo
NEILSON James
NICHOLS Mike
POLLACK Sydney
PUTTNAM Lord David
RADFORD Michael
REDFORD Robert
RESNAIS Alain
RICHTER WD
ROBBINS Brian,
  Matthew
RUSSELL Ken
SENNETT Mack
SHERMAN George,
  Vincent
SIODMAK Robert
SPIEGEL Sam
STEVENS Andrew,
  George
STURGES John,
  Preston
USTINOV Sir Peter
VAN DYKE WS
WENDERS Wim
WELLMAN William A
YOSHIDA Yoshishige

8

ANDERSON Michael
AVILDSEN John G
BEAUDINE William
BEAUMONT Harry
BERKELEY Busby
BOULTING John, Roy

BRACKETT Charles
BROCCOLI Cubby
CRICHTON Charles
CUMMINGS Irving
DIETERLE William
EASTWOOD Clint
FRIEDKIN William
GOULDING Edmund
GRIFFITH DW
HAMILTON Guy
HATHAWAY Henry
ICHIKAWA Kon
JEFFRIES Lionel
KEIGHLEY William
KERSHNER Irvin
KUROSAWA Akira
LEVINSON Barry
LUBITSCH Ernst
LUHRMANN Baz
MARSHALL George
MCLAGLEN Andrew V
MERCHANT Ismail
MINNELLI Vincente
MULLIGAN Robert
PETERSEN Wolfgang
POLANSKI Roman
SANDRICH Mark
SCORSESE Martin
SELZNICK David O
SPELLING Aaron
SUSSKIND David
THALBERG Irving
TRUFFAUT François
VISCONTI Luchino
ZEMECKIS Robert

9
ANTONIONI
  Michelangelo
BERNHARDT Kurt
CARSTAIRS John Paddy
FLEISCHER Max,
  Richard
GOLDSTONE James
HITCHCOCK Sir Alfred
MAMOULIAN Rouben
MILESTONE Lewis
MINGHELLA Anthony
NEGULESCO Jean
PASTERNAK Joe
PECKINPAH Sam
PREMINGER Otto
REINHARDT Max
ROSENBERG Max J
SCHAFFNER Franklin
SCHNEIDER Bert
SPIELBERG Steven

STEVENSON Robert
STROMBERG Hunt
WANAMAKER Sam
YOSHIMURA Kozaburo
ZINNEMANN Fred

10
BERTOLUCCI Bernardo,
  Giuseppe
CASSAVETES John
EISENSTEIN Sergei
MANKIEWICZ Herman
RICHARDSON Tony
SILLIPHANT Sterling
SODERBERGH Steven
ZEFFIRELLI Franco

11
BOGDANOVICH Peter
COSTA-GAVRAS
  Constantin

HUMBERSTONE
  H Bruce
LEE-THOMPSON J
PRESSBURGER Arnold
SCHLESINGER John
SHAUGHNESSY Alfred
SPRINGSTEEN RG

12
ATTENBOROUGH
  Lord Richard
MORE O'FERRALL
  George
SCHERTZINGER Victor
SPOTTISWOODE Roger
VON STERNBERG Josef

13
FRANKENHEIMER John

Arts – Cinema – FILM CHARACTERS

3
AMY *Chasing Amy*
BOB *Clerks*
CHE *Evita*
DIL *The Crying Game*
DIM *A Clockwork Orange*
DOC *Back to the Future,
  The Getaway,
  Wyatt Earp*
HAL *2001: A Space
  Odyssey*
HUD *Hud*

JAY *Clerks, The Great
  Gatsby*
KIP *The English Patient*
MAX *Mad Max, Max Mon
  Amour, The Producers*
NED *The Swimmer*
NEO *The Matrix*
RED *The Shawshank
  Redemption*
SAM *Casablanca*
TED *Bill and Ted's Bogus
  Journey*

4
ALEX *A Clockwork
  Orange, Fatal Attraction*
ANNA *Anna and the
  King, The King and I*
BABE *Babe, Marathon
  Man*
BILL *Bill and Ted's Bogus
  Journey, Kill Bill*
BOND Bond films
BRAD *The Rocky Horror
  Picture Show*

CATO *The Pink Panther etc*
CORA *The Postman Always Rings Twice*
DATA *Star Trek*
DAVE *2001: A Space Odyssey*
ELSA *Born Free*
ERIK *The Phantom of the Opera*
ERIN *Erin Brockovich*
GOGO *Kill Bill: Vol. 1*
IGOR *Young Frankenstein*
ILSA *Casablanca*
IRIS *Taxi Driver*
IRMA *Irma La Douce*
JANE *Tarzan etc*
JAWS *Bond villain*
KIRK *Star Trek*
LARA *Dr Zhivago*
LUKE *Cool Hand Luke*
MARY *There's Something About Mary*
PRIS *Blade Runner*
RICK *Casablanca*
RITA *Educating Rita*
ROSE *Titanic*
SARA *Two Mules for Sister Sara*
TOTO *The Wizard of Oz*
TUCO *The Good, the Bad and the Ugly*
YODA *Star Wars*

5

ALFIE *Alfie*
ARWEN *The Lord of the Rings*
BAMBI *Bambi, Diamonds Are Forever*
BLUTO *Animal House*
BUTCH *Pulp Fiction*
CLYDE *Any Which Way You Can, Bonnie and Clyde, Every Which Way but Loose*
DANNY *Grease*
DONNY *The Big Lebowski*
DORIS *The Owl and the Pussycat*
FELIX *The Odd Couple*
FREDO *The Godfather*
FRODO *The Lord of the Rings*
HARRY *Dirty Harry,* Harry Potter films, *Magnum Force*
HOGAN *Two Mules for Sister Sara*
HUTCH *Starsky & Hutch*
JANET *The Rocky Horror Picture Show*
JASON *Friday the 13th*
JERRY *Some Like It Hot*
KEVIN *Home Alone*
KURTZ *Apocalypse Now*
MAMMY *Gone with the Wind*
MARGE *Fargo*
MARGO *All About Eve*
MARIA *The Sound of Music*

MARTY *Back to the Future*
OSCAR *The Odd Couple*
PADME *Star Wars*
QUEEG *The Caine Mutiny*
QUINT *Jaws*
RAMBO *First Blood Rambo*
REGAN *The Exorcist*
RHETT *Gone with the Wind*
ROBIN *Batman*
ROCKY *Rocky*
ROXIE *Chicago*
SANDY *Grease*
SPOCK *Star Trek*
SUSAN *Desperately Seeking Susan*
UHURA *Star Trek*
VELMA *Chicago*
VIOLA *Shakespeare in Love*

6

ALMÁSY *The English Patient*
BEN-HUR *Ben-Hur*
BONNIE *Bonnie and Clyde*
BUD FOX *Wall Street*
CARRIE *Carrie*
CARTER *Get Carter*
CHANCE *Being There*
CHEETA *Tarzan etc*
CHEKOV *Star Trek*
COOGAN *Coogan's Bluff*

DAMIEN *The Omen*
DAPHNE *Some Like It Hot*
DR EVIL *Austin Powers*
FREDDY *A Nightmare on Elm Street*
GOLLUM *The Lord of the Rings*
LASSIE *Lassie*
LOUISE *Thelma and Louise*
MARTHA *Who's Afraid of Virginia Woolf?*
MAY DAY Bond girl/villain *A View to a Kill*
MR KIDD Bond villain *Diamonds Are Forever*
MR PINK *Reservoir Dogs*
MR WINT Bond villain *Diamonds Are Forever*
ODDJOB Bond villain
PICARD *Star Trek*
PINKIE *Brighton Rock*
RACHEL *The Night of the Hunter, Witness*
RENARD Bond villain *The World Is Not Enough*
RIPLEY *Alien* etc, *Ripley's Game, The Talented Mr Ripley*
SOPHIE *Sophie's Choice*
TARZAN *Tarzan* etc
THELMA *Thelma and Louise*
VERBAL *The Usual Suspects*
VIVIAN *The Big Sleep*
XAVIER *X-Men* etc

7

ARAGORN *The Lord of the Rings*
BLOFELD Bond villain
BULLITT *Bullitt*
DOROTHY *The Wizard of Oz*
DRACULA *Dracula* etc
FRENCHY *Destry Rides Again, Goodfellas, Grease*
GANDALF *The Lord of the Rings*
HAN SOLO *Star Wars*
HAWKEYE *M*A*S*H*
HOT LIPS *M*A*S*H*
KILGORE *Apocalypse Now*
LEGOLAS *The Lord of the Rings*
MAGNETO *X-Men* etc
MAX CADY *Cape Fear*
MAXIMUS *Gladiator*
MR DEEDS *Mr Deeds Goes to Town*
MR SMITH *Mr Smith Goes to Washington*
SCHMIDT *About Schmidt*
SERPICO *Serpico*
STARSKY *Starsky & Hutch*
THE DUDE *The Big Lebowski*
TOM JOAD *The Grapes of Wrath*
TRINITY *The Matrix* etc

8

BABE LEVY *Marathon Man*
BABY JANE *Whatever Happened to Baby Jane?*
CATWOMAN *Catwoman*
CLOUSEAU *The Pink Panther* etc
COMMODUS *Gladiator*
DOC BROWN *Back to the Future*
DOC MCCOY *The Getaway*
HANNIBAL *Hannibal, Hannibal Rising, Manhunter, Red Dragon, The Silence of the Lambs*
HERMIONE *Harry Potter* films
ILSA LUND *Casablanca*
JIM STARK *Rebel without a Cause*
LOIS LANE *Superman*
MARY JANE *Spider-Man*
MORPHEUS *The Matrix* etc
MR BLONDE *Reservoir Dogs*
MR ORANGE *Reservoir Dogs*
NORMA RAE *Norma Rae*
ROSEMARY *Rosemary's Baby*
SAM SPADE *The Maltese Falcon*
SCARLETT *Gone with the Wind*

SUPERMAN *Superman*
TALLULAH *Bugsy Malone*
THE BRIDE *Kill Bill*
THE JOKER *Batman*
TOM HAGEN *The Godfather*
ZACK MAYO *An Officer and a Gentleman*

9

ANNIE HALL *Annie Hall*
BILLY MACK *Love Actually*
CHEWBACCA *Star Wars*
CLARK KENT *Superman*
DANNY ZUKO *Grease*
DEMETRIUS *Demetrius and the Gladiators*
ELIOT NESS *The Untouchables*
ETHAN HUNT *Mission: Impossible*
GALADRIEL *The Lord of the Rings*
GUY HAINES *Strangers on a Train*
HARRY LIME *Home Alone, The Third Man*
JAMES BOND *Bond films*
JAY GATSBY *The Great Gatsby*
JOHN SHAFT *Shaft*
LEX LUTHOR *Superman*
MARK DARCY *Bridget Jones's Diary*
MR BRIDGER *The Italian Job*

MRS ISELIN *The Manchurian Candidate*
NINOTCHKA *Ninotchka*
O-REN ISHII *Kill Bill*
QUASIMODO *The Hunchback of Notre Dame*
ROBIN HOOD *The Adventures of Robin Hood*
ROSA KLEBB *From Russia with Love*
ROSE SAYER *The African Queen*
ROXIE HART *Chicago*
SILENT BOB *Clerks*
SUGAR KANE *Some Like It Hot*
THE TIN MAN *The Wizard of Oz*
TOM RIPLEY *Ripley's Game, The Talented Mr Ripley*
TRACY LORD *High Society, The Philadelphia Story*
WOLVERINE *X-Men* etc
YOSSARIAN *Catch-22*

10

ACE VENTURA *Ace Ventura: Pet Detective* etc
ADSO OF MELK *The Name of the Rose*
AGENT SMITH *The Matrix* etc
ALVY SINGER *Annie Hall*
BILLY FLYNN *Chicago*

BRUCE WAYNE *Batman*
DARTH VADER *Star Wars*
DUMBLEDORE *Harry Potter* films
ELLE DRIVER *Kill Bill*
EL MARIACHI *Desperado, El Mariachi, Once upon a Time in Mexico*
FELIX UNGAR *The Odd Couple*
FRANK BOOTH *Blue Velvet*
FRED C DOBBS *The Treasure of the Sierra Madre*
GOLDFINGER *Goldfinger*
GREG FOCKER *Meet the Fockers, Meet the Parents*
HONEY RYDER *Bond girl Dr No*
JACK DAWSON *Titanic*
JAKE GITTES *Chinatown*
JAMES T KIRK *Star Trek*
JEAN BRODIE *The Prime of Miss Jean Brodie*
JOSEY WALES *The Outlaw Josey Wales*
LORELEI LEE *Gentlemen Prefer Blondes*
MARTY MCFLY *Back to the Future*
MAXIMILIAN *Cabaret*
MIA WALLACE *Pulp Fiction*
MRS DANVERS *Rebecca*
NED MERRILL *The Swimmer*

PAUL KERSEY *Death Wish*
RATSO RIZZO *Midnight Cowboy*
RICK BLAINE *Casablanca*
SCARAMANGA *Bond villain*
SUSAN VANCE *Bringing Up Baby*
THE PENGUIN *Batman Returns*
THE RIDDLER *Batman Forever*
TONY MANERO *Saturday Night Fever*
VAN HELSING *Dracula etc, Van Helsing*
VELMA KELLY *Chicago*
VERBAL KINT *The Usual Suspects*
WILLY WONKA *Charlie and the Chocolate Factory*
XANDER CAGE *xXx*

11
ANNIE WILKES *Misery*
BRUCE BANNER *Hulk*
CARRIE WHITE *Carrie*
CHILI PALMER *Be Cool, Get Shorty*
CLYDE BARROW *Bonnie and Clyde*
DOLORES HAZE *Lolita*
DOROTHY GALE *The Wizard of Oz*
ELEKTRA KING *Bond girl The World Is Not Enough*

EMILIO LARGO *Bond villain*
FELIX LEITER *Bond films*
FORREST GUMP *Forrest Gump*
FRANK DREBIN *Naked Gun*
FRAN KUBELIK *The Apartment*
FRAU BLÜCHER *Young Frankenstein*
GORDON GEKKO *Wall Street*
HANS BECKERT *M*
HARRY PALMER *Billion Dollar Brain, Funeral in Berlin, The Ipcress File*
HARRY POTTER *Harry Potter films*
IRMA LA DOUCE *Irma La Douce*
JACK SPARROW *Pirates of the Caribbean*
JAR JAR BINKS *Star Wars*
JASON BOURNE *The Bourne Identity, The Bourne Supremacy*
JEFF SPICOLI *Fast Times at Ridgemont High*
JJ HUNSECKER *Sweet Smell of Success*
JUDAH BEN-HUR *Ben-Hur*
MARY POPPINS *Mary Poppins*
MATT MURDOCK *Daredevil*

MRS ROBINSON *The Graduate*
NORMAN BATES *Psycho*
NORMAN MAINE *A Star Is Born*
ODA MAE BROWN *Ghost*
PETER PARKER *Spider-Man*
PHILO BEDDOE *Any Which Way You Can, Every Which Way but Loose*
POPEYE DOYLE *The French Connection*
PUSSY GALORE *Bond girl Goldfinger*
RAYMOND SHAW *The Manchurian Candidate*
RHETT BUTLER *Gone with the Wind*
ROCKY BALBOA *Rocky*
SALLY BOWLES *Cabaret*
SANDY OLSSON *Grease*
SARAH CONNOR *The Terminator*
SETH BRUNDLE *The Fly*
SIRIUS BLACK *Harry Potter films*
TERRY MALLOY *On the Waterfront*
THOMAS CROWN *The Thomas Crown Affair*
TIFFANY CASE *Bond girl Diamonds Are Forever*
TOMMY DEVITO *Goodfellas*

TONY MONTANA
Scarface
VELVET BROWN
National Velvet
VINCENT VEGA *Pulp Fiction*
VIRGIL TIBBS *In the Heat of the Night, They Call Me MISTER Tibbs!*

12
ASHLEY WILKES *Gone with the Wind*
ATTICUS FINCH *To Kill a Mockingbird*
AUSTIN POWERS *Austin Powers*
BILBO BAGGINS *The Lord of the Rings*
BONNIE PARKER *Bonnie and Clyde*
BRIDGET JONES *Bridget Jones's Diary*
BUTCH CASSIDY *Butch Cassidy and the Sundance Kid*
CALAMITY JANE *Calamity Jane*
CAPTAIN QUINT *Jaws*
CRUELLA DE VIL *101 Dalmatians*
DR PETER BLOOD *Captain Blood*
ETHAN EDWARDS *The Searchers*
FRANK BULLITT *Bullitt*
FRANKENSTEIN *Frankenstein* etc

FRANK-N-FURTER *The Rocky Horror Picture Show*
FRODO BAGGINS *The Lord of the Rings*
GEORGE BAILEY *It's a Wonderful Life*
INDIANA JONES *Raiders of the Lost Ark* etc
JABBA THE HUTT *Star Wars*
JACK TORRANCE *The Shining*
MIRANDA FROST Bond girl *Die Another Day*
NORMA DESMOND *Sunset Boulevard*
NURSE RATCHED *One Flew over the Cuckoo's Nest*
OBI-WAN KENOBI *Star Wars*
OSCAR MADISON *The Odd Couple*
PADME AMIDALA *Star Wars*
PLENTY O'TOOLE Bond girl *Diamonds Are Forever*
PRINCESS LEIA *Star Wars*
ROBERT STROUD *Birdman of Alcatraz*
RUBEUS HAGRID Harry Potter films
RUPERT PUPKIN *The King of Comedy*
SEVERUS SNAPE Harry Potter films

SHANGHAI LILY
Shanghai Express
STELLA DALLAS *Stella Dallas*
THE SCARECROW *The Wizard of Oz*
TRAVIS BICKLE *Taxi Driver*
VERNITA GREEN *Kill Bill*
VICTOR LASZLO *Casablanca*
XENIA ONATOPP Bond girl/villain *GoldenEye*

13
ANNA LEONOWENS *Anna and the King, The King and I*
BLANCHE DUBOIS *A Streetcar Named Desire*
BLANCHE HUDSON *Whatever Happened to Baby Jane?*
CHARLES XAVIER *X-Men* etc
CHARLIE ALLNUT *The African Queen*
CHARLIE CROKER *The Italian Job*
CHARLOTTE HAZE *Lolita*
COMMANDER DATA *Star Trek*
DANIEL CLEAVER *Bridget Jones's Diary*
DARYL VAN HORNE *The Witches of Eastwick*
DR STRANGELOVE *Dr Strangelove*

DUDLEY DURSLEY Harry Potter films
FREDDY KRUEGER *A Nightmare on Elm Street*
HARRY CALLAHAN *Dirty Harry, Magnum Force*
HOLLY GOODHEAD Bond girl *Moonraker*
LESTER BURNHAM *American Beauty*
LOTTE SCHWARTZ *Being John Malkovich*
LUKE SKYWALKER *Star Wars*
MARGO CHANNING *All About Eve*
MAX BIALYSTOCK *The Producers*
MILDRED PIERCE *Mildred Pierce*
MINNESOTA FATS *The Hustler*
MONSIEUR HULOT *Monsieur Hulot's Holiday*
PHILIP MARLOWE *The Big Sleep* etc
RICHARD KIMBLE *The Fugitive*
RUFUS T FIREFLY *Duck Soup*
SCARLETT O'HARA *Gone with the Wind*
SISTER CLODAGH *Black Narcissus*
SONNY CORLEONE *The Godfather*
WARREN SCHMIDT *About Schmidt*

14
AURORA GREENWAY *Terms of Endearment*
BABY JANE HUDSON *Whatever Happened to Baby Jane?*
CAPTAIN WILLARD *Apocalypse Now*
ELIZA DOOLITTLE *My Fair Lady*
ERIN BROCKOVICH *Erin Brockovich*
ESTHER BLODGETT *A Star Is Born*
HANNIBAL LECTER *Hannibal, Hannibal Rising, Red Dragon, The Silence of the Lambs*
HENRI CHARRIERE *Papillon*
HOLLY GOLIGHTLY *Breakfast at Tiffany's*
HUMBERT HUMBERT *Lolita*
JONATHAN HARKER *Dracula* etc
JULES WINNFIELD *Pulp Fiction*
MARGE GUNDERSON *Fargo*
MARY JANE WATSON *Spider-Man*
MISS MONEYPENNY Bond films
RANDLE MCMURPHY *One Flew over the Cuckoo's Nest*
RAYMOND BABBITT *Rain Man*

ROOSTER COGBURN *Rooster Cogburn, True Grit*
THE SUNDANCE KID *Butch Cassidy and the Sundance Kid*
WILLIAM CUTTING *Gangs of New York*

15
ALBUS DUMBLEDORE Harry Potter films
AMSTERDAM VALLON *Gangs of New York*
ANAKIN SKYWALKER *Star Wars*
AURIC GOLDFINGER Bond villain
CATHERINE SLOPER *The Heiress*
CLARICE STARLING *Hannibal, The Silence of the Lambs*
COOLER KING HILTS *The Great Escape*
DICKIE GREENLEAF *The Talented Mr Ripley*
DON VITO CORLEONE *The Godfather*
DOROTHY MICHAELS *Tootsie*
HERMIONE GRANGER Harry Potter films
MARCELLUS GALLIO *The Robe*
MELANIE HAMILTON *Gone with the Wind*

MICHAEL CORLEONE *The Godfather*
NATALIA LANDAUER *Cabaret*
PROFESSOR XAVIER
  X-Men etc
STANLEY KOWALSKI *A Streetcar
  Named Desire*
THE COWARDLY LION *The Wizard
  of Oz*

16
BENJAMIN BRADDOCK *The Graduate*
CATHERINE TRAMELL *Basic Instinct*
DR CHRISTIAN SZELL *Marathon Man*
KEVIN MCCALLISTER *Home Alone*
MORTIMER BREWSTER *Arsenic and
  Old Lace*

17
BREATHLESS MAHONEY *Dick Tracy*
CAPTAIN JACK AUBREY *Master and
  Commander*
CAPTAIN JAMES T KIRK *Star Trek*
CHARLES FOSTER KANE *Citizen Kane*
INSPECTOR CLOUSEAU *The Pink
  Panther* etc
MINERVA MCGONAGALL Harry
  Potter films
TRACY SAMANTHA LORD *High
  Society, The Philadelphia Story*

18
CAPTAIN JACK SPARROW *Pirates of
  the Caribbean*
EDWARD SCISSORHANDS *Edward
  Scissorhands*
ERNST STAVRO BLOFELD Bond villain
GENERAL JACK D RIPPER
  Dr Strangelove
PHYLLIS DIETRICHSON *Double
  Indemnity*

19
COUNT LASZLO DE ALMÁSY *The
  English Patient*
REVEREND HARRY POWELL *The Night
  of the Hunter*
THOMAS BABINGTON LEVY
  Marathon Man

20
CAPTAIN JEAN-LUC PICARD *Star Trek*
GENERAL BUCK TURGIDSON
  Dr Strangelove
WILLIAM OF BASKERVILLE *The Name
  of the Rose*

Arts – Cinema – FILM COMPANIES
s = studios

3
MGM
RKO

4
BRAY *s*
RANK
SONY

5
PATHÉ
PIXAR
TROMA

6
AMICUS
CANNON
DENHAM *s*
DHARMA
EALING *s*
HAMMER

LONDON
RAMOJI *s*

7
CAROLCO
CINETIL
ELSTREE *s*
ESSANAY
GAUMONT
LIBERTY
MIRAMAX
RAJSHRI
TRISTAR
YASH RAJ

8
COLUMBIA
HANDMADE
KEYSTONE
PINEWOOD *s*
WOODFALL

9
CINECITTÀ *s*
ISLEWORTH *s*
LEAVESDEN *s*
PARAMOUNT
TWO CITIES
UNIVERSAL

10
CHURCH HILL
DREAMWORKS
SHEPPERTON *s*
WALT DISNEY

11
BOREHAMWOOD *s*
BRITISH LION

12
GAINSBOROUGH

13
ALLIED ARTISTS
INTERNATIONAL
MERCHANT IVORY
UNITED ARTISTS

14
WARNER BROTHERS

16
RANK ORGANISATION
RKO RADIO PICTURES

17
ASSOCIATED BRITISH
METRO-GOLDWYN-MAYER

19
TWENTIETH CENTURY FOX

Arts – Cinema – FILM FESTIVALS

4
KARA
  Karachi
OSLO
RIGA

5
DUBAI

HAIFA
INDIA
PUSAN
TOKYO

6
ANKARA
BERGEN

BERLIN
CANNES
HAWAII
KRAKÓW
LONDON
MOSCOW
SYDNEY
VENICE

WARSAW

7
BANGKOK
CALGARY
JAKARTA
LOCARNO
NEWPORT

NEW YORK
SEATTLE
SEMINCI
  Valladolid
TORONTO

8
ADELAIDE

CARTHAGE Tunis
CINÉFEST Greater
  Sudbury
EDMONTON
FLANDERS Ghent
GÖTEBORG
HELSINKI
HONG KONG
ISTANBUL
MONTREAL
SARAJEVO
SHANGHAI
SUNDANCE Park City/
  Salt Lake City
VIENNALE Vienna

9
CLEVELAND
DEAUVILLE
EDINBURGH
FEBIOFEST Prague
JERUSALEM
LITHUANIA
MELBOURNE
NORWEGIAN
  Haugesund
ROTTERDAM
STOCKHOLM
VANCOUVER

10
COPENHAGEN

11
GOLDEN HORSE Taipei
KARLOVY VARY

12
INDIANAPOLIS
ST PETERSBURG
THESSALONIKI

Arts – Cinema – FILM TITLES
a = animated film   *m* = musical *w* = western

3	4				
ALI	ANTZ *a*	ENVY	MAME *m*	WILT	
BIG	ARIA	FAME *m*	M*A*S*H	X-MEN	
BUG	BABE	FURY	MASK	ZULU	
ELF	BEAN	FUZZ	NARC		
EVA	BLOW	GIGI m	NUTS	**5**	
HUD *w*	CARS *a*	G MEN	PEPE *m*	ALFIE	
JFK	COMA	HAIR	REDS	ALIEN	
KES	COPS	HEAT	RENT *m*	ALIVE	
RAN	CUJO	HELP! *m*	ROPE	ANGEL	
RAY	DAVE	HOOK	RUSH	ANNIE *m*	
SAW	DIVA	HULK	SCUM	BAMBI *a*	
SHE	DR NO	IRIS	STAR!	BLADE	
XXX	DUEL	JAWS	TAPS	BORAT	
YOL	DUNE	JUDE	TESS	BUGSY	
	EDTV	KIDS	THEM!	COBRA	
	EMMA	LEON	TRON	CRASH	
		LOLA	TROY	DIGBY	

DINER
DOGMA
DUMBO *a*
EARTH
EL CID
EVITA *m*
FARGO
FREUD
FRIDA
GHOST
GIANT
GILDA
GREED
GYPSY *m*
HITCH
HOFFA
HOTEL
JULIA
KIPPS
KITTY
KLUTE
KOLYA
KOTCH
LADY L
LAURA
LENNY
MAMMY *m*
MANDY
MARTY
MULAN *a*
NAKED
NIXON
OTLEY
PINKY
RAMBO
ROCKY
RONIN
SALLY

SEVEN
SHAFT
SHANE *w*
SHINE
SHREK *a*
SIGNS
SLEEP
SPEED
TOMMY *m*
TWINS
WILDE
WINGS
YANKS
YENTL
ZELIG

6
AGATHA
ALIENS
ALWAYS
AMELIE
ARTHUR
AVALON
AVANTI!
BATMAN
BECKET
BE COOL
BEN-HUR
BLOW-UP
BRAZIL
BUSTER
CAPOTE
CARRIE
CASINO
CHARLY
CLERKS
CLOSER
COCOON

CON AIR
CONVOY
ED WOOD
ERASER
ESCAPE
EXODUS
FESTEN
FREAKS
FRENZY
GANDHI
GI JANE
GOTHIC
GREASE *m*
HAMLET
HARVEY
HENRY V
ICE AGE *a*
I, ROBOT
ISHTAR
JIGSAW
KINSEY
KISMET *m*
KUNDUN
LOLITA
MAD MAX
MARNIE
MISERY
MOTHER
ODETTE
OLIVER! *m*
ORPHÉE
PATTON
PICNIC
POPEYE
PORKY'S
PRIEST
PSYCHO
QUILLS

RIFIFI
ROBOTS *a*
ROB ROY
SCREAM
SIRENS
SLEUTH
SNATCH
SPLASH!
STRIKE
THE FLY
THE FOG
THE KID
THE NET
THE WIZ *m*
TOP GUN
TOP HAT *m*
VICTIM
WILSON
XANADU
ZARDOZ

7
AIRPORT
ALADDIN *a/m*
ALGIERS
AMADEUS
AMISTAD
ANDROID
BANANAS
BIG FISH
BIGGLES
BULLITT
BUS STOP
CABARET *m*
CAMELOT
CAMILLE
CAPRICE
CHARADE

CHICAGO *m*
CONTACT
COPYCAT
DARLING
DEAD MAN *w*
DIE HARD
DIMPLES
DRACULA
EBB TIDE
FACE OFF
FIREFOX
GI BLUES *m*
GOTHIKA
HELLBOY
HOG WILD
HOLIDAY
HOSTAGE
HOUDINI
JEZEBEL
JUBILEE
KING RAT
LANTANA
LA RONDE
LET IT BE *m*
MACBETH
MAURICE
MEMENTO
MIRANDA
MISSING
MONSTER
MOROCCO
NETWORK
NIAGARA
OCTOBER
OTHELLO
PAL JOEY *m*
PIRATES
PLATOON

POOR COW
Q PLANES
QUARTET
QUINTET
RAIN MAN
REBECCA
RED DUST
REPO MAN
RIO LOBO *w*
RIO RITA *m*
ROBOCOP
ROSALIE *m*
SABRINA
SCROOGE *m*
SERPICO
SHALAKO *w*
SHAMPOO
SIN CITY
SLEEPER
SOLARIS
SPARTAN
SPY GAME
SPY KIDS
STEPMOM
SUSPECT
THE BLOB
THE CROW
THE CURE
THE HILL
THE MASK
THE OMEN
THE RING
THE ROBE
THE ROCK
THE STUD
THE VIPs
TITANIC
TOOTSIE

TOPKAPI
TRAFFIC
TRAPEZE
TREMORS
TWISTER
ULYSSES
VALMONT
VERTIGO
WHOOPEE! *m*
WITNESS
YOJIMBO

8

ACES HIGH
ADAM'S RIB
AIRPLANE!
ALBERT RN
AMARCORD
APPLAUSE *m*
BADLANDS
BETRAYAL
BORN FREE
BOYS' TOWN
BRUBAKER
BULWORTH
CALIGULA
CAPE FEAR
CAROUSEL *m*
CASTAWAY
CAST AWAY
CATWOMAN
CHOCOLAT
CIMARRON *w*
CLOCKERS
CLUELESS
COCKTAIL
CRITTERS
CUL-DE-SAC

CURLY TOP
DARK STAR
DEAD CALM
DE-LOVELY *m*
DOGVILLE
DOWNFALL
DUCK SOUP
ELECTION
EXISTENZ
FANTASIA *a*
FIREWALL
GASLIGHT
GERMINAL
GODSPELL *m*
GODZILLA
GREMLINS
GUN CRAZY
GUNGA DIN
HANNIBAL
HIGH NOON *w*
IDENTITY
INSOMNIA
IT'S A GIFT
JANE EYRE
KEY LARGO
KHARTOUM
KILL BILL
KING KONG
KING'S ROW
LA STRADA
LIFEBOAT
MAGNOLIA
MALCOLM X
MALLRATS
MEPHISTO
MIDNIGHT
MOBY DICK
MONA LISA

MON ONCLE
MRS BROWN
MY GAL SAL *m*
NAKED GUN
NAPOLEON
NED KELLY
NORMA RAE
NOSTROMO
OKLAHOMA! *m*
OUTBREAK
PAPILLON
PETER PAN *a*
PREDATOR
PRIME CUT
QUERELLE
QUIZ SHOW
QUO VADIS
RASHOMON
RIO BRAVO *w*
RUSHMORE
SABOTAGE
SAYONARA
SCANNERS
SCARFACE
SEXTETTE
SHOW BOAT *m*
SIDEWAYS
SILKWOOD
STAR WARS
STEAMING
SUPERMAN
THE ALAMO *w*
THE BIRDS
THE BITCH
THE CHASE
THE CROWD
THE HOURS
THE KNACK

THE LIMEY
THE MUMMY
THE PIANO
THE QUEEN
THE REBEL
THE SHEIK
THE STING
THE SWARM
THE THIEF
THE THING
THE TRAMP
THE TRIAL
TIGER BAY
TO DIE FOR
TOKYO JOE
TOM JONES
TONY ROME
TOY STORY *a*
TRISTANA
TRUE GRIT *w*
TRUE LIES
TWO WOMEN
VERA CRUZ *w*
WATERLOO

9

ABOUT A BOY
A BUG'S LIFE *a*
ALEXANDER
ANASTASIA *a*
ANNIE HALL
ARABESQUE
BAD TIMING
BEAU GESTE
BEWITCHED
BILLY LIAR
BLACKMAIL
BLACK RAIN

BOOMERANG
BRIGADOON *m*
CAT BALLOU *w*
CAT PEOPLE
CAVALCADE
CHINATOWN
CHRISTINE
CITY OF GOD
CLEOPATRA
CLOCKWISE
CROSSFIRE
DAREDEVIL
DEAD AGAIN
DEATH WISH
DICK TRACY
DR CYCLOPS
EASY RIDER
ELIZABETH
EVERGREEN *m*
FIGHT CLUB
FREE WILLY
FUNNY FACE *m*
FUNNY GIRL *m*
GALLIPOLI
GENEVIEVE
GET CARTER
GET SHORTY
GLADIATOR
GOLDENEYE
GORKY PARK
HALLOWEEN
HAPPY FEET *a*
HELPMATES
HOME ALONE
HUE AND CRY
IL POSTINO
I'M NO ANGEL
INTERIORS

JOAN OF ARC
JUNGLE JIM
KAGEMUSHA
LA BALANCE
LABYRINTH
LAYER CAKE
LE BOUCHER
LIMELIGHT
LOCAL HERO
LOVE STORY
MANHATTAN
MEAN GIRLS
MIAMI VICE
MOONRAKER
MOUSEHUNT
NASHVILLE
NINOTCHKA
NOSFERATU
NOTORIOUS
OBSESSION
OCTOPUSSY
ODD MAN OUT
O LUCKY MAN!
ON THE TOWN *m*
OPEN RANGE *w*
OPEN WATER
PALE RIDER *w*
PANIC ROOM
PAPER MOON
PINOCCHIO *a*
PYGMALION
RADIO DAYS
RED DRAGON
REMBRANDT
REPULSION
ROAD TO RIO
ROSE MARIE *m*
ROXIE HART *m*

SATYRICON
SECRETARY
SEXY BEAST
SHORT CUTS
SISTER ACT
SPANGLISH
SPARTACUS
SPIDER-MAN
STAGE DOOR
STRAW DOGS
STROMBOLI
SUSPICION
TAKING OFF
TALK TO HER
THE BOWERY
THE COOLER
THE DAMNED
THE DEVILS
THE GUVNOR
THE JACKET
THE MATRIX
THE OTHERS
THE PLAYER
THE RACKET
THE TENANT
TOMBSTONE *w*
TOP SECRET
ULEE'S GOLD
UNDER FIRE
VERA DRAKE
VIRIDIANA
WAG THE DOG
WALKABOUT
WESTWORLD
WHITE HEAT
WIMBLEDON
WISE BLOOD

WOODSTOCK
ZOOLANDER

10
ABSOLUTION
ADAPTATION
AFFLICTION
ARMAGEDDON
AWAKENINGS
BACK STREET
BAGDAD CAFE
BARBARELLA
BARBERSHOP *m*
BARTON FINK
BEING THERE
BEST IN SHOW
BLOCKHEADS
BLUE HAWAII *m*
BLUE VELVET
BRAVEHEART
BULL DURHAM
CARAVAGGIO
CASABLANCA
CHASING AMY
CHICKEN RUN *a*
CITY LIGHTS
CITY OF HOPE
CITY ON FIRE
COLLATERAL
COMING HOME
COYOTE UGLY *m*
CRY FREEDOM
DEEP IMPACT
DIRTY HARRY
DISCLOSURE
DR DOLITTLE
EARTHQUAKE
EAST IS EAST

EAST OF EDEN
EASY STREET
EMMANUELLE
ENTRAPMENT
FANCY PANTS
FIRST BLOOD
FLASHDANCE *m*
FLATLINERS
FORT APACHE *w*
FRA DIAVOLO
GARDEN STATE
GEORGY GIRL
GHOST WORLD
GOING MY WAY
GOLDFINGER
GOODFELLAS
GRAND HOTEL
HALLELUJAH
HELLO DOLLY *m*
HIGHLANDER
HIGH SIERRA
HOLIDAY INN *m*
HOUSE CALLS
HOUSE OF WAX
HOWARDS END
IN HER SHOES
INTERMEZZO
JAGGED EDGE
JAMAICA INN
JOUR DE FÊTE
JUGGERNAUT
JULES ET JIM
JUNGLE BOOK *a*
KID GALAHAD
KING CREOLE *m*
KISS ME KATE *m*
KITTY FOYLE
LADY BE GOOD *m*

LADY KILLER
LAST ORDERS
L'AVVENTURA
LONDON TOWN *m*
MADAGASCAR *a*
MEN IN BLACK
METROPOLIS
MISS POTTER
MOONSTRUCK
MOONWALKER
MRS MINIVER
MY FAIR LADY *m*
MY LEFT FOOT
NACHO LIBRE
NIGHT GAMES
NIL BY MOUTH
NINE TO FIVE
NOW VOYAGER
OH MR PORTER
ON THE BEACH
OSSESSIONE
OUT OF SIGHT
PARENTHOOD
PHONE BOOTH
PILLOW TALK
POOL SHARKS
POSSESSION
PRIMAL FEAR
RAGING BULL
REAR WINDOW
RED GARTERS *m*
RED SORGHUM
ROAD TO BALI
ROLLERBALL
ROUSTABOUT *m*
RUN LOLA RUN
SAFETY LAST
SCARY MOVIE

SEABISCUIT
SEBASTIANE
SHENANDOAH *w*
SING AS WE GO *m*
SLINGBLADE
SPELLBOUND
STAGECOACH *w*
SUMMERTIME
TAXI DRIVER
THE ACCUSED
THE AVIATOR
THE BIG HEAT
THE BLUE MAX
THE BREAK-UP
THE CITADEL
THE DRESSER
THE GENERAL
THE HEIRESS
THE HUSTLER
THE INSIDER
THE KILLERS
THE KILLING
THE LEOPARD
THE LOVE BUG
THE MISFITS
THE MISSION
THE PIANIST
THE RECRUIT
THE SHINING
THE SWIMMER
THE THIN MAN
THE TIN DRUM
THE VILLAGE
THE WILD ONE
THREE KINGS
UNFAITHFUL
UNFORGIVEN *w*
UP THE FRONT

VANILLA SKY
VIVA ZAPATA!
WALL STREET
WAY OUT WEST
WHALE RIDER
WHAT'S UP DOC?

11

A CHORUS LINE *m*
A CLOSE SHAVE *a*
A FEW GOOD MEN
ALL ABOUT EVE
ALL THAT JAZZ
ANALYZE THIS
ARISE MY LOVE
A STAR IS BORN *m*
BABES IN ARMS *m*
BARRY LYNDON
BEETLE JUICE
BELLE DE JOUR
BIG BUSINESS
BILLY ELLIOT
BLADE RUNNER
BLOOD SIMPLE
BOYS DON'T CRY
BROKEN ARROW
BUGSY MALONE
CALL ME MADAM *m*
CARMEN JONES *m*
CARRY ON CLEO
CARRY ON DICK
CARRY ON JACK
CHU CHIN CHOW *m*
CITIZEN KANE
CLAIRE'S KNEE
COACH CARTER
CONSTANTINE
CORPSE BRIDE *a*

CRIMSON TIDE
DAY FOR NIGHT
DEAD OF NIGHT
DEAD RINGERS
DELIVERANCE
DOCTOR AT SEA
DONNIE DARKO
DON'T LOOK NOW
ELEPHANT BOY
ELMER GANTRY
ENDLESS LOVE
FALLING DOWN
FINDING NEMO *a*
FIRESTARTER
FLASH GORDON
FLUSHED AWAY *a*
FORREST GUMP
GOSFORD PARK
HEAT AND DUST
HELL'S ANGELS
HIGH SOCIETY *m*
HOTEL RWANDA
IN COLD BLOOD
INTOLERANCE
IRMA LA DOUCE
I WANT TO LIVE
JABBERWOCKY
JACKIE BROWN
LA DOLCE VITA
LISZTOMANIA *m*
LITTLE NICKY
LITTLE WOMEN
LORENZO'S OIL
LOST HIGHWAY
LOST HORIZON
LUST FOR LIFE
MAGNUM FORCE
MARATHON MAN

MARS ATTACKS!
MARY POPPINS *m*
MEAN STREETS
MEET JOHN DOE
MODERN TIMES
MONSTERS INC *a*
MOULIN ROUGE *m*
MYSTIC RIVER
NANNY MCPHEE
NIGHT AND DAY *m*
NO NO NANETTE *m*
NOTTING HILL
OLIVER TWIST
OUR MISS FRED
OUT OF AFRICA
PEARL HARBOR
PERFORMANCE
PEYTON PLACE
POLTERGEIST
PRÊT-À-PORTER
PRETTY WOMAN
PROOF OF LIFE
PULP FICTION
ROGER DODGER
ROME EXPRESS
ROOM SERVICE
RUNAWAY JURY
SAVING GRACE
SHADOWLANDS
SHIP OF FOOLS
SOLDIER BLUE
STRANGE DAYS
SUMMER OF SAM
SUPER SIZE ME
TEACHER'S PET
THE BANK DICK
THE BIG SLEEP
THE BLUE LAMP

THE CABLE GUY
THE CARDINAL
THE CRUEL SEA
THE DEPARTED
THE ENFORCER
THE EXORCIST
THE FUGITIVE
THE GOLD RUSH
THE GOOD GIRL
THE GRADUATE
THE GRIFTERS
THE ICE STORM
THE KING AND I *m*
THE LAST WAVE
THE LION KING *a*
THE MAGIC BOX
THE MUSIC BOX
THE OMEGA MAN
THE PALEFACE
THE QUIET MAN
THE RED SHOES
THE RESCUERS *a*
THE SHOOTIST *w*
THE TERMINAL
THE THIRD MAN
THE WAY AHEAD
THE WRONG BOX
THUNDERBALL
THUNDER ROCK
TIME BANDITS
TORN CURTAIN
TOTAL RECALL
TOUCH OF EVIL
TRAINING DAY
WAR AND PEACE
WAYNE'S WORLD
WILD AT HEART
WOMEN IN LOVE

WORKING GIRL

12
ABOUT SCHMIDT
ACE IN THE HOLE
ALMOST FAMOUS
AMORES PERROS
ANDREI RUBLEV
ANNA KARENINA
ANYTHING GOES *m*
APRIL IN PARIS *m*
ATLANTIC CITY
A VIEW TO A KILL
BAD EDUCATION
BATMAN BEGINS
BATTLEGROUND
BLITHE SPIRIT
BLOOD AND SAND
BOOGIE NIGHTS
BOYZ N THE HOOD
BREAKING AWAY
BRIGHTON ROCK
CACTUS FLOWER
CALAMITY JANE *m/w*
CAPRICORN ONE
CAPTAIN BLOOD
CARRY ON CABBY
CARRY ON GIRLS
CARRY ON HENRY
CARRY ON NURSE
CASINO ROYALE
CITY SLICKERS
COLD MOUNTAIN
COOL HAND LUKE
DAY OF THE DEAD
DAYS OF HEAVEN
DELICATESSEN
DIRTY DANCING

DOCTOR IN LOVE
DONNIE BRASCO
DONOVAN'S REEF
DRAGONSLAYER
DUEL IN THE SUN
EASTER PARADE *m*
EYES WIDE SHUT
FITZCARRALDO
FRANKENSTEIN
GHOSTBUSTERS
GREGORY'S GIRL
GROUNDHOG DAY
GUYS AND DOLLS *m*
HELLZAPOPPIN'
HIGH FIDELITY
HOUSE OF CARDS
IN THE BEDROOM
JERRY MAGUIRE
JURASSIC PARK
KEY TO THE CITY
KISS ME DEADLY
LA RÈGLE DU JEU
LE JOUR SE LÈVE
LETHAL WEAPON
LITTLE CAESAR
LOVE ACTUALLY
LOVE AND DEATH
LOVE ME TENDER *m*
MAJOR BARBARA
MEMPHIS BELLE
MONSTER-IN-LAW
MONSTER'S BALL
MRS DOUBTFIRE
MY MAN GODFREY
MYSTERY TRAIN
NEVER TOO LATE
OCEAN'S ELEVEN
OF MICE AND MEN

OLIVER'S STORY
ONE FALSE MOVE
ONE HOUR PHOTO
ON GOLDEN POND
PADRE PADRONE
PATHS OF GLORY
PATRIOT GAMES
PHILADELPHIA
PORK CHOP HILL
PRIZZI'S HONOR
QUADROPHENIA *m*
RAMBLING ROSE
RESIDENT EVIL
REUBEN REUBEN
ROAD TO UTOPIA
ROMAN HOLIDAY
ROOM AT THE TOP
RUNAWAY BRIDE
SAILOR BEWARE
SAN FRANCISCO
SANTA FÉ TRAIL *w*
SAVE THE TIGER
SCHOOL OF ROCK *m*
SERGEANT YORK
SEVEN SAMURAI
SHALLOW GRAVE
SHALL WE DANCE? *m*
SLEEPY HOLLOW
SLIDING DOORS
SONG OF NORWAY *m*
SOUTH PACIFIC *m*
SPIRITED AWAY *a*
STAYING ALIVE *m*
STUART LITTLE
SWEET CHARITY *m*
TANGO AND CASH
THE APARTMENT
THE BIG PARADE

THE BLUE ANGEL *m*
THE BOY FRIEND *m*
THE CANDIDATE
THE COLLECTOR
THE CONTENDER
THE FAMILY WAY
THE FRONT PAGE
THE FULL MONTY
THE GO-BETWEEN
THE GODFATHER
THE GOOD EARTH
THE GREAT RACE
THE GREEN MILE
THE KARATE KID
THE LAKE HOUSE
THE LAST METRO
THE MACHINIST
THE MAIN EVENT
THE NAKED CITY
THE NAVIGATOR
THE NUN'S STORY
THE ODD COUPLE
THE PRODUCERS *m*
THE UNINVITED
THE WESTERNER *w*
THE WILD BUNCH *w*
THE WILD GEESE
THE YOUNG ONES *m*
THINGS TO COME
TORA! TORA! TORA!
TOWED IN A HOLE
V FOR VENDETTA
VIVA LAS VEGAS *m*
WATERLOO ROAD
WE'RE NO ANGELS
WHISKY GALORE
WILD WILD WEST *w*
WITHNAIL AND I

YOUNG AT HEART
YOUNG WINSTON

13
A BRIDGE TOO FAR
A KIND OF LOVING
ALTERED STATES
ANCHORS AWEIGH *m*
APOCALYPSE NOW
ARE WE THERE YET?
ARLINGTON ROAD
A TASTE OF HONEY
A TOUCH OF CLASS
A WALK IN THE SUN
BABETTE'S FEAST
BASIC INSTINCT
BATMAN FOREVER
BATMAN RETURNS
BEFORE SUNRISE
BLACK HAWK DOWN
BORN YESTERDAY
BOY ON A DOLPHIN
BREAKER MORANT
BREAKING GLASS *m*
BROADCAST NEWS
BROKEN FLOWERS
BRUCE ALMIGHTY
BURNT BY THE SUN
CABIN IN THE SKY *m*
CARRY ON ABROAD
CARRY ON BEHIND
CARRY ON COWBOY
CARRY ON DOCTOR
CARRY ON MATRON
CARRY ON SPYING
CHANGING LANES
CHILDREN OF MEN
CINDERELLA MAN

COUSIN COUSINE
DADDY LONG LEGS *m*
DAWN OF THE DEAD
DAYS OF THUNDER
DEATH IN VENICE
DEMOLITION MAN
DIE ANOTHER DAY
DINNER AT EIGHT
DOCTOR AT LARGE
DOCTOR ZHIVAGO
DRESSED TO KILL
DR STRANGELOVE
DUMB AND DUMBER
EDUCATING RITA
EIGHT AND A HALF
ELIZABETHTOWN
ENGLAND MADE ME
ERIC THE VIKING
EXPRESSO BONGO
FANTASTIC FOUR
FAR FROM HEAVEN
FIELD OF DREAMS
FOR ME AND MY GAL *m*
GIVE ME A SAILOR
HALF A SIXPENCE *m*
HARRY AND TONTO
HEAVEN CAN WAIT
HIS GIRL FRIDAY
HOBSON'S CHOICE
HOLLYWOODLAND
HORSE FEATHERS
HOW I WON THE WAR
ICE COLD IN ALEX
JAILHOUSE ROCK *m*
JOHNNY BELINDA
KISSIN' COUSINS *m*
KOYAANISQATSI
LA BÊTE HUMAINE

LACOMBE LUCIEN
LAUGHING GRAVY
LEGALLY BLONDE
LES MISÉRABLES
LICENCE TO KILL
LIVE AND LET DIE
LOVE ME TONIGHT *m*
LOVE ON THE DOLE
MA AND PA KETTLE
MAN OF LA MANCHA *m*
MATCHSTICK MEN
MILDRED PIERCE
MISTER ROBERTS
MO BETTER BLUES
MONA LISA SMILE
MR AND MRS SMITH
MY COUSIN VINNY
NEVER ON SUNDAY
NORTH TO ALASKA
NOTHING SACRED
PAN'S LABYRINTH
PARADISE ALLEY
PLEASANTVILLE
POLICE ACADEMY
PRIMARY COLORS
PRIVATE ANGELO
RANDOM HARVEST
RESERVOIR DOGS
ROAD TO MOROCCO
ROMAN SCANDALS *m*
ROSEMARY'S BABY
RYAN'S DAUGHTER
SCENT OF A WOMAN
SEVENTH HEAVEN
SILK STOCKINGS *m*
SITTING PRETTY
SOME LIKE IT HOT
SOMETHING WILD

SONS AND LOVERS
SOPHIE'S CHOICE
STORMY WEATHER *m*
SUMMER HOLIDAY *m*
THE ARISTOCATS *a*
THE AWFUL TRUTH
THE BIG COUNTRY *w*
THE BLUE LAGOON
THE COTTON CLUB
THE CRYING GAME
THE DAM BUSTERS
THE DAWN PATROL
THE DEER HUNTER
THE DESERT SONG *m*
THE DIRTY DOZEN
THE FALLEN IDOL
THE FISHER KING
THE GHOST TRAIN
THE ITALIAN JOB
THE JAZZ SINGER
THE LAST DETAIL
THE LAST TYCOON
THE LONGEST DAY
THE MERRY WIDOW *m*
THE MISSIONARY
THE NAKED TRUTH
THE PAJAMA GAME *m*
THE PAPER CHASE
THE PAWNBROKER
THE RAZOR'S EDGE
THE ROSE TATTOO
THE RUNAWAY BUS
THE SIXTH SENSE
THE SOUTHERNER
THE TENDER TRAP
THE TERMINATOR
THE TRUMAN SHOW
THE WHISPERERS

THE WICKED LADY
THE WIZARD OF OZ *m*
THE WORLD OF APU
THRONE OF BLOOD
TO BE OR NOT TO BE
TO CATCH A THIEF
TO SIR WITH LOVE
TRAINSPOTTING
TROUBLE IN MIND
TWO WAY STRETCH
UNDER TWO FLAGS
UP THE JUNCTION
WATERSHIP DOWN
WEST SIDE STORY
WHITE MISCHIEF
WINGS OF DESIRE
WONDERFUL LIFE *m*
ZORBA THE GREEK

14

A BEAUTIFUL MIND
À BOUT DE SOUFFLE
A DAY AT THE RACES
A HANDFUL OF DUST
A HARD DAY'S NIGHT *m*
ALL THE KING'S MEN
ALONG CAME POLLY
AMERICAN BEAUTY
AMERICAN GIGOLO
ANIMAL CRACKERS
ANNA AND THE KING
A PLACE IN THE SUN
A ROOM WITH A VIEW
AS GOOD AS IT GETS
A SHOT IN THE DARK
A TOWN LIKE ALICE
BICYCLE THIEVES
BLACK NARCISSUS

BLAZING SADDLES
BONNIE AND CLYDE
BREAKHEART PASS *w*
BRIEF ENCOUNTER
BRINGING UP BABY
BROADWAY MELODY
CARRY ON CAMPING
CARRY ON ENGLAND
CARRY ON TEACHER
CHARIOTS OF FIRE
CHARLEY VARRICK
CHARLIE BUBBLES
CHARLIE'S ANGELS
CINEMA PARADISO
COOKIE'S FORTUNE
DEAD MAN WALKING
DEATH ON THE NILE
DIAL M FOR MURDER
DOCTOR IN CLOVER
ELECTRIC DREAMS
EMPIRE OF THE SUN
ENTER THE DRAGON
ERIN BROCKOVICH
EXECUTIVE SUITE
FINDERS KEEPERS *m*
FINIAN'S RAINBOW *m*
FIVE EASY PIECES
FOLLOW THE FLEET *m*
GANGS OF NEW YORK
GOODBYE MR CHIPS
GO WEST YOUNG MAN
HANGOVER SQUARE
HANNIBAL RISING
I'M ALL RIGHT JACK
INHERIT THE WIND
IN WHICH WE SERVE
IVAN'S CHILDHOOD
JEAN DE FLORETTE

KRAMER VS KRAMER
LA CONFIDENTIAL
LASSIE COME HOME
MEET THE FOCKERS
MEET THE PARENTS
MIDNIGHT COWBOY
MINORITY REPORT
MONKEY BUSINESS
MURIEL'S WEDDING
NATIONAL VELVET
OF HUMAN BONDAGE
ONLY TWO CAN PLAY
ORDINARY PEOPLE
OUR HOSPITALITY
OUR MAN IN HAVANA
PAINT YOUR WAGON *m/w*
PATHER PANCHALI
PLAY MISTY FOR ME
PUNCH-DRUNK LOVE
QUEEN CHRISTINA
RAISING ARIZONA
REACH FOR THE SKY
ROAD TO HONG KONG
ROAD TO ZANZIBAR
SANDS OF IWO JIMA
SCHINDLER'S LIST
SECRETS AND LIES
SEPARATE TABLES
SERGEANTS THREE
SEVEN DAYS IN MAY
SHADOW OF A DOUBT
SHAUN OF THE DEAD
SNAKES ON A PLANE
STEEL MAGNOLIAS
TALES OF HOFFMAN *m*
TEQUILA SUNRISE
THAT'LL BE THE DAY
THE BIG LEBOWSKI

THE BLACK DAHLIA
THE CAINE MUTINY
THE COLOR PURPLE
THE COMMITMENTS *m*
THE COUNTRY GIRL
THE DA VINCI CODE
THE ELEPHANT MAN
THE FIFTH ELEMENT
THE GAY DIVORCEE *m*
THE GOLD DIGGERS *m*
THE GOODBYE GIRL
THE GREAT CARUSO
THE GREAT ESCAPE
THE GREAT GATSBY
THE INCREDIBLES *a*
THE INTERPRETER
THE IPCRESS FILE
THE JOKER IS WILD
THE JOLSON STORY
THE JOY LUCK CLUB
THE LADYKILLERS
THE LAST EMPEROR
THE LAST SAMURAI
THE LIFE OF BRIAN
THE LITTLE FOXES
THE LONGEST YARD
THE LONG GOODBYE
THE LOST WEEKEND
THE L-SHAPED ROOM
THE MARK OF ZORRO
THE MASK OF ZORRO
THE MUSIC LOVERS
THE OKLAHOMA KID *w*
THE PINK PANTHER
THE PUBLIC ENEMY
THE RUSSIA HOUSE
THE SEVENTH SEAL
THE SEVENTH VEIL

THE SINGING FOOL *m*
THE THIN RED LINE
THE WAGES OF FEAR
THIS GUN FOR HIRE
THIS HAPPY BREED
TOUCHING THE VOID
TROUBLE IN STORE
TWELVE ANGRY MEN
TWO WEEKS' NOTICE
VANISHING POINT
VELVET GOLDMINE
WAR OF THE WORLDS
WOMAN OF THE YEAR
YOU ME AND DUPREE
YOUNG MR LINCOLN
Y TU MAMÁ TAMBIÉN
ZABRISKIE POINT

15

ABOVE US THE WAVES
A FACE IN THE CROWD
ALEXANDER NEVSKY
ANGER MANAGEMENT
ANNIE GET YOUR GUN *m*
A PASSAGE TO INDIA
BACK TO THE FUTURE
BEDTIME FOR BONZO
BEVERLY HILLS COP
CALIFORNIA SUITE
CARNAL KNOWLEDGE
CARRY ON CRUISING
CARRY ON SERGEANT
CATCH ME IF YOU CAN
CIRCLE OF FRIENDS
CROCODILE DUNDEE
DANCER IN THE DARK *m*
DEATH BECOMES HER
DOCTOR IN TROUBLE

DOG DAY AFTERNOON
DO THE RIGHT THING
DOUBLE INDEMNITY
ENEMY OF THE STATE
EVIL UNDER THE SUN
FAILURE TO LAUNCH
FANNY BY GASLIGHT
FANTASTIC VOYAGE
FATAL ATTRACTION
FELICIA'S JOURNEY
FLYING DOWN TO RIO *m*
FOOTLIGHT PARADE
FORBIDDEN PLANET
FOR YOUR EYES ONLY
FULL METAL JACKET
FUNERAL IN BERLIN
GIRL INTERRUPTED
GODS AND MONSTERS
GONE WITH THE WIND
GOOD WILL HUNTING
HILARY AND JACKIE
ICE STATION ZEBRA
INDEPENDENCE DAY
JESUS OF MONTREAL
JOURNEY INTO FEAR
KINDERGARTEN COP
KINGDOM OF HEAVEN
LA CAGE AUX FOLLES
LADY AND THE TRAMP *a*
LAST MAN STANDING
LEAVING LAS VEGAS
LE QUAI DES BRUMES
LES BELLES DE NUIT
LIFE IS BEAUTIFUL
LOOK WHO'S TALKING
LOVE ME OR LEAVE ME
MANON DES SOURCES
MARRIED TO THE MOB

MEET ME IN ST LOUIS *m*
MIDNIGHT EXPRESS
MIGHTY APHRODITE
MILLER'S CROSSING
MONSIEUR VERDOUX
MOVE OVER DARLING
MULHOLLAND DRIVE
MULHOLLAND FALLS
ON THE WATERFRONT
PLANET OF THE APES
PRIVATE BENJAMIN
RAISE THE TITANIC
REAP THE WILD WIND
RETURN OF THE JEDI
ROAD TO PERDITION
ROAD TO SINGAPORE
SALLY IN OUR ALLEY
SHANGHAI EXPRESS
SHE DONE HIM WRONG
SINGIN' IN THE RAIN *m*
SONS OF THE DESERT
SOUTHERN COMFORT
STATE OF THE UNION
STRIKE UP THE BAND *m*
SUNSET BOULEVARD
SUPERMAN RETURNS
TARZAN THE APE MAN
THAT TOUCH OF MINK
THE AFRICAN QUEEN
THE COLDITZ STORY
THE COLOR OF MONEY
THE CONVERSATION
THE FOUR FEATHERS
THE INVISIBLE MAN
THE KING OF COMEDY
THE LADY VANISHES
THE LEMON DROP KID
THE LION IN WINTER

THELMA AND LOUISE
THE MUMMY RETURNS
THE PARALLAX VIEW
THE PELICAN BRIEF
THE POLAR EXPRESS *a*
THE SEVEN SAMURAI
THE SHIPPING NEWS
THE SOUND OF MUSIC *m*
THE SUNSHINE BOYS
THE TAMARIND SEED
THE UNTOUCHABLES
THE VAGABOND KING *m*
THIS IS SPINAL TAP
THREE COLOURS: RED
THREE MEN IN A BOAT
UNDER THE VOLCANO
VON RYAN'S EXPRESS
WATCH ON THE RHINE
WEDDING CRASHERS
WHERE EAGLES DARE
YANGTSE INCIDENT
YELLOW SUBMARINE *a*
YIELD TO THE NIGHT
ZIEGFELD FOLLIES *m*

16
A CLOCKWORK ORANGE
A FISH CALLED WANDA
AMERICAN GRAFFITI
A NIGHT TO REMEMBER
A PRIVATE FUNCTION
BLACKBOARD JUNGLE
BREAKING THE WAVES
CLASH OF THE TITANS
CONSPIRACY THEORY
COURAGE UNDER FIRE
CRIES AND WHISPERS
CYRANO DE BERGERAC

DANCES WITH WOLVES *w*
DAVID COPPERFIELD
DEAD POETS SOCIETY
DESTRY RIDES AGAIN
DRIVING MISS DAISY
FAREWELL MY LOVELY
FINDING NEVERLAND
FRANKIE AND JOHNNY
HONEYMOON IN VEGAS
HOW THE WEST WAS WON *w*
HUSBANDS AND WIVES
INDECENT PROPOSAL
IN THE MOOD FOR LOVE
KISS KISS BANG BANG
LA GRANDE ILLUSION
LAST TANGO IN PARIS
LAWRENCE OF ARABIA
LEGENDS OF THE FALL
LILIES OF THE FIELD
MISS CONGENIALITY
NORTH BY NORTHWEST
ONCE WERE WARRIORS
RABBIT-PROOF FENCE
SHIRLEY VALENTINE
STARDUST MEMORIES
STRICTLY BALLROOM
SULLIVAN'S TRAVELS
SWEET BIRD OF YOUTH
SWEET HOME ALABAMA
THE ANDERSON TAPES
THE ASPHALT JUNGLE
THE BROTHERS GRIMM
THE CHINA SYNDROME
THE FORTUNE COOKIE
THE GRAPES OF WRATH
THE GREAT DICTATOR
THE KILLING FIELDS
THE LAST SEDUCTION

THE MALTESE FALCON
THE MIRACLE WORKER
THE MOLLY MAGUIRES
THE NAME OF THE ROSE
THE OPPOSITE OF SEX
THE PRINCE OF EGYPT *a*
THE PRINCE OF TIDES
THE PRINCESS BRIDE
THE QUIET AMERICAN
THE SEVEN YEAR ITCH
THE SHELTERING SKY
THE STEPFORD WIVES
THE STRAIGHT STORY
THE TALK OF THE TOWN
THE THIEF OF BAGDAD
THE USUAL SUSPECTS
THE WAR OF THE ROSES
THE WAY TO THE STARS
THE WEDDING SINGER
THIS SPORTING LIFE
THREE COLOURS: BLUE
TRIUMPH OF THE WILL
TWELVE O'CLOCK HIGH
UNIVERSAL SOLDIER
VALLEY OF THE DOLLS
WILD STRAWBERRIES
WORLD TRADE CENTER
WUTHERING HEIGHTS
YOU ONLY LIVE TWICE
ZAZIE DANS LE MÉTRO

17
A FISTFUL OF DOLLARS *w*
AGUIRRE WRATH OF GOD
ALIEN RESURRECTION
A MAN FOR ALL SEASONS
AN AMERICAN IN PARIS *m*
ANY WHICH WAY YOU CAN

ARSENIC AND OLD LACE
A ZED AND TWO NOUGHTS
BAD DAY AT BLACK ROCK *w*
BAREFOOT IN THE PARK
BEAUTY AND THE BEAST *a*
BEND IT LIKE BECKHAM
BIRDMAN OF ALCATRAZ
BOUDU SAUVÉ DES EAUX
BRITANNIA HOSPITAL
BROADWAY DANNY ROSE
BROKEBACK MOUNTAIN *w*
CONAN THE BARBARIAN
CONAN THE DESTROYER
DANGEROUS LIAISONS
DEFENCE OF THE REALM
DEVIL IN A BLUE DRESS
DIRTY PRETTY THINGS
DR JEKYLL AND MR HYDE
EXECUTIVE DECISION
FANNY AND ALEXANDER
FIVE GRAVES TO CAIRO
GLENGARRY GLEN ROSS
GREAT EXPECTATIONS
GROSSE POINTE BLANK
HEAVENLY CREATURES
HERE COMES MR JORDAN
HIGH PLAINS DRIFTER *w*
IT'S A WONDERFUL LIFE
LOST IN TRANSLATION
LUCKY NUMBER SLEVIN
MELINDA AND MELINDA
MILLION DOLLAR BABY
MISSION: IMPOSSIBLE
MR DEEDS GOES TO TOWN
MUTINY ON THE BOUNTY
MY BRILLIANT CAREER
PANIC IN THE STREETS
PASSPORT TO PIMLICO

PELLE THE CONQUEROR
PRIDE AND PREJUDICE
REVERSAL OF FORTUNE
ROMANCING THE STONE
SAVING PRIVATE RYAN
SEVEN YEARS IN TIBET
SHAKESPEARE IN LOVE
SINGLE WHITE FEMALE
STRANGERS ON A TRAIN
TERMS OF ENDEARMENT
THE AGE OF INNOCENCE
THE BIRTH OF A NATION
THE BOURNE IDENTITY
THE DAY OF THE JACKAL
THE DEVIL'S ADVOCATE
THE DUKES OF HAZZARD
THE ENGLISH PATIENT
THE FIRST WIVES CLUB
THE HORSE WHISPERER
THE HUDSUCKER PROXY
THE LORD OF THE RINGS
THE MATRIX RELOADED
THE MISSOURI BREAKS w
THE NUTTY PROFESSOR
THE PALM BEACH STORY
THE SCARLET EMPRESS
THE SIGN OF THE CROSS
THE WEDDING BANQUET
THE WINGS OF THE DOVE
THREE COLOURS: WHITE
TOMORROW NEVER DIES
TROUBLE IN PARADISE
WHEN HARRY MET SALLY
WHERE THE TRUTH LIES
YANKEE DOODLE DANDY
YOUNG FRANKENSTEIN

18
AU REVOIR LES ENFANTS
BATTLESHIP POTEMKIN
BEING JOHN MALKOVICH
BILLION DOLLAR BRAIN
BRIDGET JONES'S DIARY
BRINGING OUT THE DEAD
BUTTERFLIES ARE FREE
CARRY ON UP THE KHYBER
COAL MINER'S DAUGHTER
DANCE WITH A STRANGER
DIAMONDS ARE FOREVER
EDWARD SCISSORHANDS
ELECTRA GLIDE IN BLUE
FLIGHT OF THE PHOENIX
FOR A FEW DOLLARS MORE w
FROM HERE TO ETERNITY
FROM RUSSIA WITH LOVE
FUN WITH DICK AND JANE
GONE IN SIXTY SECONDS
GOOD MORNING VIETNAM
HOW TO STEAL A MILLION
INTOLERABLE CRUELTY
IT HAPPENED ONE NIGHT
IT HAPPENED TOMORROW
LAST EXIT TO BROOKLYN
MASTER AND COMMANDER
MCCABE AND MRS MILLER
MISSISSIPPI BURNING
NATURAL BORN KILLERS
NEVER SAY NEVER AGAIN
NIGHT TRAIN TO MUNICH
PEGGY SUE GOT MARRIED
REBEL WITHOUT A CAUSE
SATURDAY NIGHT FEVER
SLEEPLESS IN SEATTLE
SPLENDOR IN THE GRASS
SUNDAY BLOODY SUNDAY

THANK YOU FOR SMOKING
THE BATTLE OF ALGIERS
THE BOURNE SUPREMACY
THE CIDER HOUSE RULES
THE DEVIL WEARS PRADA
THE LAST DAYS OF DISCO
THE LAST PICTURE SHOW
THE LAVENDER HILL MOB
THE LIVING DAYLIGHTS
THE MAGIC ROUNDABOUT
THE PLOUGHMAN'S LUNCH
THE PRISONER OF ZENDA
THE REMAINS OF THE DAY
THE ROYAL TENENBAUMS
THE THIRTY-NINE STEPS
THE THREE CABALLEROS *a/m*
THE THREE FACES OF EVE
THE THREE MUSKETEERS
THE TOWERING INFERNO
TO KILL A MOCKINGBIRD

19

ALL THE PRESIDENT'S MEN
A RIVER RUNS THROUGH IT
A SLIGHT CASE OF MURDER
BOWLING FOR COLUMBINE
BREAKFAST AT TIFFANY'S
BRIDE OF FRANKENSTEIN
BULLETS OVER BROADWAY
COFFEE AND CIGARETTES
DIVORCE ITALIAN STYLE
FAREWELL MY CONCUBINE
FRIDAY THE THIRTEENTH
GENTLEMAN'S AGREEMENT
HANNAH AND HER SISTERS
HONEY I SHRUNK THE KIDS
HOW GREEN WAS MY VALLEY
IN THE HEAT OF THE NIGHT

JUDGMENT AT NUREMBERG
LARA CROFT: TOMB RAIDER
LAST YEAR IN MARIENBAD
LES ENFANTS DU PARADIS
LES ENFANTS TERRIBLES
LES QUATRE CENTS COUPS
MUCH ADO ABOUT NOTHING
MY DARLING CLEMENTINE *w*
NOT ANOTHER TEEN MOVIE *m*
ONLY ANGELS HAVE WINGS
PICNIC AT HANGING ROCK
RAIDERS OF THE LOST ARK
ROCCO AND HIS BROTHERS
SCENES FROM A MARRIAGE
SENSE AND SENSIBILITY
SEX LIES AND VIDEOTAPE
SOMETHING'S GOTTA GIVE
STRANGER THAN FICTION
SWEET SMELL OF SUCCESS
THANK YOUR LUCKY STARS *m*
THE AMITYVILLE HORROR
THE BAREFOOT CONTESSA
THE CONSTANT GARDENER
THE DIARY OF ANNE FRANK
THE FRENCH CONNECTION
THE MAN WHO WASN'T THERE
THE NIGHT OF THE HUNTER
THE NIGHT OF THE IGUANA
THE OUTLAW JOSEY WALES *w*
THE PHANTOM OF LIBERTY
THE SCARLET PIMPERNEL
THE TALENTED MR RIPLEY
THE WOMAN IN THE WINDOW
THE WORLD IS NOT ENOUGH

20

ANGELS WITH DIRTY FACES
BUENA VISTA SOCIAL CLUB

CHILDREN OF A LESSER GOD
CHITTY CHITTY BANG BANG *m*
CHRIST STOPPED AT EBOLI
DEAD MEN DON'T WEAR PLAID
EVERYONE SAYS I LOVE YOU *m*
FERRIS BUELLER'S DAY OFF
FOREIGN CORRESPONDENT
HOUSE OF FLYING DAGGERS
IN THE NAME OF THE FATHER
JASON AND THE ARGONAUTS
KISS OF THE SPIDER WOMAN
MY BEST FRIEND'S WEDDING
MY BIG FAT GREEK WEDDING
NIGHT OF THE LIVING DEAD
O BROTHER WHERE ART THOU? *m*
POSTCARDS FROM THE EDGE
SLEEPING WITH THE ENEMY
SMILES OF A SUMMER NIGHT
THE ACCIDENTAL TOURIST
THE AMERICAN PRESIDENT
THE BLAIR WITCH PROJECT

THE EMPIRE STRIKES BACK
THE FABULOUS BAKER BOYS
THE GREAT TRAIN ROBBERY
THE HUNT FOR RED OCTOBER
THE LAST OF THE MOHICANS *w*
THE LEAGUE OF GENTLEMEN
THE MAN IN THE WHITE SUIT
THE MAN WHO KNEW TOO MUCH
THE MAN WHO WOULD BE KING
THE MATRIX REVOLUTIONS
THE MOTORCYCLE DIARIES
THE PHANTOM OF THE OPERA *m*
THE PHILADELPHIA STORY
THE POSEIDON ADVENTURE
THE PURPLE ROSE OF CAIRO
THE SILENCE OF THE LAMBS
THE THOMAS CROWN AFFAIR
THE WITCHES OF EASTWICK
WHILE YOU WERE SLEEPING
WHO FRAMED ROGER RABBIT?
YOU CAN'T TAKE IT WITH YOU

Arts – Crafts – ANTIQUE NAMES
clocks = clockmaker or watchmaker furniture = furniture maker or cabinetmaker
glass = glassmaker pottery = potter or porcelain maker
silver = silversmith or goldsmith

4

ADAM Robert – furniture
AULT William – pottery
DAUM Jean – glass
HOPE Thomas – furniture
INCE William – furniture
KOPF Silas – furniture
WADE John – pottery
WEBB Thomas – glass

5

BLOOR William – pottery
CLIFF Clarice – pottery
DUCHÉ Andrew – pottery
ELERS David John – pottery
GALLÉ Emile – glass
JACOB Georges – furniture
KNIBB John – clocks
KOCKS Adrianus – pottery

LEACH Bernard – pottery
LEROY Charles – clocks
MAROT Daniel – furniture
MOSER Horst – glass
ODIOT Nicolas – silver
OEBEN Jean-François – furniture
OLSEN Jens – clocks
PHYFE Duncan – furniture
ROUBO André – furniture
SPODE Josiah – pottery
STORR Paul – silver
TERRY Eli – clocks
VEZZI Francesco – pottery

6

AVISSE Jean – furniture
BOULLE André – furniture
CHAPIN Eliphalet – furniture
COOPER Susie – pottery
DUTTON William – clocks
DWIGHT John – pottery
GILLOW Robert – furniture
GRICCI Giuseppe – pottery
JANSEN Jacob – pottery
KOOMEN Philip – furniture
KRENOV James – furniture
LINLEY Viscount David – furniture
MALOOF Sam – furniture
MINTON Thomas – pottery
SEDDON George – furniture
SØRNES Rasmus – clocks
TÉTARD Jean – silver
THOMAS Seth – clocks
THONET Michael – furniture
VALLIN Eugène – furniture
WISTAR Caspar – glass

7

AFFLECK Thomas – furniture
AMELUNG John – glass
ANDRIES Jasper – pottery
ASTBURY John – pottery
BATEMAN Hester – silver
BÖTTGER Johann – pottery
BRAMELD George – pottery
BREGUET Abraham – clocks
CARTIER Louis – clocks
CELLINI Benvenuto – silver
CRESPIN Paul –silver
DESPREZ Jean – glass
DOULTON John – pottery
FABERGÉ Peter Carl – silver
GARRARD Robert – silver
GERMAIN Thomas – silver
GODDARD John – furniture
HUYGENS Christian – clocks
KÄNDLER Johann – pottery
KUNCKEL Johannes – glass
LACROIX Roger – furniture
LALIQUE René – glass
LESSORE Emile – pottery
SCHUPPE John – silver
SHEARER Thomas – furniture
STIEGEL Henry – glass
TIFFANY Louis – glass
TOMPION Thomas – clocks
WILLARD Aaron, Benjamin, Simon – clocks

8

BERTHOUD Ferdinand – clocks
BIENNAIS Martin-Guillaume – silver
BOLSOVER Thomas – silver
CLÉRISSY Pierre – pottery
DE MORGAN William – pottery
DENNISON Aaron – clocks

DUESBURY William – pottery
GAUDREAU Antoine – furniture
HARRISON John – clocks
KETTERER Franz – clocks
KOEPPING Karl – glass
LANNUIER Charles-Honoré
  – furniture
MELCHIOR Johann – pottery
REINLEIN Anton – clocks
RIESENER Jean Henri – furniture
RIETVELD Gerrit – furniture
SHERATON Thomas – furniture
SPENGLER Adam – pottery
SPRIMONT Nicholas – silver
STICKLEY Gustav – furniture
TINWORTH George – pottery
TOWNSEND John – furniture
VULLIAMY Benjamin – clocks
WEDGWOOD Josiah – pottery
WILLAUME David – silver
WILSDORF Hans – clocks

9
DE LAMERIE Paul – silver

INGERSOLL Robert H – clocks
JAMNITZER Wenzel – silver
MAJORELLE Louis – furniture
MOORCROFT William – pottery
NAKASHIMA George – furniture
PUIFORCAT Jean – silver
VAN NOUHYS Jan – silver
VERZELINI Giacomo – glass

10
COOKWORTHY William – pottery
DELAHERCHE Auguste – pottery
MEISSONIER Juste-Aurele – silver

11
BILLINGSLEY William – pottery
CHIPPENDALE Thomas – furniture
HEPPLEWHITE George – furniture
RAVENSCROFT George – glass
VAN EENHOORN Samuel – pottery

14
JACOB-DESMALTER François
  – furniture

Arts – Crafts – **CRAFT TERMS**

3	**4**			**5**
ART	BIND	ETUI	PURL	BATIK
HEM	BUHL	FIRE	SEAM	BLOOM
PIN	(or boulle)	FRET	SLIP	BRAID
SET	CARD	FRIT	SUNG	CARVE
SEW	CAST	KILN	TURN	CHASE
TAT	CLAY	KNIT	WARP	CHINA
	CONE	LOOM	WEFT	CRAFT
	DARN	LOOP		DELFT
		MING		

DERBY
DOWEL
FLOSS
FLUTE
FRAME
GLAZE
GRAIN
HOBBY
INLAY
IVORY
JAPAN
JOINT
KYLIN
MITRE
MODEL
MOULD
MOUNT
PASTE
PEARL
PICOT
PLAIN
PLAIT
PLATE
PLEAT
QUILT
REPRO
SCARF
SPODE
TENON
THROW
WEAVE

6

BISQUE
BLUNGE
BONSAI
BOULLE
(or buhl)

EMBOSS
FAGGOT
FINISH
FIRING
GOFFER
JASPER
KAOLIN
LUSTRE
MARBLE
MOSAIC
NEEDLE
NIELLO
OFFCUT
ORMOLU
OSIERY
PATINA
PURFLE
RABBET
(or rebate)
RAFFIA
REBATE
(or rabbet)
RÉSEAU
SAGGAR
SÈVRES
SEWING
STITCH
TIE-DYE
VENEER
WICKER

7

BARBOLA
BINDING
BISCUIT
BLUNGER
BUNRAKU
BURNISH

CARVING
CASTING
CERAMIC
CHASING
COLLAGE
CROCHET
CRYSTAL
DARNING
DRESDEN
FABERGÉ
FAIENCE
GOBELIN
IKEBANA
JOINERY
LACQUER
MACRAMÉ
MATTING
MEANDER
MEISSEN
MORTISE
NAILING
NETSUKE
ORIGAMI
PASTIME
PATTERN
POTTERY
RUBBING
SAMPLER
SATSUMA
TAMBOUR
TATTING
TURNING
VARNISH
VERMEIL
WEAVING
WROUGHT

8

APPLIQUÉ
BASKETRY
BRAIDING
CERAMICS
COALPORT
DENTELLE
DOVETAIL
DOWEL PIN
EGGSHELL
EX LIBRIS
FRETWORK
GLYPTICS
GRAINING
HEELBALL
INTAGLIO
INTARSIA
IRONWARE
IRONWORK
KNITTING
KNOTTING
KNOTWORK
KOFTGARI
LAPIDARY
MAJOLICA
MANDARIN
MARBLING
MOULDING
OPENWORK
ORNAMENT
PETUNTSE
PLAITING
PLASTICS
PURFLING
REPOUSSÉ
TAPESTRY
THROWING
WEDGWOOD

WIREWORK
WOODWORK
WOOLWORK

9

BONE CHINA
CARPENTRY
CHAMPLEVÉ
CHINA CLAY
CHINAWARE
CLOISONNÉ
DELFTWARE
DRAWN WORK
FAGGOTING
FANCYWORK
FLAMEWARE
FOLK CRAFT
GLASSWARE
GOFFERING
GROS POINT
GUILLOCHE
HANDIWORK
HARD PASTE
HEM STITCH
HOMECRAFT
LETTERING
MARQUETRY
MODELLING
OBJET D'ART
OVERGLAZE
PARQUETRY
PATCHWORK
PEARLWARE
POKERWORK
PORCELAIN
SALT GLAZE
SCRIMSHAW
SCULPTURE

SGRAFFITO
SHELLWORK
SOFT PASTE
STEELWORK
STITCHING
STONEWARE
STUMPWORK
TIE-DYEING
TOP STITCH
TOREUTICS
VENEERING
VERDIGRIS
WHITEWARE
WORCESTER

10
BACK STITCH
BASKETWORK
BURNISHING
CAMEO GLASS
CREWEL WORK
CROCHETING
CROWN DERBY
EMBROIDERY
ENAMELWORK
FRENCH SEAM
GEM-CUTTING
HANDICRAFT
JASPERWARE
LITHOPHANE
LOCK STITCH
MATCHBOARD
MILLEFIORI
MOSS STITCH
NEEDLEWORK
OPEN STITCH
OVERSTITCH

PEACH-BLOOM
PENMANSHIP
PETIT POINT
PIETRA DURA
PILLOW LACE
PIN CUSHION
PLAIN WEAVE
PLASTICINE
PYROGRAPHY
QUEENSWARE
RENOVATION
REPOUSSAGE
ROPE STITCH
SAMIAN WARE
SLIP STITCH
STEM STITCH
TENT STITCH
TERRACOTTA
UNDERGLAZE
WHIP STITCH
WICKERWORK

11
BARBOLA WORK
BIAS BINDING
BLIND STITCH
BOOKBINDING
CABLE STITCH
CALLIGRAPHY
CHAIN STITCH
CHELSEA WARE
COPPERPLATE
CROCHET HOOK
CROSS STITCH
DOVETAILING
EARTHENWARE
FAMILLE ROSE

FANCY STITCH
GRANULATION
NEEDLECRAFT
NEEDLEPOINT
PLASTIC ARTS
QUEEN STITCH
RESTORATION
SATIN STITCH
SATSUMA WARE
SLIP CASTING
STEVENGRAPH
WHOLE STITCH
WROUGHT IRON

12
BASKET-MAKING
BLANC-DE-CHINE
BRASS RUBBING
CEROPLASTICS
CRACKLE GLAZE
DO-IT-YOURSELF
DRAIN CASTING
DRESDEN CHINA
FAMILLE JAUNE
FAMILLE NOIRE
FAMILLE VERTE
FRENCH POLISH
GARTER STITCH
GEM ENGRAVING
GLASS-BLOWING
GLYPTOGRAPHY
MEISSEN CHINA
PAINTED CLOTH
REPRODUCTION
SADDLE STITCH
SPIDER STITCH
VASE PAINTING

13
BLANKET STITCH
CABINET-MAKING
DARNING NEEDLE
FEATHER STITCH
FIGURE-CASTING
FLEMISH STITCH
MATCHBOARDING
MODELLING CLAY
NAIL AND THREAD
ORNAMENTATION
PASSEMENTERIE
PORCELAIN CLAY
RAILWAY STITCH
RUNNING STITCH
TORTOISESHELL
WILLOW PATTERN

14
COROMANDEL WORK
IVORY PORCELAIN
KNITTING NEEDLE
PERFECT BINDING
REDUCTION-FIRED
STOCKING STITCH
TERRA SIGILLATA
WHEATEAR STITCH

15
CLOISONNÉ ENAMEL
DRAWN-THREAD-WORK
FRENCH POLISHING

16
BUTTONHOLE STITCH

Arts – Dance – BALLET & DANCE TERMS

3
ACT
BOB
HOP
PAS
SET
TAP

4
BALL
FRIS
JAZZ
JETÉ
JUMP
PLIÉ
SKIP
STEP
TRIP
TURN
TUTU

5
BARRE
BEBOP
BRISE
DANCE
DISCO
GLIDE
PASSÉ
POISE
PUMPS
ROUND
SALSA
SWING
TWIRL

6
ADAGIO
BALLET
BALLON
CAMBRE
CHAINÉ
CHASSÉ
CHORUS
DANCER
DO-SI-DO
ENCORE
EN L'AIR
FIGURE
FRISKA
HIP HOP
HOOFER
KICK-UP
MASQUE
ODISSI
POINTE
RHYTHM
SPRING
TROUPE

7
ALLEGRO
ALLONGE
BALANCE
BARRIDA
CLASSIC
DANCING
DANSEUR
FOOTING
FOUETTÉ
LEOTARD

MAILLOT
MAYPOLE
MEASURE
PARTNER
PAS SEUL
RAGTIME
ROUNDEL
ROUTINE
SHUFFLE
TRENISE

8
ASSEMBLÉ
ATTITUDE
AUDITION
BALLROOM
BOOGALOO
CABRIOLE
CORYPHÉE
EN POINTE
ENSEMBLE
GLISSADE
HUNT BALL
ICE DANCE
MOVEMENT
ORCHESIS
PANTALON
SKIPPING
SPOTTING
STOMPING
TEA DANCE
WALTZING

9
ARABESQUE

BALLERINA
BATTEMENT
DANCE HALL
DÉVELOPPÉ
ELEVATION
ENTRECHAT
KATHAKALI
LAP DANCER
PAS DE DEUX
PIROUETTE
POUSSETTE
PROMENADE
REHEARSAL
TAP DANCER
VARIATION

10
CHORUS GIRL
CHORUS LINE
EPAULEMENT
GRAND MARCH
ICE DANCING
LAP DANCING
LINE DANCER
MASKED BALL
MASQUERADE
REPERTOIRE
TAP DANCING
THÉ DANSANT
TOUR EN L'AIR

11
BALLETOMANE
BALLET SHOES
BELLY DANCER

BREAK-DANCER
CHOREOGRAPH
DINNER DANCE
DISCOTHÉQUE
LIMBO DANCER
LINE DANCING
PASTOURELLE
PERFORMANCE
PORTE DE BRAS
ROND DE JAMBE

12
BALLETOMANIA
BELLY DANCING

BREAK-DANCING
CHASSÉ-CROISÉ
CHOREOGRAPHY
LABANOTATION
LIMBO DANCING
SKIRT DANCING

13
CORPS DE BALLET
FIGURE DANCING
MORRIS DANCING
PALAIS DE DANCE
SQUARE DANCING

14
COUNTRY DANCING
DIVERTISSEMENT
DRESS REHEARSAL
FANCY-DRESS BALL
JACK-IN-THE-GREEN

15
BALLROOM DANCING

16
FORMATION DANCING

Arts – Dance – **BALLET CHARACTERS**

4
IVAN *The Firebird*
GURN *La Sylphide*
JEAN *Raymonda*
LOYS *Giselle*

5
CLARA *The Nutcracker*
EFFIE *La Sylphide*
FRITZ *The Nutcracker*
JAMES *La Sylphide*
KITRI *Don Quixote*
ODILE *Swan Lake*
ROMEO *Romeo and Juliet*
SOLOR *La Bayadère*

6
AURORA *The Sleeping Beauty*
CONRAD *Le Corsaire*

JULIET *Romeo and Juliet*
MEDORA *Le Corsaire*
NIKIYA *La Bayadère*
ODETTE *Swan Lake*
SYLVIA *Sylvia*
TYBALT *Romeo and Juliet*

7
BASILIO *Don Quixote*
BLUE BOY *Les Patineurs*
GISELLE *Giselle*
KHVÉTIS *Les Noces*

8
ABDERMAN *Raymonda*
ALBRECHT *Giselle*
COPPÉLIA *Coppélia*
FIREBIRD *The Firebird*
GAMZATTI *La Bayadère*

HILARION *Giselle*
KASHCHEI *The Firebird*
MERCUTIO *Romeo and Juliet*
NASTASYA *Les Noces*
OLD MADGE *La Sylphide*
RAYMONDA *Raymonda*
ROTHBART *Swan Lake*
SIEGFRIED *Swan Lake*

9
ANASTASIA *Anastasia*
CARABOSSE *The Sleeping Beauty*
FLORIMUND *The Sleeping Beauty*
MOUSE KING *The Nutcracker*
RED KNIGHT *Checkmate*

10
BLACK QUEEN *Checkmate*
CINDERELLA *Cinderella*

LILAC FAIRY *The Sleeping Beauty*
PRINCE IVAN *The Firebird*

12
DROSSELMEYER *The Nutcracker*
SCHÉHÉRAZADE *Schéhérazade*

13
FRIAR LAURENCE *Romeo and Juliet*

14
CLARA STAHLBAUM *The Nutcracker*
FRITZ STAHLBAUM *The Nutcracker*
SUGAR PLUM FAIRY *The Nutcracker*

15
PRINCE FLORIMUND *The Sleeping Beauty*
PRINCE SIEGFRIED *Swan Lake*

Arts – Dance – BALLET TITLES

3
JOB Vaughan Williams

4
AGON Stravinsky
CAIN Blitzstein
JEUX Debussy
ORFA Adam

5
ARIEL Gerhard
CHOUT
  (or *The Buffoon*)
  Prokofiev

GROHG Copland
RODEO Copland

6
APOLLO
  (or *Apollon Musagète*)
  Stravinsky
BOLÉRO Ravel
CIGALE Massenet
DYBBUK Bernstein
ESPADA Massenet
FAÇADE Walton
GAYANE Khatchaturian
KHAMMA Debussy

LA PÉRI Dukas
PARADE Satie
SALOME Maxwell
  Davies
SYLVIA Delibes
THAMAR Balakirev
UNDINE Henze

7
BARABAU Rieti
ELECTRA Arnold
GISELLE Adam
ISADORA Bennett
NAMOUNA Lalo

ORPHEUS Henze Stravinsky
PAQUITA Minkus
THE LURE Holst

8
ADAM ZERO Bliss
CARD GAME (or *Jeu de Cartes*)
   Stravinsky
CARNAVAL Schumann
COPPÉLIA Delibes
KRAANERG Xenakis
LES NOCES Stravinsky
RAYMONDA Glazunov
SWAN LAKE Tchaikovsky
THE QUEST Walton

9
ANASTASIA Martinu
CHECKMATE Bliss
CLÉOPÂTRE Arensky
FANCY FREE Bernstein
LES BICHES Poulenc
PETRUSHKA (or *Petrouchka*)
   Stravinsky
SEBASTIAN Menotti
SOLITAIRE Arnold
SOUVENIRS Barber
SPARTACUS Khatchaturian
THE GUESTS Blitzstein

10
AGE OF STEEL (or *La Pas d'acier*)
   Prokofiev
AT MIDNIGHT Mahler
CINDERELLA Prokofiev
DON QUIXOTE Gerhard Minkus
LA BAYADÈRE Minkus
LA SYLPHIDE Schneitzhoeffer

LE CARILLON Massenet
LE CORSAIRE Adam
LES FORAINS Sauguet
PETROUCHKA (or *Petrushka*)
   Stravinsky
THE BUFFOON (or *Chout*)
   Prokofiev
THE DISPLAY Williamson
THE SEASONS Cage Glazunov

11
BILLY THE KID Copland
EL AMOR BRUJO Falla
JEU DE CARTES (or *Card Game*)
   Stravinsky
LA PAS D'ACIER (or *Age of Steel*)
   Prokofiev
LE TRAIN BLEU Milhaud
NOBILISSIMA Hindemith
OLD KING COLE Vaughan Williams
PULCHINELLA Stravinsky
SCHLAGOBERS R Strauss
THE FIREBIRD Stravinsky
SHÉHÉRAZADE Ravel

12
HARLEQUINADE Drigo
JAZZ CALENDAR Bennett
LES PATINEURS Meyerbeer
LES SYLPHIDES Chopin
PILLAR OF FIRE Schoenberg
SCHÉHÉRAZADE Rimksy- Korsakov
THE BOX OF TOYS (or *La Boîte à
   joujoux*) Debussy
THE DYING SWAN Saint-Saëns

13
GIFT OF THE MAGI Foss

PINEAPPLE POLL Sullivan
THE FAIRY'S KISS (or *Le Baiser de la Fée*) Stravinsky
THE FIRST SHOOT Walton
THE NUTCRACKER Tchaikovsky
THE TWO PIGEONS (or *Les Deux Pigeons*) Messager

14
BALLET IMPERIAL Tchaikovsky
DAPHNIS ET CHLOË (or *Daphnis and Chloë*) Ravel
JOSEPHSLEGENDE R Strauss
LES DEUX PIGEONS (or *The Two Pigeons*) Messager
ROMEO AND JULIET Prokofiev
SCÉNES DE BALLET Stravinsky
THE PRODIGAL SON (or *L'Enfant prodigue*) Prokofiev
THE STONE FLOWER Prokofiev
THE WISE VIRGINS Walton

15
APOLLON MUSAGÈTE (or *Apollo*) Stravinsky

DAPHNIS AND CHLOË (or *Daphnis et Chloë*) Ravel
LA BOÎTE À JOUJOUX (or *The Box of Toys*) Debussy
LE BAISER DE LA FÉE (or *The Fairy's Kiss*) Stravinsky
L'ENFANT PRODIGUE (or *The Prodigal Son*) Prokofiev
SEVEN DEADLY SINS (or *Die sieben Todsünden*) Weill
THE AGE OF ANXIETY Bernstein
THE RITE OF SPRING Stravinsky
THE WOODEN PRINCE Bartók

16
HOMAGE TO THE QUEEN Arnold
MARY QUEEN OF SCOTS McCabe

17
THE SLEEPING BEAUTY Tchaikovsky

18
DIE SIEBEN TODSÜNDEN (or *Seven Deadly Sins*) Weill
L'APRÈS-MIDI D'UN FAUNE Debussy

Arts – Dance – DANCERS & CHOREOGRAPHERS

4
NAGY Ivan
PARK Merle
WALL David

5
CHANG Yat-Sen
DOLIN Anton

GABLE Christopher
GRISI Carlotta
HAMEL Martine van
JOOSS Kurt
KELLY Gene
LABAN Rudolf von
PETIT Roland
PLATT Marc

SLEEP Wayne
TUDOR Antony

6
ARPINO Gerald
ASHTON Sir Frederick
DANIAS Lisa Starr
DOWELL Anthony

DUNCAN Isadora
FOKINE Michel
MORRIS Mark
PETIPA Marius
POWELL Eleanor
ROGERS Ginger
SIBLEY Antoinette
VALOIS Dame Ninette de
WRIGHT Rebecca

7
ASTAIRE Fred
BUJONES Fernando
BUSSELL Darcey
FARRELL Suzanne
FONTEYN Dame Margot
GREGORY Cynthia
JOFFREY Robert
MARKOVA Dame Alicia
MARTINS Peter
MASSINE Léonide

NUREYEV Rudolf
PAVLOVA Anna
RAMBERT Dame Marie
ROBBINS Jerome
SEYMOUR Lynn
SHEARER Moira
TENNANT Veronica
ULANOVA Galina

8
CHARISSE Cyd
D'AMBOISE Jacques
EGLEVSKY André
FRANKLIN Freddie
GORDEYEV Vyacheslav
HELPMANN Sir Robert
KIRKLAND Gelsey
KRONSTAM Henning
NIJINSKY Vaslav
NOVIKOFF Ivan
VASILIEV Vladimir

9
DIAGHILEV Sergei
JEANMAIRE Zizi
KARSAVINA Tamara
TALLCHIEF Maria

10
AROLDINGEN Karin von
BALANCHINE George
BORTOLUZZI Paolo
MEZENTSEVA Galina

11
BARYSHNIKOV Mikhail
PLISETSKAYA Maya

12
ANANIASHVILI Nina

Arts – Dance – DANCES

3	JUBA	GOPAK	TWIST	HUSTLE
BOP	KOLO	KWELA	VALSE	JARANA
HAY	POGO	LIMBO	VOLTE	MAXIXE
JIG	POLO	LOURE	WALTZ	MINUET
	REEL	MAMBO		NAUTCH
4	SHAG	PAVAN	**6**	PAVANE
FADO		POLKA	BAGIYE	REDOWA
GATO	**5**	RUMBA	BOLERO	SHIMMY
HAKA	CONGA	SALSA	BOOGIE	SOUSTA
HULA	FLING	SAMBA	BOSTON	TROIKA
JIVE	GALOP	STOMP	CANCAN	VELETA
JOTA	GIGUE	TANGO	CHA-CHA	WATUSI

7
BACHATA
BAMBUCA
BARYNYA
BEGUINE
BOURRÉE
CARIOCA
CSARDAS
FARRUCA
FORLANA
FOXTROT
GAVOTTE
HALLING
HOEDOWN
LAMBADA
LANCERS
LÄNDLER
LAVOLTA
MADISON
MAZURKA
MILONGA
MODINHA
MORISCO
ONE-STEP
PLANXTY
POLACCA
ROMAIKA
SARDANA
SHUFFLE
SYRTAKI
TWO-STEP

8
ALEGRIAS
BULERIAS
BUNNY HOP
BUNNY HUG
CACHUCHA

CAKEWALK
CHACONNE
COURANTE
EXCUSE-ME
FAN DANCE
FANDANGO
FLAMENCO
GALLIARD
HABAÑERA
HEY-DE-GUY
HORNPIPE
HULA-HULA
ICE DANCE
IRISH JIG
KANTIKOY
LAP DANCE
LINDY HOP
PACHANGA
RIGADOON
SARABAND
SOFT-SHOE
TAP DANCE
WAR DANCE

9
ALLEMANDE
BARN DANCE
BERGAMASK
BOSSA NOVA
BREAKDOWN
CHA-CHA-CHA
CLOG DANCE
COTILLION
ÉCOSSAISE
FARANDOLE
FOLK DANCE
GALLOPADE
JITTERBUG

LINE DANCE
PASO DOBLE
PASSEPIED
PAUL JONES
POLONAISE
QUADRILLE
QUICK-STEP
RING DANCE
ROUNDELAY
SAND DANCE
SICILIANO
SPOT DANCE
STEP DANCE
TAMBOURIN
THREESOME
TRIPUDIUM
ZAPATEADO

10
BELLY DANCE
BREAK-DANCE
CARMAGNOLE
CHARLESTON
CINQUE-PACE
CORROBOREE
HOKEY-COKEY
HULLY GULLY
PETRONELLA
ROUND DANCE
SALTARELLO
SEGUIDILLA
SEVILLANAS
SNAKE DANCE
STRATHSPEY
SWORD DANCE
TARANTELLA
TURKEY TROT
TYROLIENNE

11
ANTIKRYSTOS
CRACOVIENNE
FIGURE DANCE
LAMBETH WALK
MORRIS DANCE
PALAIS GLIDE
SCHOTTISCHE
SHIMMY-SHAKE
SQUARE DANCE
TRENCHMORES
VARSOVIENNE

12
BOOGIE-WOOGIE
COUNTRY DANCE
FOURSOME REEL
VIRGINIA REEL

13
BOSTON TWO-STEP
DOUBLE SHUFFLE
EIGHTSOME REEL
HIGHLAND FLING
VIENNESE WALTZ

14
AMERICAN SMOOTH
FORMATION DANCE
LADIES' EXCUSE-ME

15
HESITATION WALTZ
INVITATION WALTZ
MEXICAN HAT DANCE
MILITARY TWO-STEP
ROGER DE COVERLEY
SOFT-SHOE SHUFFLE

Arts – Literature – LITERARY & POETIC TERMS

3
ANA
LAY
ODE
PEN

4
BOOK
EPIC
FOOT
HERO
IAMB
LINE
MODE
MYTH
OPUS
PLOT
POEM
SAGA
TALE
TEXT
TOME
WORD
WORK

5
ARSIS
CANON
CANTO
CENTO
CONTE
CYCLE
DIARY
DRAMA
ELEGY
ENVOI

EPODE
ESSAY
FABLE
GENRE
HAIKU
ICTUS
IDYLL
LYRIC
MANGA
METRE
MOTIF
NOVEL
OCTET
PAEON
PAPER
PIECE
PROSE
QUOTE
RHYME
ROMAN
RUN-ON
SCI-FI
SQUIB
STAVE
STICH
STORY
STUDY
STYLE
SUMMA
TANKA
THEME
TITLE
VERSE
WHEEL

6
BALLAD
CRETIC
DACTYL
DONNÉE
GHAZAL
IAMBIC
IAMBUS
JINGLE
LAD LIT
LEGEND
MANUAL
MASQUE
METRIC
MONODY
MYTHOS
OCTAVE
OEUVRE
PARODY
PASSUS
PERIOD
PHRASE
POETRY
PRÉCIS
PRIMER
RHYTHM
RONDEL
SATIRE
SCAZON
SEQUEL
SESTET
SIXAIN
SONNET
STANZA
TENSON
TERCET

THESIS
VOLUME

7
ALCAICS
BALLADE
BYRONIC
CAESURA
CHAPTER
CLASSIC
COMMENT
CONTEXT
COUPLET
DIMETER
DISTICH
ECLOGUE
EPIGRAM
EPISODE
EROTICA
EXCERPT
FABLIAU
FACTION
FICTION
FUSTIAN
GEORGIC
HEROINE
HISTORY
HOMERIC
IMAGISM
LAMPOON
MEASURE
MEMOIRS
MORCEAU
NOVELLA
ODYSSEY
PANTOUM

PARABLE
PASSAGE
PEN-NAME
POETICS
PREFACE
PREQUEL
PROSODY
REFRAIN
ROMANCE
RONDEAU
SAPPHIC
SESTINA
SETTING
SPONDEE
STICHOS
STROPHE
SUBPLOT
SUMMARY
TRILOGY
TRIOLET
TROCHEE
VERSION
VILLAIN
VIRELAY
WESTERN
WRITING

8
ALLEGORY
ANALECTS
ANAPAEST
ANTI-HERO
APOLOGIA
APOLOGUE
BUCOLICS
CHICK LIT

CHOLIAMB
CLERIHEW
CRITIQUE
DOGGEREL
EPILOGUE
EPYLLION
EUPHUISM
FOLK TALE
FOREWORD
HAMARTIA
HARDBACK
LIBRETTO
LIMERICK
LIPOGRAM
LONGUEUR
LYRICISM
MILTONIC
OPUSCULE
PALINODE
PASTICHE
PASTORAL
PINDARIC
PROLOGUE
PROTASIS
QUATRAIN
SAPPHICS
SCANSION
SENARIUS
SENTENCE
SPONDAIC
SPY STORY
SYLLABLE
SYNOPSIS
TEXTBOOK
THRILLER
TREATISE
TRIBRACH
TRISTICH

TROCHAIC
TROCHICS
VERSELET
WRITINGS

9
ALLOGRAPH
ANACRUSIS
ANTHOLOGY
BIOGRAPHY
CHARACTER
DITHYRAMB
EPICEDIUM
EPINICIAN
FAIRY TALE
FLASHBACK
FREE VERSE
HAGIOLOGY
HEMISTICH
HEXAMETER
LEITMOTIF
LONG METRE
LOVE STORY
LYRIC POEM
MANNERISM
MONOGRAPH
MONOMETER
NARRATIVE
NOVELETTE
OCTAMETER
OPUSCULUM
PAPERBACK
PARAGRAPH
PENILLION
POTBOILER
POT-POURRI
PROLUSION
PSEUDONYM

QUOTATION
STORY LINE
SYMBOLISM
TERZA RIMA
TETRALOGY
VERS LIBRE
WHODUNNIT

10
AMPHIBRACH
ANAPAESTIC
BLANK VERSE
CATALECTIC
CHORIAMBUS
CLASSICISM
DÉNOUEMENT
GHOST STORY
HEPTAMETER
HEROIC POEM
LAMPOONERY
LITERATURE
MAGNUM OPUS
METAPHRASE
MISCELLANY
MOCK-HEROIC
NOM DE PLUME
NON-FICTION
OTTAVA RIMA
PAGE-TURNER
PARAPHRASE
PARNASSIAN
PENTAMETER
PERIPETEIA
PETRARCHAN
ROMAN À CLEF
SHORT METRE
STAVE RHYME
STYLISTICS

TETRAMETER
VILLAINESS
VILLANELLE

11
ALEXANDRINE
ANTI-HEROINE
ANTISTROPHE
BALLAD METRE
CAMPUS NOVEL
CLIFFHANGER
COMMON METRE
COMPOSITION
DESCRIPTION
ENJAMBEMENT
FLORILEGIUM
GALLIAMBICS
GOTHIC NOVEL
HEROIC VERSE
HORROR STORY
LIFE HISTORY
MASTERPIECE
MYTHOGRAPHY
PASTOURELLE
PROTAGONIST
PULP FICTION
PURPLE PATCH
RHYME SCHEME
ROMAN-FLEUVE
SEPTENARIUS
TRANSLATION
WORD PICTURE

12
AIRPORT NOVEL
ARCHILOCHIAN
BODICE-RIPPER
DISQUISITION

EPITHALAMIUM
LIGHT READING
NURSERY RHYME
OCTOSYLLABLE
PROLEGOMENON
PROTHALAMIUM
SPINE-CHILLER
SPRUNG RHYTHM
STORY-TELLING

13
AUTOBIOGRAPHY
BELLES-LETTRES
FEMININE RHYME
HEROIC COUPLET

NONSENSE VERSE
PENNY DREADFUL
POETIC LICENCE
POST-MODERNISM

14
ADVENTURE NOVEL
CHILDREN'S NOVEL
CONCRETE POETRY
DETECTIVE STORY
LOCUS CLASSICUS
MAGICAL REALISM
MASCULINE RHYME
RHYMING COUPLET
SCIENCE FICTION

15
EPISTOLARY NOVEL
FEMININE CAESURA
HISTORICAL NOVEL
PICARESQUE NOVEL
SERPENTINE VERSE
TRANSLITERATION

16
COMING-OF-AGE NOVEL
IAMBIC PENTAMETER
MASCULINE CAESURA

Arts – Literature – NOVEL CHARACTERS (Dickens)

3
BAR *Dorrit*
BEN *Twist*
BET (or Betsy) *Twist*
BIB Julius *Chuzzlewit*
BOB *Dorrit*
BUD Rosa (or Pussy) *Drood*
CLY Roger *Two Cities*
FAN *Carol*
FEE Doctor *Mudfog*
GAY Walter *Dombey*
JEM *Pickwick*
JOE *Carol, Dombey, Drood, Pickwick,*
  Twist, Two Cities
LIZ *Bleak*
NED *Twist*
PIP *Chuzzlewit*

PIP (or Philip Pirrip) *Expectations*
SAM *Chuzzlewit*
TIM Tiny (or Tim Cratchit) *Carol*
TIX Tom *Nickleby*
TOM *Nickleby, Pickwick, Two Cities*
TOM Captain *Expectations*
TOX Lucretia *Dombey*

4
ANNE *Dombey*
ANNY *Twist*
BAPS + Mrs *Dombey*
BELL Knight *Mudfog*
BILL *Expectations, Pickwick, Twist*
BOLO Miss *Pickwick*
BRAY Madeline, Walter *Nickleby*
CLIP *Mudfog*

COBB Tom *Rudge*
CUTE Alderman *Chimes*
DAWS Mary *Dombey*
DICK *Chuzzlewit, Nickleby, Twist*
DICK Mr (or Richard Babley) *Copperfield*
DO'EM *Mudfog*
DOZE Professor *Mudfog*
DUFF *Twist*
DULL *Mudfog*
EMMA *Pickwick*
FANG *Twist*
FERN Lilian, Will *Chimes*
FIPS *Chuzzlewit*
FISH *Chimes*
FOGG *Pickwick*
FRED *Carol*
GAMP Sarah (or Sairey) *Chuzzlewit*
GILL Mrs *Chuzzlewit*
GRUB *Mudfog*
GRUB Gabriel *Pickwick*
HAWK Sir Mulberry *Nickleby*
HEEP Mrs, Uriah *Copperfield*
HUGH *Rudge*
HUMM Anthony *Pickwick*
HUNT *Pickwick*
JACK *Chuzzlewit*
JANE *Chuzzlewit, Nickleby, Pickwick*
JODD *Chuzzlewit*
JOEY Captain *Mutual*
JOHN *Dombey, Pickwick, Uncommercial*
JOWL Joe *Curiosity*
JUPE Cecilia, Signor *Hard*
KAGS *Twist*
KATE *Dombey, Pickwick*
KITT Miss *Copperfield*
KLEM + Miss, Mrs *Uncommercial*
KNAG Miss, Mortimer *Nickleby*
LANE Miss *Nickleby*

LIST Isaac *Curiosity*
MANN Mrs *Twist*
MARY *Pickwick*
MELL Charles, Mrs *Copperfield*
MIFF Mrs *Dombey*
MIKE *Expectations*
MUFF Professor *Mudfog*
MULL Professor *Mudfog*
NOGO Professor *Mudfog*
OMER Minnie *Copperfield*
OWEN John *Curiosity*
PEAK *Rudge*
PEGG *Uncommercial*
PELL Solomon *Pickwick*
PEPS Doctor *Dombey*
PIPE Mrs *Bleak*
POTT + Mrs *Pickwick*
PRIG Betsey *Chuzzlewit*
PYKE *Nickleby*
RIAH *Mutual*
ROSA *Bleak*
RUGG + Anastasia *Dorrit*
SLUG *Mudfog*
SLUM *Curiosity*
SMIF Putnam *Chuzzlewit*
TIGG Montague *Chuzzlewit*
TIPP *Copperfield*
TOPE + Mrs *Drood*
VECK Margaret, Toby *Chimes*
WADE Miss *Dorrit*
WEGG Silas *Mutual*
WEST Dame *Curiosity*
WISK Miss *Bleak*
WOLF *Chuzzlewit*

5

ADAMS *Copperfield*
ADAMS Captain *Nickleby*

ADAMS Jack *Dombey*
ALICE *Nickleby*
ALLEN Arabella, Benjamin *Pickwick*
BATES Charley *Twist*
BECKY *Twist*
BELLE *Carol*
BENCH *Dorrit*
BERRY (or Berinthia) *Dombey, Dorrit*
BETSY *Pickwick*
BETSY (or Bet) *Twist*
BEVAN + Mrs *Chuzzlewit*
BIDDY *Expectations*
BILER *Dombey*
BLANK *Mudfog*
BLAZO Colonel *Pickwick*
BLOGG *Mutual*
BLUBB *Mudfog*
BOKUM Mrs *Dombey*
BOOTS *Mutual*
BORUM + Mrs *Nickleby*
BRASS Sally, Sampson *Curiosity*
BRICK Jefferson, Mrs *Chuzzlewit*
BROWN *Curiosity, Mudfog*
BROWN Mrs *Dombey*
BUFFY William *Bleak*
BULPH *Nickleby*
CARLO *Curiosity*
CASBY *Dorrit*
CHICK John, Mrs *Dombey*
CHIPS *Uncommercial*
CHOKE General *Chuzzlewit*
CLARE Ada *Bleak*
CLARK *Dombey*
CLARK Mrs *Nickleby*
CLIVE *Dorrit*
COBBY *Uncommercial*
CROWL *Nickleby*
CRUPP Mrs *Copperfield*

DAISY Solomon *Rudge*
DARBY *Bleak*
DARBY + Mrs *Uncommercial*
DAVID *Nickleby*
DAWES Miss *Dorrit*
DINGO Professor *Bleak*
DIVER Colonel *Chuzzlewit*
DOLLS Mr *Mutual*
DOYCE Daniel *Dorrit*
DROOD Edwin *Drood*
DUMMY *Mudfog*
EVANS Richard *Curiosity*
FAGIN *Twist*
FIERY Captain *Mudfog*
FILER *Chimes*
FLITE Miss *Bleak*
FOLEY *Dombey*
FOXEY Doctor *Mudfog*
GILES *Twist*
GILLS Solomon *Dombey*
GOODY Mrs *Mutual*
GOWAN Henry, Mrs *Dorrit*
GREEN *Bleak*
GREEN Lucy *Uncommercial*
GREEN Miss *Nickleby*
GREEN Tom *Rudge*
GRIDE Arthur *Nickleby*
GRIME Professor *Mudfog*
GUPPY William, Mrs *Bleak*
GWYNN Miss *Pickwick*
HARRY *Curiosity, Twist*
HENRY *Pickwick*
HEXAM Charley, Jesse, Lizzie *Mutual*
ISAAC *Pickwick*
JAMES Henry *Dombey*
JANET *Copperfield*
JENNY *Bleak*
JERRY *Curiosity*

JINKS *Pickwick*
JOBBA *Mudfog*
JONES *Bleak*
JONES George *Mutual*
JONES Mary *Rudge*
JOPER Billy *Dombey*
JORAM Joe, Minnie, Mrs *Copperfield*
KENGE *Bleak*
KETCH Professor *Mudfog*
KINCH Horace *Uncommercial*
KROOK *Bleak*
LOBBS Maria *Pickwick*
LORRY Jarvis *Two Cities*
LOUIS *Uncommercial*
LUCAS Solomon *Pickwick*
LUMMY Ned *Chuzzlewit*
LUPIN Mrs *Chuzzlewit*
MAGGY *Dorrit*
MELIA *Dombey*
MERCY *Uncommercial*
MIGGS Miss *Rudge*
MILLS Julia *Copperfield*
MISTY *Mudfog*
MITTS Mrs *Uncommercial*
MOBBS *Nickleby*
MOLLY *Expectations*
MONKS *Twist*
MOULD + Mrs *Chuzzlewit*
MUDGE Jonas *Pickwick*
NAMBY *Pickwick*
NANCY *Twist*
NANDY John Edward *Dorrit*
NEDDY *Pickwick*
NODDY *Pickwick*
NOGGS Newman *Nickleby*
PAYNE Doctor *Pickwick*
PEDRO *Curiosity*
PERCH + Mrs *Dombey*

PINCH Ruth, Tom *Chuzzlewit*
PIPER Professor *Chuzzlewit*
PLUCK *Nickleby*
POLLY *Bleak*
POUCH Mrs *Bleak*
PRICE *Pickwick*
PRICE Matilda *Nickleby*
PROSS Miss, Solomon (alias John
   Barsad) *Two Cities*
PUSSY (or Rosa Bud) *Drood*
QUALE *Bleak*
QUILP Daniel, Mrs *Curiosity*
ROKER Tom *Pickwick*
RUDGE Barnaby, Mrs *Rudge*
SALLY *Twist*
SAXBY Long *Dombey*
SCOTT Tom *Curiosity*
SCROO *Mudfog*
SHARP *Copperfield*
SIKES Bill *Twist*
SLOUT *Twist*
SLURK *Pickwick*
SLYME Chevy *Chuzzlewit*
SMART Tom *Pickwick*
SMIKE *Nickleby*
SMITH *Mudfog*
SNIPE Wilmot *Pickwick*
SNOBB *Nickleby*
SNORE Professor *Mudfog*
SQUOD Phil *Bleak*
STAGG *Rudge*
SUSAN *Twist*
TOMMY *Pickwick*
TOOTS *Dombey*
TOZER *Dombey*
TRABB *Expectations*
TRENT Frederick, Nell (or Little Nell)
   Curiosity

TRUCK *Mudfog*
TUGBY *Chimes*
TWIST Oliver *Twist*
VENUS *Mutual*
WATTY *Pickwick*
WHITE Betsy *Uncommercial*
WICKS *Pickwick*

6
AFFERY *Dorrit*
AMELIA *Expectations*
BABLEY Richard (or Mr Dick) *Copperfield*
BADGER Bayham, Mrs *Bleak*
BAGNET Malta, Matthew, Quebec, Woolwich *Bleak*
BAILEY Benjamin *Chuzzlewit*
BAILEY Captain *Copperfield*
BAMBER Jack *Pickwick*
BANTAM Angelo Cyrus *Pickwick*
BARKER Phil *Twist*
BARKIS *Copperfield*
BARLEY Clara, Old Bill *Expectations*
BARNEY *Twist*
BARSAD John (alias of Solomon Pross) *Two Cities*
BAYTON + Mrs *Twist*
BEADLE Harriet *Dorrit*
BEDWIN Mrs *Twist*
BELLER Henry *Pickwick*
BETSEY Jane *Dombey*
BISHOP *Dorrit*
BITZER *Hard*
BLIGHT *Mutual*
BOCKER Tom *Mutual*
BOFFER *Pickwick*
BOFFIN Nicodemus, Mrs *Mutual*
BOGLES Mrs *Uncommercial*

BOGSBY James *Bleak*
BOLDER *Nickleby*
BOLTER Morris, Mrs *Twist*
BOLTON Robert *Mudfog*
BONNEY *Nickleby*
BOODLE Lord *Bleak*
BOWLEY Sir Joseph, Lady, Master *Chimes*
BREWER *Mutual*
BRIGGS *Dombey*
BROOKS *Nickleby, Pickwick*
BUCKET Inspector, Mrs *Bleak*
BUDGER Mrs *Pickwick*
BUFFER Doctor *Mudfog*
BUFFUM Oscar *Chuzzlewit*
BULDER Colonel, Miss, Mrs *Pickwick*
BUMBLE + Mrs *Twist*
BUNSBY Captain *Dombey*
BURTON Thomas *Pickwick*
BUZFUZ Serjeant *Pickwick*
CARKER Harriet, James, John *Dombey*
CARTER *Mudfog*
CARTON Sydney *Two Cities*
CHEGGS Alick, Miss *Curiosity*
CICERO *Chuzzlewit*
CLARKE Susan *Pickwick*
COBBEY *Nickleby*
COCKER Indignation *Uncommercial*
CODGER Miss *Chuzzlewit*
CODLIN Thomas *Curiosity*
COILER Mrs *Expectations*
CONWAY General *Rudge*
CORNEY Mrs *Twist*
CRIPPS Tom *Pickwick*
CURDLE + Mrs *Nickleby*
CUTLER + Mrs *Nickleby*
CUTTLE Captain *Dombey*
DABBER *Nickleby*

DARNAY Charles (alias of Charles St
Evrémonde) *Two Cities*
DARTLE Rosa *Copperfield*
DEMPLE George *Copperfield*
DENNIS Ned *Rudge*
DEPUTY *Drood*
DIBABS Jane *Nickleby*
DIBBLE Dorothy, Sampson
Uncommercial
DODSON *Pickwick*
DOMBEY Edith, Fanny, Florence, Paul
Dombey
DORKER *Nickleby*
DORRIT Amy (or Little), Edward,
Fanny, Frederick, Little, Tip, William
Dorrit
DOWLER Captain, Mrs *Pickwick*
DUNKLE Doctor *Chuzzlewit*
ENDELL Martha *Copperfield*
FEEDER + Reverend *Dombey*
FEENIX Lord *Dombey*
FIZKIN Horatio *Pickwick*
FOLAIR *Nickleby*
GANDER *Chuzzlewit*
GEORGE *Copperfield, Curiosity, Nickleby*
GEORGE Trooper *Bleak*
GORDON Colonel, Lord *Rudge*
GORDON Emma *Hard*
GRAHAM Mary *Chuzzlewit*
GRIGGS *Pickwick*
GROPER Colonel *Chuzzlewit*
GROVES James *Curiosity*
GRUEBY John *Rudge*
GRUNDY *Pickwick*
GUNTER *Pickwick*
GUSHER *Bleak*
GUSTER *Bleak*
HANNAH *Nickleby*

HARMON John, Mrs *Mutual*
HARRIS *Curiosity, Pickwick*
HARRIS Mrs *Chuzzlewit*
HAWDON Captain *Bleak*
HIGDEN Betty *Mutual*
HOMINY Mrs *Chuzzlewit*
HOWLER Reverend *Dombey*
HUBBLE + Mrs *Expectations*
HUNTER Leo, Mrs *Pickwick*
HUTLEY Jemmy *Pickwick*
IZZARD *Chuzzlewit*
JARLEY Mrs *Curiosity*
JASPER John *Drood*
JEMIMA *Dombey*
JINGLE Alfred *Pickwick*
JOHNNY *Mutual*
KETTLE La Fayette *Chuzzlewit*
KIBBLE Jacob *Mutual*
KIMBER *Drood*
LAMMLE Alfred, Mrs *Mutual*
LEAVER *Mudfog*
LIVELY *Twist*
LOBLEY *Drood*
LOWTEN *Pickwick*
LUFFEY *Pickwick*
LUMBEY Doctor *Nickleby*
MAGNUS Peter *Pickwick*
MALDON Jack *Copperfield*
MALLET *Mudfog*
MARKER Mrs *Nickleby*
MARLEY Jacob *Carol*
MAROON Captain *Dorrit*
MARTHA *Dombey, Twist*
MARTIN Betsy, Jack (or The
Bagman's Uncle), Tom *Pickwick*
MARTIN Captain *Dorrit*
MARTON *Curiosity*
MAYDAY *Uncommercial*

MAYLIE Harry, Mrs, Rose *Twist*
MERDLE + Mrs *Dorrit*
MIGGOT *Uncommercial*
MILLER *Pickwick*
MILVEY Reverend, Mrs *Mutual*
MIVINS *Pickwick*
MODDLE Augustus *Chuzzlewit*
MOONEY *Bleak*
MORFIN *Dombey*
MORGAN Becky *Curiosity*
MR DICK (or Richard Babley)
   Copperfield
MULLIT Professor *Chuzzlewit*
MUNTLE *Nickleby*
MUZZLE *Pickwick*
NIPPER Susan *Dombey*
NOAKES *Mudfog*
ORLICK Dolge *Expectations*
PANCKS *Dorrit*
PANKEY Miss *Dombey*
PARKES Phil *Rudge*
PARKLE *Uncommercial*
PEGLER Mrs *Hard*
PEPPER *Expectations*
PERKER *Pickwick*
PHOEBE *Nickleby*
PHUNKY *Pickwick*
PIDGER *Copperfield*
PIPKIN *Mudfog*
PIPKIN Nathaniel *Pickwick*
PIRRIP Philip (or Pip) *Expectations*
POCKET Alick, Fanny, Herbert, Jane,
   Joe, Matthew, Mrs, Sarah *Expectations*
PODDER *Pickwick*
POGRAM Elijah *Chuzzlewit*
PROSEE *Mudfog*
PROVIS (alias of Abel Magwitch)
   Expectations

PUFFER Princess *Drood*
PUPKER *Nickleby*
QUINCH Mrs *Uncommercial*
RADDLE + Mrs *Pickwick*
RAMSEY *Pickwick*
RIGAUD *Dorrit*
ROGERS Miss, Mrs *Nickleby, Pickwick*
RUMMAN Professor *Mudfog*
SAPSEA Thomas *Drood*
SAWYER *Mudfog*
SAWYER Bob *Pickwick*
SCALEY *Nickleby*
SLEARY + Josephine *Hard*
SLINGO *Dorrit*
SLOPPY *Mutual*
SMOUCH *Pickwick*
SNIGGS *Mudfog*
SNIVEY *Mudfog*
SOEMUP Doctor *Mudfog*
SOPHIA *Chuzzlewit, Expectations*
SOWNDS *Dombey*
SPECKS Joe, Mrs *Uncommercial*
SPIKER Henry, Mrs *Copperfield*
SPYERS Jem *Twist*
STAPLE *Pickwick*
STRONG Doctor, Mrs *Copperfield*
STYLES *Mudfog*
SWILLS Little *Bleak*
TACKER *Chuzzlewit*
TADGER Brother *Pickwick*
TANGLE *Bleak*
TAPLEY Mark *Chuzzlewit*
TARTAR *Drood*
THOMAS *Bleak, Nickleby, Pickwick*
TICKIT Mrs *Dorrit*
TICKLE *Mudfog*
TIFFEY *Copperfield*
TISHER Mrs *Drood*

TOM TIX *Nickleby*
TOODLE Robin, Mrs *Dombey*
TOOTLE Tom *Mutual*
TOPPER *Carol*
TOPPIT Miss *Chuzzlewit*
TUCKLE *Pickwick*
TUNGAY *Copperfield*
TUPMAN Tracy *Pickwick*
VARDEN Dolly, Gabriel, Martha *Rudge*
VHOLES *Bleak*
VILLAM *Pickwick*
VUFFIN *Curiosity*
WALKER *Pickwick*
WALKER Mick *Copperfield*
WARDLE + Emily, Isabella, Mrs,
   Rachael *Pickwick*
WEEDLE Anastasia *Uncommercial*
WELLER Mrs, Sam (or Samuel), Tony
   Pickwick
WHEEZY Professor *Mudfog*
WICKAM Mrs *Dombey*
WIGSBY *Mudfog*
WILFER Bella, Lavinia, Mrs, Reginald
   Mutual
WILLET Joe, John *Rudge*
WINKLE Nathaniel *Pickwick*
WOPSLE *Expectations*
WRYMUG Mrs *Nickleby*
WUGSBY Mrs *Pickwick*
YAWLER *Copperfield*

7

AKERMAN *Rudge*
ANTONIO *Uncommercial*
BANGHAM Mrs *Dorrit*
BARBARA *Curiosity*
BARBARY Miss, Mrs *Bleak*
BARDELL Martha, Tommy *Pickwick*

BATTENS *Uncommercial*
BAZZARD *Drood*
BELLING *Nickleby*
BELLOWS Brother *Dorrit*
BLIMBER Cornelia, Doctor, Mrs
   Dombey
BLINDER Mrs *Bleak*
BLOTTON *Pickwick*
BLOWERS *Bleak*
BOBSTER + Cecilia *Nickleby*
BOLDWIG Captain *Pickwick*
BROGLEY *Dombey*
BROOKER *Nickleby*
BROWDIE John *Nickleby*
BULLAMY *Chuzzlewit*
BULLMAN *Pickwick*
CAMILLA *Expectations*
CHARLEY *Copperfield, Pickwick*
CHESTER Edward, Sir John *Rudge*
CHESTLE *Copperfield*
CHIGGLE *Chuzzlewit*
CHILLIP Doctor *Copperfield*
CHIVERY John *Dorrit*
CHOLLOP Major *Chuzzlewit*
CHOWSER Colonel *Nickleby*
CHUFFEY *Chuzzlewit*
CLEAVER Fanny *Mutual*
CLENNAM Arthur, Gilbert, Mrs *Dorrit*
CLUBBER Lady *Pickwick*
CRACKIT Toby *Twist*
CREAKLE + Miss, Mrs *Copperfield*
CREWLER Mrs, Reverend, Sophy
   Copperfield
CRIMPLE David *Chuzzlewit*
CROOKEY *Pickwick*
CROPLEY Miss *Nickleby*
DAWKINS John (or The Artful Dodger)
   Twist

DEDLOCK Lady, Sir Leicester, Volumnia *Bleak*
DEEDLES *Chimes*
DEFARGE Ernest, Madame *Two Cities*
DOLLOBY *Copperfield*
DOWDLES Miss *Nickleby*
DRAWLEY *Mudfog*
DRUMMLE Bentley *Expectations*
DUBBLEY *Pickwick*
DURDLES *Drood*
EDMUNDS John, Mrs *Pickwick*
EDWARDS Miss *Curiosity*
ESTELLA *Expectations*
FIZZGIG Don Bolaro *Pickwick*
FLASHER Wilkins *Pickwick*
FLEMING Agnes, Rose *Twist*
FLOPSON *Expectations*
FLOWERS *Dombey*
GABELLE *Two Cities*
GARGERY Joe, Mrs *Expectations*
GARLAND Abel, Mrs *Curiosity*
GASPARD *Two Cities*
GAZINGI Miss *Nickleby*
GENERAL Mrs *Dorrit*
GIGGLES Miss *Drood*
GILBERT Mark *Rudge*
GLAMOUR Bob *Mutual*
GLOBSON Bully *Uncommercial*
GOODWIN *Pickwick*
GRANGER Edith *Dombey*
GRAYPER + Mrs *Copperfield*
GREGORY *Copperfield*
GRIDLEY *Bleak*
GRIMBLE *Nickleby*
GRIMWIG *Twist*
GRINDER *Curiosity*
GROFFIN Thomas *Pickwick*

GROMPUS *Mutual*
GRUBBLE *Bleak*
GRUDDEN Mrs *Nickleby*
GRUMMER Daniel *Pickwick*
HAGGAGE Doctor *Dorrit*
HAWKINS *Mutual*
HERBERT *Rudge*
HEYLING George, Mrs *Pickwick*
HOPKINS Captain *Copperfield*
HOPKINS Jack *Pickwick*
JACKSON *Dorrit, Pickwick*
JACKSON Michael *Bleak*
JAGGERS *Expectations*
JELLYBY Caddy, Caroline, Peepy, Mrs *Bleak*
JENKINS *Nickleby*
JINIWIN Mrs *Curiosity*
JINKINS *Chuzzlewit, Pickwick*
JOBLING Doctor *Chuzzlewit*
JOBLING Tony *Bleak*
JOE JOWL *Curiosity*
JOHNSON *Nickleby*
JOHNSON Tom *Dombey*
JOLLSON Mrs *Dombey*
JORKINS *Copperfield*
KEDGICK Captain *Chuzzlewit*
KENWIGS Morleena, Mrs *Nickleby*
KWAKLEY *Mudfog*
LARKINS + Miss *Copperfield*
LEEFORD Edward, Edwin *Twist*
LEWSOME *Chuzzlewit*
LINSEED Duke of *Mutual*
MALLARD *Pickwick*
MANETTE Doctor, Lucie *Two Cities*
MANNING *Pickwick*
MARKHAM *Copperfield*
MARWOOD Alice *Dombey*
MEAGLES Minnie (or Pet), Mrs *Dorrit*

MELLOWS *Uncommercial*
MERCURY *Bleak*
MILLERS *Expectations*
MITHERS Lady *Copperfield*
MORDLIN Brother *Pickwick*
MORTAIR *Mudfog*
MOWCHER Miss *Copperfield*
MR DOLLS *Mutual*
MRS BAPS *Dombey*
MRS GILL *Chuzzlewit*
MRS HEEP *Copperfield*
MRS KLEM *Uncommercial*
MRS MANN *Twist*
MRS MELL *Copperfield*
MRS MIFF *Dombey*
MRS PIPE *Bleak*
MRS POTT *Pickwick*
MRS TOPE *Drood*
MULLINS Jack *Mutual*
NADGETT *Chuzzlewit*
NECKETT + Charlotte, Emma, Tom *Bleak*
NUBBLES Jacob, Kit, Mrs *Curiosity*
NUPKINS George, Mrs *Pickwick*
PARAGON Mary Anne *Copperfield*
PAWKINS Major, Mrs *Chuzzlewit*
PEECHER Emma *Mutual*
PERKINS Mrs *Bleak*
PESSELL *Mudfog*
PILKINS *Dombey*
PIPCHIN Mrs *Dombey*
PITCHER *Nickleby*
PODSNAP Georgiana, John, Mrs *Mutual*
POTKINS William *Expectations*
PRUFFLE *Pickwick*
QUINION *Copperfield*
RACHAEL *Hard*
RADFOOT George *Mutual*
RAYMOND *Expectations*

RICHARD *Chimes, Nickleby*
RICKITS Miss *Drood*
ROSA BUD (or Pussy) *Drood*
SAGGERS Mrs *Uncommercial*
SAMPSON George *Mutual*
SANDERS Mrs *Pickwick*
SCADDER Zephania *Chuzzlewit*
SCROOGE Ebenezer *Carol*
SIMMERY Frank *Pickwick*
SIMMONS Mrs *Curiosity*
SIMMONS William *Chuzzlewit*
SIMPSON *Pickwick*
SKEWTON Edith, Mrs *Dombey*
SKIMPIN *Pickwick*
SLAMMER Doctor *Pickwick*
SLASHER *Pickwick*
SLUMKEY Samuel *Pickwick*
SMANGLE *Pickwick*
SMAUKER John *Pickwick*
SMITHIE + Mrs *Pickwick*
SNAGSBY + Mrs *Bleak*
SNAWLEY + Mrs *Nickleby*
SNEWKES *Nickleby*
SNUBBIN Serjeant *Pickwick*
SNUFFIM *Nickleby*
SOWSTER *Mudfog*
SPARSIT + Mrs *Hard*
SPENLOW Clarissa, Dora, Francis, Lavinia *Copperfield*
SQUEERS Fanny, Mrs, Wackford *Nickleby*
SQUIRES Olympia *Uncommercial*
STABLES Bob *Bleak*
STARTOP *Expectations*
STRYVER *Two Cities*
SWEENEY Mrs *Uncommercial*
SWOSSER Captain *Bleak*
TAMAROO *Chuzzlewit*

TAPKINS Mrs *Mutual*
TIMPSON *Uncommercial*
TINKLER *Dorrit*
TINY TIM (or Tim Cratchit) *Carol*
TIPPINS Lady *Mutual*
TODGERS Mrs *Chuzzlewit*
TOM COBB *Rudge*
TOMKINS *Nickleby*
TOMKINS Miss *Pickwick*
TOORELL Doctor *Mudfog*
TROTTER Job *Pickwick*
TRUNDLE *Pickwick*
TWEMLOW Melvin *Mutual*
TWIGGER Edward (or Bottle-nosed
  Ned), Mrs *Mudfog*
UPWITCH Richard *Pickwick*
WACKLES Jane, Melissa, Mrs *Curiosity*
WAGHORN *Mudfog*
WATKINS *Nickleby*
WEMMICK John *Expectations*
WHIFFIN *Pickwick*
WHIMPLE Mrs *Expectations*
WILKINS *Pickwick*
WILKINS Dick *Carol*
WILLIAM *Copperfield, Nickleby*
WITHERS *Dombey*
WOBBLER *Dorrit*

8
ADA CLARE *Bleak*
AKERSHEM Sophronia *Mutual*
ALPHONSE *Nickleby*
ANDERSON John *Uncommercial*
ANGELICA *Uncommercial*
BAGSTOCK Major *Dombey*
BARNACLE Clarence, Lady, Lord, Tite,
  William *Dorrit*
BENJAMIN *Rudge*

BENJAMIN Thomas *Copperfield*
BILBERRY Lady *Dorrit*
BLATHERS *Twist*
BLOCKITT Mrs *Dombey*
BLOCKSON Mrs *Nickleby*
BOYTHORN Lawrence *Bleak*
BRANDLEY Mrs *Expectations*
BRAVASSA Miss *Nickleby*
BRITTLES *Twist*
BROWNLOW *Twist*
CAROLINE *Carol*
CARSTONE Richard *Bleak*
CHADBAND Mrs, Reverend *Bleak*
CHILDERS *Hard*
CHINAMAN Jack *Drood*
CHITLING Tom *Twist*
CLAYPOLE Noah *Twist*
CLEVERLY William *Uncommercial*
CLICKETT *Copperfield*
CLUPPINS Mrs *Pickwick*
CRADDOCK Mrs *Pickwick*
CRATCHIT Bob, Mrs, Tim *Carol*
CRINKLES *Mudfog*
CRIPPLES Master *Dorrit*
CRUMMLES Master, Mrs, Ninetta,
  Percy, Vincent *Nickleby*
CRUNCHER Jerry, Mrs, Young Jerry
  Two Cities
CRUSHTON *Pickwick*
DAME WEST *Curiosity*
DARK JACK *Uncommercial*
DATCHERY Dick *Drood*
FEZZIWIG + Mrs *Carol*
FINCHING Flora *Dorrit*
FLABELLA Lady *Nickleby*
FLADDOCK General *Chuzzlewit*
FLANDERS Sally *Uncommercial*
FLEDGEBY *Mutual*

FLUGGERS *Nickleby*
FLUMMERY *Mudfog*
FRANÇOIS *Dombey*
GAMFIELD *Twist*
GASHFORD *Rudge*
GLIDDERY Bob *Mutual*
GRAINGER *Copperfield*
GRANNETT *Twist*
GULPIDGE + Mrs *Copperfield*
GUMMIDGE Mrs *Copperfield*
HAREDALE Emma *Rudge*
HARRISON *Mutual*
HAVISHAM Arthur, Miss *Expectations*
HORTENSE *Bleak*
JARNDYCE John, Tom *Bleak*
JENNINGS *Mudfog, Nickleby*
JENNINGS Miss *Drood*
JOE JORAM *Copperfield*
JOHN OWEN *Curiosity*
JOLTERED *Mudfog*
JONATHAN *Mutual*
LA CREEVY Miss *Nickleby*
LANDLESS Helena, Neville *Drood*
LANGDALE *Rudge*
LEDBRAIN X *Mudfog*
LEDBROOK Miss *Nickleby*
LENVILLE Mrs, Thomas *Nickleby*
LIMBKINS *Twist*
LITTIMER *Copperfield*
LOSBERNE *Twist*
MAGWITCH Abel (alias Provis)
  Expectations
MARGARET *Pickwick*
MARY ANNE *Expectations*
MARY DAWS *Dombey*
MAUNDERS *Curiosity*
MICAWBER Emma, Wilkins
  Copperfield

MISS BOLO *Pickwick*
MISS KITT *Copperfield*
MISS KLEM *Uncommercial*
MISS KNAG *Nickelby*
MISS LANE *Nickleby*
MISS WADE *Dorrit*
MISS WISK *Bleak*
MRS BEVAN *Chuzzlewit*
MRS BOKUM *Dombey*
MRS BORUM *Nickleby*
MRS BRICK *Chuzzlewit*
MRS BROWN *Dombey*
MRS CHICK *Dombey*
MRS CLARK *Nickleby*
MRS CRUPP *Copperfield*
MRS DARBY *Uncommercial*
MRS GOODY *Mutual*
MRS GOWAN *Dorrit*
MRS GUPPY *Bleak*
MRS JORAM *Copperfield*
MRS LUPIN *Chuzzlewit*
MRS MITTS *Uncommercial*
MRS MOULD *Chuzzlewit*
MRS PERCH *Dombey*
MRS POUCH *Bleak*
MRS QUILP *Curiosity*
MRS RUDGE *Rudge*
MUDBERRY Mrs *Pickwick*
MURDERER Captain *Uncommercial*
MUTANHED Lord *Pickwick*
NED LUMMY *Chuzzlewit*
NICKLEBY Godfrey, Kate, Nicholas,
  Ralph *Nickleby*
OLD DAVID *Curiosity*
OLD GLUBB *Dombey*
OLD LOBBS *Pickwick*
PANGLOSS *Uncommercial*
PEARTREE *Drood*

PEGGOTTY Clara, Daniel, Ham, Joe
  Copperfield
PICKWICK Samuel *Pickwick*
PLORNISH Mrs, Thomas *Dorrit*
PURBLIND *Mudfog*
PYEGRAVE Charley *Copperfield*
QUICKEAR *Uncommercial*
REYNOLDS Miss *Drood*
ROBINSON *Dombey*
ROGER CLY *Two Cities*
SCADGERS Lady *Hard*
SCREWZER Tommy *Dombey*
SHARPEYE *Uncommercial*
SHEPHERD Miss *Copperfield*
SIMMONDS Miss *Nickleby*
SKETTLES Barnet, Lady *Dombey*
SKIFFINS Miss *Expectations*
SKIMPOLE Harold, Kitty, Laura, Mrs
  Bleak
SLADDERY *Bleak*
SMIGGERS Joseph *Pickwick*
SMITHERS Miss *Pickwick*
SPARKLER Edmund *Dorrit*
STIGGINS *Pickwick*
TIMBERED *Mudfog*
TIMBERRY Snittle *Nickleby*
TOBY VECK *Chimes*
TOM GREEN *Rudge*
TOM PINCH *Chuzzlewit*
TOM ROKER *Pickwick*
TOM SCOTT *Curiosity*
TOM SMART *Pickwick*
TRADDLES Thomas *Copperfield*
TREASURY *Dorrit*
TRIMMERS *Nickleby*
TROTWOOD Betsey *Copperfield*
WESTLOCK John *Chuzzlewit*
WESTWOOD *Nickleby*

WHIFFERS *Pickwick*
WILL FERN *Chimes*
WILLIAMS William *Mutual*
WRAYBURN Eugene, Mrs *Mutual*

9

AMY DORRIT (or Little Dorrit) *Dorrit*
BARRONEAU Madame *Dorrit*
BELVAWNEY Miss *Nickleby*
BERINTHIA (or Berry) *Dombey*
BILLICKIN Mrs *Drood*
BILL SIKES *Twist*
BLACK BILL *Expectations*
BLACKPOOL Mrs, Stephen *Hard*
BLUNDERUM *Mudfog*
BOB SAWYER *Pickwick*
BOUNDERBY Josiah, Mrs *Hard*
BROWNDOCK Miss *Nickleby*
BULLFINCH *Uncommercial*
CARLAVERO *Uncommercial*
CHARLOTTE *Dorrit, Twist*
CHEERYBLE Charles, Edwin, Frank
  Nickleby
CHICKWEED Conkey *Twist*
CHRISTINA Donna *Pickwick*
CHUCKSTER *Curiosity*
CLARRIKER *Expectations*
COMPEYSON + Mrs *Expectations*
DOCTOR FEE *Mudfog*
DUNSTABLE *Expectations*
FERDINAND Miss *Drood*
FIBBITSON Mrs *Copperfield*
FINCHBURY Lady *Dombey*
FLIPFIELD Mrs, Tom *Uncommercial*
GEORGIANA *Expectations*
GRADGRIND Adam Smith, Jane, Louisa,
  Malthus, Mrs, Thomas, Tom *Hard*
GRAYMARSH *Nickleby*

GREGSBURY *Nickleby*
GREWGIOUS Hiram *Drood*
GRUMMIDGE Doctor *Mudfog*
HARTHOUSE James *Hard*
HAWKINSON Aunt *Mutual*
HEADSTONE Bradley *Mutual*
ISAAC LIST *Curiosity*
JACK ADAMS *Dombey*
JEM SPYERS *Twist*
JENKINSON *Dorrit*
JOE POCKET *Expectations*
JOE SPECKS *Uncommercial*
JOE WILLET *Rudge*
JOHN CHICK *Dombey*
JULIUS BIB *Chuzzlewit*
KINDHEART *Uncommercial*
LEO HUNTER *Pickwick*
LIGHTWOOD Mortimer *Mutual*
LILLYVICK + Mrs *Nickleby*
LONG SAXBY *Dombey*
LORD MAYOR *Rudge*
LUCY GREEN *Uncommercial*
MANTALINI Alfred, Madame *Nickleby*
MARKLEHAM Mrs *Copperfield*
MARY JONES *Rudge*
MISS DAWES *Dorrit*
MISS FLITE *Bleak*
MISS GREEN *Nickleby*
MISS GWYNN *Pickwick*
MISS MIGGS *Rudge*
MISS PROSS *Two Cities*
MRS BADGER *Bleak*
MRS BAYTON *Twist*
MRS BEDWIN *Twist*
MRS BOFFIN *Mutual*
MRS BOGLES *Uncommercial*
MRS BOLTER *Twist*
MRS BUCKET *Bleak*

MRS BUDGER *Pickwick*
MRS BULDER *Pickwick*
MRS BUMBLE *Twist*
MRS COILER *Expectations*
MRS CORNEY *Twist*
MRS CURDLE *Nickleby*
MRS CUTLER *Nickleby*
MRS DOWLER *Pickwick*
MRS HARMON *Mutual*
MRS HARRIS *Chuzzlewit*
MRS HOMINY *Chuzzlewit*
MRS HUBBLE *Expectations*
MRS HUNTER *Pickwick*
MRS JARLEY *Curiosity*
MRS LAMMLE *Mutual*
MRS MARKER *Nickleby*
MRS MAYLIE *Twist*
MRS MERDLE *Dorrit*
MRS MILVEY *Mutual*
MRS PEGLER *Hard*
MRS POCKET *Expectations*
MRS QUINCH *Uncommercial*
MRS RADDLE *Pickwick*
MRS ROGERS *Pickwick*
MRS SPECKS *Uncommercial*
MRS SPIKER *Copperfield*
MRS STRONG *Copperfield*
MRS TICKIT *Dorrit*
MRS TISHER *Drood*
MRS TOODLE *Dombey*
MRS WARDLE *Pickwick*
MRS WELLER *Pickwick*
MRS WICKAM *Dombey*
MRS WILFER *Mutual*
MRS WRYMUG *Nickleby*
MRS WUGSBY *Pickwick*
MURDSTONE Edward, Jane, Mrs
    Copperfield

NED DENNIS *Rudge*
NEESHAWTS Doctor *Mudfog*
NELL TRENT (or Little Nell) *Curiosity*
NOCKEMORF *Pickwick*
PARDIGGLE + Alfred, Egbert, Felix, Francis, Mrs, Oswald *Bleak*
PASSNIDGE *Bleak*
PECKSNIFF Charity (or Cherry), Mercy (or Merry), Seth *Chuzzlewit*
PHIL SQUOD *Bleak*
PORKENHAM Mrs, Sidney *Pickwick*
POTTERSON Abbey, Job *Mutual*
PRISCILLA *Bleak*
PUGSTYLES *Nickleby*
RIDERHOOD Pleasant, Roger *Mutual*
RUTH PINCH *Chuzzlewit*
SAM WELLER (or Samuel) *Pickwick*
SARAH GAMP (or Sairey) *Chuzzlewit*
SILAS WEGG *Mutual*
SMALLWEED Bart, Joshua, Judith, Mrs *Bleak*
SMORLTORK Count *Pickwick*
SNODGRASS Augustus *Pickwick*
SPRODGKIN Sally *Mutual*
STRUGGLES *Pickwick*
SUMMERSON Esther *Bleak*
SWIVELLER Dick *Curiosity*
TAPPERTIT Simon (or Sim) *Rudge*
TAPPLETON Lieutenant *Pickwick*
THE BAGMAN *Pickwick*
THE SEXTON *Curiosity*
TIP DORRIT *Dorrit*
TOM BOCKER *Mutual*
TOM CRIPPS *Pickwick*
TOMLINSON Mrs *Bleak*
TOM MARTIN *Pickwick*
TOM TOOTLE *Mutual*
TOWLINSON Thomas *Dombey*

TRAMPFOOT *Uncommercial*
TULRUMBLE Mrs, Nicholas *Mudfog*
URIAH HEEP *Copperfield*
VENEERING Hamilton, Mrs *Mutual*
VERISOPHT Lord *Nickleby*
WALTER GAY *Dombey*
WICKFIELD Agnes *Copperfield*
WILTSHIRE *Uncommercial*
WITHERDEN *Curiosity*
WOODCOURT Doctor, Mrs *Bleak*
X LEDBRAIN *Mudfog*

10
AYRESLEIGH *Pickwick*
BANJO BONES *Uncommercial*
BETSEY JANE *Dombey*
BETSEY PRIG *Chuzzlewit*
BETSY WHITE *Uncommercial*
BILLY JOPER *Dombey*
BOB GLAMOUR *Mutual*
BOB STABLES *Bleak*
CAPTAIN TOM *Expectations*
CAVALLETTO Altro *Dorrit*
CHEVY SLYME *Chuzzlewit*
CHUZZLEWIT Anthony, Diggory, George , Jonas, Martin, Mrs, Toby *Chuzzlewit*
COPPERNOSE *Mudfog*
CRISPARKLE Canon, Mrs *Drood*
DOCTOR PEPS *Dombey*
EDWIN DROOD *Drood*
EMMA GORDON *Hard*
FLINTWINCH Ephraim, Jeremiah, Mrs *Dorrit*
GALLANBILE *Nickleby*
HENRY GOWAN *Dorrit*
HENRY JAMES *Dombey*
JACK BAMBER *Pickwick*

JACK MALDON *Copperfield*
JACK MARTIN (or The Bagman's
  Uncle) *Pickwick*
JANE BETSEY *Dombey*
JANE DIBABS *Nickleby*
JANE POCKET *Expectations*
JESSE HEXAM *Mutual*
JOB TROTTER *Pickwick*
JOE GARGERY *Expectations*
JOHN BARSAD (alias of Solomon
  Pross) *Two Cities*
JOHN CARKER *Dombey*
JOHN GRUEBY *Rudge*
JOHN HARMON *Mutual*
JOHN JASPER *Drood*
JOHN WILLET *Rudge*
JONAS MUDGE *Pickwick*
JULIA MILLS *Copperfield*
KIDGERBURY Mrs *Copperfield*
KIT NUBBLES *Curiosity*
KNIGHT BELL *Mudfog*
LADY BOWLEY *Chimes*
LILIAN FERN *Chimes*
LITTLE EM'LY *Copperfield*
LITTLE NELL (or Nell Trent) *Curiosity*
LORD BOODLE *Bleak*
LORD FEENIX *Dombey*
LORD GORDON *Rudge*
MACSTINGER Alexander, Charles,
  Juliana, Mrs *Dombey*
MARIA LOBBS *Pickwick*
MARK TAPLEY *Chuzzlewit*
MARY GRAHAM *Chuzzlewit*
MICK WALKER *Copperfield*
MINNIE OMER *Copperfield*
MISS BULDER *Pickwick*
MISS CHEGGS *Curiosity*
MISS CODGER *Chuzzlewit*

MISS PANKEY *Dombey*
MISS ROGERS *Nickleby*
MISS TOPPIT *Chuzzlewit*
MRS BANGHAM *Dorrit*
MRS BARBARY *Bleak*
MRS BLIMBER *Dombey*
MRS BLINDER *Bleak*
MRS CLENNAM *Dorrit*
MRS CREAKLE *Copperfield*
MRS CREWLER *Copperfield*
MRS EDMUNDS *Pickwick*
MRS GARGERY *Expectations*
MRS GARLAND *Curiosity*
MRS GENERAL *Dorrit*
MRS GRAYPER *Copperfield*
MRS GRUDDEN *Nickleby*
MRS HEYLING *Pickwick*
MRS JELLYBY *Bleak*
MRS JINIWIN *Curiosity*
MRS JOLLSON *Dombey*
MRS KENWIGS *Nickleby*
MRS MEAGLES *Dorrit*
MRS NUBBLES *Curiosity*
MRS NUPKINS *Pickwick*
MRS PAWKINS *Chuzzlewit*
MRS PERKINS *Bleak*
MRS PIPCHIN *Dombey*
MRS PODSNAP *Mutual*
MRS SAGGERS *Uncommercial*
MRS SANDERS *Pickwick*
MRS SIMMONS *Curiosity*
MRS SKEWTON *Dombey*
MRS SMITHIE *Pickwick*
MRS SNAGSBY *Bleak*
MRS SNAWLEY *Nickleby*
MRS SPARSIT *Hard*
MRS SQUEERS *Nickleby*
MRS SWEENEY *Uncommercial*

MRS TAPKINS *Mutual*
MRS TODGERS *Chuzzlewit*
MRS TWIGGER *Mudfog*
MRS WACKLES *Curiosity*
MRS WHIMPLE *Expectations*
MURGATROYD *Mudfog*
ONOWENEVER Miss, Mrs *Uncommercial*
PAUL DOMBEY *Dombey*
PELTIROGUS Horatio *Nickleby*
PET MEAGLES (or Minnie) *Dorrit*
PHIL BARKER *Twist*
PHIL PARKES *Rudge*
PUTNAM SMIF *Chuzzlewit*
QUEERSPECK Professor *Mudfog*
ROSA DARTLE *Copperfield*
ROSE MAYLIE *Twist*
ROUNCEWELL George, Mrs, Watt
  Bleak
SAIREY GAMP (or Sarah) *Chuzzlewit*
SALLY BRASS *Curiosity*
SIGNOR JUPE *Hard*
SLIDERSKEW Peg *Nickleby*
SNEVELLICI + Miss, Mrs *Nickleby*
SNIGSWORTH Lord *Mutual*
SNUPHANUPH Lady *Pickwick*
SOWERBERRY + Mrs *Twist*
SPOTTLETOE + Mrs *Chuzzlewit*
STARELEIGH Mr Justice *Pickwick*
STEERFORTH James, Mrs *Copperfield*
THICKNESSE *Mudfog*
TOM JOHNSON *Dombey*
TOM NECKETT *Bleak*
TONY WELLER *Pickwick*
TURVEYDROP + Prince *Bleak*
TWINKLETON Miss *Drood*
WALTER BRAY *Nickleby*
WATERBROOK + Mrs *Copperfield*
WITITTERLY Henry, Mrs *Nickleby*

11
ABEL GARLAND *Curiosity*
ALICK CHEGGS *Curiosity*
ALICK POCKET *Expectations*
ANTHONY HUMM *Pickwick*
ARTHUR GRIDE *Nickleby*
BECKY MORGAN *Curiosity*
BELLA WILFER *Mutual*
BETSY MARTIN *Pickwick*
BETTY HIGDEN *Mutual*
BITHERSTONE Master *Mutual*
BLUNDERBORE Captain *Mudfog*
BOB CRATCHIT *Carol*
BOB GLIDDERY *Mutual*
CAPTAIN JOEY *Mutual*
CECILIA JUPE *Hard*
CHARLES MELL *Copperfield*
CLARA BARLEY *Expectations*
COPPERFIELD David, Mrs *Copperfield*
DANIEL DOYCE *Dorrit*
DANIEL QUILP *Curiosity*
DICK WILKINS *Carol*
DOCTOR FOXEY *Mudfog*
DOCTOR PAYNE *Pickwick*
DOLGE ORLICK *Expectations*
DOLLY VARDEN *Rudge*
DORA SPENLOW *Copperfield*
EDITH DOMBEY *Dombey*
EMILY WARDLE *Pickwick*
EMMA NECKETT *Bleak*
EMMA PEECHER *Mutual*
FANNY DOMBEY *Dombey*
FANNY DORRIT *Dorrit*
FANNY POCKET *Expectations*
GABRIEL GRUB *Pickwick*
GEORGE JONES *Mutual*
HAM PEGGOTTY *Copperfield*
HARRY MAYLIE *Twist*

HENRY BELLER *Pickwick*
HENRY SPIKER *Copperfield*
HORACE KINCH *Uncommercial*
JACK DAWKINS or John (alias The
   Artful Dodger) *Twist*
JACK HOPKINS *Pickwick*
JACK MULLINS *Mutual*
JACOB KIBBLE *Mutual*
JACOB MARLEY *Carol*
JAMES BOGSBY *Bleak*
JAMES CARKER *Dombey*
JAMES GROVES *Curiosity*
JANE WACKLES *Curiosity*
JARVIS LORRY *Two Cities*
JEMMY HUTLEY *Pickwick*
JOE PEGGOTTY *Copperfield*
JOHN BROWDIE *Nickleby*
JOHN CHIVERY *Dorrit*
JOHN DAWKINS or Jack (alias The
   Artful Dodger) *Twist*
JOHN EDMUNDS *Pickwick*
JOHN PODSNAP *Mutual*
JOHN SMAUKER *Pickwick*
JOHN WEMMICK *Expectations*
LADY CLUBBER *Pickwick*
LADY DEDLOCK *Bleak*
LADY MITHERS *Copperfield*
LADY TIPPINS *Mutual*
LINKINWATER Miss, Tim *Nickleby*
LIZZIE HEXAM *Mutual*
LUCRETIA TOX *Dombey*
MALTA BAGNET *Bleak*
MARK GILBERT *Rudge*
MELVILLESON Miss *Bleak*
MINNIE JORAM *Copperfield*
MISS BARBARY *Bleak*
MISS CREAKLE *Copperfield*
MISS CROPLEY *Nickleby*

MISS DOWDLES *Nickleby*
MISS EDWARDS *Curiosity*
MISS GAZINGI *Nickleby*
MISS GIGGLES *Drood*
MISS LARKINS *Copperfield*
MISS MOWCHER *Copperfield*
MISS RICKITS *Drood*
MISS TOMKINS *Pickwick*
MONFLATHERS Miss *Curiosity*
MRS BLOCKITT *Dombey*
MRS BLOCKSON *Nickleby*
MRS BRANDLEY *Expectations*
MRS CHADBAND *Bleak*
MRS CLUPPINS *Pickwick*
MRS CRADDOCK *Pickwick*
MRS CRATCHIT *Carol*
MRS CRUMMLES *Nickleby*
MRS CRUNCHER *Two Cities*
MRS FEZZIWIG *Carol*
MRS GULPIDGE *Copperfield*
MRS GUMMIDGE *Copperfield*
MRS LENVILLE *Nickleby*
MRS MUDBERRY *Pickwick*
MRS PLORNISH *Dorrit*
MRS SKIMPOLE *Bleak*
MRS WRAYBURN *Mutual*
NEWMAN NOGGS *Nickleby*
OLIVER TWIST *Twist*
OSCAR BUFFUM *Chuzzlewit*
PETER MAGNUS *Pickwick*
PUMBLECHOOK Uncle *Expectations*
ROBIN TOODLE *Dombey*
ROSE FLEMING *Twist*
SARAH POCKET *Expectations*
SLACKBRIDGE *Hard*
SOLOMON PELL *Pickwick*
ST EVRÉMONDE Charles (alias Charles
   Darnay), Marquis *Two Cities*

SUSAN CLARKE *Pickwick*
SUSAN NIPPER *Dombey*
SWEEDLEPIPE Paul (or Poll) *Chuzzlewit*
THE BACHELOR *Curiosity*
THE SHEPHERD *Pickwick*
TIM CRATCHIT (or Tiny Tim) *Carol*
TOBY CRACKIT *Twist*
TOM CHITLING *Twist*
TOM JARNDYCE *Bleak*
TONY JOBLING *Bleak*
TRACY TUPMAN *Pickwick*
TULKINGHORN *Bleak*
WILMOT SNIPE *Pickwick*
WITHERFIELD Miss *Pickwick*

12

ABEL MAGWITCH *Expectations*
AGNES FLEMING *Twist*
ALDERMAN CUTE *Chimes*
ALFRED JINGLE *Pickwick*
ALFRED LAMMLE *Mutual*
ALICE MARWOOD *Dombey*
BARNABY RUDGE *Rudge*
BAYHAM BADGER *Bleak*
BULLY GLOBSON *Uncommercial*
CADDY JELLYBY *Bleak*
CAPTAIN ADAMS *Nickleby*
CAPTAIN FIERY *Mudfog*
CHARLEY BATES *Twist*
CHARLEY HEXAM *Mutual*
COLONEL BLAZO *Pickwick*
COLONEL DIVER *Chuzzlewit*
DAVID CRIMPLE *Chuzzlewit*
DICK DATCHERY *Drood*
DOCTOR BUFFER *Mudfog*
DOCTOR DUNKLE *Chuzzlewit*
DOCTOR LUMBEY *Nickleby*
DOCTOR SOEMUP *Mudfog*

DOCTOR STRONG *Copperfield*
EDITH GRANGER *Dombey*
EDITH SKEWTON *Dombey*
EDWARD DORRIT *Dorrit*
EDWIN LEEFORD *Twist*
ELIJAH POGRAM *Chuzzlewit*
EMMA HAREDALE *Rudge*
EMMA MICAWBER *Copperfield*
FANNY CLEAVER *Mutual*
FANNY SQUEERS *Nickleby*
FILLETOVILLE *Pickwick*
FRANK SIMMERY *Pickwick*
GENERAL CHOKE *Chuzzlewit*
GEORGE DEMPLE *Copperfield*
GRAZINGLANDS + Mrs
  Uncommercial
HONEYTHUNDER Luke *Drood*
JACK CHINAMAN *Drood*
JACOB NUBBLES *Curiosity*
JOB POTTERSON *Mutual*
JOHN ANDERSON *Uncommercial*
JOHN JARNDYCE *Bleak*
JOHN WESTLOCK *Chuzzlewit*
KATE NICKLEBY *Nickleby*
KUTANKUMAGEN Doctor *Mudfog*
LADY BARNACLE *Dorrit*
LADY BILBERRY *Dorrit*
LADY FLABELLA *Nickleby*
LADY SCADGERS *Hard*
LADY SKETTLES *Dombey*
LITTLE DORRIT (or Amy Dorrit) *Dorrit*
LITTLE SWILLS *Bleak*
LORD BARNACLE *Dorrit*
LORD MUTANHED *Pickwick*
LUCIE MANETTE *Two Cities*
MADELINE BRAY *Nickleby*
MAJOR CHOLLOP *Chuzzlewit*
MAJOR PAWKINS *Chuzzlewit*

MARGARET VECK *Chimes*
MARTHA ENDELL *Copperfield*
MARTHA VARDEN *Rudge*
MASTER BOWLEY *Chimes*
MATILDA PRICE *Nickleby*
MELCHISEDECH *Bleak*
MISS BRAVASSA *Nickleby*
MISS HAVISHAM *Expectations*
MISS JENNINGS *Drood*
MISS LA CREEVY *Nickleby*
MISS LEDBROOK *Nickleby*
MISS REYNOLDS *Drood*
MISS SHEPHERD *Copperfield*
MISS SIMMONDS *Nickleby*
MISS SKIFFINS *Expectations*
MISS SMITHERS *Pickwick*
MONTAGUE TIGG *Chuzzlewit*
MORRIS BOLTER *Twist*
MORTIMER KNAG *Nickleby*
MRS BILLICKIN *Drood*
MRS BLACKPOOL *Hard*
MRS BOUNDERBY *Hard*
MRS COMPEYSON *Expectations*
MRS FIBBITSON *Copperfield*
MRS FLIPFIELD *Uncommercial*
MRS GRADGRIND *Hard*
MRS LILLYVICK *Nickleby*
MRS MARKLEHAM *Copperfield*
MRS MURDSTONE *Copperfield*
MRS PARDIGGLE *Bleak*
MRS PORKENHAM *Pickwick*
MRS SMALLWEED *Bleak*
MRS TOMLINSON *Pickwick*
MRS TULRUMBLE *Mudfog*
MRS VENEERING *Mutual*
MRS WOODCOURT *Bleak*
MUDDLEBRAINS *Mudfog*
NOAH CLAYPOLE *Twist*

PEEPY JELLYBY *Bleak*
PHILIP PIRRIP (or Pip) *Expectations*
PUMPKINSKULL *Mudfog*
QUEBEC BAGNET *Bleak*
RICHARD EVANS *Curiosity*
ROBERT BOLTON *Mudfog*
SAMPSON BRASS *Curiosity*
SAMUEL WELLER (or Sam) *Pickwick*
SHINY VILLIAM *Pickwick*
SIM TAPPERTIT (or Simon) *Rudge*
SOLOMON DAISY *Rudge*
SOLOMON GILLS *Dombey*
SOLOMON LUCAS *Pickwick*
SOLOMON PROSS (alias John
  Barsad) *Two Cities*
SOPHY CREWLER *Copperfield*
STRAUDENHEIM *Uncommercial*
SYDNEY CARTON *Two Cities*
THOMAS BURTON *Pickwick*
THOMAS CODLIN *Curiosity*
THOMAS SAPSEA *Drood*
TITE BARNACLE *Dorrit*
TOLLIMGLOWER Lady *Pickwick*
TOM FLIPFIELD *Uncommercial*
TOM GRADGRIND *Hard*
TOMMY BARDELL *Pickwick*
WILLIAM BUFFY *Bleak*
WILLIAM GUPPY *Bleak*
WOODENSCONCE *Mudfog*

13

ANASTASIA RUGG *Dorrit*
ARABELLA ALLEN *Pickwick*
ARTHUR CLENNAM *Dorrit*
AUNT HAWKINSON *Mutual*
BART SMALLWEED *Bleak*
BENJAMIN ALLEN *Pickwick*
BROTHER TADGER *Pickwick*

CAPTAIN BAILEY *Copperfield*
CAPTAIN BUNSBY *Dombey*
CAPTAIN CUTTLE *Dombey*
CAPTAIN DOWLER *Pickwick*
CAPTAIN HAWDON *Bleak*
CAPTAIN MAROON *Dorrit*
CAPTAIN MARTIN *Dorrit*
CHARLES DARNAY (alias of Charles St Evrémonde) *Two Cities*
CLARA PEGGOTTY *Copperfield*
COLONEL BULDER *Pickwick*
COLONEL GORDON *Rudge*
COLONEL GROPER *Chuzzlewit*
DANIEL GRUMMER *Pickwick*
DICK SWIVELLER *Curiosity*
DOCTOR BLIMBER *Dombey*
DOCTOR CHILLIP *Copperfield*
DOCTOR HAGGAGE *Dorrit*
DOCTOR JOBLING *Chuzzlewit*
DOCTOR MANETTE *Two Cities*
DOCTOR SLAMMER *Pickwick*
DOCTOR TOORELL *Mudfog*
DOROTHY DIBBLE *Uncommercial*
DUKE OF LINSEED *Mutual*
EDWARD CHESTER *Rudge*
EDWARD LEEFORD *Twist*
EDWARD TWIGGER (or Bottle-nosed Ned) *Mudfog*
ERNEST DEFARGE *Two Cities*
FLORA FINCHING *Dorrit*
GABRIEL VARDEN *Rudge*
GENERAL CONWAY *Rudge*
GEORGE HEYLING *Pickwick*
GEORGE NUPKINS *Pickwick*
GEORGE RADFOOT *Mutual*
GEORGE SAMPSON *Mutual*
HARRIET BEADLE *Dorrit*
HARRIET CARKER *Dombey*

HERBERT POCKET *Expectations*
HORATIO FIZKIN *Pickwick*
JANE GRADGRIND *Hard*
JANE MURDSTONE *Copperfield*
JERRY CRUNCHER *Two Cities*
KIDDERMINSTER *Hard*
KITTY SKIMPOLE *Bleak*
LADY FINCHBURY *Dombey*
LAURA SKIMPOLE *Bleak*
LAVINIA WILFER *Mutual*
LORD VERISOPHT *Nickleby*
MADAME DEFARGE *Two Cities*
MAJOR BAGSTOCK *Dombey*
MARTHA BARDELL *Pickwick*
MATTHEW BAGNET *Bleak*
MATTHEW POCKET *Expectations*
M'CHOAKUMCHILD *Hard*
MELVIN TWEMLOW *Mutual*
MINNIE MEAGLES (or Pet) *Dorrit*
MISS BELVAWNEY *Nickleby*
MISS BROWNDOCK *Nickleby*
MISS FERDINAND *Drood*
MRS CHUZZLEWIT *Chuzzlewit*
MRS CRISPARKLE *Drood*
MRS FLINTWINCH *Dorrit*
MRS KIDGERBURY *Copperfield*
MRS MACSTINGER *Dombey*
MRS ONOWENEVER *Uncommercial*
MRS ROUNCEWELL *Bleak*
MRS SNEVELLICI *Nickleby*
MRS SOWERBERRY *Twist*
MRS SPOTTLETOE *Chuzzlewit*
MRS STEERFORTH *Copperfield*
MRS WATERBROOK *Copperfield*
MRS WITITTERLY *Nickleby*
OLD BILL BARLEY *Expectations*
PEG SLIDERSKEW *Nickleby*
PERCY CRUMMLES *Nickleby*

PROFESSOR DOZE *Mudfog*
PROFESSOR MUFF *Mudfog*
PROFESSOR MULL *Mudfog*
PROFESSOR NOGO *Mudfog*
RACHAEL WARDLE *Pickwick*
RALPH NICKLEBY *Nickleby*
RICHARD BABLEY (or Mr Dick)
   Copperfield
SALLY FLANDERS *Uncommercial*
SAMPSON DIBBLE *Uncommercial*
SAMUEL SLUMKEY *Pickwick*
SETH PECKSNIFF *Chuzzlewit*
SLUMMINTOWKEN *Pickwick*
SNUFFLETOFFLE QJ *Mudfog*
STILTSTALKING Lord *Dorrit*
THOMAS GROFFIN *Pickwick*
TOMMY SCREWZER *Dombey*
TROOPER GEORGE *Bleak*
WILLIAM DORRIT *Dorrit*

14

ABBEY POTTERSON *Mutual*
AGNES WICKFIELD *Copperfield*
ARTHUR HAVISHAM *Expectations*
AUGUSTUS MODDLE *Chuzzlewit*
BARNET SKETTLES *Dombey*
BENJAMIN BAILEY *Chuzzlewit*
BENTLEY DRUMMLE *Expectations*
BETSEY TROTWOOD *Copperfield*
BOTTLE-NOSED NED *Mudfog*
BROTHER BELLOWS *Dorrit*
BROTHER MORDLIN *Pickwick*
CAPTAIN BOLDWIG *Pickwick*
CAPTAIN HOPKINS *Copperfield*
CAPTAIN KEDGICK *Chuzzlewit*
CAPTAIN SWOSSER *Bleak*
CECILIA BOBSTER *Nickleby*
COLONEL CHOWSER *Nickleby*

COUNT SMORLTORK *Pickwick*
DANIEL PEGGOTTY *Copperfield*
DONNA CHRISTINA *Pickwick*
EDMUND SPARKLER *Dorrit*
EDWIN CHEERYBLE *Nickleby*
EUGENE WRAYBURN *Mutual*
FELIX PARDIGGLE *Bleak*
FLORENCE DOMBEY *Dombey*
FRANCIS SPENLOW *Copperfield*
FRANK CHEERYBLE *Nickleby*
FREDERICK TRENT *Curiosity*
GILBERT CLENNAM *Dorrit*
HAROLD SKIMPOLE *Bleak*
HELENA LANDLESS *Drood*
HIRAM GREWGIOUS *Drood*
ISABELLA WARDLE *Pickwick*
JAMES HARTHOUSE *Hard*
JEFFERSON BRICK *Chuzzlewit*
JOSEPH SMIGGERS *Pickwick*
LADY SNUPHANUPH *Pickwick*
LAVINIA SPENLOW *Copperfield*
LORD SNIGSWORTH *Mutual*
MASTER CRIPPLES *Dorrit*
MASTER CRUMMLES *Nickleby*
MELISSA WACKLES *Curiosity*
MERCANTILE JACK *Uncommercial*
MERCY PECKSNIFF (or Merry)
   Chuzzlewit
MERRY PECKSNIFF (or Mercy)
   Chuzzlewit
MICHAEL JACKSON *Bleak*
MISS ONOWENEVER *Uncommercial*
MISS SNEVELLICI *Nickleby*
MISS TWINKLETON *Drood*
MORGAN AP KERRIG *Bleak*
MRS COPPERFIELD *Copperfield*
OLYMPIA SQUIRES *Uncommercial*
PRINCESS PUFFER *Drood*

PROFESSOR DINGO *Bleak*
PROFESSOR GRIME *Mudfog*
PROFESSOR KETCH *Mudfog*
PROFESSOR PIPER *Chuzzlewit*
PROFESSOR SNORE *Mudfog*
REGINALD WILFER Mutual
REVEREND FEEDER *Dombey*
REVEREND HOWLER *Dombey*
REVEREND MILVEY *Mutual*
RICHARD UPWITCH *Pickwick*
ROGER RIDERHOOD *Mutual*
SALLY SPRODGKIN *Mutual*
SAMUEL PICKWICK *Pickwick*
SERJEANT BUZFUZ *Pickwick*
SIMON TAPPERTIT *Rudge*
SIR JOHN CHESTER *Rudge*
THE MARCHIONESS *Curiosity*
THOMAS BENJAMIN *Copperfield*
THOMAS LENVILLE *Nickleby*
THOMAS PLORNISH *Dorrit*
THOMAS TRADDLES *Copperfield*
TIM LINKINWATER *Nickleby*
TOBY CHUZZLEWIT *Chuzzlewit*
WATT ROUNCEWELL *Bleak*
WILKINS FLASHER *Pickwick*
WILLIAM POTKINS *Expectations*
WILLIAM SIMMONS *Chuzzlewit*
WOOLWICH BAGNET *Bleak*

15

ALFRED MANTALINI *Nickleby*
ALFRED PARDIGGLE *Bleak*
ALTRO CAVALLETTO *Dorrit*
ANASTASIA WEEDLE *Uncommerical*
CANON CRISPARKLE *Drood*
CAPTAIN MURDERER *Uncommercial*
CAROLINE JELLYBY *Bleak*
CHARLEY PYEGRAVE *Copperfield*

CHERRY PECKSNIFF (or Charity)
  Chuzzlewit
CLARISSA SPENLOW *Copperfield*
CONKEY CHICKWEED *Twist*
CORNELIA BLIMBER *Dombey*
DOCTOR GRUMMIDGE *Mudfog*
DOCTOR NEESHAWTS *Mudfog*
DOCTOR WOODCOURT *Bleak*
EBENEZER SCROOGE *Carol*
EDWARD MURDSTONE *Copperfield*
EGBERT PARDIGGLE *Bleak*
ESTHER SUMMERSON *Bleak*
FREDERICK DORRIT *Dorrit*
GENERAL FLADDOCK *Chuzzlewit*
GODFREY NICKLEBY *Nickleby*
HENRY WITITTERLY *Nickleby*
INSPECTOR BUCKET *Bleak*
JAMES STEERFORTH *Copperfield*
JOHN EDWARD NANDY *Dorrit*
JONAS CHUZZLEWIT *Chuzzlewit*
JOSEPHINE SLEARY *Hard*
JOSHUA SMALLWEED *Bleak*
JOSIAH BOUNDERBY *Hard*
JUDITH SMALLWEED *Bleak*
LA FAYETTE KETTLE *Chuzzlewit*
LOUISA GRADGRIND *Hard*
MADAME BARRONEAU *Dorrit*
MADAME MANTALINI *Nickleby*
MARY ANNE PARAGON *Copperfield*
MISS LINKINWATER *Nickleby*
MISS MELVILLESON *Bleak*
MISS MONFLATHERS *Curiosity*
MISS WITHERFIELD *Pickwick*
MORLEENA KENWIGS *Nickleby*
MRS GRAZINGLANDS *Uncommercial*
NATHANIEL PIPKIN *Pickwick*
NATHANIEL WINKLE *Pickwick*
NEVILLE LANDLESS *Drood*

NICODEMUS BOFFIN *Mutual*
NINETTA CRUMMLES *Nickleby*
OSWALD PARDIGGLE *Bleak*
PAUL SWEEDLEPIPE (or Poll) *Chuzzlewit*
POLL SWEEDLEPIPE (or Paul) *Chuzzlewit*
PROFESSOR MULLIT *Chuzzlewit*
PROFESSOR RUMMAN *Mudfog*
PROFESSOR WHEEZY *Mudfog*
QJ SNUFFLETOFFLE *Mudfog*
REVEREND CREWLER *Copperfield*
RICHARD CARSTONE *Bleak*
SERJEANT SNUBBIN *Pickwick*
SIDNEY PORKENHAM *Pickwick*
SIR JOSEPH BOWLEY *Chimes*
SIR MULBERRY HAWK *Nickleby*
SNITTLE TIMBERRY *Nickleby*
THE ARTFUL DODGER (alias of John
  (or Jack) Dawkins) *Twist*
THE BAGMAN'S UNCLE (or Jack
  Martin) *Pickwick*
THE YOUNG BUTCHER *Copperfield*
THOMAS GRADGRIND *Hard*
THOMAS TOWLINSON *Dombey*
VINCENT CRUMMLES *Nickleby*
VOLUMNIA DEDLOCK *Bleak*
WACKFORD SQUEERS *Nickleby*
WILKINS MICAWBER *Copperfield*
WILLIAM BARNACLE *Dorrit*
WILLIAM CLEVERLY *Uncommercial*
WILLIAM WILLIAMS *Mutual*
ZEPHANIA SCADDER *Chuzzlewit*

16
BRADLEY HEADSTONE *Mutual*
CHARITY PECKSNIFF (or Cherry)
  Chuzzlewit
CHARLES CHEERYBLE *Nickleby*
CHARLOTTE NECKETT *Bleak*

CLARENCE BARNACLE *Dorrit*
DAVID COPPERFIELD *Copperfield*
DON BOLARO FIZZGIG *Pickwick*
FRANCIS PARDIGGLE *Bleak*
GEORGE CHUZZLEWIT *Chuzzlewit*
GEORGE ROUNCEWELL *Bleak*
GEORGIANA PODSNAP *Mutual*
LADY TOLLIMGLOWER *Pickwick*
LAWRENCE BOYTHORN *Bleak*
LUKE HONEYTHUNDER *Drood*
MALTHUS GRADGRIND *Hard*
MARTIN CHUZZLEWIT *Chuzzlewit*
NICHOLAS NICKLEBY *Nickleby*
PRINCE TURVEYDROP *Bleak*
REVEREND CHADBAND *Bleak*
STEPHEN BLACKPOOL *Hard*
UNCLE PUMBLECHOOK *Expectations*

17
ANGELO CYRUS BANTAM *Pickwick*
ANTHONY CHUZZLEWIT *Chuzzlewit*
AUGUSTUS SNODGRASS *Pickwick*
CHARLES MACSTINGER *Dombey*
DIGGORY CHUZZLEWIT *Chuzzlewit*
EPHRAIM FLINTWINCH *Dorrit*
HAMILTON VENEERING *Mutual*
HORATIO PELTIROGUS *Nickleby*
INDIGNATION COCKER *Uncommercial*
JULIANA MACSTINGER *Dombey*
LORD STILTSTALKING *Dorrit*
MASTER BITHERSTONE *Mutual*
MORTIMER LIGHTWOOD *Mutual*
NICHOLAS TULRUMBLE *Mudfog*
PLEASANT RIDERHOOD *Mutual*
SOPHRONIA AKERSHEM *Mutual*

18
ADAM SMITH GRADGRIND *Hard*

CAPTAIN BLUNDERBORE *Mudfog*
CHARLES ST EVRÉMONDE (alias
   Charles Darnay) *Two Cities*
DOCTOR KUTANKUMAGEN *Mudfog*
JEREMIAH FLINTWINCH *Dorrit*
MARQUIS ST EVRÉMONDE *Two Cities*
YOUNG JERRY CRUNCHER *Two Cities*

19
ALEXANDER MACSTINGER *Dombey*
LIEUTENANT TAPPLETON *Pickwick*
MR JUSTICE STARELEIGH *Pickwick*
PROFESSOR QUEERSPECK *Mudfog*
SIR LEICESTER DEDLOCK *Bleak*

Arts – Literature – NOVEL CHARACTERS (general)

3
DAN *Puck of Pook's Hill*
IDA *Brighton Rock*
JEM *To Kill a Mockingbird*
JIM *Lord Jim*
LEE Lorelei *Gentlemen Prefer Blondes*
OAK Gabriel *Far from the Madding
   Crowd*
PYM Magnus *A Perfect Spy*
TOM *The Water Babies*
VYE Eustacia *The Return of the Native*

4
AHAB Captain *Moby Dick*
ALGY *Biggles series*
AZIZ Doctor *A Passage to India*
BEDE Adam *Adam Bede*
BOND James *James Bond series*
BOOT John *Scoop*
BULL Johnny *Billy Bunter series*
CARR Katy *What Katy Did*
CASS Eppie *Silas Marner*
CORD Jonas *The Carpetbaggers*
CUFF Sergeant *The Moonstone*
DEAN Susie *The Good Companions*
DEWY Dick *Under the Greenwood Tree*

DONN Arabella *Jude the Obscure*
EAST *Tom Brown's Schooldays*
EASY John *Mr Midshipman Easy*
EYRE Jane *Jane Eyre*
FINN Huckleberry *The Adventures of
   Huckleberry Finn*
FINN Phineas *Phineas Finn*
FOGG Phileas *Around the World in
   Eighty Days*
GARP *The World According to Garp*
GRAY Dorian *The Picture of Dorian Gray*
GREY Agnes *Agnes Grey*
GUNN Ben *Treasure Island*
HOGG Georgina *The Comforters*
HOLT Felix *Felix Holt*
HOLT Gavin *The Cruel Sea*
HYDE Mr *The Strange Case of Dr
   Jekyll and Mr Hyde*
JANE *Tarzan series*
JOAD Tom *The Grapes of Wrath*
KEMP Liza *Liza of Lambeth*
KIRK Howard *The History Man*
LAST Tony *A Handful of Dust*
LIME Harry *The Third Man*
LUCK Thomas *The Luck of Roaring
   Camp*

LUNG Wang *The Good Earth*
MOND Mustapha *Brave New World*
NEMO Captain *20,000 Leagues under the Sea*
NUNN Jimmy *The Good Companions*
PYLE Alben *The Quiet American*
REED Mrs *Jane Eyre*
RICE Sammy *The Small Back Room*
RIDD John *Lorna Doone*
ROSE *Brighton Rock*
SEAL Basil *Put Out More Flags*
SYME Gabriel *The Man Who Was Thursday*
TAJI *Mardi*
TROY Sergeant *Far from the Madding Crowd*
VANE Harriet *Strong Poison* etc
VOSS Johann *Voss*
WEIR Adam *Weir of Hermiston*

5

ALICE *Alice's Adventures in Wonderland, Through the Looking Glass*
ATHOS *The Three Musketeers*
BATES *Stalky & Co*
BLAKE Franklin *The Moonstone*
BLOOD Captain *Captain Blood*
BLOOM Leopold, Molly *Ulysses*
BOOTH Amelia, William *Amelia*
BRECK Alan *Kidnapped, Catriona*
BROWN Father *Father Brown series*
BROWN Tom *Tom Brown's Schooldays*
BROWN Velvet *National Velvet*
BROWN William *Just William series*
BUNNY *The Amateur Cracksman* etc
CAREY Philip *Of Human Bondage*
CHIPS *Goodbye Mr Chips*
CLARA *Heidi*

CLARE Angel *Tess of the D'Urbervilles*
COHEN Mirah *Daniel Deronda*
CRANE Ichabod *The Legend of Sleepy Hollow*
DARCY *Pride and Prejudice*
DAWES Baxter *Sons and Lovers*
DIXON Jim *Lucky Jim*
DOONE Carver, Lorna *Lorna Doone*
DUBBY *Phineas Finn*
DUPIN Auguste *The Murders in the Rue Morgue* etc
DUROY Georges *Bel-Ami*
ELIZA *Uncle Tom's Cabin*
FINCH Atticus *To Kill a Mockingbird*
FLORA *The Turn of the Screw*
FLYNN Father *Dubliners*
FLYTE Sebastian *Brideshead Revisited*
FOSCO Count *The Woman in White*
GESTE Beau *Beau Geste*
HEIDI *Heidi*
HOLLY Ludwig *She*
JANET *Beyond This Place*
JONES Tom *Tom Jones*
KIPPS Arthur *Kipps*
KLEIN Honor *A Severed Head*
LARCH Doctor *The Cider House Rules*
LEIGH Amyas *Westward Ho!*
LOGAN Fanny *The Pursuit of Love*
MARCH Amy, Beth, Jo, Meg *Little Women*
MASON Perry *The Case of the Velvet Claws* etc
MERCY *The Pilgrim's Progress*
MILES *The Turn of the Screw*
MITTY Walter *The Secret Life of Walter Mitty*
MOORE Mrs *A Passage to India*
M'TURK *Stalky & Co*

O'HARA Kimball *Kim*
O'HARA Scarlett *Gone with the Wind*
PAGET Jean *A Town Like Alice*
PANZA Sancho *Don Quixote*
PIGGY *Lord of the Flies*
POLLY Alfred *The History of Mr Polly*
POSTE Flora *Cold Comfort Farm*
POTTS Caractacus *Chitty Chitty Bang Bang*
PRICE Fanny *Mansfield Park*
QUEEG Captain *The Caine Mutiny*
QUEEN Ellery *Ellery Queen series*
RALPH *Lord of the Flies*
READY Masterman *Masterman Ready*
REMUS Uncle *Uncle Remus series*
RYDER Charles *Brideshead Revisited*
SAMSA Gregor *Metamorphosis*
SCOUT *To Kill a Mockingbird*
SHARP Becky *Vanity Fair*
SINAI Saleem *Midnight's Children*
SINGH Hurree *Billy Bunter series*
SLOPE Reverend *Barsetshire series*
SLOTH *The Pilgrim's Progress*
SMITH Winston *Nineteen Eighty-Four*
SNOWE Lucy *Villette*
SPADE Sam *The Maltese Falcon*
SWANN Charles *Remembrance of Things Past*
TEMPY Aunt *Uncle Remus stories*
TOPSY *Uncle Tom's Cabin*
TOWNE Langdon *Northwest Passage*
TRANT Elizabeth *The Good Companions*
TRASK Adam *East of Eden*
TRENT Philip *Trent's Last Case* etc
TWALA *King Solomon's Mines*
UNCAS *The Last of the Mohicans* etc
USHER Roderick *The Fall of the House of Usher*

VINCY Walter *Middlemarch*
WADDY *Kipps*
WAKEM Philip *The Mill on the Floss*
WELLS Homer *The Cider House Rules*
WOLFE Nero *Fer-de-Lance* etc

6

ADOLPH *Uncle Tom's Cabin*
AITKEN *Prester John*
ALLEYN Inspector *A Man Lay Dead* etc
ARAMIS *The Three Musketeers*
ARCHER Isabel *The Portrait of a Lady*
AYESHA *She*
BAINES Constance, Sophia *The Old Wives' Tale*
BEETLE *Stalky & Co*
BENBOW *Clayhanger*
BENNET Catherine, Elizabeth, Jane, Lydia, Mary, Mrs *Pride and Prejudice*
BOVARY Madame *Madame Bovary*
BOWLES Sally *Goodbye to Berlin*
BRODIE Jean *The Prime of Miss Jean Brodie*
BROOKE Dorothea *Middlemarch*
BUMPPO Natty *The Last of the Mohicans* etc
BUNTER Billy *Billy Bunter series*
BUTLER Rhett *Gone with the Wind*
CHERRY Bob *Billy Bunter series*
COOLEY Ben *Kangaroo*
CROWNE Lenina *Brave New World*
CRUSOE Robinson *Robinson Crusoe*
DAGGOO *Moby Dick*
DANTES Edmond *The Count of Monte Cristo*
DOBSON Zuleika *Zuleika Dobson*

ELLIOT Anne, Elizabeth, Sir Walter
  Persuasion
ESMOND Colonel *The History of
  Henry Esmond Esquire*
FAWLEY Jude *Jude the Obscure*
FINLAY Doctor *Beyond This Place*
FIRMIN Geoffrey *Under the Volcano*
FLOSKY *Nightmare Abbey*
FOSSIL Posy *Ballet Shoes*
FOWLER Thomas *The Quiet American*
FRIDAY *Robinson Crusoe*
GAGOOL *King Solomon's Mines*
GANTRY Elmer *Elmer Gantry*
GATSBY Jay *The Great Gatsby*
GEORGE *Of Mice and Men, Three Men
  in a Boat*
GINGER *Biggles series*
GORDON Squire *Black Beauty*
GRIMES *The Water Babies*
HANNAH *Little Women*
HANNAY Richard *The Thirty-Nine
  Steps* etc
HARKER Jonathan *Dracula*
HARPER Joe *The Adventures of Tom
  Sawyer*
HERZOG Moses *Herzog*
HOLMES Mycroft, Sherlock *Sherlock
  Holmes series*
HUDSON Mrs *Sherlock Holmes series*
JEEVES *My Man Jeeves* etc
JEKYLL Doctor *The Strange Case of Dr
  Jekyll and Mr Hyde*
JORDAN Robert *For Whom the Bell Tolls*
KETTLE Captain *The Adventures of
  Captain Kettle* etc
LARKIN Ma, Pop *The Darling Buds of
  May*
LAURIE *Little Women*

LEGREE Simon *Uncle Tom's Cabin*
LENNIE *Of Mice and Men*
LINTON Edgar *Wuthering Heights*
LOLITA *Lolita*
LYNDON Barry *The Luck of Barry
  Lyndon*
MACKAY Miss *The Prime of Miss Jean
  Brodie*
MANSON Doctor *The Citadel*
MARNER Silas *Silas Marner*
MARPLE Miss T*he Murder at the
  Vicarage* etc
MOREAU Doctor *The Island of Dr
  Moreau*
MORGAN Angharad, Huw *How
  Green Was My Valley*
MORRIS Adam *The Glittering Prizes*
MOWGLI *The Jungle Books*
MR HYDE *The Strange Case of Dr
  Jekyll and Mr Hyde*
NEWMAN Christopher *The American*
NORRIS Arthur *Mr Norris Changes
  Trains*
NUGENT Frank *Billy Bunter series*
ODDJOB *Goldfinger*
ODETTE *Remembrance of Things Past*
OSMOND Gilbert *The Portrait of a
  Lady*
PHUONG *The Quiet American*
PICKLE Peregrine *The Adventures of
  Peregrine Pickle*
PINKIE *Brighton Rock*
POIROT Hercule *The Mysterious
  Affair at Styles* etc
POOTER Carrie, Charles, Lupin *The
  Diary of a Nobody*
POTTER Harry *Harry Potter series*
PSMITH *Leave it to Psmith* etc

RADLEY Boo *To Kill a Mockingbird*
RANDOM Roderick *The Adventures of Roderick Random*
ROB ROY *Rob Roy*
ROSTOV *War and Peace*
SANGER Tessy *The Constant Nymph*
SAWYER Tom *The Adventures of Tom Sawyer*
SCOBIE Henry *The Heart of the Matter*
SEDLEY Amelia *Vanity Fair*
SHANDY Tristram *Tristram Shandy*
SILVER Long John *Treasure Island*
SIMPLE Peter *Peter Simple*
SLOPER Doctor *Washington Square*
SMEETH *Angel Pavement*
SMILEY George *Smiley's People* etc
SORREL Hetty *Adam Bede*
STALKY *Stalky & Co*
STREET Della T*he Case of the Velvet Claws* etc
TARZAN *Tarzan series*
THORNE Doctor *Doctor Thorne*
THORPE Isabella *Northanger Abbey*
TILNEY Henry *Northanger Abbey*
TOOMEY Kenneth *Earthly Powers*
TURKEY *Stalky & Co*
TURPIN Dick *Rookwood*
UMPOPA *King Solomon's Mines*
WALKER John, Roger, Susan, Titty, Vicky *Swallows and Amazons*
WATSON Doctor Sherlock Holmes series
WILCOX Henry *Howards End*
WILKES Ashley, India *Gone with the Wind*
WIMSEY Lord Peter *Whose Body?* etc
WOTTON Lord *The Picture of Dorian Gray*

7

AMERIGO Prince *The Golden Bowl*
ANDREWS Joseph *The Adventures of Joseph Andrews*
ANDREWS Pamela *Pamela*
BADGERY Herbert *Illywhacker*
BALFOUR David *Kidnapped, Catriona*
BEN GUNN *Treasure Island*
BERNERS Belle *Lavengro*
BERTRAM Allan *Guy Mannering*
BERTRAM Lady *Mansfield Park*
BIGGLES Biggles series
BINGLEY Charles *Pride and Prejudice*
BOWLING Tom *The Adventures of Roderick Random*
BRANDON Colonel *Sense and Sensibility*
CAMERON Doctor *Beyond This Place*
CAMPION Albert *The Crime at Black Dudley* etc
CLINKER Humphry *The Expedition of Humphry Clinker*
COLLINS Reverend *Pride and Prejudice*
CRAWLEY Sir Pitt *Vanity Fair*
CYPRESS *Nightmare Abbey*
DANVERS Mrs *Rebecca*
DEDALUS Stephen *Ulysses*
DERONDA Daniel *Daniel Deronda*
DE SELBY *The Third Policeman*
DETROIT Nathan *Guys and Dolls*
DINMONT Dandie *Guy Mannering*
DRACULA Count *Dracula*
DURWARD Quentin *Quentin Durward*
ENDERBY *Inside Mr Enderby* etc
FAIRFAX Jane *Emma*
FAIRFAX Mrs *Jane Eyre*
FARFRAE Donald *The Mayor of Casterbridge*

FORSYTE Fleur, Holly, James, Jolyon, Soames *The Forsyte Saga*
GRANGER Hermione Harry Potter series
GRANTLY Archdeacon Barsetshire series
GRIFFIN *The Invisible Man*
HARDING Septimus Barsetshire series
HARLOWE Clarissa *Clarissa*
HAWKEYE *The Last of the Mohicans* etc
HAWKINS Jim *Treasure Island*
HERRIES Francis *Rogue Herries*
HOPEFUL *The Pilgrim's Progress*
HUMBERT Humbert *Lolita*
ISHMAEL *Moby Dick*
IVANHOE *Ivanhoe*
JENKYNS Deborah *Cranford*
JO MARCH *Little Women*
JOSEPH K *The Trial*
KEELDAR Shirley *Shirley*
KENTUCK *The Luck of Roaring Camp*
KROESIG Anthony *The Pursuit of Love*
LAMBERT Colonel *The Virginians*
LAMPTON Joe *Room at the Top*
LATIMER Darsie *Redgauntlet*
LIVESEY Doctor *Treasure Island*
LOVEDAY John *The Trumpet-Major*
MAIGRET Maigret series
MARKHAM Gilbert *The Tenant of Wildfell Hall*
MARLOWE Philip *The Big Sleep* etc
MELLORS Oliver *Lady Chatterley's Lover*
MORLAND Catherine *Northanger Abbey*
MRS REED *Jane Eyre*
NATASHA *War and Peace*
NEWCOME Thomas *The Newcomes*

OAKROYD Jess *The Good Companions*
ORLANDO *Orlando*
OVERTON *The Way of All Flesh*
PADDOCK *The Thirty-Nine Steps*
PANURGE *Gargantua and Pantagruel*
PERKUPP Mr *The Diary of a Nobody*
PEVERIL Julian *Peveril of the Peak*
POLDARK Ross Poldark series
POPPINS Mary Mary Poppins series
PORTHOS *The Three Musketeers*
PROUDIE Bishop, Mrs Barsetshire series
QUESTED Adela *A Passage to India*
QUIXOTE Don *Don Quixote*
RADLETT Linda *The Pursuit of Love*
RAFFLES *The Amateur Cracksman* etc
RAINIER Charles *Random Harvest*
RANDALL Rebecca *Rebecca of Sunnybrook Farm*
REBECCA *Rebecca, Ivanhoe*
ROBSART Amy *Kenilworth*
RUMPOLE Horace Rumpole series
SANDERS *Sanders of the River*
ST CLAIR Eva *Uncle Tom's Cabin*
TEMPLAR Simon *Meet the Tiger* etc
TOM JOAD *The Grapes of Wrath*
UKRIDGE *Love Among the Chickens*
VALJEAN Jean *Les Misérables*
VRONSKI *Anna Karenina*
WARWICK Diana *Diana of the Crossways*
WEASLEY Ronald Harry Potter series
WESTERN Mrs, Sophia, Squire *Tom Jones*
WHARTON Harry Billy Bunter series
WICKHAM George *Pride and Prejudice*
WILLIAM *Three Men in a Boat*

WOOSTER Bertie *My Man Jeeves* etc
ZHIVAGO Doctor *Dr Zhivago*

8
ADAM BEDE *Adam Bede*
ADAM WEIR *Weir of Hermiston*
AMY MARCH *Little Women*
APOLLYON *The Pilgrim's Progress*
ARMITAGE Jacob *The Children of the New Forest*
ASHWORTH Paul *Fever Pitch*
BEVERLEY Colonel *The Children of the New Forest*
BEZUKHOV *War and Peace*
BLAKENEY Sir Percy *The Scarlet Pimpernel*
BLIND PEW *Treasure Island*
BOLDWOOD Farmer *Far from the Madding Crowd*
BRANGWEN Tom *The Rainbow, Women in Love*
BRITLING Hugh *Mr Britling Sees It Through*
CARRAWAY Nick *The Great Gatsby*
CASAUBON *Foucault's Pendulum*
CASAUBON Edward *Middlemarch*
CATRIONA *Catriona*
DALLOWAY Mrs *Mrs Dalloway*
DASHWOOD Henry *Sense and Sensibility*
DE BOURGH Lady *Pride and Prejudice*
DERRIMAN Festus *The Trumpet-Major*
DE WINTER Max *Rebecca*
DICK DEWY *Under the Greenwood Tree*
DRUMMOND Bulldog *Bulldog Drummond* etc
DRUMMOND Catriona *Catriona*

DULCINEA *Don Quixote*
EARNSHAW Catherine *Wuthering Heights*
EMMELINE *Uncle Tom's Cabin*
EVERDENE Bathsheba *Far from the Madding Crowd*
FAITHFUL *The Pilgrim's Progress*
FANDORIN Erast *The Winter Queen* etc
FFOULKES *The Scarlet Pimpernel*
FLAMBEAU Father Brown series
FLANDERS Jacob *Jacob's Room*
FLANDERS Moll *Moll Flanders*
FLASHMAN *Flashman* etc, *Tom Brown's Schooldays*
GLENCORA Lady Palliser series
GULLIVER Lemuel *Gulliver's Travels*
HALLWARD Basil *The Picture of Dorian Gray*
HASTINGS Poirot series
HENCHARD Michael *The Mayor of Casterbridge*
HOLCOMBE Marian *The Woman in White*
INJUN JOE *The Adventures of Tom Sawyer*
JANE EYRE *Jane Eyre*
JIM DIXON *Lucky Jim*
JOHN BOOT *Scoop*
JOHN EASY *Mr Midshipman Easy*
JOHN RIDD *Lorna Doone*
JORDACHE Axel *Rich Man, Poor Man*
JORROCKS Mr Jorrocks series
KARENINA Anna *Anna Karenina*
KATY CARR *What Katy Did*
LESSWAYS Hilda *Clayhanger*
LESTRADE Inspector Sherlock Holmes series

LEWISHAM George *Love and Mr Lewisham*
LIZA KEMP *Liza of Lambeth*
LOCKWOOD *Wuthering Heights*
MA LARKIN *The Darling Buds of May*
MEG MARCH *Little Women*
MORIARTY *Sherlock Holmes series*
MRS MOORE *A Passage to India*
MUSGROVE Charles *Persuasion*
O'FERRALL Trilby *Trilby*
PALLISER Admiral *Palliser series*
PANGLOSS Doctor *Candide*
PETERSEN Carl *Bulldog Drummond* etc
PRIMROSE Charles *The Vicar of Wakefield*
QUEEQUEG *Moby Dick*
ROBINSON Fritz *The Swiss Family Robinson*
SAM SPADE *The Maltese Falcon*
SCYTHROP *Nightmare Abbey*
STANDISH Lady *Palliser series*
ST BUNGAY *Phineas Finn*
SVENGALI *Trilby*
TASHTEGO *Moby Dick*
THATCHER Becky *The Adventures of Tom Sawyer*
THOMPSON Sadie *Rain*
THWACKUM *Tom Jones*
TOM BROWN *Tom Brown's Schooldays*
TOM JONES *Tom Jones*
TONY LAST *A Handful of Dust*
TULLIVER Maggie, Tom *The Mill on the Floss*
UNCLE TOM *Uncle Tom's Cabin*
VERINDER Rachel *The Moonstone*
WANG LUNG *The Good Earth*
WAVERLEY Edward *Waverley novels*

WILLIAMS Eric *Eric or Little by Little*

9

ABBEVILLE Horace *Cannery Row*
ADAM TRASK *East of Eden*
AGNES GREY *Agnes Grey*
ALAN BRECK *Kidnapped, Catriona*
ALBEN PYLE *The Quiet American*
ALLWORTHY Squire *Tom Jones*
AUNT TEMPY *Uncle Remus series*
BASIL SEAL *Put Out More Flags*
BEAU GESTE *Beau Geste*
BEN COOLEY *Kangaroo*
BETH MARCH *Little Women*
BOB CHERRY *Billy Bunter series*
BOLKONSKI Prince *War and Peace*
BOO RADLEY *To Kill a Mockingbird*
BRIDEHEAD Sue *Jude the Obscure*
CATHERICK Anne *The Woman in White*
CAULFIELD Holden *The Catcher in the Rye*
CHRISTIAN *The Pilgrim's Progress*
CONINGSBY Harry *Coningsby*
DALGLIESH Adam *Cover Her Face* etc
D'ARTAGNAN *The Three Musketeers*
DRIFFIELD Rosie *Cakes and Ale*
DRYASDUST Doctor *The Antiquary*
EARWICKER Humphrey *Finnegans Wake*
EPPIE CASS *Silas Marner*
ESMERELDA *Notre Dame de Paris*
ESTERHAZY Toby *Smiley's People*
FELIX HOLT *Felix Holt*
GARGANTUA *Gargantua and Pantagruel*
GAVIN HOLT *The Cruel Sea*
GREYSTOKE Lord *Tarzan series*
HARRY LIME *The Third Man*

HARTRIGHT Walter *The Woman in White*
HUW MORGAN *How Green Was My Valley*
INGLEWOOD Squire *Rob Roy*
JAMES BOND *James Bond series*
JAY GATSBY *The Great Gatsby*
JEAN PAGET *A Town Like Alice*
JIMMY NUNN *The Good Companions*
JOE HARPER *The Adventures of Tom Sawyer*
JOLLIFANT Inigo *The Good Companions*
JONAS CORD *The Carpetbaggers*
KNIGHTLEY George *Emma*
LUCY SNOWE *Villette*
MAGNUS PYM *A Perfect Spy*
MANNERING Guy *Guy Mannering*
MARCHMAIN Lady *Brideshead Revisited*
MERRILIES Meg *Guy Mannering*
MEURSAULT *L'Étranger*
MR PERKUPP *The Diary of a Nobody*
MRS BENNET *Pride and Prejudice*
MRS HUDSON *Sherlock Holmes series*
NERO WOLFE *Fer-de-Lance* etc
PENDENNIS Arthur *Pendennis*
PONDEREVO Edward *Tono-Bungay*
POP LARKIN *The Darling Buds of May*
QUASIMODO *Notre Dame de Paris*
ROCHESTER Edward *Jane Eyre*
SAMMY RICE *The Small Back Room*
SMALLWAYS Bert *War in the Air*
SUSIE DEAN *The Good Companions*
TOM SAWYER *The Adventures of Tom Sawyer*
TRELAWNEY Squire *Treasure Island*
UNCLE TOBY *Tristram Shandy*

WENTWORTH Captain *Persuasion*
WENTWORTH Clifford *The Europeans*
WOODHOUSE Emma *Emma*
YEOBRIGHT Clym *The Return of the Native*
YOSSARIAN *Catch-22*

10

ADAM MORRIS *The Glittering Prizes*
AMYAS LEIGH *Westward Ho!*
AMY ROBSART *Kenilworth*
ANGEL CLARE *Tess of the D'Urbervilles*
ANNE ELLIOT *Persuasion*
BECKY SHARP *Vanity Fair*
CHALLENGER Professor *The Lost World*
CHATTERLEY Lady *Lady Chatterley's Lover*
CHRISTIANA *The Pilgrim's Progress*
CLAYHANGER Edwin *Clayhanger*
COUNT FOSCO *The Woman in White*
CRIMSWORTH William *The Professor*
CROUCHBACK Guy *Men at Arms* etc
DICK TURPIN *Rookwood*
DOCTOR AZIZ *A Passage to India*
DON QUIXOTE *Don Quixote*
DORIAN GRAY *The Picture of Dorian Gray*
EVA ST CLAIR *Uncle Tom's Cabin*
FANNY LOGAN *The Pursuit of Love*
FANNY PRICE *Mansfield Park*
FAUNTLEROY Lord *Little Lord Fauntleroy*
FLORA POSTE *Cold Comfort Farm*
FRIEDEMANN Herr *Little Herr Friedemann*
GABRIEL OAK *Far from the Madding Crowd*

GOLDFINGER Auric *Goldfinger*
HEATHCLIFF *Wuthering Heights*
HOMER WELLS *The Cider House Rules*
HONOR KLEIN *A Severed Head*
HORNBLOWER Horatio Hornblower series
HOWARD KIRK *The History Man*
HUNTINGDON Helen *The Tenant of Wildfell Hall*
JANE BENNET *Pride and Prejudice*
JEAN BRODIE *The Prime of Miss Jean Brodie*
JIM HAWKINS *Treasure Island*
JOE LAMPTON *Room at the Top*
JOHANN VOSS *Voss*
JOHNNY BULL Billy Bunter series
JOHN WALKER *Swallows and Amazons*
JUDE FAWLEY *Jude the Obscure*
LORD WOTTON *The Picture of Dorian Gray*
LORELEI LEE *Gentlemen Prefer Blondes*
LORNA DOONE *Lorna Doone*
MARY BENNET *Pride and Prejudice*
MIRAH COHEN *Daniel Deronda*
MISS MACKAY *The Prime of Miss Jean Brodie*
MISS MARPLE *The Murder at the Vicarage* etc
MOLLY BLOOM *Ulysses*
MONEYPENNY Miss James Bond series
MR JORROCKS Jorrocks series
MRS DANVERS *Rebecca*
MRS FAIRFAX *Jane Eyre*
MRS PROUDIE Barsetshire series
MRS WESTERN *Tom Jones*
PANTAGRUEL *Gargantua and Pantagruel*

PERRY MASON *The Case of the Velvet Claws* etc
PETULENGRO Jasper *Lavengro*
POSY FOSSIL *Ballet Shoes*
QUATERMAIN Allan *King Solomon's Mines*
RASSENDYLL Rudolf *The Prisoner of Zenda*
STARKADDER Amos, Seth *Cold Comfort Farm*
STRICKLAND Charles *The Moon and Sixpence*
TELLWRIGHT Anna *Anna of the Five Towns*
THOMAS LUCK *The Luck of Roaring Camp*
TOM BOWLING *The Adventures of Roderick Random*
UNCLE REMUS Uncle Remus series
VAN DER VALK *Love in Amsterdam* etc
WIDMERPOOL Kenneth *A Dance to the Music of Time*
WILLOUGHBY John *Sense and Sensibility*

11

ALFRED POLLY *The History of Mr Polly*
AMELIA BOOTH *Amelia*
ARTHUR KIPPS *Kipps*
AUNT ADA DOOM *Cold Comfort Farm*
BARRY LYNDON *The Luck of Barry Lyndon*
BAXTER DAWES *Sons and Lovers*
BILLY BUNTER Billy Bunter series
CAPTAIN AHAB *Moby Dick*
CAPTAIN NEMO *20,000 Leagues under the Sea*
CARVER DOONE *Lorna Doone*

CHEROKEE SAL *The Luck of Roaring Camp*
DELLA STREET *The Case of the Velvet Claws* etc
DOCTOR LARCH *The Cider House Rules*
D'URBERVILLE Alec *Tess of the D'Urbervilles*
DURBEYFIELD Tess *Tess of the D'Urbervilles*
EDGAR LINTON *Wuthering Heights*
ELLERY QUEEN Ellery Queen series
ELMER GANTRY *Elmer Gantry*
EUSTACIA VYE *The Return of the Native*
FATHER BROWN Father Brown series
FATHER FLYNN *Dubliners*
FRANK NUGENT Billy Bunter series
GABRIEL SYME *The Man Who Was Thursday*
GREGOR SAMSA *Metamorphosis*
HARRIET VANE *Strong Poison*
HARRY POTTER Harry Potter series
HENRY SCOBIE *The Heart of the Matter*
HENRY TILNEY *Northanger Abbey*
HENRY WILCOX *Howards End*
HETTY SORREL *Adam Bede*
HURREE SINGH Billy Bunter series
INDIA WILKES *Gone with the Wind*
JANE FAIRFAX *Emma*
JEAN VALJEAN *Les Misérables*
JESS OAKROYD *The Good Companions*
JOHN LOVEDAY *The Trumpet-Major*
LADY BERTRAM *Mansfield Park*
LUDWIG HOLLY *She*
LUPIN POOTER *The Diary of a Nobody*
LYDIA BENNET *Pride and Prejudice*

MARY POPPINS Mary Poppins series
MAX DE WINTER *Rebecca*
MOSES HERZOG *Herzog*
MRS DALLOWAY *Mrs Dalloway*
NATTY BUMPPO *The Last of the Mohicans* etc
PETER SIMPLE *Peter Simple*
PHILEAS FOGG *Around the World in Eighty Days*
PHILIP CAREY *Of Human Bondage*
PHILIP TRENT *Trent's Last Case* etc
PHILIP WAKEM *The Mill on the Floss*
PHINEAS FINN *Phineas Finn*
RASKOLNIKOV *Crime and Punishment*
REDGAUNTLET *Redgauntlet*
RHETT BUTLER *Gone with the Wind*
ROGER WALKER *Swallows and Amazons*
ROSS POLDARK Poldark series
SALEEM SINAI *Midnight's Children*
SALLY BOWLES *Goodbye to Berlin*
SANCHO PANZA *Don Quixote*
SCARAMOUCHE *Scaramouche*
SILAS MARNER *Silas Marner*
SIMON LEGREE *Uncle Tom's Cabin*
SUSAN WALKER *Swallows and Amazons*
TESSY SANGER *The Constant Nymph*
TITTY WALKER *Swallows and Amazons*
TOM BRANGWEN *The Rainbow, Women in Love*
TOM TULLIVER *The Mill on the Floss*
VELVET BROWN *National Velvet*
VICKY WALKER *Swallows and Amazons*
VON STALHEIN Erich Biggles series
WALTER MITTY *The Secret Life of Walter Mitty*
WALTER VINCY *Middlemarch*

12

ADELA QUESTED *A Passage to India*
ALLAN BERTRAM *Guy Mannering*
AMELIA SEDLEY *Vanity Fair*
ANNA KARENINA *Anna Karenina*
ARABELLA DONN *Jude the Obscure*
ARTHUR NORRIS *Mr Norris Changes Trains*
ASHLEY WILKES *Gone with the Wind*
ATTICUS FINCH *To Kill a Mockingbird*
AUGUSTE DUPIN *The Murders in the Rue Morgue* etc
AXEL JORDACHE *Rich Man, Poor Man*
BELLE BERNERS *Lavengro*
BRECKINRIDGE Myra *Myra Breckinridge*
CAPTAIN BLOOD *Captain Blood*
CAPTAIN QUEEG *The Caine Mutiny*
CARL PETERSEN *Bulldog Drummond* etc
CARRIE POOTER *The Diary of a Nobody*
CHARLES RYDER *Brideshead Revisited*
CHARLES SWANN *Remembrance of Things Past*
CHINGACHGOOK *The Last of the Mohicans* etc
COUNT DRACULA *Dracula*
DAVID BALFOUR *Kidnapped, Catriona*
DIANA WARWICK *Diana of the Crossways*
DOCTOR FINLAY *Beyond This Place*
DOCTOR JEKYLL *The Strange Case of Dr Jekyll and Mr Hyde*
DOCTOR MANSON *The Citadel*
DOCTOR MOREAU *The Island of Dr Moreau*
DOCTOR SLOPER *Washington Square*
DOCTOR THORNE *Doctor Thorne*

DOCTOR WATSON Sherlock Holmes series
EDMOND DANTES *The Count of Monte Cristo*
ERIC WILLIAMS *Eric or Little by Little*
FLEUR FORSYTE *The Forsyte Saga*
FRANKENSTEIN Doctor *Frankenstein*
GEORGES DUROY *Bel-Ami*
GEORGE SMILEY *Smiley's People* etc
GEORGINA HOGG *The Comforters*
GIANT DESPAIR *The Pilgrim's Progress*
GUY MANNERING *Guy Mannering*
HARRY WHARTON Billy Bunter series
HOLLY FORSYTE *The Forsyte Saga*
HUGH BRITLING *Mr Britling Sees It Through*
ICHABOD CRANE *The Legend of Sleepy Hollow*
ISABEL ARCHER *The Portrait of a Lady*
JAMES FORSYTE *The Forsyte Saga*
KIMBALL O'HARA *Kim*
LADY DE BOURGH *Pride and Prejudice*
LADY GLENCORA Palliser series
LADY STANDISH Palliser series
LANGDON TOWNE *Northwest Passage*
LENINA CROWNE *Brave New World*
LEOPOLD BLOOM *Ulysses*
LINDA RADLETT *The Pursuit of Love*
MADAME BOVARY *Madame Bovary*
MEG MERRILIES *Guy Mannering*
MOLL FLANDERS *Moll Flanders*
MUSTAPHA MOND *Brave New World*
NICK CARRAWAY *The Great Gatsby*
OSBALDISTONE Sir Hildebrand *Rob Roy*
PASSEPARTOUT *Around the World in Eighty Days*

PAUL ASHWORTH *Fever Pitch*
PENNYFEATHER Paul *Decline and Fall*
RIP VAN WINKLE *Rip Van Winkle*
ROBERT JORDAN *For Whom the Bell Tolls*
SERGEANT CUFF *The Moonstone*
SERGEANT TROY *Far from the Madding Crowd*
SIMON TEMPLAR *Meet the Tiger* etc
SOPHIA BAINES *The Old Wives' Tale*
SQUIRE GORDON *Black Beauty*
SUE BRIDEHEAD *Jude the Obscure*
THOMAS FOWLER *The Quiet American*
WILLIAM BOOTH *Amelia*
WILLIAM BROWN Just William series
WINSTON SMITH *Nineteen Eighty-Four*

13
ADAM DALGLIESH *Cover Her Face* etc
ALBERT CAMPION *The Crime at Black Dudley* etc
ANNE CATHERICK *The Woman in White*
BASIL HALLWARD *The Picture of Dorian Gray*
BECKY THATCHER *The Adventures of Tom Sawyer*
BERTIE WOOSTER *My Man Jeeves* etc
BERT SMALLWAYS *War in the Air*
BISHOP PROUDIE Barsetshire series
CAPTAIN KETTLE *The Adventures of Captain Kettle* etc
CHARLES POOTER *The Diary of a Nobody*
CLYM YEOBRIGHT *The Return of the Native*
COLONEL ESMOND *The History of Henry Esmond Esquire*
DANDIE DINMONT *Guy Mannering*

DANIEL DERONDA *Daniel Deronda*
DARSIE LATIMER *Redgauntlet*
DOCTOR CAMERON *Beyond This Place*
DOCTOR LIVESEY *Treasure Island*
DOCTOR ZHIVAGO *Dr Zhivago*
DONALD FARFRAE *The Mayor of Casterbridge*
EMMA WOODHOUSE *Emma*
ERAST FANDORIN *The Winter Queen* etc
FRANKLIN BLAKE *The Moonstone*
FRITZ ROBINSON *The Swiss Family Robinson*
GEORGE WICKHAM *Pride and Prejudice*
GILBERT OSMOND *The Portrait of a Lady*
GUY CROUCHBACK *Men at Arms* etc
HENRY DASHWOOD *Sense and Sensibility*
HERCULE POIROT *The Mysterious Affair at Styles* etc
HILDA LESSWAYS *Clayhanger*
HORACE RUMPOLE Rumpole series
JACOB ARMITAGE *The Children of the New Forest*
JACOB FLANDERS *Jacob's Room*
JOLYON FORSYTE *The Forsyte Saga*
JOSEPH ANDREWS *The Adventures of Joseph Andrews*
JULIAN PEVERIL *Peveril of the Peak*
KENNETH TOOMEY *Earthly Powers*
LADY MARCHMAIN *Brideshead Revisited*
LORD GREYSTOKE Tarzan series
MYCROFT HOLMES Sherlock Holmes series

NATHAN DETROIT *Guys and Dolls*
OLIVER MELLORS *Lady Chatterley's Lover*
PAMELA ANDREWS *Pamela*
PHILIP MARLOWE *The Big Sleep* etc
PRINCE AMERIGO *The Golden Bowl*
REVEREND SLOPE Barsetshire series
RICHARD HANNAY *The Thirty-Nine Steps* etc
RODERICK USHER *The Fall of the House of Usher*
RONALD WEASLEY Harry Potter series
SADIE THOMPSON *Rain*
SCARLETT O'HARA *Gone with the Wind*
SOAMES FORSYTE *The Forsyte Saga*
SOPHIA WESTERN *Tom Jones*
SQUIRE WESTERN *Tom Jones*
THOMAS NEWCOME *The Newcomes*
TOBY ESTERHAZY *Smiley's People*
ZULEIKA DOBSON *Zuleika Dobson*

14
AMOS STARKADDER *Cold Comfort Farm*
ANGHARAD MORGAN *How Green Was My Valley*
ANNA TELLWRIGHT *Anna of the Five Towns*
ANTHONY KROESIG *The Pursuit of Love*
CHARLES BINGLEY *Pride and Prejudice*
CHARLES RAINIER *Random Harvest*
COLONEL BRANDON *Sense and Sensibility*
COLONEL LAMBERT *The Virginians*
DEBORAH JENKYNS *Cranford*
DOCTOR PANGLOSS *Candide*

DOROTHEA BROOKE *Middlemarch*
EDWARD CASAUBON *Middlemarch*
EDWARD WAVERLEY Waverley novels
ELIZABETH TRANT *The Good Companions*
FARMER BOLDWOOD *Far from the Madding Crowd*
FESTUS DERRIMAN *The Trumpet-Major*
FRANCIS HERRIES *Rogue Herries*
GEOFFREY FIRMIN *Under the Volcano*
GEORGE LEWISHAM *Love and Mr Lewisham*
GILBERT MARKHAM *The Tenant of Wildfell Hall*
HARRY CONINGSBY *Coningsby*
HERBERT BADGERY *Illywhacker*
HERR FRIEDEMANN *Little Herr Friedemann*
HUMBERT HUMBERT *Lolita*
HUMPHRY CLINKER *The Expedition of Humphry Clinker*
INIGO JOLLIFANT *The Good Companions*
ISABELLA THORPE *Northanger Abbey*
JOHN WILLOUGHBY *Sense and Sensibility*
JONATHAN HARKER *Dracula*
LADY CHATTERLEY *Lady Chatterley's Lover*
LEMUEL GULLIVER *Gulliver's Travels*
LONG JOHN SILVER *Treasure Island*
LORD FAUNTLEROY *Little Lord Fauntleroy*
MAGGIE TULLIVER *The Mill on the Floss*
MARIAN HOLCOMBE *The Woman in White*
MASTERMAN READY *Masterman Ready*

MISS MONEYPENNY James Bond series
QUENTIN DURWARD *Quentin Durward*
RACHEL VERINDER *The Moonstone*
REBECCA RANDALL *Rebecca of Sunnybrook Farm*
ROBINSON CRUSOE *Robinson Crusoe*
RODERICK RANDOM *The Adventures of Roderick Random*
ROSIE DRIFFIELD *Cakes and Ale*
SEBASTIAN FLYTE *Brideshead Revisited*
SETH STARKADDER *Cold Comfort Farm*
SHERLOCK HOLMES Sherlock Holmes series
SHIRLEY KEELDAR *Shirley*
SIR PITT CRAWLEY *Vanity Fair*
STEPHEN DEDALUS *Ulysses*
TRILBY O'FERRALL *Trilby*
TRISTRAM SHANDY *Tristram Shandy*
WORLDLY-WISEMAN Mr *Pilgrim's Progress*

15
ADMIRAL PALLISER Palliser series
ALEC D'URBERVILLE *Tess of the D'Urbervilles*
ALLAN QUATERMAIN *King Solomon's Mines*
ARTHUR PENDENNIS *Pendennis*
AURIC GOLDFINGER *Goldfinger*
BULLDOG DRUMMOND *Bulldog Drummond* etc
CARACTACUS POTTS *Chitty Chitty Bang Bang*
CATHERINE BENNET *Pride and Prejudice*
CHARLES MUSGROVE *Persuasion*

CHARLES PRIMROSE *The Vicar of Wakefield*
CLARISSA HARLOWE *Clarissa*
COLONEL BEVERLEY *The Children of the New Forest*
CONSTANCE BAINES *The Old Wives' Tale*
DOCTOR DRYASDUST *The Antiquary*
EDWARD PONDEREVO *Tono-Bungay*
EDWARD ROCHESTER *Jane Eyre*
EDWIN CLAYHANGER *Clayhanger*
ELIZABETH BENNET *Pride and Prejudice*
ELIZABETH ELLIOT *Persuasion*
GEORGE KNIGHTLEY *Emma*
HELEN HUNTINGDON *The Tenant of Wildfell Hall*
HERMIONE GRANGER Harry Potter series
HOLDEN CAULFIELD *The Catcher in the Rye*
HORACE ABBEVILLE *Cannery Row*
HUCKLEBERRY FINN *The Adventures of Huckleberry Finn*
INSPECTOR ALLEYN *A Man Lay Dead* etc
LORD PETER WIMSEY *Whose Body?* etc
MICHAEL HENCHARD *The Mayor of Casterbridge*
PEREGRINE PICKLE *The Adventures of Peregrine Pickle*
PRINCE BOLKONSKI *War and Peace*
REVEREND COLLINS *Pride and Prejudice*
RUPERT OF HENTZAU Ruritania series
SEPTIMUS HARDING Barsetshire series
SIR WALTER ELLIOT *Persuasion*

SQUIRE ALLWORTHY *Tom Jones*
SQUIRE INGLEWOOD *Rob Roy*
SQUIRE TRELAWNEY *Treasure Island*
TESS DURBEYFIELD *Tess of the D'Urbervilles*
WALTER HARTRIGHT *The Woman in White*

16
CAPTAIN WENTWORTH *Persuasion*
CATHERINE MORLAND *Northanger Abbey*
CATRIONA DRUMMOND *Catriona*
ERICH VON STALHEIN Biggles series
JASPER PETULENGRO *Lavengro*
MR WORLDLY-WISEMAN *The Pilgrim's Progress*
MYRA BRECKINRIDGE *Myra Breckinridge*
PAUL PENNYFEATHER *Decline and Fall*
RUDOLF RASSENDYLL *The Prisoner of Zenda*
SIR PERCY BLAKENEY *The Scarlet Pimpernel*

17
ARCHDEACON GRANTLY Barsetshire series

BATHSHEBA EVERDENE *Far from the Madding Crowd*
CATHERINE EARNSHAW *Wuthering Heights*
CHARLES STRICKLAND *The Moon and Sixpence*
CHRISTOPHER NEWMAN *The American*
CLIFFORD WENTWORTH *The Europeans*
HORATIO HORNBLOWER Hornblower series
HUMPHREY EARWICKER *Finnegans Wake*
INSPECTOR LESTRADE Sherlock Holmes series
KENNETH WIDMERPOOL *A Dance to the Music of Time*
WILLIAM CRIMSWORTH *The Professor*

18
DOCTOR FRANKENSTEIN *Frankenstein*

19
PROFESSOR CHALLENGER *The Lost World*

Arts – Literature – NOVEL TITLES

3
ADA Nabokov
BOY Hanley

CAL MacLaverty
CAT North
FEN North

FOE Coetzee
ICE J Follett
KES Hines

KIM Kipling
OIL! Sinclair
PIP North
SHE Haggard
UTZ Chatwin
WEB Wyndham

4

CELL King
CLEA L Durrell
COMA Cook
CUJO King
CUTS M Bradbury
DAWN Haggard
DRED Stowe
DR NO Fleming
DUNE F Herbert
EMMA Austen
GIGI Colette
GLUE Welsh
ICON Forsyth
JAWS Benchley
LAIR J Herbert
LAMB MacLaverty
MARY Nabokov,
  Wollstonecraft
MOON J Herbert
NANA Zola
N OR M? Christie
OMOO Melville
PNIN Nabokov
POLO J Cooper
PREY Crichton
PULP Bukowski
RAIN Maugham
RISK Francis
RUTH Gaskell
SIDO Colette

SOLO Higgins
SONS Buck
SS-GB Deighton
SWAG Leonard
TARR W Lewis
THEM Oates
TUNC L Durrell
VOSS P White
WATT Beckett
WHIT I Banks
WILT Sharpe

5

A LIFE (or *Une Vie*)
  Maupassant
ASSEZ Beckett
BAMBI Salten
BANCO Charrière
BELLA J Cooper,
  Giraudoux
BLISS Carey, Mansfield
CANDY Southern
CHÉRI Colette
CHLOE North
CHOKE Palahniuk
CLASS J Cooper
CONGO Crichton
CRASH Ballard
DIARY Palahniuk
ÉMILE Rousseau
EMILY J Cooper
FILTH Welsh
FOCUS A Miller
HEIDI Spyri
HOTEL Hailey
JUNKY Burroughs
KALKI Vidal
KIPPS Wells

LIBRA Delillo
MARDI Melville
MINGO JC Harris
MONEY M Amis
MOODS Alcott
MOTHS Ouida
MR PIM Milne
MR PYE Peake
MYRON Vidal
NEXUS H Miller
PORNO Welsh
PROOF Francis
PYLON Faulkner
ROOTS Haley
RUDIN Turgenev
SALLY North
SAPHO Daudet
SCOOP E Waugh
SEXUS H Miller
SHAME Rushdie
SMOKE Turgenev
SNOBS Fellowes
SPACE Michener
SPIES Frayn
STARK Elton
STEPS Kosinski
STICK Leonard
SYBIL Disraeli
TEXAS Michener
TO LET Galsworthy
TOPAZ Uris
TYPEE Melville
WANDA Ouida
YEAST Kingsley
ZADIG Voltaire

6

AMELIA Fielding
BEL-AMI Maupassant
BEN-HUR L Wallace
CARRIE King
CHOCKY Wyndham
DEMIAN Hesse
DORIAN Self
ECHOES Binchy,
  Mackenzie
EMPIRE Vidal
ENIGMA R Harris
ESTHER H Adams
EXODUS Uris
FERGUS B Moore
GROWTH Tarkington
HELENA E Waugh
HERZOG Bellow
HOMBRE Leonard
HUNGER Hamsun
I ROBOT Asimov
ISLAND A Huxley
JEREMY HS Walpole
JULIAN Vidal
JURGEN Cabell
LOLITA Nabokov
MEDUSA H Innes
MISERY King
MOLLOY Beckett
MOTHER Gorky
MURPHY Beckett
NAUSEA (or *La Nausée*)
  Sartre
NO NAME W Collins
OTHMAR Ouida
PAMELA Richardson
PELHAM Bulwer-Lytton
PENROD Tarkington

PHROSO Hope
PIERRE Melville
PLEXUS H Miller
PRAXIS Weldon
RIDERS J Cooper
RIENZI Bulwer-Lytton
RIVALS J Cooper
ROB ROY W Scott
ROMOLA G Eliot
ROXANA Defoe
SHOGUN Clavell
SHOSHA Singer
SLIVER Levin
SYLVIA Sinclair
TAI PAN Clavell
THE BFG Dahl
THE FOG J Herbert
THE FOX DH Lawrence
THE SEA Banville
TRILBY G Du Maurier
UNE VIE (or *A Life*)
  Maupassant
UNGAVA Ballantyne
UNLESS Shields
UTOPIA More
WALDEN Thoreau
WICKED! J Cooper

7

ADOLPHE Constant
AIRPORT Hailey
AMERIKA Kafka
ARCADIA Sidney
ARMANCE Stendhal
BABBITT S Lewis
BELOVED Morrison
BLOW FLY P Cornwell
BOUDICA M Scott

CALYPSO McBain
CAMILLA Burney
CANDIDE Voltaire
CAPRICE Firbank
CAT'S EYE Atwood
CECILIA Burney
COUPLES Updike
CRY WOLF W Smith
CURTAIN Christie
DEAD AIR I Banks
DESPAIR Nabokov
DOLORES Compton-
  Burnett, Susann
DRACULA Stoker
EMPEROR Iggulden
EREWHON Butler
EUPHUES Lyly
EVELINA Burney
FARAWAY Priestley
HARRIET J Cooper
HOW IT IS Beckett
HYPATIA Kingsley
IVANHOE W Scott
JOCELYN Galsworthy
JO'S BOYS Alcott
JUSTINE L Durrell, Sade
KING RAT Clavell
LA CHUTE (or *The Fall*)
  Camus
LA PESTE (or *The
  Plague*) Camus
LEONORA Bennett
LORD JIM Conrad
LOTHAIR Disraeli
MAURICE Forster
MINE BOY Abrahams
NEMESIS Christie
NUMQUAM L Durrell

OBLOMOV Goncharov
OCTAVIA J Cooper
ORLANDO Woolf
OUR GAME Le Carré
PAL JOEY O'Hara
PERFUME Süskind
POMPEII R Harris
POOR COW Dunn
POPCORN Elton
PUCKOON Milligan
QUARTET Rhys
RAGTIME Doctorow
REBECCA D Du Maurier
REDBURN Melville
SAVILLE Storey
SECRETS Steel
SHARDIK R Adams
SHIRLEY C Brontë
SKYLARK EE Smith
SOLARIS Lem
SUCCESS M Amis
TANCRED Disraeli
TAR BABY Morrison
THEATRE Maugham
THE BELL Murdoch
THE DEEP Benchley,
  Spillane
THE FALL (or La Chute)
  Camus
THE JOKE Kundera
THE JUMP Cole
THE LIAR Fry
THE STUD J Collins
THE TENT Atwood
TRINITY Uris
TRISTAN Mann
TYPHOON Conrad
UKRIDGE Wodehouse

ULYSSES Joyce
VENETIA Disraeli

8

ADAM BEDE G Eliot
ANTIC HAY A Huxley
ATHERTON MR Mitford
BIRDSONG Faulks
CARNIVAL Mackenzie
CATRIONA Stevenson
CHOCOLAT J Harris
CLARISSA Richardson
CONSUELO Sand
CRANFORD Gaskell
DÉJÀ DEAD Reichs
DISGRACE Coetzee
DOCTOR NO Fleming
DROP CITY Boyle
ENDYMION Disraeli
FACTOTUM Bukowski
FANSHAWE Hawthorne
FICTIONS Borges
FLASHMAN Fraser
FOOLS DIE Puzo
FREE FALL Golding
FRESCOES Ouida
GERMINAL Zola
GLORIANA Moorcock
GOLD MINE W Smith
GRIDLOCK Elton
HANNIBAL T Harris
I THE JURY Spillane
JAILBIRD Vonnegut
JANE EYRE C Brontë
KANGAROO
  DH Lawrence
KING COAL Sinclair
LADY ANNA A Trollope

LA NAUSÉE
  (or Nausea) Sartre
LAVENGRO Borrow
LIFE OF PI Martel
LUCKY JIM K Amis
MAKING DO Goodman
MOBY DICK Melville
NICE WORK Lodge
NOON WINE Porter
NOSTROMO Conrad
ON BEAUTY Z Smith
ON THE EVE Turgenev
OVERLOAD Hailey
PALE FIRE Nabokov
PAPILLON Charrière
POOR FOLK
  Dostoyevsky
PUFFBALL Weldon
RASSELAS S Johnson
ROOKWOOD
  Ainsworth
SALAMMBÔ Flaubert
SANDITON Austen
SATURDAY McEwan
SCRUPLES Krantz
SEPTIMUS Hawthorne
SEVEN MEN Beerbohm
SIR NIGEL Doyle
SPEAK NOW Yerby
SPY STORY Deighton
SWAN SONG
  Galsworthy
THE ABBOT W Scott
THE BEACH Garland
THE BETSY Robbins
THE BIRDS
  D Du Maurier
THE BITCH J Collins

THE FIXER Malamud
THE IDIOT Dostoyevsky
THE JUDGE R West
THE MAGUS Fowles
THE TRIAL Kafka
THE WAVES Woolf
TIMELINE Crichton
TOM JONES Henry
  Fielding
TRIAL RUN Francis
VALPERGA M Shelley
VILLETTE C Brontë
VITTORIA Meredith
WAVERLEY W Scott
WILLIWAW Vidal

9

AARON'S ROD
  DH Lawrence
ABOUT A BOY Hornby
AFTER DARK W Collins
AGNES GREY A Brontë
A LOT TO ASK
  PH Newby
AMSTERDAM McEwan
ARCHANGEL R Harris,
  G Seymour
ATONEMENT McEwan
BALTHAZAR L Durrell
BEAU GESTE Wren
BILLY BUDD Melville
BILLY LIAR Waterhouse
BLACK ROBE B Moore
BLACK SNOW Bulgakov
BLIND LOVE Pritchett
BLOODLINE Sheldon
BONE CRACK Francis
BRICK LANE Ali

CHILDHOOD Gorky
CHRISTINE King
CIRCUS BOY Manning-
  Sanders
CONINGSBY Disraeli
DEAD SOULS Gogol,
  Rankin
DEMOCRACY H Adams
DODSWORTH S Lewis
DREAM DAYS Grahame
DUBLINERS Joyce
EAST LYNNE Wood
FANNY HILL Cleland
FELIX HOLT G Eliot
FIRST LOVE Turgenev
FORTITUDE HS Walpole
GET SHORTY Leonard
GOOD WIVES Alcott
GORKY PARK MC Smith
GREAT APES Self
GUY RIVERS Simms
HARD TIMES Dickens
HARLEQUIN M West
HAWKSMOOR Ackroyd
I CLAUDIUS Graves
KIDNAPPED Stevenson
KINFLICKS Alther
L'ÉTRANGER (or *The
  Outsider*) Camus
LITTLE MEN Alcott
LOVE STORY Segal
MEN AT ARMS
  E Waugh
MOONRAKER Fleming
MOON TIGER Lively
NIGHTFALL Asimov
OCTOPUSSY Fleming
ON THE ROAD Kerouac

ORLEY FARM
  A Trollope
OUR STREET Thackeray
OWLS DO CRY Frame
PASSENGER Keneally
PENDENNIS Thackeray
PENMARRIC Howatch
POLAR STAR MC Smith
POTTERISM
  R Macaulay
RABBIT RUN Updike
RADCLIFFE Storey
RED DRAGON T Harris
ROGUE MALE
  Household
ROMANY RYE Borrow
SAINT JACK Theroux
'SALEM'S LOT King
SANCTUARY Faulkner,
  Wharton
SEVENTEEN Tarkington
SNOW CRASH
  Stephenson
SOME DO NOT Ford
SOUR SWEET Mo
STAYING ON P Scott
THE CASTLE Kafka
THE CHIMES Dickens
THE CLOCKS Christie
THE DEVILS
  Dostoyevsky
THE EGOIST Meredith
THE HEROES Kingsley
THE HOBBIT Tolkien
THE MEMBER Galt
THE PLAGUE (or *La
  Peste*) Camus
THE SÉANCE Singer

THE VICTIM Bellow
THE WARDEN
  A Trollope
VENUSBERG Powell
VICE VERSA Anstey
VOL DE NUIT (or
  Night Flight) Saint-
  Exupéry
WATERLAND G Swift
WHITE FANG London
WHOSE BODY? Sayers
WILD WALES Borrow
WISE BLOOD
  O'Connor
WORLD'S END Sinclair

10
A LAODICEAN Hardy
ALIAS GRACE Atwood
ALICE ADAMS
  Tarkington
ALTON LOCKE Kingsley
ANIMAL FARM Orwell
ANNABEL LEE Poe
BEAR ISLAND Maclean
BEING THERE Kosinski
BLEAK HOUSE Dickens
BULLET PARK Cheever
CANCER WARD
  Solzhenitsyn
CANNERY ROW
  Steinbeck
CASHELMARA Howatch
CAT'S CRADLE
  Vonnegut
CENTENNIAL Michener
CHATTERTON Ackroyd
CLAYHANGER Bennett

CLOUD ATLAS
  D Mitchell
COMPLICITY I Banks
DEAD BABIES M Amis
DON QUIXOTE
  Cervantes
EAST OF EDEN Steinbeck
EAST OF SUEZ
  Maugham
EFFI BRIEST Fontane
ETHAN FROME
  Wharton
EUGENE ARAM Bulwer-
  Lytton
FATHERLAND R Harris
FELIX KRULL Mann
FER-DE-LANCE Stout
FEVER PITCH Hornby
FROST IN MAY A White
GAUDY NIGHT Sayers
GOLDFINGER Fleming
GOOD AS GOLD Heller
HARRY'S GAME
  Seymour
HOTEL DU LAC
  Brookner
HOWARDS END
  Forster
IN CHANCERY
  Galsworthy
JACOB'S ROOM Woolf
JAKE'S THING K Amis
JAMAICA INN
  D Du Maurier
JOSH LAWTON Bragg
KENILWORTH W Scott
LABYRINTHS Borges
LAST ORDERS G Swift

LORNA DOONE
  Blackmore
MALONE DIES Beckett
MARTIN EDEN London
MARY BARTON Gaskell
MAXIMUM BOB
  Leonard
MELINCOURT Peacock
MOUNTOLIVE L Durrell
NOBLE HOUSE Clavell
ON THE BEACH Shute
PERELANDRA CS Lewis
PERSUASION Austen
POSSESSION Byatt
RED HARVEST
  Hammett
ROUGHING IT Twain
RURAL RIDES Cobbett
SA.LMAGUNDI
  W Irving
SAVAGE GOLD Fuller
SMALL WORLD Lodge
SUNSET PASS Grey
TAKE IT EASY Runyon
THE BELL JAR Plath
THE CITADEL Cronin
THE DEFENCE Nabokov
THE GOLD BUG Poe
THE LEOPARD (or
  Il Gattopardo)
  Lampedusa
THE MARTIAN
  G Du Maurier
THE MONSTER Crane
THE PRAIRIE JF Cooper
THE PROVOST Galt
THE RAINBOW
  DH Lawrence

THE RED PONY Steinbeck
THE SHINING King
THE THIN MAN Hammett
THE TIN DRUM Grass
THE WATSONS Austen
THE WRECKER Stevenson
THREE LIVES Stein
THREE WEEKS Glyn
TIME'S ARROW M Amis
TITUS ALONE Peake
TITUS GROAN Peake
TONO-BUNGAY Wells
UNCLE REMUS JC Harris
UNDERWORLD DeLillo
VANITY FAIR Thackeray
VESTAL FIRE Mackenzie
VILE BODIES E Waugh
VIRGIN SOIL Turgenev
VIVIAN GREY Disraeli
WESTWARD HO! Kingsley
WHITE NOISE Delillo
WHITE TEETH Z Smith
WOLF SOLENT JC Powys

11
A MAN LAY DEAD Marsh
ANN VERONICA Wells
A PAGAN PLACE E O'Brien
A PERFECT SPY Le Carré
AS I LAY DYING Faulkner
A TALE OF A TUB J Swift
BALLET SHOES Streatfield
BARRY LYNDON Thackeray
BLACK BEAUTY Sewell
BLACK BRYONY TF Powys
BLACK SPRING H Miller
BOGLE CORBET Galt
BOULE DE SUIF Maupassant

BURIED ALIVE Bennett
BURMESE DAYS Orwell
CAKES AND ALE Maugham
CLOCHEMERLE G Chevalier
COLONEL JACK Defoe
CORAL ISLAND Ballantyne
COURRIER-SUD (or *Southern Mail*)
   Saint-Exupéry
CROME YELLOW A Huxley
DAISY MILLER H James
DANGLING MAN Bellow
DEATH DU JOUR
   Reichs
ELMER GANTRY S Lewis
ELUSIVE EARL Cartland
FINGERSMITH Waters
FIRESTARTER King
GORMENGHAST Peake
GREENMANTLE Buchan
GRIFFIN'S WAY Yerby
HARRIET SAID Bainbridge
HENRY ESMOND Thackeray
HOW TO BE GOOD Hornby
ILLYWHACKER Carey
IN A PROVINCE Van Der Post
IN COLD BLOOD Capote
JUST WILLIAM Crompton
KANE AND ABEL Archer
LITTLE WOMEN Alcott
LOST HORIZON Hilton
MARATHON MAN Goldman
MARTHA QUEST Lessing
MARTIN FABER Simms
MARY POPPINS Travers
MEMENTO MORI Spark
MEN AND WIVES Compton-Burnett
MICAH CLARKE Doyle
MIDDLEMARCH G Eliot

MRS DALLOWAY Woolf
MY IDEA OF FUN Self
NEUROMANCER Gibson
NIGHT FLIGHT (or *Vol de Nuit*)
  Saint-Exupéry
NO COMEBACKS Forsyth
OLIVER TWIST Dickens
OTHER PEOPLE M Amis
OUT OF AFRICA Blixen
PETER SIMPLE Marryat
PEYTON PLACE Metalious
PHINEAS FINN A Trollope
PRESTER JOHN Buchan
RABBIT REDUX Updike
REDGAUNTLET W Scott
RESTORATION Tremain
RIPLEY'S GAME Highsmith
RODNEY STONE Doyle
SCARAMOUCHE Sabatini
SEIZE THE DAY Bellow
SHIP OF FOOLS Porter
SHORT FRIDAY Singer
SILAS MARNER G Eliot
SILVER BLAZE Doyle
SNOW COUNTRY Kawabata
STEPPENWOLF Hesse
SWITCH BITCH Dahl
TATTERED TOM Alger
THE AMERICAN H James
THE BERTRAMS A Trollope
THE BIG SLEEP Chandler
THE CROW ROAD I Banks
THE CRUEL SEA Monsarrat
THE DEAD ZONE King
THE DEER PARK Mailer
THE EXORCIST Blatty
THE HIRED MAN Bragg
THE HIRELING Hartley

THE HUMAN AGE W Lewis
THE IRON HEEL London
THE LEVANTER Ambler
THE LOVED ONE E Waugh
THE MEMORIAL Isherwood
THE MIMIC MEN Naipaul
THE NEWCOMES Thackeray
THE ODD WOMEN Gissing
THE OPEN BOAT Crane
THE OUTSIDER (or *L'Étranger*)
  Camus; C Wilson, R Wright
THE SATANIST Wheatley
THE TALISMAN W Scott
THE THIRD MAN Greene
THE TOLL GATE Heyer
THE WRONG BOX Stevenson
THE YEMASSEE Simms
THUNDERBALL Fleming
TOBACCO ROAD Caldwell
TWO ON A TOWER Hardy
ULTIMA THULE HH Richardson
UNDER THE NET Murdoch
WAR AND PEACE Tolstoy
WAR IN THE AIR Wells
WHAT KATY DID Coolidge
WHITE NIGHTS Dostoyevsky
WOMEN IN LOVE DH Lawrence

12

A BAR OF SHADOW Van Der Post
AFTERNOON MEN Powell
ANNA KARENINA Tolstoy
A SEVERED HEAD Murdoch
A SUITABLE BOY Seth
A TIME TO DANCE Bragg
BARNABY RUDGE Dickens
BEND SINISTER Nabokov
BRIGHTON ROCK Greene

BUDDENBROOKS Mann
CAPTAIN BLOOD Sabatini
CASINO ROYALE Fleming
DANIEL MARTIN Fowles
DANSE MACABRE King
DEAD MAN'S ROCK Quiller-Couch
DELTA WEDDING Welty
DOCTOR THORNE A Trollope
DOMBEY AND SON Dickens
DOUBLE DOUBLE Queen
ELEPHANT SONG W Smith
ENDURING LOVE McEwan
ESTHER WATERS G Moore
EUGENE ONEGIN Pushkin
FEAR IS THE KEY Maclean
FEAR OF FLYING Jong
FISH DEFERRED Wodehouse
FOMA GORDEYEV Gorky
FRANKENSTEIN M Shelley
GUY MANNERING W Scott
GUYS AND DOLLS Runyon
HAPPENSTANCE Shields
HEADLONG HALL Peacock
HIGH FIDELITY Hornby
HOLD THE DREAM Bradford
HOLY DEADLOCK AP Herbert
HUMAN CROQUET Atkinson
HUNTINGTOWER Buchan
IL GATTOPARDO (or *The Leopard*)
   Lampedusa
IN A FREE STATE Naipaul
ISRAEL POTTER Melville
JURASSIC PARK Crichton
KISS ME DEADLY Spillane
LE GRAND ÉCART Cocteau
LE PETIT CHOSE Daudet
LESS THAN ZERO Ellis
LIFE AT THE TOP Braine

L'IMMORALISTE (or *The Immoralist*)
   Gide
LITTLE DORRIT Dickens
LONDON FIELDS M Amis
LONESOME DOVE McMurtry
LOVE FOR LYDIA Bates
LUCIANO'S LUCK Higgins
MADAME BOVARY Flaubert
MAIDEN CASTLE JC Powys
MANON LESCAUT Prévost
MIGUEL STREET Naipaul
MOLL FLANDERS Defoe
MURDER IS EASY Christie
MY LIFE AS A MAN Roth
NEVER LET ME GO Ishiguro
NOT TO DISTURB Spark
OF MICE AND MEN Steinbeck
OLD MORTALITY W Scott
ORPHAN ISLAND R Macaulay
PHINEAS REDUX A Trollope
PRATER VIOLET Isherwood
PRECIOUS BANE Webb
REGENERATION Barker
RESURRECTION Tolstoy
ROGUE HERRIES HS Walpole
ROOM AT THE TOP Braine
SACRED HUNGER Unsworth
SISTER CARRIE Dreiser
SOUTHERN MAIL (or *Courrier-Sud*)
   Saint-Exupéry
STARS AND BARS Boyd
STRONG POISON Sayers
SWEET WILLIAM Bainbridge
THE ANTIQUARY W Scott
THE BETROTHED (or *I Promessi Sposi*)
   Manzoni
THE BORROWERS Norton
THE CHOIR BOYS Wambaugh

THE COLLECTOR Fowles
THE COMEDIANS Greene
THE DECAMERON Boccaccio
THE DOGS OF WAR Forsyth
THE EUROPEANS H James
THE FLYING INN Chesterton
THE GHOST ROAD Barker
THE GINGER MAN Donleavy
THE GO-BETWEEN Hartley
THE GODFATHER Puzo
THE GOLDEN AGE Grahame
THE GOOD EARTH Buck
THE GRASS HARP Capote
THE LOST WORLD Doyle
THE LOVING CUP Graham
THE MAN WITHIN Greene
THE MARY DEARE H Innes
THE MONASTERY W Scott
THE MOONSTONE W Collins
THE OLD DEVILS K Amis
THE PROFESSOR C Brontë
THE SCAPEGOAT D Du Maurier
THE SEA, THE SEA Murdoch
THE SNOW GOOSE Gallico
THE TWO TOWERS Tolkien
THE VOYAGE OUT Woolf
THE WATERFALL Drabble
THE WHITE DEER Thurber
TOO MANY COOKS Stout
TORTILLA FLAT Steinbeck
TRAGIC GROUND Caldwell
WATCH AND WARD H James
WESTERN UNION Grey
WHAT A CARVE UP! Coe
WHISKY GALORE Mackenzie
WILD CONQUEST Abrahams

13

A BOY'S OWN STORY E White
A BURNT-OUT CASE Greene
A HOUSE DIVIDED Buck
A KIND OF LOVING Barstow
ALMAYER'S FOLLY Conrad
A MODERN COMEDY Galsworthy
A MODERN UTOPIA Wells
ANGEL PAVEMENT Priestley
AN ICE CREAM WAR Boyd
A SPARROW FALLS W Smith
ATLAS SHRUGGED Rand
BILLY BATHGATE Doctorow
BRAVE NEW WORLD A Huxley
CALL OF THE WILD London
CARRY ON JEEVES! Wodehouse
CHARLOTTE GRAY Faulks
CHARLOTTE'S WEB EB White
CHILDHOOD'S END Clarke
COUSIN PHILLIS Gaskell
DANDELION DAYS Williamson
DANGEROUS LADY Cole
DANIEL DERONDA G Eliot
DEATH IN VENICE Mann
DER ZAUBERBERG (or *The Magic Mountain*) Mann
DOCTOR AT LARGE Gordon
DOCTOR ZHIVAGO Pasternak
DOKTOR FAUSTUS Mann
DREAMS DIE FAST Robbins
EARTHLY POWERS Burgess
ENGLAND MADE ME Greene
EYELESS IN GAZA A Huxley
FAME IS THE SPUR Spring
FEMALE FRIENDS Weldon
FINNEGANS WAKE Joyce
GIMPEL THE FOOL Singer
HATTER'S CASTLE Cronin

HELD IN BONDAGE Ouida
HILDA LESSWAYS Bennett
HUMBOLDT'S GIFT Bellow
INCONCEIVABLE Elton
JACOB FAITHFUL Marryat
JOSEPH ANDREWS Henry Fielding
JUST SO STORIES Kipling
LADDERS TO FIRE Nin
LE PETIT PRINCE (or *The Little Prince*)
   Saint-Exupéry
LES MISÉRABLES Hugo
LIGHT IN AUGUST Faulkner
LIVE AND LET DIE Fleming
LIZA OF LAMBETH Maugham
LOSER TAKES ALL Greene
LOTTE IN WEIMAR Mann
LOVE ON THE DOLE Greenwood
MANSFIELD PARK Austen
METAMORPHOSIS Kafka
NEW GRUB STREET Gissing
NORTH AND SOUTH Gaskell
PETER IBBETSON G Du Maurier
PICTURE PALACE Theroux
PINCHER MARTIN Golding
POSTERN OF FATE Christie
PRINCE CASPIAN CS Lewis
PRIVATE ANGELO Linklater
RANDOM HARVEST Hilton
RIDDLEY WALKER Hoban
RIGHT HO JEEVES! Wodehouse
SANDRA BELLONI Meredith
SCHINDLER'S ARK Keneally
SELF-CONDEMNED W Lewis
SKETCHES BY BOZ Dickens
SMILEY'S PEOPLE Le Carré
SOLDIERS THREE Kipling
SONS AND LOVERS DH Lawrence
SOPHIE'S CHOICE Styron

STAMBOUL TRAIN Greene
SWORD OF HONOUR E Waugh
SYLVIA'S LOVERS Gaskell
TARKA THE OTTER Williamson
THE ABC MURDERS Christie
THE AWKWARD AGE H James
THE BLACK ARROW Stevenson
THE BLACK TOWER PD James
THE BLUE LAGOON Stacpoole
THE BONE PEOPLE Hulme
THE BOSTONIANS H James
THE CHRYSALIDS Wyndham
THE CLAVERINGS A Trollope
THE COMFORTERS Spark
THE DAISY CHAIN Yonge
THE DEAD SECRET W Collins
THE DEERSLAYER JF Cooper
THE EBONY TOWER Fowles
THE EDWARDIANS Sackville-West
THE FISHER KING Powell
THE GOLDEN BOWL H James
THE GOLDEN KEEL Bagley
THE HIGH WINDOW Chandler
THE HISTORY MAN M Bradbury
THE HUMAN STAIN Roth
THE IMMORALIST (or *L'Immoraliste*)
   Gide
THE INHERITORS Golding
THE JEALOUS GOD Braine
THE LAST BATTLE CS Lewis
THE LAST TYCOON FS Fitzgerald
THE LOST PRINCE FH Burnett
THE MAID OF SKER Blackmore
THE MARBLE FAUN Hawthorne
THE METROPOLIS Sinclair
THE NAKED LUNCH Burroughs
THE NEGOTIATOR Forsyth
THE ODESSA FILE Forsyth

THE ONION FIELD Wambaugh
THE PATHFINDER JF Cooper
THE PERSIAN BOY Renault
THE PLAGUE DOGS R Adams
THE RAJ QUARTET P Scott
THE RAZOR'S EDGE Maugham
THÉRÈSE RAQUIN Zola
THE SCULPTRESS Walters
THE SIGN OF FOUR Doyle
THE SKETCH BOOK W Irving
THE SPOILT CITY Manning
THE THORN BIRDS McCullough
THE TRAGIC MUSE H James
THE TRIPLE ECHO Bates
THE TWO SISTERS Bates
THE VIRGINIANS Thackeray
THE WHITE HOTEL DM Thomas
THE WINDS OF WAR Wouk
THE WIZARD OF OZ Baum
THE WOMEN'S ROOM French
THE YOUNG LIONS I Shaw
TIME FOR A TIGER Burgess
TOLD BY AN IDIOT R Macaulay
TRAINSPOTTING Welsh
UNDER TWO FLAGS Ouida
UP THE JUNCTION Dunn
WATERSHIP DOWN R Adams
WINNIE-THE-POOH Milne
ZORBA THE GREEK Kazantzakis
ZULEIKA DOBSON Beerbohm

14
ABSALOM, ABSALOM! Faulkner
A HANDFUL OF DUST E Waugh
A HERO OF OUR TIME Lermontov
A MAN OF PROPERTY Galsworthy
AMERICAN PSYCHO Ellis
ANOTHER COUNTRY Baldwin

A ROOM OF ONE'S OWN Woolf
A ROOM WITH A VIEW Forster
A SHIP OF THE LINE Forester
A TASTE FOR DEATH PD James
A TEMPORARY LIFE Storey
A TOWN LIKE ALICE Shute
AT SWIM-TWO-BIRDS F O'Brien
BEFORE SHE MET ME Barnes
BEGGARMAN THIEF I Shaw
BETWEEN THE ACTS Woolf
BIRDS OF AMERICA McCarthy
CASTLE RACKRENT Edgeworth
CASTLE RICHMOND A Trollope
CHANGING PLACES Lodge
CIDER WITH ROSIE L Lee
CLAUDIUS THE GOD Graves
COMING UP FOR AIR Orwell
CROTCHET CASTLE Peacock
DALKEY ARCHIVES F O'Brien
DARKNESS AT NOON Koestler
DEAD MAN LEADING Pritchett
DEATH ON THE NILE Christie
DECEPTION POINT D Brown
DECLINE AND FALL E Waugh
EMPIRE OF THE SUN Ballard
EVAN HARRINGTON Meredith
EXCELLENT WOMEN Pym
EYE OF THE NEEDLE K Follett
FATHERS AND SONS Turgenev
FRANNY AND ZOOEY Salinger
GOD'S LITTLE ACRE Caldwell
GOODBYE MR CHIPS Hilton
HANGOVER SQUARE Hamilton
HOLLYWOOD WIVES J Collins
HUMPHRY CLINKER Smollett
I PROMESSI SPOSI (or *The Betrothed*)
  Manzoni
ISLAND IN THE SUN AR Waugh

JUDE THE OBSCURE Hardy
LE MORTE D'ARTHUR Malory
LESS THAN ANGELS Pym
LORD HORNBLOWER Forester
LORD OF THE FLIES Golding
LORD OF THE RINGS Tolkien
MASTERMAN READY Marryat
MODERN CHIVALRY Brackenridge
MY COUSIN RACHEL D Du Maurier
MY FRIEND FLICKA O'Hara
NATIONAL VELVET Bagnold
NIGHTMARE ABBEY Peacock
OF HUMAN BONDAGE Maugham
ONE PAIR OF HANDS M Dickens
OUR MAN IN HAVANA Greene
PICKWICK PAPERS Dickens
QUENTIN DURWARD W Scott
RICH MAN, POOR MAN I Shaw
RITES OF PASSAGE Golding
ROBINSON CRUSOE Defoe
RODERICK HUDSON H James
RODERICK RANDOM Smollett
SALAR THE SALMON Williamson
SEA OF FERTILITY Mishima
TALES OF THE CITY Maupin
THE ADVENTURERS Robbins
THE AMBASSADORS H James
THE BLACK PRINCE Murdoch
THE CAINE MUTINY Wouk
THE COLOR PURPLE A Walker
THE CORRECTIONS Franzen
THE DA VINCI CODE D Brown
THE DOCTOR'S WIFE B Moore
THE EDIBLE WOMAN Atwood
THE FIRST CIRCLE Solzhenitsyn
THE FORSYTE SAGA Galsworthy
THE FOUR JUST MEN E Wallace
THE GARDEN PARTY Mansfield

THE GARRICK YEAR Drabble
THE GOOD SOLDIER Ford
THE GREAT GATSBY FS Fitzgerald
THE HUMAN FACTOR Greene
THE IPCRESS FILE Deighton
THE ITALIAN GIRL Murdoch
THE JOY LUCK CLUB Tan
THE JUNGLE BOOKS Kipling
THE KRAKEN WAKES Wyndham
THE LONG GOODBYE Chandler
THE LOOM OF YOUTH AR Waugh
THE L-SHAPED ROOM LR Banks
THE MALCONTENTS Snow
THE NINE TAILORS Sayers
THE PAINTED VEIL Maugham
THE RECTOR'S WIFE J Trollope
THE ROTTERS' CLUB Coe
THE RUSSIA HOUSE Le Carré
THE SEEDS OF TIME Wyndham
THE SILVER CHAIR CS Lewis
THE SILVER SPOON Galsworthy
THE TIME MACHINE Wells
THE WASP FACTORY I Banks
THE WATER BABIES Kingsley
THE WHITE MONKEY Galsworthy
THE WOODLANDERS Hardy
TREASURE ISLAND Stevenson
TRENT'S LAST CASE Bentley
TRISTRAM SHANDY Sterne
TROPIC OF CANCER H Miller
UNCLE TOM'S CABIN Stowe
WAVERLEY NOVELS W Scott
WHAT MAISIE KNEW H James

15
A BEND IN THE RIVER Naipaul
ACCORDION CRIMES Proulx
A CHRISTMAS CAROL Dickens

A DRY WHITE SEASON Brink
A FAREWELL TO ARMS Hemingway
ALLAN QUATERMAIN Haggard
A MATTER OF HONOUR Archer
AN AMERICAN DREAM Mailer
ANGELS AND DEMONS D Brown
A PAIR OF BLUE EYES Hardy
A PASSAGE TO INDIA Forster
A STUDY IN SCARLET Doyle
BEYOND THIS PLACE Cronin
BRACEBRIDGE HALL W Irving
BULLDOG DRUMMOND Sapper
CARDS ON THE TABLE Christie
CASTLE DANGEROUS W Scott
CATCHER IN THE RYE Salinger
CIRCLE OF FRIENDS Binchy
CLOUDS OF WITNESS Sayers
COLD COMFORT FARM Gibbons
DIGITAL FORTRESS D Brown
EUSTACE AND HILDA Hartley
EVIL UNDER THE SUN Christie
FANTASTIC VOYAGE Asimov
FLAUBERT'S PARROT Barnes
FOR YOUR EYES ONLY Fleming
FRENCHMAN'S CREEK D Du Maurier
FUNERAL IN BERLIN Deighton
GONE WITH THE WIND M Mitchell
GOODBYE TO BERLIN Isherwood
GRAVITY'S RAINBOW Pynchon
HEART OF DARKNESS Conrad
HEMLOCK AND AFTER A Wilson
HENRIETTA TEMPLE Disraeli
HEREWARD THE WAKE Kingsley
ICE STATION ZEBRA Maclean
INSIDE MR ENDERBY Burgess
LEAVE IT TO PSMITH Wodehouse
LE GRAND MEAULNES Alain-Fournier
LE ROUGE ET LE NOIR Stendhal

LES BELLES IMAGES Beauvoir
LOVE IN AMSTERDAM Freeling
MY SISTER'S KEEPER Picoult
NORTHANGER ABBEY Austen
ORMEROD'S LANDING L Thomas
OSCAR AND LUCINDA Carey
OUR MUTUAL FRIEND Dickens
PATH OF DALLIANCE A Waugh
PEREGRINE PICKLE Smollett
PORTERHOUSE BLUE Sharpe
PORTRAIT OF A LADY H James
PREMATURE BURIAL Poe
PUCK OF POOK'S HILL Kipling
PUDD'NHEAD WILSON Twain
PUT OUT MORE FLAGS E Waugh
QUEEN SHEBA'S RING Haggard
QUERELLE DE BREST Genet
RETURN OF THE KING Tolkien
RIOTOUS ASSEMBLY Sharpe
RUPERT OF HENTZAU Hope
STRANGE CONFLICT Wheatley
SUMMER LIGHTNING Wodehouse
TARZAN OF THE APES Burroughs
THE ASPERN PAPERS H James
THE AUTOGRAPH MAN Z Smith
THE BEAST MUST DIE N Blake
THE CAMOMILE LAWN Wesley
THE CAVES OF STEEL Asimov
THE CEMENT GARDEN McEwan
THE COUNTRY GIRLS E O'Brien
THE DISPOSSESSED Le Guin
THE FAMISHED ROAD Okri
THE FAR PAVILIONS Kaye
THE GLASS-BLOWERS D Du Maurier
THE GREAT FORTUNE Manning
THE HIPPOPOTAMUS Fry
THE HOUSE OF MIRTH Wharton
THE INVISIBLE MAN Wells

THE KING'S GENERAL D Du Maurier
THE LINE OF BEAUTY Hollinghurst
THE LITTLE PRINCE (or *Le Petit Prince*)
  Saint-Exupéry
THE MALLEN STREAK Cookson
THE MUDFOG PAPERS Dickens
THE NURSERY ALICE Carroll
THE OLD WIVES' TALE Bennett
THEOPHILUS NORTH Wilder
THE RACHEL PAPERS M Amis
THE SECRET GARDEN FH Burnett
THE SHIPPING NEWS Proulx
THE SILMARILLION Tolkien
THE SPECKLED BAND Doyle
THE STONE DIARIES Shields
THE SUN ALSO RISES Hemingway
THE THINKING REED R West
THE TRUMPET-MAJOR Hardy
THE VALLEY OF FEAR Doyle
THE WAY WE LIVE NOW A Trollope
THE WHITE COMPANY Doyle
THE WHITE PEACOCK DH Lawrence
THE WOMAN IN WHITE W Collins
THE WOULDBEGOODS Nesbit
THREE MEN IN A BOAT Jerome
TO THE LIGHTHOUSE Woolf
TROPIC OF RUISLIP L Thomas
UNDER THE VOLCANO Lowry
UNNATURAL CAUSES PD James
VERNON GOD LITTLE Pierre
WEIR OF HERMISTON Stevenson
WHERE EAGLES DARE Maclean
WIDE SARGASSO SEA Rhys

16

A CLOCKWORK ORANGE Burgess
A GOOD MAN IN AFRICA Boyd
A KISS BEFORE DYING Levin

A PALE VIEW OF HILLS Ishiguro
A TALE OF TWO CITIES Dickens
BARCHESTER TOWERS A Trollope
BONJOUR TRISTESSE Sagan
DAVID COPPERFIELD Dickens
DESOLATION ANGELS Kerouac
DOCTOR IN THE HOUSE Gordon
FAMILY AND FRIENDS Brookner
FAREWELL MY LOVELY Chandler
FIRST AMONG EQUALS Archer
GOODBYE TO ALL THAT Graves
GULLIVER'S TRAVELS J Swift
HE KNEW HE WAS RIGHT A Trollope
HIS DARK MATERIALS Pullman
IN A GERMAN PENSION Mansfield
INDECENT EXPOSURE Sharpe
LA COMÉDIE HUMAINE Balzac
LITTLE GREY RABBIT Uttley
MARTIN CHUZZLEWIT Dickens
MEMOIRS OF A GEISHA Golden
MONSIGNOR QUIXOTE Greene
MR MIDSHIPMAN EASY Marryat
MYRA BRECKINRIDGE Vidal
NICHOLAS NICKLEBY Dickens
NORTHWEST PASSAGE Roberts
NOTRE-DAME DE PARIS Hugo
ONE FAT ENGLISHMAN K Amis
PEVERIL OF THE PEAK W Scott
PRESUMED INNOCENT Turow
SPARKLING CYANIDE Christie
TAKE A GIRL LIKE YOU K Amis
TENDER IS THE NIGHT FS Fitzgerald
THE ABBESS OF CREWE Spark
THE BALKAN TRILOGY Manning
THE BLIND ASSASSIN Atwood
THE CARPETBAGGERS Robbins
THE CONSTANT NYMPH Kennedy
THE DEVIL RIDES OUT Wheatley

THE GLASS BEAD GAME (or *Das Glasperlenspiel*) Hesse
THE GOOD TERRORIST Lessing
THE GRAPES OF WRATH Steinbeck
THE HANDMAID'S TALE Atwood
THE HISTORY OF LOVE Krauss
THE LADY IN THE LAKE Chandler
THE MAGIC MOUNTAIN (or *Der Zauberberg*) Mann
THE MALTESE FALCON Hammett
THE MOSQUITO COAST Theroux
THE NAME OF THE ROSE Eco
THE PLUMED SERPENT DH Lawrence
THE PURSUIT OF LOVE N Mitford
THE QUEEN OF SPADES Pushkin
THE QUIET AMERICAN Greene
THE SATANIC VERSES Rushdie
THE SCARLET LETTER Hawthorne
THE SECRET HISTORY Tartt
THE SECRET PILGRIM Le Carré
THE SHELTERING SKY Bowles
THE SPY WHO LOVED ME Fleming
THE STARS LOOK DOWN Cronin
THE WAY OF ALL FLESH Butler
THE YOUNG VISITERS Ashford
THIS SPORTING LIFE Storey
TIPPING THE VELVET Waters
TO HAVE AND HAVE NOT Hemingway
VALLEY OF THE DOLLS Susann
WASHINGTON SQUARE H James
WUTHERING HEIGHTS E Brontë
YOU ONLY LIVE TWICE Fleming

17

ABSOLUTE BEGINNERS MacInnes
A HOUSE FOR MR BISWAS Naipaul
ALICE IN WONDERLAND Carroll
AN AMERICAN TRAGEDY Dreiser

A NEST OF GENTLEFOLK Turgenev
ANNE OF GREEN GABLES Montgomery
A WOMAN OF SUBSTANCE Bradford
CAPTAIN HORNBLOWER RN Forester
FOUCAULT'S PENDULUM Eco
GRAND BABYLON HOTEL Bennett
GREAT EXPECTATIONS Dickens
HOLLYWOOD HUSBANDS J Collins
I CAPTURE THE CASTLE D Smith
KING SOLOMON'S MINES Haggard
LOVE AND MR LEWISHAM Wells
MIDNIGHT'S CHILDREN Rushdie
NAUGHTY AMELIA JANE Blyton
NIGHTS AT THE CIRCUS Carter
PADDY CLARKE HA HA HA Doyle
POINT COUNTER POINT A Huxley
PORTNOY'S COMPLAINT Roth
PRIDE AND PREJUDICE Austen
SOMETHING HAPPENED Heller
SUSHI FOR BEGINNERS Keyes
THE AGE OF INNOCENCE Wharton
THE BOOK OF EVIDENCE Banville
THE BULL FROM THE SEA Renault
THE CORNISH TRILOGY R Davies
THE DAY OF THE JACKAL Forsyth
THE DAY OF THE LOCUST N West
THE DIARY OF A NOBODY Grossmith
THE EAGLE HAS LANDED Higgins
THE END OF THE AFFAIR Greene
THE ENGLISH PATIENT Ondaatje
THE FOURTH PROTOCOL Forsyth
THE GOOD COMPANIONS Priestley
THE GRASS IS SINGING Lessing
THE GUNS OF NAVARONE Maclean
THE ILLUSTRATED MAN R Bradbury
THE JOKER IN THE PACK Chase
THE KREUTZER SONATA Tolstoy

THE MAGIC CHRISTIAN Southern
THE MANDELBAUM GATE Spark
THE MIDWICH CUCKOOS Wyndham
THE MILL ON THE FLOSS G Eliot
THE ROADS TO FREEDOM Sartre
THE ROAD TO WELVILLE Boyle
THE TAILOR OF PANAMA Le Carré
THE THIRD POLICEMAN F O'Brien
THE TURN OF THE SCREW H James
THE VIRGIN SOLDIERS L Thomas
THE WAR OF THE WORLDS Wells
THE WINGS OF THE DOVE H James
TRAVELS WITH MY AUNT Greene
TROPIC OF CAPRICORN H Miller
TROUBLE WITH LICHEN Wyndham
WAR AND REMEMBRANCE Wouk
WHEN WE WERE ORPHANS Ishiguro
WIVES AND DAUGHTERS Gaskell

18
ACCORDING TO QUEENEY Bainbridge
A HIGH WIND IN JAMAICA R Hughes
A MURDER IS ANNOUNCED Christie
ANNA OF THE FIVE TOWNS Bennett
BILLION-DOLLAR BRAIN Deighton
BRIDGET JONES'S DIARY H Fielding
CRIME AND PUNISHMENT
  Dostoyevsky
DAS GLASPERLENSPIEL (or *The Glass
  Bead Game*) Hesse
DIAMONDS ARE FOREVER Fleming
FROM RUSSIA WITH LOVE Fleming
KING SOLOMON'S CARPET Vine
LAST EXIT TO BROOKLYN Selby
LOVE IN A COLD CLIMATE N Mitford
NINETEEN EIGHTY-FOUR Orwell
RUMPOLE OF THE BAILEY Mortimer
SLAUGHTERHOUSE FIVE Vonnegut

SWALLOWS AND AMAZONS Ransome
THE ANDROMEDA STRAIN Crichton
THE CATCHER IN THE RYE JD Salinger
THE CIDER HOUSE RULES J Irving
THE CITY AND THE STARS AC Clarke
THE EAGLE OF THE NINTH Sutcliff
THE FAIR MAID OF PERTH W Scott
THE GETTING OF WISDOM
  HH Richardson
THE INNOCENTS ABROAD Twain
THE JEWEL IN THE CROWN P Scott
THE LITTLE MATCH GIRL Andersen
THE LOOKING-GLASS WAR Le Carré
THE MOON AND SIXPENCE Maugham
THE NAKED AND THE DEAD Mailer
THE OLD MAN AND THE SEA
  Hemingway
THE OTHER BOLEYN GIRL Gregory
THE POISONWOOD BIBLE Kingsolver
THE PORTRAIT OF A LADY H James
THE PRISONER OF ZENDA Hope
THE RAILWAY CHILDREN Nesbit
THE REMAINS OF THE DAY Ishiguro
THE SOUND AND THE FURY Faulkner
THE SPOILS OF POYNTON H James
THE SWORD IN THE STONE TH White
THE THIRTY-NINE STEPS Buchan
THE THREE MUSKETEERS Dumas
THE TORTILLA CURTAIN Boyle
THIS SIDE OF PARADISE FS Fitzgerald
TO KILL A MOCKINGBIRD H Lee
VIRGIN SOIL UPTURNED Sholokhov
WELCOME TO HARD TIMES Doctorow
WHEN EIGHT BELLS TOLL Maclean

19
AND QUIET FLOWS THE DON
  Sholokhov

ANGLO-SAXON ATTITUDES A Wilson
AN INSULAR POSSESSION Mo
A PRAYER FOR OWEN MEANY J Irving
A SENTIMENTAL JOURNEY Sterne
A SMALL TOWN IN GERMANY
 Le Carré
BREAKFAST AT TIFFANY'S Capote
BRIDESHEAD REVISITED E Waugh
DEATH IN THE AFTERNOON
 Hemingway
EATING PEOPLE IS WRONG
 M Bradbury
FOR WHOM THE BELL TOLLS
 Hemingway
HOW GREEN WAS MY VALLEY
 Llewellyn
HOW LATE IT WAS, HOW LATE Kelman
METHUSELAH'S CHILDREN Heinlein
SENSE AND SENSIBILITY Austen
THE ARMIES OF THE NIGHT Mailer
THE BLACKBOARD JUNGLE Hunter
THE BODY IN THE LIBRARY Christie
THE BUDDHA OF SUBURBIA Kureishi
THE CITY AND THE PILLAR Vidal
THE CONSTANT GARDENER Le Carré
THE CORRIDORS OF POWER Snow
THE DARLING BUDS OF MAY Bates
THE DAY OF THE TRIFFIDS Wyndham
THE GLITTERING PRIZES Raphael
THE GOD OF SMALL THINGS Roy
THE GOOD SOLDIER ŠVEJK Hašek
THE GULAG ARCHIPELAGO
 Solzhenitsyn
THE HEART OF THE MATTER Greene
THE HISTORY OF MR POLLY Wells
THE HOLCROFT COVENANT Ludlum
THE HOUSE ON THE STRAND
 D Du Maurier

THE MAID OF BUTTERMERE Bragg
THE MIRACLE OF THE ROSE Genet
THE NUMBER OF THE BEAST Heinlein
THE OLD CURIOSITY SHOP Dickens
THE PILGRIM'S PROGRESS Bunyan
THE POWER AND THE GLORY Greene
THE PRODIGAL DAUGHTER Archer
THE RIDDLE OF THE SANDS Childers
THE SCARLET PIMPERNEL Orczy
THE STARS' TENNIS BALLS Fry
THE VICAR OF WAKEFIELD Goldsmith
THE WELL OF LONELINESS Hall
THE WIND IN THE WILLOWS Grahame
TOM BROWN'S SCHOOLDAYS
 T Hughes

20

A BOUQUET OF BARBED WIRE
 Newman
A CONFEDERACY OF DUNCES Toole
A PARLIAMENTARY AFFAIR Currie
BERLIN ALEXANDERPLATZ Döblin
CRY THE BELOVED COUNTRY Paton
EMIL AND THE DETECTIVES Kästner
HOW TO SAVE YOUR OWN LIFE Jong
INVITATION TO THE WALTZ Lehmann
KISS OF THE SPIDER WOMAN Puig
LADY CHATTERLEY'S LOVER
 DH Lawrence
LITTLE LORD FAUNTLEROY FH Burnett
NOTES FROM UNDERGROUND
 Dostoyevsky
OFFICERS AND GENTLEMEN E Waugh
OTHER PEOPLE'S CHILDREN J Trollope
THE ALEXANDRIA QUARTET L Durrell
THE BRIDE OF LAMMERMOOR W Scott
THE BROTHERS KARAMAZOV
 Dostoyevsky

THE CONFIDENTIAL AGENT Greene
THE DEVIL'S ALTERNATIVE Forsyth
THE HEART OF MIDLOTHIAN W Scott
THE HOTEL NEW HAMPSHIRE J Irving
THE HOUSE AT POOH CORNER Milne
THE HOUSE OF THE SPIRITS Allende
THE HUNT FOR RED OCTOBER Clancy
THE LAST DAYS OF POMPEII Bulwer-
  Lytton
THE LAST OF THE MOHICANS
  JF Cooper
THE LITTLE DRUMMER GIRL Le Carré
THE MARTIAN CHRONICLES
  R Bradbury

THE ONCE AND FUTURE KING
  TH White
THE PIT AND THE PENDULUM Poe
THE RETURN OF THE NATIVE Hardy
THE SILENCE OF THE LAMBS T Harris
THE TIME TRAVELER'S WIFE
  Niffenegger
THE TOWERS OF TREBIZOND
  Macaulay
THE WARLORD CHRONICLES
  B Cornwell
TO SERVE THEM ALL MY DAYS
  Delderfield

Arts – Literature – PLAY CHARACTERS (general)

3
BEN *The Dumb Waiter*
CAT Captain *Under Milk Wood*
FAY *Loot*
GUS *The Dumb Waiter*
HAL *Loot*
LOB *Dear Brutus*
MAX *The Homecoming*
UBU *Ubu Roi*

4
ANYA *The Cherry Orchard*
BETH *Dry Rot*
BOON Walter *You Never Can Tell*
CARR Henry *Travesties*
CLOV *Endgame*
DAWN *Steaming*
FACE *The Alchemist*
HAMM *Endgame*

HOOK Captain *Peter Pan*
HOPE Harry *The Iceman Cometh*
JANE *The Reluctant Debutante,
  Steaming*
JEAN *Miss Julie*
KATE *Bedroom Farce*
KATH *Entertaining Mr Sloane*
KEMP *Entertaining Mr Sloane*
KITE Sergeant *The Recruiting Officer*
LAKE Diana, Kenneth *French without
  Tears*
LANE *The Importance of Being Earnest*
LOAM Earl of *The Admirable Crichton*
LUKA *The Lower Depths*
MORE Sir Thomas *A Man for All
  Seasons*
NAGG *Endgame*
NANA *Peter Pan*
NELL *Endgame*

NORA *A Doll's House*
OLGA *The Three Sisters*
PAGE Freddie *The Deep Blue Sea*
PUFF *The Critic*
RICE Archie *The Entertainer*
RITA *Educating Rita*
SMEE *Peter Pan*
WYKE Andrew *Sleuth*

5

ACRES Bob *The Rivals*
ALICE *A Woman of No Importance*
ARGAN *Le Malade imaginaire*
BLACK Jack *Under Milk Wood*
BLISS David, Judith *Hay Fever*
BOYLE Juno *Juno and the Paycock*
CLARK Willie *The Sunshine Boys*
DOYLE Larry *John Bull's Other Island*
DUMBY *Lady Windermere's Fan*
EDDIE *Entertaining Mr Sloane*
ELYOT *Private Lives*
FAUST *Faust*
FEERS *The Cherry Orchard*
FELIX *The Odd Couple*
FOWLE *The Dock Brief*
FRANK *Educating Rita*
GOOLE Inspector *An Inspector Calls*
HELEN *A Taste of Honey*
HIRST *No Man's Land*
INDRA *A Dream Play*
IRINA *The Three Sisters*
JOSIE *Steaming*
JULIE *Miss Julie*
KRAPP *Krapp's Last Tape*
LEEDS Nina *Strange Interlude*
LEWIS Al *The Sunshine Boys*
LOMAN Willy *Death of a Salesman*
LUCKY *Waiting for Godot*

MAHON Christy *The Playboy of the Western World*
MALFI Duchess of *The Duchess of Malfi*
MASHA *The Three Sisters*
MASON *An Ideal Husband*
MOSCA *Volpone*
NANCY *Steaming*
OSCAR *The Odd Couple*
PETER *A Taste of Honey*
POZZO *Waiting for Godot*
PRISM Miss *The Importance of Being Earnest*
ROWAN Richard *Exiles*
SKIPS Matthew *The Lady's Not for Burning*
SNEER *The Critic*
SONYA *Uncle Vanya*
SWABB Mrs *Habeas Corpus*
SYBIL *Private Lives*
TWINE Gertrude *Rookery Nook*
VANYA *Uncle Vanya*
VASKA *The Lower Depths*
YERMA *Yerma*

6

AMANDA *Private Lives*
ARCATI Madame *Blithe Spirit*
ARCHER Francis *The Beaux' Stratagem*
BARDIN Zakhar *Enemies*
BOSOLA *The Duchess of Malfi*
CARDEW Cecily *The Importance of Being Earnest*
DANGLE *The Critic*
DENNIS *Loot*
DUBOIS Blanche *A Streetcar Named Desire*
DYSART Martin *Equus*
EGMONT Count *Egmont*

ELVIRA *Blithe Spirit, Pizarro*
FISHER Billy *Billy Liar*
GEORGE *Who's Afraid of Virginia Woolf?*
GORING Viscount *An Ideal Husband*
GURTON Gammer *Gammer Gurton's Needle*
HORNER *The Country Wife*
HUNTER Frances, Peter *No Sex Please, We're British*
JACOMO *The Jew of Malta*
KELVIL *A Woman of No Importance*
MAGNUS King *The Apple Cart*
MANGAN Alfred *Heartbreak House*
MARKBY Lady *An Ideal Husband*
MARLOW Young *She Stoops to Conquer*
MARTHA *Who's Afraid of Virginia Woolf?*
MORELL Candida, Reverend *Candida*
MORGAN Organ *Under Milk Wood*
ONDINE *Ondine*
PARKER *Lady Windermere's Fan*
PHIPPS *An Ideal Husband*
PHIPPS Fred *Dry Rot*
PORTER Jimmy *Look Back in Anger*
SALOMÉ *Salomé*
SILVIA *The Recruiting Officer*
SLOANE *Entertaining Mr Sloane*
STRANG Alan *Equus*
TANNER John *Man and Superman*
TAPLOW *The Browning Version*
TEAZLE Lady, Sir Peter *The School for Scandal*
TINDLE Milo *Sleuth*
TYRONE James, Mary *Long Day's Journey into Night*
VICTOR *Private Lives*
VIOLET *Steaming*

WARREN Mrs *Mrs Warren's Profession*
YELENA *Uncle Vanya*

7

AIMWELL Thomas *The Beaux' Stratagem*
ALCESTE *Le Misanthrope*
AL LEWIS *The Sunshine Boys*
ALLMERS Eyolf *Little Eyolf*
ALLONBY Mrs *A Woman of No Importance*
ARSINOE *Le Misanthrope*
BARABAS *The Jew of Malta*
BELYAEV *A Month in the Country*
CANDOUR Mrs *The School for Scandal*
CHESNEY Jack *Charley's Aunt*
DARLING John, Michael, Mrs, Wendy *Peter Pan*
DIGGORY *She Stoops to Conquer*
DUDGEON Richard *The Devil's Disciple*
ELIANTE *Le Misanthrope*
FAIRFAX Gwendolen *The Importance of Being Earnest*
FAUSTUS Doctor *Doctor Faustus*
HIGGINS Henry *Pygmalion*
ISLAYEV *A Month in the Country*
LOVEWIT *The Alchemist*
LUMPKIN Tony *She Stoops to Conquer*
MALCOLM *Bedroom Farce*
MANDERS Pastor *Ghosts*
MARLENE *Top Girls*
MEADOWS Mrs *Steaming*
MOULTON *The Importance of Being Earnest*
NATALYA *A Month in the Country*

OEDIPUS *Oedipus Rex*
PROTEUS Joseph *The Apple Cart*
ROSALIE *Lady Windermere's Fan*
SOLNESS Halvard *The Master Builder*
SOLVEIG *Peer Gynt*
SPOONER *No Man's Land*
SURFACE *The School for Scandal*
TORVALD *A Doll's House*
TROTTER Sergeant *The Mousetrap*
VOLPONE *Volpone*
WINSLOW Ronnie *The Winslow Boy*
WORSLEY Hester *A Woman of No Importance*
WOYZECK *Woyzeck*
WYKEHAM Charles *Charley's Aunt*

8

ABSOLUTE Anthony *The Rivals*
ANTIGONE *Antigone*
BACKBITE Sir Benjamin *The School for Scandal*
BEVERLEY *Abigail's Party*
BEVERLEY Ensign *The Rivals*
BIG DADDY *Cat on a Hot Tin Roof*
BOB ACRES *The Rivals*
BONIFACE *Hotel Paradise*
BREWSTER Abby, Martha *Arsenic and Old Lace*
CARLISLE Lady *Lady Windermere's Fan*
CÉLIMÈNE *Le Misanthrope*
CHASUBLE Reverend *The Importance of Being Earnest*
CHILTERN Lady, Sir Robert *An Ideal Husband*
CRABTREE *The School for Scandal*
CRICHTON *The Admirable Crichton*
DELAHAYE *Spider's Web*
ESTRAGON *Waiting for Godot*

HASTINGS *She Stoops to Conquer*
JOKANAAN *Salomé*
JOURDAIN Monsieur *Le Bourgeois Gentilhomme*
LANGUISH Lydia *The Rivals*
MALAPROP Mrs *The Rivals*
MERRIMAN *The Importance of Being Earnest*
MIRABELL *The Way of the World*
MRS SWABB *Habeas Corpus*
PEER GYNT *Peer Gynt*
PETER PAN *Peter Pan*
RANEVSKY Madame *The Cherry Orchard*
ROBINSON Violet *Man and Superman*
SHOTOVER Captain *Heartbreak House*
STANHOPE Captain *Journey's End*
TRELAWNY Rose *Trelawny of the Wells*
VLADIMIR *Waiting for Godot*
VULLIAMY *The Fascinating Foundling*
WAGSTAFF Colonel, Mrs *Dry Rot*
WORTHING John *The Importance of Being Earnest*

9

ANDROCLES *Androcles and the Lion*
BABBERLEY Lord *Charley's Aunt*
BOUNTIFUL Lady *The Beaux' Stratagem*
BRACKNELL Lady *The Importance of Being Earnest*
BROADBENT Tom *John Bull's Other Island*
CAVERSHAM Earl of *An Ideal Husband*
DIANA LAKE *French without Tears*
DOOLITTLE Alfred, Eliza *Pygmalion*
ESSENDINE Garry *Present Laughter*
HARRY HOPE *The Iceman Cometh*

HENRY CARR *Travesties*
JACK BLACK *Under Milk Wood*
JUNO BOYLE *Juno and the Paycock*
KOSTILYOV *The Lower Depths*
MILLAMANT *The Way of the World*
MISS PRISM *The Importance of Being Earnest*
MONCRIEFF Algernon *The Importance of Being Earnest*
MRS WARREN *Mrs Warren's Profession*
NINA LEEDS *Strange Interlude*
PICKERING Colonel *Pygmalion*
POLYDAMUS *Marriage à la Mode*
SNEERWELL Lady *The School for Scandal*
TANQUERAY Aubrey, Paula *The Second Mrs Tanqueray*
TIGER LILY *Peter Pan*
WAYNFLETE Lady *Captain Brassbound's Conversion*
WICKSTEED Doctor *Habeas Corpus*
WINGFIELD Amanda *The Glass Menagerie*

10

ALAN STRANG *Equus*
ANDREW WYKE *Sleuth*
ARCHIE RICE *The Entertainer*
BARNARDINE *The Jew of Malta*
BLUNTSCHLI Captain *Arms and the Man*
BRASSBOUND Captain *Captain Brassbound's Conversion*
CAPTAIN CAT *Under Milk Wood*
DARLINGTON Lord *Lady Windermere's Fan*
DAVID BLISS *Hay Fever*
DONNA LUCIA *Charley's Aunt*

EARL OF LOAM *The Admirable Crichton*
FLASH HARRY *Dry Rot*
FRED PHIPPS *Dry Rot*
HARDCASTLE *She Stoops to Conquer*
HUNSTANTON Lady *A Woman of No Importance*
JOHN TANNER *Man and Superman*
KING MAGNUS *The Apple Cart*
LADY MARKBY *An Ideal Husband*
LADY TEAZLE *The School for Scandal*
LARRY DOYLE *John Bull's Other Island*
LICKCHEESE *Widowers' Houses*
MANNINGHAM Bella *Gaslight*
MARCHBANKS Eugene *Candida*
MARY TYRONE *Long Day's Journey into Night*
MILO TINDLE *Sleuth*
MORGENHALL *The Dock Brief*
MRS ALLONBY *A Woman of No Importance*
MRS CANDOUR *The School for Scandal*
MRS DARLING *Peter Pan*
MRS MEADOWS *Steaming*
PONTEFRACT Lady *A Woman of No Importance*
SEMPRONIUS *The Apple Cart*
TINKERBELL *Peter Pan*
UNDERSHAFT Barbara *Major Barbara*
WALTER BOON *You Never Can Tell*
WILLY LOMAN *Death of a Salesman*
WINDERMERE Lady, Lord *Lady Windermere's Fan*
ZARECHNAYA Nina *The Seagull*

11

BILLY FISHER *Billy Liar*
CAPTAIN HOOK *Peter Pan*
COUNT EGMONT *Egmont*

FREDDIE PAGE *The Deep Blue Sea*
ILLINGWORTH Lord *A Woman of No Importance*
JACK CHESNEY *Charley's Aunt*
JAMES TYRONE *Long Day's Journey into Night*
JIMMY PORTER *Look Back in Anger*
JOHN DARLING *Peter Pan*
JUDITH BLISS *Hay Fever*
KENNETH LAKE *French without Tears*
MRS MALAPROP *The Rivals*
MRS WAGSTAFF *Dry Rot*
ORGAN MORGAN *Under Milk Wood*
PETER HUNTER *No Sex Please, We're British*
ROSENCRANTZ *Rosencrantz and Guildenstern Are Dead*
SEREBRYAKOV *Uncle Vanya*
TAMBURLAINE *Tamburlaine*
TONY LUMPKIN *She Stoops to Conquer*
WILLIE CLARK *The Sunshine Boys*
YOUNG MARLOW *She Stoops to Conquer*

12

ABBY BREWSTER *Arsenic and Old Lace*
ALFRED MANGAN *Heartbreak House*
CECILY CARDEW *The Importance of Being Earnest*
CHRISTY MAHON *The Playboy of the Western World*
EYOLF ALLMERS *Little Eyolf*
GAMMER GURTON *Gammer Gurton's Needle*
GUILDENSTERN *Rosencrantz and Guildenstern Are Dead*
HENRY HIGGINS *Pygmalion*

JOHN WORTHING *The Importance of Being Earnest*
LADY CARLISLE *Lady Windermere's Fan*
LADY CHILTERN *An Ideal Husband*
MADAME ARCATI *Blithe Spirit*
MARTIN DYSART *Equus*
MATTHEW SKIPS *The Lady's Not for Burning*
RICHARD ROWAN *Exiles*
ROSE TRELAWNY *Trelawny of the Wells*
SERGEANT KITE *The Recruiting Officer*
TOM BROADBENT *John Bull's Other Island*
WENDY DARLING *Peter Pan*
ZACHANASSIAN Claire *The Visit*
ZAKHAR BARDIN *Enemies*

13

BLANCHE DUBOIS *A Streetcar Named Desire*
CANDIDA MORELL *Candida*
DOCTOR FAUSTUS *Doctor Faustus*
FRANCES HUNTER *No Sex Please, We're British*
FRANCIS ARCHER *The Beaux' Stratagem*
GERTRUDE TWINE *Rookery Nook*
HESTER WORSLEY *A Woman of No Importance*
JOSEPH PROTEUS *The Apple Cart*
LADY BOUNTIFUL *The Beaux' Stratagem*
LADY BRACKNELL *The Importance of Being Earnest*
LADY SNEERWELL *The School for Scandal*
LADY WAYNFLETE *Captain Brassbound's Conversion*

LORD BABBERLEY *Charley's Aunt*
LYDIA LANGUISH *The Rivals*
PASTOR MANDERS *Ghosts*
RONNIE WINSLOW *The Winslow Boy*
SIR THOMAS MORE *A Man for All Seasons*
THOMAS AIMWELL *The Beaux' Stratagem*

14

CHARLES WYKEHAM *Charley's Aunt*
DUCHESS OF MALFI *The Duchess of Malfi*
ELIZA DOOLITTLE *Pygmalion*
ENSIGN BEVERLEY *The Rivals*
GARRY ESSENDINE *Present Laughter*
HALVARD SOLNESS *The Master Builder*
INSPECTOR GOOLE *An Inspector Calls*
LADY HUNSTANTON *A Woman of No Importance*
LADY PONTEFRACT *A Woman of No Importance*
LADY WINDERMERE *Lady Windermere's Fan*
LORD DARLINGTON *Lady Windermere's Fan*
LORD WINDERMERE *Lady Windermere's Fan*
MADAME RANEVSKY *The Cherry Orchard*
MARTHA BREWSTER *Arsenic and Old Lace*
MEPHISTOPHELES *Doctor Faustus*
MICHAEL DARLING *Peter Pan*
NINA ZARECHNAYA *The Seagull*

PAULA TANQUERAY *The Second Mrs Tanqueray*
REVEREND MORELL *Candida*
RICHARD DUDGEON *The Devil's Disciple*
SIR PETER TEAZLE *The School for Scandal*
VIOLET ROBINSON *Man and Superman*
VISCOUNT GORING *An Ideal Husband*

15

ALFRED DOOLITTLE *Pygmalion*
AMANDA WINGFIELD *The Glass Menagerie*
ANTHONY ABSOLUTE *The Rivals*
AUBREY TANQUERAY *The Second Mrs Tanqueray*
BELLA MANNINGHAM *Gaslight*
CAPTAIN SHOTOVER *Heartbreak House*
CAPTAIN STANHOPE *Journey's End*
COLONEL WAGSTAFF *Dry Rot*
DOCTOR WICKSTEED *Habeas Corpus*
EARL OF CAVERSHAM *An Ideal Husband*
LORD ILLINGWORTH *A Woman of No Importance*
SERGEANT TROTTER *The Mousetrap*

16

COLONEL PICKERING *Pygmalion*
EUGENE MARCHBANKS *Candida*
GWENDOLEN FAIRFAX *The Importance of Being Earnest*
MONSIEUR JOURDAIN *Le Bourgeois Gentilhomme*
REVEREND CHASUBLE *The Importance of Being Earnest*

17
ALGERNON MONCRIEFF *The Importance of Being Earnest*
BARBARA UNDERSHAFT *Major Barbara*
CAPTAIN BLUNTSCHLI *Arms and the Man*
CAPTAIN BRASSBOUND *Captain Brassbound's Conversion*

SIR ROBERT CHILTERN *An Ideal Husband*

18
CLAIRE ZACHANASSIAN *The Visit*

Arts – Literature – PLAY CHARACTERS (Shakespeare)

3
BOY *Macbeth*
NYM *Hen V, Merry*
SAY Lord *Hen VI 2*
SLY Christopher *Taming*

4
ADAM *As You*
AJAX *Troilus*
ANNE Lady *Rich III*
BONA *Hen VI 3*
CADE Jack *Hen VI 2*
CATO Young *Julius*
DAVY *Hen IV 2*
DICK *Hen VI 2*
DION *Winter's*
DUKE *As You*
DULL *Love's*
EROS *Antony*
FANG *Hen IV 2*
FORD Mistress *Merry*
GREY Lady *Hen VI 3*
GREY Lord *Rich III*
GREY Sir Thomas *Hen V*
HERO *Much Ado*

HUME John *Hen VI 2*
IAGO *Othello*
IDEN Alexander *Hen VI 2*
IRAS *Antony*
JAMY *Hen V*
JOHN Friar *Romeo*
JOHN King *John*
JOHN Prince *Hen IV 1 & 2*
JUNO *Tempest*
LEAR King *Lear*
LENA Popilius *Julius*
LUCE *Comedy*
LUCY Sir William *Hen VI 1*
MOTH *Love's, MN Dream*
PAGE Mistress Anne, William *Merry*
PETO *Hen IV 1 & 2*
PUCK (or Robin Goodfellow) *MN Dream*
ROSS *Macbeth*
ROSS Lord *Rich II*
SNUG *MN Dream*
VAUX Sir Nicholas *Hen VIII*
VAUX Sir William *Hen VI 2*
WART Thomas *Hen IV 2*

5

AARON *Titus*
ALICE *Hen V*
ANGUS *Macbeth*
ARIEL *Tempest*
BAGOT *Rich II*
BATES *Hen V*
BELCH Sir Toby *Twelfth*
BEVIS George *Hen VI 2*
BIGOT Lord *John*
BLUNT Sir Walter *Hen IV 1 & 2*
BOULT *Pericles*
BOYET *Love's*
BUSHY *Rich II*
BUTTS Doctor *Hen VIII*
CAIUS *Titus*
CAIUS Doctor *Merry*
CASCA *Julius*
CELIA *As You*
CERES *Tempest*
CINNA *Julius*
CLEON *Pericles*
CORIN *As You*
COURT *Hen V*
CUPID *Timon*
CURAN *Lear*
CURIO *Twelfth*
DENNY Sir Anthony *Hen VIII*
DIANA *All's Well, Pericles*
EDGAR *Lear*
EGEUS *MN Dream*
ELBOW *Measure*
EVANS Sir Hugh *Merry*
FESTE *Twelfth*
FLUTE *MN Dream*
FROTH *Measure*
GOBBO Launcelot, Old *Merchant*
GOFFE Matthew *Hen VI 2*

GOWER *Hen IV 2, Hen V, Pericles*
GREEN *Rich II*
HELEN *Cymbel, Troilus*
HENRY *Rich III*
HENRY the Eighth *Hen VIII*
HENRY the Fifth *Hen V*
HENRY the Fourth *Hen IV 1 & 2*
HENRY the Sixth *Hen VI 1 2 & 3*
HENRY Prince *John*
JULIA *Two Gent*
LAFEU *All's Well*
LEWIS *Hen V, John*
LOUIS *Hen VI 3*
LOVEL Lord *Rich III*
LUCIO *Measure*
MARIA *Love's, Twelfth*
MELUN *John*
MENAS *Antony*
MOPSA *Winter's*
OSRIC *Hamlet*
PARIS *Romeo, Troilus*
PERCY *Hen IV 1 & 2*
PERCY Henry *Hen IV 1 & 2, Rich II*
PERCY Lady *Hen IV 1 & 2*
PERCY Thomas *Hen IV 1*
PETER *Hen VI 2, John, Measure,*
  Romeo
PHEBE *As You*
PHILO *Antony*
PINCH *Comedy*
POINS Edward *Hen IV 1 & 2*
PRIAM *Troilus*
REGAN *Lear*
ROBIN *Merry*
ROMEO *Romeo*
RUGBY *Merry*
SMITH *Hen VI 2*
SNARE *Hen IV 2*

SNOUT *MN Dream*
SPEED *Two Gent*
TIMON *Timon*
TITUS *Timon*
TUBAL *Merchant*
VARRO *Julius*
VIOLA *Twelfth*

6
ADRIAN *Corio, Tempest*
AEGEON *Comedy*
AENEAS *Troilus*
ALEXAS *Antony*
ALONSO *Tempest*
AMIENS *As You*
ANGELO *Comedy, Measure*
ANTONY Mark *Antony*
ARTHUR *John*
AUDREY *As You*
BANQUO *Macbeth*
BASSET *Hen VI 1*
BIANCA *Othello, Taming*
BLANCH *John*
BLOUNT Sir James *Rich III*
BOTTOM *MN Dream*
BRUTUS Decius, Marcus *Julius*
BRUTUS Junius *Corio*
BULLEN Anne *Hen VIII*
CAESAR Julius, Octavius *Antony, Julius*
CAPHIS *Timon*
CASSIO *Othello*
CHIRON *Titus*
CICERO *Julius*
CIMBER Metellus *Julius*
CLITUS *Julius*
CLOTEN *Cymbel*
COBWEB *MN Dream*
CURTIS *Taming*

DENNIS *As You*
DORCAS *Winter's*
DROMIO of Ephesus, of Syracuse
    Comedy
DUMAIN *Love's*
DUNCAN *Macbeth*
EDMUND *Hen VI 3, Lear*
EDWARD *Hen VI 2 & 3*
EDWARD the Fourth *Rich III*
ELINOR Queen *John*
EMILIA *Othello, Winter's*
FABIAN *Twelfth*
FEEBLE Francis *Hen IV 2*
FENTON *Merry*
GALLUS *Antony*
GEORGE *Hen VI 3, Rich III*
GREMIO *Taming*
GRUMIO *Taming*
GURNEY James *John*
HAMLET *Hamlet*
HECATE *Macbeth*
HECTOR *Troilus*
HELENA *All's Well, MN Dream*
HERMIA *MN Dream*
HORNER Thomas *Hen VI 2*
HUBERT *John*
IMOGEN *Cymbel*
ISABEL *Hen V*
JAQUES *As You*
JULIET *Measure, Romeo*
LAUNCE *Two Gent*
LE BEAU *As You*
LENNOX *Macbeth*
LOVELL Sir Thomas *Hen VIII*
LUCIUS *Julius, Timon*
LUCIUS Caius *Cymbel*
LUCIUS Young *Titus*
MARINA *Pericles*

MINOLA Baptista *Taming*
MORTON *Hen IV 2*
MORTON John *Rich III*
MOULDY Ralph *Hen IV 2*
MUTIUS *Titus*
NESTOR *Troilus*
OBERON *MN Dream*
OLIVER *As You*
OLIVIA *Twelfth*
ORSINO *Twelfth*
OSWALD *Lear*
PIERCE Sir *Rich II*
PISTOL *Hen IV 2, Hen V, Merry*
POMPEY *Measure*
PORTIA *Julius, Merchant*
QUINCE *MN Dream*
RIVERS Earl *Rich III*
RIVERS Lord *Hen VI 3*
RUMOUR *Hen IV 2*
SANDYS Lord *Hen VIII*
SCALES Lord *Hen VI 2*
SCARUS *Antony*
SCROOP *Hen IV 1 & 2*
SCROOP Lord *Hen V*
SCROOP Sir Stephen *Rich II*
SEYTON *Macbeth*
SHADOW Simon *Hen IV 2*
SILIUS *Antony*
SILVIA *Two Gent*
SIMPLE *Merry*
SIWARD Young *Macbeth*
STRATO *Julius*
TALBOT Lord *Hen VI 1*
TAMORA *Titus*
TAURUS *Antony*
THAISA *Pericles*
THOMAS *Hen IV 2, Measure*
THURIO *Two Gent*

TRANIO *Taming*
TYBALT *Romeo*
TYRREL Sir James *Rich III*
URSULA *Much Ado*
VERGES *Much Ado*
VERNON Sir Richard *Hen IV 1,
   Hen VI 1*
WOLSEY Cardinal *Hen VIII*
YORICK *Hamlet*

7

ABRAHAM *Romeo*
ADRIANA *Comedy*
AEMILIA *Comedy*
AGRIPPA *Antony*
AGRIPPA Menenius *Corio*
ALARBUS *Titus*
AMAZONS *Timon*
ANTENOR *Troilus*
ANTONIO *Merchant, Much Ado,
   Tempest, Twelfth*
BEROWNE *Love's*
BERTRAM *All's Well*
BRANDON *Hen VIII*
BRANDON Sir William *Rich III*
CALCHAS *Troilus*
CALIBAN *Tempest*
CAMILLO *Winter's*
CAPULET + Lady *Romeo*
CASSIUS *Julius*
CATESBY Sir William *Rich III*
CERIMON *Pericles*
CHARLES *As You, Hen VI*
CHARLES the Sixth *Hen V*
CLAUDIO *Measure, Much Ado*
CONRADE *Much Ado*
COSTARD *Love's*
CRANMER *Henry VIII*

DE BURGH Hubert *John*
DIONYZA *Pericles*
DON JOHN *Much Ado*
ELEANOR *Hen VI 2*
ESCALUS *Measure, Romeo*
ESCANES *Pericles*
FLAVIUS *Julius, Timon*
FLEANCE *Macbeth*
FRANCIS *Hen IV 2*
FRANCIS Friar *Much Ado*
GONERIL *Lear*
GONZALO *Tempest*
GREGORY *Romeo*
HELENUS *Troilus*
HERBERT Sir Walter *Rich III*
HOLLAND John *Hen VI 2*
HOTSPUR Henry *Hen IV 1*
IACHIMO *Cymbel*
JESSICA *Merchant*
LAERTES *Hamlet*
LARTIUS Titus *Corio*
LAVACHE *All's Well*
LAVINIA *Titus*
LEONATO *Much Ado*
LEONINE *Pericles*
LEONTES *Winter's*
LEPIDUS M Aemilius *Antony, Julius*
LORD SAY *Hen VI 2*
LORENZO *Merchant*
LUCETTA *Two Gent*
LUCIANA *Comedy*
LYMOGES *John*
MACBETH + Lady *Macbeth*
MACDUFF + Lady *Macbeth*
MALCOLM *Macbeth*
MARCADE *Love's*
MARCIUS Caius, Young *Corio*
MARDIAN *Antony*

MARIANA *All's Well, Measure*
MARSHAL Lord *Rich II*
MARTEXT Sir Oliver *As You*
MARTIUS *Titus*
MESSALA *Julius*
MICHAEL *Hen VI 2*
MICHAEL Sir *Hen IV 1*
MIRANDA *Tempest*
MONTANO *Othello*
MONTJOY *Hen V*
MOWBRAY Lord *Hen IV 2*
MOWBRAY Thomas *Rich II*
NERISSA *Merchant*
NICANOR *Corio*
OCTAVIA *Antony*
OPHELIA *Hamlet*
ORLANDO *As You*
OTHELLO *Othello*
PAULINA *Winter's*
PERDITA *Winter's*
PHYRNIA *Timon*
PISANIO *Cymbel*
PROTEUS *Two Gent*
PUBLIUS *Julius, Titus*
QUICKLY Hostess *Hen IV 1 & 2*
QUICKLY Mistress *Merry*
QUINTUS *Titus*
RICHARD *Hen VI 2 & 3*
RICHARD Plantagenet *Hen VI 1 & 2*
RICHARD the Second *Richard II*
RICHARD the Third *Rich III*
SALERIO *Merchant*
SAMPSON *Romeo*
SHALLOW *Merry*
SHALLOW Robert *Hen IV 2*
SHYLOCK *Merchant*
SILENCE *Hen IV 2*
SILVIUS *As You*

SIMPCOX Saunder *Hen VI 2*
SLENDER *Merry*
SOLANIO *Merchant*
SOLINUS *Comedy*
STANLEY Lord *Rich III*
STANLEY Sir John *Hen VI 2*
STANLEY Sir William *Hen VI 3*
SYCORAX *Tempest*
THESEUS *MN Dream*
THYREUS *Antony*
TITANIA *MN Dream*
TRAVERS *Hen IV 2*
TRESSEL *Rich III*
TROILUS *Troilus*
ULYSSES *Troilus*
URSWICK Christopher *Rich III*
VALERIA *Corio*
VARRIUS *Antony, Measure*
VAUGHAN Sir Thomas *Rich III*
VELUTUS Sicinius *Corio*
WILLIAM *As You*

8

ABHORSON *Measure*
ACHILLES *Troilus*
AEMILIUS *Titus*
ANTONIUS Marcus *Julius*
AUFIDIUS Tullus *Corio*
BARDOLPH *Hen IV 1, Hen V, Merry*
BARDOLPH Lord *Hen IV 2*
BASSANIO *Merchant*
BEATRICE *Much Ado*
BEAUFORT Cardinal *Hen VI 2*
BEAUFORT Henry, Thomas *Hen VI 1*
BEAUFORT John *Hen VI 1, 2 & 3*
BELARIUS *Cymbel*
BENEDICK *Much Ado*
BENVOLIO *Romeo*

BERKELEY *Rich III*
BERKELEY Earl *Rich II*
BERNARDO *Hamlet*
BORACHIO *Much Ado*
BULLCALF Peter *Hen IV 2*
CAMPEIUS Cardinal *Hen VIII*
CANIDIUS *Antony*
CAPUCIUS *Hen VIII*
CHARMIAN *Antony*
CLAUDIUS *Hamlet, Julius*
CLIFFORD Lord *Hen VI 2 & 3*
CLIFFORD Young *Hen VI 2*
COLVILLE Sir John *Hen IV 2*
COMINIUS *Corio*
CORDELIA *Lear*
CRESSIDA *Troilus*
CROMWELL *Hen VIII*
DERCETAS *Antony*
DIOMEDES *Antony, Troilus*
DOGBERRY *Much Ado*
DON PEDRO *Much Ado*
EGLAMOUR *Two Gent*
FALSTAFF Sir John *Hen IV 1 & 2, Merry*
FASTOLFE Sir John *Hen VI 1*
FLORIZEL *Winter's*
FLUELLEN *Hen V*
GADSHILL *Hen IV 1*
GARDINER *Hen VIII*
GARGRAVE Sir Thomas *Hen VI 1*
GERTRUDE *Hamlet*
GRANDPRÉ *Hen V*
GRATIANO *Merchant, Othello*
GRIFFITH *Hen VIII*
HARCOURT *Hen IV 2*
HASTINGS Lord *Hen IV 2, Hen VI 3, Rich III*
HERMIONE *Winter's*
HUMPHREY Prince *Hen IV 2*

ISABELLA Measure
JACK CADE *Hen VI 2*
JOHN HUME *Hen VI 2*
JOURDAIN Margery *Hen VI 2*
KING JOHN *John*
KING LEAR *Lear*
LADY ANNE *Rich III*
LADY GREY *Hen VI 3*
LAWRENCE Friar *Romeo*
LEONARDO *Merchant*
LEONATUS Posthumus *Cymbel*
LIGARIUS *Julius*
LODOVICO *Othello*
LORD GREY *Rich III*
LORD ROSS *Rich II*
LUCENTIO *Taming*
LUCILIUS *Julius, Timon*
LUCULLUS *Timon*
LYSANDER *MN Dream*
MAECENAS *Antony*
MALVOLIO *Twelfth*
MARGARET *Much Ado, Rich III*
MARGARET Queen *Hen VI 1, 2 & 3*
MARULLUS *Julius*
MENELAUS *Troilus*
MENTEITH *Macbeth*
MERCUTIO *Romeo*
MONTAGUE + Lady *Romeo*
MORTIMER Edmund *Hen IV 1,*
  Hen VI 1
MORTIMER Lady *Hen IV 1*
MORTIMER Sir Hugh, Sir John
  Hen VI 3
OLD GOBBO *Merchant*
OVERDONE Mistress *Measure*
PANDARUS *Troilus*
PANDULPH Cardinal *John*
PANTHINO *Two Gent*

PAROLLES *All's Well*
PATIENCE *Hen VIII*
PERICLES *Pericles*
PHILARIO *Cymbel*
PHILEMON *Pericles*
PHILOTUS *Timon*
PINDARUS *Julius*
POLONIUS *Hamlet*
POMPEIUS Sextus *Antony*
PROSPERO *Tempest*
RAMBURES *Hen V*
RATCLIFF Sir Richard *Rich III*
REIGNIER *Hen VI 1*
REYNALDO *Hamlet*
RODERIGO *Othello*
ROSALIND *As You*
ROSALINE *Love's*
SELEUCUS *Antony*
STAFFORD Lord *Hen VI 3*
STAFFORD Sir Humphrey, William
  Hen VI 2
STEPHANO *Merchant, Tempest*
THALIARD *Pericles*
TIMANDRA *Timon*
TITINIUS *Julius*
TRINCULO *Tempest*
VIOLENTA *All's Well*
VIRGILIA *Corio*
VOLUMNIA *Corio*
WHITMORE Walter *Hen VI 2*
WILLIAMS *Hen V*

9

AGAMEMNON *Troilus*
AGUECHEEK Sir Andrew *Twelfth*
ALEXANDER *Troilus*
ANTIGONUS *Winter's*
ANTIOCHUS *Pericles*

APEMANTUS *Timon*
ARCHIBALD *Hen IV 1*
ARVIRAGUS *Cymbel*
AUTOLYCUS *Winter's*
BALTHASAR *Merchant, Much Ado, Romeo*
BALTHAZAR *Comedy*
BASSIANUS *Titus*
BIONDELLO *Taming*
BOURCHIER Cardinal *Rich III*
BRABANTIO *Othello*
CAITHNESS *Macbeth*
CASSANDRA *Troilus*
CHATILLON *John*
CLEOMENES *Winter's*
CLEOPATRA *Antony*
CONSTANCE *John*
CORNELIUS *Cymbel, Hamlet*
CYMBELINE *Cymbel*
DARDANIUS *Julius*
DEIPHOBUS *Troilus*
DEMETRIUS *Antony, MN Dream, Titus*
DESDEMONA *Othello*
DOLABELLA *Antony*
DONALBAIN *Macbeth*
ELIZABETH *Rich III*
ENOBARBUS Domitius *Antony*
ERPINGHAM Sir Thomas *Hen V*
FERDINAND *Love's, Tempest*
FITZWATER Lord *Rich II*
FLAMINIUS *Timon*
FRANCISCA *Measure*
FRANCISCO *Hamlet, Tempest*
FREDERICK *As You*
FRIAR JOHN *Romeo*
GLANSDALE Sir William *Hen VI 1*
GLENDOWER Owen *Hen IV 1*
GUIDERIUS *Cymbel*

GUILDFORD Sir Henry *Hen VIII*
HELICANUS *Pericles*
HIPPOLYTA *MN Dream*
HORTENSIO *Taming*
KATHARINA *Taming*
KATHARINE *Love's*
KATHARINE Queen *Hen VIII*
KATHERINE *Hen V*
LADY PERCY *Hen IV 1 & 2*
LORD BIGOT *John*
LORD LOVEL *Rich III*
LYCHORIDA *Pericles*
MACMORRIS *Hen V*
MAMILLIUS *Winter's*
MARCELLUS *Hamlet*
NATHANIEL Sir *Love's*
PATROCLUS *Troilus*
PETRUCHIO *Taming*
POLIXENES *Winter's*
ROTHERHAM Thomas *Rich III*
SEBASTIAN *Tempest, Twelfth*
SERVILIUS *Timon*
SIMONIDES *Pericles*
SIR PIERCE of Exton *Rich II*
SOUTHWELL John *Hen VI 2*
TEARSHEET Doll *Hen IV 2*
THERSITES *Troilus*
TREBONIUS *Julius*
VALENTINE *Titus, Twelfth, Two Gent*
VENTIDIUS *Antony, Timon*
VINCENTIO *Measure, Taming*
VOLTEMAND *Hamlet*
VOLUMNIUS *Julius*
WOODVILLE *Hen VI 1*
YOUNG CATO *Julius*

10
ALCIBIADES *Timon*

ANDROMACHE *Troilus*
ANDRONICUS Marcus, Titus *Titus*
ANNE BULLEN *Hen VIII*
ANTIPHOLUS of Ephesus, of Syracuse
  Comedy
ARCHIDAMUS *Winter's*
BARNARDINE *Measure*
BRAKENBURY Sir Robert *Rich III*
CALPHURNIA *Julius*
CORIOLANUS *Corio*
DON ADRIANO *Love's*
DUKE OF YORK *Hen V*
EARL OF KENT *Hen IV 2, Lear*
EARL RIVERS *Rich III*
EUPHRONIUS *Antony*
FORTINBRAS *Hamlet*
GOODFELLOW Robin (or Puck)
  MN Dream
HENRY PERCY *Hen IV 1 & 2, Rich II*
HOLOFERNES *Love's*
JAQUENETTA *Love's*
JOHN MORTON *Rich III*
LONGAVILLE *Love's*
LORD RIVERS *Hen VI 3*
LORD SANDYS *Hen VIII*
LORD SCALES *Hen VI 2*
LORD SCROOP Hen V
LORD TALBOT *Hen VI 1*
LYSIMACHUS *Pericles*
MARGARELON *Troilus*
MARK ANTONY *Antony*
MENECRATES *Antony*
MONTGOMERY Sir John *Hen VI 3*
PRINCE JOHN *Hen IV 1 & 2*
PROCULEIUS *Antony*
SATURNINUS *Titus*
SEMPRONIUS *Timon, Titus*
SIR MICHAEL *Hen IV 1*

SOMERVILLE Sir John *Hen VI 3*
STARVELING *MN Dream*
THOMAS WART *Hen IV 2*
TOUCHSTONE *As You*
WILLOUGHBY Lord *Rich II*

11
ABERGAVENNY Lord *Hen VIII*
ARTEMIDORUS *Julius*
BISHOP OF ELY *Hen V*
BOLINGBROKE Henry *Rich II*
BOLINGBROKE Roger *Hen VI 2*
CAIUS LUCIUS *Cymbel*
DOCTOR BUTTS *Hen VIII*
DOCTOR CAIUS *Merry*
DUKE OF MILAN *Merry*
EARL OF ESSEX *John*
EDWARD POINS *Hen IV 1 & 2*
GEORGE BEVIS *Hen VI 2*
JAMES GURNEY *John*
JOHN HOLLAND *Hen VI 2*
JOHN OF GAUNT *Rich II*
LADY CAPULET *Romeo*
LADY MACBETH *Macbeth*
LADY MACDUFF *Macbeth*
LORD MARSHAL *Rich II*
LORD MOWBRAY *Hen IV 2*
LORD STANLEY *Rich III*
MUSTARDSEED *MN Dream*
PHILOSTRATE *MN Dream*
PLANTAGENET Richard *Hen VI 1 & 2*
PRINCE HENRY *John*
QUEEN ELINOR *John*
RALPH MOULDY *Hen IV 2*
ROSENCRANTZ *Hamlet*
SIMON SHADOW *Hen IV 2*
THOMAS PERCY *Hen IV 1*
WILLIAM PAGE *Merry*

YOUNG LUCIUS *Titus*
YOUNG SIWARD *Macbeth*

TITUS LARTIUS *Corio*
WEIRD SISTERS *Macbeth*
YOUNG MARCIUS *Corio*

12

CAIUS MARCIUS *Corio*
DECIUS BRUTUS *Julius*
DUKE OF ALBANY *Lear*
DUKE OF EXETER *Hen V, Hen VI 3*
DUKE OF SURREY *Rich II*
DUKE OF VENICE *Merchant, Othello*
EARL BERKELEY *Rich II*
EARL OF OXFORD *Hen VI 3, Rich III*
EARL OF SURREY *Hen IV 2, Hen VIII,*
 Rich III
FRIAR FRANCIS *Much Ado*
GUILDENSTERN *Hamlet*
HENRY HOTSPUR *Hen IV 1*
JOHN BEAUFORT *Hen VI 1, 2 & 3*
JULIUS CAESAR *Antony, Julius*
JUNIUS BRUTUS *Corio*
KING OF FRANCE *All's Well, Lear*
LADY MONTAGUE *Romeo*
LADY MORTIMER *Hen IV 1*
LORD BARDOLPH *Hen IV 2*
LORD CLIFFORD *Hen VI 2 & 3*
LORD HASTINGS *Hen IV 2, Hen VI 3,*
 Rich III
LORD STAFFORD *Hen VI 3*
MARCUS BRUTUS *Julius*
MATTHEW GOFFE *Hen VI 2*
MISTRESS FORD *Merry*
MISTRESS PAGE *Merry*
PEASEBLOSSOM *MN Dream*
POPILIUS LENA *Julius*
SIR HUGH EVANS *Merry*
SIR NATHANIEL *Love's*
SIR TOBY BELCH *Twelfth*
THOMAS HORNER *Hen VI 2*

13

ALEXANDER IDEN *Hen VI 2*
DOLL TEARSHEET *Hen IV 2*
DUCHESS OF YORK *Rich II, Rich III*
DUKE OF ALENÇON *Hen VI 1*
DUKE OF AUMERLE *Rich II*
DUKE OF BEDFORD *Hen V, Hen VI 1*
DUKE OF BOURBON *Hen V*
DUKE OF NORFOLK *Hen VI 3,*
 Hen VIII, Rich III
DUKE OF ORLEANS *Hen V*
DUKE OF SUFFOLK *Hen VI 2, Hen VIII*
EARL OF SUFFOLK *Hen VI 1*
EARL OF WARWICK *Hen IV 2, Hen V,*
 Hen VI 1, 2 & 3
FAULCONBRIDGE *Lady, Robert John*
FRANCIS FEEBLE *Hen IV 2*
FRIAR LAWRENCE *Romeo*
HENRY BEAUFORT *Hen VI 1*
HENRY THE FIFTH *Hen V*
HENRY THE SIXTH *Hen VI 1, 2 & 3*
HUBERT DE BURGH *John*
JOAN LA PUCELLE *Hen VI 1*
JOHN SOUTHWELL *Hen VI 2*
LORD FITZWATER *Rich II*
OWEN GLENDOWER *Hen IV 1*
PETER BULLCALF *Hen IV 2*
QUEEN MARGARET *Hen VI 1, 2 & 3*
ROBERT SHALLOW *Hen IV 2*
SIR THOMAS GREY *Hen V*
THOMAS MOWBRAY *Rich II*
YOUNG CLIFFORD *Hen VI 2*

14

BAPTISTA MINOLA *Taming*
CARDINAL WOLSEY *Hen VIII*
CHRISTOPHER SLY *Taming*
DUKE OF BRITAINE *Hen V*
DUKE OF BURGUNDY *Hen V,*
  Hen VI 1, Lear
DUKE OF CORNWALL *Lear*
DUKE OF FLORENCE *All's Well*
EARL OF PEMBROKE *Hen VI 3,*
  John
EDMUND MORTIMER *Hen IV 1,*
  Hen VI 1
HENRY THE EIGHTH *Hen VIII*
HENRY THE FOURTH *Hen IV 1 & 2*
HOSTESS QUICKLY *Hen IV 1 & 2*
LAUNCELOT GOBBO *Merchant*
LORD WILLOUGHBY *Rich II*
MARCUS ANTONIUS *Julius*
METELLUS CIMBER *Julius*
NORTHUMBERLAND Lady *Hen IV 2*
OCTAVIUS CAESAR *Antony, Julius*
PHILIP OF FRANCE *John*
PRINCE HUMPHREY *Hen IV 2*
QUEEN KATHARINE *Hen VIII*
SAUNDER SIMPCOX *Hen VI 2*
SEXTUS POMPEIUS *Antony*
SIR JAMES BLOUNT *Rich III*
SIR JAMES TYRREL *Rich III*
SIR JOHN STANLEY *Hen VI 2*
SIR WALTER BLUNT *Hen IV 1 & 2*
SIR WILLIAM LUCY *Hen VI 1*
SIR WILLIAM VAUX *Hen VI 2*
THOMAS BEAUFORT *Hen VI 1*
TULLUS AUFIDIUS *Corio*
WALTER WHITMORE *Hen VI 2*

15

CHARLES THE SIXTH *Hen V*
DROMIO OF EPHESUS *Comedy*
EARL OF CAMBRIDGE *Hen V*
EARL OF SALISBURY *Hen V,*
  Hen VI 1 & 2, John, Rich II
EDMUND OF LANGLEY *Rich II*
EDWARD THE FOURTH *Rich III*
LORD ABERGAVENNY *Hen VIII*
MARGERY JOURDAIN *Hen VI 2*
MARQUIS OF DORSET *Rich III*
MENENIUS AGRIPPA *Corio*
MISTRESS QUICKLY *Merry*
PRINCE OF ARRAGON *Merchant*
PRINCE OF MOROCCO *Merchant*
RICHARD THE THIRD *Rich III*
ROBIN GOODFELLOW (or Puck)
  MN Dream
SICINIUS VELUTUS *Corio*
SIR ANTHONY DENNY *Hen VIII*
SIR HUGH MORTIMER *Hen VI 3*
SIR JOHN COLVILLE *Hen IV 2*
SIR JOHN FALSTAFF *Hen IV 1 & 2,*
  Merry
SIR JOHN FASTOLFE *Hen VI 1*
SIR JOHN MORTIMER *Hen VI 3*
SIR NICHOLAS VAUX *Hen VIII*
SIR THOMAS LOVELL *Hen VIII*
THOMAS ROTHERHAM *Rich III*
TITUS ANDRONICUS *Titus*
WILLIAM STAFFORD *Hen VI 2*

16

BASTARD OF ORLEANS *Hen VI 1*
BISHOP OF CARLISLE *Rich II*
CARDINAL BEAUFORT *Hen VI 2*
CARDINAL CAMPEIUS *Hen VIII*
CARDINAL PANDULPH *John*
DROMIO OF SYRACUSE *Comedy*

DUKE OF BUCKINGHAM *Hen VI,
    Rich III*
DUKE OF GLOUCESTER *Hen V,
    Hen VI 1*
EARL OF GLOUCESTER *Lear*
HENRY BOLINGBROKE *Rich II*
LORD CHIEF JUSTICE *Hen IV 2*
M AEMILIUS LEPIDUS *Antony, Julius*
MARCUS ANDRONICUS *Titus*
MISTRESS ANNE PAGE *Merry*
MISTRESS OVERDONE *Measure*
PHILIP THE BASTARD *John*
PRINCESS OF FRANCE *Love's*
RICHARD THE SECOND *Rich II*
ROGER BOLINGBROKE *Hen VI 2*
SIR OLIVER MARTEXT *As You*
SIR PIERCE OF EXTON *Rich II*
SIR RICHARD VERNON *Hen IV 1*
SIR STEPHEN SCROOP *Rich II*
SIR THOMAS VAUGHAN *Rich III*
SIR WALTER HERBERT *Rich III*

17

CARDINAL BOURCHIER *Rich III*
DOMITIUS ENOBARBUS *Antony*
LADY FAULCONBRIDGE *John*
LORD MAYOR OF LONDON *Rich III*
MARQUIS OF MONTAGUE *Hen VI 3*
POSTHUMUS LEONATUS *Cymbel*
SIR HENRY GUILDFORD *Hen VIII*
SIR JOHN MONTGOMERY *Hen VI 3*
SIR JOHN SOMERVILLE *Hen VI 3*

SIR THOMAS GARGRAVE *Hen VI 1*
SIR WILLIAM BRANDON *Rich III*
SIR WILLIAM CATESBY *Rich III*
SIR WILLIAM STANLEY *Hen VI 3*

18

ABBOT OF WESTMINSTER *Rich II*
CHRISTOPHER URSWICK *Rich III*
COUNTESS OF AUVERGNE *Hen VI 1*
DON ADRIANO DE ARMADO *Love's*
EARL OF WESTMORELAND
    Hen IV 1 & 2, Hen V, Hen VI 3
LADY NORTHUMBERLAND *Hen IV 2*
RICHARD PLANTAGENET
    Hen VI 1 & 2
SIR ANDREW AGUECHEEK *Twelfth*
SIR RICHARD RATCLIFF *Rich III*
SIR THOMAS ERPINGHAM *Hen V*

19

ANTIPHOLUS OF EPHESUS *Comedy*
COUNTESS OF ROUSILLON *All's Well*
DUCHESS OF GLOUCESTER *Rich II*
ROBERT FAULCONBRIDGE *John*
SIR HUMPHREY STAFFORD *Hen VI 2*
SIR ROBERT BRAKENBURY *Rich III*
SIR WILLIAM GLANSDALE *Hen VI 1*

20

ANTIPHOLUS OF SYRACUSE *Comedy*
EARL OF NORTHUMBERLAND
    Hen IV 2, Hen VI 3

Arts – Literature – PLAY TITLES

3

FEN C Churchill
ION Euripides
RUR Capek
SUS Keeffe

4

AJAX Gide, Sophocles
BAAL Brecht
BENT Sherman
FAME A Miller
GOOD CP Taylor
HOME Storey
IRIS Pinero
KEAN Sartre
LEAR Bond
LENZ Büchner
LOOT Orton
NOT I Beckett
PIAF Gems
PLAY Beckett
QUAD Beckett
ROPE Hamilton
ROSS Rattigan
VERA Wilde
ZACK Brighouse

5

ASHES Rudkin
BETZI Douglas-Home
BRAND Ibsen
CINNA Corneille
EH JOE Beckett
ENJOY Alan Bennett
EQUUS P Shaffer

FAUST Goethe
GREEK Berkoff
HELEN Euripides
LE CID Corneille
LIOLA Pirandello
MEDEA Euripides, Seneca
MÉDÉE Anouilh
POLLY Gay
ROOTS Wesker
SAVED Bond
TANYA Arbuzov
THARK Travers
YERMA Lorca

6

ADVENT Strindberg
ANDRIA Terence
BECKET Anouilh
BREATH Beckett
BUTLEY S Gray
CLIZIA Machiavelli
CLOUDS Frayn
DRY ROT J Chapman
EASTER Strindberg
EGMONT Goethe
EMBERS Beckett
ESCAPE Galsworthy
EXILED Galsworthy
EXILES Joyce
GENEVA GB Shaw
GHOSTS Ibsen
HAMLET Shakespeare
IVANOV Chekhov
LUTHER Osborne
MÉLITE Corneille

MOTHER Capek
ONDINE Giraudoux
ORPHÉE Cocteau
OWNERS C Churchill
PHÈDRE Racine
PLENTY Hare
PRAVDA Hare & Brenton
SALOMÉ Wilde
SLEUTH A Shaffer
STRIFE Galsworthy
TARARE Beaumarchais
UBU ROI Jarry
WELDED O'Neill

7

ALL OVER Albee
AMADEUS P Shaffer
ARCADIA Stoppard
ATHALIE Racine
CALVARY Yeats
CANDIDA GB Shaw
CLAVIGO Goethe
DEIRDRE Yeats
DESTINY Edgar
ELECTRA Euripides,
  Sophocles
ENDGAME Beckett
ENEMIES Gorky
EPICENE Jonson
EUGÉNIE Beaumarchais
HAPGOOD Stoppard
JUMPERS Stoppard
JUSTICE Galsworthy
KNUCKLE Hare
MACBETH Shakespeare

MARTINE Bernard
OEDIPUS Seneca
OLEANNA Mamet
ORESTES Euripides
OTHELLO Shakespeare
OUR TOWN T Wilder
PHAEDRA Seneca
PIMPLES Bleasdale
PIZARRO Sheridan
PLUNDER Travers
REVENGE Brenton
ROCKABY Beckett
SEJANUS Jonson
SHEPPEY Maugham
SILENCE Pinter
THE BEAR Chekhov
THE LARK (or *L'Alouette*)
   Anouilh
THE ROCK TS Eliot
THE ROOM Pinter
VERDICT Christie
VICTORY Barker
VOLPONE Jonson
WOYZECK Büchner
YONADAB P Shaffer

8

ALCESTIS Euripides
ANTIGONE Anouilh,
   Cocteau, Sophocles
BÉRÉNICE Racine
BETRAYAL Pinter
CATALINA Ibsen
CLARENCE Tarkington
CRACKERS Bleasdale
DUTCHMAN Baraka
FOCO NOVO Pomerance
GASLIGHT Hamilton

HAY FEVER Coward
IRONHAND Arden
KATHLEEN Babe
KING JOHN Shakespeare
KING LEAR Shakespeare
LAKEBOAT Mamet
LE BALCON (or *The
   Balcony*) Genet
LE DINDON (or *Sauce
   for the Goose*) Feydeau
MARY ROSE Barrie
OLD TIMES Pinter
OPERETTE Coward
PEER GYNT Ibsen
PENELOPE Maugham
PETER PAN Barrie
PLATONOV Chekhov
SALONIKA Page
SKYLIGHT Hare
STEAMING Dunn
TARTUFFE Molière
TEA PARTY Pinter
THE BIRDS Aristophanes
THE CENCI Shelley
THE FLIES (or *Les
   Mouches*) Sartre
THE FROGS Aristophanes
THE MAIDS (or *Les
   Bonnes*) Genet
THE ROVER Behn
THE SHAWL Mamet
THE TANGO Mrozek
THE TUTOR Brecht
THE VISIT Dürrenmatt
THE WASPS
   Aristophanes
TOP GIRLS C Churchill
WRECKERS Edgar

9

AGAMEMNON
   Aeschylus, Berkoff
ALL MY SONS A Miller
A NIGHT OUT Pinter
BILLY LIAR Hall &
   Waterhouse
BLOOD KNOT Fugard
CAVALCADE Coward
CITY SUGAR Poliakoff
CYMBELINE Shakespeare
DANDY DICK Pinero
DIE RÄUBER (or *The
   Robbers*) Schiller
DIRTY WORK Travers
ELIZABETH Fo
FLAREPATH Rattigan
GETTING ON Alan
   Bennett
HAPPY DAYS Beckett
INDIAN INK Stoppard
IPHIGÉNIE Goethe,
   Racine
L'ALOUETTE (or *The
   Lark*) Anouilh
LA SAUVAGE (or *Restless
   Heart*) Anouilh
LES BONNES (or *The
   Maids*) Genet
LISTENING Albee
LUNCH HOUR Mortimer
MISS JULIE Strindberg
MR WHATNOT
   Ayckbourn
NOISES OFF Frayn
OVERHEARD Ustinov
OVERRULED GB Shaw
PARTY TIME Pinter

PHILASTER Beaumont & Fletcher
POETASTER Jonson
PYGMALION GB Shaw
QUADRILLE Coward
SAINT JOAN GB Shaw
SANTA CRUZ Frisch
SQUIRRELS Mamet
THE CASTLE Barker
THE CHAIRS Ionesco
THE CIRCLE Maugham
THE CLOUDS Aristophanes
THE CRITIC Sheridan
THE DEVILS Whiting
THE FATHER Strindberg
THE LESSON Ionesco
THE RIVALS Sheridan
THE VORTEX Coward
TOM AND VIV Hastings
WHITE LIES P Shaffer

10
ACT OF UNION Finnegan
ALCIBIADES Otway
ALL FOR LOVE Dryden
AMPHITRYON Giraudoux, Plautus
ANDROMACHE Euripides, Racine
AURENG-ZEBE Dryden
BORSTAL BOY Behan
CAMINO REAL T Williams
CHAPTER TWO Simon
CONFUSIONS Ayckbourn
CORIOLANUS Shakespeare
CURTMANTLE Fry
DEAR BRUTUS Barrie
DIRTY LINEN Stopppard
EAST OF SUEZ Maugham
EASY VIRTUE Coward
GENTLE JACK Bolt

GHOST TRAIN Ridley
GUSTAF VASA Strindberg
HIPPOLYTUS Euripides
INTERMEZZO Giraudoux
JAKE'S WOMEN Simon
LES MOUCHES (or *The Flies*) Sartre
LYSISTRATA Aristophanes
MARY STUART (or *Maria Stuart*)
   Schiller
OEDIPUS REX Sophocles
ON THE ROCKS GB Shaw
PLAZA SUITE Simon
PURPLE DUST O'Casey
RHINOCEROS Ionesco
TEMPTATION Havel
THE BACCHAE Euripides
THE BALCONY (or *Le Balcon*) Genet
THE CHANCES Fletcher
THE DRESSER Harwood
THE DYNASTS Hardy
THE HOSTAGE Behan
THE KITCHEN Wesker
THE OLD ONES Wesker
THE RELAPSE Vanbrugh
THE ROBBERS (or *Die Räuber*) Schiller
THE SANDBOY Frayn
THE SEAGULL Chekhov
THE TEMPEST Shakespeare
THE WEDDING Chekhov
TRAVESTIES Stoppard
TURKEY TIME Travers
UNCLE VANYA Chekhov
WEST OF SUEZ Osborne

11
A DOLL'S HOUSE Ibsen
ALL FALL DOWN Arden
ALL THAT FALL Beckett

A SLIGHT ACHE Pinter
AS YOU LIKE IT Shakespeare
BENEFACTORS Frayn
BITTER SWEET Coward
BLACK COFFEE Christie
BRITANNICUS Racine
CATASTROPHE Beckett
CELEBRATION Pinter
DEAR OCTOPUS D Smith
HEDDA GABLER Ibsen
IBSEN'S GHOST Barrie
IT IS WRITTEN Dürrenmatt
JOKING APART Ayckbourn
JOURNEY'S END Sherriff
LES DEUX AMIS (or *The Two Friends*)
  Beaumarchais
LITTLE EYOLF Ibsen
LOVE FOR LOVE Congreve
LOVE IN A WOOD Wycherley
LOVE'S COMEDY Ibsen
MARIA STUART (or *Mary Stuart*)
  Schiller
MISALLIANCE GB Shaw
NIGHT AND DAY Stoppard
PANDORA'S BOX Wedekind
PHILOCTETES Sophocles
PHOTO FINISH Ustinov
RACING DEMON Hare
ROOKERY NOOK Travers
ROSMERSHOLM Ibsen
TAKING STEPS Ayckbourn
TAMBURLAINE Marlowe
THE BANKRUPT Ostrovsky
THE BOY DAVID Barrie
THE CRUCIBLE A Miller
THE GAMBLERS Stoppard
THE HOTHOUSE Pinter
THE PERSIANS Aeschylus

THE PROPOSAL Chekhov
THE SKIN GAME Galsworthy
THE STRONGER Strindberg
THE TAX EXILE P Gems
THE WILD DUCK Ibsen
THE ZOO STORY Albee
TIME PRESENT Osborne
WAY UPSTREAM Ayckbourn
WOMAN IN MIND Ayckbourn

12

A FAIR QUARREL Middleton & Rowley
AFTER THE FALL A Miller
A MAN OF HONOUR Maugham
ANNA CHRISTIE O'Neill
ASHES TO ASHES Pinter
AUTUMN CROCUS D Smith
BEDROOM FARCE Ayckbourn
BLITHE SPIRIT Coward
BLOOD WEDDING Lorca
BORIS GODUNOV Pushkin
BUSSY D'AMBOIS G Chapman
CAUSE CÉLÈBRE Rattigan
CHARLEY'S AUNT B Thomas
DOCTOR BOLFRY Bridie
DONKEY'S YEARS Frayn
FALLEN ANGELS Coward
FAMILY VOICES Pinter
FORTY YEARS ON Alan Bennett
FUNERAL GAMES Orton
GOOSE PIMPLES Leigh
HABEAS CORPUS Alan Bennett
IT'S A MADHOUSE Bleasdale
JULIUS CAESAR Shakespeare
LA MANDRAGOLA Machiavelli
LES PLAIDEURS (or *The Litigants*)
  Racine
MAJOR BARBARA GB Shaw

MAKE AND BREAK Frayn
MAKING TRACKS Ayckbourn
MISTERO BUFFO Fo
ONE FOR THE POT Cooney
PRIVATE LIVES Coward
SARDANAPALUS Byron
SIMPLE SPYMEN J Chapman
STAGS AND HENS W Russell
STUFF HAPPENS Hare
THE ALCHEMIST Jonson
THE ANATOMIST Bridie
THE APPLE CART GB Shaw
THE BORDERERS Wordsworth
THE BROKEN JUG Kleist
THE CARETAKER Pinter
THE DOCK BRIEF Mortimer
THE EMIGRANTS Mrozek
THE EUMENIDES Aeschylus
THE HOUR GLASS Yeats
THE LITIGANTS (or *Les Plaideurs*)
   Racine
THE MOUSETRAP Christie
THE ODD COUPLE Simon
THE PUBLIC EYE P Shaffer
THE SILVER BOX Galsworthy
THE WOOD DEMON Chekhov
THE YOUNG IDEA Coward
TOTAL ECLIPSE Hampton
TRANSLATIONS Friel
TWELFTH NIGHT Shakespeare
TYRANNIC LOVE Dryden
ZIGGER ZAGGER Terson

13

ABIGAIL'S PARTY Leigh
ABSENT FRIENDS Ayckbourn
AFTER MAGRITTE Stoppard
AFTER THE DANCE Rattigan

A KIND OF ALASKA Pinter
A PATRIOT FOR ME Osborne
ARMS AND THE MAN GB Shaw
A TASTE OF HONEY Delaney
A WINTER COMEDY Fry
BLOOD BROTHERS W Russell
DESERT HIGHWAY Priestley
DOCTOR FAUSTUS Marlowe
EDUCATING RITA W Russell
FIDDLERS THREE Christie
GOODBYE HOWARD Linney
HENRY THE FIFTH Shakespeare
HENRY THE SIXTH (Part I, II & III)
   Shakespeare
HOBSON'S CHOICE Brighouse
HOTEL PARADISO Feydeau
IN CELEBRATION Storey
LABURNUM GROVE Priestley
LA VOIX HUMAINE (or *The Human
   Voice*) Cocteau
LE MISANTHROPE (or *The
   Misanthrope*) Molière
LOST IN YONKERS Simon
MADE IN BANGKOK Minghella
MARCO MILLIONS O'Neill
NIGHT MUST FALL E Williams
ONE FOR THE ROAD Pinter
ON THE HIGH ROAD Chekhov
PRESS CUTTINGS GB Shaw
QUALITY STREET Barrie
RESTLESS HEART (or *La Sauvage*)
   Anouilh
TEN TIMES TABLE Ayckbourn
THE ACHARNIANS Aristophanes
THE AMEN CORNER Baldwin
THE CHANGELING Middleton &
   Rowley
THE COLLECTION Pinter

THE DUMB WAITER Pinter
THE HUMAN VOICE (or *La Voix humaine*) Cocteau
THE INSECT PLAY Capek
THE JEW OF MALTA Marlowe
THE KINGFISHER Douglas-Home
THE LINDEN TREE Priestley
THE MAGISTRATE Pinero
THE MATCHMAKER T Wilder
THE OLD COUNTRY Alan Bennett
THE PRIVATE EAR P Shaffer
THE ROSE TATTOO T Williams
THE SPIDER'S WEB Christie
THE TWIN RIVALS Farquhar
THE TWO FOSCARI Byron
THE TWO FRIENDS (or *Les Deux Amis*) Beaumarchais
THE WHITE DEVIL Webster
THE WINSLOW BOY Rattigan
TIMON OF ATHENS Shakespeare
TORQUATO TASSO Goethe
UNDER MILK WOOD D Thomas
VENUS OBSERVED Fry

14

AFORE NIGHT COME Rudkin
AN IDEAL HUSBAND Wilde
A PIECE OF MY MIND Nichols
BOESMAN AND LENA Fugard
BOSTON MARRIAGE Mamet
GETTING MARRIED GB Shaw
GREAT CATHERINE GB Shaw
HENRY THE EIGHTH Shakespeare
HENRY THE FOURTH (Part I & II) Shakespeare
KRAPP'S LAST TAPE Beckett
LOVE AND A BOTTLE Farquhar
MAN AND SUPERMAN GB Shaw

RELATIVE VALUES Coward
RIDERS TO THE SEA Synge
ROMEO AND JULIET Shakespeare
SEPARATE TABLES Rattigan
THE CORN IS GREEN E Williams
THE COUNTRY GIRL Odets
THE COUNTRY WIFE Wycherley
THE DEEP BLUE SEA Rattigan
THE ENTERTAINER Osborne
THE FIRE RAISERS Frisch
THE GHOST SONATA Strindberg
THE LITTLE FOXES Hellman
THE LOWER DEPTHS Gorky
THE LUCKY CHANCE Behn
THE MAN FROM HOME Tarkington
THE MISANTHROPE (or *Le Misanthrope*) Molière
THE OLD BACHELOR Congreve
THE PHILANDERER GB Shaw
THE PLAIN DEALER Wycherley
THE QUARE FELLOW Behan
THE SON OF LIGHT Rudkin
THE TROJAN WOMEN Euripides
THE WINTER'S TALE Shakespeare
THIS HAPPY BREED Coward
TOAD OF TOAD HALL Milne
VENICE PRESERV'D Otway
WIDOWERS' HOUSES GB Shaw
WITHIN THE GATES O'Casey
WURZEL-FLUMMERY Milne

15

AMERICAN BUFFALO Mamet
BARTHOLOMEW FAIR Jonson
CALIFORNIA SUITE Simon
DANGEROUS CORNER Priestley
DESIGN FOR LIVING Coward
DOWN THE DOCK ROAD Bleasdale

EACH IN HIS OWN WAY Pirandello
EDWARD THE SECOND Marlowe
FLOWERING CHERRY Bolt
HEARTBREAK HOUSE GB Shaw
IN FIVE YEARS' TIME Lorca
LOOK BACK IN ANGER Osborne
MARRIAGE À LA MODE Dryden
MURMURING JUDGES Hare
PAID ON BOTH SIDES Auden
PRESENT LAUGHTER Coward
RICHARD CORK'S LEG Behan
RICHARD THE THIRD Shakespeare
SHOOTING THE PAST Poliakoff
SPRING AWAKENING Wedekind
TAKEN IN MARRIAGE Babe
THE AMOROUS PRAWN Kimmins
THE BEGGAR'S OPERA Gay
THE CONSTANT WIFE Maugham
THE DEVIL IS AN ASS Jonson
THE DOUBLE-DEALER Congreve
THE ICEMAN COMETH O'Neill
THE MAN OF DESTINY GB Shaw
THE POPE'S WEDDING Bond
THE PROVOKED WIFE Vanbrugh
THE SAVAGE PARADE A Shaffer
THE SILVER TASSIE O'Casey
THE SUNSHINE BOYS Simon
THE THREE SISTERS Chekhov
TITUS ANDRONICUS Shakespeare
TWO NOBLE KINSMEN Shakespeare
VASSA SHELESNOVA Gorky
WAITING FOR GODOT Beckett
WATCH IT COME DOWN Osborne
WATCH ON THE RHINE Hellman
YOU NEVER CAN TELL GB Shaw

16
A CUCKOO IN THE NEST Travers

A MOUTHFUL OF BIRDS C Churchill
AN INSPECTOR CALLS Priestley
BACK TO METHUSELAH GB Shaw
BEYOND THE HORIZON O'Neill
CAT ON A HOT TIN ROOF T Williams
LOVE'S LABOUR'S LOST Shakespeare
NIGHT OF THE IGUANA T Williams
RICHARD THE SECOND Shakespeare
SAUCE FOR THE GOOSE (or *Le Dindon*) Feydeau
SHIRLEY VALENTINE W Russell
THE BIRTHDAY PARTY Pinter
THE COAST OF UTOPIA Stoppard
THE COCKTAIL PARTY TS Eliot
THE WAY OF THE WORLD Congreve
WHAT THE BUTLER SAW Orton

17
A MAN FOR ALL SEASONS Bolt
LE MARIAGE DE FIGARO (or *The Marriage of Figaro*) Beaumarchais
MEASURE FOR MEASURE Shakespeare
ROMANOFF AND JULIET Ustinov
THE BEAUX' STRATAGEM Farquhar
THE COMEDY OF ERRORS
    Shakespeare
THE DEVIL'S DISCIPLE GB Shaw
THE DOCTOR'S DILEMMA GB Shaw
THE DUCHESS OF MALFI Webster
THE GLASS MENAGERIE T Williams
THE LITTLE MINISTER Barrie
THE PHILANTHROPIST Hampton
THE SPANISH TRAGEDY Kyd

18
ANTONY AND CLEOPATRA
    Shakespeare
FRENCH WITHOUT TEARS Rattigan

LADY WINDERMERE'S FAN Wilde
LE BARBIER DE SÉVILLE (or *The Barber
of Seville*) Beaumarchais
THE BARBER OF SEVILLE (or *Le Barbier
de Séville*) Beaumarchais
THE NORMAN CONQUESTS
Ayckbourn
THE THREEPENNY OPERA Brecht
THE UNEXPECTED GUEST Christie
TROILUS AND CRESSIDA Shakespeare

19
ANDROCLES AND THE LION
GB Shaw
CHIPS WITH EVERYTHING Wesker
EVERY MAN IN HIS HUMOUR Jonson
THE DEATH OF CUCHULAIN Yeats
THE MARRIAGE OF FIGARO (or *Le
Mariage de Figaro*) Beaumarchais
THE MERCHANT OF VENICE
Shakespeare

THE SCHOOL FOR SCANDAL
Sheridan
THE TAMING OF THE SHREW
Shakespeare

20
ALL'S WELL THAT ENDS WELL
Shakespeare
A WOMAN OF NO IMPORTANCE
Wilde
BRIGHTON BEACH MEMOIRS Simon
HOW THE OTHER HALF LOVES
Ayckbourn
JOHN BULL'S OTHER ISLAND
GB Shaw
MRS WARREN'S PROFESSION
GB Shaw
MURDER IN THE CATHEDRAL TS Eliot
PERICLES, PRINCE OF TYRE
Shakespeare
THE RECRUITING OFFICER Farquhar

Arts – Literature – POEM TITLES

3
BAT Lawrence
EVE Hodgson
FOG Sandburg
GOG Hughes
MAY Barnes
NAN Masefield
NOW Thwaite
WAR Apollinaire, Dryden
YES Joyce

4
ALMA Prior
CROW Hughes
DAWN Lorca
DAYS Larkin
DIDO Ashbery
DUST Brooke
HERE Larkin, RS Thomas
JEAN Burns
LARA Byron
LOVE Coleridge

MAUD Tennyson
ODES Horace, Pindar
PIKE Hughes
POEM Armitage
RAIN E Thomas
SAUL Browning
SNOW Macneice
SONG Donne
THAW E Thomas
THEY RS Thomas
WIND Hughes, Fenton

5
AARON Herbert
A COAT Yeats
A SONG Shakespeare
ATLAS Fanthorpe
A WAVE Ashbery
BABEL De La Mare
BOOKS Crabbe
BOOTS Kipling
CAIRO Thwaite
COMUS Milton
DADDY Plath
DAISY Thompson
DELAY Jennings
DORIS Congreve
DRAKE Noyes
ELEGY Gray
EVANS RS Thomas
FANCY Keats
FOOLS Jonson
GOING Larkin
GREEN Barnes
HÉLAS! Wilde
ILIAD Homer
IMAGE Hulme
ITALY Byron
LAMIA Keats
LIMBO Coleridge
PIANO Lawrence
ROADS E Thomas
SNAKE Lawrence
TOADS Larkin
TOMMY Kipling
WANTS Larkin
WATER Larkin
WORDS Plath
YPRES Binyon
ZIMIR Dryden

6
A DITTY Sidney
ADVICE Bierce
A FEVER Donne
AFRICA Plutarch
ANGELS Abse
APPLES Swift
ARABIA De La Mare
ASLEEP Owen
ATTACK Sassoon
AUGUST Macneice
AUTUMN De La Mare
BADGER Clare
BEAUTY Sappho
BRAHMA Emerson
CANTOS Pound
CLOUDS Brooke
COMING Larking
DAPHNE Lyly
DREAMS Breton
DUBLIN Macneice
HASSAN Flecker
HUNGER Binyon
LAMENT Flint
LEAVES Binyon
LESBIA Catullus
LONDON Blake, Jonson
MARINA Eliot
MILTON Blake
NATURE Emerson
ONE ART Bishop
OXFORD Lovatt-
  Williams
RETURN Cavafy
RÌZPAH Tennyson
SENLIN Aiken
SLOUGH Betjeman
SPLEEN Baudelaire

THE ANT Nash
THE DAY Fuller
TOKENS Barnes
UPHILL C Rossetti
WOLVES Macneice

7
ABISHAG Rilke
ADONAIS Shelley
ALASTOR Shelley
AMERICA Ginsberg
ANIMULA Eliot
ARCADES Milton
AT GRASS Larkin
A VISION Clare
A WREATH Herbert
BEOWULF ?
BIRCHES Frost
BRUMANA Flecker
CAELICA Greville
CALAMUS Whitman
CARGOES Masefield
CHICAGO Sandburg
DOLORES Swinburne
DON JUAN Byron
ELEGIES Donne
FATIGUE Belloc
FLORIDA Abse
FOREVER Carver
INFERNO Dante
IT RAINS E Thomas
JANUARY RS Thomas
KILMENY Hogg
LEISURE Davies
LEPANTO Chesterton
LIMITED Sandburg
LULLABY Auden
LYCIDAS Milton

187

MANFRED Auden
MARIANA Eliot
MARMION Scott
MAZEPPA Byron
MICHAEL Wordsworth
MISS GEE Auden
MISS LOO De La Mare
MISSING Auden
MORNING Clare
MUSEUMS Macneice
NEW YORK Lorca
NOTHING Fenton
OCTOBER D Thomas
ODYSSEY Homer
PAULINE Browning
REMAINS Greville
SERIOUS Fenton
SHINGLE Nicholson
SONNETS Shakespeare
SUCCESS Brooke
TARTARY De La Mare
THE BAIT Donne
THE BARD Gray
THE BULL Hodgson
THE CALL Mew
THE DEAD Brooke
THE FLEA Donne
THE HILL Brooke
THE LAMB Blake
THE OXEN Hardy
THE PIKE Hughes
THE SKIP Fenton
THE TASK Cowper
THE TOYS Patmore
TO A LADY Pope
TZIGANY Pushkin
ULYSSES Tennyson
UP THERE Auden

WARNING Joseph

8

A PEASANT RS Thomas
A RAPTURE Carew
AUGURIES Blake
CADENCES Flint
CUT GRASS Larkin
DISABLED Owen
ENDYMION Keats
FAIR INES Hood
FAREWELL A Brontë
FERN HILL D Thomas
FULL MOON Sappho
FUTILITY Owen
GEDICHTE Heine
GOD, A POEM Fenton
GUNGA DIN Kipling
HESPERUS Clare
HIAWATHA Longfellow
HUDIBRAS Butler
HYPERION Keats
I SAW A MAN Crane
ISABELLA Keats
KANGAROO Lawrence
L'ALLEGRO Milton
LUCY GRAY Wordsworth
LUPERCAL Hughes
MALACODA Beckett
MANDALAY Kipling
MILKMAID Lee
MRS AESOP Duffy
MRS BEAST Duffy
ONE FLESH Jennings
PARADISO Dante
POLITICS Yeats
POOR POLL Bridges
PORTRAIT Cummings

PRELUDES Eliot
PROSPICE Browning
RELIGION Vaughan
SEA FEVER Masefield
SELF-PITY Lawrence
SNOWDROP Hughes
SORDELLO Browning
THE ALTAR Herbert
THE BRIDE Lawrence
THE CLOUD Shelley
THE CURSE Berryman
THE DREAM Donne
THE GHOST De La Mare
THE GLORY E Thomas
THE GLOVE Browning
THE HEART Crane
THE MOUND Hardy
THE PEARL Herbert
THE RAVEN Poe
THE RELIC Donne
THE ROVER Scott
THE SNAIL Lovelace
THE SWARM Plath
THE TAXIS Macneice
THE TYGER Blake
THE WORLD Raine,
   Vaughan
THE WOUND Gunn
THE YACHT Catullus
THISTLES Hughes
TO A MOUSE Burns
TO AUTUMN Keats
VALUABLE Smith

9

A BOY'S WILL Frost
ADLESTROP E Thomas
ALMSWOMEN Blunden

A PASSER-BY Bridges
A PASTORAL Daniel
BIOGRAPHY Masefield
BLOODY MEN Cope
BYZANTIUM Yeats
CELANDINE E Thomas
CHRISTMAS Betjeman
CYPRESSES Lawrence
DEJECTION Coleridge
EAST COKER Eliot
EXCELSIOR Longfellow
EXECUTIVE Betjeman
FIAMMETTA Boccaccio
GERONTION Eliot
GROWING UP Fanthorpe
HER PRAISE Yeats
JERUSALEM Blake, Fenton
KUBLA KHAN Coleridge
LAST LINES E Brontë
MARRIAGES Thwaite
MIDDLESEX Betjeman
MID-WINTER Rossetti
MONT BLANC Shelley
MOONLIGHT Apollinaire
MR BLEANEY Larkin
MRS MALONE Farjeon
NIGHT MAIL Auden
ROSABELLE Scott
ROSALYNDE Lodge
RURAL LIFE Crabbe
SKUNK HOUR Lowell
SNOW-BOUND Whittier
THE CHOICE Herbert
THE DONKEY Chesterton
THE 'EATHEN Kipling
THE EXILES Auden
THE GARDEN Marvell
THE HORSES Muir

THE OUTLAW Scott
THE PULLEY Herbert
THE TEMPLE Herbert
VALENTINE Duffy

10
AE FOND KISS Burns
ANNABEL LEE Poe
ARS POETICA Macleish
BRIGHT STAR Keats
CASABLANCA Hemans
CHERRY RIPE Campion
CHRISTABEL Coleridge
CORRUPTION Vaughan
CRADLE SONG Macneice
DESIDERATA Ehrmann
DOVER BEACH Arnold
ENOCH ARDEN
  Tennyson
EVANGELINE Longfellow
FAMOUS POET Hughes
GENTILESSE Chaucer
GETHSEMANE Kipling
HESPERIDES Herrick
IN A GONDOLA
  Browning
IN MEMORIAM
  Tennyson, E Thomas
IN TENEBRIS Hardy
JOHN GILPIN Cowper
LONDON SNOW Bridges
MAN AND WIFE Lowell
MUTABILITY Wordsworth
NEXT, PLEASE Larkin
OZYMANDIAS Shelley
PIED BEAUTY Hopkins
POLY-OLBION Drayton
PROMETHEUS Goethe

PURGATORIO Dante
ROSE AYLMER Landor
ST AGNES EVE Tennyson
STILL I RISE Angelou
TARANTELLA Belloc
THE BOROUGH Crabbe
THE COOL WEB Graves
THE CORSAIR Byron
THE DUNCIAD Pope
THE ECSTASY Donne
THE FLOWERS Kipling
THE FUNERAL Donne
THE GENERAL Sassoon
THE LAST LAP Kipling
THE PANTHER Rilke
THE PRELUDE
  Wordsworth
THE RETREAT Vaughan
THE SCHOLAR Southey
THE SEASONS Thomson
THE SKATERS Ashbery
THE SOLDIER Brooke
THE TEMPEST Vaughan
THE VILLAGE Crabbe
TO THE MUSES Blake
UP THE RHINE Hood
VIEW OF A PIG Hughes
WHOROSCOPE Beckett

11
A LOVER'S PLEA
  Campion
AND YOU, HELEN
  Hughes
A RED RED ROSE Burns
AURORA LEIGH Barrett-
  Browning
BASE DETAILS Sassoon

CHURCH GOING Larkin
CLAIR DE LUNE Verlaine
DANNY DEEVER Kipling
DUBLINESQUE Larkin
FELIX RANDAL Hopkins
HIGH WINDOWS Larkin
HOME IS SO SAD Larkin
IL PENSEROSO Milton
INTIMATIONS Wordsworth
JABBERWOCKY Carroll
JODRELL BANK P Dickinson
LADY LAZARUS Plath
MAC-FLECKNOE Dryden
MARY MORISON Burns
MATLOCK BATH Betjeman
MEN AND WOMEN Browning
MORNING SONG Plath
MR APPOLINAX Eliot
MRS TIRESIAS Duffy
NICHOLAS NYE De La Mare
OCTOBER DAWN Hughes
ON BEN JONSON Shakespeare
ON MERE BEING Stevens
PETER GRIMES Crabbe
PIPPA PASSES Browning
RESIGNATION Chatterton
SCAFELL PIKE Nicholson
SCOTS WHA HAE Burns
SISTER HELEN Rossetti
SONG TO CELIA Jonson
STONY LIMITS Macdiarmid
TALL NETTLES Larkin, E Thomas
TAM O'SHANTER Burns
THE BAD THING Wain
THE BALL POEM Berryman
THE CASTAWAY Cowper
THE COLOSSUS Plath
THE DESERTER Housman

THE FOUR ZOAS Blake
THE HOCK CART Herrick
THE JUMBLIES Lear
THE OLD FOOLS Larkin
THE RUBAIYAT Omar Khayyám
THE SICK ROSE Blake
THE SUNSHADE Hardy
THE TWO TREES Yeats
THE VAGABOND Stevenson
TO AN OLD LADY Empson
TO DAFFODILS Herrick
VIRGIL'S GNAT Spenser

12
ABOU BEN ADHEM Hunt
ABOVE THE DOCK Hulme
A GAME OF CHESS Eliot
AIR AND ANGELS Donne
ANCIENT MUSIC Pound
AN ESSAY ON MAN Pope
ASH WEDNESDAY Eliot
AULD LANG SYNE Burns
BAGPIPE MUSIC Macneice
BLACK JACKETS Gunn
BLOOD AND LEAD Fenton
BONNIE LESLEY Burns
CHILDE HAROLD Byron
DEATH AND LOVE Jonson
DEATH BY WATER Eliot
DOES IT MATTER Sassoon
DRUMMER HODGE Hardy
DUINO ELEGIES Rilke
EPITHALAMION Spenser
EVERYONE SANG Sassoon
FAREWELL LOVE Wyatt
FLOWER-DE-LUCE Tennyson
HA'NACKER HILL Belloc
HAWK ROOSTING Hughes

HOLY THURSDAY Blake
INFANT SORROW Blake
LE BATEAU IVRE Rimbaud
LOCKSLEY HALL Tennyson
LOVE AND SLEEP Swinburne
LOVE'S ALCHEMY Donne
LOVE'S FAREWLL Drayton
MAGGIE LAUDER Burns
MEG MERRILIES Keats
MORTE D'ARTHUR Tennyson
NOBLE NUMBERS Herrick
NO SECOND TROY Yeats
OLD FURNITURE Hardy
OUT OF THE EAST Fenton
PARADISE LOST Milton
PIERS PLOWMAN Langland
PROTHALAMION Spenser
RABBI BEN EZRA Browning
REINEKE FUCHS Goethe
RENOUNCEMENT Maynell
SCOTS UNBOUND Macdiarmid
SONG OF MYSELF Whitman
SWEET CONTENT Dekker
THE ALBATROSS Herbert
THE BLACKBIRD Drinkwater
THE COOK'S TALE Chaucer
THE EXCURSION Wordsworth
THE EXPLOSION Larkin
THE FISHERMAN Yeats
THE HOLLOW MEN Eliot
THE HOURGLASS Jonson
THE LONG TRAIL Kipling
THE MONK'S TALE Chaucer
THE QUIET LIFE Pope
THE TRAVELLER Berryman
THE WASTE LAND Eliot
THE WINDHOVER Hopkins
THE WITNESSES Auden

TINTERN ABBEY Wordsworth
TULLOCHGORUM Burns
VITAI LAMPADA Newbolt
YELLOW TULIPS Fenton

13

AN ARUNDEL TOMB Larkin
A SEASON IN HELL Rimbaud
A SUPPLICATION Wyatt
AUTUMN JOURNAL Macneice
BINSEY POPLARS Hopkins
CHANNEL FIRING Hardy
DOCKERY AND SON Larkin
EPIPSYCHIDION Shelley
FATHER WILLIAM Carroll
FÊTES GALANTES Verlaine
FOR SAINT PETER Fanthorpe
HOUSEBOAT DAYS Ashbery
IN PARENTHESIS Jones
INSENSIBILITY Owen
JAMES HONEYMAN Auden
LEAVES OF GRASS Whitman
LINES ON MILTON Dryden
LITTLE GIDDING Eliot
LONG-LEGGED FLY Yeats
METAMORPHOSES Ovid
MINSTREL'S SONG Chatterton
MY LAST DUCHESS Browning
NAMING OF PARTS Reed
NEW YEAR LETTER Auden
NORTH OF BOSTON Frost
NOT MY BEST SIDE Fanthorpe
ODE TO A SKYLARK Shelley,
    Wordsworth
ON WENLOCK EDGE Housman
PASTORAL POESY Clare
REYNARD THE FOX Masefield
RULE BRITANNIA Thomson

SUBURBAN DREAM Muir
THE APPARITION Donne
THE CHERRY TREE Housman
THE CLERK'S TALE Chaucer
THE CLOTHES PIT Dunn
THE DREAM SONGS Berryman
THE EMBANKMENT Hulme
THE FIRE SERMON Eliot
THE FRIAR'S TALE Chaucer
THE GIFTS OF GOD Herbert
THE HIGHWAYMAN Noyes
THE INVITATION Shelley
THE QUEEN'S WAKE Hogg
THE REEVE'S TALE Chaucer
THE RHINOCEROS Nash
THE RUINED MAID Hardy
THE UNNAMEABLE Thwaite
TO MY VALENTINE Nash
VERS DE SOCIÉTÉ Larkin
WELSH INCIDENT Graves
WHEN YOU ARE OLD Yeats
WINDSOR FOREST Pope

14

A GERMAN REQUIEM Fenton
A SHROPSHIRE LAD Betjeman,
  Housman
ABOUT HIS PERSON Armitage
ANNUS MIRABILIS Dryden, Larkin
AWAY MELANCHOLY Smith
BLAME NOT MY LUTE Wyatt
CARRION COMFORT Hopkins
COUNSEL TO GIRLS Herrick
DIVINA COMMEDIA Dante
DOWN, WANTON, DOWN Graves
HEARTBREAK CAMP Campbell
HERO AND LEANDER Chapman,
  Marlowe

IN A BATH TEASHOP Betjeman
IN PARIS WITH YOU Fenton
LEDA AND THE SWAN Yeats
LES FLEURS DU MAL Baudelaire
LOVE SONGS IN AGE Larkin
ONE PERFECT ROSE Parker
SLEEP AND BEAUTY Keats
SUNNY PRESTATYN Larkin
THE AEOLIAN HARP Coleridge
THE ANNIVERSARY Donne
THE DRUNKEN BOAT Rimbaud
THE DRY SALVAGES Eliot
THE GRASSHOPPER Lovelace
THE HOUSE OF FAME Chaucer
THE KNIGHT'S TALE Chaucer
THE LOTUS EATERS Tennyson
THE MILLER'S TALE Chaucer
THE NIGHTINGALE Petrarch
THE PARSON'S TALE Chaucer
THE POPLAR FIELD Cowper
THE POT GERANIUM Nicholson
THE SINGLE HOUND E Dickinson
THE SQUIRE'S TALE Chaucer
THIS BE THE VERSE Larkin
TIMOTHY WINTERS Causley
UNDER BEN BULBEN Yeats
VENUS AND ADONIS Shakespeare
WELSH LANDSCAPE RS Thomas

15

ALEXANDER'S FEAST Dryden
CHANSON DE ROLAND ?
EARTH TRIUMPHANT Aiken
ELOISA TO ABELARD Pope
FAIRGROUND MUSIC Fuller
FROST AT MIDNIGHT Coleridge
GIVING UP SMOKING Cope
HARROW-ON-THE-HILL Betjeman

IDYLLS OF THE KING Tennyson
LORD COZENS HARDY Betjeman
LOVE'S PHILOSOPHY Shelley
MEN WHO MARCH AWAY Hardy
MID-WINTER WAKING Graves
NO CHANGE OF PLACE Auden
PORTRAIT OF A LADY Eliot
SAMSON AGONISTES Milton
STELLA'S BIRTHDAY Swift
STUDY OF TWO PEARS Stevens
SUMMONED BY BELLS Betjeman
THE DIVINE COMEDY Dante
THE EVE OF ST AGNES Keats
THE FAERIE QUEENE Spenser
THE FOUR QUARTETS Eliot
THE HIPPOPOTAMUS Eliot
THE ILLUSIONISTS Fuller
THE INCHCAPE ROCK Southey
THE PAINS OF SLEEP Coleridge
THE PRIORESS' TALE Chaucer
THE ROAD NOT TAKEN Frost
THE SCHOLAR GIPSY Arnold
THE SECOND COMING Yeats
THE SHIPMAN'S TALE Chaucer
THE SORROW OF LOVE Yeats
THE WHITE GODDESS Graves
THIS LUNAR BEAUTY Auden
WAKING IN THE BLUE Lowell
WINTER LANDSCAPE Berryman
YOU, NEIGHBOUR GOD Rilke

16
GUS: THE THEATRE CAT Eliot
JOURNEY OF THE MAGI Eliot
ODE ON A GRECIAN URN Keats
ODE TO THE WEST WIND Shelley
PARADISE REGAINED Milton
SHE WALKS IN BEAUTY Byron

THE BRIDE OF ABYDOS Byron
THE FAITHLESS WIFE Lorca
THE FRANKLIN'S TALE Chaucer
THE LADY OF SHALOTT Tennyson
THE MANCIPLE'S TALE Chaucer
THE MAN OF LAW'S TALE Chaucer
THE MERCHANT'S TALE Chaucer
THE PARDONER'S TALE Chaucer
THE RAPE OF THE LOCK Pope
THE SUMMONER'S TALE Chaucer
TO A MOUNTAIN DAISY Burns
TO HIS COY MISTRESS Marvell
VERGISSMEINNICHT Douglas

17
DIRGE WITHOUT MUSIC
    St Vincent Millay
IN MEMORY OF WB YEATS Yeats
ODE TO A NIGHTINGALE Keats
PRAYER BEFORE BIRTH Macneice
THE DARKLING THRUSH Hardy
THE PHYSICIAN'S TALE Chaucer
THE POET'S COMPANION Fanthorpe
THE SONG OF THE SHIRT Hood

18
AN ESSAY ON CRITICISM Pope
HE FELL AMONG THIEVES Newbolt
LORD ULLIN'S DAUGHTER Campbell
SAILING TO BYZANTIUM Yeats
THE CANTERBURY TALES Chaucer
THE GENERAL PROLOGUE Chaucer
THE NUN'S PRIEST'S TALE Chaucer
THE SEA AND THE MIRROR Auden
THE WHITSUN WEDDINGS Larkin
THE WIFE OF BATH'S TALE Chaucer
TROILUS AND CRISEYDE Chaucer

19

A SLICE OF WEDDING CAKE Graves
A SUBALTERN'S LOVE SONG Betjeman
AUGURIES OF INNOCENCE Blake
BALLAD OF READING GAOL Wilde
DIARY OF A CHURCH MOUSE
  Betjeman

IN PRAISE OF LIMESTONE Auden
LAKE ISLE OF INNISFREE Yeats
TEA AT THE PALAZ OF HOON Stevens
THE CANON YEOMAN'S TALE
  Chaucer
THE GLORY OF THE GARDEN Kipling

Arts – Literature – THEATRICAL TERMS

3	MIKE	ASIDE	STALL	LINE-UP	CIRCUIT
ACT	MIME	CLOTH	STAND	MAKE-UP	CLASSIC
BOX	OLIO	CYCLE	STORY	MASQUE	COMPANY
CUE	PART	DÉCOR	STUDY	MIMING	CURTAIN
HIT	PLAY	DRAMA	TITLE	NUMBER	EFFECTS
NOH	PLOT	ENTRY	TRICK	PARODY	EPISODE
PIT	PROP	FARCE	WINGS	PERIOD	GALLERY
REP	ROLE	FIT-UP		PROMPT	GUIGNOL
RIG	SEAT	FLIES	**6**	PUPPET	HISTORY
RUN	SHOW	FOOTS	ACTING	REVIEW	MATINÉE
SET	SKIT	FOYER	BOARDS	SCRIPT	MUMMERY
	SOLO	HOUSE	BRIDGE	SHTICK	MUMMING
4	SPOT	LINES	BY-PLAY	SKETCH	MUSICAL
BOOK	STAR	PANTO	CHORUS	STALLS	MYSTERY
BOOM	TABS	PAPER	CIRCLE	STOOGE	ONSTAGE
CAST	TONY	PIECE	CLAQUE	TROUPE	OVATION
CLAP	TOUR	PROPS	COMEDY		PERFORM
DAME	TRAP	PUNCH	CO-STAR	**7**	PLAYLET
DROP	TURN	REVUE	DRAPES	ACTRESS	PREVIEW
EXIT	WING	SCENA	DRY ICE	APPLAUD	READING
FLOP		SCENE	DRY RUN	BALCONY	REVIVAL
GODS	**5**	SLIPS	ENCORE	BENEFIT	RIGGING
JUDY	ACTOR	SMASH	EQUITY	BIT PART	SCENERY
LEAD	AD LIB	SOUND	EXEUNT	BUNRAKU	SEATING
LOGE	APRON	STAGE	FINALE	CABARET	SELL-OUT
MASK	ARENA	STAGY	KABUKI	CASTING	SETTING

SHOWBIZ
STAGERY
STARDOM
SUBPLOT
TABLEAU
TAKE-OFF
THEATRE
THE GODS
TRAGEDY
TRILOGY
UPSTAGE
VARIETY

8

APPLAUSE
AUDIENCE
AUDITION
BACKDROP
CLAPPING
COSTUMES
COULISSE
CRITIQUE
CRUSH BAR
DIALOGUE
DRESSER
DROLLERY
DUMB SHOW
DUOLOGUE
ENSEMBLE
ENTR'ACTE
ENTRANCE
EPILOGUE
FESTIVAL
INTERACT
INTERVAL
JUVENILE
LIGHTING
NAME PART

OFFSTAGE
PARTERRE
PASTORAL
PLAYBILL
PREMIERE
PROLOGUE
PROMPTER
PROPERTY
PUPPETRY
SCENARIO
SET PIECE
SMASH HIT
STAR TURN
THE HALLS
THESPIAN
THRILLER
TRAVESTY
VIGNETTE
WARDROBE

9

BACKCLOTH
BACKLIGHT
BACKSTAGE
BAIGNOIRE
BOX OFFICE
BURLESQUE
CHARACTER
CLOAKROOM
COLUMBINE
CURTAIN-UP
DEPICTION
DRAMATICS
DRAMATIST
DROP SCENE
FLOOR SHOW
FOOTLIGHT
FULL HOUSE

GREEN ROOM
HAPPENING
HARLEQUIN
HYPNOTISM
INTERLUDE
LIMELIGHT
LOW COMEDY
MELODRAMA
MESMERISM
MEZZANINE
MONODRAMA
MONOLOGUE
MUSIC HALL
NIGHT-CLUB
NOISES OFF
ORCHESTRA
PANTALOON
PANTOMIME
PARABASIS
PERSONAGE
PLAYHOUSE
PORTRAYAL
PROGRAMME
PROMPT BOX
PROMPTING
REHEARSAL
REPERTORY
SCENE DOCK
SET DESIGN
SLAPSTICK
SOLILOQUY
SPIRIT GUM
SPOTLIGHT
STAGE DOOR
STAGE HAND
STAGE NAME
STAGE PLAY
STAGINESS

STORY LINE
STRIP CLUB
THEATRICS
TITLE ROLE
TRIALOGUE
TWO-HANDER
UNDERPLOT
WHODUNNIT

10

APRON STAGE
AUDITORIUM
CHORUS GIRL
CHORUS LINE
CLOSET PLAY
DÉNOUEMENT
DRAMATURGY
FIRST HOUSE
FIRST NIGHT
FOOTLIGHTS
FOURTH WALL
HIPPODROME
HISTRIONIC
IMPRESSION
MARIONETTE
MICROPHONE
PASQUINADE
PLAYWRIGHT
PRODUCTION
PROMPT SIDE
PROSCENIUM
PUPPET SHOW
REHEARSING
REPERTOIRE
STAGECRAFT
STRIPTEASE
THEATRICAL
UNDERSTUDY

VAUDEVILLE
WALK-ON PART

11
BLACK COMEDY
CENTRE STAGE
CLIFFHANGER
CLOSET DRAMA
CURTAIN CALL
DRAMATICISM
DRESS CIRCLE
DROP CURTAIN
GREASEPAINT
HISTRIONICS
HOUSE LIGHTS
LIVE THEATRE
MIRACLE PLAY
MISE-EN-SCÈNE
MYSTERY PLAY
PASSION PLAY
PERFORMANCE
PROBLEM PLAY
PUNCHINELLO
RIGGING LOFT
SECOND HOUSE
STAGE FRIGHT
STAGE-STRUCK
THEATRICALS
TRAGI-COMEDY
UPPER CIRCLE
VARIETY SHOW
VENTRILOQUY

12
AMPHITHEATRE
DRESSING ROOM
EXTRAVAGANZA
GRAND GUIGNOL
HARLEQUINADE
INTERMISSION
METHOD ACTING
MORALITY PLAY
NATIVITY PLAY
PEPPER'S GHOST
PROMPT CORNER
PUNCH AND JUDY
SHOW BUSINESS
STAGE EFFECTS
STAGE WHISPER
STOCK COMPANY
STRAIGHT PLAY
SUMMER SEASON
TOTAL THEATRE

13
CHARACTER PART
COUP DE THÉÂTRE
CURTAIN SPEECH
DEUS EX MACHINA
DRAMATISATION
IMPERSONATION
LITTLE THEATRE
MUSICAL COMEDY
SAFETY CURTAIN
SHADOW THEATRE

STAGE PRESENCE
TABLEAU VIVANT
THEATRE TICKET
THEATRICALITY
VENTRILOQUISM

14
CHARACTER ACTOR
DRESS REHEARSAL
INTERPRETATION
PROSCENIUM ARCH
REPRESENTATION
STAGE DIRECTION
SUPPORTING ROLE

15
CHARACTER ACTING
COMEDY OF MANNERS
FRONT OF THE HOUSE
LEGITIMATE DRAMA
ORCHESTRA STALLS
PHYSICAL THEATRE
SHADOW PANTOMIME
STANDING OVATION

16
AMATEUR DRAMATICS
DRAMATIS PERSONAE
KITCHEN-SINK DRAMA
PERFORMING RIGHTS

Arts – Literature – WRITERS (non-fiction writers)

3
KEE Robert

4
HALL Edward
HUME David
HUNT Leigh
JUNG Carl
LAMB Charles
LIVY
MANN Thomas
MUIR Frank
NASH Ogden
POPE Alexander
READ Sir Herbert
SADE Marquis de
WARD Artemus – (pen-
    name of Charles Farrar
    Browne)
WEIR Arabella

5
ADAMS Hannah James
BACON Baron Francis,
    Roger
BURKE Edmund
CLARK Sir Kenneth,
    Manning Hope
FREUD Sigmund
GOSSE Sir Edmund
HEINE Heinrich
HULME TE
MAGEE Brian
NEWBY Eric
PAINE Thomas

PEPYS Samuel
STARK Dame Freya
SWIFT Jonathan
TRUSS Lynne
VIDAL Gore

6
ASCHAM Roger
BRYANT Arthur
BRYSON Bill
BURTON Sir Richard
DARWIN Charles
EVELYN John
FRASER Lady Antonia
GIBBON Edward
GRAVES Robert
HOBBES Thomas
HUXLEY Sir Julian
KIRKUP James
LOWELL James
NEWMAN John
ORWELL George
PARKER Dorothy
PASCAL Blaise
RUSKIN John
SARTRE Jean-Paul
SMILES Samuel
STEELE Sir Richard
TAYLOR AJP, Bayard
VALÉRY Paul
WALTON Izaak
WILSON AN
WOTTON Sir Henry

7
ADDISON Joseph
BLUNDEN Edmund
CAMERON James
CARLYLE Thomas
COBBETT William
DAWKINS Richard
DIDEROT Denis
DURRELL Gerald
ELLMANN Richard
EMERSON Ralph Waldo
GOODMAN Ellen
HAWKING Stephen
HAZLITT William
HERBERT AP
HILLIER Bevis
HOLROYD Michael
JOHNSON Dr Samuel
KENNEDY Sir Ludovic
LAMARCK Jean-Baptiste
LINDSAY Philip
MENCKEN HL
MITFORD Jessica, Nancy
PREBBLE John
SITWELL Sacheverell
SPENDER Sir Stephen
THEROUX Paul
THOREAU Henry
THURBER James
TOYNBEE Arnold

8
APULEIUS
BEAUVOIR Simone de
CONNOLLY Cyril

DALRYMPLE William
KOESTLER Arthur
LAWRENCE TE
LOCKHART John
MACAULAY Thomas
   Babington
MICHELET Jules
PERELMAN SJ
ROUSSEAU Jean-Jacques
SCHILLER Friedrich
STRACHEY Lytton
VOLTAIRE (pen-name of
   François Marie Arouet)
WEDGWOOD Dame
   Veronica
XENOPHON

9
ALDINGTON Richard
ARBUTHNOT John

BRONOWSKI Jacob
CHURCHILL Sir Winston
DE QUINCEY Thomas
ECKERMANN Johann
FROISSART Jean
LA BRUYÈRE Jean de
LAMARTINE Alphonse
MARTINEAU Harriet
MONTAIGNE Michel
PARKINSON Cyril

10
CHESTERTON GK
DIO CASSIUS
FITZGERALD Edward
MUGGERIDGE Malcolm
THUCYDIDES

11
BLESSINGTON Countess

CASTIGLIONE Count
   Baldassare

12
QUILLER-COUCH Sir
   Arthur

13
CHATEAUBRIAND
   Vicomte de
ORTEGA Y GASSET José

14
BRILLAT-SAVARIN
   Anthelme

15
DIODORUS SICULUS

Arts – Literature – WRITERS (Novelists, Poets & Dramatists)

3
ADE George
ALI Monica
ECO Umberto
FRY Christopher
GAY John
GYP (pen-name
   of Comtesse
   de Mirabeau)
KYD Thomas
LEE Harper,
   Laurie
NIN Anaïs

NYE Robert
POE Edgar Allan
PYE Henry
PYM Barbara
TEY Josephine
TYL Josef

4
ABSE Dannie
ADAM Paul
AMIS Sir Kingsley,
   Martin
ASCH Sholem

AUEL Jean M
BABE Thomas
BALL John
BAUM L Frank,
   Vicki
BEHN Aphra
BÖLL Heinrich
BOLT Robert
BOND Edward,
   Michael
BOYD William
BUCK Pearl
CAIN James M

CARY Joyce
CELA Camilo José
COLE Martina
COOK Robin
DAHL Roald
DUNN Douglas, Nell
FAST Howard
FORD Ford Madox,
   John
GALT John
GASH Jonathan
GEMS Pam
GIDE André

GORE Catherine
GRAY Alasdair, David, Simon, Thomas
GREY Zane
GUNN Neil, Thom
HABE Hans
HALL Adam, Radclyffe, Willis
HARE David
HART Moss
HILL Susan
HOAG Tami
HOEG Peter
HOGG James
HOLT Victoria
HOOD Thomas
HOPE Anthony
HUGO Victor
HUNT E Howard, Leigh
HYNE Charles
ILES Francis
INGE William
JONG Erica
KAYE MM
KENT Alexander
KING Francis, Stephen
KNOX Ross
LAMB Charles, Mary
LEAR Edward
LENZ Siegfried
LOOS Anita
LOTI Pierre
LYLY John
MANN Heinrich, Jessica, Thomas
MUIR Edwin
NASH Ogden
OKRI Ben

OVID
OWEN Wilfred
PAGE Louise, Thomas
POPE Alexander
PUZO Mario
RAND Ayn
READ Miss, Piers Paul
REID Forrest, Mayne
RHYS Jean
RICE Elmer
ROTH Philip
ROWE Nicholas
SAKI (pen-name of HH Munro)
SAND George (pen-name of Baronne Dudevant)
SHAW GB, Irwin
SNOW Baron CP
TATE Allen
TODD Barbara
URIS Leon
VEGA Lope de
WAIN John
WARD Mary, Augusta
WEBB Mary
WEST Morris, Nathanael, Dame Rebecca
WOOD Ellen
WOUK Herman
WREN PC
WYSS Johann
ZOLA Émile

5

ADAMS Douglas, Richard
AIKEN Conrad, Joan
ALBEE Edward

ALGER Horatio
ANAND Mulk Raj
ARDEN John
AUDEN WH
AVERY Gillian
AWDRY WV
AYRES Pam
BANKS Iain, Lynne Reid
BARTH John
BATES HE
BEHAN Brendan
BENÉT Stephen
BLAKE Nicholas (pen-name of Cecil Day-Lewis), William
BLOCH Robert
BLUME Judy
BOWEN Elizabeth
BRAGG Melvyn
BRETT Simon
BROWN Dan
BUNIN Ivan
BURNS Robert
BYATT AS
BYRON Lord
CAINE Sir Hall
CAMUS Albert
ČAPEK Karel
CAREW Thomas
CAREY Peter
CHASE James Hadley
CLARE John
CLARK Mary Higgins
COHEN Leonard
CRANE Stephen
DANTE Alighieri
DEFOE Daniel
DESAI Anita

DONNE John
DOYLE Sir Arthur
  Conan, Roddy
DUFFY Maureen
DUMAS Alexandre
EDGAR David
EDSON JT
ELIOT George (pen-name
  of Mary Ann Evans), TS
ELLIS Alice Thomas (pen-
  name of Anna Haycroft)
EWING Juliana
FIGES Eva
FLINT Frank
FRAME Janet
FRAYN Michael
FRIEL Brian, George
FROST Robert
GENET Jean
GLOAG John
GOGOL Nikolai
GORKY Maxim
GOSSE Sir Edmund
GRASS Günter
GREEN Henry, Julien
GRIMM Jacob, Wilhelm
HALEY Alex
HARDY Thomas
HARTE Bret
HAVEL Václav
HECHT Ben
HEINE Heinrich
HENRY O (pen-name of
  William Sydney Porter)
HENTY GA
HESSE Hermann
HEYER Georgette
HINES Barry

HOMER
HULME TE
IBSEN Henrik
INNES Hammond
JACOBS WW
JAMES Henry,
  Baroness PD
JARRY Alfred
JOHNS WE
JÓKAI Mór
JONES Ernest, James
JOYCE James
KAFKA Franz
KEATS John
KESEY Ken
KEYES Frances Parkinson
KLEIN AM
KOPIT Arthur
LEIGH Mike
LEVIN Ira
LEWIS CS, MG, Sinclair,
  Wyndham
LLOSA Mario Vargas
LODGE David, Thomas
LOFTS Norah
LOGUE Christopher
LOWRY Malcolm
LYALL Edna, Gavin
MAMET David
MARSH Dame Ngaio
MILNE AA
MOORE Brian, George
MOSSE Kate
MUNRO Neil
MYERS LH
NASHE Thomas
NEWBY PH
NIVEN Larry

NOBBS David
NOYES Alfred
OATES Joyce Carol
ODETS Clifford
O'HARA John, Mary
ORCZY Baroness
ORTON Joe
OTWAY Thomas
OUIDA (pen-name of
  Maria Louise de la
  Ramée)
OZICK Cynthia
PATON Alan
PEAKE Mervyn
PÉGUY Charles
PERCY Walter
PETERS Ellis (pen-name
  of Edith Pargeter)
PLATH Sylvia
POUND Ezra
POWYS John Cowper,
  Llewellyn, TF
PRIOR Matthew
QUEEN Ellery (joint
  pen-name of Frederick
  Dannay & Manfred
  Lee)
RAABE Wilhelm
RAINE Craig
RASPE RE
READE Charles
RILKE Rainer
SACHS Hans, Nelly
SAGAN Françoise
SAYLE Alexei
SCOTT Paul, Sir Walter
SEGAL Erich
SELBY Hubert

SHUTE Nevil
SIMMS William Gilmour
SIMON Claude, Neil
SMITH Betty, Charlotte,
  Dodie, EE Doc, Martin
  Cruz, Stevie, Wilbur
SPARK Dame Muriel
SPYRI Johanna
STAËL Madame de
STEEL Danielle
STEIN Gertrude
STONE Irving
STORM Theodor
STOUT Rex
STOWE Harriet Beecher
SVEVO Italo
SWIFT Graham, Jonathan
SYNGE JM
TASSO Bernardo,
  Torquato
TUOHY Frank
TUROW Scott
TWAIN Mark (pen-name
  of Samuel Langhorne
  Clemens)
UDALL Nicholas
VERGA Giovanni
VERNE Jules
VIDAL Gore
WAUGH Alec, Auberon,
  Evelyn
WELLS HG
WELSH Irvine
WELTY Eudora
WHITE Antonia,
  Edmund, Patrick, TH
WILDE Oscar
WOLFE Charles,

Thomas, Tom
WOOLF Leonard, Virginia
WYATT Sir Thomas
YATES Dornford (pen-
  name of Cecil Mercer)
YEATS WB
YERBY Frank
YONGE Charlotte M
YOUNG Francis
ZAFÓN Carlos Ruiz
ZWEIG Stefan

6

ACHEBE Chinua
AKUNIN Boris (pen-name
  of Grigory Chkhartishvili)
ALCOTT Louisa M
ALDISS Brian W
ALEXIS Willibald (pen-
  name of Georg Häring)
ALGREN Nelson
AMBLER Eric
ANSTEY F (pen-name of
  Thomas Anstey Guthrie)
ARAGON Louis
ARCHER Jeffrey
ARNOLD Matthew
ASIMOV Isaac
ATWOOD Margaret
AUSTEN Jane
AUSTER John
AUSTIN Alfred
BAGLEY Desmond
BALZAC Honoré de
BARAKA Amiri
BARHAM Richard
BARNES Djuna, Julian,
  Peter, William

BAROJA Pia
BARRIE JM
BAWDEN Nina
BECQUE Henry
BELLOC Hilaire
BELLOW Saul
BENSON EF, RH, Stella
BERGER Thomas
BESANT Sir Walter
BESTER Alfred
BIERCE Ambrose
BINCHY Maeve
BINYON Laurence
BLIXEN Baroness Karen
BLYTON Enid
BORGES Jorge Luis
BORROW George
BOULLE Pierre
BRAINE John
BRECHT Bertolt
BRETON Nicholas
BRIDIE James
BRONTË Anne,
  Charlotte, Emily
BROOKE Rupert
BROPHY Brigid
BUCHAN John
BUNYAN John
BURNEY Fanny
BUTLER Samuel
CABELL James Branch
CAPOTE Truman
CARTER Angela
CARVER Raymond
CATHER Willa
CAVAFY Constantine
  (pen-name of
  Konstantinos Kaváfis)

CÉLINE Louis-Ferdinand
   (pen-name of LF
   Destouches)
CIBBER Colley
CLANCY Tom
CLARKE Arthur C
CLEARY Jon
CONDON Richard
CONRAD Joseph
COONEY Ray
COOPER James
   Fenimore, Jilly, William
COWARD Sir Noël
COWPER William
CRABBE George
CRONIN AJ
DANIEL Samuel
DAUDET Alphonse
DAVIES Idris, Robertson,
   William
DEKKER Thomas
DE VERE Aubrey
DEXTER Colin
DIDION Joan
DOWSON Ernest
DRYDEN John
DUNBAR Paul, William
ÉLUARD Paul
EMPSON Sir William
FARRAR Frederick
FAULKS Sebastian
FERBER Edna
FISHER Dorothea Frances
FOUQUÉ Friedrich
FOWLES John
FRANCE Anatole
FRASER Lady Antonia,
   George Macdonald

FRISCH Max
FUGARD Athol
FULLER Henry, John, Roy
GARNER Alan
GIBBON Lewis
GODDEN Rumer
GODWIN William
GOETHE Johann
GORDON Richard
GRAHAM Winston
GRAVES Robert
GREENE Graham
HAILEY Arthur
HAMSUN Knut (pen-
   name of Knut Pedersen)
HANLEY James
HARRIS Joel Chandler,
   Robert, Thomas, Wilson
HELLER Joseph
HEMANS Felicia
HESIOD
HILTON James
HOLMAN Robert
HOLMES Oliver Wendell
HORACE
HORNBY Nick
HUGHES Richard, Ted,
   Thomas
HUXLEY Aldous
IBÁÑEZ Vicente Blasco
IRVING John, Washington
JEROME Jerome K
JONSON Ben
KEEFFE Barrie
KELLER Gottfried
KELMAN James
KIRKUP James
KLEIST Heinrich von

KOONTZ Dean
KRANTZ Judith
L'AMOUR Louis
LANDOR Walter Savage
LARKIN Philip
LEASOR James
LE FANU Sheridan
LEROUX Gaston
LEVINE Philip
LINNEY Romulus
LIVELY Penelope
LONDON Jack
LOWELL Robert
LUCIAN
LUDLUM Robert
MAILER Norman
MALORY Sir Thomas
MCBAIN Ed (pen-name
   of Evan Hunter)
MCEWAN Ian
MCKUEN Rod
MERCER David
MILLER Arthur, Henry
MILTON John
MOONEY Bel
MORGAN Charles
MORRIS William
MOTION Andrew
MROZEK Slawomir
MURRAY Melissa
NERVAL Gérard de
NESBIT E
NEWMAN Andrea
NORRIS Frank
NORTON Mary
O'BRIEN Edna, Flann
O'CASEY Sean
O'NEILL Eugene

ORWELL George (pen-name of Eric Blair)
PARKER Dorothy
PARKIN Molly
PETÖFI Sándor
PINDAR
PINERO Sir Arthur Wing
PINTER Harold
PLAIDY Jean
PORTER Anne Maria, Jane, Kathleen, Peter
POTTER Beatrix, Dennis
POWELL Anthony
PROULX E Annie
PROUST Marcel
RACINE Jean
RIDLEY Arnold
ROHMER Sax {pen-name of Arthur Ward)
ROWLEY William
RUDKIN David
RUNYON Damon
SALTEN Felix
SAPPER (pen-name of Herman Cyril McNeile)
SAPPHO
SARDOU Victorien
SARTRE Jean-Paul
SAVAGE Richard
SAYERS Dorothy L
SENECA
SEWELL Anna
SHANGE Ntozake
SHARPE Tom
SHREVE Anita
SIDNEY Sir Philip
SINGER Isaac
SPRING Howard

STEELE Sir Richard
STERNE Laurence
STOKER Bram
STOREY David
STYRON William
SYMONS Julian
TAGORE Rabindranath
TAYLOR Edward, Elizabeth, Sir Henry, Peter
TERSON Peter
THOMAS Craig, DM, Dylan, Edward, Leslie, RS
TREECE Henry
TREVOR William
UNDSET Sigrid
UPDIKE John
UPWARD Edward
UTTLEY Alison
VALÉRY Paul
VIRGIL
WALLER Edmund
WANDOR Michelene
WARNER CD, Rex, Sylvia Townsend
WARTON Thomas
WATERS Sarah
WELDON Fay
WERFEL Franz
WESKER Arnold
WESLEY Mary
WIGGIN Kate
WILCOX Ella Wheeler
WILDER Laura Ingalls, Thornton
WILLIS Lord
WILSON AN, Sir Angus, Colin

WINSOR Kathleen
WOTTON Sir Henry
WRIGHT Judith, Richard

7

ACKROYD Peter
ALCAEUS
ÁLVAREZ Joaquín, Serafin
ANOUILH Jean
ANTHONY Evelyn, Piers
ARBUZOV Aleksei
ARIOSTO Ludovico
ARRABAL Fernando
ASHBERY John
BAGNOLD Enid
BALCHIN Nigel
BALDWIN James
BARSTOW Stan
BECKETT Samuel
BEDDOES Thomas
BENNETT Alan, Arnold
BENTLEY EC
BERKOFF Steven
BERNARD Tristan
BIGGERS Earl Derr
BLUNDEN Edmund
BOSWELL James
BRENTON Howard
BRIDGES Robert
BÜCHNER Georg
BURGESS Anthony
BURNETT Francis Hodgson
CAEDMON
CAMPION Thomas
CARROLL Lewis (pen-name of Charles Lutwidge Dodgson)

CHAPMAN George
CHAUCER Geoffrey
CHEKHOV Anton
CLAVELL James
CLELAND John
COCTEAU Jean
COETZEE JM
COLETTE (pen-name
   of Sidonie-Gabrielle
   Colette)
COLLINS Jackie, Wilkie
COOKSON Catherine
CORELLI Marie
COZZENS James Gould
CREASEY John
CURTEIS Ian
CUSSLER Clive
DEEPING Warwick
DELANEY Shelagh
DELEDDA Grazia
DELILLO Don
DEUTSCH Babette
   (pen-name of Avrahm
   Yarmolinsky)
DE VRIES Peter
DICKENS Charles, Monica
DIDEROT Denis
DOUGLAS Lloyd C, Lord
DOWLING Finuala
DRABBLE Margaret
DRAYTON Michael
DREISER Theodore
DUHAMEL Georges
DUNNETT Dorothy
DUNSANY Edward
DURRELL Lawrence
EMERSON Ralph Waldo
ENRIGHT DJ

FARRELL James T
FEYDEAU Georges
FIRBANK Ronald
FLECKER James Elroy
FLEMING Ian
FOLLETT Ken
FORSTER EM
FORSYTH Frederick
FOSCOLO Ugo
FRANCIS Dick
FRENEAU Philip
FUENTES Carlos
GALLICO Paul
GARDNER Erle Stanley
GARLAND Hamlin
GARNETT David, Eve
GASKELL Elizabeth
GAUTIER Théophile
GIBBONS Stella
GILBERT Sir William
GISSING George
GLASGOW Ellen
GOLDING Sir William
GOLDMAN William
GOLDONI Carlo
GRAHAME Kenneth
GRISHAM John
GUNTHER John
HAGGARD Sir H Rider
HAMMETT Dashiell
HAMPTON Christopher
HARTLEY LP
HARWOOD Gwen,
   Harold
HAZZARD Shirley
HELLMAN Lillian
HERBERT Sir AP, Frank,
   James

HERRICK Robert
HEYWOOD Thomas
HIGGINS George V, Jack
   (pen-name of Harry
   Patterson)
HODGSON Ralph
HOLBERG Ludvig
HOPKINS Gerard Manley
HORNUNG EW
HOUSMAN AE
HOWATCH Susan
HOWELLS William Dean
HUBBELL Patricia
IONESCO Eugène
JACKSON Helen
JANSSON Tove
JIMÉNEZ Juan Ramón
JOHNSON BS, Samuel
KÄSTNER Erich
KAUFMAN George S
KEATING HRF
KENNEDY Margaret
KEROUAC Jack
KIMMINS Anthony
KIPLING Rudyard
KITCHIN CHB
LABICHE Eugène
LARDNER Ring
LAXNESS Halldór
LEACOCK Stephen
LE CARRÉ John (pen-
   name of David
   Cornwell)
LEHMANN Rosamund
LEONARD Elmore,
   Hugh, Tom
LESSING Doris
LINDSAY Vachel

LOFTING Hugh
MACLEAN Alistair
MALAMUD Bernard
MALRAUX André
MANKELL Henning
MANNING Olivia
MARLOWE Christopher
MÁRQUEZ Gabriel García
MARQUIS Don
MARRYAT Captain
 Frederick
MARVELL Andrew
MASTERS John
MATURIN Charles
MAUGHAM Robin,
 W Somerset
MAURIAC François
MAUROIS André
MCGOUGH Roger
MCGRATH John Peter
MÉRIMÉE Prosper
MISHIMA Yukio
MITFORD Mary Russell,
 Nancy
MOLIÈRE (pen-name of
 Jean Baptiste Poquelin)
MORAVIA Alberto
MUMFORD Lewis
MURDOCH Dame Iris
NABOKOV Vladimir
NAIPAUL Sir VS
NARAYAN RK
NEWBOLT Sir Henry
NICHOLS Peter
O'CONNOR Edwin, Frank
OSBORNE John
PATMORE Coventry
PEACOCK Thomas Love

PICOULT Jodi
PILCHER Rosamunde
PLAUTUS
PRÉVOST Abbé
PUSHKIN Alexander
PYNCHON Thomas
QUENEAU Raymond
RANSOME Arthur
RAPHAEL Frederic
RENAULT Mary (pen-
 name of Mary Challans)
RENDELL Baroness Ruth
REYMONT WS
RICHLER Mordecai
RIDDELL Henry
RIMBAUD Arthur
ROBBINS Harold, Tom
ROBERTS Kenneth
ROLLAND Romain
ROMAINS Jules (pen-
 name of Louis Farigoule)
ROSTAND Edmond
ROWLING JK
RUSHDIE Salman
SAROYAN William
SASSOON Siegfried
SERVICE Robert William
SEYMOUR Gerald
SHAFFER Anthony, Peter
SHELDON Sidney
SHELLEY Mary, Percy
SHEPARD Sam
SHERMAN Martin
SIMENON Georges
SIMPSON Helen, NF
SITWELL Dame Edith, Sir
 Osbert
SKELTON John

SOLOGUB Fyodor
 (pen-name of Fyodor
 Teternikov)
SOUTHEY Robert
SOYINKA Wole
SPENDER Sir Stephen
SPENSER Edmund
STEVENS Wallace
STEWART JIM, Lady Mary
SURTEES RS
TENNANT Emma
TERENCE
THEROUX Paul
THESPIS
THIONG'O Ngugi
THOMSON Derick S,
 James
THOREAU Henry
THWAITE Anthony
TOLKIEN JRR
TOLSTOY Count Leo
TOMALIN Claire
TOURGÉE Albion W
TRAVERS Ben, PL
TUTUOLA Amos
USTINOV Sir Peter
VAN DINE SS
VAN VOGT AE
VAUGHAN Henry
VICENTE Gil
VINAVER Michel
WALLACE Edgar
WALPOLE Horace,
 Sir Hugh
WALTERS Minette
WEBSTER John
WHARTON Edith
WHITING John

WHITMAN Walt
WIELAND Christoph
WYNDHAM John

8
ABRAHAMS Peter
ALLBEURY Ted
ANDERSEN Hans
  Christian
ANDERSON Sherwood
AUERBACH Berthold
BANVILLE John, Théodore
BARBUSSE Henri
BEAUMONT Francis,
  Sir John
BEAUVOIR Simone de
BEERBOHM Sir Max
BENCHLEY Peter
BERNANOS Georges
BETJEMAN Sir John
BJØRNSON Bjørnstjerne
BRADBURY Sir Malcolm,
  Ray
BRADFORD Barbara
  Taylor
BROOKNER Anita
BROWNING Robert,
  Elizabeth Barrett
BRUNHOFF Jean de
BULGAKOV Mikhail
CALDWELL Erskine
CAMPBELL Roy, Thomas
CARTLAND Barbara
CATULLUS
CHANDLER Raymond
CHRISTIE Dame Agatha
CLAUDIAN
CONGREVE William

COOLIDGE Susan
CORNWELL Bernard,
  Patricia
CRAWFORD F Marion
CRICHTON Michael
CROMPTON Richmal
CUMMINGS EE
D'AVENANT Sir William
DAVIDSON Lionel
DAY-LEWIS Cecil
DE FOREST John William
DEIGHTON Len
DE LA MARE Walter
DISRAELI Benjamin
DOCTOROW EL
DONLEAVY JP
ETHEREGE Sir George
FARQUHAR George
FAULKNER William
FIELDING Henry
FLANNERY Peter
FLAUBERT Gustave
FLETCHER John
FORESTER CS
FREELING Nicholas
GABORIAU Émile
GINSBERG Allen
GONCOURT Edmond
  de, Jules de
GORDIMER Nadine
GREVILLE Sir Fulke
HAMILTON Donald,
  Patrick
HASTINGS Michael
HEINLEIN Robert A
HUYSMANS Joris-Karl
INCHBALD Elizabeth
ISHIGURO Kazuo

JENNINGS Elizabeth
JHABVALA Ruth Prawer
KÁLIDÁSA
KAVANAGH Julia, Patrick
KAWABATA Yasunari
KENEALLY Thomas
KINGSLEY Charles, Henry
KOESTLER Arthur
KOSINSKI Jerzy
KOTZEBUE August
LAGERLÖF Selma
LANGLAND William
LAURENCE Margaret
LAWRENCE DH
LEOPARDI Giacomo
LOCKHART John
LOVELACE Richard
MACAULAY Dame Rose
MACINNES Colin
MACNEICE Louis
MALLARMÉ Stéphane
MARIVAUX Pierre
MARQUAND John P
MCMURTRY Larry
MELVILLE Herman
MENANDER
MEREDITH George, Hal
MICHENER James A
MITCHELL Julian,
  Margaret
MOORCOCK Michael
MORRISON Toni
MORTIMER Sir John,
  Penelope
NEKRASOV Nikolai
NORDHOFF Charles
OLIPHANT Margaret
OSBOURNE Lloyd

PERRAULT Charles
PETRARCH
PRICHARD Katharine
QUENNELL Sir Peter
RABELAIS François
RATTIGAN Sir Terence
REMARQUE Erich Maria
 (pen-name of Erich
 Paul Remark)
RICHARDS Frank
 (pen-name of Charles
 Hamilton)
ROSSETTI Christina,
 Dante Gabriel
ROUSSEAU Jean
 Baptiste, Jean-Jacques
RUNEBERG Johan
SABATINI Rafael
SALINGER JD
SANDBURG Carl
SARRAUTE Nathalie
SCHILLER Friedrich von
SHADWELL Thomas
SHERIDAN Richard
 Brinsley
SHERRIFF RC
SILLITOE Alan
SINCLAIR May, Upton
SMOLLETT Tobias
SOUPAULT Philippe
SPILLANE Mickey
STAFFORD Jean
STENDHAL (pen-name
 of Henri Beyle)
STOPPARD Sir Tom
SUCKLING Sir John
TEASDALE Sara
TENNYSON Lord Alfred

TIBULLUS
TRAHERNE Thomas
TREMBLAY Michel
TRESSELL Robert
TRIGIANI Adriana
TROLLOPE Anthony,
 Joanna
TULSĪDĀS
TURGENEV Ivan
UNSWORTH Barry
VANBRUGH Sir John
VERLAINE Paul
VOLTAIRE (pen-name of
 François-Marie Arouet)
VONNEGUT Kurt
WAMBAUGH Joseph
WEDEKIND Frank
WHEATLEY Dennis
WHITTIER John Greenleaf
WILLIAMS Raymond,
 Tennessee, William
 Carlos
ZAMYATIN Evgeny

9
AESCHYLUS
AINSWORTH William
 Harrison
AKHMATOVA Anna (pen-
 name of Anna Gorenko)
ALDINGTON Richard
ALLINGHAM Margery,
 William
AYCKBOURN Sir Alan
BEMELMANS Ludwig
BERESFORD Elizabeth
BLACKMORE RD
BLEASDALE Alan

BOCCACCIO Giovanni
BRICKHILL Paul
BRIGHOUSE Harold
BROMFIELD Louis
BURROUGHS Edgar
 Rice, William
CALLAGHAN Morley
CALVERLEY Charles
CERVANTES Miguel de
CHARTERIS Leslie (pen-
 name of Leslie Yin)
CHURCHILL Caryl,
 Winston, Sir Winston
COLERIDGE Samuel
 Taylor
CORNEILLE Pierre,
 Thomas
CRESSWELL Helen
D'ANNUNZIO Gabriele
DE FILIPPO Eduardo
DE LA ROCHE Mazo
DICKINSON Emily
DOS PASSOS John
DU MAURIER Dame
 Daphne, George
DURBRIDGE Francis
EDGEWORTH Maria
EGGLESTON Edward
EURIPIDES
FEINSTEIN Elaine
FROISSART Jean
GIRAUDOUX Jean
GOLDSMITH Oliver
GONCHAROV Ivan
GREENWOOD Walter
GROSSMITH George,
 Weedon
HAUPTMANN Gerhart

HAWTHORNE Nathaniel
HEMINGWAY Ernest
HIGHSMITH Patricia
HÖLDERLIN Friedrich
HOUSEHOLD Geoffrey
INNAURATO Albert
ISHERWOOD
  Christopher
KELLERMAN Jonathan
KLOPSTOCK Friedrich
LA FRENAIS Ian
LAMARTINE Alphonse
LAMPEDUSA Giuseppe di
LERMONTOV Mikhail
LINKLATER Eric
LLEWELLYN Richard
  (pen-name of Richard
  Lloyd)
LOVECRAFT HP
LUCRETIUS
MACDONALD George,
  John D, Ross (pen-
  name of Kenneth
  Millar)
MACKENZIE Sir
  Compton
MANKOWITZ Wolf
MANSFIELD Katherine
MARTINEAU Harriet
MASEFIELD John
MASSINGER Philip
METALIOUS Grace
MIDDLETON Thomas
MINGHELLA Anthony
MITCHISON Naomi
MONSARRAT Nicholas
NICHOLSON Peter
O'FLAHERTY Liam

OSTROVSKY Aleksandr
PASTERNAK Boris
PATTERSON James
POLIAKOFF Stephen
POMERANCE Bernard
PRIESTLEY JB
PRITCHETT Sir VS
RADCLIFFE Ann
ROSENTHAL Jack
SACKVILLE Thomas
SCHREINER Olive
SHENSTONE William
SHOLOKHOV Mikhail
SILLANPÄÄ Frans
SIMONIDES
SLAUGHTER Frank
SOPHOCLES
SOUTHWELL Robert
STACPOOLE Henry
STEINBECK John
STEVENSON RL
STRIBLING TS
SWINBURNE Algernon
THACKERAY William
  Makepeace
UNGARETTI Giuseppe
VERHAEREN Émile
VITTORINI Elio
WERGELAND Hendrik
WHITEHEAD Charles
WINTERSON Jeanette
WODEHOUSE Sir PG
WYCHERLEY William
YANKOWITZ Susan
ZEPHANIAH Benjamin

10
AUCHINLOSS Louis

BAINBRIDGE Dame Beryl
BALLANTYNE RM
BAUDELAIRE Charles
BENEDICTUS David
BUCKERIDGE Anthony
CHATTERTON Thomas
CHESTERTON GK
DOSTOEVSKY Fyodor
DRINKWATER John
DÜRRENMATT Friedrich
FITZGERALD Edward,
  F Scott
GALSWORTHY John
KESSELRING Joseph
LA FONTAINE Jean de
LAGERKVIST Pär
LONGFELLOW Henry
  Wadsworth
MACDIARMID Hugh
  (pen-name of
  Christopher Grieve)
MARKANDAYA Kamala
MAUPASSANT Guy de
MAYAKOVSKY Vladimir
MCGONAGALL William
MONTGOMERY LM
PIRANDELLO Luigi
PROPERTIUS
RICHARDSON Samuel
SCHNITZLER Arthur
SOMERVILLE Edith
STRINDBERG August
TARKINGTON Booth
THEOCRITUS
VAN DER POST Sir
  Laurens
VANSITTART Peter
WASSERMANN Jakob

WATERHOUSE Keith
WILLIAMSON Henry
WORDSWORTH William
XENOPHANES

11
ANZENGRÜBER Ludwig
APOLLINAIRE Guillaume (pen-name
  of Wilhelm Kostrowitzky)
ARCHILOCHUS
BARING-GOULD Sabine
BACCHYLIDES
BLESSINGTON Countess
CALLIMACHUS
CASTIGLIONE Count Baldassare
DELDERFIELD RF
DOUGLAS-HOME William
EICHENDORFF Joseph
GARCÍA LORCA Federico
GRILLPARZER Franz
KAZANTZAKIS Nikos
MAETERLINCK Count Maurice
MONTHERLANT Henri de
OMAR KHAYYÁM
O'SHAUGNESSY Arthur
PÉREZ GALDÓS Benito
PONTOPPIDAN Henrik
SHAKESPEARE William
SIENKIEWICZ Henryk
STREATFEILD Noel
YEVTUSHENKO Yevgeni

12
ARISTOPHANES
BEAUMARCHAIS Pierre
BULWER-LYTTON Baron Edward

FEUCHTWANGER Lion
HOFMANNSTHAL Hugo von
MARTIN DU GARD Roger
MITTELHOLZER Edgar
PÉREZ DE AYALA Ramón
QUILLER-COUCH Sir Arthur
ROBBE-GRILLET Alain
SAINT-EXUPÉRY Antoine de
SOLZHENITSYN Aleksandr

13
ALAIN-FOURNIER (pen-name of
  Henri-Alban Fournier)
ČSOKONAI VITÉZ Mihály
HARISHCHANDRA Bharatendu
SACKVILLE-WEST Vita
TIRSO DE MOLINA (pen-name of
  Gabriel Téllez)

14
COMPTON-BURNETT Dame Ivy
ERCILLA Y ZÚÑIGA Alonso de
GRIMMELSHAUSEN Johann
LECONTE DE LISLE Charles
OEHLENSCHLÄGER Adam
SULLY-PRUDHOMME (pen-name of
  René Prudhomme)
WOLLSTONECRAFT Mary
ZORRILLA Y MORAL José

15
GRANVILLE-BARKER Harley
HANSFORD-JOHNSON Pamela

16
BARBEY D'AUREVILLY Jules

Arts – Media – COMMUNICATIONS

3
DOT
DVD
FAX
GEN
KEY
NET
PIP
SOS
STD
WEB
WWW

4
BLIP
CALL
CARD
CHIT
CODE
DASH
DATA
DIAL
LINE
LINK
MAIL
MEMO
NEWS
NOTE
PIPS
POST
SCAN
SEND
SIGN
SPAM
TAPE

TEXT
WIRE

5
BLEEP
CABLE
CODEX
E-MAIL
FLASH
INPUT
MEDIA
MODEM
MORSE
ORGAN
PAGER
PHONE
PO BOX
RADAR
RADIO
RELAY
SKYPE
STAMP
TELEX
TRACT
TRUNK
VIDEO

6
AERIAL
BEACON
BLOWER
CIPHER
ERRAND
HOMING
HOOK-UP

LETTER
LINK-UP
MAYDAY
MEDIUM
MOBILE
NOTICE
OUTPUT
PEN PAL
PINGER
POSTER
REPORT
RUNNER
SENDER
SIGNAL
SPARKS
TANNOY
TICKER
TIC-TAC
WIGWAG

7
ADDRESS
AIR MAIL
ANTENNA
BLEEPER
CARRIER
CB RADIO
CHANNEL
COURIER
EPISTLE
EXPRESS
FAN MAIL
HANDSET
HOTLINE
LOW-DOWN

MAILBAG
MAILBOX
MAIL VAN
MESSAGE
MISSIVE
MONITOR
NETWORK
NOTELET
PHONE-IN
POSTAGE
POSTBAG
SCANNER
SIMPLEX
SPUTNIK
TEXTING
TIDINGS
WAR DRUM
ZIP CODE

8
AGITPROP
AREA CODE
BULLETIN
CALLBACK
CIRCULAR
DIALLING
DISPATCH
ENVELOPE
EXCHANGE
INTELSAT
INTERCOM
INTERNET
JUNK MAIL
LANDLINE
LAST POST

LIFELINE
MAILBOAT
MAIL CART
MAILSHOT
NEWSCAST
NEWSROOM
OPERATOR
PAMPHLET
PAYBOOTH
PAY CABLE
PAYPHONE
PIPELINE
POSTCARD
POSTCODE
POSTMARK
RECEIVER
REPEATER
SCANNING
TALKBACK
TELECAST
TELEGRAM
TELETEXT
TELETYPE
TICK-TACK
TRACKING
TRANSMIT
VIEWDATA
WIRELESS

9
AIR LETTER
BLUETOOTH
BROADBAND
BROADCAST
CABLEGRAM

DICTATION
EARPHONES
ERRAND BOY
EXTENSION
FIRST POST
GO-BETWEEN
GRAPEVINE
HELIOGRAM
INTERPRET
LETTER BOX
LOCAL CALL
MAIL MERGE
MAIL ORDER
MAIL TRAIN
MASS MEDIA
MEGAPHONE
MESSENGER
MORSE CODE
NEWSFLASH
NEWSPAPER
NEWS-SHEET
PARTY LINE
PENFRIEND
PENNY POST
PILLAR BOX
RADIOGRAM
SATELLITE
SCRAMBLER
SEMAPHORE
SIGNALLER
TELEGRAPH
TELEPHONE
TELEPHONY
TOWN CRIER
TRANSLATE
TRUNK CALL
VERY LIGHT

10
AEROGRAMME
BILLET-DOUX
BLACKBERRY
COMMUNIQUÉ
CRYPTOGRAM
DICTAPHONE
ENCYCLICAL
HEADPHONES
HELIOGRAPH
HYDROPHONE
LETTER-CARD
LOUDHAILER
LOVE LETTER
MICROPHONE
NEWSCASTER
NEWSLETTER
NEWSREADER
OPEN LETTER
PARCEL POST
PAY CHANNEL
PAY STATION
PHONE BOOTH
PIGEON POST
POSTAL CODE
POST OFFICE
POSTSCRIPT
PROPAGANDA
RADIOPHONE
RADIO WAVES
ROUND ROBIN
SECOND POST
SIGNALLING
SIGNALMAN
TELEGRAPHY
TELEVISION
TICKER TAPE
TIME SIGNAL

TRANSLATOR
VIDEOPHONE
WIGWAGGING

11
CHAIN LETTER
COMMUNICATE
CRYPTOGRAPH
ENGAGED TONE
HELIOGRAPHY
INFORMATION
INTERPRETER
LOUDSPEAKER
MAIL CARRIER
MAILING LIST
MOBILE PHONE
NEWSCASTING
NOTICE BOARD
PIRATE RADIO
RADIO BEACON
SMOKE SIGNAL
SWITCHBOARD
TAPE MACHINE
TELECOTTAGE
TELEMESSAGE
TELEPHONIST
TELEPRINTER
TRANSLATION
TRANSPONDER
TWO-WAY RADIO
WORD OF MOUTH
WRONG NUMBER

12
BROADCASTING
CITIZENS' BAND
COMMUNICATOR
DIALLING CODE

DIALLING TONE
INTERNET CAFÉ
INTERPRETING
NEWS BULLETIN
NOTIFICATION
POSTAGE STAMP
RADAR SCANNER
RADIO STATION
RECEIVING SET
SIGN LANGUAGE
SPEAKING TUBE
TAPE RECORDER
TELEPHONE BOX
TELESHOPPING
TRANSMISSION
WALKIE-TALKIE
WORLD WIDE WEB

13
BEGGING LETTER
BUSH TELEGRAPH
CARRIER PIGEON
COMMUNICATION
DISTRESS FLARE
EXPRESS LETTER
EXPRESS PARCEL
HERTZIAN WAVES
LETTER MISSIVE
PIRATE STATION
POSTE RESTANTE
POST OFFICE BOX
RADIOLOCATION
RADIOTELEGRAM
REMOTE CONTROL
SPEAKING CLOCK
TAPE RECORDING
TELEGRAPH POLE

TELEGRAPH WIRE
TELEPHONE CALL
TELERECORDING
VIDEO RECORDER

14
CIRCULAR LETTER
CLOCKWORK RADIO
CORRESPONDENCE
COVERING LETTER

DISTRESS SIGNAL
FINGER ALPHABET
FIRST CLASS MAIL
PASTORAL LETTER
RADIO-TELEPHONY
TELETYPEWRITER
VIDEO RECORDING

15
CABLE TELEVISION
EXPRESS DELIVERY
PERSONAL SERVICE
POISON PEN LETTER
SECOND CLASS MAIL
SPEAKING TRUMPET
TELEPHONE NUMBER
TRANSISTOR RADIO
WIRELESS STATION

Arts – Media – COMPUTERS

3	CORE	PLUG	BATCH	INPUT	**6**
BIT	DATA	PORT	BLANK	LABEL	ACCESS
BOX	DECK	REEL	BLOCK	LOGIC	A DRIVE
BUG	DISK	SAVE	CABLE	MODEM	ANALOG
KEY	DUMP	SCAN	CARRY	MOUSE	ALT KEY
LEG	EDIT	SKIP	CHAIN	ORDER	BACK-UP
ROW	EXIT	STEP	CHART	PATCH	BINARY
RUN	FILE	TAPE	CHECK	PIXEL	BITMAP
SET	FILM	TEXT	CLICK	RADIX	BRANCH
TAB	FONT	TIFF	COBOL	RANGE	BUCKET
	GATE	TYPE	CORAL	ROUTE	BUFFER
4	HELP	VIEW	CYCLE	SCALE	CATENA
AREA	JACK	WI-FI	DEBUG	SCART	C DRIVE
BAND	JAVA	WORD	DIGIT	STACK	CODING
BASE	JPEG	WRAP	DIODE	STORE	COLUMN
BAUD	LINK	ZERO	DRIFT	TABLE	CURSOR
BIAS	LOOP	ZONE	DRIVE	TALLY	D DRIVE
BOOT	MARK		ENTER	TIMER	DELETE
BYTE	MASK	**5**	ENTRY	TOWER	E DRIVE
CARD	MENU	ADDER	ERROR	TRACK	FACTOR
CELL	MODE	ALGOL	FAULT	VIDEO	FILTER
CHAD	PACK	ARRAY	GROUP	VIRUS	FORMAT
CODE	PAGE	BASIC	INDEX		HEADER

INSERT
LAPTOP
MATRIX
MEMORY
MODULE
OUTPUT
PASCAL
REBOOT
RECALL
RECORD
REPORT
RESULT
SCREEN
SCROLL
SEARCH
SOCKET
SORTER
STREAM
STRING
SUBSET
SYMBOL
SYSTEM
TOGGLE
UPDATE
VOLUME
WINDOW

7

ADDRESS
ARCHIVE
CHANNEL
CHOPPER
CIRCUIT
CONSOLE
CONTROL
DATA SET
DECODER
DESKTOP

DIGITAL
DISPLAY
DUMPING
EMITTER
ENCODER
FAILURE
FORTRAN
GARBAGE
HACKING
JOURNAL
KEYWORD
LIBRARY
LIMITER
MASKING
MESSAGE
MONITOR
NETWORK
NOTEPAD
OPERAND
OVERLAY
PACKAGE
PRINTER
PROCESS
PROGRAM
READ-OUT
ROUTINE
ROUTING
RUN TIME
SCANNER
SECTION
SIMPLEX
SORTING
STACKER
START-UP
STORAGE
SUMMARY
TEST-RUN
TOOLBAR

UTILITY

8

ANALYSIS
ARGUMENT
ASSEMBLY
AUTOTEXT
BLOCKING
CAPACITY
COLLATOR
COMPILER
CORE DUMP
DATABANK
DATABASE
DATA TYPE
DOCUMENT
EMULATOR
FLIP-FLOP
FUNCTION
HARDWARE
INDEXING
KEYBOARD
LANGUAGE
LIGHT PEN
MOUSE MAT
OPERATOR
PASSWORD
PRINT-OUT
REAL TIME
RECOVERY
REGISTERED
SAMPLING
SCANNING
SCHEDULE
SECURITY
SEEK TIME
SEQUENCE
SETTINGS

SOFTWARE
TERMINAL
TYPEFACE
UPDATING

9

ARCHIVING
ASSEMBLER
BENCHMARK
BITSTREAM
BOOTSTRAP
BREAKDOWN
CHARACTER
CONFIGURE
CONNECTOR
CONVERTER
DEBUGGING
DIGITISER
DISK DRIVE
FLOWCHART
GENERATOR
HYPERLINK
INTERFACE
LEFT-CLICK
OPERATION
PAGE SET-UP
PARITY BIT
PERIPHERY
PROCESSOR
QUANTISER
QUICKTRAN
RETRIEVAL
TABULATOR
TOGGLE KEY
WRITE-ONCE

10

ACCESS TIME
ADDRESSING
AUTOFORMAT
BINARY CODE
BINARY TREE
CALCULATOR
COMPARATOR
CONTROL KEY
DATA MINING
FLOPPY DISK
MACHINE RUN
NETWORKING
PATCHBOARD
PROCESSING
PROPERTIES
PSEUDOCODE
RIGHT-CLICK
SCHEDULING
SUBROUTINE
TABULATION
THROUGHPUT
TRANSLATOR
TYPEWRITER

11

BINARY DIGIT
COMPUTERESE
DATA CAPTURE
DATA STORAGE
INFORMATION

MACHINE CODE
MEMORY STICK
MOTHERBOARD
OPTICAL DISK
PROGRAMMING
SCREEN SAVER
TIME-SHARING
TRANSACTION

12

BINARY SEARCH
COMPUTER GAME
CONTROL PANEL
DATA TERMINAL
DISASSEMBLER
ERROR MESSAGE
FILE RECOVERY
INPUT PROGRAM
MAGNETIC DISK
PRINT PREVIEW
RANDOM ACCESS
RESPONSE TIME
TAPE STREAMER
TOGGLE SWITCH
WRITE-PROTECT

13

BASIC LANGUAGE
CONFIGURATION
DATA PROCESSOR
DATA WAREHOUSE

DOCUMENTATION
INK-JET PRINTER
JUSTIFICATION
MATRIX PRINTER
MICROCOMPUTER
SHIFT REGISTER
SOURCE PROGRAM
SPECIFICATION
SYSTEMS DESIGN
VIRTUAL MEMORY
WORD PROCESSOR

14

ANALOG COMPUTER
DATA MANAGEMENT
DATA PROCESSING
INSTRUCTION SET
MICROPROCESSOR
WORD PROCESSING

15

COMPUTERISATION
COMPUTER PROGRAM
COMPUTER SCIENCE
DEFRAGMENTATION
DIGITAL COMPUTER
ERROR CORRECTION
INSTRUCTION CODE
MACHINE LANGUAGE
OPERATING SYSTEM
SYSTEMS ANALYSIS

Arts – Media – Publication – COMIC & CARTOON CHARACTERS

3
DOC Disney
   dwarf
TOM

4
CHIP
DALE
HUEY
JANE
JEFF
MUTT
ODIE
PLUG

5
BABAR
BAMBI
BLUTO
BUTCH
DEWEY
DIGBY
DIXIE
DOPEY Disney
   dwarf
DUMBO
FLOOK
GOOFY
HAPPY Disney
   dwarf
JERRY
LOUIE
NANCY
PIXIE
ROBIN

SNOWY
SPIKE
WIMPY

6
BATMAN
BOO-BOO
CALVIN
EUDORA
GINGER
GRUMPY Disney
   dwarf
HOBBES
OBELIX
POPEYE
SLEEPY Disney
   dwarf
SMIFFY
SMUDGE
SNEEZY Disney
   dwarf
SNOOPY
TINTIN

7
ASTERIX
BASHFUL Disney
   dwarf
BLONDIE
DAGWOOD
DAN DARE
DILBERT
GNASHER
JESSICA
MR MAGOO

MUTTLEY
PEBBLES
RAPHAEL
SWEE'PEA

8
ANDY CAPP
BAMM-BAMM
BATWOMAN
BLACK BOB
CATWOMAN
CUTHBERT
GARFIELD
LEONARDO
L'IL ABNER
LOIS LANE
OLIVE OYL
PORKY PIG
SUPERMAN
THE JOKER
THE MEKON
YOGI BEAR

9
ALF TUPPER
BANANAMAN
BETTY BOOP
BUGS BUNNY
DAFFY DUCK
DALE ARDEN
DICK TRACY
DONATELLO
ELMER FUDD
LEX LUTHOR
OOR WULLIE

SNOW WHITE
SPIDER-MAN
SYLVESTER
THE SMURFS
TWEETY PIE
WOODSTOCK

10
ALLY SLOPER
BUCK ROGERS
DEPUTY DAWG
DONALD DUCK
FRED BASSET
HEATHCLIFF
LITTLE PLUM
LORD SNOOTY
ROAD RUNNER
THE GAMBOLS
THE MOOMINS
THE PENGUIN
THE RIDDLER

11
BETTY RUBBLE
CHIP AND DALE
FELIX THE CAT
FLASH GORDON
FRITZ THE CAT
KORKY THE CAT
MUTT AND JEFF
PINK PANTHER
ROGER MELLIE
ROGER RABBIT
SNAGGLEPUSS
THE FAT SLAGS

TOM AND JERRY
WILE E COYOTE
WONDER WOMAN

12
BARNEY RUBBLE
BIFFO THE BEAR
BILLY THE FISH
CHARLIE BROWN
COLONEL BLIMP
DESPERATE DAN
DOCTOR ZARKOV
HUNGRY HORACE
MICHELANGELO
MICKEY MOUSE
MIGHTY MOUSE
MINNIE MOUSE
THE PERISHERS

13
BERYL THE PERIL
CAPTAIN MARVEL
CHICKEN LITTLE
DICK DASTARDLY
JIMINY CRICKET
MINNIE THE MINX
MODESTY BLAISE
PIXIE AND DIXIE
POOPDECK PAPPY
RUPERT THE BEAR

14
BASH STREET KIDS
CAPTAIN HADDOCK
DAISY MAE SCRAGG
FOGHORN LEGHORN
FRED FLINTSTONE

ROY OF THE ROVERS
SPEEDY GONZALEZ

15
CALVIN AND HOBBES
DENNIS THE MENACE
TOM, DICK AND HARRY
WILMA FLINTSTONE
WOODY WOODPECKER

16
HAGAR THE HORRIBLE
HUCKLEBERRY HOUND

17
BLONDIE AND DAGWOOD
PROFESSOR CALCULUS

Arts – Media – Publication – MAGAZINES & COMICS

3
EVE
FHM
MAD
MCN
NME
NOW
RED
SHE
VIZ
ZOO

4
BEST
CHAT

ELLE
HEAT
LIFE
LION
MIZZ
MOJO
MORE
NUTS
REAL
TIME

5
ARENA
BEANO
BELLA

BLISS
BLUSH!
BUNTY
CLASH
DANDY
EAGLE
HELLO!
MATCH
MAXIM
PRIMA
PUNCH
SHOUT
STERN
SUGAR
TIGER

VOGUE
WHICH?
WOMAN
YOURS

6
BEEZER
BRIDES
BUSTER
CANDIS
CLOSER
EMPIRE
GRANTA
GRAZIA
JACKIE

LOADED
LOOK-IN
REVEAL
SUDOKU
TATLER
TOPPER
TV HITS

7
AUTOCAR
COMPANY
ESQUIRE
FLYPAST
GLAMOUR
HOTSPUR

KERRANG!
MAJESTY
PLAYBOY
PUZZLER
STRIKER
THE FACE
THE LADY
TIME OUT
TOP GEAR
TV QUICK
TV TIMES
TWINKLE
VALIANT
WHAT CAR?

8
GAY TIMES
KNOCKOUT
MY WEEKLY
NEWSWEEK
SPARE RIB
THE FIELD
THE IDLER
THE OLDIE
THE STAGE
TOP SANTÉ
TV CHOICE

9
COMPUTING
CUSTOM CAR
GOLF WORLD
GOOD HOMES
IDEAL HOME
PENTHOUSE

SMASH HITS
THAT'S LIFE
THE GROCER
THE LANCET
THE VICTOR
WHAT'S ON TV
WOMAN'S OWN

10
AUTO TRADER
DER SPIEGEL
INSIDE SOAP
LLOYD'S LIST
MEN'S HEALTH
PARIS MATCH
PRIVATE EYE
RADIO TIMES
TAKE A BREAK
VANITY FAIR
WATCHTOWER

11
CLASSIC CARS
COUNTRY LIFE
MARIE CLAIRE
MELODY MAKER
SEARCHLIGHT
THE LISTENER

12
ANGLING TIMES
COSMOPOLITAN
FAMILY CIRCLE
LOOK AND LEARN
ROLLING STONE

THE ECONOMIST
THE NEW YORKER
WOMAN'S WEEKLY

13
COUNTRY LIVING
DALTON'S WEEKLY
GARDEN ANSWERS
HARPER'S BAZAAR
HORSE AND HOUND
READER'S DIGEST

14
COMPUTER WEEKLY
GARDENERS' WORLD
HOUSE AND GARDEN

15
AMATEUR GARDENER
EXCHANGE AND MART
HARPERS AND QUEEN
HOMES AND GARDENS
NATIONAL LAMPOON
THE BOY'S OWN PAPER
THE NEW SCIENTIST

16
AMATEUR GARDENING
GOOD HOUSEKEEPING
NATIONAL ENQUIRER

18
NATIONAL GEOGRAPHIC

Arts – Media – Publication – NEWSPAPERS
British unless stated

4
BILD Germany
TRUD Russia
VLAN Belgium

5
ARGUS South Africa
ASAHI Japan

6
EL PAIS Spain
PRAVDA Russia
THE SUN

7
DIE ZEIT Germany
GROEP AZ Belgium
LE MONDE France

8
GROUPE AZ Belgium
ICI PARIS France
IZVESTIA Russia
LA STAMPA Italy
LE FIGARO France
LE SOLEIL Canada
THE TIMES

9
DAILY MAIL
DAILY NEWS USA
DAILY STAR
THE PEOPLE

10
DAILY SPORT
LE PARISIEN France

11
AFTENPOSTEN
  Norway
AFTONBLADET
  Sweden
DAILY MIRROR
DAILY RECORD
DE TELEGRAAF
  Netherlands
OUEST-FRANCE
  France
SUNDAY SPORT
THE BIG ISSUE
THE GUARDIAN
THE OBSERVER
THE SCOTSMAN

12
DAILY EXPRESS
LA REPUBBLICA Italy
SUNDAY MIRROR
THE SPECTATOR
THE SPORTSMAN

13
THE RACING POST

14
FINANCIAL TIMES
NEWS OF THE WORLD
SONNTAG AKTUELL Germany
SUNDAY EXPRESS
THE INDEPENDENT
THE SUNDAY TIMES

15
BERLINER ZEITUNG Germany
EVENING STANDARD
THE MAIL ON SUNDAY
THE NEW YORK TIMES USA
THE SPORTING LIFE

16
NEW ZEALAND HERALD
  New Zealand
THE YORKSHIRE POST

17
THE BIRMINGHAM POST
THE DAILY TELEGRAPH
THE NEW YORK TRIBUNE USA
THE WASHINGTON POST USA
WALL STREET JOURNAL USA

18
THE SUNDAY TELEGRAPH

19
SYDNEY MORNING HERALD
  Australia

Arts – Media – Publication – PRINTING & JOURNALISM

3
DIE
GUM
INK
MAG
PAD
RAG
RUN
WAX
WEB

4
BILL
BIND
BODY
BOLD
BOOK
BULL
BUMF
CAPS
CARD
CASE
COPY
CYAN
DEMY
EDIT
ETCH
FACE
FILE
FILM
FONT
FORM
GLUE
GRID
HACK
HEAD
ITEM

JPEG
KERN
LEAD
LEAF
LINE
LIST
LOGO
MARK
MASK
MPEG
NEWS
PAGE
PICA
PLUG
PULP
REAM
ROLL
RUBY
RULE
SIDE
SLUG
SORT
STAR
STET
TEXT
TIFF
TINT
TOME
TURN
TYPE
TYPO
WORD
YAPP

5
ALBUM
ANNAL

ATLAS
BIBLE
BLACK
BLANK
BLEED
BLOCK
BLURB
BOARD
BRACE
CANON
CARET
CHART
CHASE
CODEX
COMIC
COVER
DAILY
DEVIL
DIARY
DRAFT
DUMMY
ÉLITE
EXTRA
FOLIO
FORME
FOUNT
FUDGE
GLOSS
GUARD
GUIDE
INDEX
INSET
ISSUE
LITHO
NOVEL
PAPER
PATCH

PEARL
PLATE
POINT
PRESS
PRINT
PROEM
PROOF
QUIRE
QUOTE
RECTO
ROMAN
ROUGH
ROYAL
SCOOP
SCRIP
SERIF
SHEET
SLICK
SPACE
SPINE
STATE
STORY
STRIP
STYLE
SWASH
TABLE
TITLE
TRACT
TUTOR
VERSO
WIDOW
XEROX
ZINCO

6
ADVERT
ANNUAL

BINDER
BORDER
BYLINE
CAHIER
CENSOR
CHROMO
COCK-UP
COLUMN
COUPON
DAGGER
DECKLE
DIGEST
EDITOR
ERRATA
EXPOSÉ
FLIMSY
FOLDER
FOOTER
FORMAT
GALLEY
GLOSSY
GOBBET
GUTTER
HEADER
HERBAL
INDENT
INK-JET
INSERT
ITALIC
JACKET
JOURNO
LAYOUT
LEADER
LEGEND
LETTER
MACKLE
MAKE-UP

MANUAL
MARGIN
MATTER
MISSAL
MOCK-UP
MORGUE
NOTICE
NUMBER
OBELUS
OCTAVO
OFFSET
ORPHAN
OZALID
PAGING
PLATEN
PRIMER
QUARTO
READER
RECORD
RED TOP
REGLET
REHASH
REPORT
REVIEW
RUBRIC
SCREEN
SCRIPT
SCROLL
SERIES
SIGLUM
SOURCE
SPACER
SPREAD
STAPLE
TABLET
TICKET
TYMPAN
TYPING
UNCIAL

VELLUM
VERSAL
VOLUME
WEEKLY
YELLOW

7
ADDENDA
ALMANAC
ARTICLE
ARTWORK
BALLOON
BANDING
BINDING
BOOKLET
BRACKET
BRAILLE
CAPITAL
CAPTION
CARTOON
CHAPTER
CUTTING
D NOTICE
DOSSIER
EDITING
EDITION
ENGRAVE
ERRATUM
ETCHING
EXAMPLE
EXTRACT
FEATURE
FICTION
FLYLEAF
FRAKTUR
FRISKET
GAZETTE
GRAVURE
HANDOUT

HEADING
IMPRINT
INK-FEED
INSIDES
ITALICS
JOURNAL
KERNING
LAW BOOK
LEXICON
LITERAL
MASKING
MEASURE
MEMOIRS
MISCOPY
MONTHLY
NOVELLA
OMNIBUS
OPENING
OVERLAY
OVERRUN
PAPYRUS
PARAGON
PASTE-UP
PREFACE
PRELIMS
PRINTER
PROCESS
PROFILE
PUBLISH
REISSUE
RELEASE
REPRINT
REVERSO
REWRITE
ROYALTY
SHOCKER
SNIPPET
SPECIAL
SUBBING

SUBEDIT
TABLOID
TRINDLE
TYPESET
WEBBING
WRITE-UP
WRITING

8
ADDENDUM
ANNOTATE
APPENDIX
ASCENDER
ASTERISK
BACK PAGE
BESTIARY
BIWEEKLY
BLEEDING
BLEED-OFF
BRACKETS
BREVIARY
BROCHURE
CALENDAR
CASEBOOK
CHAPBOOK
CITY DESK
CLIPPING
COLOPHON
CONTENTS
COPYBOOK
DATELINE
DEADLINE
ELEPHANT
ENDPAPER
EPIGRAPH
EX LIBRIS
FAIR COPY
FASCICLE
FILE COPY

FOOLSCAP
FOOTNOTE
FOREWORD
GLASSINE
GLOSSARY
HACKWORK
HALF-TONE
HANDBILL
HANDBOOK
HARDBACK
HEADLINE
HEADNOTE
HEADWORD
HORNBOOK
IDEOGRAM
IMPERIAL
INTAGLIO
KEYBOARD
LEXIGRAM
LIGATURE
LINOTYPE
LOGOGRAM
LOGOTYPE
LONGHAND
MAGAZINE
MAQUETTE
MISPRINT
MONGRAM
MONOTYPE
NEWSDESK
NEWSROOM
OBITUARY
OUTSIDES
PAMPHLET
POSTCARD
PREAMBLE
PRE-PRINT
PRESS BOX
PRINTING

PRINT RUN
RATE CARD
REGISTER
REPORTER
SENTENCE
SNIPPING
STREAMER
SUBTITLE
TEXTBOOK
THRILLER
TRANSFER
TYPEFACE
VARIORUM
WOOD PULP
WORDBOOK
YEARBOOK

9

AMPERSAND
ANTHOLOGY
ATTRIBUTE
BACK COVER
BIMONTHLY
BIOGRAPHY
BLOCK TYPE
BLUEPRINT
BOOKPLATE
BOOK TRADE
BROADSIDE
CATALOGUE
CENSORING
CHARACTER
CHRONICLE
CLARENDON
COLLATION
COLUMNIST
COMPOSING
COPYRIGHT
CROP MARKS

CROSS HEAD
CROSSWORD
CUNEIFORM
DESCENDER
DESK DIARY
DIME NOVEL
DIRECTORY
DUODECIMO
DUPLICATE
DUST COVER
EDITORIAL
ENGRAVING
EXCLUSIVE
EXPURGATE
FORMULARY
FREELANCE
FRONT PAGE
FURNITURE
GAZETTEER
GUIDEBOOK
HALF-TITLE
HEADPIECE
HELVETICA
HIEROGRAM
INDENTION
INDIAN INK
INSERTION
INTERLEAF
ITINERARY
LETTERING
LETTERSET
LOWER CASE
MAJUSCULE
MAKE-READY
MEMORIALS
MINUSCULE
NEWSPAPER
NEWSPRINT
NEWS-SHEET

NEWS TRADE
NONPAREIL
NOVELETTE
ORDER BOOK
OVERPRINT
PAGE PROOF
PAPARAZZI
PAPERBACK
PARAGRAPH
PARCHMENT
PHOTOCOPY
PHOTOSTAT
PICTOGRAM
PICTORIAL
POINT SIZE
PRESS CARD
PROGRAMME
PROOF-READ
PUBLISHER
QUARTERLY
QUOTATION
RECENSION
REDACTION
REPORTAGE
REPORTING
ROYALTIES
SCRAPBOOK
SECRETARY
SHORTHAND
SMALL CAPS
STITCHING
STOP PRESS
STORYBOOK
STRAPLINE
STYLE BOOK
SUBEDITOR
SYNDICATE
TAILPIECE
THESAURUS

TITLE PAGE
UPPER CASE
VADE MECUM
WATERLINE
WATERMARK
WEB OFFSET
WOODBLOCK

10
ANNOTATION
ASSIGNMENT
BACK NUMBER
BESTSELLER
BIBLIOLOGY
BOOKBINDER
BOWDLERISE
BOWDLERISM
BROADSHEET
CARICATURE
CENTREFOLD
CITY EDITOR
COLLECTION
COLPORTAGE
COLPORTEUR
COMMENTARY
COMPENDIUM
COPYWRITER
CORRIGENDA
DAILY PAPER
DECKLE EDGE
DEDICATION
DICTIONARY
DIE CUTTING
DISCLAIMER
DUST JACKET
EDITORSHIP
FEUILLETON
FREELANCER
FRONT COVER

GRANGERISE
GRANGERISM
HIEROGLYPH
HOUSE STYLE
IMPOSITION
IMPRESSION
IMPRIMATUR
INCUNABULA
JOURNALESE
JOURNALISM
LEADER PAGE
LETTERHEAD
LITERATURE
LITHOGRAPH
MANUSCRIPT
MARGINALIA
NEWS AGENCY
NEWSLETTER
NEWSWORTHY
OCTODECIMO
OVERMATTER
PAGINATION
PALIMPSEST
PERIODICAL
PHRASE BOOK
PICTOGRAPH
PLAGIARISM
PLATEMAKER
PROPRIETOR
PUBLISHING
READERSHIP
RETRACTION
REVIEW COPY
SCHOOLBOOK
SEPARATION
SKETCHBOOK
SOURCEBOOK
SPORTS PAGE
SUBEDITING

SUB-HEADING
SUPPLEMENT
THUMB INDEX
TITLE SHEET
TRADE PAPER
TRADE PRESS
TYPESCRIPT
TYPESETTER
TYPEWRITER
VOCABULARY
WOODEN TYPE
XEROGRAPHY
YELLOWBACK

11
ADVANCE COPY
ADVERTORIAL
AGONY COLUMN
AIDE-MEMOIRE
ANTIQUARIAN
BASKERVILLE
BLOCK LETTER
BOOKBINDING
CALLING CARD
CIRCULATION
COMPILATION
CONCORDANCE
CONTRIBUTOR
COOKERY BOOK
COPYWRITING
CORRIGENDUM
CUB REPORTER
CYCLOPAEDIA
DECKLE-EDGED
DISTRIBUTOR
DUPLICATION
ELECTROTYPE
ENCHIRIDION
EXPURGATION

GALLEY PROOF
GRAMMALOGUE
GUTTER PRESS
HALF BINDING
ILLUSTRATED
INSCRIPTION
INTERPOLATE
LETTERPRESS
LITHOGRAPHY
ONOMASTICON
ON THE RECORD
PARENTHESES
PARENTHESIS
PICTOGRAPHY
PICTURE BOOK
PLATEMAKING
PRINTER'S INK
PROOF-READER
PUBLICATION
READING BOOK
ROTOGRAVURE
RUNNING FOOT
RUNNING HEAD
SILLY SEASON
SLOW NEWS DAY
STATUTE BOOK
STENOGRAPHY
SYNDICATION
TYPE FOUNDER
TYPE FOUNDRY
TYPESETTING
TYPEWRITING

12
BIBLIOGRAPHY
BIRTHDAY CARD
BLOCK CAPITAL
BLOCK LETTERS
BREAKING NEWS

BUSINESS CARD
CONTRIBUTION
DEPUTY EDITOR
DISTRIBUTION
DOUBLE DAGGER
DOUBLE OBELUS
EXERCISE BOOK
FEATURES PAGE
FOURTH ESTATE
FRONTISPIECE
GLOSSOGRAPHY
GOSSIP COLUMN
HIEROGLYPHIC
ILLUMINATION
ILLUSTRATION
INTRODUCTION
LEADER WRITER
MARGINAL NOTE
OFF THE RECORD
PERFECT BOUND
PHOTOCOPYING
PHOTOGRAVURE
PHOTOSETTING
PRESS CUTTING
PRESS GALLERY
PRESS RELEASE
PRINTER'S MARK
PROOF-READING
RUNNING TITLE
SADDLE STITCH
SCANDAL SHEET
SMALL CAPITAL
STENOGRAPHER
STRIP CARTOON
TRANSPARENCY
VISITING CARD
VISITORS' BOOK

13
AUTOBIOGRAPHY
BLOCK CAPITALS
CHRISTMAS CARD
CONDENSED TYPE
ENCYCLOPAEDIA
GREETINGS CARD
HIEROGLYPHICS
INTERPOLATION
JUSTIFICATION
LEFT JUSTIFIED
PENNY DREADFUL
PLATE PRINTING
PRELIMINARIES
PRINTING PAPER
PRINTING PRESS
QUESTIONNAIRE
READING MATTER
READY RECKONER
REFERENCE BOOK
SPIRAL BINDING
SUBJECT MATTER
VALENTINE CARD

14
BANNER HEADLINE
COMPOSING STICK
CROSS-REFERENCE
FEATURES EDITOR
GLOSSY MAGAZINE
INVITATION CARD
LATE-NIGHT FINAL
NEWSWORTHINESS
OFFSET PRINTING
OMNIBUS EDITION
PERFECT BINDING
PERSONAL COLUMN
RIGHT JUSTIFIED
SCREEN PRINTING

SPECIAL EDITION

15
ACKNOWLEDGEMENT
CAMERA-READY COPY
CROSSWORD PUZZLE

LOOSE-LEAF BINDER
NAUTICAL ALMANAC
PICTURE POSTCARD
PROOF CORRECTING
PROOF CORRECTION
RUNNING HEADLINE

16
CHROMOLITHOGRAPH
COLOUR SEPARATION
COLOUR SUPPLEMENT

Arts – Media – Television – TV & RADIO PERSONALITIES
Also see Actors & Actresses, Celebrity Chefs, Comedians

3
AIR Donna
COX Doc, Sara
DAY Sir Robin
DEE Simon
DON Monty
FOX Neil
FRY Stephen
GEE Dustin
HAY Alex
JAY Peter
KAY Vernon
RAY Robin, Ted
WAX Ruby

4
ADIE Kate
ALAN Ray
BALL Bobby,
 Johnny, Zoë
BEER Alice
BIRD John
BOND Jennie
BOYD Tommy
CANT Brian
CASH Dave

COLE John
COOK Peter,
 Roger, Sue
DALY Tess
DODD Ken
DUNN John
FISH Michael
FORD Anna
GALL Sandy
GRAY Muriel
HALE Gareth
HALL Stuart, Terry
HANN Judith
HART Tony
HILL Benny, Harry,
 Jane, Jimmy
HUDD Roy
IDLE Eric
JUDD Lesley
KING Larry
KYLE Jeremy
LAKE Ricki
LAMB Amanda
LONG Janice
LOWE Chris, Ted
MARR Andrew

MAYO Simon
MUIR Frank
NEAL Andrew
OWEN Nicholas,
 Nick
PACE Norman
PEEL John
READ Al, Mike
REES Nigel
RICE Anneka
ROSS Jonathan,
 Nick, Paul
SHAW Adam
SNOW Jon, Peter
SYAL Meera
TONG Pete
TOOK Barry
TUSA John
VINE David, Jeremy
WALL Max
WARK Kirsty
WEST Peter
WISE Ernie
WOOD Victoria

5

ABBOT Russ
AGNEW Jonathan
ASKEY Arthur
ASPEL Michael
BAKER Danny, Richard
BANKS Jeff
BATES Simon
BLACK Cilla
BLAIR Lionel
BORGE Victor
BOUGH Frank
BOWEN Jeremy, Jim
BRAGG Baron Melvyn
BROWN Faith, Janet
BRUCE Fiona, Ken
BUERK Michael
BURKE James, Kathy
BURNS Gordon
CAINE Marti
CLARY Julian
COHEN Sasha Baron
COOKE Alistair
CRANE Andy
CRYER Barry
CURRY Mark
DANDO Jill
DAVIS Evan
DAVRO Bobby
DOYLE Craig
DRAKE Charlie
ELTON Ben
EMERY Dick
EMNEY Fred
ESLER Gavin
EVANS Chris
FELTZ Vanessa
FOGLE Ben

FREUD Emma
FROST Sir David
GAVIN Diarmuid
GILES Bill
GOODY Jade
GRANT Russell
GREEN Benny, Tony
GREGG Anne
GUBBA Tony
HARTY Russell
HENRY Lenny
HORNE Kenneth
JAMES Clive
JONES Ann, Clay,
  Peter, Terry
JUNOR Penny
KELLY Barbara, Chris,
  Henry, Lorraine,
  Matthew
LARGE Eddie
LA RUE Danny
LEWIS Martyn, Paul,
  Tony
LLOYD Sian
LOGAN Gabby
LYNAM Des
MCGEE Debbie
MEARS Ray
MILES Michael
MOORE Brian, Dudley,
  Sir Patrick, Ray
NEGUS Arthur
NIXON David
ODDIE Bill
PALIN Michael
PARRY Alan
RIDER Steve
ROWAN Dan

SACHS Leonard
SAYLE Alexei
SCOTT Brough, Selina
SERLE Chris
SMITH Arthur, Linda,
  Mel
SOPEL Jon
SYKES Eric, Melanie
TULLY Mark
WAITE John
WALSH Tommy
WEEKS Alan
WELLS John
WHITE Peter
WOLFF Heinz
WOODS Peter
WORTH Harry
YATES Paula
YOUNG Jimmy, Kirsty,
  Muriel

6

ALLISS Peter
AL READ
ARLOTT John
ARTHUR Toni
AUSTIN Mark
BARKER Ronnie, Sue
BARNES Carol
BASHIR Martin
BAXTER Raymond,
  Stanley
BEADLE Jeremy
BENAUD Richie
BHASKAR Sanjeev
BRADEN Bernard
BROUGH Peter
BRYDON Rob

BURNET Sir Alastair
BUTLER Brian
CANNON Tommy
CARSON Johnny, Willie
CARTER John
CASTLE Andrew, Roy
CHILES Adrian
CLARKE Nick, Oz
CLEESE John
CLOUGH Gordon
CONLEY Brian
COOGAN Steve
COOPER Joseph,
  Tommy
COTTON Billy, Fearne
COWELL Simon
CRAVEN John
DAVIES Barry, Dickie
DAWSON Les
DEELEY Cat
DENNIS Les
DERHAM Katie
DIBNAH Fred
DOC COX
DOUGAL Robert
DUNCAN Peter
EMBERG Bella
FOSTER Brendan
FRENCH Dawn
GARDEN Graeme
GARVEY Jane
GLOVER Fi
GREENE Hughie, Sarah
GUYLER Deryck
HANSEN Alan
HARRIS Bob, Keith, Rolf
HAYNES Arthur
HAYTON Philip

HEARNE Richard
HEINEY Paul
HELVIN Marie
HISLOP Ian
HOBDAY Peter
HOBLEY McDonald
HOLMES Eamonn
HOWARD Margaret
HOWERD Frankie
HUMBLE Kate
IRVINE Hazel
JACOBS David
JENSEN David
JORDON Darren
JUNKIN John
KIELTY Patrick
LAMARR Mark
LAURIE Hugh
LAWLEY Sue
LAWSON Mark
LEGARD Jonathan
LITTLE Syd
MARTIN Dick, Paul
MAYALL Rik
MCCALL Davina
MERTON Paul
MILLER Max
MORGAN Cliff, Piers
MORRIS Johnny, Juliet,
  Mike
MOTSON John
MOYLES Chris
MURRAY Jenni, Pete
MURROW Ed
NOAKES John
NORDEN Denis
NORMAN Barry
NORTON Graham

OAKSEY John
O'GRADY Paul
O'LEARY Dermot
PARKIN Leonard
PAXMAN Jeremy
PETERS Andi, Sylvia
PILGER John
PORTER Gail
POWELL Peter, Sandy
PURVES Libby, Peter
RAVENS Jan
RAYNER Claire
RIPPON Angela
RIVERS Joan
ROGERS Ted
ROSLIN Gaby
SAVILE Sir Jimmy
SCULLY Hugh
SEWELL Brian
SNAGGE John
SPICER Lorne
STUART Moira
STUBBS Ray
SUCHET John
TAYLOR Shaw
TED RAY
TRAVIS Dave Lee
TURNER Anthea
WALDEN Brian
WALKER Johnnie,
  Murray, Roy
WALTON Kent
WARING Eddie
WILCOX Desmond
WILLIS Wincey
WILMOT Gary
WILSON Bob, Francis,
  Julian, Quentin

WINTON Dale
WISDOM Sir Norman
WRIGHT Matthew,
  Steve
YENTOB Alan

7
ADAMSON Tony
ALAGIAH George
ALEX HAY
ALLSOPP Kirstie
ANDREWS Eamonn
BADDIEL David
BALDING Clare
BARNETT Lady Isobel
BELLAMY David
BENNETT Lennie
BENTINE Michael
BIGGINS Christopher
BLOFELD Henry
BOTTING Louise
BREMNER Rory
BRITTON Fern
BROMLEY Peter
CARROTT Jasper
CHAPMAN Graham,
  Nicki
CHEGWIN Keith
CHESTER Charlie
COLEMAN David
COLLIER Norman
CORBETT Harry,
  Matthew, Ronnie
CULSHAW Jon
DANIELS Paul
DEAYTON Angus
DELANEY Frank
DIAMOND Anne

DIGANCE Richard
DIMMOCK Charlie,
  Peter
DRABBLE Phil
EDMONDS Noël
EDWARDS Huw
ENFIELD Harry
EVERETT Kenny
EVERTON Clive
FORDYCE Keith
FORSYTH Bruce
FORTUNE John
FREEMAN Alan,
  John
GODDARD Trisha
GOODIER Mark
GOOLDEN Jilly
GOSLING Ray
GRAYSON Larry
HANCOCK Nick, Tony
HANDLEY Tommy
HARDING Gilbert,
  Mike
HOLLAND Jools
HOLNESS Bob
HOUSEGO Fred
JACKSON Jack
JON SNOW
JONSSON Ulrika
JUPITUS Phill
KENDALL Kenneth
KEN DODD
KENNEDY Sir Ludovic,
  Sarah
KERSHAW Andy
KETTLEY John
KNOWLES Nick
LINDLEY Jimmy

LINEKER Gary
MADELEY Richard
MASKELL Dan
MATTHEW Brian
MCCLOUD Kevin
MCGOWAN Alistair,
  Cathy
MCGRATH Rory
NEIL FOX
O'BRIAIN Dara
O'CONNOR Des, Tom
PARSONS Nicholas
PEEBLES Andy
PHILBIN Maggie
PICKLES Wilfred
PLOMLEY Roy
RANTZEN Esther
RAWORTH Sophie
REDFERN Anthea
REDHEAD Brian
RUSHTON Willie
SARA COX
SAWALHA Nadia
SECOMBE Sir Harry
SELLERS Peter
SHERRIN Ned
SIMPSON John
SISSONS Peter
SKINNER Frank
SMILLIE Carol
SPENCER Phil
ST CLAIR Isla
STEWART Alastair, Ed
STILGOE Richard
SUE COOK
SWEENEY Claire
TARRANT Chris
TED LOWE

THEROUX Louis
THROWER Debbie, Percy
TOKSVIG Sandi
VAUGHAN Johnny,
  Norman
VINCENT Robbie
WEBSTER Mark
WHEELER Charles,
  Sir Mortimer
WHICKER Alan
WINFREY Oprah
WOODALL Trinny
YARWOOD Mike
ZOË BALL

8

ADAM SHAW
ANDERSON Clive
ANNA FORD
ANN JONES
ATKINSON Rowan
BAKEWELL Joan
BEN ELTON
BEN FOGLE
BENJAMIN Floella
BYGRAVES Max
CAMPBELL Nicky
CHALMERS Judith
CLARKSON Jeremy
CROWTHER Leslie
DAN ROWAN
DAVIDSON Jim
DES LYNAM
DIMBLEBY David,
  Jonathan, Richard
DINENAGE Fred
DONNA AIR
DONNELLY Declan

DUGGLEBY Vincent
ED MURROW
ERIC IDLE
FI GLOVER
FINNIGAN Judy
FLETCHER Cyril
FRINDALL Bill
FROSTRUP Mariella
GROSSMAN Loyd
HAMILTON David
HANRAHAN Brian
HARRIOTT Ainsley
HUMPHRYS John
JANE HILL
JIM BOWEN
JOHN BIRD
JOHN COLE
JOHN DUNN
JOHN PEEL
JOHNSTON Brian
JOHN TUSA
JON SOPEL
KATE ADIE
KEN BRUCE
KRONKITE Walter
MARSHALL Arthur
MCDONALD Sir Trevor
MEL SMITH
METCALFE Jean
MIKE READ
MILLIGAN Spike
MITCHELL Leslie
MONTAGUE Sarah
MONTEITH Kelly
MONTY DON
NAUGHTIE James
NICHOLAS Mark
NICK OWEN

NICK ROSS
OSBOURNE Sharon
OZ CLARKE
PASQUALE Joe
PAUL ROSS
PETER JAY
PETE TONG
PETTIFER Julian
RAY MEARS
RAY MOORE
ROBIN DAY Sir
ROBIN RAY
ROBINSON Anne, Nick,
  Robert, Tony
SAUNDERS Jennifer
SERGEANT John
SIMON DEE
SPRINGER Jerry
STOPPARD Miriam
STOURTON Edward
SULLIVAN Ed
TIM EWART
TONY HART
TURNBULL Bill
VAN OUTEN Denise
WHITELEY Richard
WILLIAMS Dorian,
  Kenneth, Sian
WITCHELL Nicholas

9

ALAN PARRY
ALAN WEEKS
ALICE BEER
ANDY CRANE
ANNE GREGG
ARMSTRONG Fiona,
  Pamela

BARRYMORE Michael
BARRY TOOK
BEARDSHAW Chris
BENNY HILL
BILL GILES
BILL ODDIE
BLACKBURN Tony
BOBBY BALL
BOB HARRIS
BOB WILSON
BOSANQUET Reginald
BRANDRETH Gyles
BRIAN CANT
CARPENTER Harry
CAT DEELEY
CHRIS LOWE
CLAY JONES
DAVID VINE
DECOURCEY Roger
DICK EMERY
DICKINSON David
DUSTIN GEE
ED STEWART
EMMA FREUD
ERIC SYKES
ERNIE WISE
EVAN DAVIS
FORRESTER Philippa
FRANK MUIR
FRED EMNEY
GASCOIGNE Bamber
HARRY HILL
HART-DAVIS Adam
HENDERSON Dickie
HUMPHRIES Barry
HUNNIFORD Gloria
IAN HISLOP
INVERDALE John

JADE GOODY
JAN RAVENS
JEFF BANKS
JILL DANDO
JIMMY HILL
JOHN WAITE
JOHN WELLS
KAPLINSKY Natasha
KNOX-MAWER June
LARRY KING
LAWRENSON Mark
LES DAWSON
LES DENNIS
LONGHURST Henry
LYTTELTON Humphrey
MACGREGOR Sue
MAGNUSSON
   Magnus, Sally
MARK CURRY
MARK TULLY
MAX MILLER
MCCASKILL Ian
MCCRIRICK John
MCPARTLIN Anthony
MEERA SYAL
MIKE SMITH
MONKHOUSE Bob
MORECAMBE Eric
MURNAGHAN Dermot
NICHOLSON Michael
NIGEL REES
O'SULLEVAN Peter
PARKINSON Michael
PAUL LEWIS
PETER COOK
PETER SNOW
PETER WEST
PICKERING Ron

RAY STUBBS
RHYS-JONES Griff
RICKI LAKE
RIK MAYALL
ROBERTSON Max,
   Mick
ROGER COOK
ROLLINSON Helen
ROSENTHAL Jim
ROY CASTLE
ROY WALKER
RUSS ABBOT
SANDY GALL
SCHOFIELD Phillip
SIAN LLOYD
SIMON MAYO
SINGLETON Val
STAPLETON John
SUE BARKER
SUE LAWLEY
SYD LITTLE
TED ROGERS
TERRY HALL
THEAKSTON Jamie
TOMMY BOYD
TONY GREEN
TONY GUBBA
TONY LEWIS
VORDERMAN Carol
WINKLEMAN Claudia
WONNACOTT Tim

10
ALAN HANSEN
ALAN YENTOB
AMANDA LAMB
ANDI PETERS
ANDREW MARR

ANDREW NEAL
ANNEKA RICE
BARRY CRYER
BENNY GREEN
BOBBY DAVRO
BOB HOLNESS
BRIAN MOORE
BRIGSTOCKE Marcus
CATHERWOOD Andrea
CHRIS EVANS
CHRIS KELLY
CHRIS SERLE
CLIVE JAMES
CRAIG DOYLE
DALE WINTON
DAN MASKELL
DANNY BAKER
DANNY LA RUE
DAVID FROST Sir
DAVID NIXON
DAWN FRENCH
DES O'CONNOR
DICK MARTIN
ED SULLIVAN
FAITH BROWN
FIONA BRUCE
FRANK BOUGH
FRED DIBNAH
GABBY LOGAN
GABY ROSLIN
GAIL PORTER
GAMBACCINI Paul
GARETH HALE
GARY WILMOT
GAVIN ESLER
HARGREAVES Jack
HARRY WORTH
HEINZ WOLFF

HENRY KELLY
HUGH LAURIE
HUGH SCULLY
HUW EDWARDS
JAMES BURKE
JANE GARVEY
JANET BROWN
JANICE LONG
JENNIE BOND
JEREMY KYLE
JEREMY VINE
JIMMY YOUNG
JOAN RIVERS
JOHN ARLOTT
JOHN CARTER
JOHN CLEESE
JOHN CRAVEN
JOHN JUNKIN
JOHN MOTSON
JOHN NOAKES
JOHNNY BALL
JOHN OAKSEY
JOHN PILGER
JOHN SNAGGE
JOHN SUCHET
JON CULSHAW
JUDITH HANN
KATE HUMBLE
KATHY BURKE
KENT WALTON
KILROY-SILK Robert
KIRSTY WARK
LENNY HENRY
LESLEY JUDD
LINDA SMITH
MACPHERSON Sandy
MARK AUSTIN
MARK LAMARR

MARK LAWSON
MARTI CAINE
MICHELMORE Cliff
MIKE MORRIS
MUGGERIDGE Malcolm
MURIEL GRAY
NED SHERRIN
NICK CLARKE
NORMAN PACE
PAULA YATES
PAUL HEINEY
PAUL MARTIN
PAUL MERTON
PAUL O'GRADY
PENNY JUNOR
PETE MURRAY
PETER JONES
PETER WHITE
PETER WOODS
RAY GOSLING
ROLF HARRIS
ROY PLOMLEY
SHAW TAYLOR
SIMON BATES
SOMERVILLE Julia
STEPHEN FRY
STEPHENSON Pamela
STUART HALL
TERRY JONES
TERRY WOGAN
TITCHMARSH Alan
TOMMY WALSH
TOM O'CONNOR
TONI ARTHUR

11
ALAN FREEMAN
ALAN WHICKER

ALEXEI SAYLE
ANDY KERSHAW
ANDY PEEBLES
ANNE DIAMOND
ARTHUR ASKEY
ARTHUR NEGUS
ARTHUR SMITH
BARRY DAVIES
BARRY NORMAN
BELLA EMBERG
BILLY COTTON
BRIAN BUTLER
BRIAN CONLEY
BRIAN SEWELL
BRIAN WALDEN
BROUGH SCOTT
CAROL BARNES
CLIFF MORGAN
CONSTANTINE
  Susannah
CRUICKSHANK Dan
DARA O'BRIAIN
DAVID JACOBS
DAVID JENSEN
DEBBIE MCGEE
DENIS NORDEN
DUDLEY MOORE
DURDEN-SMITH Mark,
  Neil
EDDIE WARING
FERN BRITTON
FRED HOUSEGO
GARY LINEKER
GLENDENNING
  Raymond
GORDON BURNS
HAZEL IRVINE
ISLA ST CLAIR

JACK JACKSON
JENNI MURRAY
JEREMY BOWEN
JIM DAVIDSON
JIMMY SAVILE Sir
JOE PASQUALE
JOHN FORTUNE
JOHN FREEMAN
JOHN KETTLEY
JOHN SIMPSON
JULIAN CLARY
KATIE DERHAM
KEITH HARRIS
KIRSTY YOUNG
LIBBY PURVES
LIONEL BLAIR
LORNE SPICER
MARIE HELVIN
MARK GOODIER
MARK WEBSTER
MARTYN LEWIS
MAX BYGRAVES
MELVYN BRAGG Baron
MICHAEL FISH
MIKE HARDING
MIKE YARWOOD
MOIRA STUART
MURIEL YOUNG
NICK HANCOCK
NICK KNOWLES
NIGHTINGALE Annie
NOËL EDMONDS
PAUL DANIELS
PETER ALLISS
PETER BROUGH
PETER DUNCAN
PETER HOBDAY
PETER POWELL

PETER PURVES
PHIL DRABBLE
PHIL SPENCER
PIERS MORGAN
PRENDEVILLE Kieran
RORY BREMNER
RORY MCGRATH
SANDY POWELL
SARAH GREENE
SELINA SCOTT
SIMON COWELL
STEVE COOGAN
STEVE WRIGHT
TOMMY CANNON
TOMMY COOPER
TONY ADAMSON
TONY HANCOCK
VICTOR BORGE

12
ADRIAN CHILES
ANDREW CASTLE
ANGELA RIPPON
ANGUS DEAYTON
ANNE ROBINSON
ANNETTE MILLS
ANTHEA TURNER
ARTHUR HAYNES
ATTENBOROUGH
  Sir David
BARBARA KELLY
BILL FRINDALL
BILL TURNBULL
BOB MONKHOUSE
BRIAN MATTHEW
BRIAN REDHEAD
BROOKE-TAYLOR Tim
BRUCE FORSYTH

CAROL SMILLIE
CATHY MCGOWAN
CHARLIE DRAKE
CHRIS TARRANT
CLAIRE RAYNER
CLARE BALDING
CLIVE EVERTON
DARREN JORDON
DAVID BADDIEL
DAVID BELLAMY
DAVID COLEMAN
DAVINA MCCALL
DERMOT O'LEARY
DERYCK GUYLER
DICKIE DAVIES
EAMONN HOLMES
FEARNE COTTON
FRANK DELANEY
FRANK SKINNER
FRED DINENAGE
GORDON CLOUGH
GRAEME GARDEN
GRAHAM NORTON
HARRY CORBETT
HARRY ENFIELD
HARRY SECOMBE Sir
HENRY BLOFELD
HUGHIE GREENE
IAN MCCASKILL
JEAN METCALFE
JEREMY BEADLE
JEREMY PAXMAN
JILLY GOOLDEN
JIMMY LINDLEY
JIMMY TARBUCK
JIM ROSENTHAL
JOAN BAKEWELL
JOHN HUMPHRYS

JOHNNY CARSON
JOHNNY MORRIS
JOHN SERGEANT
JONATHAN ROSS
JOOLS HOLLAND
JOSEPH COOPER
JUDY FINNIGAN
JULIAN WILSON
JULIET MORRIS
KEITH CHEGWIN
KEITH FORDYCE
KENNETH HORNE
KENNY EVERETT
KEVIN MCCLOUD
LARRY GRAYSON
LEONARD SACHS
LOUIS THEROUX
LOYD GROSSMAN
MARK NICHOLAS
MARTIN BASHIR
MATTHEW KELLY
MAX ROBERTSON
MELANIE SYKES
MICHAEL ASPEL
MICHAEL BUERK
MICHAEL MILES
MICHAEL PALIN
MURRAY WALKER
NADIA SAWALHA
NICHOLAS OWEN
NICKI CHAPMAN
NICK ROBINSON
NORMAN WISDOM Sir
OPRAH WINFREY
PATRICK MOORE Sir
PERCY THROWER
PETER BROMLEY
PETER DIMMOCK

PETER SELLERS
PETER SISSONS
PHILL JUPITUS
RICHARD BAKER
RICHIE BENAUD
ROBERT DOUGAL
RONNIE BARKER
RON PICKERING
RUSSELL GRANT
RUSSELL HARTY
SANDI TOKSVIG
SARAH KENNEDY
SIAN WILLIAMS
STARMER-SMITH Nigel
STREET-PORTER Janet
SYLVIA PETERS
TIM WONNACOTT
TOMMY HANDLEY
TONY ROBINSON
VAL SINGLETON
VANESSA FELTZ
VICTORIA WOOD
WINCEY WILLIS
WOLSTENHOLME
  Kenneth

13
ADAM HART-DAVIS
ALISTAIR COOKE
ANTHEA REDFERN
BERNARD BRADEN
BRENDAN FOSTER
BRIAN JOHNSTON
CLAIRE SWEENEY
CLIVE ANDERSON
CYRIL FLETCHER
DANVERS-WALKER Bob
DAVE LEE TRAVIS

DAVID DIMBLEBY
DAVID HAMILTON
DIARMUID GAVIN
DEBBIE THROWER
DESMOND WILCOX
EAMONN ANDREWS
ERIC MORECAMBE
ESTHER RANTZEN
FRANCIS WILSON
FRANKIE HOWERD
GEORGE ALAGIAH
GRAHAM CHAPMAN
ISOBEL BARNETT Lady
JAMES NAUGHTIE
JASPER CARROTT
JERRY SPRINGER
JOHN INVERDALE
JOHN MCCRIRICK
JOHNNIE WALKER
JOHNNY VAUGHAN
JOHN STAPLETON
JONATHAN AGNEW
JUNE KNOX-MAWER
KELLY MONTEITH
LENNIE BENNETT
LEONARD PARKIN
LORRAINE KELLY
LOUISE BOTTING
MAGGIE PHILBIN
MARK LAWRENSON
MARTIN-JENKINS
   Christopher
MATTHEW WRIGHT
MICK ROBERTSON
NICKY CAMPBELL
NORMAN COLLIER
NORMAN VAUGHAN
PATRICK KIELTY

QUENTIN WILSON
RAYMOND BAXTER
RICHARD HEARNE
ROBBIE VINCENT
RONNIE CORBETT
ROWAN ATKINSON
SARAH MONTAGUE
SOPHIE RAWORTH
SPIKE MILLIGAN
STANLEY BAXTER
TONY GODDARD
TRINNY WOODALL
TRISHA GODDARD
ULRIKA JONSSON
WILLIE RUSHTON

14
ALAN TITCHMARSH
ALASTAIR BURNET Sir
ARTHUR MARSHALL
BARRY HUMPHRIES
CAROL VORDERMAN
CHARLES WHEELER
CHARLIE CHESTER
CHARLIE DIMMOCK
CHRIS BEARDSHAW
DAN CRUICKSHANK
DAVID DICKINSON
DECLAN DONNELLY
DENISE VAN OUTEN
DORIAN WILLIAMS
EDWARD STOURTON
FIONA ARMSTRONG
GILBERT HARDING
GRIFF RHYS-JONES
GYLES BRANDRETH
HARRY CARPENTER
HELEN ROLLINSON

HENRY LONGHURST
JACK HARGREAVES
JAMIE THEAKSTON
JEREMY CLARKSON
JONATHAN LEGARD
JUDITH CHALMERS
JULIAN PETTIFER
KENNETH KENDALL
KIRSTIE ALLSOPP
LESLIE CROWTHER
LESLIE MITCHELL
LUDOVIC KENNEDY Sir
MARGARET HOWARD
MATTHEW CORBETT
MCDONALD HOBLEY
MICHAEL BENTINE
MIRIAM STOPPARD
PAUL GAMBACCINI
PETER O'SULLEVAN
RICHARD MADELEY
RICHARD STILGOE
ROBERT ROBINSON
ROGER DECOURCEY
SALLY MAGNUSSON
SANJEEV BHASKAR
SHARON OSBOURNE
TREVOR MCDONALD Sir
WALTER KRONKITE
WILFRED PICKLES

15
AINSLEY HARRIOTT
ALASTAIR STEWART
ALISTAIR MCGOWAN
BAMBER GASCOIGNE
DERMOT MURNAGHAN
DICKIE HENDERSON
FLOELLA BENJAMIN

GLORIA HUNNIFORD
JULIA SOMERVILLE
KENNETH WILLIAMS
MAGNUS MAGNUSSON
MARK DURDEN-SMITH
NEIL DURDEN-SMITH
NICHOLAS PARSONS
PAMELA ARMSTRONG
RICHARD DIMBLEBY
RICHARD WHITELEY
SANDY MACPHERSON
SASHA BARON COHEN
TIM BROOKE-TAYLOR
VINCENT DUGGLEBY
WORRALL THOMPSON
  Antony

16
ANDREA CATHERWOOD

ANNIE NIGHTINGALE
ANTHONY MCPARTLIN
BOB DANVERS-WALKER
CLAUDIA WINKLEMAN
JENNIFER SAUNDERS
JONATHAN DIMBLEBY
MARCUS BRIGSTOCKE
MICHAEL BARRYMORE
MICHAEL NICHOLSON
MICHAEL PARKINSON
NATASHA KAPLINSKY
NICHOLAS WITCHELL
PAMELA STEPHENSON
PHILLIP SCHOFIELD
ROBERT KILROY-SILK

17
DAVID ATTENBOROUGH
  Sir

HUMPHREY LYTTELTON
JANET STREET-PORTER
KIERAN PRENDEVILLE
MALCOLM MUGGERIDGE
NIGEL STARMER-SMITH
PHILIPPA FORRESTER
REGINALD BOSANQUET

18
CHRISTOPHER BIGGINS
RAYMOND GLENDENNING

19
KENNETH WOLSTENHOLME
SUSANNAH CONSTANTINE

Arts – Media – Television – TV & RADIO TERMS

3	DIAL	SLOT	GHOST	**6**	REMOTE
DUB	DISH	SNOW	HERTZ	ADMASS	REPEAT
DVD	EMMY	SOAP	NICAM	ADVERT	SCREEN
PAN	GAIN	TAPE	NOISE	AERIAL	SCRIPT
PAP	HOST	TONE	PANEL	BEACON	SERIAL
SET	KNOB	VIEW	PULSE	CAMERA	SERIES
	LINE	WAVE	RADIO	COMEDY	SIGNAL
4	MIKE		RELAY	DIPOLE	SITCOM
BAND	NEWS	**5**	RERUN	FADE-IN	SKETCH
BAUD	PIPS	BLEEP	SCART	FILTER	STATIC
BOOM	PLAY	CABLE	SOUND	FORMAT	STUDIO
CAST	QUIZ	DRAMA	TELLY	LEAD-IN	VIEWER
CCTV	SCAN	FIELD	TRACK	NEEDLE	VISION
CLIP	SHOW	FRAME	VIDEO	RASTER	WOOFER

7
ANTENNA
AUTOCUE
BLEEPER
BLOOPER
CARRIER
CATHODE
CB RADIO
CHANNEL
CLOSE-UP
CONSOLE
DIGITAL
DISPLAY
DUBBING
EPISODE
EXCERPT
FADE-OUT
MONITOR
NETWORK
OUT-TAKE
PANNING
PHONE-IN
PICTURE
RATINGS
SCANNER
SKY WAVE
SPEAKER
STATION
TWEETER
VARIETY
VIEWING

8
AUDITION
BULLETIN
CALL SIGN
CASSETTE
CHAT SHOW

DIALOGUE
EPILOGUE
GAME SHOW
LONG WAVE
MAGIC EYE
NARRATOR
NEWSCAST
RECEIVER
SATELLITE
SCANNING
TALK SHOW
TELECAST
TELECINE
TELEFILM
TELETHON
TELEVISE
TRACKING
TRANSMIT
WAVEBAND
WIRELESS

9
AMPLIFIER
ANNOUNCER
BANDWIDTH
BLIND SPOT
BROADCAST
DOCUDRAMA
EARPHONES
FREQUENCY
IDIOT CARD
INTERVIEW
MASS MEDIA
MEGAHERTZ
MICROWAVE
MODULATOR
NARRATION
OSCILLATE

PANEL GAME
PRESENTER
PRIME TIME
PROGRAMME
RADIO WAVE
RECEPTION
SCREENING
SET-TOP BOX
SHORT WAVE
SIMULCAST
SOAP OPERA
VIDEOPLUS
VIDEOTAPE

10
COMMENTARY
COMMERCIAL
CONTINUITY
CRYSTAL SET
DISC JOCKEY
DISTORTION
EUROVISION
FAMILY SHOW
FLAT SCREEN
FREE-TO-VIEW
GOLDEN ROSE
HEADPHONES
IDIOT BOARD
INSTALMENT
LOCAL RADIO
MEDIUM WAVE
MICROPHONE
MODULATION
MULTIMEDIA
NEWSCASTER
NEWSREADER
OSCILLATOR
PAY-PER-VIEW

RESOLUTION
SUPPRESSOR
TELEVISION
TELEVISUAL
TIME SIGNAL
TRANSCRIPT
WAVELENGTH

11
ASPECT RATIO
CATCHPHRASE
CAT'S WHISKER
DOCUMENTARY
DVD RECORDER
FREEZE FRAME
LOUDSPEAKER
NEWSCASTING
OSCILLATION
REALITY SHOW
SMALL SCREEN
SPECTACULAR
TRANSCEIVER
TRANSMITTER
TRANSPONDER

12
ACTION REPLAY
ANNOUNCEMENT
ATMOSPHERICS
BROADCASTING
CITIZENS' BAND
EXTRAVAGANZA
INTERFERENCE
RADIO STATION
RECEIVING SET
SATELLITE DISH
SOUND EFFECTS
TELEPROMPTER

TRANSMISSION

13
AMPLIFICATION
BREAKFAST SHOW
CLOSED CIRCUIT
DRAMATISATION
LAUGHTER TRACK
PIRATE STATION
REMOTE CONTROL
SIGNATURE TUNE

SURROUND SOUND
TELERECORDING
VIDEO RECORDER

14
AUDIO FREQUENCY
CATHODE RAY TUBE
CHANNEL SURFING
RADIO FREQUENCY
VIDEO FREQUENCY
VIDEO RECORDING

15
CABLE TELEVISION
COMMERCIAL BREAK
DIRECTION-FINDER
SITUATION COMEDY

16
OUTSIDE BROADCAST

Arts – Media – Television – TV CHARACTERS

3
ADA *For the Love of Ada, The Larkins*
ALF *Coronation Street, Heartbeat, Home and Away, The Larkins, Till Death Us Do Part*
AMY *Crossroads*
ANN *Ever Decreasing Circles, George and Mildred*
ASH *Casualty*
BAZ *Casualty*
BEA *House of Eliott, Prisoner: Cell Block H*
BEN *Bonanza, Butterflies, Flower Pot Men, Hollyoaks, My Family, 2Point4 Children*
BET *Coronation Street*

BOB *Bob the Builder, Emmerdale, The Likely Lads*
BOD *Bod*
CAT *Red Dwarf*
DAN *Roseanne*
DEN *EastEnders*
DEV *Coronation Street*
DOC *Gunsmoke*
DON *The Bill*
DOT *EastEnders*
ELI *Last of the Summer Wine*
ENA *Coronation Street*
FIZ *Coronation Street*
GIL *CSI: Crime Scene Investigation, Rawhide*
IAN *EastEnders*
IVY *Coronation Street, In Loving Memory, Last of the Summer Wine*
JAN *Howards' Way*

JED *The Beverly Hillbillies, Crocodile Shoes*
JIM *EastEnders, Neighbours, The Rockford Files, The Royle Family, The Vicar of Dibley*
JOE *Emmerdale, Grafters, Neighbours*
KAT *EastEnders*
KEN *Common As Muck, Coronation Street, Howards' Way*
LEN *Coronation Street*
LES *Coronation Street*
LIZ *Rumpole of the Bailey*
LOU *EastEnders, Little Britain, Neighbours*
MAC *Doctors*
MAX *Hart to Hart, Hollyoaks, Tweenies*
MEG *Crossroads*

MIA *Cutting It*
NEV *Common As Muck*
PAT *EastEnders*
RAY *Dallas*
REG *Goodnight Sweetheart, The Rag Trade, The Bill*
RIA *Butterflies*
RIC *Holby City*
RON *Goodnight Sweetheart*
ROS *Bugs*
ROY *EastEnders*
ROZ *Frasier, Last of the Summer Wine*
SAM *Cheers, Silent Witness*
SID *Bless This House*
TED *Hi-de-Hi!*
TIM *The Office*
TOM *Don't Wait Up, The Fall and Rise of Reginald Perrin, Gimme Gimme Gimme, The Good Life, Howards' Way, Last of the Summer Wine, Midsomer Murders, Tom and Jerry, Waiting for God*
VIC *Where the Heart Is*
VIV *The Bill, Emmerdale*
ZAK *Emmerdale*
ZOE *Emmerdale*

4

ADAM *Bonanza, Cold Feet, Crossroads*
ALAN *Emmerdale, Rising Damp*
ALEC *Coronation Street, May to December*
ALEX *Holby City*
AMOS *Emmerdale*
ANDY *Little Britain*
BART *Maverick, The Simpsons*
BILL *Flower Pot Men, 2Point4 Children*
BOON *Boon*
BREN *Dinnerladies*
BRET *Maverick*
CAIN *Emmerdale*
DAVE *Family Affairs, Minder, Red Dwarf, The Royle Family, The Sullivans*
DAWN *The Office*
DINO *The Flintstones*
EDIE *Last of the Summer Wine*
EDNA *Emmerdale*
ELSE *Till Death Us Do Part*
ERIC *Emmerdale, Lovejoy*
EVIE *House of Eliott*
FINN *Cutting It*
FITZ *Cracker*
FIZZ *Tweenies*
FOXY *Common As Muck*
FRED *Coronation Street, The Flintstones, Hi-de-Hi!, I Love Lucy*
GAIL *Coronation Street*
GARY *Dallas, Goodnight Sweetheart, Knots Landing, Men Behaving Badly*
GINA *Heartbeat*

GREG *Hollyoaks*
HOSS *Bonanza*
HUGO *The Vicar of Dibley*
JACK *Bread, Coronation Street, Emmerdale, Hollyoaks, Howards' Way, On the Buses, When the Boat Comes In*
JAKE *Tweenies*
JANE *Waiting for God*
JEAN *As Time Goes By, Bless This House*
JEFF *The Colbys, Dynasty*
JESS *Postman Pat*
JILL *Crossroads*
JOAN *The Fall and Rise of Reginald Perrin*
JOEY *Bread, Friends*
JOHN *Dear John, The Waltons*
JOSS *Casualty, Tenko*
JUDY *Tweenies*
JUNE *Terry and June*
KATE *Kate, Tenko*
KURT *Hollyoaks*
KYLE *Footballers' Wives, South Park*
LILY *The Munsters*
LISA *The Simpsons*
LUCY *Dallas, I Love Lucy*
LUKE *The Dukes of Hazzard*
LYNN *I'm Alan Partridge*
MAPP *Mapp & Lucia*
MIKE *Coronation Street, A Fine Romance, Only Fools and Horses, Till Death Us Do Part*

MILO *Tweenies*
MIMI *'Allo 'Allo*
MORK *Mork and Mindy*
MUCK *Bob the Builder*
NEIL *The Young Ones*
NICK *Bugs, Heartbeat, My Family*
NORA *Last of the Summer Wine*
NORM *Cheers*
OWEN *Holby City, The Vicar of Dibley*
PAUL *Ever Decreasing Circles, Neighbours*
PETE *Cold Feet*
PHIL *EastEnders*
PIKE *Dad's Army*
PUGH Camberwick Green series
RENÉ *'Allo 'Allo*
RICK *The Young Ones*
RITA *Coronation Street, Till Death Us Do Part*
RONA *2Point4 Children*
ROSE *The Golden Girls, Keeping Up Appearances, Tenko, Upstairs Downstairs*
ROSS *Friends*
RUBY *Upstairs, Downstairs*
RUTH *Where the Heart Is*
SETH *Emmerdale*
SPUD *Bob the Builder*
STAN *Coronation Street, Dinnerladies, On the Buses, South Park*
STIG *Stig of the Dump*

SUZI *Tutti Frutti*
TOBY *Don't Wait Up*
TONY *Dinnerladies, Hollyoaks, Men Behaving Badly, The Sopranos*
TOSH *The Bill*
TROY *Midsomer Murders*
URKO *The Planet of the Apes*
VERA *Coronation Street, Prisoner: Cell Block H*
WEED *Flower Pot Men*
WILL *Will & Grace*
XENA *Xena: Warrior Princess*
YOGI *Yogi Bear*
ZARA *Hollyoaks*
ZAZA *Hector's House*
ZOOT *The Muppet Show*

5

AILSA *Home and Away*
ALFIE *EastEnders*
ALICE *The Vicar of Dibley*
ALLIE *Cutting It*
ANGIE *EastEnders*
ANITA *Dinnerladies*
ANNIE *Coronation Street*
ANTON *Holby City*
BARRY *Brookside, Hi-de-Hi!, Last of the Summer Wine*
BASIL *Fawlty Towers*
BELLA *Tweenies, Widows*
BENNY *Crossroads*
BERYL *The Liver Birds, The Lovers*

BETTY *Coronation Street, Emmerdale, The Flintstones, Some Mothers Do 'Ave 'Em*
BILKO *The Phil Silvers Show*
BILLY *Bread, EastEnders, In Loving Memory*
BLAKE *Dynasty*
BLOTT *Blott on the Landscape*
BOBBY *Dallas*
BODIE *The Professionals*
BONES *Star Trek*
BRIAN *The Magic Roundabout*
BUFFY *Buffy the Vampire Slayer*
BUNGO *The Wombles*
BURKE *Burke's Law*
CARLA *Cheers*
CHASE *Falcon Crest*
CHRIS *The Cuckoo Waltz, Emmerdale*
CLIFF *Cheers, The Cosby Show, Dallas*
CLIVE *Singles*
COLIN *Colin's Sandwich*
COMPO *Last of the Summer Wine*
CRANE *Crane*
CURLY *Coronation Street*
DADDY *Keeping Up Appearances*
DAISY *Keeping Up Appearances, Upstairs, Downstairs*
DANNO *Hawaii Five-O*

DANNY *The Paradise Club, Tutti Frutti*
DAVID *At Home with the Braithwaites, Cold Feet, Crossroads, Heartbeat, Moonlighting, The Office, The Vicar of Dibley*
DIANA *Waiting for God*
DIANE *Cheers, Emmerdale*
DIPSY *Teletubbies*
DOLLY *Dinnerladies, Widows*
DORIS *Crossroads*
DOYLE *The Professionals*
DUFFY *Casualty*
DYLAN *The Magic Roundabout*
EDDIE *Bottom, Filthy Rich and Catflap, The Munsters*
EDINA *Absolutely Fabulous*
EDITH *'Allo 'Allo*
ELLEN *Ellen*
ELSIE *Coronation Street*
EMILY *Coronation Street, Emmerdale, Little Britain*
EMMET *Keeping Up Appearances*
ERNIE *Cheers*
ETHEL *I Love Lucy*
FANNY *'Allo 'Allo*
FLEUR *The Forsyte Saga*
FLISS *The Cuckoo Waltz*
FOGGY *Last of the Summer Wine*

FOYLE *Foyle's War*
FRANK *EastEnders, Love Hurts, Some Mothers Do 'Ave 'Em, The Vicar of Dibley*
FROST *A Touch of Frost*
GALEN *The Planet of the Apes*
GAVIN *Cutting It*
GERDA *Tenko*
GOLLY *Monarch of the Glen*
GONZO *The Muppet Show*
GOODY *The Thin Blue Line*
GRACE *The Sullivans, Will & Grace*
GRANT *EastEnders, Home and Away*
GRUBB *Camberwick Green series*
HABIB *The Thin Blue Line*
HELEN *Neighbours*
HELGA *'Allo 'Allo*
HENRY *Emmerdale, Pie in the Sky, Rumpole of the Bailey*
HETTY *Hetty Wainthropp Investigates*
HILDA *Coronation Street, Ever Decreasing Circles, Rumpole of the Bailey*
HOGAN *Hogan's Heroes*
HOLLY *Red Dwarf*
HOMER *The Simpsons*
HUTCH *Starsky and Hutch*

IRENE *The Forsyte Saga*
JAMBO *Hollyoaks*
JANET *Dr Finlay's Casebook*
JANEY *My Family*
JASON *The Colbys*
JENNA *Dallas*
JENNY *Cold Feet*
JERRY *The Good Life, Tom and Jerry*
JIMMY *Brookside, The Fall and Rise of Reginald Perrin*
JONNO *Common As Muck*
JULIE *Byker Grove*
KAREN *Cold Feet*
KARIM *The Buddha of Suburbia*
KENNY *South Park*
KEVIN *Coronation Street, Harry Enfield shows*
KITTY *Gunsmoke*
KOJAK *Kojak*
KUZAK *LA Law*
LACEY *Cagney and Lacey*
LAURA *A Fine Romance*
LEWIS *Inspector Morse*
LEXIE *Monarch of the Glen*
LINDA *The Fall and Rise of Reginald Perrin, Gimme Gimme Gimme, Linda Green, Widows*
LOFTY *Bob the Builder, EastEnders, It Ain't Half Hot Mum*

LOGAN *Logan's Run*
LOUIE *Taxi*
LUCAS *Maigret*
LUCIA *Mapp & Lucia*
LURCH *The Addams Family*
MADGE *Neighbours*
MANDY *Hollyoaks*
MARGE *The Simpsons*
MARGO *The Good Life*
MEGAN *Casualty, The District Nurse*
MINDY *Mork and Mindy*
MITCH *Baywatch*
MOLLY *Monarch of the Glen*
MORSE *Inspector Morse*
NILES *Frasier*
OLIVE *On the Buses*
OSCAR *Heartbeat*
PADDY *Emmerdale, The Rag Trade*
PATSY *Absolutely Fabulous*
PATTY *The Simpsons*
PEARL *Last of the Summer Wine*
PEGGY *EastEnders, Hi-de-Hi!, Where the Heart Is*
PENNY *Just Good Friends*
PERRY Harry Enfield shows
PIPPA *One Foot in the Grave*
POLLY *Fawlty Towers*
QUINN *Spooks*
RADAR *M*A*S*H*

RALPH *Filthy Rich and Catflap*
REBUS *Rebus*
REGAN *The Sweeney*
RHODA *Rhoda*
RICKY *EastEnders, I Love Lucy*
ROBIN *Batman, Man about the House, Robin's Nest*
ROCKY *The Rockford Files*
ROLEY *Bob the Builder*
ROWDY *Rawhide*
ROWLF *The Muppet Show*
SABLE *The Colbys*
SALLY *Coronation Street*
SARAH *Upstairs, Downstairs*
SANDY *Crossroads*
SCOOP *Bob the Builder*
SCOTT *Neighbours*
SELMA *The Simpsons*
SHELL *Bad Girls*
SPIKE *Hi-de-Hi!*
SPOCK *Star Trek*
STEED *The Avengers, The New Avengers*
STEEL *Sapphire and Steel*
STEPH *Emmerdale, Hollyoaks*
STEVE *Coronation Street*
SUNIL *Common As Muck*
SUSAN *My Family*
SYBIL *Fawlty Towers*
TAFFY *The Bill*
TANYA *Footballers' Wives*

TEDDY *Andy Pandy*
TERRY *Fawlty Towers, The Likely Lads, Minder, Terry and June*
TESSA *Love Hurts*
TILLY *The Flame Trees of Thika*
TOMSK *The Wombles*
TONTO *The Lone Ranger*
TRULY *Last of the Summer Wine*
TUBBS *Miami Vice*
UHURA *Star Trek*
VICKY *Little Britain*
VINCE *Deputy Dawg, Just Good Friends*
WAYNE *Auf Wiedersehen, Pet*, Harry Enfield shows
WENDY *Bob the Builder*
WILMA *The Flintstones*
ZAIUS *The Planet of the Apes*
ZUBIN *Holby City*

6

ADRIAN *Bread*
ALBERT *Coronation Street, Steptoe and Son*
ALEXIS *Dynasty*
ALISON *At Home with the Braithwaites*
ANGELA *Falcon Crest*
ANIMAL *The Muppet Show*
ANTONY *The Royle Family*

ARCHIE *Only When I Laugh*
ARNOLD *Diff'rent Strokes*
ARTHUR *EastEnders, Minder, On the Buses*
ASHLEY *Coronation Street, Emmerdale*
AUDREY *Coronation Street, To the Manor Born*
BARNEY *The Flintstones, Stig of the Dump*
BATMAN *Batman*
BEAKER *The Muppet Show*
BENSON *Benson*
BERNIE *Heartbeat*
BIANCA *EastEnders*
BLAKEY *On the Buses*
BO DUKE *The Dukes of Hazzard*
BOO-BOO *Yogi Bear*
BOYCIE *Only Fools and Horses*
BUBBLE *Absolutely Fabulous*
BUDGIE *Budgie*
CAGNEY *Cagney and Lacey*
CALLAN *Callan*
CANNON *Cannon*
CARRIE *Sex and the City*
CARTER *The Sweeney*
CEDRIC *The Darling Buds of May*
CLAUDE *Heartbeat*
CLEGGY *Last of the Summer Wine*

CONNIE *Connie*
COWLEY *The Professionals*
DAFYDD *Little Britain*
DAMIEN *Only Fools and Horses*
DAPHNE *Frasier*
DARRIN *Bewitched*
DEL BOY *Only Fools and Horses*
DENISE *The Royle Family*
DENNIS *Auf Wiedersehen, Pet*
DENZIL *Only Fools and Horses*
DIBBLE *Camberwick Green series*
DONALD *Home and Away*
DOOGIE *Doogie Howser MD*
DORIEN *Birds of a Feather*
DOUGAL *The Magic Roundabout*
DUNCAN *Monarch of the Glen*
EDWARD *Edward and Mrs Simpson, Edward the Seventh, Upstairs Downstairs*
ENDORA *Bewitched*
FALLON *Dynasty*
FIGGIS *Only When I Laugh*
FINCHY *The Office*
FLETCH *Porridge*

FONZIE *Happy Days*
GAMBIT *The New Avengers*
GARETH *The Office*
GEORGE *George and Mildred, Man about the House*
GLADYS *Hi-de-Hi!, Open All Hours*
GLENDA *Last of the Summer Wine*
GLORIA *It Ain't Half Hot Mum*
GODBER *Porridge*
GRAMPA *The Simpsons*
GROMIT *Wallace and Gromit*
GRUBER *'Allo 'Allo*
HAMISH *Hamish Macbeth*
HAROLD *Neighbours, Steptoe and Son*
HAROON *The Buddha of Suburbia*
HARVEY *Waiting for God*
HAZELL *Hazell*
HECTOR *Hector's House, Monarch of the Glen*
HEDGES *Please Sir!*
HERMAN *The Munsters*
HESTER *Fresh Fields*
HODGES *Dad's Army*
HOWARD *The Bounder, Ever Decreasing Circles, Last of the Summer Wine*
HUDSON *Upstairs, Downstairs*

JACKIE *Footballers'*
Wives, Singles
JOLYON *The Forsyte*
Saga
KERMIT *The Muppet*
Show
KRYTEN *Red Dwarf*
LAA-LAA *Teletubbies*
LAUREN *The Catherine*
Tate Show
LIONEL *As Time Goes By*
LONELY *Callan*
LOUISE *Hollyoaks*
LURCIO *Up Pompeii!*
LYTTON *Lytton's Diary*
MADDIE *Moonlighting*
MAGGIE *The Simpsons*
MAGNUM *Magnum PI*
MANNIX *Mannix*
MANUEL *Fawlty Towers*
MARINA *Last of the*
Summer Wine
MARION *Tenko*
MARKER *Public Eye*
MARLON *Emmerdale*
MARTHA *Coronation*
Street
MARTIN *Coronation*
Street, Ever Decreasing
Circles
MATTIE *House of Cards*
series
MAXINE *The Mistress*
MCGILL *Man in a*
Suitcase
MINNIE *Coronation*
Street
MONICA *Friends*

MOTHER *The Avengers*
MR BEAN *Mr Bean*
MR BENN *Mr Benn*
MR SULU *Star Trek*
MULDER *The X-Files*
MUSKIE *Deputy Dawg*
NELLIE *Bread, Tenko*
NOO-NOO *Teletubbies*
NORMAN *Only When I*
Laugh
NURSIE *Blackadder II*
OLIVIA *The Waltons*
ONSLOW *Keeping Up*
Appearances
PAMELA *Dallas, Singles*
PANCHO *The Cisco Kid*
PARKER *Thunderbirds*
PASCOE *Dalziel and*
Pascoe
PEPPER *Police Woman*
PETULA *Dinnerladies*
PHELPS *Mission:*
Impossible
PHILIP *Rising Damp*
PHOEBE *Friends,*
Goodnight Sweetheart
PURDEY *The New*
Avengers
QUINCY *Quincy*
RACHEL *Cold Feet,*
Friends
RAQUEL *Only Fools and*
Horses
REGGIE *The Fall and Rise*
of Reginald Perrin
REILLY *Reilly – Ace of*
Spies
RICHIE *Bottom*

RIGSBY *Rising Damp*
RIMMER *Red Dwarf*
RODNEY *Emmerdale,*
Only Fools and Horses
SANDRA *The Liver Birds*
SCOOBY *Scooby Doo,*
Where Are You?
SCOTTY *Star Trek*
SCULLY *The X-Files*
SHAGGY *Scooby Doo,*
Where Are You?
SHARON *Birds of a*
Feather, EastEnders
SHARPE *Sharpe*
SINBAD *Brookside*
SKIPPY *Skippy, the Bush*
Kangaroo
SNUDGE *Bootsie and*
Snudge
SOAMES *The Forsyte*
Saga
SOPHIA *The Golden Girls*
STEELE *Remington Steele*
SYLVIA *Hi-de-Hi!*
TATTOO *Fantasy Island*
THOMAS *Thomas the*
Tank Engine
TINKER *Lovejoy*
TOP CAT *Boss Cat*
TRACEY *Birds of a*
Feather
TREVOR *Brookside,*
Grafters
TRICIA *Heartbeat*
TUCKER *Grange Hill*
TYRONE *Coronation*
Street
VERNON *Heartbeat*

VICTOR *One Foot in the Grave*
VYVYAN *The Young Ones*
WALTER *For the Love of Ada*
WESLEY *Last of the Summer Wine*
WILLIS *Diff'rent Strokes*
WOLFIE *Citizen Smith*
YOSSER *Boys from the Blackstuff*
YVETTE *'Allo 'Allo, Secret Army*
YVONNE *Goodnight Sweetheart, Hi-de-Hi!*

7

AVELINE *Bread*
BAGPUSS *Bagpuss*
BANACEK *Banacek*
BARBARA *The Good Life, The Royle Family*
BAYLEAF *London's Burning*
BERNARD *Common As Muck, Yes, Minister*
BLANCHE *Coronation Street, The Golden Girls*
BOB HOPE *Emmerdale*
BOOTSIE *Bootsie and Snudge*
BRAINS *Thunderbirds*
CADFAEL *Cadfael*
CARTMAN *South Park*
CHARITY *Emmerdale*
CHARLES *Howards' Way*

CHARLIE *Bergerac, Casualty, EastEnders, Lovejoy*
CHESTER *Gunsmoke*
CHRISSY *Man about the House*
COLUMBO *Columbo*
CUSTARD *Roobarb*
DALZIEL *Dalziel and Pascoe*
DEBORAH *Men Behaving Badly*
DEMELZA *Poldark*
DEMPSEY *Dempsey and Makepeace*
DESMOND *Desmond's*
DIERDRE *Coronation Street*
DOODLES *Tweenies*
DOROTHY *The Golden Girls, Men Behaving Badly*
FACEMAN *The A-Team*
FAIRFAX *'Allo 'Allo*
FRASIER *Cheers, Frasier*
FREDDIE *Bread*
GRANDAD *Bread, Only Fools and Horses*
GRANDPA *The Munsters*
HAWKEYE *M*A*S*H*
HOPKIRK *Randall and Hopkirk Deceased*
HOT LIPS *M*A*S*H*
JEFFREY *George and Mildred, Hi-de-Hi!*
JESSICA *Murder, She Wrote, Some Mothers Do 'Ave 'Em*

JOHN BOY *The Waltons*
JR EWING *Dallas*
KAT MOON (+ SLATER) *EastEnders*
KEN BOON *Boon*
KLINGER *M*A*S*H*
KRYSTLE *Dynasty*
LAVERNE *Laverne and Shirley*
LECLERC *'Allo 'Allo*
LEONARD *Butterflies*
LETITIA *The Vicar of Dibley*
LILO LIL *Bread*
LOVEJOY *Lovejoy*
MAIGRET *Maigret*
MALCOLM *Singles*
MARJORY *To the Manor Born*
MARLENE *Only Fools and Horses*
MCCLOUD *McCloud*
MICHAEL *My Family*
MILDRED *George and Mildred, Man about the House*
MR BURNS *The Simpsons*
MR LUCAS *Are You Being Served?*
MR PLATT *Camberwick Green series*
MR RUSTY *The Magic Roundabout*
MRS HALL *All Creatures Great and Small*
MR SPOCK *Star Trek*
MR TROOP *Camberwick Green series*

MUTTLEY *Wacky Races*
NEVILLE *Auf Wiedersehen, Pet*
ORINOCO *The Wombles*
PALADIN *Have Gun Will Travel*
PATRICK *One Foot in the Grave*
PAULINE *EastEnders*
PEBBLES *The Flintstones*
PENFOLD *Dangermouse*
POLDARK *Poldark*
RANDALL *Randall and Hopkirk Deceased*
RICHARD *Coronation Street, Filthy Rich and Catflap, Keeping Up Appearances, To the Manor Born*
ROOBARB *Roobarb*
RUMPOLE *Rumpole of the Bailey*
SAFFRON *Absolutely Fabulous*
SAM RYAN *Silent Witness*
SCOOTER *The Muppet Show*
SEYMOUR *Last of the Summer Wine*
SHELLEY *Shelley*
SHIRLEY *Laverne and Shirley, Widows*
SPENDER *Spender*
STARSKY *Starsky and Hutch*
STATLER *The Muppet Show*
STAVROS *Harry Enfield shows*
TABITHA *Bewitched*
TAGGART *Taggart*
TIMOTHY *Sorry!*
TOM GOOD *The Good Life*
TRIGGER *Only Fools and Horses*
TRISTAN *All Creatures Great and Small*
TWINKLE *Dinnerladies*
TWIZZLE *The Adventures of Twizzle*
VIV HOPE (+ WINDSOR) *Emmerdale*
WALDORF *The Muppet Show*
WALLACE *Wallace and Gromit*
WEXFORD *The Ruth Rendell Mysteries*

WILLIAM *Fresh Fields*
ZEBEDEE *The Magic Roundabout*
ZOE TATE *Emmerdale*

8

ALISTAIR *Crystal Tipps and Alistair*
ALPHONSE *'Allo 'Allo*
BALDRICK *Blackadder series*
BAMM BAMM *The Flintstones*
BEATRICE *Tenko*
BEN CASEY *Ben Casey*
BERGERAC *Bergerac*
BET LYNCH (+ GILROY) *Coronation Street*
BOB CRYER *The Bill*
BRACKETT *Camberwick Green series*
BRACKMAN *LA Law*
CATWOMAN *Batman*
CHAMPION *Champion the Wonder Horse*
CHANDLER *Friends*
CHARISMA *London's Burning*
CHARLENE *Neighbours*
CHEYENNE *Cheyenne*
CHRISSIE *Holby City*
CJ PARKER *Baywatch*
CRABTREE *'Allo 'Allo*
CROCKETT *Miami Vice*
CUTHBERT *Camberwick Green series*
DAVE NICE *Harry Enfield shows*
DIRTY DEN *EastEnders*
DON BEECH *The Bill*
DOUG ROSS *ER*
ELLY MAY *The Beverly Hillbillies*
EMMA PEEL *The Avengers*
FLORENCE *The Magic Roundabout*
GEOFFREY *The Lovers*
GEORGINA *Upstairs, Downstairs*

GIL FAVOR *Rawhide*
GINA WARD *Heartbeat*
HADLEIGH *Hadleigh*
HANNIBAL *The A-Team*
HYACINTH *Keeping Up Appearances*
IAN BEALE *EastEnders*
IRONSIDE *A Man Called Ironside*
JACK FORD *When the Boat Comes In*
JENNIFER *Hart to Hart*
JIM ROYLE *The Royle Family*
JOHNNY HO *The Chinese Detective*
JONATHAN *Hart to Hart*
KAVANAGH *Kavanagh QC*
LADY JANE *Lovejoy*
LOCKHART *No Hiding Place*
LOOBY LOO *Andy Pandy*
LOU BEALE *EastEnders*
LOU GRANT *Lou Grant*
LUKE DUKE *The Dukes of Hazzard*
MACGYVER *MacGyver*
MA LARKIN *The Darling Buds of May*
MARGARET *One Foot in the Grave, Pie in the Sky*
MARIETTE *The Darling Buds of May*
MARJORIE *Little Britain*
MCKENZIE *LA Law*
MILHOUSE *The Simpsons*
MISTER ED *Mister Ed*
MR BLOBBY *Noel's House Party*
MR FENNER *The Rag Trade*
MR MACKAY *Porridge*
MR RIGSBY *Rising Damp*
MR ROARKE *Fantasy Island*
MRS AVERY *Last of the Summer Wine*
MRS DOYLE *Father Ted*
PAT EVANS (+ WICKS/BUTCHER) *EastEnders*
PAT WICKS (+ BUTCHER/EVANS) *EastEnders*
PHILIPPA *Dinnerladies*
PHYLLIDA *Rumpole of the Bailey*
PILCHARD *Bob the Builder*
RANGI RAM *It Ain't Half Hot Mum*
ROBBY BOX *Big Deal*
ROJ BLAKE *Blake's 7*
ROSEANNE *Roseanne*
ROY EVANS *EastEnders*
SAMANTHA *Bewitched*
SAPPHIRE *Sapphire and Steel*
SICKNOTE *London's Burning*
SNOWBALL *The Simpsons*
SUE ELLEN *Dallas*
SUPERTED *Superted*
SWEETUMS *The Muppet Show*
TARA KING *The Avengers*
TED BOVIS *Hi-de-Hi!*
THE JOKER *Batman*
THE SAINT *The Saint, Return of the Saint*
TJ HOOKER *TJ Hooker*
TOADFISH *Neighbours*
TOM QUINN *Spooks*
TRISTRAM *George and Mildred*
UNCLE TOM *Rumpole of the Bailey*
URQUHART House of Cards series
VASELINE *London's Burning*
WAYNETTA Harry Enfield shows
WYCLIFFE *Wycliffe*
YAMAUCHI *Tenko*
YOGI BEAR *Yogi Bear*

9
ALEX ADAMS *Holby City*
ALFIE MOON *EastEnders*
AMY TURTLE *Crossroads*

ANDY PANDY *Andy Pandy*
ARKWRIGHT *Open All Hours*
AUNT SALLY *Worzel Gummidge*
BA BARACAS *The A-Team*
BABY DAVID *The Royle Family*
BANANAMAN *Bananaman*
BEA ELIOTT *House of Eliott*
BEN DAVIES *Hollyoaks*
BEN HARPER *My Family*
BET GILROY (+ LYNCH) *Coronation Street*
BOB FERRIS *The Likely Lads*
BRABINGER *To the Manor Born*
CARSTAIRS *'Allo 'Allo*
CASSANDRA *Only Fools and Horses*
CATHY GALE *The Avengers*
CATWEAZLE *Catweazle*
CHRIS TATE *Emmerdale*
DAN CONNER *Roseanne*
DANNY KANE *The Paradise Club*
DOCTOR WHO *Doctor Who*
DORIS LUKE *Crossroads*
DOT COTTON (+ BRANNING) *EastEnders*
EDNA BIRCH *Emmerdale*
ELIOT NESS *The Untouchables*
ELIZABETH *The Fall and Rise of Reginald Perrin, Keeping Up Appearances*
FATHER TED *Father Ted*
GARY EWING *Dallas, Knots Landing*
GERALDINE *The Vicar of Dibley*
GLADSTONE *The Thin Blue Line*
GRANVILLE *Open All Hours*
HERR FLICK *'Allo 'Allo*
HUGGY BEAR *Starsky and Hutch*
JACK BAUER *24*
JACK FROST *A Touch of Frost*

JACK REGAN *The Sweeney*
JACK ROLFE *Howards' Way*
JAN HOWARD *Howards' Way*
JASON KING *Department S, Jason King*
JEFF COLBY *The Colbys, Dynasty*
JEFF TRACY *Thunderbirds*
JENNA WADE *Dallas*
JIM PHELPS *Mission: Impossible*
JOE FRIDAY *Dragnet*
JOE MANGEL *Neighbours*
JOE MANNIX *Mannix*
JOE PURVIS *Grafters*
JOE SUGDEN *Emmerdale*
JOHN DRAKE *Danger Man*
JOHN KELLY *NYPD Blue*
JOHN REBUS *Rebus*
JOHN STEED *The Avengers, The New Avengers*
KARIM AMIR *The Buddha of Suburbia*
KAT SLATER (+ MOON) *EastEnders*
KEN BARLOW *Coronation Street*
LITTLE JOE *Bonanza*
LUCY EWING *Dallas*
MAGNUS PYM *A Perfect Spy*
MAKEPEACE *Dempsey and Makepeace*
MATT BURKE *Taggart*
MIKE SMASH Harry Enfield shows
MISS DIANE *Crossroads*
MISS ELLIE *Dallas*
MISS JONES *Rising Damp*
MISS PIGGY *The Muppet Show*
MISS TIBBS *Fawlty Towers*
MR BRITTAS *The Brittas Empire*
MR MAJEIKA *Mr Majeika*
MR RUMBOLD *Are You Being Served?*
MRS COBBIT Camberwick Green series
MRS DINGLE Camberwick Green series

MRS MERTON *The Mrs Merton Show*
MR WAVERLY *The Man from UNCLE*
NICK ROWAN *Heartbeat*
NORA BATTY *Last of the Summer Wine*
OWEN DAVIS *Holby City*
PADDY KIRK *Emmerdale*
PC MCGARRY Camberwick Green series
POP LARKIN *The Darling Buds of May*
RAY KREBBS *Dallas*
REG HOLLIS *The Bill*
SCOOBY DOO *Scooby Doo, Where Are You?*
SETH ADAMS *Wagon Train*
SID ABBOTT *Bless This House*
SIEGFRIED *All Creatures Great and Small*
STAN OGDEN *Coronation Street*
STEPH DEAN *Hollyoaks*
SUPERGRAN *Supergran*
THEO KOJAK *Kojak*
THE RANGER *Yogi Bear*
THERMOMAN *My Hero*
TOBERMORY *The Wombles*
TOM HOWARD *Howards' Way*
UNCLE MORT *I Didn't Know You Cared*
ZAK DINGLE *Emmerdale*

10

ADA LARKINS *The Larkins*
ADAM CHANCE *Crossroads*
ALAN B'STARD *The New Statesman*
ALAN TURNER *Emmerdale*
ALEC GILROY *Coronation Street*
ALF GARNETT *Till Death Us Do Part*
ALF LARKINS *The Larkins*
ALF ROBERTS *Coronation Street*
ALF STEWART *Home and Away*
ALLY MCBEAL *Ally McBeal*

ANTON MEYER *Holby City*
BARRY GRANT *Brookside*
BASIL BRUSH *The Basil Brush Show*
BEAUREGARD *The Muppet Show*
BLACKADDER Blackadder series
BOBBY EWING *Dallas*
BRUCE WAYNE *Batman*
BUCK ROGERS *Buck Rogers in the 25th Century*
CAIN DINGLE *Emmerdale*
CHARDONNAY *Footballers' Wives*
CURLY WATTS *Coronation Street*
DAISY MOSES *The Beverly Hillbillies*
DAVE CALLAN *Family Affairs*
DAVE LISTER *Red Dwarf*
DAVID BRENT *The Office*
DEEP THROAT *The X-Files*
DEPUTY DAWG *Deputy Dawg*
DOCTOR LEGG *EastEnders*
EDIE PEGDEN *Last of the Summer Wine*
ERMINTRUDE *The Magic Roundabout*
EVIE ELIOTT *House of Eliott*
FATHER JACK *Father Ted*
FIREMAN SAM *Fireman Sam*
FOZZIE BEAR *The Muppet Show*
GIL GRISSOM *CSI: Crime Scene Investigation*
GLADYS PUGH *Hi-de-Hi!*
HAROON AMIR *The Buddha of Suburbia*
HARVEY MOON *Shine On Harvey Moon*
HENRY WILKS *Emmerdale*
HILDA OGDEN *Coronation Street*
HUGO HORTON *The Vicar of Dibley*
JACKIE REID *Taggart*
JACK SUGDEN *Emmerdale*
JACK WALKER *Coronation Street*

JAMES T KIRK *Star Trek*
JASON COLBY *The Colbys*
JEAN ABBOTT *Bless This House*
JIM TAGGART *Taggart*
JOHN WALTON *The Waltons*
KATE GRAHAM *Kate*
KEN MASTERS *Howards' Way*
KUNTA KINTE *Roots*
KURT BENSON *Hollyoaks*
LINDA GREEN *Linda Green*
LORD PERCY *Blackadder II*
MAJOR GOWEN *Fawlty Towers*
MARK GREENE *ER*
MARK HARRIS *Man from Atlantis*
MATT DILLON *Gunsmoke*
MIKE GAMBIT *The New Avengers*
MIKE HAMMER *Mike Hammer*
MIKE SELWAY *A Fine Romance*
MISS BRAHMS *Are You Being Served?*
MISS GATSBY *Fawlty Towers*
MISS MARPLE *Miss Marple*
MONICA BING (+ GELLER) *Friends*
MR CARRAWAY Camberwick Green
   series
MR CROCKETT Camberwick Green
   series
MR DAGENHAM Camberwick Green
   series
MR GRAINGER *Are You Being Served?*
MR MACHENRY *The Magic
   Roundabout*
MRS BRADLEY *The Mrs Bradley
   Mysteries*
MRS BRIDGES *Upstairs, Downstairs*
MRS GOGGINS *Postman Pat*
MRS SIMPSON *Edward and Mrs
   Simpson*
MRS WARBOYS *One Foot in the Grave*

NILES CRANE *Frasier*
NURSE GUPTE *Only When I Laugh*
PADDINGTON *Paddington*
PADEREWSKI *It Ain't Half Hot Mum*
PAT BUTCHER (+ WICKS/EVANS)
   EastEnders
PATSY STONE *Absolutely Fabulous*
PERRY MASON *Perry Mason*
PETER HAZEL Camberwick Green series
PETROCELLI *Petrocelli*
POSTMAN PAT *Postman Pat*
QUATERMASS *Quatermass*
RALPH GORSE *The Charmer*
REG WEXFORD *The Ruth Rendell
   Mysteries*
RENÉ ARTOIS *'Allo 'Allo*
RIC GRIFFIN *Holby City*
ROBIN TRIPP *Man about the House,
   Robin's Nest*
RON MANAGER *The Fast Show*
ROSS GELLER *Friends*
ROWDY YATES *Rawhide*
SABLE COLBY *The Colbys*
SAM BECKETT *Quantum Leap*
SAM MCCLOUD *McCloud*
SCOTT TRACY *Thunderbirds*
SHOESTRING *Shoestring*
SPIKE DIXON *Hi-de-Hi!*
THE PENGUIN *Batman*
THE RIDDLER *Batman*
TILLY GRANT *The Flame Trees of Thika*
TINKY WINKY *Teletubbies*
TOM BARNABY *Midsomer Murders*
TOM LATIMER *Don't Wait Up*
VAN DER VALK *Van der Valk*
VIV WINDSOR (+ HOPE) *Emmerdale*
WELLINGTON *The Wombles*
ZARA MORGAN *Hollyoaks*

11

ADAM ADAMANT *Adam Adamant Lives!*
AGENT COOPER *Twin Peaks*
AGENT MULDER *The X-Files*
AGENT SCULLY *The X-Files*
ALF VENTRESS *Heartbeat*
AMOS BREARLY *Emmerdale*
ANN FOURMILE *George and Mildred*
ANNIE WALKER *Coronation Street*
APRIL DANCER *The Girl from UNCLE*
ARTHUR DALEY *Minder*
BARBARA GOOD *The Good Life*
BART SIMPSON *The Simpsons*
BASIL FAWLTY *Fawlty Towers*
BETTY RUBBLE *The Flintstones*
BETTY TURPIN *Coronation Street*
CAPTAIN KIRK *Star Trek*
CHARITY TATE (+ DINGLE) *Emmerdale*
CHIN HO KELLY *Hawaii Five-O*
CLIFF BARNES *Dallas*
COLONEL HALL *The Phil Silvers Show*
COLT SEAVERS *The Fall Guy*
DANGERMOUSE *Dangermouse*
DAVE CREEGAN *Touching Evil*
DAVID BANNER *The Incredible Hulk*
DAVID HORTON *The Vicar of Dibley*
DAVID HUNTER *Crossroads*
DELLA STREET *Perry Mason*
DENNIS WATTS *EastEnders*
DIANA PRINCE *Wonder Woman*
DIANE SUGDEN (+ BLACKSTOCK) *Emmerdale*
DICK SOLOMON *Third Rock from the Sun*
DOCTOR DAKER *A Very Peculiar Practice*
DORIEN GREEN *Birds of a Feather*

DOT BRANNING (+ COTTON) *EastEnders*
EDDIE HITLER *Bottom*
EDITH ARTOIS *'Allo 'Allo*
ELLEN MORGAN *Ellen*
ELSIE HOWARD (+ TANNER) *Coronation Street*
ELSIE TANNER (+ HOWARD) *Coronation Street*
EMILY BISHOP (+ NUGENT) *Coronation Street*
EMILY HOWARD *Little Britain*
EMILY NUGENT (+ BISHOP) *Coronation Street*
ENA SHARPLES *Coronation Street*
ERIC POLLARD *Emmerdale*
FRANK CANNON *Cannon*
FRANK MARKER *Public Eye*
FRANK STUBBS *Frank Stubbs Promotes*
FRED ELLIOTT *Coronation Street*
FRED QUILLEY *Hi-de-Hi!*
GARY SPARROW *Goodnight Sweetheart*
GEORGE DIXON *Dixon of Dock Green*
GEORGE ROPER *George and Mildred, Man about the House*
HARRY ORWELL *Harry O*
HELEN HEWITT *The Governor*
HENNO GARVIE *Ultimate Force*
HENRY CRABBE *Pie in the Sky*
IVY UNSWORTH *In Loving Memory*
JACK BOSWELL *Bread*
JACK OSBORNE *Hollyoaks*
JAMBO BOLTON *Hollyoaks*
JAMES HACKER *Yes, Minister*
JAMES HAZELL *Hazell*
JEAN DARBLAY *Juliet Bravo*
JED CLAMPETT *The Beverly Hillbillies*
JED SHEPPERD *Crocodile Shoes*

JEMIMA SHORE *Jemima Shore Investigates*
JIM BERGERAC *Bergerac*
JIM BRANNING *EastEnders*
JIM ROBINSON *Neighbours*
JIM ROCKFORD *The Rockford Files*
JOEY BOSWELL *Bread*
KATE LONGTON *Juliet Bravo*
LADY BELLAMY *Upstairs, Downstairs*
LAURA DALTON *A Fine Romance*
LAURA PALMER *Twin Peaks*
LEONARD DUNN *Butterflies*
LILY MUNSTER *The Munsters*
LISA SIMPSON *The Simpsons*
LOADSAMONEY Harry Enfield shows
LORD BELLAMY *Upstairs, Downstairs*
MAX HEADROOM *Max Headroom*
MEG MORTIMER (+ RICHARDSON) *Crossroads*
METAL MICKEY *Metal Mickey*
MIKE BALDWIN *Coronation Street*
MIKE BRADLEY *Heartbeat*
MIKE JARDINE *Taggart*
MR HUMPHRIES *Are You Being Served?*
MR PARTRIDGE *Hi-de-Hi!*
MRS HONEYMAN Camberwick Green series
MRS SLOCOMBE *Are You Being Served?*
NORMAN CLEGG *Last of the Summer Wine*
PERCY TOPLIS *The Monocled Mutineer*
PHIL BELLAMY *Heartbeat*
PRIVATE PIKE *Dad's Army*
RAB C NESBITT *Rab C Nesbitt*
RACHEL GREEN *Friends*
RALPH FILTHY *Filthy Rich and Catflap*
RICHARD BOYD *Boyd QC*

RICHARD RICH *Filthy Rich and Catflap*
ROGER VARLEY Camberwick Green series
ROSS POLDARK *Poldark*
ROY GALLOWAY *The Bill*
SAM THE EAGLE *The Muppet Show*
SIR HUMPHREY *Yes, Minister*
SMALLHAUSEN *'Allo 'Allo*
STEPH STOKES *Emmerdale*
STEVE AUSTIN *The Six Million Dollar Man*
SUSAN HARPER *My Family*
SUZI KETTLES *Tutti Frutti*
SYBIL FAWLTY *Fawlty Towers*
TERRY MCCANN *Minder*
THE CISCO KID *The Cisco Kid*
THOMAS TRIPP Camberwick Green series
TOBY LATIMER *Don't Wait Up*
TONY SOPRANO *The Sopranos*
TRAPPER JOHN *M*A*S*H*
TROY TEMPEST *Stingray*
UNCLE ALBERT *Only Fools and Horses*
VIRGIL TRACY *Thunderbirds*
VIV MARTELLA *The Bill*
WINDY MILLER Camberwick Green series
WONDER WOMAN *Wonder Woman*

12

AILSA STEWART *Home and Away*
ALBERT FOIRET *Secret Army*
ARTHUR FOWLER *EastEnders*
ASHLEY THOMAS *Emmerdale*
BARBARA ROYLE *The Royle Family*
BARNABY JONES *Barnaby Jones*
BARNEY MCGREW Camberwick Green series

BARNEY RUBBLE *The Flintstones*
BART MAVERICK *Maverick*
BEN PARKINSON *Butterflies*
BENTON FRASER *Due South*
BILLY BOSWELL *Bread*
BILLY HENSHAW *In Loving Memory*
BRET MAVERICK *Maverick*
CAPTAIN FLACK Camberwick Green series
CAPTAIN SNORT Camberwick Green series
CHANDLER BING *Friends*
CHARLES FRERE *Howards' Way*
CHIPPY MINTON Camberwick Green series
COLONEL HOGAN *Hogan's Heroes*
CORPORAL MARSH *Get Some In!*
CRYSTAL TIPPS *Crystal Tipps and Alistair*
DANNY BALDWIN *Coronation Street*
DANNY MCGLONE *Tutti Frutti*
DAVE SULLIVAN *The Sullivans*
DEREK TROTTER *Only Fools and Horses*
DOCTOR FINLAY *Doctor Finlay, Dr Finlay's Casebook*
DOCTOR THORPE *Only When I Laugh*
DONALD FISHER *Home and Away*
EDDIE CATFLAP *Filthy Rich and Catflap*
EDINA MONSOON *Absolutely Fabulous*
ERSKINE-BROWN *Rumpole of the Bailey*
FATHER DOUGAL *Father Ted*
FRANK BUTCHER *EastEnders*
FRANK FURILLO *Hill Street Blues*
FRANK SPENCER *Some Mothers Do 'Ave 'Em*
FRASIER CRANE *Cheers, Frasier*
GEORGE CARTER *The Sweeney*

GREG ANDERSEN *Hollyoaks*
HAROLD BISHOP *Neighbours*
HELEN DANIELS *Neighbours*
HESTER FIELDS *Fresh Fields*
HOMER SIMPSON *The Simpsons*
JAIME SOMMERS *The Bionic Woman*
JAMES HERRIOT *All Creatures Great and Small*
JANE TENNISON *Prime Suspect*
JENNIFER HART *Hart to Hart*
JONATHAN BELL Camberwick Green series
JONATHAN HART *Hart to Hart*
KEVIN WEBSTER *Coronation Street*
LADY PENELOPE *Thunderbirds*
LENNY THE LION *The Lenny the Lion Show*
LES BATTERSBY *Coronation Street*
LORD MELCHETT *Blackadder II*
LOU CARPENTER *Neighbours*
LOUIE DE PALMA *Taxi*
LOUISE TAYLOR *Hollyoaks*
MADAME CHOLET *The Wombles*
MAGGIE FORBES *The Gentle Touch*
MARGE SIMPSON *The Simpsons*
MARLON DINGLE *Emmerdale*
MATTIE STORIN House of Cards series
MEGAN ROBERTS *The District Nurse*
MICKEY MURPHY Camberwick Green series
MICKEY PEARCE *Only Fools and Horses*
MILDRED ROPER *George and Mildred, Man about the House*
MIMI LA BONQUE *'Allo 'Allo*
MISS LOVELACE Camberwick Green series
MONICA GELLER (+ BING) *Friends*

NAPOLEON SOLO *The Man from UNCLE*
OLIVIA WALTON *The Waltons*
PAUL ROBINSON *Neighbours*
PEGGY BUTCHER (+ MITCHELL) *EastEnders*
PHIL MITCHELL *EastEnders*
PHOEBE BUFFAY *Friends*
POLLY SHERMAN *Fawlty Towers*
REGGIE PERRIN *The Fall and Rise of Reginald Perrin*
RIA PARKINSON *Butterflies*
ROBERT MCCALL *The Equalizer*
SERGEANT TROY *Midsomer Murders*
SERGEANT WATT *Z Cars*
SIMON TEMPLAR *The Saint, Return of the Saint*
TERRY COLLIER *The Likely Lads*
THE VIRGINIAN *The Virginian*
TRACEY STUBBS *Birds of a Feather*
TREVOR PURVIS *Grafters*
VICKY POLLARD *Little Britain*
WESLEY PEGDEN *Last of the Summer Wine*
YOSSER HUGHES *Boys from the Blackstuff*
YOUNG MR GRACE *Are You Being Served?*

13

ADRIAN BOSWELL *Bread*
ALAN PARTRIDGE *I'm Alan Partridge, Knowing Me, Knowing You…*
ALBERT STEPTOE *Steptoe and Son*
ALBERT TATLOCK *Coronation Street*
ALEC CALLENDER *May to December*
ARNOLD J RIMMER *Red Dwarf*
ASHLEY PEACOCK *Coronation Street*

AUDREY ROBERTS *Coronation Street*
BEN CARTWRIGHT *Bonanza*
BERNARD HEDGES *Please Sir!*
BERNIE SCRIPPS *Heartbeat*
BIG JOHN CANNON *The High Chaparral*
BILLY MITCHELL *EastEnders*
CAPTAIN ONEDIN *The Onedin Line*
CAPTAIN PICARD *Star Trek: the Next Generation*
CHARITY DINGLE (+ TATE) *Emmerdale*
CHARLIE SLATER *EastEnders*
CHASE GIOBERTI *Falcon Crest*
CHEYENNE BODIE *Cheyenne*
CLIFF HUXTABLE *The Cosby Show*
COLONEL POTTER *M*A*S*H*
CORPORAL JONES *Dad's Army*
DICK DASTARDLY *Wacky Races*
DOCTOR CAMERON *Doctor Finlay, Dr Finlay's Casebook*
DOCTOR KILDARE *Dr Kildare*
DOCTOR SNODDIE *Dr Finlay's Casebook*
FOGGY DEWHURST *Last of the Summer Wine*
FRANK BURNSIDE *The Bill*
GORDON BRITTAS *The Brittas Empire*
GRACE SULLIVAN *The Sullivans*
GRANT MITCHELL *EastEnders, Home and Away*
HAROLD STEPTOE *Steptoe and Son*
HAMISH MACBETH *Hamish Macbeth*
HAWKEYE PIERCE *M*A*S*H*
HERMAN MUNSTER *The Munsters*
HORACE RUMPOLE *Rumpole of the Bailey*
ILLYA KURYAKIN *The Man from UNCLE*
IVOR THE ENGINE *Ivor the Engine*

JACK DUCKWORTH *Coronation Street*
JAMES HADLEIGH *Hadleigh*
JEAN-LUC PICARD *Star Trek: the Next Generation*
JIMMY CORKHILL *Brookside*
JOEY TRIBBIANI *Friends*
JOLYON FORSYTE *The Forsyte Saga*
JONATHAN CREEK *Jonathan Creek*
JONES THE STEAM *Ivor the Engine*
JUDGE JOHN DEED *Judge John Deed*
KERMIT THE FROG *The Muppet Show*
KLINKERHOFFEN *'Allo 'Allo*
LEN FAIRCLOUGH *Coronation Street*
MAGGIE SIMPSON *The Simpsons*
MARJORIE DAWES *Little Britain*
MARY BETH LACEY *Cagney and Lacey*
MAX CUNNINGHAM *Hollyoaks*
MEG RICHARDSON (+ MORTIMER) *Crossroads*
MICHAEL KNIGHT *Knight Rider*
MUFFIN THE MULE *Muffin the Mule*
NELLIE BOSWELL *Bread*
NEVILLE LYTTON *Lytton's Diary*
OSCAR BLAKETON *Heartbeat*
PAULINE FOWLER *EastEnders*
PEGGY MITCHELL (+ BUTCHER) *EastEnders*
PHIL ESTERHAUS *Hill Street Blues*
PHILIP E MARLOW *The Singing Detective*
PRIVATE FRASER *Dad's Army*
PRIVATE WALKER *Dad's Army*
RICHARD BUCKET *Keeping Up Appearances*
RICHARD DEVERE *To the Manor Born*
RICHIE RICHARD *Bottom*
RODNEY TROTTER *Only Fools and Horses*

SERGEANT BILKO *The Phil Silvers Show*
SERGEANT LEWIS *Inspector Morse*
SETH ARMSTRONG *Emmerdale*
SOAMES FORSYTE *The Forsyte Saga*
STEVE MCDONALD *Coronation Street*
THE LONE RANGER *The Lone Ranger*
THOMAS BANACEK *Banacek*
TIM NICE-BUT-DIM *Harry Enfield shows*
TRISTAN FARNON *All Creatures Great and Small*
TUCKER JENKINS *Grange Hill*
VERA DUCKWORTH *Coronation Street*
VERNON SCRIPPS *Heartbeat*
VICTOR MELDREW *One Foot in the Grave*
WILLIAM FIELDS *Fresh Fields*
YVONNE SPARROW *Goodnight Sweetheart*

14
ADAM CARTWRIGHT *Bonanza*
ANGELA CHANNING *Falcon Crest*
AVELINE BOSWELL *Bread*
BRENDAN MCGUIRE *Doctors*
BROTHER CADFAEL *Cadfael*
CAPTAIN BELLAMY *Upstairs, Downstairs*
CAPTAIN DARLING *Blackadder Goes Forth*
CAPTAIN FURILLO *Hill Street Blues*
CAPTAIN PEACOCK *Are You Being Served?*
CAPTAIN SCARLET *Captain Scarlet and the Mysterons*
CARRIE BRADSHAW *Sex and the City*
DESMOND AMBROSE *Desmond's*
FREDDIE BOSWELL *Bread*

FRED FLINTSTONE *The Flintstones*
GLADYS EMMANUEL *Open All Hours*
HOSS CARTWRIGHT *Bonanza*
HYACINTH BUCKET *Keeping Up Appearances*
INSPECTOR FROST *A Touch of Frost*
INSPECTOR MORSE *Inspector Morse*
JOAN GREENGROSS *The Fall and Rise of Reginald Perrin*
JONATHAN CREEK *Jonathan Creek*
KRUSTY THE CLOWN *The Simpsons*
KWAI CHANG CAINE *Kung Fu*
LORD BELBOROUGH *Camberwick Green series*
MARGARET CRABBE *Pie in the Sky*
MINNIE CALDWELL *Coronation Street*
MITCH BUCHANNON *Baywatch*
MOLLY MACDONALD *Monarch of the Glen*
MR BARROWCLOUGH *Porridge*
PEPPER ANDERSON *Police Woman*
PHILIP BOSINNEY *The Forsyte Saga*
PRIVATE GODFREY *Dad's Army*
RICHARD HILLMAN *Coronation Street*
ROSEANNE CONNER *Roseanne*
SAFFRON MONSOON *Absolutely Fabulous*
SERGEANT WILSON *Dad's Army*
SIR EDWARD FRERE *Howards' Way*
STEVE MCGARRETT *Hawaii Five-O*
THE SWEDISH CHEF *The Muppet Show*
TIMOTHY LUMSDEN *Sorry!*
TONY HUTCHINSON *Hollyoaks*
TREVOR JORDACHE *Brookside*
WORZEL GUMMIDGE *Worzel Gummidge*

15

BLAKE CARRINGTON *Dynasty*
CAPTAIN HOGTHROB *The Muppet Show*
CHARLIE FAIRHEAD *Casualty*
CHRISTINE CAGNEY *Cagney and Lacey*
DAVID BRAITHWAITE *At Home with the Braithwaites*
DIANE BLACKSTOCK (+ SUGDEN) *Emmerdale*
DOCTOR GILLESPIE *Dr Kildare*
EDDIE SHOESTRING *Shoestring*
ELIZABETH PERRIN *The Fall and Rise of Reginald Perrin*
ELLY MAY CLAMPETT *The Beverly Hillbillies*
FATHER TED CRILLY *Father Ted*
FRANCIS URQUHART *House of Cards series*
HECTOR MACDONALD *Monarch of the Glen*
HERBERT TRUELOVE *Last of the Summer Wine*
HETTY WAINTHROPP *Hetty Wainthropp Investigates*
HOT LIPS HOULIHAN *M*A*S*H*
INSPECTOR BARLOW *Z Cars*
INSPECTOR FOWLER *The Thin Blue Line*
INSPECTOR LYNLEY *The Inspector Lynley Mysteries*
JEFFREY FAIRMILE *George and Mildred*
JERRY LEADBETTER *The Good Life*
JESSICA FLETCHER *Murder, She Wrote*
LIEUTENANT KOJAK *Kojak*
MANDY HUTCHINSON *Hollyoaks*
MARGARET MELDREW *One Foot in the Grave*

MARGO LEADBETTER *The Good Life*
MARTHA LONGHURST *Coronation Street*
MONSIEUR LECLERC *'Allo 'Allo*
OFFICER CRABTREE *'Allo 'Allo*
PAUL DANGERFIELD *Dangerfield*
PENELOPE PITSTOP *Wacky Races*
PRIVATE DOBERMAN *The Phil Silvers Show*
REMINGTON STEELE *Remington Steele*
SANDY RICHARDSON *Crossroads*
SIEGFRIED FARNON *All Creatures Great and Small*
SISTER BERTRILLE *The Flying Nun*
TRICIA SUMMERBEE *Heartbeat*
WILMA FLINTSTONE *The Flintstones*

16

ALISON BRAITHWAITE *At Home with the Braithwaites*
AUNTIE WAINWRIGHT *Last of the Summer Wine*
BUFFY ANNE SUMMERS *Buffy the Vampire Slayer*
CAPTAIN AMOS BURKE *Burke's Law*
CHIEF DAN MATTHEWS *Highway Patrol*
CLAUDE GREENGRASS *Heartbeat*
EDMUND BLACKADDER *Blackadder series*

GARETH BLACKSTOCK *Chef!*
GERALDINE GRANGER *The Vicar of Dibley*
INSPECTOR BARNABY *Midsomer Murders*
INSPECTOR MAIGRET *Maigret*
INSPECTOR WEXFORD *The Ruth Rendell Mysteries*
MONSIEUR ALPHONSE *'Allo 'Allo*
PEGGY OLLERENSHAW *Hi-de-Hi!*
PRESIDENT BARTLET *The West Wing*
RODNEY BLACKSTOCK *Emmerdale*
SERGEANT ANDERSON *Police Woman*
SERGEANT BLAKETON *Heartbeat*
SERGEANT CRADDOCK *Heartbeat*
TRISTRAM FOURMILE *George and Mildred*

17

CHARLIE HUNGERFORD *Bergerac*
FATHER DUDDLESWELL *Bless Me Father*

18

CLAUDE ERSKINE-BROWN *Rumpole of the Bailey*
GREAT UNCLE BULGARIA *The Wombles*
SIR HUMPHREY APPLEBY *Yes, Minister*

Arts – Media – Television – TV PROGRAMMES

3
ALF
BOD
DAD
FOX
GBH
HOW!
JOE
LUV
OTT
QED
SAM
UFO

4
BOON
BUGS
CHEF!
FAME
I SPY
KYTV
LOOK
M*A*S*H
MAYO
SOAP
SOLO
TAXI

5
AGONY
ARENA
BABAR
BRASS
BREAD
CHALK

CHIPS
COAST
CRANE
CRIBB
DOTTO
HOTEL
JULIA
KOJAK
LA LAW
NANNY
OH BOY!
PARIS
REBUS
RHODA
ROOTS
SORRY!
SPACE
SYKES
TEMPO
TENKO
TV EYE
WINGS
WOGAN
Z CARS
ZORRO

6
ANGELS
BADGER
BATMAN
BENSON
BOTTOM
BOYD QC
BUDGIE
CALLAN

CANNON
CHEERS
CHOCKY
CINEMA
CLUEDO
CONNIE
CYBILL
DALLAS
EXTRAS
FLOG IT!
F TROOP
GAME ON
HANNAY
HARRY O
HAZELL
HI-DE-HI!
HUSTLE
JIMMY'S
KUNG FU
LASSIE
LILLIE
MAGPIE
MANNIX
MEDICS
MINDER
MR BEAN
MR BENN
MY HERO
POPEYE
QUINCY
REDCAP
RHODES
SAHARA
SHARPE
SHOGUN

SORTED
SPOOKS
TARGET
TARZAN
TISWAS
TOP CAT
WHACK-O!
WIDOWS
YOU BET!

7
AIRLINE
AIRPORT
AIRWOLF
BAGPUSS
BANACEK
BIG DEAL
BONANZA
BOSS CAT
CADFAEL
CAMPION
CHANCER
CHIGLEY
COLDITZ
COLUMBO
COMPACT
CRACKER
DAKTARI
DEE TIME
DOCTORS
DRAGNET
DREAM ON
DYNASTY
FIMBLES
FLIPPER

FRASIER
FRIENDS
GRANDAD
HANCOCK
HIGHWAY
HOLIDAY
HORIZON
IVANHOE
JERICHO
JUSTICE
KARAOKE
LARAMIE
LEAVING
LOVEJOY
MADIGAN
MAIGRET
MANHUNT
MATLOCK
MCCLOUD
MONITOR
NEWHART
OMNIBUS
ON THE UP
ORLANDO
POLDARK
POP IDOL
QUILLER
RAFFLES
RAINBOW
RAWHIDE
RESNICK
RUGRATS
SEA HUNT
SHELLEY
SINGLES

SPENDER
SUNBURN
TAGGART
THE BILL
THE COPS
THE TUBE
THE VICE
THE WORD
TONIGHT
TOP GEAR
TRAINER
WARSHIP
ZOO TIME

8
'ALLO 'ALLO
AQUARIUS
ASK ASPEL
BAD GIRLS
BALAMORY
BAYWATCH
BEN CASEY
BERGERAC
BIG BREAK
BRAMWELL
BULLSEYE
CAR BOOTY
CASANOVA
CASUALTY
CHEYENNE
CLARENCE
COLD FEET
COUPLING
DAD'S ARMY
DEAR JOHN

DESMOND'S
DUE SOUTH
DUTY FREE
EGGHEADS
ELDORADO
FOXY LADY
GRAFTERS
GUNSMOKE
HADLEIGH
HOT METAL
HUGH AND I
LOU GRANT
MACGYVER
MAGNUM PI
MAN ALIVE
MAVERICK
MCCALLUM
MISTER ED
MR AND MRS
MY FAMILY
NEW FACES
NYPD BLUE
PANORAMA
PLAY AWAY
PORRIDGE
POT BLACK
QUIZ BALL
RECKLESS
RED DWARF
ROSEANNE
SEINFELD
SPIN CITY
STAR TREK
STINGRAY
SUPERTED
SURVIVAL
SURVIVOR
THE A-TEAM

THE BARON
THE BRIEF
THE CHIEF
THE GRAND
THE HERBS
THE KNOCK
THE LAKES
THE SAINT
THIS WEEK
TJ HOOKER
TRIANGLE
TRUMPTON
TWEENIES
VISION ON
WATCHDOG
WATCHING
WHIPLASH
WILD WEST
WYCLIFFE
YOGI BEAR
ZOO QUEST

9

A BIT OF A DO
AMOS 'N' ANDY
ANDY PANDY
ART ATTACK
BANANAMAN
BERYL'S LOT
BEWITCHED
BLIND DATE
BLUE PETER
BREAKFAST
BROOKSIDE
BURKE'S LAW
CATCHWORD
CATWEAZLE
CHRONICLE

CIRCUS BOY
COUNTDOWN
CROSS WITS
CUTTING IT
DAN AUGUST
DANGER MAN
DANGER UXB
DARK SKIES
DID YOU SEE?
DOCTOR WHO
DOOMWATCH
DR KILDARE
EMMERDALE
EMPTY NEST
EUROTRASH
FATHER TED
FOYLE'S WAR
GENTLE BEN
GET SOME IN!
GOING LIVE!
HAPPINESS
HAPPY DAYS
HEARTBEAT
HENRY'S CAT
HOLBY CITY
HOLLYOAKS
I, CLAUDIUS
I LOVE LUCY
JACKANORY
JASON KING
LOGAN'S RUN
LOVE HURTS
MAKING OUT
MIAMI VICE
MISS WORLD
MR MAJEIKA
MURDER BAG
MURDER ONE

NAKED CITY
NEWS AT TEN
NEWSNIGHT
NEWSROUND
NEW TRICKS
NEXT OF KIN
NO BANANAS
PLEASE SIR!
POKERFACE
PUBLIC EYE
REAL WOMEN
ROBOT WARS
RUNAROUND
SCREAMING
SO HAUNT ME
SOUTH PARK
STAY LUCKY
SUPERGRAN
TFI FRIDAY
THAT'S LIFE
THE COLBYS
THE CRUISE
THE FAMILY
THE GAFFER
THE LOVERS
THE OFFICE
THE WORKER
THE X-FILES
TIMEWATCH
TORCHWOOD
TURNABOUT
TWIN PEAKS
UGLY BETTY
ULTRA QUIZ
UP POMPEII!

10

AFTER HENRY

ALL YOUR OWN
ALLY MCBEAL
AMBASSADOR
BAND OF GOLD
BIG BROTHER
BOB AND ROSE
BOTANIC MAN
BYKER GROVE
CANNONBALL
CASEY JONES
CHILD'S PLAY
CLAYHANGER
CROSSROADS
CROWN COURT
DEAR LADIES
DEPARTMENT S
DEPUTY DAWG
DON'T WAIT UP
EASTENDERS
ELIZABETH R
FACE TO FACE
FAMILY TIES
FIREMAN SAM
FULL CIRCLE
GIDEON'S WAY
GIRLS ON TOP
GLADIATORS
GRANDSTAND
GRANGE HILL
HART TO HART
HORNBLOWER
HOWARDS' WAY
JIM'LL FIX IT
KAVANAGH QC
KEEPING MUM
KISS ME KATE
LIFE ON MARS
LINDA GREEN

LOOSE WOMEN
MASTERCHEF
MASTERMIND
MASTERTEAM
MERSEYBEAT
MIKE HAMMER
MISS MARPLE
MOTORMOUTH
NAKED VIDEO
NATIONWIDE
NEIGHBOURS
NO, HONESTLY
ON THE BUSES
PADDINGTON
PERRY MASON
PETROCELLI
PLAY SCHOOL
POGLES' WOOD
POLE TO POLE
POLICE FIVE
POSTMAN PAT
QUATERMASS
RENTAGHOST
RISING DAMP
ROBIN'S NEST
ROGER ROGER
SCREEN TEST
SECRET ARMY
SHOESTRING
SPORTSVIEW
STYLE TRIAL
TERRAHAWKS
THAT'S MY BOY
THE BIG TIME
THE BOUNDER
THE CHARMER
THE FALL GUY
THE GOODIES

THE IRISH RM
THE LARKINS
THE MONKEES
THE ONE SHOW
THE PLANETS
THE SWEENEY
THE WALTONS
THE WAR GAME
THE WOMBLES
THE X FACTOR
VAN DER VALK
WACKY RACES
WAGON TRAIN
WELLS FARGO
WHO DO YOU DO?
WHY DON'T YOU?
WISH ME LUCK

11
ANIMAL MAGIC
BARGAIN HUNT
BRADEN'S WEEK
BUTTERFLIES
CALL MY BLUFF
CATCHPHRASE
CHICAGO HOPE
CITY CENTRAL
CLOCKING OFF
COLD LAZARUS
COME DANCING
COMIC RELIEF
CONFESSIONS
COUNTRYFILE
CRACKERJACK
DANGERFIELD
DANGERMOUSE
DANIEL BOONE
DEPARTMENT S

DINNERLADIES
DOWN TO EARTH
FALCON CREST
FRAGGLE ROCK
FRESH FIELDS
GIVE US A CLUE
GORMENGHAST
GROUND FORCE
HAWAII FIVE-O
HOME AND AWAY
HOME TO ROOST
JUKE BOX JURY
JULIET BRAVO
JUST WILLIAM
KNIGHT RIDER
LATE STARTER
LEAD BALLOON
LIFE ON EARTH
LOST IN SPACE
MAISIE RAINE
MATT HOUSTON
MAX HEADROOM
METAL MICKEY
MY THREE SONS
NIGHTY NIGHT
OUTSIDE EDGE
PEYTON PLACE
PIE IN THE SKY
POLICE WOMAN
QUANTUM LEAP
RAB C NESBITT
ROCK FOLLIES
ROSIE AND JIM
SHADOWLANDS
SLINGER'S DAY
SPORTSNIGHT
SPOT THE TUNE
ST ELSEWHERE

TED AND ALICE
TELETUBBIES
THE ARMY GAME
THE AVENGERS
THE BROTHERS
THE BUMBLIES
THE CAZALETS
THE CISCO KID
THE FAST SHOW
THE FUGITIVE
THE GOOD LIFE
THE GRIMLEYS
THE INFORMER
THE LOVE BOAT
THE LUCY SHOW
THE MEN'S ROOM
THE MISTRESS
THE MUNSTERS
THE OTHER 'ARF
THE PRISONER
THE RAG TRADE
THE RIFLEMAN
THE SIMPSONS
THE SOPRANOS
THE WEST WING
THIS MORNING
TOM AND JERRY
TRIPPER'S DAY
TUCKER'S LUCK
TUTTI FRUTTI
TWO'S COMPANY
WHAT'S MY LINE?
WHIRLYBIRDS
WONDER WOMAN
YES, MINISTER

12
A FAMILY AT WAR

A FINE ROMANCE
ALBION MARKET
A LIFE OF GRIME
ASK THE FAMILY
AS TIME GOES BY
BARNABY JONES
BARNEY MILLER
BLOCKBUSTERS
BRUSH STROKES
CANDID CAMERA
CITIZEN SMITH
CITY HOSPITAL
CIVILIZATION
CLAPPERBOARD
COMMON AS MUCK
CRIMEWATCH UK
DAWSON'S CREEK
DEAL OR NO DEAL
DOCTOR FINLAY
FACE THE MUSIC
FAWLTY TOWERS
FIFTEEN TO ONE
FLOWERPOT MEN
FOOD AND DRINK
FOREVER GREEN
FORTY MINUTES
GOING FOR GOLD
GRAND DESIGNS
GRUMPY OLD MEN
HARK AT BARKER
HEARTS OF GOLD
HECTOR'S HOUSE
HELL'S KITCHEN
HOGAN'S HEROES
HOPE AND GLORY
HOUSE OF CARDS
I MARRIED JOAN
IT'S A KNOCKOUT

JOINT ACCOUNT
KNOTS LANDING
LYTTON'S DIARY
MOONLIGHTING
MORK AND MINDY
MURDER IN MIND
NAME THAT TUNE
NEW STREET LAW
NIGHTINGALES
OPEN ALL HOURS
PEAK PRACTICE
PLAY FOR TODAY
POINTS OF VIEW
PRESTON FRONT
PRIME SUSPECT
QUESTION TIME
RIPPING YARNS
ROUGH JUSTICE
ROVING REPORT
SERGEANT CORK
SESAME STREET
SIX FEET UNDER
SOFTLY, SOFTLY
STELLA STREET
TAKE YOUR PICK
TALKING HEADS
TELLY ADDICTS
TERRY AND JUNE
THE BORROWERS
THE CHAMPIONS
THE COMEDIANS
THE COSBY SHOW
THE EQUALIZER
THE FAMILY MAN
THE FLYING NUN
THE NEWCOMERS
THE OSBOURNES
THE PALLISERS

THE POWER GAME
THE SOOTY SHOW
THE SULLIVANS
THE THICK OF IT
THE VIRGINIAN
THE YOUNG ONES
THREE OF A KIND
THUNDERBIRDS
TOP OF THE POPS
TOUCHING EVIL
TREASURE HUNT
WATERLOO ROAD
WEEKEND WORLD
WORKING LUNCH
WORLD OF SPORT
YOU RANG, M'LORD?

13

ABIGAIL'S PARTY
A SENSE OF GUILT
A TOUCH OF FROST
BAR MITZVAH BOY
BLANKETY BLANK
BLESS ME, FATHER
BOB THE BUILDER
CARDIAC ARREST
CATHY COME HOME
CHANDLER AND CO
CHANGING ROOMS
CHILDREN'S WARD
CHUCKLEVISION
CURRY AND CHIPS
FAMILY AFFAIRS
FANTASY ISLAND
GAME FOR A LAUGH
GOING FOR A SONG
GOING STRAIGHT
HAMISH MACBETH

HARBOUR LIGHTS
HIGHWAY PATROL
IT TAKES A THIEF
IVOR THE ENGINE
JONATHAN CREEK
JUDGE JOHN DEED
LITTLE BRITAIN
LOOKS FAMILIAR
MARCUS WELBY MD
MATCH OF THE DAY
MAY TO DECEMBER
MUFFIN THE MULE
NEVER THE TWAIN
NO HIDING PLACE
NORTH AND SOUTH
PINKY AND PERKY
READY, STEADY, GO!
SEX AND THE CITY
SHOOTING STARS
SILENT WITNESS
SMILEY'S PEOPLE
SONGS OF PRAISE
SPECIAL BRANCH
SPITTING IMAGE
STARS ON SUNDAY
STEPTOE AND SON
STRIKE IT LUCKY
THE APPRENTICE
THE BLACKADDER
THE BLUE PLANET
THE BRADY BUNCH
THE BROKER'S MAN
THE BUCCANEERS
THE DETECTIVES
THE GOLDEN SHOT
THE HELLO GIRLS
THE LIKELY LADS
THE LIVER BIRDS

THE LONE RANGER
THE MAIN CHANCE
THE MANAGERESS
THE MUPPET SHOW
THE ONEDIN LINE
THE PERSUADERS
THE SKY AT NIGHT
THE SUPERSTARS
THE TWO RONNIES
THE UPCHAT LINE
THE WINDS OF WAR
THE WOODENTOPS
THE WORLD AT WAR
ULTIMATE FORCE
WAITING FOR GOD
WAKING THE DEAD
WHAT NOT TO WEAR
WHICKER'S WORLD
WILDLIFE ON ONE
WORLD IN ACTION

14

A BRUSH WITH FAME
AIN'T MISBEHAVIN'
ALL IN GOOD FAITH
ALL IN THE FAMILY
ANIMAL HOSPITAL
A PLACE IN THE SUN
BALLYKISSANGEL
BAND OF BROTHERS
BLESS THIS HOUSE
BUSMAN'S HOLIDAY
CAGNEY AND LACEY
CAPTAIN PUGWASH
CARRIE AND BARRY
CASH IN THE ATTIC
CHARLIE'S ANGELS
CHILD OF OUR TIME

CHILDREN IN NEED
COLIN'S SANDWICH
CRISS CROSS QUIZ
CROCODILE SHOES
DOOGIE HOWSER MD
EDGE OF DARKNESS
ENEMY AT THE DOOR
FAMILY FORTUNES
FROCKS ON THE BOX
GARDENERS' WORLD
GRACE UNDER FIRE
GRUMPY OLD WOMEN
HAPPY EVER AFTER
HEARTBURN HOTEL
HIGHWAY PATROL
IN AT THE DEEP END
IN LOVING MEMORY
INSPECTOR MORSE
LIZZIE DRIPPING
LONDON'S BURNING
MAN IN A SUITCASE
MIXED BLESSINGS
MURDER, SHE WROTE
MY WIFE NEXT DOOR
NOT ONLY, BUT ALSO
ONLY WHEN I LAUGH
PAT AND MARGARET
PEOPLE'S CENTURY
PROPERTY LADDER
QUEENIE'S CASTLE
RECORD BREAKERS
RICHARD AND JUDY
SECOND THOUGHTS
SIX-FIVE SPECIAL
SOLDIER, SOLDIER
SURGICAL SPIRIT
SUTHERLAND'S LAW
SYLVANIA WATERS

TELFORD'S CHANGE
THE ASCENT OF MAN
THE BIONIC WOMAN
THE CLOTHES SHOW
THE CRYSTAL MAZE
THE CUCKOO WALTZ
THE FLINTSTONES
THE FORSYTE SAGA
THE FOUR JUST MEN
THE GENTLE TOUCH
THE GOLDEN GIRLS
THE GOOD OLD DAYS
THE GROVE FAMILY
THE HOT SHOE SHOW
THE HUMAN JUNGLE
THE NEW AVENGERS
THE OUTER LIMITS
THE PIGLET FILES
THE PLANE MAKERS
THE PYRAMID GAME
THE ROYLE FAMILY
THE SMOKING ROOM
THE WATER MARGIN
THE WEAKEST LINK
THE WONDER YEARS
THIS IS YOUR LIFE
THREE UP, TWO DOWN
TOMORROW'S WORLD
TO THE MANOR BORN
WHEEL OF FORTUNE
WINNER TAKES ALL
WORZEL GUMMIDGE

15

ARMCHAIR THEATRE
AUNTIE'S BLOOMERS
BETWEEN THE LINES
BIRDS OF A FEATHER

CAMBERWICK GREEN
CHALLENGE ANNEKA
COMEDY PLAYHOUSE
DIFF'RENT STROKES
DOUBLE YOUR MONEY
EXECUTIVE STRESS
FOR THE LOVE OF ADA
GENERAL HOSPITAL
GIMME GIMME GIMME
HILL STREET BLUES
HOW DO THEY DO
 THAT?
I'M ALAN PARTRIDGE
INTERPOL CALLING
IT'S A SQUARE WORLD
JESUS OF NAZARETH
JUST GOOD FRIENDS
LAND OF THE GIANTS
LATE NIGHT LINE-UP
MAN FROM ATLANTIS
MCMILLAN AND WIFE
MIDSOMER MURDERS
NOEL'S HOUSE PARTY
ONE MAN AND HIS
 DOG
PEBBLE MILL AT ONE
PLAYING THE FIELD
REMINGTON STEELE
ROBIN OF SHERWOOD
SPEND, SPEND, SPEND
STARSKY AND HUTCH
TAKE THE HIGH ROAD
THE ADDAMS FAMILY
THE BIG BREAKFAST
THE FLYING DOCTOR
THE GREAT EGG RACE
THE INVISIBLE MAN
THE LIVING PLANET

THE MAN FROM UNCLE
THE NEW STATESMAN
THE PARADISE CLUB
THE PRICE IS RIGHT
THE THIN BLUE LINE
THE TWILIGHT ZONE
THE UNTOUCHABLES
THIRTYSOMETHING
WATCH WITH MOTHER
WHERE THE HEART IS
WHERE THERE'S LIFE
WISH YOU WERE HERE?
YOU'VE BEEN FRAMED!

16
ADAM ADAMANT LIVES!
ALL GAS AND GAITERS
ALL OUR YESTERDAYS
ANTIQUES ROADSHOW
A QUESTION OF SPORT
BOOTSIE AND SNUDGE
CELEBRITY SQUARES
CORONATION STREET
DALZIEL AND PASCOE
DEATH OF A PRINCESS
DIXON OF DOCK GREEN
FAIRLY SECRET ARMY
FAITH IN THE FUTURE
FATHER, DEAR FATHER
FOOTBALLERS' WIVES
GEORGE AND MILDRED
HOPALONG CASSIDY
IT AIN'T HALF HOT MUM
JEEVES AND WOOSTER
LOVE THY NEIGHBOUR
MAN ABOUT THE HOUSE
MEN BEHAVING BADLY
MIND YOUR LANGUAGE

MONARCH OF THE GLEN
MURDER MOST HORRID
NORTHERN EXPOSURE
PERFECT STRANGERS
RAG TAG AND BOBTAIL
REILLY, ACE OF SPIES
RETURN OF THE SAINT
SALE OF THE CENTURY
SAPPHIRE AND STEEL
STARS IN THEIR EYES
SURPRISE, SURPRISE
THE BRITTAS EMPIRE
THE DISTRICT NURSE
THE GIRL FROM UNCLE
THE HIGH CHAPARRAL
THE HOUSE OF ELIOTT
THE KRYPTON FACTOR
THE MARRIAGE LINES
THE MRS MERTON SHOW
THE PROFESSIONALS
THE ROCKFORD FILES
THE SOUTH BANK SHOW
THE VICAR OF DIBLEY
TIPPING THE VELVET
WHAT THE PAPERS SAY
WITHIN THESE WALLS
YES, PRIME MINISTER

17
ALAS SMITH AND JONES
ARE YOU BEING SERVED?
AUF WIEDERSEHEN, PET
DR FINLAY'S CASEBOOK
DROP THE DEAD DONKEY
EVERY SECOND COUNTS
HAVE GUN WILL TRAVEL
LAVERNE AND SHIRLEY
MISSION: IMPOSSIBLE

ONE FOOT IN THE GRAVE
OPPORTUNITY KNOCKS
PENNIES FROM HEAVEN
SHINE ON HARVEY MOON
THE DUKES OF HAZZARD
THE FLYING GARDENER
THE GENERATION GAME
THE INCREDIBLE HULK
THROUGH THE KEYHOLE
TILL DEATH US DO PART
WE ARE THE CHAMPIONS

18
ABSOLUTELY FABULOUS
ALIAS SMITH AND JONES
A MAN CALLED IRONSIDE
CASTLE IN THE COUNTRY

GOODNESS GRACIOUS ME
HAVE I GOT NEWS FOR YOU
I DIDN'T KNOW YOU CARED
JEUX SANS FRONTIÈRES
ONLY FOOLS AND HORSES
PLAY YOUR CARDS RIGHT
PRISONER: CELL BLOCK H
SOME MOTHERS DO 'AVE 'EM
THE JEWEL IN THE CROWN
THE MAGIC ROUNDABOUT
THE PHIL SILVERS SHOW
THE PINK PANTHER SHOW
THE PLANET OF THE APES
THE RIFF RAFF ELEMENT
UPSTAIRS, DOWNSTAIRS
WHEN THE BOAT COMES IN

Arts – Music & Entertainment – COMEDIANS

3
FRY Stephen
GEE Dustin
KAY Peter
RAY Ted
ROY Derek
WAX Ruby

4
ALAN Ray
BALL Bobby
BIRD John
CARR Jimmy
COOK Peter
DODD Ken
GOLD Jimmy

GRAY Eddie
HALE Gareth
HALL Terry
HILL Benny, Harry
HOPE Bob
HUDD Roy
HULL Rod
IDLE Eric
KING Dave
KNOX Teddy
PACE Norman
READ Al
REID Mike
TODD Bob
WALL Max
WISE Ernie

WOOD Victoria

5
ABBOT Russ
ALLEN Chesney, Gracie
ASKEY Arthur
BAKER Hylda
BENNY Jack
BORGE Victor
BOWEN Jim
BROWN Duggie,
   Faith, Janet
BRUCE Lenny
BURNS George
CHASE Charlie
CRYER Barry

DAVRO Bobby
DIXON Reg
DRAKE Charlie
ELTON Ben
EMERY Dick
EMNEY Fred
EVANS Lee, Norman
FYFFE Will
HENRY Lenny
HORNE Kenneth
JAMES Jimmy
JEWEL Jimmy
JONES Terry
KLEIN Robert
LARGE Eddie
MASON Jackie

MOORE Dudley
MORAN Dylan
NERVO Jimmy
ODDIE Bill
PALIN Michael
PLATT Ken
ROBEY Sir George
ROWAN Dan
SAYLE Alexei
SMITH Mel
STARR Freddie
SYKES Eric
VEGAS Johnny
WELLS John
WORTH Harry

6

AL READ
ANCONA Ronni
BAILEY Bill
BARKER Ronnie
BAXTER Stanley
BERMAN Shelley
BROUGH Peter
CAESAR Sid
CANNON Tommy
CARSON Frank
CLEESE John
COOGAN Steve
COOPER Tommy
DAWSON Les
DENNIS Les
EMBERG Bella
FORMBY George
FRENCH Dawn
GARDEN Graeme
GUYLER Deryck
HARRIS Keith

HAYNES Arthur
HEARNE Richard
HOWERD Frankie
IZZARD Eddie
JETHRO
JUNKIN John
LAURIE Hugh
LITTLE Syd
MARTIN Dick
MAYALL Rik
MILLER Max
MODLEY Albert
MURRAY Chic
O'GRADY Paul
OLIVER Vic
POWELL Sandy
REEVES Vic
RIVERS Joan
ROGERS Ted
RUDNER Rita
TED RAY
WALKER Roy
WATERS Doris, Elsie
WILMOT Gary
WILTON Robb
WISDOM Sir Norman

7

BENNETT Lennie
BENTINE Michael
BOB HOPE
BOB TODD
BREMNER Rory
CARROTT Jasper
CHAPMAN Graham
CHESTER Charlie
CLIFTON Bernie
COLLIER Norman

CORBETT Ronnie
CRICKET Jimmy
DIGANCE Richard
DOUGLAS Jack
EDWARDS Jimmy
ENFIELD Harry
ENGLISH Arthur
FELDMAN Marty
FORTUNE John
FRINTON Freddie
GERVAIS Ricky
GOODWIN Ken
GRAYSON Larry
HANCOCK Tony
HANDLEY Tommy
KEN DODD
MACLEAN Don
MAX WALL
MCGOWAN Alistair
MURDOCH Richard
NEWHART Bob
O'CONNOR Tom
RAY ALAN
ROD HULL
ROY HUDD
RUBY WAX
SECOMBE Sir Harry
SELLERS Peter
STILGOE Richard
TARBUCK Jimmy
TRINDER Tommy
WARRISS Ben
WHEELER Jimmy
WINTERS Bernie, Mike
YARWOOD Mike

8

ATKINSON Rowan

BEN ELTON
BOARDMAN Stan
BYGRAVES Max
CAVANAGH Peter
CONNOLLY Billy
DAN ROWAN
DAVE KING
DAVIDSON Jim
DEREK ROY
ERIC IDLE
FLANAGAN Bud
FLETCHER Cyril
JIM BOWEN
JOHN BIRD
KEN PLATT
MEL SMITH
MIKE REID
MILLIGAN Spike
MORTIMER Bob
NAUGHTON Charlie
PASQUALE Joe
PETER KAY
REG DIXON
STENNETT Stan

9
BENNY HILL
BILL ODDIE
BOBBY BALL
CLITHEROE Jimmy
DICK EMERY
DUSTIN GEE
EDDIE GRAY
ERIC SYKES
ERNIE WISE
FRED EMNEY
HARRY HILL
JACK BENNY

JIMMY CARR
JIMMY GOLD
JOHN WELLS
LES DAWSON
LES DENNIS
MAX MILLER
MONKHOUSE Bob
MORECAMBE Eric
PETER COOK
RHYS-JONES Griff
RIK MAYALL
ROY WALKER
RUSS ABBOT
SHANDLING Garry
SID CAESAR
SYD LITTLE
TEDDY KNOX
TED ROGERS
TERRY HALL
VIC OLIVER
VIC REEVES
WILL FYFFE

10
BARRY CRYER
BEN WARRISS
BILL BAILEY
BOBBY DAVRO
BOB NEWHART
CHIC MURRAY
DAWN FRENCH
DICK MARTIN
DON MACLEAN
DYLAN MORAN
EDDIE LARGE
FAITH BROWN
GARETH HALE
GARY WILMOT

HARRY WORTH
HUGH LAURIE
HYLDA BAKER
JANET BROWN
JIMMY JAMES
JIMMY JEWEL
JIMMY NERVO
JOAN RIVERS
JOHN CLEESE
JOHN JUNKIN
KEN GOODWIN
LENNY BRUCE
LENNY HENRY
NORMAN PACE
PAUL O'GRADY
RITA RUDNER
ROBB WILTON
STEPHEN FRY
TERRY JONES
TOM O'CONNOR

11
ALEXEI SAYLE
ARTHUR ASKEY
BELLA EMBERG
BOB MORTIMER
BUD FLANAGAN
DORIS WATERS
DUDLEY MOORE
DUGGIE BROWN
EDDIE IZZARD
ELSIE WATERS
FRANK CARSON
GEORGE BURNS
GEORGE ROBEY Sir
GRACIE ALLEN
JACK DOUGLAS
JACKIE MASON

JIM DAVIDSON
JOE PASQUALE
JOHN FORTUNE
KEITH HARRIS
MAX BYGRAVES
MIKE WINTERS
MIKE YARWOOD
NORMAN EVANS
PETER BROUGH
ROBERT KLEIN
RONNI ANCONA
RORY BREMNER
SANDY POWELL
STEVE COOGAN
TOMMY CANNON
TOMMY COOPER
TONY HANCOCK
VICTOR BORGE

12
ALBERT MODLEY
ARTHUR HAYNES
BOB MONKHOUSE
CHARLIE CHASE
CHARLIE DRAKE
CHESNEY ALLEN
DERYCK GUYLER
FREDDIE STARR

GEORGE FORMBY
GRAEME GARDEN
HARRY ENFIELD
HARRY SECOMBE Sir
JIMMY CRICKET
JIMMY EDWARDS
JIMMY TARBUCK
JIMMY WHEELER
JOHNNY VEGAS
KENNETH HORNE
LARRY GRAYSON
MARTY FELDMAN
NORMAN WISDOM Sir
PETER SELLERS
RICKY GERVAIS
RONNIE BARKER
STAN BOARDMAN
STAN STENNETT
TOMMY HANDLEY
TOMMY TRINDER
VICTORIA WOOD

13
ARTHUR ENGLISH
BERNIE CLIFTON
BERNIE WINTERS
CYRIL FLETCHER
ERIC MORECAMBE

FRANKIE HOWERD
GRAHAM CHAPMAN
JASPER CARROTT
LENNIE BENNETT
NORMAN COLLIER
PETER CAVANAGH
RICHARD HEARNE
RONNIE CORBETT
ROWAN ATKINSON
SHELLEY BERMAN
SPIKE MILLIGAN
STANLEY BAXTER

14
CHARLIE CHESTER
FREDDIE FRINTON
GARRY SHANDLING
GRIFF RHYS-JONES
JIMMY CLITHEROE
MICHAEL BENTINE
RICHARD DIGANCE
RICHARD MURDOCH
RICHARD STILGOE

15
ALISTAIR MCGOWAN
CHARLIE NAUGHTON

Arts – Music & Entertainment – COMPOSERS

3
BAX Sir Arnold
CUI César
FRY William
SOR Fernando
TYE Christopher

4
ADAM Adolphe
ARNE Thomas
BACH Johann, Christian,
    Johann, Christoph,
    Johann Sebastian

BART Lionel
BERG Alban
BLOW John
BYRD William
CAGE John
FOSS Lukas

GADE Niels
IVES Charles
KERN Jerome
LALO Édouard
LOBO Duarte
LYTE Henry

MITI Luca
NONO Luigi
ORFF Carl
PERI Jacopo
TOCH Ernst
WOLF Hugo

5

AGNEW Roy
ANSON Egbert
AUBER Daniel
AURIC Georges
BERIO Luciano
BINET Jean
BIZET Georges
BLISS Sir Arthur
BLOCH Ernest
BOITO Arrigo
COWEN Sir Frederick
DAVIS Carl
DUFAY Guillaume
DUKAS Paul
ELGAR Sir Edward
FALLA Manuel de
FAURÉ Gabriel
FRANZ Robert
GLUCK Christoph
GRIEG Edvard
GROFÉ Ferde
HAYDN Franz
HENZE Hans
HOLST Gustav
HUBER Hans
IBERT Jacques
KOVEN Reginald de
LEHÁR Franz
LISZT Franz
LOEWE Frederick, Karl
LULLY Jean-Baptiste

NUNES Emmanuel
NYMAN Michael
PARRY Sir Charles
RAVEL Maurice
REGER Max
RIETI Vittorio
SATIE Erik
SOUSA John Philip
SPOHR Ludwig
SUPPÉ Franz von
TOSTI Sir Francesco
VERDI Giuseppe
WEBER Carl
WEILL Kurt
WIDOR Charles

6

ALFANO Franco
ARNOLD Sir Malcolm
BARBER Samuel
BERTÓK Béla
BERLIN Irving
BOULEZ Pierre
BRAHMS Johannes
BRIDGE Frank
BUSONI Ferruccio
CHOPIN Frédéric
CLARKE Jeremiah
COATES Eric
COWARD Sir Noël
CZERNY Karl
DAVIES Peter Maxwell
DELIUS Frederick
DUPARC Henri
DVOŘÁK Antonin
ENESCO Georges
FLOTOW Friedrich
FOSTER Stephen
FRANCK César

GERMAN Edward
GLINKA Mikhail
GOUNOD Charles
HADLEY Patrick
HANDEL George
  Frederick
HANSON Howard
HUMMEL Johann
JOPLIN Scott
JUTRAS Benoît
KODÁLY Zoltán
LIADOV Anatol
MAHLER Gustav
MINKUS Léon
MOZART Wolfgang
  Amadeus
O'RIADA Sean
PLEYEL Ignaz
PORTER Cole
QUANTZ Johann
RAMEAU Jean-Philippe
RUBBRA Edmund
SCELSI Giacinto
SCHÜTZ Heinrich
SEIBER Mátyás
TALLIS Thomas
THOMAS Ambroise
VARÈSE Edgar
WAGNER Richard
WALTON Sir William
WEBERN Anton von
WESLEY Charles

7

ADDISON John
ALBÉNIZ Isaac
ARENSKY Anton
BANTOCK Sir Granville
BELLINI Vincenzo

BENNETT Richard
Rodney
BERGSMA William
BERLIOZ Hector
BORODIN Alexander
BRITTEN Sir Benjamin
COPLAND Aaron
CORELLI Arcangelo
DEBUSSY Claude
DELIBES Léo
DES PRÉS Josquin
DOWLAND John
EINAUDI Ludovico
FRANKEL Benjamin
GIBBONS Orlando
HERBERT Victor
IRELAND John
JANÁČEK Leoš
JOACHIM Joseph
LAMBERT Constant
LEGRAND Michel
MACCUNN Hamish
MARTINU Bohuslav
MENOTTI Gian-Carlo
MILHAUD Darius
NIELSEN Carl
NOVELLO Ivor
PEPUSCH Johann
POULENC Francis
PUCCINI Giacomo
QUILTER Roger
RODGERS Richard
RODRIGO Joaquin
ROMBERG Sigmund
ROSSINI Gioacchino
RUGGLES Carl
SAUGUET Henri
SINDING Christian
SMETANA Bedřich

STAINER Sir John
STRAUSS Johann, Oskar,
Richard
TANSMAN Aleksander
TARTINI Giuseppe
TAVENER John
TIPPETT Sir Michael
TOPLADY Augustus
TORELLI Giuseppe
VIVALDI Antonio
WALLACE Vincent
WEELKES Thomas
XENAKIS Iannis

8

AKIMENKO Fyodor
ALBINONI Tommaso
BOUGHTON Rutland
BRUCKNER Anton
CHABRIER Alexis
COUPERIN Charles
DOHNÁNYI Ernst von
GERSHWIN George
GIORDANI Giuseppe,
Tommaso
GLAZUNOV Alexander
GRAINGER Percy
GRANADOS Enrique
HAMLISCH Marvin
HONEGGER Arthur
KETÈLBEY Albert W
MAILLART Aimé
MASCAGNI Pietro
MASSENET Jules
MESSAGER André
MESSIAEN Olivier
PAGANINI Nicolo
PALMGREN Selim
PHILIDOR François

RAYBOULD Jon
RESPIGHI Ottorino
SCHNABEL Artur
SCHUBERT Franz
SCHUMANN Robert
SCRIABIN Alexander
SIBELIUS Jean
SONDHEIM Stephen
SPONTINI Gasparo
STANFORD Sir Charles
SULLIVAN Sir Arthur
TAVERNER John
TELEMANN Georg
VICTORIA Tomás
WAGENAAR Bernard
WILLIAMS John

9

ADDINSELL Richard
BALAKIREV Mili
BEETHOVEN Ludwig van
BERNSTEIN Leonard
BUXTEHUDE Diderik
CHERUBINI Maria Luigi
DONIZETTI Gaetano
DUNSTABLE John
FITELBERG Jerzy
GRUENBERG Louis
HINDEMITH Paul
LOCATELLI Pietro
MACDOWELL Edward
MACKENZIE
Sir Alexander
MAZZOCCHI Domenico
MEYERBEER Giacomo
MONIUSZKO Stanislaw
OFFENBACH Jacques
PAISIELLO Giovanni
PERGOLESI Giovanni

PROKOFIEV Sergei
RODRIGUEZ Robert
SCARLATTI Alessandro
SCHÖNBERG Arnold
STEINBERG Ben
TOMMASINI Matthew

10
BLITZSTEIN Marc
BOCCHERINI Luigi
FERRABOSCO Alfonso,
   Domenico
KABALEVSKY Dmitri
MIASKOVSKY Nikolai
MONTEVERDI Claudio
MUSSORGSKY Modest
PALESTRINA Giovanni
PENDERECKI Christoph
PONCHIELLI Amilcare
RUBINSTEIN Anton
SAINT-SAËNS Camille
SKALKOTTAS Nikos
STRAVINSKY Igor

TOURNEMIRE Charles
VILLA-LOBOS Heitor
WALDTEUFEL Émile
WILLIAMSON Malcolm

11
BARING-GOULD Sabine
CHARPENTIER Gustave
DITTERSDORF Karl
HUMPERDINCK
   Engelbert
LEONCAVALLO Ruggiero
LLOYD WEBBER Lord
   Andrew
MENDELSSOHN Felix
NIEDERMEYER Louis
RACHMANINOV Sergei
STOCKHAUSEN
   Karlheinz
TCHAIKOVSKY Peter
   Ilyich
WOLF-FERRARI Ermanno

12
DALLAPICCOLA Luigi
KOUSSEVITSKY Sergei
ROSTROPOVICH
   Mstislav
SHOSTAKOVICH Dmitri

13
KHATCHATURIAN Aram
ROUGET DE LISLE Claude

14
RIMSKY-KORSAKOV
   Nikolai

15
ALBRECHTSBERGER
   Johann
COLERIDGE-TAYLOR
   Samuel
SCHNEITZHOEFFER Jean
VAUGHAN WILLIAMS
   Ralph

Arts – Music & Entertainment – CONDUCTORS

3
GUI Vittorio

4
BÖHM Karl
HALL Henry
LEVI Hermann
MUTI Riccardo
ROTH Arnie
WOOD Henry

5
BOULT Sir Adrian
BÜLOW Hans
BUSCH Fritz
CHUNG Myung-
   Whun
DAVIS Sir Andrew,
   Colin
EREDE Alberto
HALLÉ Charles
HEGER Robert

JORDÁ Enrique
KEMPE Rudolf
KRIPS Joseph
MEHTA Zubin
MUNCH Charles
RANKL Karl
SOLTI Sir Georg
SZELL George
VOTTO Antonino

6
ABBADO Claudio
BOULEZ Pierre
DUTOIT Charles
ITURBI José
JACOBI Frederick
JACOBS René
JOCHUM Eugen
KRAUSS Clemens
LEVINE James
MAAZEL Lorin

NAGANO Kent
PRÊTRE Georges
PREVIN André
RATTLE Sir Simon
REINER Fritz
TAUSKY Vilem

7
BEECHAM Sir Thomas
BONYNGE Richard
CHAILLY Ricardo
FRICSAY Ferenc
GERGIEV Valery
GIULINI Carlo Maria
HAITINK Bernard
HARDING Daniel
JOCHUM Eugen
KARAJAN Herbert von
KLEIBER Carlos, Erich
KUBELIK Rafael
LAMBERT Constant
NIKISCH Arthur
PAPPANO Antonio
PINNOCK Trevor
PLASSON Michel
SALONEN Esa-Pekka
SARGENT Sir Malcolm
SCHWARZ Gerard
SERAFIN Tullio
SLATKIN Felix, Leonard

8
ALBRECHT Gerd

ANSERMET Ernest
BODANSKY Artur
CHRISTIE William
CLUYTENS André
DE SABATA Victor
DOHNÁNYI Christoph
  von
GARDELLI Lamberto
GARDINER John Eliot
GOOSSENS Sir Eugene
HERRMANN Bernard
MARÉCHAL Maurice
MARRINER Sir Neville
ROBINSON Christopher
ROTHWELL Walter
SINOPOLI Giuseppe
SMALLENS Alexander

9
ABENDROTH Hermann
ASHKENAZY Vladimir
BARENBOIM Daniel
BERNSTEIN Leonard
GAVAZZENI Gianandrea
HAUSEGGER
  Siegmund von
KEILBERTH Joseph
KLEMPERER Otto
LEINSDORF Erich
MACKERASS Charles
MANTOVANI Annunzio
MATHIESON Muir
MINKOWSKI Marc

PREVITALI Fernando
PRITCHARD Sir John
SCHIPPERS Thomas
STOKOWSKI Leopold
SYLVESTER Victor
TOSCANINI Arturo

10
BARBIROLLI Sir John
CHEVILLARD Camille
FISTOULARI Anatole
KONDRASHIN Kyril
MANCINELLI Luigi
SAWALLISCH Wolfgang

11
FÜRTWÄNGLER Wilhelm
HARNONCOURT Nikolaus
HOOGSTRATEN Willem van
KOSTELANETZ André
PERSICHETTI Vincent

12
INGHELBRECHT Désiré
KOUSSEVITSKY Serge
ROSTROPOVICH Mstislav

13
HOLLINGSWORTH John

14
KNAPPERTSBUSCH Hans

Arts – Music & Entertainment – ENTERTAINERS (types)

3
ACT
DUO
HAM
PRO

4
BARD
CAST
IDOL
LEAD
STAR
TURN

5
ACTOR
CLOWN
COMIC
DROLL
EXTRA
MIMER
MIMIC

6
ARTIST
DANCER
DISEUR
GEISHA
GUISER
JESTER
MUMMER
STOOGE
TROUPE

7
ACROBAT

ACTRESS
ARTISTE
AUGUSTE
BUFFOON
COMMÈRE
COMPANY
COMPÈRE
DISEUSE
FARCEUR
HETAERA
JUGGLER
PIERROT
SHOWMAN
STARLET
TROUPER
TUMBLER

8
BALANCER
COMEDIAN
CONJUROR
DANSEUSE
FARCEUSE
FIGURANT
FILM STAR
MAGICIAN
MIMESTER
MIMICKER
POSTURER
SHOWGIRL
STAR TURN
STRIPPER
STUNTMAN
THESPIAN
TOP-LINER
WALKER-ON

9
ANCHORMAN
ANNOUNCER
BALLERINA
CELEBRITY
ECDYSIAST
FAN DANCER
FIGURANTE
FIRE-EATER
HYPNOTIST
LAP DANCER
LION TAMER
MESMERIST
MOVIE STAR
PANELLIST
PANTALOON
PERFORMER
POSTURIST
PRESENTER
PRINCIPAL
PUPPETEER
SOUBRETTE
TAP DANCER
TRAGEDIAN
WARM-UP ACT

10
CHORUS GIRL
CHORUS LINE
COMÉDIENNE
DRAG ARTIST
FIRE-WALKER
FOLK DANCER
GEISHA GIRL
GO-GO DANCER
LEADING MAN

NAUTCH GIRL
POLE DANCER
RINGMASTER
ROPE-WALKER
TAXI DANCER
TROUBADOUR
UNDERSTUDY
UNICYCLIST
WIRE-WALKER

11
BARNSTORMER
BELLY DANCER
BROADCASTER
COMEDY ACTOR
COURT JESTER
DANCING GIRL
ENTERTAINER
FUNAMBULIST
ILLUSIONIST
LEADING LADY
LIMBO DANCER
MATINÉE IDOL
MONOLOGUIST
PANTOMIMIST
STILT-WALKER
STRAIGHT MAN
STRIPTEASER
TRAGEDIENNE

12
ACTOR-MANAGER
BALLET DANCER
ESCAPOLOGIST
IMPERSONATOR
JUVENILE LEAD

KNIFE-THROWER
MORRIS DANCER
PRINCIPAL BOY
SNAKE CHARMER
STAND-UP COMIC
VAUDEVILLIAN

IMPRESSIONIST
PANTOMIME DAME
PRINCIPAL GIRL
STRAIGHT ACTOR
TRAPEZE ARTIST
VENTRILOQUIST

SWORD-SWALLOWER

15
PRESTIDIGITATOR
SONG-AND-DANCE MAN
STRAIGHT ACTRESS
STROLLING PLAYER
SUPPORTING ACTOR
TIGHTROPE WALKER

13
COMEDY ACTRESS
CONTORTIONIST
CORPS DE BALLET

14
CHARACTER ACTOR
FLAMENCO DANCER
PRIMA BALLERINA

Arts – Music & Entertainment – MUSICAL INSTRUMENTS
* = orchestra section

3	**VIOL**	PIANO	CYMBAL	BANDURA	MUSETTE
KIT		PIPES	FIDDLE	BARYTON	OCARINA
LUR	**5**	REBAB	GUITAR	BASSOON	PANDORA
OUD	BANJO	REBEC	LITUUS	BAZOOKA	PIANINO
SAX	BELLS	SHAWM	MARACA	BODHRÁN	PIANOLA
SAZ	BONGO	SHENG	RATTLE	BUCCINA	PICCOLO
	BRASS*	SITAR	SANTIR	CELESTA	SACKBUT
4	BUGLE	TABLA	SHOFAR	CELESTE	SALPINX
BELL	CELLO	TABOR	SPINET	CEMBALO	SAMISEN
DRUM	CHIME	TAIKO	SPOONS	CITTERN	SARANGI
ERHU	CRWTH	VEENA	SYRINX	CLARION	SAXHORN
FIFE	DOBRO	VIBES	TAM-TAM	CLAVIER	SERPENT
GONG	DRONE	VIOLA	TOM-TOM	CLOG BOX	SISTRUM
HARP	FLUTE		VIELLE	COWBELL	STRINGS*
HORN	GAITA	**6**	VIOLIN	CROTALE	TAMBOUR
KOTO	GAMBA	ATABAL	ZITHER	FAGOTTO	THEORBO
LUTE	GRAND	BONGOS		GITTERN	TIMBREL
LYRE	KAZOO	CHIMES	**7**	HAUTBOY	TIMPANI
OBOE	MBIRA	CITOLE	ALPHORN	MANDOLA	TRUMPET
PIPE	NAKER	CLAVES	ALTHORN	MANDORA	UKULELE
REED	NGONI	CORNET	BAGPIPE	MARACAS	UPRIGHT
TUBA	ORGAN	CURTAL	BANDORA	MARIMBA	VIHUELA

VIOLONE
WHISTLE

8
ALTO OBOE
ARCHLUTE
AUTOHARP
BAGPIPES
BANJOLIN
BASS DRUM
BASS VIOL
BOMBARDE
BOUZOUKI
CALLIOPE
CARILLON
CLARINET
CRUMHORN
DULCIMER
HANDBELL
JEW'S HARP
MANDOLIN
MELODEON
MELODICA
MIRLITON
OLIPHANT
OTTAVINO
PAN PIPES
POST HORN
PSALTERY
RECORDER
SIDE DRUM
TAMBOURA
TENOR COR
TIMBALES
TRIANGLE
TROMBONE
VIRGINAL
VOCALION
WALDHORN

WOODWIND*
ZAMPOGNA

9
ACCORDION
ALPENHORN
ALTO FLUTE
BABY GRAND
BALALAIKA
BOMBARDON
CASTANETS
CHALUMEAU
CHIME BARS
CORNEMUSE
CORNO ALTO
DRONE PIPE
EUPHONIUM
FLAGEOLET
FLÛTE-À-BEC
HARMONICA
HARMONIUM
KRUMMHORN
LANGSPIEL
MRIDANGAM
NOSE FLUTE
ORPHARION
PIPE ORGAN
PITCH-PIPE
REED ORGAN
SAXOPHONE
SNARE DRUM
TAMBOURIN
UNIT ORGAN
VIOLA ALTA
WASHBOARD
WELSH HARP
WURLITZER
XYLOPHONE
XYLORIMBA

10
BASSET HORN
BASS GUITAR
BONGO DRUMS
CHITARRONE
CLAVICHORD
CONCERTINA
CONTRABASS
COR ANGLAIS
CORNO BASSO
DIDGERIDOO
DOUBLE BASS
FLUGELHORN
FORTEPIANO
FRENCH HORN
GRAND PIANO
HURDY-GURDY
KETTLEDRUM
MELLOPHONE
MOUTH ORGAN
MUSICAL BOX
MUSICAL SAW
OBOE D'AMORE
OPHICLEIDE
PERCUSSION*
PIANOFORTE
PIANO ORGAN
SLEIGH BELL
SOUSAPHONE
SQUEEZE BOX
TAMBOURINE
THUMB PIANO
TIN WHISTLE
TRIPLE HARP
VIBRAPHONE

11
AEOLIAN HARP
ALTO SAXHORN

BARREL ORGAN
CHORDOPHONE
CHURCH ORGAN
CINEMA ORGAN
FIPPLE FLUTE
FLÛTE D'AMOUR
HARPSICHORD
HECKELPHONE
HUNTING HORN
OCTAVE FLUTE
ORCHESTRINA
ORCHESTRION
PLAYER-PIANO
SLEIGH BELLS
VIOLA D'AMORE
VIOLONCELLO
WOBBLE-BOARD
ZITHER BANJO

12
ALTO CLARINET
ALTO TROMBONE
BASS TROMBONE
CHAMBER ORGAN
CONCERT GRAND
CORNO VENTILE
GLOCKENSPIEL
HAMMOND ORGAN
HI-HAT CYMBALS
METALLOPHONE
PENNY WHISTLE
RHYTHM GUITAR
SARRUSOPHONE
SIZZLE CYMBAL
THEATRE ORGAN
TROMBA MARINA
TUBULAR BELLS
UILLEAN PIPES
VIOLA DA GAMBA

VIOLA POMPOSA

13
ALTO SAXOPHONE
AMERICAN ORGAN
CLARINET FLUTE
CONTRABASSOON
CORNO A PISTONI
DOUBLE BASSOON
ELECTRIC ORGAN
HAMMERKLAVIER
PANHARMONICON
POSITIVE ORGAN
SLIDE TROMBONE
SWANEE WHISTLE

TENOR TROMBONE
TINTINNABULUM
VIHUELA DE ARIO
VIHUELA DE MANO
VIOLA BASTARDA

14
CLAVICYTHERIUM
CORNO A MACCHINA
ELECTRIC GUITAR
JINGLING JOHNNY
MUSICAL GLASSES
PIANO ACCORDION
PORTATIVE ORGAN
REED INSTRUMENT

TENOR SAXOPHONE
VIOLA DA BRACCIO
WIND INSTRUMENT

15
BRASS INSTRUMENT
CHINESE PAVILION
CLASSICAL GUITAR
CORNO DI BASSETTO
MOOG SYNTHESIZER
TROMBA DA TIRARSI
TURKISH CRESCENT

16
CHINESE WOOD BLOCK

Arts – Music & Entertainment – MUSICAL TERMS

3	SKA	FRET	OPUS	SLUR	BASSO	DIRGE
AIR	SOH	FROG	PART	SOLO	BATON	DITTY
BAR	TIE	GLEE	PEAL	SONG	BEBOP	DOLCE
BOB		HEAD	PIPE	SOUL	BELLY	DRONE
BOW	**4**	HEEL	PLAY	STOP	B FLAT	DUMKA
DOH	ALTO	HYMN	PORT	TAIL	BLUES	E FLAT
DUO	ARIA	JACK	PUNK	TIME	BRASS	ÉTUDE
FAH	BAND	JAZZ	RAGA	TONE	BREVE	F FLAT
KEY	BASS	JIVE	RALL	TOP C	BUFFO	FIFTH
LAH	BEAT	LIED	REED	TRAD	CANON	FORTE
LAY	BELL	LILT	REST	TRIO	CANTO	FUGUE
MIX	BOOK	LONG	RIFF	TUNE	CAROL	GAMUT
NUT	CLEF	MASS	RING	TURN	CATCH	G FLAT
PEG	CODA	MODE	RISE	VAMP	C FLAT	GIGUE
PIN	DESK	MONO	ROCK	WOLF	CHANT	HOUSE
POP	DUET	MOOD	ROLL	WORK	CHIME	INTRO
RAG	FADO	MUTE	ROOT		CHORD	KWELA
RIB	FLAT	NECK	SCAT	**5**	COMMA	LARGO
RUN	FORM	NOTE	SING	A FLAT	D FLAT	LENTO

LYRIC	STAVE	AUBADE	OCTAVE	**7**
MARCH	STICK	BALLAD	PAVANE	AGITATO
MESTO	STOMP	BOLERO	PEG-BOX	ALLEGRO
METER	STRUM	BOOGIE	PERIOD	AMOROSO
MINIM	STYLE	BRIDGE	PHRASE	ANDANTE
MIXER	SUITE	B SHARP	PIPING	ANIMATO
MOLTO	SWELL	BURDEN	PISTON	ARIETTA
MOTET	SWING	CANTUS	PODIUM	BACKING
MOTIF	TANGO	CATGUT	PRESTO	BALLADE
MUSIC	TEMPO	CHORAL	QUAVER	BAROQUE
MUZAK	TENOR	CHORUS	REGGAE	BOURDON
NEUME	TENTH	COURSE	REPEAT	BRAVURA
NINTH	THEME	C SHARP	RHYTHM	CADENCE
NONET	THIRD	DAMPER	SECOND	CALANDO
OCTET	TITLE	D SHARP	SEPTET	CALYPSO
OPERA	TONAL	EIGHTH	SERIES	CANTATA
PAEAN	TONIC	ENCORE	SEXTET	CANZONE
PAUSE	TOUCH	ENTRÉE	SHANTY	CELESTE
PAVAN	TRIAD	E SHARP	SNATCH	CHANSON
PEDAL	TRILL	FIGURE	SONATA	CHANTER
PIANO	TROLL	FINALE	STEREO	CHORALE
PIECE	TUNER	FIPPLE	STRAIN	CLAPPER
PITCH	TUTTI	FOURTH	STRING	CLASSIC
POLKA	TWANG	F SHARP	TATTOO	CON BRIO
PSALM	VALUE	GARAGE	TENUTO	CONCERT
RONDO	VALVE	G SHARP	TIERCE	CONCORD
ROUND	VOCAL	HAMMER	TIMBRE	CONSOLE
SAMBA	VOICE	JINGLE	TONGUE	COUPLER
SCALE	WAIST	LAMENT	TREBLE	DESCANT
SCORE	WALTZ	LEGATO	TRIPLE	DISCORD
SEGNO	YODEL	LIEDER	TUNING	EPISODE
SHARP	ZOPPA	LYRICS	UNISON	FANFARE
SHIFT		MEDLEY	UPBEAT	FERMATA
SIXTH	**6**	MELODY	VENTIL	GAVOTTE
SLIDE	ACCORD	MINUET	VERSET	HARMONY
SOL-FA	ADAGIO	MONODY	WARBLE	HEMIOLA
SOUND	ANTHEM	MOTION		KARAOKE
SPACE	ARIOSO	NIENTE		KEYNOTE
STAFF	A SHARP	NUMBER		LULLABY

MARCATO	STRETTO	CROTCHET	OPERETTA
MEASURE	STRINGS	DIAPASON	OPUSCULE
MEDIANT	TOCCATA	DIATONIC	ORATORIO
MELISMA	TRACKER	DOMINANT	OSTINATO
MELODIC	TREMOLO	DOWNBEAT	OVERTONE
MIDDLE C	TRITONE	DRUMHEAD	OVERTURE
MIXTURE	TRUMPET	DULCIANA	PART-SONG
MORDENT	TWELFTH	ENSEMBLE	PASTICHE
MUSETTE	VAMPING	ENTR'ACTE	PHRASING
MUSICAL	VIBRATO	EVENSONG	PIPEWORK
NATURAL	VOICING	FABURDEN	PLECTRUM
NEW RAVE		FALSETTO	POP MUSIC
ORGANUM	**8**	FANTASIA	PORTANDO
PARTITA	A BATTUTA	FESTIVAL	POSITION
PASSAGE	AGNUS DEI	FLAMENCO	POSTLUDE
PIANISM	ALLELUIA	FLOURISH	PRACTICE
PIBROCH	ANTIPHON	FLUE PIPE	REED PIPE
PLAYING	ARPEGGIO	FOLDEROL	REED STOP
POP SONG	BARITONE	FOLK ROCK	REGISTER
PRELUDE	BASS CLEF	FOLK SONG	REPETEND
QUARTET	BEL CANTO	FUGHETTA	RHAPSODY
QUINTET	BELL-ROPE	HALF-NOTE	RHYTHMIC
RAGTIME	BERCEUSE	HALF-TONE	RICERCAR
RECITAL	BLUE NOTE	HARMONIC	RITENUTO
REFRAIN	BOAT SONG	HYMN TUNE	ROOT NOTE
REPRISE	BOB MAJOR	INTERVAL	SARABAND
REQUIEM	BOB MINOR	KEYBOARD	SCHMALTZ
REVERIE	BOB ROYAL	LIGATURE	SEMITONE
RIPIENO	CANTICLE	LOVE SONG	SEQUENCE
ROMANCE	CARILLON	MADRIGAL	SERENADE
ROULADE	CASTRATO	MAESTOSO	SERENATA
SANCTUS	CAVATINA	MAJOR KEY	SINFONIA
SCHERZO	CHACONNE	MINOR KEY	SING-SONG
SETTING	CHEVALET	MODULATE	SONATINA
SEVENTH	CHEVILLE	MOVEMENT	SONG FORM
SINGING	CONCERTO	MUSICALE	SOUNDBOX
SKIFFLE	CORONACH	NOCTURNE	SOURDINE
SOPRANO	COURANTE	NOTATION	SPICCATO
SORDINO	CROMORNE	OPEN NOTE	STACCATO

STANDARD
STOPPING
SUBTONIC
SYMPHONY
TERZETTO
THRENODY
TONALITY
TONE POEM
TONICITY
TRAD JAZZ
UNA CORDA
VOCALISM
WOODWIND
WREST PIN
ZARZUELA

9
A CAPPELLA
ALLEMANDE
ALTISSIMO
ANDANTINO
ARABESQUE
BAGATELLE
BANDSTAND
BARCAROLE
BEAT MUSIC
BRASS BAND
BUGLE CALL
CANTABILE
CANTILENA
CAPRICCIO
CASSATION
CHARIVARI
CHROMATIC
CONTRALTO
CRESCENDO
DANCE TUNE
DITHYRAMB
DIXIELAND

DOUBLE BAR
DRUMSTICK
DUMB PIANO
EXTEMPORE
FINGERING
FIORITURA
FOLK MUSIC
FULL SCORE
GLISSANDO
GONG STICK
GRACE NOTE
GRANDSIRE
GRUPPETTO
HEXACHORD
HONKY-TONK
IMPROMPTU
IMPROVISE
INTERLUDE
INVENTION
LARGHETTO
LEGER LINE
LEITMOTIF
METRONOME
MICROTONE
MODULATOR
MOOD MUSIC
MUSIC ROLL
OBBLIGATO
OCTACHORD
OPEN SCORE
OPUSCULUM
ORCHESTRA
ORGAN PIPE
PARAMETER
PARTITURA
PASO DOBLE
PASTORALE
PIANO WIRE
PIZZICATO

PLAINSONG
POLONAISE
POLYPHONY
POT-POURRI
PRINCIPAL
QUADRILLE
QUODLIBET
REHEARSAL
RENDERING
RENDITION
REPLICATE
RESONATOR
ROCK 'N' ROLL
ROUNDELAY
SELECTION
SEMIBREVE
SERIALISE
SFORZANDO
SICILIANO
SIGHT-PLAY
SIGHT-READ
SIGHT-SING
SIGNATURE
SLENTANDO
SOFT PEDAL
SOLFEGGIO
SONG CYCLE
SOPRANINO
SOSTENUTO
SOTTO VOCE
SOUNDHOLE
SPIRITUAL
STRUMMING
TABLATURE
TAILPIECE
TENOR CLEF
TESSITURA
THEME SONG
THEME TUNE

TOCCATINA
TONOMETER
TORCH SONG
TUNING PEG
UNDERTONE
VARIATION
VOLUNTARY
VOX HUMANA
WHOLE-NOTE
WHOLE-TONE
WIND-CHEST

10
ACCIDENTAL
AFFRETANDO
BACCHANALE
ATTUNEMENT
BITONALITY
BOB MAXIMUS
CANTO FERMO
CHEST VOICE
CLARABELLA
CLASSICISM
COLORATURA
COMIC OPERA
COMMON TIME
CONCERTINO
CONSONANCE
DANCE MUSIC
DIGITORIUM
DIMINUENDO
DISSONANCE
DORIAN MODE
DOTTED NOTE
DOUBLE FLAT
DOUBLE TIME
EISTEDDFOD
EMBOUCHURE
EXPOSITION

FINGERHOLE
GARAGE ROCK
GRAND OPERA
GROUND BASS
HEPTACHORD
HOUSE MUSIC
HUMORESQUE
INSTRUMENT
INTERMEZZO
INTONATION
JAM SESSION
LIGHT MUSIC
LIGHT OPERA
LYDIAN MODE
MAINSTREAM
MAJOR SCALE
MASTERWORK
MEDITATION
MINOR SCALE
MODULATION
MOUTHPIECE
MUSICALITY
MUSIC STAND
MUSIC STOOL
NACHSCHLAG
OPERA SERIA
PARADIDDLE
PATTER SONG
PEDALBOARD
PENTACHORD
PERCUSSION
PIANO STOOL
PIPED MUSIC
PLAIN-CHANT
POLYPHONIC
PORTAMENTO
PORT DE VOIX
RECITATIVE
RECITATIVO

REHEARSING
REPERTOIRE
RESOLUTION
RITARDANDO
RITORNELLO
ROCKABILLY
SALICIONAL
SCHERZANDO
SCORDATURA
SCOTCH SNAP
SEMIQUAVER
SILVER BAND
SONATA FORM
SOUNDBOARD
STRATHSPEY
SUBMEDIANT
SUPERTONIC
SWING MUSIC
TARANTELLA
TETRACHORD
THE IVORIES
THEME MUSIC
TOCCATELLA
TONIC SOL-FA
TRANSCRIBE
TRANSITION
TREBLE CLEF
TREMOLANDO
TRIPLE TIME
TUNING FORK
TWELVE-NOTE
VIOLIN CASE
VIRTUOSITY

11

ACCELERANDO
AEOLIAN MODE
ARRANGEMENT
CAPRICCIOSO

CHANTERELLE
COMMON CHORD
COMPOSITION
CONCERTANTE
DECRESCENDO
DEVELOPMENT
DISCOGRAPHY
DOUBLE SHARP
FANFARONADE
FIDDLESTICK
FIGURED BASS
FINGERBOARD
FUNDAMENTAL
GREAT OCTAVE
HUNTING SONG
LEADING NOTE
LOCRIAN MODE
MASTERPIECE
MIXTURE STOP
MUSIC HOLDER
OPEN HARMONY
OPÉRA BOUFFE
ORCHESTRATE
PARTIAL NOTE
PASSACAGLIA
PASSING NOTE
PEDAL ACTION
PERFORMANCE
PRESTISSIMO
PROGRESSION
QUARTER-NOTE
QUARTER-TONE
RALLENTANDO
RECESSIONAL
RIFACIMENTO
RINFORZANDO
SCOTCH CATCH
SERIAL MUSIC
SMALL OCTAVE

STEREOPHONY
SUBDOMINANT
SYNCOPATION
TEMPERAMENT
TRUMPET TUNE
VOIX CELESTE
VOX ANGELICA

12

ACCIACCATURA
ALTALTISSIMO
ANTICIPATION
APPOGGIATURA
AUGMENTATION
BOOGIE-WOOGIE
CANTUS FIRMUS
CHAMBER MUSIC
CHROMATICISM
CLOSE HARMONY
COMPOUND TIME
CONCERT PITCH
COUNTERPOINT
COUNTER-TENOR
DIVERTIMENTO
EPITHALAMIUM
EXTRAVAGANZA
HEAD REGISTER
INTERMISSION
INTRODUCTION
KEY SIGNATURE
MEZZO-SOPRANO
MOTO PERPETUO
MUSICAL DRAMA
NATURAL SCALE
OPÉRA COMIQUE
PERFECT FIFTH
PERFECT PITCH
PHILHARMONIC
PHRYGIAN MODE

PRALLTRILLER
REGISTRATION
RESONANCE BOX
SESQUIALTERA
SIGHT-PLAYING
SIGHT-READING
SIGHT-SINGING
SUSTAIN PEDAL
THOROUGH BASS
VIOLIN-STRING
WEDDING MARCH

13
ABSOLUTE MUSIC
ABSOLUTE PITCH
ACCOMPANIMENT
BALLAD CONCERT
BASSO PROFONDO
CHEST REGISTER
COMMON MEASURE
GREGORIAN MODE
HARMONIC MINOR
IMPROVISATION

NEOCLASSICISM
ORCHESTRATION
PERFECT FOURTH
PLAGAL CADENCE
RANZ DES VACHES
SERIALISATION
SIGNATURE TUNE
SOUNDING BOARD
STAFF NOTATION
STRING QUARTET
SUPERDOMINANT
SYMPHONIC POEM
TIME SIGNATURE
TRANSCRIPTION
TRANSPOSITION

14
CHROMATIC SCALE
CLASSICAL MUSIC
CONTRARY MOTION
COUNTERSUBJECT
DEMISEMIQUAVER
DOUBLE-STOPPING

GREGORIAN CHANT
INTERPRETATION
JANISSARY MUSIC
JUST INTONATION
MIXOLYDIAN MODE
NATIONAL ANTHEM
PERFECT CADENCE
PROGRAMME MUSIC
RECAPITULATION
SONATA DA CAMERA

15
CONCERT OVERTURE
ELECTRONIC MUSIC
INCIDENTAL MUSIC
INSTRUMENTATION
MUSIQUE CONCRÈTE
NEAPOLITAN SIXTH
PERFECT INTERVAL
SERIAL TECHNIQUE
TRADITIONAL JAZZ

Arts – Music & Entertainment – MUSICIANS (types)

4	**6**	SEXTET	JUG BAND	DUETTIST
BAND	BUGLER	TOOTER	MAESTRO	ENSEMBLE
TRIO	BUSKER	VIBIST	PIANIST	JAZZ BAND
	HARPER		QUARTET	LUTANIST
5	HORNER	**7**	QUINTET	MINSTREL
COMBO	LEADER	BOY BAND	SOLOIST	ORGANIST
FIFER	LUTIST	CELLIST	VIOLIST	POP GROUP
GROUP	LYRIST	DRUMMER		ROCK BAND
OCTET	OBOIST	FIDDLER	**8**	SITARIST
PIPER	PLAYER	GAMELAN	BAGPIPER	TENORIST
	SEPTET	HARPIST	BANJOIST	VIRTUOSO

9
BRASS BAND
CEMBALIST
CONDUCTOR
CYMBALIST
DANCE BAND
GUITARIST
ORCHESTRA
PICCOLIST
PRINCIPAL
ROCK GROUP
SERENADER
STEEL BAND
TIMPANIST
TRUMPETER
VIOLINIST

10
BANDLEADER
BANDMASTER

BASSOONIST
BELL-RINGER
CORNETTIST
ONE-MAN BAND
SYNCOPATOR
TROMBONIST

11
ACCOMPANIST
CARILLONEUR
POLYPHONIST
SAXOPHONIST
XYLOPHONIST

12
ACCORDIONIST
CLARINETTIST
MILITARY BAND
ORGAN-GRINDER
VIBRAPHONIST

13
BASS GUITARIST
CAMPANOLOGIST
CONTRAPUNTIST
KETTLEDRUMMER
LEAD GUITARIST
LEAD VIOLINIST
PERCUSSIONIST
RHYTHM SECTION
VIOLONCELLIST

14
FIRST VIOLINIST

15
HARMONICA PLAYER
INSTRUMENTALIST
RECORDING ARTIST
RHYTHM GUITARIST
SECOND VIOLINIST

Arts – Music & Entertainment – OPERA CHARACTERS

3
IDA *Princess Ida*
LIÙ *Turandot*
MAX *The Marksman*
MEG *Falstaff*
TOM *The Rake's Progress*

4
ACIS *Acis and Galatea*
AÏDA *Aïda*
ALWA *Lulu*
ANNA *The White Lady*
ANNE *The Rake's Progress*
ATYS *Atys*

BABA *The Medium*
BESS *Porgy and Bess*
CUNO *The Marksman*
DIDO *Dido and Aeneas*
ELSA *Lohengrin*
EMMA *Fierrabras*
ERDA *Das Rheingold,
    Die Walküre, Siegfried,
    Götterdämmerung*
GOLO *Genovevo*
HÁRY *Háry János*
HUGH *Hugh the Drover*
IGOR *Prince Igor*
INEZ *The Gondoliers*

KATE *Madama Butterfly*
KO-KO *The Mikado*
LISA *The Queen of Spades*
LOLA *Cavalleria rusticana*
LUCY *The Beggar's Opera*
LUIZ *The Gondoliers*
LULU *Lulu*
MACK *The Threepenny
    Opera*
MARY *Hugh the Drover*
MIMI *La Bohème*
NERO *Agrippina*
OCHS *Der Rosenkavalier*
OLGA *The Maid of Pskov*

PACO *La vida breve*
ROSE *Ruddigore*
RUTH *The Pirates of Penzance*
THEA *The Knot Garden*
VERE *Billy Budd*

5

ADINA *The Elixir of Love*
ALEKO *Aleko*
ALICE *Falstaff*
AMINA *The Sleepwalker*
CALAF *Turandot*
CANIO *I pagliacci*
CROWN *Porgy and Bess*
EDWIN *Trial by Jury*
FABER *The Knot Garden*
FALKE *Die Fledermaus*
FAUST *Doktor Faust, Faust*
GILDA *Rigoletto*
HAGEN *Götterdämmerung*
LAKMÉ *Lakmé*
LEÏLA *The Pearl Fishers*
LUCIA *Lucia di Lammermoor*
MABEL *The Pirates of Penzance*
MANON *Manon, Manon Lescaut*
MARCO *The Gondoliers*
MARIE *Wozzeck*
MÉDÉE *Médée*
NADIR *The Pearl Fishers*
NEDDA *I pagliacci*
NORMA *Norma*
ORFEO *Orfeo, Orfeo ed Eurydice*

POLLY *The Beggar's Opera, The Threepenny Opera*
PORGY *Porgy and Bess*
RALPH *HMS Pinafore*
ROMEO *Romeo and Juliet*
SADKO *Sadko*
SALUD *La vida breve*
SELIM *The Turk in Italy*
SENTA *The Flying Dutchman*
SERSE *Serse*
THAÏS *Thaïs*
TONIO *I pagliacci*
TOSCA *Tosca*
VENUS *Venus and Adonis*
WOTAN *Das Rheingold, Die Walküre, Siegfried, Götterdämmerung*
ZAIDA *The Turk in Italy*
ZURGA *The Pearl Fishers*

6

ADMÈTE *Alceste*
ADOLAR *Euryanthe*
ADONIS *Venus and Adonis*
AENEAS *Dido and Aeneas*
AEOLUS *Idoménée*
AGATHE *The Marksman*
ALCINA *Alcina*
AMELIA *A Masked Ball*
ARMIDE *Armide*
BANQUO *Macbeth*
CADMUS *Semele*
CARMEN *Carmen*

CASPAR *The Marksman*
CASTOR *Castor et Pollux*
DALAND *The Flying Dutchman*
DANAUS *Les Danaïdes*
DORVIL *The Silken Ladder*
ELVINO *The Sleepwalker*
ELVIRA *Don Giovanni*
FIGARO *The Barber of Seville, The Marriage of Figaro*
GIULIA *The Silken Ladder*
GRETEL *Hänsel und Gretel*
HÄNSEL *Hänsel und Gretel*
HÉLÈNE *La belle Hélène*
ISOLDE *Tristan und Isolde*
JULIEN *Louise*
JULIET *Romeo and Juliet*
KUNDRY *Parsifal*
LOUISE *Louise*
NOTUNG *Die Walküre, Siegfried*
OBERON *Oberon*
OTELLO (or *Othello*) *Otello*
PAMINA *The Magic Flute*
PLATÉE *Platée*
POLLUX *Castor et Pollux*
POPOVA *The Bear*
RENATO *A Masked Ball*
ROSINA *The Barber of Seville*
RUSLAN *Ruslan and Lyudmila*

SAMSON *Samson and Delilah*
SEMELE *Semele*
SOPHIE *Der Rosenkavalier*
SUZUKI *Madama Butterfly*
SYLVIA *Orfeo*
TAMINO *The Magic Flute*
THISBE *Cinderella*
UBERTO *La serva padrona*
UNDINE *Undine*
YUM-YUM *The Mikado*

7

ALCESTE *Alceste*
ALFREDO *La traviata*
ASTERIA *Tamerlano*
ATHAMAS *Semele*
BACULUS *The Poacher*
BAJAZET *Tamerlano*
BARNABA *La gioconda*
BARTOLO *The Barber of Seville, The Marriage of Figaro*
CANDIDE *Candide*
CARMELA *La vida breve*
CEPRANO *Rigoletto*
DANDINI *Cinderella*
DELILAH *Samson and Delilah*
DON JOSÉ *Carmen*
DORMONT *The Silken Ladder*
EDGARDO *Lucia di Lammermoor*
ELÉAZAR *La Juive*

FIDELIO *Fidelio*
GALATEA *Acis and Galatea*
GESSLER *William Tell*
GINEVRA *Ariodante*
HUNDING *Die Walküre*
KATISHA *The Mikado*
LEONORA *Fidelio, Il trovatore*
LORENZO *Fra Diavolo*
MACBETH *Macbeth*
MACDUFF *Macbeth*
MANRICO *Il trovatore*
MAŘENKA *The Bartered Bride*
NABUCCO *Nabucco*
NINETTA *The Love for Three Oranges, The Thieving Magpie*
ORPHEUS *Orpheus, Orpheus in the Underworld*
OTHELLO (or *Otello*) *Othello*
PEACHUM *The Beggar's Opera, The Threepenny Opera*
PHYLLIS *Iolanthe*
POOH-BAH *The Mikado*
RADAMÈS *Aïda*
RINALDO *Rinaldo*
RODOLFO *La bohème, Luisa Miller*
RUSALKA *Rusalka*
RUTHVEN *The Vampire*
SCARPIA *Tosca*
SERPINA *La serva padrona*
SMIRNOV *The Bear*

SUSANNA *The Marriage of Figaro*
TATYANA *Eugene Onegin*
TCHELIO *The Love for Three Oranges*
TELAIRA *Castor et Pollux*
TITANIA *Oberon*
TRISTAN *Tristan und Isolde*
TURIDDÙ *Cavalleria rusticana*
WOLFRAM *Tannhäuser*
WOZZECK *Wozzeck*
ZERLINA *Don Giovanni*
ZERLINE *Fra Diavolo*

8

ADALGISA *Norma*
ALBERICH *Das Rheingold, Siegfried*
ALMIRENA *Rinaldo*
AMFORTAS *Parsfial*
ANGELINA *Trial by Jury*
ATHENAËL *Thaïs*
CLAGGART *Billy Budd*
CLAUDIUS *Agrippina*
CLORINDA *Cinderella*
COUNT ORY *Count Ory*
EURYDICE *Orfeo, Orfeo ed Eurydice*
FALSTAFF *Falstaff*
FERRANDO *Così fan tutte*
FREDERIC *The Pirates of Penzance*
GENOVEVA *Genoveva*
GIOCONDA *La gioconda*

GIUSEPPE *The Gondoliers*
GOFFREDO *Rinaldo*
HOFFMANN *The Tales of Hoffmann*
IDOMÉNÉE *Idoménée*
IDOMENEO *Idomeneo*
IOLANTHE *Iolanthe*
JESSONDA *Jessonda*
KOVALYOV *The Nose*
LUCREZIA *Lucrezia Borgia*
LYUDMILA *Ruslan and Lyudmila*
MACHEATH *The Beggar's Opera*
MARCELLO *La bohème*
NANKI-POO *The Mikado*
NEMORINO *The Elixir of Love*
OCTAVIAN *Der Rosenkavalier*
PANGLOSS *Candide*
PAPAGENO *The Magic Flute*
PARSIFAL *Parsifal*
PATIENCE *Patience*
POLLIONE *Norma*
RICCARDO *A Masked Ball*
RUGGIERO *Alcina*
SARASTRO *The Magic Flute*
SIEGMUND *Die Walküre*
STREPHON *Iolanthe*
TANCREDI *Tancredi*
TURANDOT *Turandot*
VESPETTA *Pimpinone*
VIOLETTA *La traviata*

9

AGRIPPINA *Agrippina*
ARIODANTE *Ariodante*
BARBARINA *The Marriage of Figaro*
BILLY BUDD *Billy Budd*
BLUEBEARD *Bluebeard's Castle*
BUNTHORNE *Patience*
BUTTERFLY *Madama Butterfly*
CHERUBINO *The Marriage of Figaro*

CUNEGONDE *Candide*
DES GRIEUX *Manon Lescaut*
DON CARLOS *Don Carlos*
DONNA ANNA *Don Giovanni*
DORABELLA *Così fan tutte*
ESCAMILLO *Carmen*
ELISABETH *Tannhäuser*
EURYANTHE *Euryanthe*
FLORESTAN *Fidelio*
GUALTIERO *The Pirate*
GUGLIELMO *Così fan tutte*
JOSEPHINE *HMS Pinafore*
LEPORELLO *Don Giovanni*
LOHENGRIN *Lohengrin*
MADELEINE *Capriccio*
MRS CRIPPS *HMS Pinafore*
PIMPINONE *Pimpinone*
PINKERTON *Madama Butterfly*
RIGOLETTO *Rigoletto*
SHARPLESS *Madama Butterfly*
SIEGFRIED *Genoveva, Siegfried,
    Götterdämmerung*
SIEGLINDE *Die Walküre*
TAMERLANO *Tamerlano*
THE MIKADO *The Mikado*

10

BRADAMANTE *Alcina*
BRÜNNHILDE *Die Walküre, Siegfried,
    Götterdämmerung*
CINDERELLA *Cinderella*
DON ALFONSO *Così fan tutte*
DON BASILIO *The Barber of Seville, The
    Marriage of Figaro*
DON OTTAVIO *Don Giovanni*
EISENSTEIN *Die Fledermaus*
FIERRABRAS *Fierrabras*
FIORDILIGI *Così fan tutte*
FRA DIAVOLO *Fra Diavolo*

MARCELLINA *The Marriage of Figaro*
MARGARETHA *Genovevo*
MONOSTATOS *The Magic Flute*
TANNHÄUSER *Tannhäuser*
YAROSLAVNA *Prince Igor*

11
CAVARADOSSI *Tosca*
DICK DEADEYE *HMS Pinafore*
DON GIOVANNI *Don Giovanni*
DON PASQUALE *Don Pasquale*
LADY MACBETH *Macbeth*
LUISA MILLER *Luisa Miller*
PETER GRIMES *Peter Grimes*
SPARAFUCILE *Rigoletto*
WILLIAM TELL *William Tell*

12
BORIS GODUNOV *Boris Godunov*
DON MAGNIFICO *Cinderella*
EUGENE ONEGIN *Eugene Onegin*

HANNA GLAWARI *The Merry Widow*
PRINCE GREMIN *Eugene Onegin*

13
ALBERT HERRING *Albert Herring*
CAPTAIN ZUNIGA *Carmen*
COUNT ALMAVIVA *The Barber of
    Seville, The Marriage of Figaro*
ROBIN OAKAPPLE *Ruddigore*

14
COLONEL FAIRFAX *The Yeomen of the
    Guard*
LORD CHANCELLOR *Iolanthe*
MEPHISTOPHELES *Doktor Faust,
    Faust*
SERGEANT MERYLL *The Yeomen of the
    Guard*

15
CAPTAIN CORCORAN *HMS Pinafore*

Arts – Music & Entertainment – OPERA TITLES

3
JOB Dallapiccola
NOS (or *The Nose*)
    Shostakovich

4
AÏDA Verdi
ATYS Lully
FATE (or *Osud*)
    Janáček
IRIS Mascagni
LEAR Reimann
LULU Berg

NERO (or *Nerone*)
    Boito, Mascagni
NINA Paisiello
OSUD (or *Fate*)
    Janáček
RUTH Berkeley
ZAZÀ Leoncavallo

5
ADINA Rossini
ALEKO Rachmaninov
EDGAR Puccini
FAUST Gounod, Spohr

GOLEM Casken
GREEK Turnage
HALKA Moniuszko
IZAHT Villa-Lobos
LAKMÉ Delibes
LE CID Massenet
MANON Massenet
MAVRA Stravinsky
MÉDÉE Charpentier,
    Cherubini
MLADA Rimsky-
    Korsakov
NORMA Bellini

ORFEO Monteverdi
SADKO Rimsky-
  Korsakov
SAPHO Gounod
SERSE Handel
TESEO Handel
THAÏS Massenet
TOSCA Puccini
YERMA Villa Lobos
ZAIDE Mozart

6

ALCINA Handel
ALMIRA Handel
ARMIDE Gluck,
  Lully
ATTILA Verdi
CARMEN Bizet
DAPHNE R Strauss
DIDONE Cavalli
EGISTO Cavalli
ERNANI Verdi
FEDORA Giordano
FLAMES (or *Flammen*)
  Schulhoff
GAWAIN Birtwistle
HAMLET Thomas
IGROKI (or *The
  Gamblers*)
  Shostakovich
JENŮFA Janáček
KOANGA Delius
LIBUŠE Smetana
LOUISE Charpentier
MARTHA Flotow
MIGNON Thomas
NATOMA Herbert
NELSON Berkeley
NERONE (or *Nero*)

Boito, Mascagni
OBERON Weber
OTELLO (or *Othello*)
  Rossini, Verdi
OTTONE Handel
PLATÉE Rameau
RIENZI Wagner
SALOME R Strauss
SEMELE Handel
TARARE Salieri
THE BAT (or *Die
  Fledermaus*)
  J Strauss II
THE ZOO Sullivan
UNDINE Hoffmann,
  Lortzing

7

ALCESTE Gluck
ARIANNA Handel
BOMARZO Ginastera
CALISTO Cavalli
CANDIDE Bernstein
DALIBOR Smetana
DIARMID MacCunn
DINORAH Meyerbeer
ELEKTRA R Strauss
FARNACE Vivaldi
FIDELIO Beethoven
FLAMMEN (or *Flames*)
  Schulhoff
GIASONE Cavalli
GUNTRAM R Strauss
IRMELIN Delius
IVANHOE Sullivan
LA JUIVE Halévy
LA WALLY Catalani
LEONORA Fry
LE VILLI Puccini

MACBETH Bloch,
  Verdi
MAZEPPA
  Tchaikovsky
NABUCCO (or
  Nebuchadnezzar)
  Verdi
NEW YEAR Tippett
ORLANDO Handel
ORMINDO Cavalli
ORPHEUS Telemann
OTHELLO (or *Otello*)
  Rossini, Verdi
POLIUTO Donizetti
RINALDO Handel
RUSALKA Dvořák
SAVITRI Holst
TEODORA Scarlatti
THE BEAR Walton
THE NOSE (or *Nos*)
  Shostakovich
THESPIS Sullivan
VANESSA Barber
WERTHER Massenet
WOZZECK Berg
YOLANTA
  Tchaikovsky

8

AKHNATEN Glass
ANACRÉON
  Cherubini
ARABELLA R Strauss
BERENICE Handel
CHÉRUBIN Massenet
CLARISSA Holloway
COUNT ORY (or *Le
  Comte Ory*) Rossini
DARDANUS Rameau

DER ZWERG (or *The Dwarf*)
  Zemlinsky
DIMITRIJ Dvořák
DJAMILEH Bizet
FALSTAFF Salieri, Verdi
GENOVEVA (or *Genevieve*)
  Schumann
GLORIANA Britten
GOYESCAS Granados
GRISELDA Vivaldi
HERODIAS (or *Hérodiade*)
  Massenet
IDOMÉNÉE Campra
IDOMENEO Mozart
IL PIRATA (or *The Pirate*) Bellini
IOLANTHE Sullivan
JESSONDA Spohr
JULIETTA Martinů
KULLERVO Sallinen
LA BOHÈME Puccini
LE CINESI Gluck
LE COQ D'OR (or *The Golden
  Cockerel*) Rimsky-Korsakov
LE ROI D'YS Lalo
LODOÏSKA Cherubini
MARITANA Wallace
MAY NIGHT (or *Mayskaya Noch*)
  Rimsky-Korsakov
MIREILLE Gounod
PARSIFAL Wagner
PATIENCE Sullivan
PÉNÉLOPE Fauré
TANCREDI Rossini
TAVERNER Maxwell Davies
THE DWARF (or *Der Zwerg*)
  Zemlinsky
TOM JONES German
TURANDOT Busoni, Puccini

9
ABU HASSAN Weber
AGRIPPINA Handel
ARIODANTE Handel
BILLY BUDD Britten
BOCCACCIO Suppé
CAPRICCIO R Strauss
CARDILLAC Hindemith
COX AND BOX Sullivan
DER VAMPYR (or *The Vampire*)
  Marschner
DON CARLOS Verdi
EURYANTHE Weber
FEUERSNOT R Strauss
GENEVIEVE (or *Genoveva*) Schumann
HÁRY JÁNOS Kodály
HÉRODIADE (or *Herodias*) Massenet
IL TABARRO (part of *Il Trittico*) Puccini
I PURITANI (or *The Puritans*) Bellini
KING PRIAM Tippett
KING ROGER Szymanowski
LA RONDINE Puccini
LA VESTALE Spontini
LOHENGRIN Wagner
MADDALENA Prokofiev
MADELEINE Herbert
MASKARADE (or *Masquerade*)
  Nielsen
NOTRE DAME Schmidt
PARTENOPE Handel
PIMPINONE Telemann
PIQUE DAME (or *Pikovaya Dama; The
  Queen of Spades*) Tchaikovsky
PURGATORY Crosse
RADAMISTO Handel
RIGOLETTO Verdi
RUDDIGORE Sullivan
SIEGFRIED (part of *Der Ring des
  Nibelungen*) Wagner

TAMERLANO Handel
THE CLOWNS (or *I pagliacci*)
  Leoncavallo
THE CONSUL Menotti
THE CRITIC Stanford
THE DUENNA Gerhard
THE MEDIUM Menotti
THE MIKADO Sullivan
THE PIRATE (or *Il Pirata*) Bellini
VÉRONIQUE Messager

10

ANNA BOLENA Donizetti
ARLECCHINO Busoni
ARTAXERXES Arne
CENDRILLON (or *Cinderella*)
  Massenet
CINDERELLA (or *Cendrillon*)
  Massenet, (or *La Cenerentola*)
  Rossini
DIE WALKÜRE (part of *Der Ring des
  Nibelungen*) Wagner
FANNY ROBIN Harper
FIERRABRAS Schubert
FRA DIAVOLO Auber
IL FLAMINIO Pergolesi
IL TRITTICO Puccini
INTERMEZZO R Strauss
I PAGLIACCI (or *The Clowns*)
  Leoncavallo
LA FAVORITE Donizetti
L'AFRICAINE Meyerbeer
LA GIOCONDA Ponchielli
LA GRISELDA Scarlatti
LA TRAVIATA Verdi
LE COMTE ORY (or *Count Ory*)
  Rossini
LE PROPHÈTE Meyerbeer
LES TROYENS (or *The Trojans*) Berlioz

MASANIELLO Auber
MASQUERADE (or *Maskarade*) Nielsen
MERRY MOUNT Hanson
OEDIPUS REX Stravinsky
PALESTRINA Pfitzner
PRINCE IGOR Borodin
SAVONAROLA Stanford
SEMIRAMIDE Rossini
TANNHÄUSER Wagner
THE POACHER (or *Der Wildschütz*)
  Lortzing
THE TROJANS (or *Les Troyens*) Berlioz
THE VAMPIRE (or *Der Vampyr*)
  Marschner

11

A MASKED BALL (or *Un Ballo in
  maschera*) Verdi
CHEREVICHKI (or *The Slippers*)
  Tchaikovsky
DOKTOR FAUST (or *Doctor Faust*)
  Busoni
DON GIOVANNI Mozart
DON PASQUALE Donizetti
ESCLARMONDE Massenet
HANS HEILING Marschner
HMS PINAFORE Sullivan
IL TROVATORE Verdi
JEANIE DEANS MacCunn
L'AMICO FRITZ Mascagni
LA PÉRICHOLE Offenbach
LA VIDA BREVE Falla
LES BORÉADES Rameau
LES DANAÏDES Salieri
LUISA MILLER Verdi
MARY OF EGYPT Tavener
MEFISTOFELE (or *Mephistopheles*)
  Boito
PETER GRIMES Britten

PRINCESS IDA Sullivan
QUINTO FABIO Cherubini
SAUL OG DAVID (or *Saul and David*)
  Nielsen
SNEGUROCHKA (or *The Snow
  Maiden*) Rimsky-Korsakov
STREET SCENE Weill
THE GAMBLERS (or *Igroki*)
  Shostakovich
THE ICE BREAK Tippett
THE MARKSMAN (or *Der Freischütz*)
  Weber
THE PURITANS (or *I puritani*) Bellini
THE SLIPPERS (or *Cherevichki*)
  Tchaikovsky
THE SORCERER Sullivan
TRIAL BY JURY Sullivan
WAR AND PEACE Prokofiev
WILLIAM TELL (or *Guillaume Tell*)
  Rossini

12

BORIS GODUNOV Mussorgsky
CHRISTMAS EVE Rimsky-Korsakov
COSÌ FAN TUTTE Mozart
DAS RHEINGOLD (part of *Der Ring
  des Nibelungen*) Wagner
DIDO AND AENEAS Purcell
EUGENE ONEGIN Tchaikovsky
INTOLLERANZA Nono
KÁTA KABANOVÁ Janáček
KÖNIGSKINDER (or *The King's
  Children*) Humperdinck
LA GAZZA LADRA (or *The Thieving
  Magpie*) Rossini
LA SONNAMBULA (or *The
  Sleepwalker*) Bellini
LE DOMINO NOIR (or *The Black
  Domino*) Auber

LES HUGUENOTS Meyerbeer
MANON LESCAUT Puccini
MAYSKAYA NOCH (or *May Night*)
  Rimsky-Korsakov
MOSÈ IN EGITTO (or *Moses in Egypt*)
  Rossini
MOSES IN EGYPT (or *Mosè in Egitto*)
  Rossini
MOSES UND ARON (or *Moses and
  Aaron*) Schoenberg
OWEN WINGRAVE Britten
PARADISE LOST Penderecki
PIKOVAYA DAMA (or *Pique Dame; The
  Queen of Spades*) Tchaikovsky
PORGY AND BESS Gershwin
PUNCH AND JUDY Birtwistle
SAUL AND DAVID (or *Saul og David*)
  Nielsen
SUOR ANGELICA (part of *Il Trittico*)
  Puccini
THE GRAND DUKE Sullivan
THE NORTH STAR Meyerbeer
THE OLYMPIANS Bliss
THE WHITE LADY (or *La Dame
  blanche*) Boïeldieu

13

ALBERT HERRING Britten
ANDREA CHÉNIER Giordano
COLAS BREUGNON Kabalevsky
DEATH IN VENICE Britten
DER CORREGIDOR (or *The
  Magistrate*) Wolf
DER FERNE KLANG (or *The Distant
  Sound*) Schreker
DER FREISCHÜTZ (or *The Marksman*)
  Weber
DER WILDSCHÜTZ (or *The Poacher*)
  Lortzing

DIABLY Z LOUDUN (or *The Devils of Loudun*) Penderecki
DIDO AND AENEAS Purcell
DIE FLEDERMAUS (or *The Bat*) J Strauss II
DOCTOR MIRACLE (or *Le Docteur Miracle*) Bizet
GUILLAUME TELL (or *William Tell*) Rossini
HUGH THE DROVER Vaughan Williams
KHOVANSHCHINA Mussorgsky
LA BELLE HÉLÈNE Offenbach
LA CENERENTOLA (or *Cinderella*) Rossini
LA DAME BLANCHE (or *The White Lady*) Boïeldieu
LA SCALA DI SETA (or *The Silken Ladder*) Rossini
LA VOIX HUMAINE (or *The Human Voice*) Poulenc
L'ELISIR D'AMORE (or *The Elixir of Love*) Donizetti
L'ÉTOILE DU NORD (or *The North Star*) Meyerbeer
MERRIE ENGLAND German
MOSES AND AARON (or *Moses und Aron*) Schoenberg
OTTONE IN VILLA Vivaldi
SIR JOHN IN LOVE Vaughan Williams
THE FIERY ANGEL Prokofiev
THE GONDOLIERS Sullivan
THE HUMAN VOICE (or *La Voix humaine*) Poulenc
THE KNOT GARDEN Tippett
THE LIGHTHOUSE Maxwell Davies
THE MAGIC FLUTE (or *Die Zauberflöte*) Mozart
THE MAGISTRATE (or *Der Corregidor*) Wolf

THE MERRY WIDOW (or *Die lustige Witwe*) Léhar
THE SNOW MAIDEN (or *Snegurochka*) Rimsky-Korsakov
THE TENDER LAND Copland
THE TSAR'S BRIDE Rimsky-Korsakov
UTOPIA LIMITED Sullivan

14

ARIADNE ON NAXOS (or *Ariadne auf Naxos*) R Strauss
AT THE BOAR'S HEAD Holst
CASTOR ET POLLUX (or *Castor and Pollux*) Rameau
CONTRABANDISTA Sullivan
DIE ZAUBERFLÖTE (or *The Magic Flute*) Mozart
GIANNI SCHICCHI (part of *Il Trittico*) Puccini
LA SERVA PADRONA Pergolesi
LA VERA COSTANZA Haydn
LE ROI MALGRÉ LUI Chabrier
LES ABENCÉRAGES Cherubini
LUCREZIA BORGIA Donizetti
MEPHISTOPHELES (or *Mefistofele*) Boito
NEBUCHADNEZZAR (or *Nabucco*) Verdi
ORLANDO FURIOSO Vivaldi
OUR MAN IN HAVANA Williamson
RIDERS TO THE SEA Vaughan Williams
ROBERT LE DIABLE (or *Robert the Devil*) Meyerbeer
ROBERT THE DEVIL (or *Robert le Diable*) Meyerbeer
ROMEO AND JULIET (or *Roméo et Juliette*) Gounod
SAMSON ET DALILA (or *Samson and Delilah*) Saint-Saëns

THE BEAUTY STONE Sullivan
THE BLACK DOMINO (or *Le Domino noir*) Auber
THE MAID OF PSKOV Rimsky-Korsakov
THE NIGHTINGALE Stravinsky
THE PERFECT FOOL Holst
THE SLEEPWALKER (or *La Sonnambula*) Bellini
THE SPANISH HOUR (or *L'Heure espagnole*) Ravel
THE TURK IN ITALY (or *Il Turco in Italia*) Rossini

15

ARIADNE AUF NAXOS (or *Ariadne on Naxos*) R Strauss
CASTOR AND POLLUX (or *Castor et Pollux*) Rameau
DIE LUSTIGE WITWE (or *The Merry Widow*) Léhar
GÖTTERDÄMMERUNG (part of *Der Ring des Nibelungen*) Wagner
HANSEL AND GRETEL (or *Hänsel und Gretel*) Humperdinck
HÄNSEL UND GRETEL (or *Hansel and Gretel*) Humperdinck
IL TURCO IN ITALIA (or *The Turk in Italy*) Rossini
LA FINTA SEMPLICE Mozart
LA VIE PARISIENNE Offenbach
LE NOZZE DI FIGARO (or *The Marriage of Figaro*) Mozart
L'HEURE ESPAGNOLE (or *The Spanish Hour*) Ravel
MADAMA BUTTERFLY (or *Madame Butterfly*) Puccini
MADAME BUTTERFLY (or *Madama Butterfly*) Puccini

ORFEO ED EURIDICE Gluck
ORLANDO PALADINO Haydn
ORPHÉE AUX ENFERS (or *Orpheus in the Underworld*) Offenbach
ROMÉO ET JULIETTE (or *Romeo and Juliet*) Gounod
RUSLAN AND LYUDMILA Glinka
SIMON BOCCANEGRA Verdi
THE BEGGAR'S OPERA Pepusch/Gay
THE BOHEMIAN GIRL Balfe
THE DISTANT SOUND (or *Der ferne Klang*) Schreker
THE ELIXIR OF LOVE (or *L'Elisir d'Amore*) Donizetti
THE PEARL FISHERS (or *Les Pêcheurs de perles*) Bizet
THE ROSE OF PERSIA Sullivan
THE SILKEN LADDER (or *La Scala di seta*) Rossini

16

BLUEBEARD'S CASTLE Bartók
DER ROSENKAVALIER R Strauss
LE DOCTEUR MIRACLE (or *Doctor Miracle*) Bizet
SAMSON AND DELILAH (or *Samson et Dalila*) Saint-Saëns
THE BARTERED BRIDE Smetana
THE KING'S CHILDREN (or *Königskinder*) Humperdinck
THE MAGIC FOUNTAIN Delius
THE MASK OF ORPHEUS Birtwistle
THE QUEEN OF SPADES (or *Pikovaya Dama; Pique Dame*) Tchaikovsky
THE RAKE'S PROGRESS Stravinsky
TRISTAN UND ISOLDE Wagner
WUTHERING HEIGHTS Herrmann

Arts – Music & Entertainment – Singers & Musicians – CHART PERFORMERS
* = group

3
ABC*
A-HA*
AIR*
AMA Shola
ANT Adam
ASH*
ATB
DAY Doris
DEE Dave, Joey, Kiki
DIO*
DNA*
ELO*
EMF*
FOX Samantha
GUN*
JAM*
JOE
KIM Andy
KWS*
LEE Benny, Brenda,
    Dee C, Leapy, Peggy
MAY Brian, Simon
MUD*
MYA
NAS
OMC
ONO Yoko
OPM*
OTT*
PHD*
POP Iggy
RAY Johnnie
REA Chris
REM*
ROE Tommy

ROS Edmundo
ROY Harry
SKY*
SWV*
TEX Joe
TLC*
UFO*
URE Midge
VEE Bobby
WAH!*
WHO*
XTC*
YES*

4
ABBA*
AC/DC*
AMOS Tori
ANKA Paul
ANTS*
AQUA*
BAEZ Joan
BALL Michael
BAND*
BATT Mike
BEAT*
BECK Jeff
BELL Madeleine,
    Maggie
BLUE* Barry
BLUR*
BONN Issy
BONO
BROS*
BUSH Kate
CARA Irene

CARR Pearl, Vikki
CARS*
CASH Johnny
CASS Mama
CAST*
CHER
CHIC*
COLE Lloyd, MC,
    Natalie, Nat 'King'
COMO Perry
CROW Sheryl
CULT*
CURE*
D'ABO Mike
DANA
DAWN*
DEAN Hazell, Jimmy
DENE Terry
DEVO*
DIDO
DION + Celine
DODD Ken
DOGG Nate
DUNN Clive
DURY Ian
ECHO
EDDY Duane, Nelson
EELS*
ENYA
FAME Georgie
FARM*
FAWN James
FIRM*
FIVE*
FORD Emile, Clinton
FOXX Charlie, Inez

FRED John
FREE*
FURY Billy
GAME*
GAYE Marvin
GIBB Andy, Barry,
  Maurice, Robin
GORE Lesley
GRAY Dobie
HALL Daryl
HEBB Bobby
HERD*
HILL Benny, Faith,
  Lauryn, Vince
HOLE*
HOLT John
HUNT Marsha
IDOL Billy
INXS*
IVES Burl
JAY-Z
JEAN Wyclef
JETS*
JOEL Billy
JOHN Sir Elton
KANE Eden
KAYE Danny
KEEL Howard
KEYS Alicia
KHAN Chaka
KIDD Johnny
KING Ben E, Carole,
  Evelyn, Hetty,
  Jonathan, Solomon
KITT Eartha
KORN*
KUNZ Charlie
LANG Don, KD
LAST James

LIND Bob
LINX*
LOBO
LOSS Joe
LOVE Geoff
LULU
LYNN Dame Vera
MANN Johnny
MARX Richard
MA$E
MIKE
MOBY
MOON Keith
MOVE*
MUSE*
MYLO
NAIL Jimmy
NASH Graham, Johnny
NATÉ Ultra
NEIL
NENA
NEWS*
NICE*
OPUS*
OWEN Mark
PACE Thom
PAGE Jimmy, Patti
PARK Simon
PARR John
PAUL Billy, Owen, Sean
PIAF Edith
PINK
PIPS*
PULP*
Q-TIP*
REED Lou
REEF*
REID Neil
RICH Buddy, Charlie

RIDE*
ROSE Axl
ROSS Annie, Diana
ROY C
ROZA Lita
RUSH Jennifer
RUTS*
RYAN Barry, Marion,
  Paul
SADE
SANG Samantha
SASH!*
SEAL
SHAW Sandie
SLIK*
SNAP*
SOUL David
STYX*
SWAN Billy
TAMS*
THEM*
TOTO*
TOYS*
T'PAU*
T REX*
TRIO*
VEGA Suzanne
WARD Anita, Clifford T
WASH Martha
WASP*
WEBB Marti
WEST Kanye, Keith
WHAM!*
WINK Josh
WOOD Ron, Roy
YAZZ
YORK*

5
ABBOT Russ
ABDUL Paula
ADAMS Bryan
ALARM*
ALLEN Chesney
ANDRE Peter
ASWAD*
AUGER Brian
AUTRY Gene
AVONS*
BAKER Ginger
BARRY John, Len
BASIL Toni
BERRY Chuck, Dave,
  Mike, Nick
BIGGS Barry
BJÖRK
BLACK Cilla
BLIGE Mary J
BLOOM Bobby
BLUNT James
BLYTH Ann
BOLAN Marc
BONDS Gary 'US'
BOONE Pat
BOOTH Webster
BOWIE David
BRAGG Billy
BREAD*
BRENT Tony
BROWN Arthur, Bobby,
  Ian, James, Jocelyn,
  Joe, Sam
BRUCE Jack, Tommy
BUBLÉ Michael
BYRDS*
CAMEO*
CAREY Mariah

CLARK Petula
CLASH*
CLIFF Jimmy
CLINE Patsy
CLOCK*
COGAN Alma
COOKE Sam
CORAL*
CORRS*
CREAM*
CRUSH Bobby
D'ARBY Terence Trent
DAREY Matt
DARIN Bobby
DARTS*
DAVID Craig, FR
DAVIS Billie, Sammy,
  Skeeter
DAYNE Taylor
DEENE Carol
DIXON Reg
DODGY*
DOLAN Joe
DOLCE Joe
DOORS*
DOVES*
DR DRE
D:REAM*
DUFFY Stephen
DUSTY Slim
DYLAN Bob
ELLIS Shirley
ESSEX David
EVANS Maureen
EXILE*
FACES*
FAGIN Joe
FAITH Adam, Percy
FALCO

FELIX Julie
FERRY Bryan
FLACK Roberta
FLOYD Eddie
FOCUS*
GATES Gareth
GAYLE Crystal
GINA G
GOONS*
GORMÉ Eydie
GRANT Eddy
GRECO Buddy
GREEN Al, Peter
HALEY Bill
HARDY Françoise
HARRY Debbie/
  Deborah
HAYES Darren, Isaac
HEART*
HEATH Ted
HEINZ
HELLO*
HENRY Clarence
  'Frogman'
HOLLY Buddy
HORNE Lena
HUTCH
HYNDE Chrissie
IRWIN Big Dee
JACKS Terry
JAMES* Tommy
JAPAN*
JARRE Jean-Michel
JONES Aled, Allan,
  Brian, Grace, Howard,
  Jimmy, Paul, Shirley,
  Sir Tom
KAMEN Nick
KELIS

KELLY Gene, R
KENNY*
KINKS*
KIRBY Kathy
LAINE Frankie
LA MIX*
LE BON Simon
LEMAR
LE ROC Kele
LEWIS CJ, Huey, Jerry
   Lee, Leona, Linda,
   Ramsey
LOCKE Joseph
LOGAN Jimmy, Johnny
LOLLY
LOPEZ Jennifer, Trini
LOTIS Dennis
LUMAN Bob
LYDON John
LYMON Frankie
LYNCH Kenny
MARIE Kelly
MARIO
MCCOY Van
MCFLY*
MCKEE Maria
MELUA Katie
MILES John, Robert
MILLS Hayley, Mrs,
   Stephanie
MOJOS*
MONEY Zoot
MONRO Matt
MOONE Maggie
MOORE Gary
MOYET Alison
MR BIG*
MUMBA Samantha
NELLY

NOBLE Dennis
NOMAD*
NOONE Peter
'N SYNC*
NUMAN Gary
OASIS*
OATES John
OCEAN Billy
O'JAYS*
O'NEAL Alexander
ORBIT William
O-TOWN*
O-ZONE*
PAIGE Elaine, Jennifer
PARIS Mica, Ryan
PAYNE Freda
PEERS Donald
PETTY Tom
PILOT*
PIPER Billie
PLANT Robert
POOLE Brian
PRADO Perez
PRICE Alan, Lloyd
PROBY PJ
QUAYE Finley
QUEEN*
RACEY*
RAKIM
RANKS Shabba
RAWLS Lou
REDDY Helen
REGAN Joan
RILEY Jeannie C
RIMES LeAnn
ROMEO Max
ROSSO Nini
RUFUS*
SARNE Mike

SAXON*
SAYER Leo
SCOTT Jack, Linda
SHAND Jimmy
SIMON Carly, Paul
SISKO
SKIDS*
SLADE*
SMITH OC, Will
SONIA
SOUTH Joe
SPACE*
STARR Edwin, Kay,
   Ringo
STEAM*
STEPS*
STING
STONE Joss
SUEDE*
SUGGS
SWANN Donald
SWEET*
SYBIL
TEMPO Nina
TERRY Todd
TEXAS*
TOPOL
TORMÉ Mel
TOYAH
TRENT Jackie
TRUTH*
TWAIN Shania
TYLER Bonnie
TYMES*
USHER
VALLI Frankie
VERVE*
VRIES Jurgen
WAITE John

WALSH Joe
WATTS Charlie
WELLS Mary
WELSH Bruce
WHITE Barry
WILDE Kim, Marty
WINGS*
WYLIE Pete
WYMAN Bill
YAZOO*
YELLO*
YOUNG Jimmy, Karen,
  Lester, Neil, Paul
ZAGER Michael
ZZ TOP*

6
ALMOND Marc
ALPERT Herb
ANGELS*
ARNOLD David, PP
ARTHUR Davey
ASTLEY Rick
ATKINS Chet
ATWELL Winifred
AVALON Frankie
BAILEY Pearl
BALDRY Long John
BARLOW Gary
BASSEY Dame Shirley
BENSON George
BENTON Brook
BERLIN*
BIRKIN Jane
BOLTON Michael
BONEY M*
BOWLLY Al
BOW WOW*
BRANDY

BREWER Teresa
BROOKS Elkie
BRYSON Peabo
BUNTON Emma
BURDON Eric
BUSTED*
CAM'RON
CANNON Freddy
CANTOR Eddie
CARMEN Eric
CARNEY Kate
CARTER Aaron
CHERRY Eagle-Eye,
  Neneh
CHINGY
CHURCH Charlotte
CLARKE Allan
COCKER Jarvis, Joe
COMETS*
CONRAD Jess
CONWAY Russ
COOLIO
COOPER Alice
COTTON Billy
COWARD Sir Noël
CRAMER Floyd
CRAVEN Beverley
CREOLE Kid
CROSBY Bing
CUTLER Adge
DAMAGE*
DAMNED*
DAMONE Vic
DARIO G*
DARREN James
DAVIES Dave, Ray
DEKKER Desmond
DENNIS Kathy
DENVER John, Karl

DE PAUL Lynsey
DES'REE
DISTEL Sacha
DIVINE
DJ OTZI
DOLLAR*
DORSEY Lee
DR HOOK*
DUNCAN Johnny
DUNDAS David
DUPREE Simon
DURHAM Judith
EAGLES*
EASTON Sheena
EMINEM
ENIGMA*
EQUALS*
EUROPE*
EVERLY Don, Phil
FABIAN
FAMILY*
FEARON Phil
FEEDER*
FENTON Shane
FERRER José
FIELDS Dame Gracie
FISHER Eddie
FORMBY George
FUGEES*
FUREYS*
GASKIN Barbara
GAYNOR Gloria
GELDOF Bob
GENTRY Bobbie
GIBSON Debbie, Don,
  Wayne
GILLAN*
GO WEST*
GRACIE Charlie

GRAHAM Jaki
HANSON* John
HARDIN Ty
HARLEY Steve
HARRIS Anita,
  Emmylou, Jet, Phil,
  Richard, Rolf
HARVEY Alex
HAWKES Chesney
HILTON Ronnie
HODGES Johnny
HOLDER Noddy
HONEYZ*
HOPKIN Mary
HORTON Johnny
HUNTER Tab
HYLAND Brian
IFIELD Frank
JAGGER Sir Mick
JA RULE
JOLSON Al
JOPLIN Janis
KENNY G
KEPURA Jan
KNIGHT Beverley,
  Gladys
KRAMER Billy J
LAUPER Cyndi
LAYTON Lindy
LENNON John, Julian
LENNOX Annie
LESTER Ketty
LEYTON John
LIL' KIM
LIMAHL
LIMMIE
LINDON Millie
LONDON Julie, Laurie
LOUISE

LOVICH Lena
LYNOTT Phil
LYTTLE Kevin
MACRAE Gordon
MAI TAI*
MANSUN*
MARINI Marino
MARLEY Bob
MARTIN Dean, Mary,
  Millicent, Ray, Tony
MARVIN Hank, Lee
MATHIS Johnny
MAYALL John
MCCRAE George
MCLEAN Bitty, Don
MCNEAL Patricia
MCTELL Ralph
MEEHAN Tony
MELVIN Harold
MENDES Sergio
MERMAN Ethel
MICHEL Pras
MIDLER Bette
MILLER Gary, Glenn,
  Ned, Roger
MILLIE
MINOTT Sugar
MIRAGE*
MOLOKO*
MONICA
MONROE Gerry
MONTEZ Chris
MORGAN Helen, Jane
MORRIS Lily
MOTORS*
MURPHY Rose
MURRAY Ruby
NELSON Rick/Ricky,
  Sandy, Willie

NEVINS Jason
NEWLEY Anthony
NICOLE
NOLANS*
NUTINI Paolo
OFARIM Abi, Esther
OLIVER
ORRICO Stacie
OSMOND Donny,
  Little Jimmy, Marie
OUR KID*
PALMER Robert
PARKER Ray
PARTON Dolly
P DIDDY
PEARLS*
PELLOW Marti
PIGBAG*
PITNEY Gene
POGUES*
POISON*
POLICE*
POWELL Cozy
PRIEST Maxi
PRINCE
QUATRO Suzi
RAGHAV
RASMUS*
RAYDIO*
RED BOX*
REDMAN
REEVES Jim, Martha,
  Vic
RHYMES Busta
RICHIE Lionel
RITTER Tex
ROGERS Ginger, Julie,
  Kenny
ROTTEN Johnny

ROWLES John
RUFFIN Jimmy
RUMOUR*
RUN-DMC*
RYDELL Bobby
SAILOR*
SAMMES Mike
SAVAGE Edna
SCAGGS Boz
SECADA Jon
SEDAKA Neil
SEEGER Pete
SHAGGY
SHAMEN*
SHARPE Rocky
SIFFRE Labi
SIMONE Nina
SLEDGE Percy
SMITHS*
SMOKIE*
SMURFS*
SOURCE*
SPARKS*
SPEARS Billie Jo,
  Britney
STATON Candi
STEELE Tommy
STRIKE*
SUMMER Donna
SYLVIA
TAYLOR James, Mick, R
  Dean, Roger
TEMPLE Shirley
THOMAS Evelyn,
  Kenny, Rob, Rufus
TRACIE
TRANS-X*
TRAVIS*
TROGGS*

TUCKER Sophie,
  Tommy
TURNER Ike, Joan, Tina
TWEETS*
TWISTA
TWITTY Conway
UK SUBS*
ULLMAN Tracey
VALENS Ritchie
VALLEE Rudy
VAN DYK Paul
VAPORS*
VINTON Bobby
VIPERS*
VISAGE*
WALKER John, Junior,
  Scott
WARNES Jennifer
WATERS Crystal, Ethel
WATSON Russell
WEEDON Bert
WEEZER*
WELLER Paul
WESTON Kim
WILLIS Bruce
WILSON Brian, Dooley,
  Jackie, Mari
WISDOM Sir Norman
WONDER Stevie
WOOLEY Sheb
WRIGHT Ruby
WYNTER Mark
XZIBIT
ZAMFIR Gheorghe

7

AALIYAH
ADAMSKI
AMAZULU*

AMERICA*
ANDREWS Chris
ANIMALS*
ARCHIES*
ARRIVAL*
ASHANTI*
ASTAIRE Fred
BAND AID*
BANGLES*
BAUHAUS*
BEATLES*
BEE GEES*
BELOVED*
BENATAR Pat
BENNETT Cliff, Tony
BEYONCÉ
BLONDIE*
BON JOVI* Jon
BOSWELL Eve
BOX TOPS*
BOYZONE*
BRANDON Johnny
BRAXTON Toni
BROOKER Gary
BUGGLES*
CALVERT Eddie
CARROLL Dina, Ronnie
CASSIDY David, Eva
CASUALS*
CHAPMAN Tracy
CHARLES Ray, Tina
CHECKER Chubby
CHICAGO*
CHICANE*
CLAPTON Eric
CLOONEY Rosemary
COCHRAN Eddie
COLLINS Judy, Phil
COLONNA Jerry

CORNELL Don, Lena
COUSINS Tina
DAKOTAS*
DALTREY Roger
DANIELS Billy
DE BURGH Chris
DELRONS*
DIAMOND Neil
DICKSON Barbara
DIDDLEY Bo
DJ SAMMY
DONEGAN Lonnie
DONOVAN + Jason
DOOLIES*
DOUGLAS Carl, Craig
DR ALBAN
DRU HILL*
DURANTE Jimmy
DYNASTY*
EDMUNDS Dave
EDWARDS Tommy
ELLIMAN Yvonne
ELLIOTT Missy
  'Misdemeanour'
EN VOGUE*
ERASURE*
ESTEFAN Gloria
ETERNAL*
EXTREME*
FARLOWE Chris
FAT BOYS*
FONTANA Wayne
FORDHAM Julia
FRANCIS Connie
FREEMAN Bud
FURTADO Nelly
GABRIEL Peter
GAP BAND*
GARBAGE*

GARRETT Leif
GENESIS*
GEORDIE*
GLITTER Gary
GOODIES*
GOODREM Delta
GOODWIN Ron
GUTHRIE Arlo, Gwen,
  Woody
HANCOCK Herbie
HAYWARD Justin
HEAR'SAY*
HENDRIX Jimi
HEYWARD Nick
HOLLIES*
HOUSTON Whitney
ICE CUBE
IT BITES*
JACKSON Janet,
  Jermaine, Joe,
  Michael
JAMELIA
JESTERS*
JOHNSON Holly,
  Johnny, Laurie, Marv,
  Teddy
JUSTICE Jimmy
KEATING Ronan
KERSHAW Nik
KILLERS*
KOSHEEN*
KRAVITZ Lenny
LAVIGNE Avril
LEGRAND Michel
LL COOL J
LOCKLIN Hank
LOGGINS Kenny
LOVE INC*
LUVVERS*

MACCOLL Kirsty
MADNESS*
MADONNA
MAGUIRE Sean
MALCOLM Carl
MANCINI Henry
MANILOW Barry
MARBLES*
MARCELS*
MARILYN
MARKHAM Pigmeat
MAROONS*
MARSDEN Gerry
MARTELL Lena
MARTIKA
MARTINO Al
MATHIEU Mirielle
MAUGHAN Susan
MAURIAT Paul
MAZELLE Kim
MCGUIRE Barry
MCLAREN Malcolm
MELANIE
MERCURY Freddie
MERSEYS*
MICHAEL George
MICHELL Keith
MINOGUE Dannii,
  Kylie
MIRANDA Carmen
MISSION*
MIS-TEEQ*
MOMENTS*
MONKEES*
MONSOON*
M PEOPLE*
NATASHA
NILSSON
NIRVANA*

NO DOUBT*
NO MERCY*
N-TRANCE*
O'CONNOR Des,
   Hazel, Sinead
ODYSSEY*
ORBISON Roy
ORBITAL*
ORLANDO Tony
OSMONDS*
OTTAWAN*
OUTKAST*
OUTLAWS*
PARADIS Vanessa
PEARSON Johnny
PEPPERS*
PERKINS Carl
PICKETT Bobby 'Boris',
   Wilson
PIGLETS*
PINKIES*
PIRATES*
PLACEBO*
POLLARD Su
PRESLEY Elvis, Reg
PRESTON Billy, Mike,
   Johnny
PRODIGY*
PROVINE Dorothy
PUCKETT Gary
RAH BAND*
RAINBOW*
RAMONES*
RAMRODS*
RATTLES*
REBEL MC
REDBONE*
REDDING Otis
REGENTS*

REPLAYS*
RICHARD Sir Cliff
RICHMAN Jonathan
RICKITT Adam
ROBBINS Kate, Marty
ROBERTS Juliet,
   Malcolm
ROBESON Paul
RODGERS Clodagh,
   Jimmie
ROUSSOS Demis
ROXETTE*
ROZALLA*
SAD CAFÉ*
SANCHEZ Roger
SANTANA*
SAVALAS Telly
SECOMBE Sir Harry
SEEKERS*
SELLERS Peter
SHADOWS*
SHAKIRA
SHANNON + Del
SHAPIRO Helen
SHARKEY Feargal
SHELDON Doug
SHELTON Anne
SHERBET*
SHERMAN Allan
SIMPSON Jessica
SINATRA Frank,
   Nancy
SINITTA
SLEEPER*
SONIQUE
SOS BAND*
SQUEEZE*
SQUIRES Dorothy
STEFANI Gwen

STEVENS April, Cat,
   Connie, Rachel, Ray,
   Ricky, Shakin'
STEWART Amii, Andy,
   Dave, Jermaine, Rod
STRAWBS*
STREETS
STROKES*
SYLVIAN David
SYREETA
TAVARES*
TERRELL Tammy
THERAPY?*
THUNDER*
TIFFANY
TIKARAM Tanita
TONIGHT*
TRAFFIC*
TRAMMPS*
TURTLES*
TWINKLE
VALANCE Holly, Ricky
VALENTE Caterina
VAN DYKE Leroy
VAUGHAN Frankie,
   Malcolm, Sarah
VICIOUS Sid
VINCENT Gene
WAILERS*
WAKELIN Johnny
WAKEMAN Rick
WALTERS Trevor
WARREN G
WARWICK Dionne
WEAVERS*
WEDLOCK Fred
WHEELER Caron
WHISTLE*
WINTERS Ruby

WINWOOD Steve
WITHERS Bill
WIZZARD*
WOMBLES*
WURZELS*
WYNETTE Tammy
ZEIGLER Anne
ZODIACS*
ZOMBIES*

8
AGUILERA Christina
ALLISONS*
ALL-STARS*
ANDERSON Moira
AZNAVOUR Charles
BABYBIRD*
BANSHEES*
BIG THREE*
BLACK BOX*
BLUE MINK*
BUCHANAN Jack
BUNNYMEN*
BURNETTE Johnny
B*WITCHED*
BYGRAVES Max
CAMPBELL Glen
CARLISLE Belinda
CASCADES*
CHIFFONS*
CHI-LITES*
CHRISTIE* Lou, Tony
COASTERS*
COLDPLAY*
COOLIDGE Rita
COSTELLO Elvis
CRAWFORD Randy
CREW CUTS*
CRICKETS*

CRYSTALS*
DAFT PUNK*
DE LA SOUL*
DIAMONDS*
DIETRICH Marlene
DJ CASPER
DOONICAN Val
DREAMERS*
DRIFTERS*
DRISCOLL Julie
ECKSTINE Billy
FENTONES*
FIVE STAR*
FLANAGAN Bud
FLANDERS Michael
FLOATERS*
FORTUNES*
FOUR ACES*
FOURMOST*
FOUR TOPS*
FRAMPTON Peter
FRANKLIN Aretha
GARDINER Boris
GARRITTY Freddie
GORILLAZ*
GREEN DAY*
HAMILTON George,
  Russ
HARRISON George
HAWKWIND*
HEATWAVE*
HOLLIDAY Michael
HOLLOWAY Stanley
HONEYBUS*
HOTSHOTS*
HUCKNALL Mick
IGLESIAS Enrique, Julio
INK SPOTS*
JACKSONS*

JOBOXERS*
JUNKIE XL
KNOPFLER Mark
LAWRENCE Katie,
  Steve
LEANDROS Vicky
LET LOOSE*
LIBERACE
LIBERTY X*
LIMERICK Alison
LIPPS INC*
LLORENNA Kelly
LOS LOBOS*
LUDACRIS
MATCHBOX*
MATTHEWS Cerys
MAYFIELD Curtis
MCDONALD Jane,
  Michael
MCFADDEN Brian
MC HAMMER
MCKELLAR Kenneth
MCKENZIE Scott
MEAT LOAF*
MELANIE B
MELANIE C
MENSWEAR*
MICHELLE
MIRACLES*
MITCHELL Guy, Joni
MIXTURES*
MORRISON Mark, Van
MR MISTER*
MUDLARKS*
NAZARETH*
NEWBEATS*
NEW ORDER*
NEW WORLD*
NICHOLAS Paul

O'DONNELL Daniel
OLDFIELD Mike
OLYMPICS*
OSBOURNE Ozzy
PEARL JAM*
PEDDLERS*
PENISTON Ce Ce
PHARAOHS*
PHARRELL
PHILLIPS Esther, Sid
PIONEERS*
PIRANHAS*
PLATTERS*
PRINCESS
PUSSYCAT*
RAFFERTY Gerry
REPARATA
REYNOLDS Debbie
RICHARDS Keith
RIPERTON Minnie
ROBINSON Smokey,
   Tom
ROCKWELL
RONETTES*
RONSTADT Linda
RUBETTES*
SAKAMOTO Kyu
SARSTEDT Peter, Robin
SCAFFOLD*
SCOTT-LEE Lisa
S-EXPRESS*
SHAKATAK*
SHALAMAR*
SHEARING George
SHERIDAN Mark
SIMPSONS*
SIOUXSIE
SKELLERN Peter
SLIPKNOT*

SOFT CELL*
SPECIALS*
SPINNERS*
STAFFORD Jo
STARDUST Alvin
ST PETERS Crispian
STRATTON Eugene
SUPREMES*
SURFARIS*
SURVIVOR*
TAKE THAT*
TALK TALK*
THURSTON Bobby
TIGHT FIT*
TORNADOS*
TOURISTS*
TOY DOLLS*
TRAVOLTA John
TUNSTALL KT
ULTRAVOX*
UMILIANI Piero
UNION GAP*
VANDROSS Luther
VANGELIS
VAN HALEN*
VAN OUTEN Denise
VENTURES*
WATERMAN Dennis
WESTLIFE*
WHISPERS*
WILLIAMS Alyson,
   Andy, Danny,
   Deniece, Don, Hank,
   Iris, John, Mason,
   Maurice, Robbie,
   Vanessa
ZAVARONI Lena

9
ACE OF BASE*
AEROSMITH*
ALL SAINTS*
ANASTACIA
BACHELORS*
BADFINGER*
BEACH BOYS*
BEENIE MAN
BELAFONTE Harry
BIG BOPPER
BLACK LACE*
BLUEBELLS*
BLUENOTES*
BLUETONES*
BLUNSTONE Colin
BOW WOW WOW*
BOY GEORGE
BRIGHTMAN Sarah
BUCKS FIZZ*
BUZZCOCKS*
CARDIGANS*
CARPENTER Karen,
   Richard
CATATONIA*
CLEOPATRA*
COVINGTON Julie
CRUSADERS*
CUFFLINKS*
DEL AMITRI*
DICKINSON Bruce
DIXIE CUPS*
DUBLINERS*
EASYBEATS*
FAITHFULL Marianne
FAITHLESS*
FELICIANO José
FOREIGNER*
FOUR PREPS*

GABRIELLE
GALLAGHER Liam,
　Noel
GARFUNKEL Art
GOLDFRAPP*
GOLDSBORO Bobby
GREENBAUM Norman
GREYHOUND*
HALLIWELL Geri
HAZLEWOOD Lee
HENDERSON Joe
HOCKRIDGE Edmund
HOT BUTTER*
IMBRUGLIA Natalie
INNER CITY*
IVY LEAGUE*
JANKOWSKI Horst
JEFFERSON
KAEMPFERT Bert
KRAFTWERK*
LANDSCAPE*
LEVELLERS*
LITTLE EVA
LOOSE ENDS*
LOS BRAVOS*
MANTRONIX*
MARILLION*
MARMALADE*
MCCARTNEY Sir Paul
MCCORMACK John
MCLACHLAN Craig
MCPHATTER Clyde
MECHANICS*
MEL AND KIM*
MEN AT WORK*
METALLICA*
METHOD MAN
MIGIL FIVE*
MORRICONE Ennio

MORRISSEY
MOTÖRHEAD*
MOUSKOURI Nana
OFFSPRING*
O'SULLIVAN Gilbert
PAPER LACE*
PARKINSON Jimmy
PARTRIDGE Don
PASADENAS*
PINK FLOYD*
PONI-TAILS*
RADIOHEAD*
RAINWATER Marvin
REAL MCCOY*
REAL THING*
REPUBLICA*
ROBERTSON BA
ROSE ROYCE*
ROXY MUSIC*
SALT-N-PEPA*
SCORPIONS*
SEARCHERS*
SHED SEVEN*
SHIRELLES*
SHONDELLS*
SIMPLY RED*
SNOOP DOGG
SPOTNICKS*
STAPLETON Cyril
STATUS QUO*
STEELY DAN*
STRAY CATS*
STREISAND Barbra
SUGABABES*
SYLVESTER
TEENAGERS*
THIN LIZZY*
TILLOTSON Johnny
TIN TIN OUT*

TOPLOADER*
TOWNSHEND Pete
TREMELOES*
UPSETTERS*
VALENTINE Dickie
VANDELLAS*
VAN HELDEN Armand
VENGABOYS*
WAS (NOT WAS)*
WATERBOYS*
WET WET WET*
WHITFIELD David
WHITTAKER Roger
WILDCHILD
YARDBIRDS*
YELLOW DOG*
YOUNG ONES*
ZACHARIAS Helmut

10
AMEN CORNER*
APPLEJACKS*
ART OF NOISE*
BAD MANNERS*
BANANARAMA*
BELLE STARS*
BIG COUNTRY*
BLANCMANGE*
BLOCKHEADS*
BOB AND EARL*
CANNED HEAT*
CARAVELLES*
CARPENTERS*
CHARLATANS*
CHECKMATES*
CHICORY TIP*
CHORDETTES*
CHRISTIANS*
CLAYDERMAN Richard

COMMODORES*
COMMUNARDS*
DEACON BLUE*
DEEP PURPLE*
DEF LEPPARD*
DR FEELGOOD*
DURAN DURAN*
ELECTRONIC*
EURYTHMICS*
FATBOY SLIM
GAINSBOURG Serge
GIRLS ALOUD*
GUNS N' ROSES*
HARDCASTLE Paul
HIGHWAYMEN*
HONEYCOMBS*
HURRICANES*
IRON MAIDEN*
JAMIROQUAI*
JAN AND DEAN*
JETHRO TULL*
JUDGE DREAD
KAJAGOOGOO*
KALIN TWINS*
KRISS KROSS*
KULA SHAKER*
LAMBRETTAS*
LAS KETCHUP*
LIMP BIZKIT*
LINKIN PARK*
LIQUID GOLD*
LOUDERMILK John D
LOVE AFFAIR*
MACKINTOSH Ken
MARTINDALE Wink
MATT BIANCO*
MAXÏMO PARK*
MCCUTCHEON
  Martine

MELACHRINO George
MONTENEGRO Hugo
MOODY BLUES*
MORISSETTE Alanis
MÖTLEY CRÜE*
MS DYNAMITE
MUNGO JERRY*
NEW EDITION*
NEW SEEKERS*
NEWTON-JOHN Olivia
NICKELBACK*
PACEMAKERS*
PORTISHEAD*
PRETENDERS*
RACING CARS*
RAM JAM BAND*
RAZORLIGHT*
SAM AND DAVE*
SAM THE SHAM
SANDPIPERS*
SAW DOCTORS*
SEX PISTOLS*
SHANGRI-LAS*
SMALL FACES*
SOMERVILLE Jimmy
SOUL II SOUL*
SPICE GIRLS*
STANSFIELD Lisa
STARGAZERS*
STARSAILOR*
STONE ROSES*
STRANGLERS*
STYLISTICS*
SUPERGRASS*
SUPERTRAMP*
TEDDY BEARS*
THIRD WORLD*
TIMBERLAKE Justin
TOM TOM CLUB*

UGLY KID JOE*
UNDERTONES*
UNDERWORLD*
UTAH SAINTS*
VANILLA ICE
VANITY FARE*
WASHINGTON Geno
WAVELENGTH*
WHITESNAKE*
WILDHEARTS*
YOUNGBLOOD
  Sydney

11
ALICE DEEJAY*
ARMATRADING Joan
AZTEC CAMERA*
BEASTIE BOYS*
BEATMASTERS*
BEDINGFIELD Daniel
BIG ROLL BAND*
BLACKSTREET*
BLAZIN' SQUAD*
BLOW MONKEYS*
BOMB THE BASS*
BRONSKI BEAT*
CHACKSFIELD Frank
CHAS AND DAVE*
CHEEKY GIRLS*
CHINA CRISIS*
CHUMBAWAMBA*
CULTURE CLUB*
CYPRESS HILL*
DEAD OR ALIVE*
DEPECHE MODE*
DIRE STRAITS*
ELLIS-BEXTOR Sophie
FAITH NO MORE*
FATBACK BAND*

FOO FIGHTERS*
FOUNDATIONS*
FOUR PENNIES*
FOUR SEASONS*
FUN BOY THREE*
GENERATION X*
GLITTER BAND*
HILLTOPPERS*
HUMAN LEAGUE*
HUMPERDINCK
  Engelbert
IMAGINATION*
JACKSON FIVE*
JORDONAIRES*
JUDAS PRIEST*
KAYE SISTERS*
KILLING JOKE*
LINDISFARNE*
MANFRED MANN*
MARVELETTES*
MELKY SEDECK*
MERSEYBEATS*
MINDBENDERS*
MODERNAIRES*
NAPOLEON XIV
OHIO EXPRESS*
ORANGE JUICE*
OVERLANDERS*
PET SHOP BOYS*
PILTDOWN MEN*
PLAYBOY BAND*
POPPY FAMILY*
PROCOL HARUM*
PUBLIC ENEMY*
QUANTUM JUMP*
RHYTHM KINGS*
SAINTE-MARIE Buffy
SIMPLE MINDS*
SO SOLID CREW*

SOUNDGARDEN*
SPIN DOCTORS*
SPRINGFIELD Dusty
SPRINGSTEEN Bruce
STEPPENWOLF*
T CONNECTION*
TEMPTATIONS*
TURIN BRAKES*
WHITE PLAINS*
WONDER STUFF*

12
ALISHA'S ATTIC*
ARTFUL DODGER*
ATOMIC KITTEN*
BASEMENT JAXX*
BLACK SABBATH*
BOB AND MARCIA*
BOOMTOWN RATS*
BOYSTOWN GANG*
COCKNEY REBEL*
CROWDED HOUSE*
CRYPT-KICKERS*
DANDY WARHOLS*
DIZZEE RASCAL
DREAMWEAVERS*
FIDDLER'S DRAM*
FIRST EDITION*
FLEETWOOD MAC*
FLOWERPOT MEN*
FOUR FRESHMEN*
GRATEFUL DEAD*
GUYS AND DOLLS*
HAPPY MONDAYS*
HOT CHOCOLATE*
HOUSEMARTINS*
KAISER CHIEFS*
KING BROTHERS*
KINGSTON TRIO*

LITTLE ANGELS*
LIVING IN A BOX*
MEDICINE HEAD*
MIDNIGHT STAR*
MIKI AND GRIFF*
MILLI VANILLI*
MODERN LOVERS*
MUSICAL YOUTH*
NOTORIOUS BIG
PAUL AND PAULA*
PETERS AND LEE*
PLASTIC PENNY*
POWER STATION*
PREFAB SPROUT*
PRETTY THINGS*
PRIMAL SCREAM*
SAINT ETIENNE*
SAVAGE GARDEN*
SECRET AFFAIR*
SHOCKING BLUE*
SHOWSTOPPERS*
SISTER SLEDGE*
SKUNK ANANSIE*
SONNY AND CHER*
SPRINGFIELDS*
STEELEYE SPAN*
ST LOUIS UNION*
STYLE COUNCIL*
SUNSHINE BAND*
TALKING HEADS*
TECHNOTRONIC*
TENPOLE TUDOR*
TERRORVISION*
THREE DEGREES*
ULTIMATE KAOS*
VERNONS GIRLS*
WEATHER GIRLS*
WHITE STRIPES*
YOUNG RASCALS*

13
ALTERED IMAGES*
ARCTIC MONKEYS*
ATOMIC ROOSTER*
BADLY DRAWN BOY
BARRON KNIGHTS*
BLACK EYED PEAS*
BROOK BROTHERS*
BROTHER BEYOND*
DAVE CLARK FIVE*
DEEP RIVER BOYS*
DESTINY'S CHILD*
FAT LARRY'S BAND*
FLYING LIZARDS*
FLYING PICKETS*
HEARTBREAKERS*
ISLEY BROTHERS*
LITTLE RICHARD
LOVIN' SPOONFUL*
MAGIC LANTERNS*
MARILYN MANSON*
MASSIVE ATTACK*
MILLS BROTHERS*
MODERN ROMANCE*
MODERN TALKING*
MOTT THE HOOPLE*
NIGHTCRAWLERS*
NINE INCH NAILS*
OLLIE AND JERRY*
PICKETTYWITCH*
REO SPEEDWAGON*
RIGHT SAID FRED*
ROCKIN' BERRIES*
ROLLING STONES*
SHOWADDYWADDY*
SPANDAU BALLET*
STEALER'S WHEEL*
STEREOPHONICS*
TEARS FOR FEARS*

THOMPSON TWINS*
THREE DOG NIGHT*
TWISTED SISTER*
VILLAGE PEOPLE*
ZAGER AND EVANS*

14
ALTHEA AND DONNA*
ANDREWS SISTERS*
BACKSTREET BOYS*
BAY CITY ROLLERS*
BEAUTIFUL SOUTH*
DOOBIE BROTHERS*
EVERLY BROTHERS*
FAIRWEATHER-LOW
   Andy
FIFTH DIMENSION*
FOSTER AND ALLEN*
FRANZ FERDINAND*
GIBSON BROTHERS*
GODLEY AND CREME*
HAYSI FANTAYZEE*
HERMAN'S HERMITS*
JON AND VANGELIS*
KOOL AND THE GANG*
LIGHTNING SEEDS*
LORD ROCKINGHAM
LYTE FUNKIE ONES*
MADISON AVENUE*
MCGUIRE SISTERS*
NASHVILLE TEENS*
PEACHES AND HERB*
PETER AND GORDON*
PLASTIC ONO BAND*
POINTER SISTERS*
PROPELLERHEADS*
PUBLIC IMAGE LTD*
RENÉE AND RENATO*
ROCKSTEADY CREW*

ROOFTOP SINGERS*
SCRITTI POLITTI*
SISTERS OF MERCY*
SWEET SENSATION*
SWING OUT SISTER*
TANGERINE DREAM*
WALKER BROTHERS*
WEDDING PRESENT*

15
APOLLO FOUR FORTY*
BELLAMY BROTHERS*
BEVERLEY SISTERS*
BIG BEN BANJO BAND*
BRAND NEW HEAVIES*
CAPTAIN SENSIBLE
CHARLES AND EDDIE*
CLASSIC NOUVEAUX*
DELTA RHYTHM BOYS*
DETROIT EMERALDS*
DETROIT SPINNERS*
GHOSTFACE KILLAH
HOTHOUSE FLOWERS*
INSPIRAL CARPETS*
MCGUINNESS FLINT*
MIDDLE OF THE ROAD*
OUTHERE BROTHERS*
PARTRIDGE FAMILY*
PEPSI AND SHIRLIE*
PLASTIC BERTRAND
PSYCHEDELIC FURS*
ROBSON AND JEROME*
TEMPERANCE SEVEN*
TRANSVISION VAMP*
UNIT FOUR PLUS TWO*
WOMACK AND WOMACK*

16
AVERAGE WHITE BAND*
CHEMICAL BROTHERS*
CRASH TEST DUMMIES*
EARTH WIND AND FIRE*

GALLAGHER AND LYLE*
GRANDMASTER FLASH
JOHNSTON BROTHERS*
LIGHTHOUSE FAMILY*
MAMAS AND THE PAPAS*

OCEAN COLOUR SCENE*
PETER, PAUL AND MARY*
POP WILL EAT ITSELF*
SMASHING PUMPKINS*
TEARDROP EXPLODES*

Arts – Music & Entertainment – Singers & Musicians – CLASSICAL PERFORMERS * = musician

3
BÄR Olaf
MAE* Vanessa
SUK* Josef

4
AMIS John
AUER* Leopold
BEST* William
BUTT Dame Clara
BYRD* William
CULP Julia
DOWD Ronald
DYER Charles
FOLI Allan 'Signor'
HESS* Dame Myra
HILL Martyn
KURZ Selma
LIND Jenny
MÖDL Martha
PYNE Louisa
RALF Torsten
RIES* Ferdinand, Franz
VOGL Heinrich
WYSS Sophie

5
ABACO* Evaristo

ACKTÉ Aïno
ADAMS Donald
ALARD* Jean-Delphin
ALLIN Norman
ANDRÉ* Franz
ARRAU* Claudio
BAKER Dame Janet
BOEHM* Theobald
BRAIN* Alfred, Aubrey, Dennis
BREAM* Julian
CROSS Joan
DU PRÉ* Jacqueline
EVANS Sir Geraint, Nancy, Rebecca
GEDDA Nicolai
GIGLI Beniamino
GOBBI Tito
GRISI Giuditta, Giulia, Reri
LANZA Mario
LLOYD Edward
MEILI Max
MELBA Dame Nellie
OGDON* John
PATEY Janet
PATTI Adelina
PEARS Sir Peter

PINZA Ezio
RAISA Rosa
SPOHR* Ludwig
STEAR Ronald
STERN* Isaac
TEYTE Dame Maggie
TUDOR* David
VIÑES* Ricardo
WERBA* Erik
YSAŸE* Eugène

6
ABBOTT Emma
ACHRON* Joseph
ALBANI Dame Emma
ALCOCK* Sir Walter
BARATI* George
BÉRIOT* Charles-Auguste de
BOCHSA* Nicolas
CALLAS Maria
CARUSO Enrico
CASALS* Pablo
COATES John
DAWSON Peter
DRAPER* Haydn
ENESCU* George
FARRAR Geraldine

GALWAY* Sir James
HEMPEL Frieda
HEROLD Vilhelm
JANSEN* Janine
KEMBLE Adelaide
KIPNIS Alexander
KÖHLER* Wolfgang
LUSSAN Zélie de
MORRIS James*, Gareth
PAPINI* Guido
QUANTZ* Johann
REEVES Sims
SCHIPA Tito
SLADEN Victoria
SQUIRE* William
TALLIS* Thomas
TAUBER Richard
TERTIS* Lionel
WILSON Catherine

7

AGUJARI Lucrezia
BAZZINI* Antonio
BOBESCO* Lola
BOCELLI Andrea
CABALLÉ Montserrat
CARREÑO* Teresa
CORELLI* Arcangelo
D'ÁRANYI* Jelly
DEERING* Richard
DESMOND Astra
DOMINGO Placido
DOWLAND* John
FARRELL Eileen
FERRIER Kathleen
GARRETT Lesley
GIBBONS* Orlando
HAMMOND
    Dame Joan

JANSSEN Herbert
JURINAC Sena
KENNEDY* Nigel
LEHMANN Lilli
MENUHIN* Hephzibah,
    Lord Yehudi
MILKINA* Nina
ROBESON Paul
SEGOVIA* Andrés
STABILE Mariano
STAMITZ* Karl
TEBALDI Renata
THIBAUD* Jacques
TIBBETT Lawrence
TRAUBEL Helen
WALLACE Ian

8

BACKHAUS* Wilhelm
BERINGER* Oscar
BJÖRLING Jussi
BLAGROVE* Henry
BORGATTI Giuseppe
CARRERAS José
CARRODUS* John
    Tiplady
FLAGSTAD Kirsten
FOURNIER Pierre
GOOSSENS* Leon,
    Marie, Sidonie
GRANADOS* Enrique
HABENECK* François
HOROWITZ* Vladimir
KREISLER* Fritz
LABLACHE Luigi
MILSTEIN* Nathan
PAGANINI* Niccolò
RAISBECK Rosina
ROTHWELL* Evelyn

STEPHENS Emery,
    Susan
STERLING Antoinette
TE KANAWA Dame Kiri
WILLIAMS* John

9

ASHKENAZY* Vladimir
BARENBOIM* Daniel
BRANNIGAN Owen
BURROUGHS Bruce
CAMPANINI Italo*,
    Cleofonte
CHALIAPIN Fyodor
FARINELLI
FRANSELLA* Albert
MCCORMACK John
OLCZEWSKA Maria
PAVAROTTI Luciano
TAGLIABUE Carlo
TORTELIER* Paul
WHITEHILL Clarence
ZIMBALIST* Efrem

10

BATTISTINI Mattia
BILLINGTON Elizabeth
DEMESSIEUX* Jeanne
GALLI-CURCI Amelita
PADEREWSKI* Ignacy
    Jan
RUBINSTEIN* Arthur
SUTHERLAND Dame
    Joan
TAGLIAVINI Ferruccio
TETRAZZINI Eva, Luisa
VIEUXTEMPS* Henri

11
LESCHETIZKY* Theodor
LLOYD WEBBER* Julian
SCHWARZKOPF Dame Elisabeth
STILES ALLEN Lilian
STOCKHAUSEN Julian*, Franz

12
ROSTROPOVICH* Mstislav

14
BAHR-MILDENBURG Anna von

Arts – Music & Entertainment – Singers & Musicians – JAZZ PERFORMERS

3
GUY Buddy
LEE Peggy
ORY Kid

4
BALL Kenny
BILK Acker
BLEY Carla
COLE Nat King
CRAY Robert
GETZ Stan
KING Albert, BB
MONK Thelonious
PASS Joe
PINE Courtney
REED Jimmy
RICH Buddy
RUSH Otis
SHAW Artie
SLIM Memphis
WEBB Chick

5
BAKER Chet
BASIE Count
BLAND Bobby
BOWIE Lester

BROWN Clifford
COREA Chick
DAVIS Miles
DIXON Willie
EVANS Bill
HAYES Tubby
HEATH Ted
HINES Earl
HOUSE Son
JAMES Etta, Harry,
    Elmore
JONES Quincy
KRALL Diana
KRUPA Gene
LAINE Dame Cleo
MOORE Dudley
MELLY George
PRIMA Louis
RAITT Bonnie
ROACH Max
SCOTT Ronnie
SMITH Bessie, Jimmy
TATUM Art
TERRY Clark
TYNER McCoy
WELSH Alex
YOUNG Lester

6
BARBER Chris
BECHET Sidney
BLAKEY Art
BOLDEN Buddy
CARTER Benny
CARTER Betty
CHERRY Don
COLYER Ken
COODER Ry
CULLUM Jamie
DOLPHY Eric
DOMINO Fats
DORSEY Jimmy, Tommy
DR JOHN
EDISON Harry
GARNER Erroll
GORDON Dexter
HERMAN Woody
HODGES Johnny
HOOKER John Lee
JOPLIN Scott
JORDAN Louis
JOSEPH Julian
KENTON Stan
KORNER Alexis
LUSHER Don
MILLER Glenn

MINGUS Charles
MORTON Jelly Roll
OLIVER King
PARKER Charlie
POWELL Bud
RAINEY Ma
RIDDLE Nelson
SILVER Horace
SIMONE Nina
TAYLOR Cecil
TRACEY Stan
TURNER Big Joe
WALKER T-Bone
WALLER Fats
WATERS Muddy

7
BROONZY Big Bill
BRUBECK Dave
CHARLES Ray
COLEMAN Ornette
COLLINS Albert
CONNICK Harry
GOODMAN Benny
HAMPTON Lionel
HANCOCK Herbie
HAWKINS Coleman
HOLIDAY Billie
HOLLAND Jools
HOPKINS Lightnin'
JACKSON Milt

JARRETT Keith
JOHNSON Lonnie,
  Robert
METHENY Pat
PARNELL Jack
ROLLINS Sonny
RUSHING Jimmy
RUSSELL Pee Wee
SANDERS Pharoah
VAUGHAN Sarah, Stevie
  Ray
WEBSTER Ben
WILSON Teddy

8
ADDERLEY Cannonball
CALLOWAY Cab
COLTRANE John
ELDRIDGE Roy
GARBAREK Jan
GILBERTO Astrud
MARSALIS Branford,
  Wynton
MULLIGAN Gerry
PETERSON Oscar
SHEARING George
THORNTON Big Mama
WILLIAMS Mary Lou

9
ARMSTRONG Louis

CHRISTIAN Charlie
DANKWORTH Sir John
ELLINGTON Duke
GILLESPIE Dizzy
GRAPPELLI Stéphane
HENDERSON Fletcher
JEFFERSON Blind Lemon
LEADBELLY
LYTTELTON Humphrey
REINHARDT Django
TEAGARDEN Jack

10
FITZGERALD Ella
HOWLIN' WOLF
MONTGOMERY Marion
WASHINGTON Dinah
WILLIAMSON Sonny
  Boy

11
BEIDERBECKE Bix
WITHERSPOON Jimmy

12
CHARLESWORTH Dick
LITTLE WALTER

17
PROFESSOR LONGHAIR

Arts – Music & Entertainment – SINGERS (types)

3	**7**	VOCALIST	SCAT SINGER
DUO	BOY BAND	WHISTLER	SONGSTRESS
	CROONER	YODELLER	TROUBADOUR
4	GLEEMAN		
ALTO	POP STAR	**9**	**11**
BASS	SECONDO	BALLADEER	CAROL SINGER
DIVA	SOLOIST	CHANTEUSE	MINNESINGER
	SOPRANO	CONTRALTO	OPERA SINGER
5	WARBLER	HARMONIST	TORCH SINGER
BASSO		POP SINGER	
GROUP	**8**	PRINCIPAL	**12**
MEZZO	BARITONE	SERENADER	COUNTER-TENOR
PRIMO	CAROLLER		MEZZO-SOPRANO
TENOR	CASTRATO	**10**	
WAITS	CHANTEUR	BOY SOPRANO	**13**
	DUETTIST	CHORUS GIRL	BASSO PROFUNDO
6	FALSETTO	CHORUS LINE	CALYPSO SINGER
BUSKER	FRONTMAN	COLORATURA	MEISTERSINGER
CHORUS	JONGLEUR	FOLK SINGER	
SINGER	MELODIST	GLEEMAIDEN	**15**
TREBLE	MINSTREL	HARMONISER	RECORDING ARTIST
	POP GROUP	LEAD SINGER	SONG-AND-DANCE MAN
	SONGSTER	PRIMA DONNA	

Arts – Music & Entertainment – SONGS (No.1 UK hits)
* = double-sided No.1

3
SHE Charles Aznavour
WHY Anthony Newley

4
BABE Take That
BLUE Eiffel 65
BURN Usher

CARS Gary Numan
DARE Gorillaz
DOOP Doop
FAME Irene Cara
FIRE The Crazy World
  of Arthur Brown
FREE Deniece
  Williams

GENO Dexy's
  Midnight Runners
HELP! The Beatles
HERO Enrique
LADY Modjo
LYLA Oasis
MAMA* Spice Girls
PRAY Take That

RISE Gabrielle
SLOW Kylie Minogue
STAN Eminem
STAY Shakespear's
  Sister
SURE Take That
TRUE Spandau Ballet
WHEN The Kalin Twins
YEAH! Usher with Lil'
  Jon & Ludacris
YMCA Village People

5

ANGEL Shaggy with
  Rayvon
AXEL F Crazy Frog
CLAIR Gilbert
  O'Sullivan
CRAZY Gnarls Barkley
DIANA Paul Anka
DIANE The Bachelors
DIZZY Vic Reeves and
  the Wonder Stuff,
  Tommy Roe
ERNIE Benny Hill
FLAVA Peter Andre
GO NOW The Moody
  Blues
HEART Pet Shop Boys
HELLO Lionel Richie
MANDY Westlife
MARIA Blondie
MUSIC Madonna
OH BOY Mud
RADIO Robbie Williams
RELAX Frankie Goes to
  Hollywood
SMILE Lily Allen
SORRY Madonna

START The Jam
STOMP Steps
TEARS Ken Dodd
TOXIC Britney Spears
VOGUE Madonna
WOMAN John Lennon
WORDS Boyzone

6

ANGELO Brotherhood
  of Man
APACHE The Shadows
ATOMIC Blondie
CALL ME Blondie
CRYING Don McLean
DAKOTA
  Stereophonics
DÉJÀ VU Beyoncé with
  Jay-Z
DESIRE U2
DIRRTY Cristina
  Aguilera with Redman
DREAMS Gabrielle
FEEL IT The Tamperer
  with Maya
FIGARO Brotherhood
  of Man
FROZEN Madonna
HEAVEN DJ Sammy
  and Yanou with Do
HEY JOE! Frankie Laine
HOLLER* Spice Girls
HUNG UP Madonna
IF I WAS Midge Ure
INSIDE Stiltskin
JULIET The Four
  Pennies
KILLER Adamski
LONELY Akon

MMMBOP Hanson
MR VAIN Culture Beat
MY LOVE Westlife
POOR ME Adam Faith
ROCK DJ Robbie
  Williams
ROLLIN' Limp Bizkit
SAILOR Petula Clark
SO SICK Ne-Yo
THE FLY U2
TOO SHY Kajagoogoo
XANADU Olivia
  Newton-John and
  the ELO
YEH, YEH* Georgie
  Fame and the Blue
  Flames

7

AMERICA Razorlight
ANITINA* M/A/R/R/S
BAD TO ME Billy J
  Kramer and the
  Dakotas
BAG IT UP Geri Halliwell
BELIEVE Cher
BREATHE Blu Cantrell
  with Sean Paul, The
  Prodigy
CABARET* Louis
  Armstrong Orchestra
CARA MIA David
  Whitfield
CHANGES Kelly and
  Ozzy Osbourne
DANCE ON! The
  Shadows
DILEMMA Nelly with
  Kelly Rowland

DIVORCE Billy
  Connolly
DON'T CHA Pussycat
  Dolls with Busta
  Rhymes
FLOAT ON The Floaters
FLY AWAY Lenny
  Kravitz
FRANKIE Sister Sledge
FREAK ME Another
  Level
FREEDOM Wham!
GAME BOY* KWS
GET AWAY Georgie
  Fame and the Blue
  Flames
GET BACK The Beatles
  with Billy Preston
GET DOWN Gilbert
  O'Sullivan
GET IT ON T Rex
GOODBYE Spice Girls
GOODIES Clara with
  Petey Pablo
GRANDAD Clive Dunn
HEY BABY DJ Otzi
HEY JUDE The Beatles
HOT LOVE T Rex
I LIKE IT Gerry and the
  Pacemakers
I'LL BE OK McFly
IMAGINE John Lennon
I'M ALIVE The Hollies
IT'S A SIN Pet Shop
  Boys
IT'S OVER Roy Orbison
JANUARY Pilot
JCB SONG Nizlopi
KON-TIKI The Shadows

LA BAMBA Los Lobos
LET IT BE Ferry Aid
LUCILLE Kenny Rogers
MAKE LUV Room 5 with
  Oliver Cheatham
MICHAEL The
  Highwaymen
MS GRACE The Tymes
MY PLACE* Nelly
NO LIMIT 2 Unlimited
OH JULIE Shakin'
  Stevens
ONLY YOU The Flying
  Pickets
RAT TRAP The
  Boomtown Rats
RUNAWAY Del
  Shannon
SAILING Rod Stewart
TELSTAR The Tornados
THE ROSE Westlife
TOO MUCH Spice Girls
TOUCH ME Rui Da
  Silva with Cassandra
TRAGEDY The Bee
  Gees,* Steps
VERTIGO U2
VINCENT Don McLean
WANNABE Spice Girls
WAY DOWN Elvis
  Presley

8
AMARILLO Tony
  Christie with Peter
  Kay
ANSWER ME Frankie
  Laine, David
  Whitfield

BABY JANE Rod
  Stewart
BABY JUMP Mungo
  Jerry
BABY LOVE The
  Supremes
BACK HOME England
  World Cup Squad
BARBADOS Typically
  Tropical
BLUE MOON The
  Marcels
CALL ON ME Eric
  Prydz
DIAMONDS Jet Harris
  and Tony Meehan
DON'T STOP The
  Outhere Brothers
DOWN DOWN Status
  Quo
ETERNITY* Robbie
  Williams
EYE LEVEL The Simon
  Park Orchestra
FASTLOVE George
  Michael
FERNANDO Abba
FILL ME IN Craig David
FIVE LIVE George
  Michael with Queen
  and Lisa Stansfield
  – EP
FLAT BEAT Mr Oizo
GET RIGHT Jennifer
  Lopez
GIVE IT UP KC and the
  Sunshine Band
HOOTS MON Lord
  Rockingham's XI

I BELIEVE Robson Green
and Jerome Flynn*,
Frankie Laine
I FEEL YOU Peter Andre
IGNITION R Kelly
I LOVE YOU Cliff
Richard and the
Shadows
INNUENDO Queen
I PRETEND Des
O'Connor
KISS KISS Holly Valance
MAD WORLD Michael
Andrews with Gary
Jules
MAMMA MIA Abba
MANEATER Nelly
Furtado
MICHELLE The
Overlanders
MONY MONY Tommy
James and the
Shondells
MR BLOBBY Mr Blobby
NO CHARGE JJ Barrie
ONE NIGHT* Elvis
Presley
PATIENCE Take That
PRECIOUS* The Jam
REAL TO ME Brian
McFadden
ROULETTE Russ Conway
SEXYBACK Justin
Timberlake
SPACEMAN Babylon
Zoo
STAR GIRL McFly
SURVIVOR Destiny's
Child

TAKE ON ME a1
THE JOKER Steve Miller
Band
THE MODEL*
Kraftwerk
THE POWER Snap!
THE STONK Hale and
Pace and the Stonkers
TOO CLOSE Blue
TRUE BLUE Madonna
WATERLOO Abba
YOU GOT IT New Kids
on the Block

9
ABBA-ESQUE Erasure
– EP
ALBATROSS Fleetwood
Mac
BABY CAKES 3 of a Kind
BEAUTIFUL Christina
Aguilera
BEETLEBUM Blur
BRIGHT EYES Art
Garfunkel
BUTTERFLY Andy
Williams
CANDY GIRL New
Edition
CAN THE CAN Suzi
Quatro
C'EST LA VIE B*Witched
CLAUDETTE* The Everly
Brothers
CONFESSIN' Frank Ifield
DO IT AGAIN The
Beach Boys
DON'T SPEAK No
Doubt

DO YOU MIND
Anthony Newley
DOWN UNDER Men at
Work
DREAMBOAT Alma
Cogan
EARTH SONG Michael
Jackson
EASY LOVER Philip
Bailey and Phil Collins
EBONY EYES* The Everly
Brothers
EVERGREEN* Will Young
EVERYTIME Britney
Spears
FOOL AGAIN Westlife
GHOST TOWN The
Specials
GOOD TIMIN' Jimmy
Jones
GREEN DOOR Shakin'
Stevens
GROOVEJET Spiller
HAPPY TALK Captain
Sensible
HEARTBEAT* Steps
I FEEL FINE The Beatles
I FEEL LOVE Donna
Summer
I GOT STUNG* Elvis
Presley
I'LL BE HOME Pat
Boone
I'M YOUR MAN Wham!
IT'S ONLY US* Robbie
Williams
IT WASN'T ME Shaggy
with Ricardo 'Rikrok'
Ducent

LET'S DANCE David Bowie, Five
LET'S PARTY Jive Bunny and the Mastermixers
LIFT ME UP Geri Halliwell
LOVE GROWS Edison Lighthouse
MAGGIE MAY Rod Stewart
METAL GURU T Rex
MOON RIVER Danny Williams
NEVER EVER All Saints
NUT ROCKER B Bumble and the Stingers
OBVIOUSLY McFly
OUT OF TIME Chris Farlowe and the Thunderbirds
PRAISE YOU Fatboy Slim
PRETTY FLY The Offspring
PUPPY LOVE Donny Osmond
RELEASE ME Engelbert Humperdinck
ROSE MARIE Slim Whitman
SACRIFICE* Elton John
SMACK THAT Akon with Eminem
STAND BY ME Ben E King
STICKWITU The Pussycat Dolls
SURRENDER Elvis Presley and the Jordanaires
THE REFLEX Duran Duran

THE STREAK Ray Stevens
TIGER FEET Mud
TWO TRIBES Frankie Goes to Hollywood
WHO'S DAVID Busted
WITHOUT ME Eminem
WONDERFUL Ja Rule with R Kelly and Ashanti
WOODSTOCK Matthews' Southern Comfort
YOUNG GIRL Gary Puckett and the Union Gap
YOUNG LOVE Tab Hunter, Donny Osmond
YOUR WOMAN White Town
YOU SAID NO Busted

10

A GOOD HEART Feargal Sharkey
ALL SHOOK UP Elvis Presley and the Jordanaires
ANNIE'S SONG John Denver
ANYONE OF US Gareth Gates
AS I LOVE YOU Shirley Bassey
BACK FOR GOOD Take That
BACK TO LIFE Soul II Soul with Caron Wheeler

BAND OF GOLD Freda Payne
BARBIE GIRL Aqua
BE FAITHFUL Fatman Scoop with the Crooklyn Clan
BILLIE JEAN Michael Jackson
BOOMBASTIC Shaggy
BOOTIE CALL All Saints
BREATHLESS The Corrs
BYE BYE BABY Bay City Rollers
CAN WE FIX IT? Bob the Builder
COZ I LUV YOU Slade
CROSSROADS Blazin' Squad
DAYDREAMER* David Cassidy
DAY TRIPPER* The Beatles
DON'T GIVE UP Chicane with Bryan Adams
DREAM LOVER Bobby Darin
FAIRGROUND Simply Red
FOOT TAPPER The Shadows
GAMBLIN' MAN* Lonnie Donegan and his Skiffle Group
GIRLFRIEND Billie
GO LET IT OUT Oasis
HALF AS NICE Amen Corner
HOLD MY HAND Don Cornell

HOUSE OF FUN Madness
ICE ICE BABY Vanilla Ice
ISRAELITES Desmond
 Dekker and the Aces
IT'S MY PARTY Dave
 Stewart and Barbara
 Gaskin
I TURN TO YOU
 Melanie C
JEALOUS GUY Roxy
 Music
JUST LOSE IT Eminem
LIVING DOLL Cliff
 Richard and the
 Drifters, Cliff Richard
 and the Young Ones
LOLA'S THEME
 Shapeshifters
LONELINESS Tomcraft
MEN IN BLACK Will
 Smith
MILLENNIUM Robbie
 Williams
MOVE CLOSER Phyllis
 Nelson
MY SON, MY SON Vera
 Lynn with Frank Weir
NIGHT FEVER The Bee
 Gees
NO TOMORROW Orson
OH CAROLINA Shaggy
OH, MEIN PAPA Eddie
 Calvert
PERFECT DAY various
 artists
PERFECTION Fairground
 Attraction
PLEASE PLEASE McFly
PURE SHORES All Saints

READY OR NOT Fugees
RED RED WINE UB40
REET PETITE Jackie
 Wilson
RIDE ON TIME Black Box
RING MY BELL Anita
 Ward
ROCK-A-BILLY Guy
 Mitchell
ROUND ROUND
 Sugababes
SCHOOL'S OUT Alice
 Cooper
SECRET LOVE Doris Day
SETTING SUN The
 Chemical Brothers
SEVEN TEARS Goombay
 Dance Band
SHE'S NOT YOU Elvis
 Presley and the
 Jordanaires
SHE'S THE ONE* Robbie
 Williams
SIDE SADDLE Russ
 Conway
SILVER LADY David Soul
STARRY EYED Michael
 Holliday
SUCH A NIGHT Johnnie
 Ray
SUGAR, SUGAR The
 Archies
SUNDAY GIRL Blondie
TEMPTATION The Everly
 Brothers
THESE WORDS Natasha
 Bedingfield
THINK TWICE Celine
 Dion

THREE LIONS Baddiel
 and Skinner and the
 Lightning Seeds
UPTOWN GIRL Billy Joel,
 Westlife
WHOLE AGAIN Atomic
 Kitten
WITHOUT YOU Mariah
 Carey, Nilsson

11
AIN'T NOBODY
 LL Cool J
AIN'T NO DOUBT
 Jimmy Nail
A LITTLE TIME The
 Beautiful South
ALL ABOUT YOU* McFly
ALL THIS TIME Michelle
ALWAYS YOURS Gary
 Glitter
AMERICAN PIE
 Madonna
BACHELOR BOY* Cliff
 Richard and the
 Shadows
BLACK COFFEE All Saints
BLOCKBUSTER! The
 Sweet
BROKEN WINGS The
 Stargazers
CATHY'S CLOWN The
 Everly Brothers
CHA CHA SLIDE DJ
 Casper
COLOURBLIND Darius
COME OUTSIDE Mike
 Sarne and Wendy
 Richard

CRAZY IN LOVE Beyoncé
DAY AND NIGHT Billie Piper
DEEPLY DIPPY Right Said Fred
DISCOTHEQUE U2
DOCTOR JONES Aqua
DO YOU LOVE ME Brian Poole and the Tremeloes
DRY YOUR EYES The Streets
FIRESTARTER The Prodigy
FOREVER LOVE Gary Barlow
FREAK LIKE ME Sugababes
FROM ME TO YOU The Beatles
GIRLS' SCHOOL* Wings
GLAD ALL OVER The Dave Clark Five
GYM AND TONIC Spacedust
HANGIN' TOUGH New Kids on the Block
HAVE YOU EVER S Club 7
HIPS DON'T LIE Shakira with Wyclef Jean
HOLD ME CLOSE David Essex
I DO IT FOR YOU Bryan Adams
I FEEL FOR YOU Chaka Khan
IF I LET YOU GO Westlife
I GOT YOU BABE Sonny and Cher, UB40 with Chrissie Hynde

I HAVE A DREAM* Westlife
I LOVE TO LOVE Tina Charles
I'M A BELIEVER The Monkees
I'M NOT IN LOVE 10cc
I SEE THE MOON The Stargazers
IT'S LIKE THAT Run-DMC vs Jason Nevins
JAPANESE BOY Aneka
JEALOUS MIND Alvin Stardust
JUST A LITTLE Liberty X
KEEP ON MOVIN' Five
LADY MADONNA The Beatles
LIGHT MY FIRE Will Young
LIKE A PRAYER Madonna
LILY THE PINK Scaffold
MAKE ME SMILE Steve Harley and Cockney Rebel
MIGHTY QUINN Manfred Mann
MISSISSIPPI Pussycat
MY DING-A-LING Chuck Berry
MY SWEET LORD George Harrison
NEVER FORGET Take That
NO OTHER LOVE Ronnie Hilton
ONLY SIXTEEN Craig Douglas
ORINOCO FLOW Enya

OVER AND OVER Nelly with Tim McGraw
RESPECTABLE Mel and Kim
RUNNING BEAR Johnny Preston
SAVIOUR'S DAY Cliff Richard
SHE LOVES YOU The Beatles
SIXTEEN TONS Tennessee Ernie Ford
SPACE ODDITY David Bowie
STAR TREKKIN' The Firm
STUPID CUPID* Connie Francis
TAINTED LOVE Soft Cell
TELEGRAM SAM T Rex
THAT'S MY GOAL Shayne Ward
THE LAST TIME The Rolling Stones
THE NEXT TIME* Cliff Richard and the Shadows
TURTLE POWER Partners in Kryme
UNBREAKABLE Westlife
UP ON THE ROOF* Robson Green and Jerome Flynn
VIVA FOREVER Spice Girls
VOODOO CHILE Jimi Hendrix
WAND'RIN' STAR Lee Marvin
WELCOME HOME Peters and Lee

WELL I ASK YOU Eden Kane
WOMAN IN LOVE Barbra Streisand
WOODEN HEART Elvis Presley
YELLOW RIVER Christie
YOU DON'T KNOW Helen Shapiro
YOU NEEDED ME Boyzone
YOU WIN AGAIN The Bee Gees

12
A FOOL SUCH AS I* Elvis Presley and the Jordanaires
A LITTLE PEACE Nicole
ALL OR NOTHING The Small Faces
ALL THAT I NEED Boyzone
AMAZING GRACE Royal Scots Dragoon Guards
ANGEL FINGERS Wizzard with the Suedettes and the Beach Boys
ASHES TO ASHES David Bowie
A WOMAN IN LOVE Frankie Laine
BABY COME BACK Pato Banton, The Equals
BEAUTIFUL DAY U2
BEING WITH YOU Smokey Robinson

BELFAST CHILD Simple Minds
BLACK OR WHITE Michael Jackson
BOOM BOOM BOOM The Outhere Brothers
CAROLINA MOON* Connie Francis
COME ON EILEEN Dexy's Midnight Runners with the Emerald Express
COMPUTER LOVE* Kraftwerk
COTTON EYE JOE Rednex
COUNTRY HOUSE Blur
DANCING QUEEN Abba
DISTANT DRUMS Jim Reeves
DO THE BARTMAN The Simpsons
DOUBLE BARREL Dave and Ansil Collins
ELEANOR RIGBY* The Beatles
END OF THE ROAD Boyz II Men
ETERNAL FLAME Atomic Kitten, The Bangles
GHETTO GOSPEL 2Pac with Elton John
HEALING HANDS* Elton John
HEART OF GLASS Blondie
HELLO, GOODBYE The Beatles

HOW DO YOU DO IT? Gerry and the Pacemakers
I REMEMBER YOU Frank Ifield
IT'S CHICO TIME Chico
I WANT YOU BACK Mel C with Missy 'Misdemeanour' Elliott
I WILL SURVIVE Gloria Gaynor
JACK YOUR BODY Steve 'Silk' Hurley
LA ISLA BONITA Madonna
LITTLE SISTER* Elvis Presley
LONG LIVE LOVE Sandie Shaw
LOSE YOURSELF Eminem
LOVE WON'T WAIT Gary Barlow
MACK THE KNIFE Bobby Darin
MAGIC MOMENTS Perry Como
NO MATTER WHAT Boyzone
NOTORIOUS BIG Nasty Girl with P Diddy, Nelly, Jagged Edge and Avery Storm
OB-LA-DI, OB-LA-DA Marmalade
ON THE REBOUND Floyd Cramer
PAINT IT BLACK The Rolling Stones

PIPES OF PEACE Paul McCartney
PLEASE DON'T GO* KWS
ROCK YOUR BABY George McCrae
SAN FRANCISCO Scott McKenzie
SATISFACTION The Rolling Stones
SAVE YOUR LOVE Renée and Renato
SHOW ME HEAVEN Maria McKee
SOFTLY, SOFTLY Ruby Murray
SOME MIGHT SAY Oasis
STARTING OVER John Lennon
SUMMER NIGHTS John Travolta and
  Olivia Newton-John
SUPER TROUPER Abba
SWEAR IT AGAIN Westlife
SWING THE MOOD Jive Bunny and
  the Mastermixers
TAKE ME BAK 'OME Slade
THE FIRST TIME Robin Beck
THE LADY IN RED Chris De Burgh
THE LAST WALTZ Engelbert
  Humperdinck
THEME FROM MASH Mash
THE PUPPY SONG* David Cassidy
THE REAL THING Toni Di Bart
THE YOUNG ONES Cliff Richard and
  the Shadows
THIS IS MY SONG Petula Clark
THIS OLE HOUSE Rosemary Clooney,
  Shakin' Stevens
THUNDERBIRDS* Busted
TICKET TO RIDE The Beatles
TOCA'S MIRACLE Fragma with Co Co
TO YOU I BELONG B*Witched
TURN BACK TIME Aqua
WEST END GIRLS Pet Shop Boys
WHEN I NEED YOU Leo Sayer
WHO'S SORRY NOW? Connie Francis
WHO'S THAT GIRL Madonna
YOUNG AT HEART The Bluebells

YOU RAISE ME UP Westlife
YOU'RE MY WORLD Cilla Black

13

ANOTHER CHANCE Roger Sanchez
BAD MOON RISING Creedence
  Clearwater Revival
BEAT SURRENDER The Jam
BLACKBERRY WAY The Move
BRASS IN POCKET The Pretenders
BRIMFUL OF ASHA Cornershop
BRING ME TO LIFE Evanescence with
  Paul McCoy
CAN'T BUY ME LOVE The Beatles
CARAVAN OF LOVE The Housemartins
CHAIN REACTION Diana Ross
CHANSON D'AMOUR Manhattan
  Transfer
COME ON YOU REDS Manchester
  United Football Club
CUMBERLAND GAP Lonnie Donegan
  and his Skiffle Group
DON'T STOP MOVIN' S Club 7
DON'T YOU WANT ME Human
  League
DUB ME GOOD TO YOU Beats
  International with Lindy Layton
EBONY AND IVORY Paul McCartney
  and Stevie Wonder
EYE OF THE TIGER Survivor
FLAP YOUR WINGS* Nelly
GOOD LUCK CHARM Elvis Presley
  and the Jordanaires
GOODNIGHT GIRL Wet Wet Wet
GOODY TWO SHOES Adam Ant
HAVE I THE RIGHT The Honeycombs
HERE IN MY HEART Al Martino
HOLE IN THE HEAD Sugababes
HOW CAN I BE SURE David Cassidy

IF YOU COME BACK Blue
I'LL STAND BY YOU Girls Aloud
INTO THE GROOVE Madonna
IT FEELS SO GOOD Sonique
IT'S ALL OVER NOW The Rolling
  Stones
IT'S NOT UNUSUAL Tom Jones
IT'S NOW OR NEVER Elvis Presley
IT'S RAINING MEN Geri Halliwell
JAILHOUSE ROCK Elvis Presley
JESUS TO A CHILD George Michael
JUST LIKE A PILL Pink
KEEP ON RUNNING Spencer Davis
  Group
KING OF THE ROAD Roger Miller
LADY MARMALADE Christina
  Aguilera, Lil' Kim, Mya and Pink,
  All Saints*
LEAVE RIGHT NOW Will Young
LIVING ON MY OWN Freddie
  Mercury
LOVESICK BLUES Frank Ifield
MAMBO ITALIANO Rosemary
  Clooney and the Mellomen
MARY'S BOY CHILD Harry Belafonte
MASSACHUSETTS The Bee Gees
MEASURE OF A MAN* Sam & Mark
MI CHICO LATINO Geri Halliwell
MULL OF KINTYRE* Wings
OH, PRETTY WOMAN Roy Orbison
ONE DAY AT A TIME Lena Martell
ONLY THE LONELY Roy Orbison
PERFECT MOMENT Martine
  McCutcheon
PURE AND SIMPLE Hear'Say
PUSH THE BUTTON Sugababes
RELIGHT MY FIRE Take That with Lulu
ROCK-A-HULA BABY* Elvis Presley
ROCK ME AMADEUS Falco

ROLLERCOASTER B*Witched
RUBBER BULLETS 10cc
SATURDAY NIGHT Whigfield
SEE MY BABY JIVE Wizzard with the
  Suedettes
SHAKIN' ALL OVER Johnny Kidd and
  the Pirates
SON OF MY FATHER Chicory Tip
SO YOU WIN AGAIN Hot Chocolate
SUGAR BABY LOVE The Rubettes
SUMMER HOLIDAY Cliff Richard and
  the Shadows
THE HINDU TIMES Oasis
THE ONE AND ONLY Chesney
  Hawkes
THE TIDE IS HIGH Atomic Kitten,
  Blondie
TWIST AND SHOUT Chaka Demus
  and Pliers with Jack Radics and Taxi
  Gang
TWO LITTLE BOYS Rolf Harris
UNDER PRESSURE Queen and David
  Bowie
WALK RIGHT BACK* The Everly
  Brothers
WE ARE THE WORLD USA for Africa
WE WILL ROCK YOU Five and Queen
WHAT DO YOU WANT? Adam Faith
WONDERFUL LAND The Shadows
WORLD IN MOTION…
  Englandneworder
WORLD OF OUR OWN Westlife
YOU BELONG TO ME Jo Stafford
YOU DON'T KNOW ME Armand Van
  Helden with Duane Harden
YOU'RE NOT ALONE Olive
YOU WEAR IT WELL Rod Stewart

14

A DIFFERENT BEAT Boyzone

AGAINST ALL ODDS Steve Brookstein, Mariah Carey with Westlife

A HARD DAY'S NIGHT The Beatles

A LITTLE BIT MORE 911

ALWAYS ON MY MIND Pet Shop Boys

ANY DREAM WILL DO Jason Donovan

BRING IT ALL BACK S Club 7

DEVIL GATE DRIVE Suzi Quatro

DON'T CALL ME BABY Madison Avenue

DON'T GIVE UP ON US David Soul

DON'T TURN AROUND Aswad

EBENEEZER GOODE The Shamen

EVERYBODY'S FREE Baz Luhmann

EVERY LOSER WINS Nick Berry

EVERYTHING I OWN Ken Boothe, Boy George

FOREVER AND EVER Slik

GENIE IN A BOTTLE Christina Aguilera

GIVE ME YOUR WORD Tennessee Ernie Ford

GOOD VIBRATIONS The Beach Boys

HIS LATEST FLAME* Elvis Presley

HONKY TONK WOMEN The Rolling Stones

I DON'T WANNA KNOW Mario Winans with Enya & P Diddy

I KNOW HIM SO WELL Elaine Paige and Barbara Dickson

I'M STILL WAITING Diana Ross

I WANNA SEX YOU UP Color Me Badd

I WANT IT THAT WAY Backstreet Boys

KARMA CHAMELEON Culture Club

KING OF MY CASTLE Wamdue Project

KUNG FU FIGHTING Carl Douglas

LITTLE CHILDREN Billy J Kramer and the Dakotas

LOOK AT THAT GIRL Guy Mitchell

MORE THAN A WOMAN Aaliyah

MOULDY OLD DOUGH Lieutenant Pigeon

MYSTERIOUS GIRL Peter Andre

NEEDLES AND PINS The Searchers

ONE DAY IN YOUR LIFE Michael Jackson

PAPA DON'T PREACH Madonna

PASS THE DUTCHIE Musical Youth

POETRY IN MOTION Johnny Tillotson

PRETTY FLAMINGO Manfred Mann

PRINCE CHARMING Adam and the Ants

QUEEN OF MY HEART Westlife

RETURN TO SENDER Elvis Presley and the Jordanaires

SHADDUP YOU FACE Joe Dolce Music Theatre

SOMEBODY HELP ME Spencer Davis Group

SOMETHIN' STUPID Nancy and Frank Sinatra, Robbie Williams and Nicole Kidman

SPINNING AROUND Kylie Minogue

SPIRIT IN THE SKY Doctor and the Medics, Gareth Gates with the Kumars, Norman Greenbaum

STAND BY YOUR MAN Tammy Wynette

STAY ANOTHER DAY East 17

SUNNY AFTERNOON The Kinks

THAT'LL BE THE DAY The Crickets

THAT'S WHAT I LIKE Jive Bunny and the Mastermixers

THE CHICKEN SONG Spitting Image
THE KETCHUP SONG Las Ketchup
THE ONLY WAY IS UP Yazz and the Plastic Population
THE POWER OF LOVE Frankie Goes to Hollywood, Jennifer Rush
THE WAYWARD WIND Frank Ifield
THE WONDER OF YOU Elvis Presley
TRAVELLIN' LIGHT Cliff Richard and the Shadows
UNDER THE BRIDGE* All Saints
WE CAN WORK IT OUT* The Beatles
WHERE ARE YOU NOW Jackie Trent
WHERE DO YOU GO TO Peter Sarstedt
WHERE IS THE LOVE? Black Eyed Peas
WOULD I LIE TO YOU Charles and Eddie
YOU ARE NOT ALONE Michael Jackson
YOU MAKE ME WANNA... Usher
YOU REALLY GOT ME The Kinks
YOU'RE BEAUTIFUL James Blunt
YOU SPIN ME ROUND Dead or Alive

15

ALL THAT SHE WANTS Ace of Base
A MOMENT LIKE THIS Leona Lewis
...BABY ONE MORE TIME Britney Spears
BECAUSE I GOT HIGH Afroman
BECAUSE WE WANT TO Billie
BEGIN THE BEGUINE Julio Iglesias
CARELESS WHISPER George Michael
CHINA IN YOUR HAND T'Pau
COMES A-LONG A-LOVE Kay Starr
CONCRETE AND CLAY Unit Four Plus Two
CONGRATULATIONS Cliff Richard
DA YA THINK I'M SEXY? Rod Stewart

DEVIL IN DISGUISE Elvis Presley and the Jordanaires
DO WAH DIDDY DIDDY Manfred Mann
EVERLASTING LOVE Love Affair
GET OFF OF MY CLOUD The Rolling Stones
GIVE A LITTLE LOVE Bay City Rollers
HAND ON YOUR HEART Kylie Minogue
HERE COMES SUMMER Jerry Keller
I BELIEVE I CAN FLY R Kelly
I DON'T WANNA DANCE Eddy Grant
IF YOU LEAVE ME NOW Chicago
I'LL BE MISSING YOU Puff Daddy and Faith Evans with U2
IN THE SUMMERTIME Mungo Jerry
I OWE YOU NOTHING Bros
IT'S ALL IN THE GAME Tommy Edwards
JUMPIN' JACK FLASH The Rolling Stones
KILLING ME SOFTLY Fugees
KNOCK THREE TIMES Dawn
LAY DOWN YOUR ARMS Anne Shelton
LIKE TOY SOLDIERS Eminem
LIVIN' LA VIDA LOCA Ricky Martin
LOVE IS ALL AROUND Wet Wet Wet
MR TAMBOURINE MAN The Byrds
MY HEART WILL GO ON Celine Dion
ONE MOMENT IN TIME Whitney Houston
OOPS! ... I DID IT AGAIN Britney Spears
OUTSIDE OF HEAVEN Eddie Fisher
PAPERBACK WRITER The Beatles
PLEASE DON'T TEASE Cliff Richard and the Shadows
PUMP UP THE VOLUME* M/A/R/R/S

PUPPET ON A STRING Sandie Shaw
RETURN OF THE MACK Mark
    Morrison
RHYTHM IS A DANCER Snap!
RIVERS OF BABYLON* Boney M
SAD SWEET DREAMER Sweet
    Sensation
SAY YOU'LL BE THERE Spice Girls
SEALED WITH A KISS Jason Donovan
SEASONS IN THE SUN Terry Jacks,
    Westlife*
SHE'S LEAVING HOME* Billy Bragg
    with Cara Tivey
SILENCE IS GOLDEN The Tremeloes
SINGING THE BLUES Guy Mitchell,
    Tommy Steele and the Steelmen
SPICE UP YOUR LIFE Spice Girls
STAND AND DELIVER Adam and the
    Ants
SUSPICIOUS MINDS* Gareth Gates
TAKE A CHANCE ON ME Abba
TEARS ON MY PILLOW Kylie
    Minogue, Johnny Nash
THE EDGE OF HEAVEN* Wham!
THE GARDEN OF EDEN Frankie
    Vaughan
THREE TIMES A LADY The
    Commodores
TOWER OF STRENGTH Frankie
    Vaughan
UNCHAINED MELODY Gareth Gates,
    Robson Green and Jerome Flynn*,
    The Righteous Brothers, Jimmy
    Young
WHISPERING GRASS Windsor Davies
    and Don Estelle
WHOLE LOTTA WOMAN Marvin
    Rainwater
YELLOW SUBMARINE* The Beatles

YOU'VE GOT A FRIEND* McFly

16
A DIFFERENT CORNER George
    Michael
ALL YOU NEED IS LOVE The Beatles
A WHITER SHADE OF PALE Procol
    Harum
BILLY DON'T BE A HERO Paper Lace
BLOCK ROCKIN' BEATS The
    Chemical Brothers
BOHEMIAN RHAPSODY Queen
BOOM, BOOM, BOOM, BOOM!! The
    Vengaboys
BOOM! SHAKE THE ROOM Jazzy Jeff
    and the Fresh Prince
DREADLOCK HOLIDAY 10cc
DREAMS OF CHILDREN* The Jam
ESPECIALLY FOR YOU Kylie Minogue
    and Jason Donovan
GANGSTA'S PARADISE Coolio with LV
GOING UNDERGROUND* The Jam
GOTTA GET THRU THIS Daniel
    Bedingfield
GREAT BALLS OF FIRE Jerry Lee Lewis
I DON'T LIKE MONDAYS The
    Boomtown Rats
IF YOU'RE NOT THE ONE Daniel
    Bedingfield
I HEAR YOU KNOCKING Dave
    Edmunds' Rockpile
I SHOULD BE SO LUCKY Kylie
    Minogue
I'VE NEVER BEEN TO ME Charlene
JOHNNY REMEMBER ME John Leyton
LITTLE RED ROOSTER The Rolling
    Stones
LOVE ME FOR A REASON The
    Osmonds

MAKING YOUR MIND UP Bucks Fizz
MESSAGE IN A BOTTLE The Police
MISTLETOE AND WINE Cliff Richard
PUTTIN' ON THE STYLE* Lonnie Donegan and his Skiffle Group
REACH FOR THE STARS* Shirley Bassey
ROCK AND ROLL WALTZ Kay Starr
SLEEPING SATELLITE Tasmin Archer
STOP LIVING THE LIE David Sneddon
SWEETS FOR MY SWEET The Searchers
TAKE MY BREATH AWAY Berlin
THE DRUGS DON'T WORK The Verve
THE NAME OF THE GAME Abba
THE REAL SLIM SHADY Eminem
THE STORY OF MY LIFE Michael Holliday
THE TEARS OF A CLOWN Smokey Robinson and the Miracles
THE WAY TO YOUR LOVE Hear'Say
THOSE WERE THE DAYS Mary Hopkin
THUNDER IN MY HEART Meck with Leo Sayer
TOWN CALLED MALICE* The Jam
UPTOWN TOP RANKING Althea and Donna
WALKING ON THE MOON The Police
WE'RE GOING TO IBIZA! The Vengaboys
WHAT'S ANOTHER YEAR Johnny Logan
WHEN A CHILD IS BORN Johnny Mathis
WITH A GIRL LIKE YOU The Troggs
WUTHERING HEIGHTS Kate Bush
YES SIR, I CAN BOOGIE Baccara
YOU CAN'T HURRY LOVE Phil Collins

17

A GROOVY KIND OF LOVE Phil Collins
ALL AROUND THE WORLD Oasis, Lisa Stansfield
A WORLD WITHOUT LOVE Peter and Gordon
CHRISTMAS ALPHABET Dickie Valentine
CLIMB EV'RY MOUNTAIN* Shirley Bassey
COWARD OF THE COUNTY Kenny Rogers
CRASHED THE WEDDING Busted
CRYING IN THE CHAPEL Elvis Presley and the Jordanaires
CUM ON FEEL THE NOIZE Slade
DEEPER UNDERGROUND Jamiroquai
DOCTORIN' THE TARDIS The Timelords
DO YOU REALLY LIKE IT DJ Pied Piper and the Masters of Ceremonies
D'YOU KNOW WHAT I MEAN? Oasis
EVERYTHING CHANGES Take That
FEELS LIKE I'M IN LOVE Kelly Marie
GONNA MAKE YOU A STAR David Essex
HERNANDO'S HIDEAWAY The Johnston Brothers
HOW DEEP IS YOUR LOVE Take That
IT'S ALMOST TOMORROW The Dreamweavers
JE T'AIME...MOI NON PLUS Jane Birkin and Serge Gainsbourg
LET LOVE LEAD THE WAY* Spice Girls
MY CAMERA NEVER LIES Bucks Fizz
MY OLD MAN'S A DUSTMAN Lonnie Donegan and his Group
PROFESSIONAL WIDOW Tori Amos

SHOW YOU THE WAY TO GO The
  Jacksons
SKWEEZE ME PLEEZE ME Slade
SOMETHING IN THE AIR
  Thunderclap Newman
TELL LAURA I LOVE HER Ricky Valance
THE CARNIVAL IS OVER The Seekers
THE FINAL COUNTDOWN Europe
THE LEGEND OF XANADU Dave Dee,
  Dozy, Beaky, Mick and Tich
THE MAN FROM LARAMIE Jimmy
  Young
THEME FROM S-EXPRESS S-Express
THE ROAD TO MANDALAY* Robbie
  Williams
THE SHOOP SHOOP SONG Cher
THE SPECIAL AKA LIVE! The Specials
  – EP
THE TWELFTH OF NEVER Donny
  Osmond
WE DON'T TALK ANYMORE Cliff
  Richard
WHAT TOOK YOU SO LONG Emma
  Bunton
WHEREVER I LAY MY HAT Paul Young

18
ANYTHING IS POSSIBLE Will Young
ARE 'FRIENDS' ELECTRIC? Tubeway
  Army
ARE YOU READY FOR LOVE Elton John
BORN TO MAKE YOU HAPPY Britney
  Spears
BROWN GIRL IN THE RING* Boney M
DANCING IN THE STREET David
  Bowie and Mick Jagger
DON'T LEAVE ME THIS WAY The
  Communards with Sarah Jane Morris
EVERY BREATH YOU TAKE The Police

FLYING WITHOUT WINGS Westlife
I CAN'T STOP LOVING YOU Ray
  Charles
I LOVE YOU LOVE ME LOVE Gary
  Glitter
I'M WALKING BEHIND YOU Eddie
  Fisher with Sally Sweetland
I THINK WE'RE ALONE NOW Tiffany
IT'S ONLY MAKE BELIEVE Conway
  Twitty
I WANNA BE THE ONLY ONE Eternal
  with BeBe Winans
I WILL ALWAYS LOVE YOU Whitney
  Houston
LET ME BE YOUR FANTASY Baby D
LOVE DON'T COST A THING
  Jennifer Lopez
MERRY XMAS EVERYBODY Slade
REACH OUT I'LL BE THERE The Four
  Tops
ROCK AROUND THE CLOCK Bill Haley
  and his Comets
SAME OLD BRAND NEW YOU a1
STRANGER IN PARADISE Tony Bennett
SWEET LIKE CHOCOLATE Shanks &
  Bigfoot
TELETUBBIES SAY EH-OH! Teletubbies
THE DAY THE RAINS CAME Jane
  Morgan
THE MINUTE YOU'RE GONE Cliff
  Richard
THERE MUST BE AN ANGEL The
  Eurythmics
THREE STEPS TO HEAVEN Eddie
  Cochran
THROW THESE GUNS AWAY*
  Dunblane
UNDER THE MOON OF LOVE
  Showaddywaddy

WHEN THE SUN GOES DOWN Arctic Monkeys

19

ALL I HAVE TO DO IS DREAM* The Everly Brothers

ALL THE THINGS SHE SAID tATu

ANYONE WHO HAD A HEART Cilla Black

BREAKFAST AT TIFFANY'S Deep Blue Something

CAN'T GIVE YOU ANYTHING The Stylistics

CHOCOLATE SALTY BALLS Chef

DON'T LOOK BACK IN ANGER Oasis

FERRY 'CROSS THE MERSEY The Christians with Holly Johnson, Paul McCartney, Gerry Marsden and Stock Aitken Waterman

HEY GIRL DON'T BOTHER ME The Tams

I'D DO ANYTHING FOR LOVE Meat Loaf

I KNEW YOU WERE WAITING Aretha Franklin and George Michael

I'M INTO SOMETHING GOOD Herman's Hermits

I ONLY HAVE EYES FOR YOU Art Garfunkel

I WANT TO HOLD YOUR HAND The Beatles

KNOWING ME, KNOWING YOU Abba

LONELY THIS CHRISTMAS Mud

LOVE CAN BUILD A BRIDGE Cher, Chrissie Hynde and Neneh Cherry with Eric Clapton

NEVER BE THE SAME AGAIN Melanie C with Lisa 'Left Eye' Lopes

NEVER GONNA GIVE YOU UP Rick Astley

SAVE YOUR KISSES FOR ME Brotherhood of Man

SHE WEARS RED FEATHERS Guy Mitchell

SMOKE GETS IN YOUR EYES The Platters

STRANGERS IN THE NIGHT Frank Sinatra

THE COMBINE HARVESTER The Wurzels

THE MILLENNIUM PRAYER Cliff Richard

THE WINNER TAKES IT ALL Abba

TOO MANY BROKEN HEARTS Jason Donovan

USE IT UP AND WEAR IT OUT Odyssey

WHAT A WONDERFUL WORLD* Louis Armstrong Orchestra

WHERE DID YOUR HEART GO* Wham!

WHO DO YOU THINK YOU ARE* Spice Girls

YES TONIGHT, JOSEPHINE Johnnie Ray

YOU'LL NEVER WALK ALONE The Crowd, Gerry and the Pacemakers, Robson Green and Jerome Flynn*

YOU'RE DRIVING ME CRAZY The Temperance Seven

20

ALL KINDS OF EVERYTHING Dana

BLOOD ON THE DANCE FLOOR Michael Jackson

CINDERELLA ROCKEFELLA Esther and Abi Ofarim

DON'T STAND SO CLOSE TO ME
The Police
FALLING IN LOVE WITH YOU UB40
FIRST CUT IS THE DEEPEST* Rod
Stewart
I DON'T FEEL LIKE DANCING Scissor
Sisters
IF TOMORROW NEVER COMES
Ronan Keating
I'M THE LEADER OF THE GANG Gary
Glitter
I NEED YOUR LOVE TONIGHT* Elvis
Presley and the Jordanaires
I WANT TO WAKE UP WITH YOU
Boris Gardiner
I WISH I WAS A PUNK ROCKER Sandi
Thom
JUST WALKING IN THE RAIN Johnnie
Ray
KNOCKIN' ON HEAVEN'S DOOR*
Dunblane
LET'S HAVE ANOTHER PARTY
Winifred Atwell
LIFE IS A ROLLERCOASTER Ronan
Keating
LITTLE THINGS MEAN A LOT Kitty
Kallen

MAKE IT EASY ON YOURSELF The
Walker Brothers
MAMA WEER ALL CRAZEE NOW Slade
OOH AAH...JUST A LITTLE BIT Gina G
THE FINGER OF SUSPICION Dickie
Valentine with the Stargazers
THE LAND OF MAKE BELIEVE Bucks
Fizz
THE LION SLEEPS TONIGHT Tight Fit
THE POOR PEOPLE OF PARIS Winifred
Atwell
THE ROUSSOS PHENOMENON
Demis Roussos – EP
THE WHITE CLIFFS OF DOVER*
Robson Green and Jerome Flynn
TIRED OF WAITING FOR YOU The
Kinks
WHATEVER WILL BE, WILL BE Doris
Day
WHEN WILL I SEE YOU AGAIN The
Three Degrees
WHY DO FOOLS FALL IN LOVE?
Frankie Lymon and the Teenagers
YOU'RE THE ONE THAT I WANT John
Travolta and Olivia Newton-John
YOU TO ME ARE EVERYTHING The
Real Thing

Arts – Visual Arts – ARTISTS

3
APT Ulricht
ARP Hans
BOL Ferdinand
COX David
DIX Otto
DOU Gerard

LAM Wilfredo
MOR Anthonis
RAY Man
UGO da Carpi
VOS Cornelis de

4
AVED Jacques
BLOW Godfrey
BOTH Jan
CANO Alonso
CARO Sir Anthony
CARR Emily

CIMA da Conegliano
COLE Thomas
COOK Beryl
CUYP Albert
DALI Salvador
DORÉ Gustave
DUFY Raoul
EMIN Tracey
ETTY William
FEKE Robert
GABO Naum
GILL Eric
GOES Hugo van der
GOYA Francisco
GROS Baron Antoine
HALS Frans
HEEM Jan
HONE Nathaniel
HUNT Holman
JOHN Augustus
JUEL Jens
KALF Willem
KLEE Paul
KOCH Joseph
LELY Sir Peter
MAES Nicolaes
MARC Franz
MASO di Banco
MIRÓ Joán
NASH John, Paul
OPIE John
PETO John
RENI Guido
ROSA Salvator
RUDE François
TROY Jean
TURA Cosima
VIEN Joseph
WEST Benjamin

WINT Peter de
WITZ Konrad
WOOD Christopher
ZICK Januarius

5
ALLAN David
ANDRE Carl
APPEL Karel
BACON Francis
BALLA Giacomo
BANKS Thomas
BARRY James
BARYE Antoine
BAZZI Giovanni
(or Sodoma)
BLAKE Sir Peter,
William
BOEHM Sir Joseph
BOSCH Hieronymus
BOUTS Dierick
BROWN Ford Madox,
Mather
BRUYN Barthel
BURRA Edward
CARRÀ Carlo
COROT Camille
COSTA Lorenzo
COTES Francis
CROME John
DACRE Winifred
DANBY Francis
DAVID Gerhard,
Jacques
DEGAS Edgar
DEVIS Arthur
DOLCI Carlo
DÜRER Albrecht
ERNST Max

FOLEY John Henry
FOPPA Vincenzo
FREUD Lucian
FRITH William
GELÉE Claude
(or Claude le Lorrain)
GOYEN Jan van
GROSZ George
HAYEZ Francesco
HIRST Damien
HOOCH Pieter de
(or Hoogh)
HOOGH Pieter de
(or Hooch)
ITTEN Johannes
JOHNS Jasper
KLIMT Gustav
LÉGER Fernand
LEWIS Wyndham
LIPPI Fra Filippo
LOTTO Lorenzo
LOWRY LS
LUINI Bernardino
(or Lovino)
MANET Édouard
MENGS Anton
METSU Gabriel
MONET Claude
MOORE Sir Henry
MOSES Anna Mary
(or Grandma Moses)
MUCHA Alphonse
MUNCH Edvard
NAVEZ François-Jospeh
NOLAN Sir Sidney
NOTKE Bernt
ORGAN Bryan
ORPEN Sir William
OUDRY Jean Baptiste

PALMA Jacopo
PEALE Charles
PENCZ Georg
PIERO della Francesca,
  di Cosimo
PIPER John
POZZO Andrea
PUGET Pierre
REDON Odilon
RICCI Marco,
  Sebastano
RILEY Bridget
RODIN Auguste
ROSSO Fiorentino
RUNGE Philipp Otto
SANTI Raffaello
  (or Raphael)
SARTO Andrea del
SCOTT David, Sir
  Peter, William
STAËL Nicolas de
STEEN Jan
SUVÉE Joseph-Benoît
TACCA Pietro
TOBEY Mark
TONKS Henry
VOUET Simon
VROOM Hendrick
WATTS George
ZOPPO Marco

6

ALBANI Francesco
BARKER Robert,
  Thomas
BATONI Pompeo
BEWICK Thomas
BOUDIN Eugène
BRAQUE Georges

BREGNO Andrea
BROWNE Hablot
  Knight
BUTLER Elizabeth,
  Reginald
CALLOT Jacques
CANOVA Antonio
CASSON AJ
CIBBER Caius Gabriel
CLOUET François
COELLO Claudio
COOPER Eileen
COPLEY John Singleton
COSWAY Richard
COTMAN John Sell
COYPEL Antoine
COZENS Alexander
CRESPI Giuseppe
DAWSON Henry
DERAIN André
DOBELL Sir William
DURAND Asher Brown
ERHART Gregor
FILDES Sir Luke
FOSTER Birket
FUSELI Henry
GEDDES Andrew
GIOTTO di Bondone
GIRTIN Thomas
GIULIO Romano
GLEYRE Charles
GLOVER John
GOUJON Jean
GREUZE Jean Baptiste
GUARDI Francesco
HECKEL Erich
HOUDON Jean Antoine
INGRES Jean
JAGGER Charles

KNIGHT Dame Laura
KRÜGER Franz
LÁSZLO Sir Philip
LA TOUR Georges de
LEGROS Alphonse
LESLIE Charles, Frank
LOVINO Bernardino
  (or Luini)
MARINI Marino
MARTIN Agnes,
  Homer Dodge, John,
  Kenneth, Mary
MERYON Charles
MICHEL Claude (or
  Clodion)
MILLES Carl
MILLET Jean François
MORONI Giovanni
MORRIS William
MYTENS Daniel
NEWMAN Barnett
OLIVER Isaac
OSTADE Adriaan van
PACHER Michael
PALMER Samuel
PANINI Giovanni
PIETRO Berrettini
PISANO Andrea,
  Giovanni, Nicola
RAMSAY Allan
RENOIR Pierre Auguste
RIBERA Jusepe de
RIVERA Diego
ROMNEY George
ROTHKO Mark
RUBENS Peter Paul
SACCHI Andrea
SANDBY Paul, Thomas
SERGEL Johan

SEURAT Georges
SIGNAC Paul
SISLEY Alfred
SLUTER Claus
SODOMA (or Giovanni
  Bazzi)
STOMER Matthias
STRANG William
STUBBS George
TANGUY Yves
TATLIN Vladimir
TISSOT James
TITIAN (or Tiziano
  Vecelli)
TOCQUÉ Louis
TROOST Cornelis
TURNER JMW
VANLOO Charles, Jean
  Baptiste
VASARI Giorgio
VERNET Claude,
  Horace
VERRIO Antonio
VERTUE George
VILLON Jacques
WALKER Dame Ethel
WARHOL Andy
WEENIX Jan
WEYDEN Rogier van
  der
WILKIE Sir David
WILSON Richard,
  Scottie
WITTEL Gaspar van
WRIGHT Joseph,
  Patience Lovell
YEAMES William

7

ALGARDI Alessandro
ALLSTON Washington
AMIGONI Jacopo
APPIANI Andrea
ASSELYN Jan
AUDUBON John
  James
BALDUNG Hans
BARBARI Jacopo de
BARLACH Ernst
BAROCCI Federico
BASSANO Jacopo da
BELLINI Giovanni
BERCHEM Nicholas
BERNINI Gian-Lorenzo
BINGHAM George
BÖCHLIN Arnold
BOLOGNA Giovanni
BONHEUR Rosa
BONNARD Pierre
BOUCHER François
BOURDON Sébastien
BROUWER Adriaen
BRUEGEL Pieter (or
  Brueghel)
CALIARI Paolo (or
  Veronese)
CALVERT Edward
CASSATT Mary
CELLINI Benvenuto
CÉZANNE Paul
CHAGALL Marc
CHARDIN Jean
CIMABUÉ Giovanni
CLODION (or Claude
  Michel)
CORINTH Lovis
COURBET Gustave

CRANACH Lucas
DALZIEL Edward
DAUMIER Honoré
DA VINCI Leonardo (or
  Leonardo)
DE VRIES Peter
EL GRECO
  (or Domenico
  Theotocopoulos)
EPSTEIN Sir Jacob
FERRARI Gaudenzio
FLAXMAN John
FOUQUET Jean
GAUGUIN Paul
GENTILE (or Gentile da
  Fabriano)
GIBBONS Grinling
GLEIZES Albert
GORMLEY Antony
HARTUNG Hans
HOBBEMA Meindert
HOCKNEY David
HOKUSAI Katsushika
HOLBEIN Hans
HOPPNER John
ISRAËLS Josef
KNELLER Sir Godfrey
LANCRET Nicolas
LAURANA Francesco
MACLISE Daniel
MAILLOL Aristide
MARTINI Simone
MATISSE Henri
MAZZOLA Girolamo
  (or Parmigiano)
MEMLINC Hans (or
  Hans Memling)
MEMLING Hans (or
  Hans Memlinc)

MILLAIS Sir John Everett
MORISOT Berthe
MORLAND George
MURILLO Bartolomé
NATTIER Jean Marc
ORCAGNA (or Andrea
  de Cione)
PASMORE Victor
PEETERS Clara
PHIDIAS
PICABIA Francis
PICASSO Pablo
PIGALLE Jean Baptiste
PITTONI Giovanni
POLLOCK Jackson
POURBUS Pieter
POUSSIN Nicolas
POYNTER Sir Edward
PRADIER James
QUARTON Enguerrand
QUELLIN Arnold
RAEBURN Sir Henry
RAPHAEL (or Raffaello
  Santi)
RIBALTA Francisco de
ROBUSTI Jacopo
  (or Tintoretto)
ROUAULT Georges
SARGENT John Singer
SICKERT Walter
SLEVOGT Max
SPENCER Sir Stanley
STEVENS Alfred
STROZZI Bernardo
TENIERS David
TENNIEL Sir John
TERBURG Gerard
  (or Gerard Terborch)
TIBALDI Pellegrino

TIEPOLO Giovanni
UCCELLO Paulo
UTRILLO Maurice
VALADON Suzanne
VAN DYCK Sir Anthony
  (or Sir Anthony
  Vandyke)
VANDYKE Sir Anthony
  (or Sir Anthony Van
  Dyck)
VAN EYCK Hubert
VAN GOGH Vincent
VAN RIJN Rembrandt
  (or Rembrandt)
VECELLI Tiziano
  (or Titian)
VERMEER Jan
VISCHER Peter
WATTEAU Antoine
WOOTTON John
WYNANTS Johannes
ZOFFANY Johann
ZUCCARO Federigo,
  Taddeo

8

AGOSTINO (or Agostino
  di Duccio)
AMMANATI
  Bartolommeo
ANNIGONI Pietro
ARMITAGE Edward,
  Kenneth
AVERCAMP Hendrik
BACICCIA Giovanni
BECKMANN Max
BELLOTTO Bernardo
BERTOLDO di Giovanni
BRABAZON Hercules

BRANCUSI Constantin
BRANGWYN Sir Frank
BRONZINO Agnolo
BRUEGHEL Pieter
  (or Pieter Bruegel)
CALLCOTT Sir Augustus
CARPEAUX Jean Baptiste
CARRACCI Annibale
CASTAGNO Andrea del
CHANTREY Sir Francis
CHRISTUS Petrus
CONTUCCI Andrea
  (or Sansovino)
COYSEVOX Antoine
DELAUNAY Sonia Terk
DRYSDALE Sir Russell
EASTLAKE Sir Charles
FALCONET Étienne
FRAMPTON Sir George
GHIBERTI Lorenzo
GIORDANO Luca
GIOVANNI (or Giovanni
  di Paolo)
GIRARDON François
GUERCINO (or Gian-
  Francesco Barbieri)
HEPWORTH Dame
  Barbara
HILLIARD Nicholas
JORDAENS Jacob
KIRCHNER Ernst Ludwig
LANDSEER Sir Edwin
LAWRENCE Jacob, Sir
  Thomas
LEONARDO
  (or Leonardo da Vinci)
LOMBARDO Pietro
MAGRITTE René
MALEVICH Kasimir

MANTEGNA Andrea
MARSHALL William
MASACCIO
MEEGEREN Han
MONTAGNA
Bartolomeo
MUNNINGS Sir Alfred
NEVINSON
Christopher
PERUGINO
PIRANESI Giambattista
PISSARRO Camille
PONTORMO Jacopo da
PURRMANN Hans
PYNACKER Adam
REYNOLDS Sir Joshua
RICHARDS Ceri
ROSSETTI Dante
Gabriel
ROTTMAYR Johann
ROUSSEAU Henri,
Théodore
RUÏSDAEL Jacob van
SARACENI Carlo
SASSETTA
SCHLÜTER Andreas
SERPOTTA Giacomo
SÉRUSIER Paul
SEVERINI Gino
SOLIMENA Francesco
SPRANGER
Bartholomeus
TERBORCH Gerard
(or Gerard Terburg)
TOPOLSKI Feliks
VERMEYEN Jan
VERONESE
(or Paolo Caliari)
VITTORIA Tommaso

VIVARINI Antonio,
Bartolommeo
VLAMINCK Maurice de
VUILLARD Édouard
WHISTLER James
McNeill, Rex
WHITELEY Brett
ZAMPIERI Domenico
(or Domenichino)
ZURBARÁN
Francisco de

9
ANTONELLO
(or Antonello
da Messina)
BARTHOLDI Auguste
BEARDSLEY Aubrey
BECCAFUMI Domenico
BLOEMAERT Abraham
CANALETTO
CONSTABLE John
CORREGGIO Antonio
DELACROIX Eugène
DELAROCHE Paul
DONATELLO
ELSHEIMER Adam
FABRITIUS Carel
FEUERBACH Anselm
FRAGONARD Jean
Honoré
GÉRICAULT Théodore
GHISLANDI Vittore
GIORGIONE
GREENAWAY Kate
GRÜNEWALD Isaak,
Matthias
HONTHORST Gerrit
KANDINSKY Wassily

KAUFFMANN Angelica
KOKOSCHKA Oskar
LANDOWSKI Paul
LANFRANCO Giovanni
MEŠTROVIĆ Ivan
MULTSCHER Hans
NICHOLSON Ben
NOLLEKENS Joseph
NORTHCOTE James
PECHSTEIN Max
PIAZZETTA Giovanni
PISANELLO Antonio
POLIAKOFF Serge
REMBRANDT
(or Rembrandt Van
Rijn)
ROUBILIAC Louis
SAENREDAM Pieter
SANSOVINO
(or Andrea Contucci)
SIQUEIROS David
Alfaro
STANFIELD Clarkson
STANZIONE Massimo
THORNHILL Sir James
TISCHBEIN Johann
VANDERLYN John
VELÁSQUEZ Diego
(or Diego Velázquez)
VELÁZQUEZ Diego
(or Diego Velásquez)
VETTRIANO Jack

10
ALMA-TADEMA Sir
Lawrence
ARCHIPENKO
Alexander
BANDINELLI Baccio

BAUMEISTER Willi
BERRUGUETE Pedro
BOTTICELLI Sandro
BOUGUEREAU William
BUONARROTI
  Michelangelo
  (or Michelangelo)
BURNE-JONES Sir
  Edward
CARAVAGGIO
CHAMPAIGNE
  Philippe de
DELLA PORTA Baccio
  (or Fra Bartolommeo)
GIACOMETTI Alberto
KENNINGTON Eric
  Henri
LIEBERMANN Max
LORENZETTI
  Ambrogio, Pietro
MODIGLIANI Amedeo
ORCHARDSON Sir
  William
PARMIGIANO (or
  Girolamo Mazzola)
PELLEGRINI Giovanni
POLLAIUOLO Antonio
POLYCLITUS
PRAXITELES
ROSSELLINO Antonio,
  Bernardo
ROWLANDSON Thomas
SCHWITTERS Kurt
SEBASTIANO
  (or Sebastiano del
  Piombo)
SIGNORELLI Luca
SQUARCIONE
  Francesco

SUTHERLAND Graham
TINTORETTO
  (or Jacopo Robusti)
TORRIGIANO Pietro
VANDERBANK John
VECCHIETTA
VERROCCHIO
  Andrea del
WALDMÜLLER
  Ferdinand
WESSELMANN Tom
WESTMACOTT Sir
  Richard
WINSTANLEY Henry
ZUCCARELLI Francesco

11
BARTOLOMMEO Fra
  (or Baccio della Porta)
DELLA ROBBIA Luca
DOMENICHINO (or
  Domenico Zampieri)
GENTILESCHI Orazio
PRIMATICCIO Francesco
SCHEEMAKERS Pieter
TERBRUGGHEN
  Hendrik
THORNYCROFT Sir
  Hamo
THORVALDSEN Bertel
VIGÉE LEBRUN Élisabeth

12
ALBERTINELLI Mariotto
DAVID D'ANGERS
  Pierre
FANTIN-LATOUR Henri
GAINSBOROUGH
  Thomas

LICHTENSTEIN Roy
MICHELANGELO
  (or Michelangelo
  Buonarroti)
PLEYDENWURFF Hans
RYSSELBERGHE
  Théo van
SASSOFERRATO
  Giovanni
WINTERHALTER Franz

13
ANDREA DE CIONE
  (or Orcagna)
DUCHAMP-VILLON
  Raymond
SÁNCHEZ COELLO
  Alonso

14
THEOTOCOPOULOS
  Domenico
  (or El Greco)
VALLAYER-COSTER Anne

15
ANDREA DA FIRENZE
CLAUDE LE LORRAIN
  (or Claude Gelée)
GIOVANNI DI PAOLO
  (or Giovanni)
LEONARDO DA VINCI
  (or Leonardo)
MODERSOHN-BECKER
  Paula
SCHMIDT-ROTTLUFF
  Karl
TOULOUSE-LAUTREC
  Henri de

16
AGOSTINO DI DUCCIO
PUVIS DE CHAVANNES Pierre
REMBRANDT VAN RIJN
(or Rembrandt)

17
GENTILE DA FABRIANO   (or Gentile)

18
ANTONELLO DA MESSINA
(or Antonello)

19
DUCCIO DE BUONINSEGNA
SEBASTIANO DEL PIOMBO
(or Sebastiano)

Arts – Visual Arts – ART TERMS

3
ART
GUM
HUE
INK
PEN

4
BUST
CARD
CHIP
DADA
DAUB
DRAW
ETCH
FORM
GLUE
ICON
IDOL
IKON
LIMN
NUDE
OILS
PLAN
POSE
TINT
TONE

VIEW
WASH

5
BOARD
BRUSH
CARVE
CHALK
CHART
CONTÉ
DECAL
DRAFT
DRYER
EASEL
FRAME
GENRE
GESSO
GLAZE
GRAPH
GROUP
HATCH
IDYLL
IMAGE
LIGHT
LINER
MODEL
MOUNT

MURAL
OP ART
PAINT
PANEL
PAPER
PASTE
PIN-UP
PRINT
PUTTO
ROUGH
ROUND
SCAPE
SCENE
SECCO
SEPIA
SHADE
SPECK
STUDY
STUMP
TITLE
TONDO
TRACE
UMBRA
VALUE
VIRTU
VOLET

6
BRONZE
CANVAS
CHROMA
COLOUR
CRAYON
CUBISM
DESIGN
DOODLE
FIGURE
FRESCO
GROUND
KIT-CAT
KITSCH
MARBLE
MARINE
MEDIUM
MEGILP
MOBILE
MOSAIC
NEEDLE
NIELLO
PALLET
PARIAN
PASTEL
PENCIL
POP ART

POSING
POSTER
RELIEF
ROCOCO
SCULPT
SHADOW
SKETCH
STATUE
STROKE
STUDIO
VALUES
VEDUTA

7
ACRYLIC
ART DECO
ATELIER
AUREOLE
BAROQUE
BAUHAUS
BOTTEGA
CAMAÏEU
CARTOON
CARVING
CLASSIC
COLLAGE
DADAISM

DIAGRAM	SCRAPER	KAKEMONO	CARDBOARD	STIPPLING
DIORAMA	SCUMBLE	LIKENESS	COLOURING	STRETCHER
DIPTYCH	SFUMATO	MANDORLA	DEPICTION	SYMBOLISM
DRAWING	SHADING	MAQUETTE	DESIGNING	TOWNSCAPE
ÉCORCHÉ	SITTING	MONOTINT	DISTEMPER	UNDERTINT
ENGRAVE	SPECKLE	MORESQUE	ENCAUSTIC	UNDERTONE
ETCHING	STABILE	MOVEMENT	ENGRAVING	VORTICISM
EXHIBIT	STENCIL	NAÏVE ART	FRESCOING	WOODBLOCK
FAUVISM	STIPPLE	NOCTURNE	GRISAILLE	WORK OF ART
FINE ART	SUBJECT	OIL PAINT	GROTESQUE	
FOLK ART	TABLEAU	ORIGINAL	LANDSCAPE	**10**
FRAMING	TACHISM	PAINTBOX	LAY FIGURE	ALTARPIECE
GALLERY	TEMPERA	PAINTING	LETTERING	ART NOUVEAU
GLAZING	TINTING	PASTORAL	LOW RELIEF	ASSEMBLAGE
GLYPTIC	TRACING	PENUMBRA	(or bas-relief)	AUTOMATISM
GOUACHE	VARNISH	PORTRAIT	MANNERISM	AVANT-GARDE
IMPASTO	VEHICLE	PREDELLA	MAULSTICK	BACKGROUND
LIMNING	VERISMO	SANGUINE	MEDALLION	CARICATURE
LINOCUT	WOODCUT	SEASCAPE	MEZZOTINT	CIRE PERDUE
MIMESIS		SKYSCAPE	MINIATURE	CLASSICISM
MONTAGE	**8**	STAFFAGE	MODERN ART	COMMISSION
MORDANT	ABSTRACT	STATUARY	MODERNISM	CROSS-HATCH
ORPHISM	ANAGLYPH	SYMMETRY	OBJET D'ART	DEFINITION
PALETTE	AQUATINT	TONALITY	OIL COLOUR	DOWNSTROKE
PATTERN	BOZZETTO	TRECENTO	OLD MASTER	DRAWING PIN
PAYSAGE	CHARCOAL	TRIPTYCH	OLEOGRAPH	FIGURATION
PICTURE	COLOSSUS	UPSTROKE	PEN-AND-INK	FOREGROUND
PIGMENT	DOODLING	WATERING	PORTRAYAL	HALF-LENGTH
PLASTIC	DRY POINT		POTBOILER	HIGH RELIEF
PREVIEW	ECCE HOMO	**9**	PRIMITIVE	KINETIC ART
PROFILE	FIGURINE	ALLA PRIMA	SCULPTING	MAINSTREAM
REALISM	FIXATIVE	ANTHEMION	SCULPTURE	MASTERWORK
RELIEVO	FROTTAGE	AQUARELLE	SCUMBLING	MINIMALISM
(or rilievo)	GRAFFITI	ARABESQUE	SERIGRAPH	MONOCHROME
RILIEVO	GRAPHICS	BAS-RELIEF	SKETCHING	MORBIDEZZA
(or	GROUPING	(or low	SKETCH PAD	OLEOGRAPHY
relievo)	HALF-TINT	relief)	SNOWSCAPE	ORDONNANCE
SCENERY	HATCHING	BEAUX ARTS	STATUETTE	PAINTBRUSH
SCOOPER	INTIMISM	BRUSHWORK	STILL LIFE	PENCILLING

PLASTICINE
PLASTICITY
POLYCHROME
RESOLUTION
RIVERSCAPE
SERIGRAPHY
SILHOUETTE
SILK SCREEN
SUPREMATISM
SURREALISM
TERRACOTTA
XYLOGRAPHY

11
ABSTRACT ART
ALTO-RILIEVO
BRUSH-STROKE
CAVO-RILIEVO
CEROPLASTIC
CHIAROSCURO
CINQUECENTO
COMPOSITION
DIVISIONISM
FÊTE GALANTE
FINGER-PAINT
GRAPHIC ARTS
LINE DRAWING
LOCAL COLOUR
MASTERPIECE
OIL PAINTING
PAPIÉR COLLÉ
PAPIÉR MÂCHÉ
PERSPECTIVE
PLASTER CAST
PLASTIC ARTS
POINTILLISM
PORTE-CRAYON
PORTRAITURE
POSTER PAINT

PRIMITIVISM
RENAISSANCE
RETROUSSAGE
ROMANTICISM
SCENOGRAPHY
SCULPTURING
SILVERPOINT
SOLID COLOUR
STENCILLING
TROMPE L'OEIL
WATERCOLOUR
WHOLE-LENGTH
WOODCARVING
ZOOMORPHISM

12
CHROMATICITY
COLOUR SCHEME
COUNTERPROOF
CREATIVE ARTS
DRAWING BOARD
DRAWING PAPER
DRAWING TABLE
ILLUMINATION
ILLUSTRATION
MEZZO-RILIEVO
MIDDLE GROUND
PALETTE KNIFE
PARIAN MARBLE
PASSEPARTOUT
PENCIL SKETCH
PICTURE FRAME
QUATTROCENTO
REPRODUCTION
SCRAPERBOARD
SELF-PORTRAIT
TRACING PAPER
VESICA PISCIS
WALL PAINTING

13
CROSS-HATCHING
EXPRESSIONISM
FLEMISH SCHOOL
IMPRESSIONISM
LINE ENGRAVING
NEOCLASSICISM
NEOPLASTICISM
POST-MODERNISM
RHYPAROGRAPHY
WOOD ENGRAVING

14
ACTION PAINTING
CONSTRUCTIVISM
FINGER-PAINTING
FORESHORTENING
KIT-KAT PORTRAIT
MIDDLE DISTANCE
PLASTER CASTING
PLASTER OF PARIS
REPRESENTATION
STEEL ENGRAVING
VANISHING POINT

15
CANVAS-STRETCHER
PRE-RAPHAELITISM
SELF-PORTRAITURE
THUMBNAIL SKETCH

16
ANTHROPOMORPHISM
PEN-AND-INK DRAWING
PORTRAIT PAINTING

17
POST-IMPRESSIONISM

Arts – Visual Arts – COLOURS & DYES

3	5	TAUPE	ROUCOU	VERMEIL
BAY	AMBER	TAWNY	RUSSET	XANTHIN
DUN	AZURE	TINGE	SALMON	
DYE	BEIGE	UMBER	SIENNA	**8**
HUE	BLACK	WHITE	SILVER	ALIZARIN
JET	BLUSH		SORREL	AMETHYST
RED	BROWN	**6**	TITIAN	BLOOD-RED
TAN	CORAL	ARGENT	VIOLET	BRICK-RED
	CREAM	AUBURN	YELLOW	BURGUNDY
4	EOSIN	AZO DYE		CARDINAL
ANIL	GRAIN	BISTRE	**7**	CAROTENE
BLUE	GREEN	BRONZE	ANILINE	CERULEAN
BUFF	GULES	CANARY	ANNATTO	CHESTNUT
CYAN	HAZEL	CERISE	BISCUIT	CINNAMON
DRAB	HENNA	CHROME	CARMINE	COLORANT
ECRU	IVORY	CLARET	CELADON	CONGO RED
FAWN	KHAKI	COBALT	CITRINE	DOVE GREY
GOLD	LEMON	COLOUR	CRIMSON	DYESTUFF
GREY	LILAC	COPPER	EMERALD	EAU DE NIL
JADE	LIVER	CYANIN	ETIOLIN	GUNMETAL
LAKE	LOVAT	DAMASK	FUCHSIN	HYACINTH
LIME	MAUVE	FALLOW	GAMBOGE	INDULINE
PINK	MOUSY	FLAVIN	GRIZZLE	IRON GREY
PLUM	OCHRE	INDIGO	JACINTH	JET BLACK
PUCE	OLIVE	KERMES	MAGENTA	LAVENDER
ROAN	PEACH	MADDER	MELANIN	LUTEOLIN
ROSE	ROUGE	MAROON	MUSTARD	MAGNOLIA
RUST	SABLE	MURREY	NACARAT	MAHOGANY
SAXE	SANDY	ORANGE	OLD GOLD	MAZARINE
TEAL	SEPIA	ORCEIN	OLD ROSE	MUSHROOM
TINT	SHADE	ORCHIL	PIGMENT	NAVY BLUE
TONE	SLATE	PASTEL	SAFFRON	ORPIMENT
VERT	SMALT	PURPLE	SINOPIA	PEA GREEN
WELD	STAIN	REDDLE	SKY BLUE	PRIMROSE
WOAD	SUEDE	RESEDA	TURACIN	PURPURIN

SANGUINE
SAP GREEN
SAPPHIRE
TINCTURE
VERDITER
VIRIDIAN

9
ALICE BLUE
AUBERGINE
BILIRUBIN
BLUE-BLACK
CARNATION
CHAMPAGNE
CHOCOLATE
COCHINEAL
COLOURANT
COLOURING
CURCUMINE
DYER'S WOAD
EUMELANIN
FIELD GREY
FLESH PINK
INDIAN RED
LAMP BLACK
LITHOPONE
MOSS GREEN
OLIVE DRAB
PEARL GREY
PHTHALEIN
PRIMULINE
RAW SIENNA
RHODAMINE
RHODOPSIN
ROYAL BLUE
SAGE GREEN
SLATE GREY
STEEL BLUE

STEEL GREY
TANGERINE
TURKEY RED
TURQUOISE
VERMILION
WHITE LEAD
ZINC WHITE

10
ANILINE DYE
AQUAMARINE
BILIVERDIN
BURNT OCHRE
BURNT UMBER
CHARTREUSE
COBALT BLUE
COQUELICOT
FLAKE WHITE
HELIOTROPE
MADDER-LAKE
OXFORD BLUE
PARIS GREEN
PEACH-BLOOM
RIFLE GREEN
ROSANILINE
SALMON PINK
TERRACOTTA

11
ANTHOCYANIN
BOTTLE GREEN
BURNT SIENNA
CARDINAL RED
CHLOROPHYLL
FLUORESCEIN
LAPIS LAZULI
NATTIER BLUE
PEACOCK BLUE

PHYCOCYANIN
SANG-DE-BOEUF
ULTRAMARINE
VENETIAN RED

12
AIR-FORCE BLUE
CANARY YELLOW
CHINESE WHITE
CHROME YELLOW
DAY-GLO COLOUR
ELECTRIC BLUE
EMERALD GREEN
LINCOLN GREEN
MIDNIGHT BLUE
NAPLES YELLOW
PRUSSIAN BLUE
QUINACRIDONE
TYRIAN PURPLE
VANDYKE BROWN
VISUAL PURPLE

13
CAMBRIDGE BLUE
GENTIAN VIOLET
MONASTRAL BLUE
PHYCOERYTHRIN
SCHEELE'S GREEN
TITANIUM WHITE

14
MONASTRAL GREEN
PHTHALOCYANINE

15
ALIZARIN CRIMSON

Arts – Visual Arts – PHOTOGRAPHERS

3
FOX Anna
ORR J Stephens
RAY Man

4
ARON Bill
BOWN Jane
CAPA Cornell, Robert
HAAS Ernst
KORN Arthur
LAND Edwin
MANN Sally
PAGE Tim
PENN Irving
PRAN Dith
RUFF Thomas

5
ADAMS Ansel, Eddie
ARBUS Diane
BALCH Reg
BARTH Uta
BLANK Gil
CAHUN Claude
CALLE Sophie
EVANS Walker
FISKE George
GÜLER Ara
HARDY Bert
JONES Steve
KARSH Yousuf
KORDA Alberto
MAYNE Roger
SIEFF Jeanloup
SUDEK Josef

YASUI Nakaji
ZERBE Jerome

6
ABBOTT Berenice
ARCHER Frederick
   Scott
ARNOLD Eve
AVEDON Richard
BAILEY David
BEATON Sir Cecil
BENSON Harry
DUPAIN Max
ERWITT Elliott
FENTON Roger
GENTHE Arnold
HIKOMA Ueno
LEIFER Neil
MADDOX Richard
MILLER Lee
MYDANS Carl
NIEPCE Nicéphore
PLICKA Frank
TALBOT William Fox
ULMANN Doris
WESTON Edward

7
BELLOCQ EJ
BURROWS Larry
CARROLL Lewis
CHAMOUX Jean
EASTMAN George
GOSSAGE John
HURRELL George
JUMONJI Bishin

NILSSON Lennart
SALOMON Erich
SEYMOUR David
SISKIND Aaron
TOSCANI Oliviero
WATKINS Carleton E

8
CREWDSON Gregory
DAGUERRE Louis
DOISNEAU Robert
ISHIMOTO Yasuhiro
KUWABARA Kineo
MATHEISL Willy
NACHTWEY James
PLÜSCHOW Guglielmo
SKOGLUND Sandy
VISHNIAC Roman

9
DAHL-WOLFE Louise
EGGLESTON William
FELDSTEIN Mark
LICHFIELD Earl Patrick
MCCARTNEY Linda
   – née Eastman
MUYBRIDGE Eadweard
PARKINSON Norman
ROBERTSON James
ROSENTHAL Joe
ROTHSTEIN Arthur
STIEGLITZ Alfred
VAN DER ZEE James

10
BOURBOULON Jacques

CUNNINGHAM
  Imogen
	12
	DEMARCHELIER Patrick
		14
		CARTIER-BRESSON
		  Jacques

11
FRIEDLANDER
  Lee
	13
	RENGER-PATZSCH
	  Albert	

Arts – Visual Arts – PHOTOGRAPHIC TERMS

4	METOL	BURNING	EXPOSURE
FILM	PHOTO	CLOSE-UP	FLASH-GUN
HYPO	PLATE	CYANINE	FOCUSING
IRIS	PRINT	DEVELOP	GELATINE
JPEG	PROOF	DODGING	HALATION
LENS	SHEET	ENPRINT	HOLOGRAM
MASK	SHOOT	FISHEYE	MOUNTANT
PACK	SLIDE	MONTAGE	NEGATIVE
REEL	SPOOL	OPALINE	PANORAMA
ROLL	STILL	PHOTO CD	PARALLAX
SCAN	XEROX	PICTURE	PHOTOFIT
SHOT		REPRINT	POLAROID
SNAP	**6**	RETOUCH	PORTRAIT
TAKE	CAMERA	SHUTTER	POSITIVE
TIFF	EXPOSE	TINTYPE	ROLL FILM
TINT	FILTER	VIDICON	SCANNING
X-RAY	QUINOL		SNAPSHOT
ZOOM	RED-EYE	**8**	SOLARISE
	RÉSEAU	AIRBRUSH	SQUEEGEE
5	RETAKE	APERTURE	VIGNETTE
ALBUM	SCREEN	CALOTYPE	WET PLATE
BLIMP	STUDIO	CASSETTE	ZOOM LENS
FIXER	TRIPOD	CONTRAST	
FLASH	UNIPOD	DARKROOM	**9**
FOCUS	VIEWER	DISC FILM	AIR BUBBLE
F-STOP		DRY PLATE	BOX CAMERA
IMAGE	**7**	EMULSION	CELLULOID
INSET	BELLOWS	ENLARGER	CHROMATIC

COLLODION
DEVELOPER
FLASH BULB
FLASH LAMP
HALF-PLATE
IMAGE FILE
MAGNIFIER
MEZZOTINT
MICROCOPY
MICROFILM
PAPARAZZI
PHOTOCALL
PHOTOCOPY
PHOTOGRAM
PHOTOSTAT
SAY CHEESE
SHEET FILM
SUBSTRATE
TELEPHOTO
WIDE-ANGLE
XENON LAMP

10
ACHROMATIC
ANASTIGMAT
ASTIGMATIC
CINE CAMERA
COLOUR FILM
DEVELOPING
DISC CAMERA
FLASHLIGHT
HELIOGRAPH
MEMORY CARD
MICRODRIVE
MICROFICHE
MONOCHROME
OVEREXPOSE
PHOTOGENIC

PHOTOGRAPH
PHOTOLITHO
PROCESSING
RESOLUTION
STANNOTYPE
VIEWFINDER
WHOLE PLATE
XEROGRAPHY

11
ACHROMATISM
ASTIGMATISM
AUTOGRAVURE
CHROMOGENIC
COMPOSITION
DEVELOPMENT
DIAPOSITIVE
DIGITAL FILE
ENLARGEMENT
FISHEYE LENS
HELIOGRAPHY
INTENSIFIER
PHOTOCOPIER
PHOTO FINISH
PHOTOGRAPHY
PHOTOMOSAIC
RANGEFINDER
ROTOGRAVURE
SILVER PRINT
SPEED CAMERA
UNDEREXPOSE

12
ANASTIGMATIC
BROMIDE PAPER
CAMERA LUCIDA
COLOUR FILTER
COLOUR SCREEN

CONTACT PRINT
DIGITAL IMAGE
DIGITAL PRINT
HELIOGRAVURE
MICROCOPYING
OVEREXPOSURE
PANCHROMATIC
PHOTOCOPYING
PHOTOGRAPHER
PHOTOGRAPHIC
PHOTOGRAVURE
PHOTOMONTAGE
PHOTO SESSION
QUARTER-PLATE
REPRODUCTION
SHUTTER SPEED
SOLARISATION
TIME EXPOSURE
TRANSPARENCY

13
ANASTIGMATISM
CAMERA OBSCURA
DAGUERREOTYPE
DIGITAL CAMERA
IRIS DIAPHRAGM
PINHOLE CAMERA
TELEPHOTO LENS
UNDEREXPOSURE
WIDE-ANGLE LENS

14
ALL-ROUND CAMERA
AUTOMATIC FOCUS
ORTHOCHROMATIC
POLAROID CAMERA
PUSH PROCESSING
SHUTTER RELEASE

SLIDE PROJECTOR
TELEPHOTOGRAPH
WATCH THE BIRDIE

15
ELECTRONIC FLASH
MICROPHOTOGRAPH

PHOTOGRAPH ALBUM
PHOTOJOURNALISM
PHOTOLITHOGRAPH
PHOTOMICROGRAPH
SHUTTER PRIORITY
TELEPHOTOGRAPHY

16
MICROPHOTOGRAPHY
PHOTOGRAPHIC FILM
PHOTOLITHOGRAPHY
PHOTO OPPORTUNITY

Arts – Visual Arts – **WORKS OF ART**
var = various artists

3
DAY Epstein
GAZ Freud
LIZ Warhol
PAN Epstein

4
BANC Manet
DAWN Michelangelo
HEAD Modigliani
MARS Velazquez
NOAH Bellini
NOON Michelangelo
RIMA Epstein

5
ASHES Munch
CACUS Poussin
CUPID Michelangelo,
  var
DANAË Klimt, Titian
DAVID Donatello,
  Michelangelo, var
DIANA Houdon
DOVES Hepworth

ENNUI Sickert
FUGUE Kandinsky
LA PIE Monet
MONEY Warhol
MOSES Michelangelo
MY BED Emin
NIGHT Epstein
PIÈTA Bellini,
  Michelangelo, var
SPRAY Lichtenstein
VENUS var
WHAAM! Lichtenstein

6
AURORA Guercino,
  Reni
DELUGE Uccello
FRIEZE Pollock
GALAXY Pollock
IRISES Van Gogh
LA RÊVE (or *The Dream*)
  Picasso
PINKIE Sir T Lawrence
SALOMÉ Donatello, var
SEARCH Pollock

SLAVES Michelangelo
SPRING Botticelli
TENORA Braque
THE KEY Pollock
THE WAR Dix
TORERO Picasso

7
ANGELUS Millet
ARCHAEON Hepworth
AREAREA Gauguin
ARTEMIS Rembrandt
AU PIANO Whistler
BACCHUS
  Michelangelo, var
BUBBLES Millais
CALVARY Chagall
CARBIDE Arp
DIPTYCH Poliakoff
ECSTASY Gill
GIRAFFE Dali
LA BELLA Titian
LA DANSE Carpeaux
LAOCOÖN El Greco,
  var

LE REPOS Manet
MADONNA var
MERCURY Bologna
NEPTUNE Ammanati
OLYMPIA Manet
OPHELIA Millais
PERSEUS Burne-Jones,
  Cellini
PIERROT Watteau
QUERINI Tiepolo
RAINBOW Rubens
REQUIEM Hepworth
SILENCE Fuseli
SPASIMO Raphael
SUICIDE Grosz
THE KISS Hayez, Klimt,
  Picasso, Rodin
THE LOCKS Constable
THE MILL Rembrandt
THE RAPE Cézanne
UGOLINO Carpeaux
VAMPIRE Munch
VENTANA Dali

8

ADMIRALS Lely
BLUE NUDE Picasso
CRUISING Cook
DORA MAAR Picasso
FESTIVAL Moore
GUERNICA Picasso
HERCULES Titian
HIGH LIFE Landseer
IN THE BOX Cassatt
LANDLADY Cook
LILY POND Monet
LION HUNT Delacroix
MILLBANK Turner

MISERERE Rouault
MONA LISA (or *La
  Gioconda*) Leonardo
MORPHEUS Houdon
PARADISE Tintorettto
TA MATETE Gauguin
THE CHAIR Van Gogh
THE DREAM (or *La Rêve*)
  Picasso,
  H Rousseau
THE ROOKS Staël
THE ROUND Pissarro
THE SNAIL Matisse
THE SWING Renoir
TRIPTYCH F Bacon
TWO FLAGS Johns
TWO NUDES Picasso
VOLTAIRE Houdon

9

A NEAT LAWN Hockney
ATOM PIECE Moore
CHURCHILL Sutherland
DINING OUT Cook
DONI TONDO
  Michelangelo
FISH MAGIC Klee
FORTITUDE Botticelli
HAYSTACKS Monet
HENRY VIII Holbein
HET PELSKE Rubens
LA MUSIQUE Matisse
LE GOURMET Picasso
LONGCHAMP Picasso
NORTH WIND Moore
ODALISQUE Ingres,
  Matisse
PARNASSUS Appiani

PRIMAVERA Botticelli
PYGMALION Burne-
  Jones
SAND HEAPS Sisley
SHIPWRECK Turner
STAG AT BAY Landseer
THE BRICKS
  (or *Equivalent VIII*)
  Andre
THE BRIDGE Munch
THE JOCKEY Toulouse-
  Lautrec
THE MACNAB Raeburn
THE MURDER Cézanne
THE READER Fragonard
THE SCREAM Munch
THE WINDOW Bonnard

10

ADAM AND EVE var
AN INTERIOR Hooch
AT THE PIANO
  Whistler
AT THE RACES Degas
BUCHENWALD Klimt
CALAIS PIER Turner
CONFESSION Poussin
DEDHAM VALE
  Constable
DEPOSITION Raphael,
  var
DULLE GRIET Brueghel
DYING SLAVE
  Michelangelo
FALSE START Johns
INSPIRATION Fragonard
LADY BRISCO
  Gainsborough

LA GIOCONDA Leonardo
  (or *Mona Lisa*)
LAPIN AGILE Utrillo
LAS MENINAS Velazquez
MISS FARREN Sir T Lawrence
MISS LINLEY Gainsborough
MRS SIDDONS Gainsborough
PEASANT MAN Van Gogh
SINGLE FORM Hepworth
STONEHENGE Turner
SUNFLOWERS Van Gogh
THE BATHERS Cézanne, Fragonard,
  Renoir
THE BLUE BOY Gainsborough
THE HAY WAIN Constable
THE REAPERS Monet
THE SKATERS Brueghel
THE THINKER Rodin
TWO FIGURES F Bacon
VISITATION Albertinelli

11

AU CHAT BOTTÉ Nicholson
CORNARD WOOD Gainsborough
CRUCIFIXION Dali, Michelangelo, var
DEMOISELLES Picasso
DOG ON A LEASH Balla
FAMILY OF MAN Hepworth
GATTAMELATA Donatello
JOIE DE VIVRE Matisse
LE JARDINIER Cézanne
MALVERN HALL Constable
MORNING HAZE Monet
MOULIN ROUGE Toulouse-Lautrec
OVER VITEBSK Chagall
PEACE AND WAR Rubens
SHIP OF FOOLS Bosch
STARRY NIGHT Van Gogh

THE MILKMAID Vermeer
THE NUDE MAJA Goya
VIEW OF DELFT Vermeer
WATERLILIES Monet

12

A STREET SCENE Lowry
AUTUMN RHYTHM Pollock
BEATA BEATRIX Rossetti
CAPTAIN CORAM Hogarth
CHILL OCTOBER Millais
CREOLE DANCER Matisse
FISHING BOATS Braque
FLATFORD MILL Constable
GRRRRRRRRRRR! Lichtenstein
ICONOGRAPHIA Van Dyck
JEANNE SAMARY Renoir
LOS CAPRICHOS Goya
MRS DAVENPORT Romney
OÙ ALLONS-NOUS? Gauguin
PEASANT DANCE Brueghel
RAPE OF EUROPA Titian
THE ANGRY SWAN Asselyn
THE BLIND GIRL Millais
THE CORNFIELD Constable
THE HORSE FAIR Bonheur
THE NAKED MAJA Goya
THE NIGHTMARE Fuseli
THE PIAZZETTA Canaletto
THE REHEARSAL Degas
THE SCAPEGOAT Hunt
THE SLAVE SHIP Turner
THE VIOLINIST Chagall
THE WATER MILL Hobbema
THREE DANCERS Picasso
TWO GENTLEMEN Reynolds
WINGED FIGURE Hepworth

13
A BIGGER SPLASH Hockney
AROUND THE FISH Klee
BENOIS MADONNA Leonardo
D'OÙ VENONS-NOUS? Gauguin
I AND THE VILLAGE Chagall
LES PARAPLUIES Renoir
MADDALENA DONI Raphael
MAISON DE PENDU Cézannne
PLACE DU TERTRE Utrillo
QUE SOMMES-NOUS? Gauguin
SIR THOMAS MORE Holbein
THE ASSUMPTION Titian, var
THE BLACK CLOCK Cézanne
THE DANCE CLASS Degas
THE DEPOSITION Rubens, var
THE ENTIRE CITY Ernst
THE HOLY FAMILY Murillo
THE LAST SUPPER Leonardo, var
THE NIGHT WATCH Rembrandt
THE PRAYING JEW Chagall
THE SHRIMP GIRL Hogarth
THREE MUSICIANS Picasso
WOMAN WITH A FAN Rembrandt

14
ANSIDEI MADONNA Raphael
A RAKE'S PROGRESS Hogarth
BEASTS OF THE SEA Matisse
BLACK AND VIOLET Kandinsky
DANCER AT THE BAR Degas
EQUIVALENT VIII (or *The Bricks*)
  Andre
FEMMES DE TAHITI Gauguin
HALT IN THE CHASE Watteau
LA DESSERTE ROSE Matisse
LA FOUGÈRE NOIRE Matisse
L'ÉGLISE D'AUVERS Van Gogh

MISS WILLOUGHBY Romney
MYSTIC NATIVITY Botticelli
NEBUCHADNEZZAR Blake
PEASANT WEDDING Brueghel
PORT OF ST MARTIN Utrillo
ROUEN CATHEDRAL Monet
SHOT RED MARILYN Warhol
SISTINE MADONNA Raphael
THE CAFÉ CONCERT Manet
THE CARD PLAYERS Cézanne
THE DANCE OF LIFE Munch
THE MORNING WALK Gainsborough
THE ROKEBY VENUS Velazquez
THE THREE GRACES Reynolds
THE YELLOW HOUSE Van Gogh
VENUS AND ADONIS Titian
VIEW ON THE STOUR Constable

15
APOLLO AND DAPHNE Bellini
AUTUMN IN BAVARIA Kandinsky
CORPSE AND MIRROR Johns
DEEP AND WET WATER Hockney
EARTHLY PARADISE Bosch
HEAD OF A YOUNG MAN Andrea
JUNGLE WITH A LION H Rousseau
LA GRANDE FAMILLE Magritte
MADONNA AND CHILD Leonardo,
  Moore, var
MARRIAGE À LA MODE Hogarth
MASSACRE AT CHIOS Delacroix
MR AND MRS ANDREWS
  Gainsborough
SEVEN SACRAMENTS Poussin
THE ANNUNCIATION Leonardo, var
THE BIRTH OF VENUS Botticelli,
  Rubens, var
THE DEATH OF WOLFE West

THE FEAST OF HEROD Donatello
THE GARDEN OF LOVE Rubens
THE GUITAR PLAYER Vermeer
THE HAPPY QUARTET H Rousseau
THE POTATO EATERS Van Gogh
THE THREE DANCERS Picasso
THE TOWER OF BABEL Brueghel
THE TRIBUTE MONEY Titian
TRANSFIGURATION Raphael, var
WHISTLER'S MOTHER Whistler
WINDSOR BEAUTIES Lely

16

A HARLOT'S PROGRESS Hogarth
AT THE MOULIN ROUGE Toulouse-
  Lautrec
CAMPBELL'S SOUP CAN Warhol
MONARCH OF THE GLEN Landseer
RESERVOIR AT HORTA Picasso
THE ANATOMY LESSON Rembrandt
THE DUCHESS OF ALBA Goya
THE FALL OF PHAETON Rubens
THE FORGE OF VULCAN Velazquez
THE GROSVENOR HUNT Stubbs
THE LAST JUDGEMENT
  Michelangelo, var
THE SINGING BUTLER Vettriano
THE SLEEPING GYPSY H Rousseau
THE VENUS OF URBINO Titian
TURQUOISE MARILYN Warhol

17

APOTHEOSIS OF SPAIN Tiepolo
CHRIST THE REDEEMER Landowski
COMING FROM THE MILL Lowry
COMING OUT OF SCHOOL Lowry

RAIN, STEAM AND SPEED Turner
THE DISASTERS OF WAR Goya
THE PROGRESS OF LOVE Fragonard

18

CECI N'EST PAS UNE PIPE Magritte
PAN AMONGST THE REEDS Böcklin
SALISBURY CATHEDRAL Constable
THE ABSINTHE DRINKER Manet
THE ANGEL OF THE NORTH
  Gormley
THE LIFE OF ST FRANCIS Giotto
THE LIGHT OF THE WORLD Hunt
THE STATUE OF LIBERTY Bartholdi

19

DEATH OF SARDANAPALUS Delacroix
LE DÉJEUNER SUR L'HERBE Manet
MUSIC IN THE TUILERIES Manet
THE BOYHOOD OF RALEIGH Millais
THE JUDGEMENT OF PARIS Etty,
  Rubens, var
THE LAUGHING CAVALIER Hals
THE SURRENDER OF BREDA
  Velazquez
THE VIRGIN OF THE ROCKS
  Leonardo
VIEW AND PLAN OF TOLEDO
  El Greco
WHEATFIELD WITH CROWS Van
  Gogh

20

THE ARNOLFINI PORTRAIT Van Eyck
THE FIGHTING TÉMÉRAIRE Turner

Buildings

Buildings – BUILDING & ARCHITECTURAL TERMS

3	BASE	NOOK	VOID	EAVES	OGIVE
BAY	BEAD	OGEE	WALL	ERECT	ORDER
COB	BEAM	PANE	WING	FLOOR	ORIEL
EYE	BOND	PIER		FLUTE	OVOLO
FUR	COVE	PILE	**5**	FRAME	PLATE
HIP	CUSP	PISÉ	ADOBE	GABLE	PORCH
KEY	DADO	PLAN	ANCON	GLASS	PUTTY
LAG	DECK	PLOT	ANNEX	GLYPH	PYLON
LUM	DOME	RAFT	ATTIC	GROIN	QUIRK
PUG	DOOR	REED	BAULK	GROUT	QUOIN
RAG	DRIP	ROOF	BLOCK	HELIX	RIDGE
RIB	DRUM	ROOM	BOARD	IONIC	ROUND
SET	FLAG	SITE	BRICK	JOIST	SHAFT
TIE	FOIL	SLAB	BUILD	LABEL	SLATE
	FRET	SLAT	COMPO	LEDGE	SLYPE
4	GROG	SPAR	CROWN	LEVEL	SOCLE
ADIT	JAMB	STOA	CRUCK	MOULD	SPIRE
APSE	LATH	STUD	CRYPT	NEWEL	SPLAY
ARCH	LEAD	TILE	DORIC	NICHE	STONE

STYLE	FILLET	PORTAL	**7**	LATHING
TABLE	FINIAL	PURLIN	ANNULET	LATTICE
TALON	FRIEZE	QUARRY	ARCHLET	LOW-RISE
TORUS	GIRDER	RAFTER	ARCHWAY	LUNETTE
TOWER	GOTHIC	RECESS	ART DECO	MANSARD
TRUNK	GUNITE	REGLET	AZULEGO	MASONRY
TUDOR	GUTTER	RETURN	BALCONY	MINARET
VAULT	GYPSUM	REVEAL	BAROQUE	MIRADOR
VERGE	HAUNCH	ROCOCO	BAUHAUS	MULLION
	HEADER	ROSACE	BONDING	NECKING
6	IMPOST	RUBBLE	CABLING	NOGGING
ABACUS	INFILL	RUSTIC	CAISSON	OUTWALL
ALCOVE	INVERT	SCOTIA	CAPITAL	PANTILE
ANNEXE	LANCET	SCREED	CEILING	PARAPET
ARCADE	LEDGER	SCROLL	CHIMNEY	PARQUET
ASHLAR	LIERNE	SEVERY	CLINKER	PLAFOND
ATRIUM	LINTEL	SOFFIT	CORBEIL	PLASTER
BATTEN	LISTEL	STAIRS	CORNICE	PLYWOOD
BILLET	LOGGIA	STOREY	COVELET	PORTICO
CASING	LOUVRE	STRING	CROCKET	PUGGING
CEMENT	MARBLE	STUCCO	DECKING	REEDING
COFFER	MATRIX	SUMMER	DIAGRAM	RESPOND
COLUMN	METOPE	TAENIA	DOORWAY	RIBBING
COPING	MODULE	TASSEL	DOUCINE	RIBWORK
CORBEL	MONIAL	THATCH	ECHINUS	RIDGING
CORNER	MORTAR	THRUST	ENTASIS	ROOFING
CORONA	MUTULE	TIE ROD	FEATHER	ROOFTOP
COURSE	NEEDLE	TILING	FESTOON	ROSETTE
COVING	NOSING	TIMBER	FLETTON	SEXFOIL
CRENEL	OFFSET	TORSEL	FLEURON	SHINGLE
CUPOLA	PALLET	TURRET	FRONTON	SHUTTER
DENTIL	PARGET	VALLEY	FURRING	SLATING
DRY ROT	PARPEN	VOLUTE	GAMBREL	SOLDIER
EXEDRA	PATERA	WATTLE	GLAZING	SQUINCH
FAÇADE	PERRON	WINDOW	HIP ROOF	STEEPLE
FACING	PILLAR	XYSTUS	HOUSING	SUPPORT
FASCIA	PLINTH		LACUNAR	TAILING
FILLER	PODIUM		LAGGING	TAMBOUR

TELAMON
TERRACE
TESSERA
TIE BEAM
TRACERY
TRANSOM
TREFOIL
TRIMMER
TRUMEAU
VERANDA
WALLING

8
ABUTMENT
AIR BRICK
AIRSHAFT
ASBESTOS
ASTRAGAL
BAGUETTE
BALUSTER
BRATTICE
BUILDING
BUTTRESS
CARYATID
CASEMENT
CENTRING
CINCTURE
CLOISTER
COLONIAL
CONCRETE
DOG-TOOTH
ENTRESOL
EPISTYLE
ERECTION
EXTRADOS
FIRE CLAY
FLAT ROOF
FLOORING

FOLIATED
FOOTINGS
FRONTAGE
GABLE END
GARGOYLE
GEORGIAN
GROINING
GROUTING
HIGH-RISE
HOUSETOP
INTRADOS
KEYSTONE
KING POST
MOULDING
OGEE ARCH
OPEN-PLAN
OVERSAIL
PALMETTE
PEDESTAL
PEDIMENT
PENT ROOF
PILASTER
PILEWORK
PINNACLE
PLATFORM
PROPYLON
PROSTYLE
PUNCHEON
RAGSTONE
RED-BRICK
ROCAILLE
ROCK WOOL
ROOF-TREE
SEMI-DOME
SHUTTERS
SKEW ARCH
SKEWBACK
SKYLIGHT

SPANDREL
SPRINGER
STAIRWAY
STRINGER
STUDDING
TECTONIC
TERRAZZO
TOPSTONE
TRIGLYPH
TYMPANUM
VAULTING
VERANDAH
VICTORIAN
VOMITORY
VOUSSOIR

9
AGGREGATE
ALABASTER
ANGLE IRON
ARCHIVOLT
ASHLARING
BANQUETTE
BATH STONE
BAY WINDOW
BONDSTONE
BOW WINDOW
BRICKWORK
BRUTALISM
CAPE DUTCH
CARTOUCHE
CHIPBOARD
CLAPBOARD
COLONNADE
CONSTRUCT
CROSS-BEAM
CROWN POST
CROW STEPS

CURTILAGE
CYMA RECTA
DECASTYLE
DECORATED
DRIPSTONE
DUCKBOARD
DUTCH TILE
EARTHWORK
ELEVATION
EMBRASURE
EXTENSION
FIRE BRICK
FLOOR PLAN
FREESTONE
GOTHICISM
GUTTERING
HARDBOARD
HEXASTYLE
HOOD MOULD
HYPOCAUST
IMBRICATE
INFILLING
LINENFOLD
MEZZANINE
MODILLION
MULTIFOIL
NEO-GOTHIC
OCTASTYLE
ONION DOME
PALLADIAN
PANTILING
PARGETING
PARTITION
PARTY WALL
PERISTYLE
PINEAPPLE
POZZOLANA
PRINCIPAL

QUEEN ANNE
QUEEN POST
RIDGE TILE
ROOF LIGHT
ROUGHCAST
SANDSTONE
SCAGLIOLA
SHINGLING
STAIRCASE
STAIRWELL
STANCHION
STONEWORK
STRETCHER
STRUCTURE
STYLOBATE
THATCHING
TROCHILUS
WAGON-ROOF
WALLBOARD
WALL PLATE

10
ARCHITRAVE
ART NOUVEAU
ATTIC ORDER
BALUSTRADE
BARGEBOARD
BRICK-BUILT
BROWNSTONE
CAVITY WALL
CHIMNEY POT
CINQUEFOIL
CLERESTORY
COLLAR BEAM
CORBELLING
CORINTHIAN
DAMP COURSE
DORIC ORDER

DUCKBOARDS
FAN TRACERY
FEATHERING
FENESTELLA
FIBREBOARD
FIELDSTONE
FIRST FLOOR
FLOORBOARD
FOUNDATION
FRENCH ROOF
GROUND PLAN
HAMMER BEAM
HIPPED ROOF
INSULATION
IONIC ORDER
ITALIANATE
JERKIN HEAD
JERRY-BUILT
LANCET ARCH
NORMAN ARCH
ORDONNANCE
PEBBLE-DASH
PENDENTIVE
PENTASTYLE
PLATE GLASS
PROJECTION
PROPYLAEUM
QUATREFOIL
RIDGE PIECE
ROMANESQUE
ROSE WINDOW
SADDLEBACK
SASH WINDOW
SCROLLWORK
SETTLEMENT
SHEET GLASS
SHUTTERING
SPLIT-LEVEL

STEREOBATE
SUBSIDENCE
SUMMER TREE
TETRASTYLE
THIRD FLOOR
TRABEATION
VOMITORIUM
WAGON VAULT
WATER SPOUT
WINDOWPANE
WINDOW SILL

11
BARREL VAULT
BEAVERBOARD
BROACH SPIRE
CINQUECENTO
COPING STONE
CORBEL TABLE
CORNERSTONE
CURTAIN WALL
CYMA REVERSA
DODECASTYLE
ENGLISH BOND
ENTABLATURE
FAN VAULTING
FIRST STOREY
FLEMISH BOND
FLOORBOARDS
FRENCH DOORS
FOUNDATIONS
GAMBREL ROOF
GROUND FLOOR
GUTTA PERCHA
ICHNOGRAPHY
IMBRICATION
MANSARD ROOF
NEO-GEORGIAN

OEIL-DE-BOEUF
ORIEL WINDOW
PLASTERWORK
RIB VAULTING
ROOFING TILE
SCAFFOLDING
SECOND FLOOR
STILTED ARCH
STORM WINDOW
STRINGBOARD
THIRD STOREY
WINDOW FRAME
WINDOW GLASS

12
ARCHITECTURE
BUILDING LINE
BUILDING SITE
BREASTSUMMER
CHIMNEY STACK
CLINKER BLOCK
CLINKER BRICK
CONSTRUCTION
DILAPIDATION
DORMER WINDOW
EARLY ENGLISH
FENESTRATION
FRONTISPIECE
FROSTED GLASS
GEODESIC DOME
HOOD MOULDING
INVERTED ARCH
LANCET WINDOW
LATTICE FRAME
LOUVRE WINDOW
PALLADIANISM
PLASTERBOARD
PREFABRICATE

RECESSED ARCH
SECOND STOREY
SPANDREL WALL
STAINED GLASS
STRING COURSE
WEATHERBOARD

13
ARCHITECTURAL
CHIMNEY BREAST
COMPASS WINDOW
CRENELLATIONS
DILAPIDATIONS
DOUBLE GLAZING
ENCAUSTIC TILE
FRENCH WINDOWS
FERRO-CONCRETE
GOTHIC REVIVAL

LATTICE GIRDER
MACHICOLATION
PERPENDICULAR
PORTLAND STONE
SEGMENTAL ARCH
SOUNDPROOFING
STRETCHER BOND
TRIUMPHAL ARCH
WATTLE AND DAUB

14
BROWNFIELD SITE
CASEMENT WINDOW
CENTRAL HEATING
CORRUGATED IRON
ENCAUSTIC BRICK
FLYING BUTTRESS
GREENFIELD SITE

LONGS AND SHORTS
PORTLAND CEMENT
PREFABRICATION
SHOULDERED ARCH
SUPERSTRUCTURE
WORKING DRAWING

15
CORINTHIAN ORDER
DAMP-PROOF COURSE
FOUNDATION STONE
HANGING BUTTRESS
INSULATING BOARD
LOAD-BEARING WALL
PARQUET FLOORING
WEATHERBOARDING

Buildings – DWELLINGS & SHELTERS

3
COT
DEN
HUT
PAD

4
BARN
BUTT
CASA
CAVE
CRIB
DIGS
DRUM
FARM

FLAT
GÎTE
HALL
HIDE
HOLE
HOME
LOFT
PILE
SEAT
SEMI
SHED
TENT
YURT

5
ABODE
ADOBE
BOOTH
BOTHY
CABIN
CONDO
CROFT
DACHA
FINCA
HOUSE
HOVEL
IGLOO
KIOSK
LODGE

MANOR
MANSE
PLACE
RANCH
ROOMS
SHACK
STALL
STAND
TEPEE
TUPIK
VILLA

6
BEDSIT
BILLET

BUNKER
CABANA
CASTLE
CHALET
DUGOUT
DUPLEX
GARAGE
GAZEBO
GRANGE
GUNYAH
LEAN-TO
MAISON
MUD HUT
PALACE
PREFAB

QUINTA
REFUGE
SHANTY
TEEPEE
WIGWAM

7
BASTIDE
CABOOSE
CARAVAN
CARPORT
CHÂTEAU
COTTAGE
FLATLET
GRANARY

HIDEOUT
KIBBUTZ
KIBITKA
KOLKHOZ
MANSION
MARQUEE
PENSION
PUP TENT
RECTORY
RETREAT
SCHLOSS
SHELTER

8
BARRACKS
BELL TENT
BUILDING
BUNGALOW
CRASH PAD
DIGGINGS
DOMICILE
DWELLING
HACIENDA
HIDEAWAY
HOME FARM
HOTHOUSE
ICE HOUSE
LODGINGS
LOG CABIN
LOVE NEST
OUTHOUSE
PAVILION
QUARTERS
RONDAVEL

SHAMIANA
TENEMENT
VICARAGE
WOODSHED

9
ALMSHOUSE
APARTMENT
BEDSITTER
BELVEDERE
BOATHOUSE
BUNKHOUSE
COALHOUSE
DOSSHOUSE
DUTCH BARN
FARMHOUSE
FARMSTEAD
FLOPHOUSE
GATEHOUSE
HERMITAGE
HOMESTEAD
HOUSE-BOAT
LONGHOUSE
NISSEN HUT
PALAFITTE
PARSONAGE
PENTHOUSE
RESIDENCE
REST-HOUSE
SANCTUARY
SENTRY BOX
TITHE BARN
TOLLBOOTH
TOLLHOUSE

TOWN HOUSE
TREE HOUSE

10
BATHING HUT
BUS SHELTER
COACH HOUSE
DOWER HOUSE
FRAME HOUSE
GARDEN SHED
GLASSHOUSE
GREENHOUSE
GUEST HOUSE
HABITATION
LIGHTHOUSE
MAISONETTE
MANOR HOUSE
PIED-À-TERRE
PRESBYTERY
QUONSET HUT
TABERNACLE

11
CONDOMINIUM
COUNTRY SEAT
DAK BUNGALOW
HUNTING SEAT
OUTBUILDING
SCHOOLHOUSE
SERVICE FLAT
SHOOTING BOX
STATELY HOME
SUMMERHOUSE
TIED COTTAGE

12
BACHELOR FLAT
COUNCIL HOUSE
COUNTRY HOUSE
HIGH-RISE FLAT
HUNTING LODGE
LAKE DWELLING
LODGING HOUSE
MANSION HOUSE
PILE DWELLING
PORTER'S LODGE
ROOMING HOUSE
TELEPHONE BOX

13
ACCOMMODATION
ANCESTRAL HOME
BOARDING HOUSE
DWELLING HOUSE
HIGH-RISE BLOCK
OPEN-PLAN HOUSE
SHOOTING LODGE

14
AIR-RAID SHELTER
BATHING MACHINE
BED-SITTING ROOM
FALLOUT SHELTER
TELEPHONE KIOSK

15
ANDERSON SHELTER
DUPLEX APARTMENT
SPLIT-LEVEL HOUSE

Buildings – EATING & DRINKING PLACES

3	POSADA	POT-HOUSE	RESTAURANT
BAR	SALOON	SNACK BAR	ROTISSERIE
INN	TAVERN		STEAKHOUSE
PUB		**9**	
	7	BEERHOUSE	**11**
4	AUBERGE	BRASSERIE	COACHING INN
CAFÉ	CANTEEN	CAFETERIA	COFFEE HOUSE
DIVE	CARVERY	CHOPHOUSE	EATING HOUSE
KHAN	CHINESE	COFFEE BAR	PUBLIC HOUSE
	GIN MILL	ESTAMINET	
5	MILK BAR	FREE HOUSE	**12**
GRILL	SHEBEEN	GIN PALACE	CARAVANSERAI
HOWFF	TAVERNA	GRILL ROOM	
JOINT	TEA ROOM	ROADHOUSE	**13**
LOCAL	TEA SHOP	SPEAKEASY	TRANSPORT CAFÉ
SERAI	WINE BAR	TAP-HOUSE	
		TEA HOUSE	**15**
6	**8**	TEA ROOMS	ICE-CREAM PARLOUR
BISTRO	ALEHOUSE	TRATTORIA	
BOOZER	CRÊPERIE		**16**
EATERY	GIN JOINT	**10**	LICENSED PREMISES
INDIAN	HOSTELRY	COFFEE SHOP	
KNEIPE	PIZZERIA	CURRY HOUSE	

Buildings – Famous Buildings & Sites – ANCIENT STONE MONUMENTS
In England unless stated. Also see Archaeological Sites

5	HAFOTY Wales	DROMROE S Ireland
AVISO Italy	ORWELL Scotland	GURTEEN S Ireland
COATE	PLANÀS France	HIRNANT Wales
FOSSA Italy		LONG MEG
	7	NEWTYLE Scotland
6	ACHMORE Scotland	PORLOCK
CARNAC France	AVEBURY	TEERGAY S Ireland
FORGES France	BERCUÍN Spain	TISBURY

WENDRON

8
ARBOR LOW
ARDBLAIR Scotland
ARDGROOM S Ireland
BALLYNOE N Ireland
BOHONAGH S Ireland
DRUMMORE Scotland
HAMNA VOE Scotland
LLANBEDR Wales
FERNACRE
STENEHED Sweden
STENNESS Scotland
SWINSIDE
WOODSIDE Scotland

9
ALMENDRES Portugal
BEAGHMORE N Ireland
BROOMRIGG
CALLANISH Scotland
CHEW STOKE
DANBY RIGG
DOOM RINGS Scotland
GLASSONBY
HALTADANS Scotland

KILCASKAN S Ireland
LEIGH DOWN
LITTLE MEG
SHIAN BANK Scotland
STANYDALE Scotland

10
BJØRKETORP Sweden
BROUGHDERG
   N Ireland
CAIRNFAULD Scotland
FORTINGALL Scotland
KILSPINDIE Scotland
SAINT-DENEC France
SHERBERTON
STONEHENGE
TROED Y RHIW Wales
UPPER EARME
YELLOWMEAD

11
COOLCLEVANE
   S Ireland
PITSCANDLIE Scotland
POBULL FHINN
   Scotland
TORHOUSEKIE Scotland

TREEN COMMON

12
DRIZZLECOMBE
MERRY MAIDENS
OFFERTON MOOR
REANASCREENA
   S Ireland

13
MITCHELL'S FOLD
RING OF BRODGAR
   Scotland
SHRONEBIRRANE
   S Ireland

14
CLOGHASTUKANE
   S Ireland
TWELVE APOSTLES

15
KINGSTON RUSSELL
NETTLEHOLE RIDGE
ROLLRIGHT STONES
STEINTANZ BELLIN
   Germany

Buildings – Famous Buildings & Sites – CASTLES (British Isles)
In England unless stated

4
BIRR S Ireland
COCH Wales
COWD N Ireland
DEAL

DEAN Scotland
DRUM Scotland
ETAL
FAST Scotland
HOLT

LEAP S Ireland
O'DEA S Ireland
PEEL Isle of Man
RABY
ROSS S Ireland

TRIM S Ireland

5
ADAIR N Ireland
AYDON

BARRA Scotland
BLAIR Scotland
BOWES
BURGH
CAHIR S Ireland
CAREW Wales
CHIRK Wales
CLARA S Ireland
COITY Wales
CONWY Wales
CORBY
CORFE
CROFT
DOUNE Scotland
DOVER
DUART Scotland
ELCHO Scotland
EWLOE Wales
FLINT Wales
FYVIE Scotland
HAGGS Scotland
HEVER
HOWTH S Ireland
HURST
LEEDS
LEWES
MOYRY N Ireland
POWIS Wales
SLANE S Ireland
TENBY Wales
TULLY N Ireland
UPNOR
WHITE Wales

6
AIRLIE
BODIAM
BOLTON

BRODIE Scotland
BROUGH
BUNGAY
BUTLER S Ireland
CAMBER
CASHEL S Ireland
CAWDOR Scotland
DUBLIN S Ireland
DUDLEY
DUFFUS Scotland
DUNBOY S Ireland
DURHAM
EDZELL Scotland
GLAMIS Scotland
GWYDYR Wales
HAILES Scotland
HUNTLY Scotland
LUDLOW
LUMLEY
LYMPNE
MAIDEN
MALLOW S Ireland
MORTON Scotland
NENAGH S Ireland
NEWARK + Scotland
NORHAM
NORRIS
NUNNEY
OAKHAM
ODIHAM
OGMORE Wales
ORFORD
PENHOW Wales
PICTON Wales
RAGLAN Wales
RIPLEY
ROSLIN Scotland
ROTHES Scotland

RUTHIN Wales
SKREEN N Ireland
SPYNIE Scotland
STROME Scotland
TIORAM Scotland
TOTNES
WALDEN
WALMER
WEOLEY

7
AFFLECK Scotland
ALNWICK
APPLEBY
ARUNDEL
ATHENRY S Ireland
BALLOCK Scotland
BARNARD
BEESTON
BELFAST N Ireland
BELVOIR
BERWICK
BLARNEY S Ireland
BRAEMAR Scotland
BRAMBER
BRODICK Scotland
BULLOCK S Ireland
CADBURY
CAISTER
CARBURY S Ireland
CARDIFF Wales
CHILHAM
COMPTON
CRATHES Scotland
CULZEAN Scotland
DENBIGH Wales
DESMOND S Ireland
DINEFWR Wales

DONEGAL S Ireland
DOUGLAS Scotland
DROMORE S Ireland
DUNDRUM N Ireland
DUNLUCE N Ireland
DUNSTER
EASTNOR
FARNHAM
GILLING
GLENAPP Scotland
GROSNEZ Channel Is
HARLECH Wales
KISIMUL Scotland
LINCOLN
LISMORE S Ireland
LYDFORD
MAYBOLE Scotland
NORWICH
PENRHYN Wales
PENRICE Wales
PENRITH
PRUDHOE
QUINTIN N Ireland
SCOTNEY
SIZERGH
SKIPSEA
SKIPTON
ST MAWES
SUDELEY
TAUNTON
THREAVE Scotland
TOROSAY Scotland
TUTBURY
WARDOUR
WARWICK
WEOBLEY Wales
WINDSOR

8
ABERDOUR Scotland
ARDGLASS N Ireland
ARDVRECK Scotland
BALMORAL Scotland
BALVENIE Scotland
BAMBURGH
BERKELEY
BOLSOVER
BOTHWELL Scotland
BROUGHAM
BROUGHTY Scotland
BRYN BRAS Wales
BUNCRANA S Ireland
BUNRATTY S Ireland
BURLEIGH Scotland
CARLISLE
CHEPSTOW Wales
CORGARFF Scotland
CRICHTON Scotland
DELGATIE Scotland
DRYSLWYN Wales
DUNROBIN Scotland
DUNVEGAN Scotland
EYNSFORD
FARLEIGH
GIRNIGOE Scotland
GOODRICH
GROSMONT Wales
HADLEIGH
HASTINGS
HELMSLEY
HERTFORD
KIDWELLY Wales
KILCHURN Scotland
KILKENNY S Ireland
KILLINEY S Ireland
LEAMANEH S Ireland

LONGTOWN
MALAHIDE S Ireland
MAYNOOTH S Ireland
MENSTRIE Scotland
MONMOUTH Wales
MOUNTJOY N Ireland
MUCHALLS Scotland
NEIDPATH Scotland
PEMBROKE Wales
PEVENSEY
PITCAPLE Scotland
PORTLAND
RHUDDLAN Wales
RICHMOND
ROTHESAY Scotland
SALTWOOD
SINCLAIR Scotland
SOUTHSEA
ST DONAT'S Wales
STIRLING Scotland
STOKESAY
STORMONT N Ireland
TAMWORTH
THETFORD
TINTAGEL
TIVERTON
TOLQUHON Scotland
URQUHART Scotland
YARMOUTH

9
ALLINGTON
ARDTERMON S Ireland
BALLYMOON S Ireland
BALLYMOTE S Ireland
BEAUMARIS Wales
BICKLEIGH
BLACKBURY

BLACKNESS Scotland
BORTHWICK Scotland
BROUGHTON
CARDONESS Scotland
CARSLUITH Scotland
CILGERRAN Wales
CLAYPOTTS Scotland
CLEARWELL
CLITHEROE
CRAIGSTON Scotland
CRICCIETH Wales
CROOKSTON Scotland
CULCREUCH Scotland
DARTMOUTH
DOLBADARN Wales
DONINGTON
DRUMINNOR Scotland
DUMBARTON Scotland
DUNGUAIRE Scotland
DUNIMARIE Scotland
DUNKERRON S Ireland
DUNNOTTAR Scotland
EDINBURGH Scotland
ELIZABETH Channel Is
FINDLATER Scotland
GLENVEAGH S Ireland
GUILDFORD
HERMITAGE Scotland
INVERARAY Scotland
INVERNESS Scotland
KILDRUMMY Scotland
KIMBOLTON
KINGSWEAR
LANCASTER
LAUGHARNE Wales
LAURISTON Scotland
LLAWHADEN Wales
LOCH LEVEN Scotland

LOUGHMORE S Ireland
MANORBIER Wales
MIDDLEHAM
MUNCASTER
PEMBRIDGE
PENDENNIS
PENDRAGON
PICKERING
POWDERHAM
RESTORMEL
ROCHESTER
SCALLOWAY Scotland
SHERBORNE
SKENFRITH Wales
SPOFFORTH
ST ANDREWS Scotland
STRANRAER Scotland
TANTALLON Scotland
TONBRIDGE
URLANMORE S Ireland
WARKWORTH

10

AUCHINDOUN
   Scotland
AUGHNANURE S Ireland
BALLYNAHOW S Ireland
CAERNARFON Wales
CAERPHILLY Wales
CARROWDORE
   N Ireland
CASTLE ACRE
COLCHESTER
CRAIGIEVAR Scotland
DEDDINGTON
DONNINGTON
DRUMLANRIG Scotland
FOULKSRATH S Ireland

GLENBUCHAT Scotland
HARTLEBURY
HUNTERSTON Scotland
INVERLOCHY Scotland
KENILWORTH
KIRKISTOWN N Ireland
LAUNCESTON
LLANSTEFAN Wales
MACLELLAN'S Scotland
NOTTINGHAM
OKEHAMPTON
OLDERFLEET N Ireland
ORCHARDTON Scotland
PORCHESTER
ROCKINGHAM
SHREWSBURY
ST BRIAVELS
TULLYNALLY S Ireland
WATERMOUTH
WINCHESTER

11

ABERYSTWYTH Wales
BALLINLOUGH S Ireland
BERKHAMSTED
CARISBROOKE
CARNASSERIE Scotland
CASTLE DROGO
CASTLE KIRKE S Ireland
CASTLE OF MEY
   Scotland
CASTLE UPTON
   N Ireland
CHARLEVILLE S Ireland
CONISBROUGH
CRAIGMILLAR Scotland
CRAIGNETHAN Scotland
DOLWYDDELAN Wales

EILEAN DONAN Scotland
ENNISKILLEN N Ireland
FRAMLINGHAM
GRIMSTHORPE
LINDISFARNE
LUDGERSHALL
MONT ORGUEIL Channel Is
OYSTERMOUTH
RAVENSBURGH
RAVENSCRAIG Scotland
SCARBOROUGH
TATTERSHALL
THIRLESTANE Scotland

12
BACONSTHORPE
BALLINCOLLIG S Ireland
BALLYGRENNAN S Ireland
CAERLAVEROCK Scotland
CARREG CENNEN Wales
CASTLE CORNET Channel Is
CASTLE FRASER Scotland
CASTLE HOWARD
CASTLE RISING
CHOLMONDELEY
CHRISTCHURCH
DUNSTAFFNAGE Scotland

DUNSTANBURGH
FOTHERINGHAY
HERSTMONCEUX
HUNTINGTOWER Scotland
LULLINGSTONE
SISSINGHURST
ST CATHERINE'S

13
BALLYNALACKEN S Ireland
CARRICKFERGUS N Ireland
CASTLE BALFOUR N Ireland
CASTLE STALKER Scotland
CHIDDINGSTONE
HAVERFORDWEST Wales
KNARESBOROUGH
SHERIFF HUTTON
TOWER OF LONDON

14
ASHBY-DE-LA-ZOUCH
BALLYNACARRIGA S Ireland
CASTLE CAMPBELL Scotland

15
CASTLE OF OLD WICK Scotland
DALTON-IN-FURNESS

Buildings – Famous Buildings & Sites – CASTLES (World)

4
BRAN Romania
EGER Hungary
HÄME Finland
LVIV Ukraine
RIGA Latvia

5
BABAK Iran
BOHUS Sweden
BOLDT USA
BREDA Netherlands
FREYR Belgium

GNIEW Poland
KARAK Jordan
NAMUR Belgium
ORAVA Slovakia
RAYEN Iran
TARTU Estonia

TOMAR Portugal
TORUN Poland
TURKU Finland

6
ALAMUT Iran
GORMAZ Spain
HEARST USA
KYBURG Switzerland
MASYAF Syria
OLESKO Ukraine
PRAGUE Czech Rep
SOROCA Moldova
TARIFA Spain
VYBORG Russia

7
BEERSEL Belgium
BOURTZI Greece
CHILLON Switzerland
COLDITZ Germany
CURWOOD USA
DUNDURN Canada
EGESKOV Denmark
KANTARA Cyprus
KOPORYE Russian
KREMLIN Russia
LARNACH New
  Zealand
MALBORK Poland
OOIDONK Belgium
RUDKHAN Iran
RUMBEKE Belgium
ST OLAF'S Finland
UPPSALA Sweden

8
AKERSHUS Norway
ALMOUROL Portugal
AUERBACH Germany
BELCOURT USA
BORGHOLM Sweden
BOUILLON Belgium
BURG ELTZ Germany
BURG MAUS Germany
GANDOLFO Italy
GATCHINA Russia
GILLETTE USA
GLEICHEN Germany
KRONBORG Denmark
SZCZECIN Poland
YENIKALE Ukraine

9
ARAGONESE Italy
BELVEDERE USA
BERGENHUS Norway
GEDIMINAS Lithuania
SAN JAVIER Spain
SFORZESCO Italy

10
BRATISLAVA Slovakia
CHÂTEAU D'IF France
CHENONCEAU France
HEIDELBERG Germany
MUIDERSLOT
  Netherlands
ST HILARION Cyprus

11
CHAPULTEPEC Mexico

GRAVENSTEEN
  Belgium
RAMBOUILLET France
VORDINGBORG
  Denmark

12
CHÂTEAU D'USSÉ
  France

13
ALBRECHTSBURG
  Germany
CHÂTEAU D'OIRON
  France

14
CASTRO URDIALES
  Spain
CASTRUM DANORUM
  Estonia
CHÂTEAU D'ANGERS
  France
CHÂTEAU DE BLOIS
  France
CHRISTIANSBORG
  Denmark
NEUSCHWANSTEIN
  Germany

15
CHÂTEAU D'AMBOISE
  France
CHÂTEAU DE CHINON
  France

Buildings – Famous Buildings & Sites – CATHEDRALS (British Isles)
In England unless stated

3
ELY

4
COBH S Ireland
CORK S Ireland
PEEL Isle of Man
TRIM S Ireland
TUAM S Ireland

5
DERBY
DERRY N Ireland
ENNIS S Ireland
FERNS S Ireland
NEWRY N Ireland
RIPON
SLIGO S Ireland
TRURO
WELLS

6
ARMAGH N Ireland
BANGOR Wales
BRECON Wales
CARLOW S Ireland
CASHEL S Ireland
DUBLIN S Ireland
DURHAM
EXETER
GALWAY S Ireland
OXFORD
RAPHOE S Ireland

7
ARUNDEL
BALLINA S Ireland
BRECHIN Scotland
BRISTOL
CARDIFF Wales
CHESTER
CLOGHER S Ireland
DORNOCH Scotland
DROMORE N Ireland
DUNKELD Scotland
GLASGOW Scotland
KILDARE S Ireland
KILLALA S Ireland
NEWPORT Wales
LINCOLN
LISBURN N Ireland
LISMORE S Ireland
NORWICH
SALFORD
ST ASAPH Wales
ST PAUL'S
THURLES S Ireland
WREXHAM Wales

8
ABERDEEN Scotland
BRADFORD
CARLISLE
COVENTRY
DUNBLANE Scotland
HEREFORD
KILKENNY S Ireland
KILLALOE S Ireland
KIRKWALL Scotland

LEIGHLIN S Ireland
LIMERICK S Ireland
LLANDAFF Wales
LONGFORD S Ireland
LOUGHREA S Ireland
MONAGHAN S Ireland
PLYMOUTH
ST ALBAN'S
ST DAVID'S Wales

9
BLACKBURN
BRENTWOOD
EDINBURGH Scotland
GUILDFORD
KILFENORA S Ireland
KILLARNEY S Ireland
LANCASTER
LEICESTER
LICHFIELD
LIVERPOOL
MULLINGAR S Ireland
NEWCASTLE
ROCHESTER
SALISBURY
SHEFFIELD
SOUTHWARK
ST ANDREWS Scotland
WAKEFIELD
WATERFORD S Ireland
WORCESTER

10
BIRMINGHAM
CANTERBURY

CHELMSFORD
CHICHESTER
GLOUCESTER
MANCHESTER
NOTTINGHAM
PORTSMOUTH
SKIBBEREEN S Ireland
WINCHESTER

11
DOWNPATRICK
  N Ireland

ENNISCORTHY
  S Ireland
ENNISKILLEN N Ireland
LETTERKENNY S Ireland
NORTHAMPTON
ROSSCARBERY
  S Ireland
WESTMINSTER

12
CLONMACNOISE
  S Ireland

PETERBOROUGH

13
BURY ST EDMUNDS

15
BALLAGHADERREEN
  S Ireland

Buildings – Famous Buildings & Sites – MUSEUMS & ART GALLERIES

3
JOS Jos, Nigeria
URE Reading

4
BODE Berlin
FOGG Cambridge,
  Mass
HUNT Limerick
TATE Liverpool, St Ives

5
ALAMO San Antonio,
  Texas
BOWES Durham
BRERA Milan
BURKE Seattle, Wash
CLUNY Paris
CONDÉ Chantilly
FREER Washington
  DC

PRADO Madrid
RÖHSS Gothenburg
USHER Lincoln

6
BENAKI Athens
DAHESH New York
DELPHI Delphi
EUREKA! Halifax
FERENS Hull
GANDHI Delhi
HARRIS Preston
JÓRVIK York
KIASMA Helsinki
LOUVRE Paris
MAEGHT Paris
SUDLEY Liverpool
UFFIZI Florence
ULSTER Belfast
WALKER Liverpool

7
BEAMISH nr Gateshead
BRITISH London
DULWICH London
EPHESUS Seljuk, Turkey
HAYWARD London
HERBERT Coventry
OLYMPIC Lausanne
PICASSO Barcelona
PUSHKIN Moscow
SAATCHI London
SCIENCE London
SHAANXI Xian
TOPKAPI Istanbul
VATICAN Rome
WHITNEY New York
ZWINGER Dresden

8
ATKINSON Southport
BARBICAN London

BROOKLYN New York
CABLE CAR San Francisco
CORINIUM Cirencester
CROMWELL Huntingdon
FOLKWANG Essen
HUMBOLDT Berlin
PERGAMON Berlin
THACKRAY Leeds

9
ACROPOLIS Athens
ASHMOLEAN Oxford
COURTAULD London
CRANBROOK Detroit, Mich
FITCHBURG Fitchburg, Mass
FORT CONDE Mobile, Alabama
GROSVENOR Chester
HENRY FORD Dearborn, Mich
HERMITAGE St Petersburg
MARMOTTAN Paris
NICHOLSON Sydney
STEDELIJK Amsterdam
TRETYAKOV Moscow
WHITWORTH Manchester

10
AMBROSIANA Milan
BLISTS HILL nr Ironbridge
CAPITOLINE Rome
GUGGENHEIM Bilbao, New York
GULBENKIAN Lisbon
MILESTONES Basingstoke
MUSÉE RODIN Paris
PITT RIVERS Oxford
POWERHOUSE Sydney
TATE MODERN London
VERSAILLES Paris

11
BRIDGESTONE Tokyo
FITZWILLIAM Cambridge
GETTY CENTER Los Angeles
IMPERIAL WAR Duxford, London
KETTLE'S YARD Cambridge
MUSÉE D'ORSAY Paris
RIJKSMUSEUM Amsterdam
TATE BRITAIN London

12
METROPOLITAN New York
NATIONAL ARMY London
POLDI PEZZOLI Milan
ROYAL ONTARIO Toronto
RUSSELL-COTES Bournemouth
SCIENCEWORKS Melbourne

13
BOVINGTON TANK Bovington,
    Dorset
EXPLORATORIUM San Francisco
GAYER-ANDERSON Cairo
NATIONAL MOTOR Beaulieu
NATIONAL PRINT Dublin
OSKAR REINHART Winterthur
ROYAL AIR FORCE Cosford,
    Shropshire, Hendon
STAATSGALERIE Stuttgart

14
ALTE PINAKOTHEK Munich
CARTWRIGHT HALL Bradford
NATIONAL PALACE Taipei
NATURAL HISTORY London
POMPIDOU CENTRE Paris

15
BARBER INSTITUTE Birmingham
CABINET WAR ROOMS London
FRICK COLLECTION New York
NATIONAL GALLERY London
NATIONAL RAILWAY York
NATIONAL TRAMWAY Crich,
  Derbyshire

16
GALLERIA BORGHESE Rome
NATIONAL MARITIME London

17
ACCADEMIA DELL'ARTE Florence
BURRELL COLLECTION Glasgow
KUNSTHISTORISCHES Vienna

MUSÉE DE L'ORANGERIE Paris
NATIONAL WATERWAYS Gloucester
VICTORIA AND ALBERT London
WALLACE COLLECTION London

18
DEUTSCHE GUGGENHEIM Berlin
NATIONAL WATERFRONT Swansea
PHILLIPS COLLECTION Washington
  DC

19
ALBERTINE COLLECTION Vienna

20
SMITHSONIAN INSTITUTE
  Washington DC

Buildings – Famous Buildings & Sites – NATIONAL PARKS

3
BUI Ghana

4
BUKK Hungary
KRKA Croatia
MERU Kenya
MOLE Ghana
SAPO Liberia
TARA Yugoslavia
YOHO Canada
ZION USA

5
AINOS Greece
AWASH Ethiopia

BANFF Canada
CHOBE Botswana
GAUJA Latvia
GOMBE Tanzania
HAMRA Sweden
KAFUE Zambia
KAROO South Africa
MLJET Croatia
NYIKA Malawi
PIRIN Bulgaria
REISA Norway
TSAVO Kenya

6
ABISKO Sweden
ACADIA USA

ARCHES USA
BROADS UK
CIRCEO Italy
DINDER Sudan
ÉCRINS France
ETOSHA Namibia
EXMOOR UK
JASPER Canada
KRUGER South Africa
MUDDUS Sweden
MÜRITZ Germany
ORDESA Spain
PINDOS Greece
PRÉSPA Greece
SIMIEN Ethiopia
TRAKAI Lithuania

VITOSA Bulgaria
VUNTUT Canada
WAPUSK Canada

7
ABRUZZO Italy
AULAVIK Canada
BIG BEND USA
DJERDAP Yugoslavia
GLACIER USA,
   Canada
JASMUND Germany
KASUNGU Malawi
KISMAYO Somali
KORNATI Croatia
LAHEMAA Estonia
LLOGARA Albania
OLYMPIC USA
OLYMPUS Greece
OULANKA Finland
REDWOOD USA
RETEZAT Romania
RONDANE Norway
SAGUARO USA
SIBILOI Kenya
SOÚNION Greece
STELVIO Italy
TIVEDEN Sweden
TRIGLAV Slovenia
VANOISE France
YANKARI Nigeria
ZAKOUMA Chad
ZAMBEZI Zimbabwe

8
AGGTELEK Hungary
BADLANDS USA
BISCAYNE USA

BONTEBOK South
   Africa
CALABRIA Italy
CATOCTIN USA
CÉVENNES France
DARTMOOR UK
FORILLON Canada
HARGEYSA Somali
HOCH HARZ Germany
KOOTENAY Canada
KRKONOSE Czech Rep
MARSABIT Kenya
PORT-CROS France
SIRMILIK Canada
SUTJESKA Bosnia-
   Herzegovina
WIND CAVE USA
WOLINSKI Poland
YOSEMITE USA

9
CAVADONGA Spain
CONNEMARA Irish Rep
ELK ISLAND Canada
GARAJONAY Spain
GLENVEAGH Irish Rep
GROS MORNE Canada
HALEAKALA USA
KIANG WEST Gambia
KILLARNEY Irish Rep
MASAI MARA Kenya
MESA VERDE USA
NEW FOREST UK
NOCKBERGE Austria
RUWENZORI Uganda
SERENGETI Tanzania
SNOWDONIA UK
TIMANFAYA Spain

VOYAGEURS USA
ZEMAITIJA Lithuania

10
ÅNDERDALEN Norway
BØRGEFJELL Norway
CAIRNGORMS UK
CRATER LAKE USA
CROSS RIVER Nigeria
DOVREFJELL Norway
EVERGLADES USA
GARPHYTTAN Sweden
GRAND TETON USA
GRASSLANDS Canada
GREAT BASIN USA
HOHE TAUERN Austria
HOT SPRINGS USA
ISLE ROYALE USA
JOSHUA TREE USA
KAMPINOSKI Poland
LA MAURICIE Canada
LEMMENJOKI Finland
LOCH LOMOND UK
MERCANTOUR France
ØVRE PASVIK Norway
PACIFIC RIM Canada
POINT PELÉE Canada
SHENANDOAH USA
SKAFTAFELL Iceland
SOUTH DOWNS UK
VELUWEZOOM
   Netherlands

11
BIEBRZANSKI Poland
CAPITOL REEF USA
DEATH VALLEY USA
DRY TORTUGAS USA

GRAND CANYON USA
JOTUNHEIMEN Norway
KOBUK VALLEY USA
LINNANSAARI Finland
MAMMOTH CAVE USA
ØVRE DIVIDAL Norway
PINEDA-GERÊS Portugal
RUSENSKI LOM Bulgaria
SKULESKOGEN Sweden
VYSOKÉ TATRY Slovakia
YELLOWSTONE USA

12
COTO DE DOÑANA Spain
GRAN PARADISO Italy
LAKE DISTRICT UK
MOUNT RAINIER USA
PEAK DISTRICT UK
SEHLABATHEBE South Africa
URHO KEKKONEN Finland

13
BERCHTESGADEN Germany
BRECON BEACONS UK
HORSESHOE BEND USA
NORTH CASCADES USA
ØVRE ANARJOKKA Norway

ROCKY MOUNTAIN USA
STABBURSDALEN Norway
VIRGIN ISLANDS USA

14
BRUCE PENINSULA Canada
DWINGELDERVELD Netherlands
HARDANGERVIDDA Norway
NORTHUMBERLAND UK
QUEEN ELIZABETH Uganda
UNTERES ODERTAL Germany/Poland
YORKSHIRE DALES UK

15
CARLSBAD CAVERNS USA
JOKULSARGLJUFUR Iceland
NORTH YORKS MOORS UK
PETRIFIED FOREST USA
TABLAS DE DAIMIEL Spain

16
MANYAS-KUSCENNETI Turkey
WICKLOW MOUNTAINS Irish Rep

18
PEMBROKESHIRE COAST UK

Buildings – Famous Buildings & Sites – STATELY HOMES (British Isles)
In England unless stated

5
DEENE Brudenell
    family
KNOLE Sackville family
STOWE

6
ASCOTT
CADHAY
ERDDIG
    Wales

FASQUE Gladstone family
UPPARK

7
ALTHORP Earl Spencer

BOWHILL Duke of
  Buccleuch
COPPINS
GIBSIDE
HAWORTH Brontë
  Sisters
HILL TOP Beatrix Potter
MAX GATE Thomas
  Hardy
OWLETTS
PLAS TEG Wales
STANDEN
THE VYNE
TOWNEND
TRERICE

8
ASHRIDGE
ASKE HALL Dundas
  family
BATEMAN'S Rudyard
  Kipling
BEAUPARC S Ireland
CHEQUERS Prime
  Minister
CLIVEDEN
COTEHELE
CRAGSIDE
DALEMAIN
EYE MANOR
EYTHROPE
HALE PARK
HAM HOUSE
ICKWORTH
ILAM HALL
LANGWELL Scotland
LONGLEAT Marquess
  of Bath

LUTON HOO
LYME PARK
MOOR PARK
PLAS MAWR Wales
RED HOUSE William
  Morris
SOMERLEY Earl of
  Normanton
TONG HALL
UGBROOKE Clifford
  family
WELL VALE

9
ASTON HALL
BECCA HALL
BRANTWOOD John
  Ruskin
CHARTWELL Sir Winston
  Churchill
CHAVENAGE
CHEVENING Foreign
  Secretary
CLAREMONT Robert
  Clive
DOWN HOUSE
  Charles Darwin
DUFF HOUSE Scotland
EATON HALL Duke of
  Westminster
ELTON HALL
FOTA HOUSE S Ireland
GUNBY HALL
HALL PLACE
HIGHCLERE Earl of
  Carnarvon
HIGHGROVE Prince
  Charles

KEW PALACE Royal
  Family
KILLERTON
KIRBY HALL
LYTES CARY
MOYNS PARK
NEWBY HALL
  Compton family
OXON HOATH
SPEKE HALL
SYON HOUSE Duke of
  Northumberland
TYTUP HALL

10
ABBOTSFORD Scotland,
  Sir Walter Scott
ALBURY PARK
  Newdegate family
ARBURY HALL
ASTLEY HALL
BLEAK HOUSE
  Charles Dickens
  (formerly Fort
  House)
BRETBY HALL Earl of
  Chesterfield
BROADLANDS Earl
  Mountbatten
CANNON HALL
CHATSWORTH
  Duke of Devonshire
CLOUDS HILL
  TE Lawrence
COBHAM HALL
DORNEYWOOD
  Cabinet Minister
DYRHAM PARK

EUSTON HALL
FIRLE PLACE Gage family
GORHAMBURY
GREYS COURT
HADDO HOUSE Scotland
HADDON HALL Duke of Rutland
HAGLEY HALL Baron Lyttelton
HALL'S CROFT Shakespeare's
  daughter Susanna
HEATON HALL
HOLKER HALL
LEVENS HALL Bagot family
LUCAN HOUSE S Ireland
MANDERSTON Scotland
  Baron Palmer
PLAS NEWYDD Wales
  Marquess of Anglesey
QUENBY HALL
RAGLEY HALL Marquess of Hertford
RYDAL MOUNT William Wordsworth
SANDON HALL Earl of Harrowby
SHANDY HALL Laurence Sterne
SHARDELOES
SPRINGHILL N Ireland
STARGROVES
SUTTON PARK
TATTON HALL
TREGOTHNAN Boscawen family
UPTON HOUSE
WALCOT HALL Robert Clive
WESTON PARK

11
ALTON TOWERS
ANTONY HOUSE
APSLEY HOUSE Duke of Wellington
AUBOURN HALL
BAGSHOT PARK Earl of Wessex

BANTRY HOUSE S Ireland
BARDON MANOR
BASING HOUSE
BEESTON HALL
BELTON HOUSE
BOWOOD HOUSE Lansdowne family
BOYNTON HALL
BRAMALL HALL
BREDE PALACE
BROCKET HALL
CAVICK HOUSE
CHINGLE HALL
CLANDON PARK
CULTRA MANOR N Ireland
DOVE COTTAGE William Wordsworth
FENTON HOUSE
GAYTON MANOR
GLYNDE PLACE
GREAT DIXTER
HALTON HOUSE Royal Air Force
HOLKHAM HALL Coke family
HORTON COURT
LAMPORT HALL Isham family
LANGLEY HALL
MARSTON HALL
OAKWELL HALL
ORDSALL HALL
ORMESBY HALL
OXBURGH HALL
PALACE HOUSE Lord Montagu
PARHAM HOUSE
PAXTON HOUSE Scotland
PINKIE HOUSE Scotland
PRESTON HALL
QUEBEC HOUSE General Wolfe
RIBSDEN HOLT
SANDRINGHAM Royal Family
SAWSTON HALL

SCONE PALACE Scotland, Earl of
    Mansfield
SEWERBY HALL
SHAW'S CORNER GB Shaw
SHIBDEN HALL
SHIPTON HALL
SHUTE BARTON
STONOR HOUSE Stonor family
SUDBURY HALL
SUTTON COURT
TABLEY HOUSE
TAPLOW COURT
TAPTON HOUSE George Stephenson
TARVIT HOUSE Scotland
TYNTESFIELD
URRAND HOUSE
WILTON HOUSE
WINTON HOUSE Scotland
WIMPOLE HALL
WINSLOW HALL
WOBURN ABBEY Duke of Bedford
WOTTON HOUSE

12
ACHESON HOUSE Scotland
ARRETON MANOR
ASHDOWN HOUSE
ATHELHAMPTON
BASILDON PARK
BENTHALL HALL
BURNS COTTAGE Robert Burns
CAMERON HOUSE Tobias Smollett
CLAYDON HOUSE
CLIFTON HOUSE N Ireland
CORSHAM COURT
CROXTETH HALL
DITCHLEY PARK
DRAYTON MANOR Sir Robert Peel

FELBRIGG HALL
FULHAM PALACE Bishop of London
    (until 1973)
GATCOMBE PARK Princess Anne
GAULDEN MANOR
GLYNDEBOURNE John Christie
HAMPTON COURT Cardinal Wolsey,
    Henry VIII
HARDWICK HALL
HEWELL GRANGE
HOUGHTON HALL Sir Robert Walpole
IGHTHAM MOTE
KENTWELL HALL
KENWOOD HOUSE
KINGSTON LACY Bankes family
KIRKLEES HALL
LICKEY GRANGE Herbert Austin
MAESMAWR HALL Wales
MANSION HOUSE Lord Mayor of
    London
NORMANBY HALL
OSBORNE HOUSE Queen Victoria
PARNHAM HOUSE
RAMMERSCALES Scotland
RENISHAW HALL Sitwell family
ROUSHAM HOUSE
SALTRAM HOUSE
SHELDON MANOR
STANFORD HALL Cave family
TEMPLE NEWSAM Ingram family
THURNHAM HALL
TOSELAND HALL
WEST STOW HALL
WHITTON COURT
WOLLATON HALL
WORTHAM MANOR
WROXTON ABBEY
WYNNSTAY HALL

13
ADLINGTON HALL
ATTINGHAM PARK
BLETCHLEY PARK
BLICKLING HALL
BOSCOBEL HOUSE
BREAMORE HOUSE Hulse family
BURGHLEY HOUSE Marquess of Exeter
CARLTON TOWERS Duke of Norfolk
CARLYLE'S HOUSE Thomas Carlyle
CHISWICK HOUSE
CLARENCE HOUSE Royal Family
CLEVEDON COURT
CLONALIS HOUSE S Ireland,
   O'Conor family
COUGHTON COURT
CULROSS PALACE Scotland
DUNSLAND HOUSE
EDNASTON MANOR
FLORENCE COURT N Ireland
FOXDENTON HALL
FROGMORE HOUSE
GAD'S HILL PLACE Charles Dickens
GAWSWORTH HALL Richards family
GAWTHORPE HALL
GOODWOOD HOUSE Duke of
   Richmond
HARDY'S COTTAGE Thomas Hardy
HAREWOOD HOUSE Earl of Harewood
HARTWELL HOUSE
HATFIELD HOUSE Marquess of
   Salisbury
HOGARTH'S HOUSE William Hogarth
HOLYROOD HOUSE Scotland
   Royal Family
HOPETOUN HOUSE Scotland
   Marquess of Linlithgow
HOUGHTON HOUSE

KEDLESTON HALL Lord Curzon
LAMBETH PALACE Archbishop of
   Canterbury
LEIGHTON HOUSE
MELBOURNE HALL
MIDDLETON HALL
NEWSTEAD ABBEY Lord Byron
PACKWOOD HOUSE
PECKOVER HOUSE
PETWORTH HOUSE
POLESDEN LACEY
ROYAL PAVILION Prince Regent
SLEDMERE HOUSE
SMEDMORE HOUSE
SMITHILLS HALL
SOMERSET HOUSE
SULGRAVE MANOR Washington
   family
THRUMPTON HALL
TRAQUAIR HOUSE Scotland
TREDEGAR HOUSE Wales,
   Morgan family
TRETOWER COURT Wales
TYRINGHAM HALL
WESTWOOD MANOR
WOLTERTON HALL

14
ADMIRALTY HOUSE
ARLINGTON COURT
AUDLEY END HOUSE
BADMINTON HOUSE Duke of
   Beaufort
BALBITHAN HOUSE Scotland
BELLAMONT HOUSE S Ireland
BERRINGTON HALL
BLENHEIM PALACE Duke of
   Marlborough

BOARSTALL MANOR
BODRHYDDAN HALL Wales
BRODSWORTH HALL
BROUGHTON HOUSE
CHARLECOTE PARK
CHILLINGTON HALL
CLARENDON HOUSE
DALKEITH PALACE Scotland
DARTINGTON HALL
DODDINGTON HALL
GODOLPHIN HOUSE
HARLAXTON MANOR
HARVINGTON HALL
HUGHENDEN MANOR Benjamin
   Disraeli
KELMSCOTT MANOR William
   Morris
KNEBWORTH HOUSE Lytton family
LANCASTER HOUSE
MAXWELTON HOUSE Scotland,
   Laurie family
MENTMORE TOWERS
MOMPESSON HOUSE
MONTACUTE HOUSE
PAINSWICK HOUSE
PENSHURST PLACE Sidney family
RUFFORD OLD HALL
SHERINGHAM HALL
SNOWSHILL MANOR Charles
   Wade
SQUERRYES COURT
ST JAMES'S PALACE Royal Family
STOURHEAD HOUSE Hoare family
STRAWBERRY HILL Sir Robert Walpole
SYDMONTON COURT Lord Lloyd
   Webber
WADDESDON MANOR Rothschild
   family

WAKEHURST PLACE
WALLINGTON HALL
WATERSTON MANOR
WHITE VINE HOUSE
WIGHTWICK MANOR
WINDLESHAM MOOR
WINGFIELD MANOR
WORLINGHAM HALL

15
BANQUETING HOUSE
BARRINGTON COURT
BURLINGTON HOUSE
CAPESTHORNE HALL Bromley-
   Davenport family
CASTLETOWN HOUSE S Ireland
CHARLESTON MANOR Sir Oswald
   Birley
COMPTON WYNYATES
FARNBOROUGH HALL
HEVENINGHAM HALL
INGATESTONE HALL Petre family
LANHYDROCK HOUSE
LENNOXLOVE HOUSE Scotland
LEVERINGTON HALL
LITTLECOTE HOUSE
LUDDESDOWN COURT
MARY ARDEN'S HOUSE
   Shakespeare's mother
MOTTISFONT ABBEY
REVOLUTION HOUSE
SCARISBRICK HALL
SHUGBOROUGH HALL
SOMERLEYTON HALL Somerleyton
   family
STIBBINGTON HALL
SUNNINGHILL PARK Duke of York
TINTINHULL HOUSE

TODDINGTON MANOR
WATERFALL ESTATE Sir Paul
  McCartney
WESTONBIRT HOUSE
WILDERHOPE MANOR
WIMBORNE ST GILES Earl of
  Shaftesbury
WYTHENSHAWE HALL

16
ALDERMASTON COURT
BUCKINGHAM PALACE Royal Family
MARLBOROUGH HOUSE
MELLERSTAIN HOUSE Scotland,
  Earl of Haddington
WILBERFORCE HOUSE William
  Wilberforce

WOOLVERSTONE HALL

17
LITTLE MORETON HALL
LONDESBOROUGH HALL
SEATON DELAVAL HALL Delaval
  family

18
APPULDURCOMBE HOUSE

19
HINCHINGBROOKE HOUSE
STRATFIELD SAYE HOUSE Duke of
  Wellington

Buildings – Famous Buildings & Sites – THEATRES & CONCERT HALLS

4
GATE Dublin, London
OHIO Columbus, USA
PARK New York
SOHO London

5
ABBEY Dublin
ANVIL Basingstoke
BOOTH New York
CIVIC Chicago, Leeds
FORD'S Washington
  DC
GLOBE London

SAVOY London

6
ALBERY London
ALLAMI Budapest
APOLLO London
ARCOLA London
BOWERY New York
COMEDY London
LYCEUM London,
  New York
L'OPÉRA Paris
MINACK Porthcurno,
  Cornwall

OLD VIC Bristol,
  London
PALACE London,
  Manchester
QUEEN'S London
STRAND London

7
ADELPHI London
ALDWYCH London
ALMEIDA London
ASTORIA London
BOLSHOI Moscow
CENTURY New York

DUCHESS London
FORTUNE London
GARRICK London
GIELGUD London
HEXAGON Reading
LA SCALA Milan
MARQUIS New York
MAYFAIR London
NEPTUNE Liverpool
NOVELLO London
OLIVIER London
PHOENIX London
PIER SIX Baltimore
UNICORN London

8
ALTE OPER Frankfurt
BARBICAN London
CITIZENS Glasgow
COLISEUM London
CRESCENT
  Birmingham
CRUCIBLE Sheffield
DE DOELEN
  Rotterdam
DOMINION London
FESTIVAL Chichester,
  Edinburgh, Stratford,
  Canada
LA FENICE Venice
MAJESTIC New York
NATIONAL London
SAN CARLO Naples
TONHALLE Zurich
WYNDHAM'S London
YOUNG VIC London

9
COTTESLOE London
CRITERION London
DRURY LANE London
ESPLANADE Singapore
HAYMARKET London
HEINZ HALL
  Pittsburgh
JONES HALL Houston
KLEINHANS Buffalo,
  USA
L'AUDITORI Barcelona
LYTTELTON London
MARYINSKY
  St Petersburg
NEW LONDON
  London
PALLADIUM London
SOUTHWARK London,
  Philadelphia
ST MARTIN'S London
USHER HALL
  Edinburgh

10
ALBERT HALL London
  – or Royal Albert Hall
FUNAMBULES Paris
GEWANDHAUS
  Leipzig
HULT CENTER Eugene,
  USA
MASSEY HALL Toronto
PICCADILLY London
ROYAL COURT
  London
STAATSOPER Berlin,
  Munich, Vienna

TANGLEWOOD
  Stockbridge, USA
WIGMORE HALL
  London

11
BURGTHEATER Vienna
CHICKEN SHED
  London
DUKE OF YORK'S
  London
HER MAJESTY'S
  London
MUSIKVEREIN Vienna
ORCHARD HALL Tokyo
SHAFTESBURY London
WÜRTTEMBERG
  Stuttgart

12
BENAROYA HALL
  Seattle
CARNEGIE HALL New
  York
COVENT GARDEN
  London – or Royal
  Opera House
DEUTSCHE OPER
  Berlin
DENVER CENTER
  Denver
FESTIVAL HALL
  London – or Royal
  Festival Hall
FLAGEY STUDIO
  Brussels
ISTANA BUDAYA Kuala
  Lumpur

METROPOLITAN New York
REDOUTENSAAL Vienna
SADLER'S WELLS London
ST DAVID'S HALL Cardiff
WALNUT STREET Philadelphia
YVONNE ARNAUD Guildford

13
ABRAVANEL HALL Salt Lake City
CITY VARIETIES Leeds
CONCERTGEBOUW Amsterdam
FESTSPIELHAUS Bayreuth, Salzburg
HACKNEY EMPIRE London
LINCOLN CENTER New York
PRINCE OF WALES London
THE OTHER PLACE Stratford-on-Avon

14
ALICE TULLY HALL New York
ARLINGTON CENTER Santa Barbara
BRIDGEWATER HALL Manchester
HILL AUDITORIUM Ann Arbor

NEW AMBASSADORS London
VICTORIA PALACE London

15
RAVINIA PAVILION Chicago
ROYAL ALBERT HALL London –
  or Albert Hall
ROYAL OPERA HOUSE London –
  or Covent Garden

16
AVERY FISHER HALL New York
BUXTON OPERA HOUSE Buxton
LOUISVILLE PALACE Louisville
ROYAL SHAKESPEARE Stratford-on-
  Avon
SYDNEY OPERA HOUSE Sydney
TRAFALGAR STUDIOS London

17
ROYAL FESTIVAL HALL London –
  or Festival Hall

Buildings – PRISONS In England unless stated   * = former prison

3
USK Wales

4
CORK S Ireland
FORD
HULL
MAZE*
  (or Long Kesh)
  N Ireland
PARC Wales

SEND
WERL Germany

5
CLINK*
FLEET*
GARTH
LEEDS
LEWES
ONLEY
PERTH Scotland

RANBY
STYAL
VERNE
WEARE
WOLDS
YODOK
  N Korea

6
ALBANY
ATTICA USA

CALTON*
  Scotland
CHANGI
  Singapore
DURHAM
ELMLEY
EXETER
FOLSOM USA
INSEIN
  Myanmar
JOLIET USA

OXFORD*
RISLEY
SHOTTS Scotland
WYMOTT

7
ASHWELL
BEDFORD
BELFAST* (or Crumlin
  Road) N Ireland
BRISTOL
BRIXTON
BUTYRKA* Russia
CARDIFF Wales
CURRAGH S Ireland
FELTHAM
FRESNES France
GARTREE
GRENDON
HINDLEY
KIRKHAM
LA SANTÉ France
LEYHILL
LINCOLN
LOW MOSS Scotland
NEWGATE*
NEW HALL
NORWICH
PRESTON
READING
SPANDAU* Germany
STOCKEN
SUDBURY
SWANSEA Wales
WAYLAND
WHATTON

8
ABERDEEN Scotland
ALCATRAZ* USA
ASHFIELD
BASTILLE* France
BELMARSH
CAMP HILL
DARTMOOR
DEERBOLT
DOWNVIEW
DUMFRIES Scotland
DUNGAVEL Scotland
GREENOCK Scotland
HAVERIGG
HIGHDOWN
HOLLOWAY
KINGSTON
LIMERICK S Ireland
LONG KESH*
  (or Maze) N Ireland
LUBYANKA* Russia
MILLBANK*
MOUNTJOY S Ireland
PORTLAND
PRESCOED Wales
QINCHENG China
SAUGHTON Scotland
SING SING USA
STAFFORD
THE MOUNT
WETHERBY

9
ABU GHRAIB Iraq
AYLESBURY
BARLINNIE Scotland
BRINSFORD
BROCKHILL

CASTLEREA S Ireland
CLAIRVAUX France
DONCASTER
DRAKE HALL
EDINBURGH Scotland
ERLESTOKE
FRANKLAND
GLEN PARVA
GUYS MARSH
HIGHPOINT
INVERNESS
  (or Porterfield)
  Scotland
KILMARNOCK
  Scotland
LANCASTER
LEICESTER
LINDHOLME
LITTLEHEY
LIVERPOOL
LOW NEWTON
MAIDSTONE
MILLHAVEN Canada
PARKHURST
PETERHEAD Scotland
POLLSMOOR S Africa
ROCHESTER
VACAVILLE USA
WAKEFIELD
WARKWORTH Canada
WHITEMOOR
YARLSWOOD

10
ACKLINGTON
ANGOLA FARM USA
BIRMINGHAM
BLUNDESTON

CANTERBURY
CASTINGTON
CHÂTEAU D'IF* France
CHELMSFORD
CLOVERHILL S Ireland
COLDINGLEY
DORCHESTER
EVERTHORPE
FOREST BANK
FOSTON HALL
FULL SUTTON
GLOUCESTER
KILMAINHAM*
  S Ireland
KILMARNOCK
  Scotland
LÅNGHOLMEN*
  Sweden
LONG LARTIN
MAGHABERRY
  S Ireland
MAGILLIGAN S Ireland
MANCHESTER
  (or Strangeways)
MARSHALSEA*
MORTON HALL
NOTTINGHAM
PELICAN BAY USA
PORTLAOISE S Ireland
SAN QUENTIN USA
SHREWSBURY
SPRING HILL
STOKE HEATH
THORN CROSS

WANDSWORTH
WARREN HILL
WERRINGTON
WHEATFIELD S Ireland
WINCHESTER

11
BLAKENHURST
BRONZEFIELD
BUCKLEY HALL
CARABANCHEL* Spain
COOKHAM WOOD
CORNTON VALE
  Scotland
CRUMLIN ROAD*
  (or Belfast) N Ireland
FORT MITCHEL
  S Ireland
HUNTERCOMBE
PENTONVILLE
PORTERFIELD
  (or Inverness)
  Scotland
STRANGEWAYS
  (or Manchester)
SWINFEN HALL

12
ASKHAM GRANGE
BULLWOOD HALL
CASTLE HUNTLY
  Scotland
DEVIL'S ISLAND*
  French Guiana

EASTWOOD PARK
FEATHERSTONE
HOLLESLEY BAY
HOWELL GRANGE
PETERBOROUGH
RIKERS ISLAND USA
ROBBEN ISLAND*
  S Africa

13
BLANTYRE HOUSE
CHANNINGS WOOD
GUANTANAMO BAY
  Cuba
KIRKLEVINGTON
LOUGHLAN HOUSE
  S Ireland
LOWDHAM GRANGE
NORTHALLERTON
SHEPTON MALLET
STANDFORD HILL
TOWER OF LONDON*

14
EAST SUTTON PARK
LATCHMERE HOUSE
WELLINGBOROUGH
WORMWOOD SCRUBS

15
LANCASTER COUNTY
  USA

Buildings – PUBLIC BUILDINGS & INSTITUTIONS

3
GYM
INN
SPA

4
BANK
CLUB
GAOL
HALL
HOME
JAIL
KIRK
SHUL
TOPE

5
ABBEY
BATHS
COURT
DUOMO
HOTEL
HOUSE
HYDRO
LYCÉE
MOTEL
SERAI
STUPA

6
ASHRAM
ASYLUM
CHAPEL
CHURCH
CINEMA
CLINIC

CRÈCHE
DAGOBA
FRIARY
HAMMAM
HOSTEL
HUMMUM
LYCEUM
MANDIR
MANÈGE
MASJID
MORGUE
MOSQUE
MUSEUM
PAGODA
PALACE
POSADA
PRIORY
PRISON
SCHOOL
TEMPLE
VIHARA

7
ACADEMY
AIRPORT
ALMONRY
BORSTAL
COLLEGE
CONVENT
DRIVE-IN
EDIFICE
EMBASSY
HOSPICE
KURSAAL
LIBRARY
MADRASA

MINSTER
MISSION
NUNNERY
NURSERY
ORATORY
RETREAT
SOCIETY
STATION
SURGERY
THEATRE

8
BASILICA
DELUBRUM
EXCHANGE
GURDWARA
HOSPITAL
KACHAHRI
LAMASERY
LAW COURT
MORTUARY
PANTHEON
PECULIAR
REGISTRY
REST HOME
SACELLUM
SEMINARY
TEOCALLI
TOWN HALL
ZIGGURAT

9
ALMA MATER
ATHENAEUM
BÉGUINAGE
CATHEDRAL

CLUBHOUSE
CONSULATE
DAY CENTRE
DAY SCHOOL
DHARMSALA
DRILL HALL
FIREHOUSE
GUILDHALL
GYMNASIUM
HERMITAGE
HIGH COURT
INFIRMARY
INSTITUTE
JOB CENTRE
JOSS HOUSE
LAW CENTRE
LAZARETTO
MAUSOLEUM
MONASTERY
MUSIC HALL
ORPHANAGE
PALAESTRA
PLAYHOUSE
POORHOUSE
PRE-SCHOOL
REST HOUSE
SANCTUARY
SKI SCHOOL
SUCCURSAL
SYNAGOGUE
WORKHOUSE

10
BUS STATION
CHURCH HALL
COURTHOUSE

COURT OF LAW
CROWN COURT
HIGH SCHOOL
LIGHTHOUSE
MARKET HALL
MENTAL HOME
MONOPTEROS
OBSERVANCY
OPERA HOUSE
OUTSTATION
PANOPTICON
PARLIAMENT
POLYCLINIC
POST OFFICE
PREP SCHOOL
SANATORIUM
SPORTS HALL
STATE HOUSE
SUBSTATION
TABERNACLE
UNIVERSITY
WATERWORKS

11
APPEAL COURT
CHAPEL ROYAL
COACHING INN
CONCERT HALL
CONVENIENCE
COUNTRY CLUB
CREMATORIUM
CUSTOM HOUSE
DHARMASHALA
FIRE STATION
INSTITUTION
MISSION HALL

NIGHT SCHOOL
NURSING HOME
OBSERVATORY
POLYTECHNIC
PUBLIC BATHS
SAVINGS BANK
STATELY HOME
STAVE CHURCH
VILLAGE HALL
YOUTH HOSTEL

12
AMPHITHEATRE
CARAVANSERAI
CHAPEL OF EASE
CHAPEL OF REST
CHAPTER HOUSE
CHURCH SCHOOL
COUNTY SCHOOL
DIVORCE COURT
HEADQUARTERS
HEALTH CENTRE
HÔTEL DE VILLE
INFANT SCHOOL
JUNIOR SCHOOL
KINDERGARTEN
MEETING HOUSE
MERCHANT BANK
MIDDLE SCHOOL
NORMAL SCHOOL
PARISH CHURCH
PENITENTIARY
PROCATHEDRAL
PUBLIC SCHOOL
RECORD OFFICE
REFORM SCHOOL
REMAND CENTRE

RIDING SCHOOL
SENIOR SCHOOL
SPORTS CENTRE
STAFF COLLEGE
STATION HOUSE
SUNDAY SCHOOL
TRAIN STATION
TURKISH BATHS

13
CHARITY SCHOOL
COMMUNITY HOME
CONSERVATOIRE
CORONER'S COURT
COUNTING HOUSE
COURT OF APPEAL
COURT OF RECORD
COURT OF REVIEW
DAY-CARE CENTRE
ESTABLISHMENT
GRAMMAR SCHOOL
HOUSE OF REFUGE
LEISURE CENTRE
MEDICAL CENTRE
MEDICAL SCHOOL
MOBILE LIBRARY
NURSERY SCHOOL
PICTURE PALACE
POLICE STATION
PRIMARY SCHOOL
PRIVATE SCHOOL
PUBLIC TOILETS
RIDING ACADEMY
STOCK EXCHANGE
SWIMMING BATHS

14
BOARDING SCHOOL
CONFERENCE HALL
COURT OF INQUIRY
LABOUR EXCHANGE
LENDING LIBRARY
MENTAL HOSPITAL
RAILWAY STATION
REGISTER OFFICE
REGISTRY OFFICE
WEATHER STATION

15
BANKRUPTCY COURT
BUILDING SOCIETY
COMMUNITY CENTRE
COTTAGE HOSPITAL
DETENTION CENTRE
FRIENDLY SOCIETY
RECEPTION CENTRE
SECONDARY SCHOOL
TEMPERANCE HOTEL
TRACKING STATION
TRAINING COLLEGE
VOLUNTARY SCHOOL

16
AMBULANCE STATION
COLLEGIATE CHURCH
COMMUNITY COLLEGE
CONFERENCE CENTRE
TEACHING HOSPITAL

17
COMMUNITY HOSPITAL
MATERNITY HOSPITAL
PREPARATORY SCHOOL

Buildings – ROOMS & INDOOR AREAS

3
BAR
BOX
DEN
LAB
LOO

4
CELL
DECK
HALL
JOHN
LOFT
MESS
NOOK
ROOM
SNUG
WARD
WELL

5
ATTIC
BERTH
BOWER
CABIN
ENTRY
FLOOR
FOYER
HAREM
LOBBY
NICHE
ORIEL
PRIVY
SALON
SAUNA
SOLAR

STAGE
STUDY
SUITE
VAULT

6
ATRIUM
BUREAU
CAMERA
CARREL
CELLAR
CHAPEL
CLOSET
DONJON
EXEDRA
FRATER
GARRET
LARDER
LOUNGE
OFFICE
PANTRY
SALOON
STOREY
STUDIO
TOILET
URINAL
VESTRY
ZENANA

7
ATELIER
BAR ROOM
BEDROOM
BOUDOIR
BOXROOM
BUTLERY

BUTTERY
CABOOSE
CENACLE
CHAMBER
CUBICLE
DAY ROOM
DINETTE
DUNGEON
GALLERY
GUNROOM
HALLWAY
HAYLOFT
KITCHEN
LANDING
LIBRARY
NURSERY
PARLOUR
PASSAGE
PRONAOS
SANCTUM
SERVERY
SICK BAY
TAPROOM
THEATRE

8
ANTEROOM
BACK ROOM
BALLROOM
BASEMENT
BASILICA
BATHROOM
CLUBROOM
COAL-HOLE
COCK LOFT
CORRIDOR

CRUSH BAR
DARKROOM
ENFILADE
FORM ROOM
INTERIOR
LAVATORY
MESS HALL
NEWSROOM
PAY BOOTH
PLAYROOM
PRESS BOX
PUMP ROOM
RESTROOM
ROYAL BOX
SACRISTY
SALEROOM
SCULLERY
SERAGLIO
SHOWROOM
SICKROOM
SNUGGERY
SOLARIUM
TRAVERSE
UPSTAIRS
WARDROBE
WARDROOM
WORKROOM
WORKSHOP

9
BOX OFFICE
CHARTROOM
CHECKROOM
CLASSROOM
CLOAKROOM
CONCOURSE

COURTROOM
CUBBY-HOLE
DORMITORY
FORECABIN
FRONT ROOM
GARDEROBE
GLORY HOLE
GREEN ROOM
GUARDROOM
GUEST ROOM
GYNAECEUM
HIDEY-HOLE
INGLENOOK
LINEN ROOM
MEZZANINE
MUSIC ROOM
ORGAN LOFT
OUBLIETTE
PRESS ROOM
PUBLIC BAR
REFECTORY
SACRARIUM
SALOON BAR
SPARE ROOM
STAFFROOM
STAIRWELL
STATEROOM
STEAM ROOM
STILL ROOM
STOCKROOM
STOREROOM
SUN LOUNGE
TRIFORIUM
VESTIBULE
WASH HOUSE

10
APARTMENTS
AUDITORIUM
BACKSTAIRS
BAR PARLOUR
BEDCHAMBER
BOILER ROOM
CASUAL WARD
COAL-CELLAR
COMMON ROOM
DEPARTMENT
DINING HALL
DINING ROOM
DISPENSARY
DOWNSTAIRS
ENGINE ROOM
FIRST FLOOR
LABORATORY
LIVING ROOM
LOCKER ROOM
LUMBER ROOM
MISERICORD
PADDED CELL
PASSAGEWAY
PENETRALIA
POWDER ROOM
ROBING ROOM
STATE CABIN
STRONGROOM
SUDATORIUM
TEPIDARIUM
THIRD FLOOR
WINE CELLAR

11
ANTECHAMBER
AUCTION ROOM
BARRACK-ROOM

BARRELHOUSE
BRIDAL SUITE
BOOKING HALL
CHAPEL ROYAL
COCKTAIL BAR
COMPARTMENT
CONTROL ROOM
DRAWING ROOM
ECHO CHAMBER
FIRST STOREY
FITTING ROOM
FRIGIDARIUM
GROUND FLOOR
HALF-LANDING
KITCHENETTE
MORNING ROOM
ORDERLY ROOM
PRIEST'S HOLE
READING ROOM
SCRIPTORIUM
SECOND FLOOR
SITTING ROOM
SMOKING ROOM
SOUP KITCHEN
THIRD STOREY
UTILITY ROOM
WAITING ROOM
WATER CLOSET

12
ASSEMBLY HALL
ASSEMBLY ROOM
BILLIARD-ROOM
CASUALTY WARD
CHANGING ROOM
CONSERVATORY
DELIVERY ROOM
DRESSING ROOM

INCIDENT ROOM
PRESS GALLERY
PRIVY CHAMBER
PROPERTY ROOM
SECOND STOREY
SERVANTS' HALL

13
BOOKING OFFICE
CONDEMNED CELL
EMERGENCY WARD
GALLEY KITCHEN
LINEN CUPBOARD
MATERNITY WARD
RECEPTION ROOM
TRANSIT LOUNGE
TREATMENT ROOM

14
BANQUETING HALL
CHAINED LIBRARY
CONSULTING ROOM
COUNCIL CHAMBER
FUNERAL PARLOUR
OPERATIONS ROOM
UNSADDLING ROOM

15
BARGAIN BASEMENT
DEPARTURE LOUNGE
PRESENCE CHAMBER
RESIDENTS' LOUNGE
SHOOTING GALLERY
WITHDRAWING ROOM

16
MINSTRELS' GALLERY
OPERATING THEATRE

Buildings – SHOPS (High Street) * = bank/building society

3
BHS
GAP
HMV
KFC
MFI
MVC

4
ALDO
ASDA
EAST
FCUK
GAME
HSBC*
IKEA
LUSH
MUJI
NEXT
QUBE
QUIZ
YOOX
ZARA

5
ABBEY*
ADAMS
ARGOS
BOOTS
CARGO
COAST
COMET
CORAL
EVANS
FAITH
HEAL'S

JONES
LINKS
MANGO
OASIS
REISS
RYMAN
SCHUH
TESCO

6
ANIMAL
BUDGEN
BURTON
CLARKS
COURTS
CURRY'S
DIXONS
HENNES
JAEGER
JIGSAW
KOOKAI
OPTIKA
ORANGE
TCHIBO
TK MAXX
TOP MAN
UNWINS
VIRGIN

7
ALLDAYS
DEXTERS
FAT FACE
HABITAT
HALIFAX*
HAMLEYS

HARRODS
H SAMUEL
ICELAND
JESSOPS
JEWSONS
LA SENZA
LIBERTY
MATALAN
MONSOON
NATWEST*
NEW LOOK
ODDBINS
PC WORLD
PRIMARK
STAPLES
THE LINK
THE PIER
THOMSON
TIE RACK
T-MOBILE
TOP SHOP
TOYS R US
WH SMITH

8
BARCLAYS*
BARRATTS
BEATTIES
BENETTON
BODY SHOP
CLINTONS
CONFETTI
CONTESSA
HALFORDS
HOMEBASE
JD SPORTS

LUNN POLY
NINE WEST
OTTAKARS
PETSMART
PETWORLD
PIZZA HUT
PLUMBASE
SUITS YOU
TJ HUGHES
VODAFONE
WAGAMAMA
WAITROSE
WOOLWICH*

9
BON MARCHÉ
DEBENHAMS
JJB SPORTS
JOHN LEWIS
LADBROKES
LLOYDS TSB*
MCDONALD'S
MORRISONS
PAST TIMES
STARBUCKS
SUPERDRUG
THORNTONS

10
ANN SUMMERS
AUSTIN REED
BLACKWELLS
BURGER KING
GOLDSMITHS
KNICKERBOX
MOTHERCARE

NATIONWIDE*
PADDY POWER
PLUMB WORLD
PRINCIPLES
ROBERT DYAS
SAINSBURY'S
SELFRIDGES
SONY CENTRE
SPECSAVERS
THOMAS COOK
TONI AND GUY
WOOLWORTHS

11
ACCESSORIZE
BLOCKBUSTER
COSTA COFFEE
GOING PLACES
LAURA ASHLEY
LITTLEWOODS
PRET A MANGER
RIVER ISLAND
WATERSTONES

12
DOMINO'S PIZZA
PIZZA EXPRESS

13
COTTON TRADERS
HARRY RAMSDENS
HOUSE OF FRASER
MAMAS AND PAPAS
MISS SELFRIDGE
VISION EXPRESS

14
BANK OF SCOTLAND*
COUNTRY CASUALS
DOROTHY PERKINS
THE BEAR FACTORY

15
MARKS AND SPENCER

17
BAY TRADING COMPANY
CARPHONE WAREHOUSE

HOLLAND AND BARRETT
WHITTARD OF CHELSEA

18
EARLY LEARNING CENTRE

Buildings – SHOPS & FACTORIES (types)

3	**6**	KENNELS	GASWORKS	CHANDLERY
PIT	AGENCY	LAUNDRY	GIFT SHOP	COOKHOUSE
	ARCADE	NAILERY	GOLD MINE	COOPERAGE
4	BAKERY	NURSERY	IRON MINE	CYCLE SHOP
CO-OP	BAZAAR	PET SHOP	JUNKSHOP	DRUGSTORE
FARM	BODEGA	PIE SHOP	MAGAZINE	FLOUR MILL
MART	BRANCH	POP SHOP	MALTINGS	GRIST MILL
MILL	BUREAU	POTTERY	PAWNSHOP	IRONWORKS
MINE	GARAGE	SALTERN	PHARMACY	MALTHOUSE
MINT	GODOWN	SAWMILL	PREMISES	MEGASTORE
SHOP	MARKET	SEX SHOP	REFINERY	MUSIC SHOP
SOUK	OFFICE	STATION	SADDLERY	NEWS-STAND
	OUTLET	TANNERY	SALT MINE	PAINT-SHOP
5	QUARRY	TIN MINE	SHOE SHOP	PAPER MILL
BOOTH	ROPERY	TOYSHOP	STANNARY	PAPER SHOP
DAIRY	SMITHY		TIDE MILL	SHALE MINE
DEPOT	TILERY	**8**	TUCKSHOP	SLATE MINE
FORGE		ABATTOIR	WINESHOP	STRIP MINE
HOUSE	**7**	BODY SHOP	WOOL MILL	SWEATSHOP
KIOSK	ARSENAL	BOOKSHOP	WORKSHOP	SWEETSHOP
PLANT	BINDERY	BOUTIQUE		TOLLBOOTH
SALON	BREWERY	BUTCHERY	**9**	WAREHOUSE
STALL	BUVETTE	COAL MINE	BAKEHOUSE	WATERMILL
STORE	CANNERY	COOKSHOP	BLEACHERY	
WORKS	CATTERY	CREAMERY	BOOKSTALL	**10**
	FACTORY	EMPORIUM	BOOKSTAND	BAKER'S SHOP
	FOUNDRY	FILATURE	BREWHOUSE	BARBER SHOP

BRICKWORKS
BUCKET SHOP
CHAIN STORE
COPPER MINE
CORNER SHOP
COTTON MILL
DISTILLERY
FISH MARKET
GADGET SHOP
GLASSWORKS
GROCETERIA
LAUNDROMAT
MEAT MARKET
MOBILE SHOP
OFF-LICENCE
OPEN MARKET
PATISSERIE
POWER PLANT
PRINTWORKS
REPAIR SHOP
REPOSITORY
SMOKEHOUSE
SPORTS SHOP
STEELWORKS
STOREHOUSE
SUBSTATION
THRIFT SHOP
TIMBERYARD

11
ANTIQUE SHOP
BEAUTY SALON
BETTING SHOP
BONDED STORE
BOULANGERIE
CHARCUTERIE
CHARITY SHOP
CLOTHES SHOP

DRAPER'S SHOP
FACTORY SHOP
FITTING SHOP
GROCER'S SHOP
HYPERMARKET
IRON FOUNDRY
LAUNDERETTE
MACHINE SHOP
OFFICE BLOCK
OIL REFINERY
ROLLING MILL
SUPERMARKET
TAILOR'S SHOP
TYPE FOUNDRY
WOOLLEN MILL

12
BUTCHER'S SHOP
CHEMIST'S SHOP
CORN EXCHANGE
DELICATESSEN
DUTY-FREE SHOP
FASHION HOUSE
FLORIST'S SHOP
GARDEN CENTRE
GENERAL STORE
HABERDASHERY
HEADQUARTERS
MARKET GARDEN
POWER STATION
RETAIL OUTLET
SPINNING MILL
TICKET AGENCY
TRADING HOUSE
TRAVEL AGENCY

13
BEAUTY PARLOUR

COVERED MARKET
ESTABLISHMENT
EXHAUST CENTRE
JEWELLER'S SHOP
PETROL STATION
PRINTING HOUSE
SMELTING HOUSE
SUGAR REFINERY

14
BUREAU DE CHANGE
FILLING STATION
FUNERAL PARLOUR
FURNITURE STORE
MASSAGE PARLOUR
NEWSAGENT'S SHOP
OUTFITTER'S SHOP
PRINTING OFFICE
PUMPING STATION
SERVICE STATION
SHOPPING CENTRE
SLAUGHTERHOUSE
STATIONER'S SHOP

15
BONDED WAREHOUSE
DEPARTMENT STORE
DRY CLEANER'S SHOP
FISH-AND-CHIP SHOP
FISHMONGER'S SHOP
IRONMONGER'S SHOP
PAWNBROKER'S SHOP
VEGETABLE MARKET

16
CONVENIENCE STORE
HAIRDRESSER'S SHOP

Buildings – UNIVERSITIES (British Isles)

3
UCE Birmingham
UEL East London

4
BATH
CITY London
HULL
KENT
OPEN Milton Keynes
YORK

5
ASTON Birmingham
DERBY
ESSEX Colchester
KEELE Newcastle-
   under-Lyme
LEEDS
LUTON
UCLAN Preston
WALES Aberystwyth,
   Bangor, Cardiff,
   Carmarthen,
   Lampeter, Newport,
   Swansea, Wrexham

6
BOLTON
BRUNEL London
DUBLIN
DUNDEE
DURHAM
EXETER
LONDON
NAPIER Edinburgh

OXFORD
QUEEN'S Belfast
SURREY Guildford
SUSSEX Falmer
ULSTER Belfast,
   Coleraine, Derry,
   Jordanstown

7
ABERTAY Dundee
BATH SPA
BRISTOL
CARDIFF
CHESTER
GLASGOW
IRELAND
LINCOLN
PAISLEY
READING
SALFORD
SWANSEA
WARWICK

8
ABERDEEN
BRADFORD
BRIGHTON
COVENTRY
EDGE HILL Ormskirk
KINGSTON
LIMERICK
PLYMOUTH
STIRLING
TEESSIDE
   Middlesbrough

9
CAMBRIDGE
CRANFIELD Beds &
   Oxon
EDINBURGH
GLAMORGAN
GREENWICH
LANCASTER
LEICESTER
LIVERPOOL
MIDDLESEX
SHEFFIELD
ST ANDREWS
WORCESTER

10
BIRMINGHAM
BUCKINGHAM
CHICHESTER
DE MONTFORT
   Leicester
DUBLIN CITY
EAST ANGLIA
HERIOT-WATT
   Edinburgh
MANCHESTER
NOTTINGHAM
PORTSMOUTH
ROEHAMPTON
SUNDERLAND
WINCHESTER

11
BOURNEMOUTH
NORTHAMPTON
NORTHUMBRIA

SOUTHAMPTON
STRATHCLYDE Glasgow
WESTMINSTER

LONDON SOUTH BANK
NOTTINGHAM TRENT
SHEFFIELD HALLAM

12
ANGLIA RUSKIN Chelmsford/
  Cambridge
HUDDERSFIELD
LOUGHBOROUGH
ROBERT GORDON Aberdeen
THAMES VALLEY

17
GLASGOW CALEDONIAN
LEEDS METROPOLITAN
NEWCASTLE-UPON-TYNE
SOUTHAMPTON SOLENT

13
LIVERPOOL HOPE
OXFORD BROOKES
STAFFORDSHIRE
WOLVERHAMPTON

18
LONDON METROPOLITAN

19
LIVERPOOL JOHN MOORES
UNIVERSITY OF THE ARTS   London

15
GLOUCESTERSHIRE

22
CANTERBURY CHRIST CHURCH
MANCHESTER METROPOLITAN

Buildings – UNIVERSITIES (World)

4
BONN Germany
KIEV Ukraine
LUND Sweden
OSLO Norway
YALE New Haven, USA

KAZAN Russia
LAVAL Quebec,
  Canada
SOFIA Bulgaria
TOKYO Japan
TOMSK Russia

NANTES France
PRAGUE Czech Rep
SYDNEY Australia
TEHRAN Iran
VIENNA Austria
WARSAW Poland

5
BEIDA Beijing, China
BROWN Providence,
  USA
CAIRO Egypt
DELHI India

6
HEBREW Jerusalem,
  Israel
LEIDEN Netherlands
LISBON Portugal
MOSCOW Russia

7
ALLIANT Mexico City,
  Mexico
BANGKOK Thailand
BOLOGNA Italy
COIMBRA Portugal

COLOGNE Germany
CORNELL Ithaca, USA
GRANADA Spain
HARVARD Cambridge,
 USA
LEIPZIG Germany
NAIROBI Kenya
SEVILLE Spain
TORONTO Canada
UPPSALA Sweden
UTRECHT Netherlands
WROCLAW Poland

8
CAPE TOWN S Africa
COLUMBIA New York,
 USA
HELSINKI Finland
HUMBOLDT Berlin,
 Germany
ISTANBUL Turkey
KHARTOUM Sudan
SÃO PAULO Brazil
SORBONNE Paris

STANFORD USA
VIADRINA Frankfurt,
 Germany

9
ARISTOTLE
 Thessaloniki, Greece
BARCELONA Spain
DARTMOUTH
 Hanover, USA
MELBOURNE Australia
PRINCETON USA
SALAMANCA Spain
STOCKHOLM Sweden

10
COPENHAGEN
 Denmark
GOTHENBURG
 Sweden
HEIDELBERG Germany
KAIRAOUINE Fez,
 Morocco
LA SAPIENZA Rome

11
BUENOS AIRES
 Argentina
COMPLUTENSE
 Madrid, Spain
MONTPELLIER France

12
EÖTVÖS LORÁND
 Budapest, Hungary
LOUIS PASTEUR
 Strasbourg, France
PENNSYLVANIA
 Philadelphia, USA
ST PETERSBURG Russia

13
CLAUDE BERNARD
 Lyons, France
WITWATERSRAND
 Johannesburg,
 S Africa

Buildings – UNIVERSITY COLLEGES

3
LBS London
LCC University of the
 Arts
LCF University of the
 Arts
LSE London
UCL London

4
CORK S Ireland

5
CLARE Cambridge
GREEN Oxford
JESUS Cambridge,
 Oxford
KEBLE Oxford

KING'S Cambridge
ORIEL Oxford

6
BANGOR Wales
CHRIST'S Cambridge
DARWIN Cambridge
DUBLIN S Ireland
EXETER Oxford

GALWAY S Ireland
GIRTON Cambridge
MERTON Oxford
QUEEN'S Oxford
QUEENS' Cambridge
SELWYN Cambridge
WADHAM Oxford

7
BALLIOL Oxford
CHELSEA University of
   the Arts
DOWNING Cambridge
KELLOGG Oxford
LINACRE Oxford
LINCOLN Oxford
NEW HALL Cambridge
NEWNHAM Cambridge
NEWPORT Wales
ST ANNE'S Oxford
ST CROSS Oxford
ST HUGH'S Oxford
ST JOHN'S Cambridge,
   Oxford
ST MARY'S Queen's
TRINITY Cambridge,
   Dublin, Oxford,
   Wales
WOLFSON Cambridge,
   Oxford

8
ALL SOULS Oxford
EMMANUEL
   Cambridge
HERTFORD Oxford
HOMERTON
   Cambridge

IMPERIAL London
LAMPETER Wales
MAGDALEN Oxford
MAYNOOTH S Ireland
NUFFIELD Oxford
PEMBROKE
   Cambridge, Oxford
ROBINSON Cambridge
ST PETER'S Oxford

9
BRASENOSE Oxford
CHURCHILL
   Cambridge
CLARE HALL
   Cambridge
COURTAULD London
MAGDALENE
   Cambridge
MANSFIELD Oxford
ST EDMUND'S
   Cambridge
TEMPLETON Oxford
WORCESTER Oxford

10
CAMBERWELL
   University of the Arts
HUGHES HALL
   Cambridge
NEW COLLEGE Oxford
PETERHOUSE
   Cambridge
SOMERVILLE Oxford
ST ANTHONY'S Oxford

11
ABERYSTWYTH Wales
CAMPION HALL
   Oxford
FITZWILLIAM
   Cambridge
REGENT'S PARK Oxford
STRANMILLIS Queen's
TRINITY HALL
   Cambridge

12
CHRIST CHURCH
   Oxford
SIDNEY SUSSEX
   Cambridge
ST CATHARINE'S
   Cambridge
ST CATHERINE'S
   Oxford
ST BENET'S HALL
   Oxford
ST EDMUND HALL
   Oxford

13
CORPUS CHRISTI
   Cambridge, Oxford
LUCY CAVENDISH
   Cambridge
ROYAL HOLLOWAY
   London

14
GREYFRIAR'S HALL
   Oxford

15
ROYAL VETERINARY London

16
CENTRAL ST MARTIN'S University of
   the Arts

GONVILLE AND CAIUS Cambridge
HARRIS MANCHESTER Oxford
LADY MARGARET HALL Oxford

17
UNIVERSITY COLLEGE Oxford

Clothing & Fashion

Clothing & Fashion – CLOTHES

3	TOP	GEAR	PINK	TOPI	CHAPS	GILET
ALB		GOWN	PUMP	(or topee)	CHOLI	GLOVE
BIB	4	HAIK	RAGS	TUTU	CLOAK	G-SUIT
BOA	AGAL	HOOD	ROBE	VEIL	CORDS	HABIT
BOW	BAGS	HOSE	RUFF	VEST	COTTA	JEANS
BOX	BAND	KEPI	SACK	WEAR	CREST	JUPON
BRA	BELT	KILT	SARI	WRAP	CROWN	KANZU
CAP	BOOT	MAIL	SASH	ZORI	CYMAR	LEVIS
DAP	BUSK	MASK	SHOE		DERBY	LONGS
FEZ	CAPE	MAXI	SLIP	5	DHOTI	LUNGI
HAT	CAUL	MIDI	SLOP	ABAYA	DICKY	MITRE
LID	COAT	MINI	SOCK	AMICE	(or dickey)	MUFTI
MAC	COIF	MINK	SPAT	APRON	DRESS	MUTCH
OBI	CLOG	MITT	SPUR	ASCOT	DUCKS	NAPPY
RIG	COPE	MUFF	SUIT	BANDS	EPHOD	PAGRI
SKI	COWL	MULE	TABI	BERET	FICHU	PANTS
TAJ	DRAG	OILS	TILE	BURKA	FROCK	PARKA
TAM	DUDS	PADS	TOGA	(or burkha)	GET-UP	PINNY
TIE	GARB	POKE	TOGS	BUSBY	GIBUS	PLAID

PLUME
ROMAL
SABOT
SCARF
SHAKO
SHAWL
SHIFT
SHIRT
SKATE
SKIRT
SLOPS
SMOCK
SNOOD
STAYS
STOCK
STOLE
TAILS
TAMMY
TANGA
TEDDY
TERAI
TIARA
TOPEE
 (or topi)
TOQUE
TOWER
TRAIN
TREWS
TRUSS
TUNIC
TUQUE
VISOR
 (or visor)
VIZOR
 (or visor)
V-NECK
WADER
WEDGE

WEEDS

6
ABOLLA
ACHKAN
ANORAK
ARCTIC
ARMLET
ARMOUR
ATTIRE
BANYAN
BASQUE
BEAVER
BERTHA
BIKINI
BLAZER
BLOUSE
BOATER
BODICE
BOLERO
BONNET
BOOTEE
BOWLER
BOW TIE
BOXERS
BRACES
BRIEFS
BROGUE
BURKHA
 (or burka)
BUSKIN
CAFTAN
 (or kaftan)
CALASH
 (or caleche)
CAPOTE
CASQUE
CHADOR

 (or chuddar)
CHIMER
CHINOS
CHITON
CHOKER
CHOPIN
CILICE
CLOCHE
COLLAR
CORSET
COSSIE
 (or cozzie)
COZZIE
 (or cossie)
CRAVAT
CUISSE
DENIMS
DIADEM
DIAPER
DICKEY
 (or dicky)
DIRNDL
DOLMAN
DOMINO
EXOMIS
FEDORA
FILLET
FLARES
GAITER
GALOSH
GANSEY
GARTER
GIRDLE
GORGET
GREAVE
HALTER
HELMET
HOODIE

INFULA
JACKET
JEMIMA
JERKIN
JERSEY
JUMPER
KABAYA
KAGOUL
 (or cagoule)
KAROSS
KAFTAN
 (or caftan)
KIMONO
KIRTLE
KNICKS
LIVERY
LOAFER
LORICA
MANTLE
MANTUA
MITTEN
MOB CAP
MORION
MOTLEY
MUKLUK
MUUMUU
NYLONS
OILERS
OUTFIT
OXFORD
PANAMA
PEPLOS
PEPLUM
PONCHO
PUTTEE
RACKET
RAGLAN
RED HAT

REEFER
RIG-OUT
ROLL-ON
SALLET
SANDAL
SARONG
SERAPE
SHORTS
SHROUD
SLACKS
SMALLS
SPIKES
SUN HAT
TABARD
TIGHTS
TIN HAT
TIPPET
TITFER
TOP HAT
TOPPER
TRILBY
TRUNKS
T-SHIRT
TUCKER
TURBAN
TUXEDO
TWEEDS
ULSTER
UNDIES
VIZARD
WEEPER
WHITES
WIMPLE
WOOLLY
ZEPHYR

7
APPAREL
ARMBAND
BALDRIC
BANDEAU
BARBOUR
BASHLYK
BASINET
BELCHER
BIRETTA
BLOUSON
BOXCOAT
BURNOUS
BUSH HAT
BUSTIER
CAGOULE
 (or kagoul)
CALECHE
 (or calash)
CAR COAT
CASSOCK
CASUALS
CATSUIT
CAUBEEN
CHAPEAU
CHAPLET
CHEMISE
CHLAMYS
CHUDDAR
 (or chador)
CIRCLET
CIVVIES
CLOBBER
CLOTHES
CORONET
COSTUME
CROP TOP
CUIRASS

CUTAWAY
DAYWEAR
DOUBLET
DRAWERS
DUPATTA
FILIBEG
FLAT CAP
FUR COAT
GARMENT
GAS MASK
G-STRING
GUMBOOT
GYM SHOE
GYMSLIP
HAUBERK
HIGH-LOW
HOMBURG
HOSIERY
HUMERAL
JAMBEAU
JELLABA
 (or djellaba)
LACE-UPS
LAURELS
LAYETTE
LEGHORN
LEOTARD
MAE WEST
MAILLOT
MANIPLE
MANTEAU
MANTLET
 (or mantelet)
MOZETTA
 (or mozzetta)
MUFFLER
NECKTIE
NIGHTIE

OVERALL
PALETOT
PALLIUM
PANOPLY
PANTIES
PEA COAT
PEEP-TOE
PELISSE
PETASUS
PILLBOX
PYJAMAS
RAIMENT
RAMMIES
ROMPERS
RUBBERS
SABATON
SARAFAN
SILK HAT
SINGLET
SKI BOOT
SKID LID
SLICKER
SLIP-ONS
SLIPPER
SNEAKER
SOUTANE
SPENCER
SPORRAN
STEP-INS
STETSON
SUNSUIT
SURCOAT
SURTOUT
SWEATER
TALL HAT
TALLITH
TANK TOP
TEA GOWN

TOP BOOT
TOPCOAT
TRICORN
 (or tricorne)
TUNICLE
TWIN SET
UNIFORM
VANDYKE
VESTURE
WEEPERS
WETSUIT
WRAPPER
YASHMAK
Y-FRONTS
ZAMARRA

8

AIGRETTE
ALL-IN-ONE
BABOUCHE
BABUSHKA
BALL GOWN
BALMORAL
BANDANNA
BATHROBE
BEARSKIN
BEDSOCKS
BLACK CAP
BLOOMERS
BLUCHERS
BOOB TUBE
BRASSARD
BREECHES
CAMISOLE
CAPELINE
CAPUCHIN
CARDIGAN
CHASUBLE

CHAUSSES
CINCTURE
CLOTH CAP
CLOTHING
CODPIECE
CORSELET
 (or corselette)
COVERALL
CRUSH HAT
CULOTTES
DALMATIC
DJELLABA
 (or jellaba)
DUSTCOAT
DUTCH CAP
EARMUFFS
ENSEMBLE
FALDETTA
FATIGUES
FINNESKO
FLANNELS
FLIP-FLOP
FOOL'S CAP
FOOTWEAR
FRILLIES
FRONTLET
GAUNTLET
GLAD RAGS
GOLF SHOE
GUERNSEY
HALF-BOOT
HEADBAND
HEADGEAR
HIMATION
HIPSTERS
JACKBOOT
JODHPURS
JUMPSUIT

KAFFIYEH
 (or keffiyeh)
KEFFIYEH
 (or kaffiyeh)
KERCHIEF
KNICKERS
KNITWEAR
LEATHERS
LEGGINGS
LIFEBELT
LINGERIE
MACKINAW
MANTELET
 (or mantlet)
MANTILLA
MENSWEAR
MILLINERY
MINK COAT
MOCCASIN
MOON BOOT
MOZZETTA
 (or mozetta)
NANKEENS
NECKBAND
NECKWEAR
NEGLIGEE
NIGHTCAP
OILSKINS
OPERA HAT
OVERALLS
OVERCOAT
OVERSHOE
PAPER HAT
PEARLIES
PECTORAL
PEIGNOIR
PELERINE
PINAFORE

PLASTRON
PLIMSOLL
POLO NECK
PUFFBALL
PUGGAREE
PULLOVER
RAINCOAT
SACK COAT
SACK SUIT
SANDSHOE
SCAPULAR
SKULLCAP
SLIPOVER
SLIP-SLOP
SMOCK TOP
SNOW BOOT
SNOWSHOE
SOLA TOPI
SOMBRERO
STOCKING
STRAW HAT
SURPLICE
SWIMSUIT
SWIMWEAR
TAILCOAT
TARBOOSH
TRAINERS
TRICORNE
 (or tricorn)
TROUSERS
TWO-PIECE
VAMBRACE
VESTMENT
WOOLLENS
WRAP-OVER
ZOOT SUIT

9

ALPARGATA
ANKLE SOCK
BALACLAVA
BEDJACKET
BILLYCOCK
BLINDFOLD
BOBBLE HAT
BOBBY SOCK
BOWLER HAT
BRASSIERE
BUSH SHIRT
CHAIN MAIL
CHEONGSAM
CLOCHE HAT
COAT DRESS
COCKED HAT
COMFORTER
CORDUROYS
COURT SHOE
CRINOLINE
DOG COLLAR
DRESS COAT
DUNGAREES
DUNSTABLE
FIELD BOOT
FLESHINGS
FORAGE CAP
FROCK COAT
FUR COLLAR
GABERDINE
GARIBALDI
GLENGARRY
GREATCOAT
HABERGEON
HAIR SHIRT
HEAD-DRESS
HEADPIECE

HEADSCARF
HOUSECOAT
HULA SKIRT
INVERNESS
JOCKEY CAP
JOCKSTRAP
JULIET CAP
KNEE-HIGHS
LOINCLOTH
LONG JOHNS
MACINTOSH
 (or mackintosh)
MINI-SKIRT
MOLESKINS
NECKCLOTH
NEWMARKET
NIGHTGOWN
OUTERWEAR
OVERDRESS
OVERSKIRT
PANAMA HAT
PANTYHOSE
PEA JACKET
PEAKED CAP
PETTICOAT
PLUS FOURS
POLONAISE
POLO SHIRT
RA-RA SKIRT
REDINGOTE
SACK DRESS
SAILOR HAT
SAM BROWNE
SANBENITO
SCHOOL TIE
SEPARATES
SHOVEL HAT
SHOWER CAP

SIREN SUIT
SLEEPSUIT
SLINGBACK
SLOPPY JOE
SLOUCH HAT
SOU'WESTER
SPACESUIT
STOCKINGS
STOMACHER
STRING TIE
STUFF GOWN
SUN BONNET
SWEATBAND
TENT DRESS
THIGH BOOT
TRACKSUIT
TROUSSEAU
UNDERVEST
UNDERWEAR
UNION SUIT
VELDSKOEN
WAISTBAND
WAISTCOAT
WIDEAWAKE
WITCH'S HAT
WRISTBAND
ZUCCHETTO

10

ARGYLE SOCK
BALLET SHOE
BATHING CAP
BODY WARMER
BOILER SUIT
BRIGANDINE
BUSH JACKET
CANONICALS
CAPRI PANTS

CHAPARAJOS
CHEMISETTE
COAT OF MAIL
COLLEGE CAP
CORSELETTE
  (or corselet)
COSSACK HAT
COTE-HARDIE
COURT DRESS
COVERT COAT
CUMMERBUND
DOC MARTENS
DRAINPIPES
DRESS SHIRT
DUFFEL COAT
ESPADRILLE
ETON COLLAR
ETON JACKET
FANCY DRESS
FEATHER BOA
FLYING SUIT
FOUR-IN-HAND
FUSTANELLA
GRASS SKIRT
HABILIMENT
HALTER-NECK
HEADSQUARE
KILMARNOCK
LADIESWEAR
LAMBREQUIN
LEDERHOSEN
LEG WARMERS
LIBERTY CAP
LIFE JACKET
LOUNGE SUIT
MACKINTOSH
  (or macintosh)
MONKEY SUIT

NIGHTDRESS
NIGHTSHIRT
OPERA CLOAK
OXFORD BAGS
OXYGEN MASK
PANTALOONS
PICTURE HAT
PITH HELMET
PLASTIC MAC
POKE BONNET
PORK-PIE HAT
RESPIRATOR
REVERSIBLE
RIDING BOOT
ROMPER SUIT
SAFARI SUIT
SALOPETTES
SHELL SUIT
SPORTS COAT
SPORTSWEAR
STEEPLE HAT
SUSPENDERS
SWEATSHIRT
TENNIS SHOE
THREE-PIECE
TRENCH COAT
TURTLE-NECK
UNDERPANTS
UNDERSHIRT
UNDERSKIRT
WAIST CLOTH
WATERPROOF
WELLINGTON
WINDJAMMER
WINDSOR TIE
WING COLLAR

11
BABY HARNESS
BASEBALL CAP
BATHING SUIT
BATTLEDRESS
BELL-BOTTOMS
BOILED SHIRT
BOXER SHORTS
BREASTPLATE
BRITISH WARM
CHAPEAU-BRAS
COMBAT DRESS
COONSKIN HAT
CO-ORDINATES
COSSACK BOOT
CRASH HELMET
DEERSTALKER
DOLLY VARDEN
FARTHINGALE
GENEVA BANDS
HAND-ME-DOWNS
HESSIAN BOOT
HOBBLE SKIRT
HOBNAIL BOOT
KISS-ME-QUICK
LEATHERWEAR
MATINEE COAT
MORNING COAT
MORTAR BOARD
NECKERCHIEF
NIGHT ATTIRE
OVERGARMENT
PANTALETTES
PANTY GIRDLE
PENGUIN SUIT
PHRYGIAN CAP
PICKELHAUBE
PILOT JACKET

PLATE ARMOUR
RIDING HABIT
RUBBER GLOVE
RUNNING SHOE
SCALE ARMOUR
SHELL JACKET
SPATTERDASH
SWAGGER COAT
TAM O'SHANTER
TANGA BRIEFS
TRIPLE CROWN
TROUSER SUIT
TYROLEAN HAT
UNDERTHINGS
WEDDING VEIL
WELLINGTONS
WIDOW'S WEEDS
WINDBREAKER
WINDCHEATER

12
ACCOUTREMENT
BODY STOCKING
BUSINESS SUIT
CAMIKNICKERS
CHASTITY BELT
CHEESE-CUTTER
CHESTERFIELD
CHRISOM-CLOTH
COMBAT JACKET
COMBINATIONS
CROPPED JEANS
DINNER JACKET
DIVIDED SKIRT
DONKEY JACKET
DRESSING GOWN
DRESS UNIFORM
EASTER BONNET

EVENING DRESS
FLYING JACKET
GALLIGASKINS
KLETTERSCHUH
KNEE BREECHES
LONG TROUSERS
LUMBERJACKET
MONKEY JACKET
MORNING DRESS
MOURNING BAND
NIGHTCLOTHES
OLD SCHOOL TIE
PEDAL PUSHERS
PRESSURE SUIT
PYJAMA JACKET
REACH-ME-DOWNS
SAFARI JACKET
SCOTCH BONNET
SHIRTWAISTER
SHOULDER BELT
SKELETON SUIT
SPORTS JACKET
STOVEPIPE HAT
SUIT OF ARMOUR
SURGICAL BOOT
TEN-GALLON HAT
UNDERCLOTHES
UNDERGARMENT
WEDDING DRESS
WINKLE-PICKER

13
ARGYLE SWEATER
BEETLE-CRUSHER
BERMUDA SHORTS
BUTTON-THROUGH
CAMEL-HAIR COAT
CARPET SLIPPER
CHILDRENSWEAR
COCKTAIL DRESS
HACKING JACKET
HAWAIIAN SKIRT
HIGHLAND DRESS
LEATHER JACKET
LIBERTY BODICE
LIFE PRESERVER
MATINEE JACKET
MOTHER HUBBARD
NORFOLK JACKET
PINAFORE DRESS
PUFFBALL SKIRT
SAM BROWNE BELT
SHEEPSKIN COAT
SHORT TROUSERS
SMOKING JACKET
SOCK SUSPENDER
SUSPENDER BELT
UNDERCLOTHING

14
BATHING COSTUME
CAMOUFLAGE GEAR

CLERICAL COLLAR
DETACHED COLLAR
FAIR ISLE JUMPER
FIREMAN'S HELMET
GOING-AWAY DRESS
KNICKERBOCKERS
MANDARIN COLLAR
PHRYGIAN BONNET
PYJAMA TROUSERS
RIDING BREECHES
SHOOTING JACKET
SWIMMING TRUNKS
WELLINGTON BOOT

15
BALACLAVA HELMET
BULLETPROOF VEST
DAVY CROCKETT HAT
FAIR ISLE SWEATER
ORTHOPAEDIC SHOE
POLO-NECK SWEATER
SWIMMING COSTUME

16
BUTTON-DOWN COLLAR
SWADDLING CLOTHES

17
CONFIRMATION DRESS
DRAINPIPE TROUSERS
FOUNDATION GARMENT

Clothing & Fashion – CLOTHING TERMS

3
ARM
CUP
CUT
EYE
FIT
FLY
FOB
HEM
LAP
LEG
NAP
PAD
PIN
RAG
RIB
RUN
SET
TAB
TAG
TAT
TOE
TON
WEB
ZIP

4
BAND
BONE
BURL
BUST
CUFF
DART
ETUI
FEEL
FLAP

FOLD
GORE
HANG
HANK
HEEL
HIPS
HOOK
HOOP
KNEE
KNOT
LIFT
LINE
LOOM
MODE
NECK
PEAK
PILE
POUF
PUFF
REEL
RUCK
SEAM
SEAT
SIZE
SLIT
SNIP
SOLE
STUD
TACK
TAIL
TAPE
TRIM
TUCK
TUFT
VAMP
VENT

WALE
WARP
WEAR
WEFT
WELT
YARN
YOKE

5
BUGLE
CHECK
CHEST
CLASP
CLOCK
CLUMP
DUMMY
FLARE
FLASH
FRILL
GODET
INLET
INSET
JABOT
LABEL
LAPEL
MATCH
MODEL
PANEL
PATCH
PICOT
PLEAT
RUCHE
SHANK
SHARP
SHIRR
SKEIN

SLASH
SPOOL
STRAP
STRIP
STYLE
TWIST
UPPER
V-NECK
VOGUE
WAIST
WEAVE

6
ARGYLE
BOBBIN
BOBBLE
BUCKLE
BUSTLE
BUTTON
CREASE
DESIGN
EYELET
FRINGE
GATHER
GUSSET
HANDLE
INSOLE
LACING
LADDER
LAPPET
LINING
NEEDLE
NUMBER
PIPING
POCKET
POMPOM

REVERS
RIBBON
RUFFLE
RUMPLE
SEQUIN
SLEEVE
STAPLE
STITCH
STRAND
STRING
TAILOR
TASSEL
TEASEL
THREAD
TOECAP
TOGGLE
TONGUE
TURN-UP
UPLIFT
WOGGLE
ZIPPER

7
ARMHOLE
CATWALK
CORSAGE
COUTURE
ELASTIC
FALSIES
FASHION
FITTING
FLOUNCE
GALLOON
HATBAND
HEELTAP
HEMLINE

MEASURE
MIDRIFF
NETSUKE
NEW LOOK
ODDMENT
ORPHREY
OUTSOLE
PADDING
PAISLEY
PANNIER
PATTERN
PICKING
PIN-TUCK
PLACKET
REMNANT
RIBBING
RUCHING
SEATING
SELVAGE
  (or selvedge)
SNIPPET
SPANGLE
SUITING
TACKING
TEXTURE
THIMBLE
TOGGERY
VEILING
WEAVING
WEBBING

8
BOOTJACK
BOOTLACE
BOX PLEAT
CREATION

DESIGNER
DOG-TOOTH
FASTENER
FROU-FROU
FURBELOW
LIRIPOOP
NECKLINE
POLKA DOT
QUILLING
RAG TRADE
RIBBONRY
RICKRACK
SELVEDGE
 (or selvage)
SHIRRING
SHOEHORN
SHOELACE
SHOULDER
SLASHING
SMOCKING
SNIPPING
SOUTACHE
TIGHT FIT
TRIMMING
TURNBACK
WARDROBE

9
CHINSTRAP
CUBAN HEEL
CYCLE CLIP
DÉCOLLETÉ

DESIGNING
FANDANGLE
FASTENING
GATHERING
HIP POCKET
INSERTION
INSIDE LEG
MANNEQUIN
MILLINERY
OVERCHECK
PAILLETTE
PETERSHAM
PINSTRIPE
PRESS STUD
SAFETY PIN
SEWING PIN
SHIRT TAIL
SPIKE HEEL
STIFFENER
STITCHING
SUSPENDER
TAILORING

10
BACK POCKET
BOONDOGGLE
BUTTONHOLE
BUTTONHOOK
COLLAR STUD
CONFECTION
COTTON REEL
DERNIER CRI

DÉSHABILLÉ
DRAWSTRING
EMPIRE LINE
ENLACEMENT
FRENCH CUFF
FRENCH HEEL
HALTER-NECK
LAVALLIÈRE
OUTFITTING
PIECE GOODS
SHIRT FRILL
SHIRT FRONT
SHOESTRING
SLIT POCKET
STIFFENING
SUPERMODEL
TASSELLING
TROUSER LEG
TURTLE-NECK

11
BIAS BINDING
DÉCOLLETAGE
DRESS LENGTH
FASHION SHOW
HERRINGBONE
HOUNDSTOOTH
LOW NECKLINE
MEASUREMENT
PATCH POCKET
PEARL BUTTON
SHIRT BUTTON

SHIRT SLEEVE
SHOULDER PAD
TAPE MEASURE
THIMBLE CASE
TROUSER CLIP
WATCH POCKET
ZIP FASTENER

12
APRON STRINGS
BUTTERFLY BOW
HABERDASHERY
HAUTE COUTURE
KIMONO SLEEVE
RAGLAN SLEEVE
SHOULDER KNOT
STILETTO HEEL
TAILOR'S CHALK
TAILOR'S DUMMY
TAILOR'S TWIST

13
BATWING SLEEVE
DARNING NEEDLE
MEASURING TAPE
PASSEMENTERIE
RATIONAL DRESS
SEWING MACHINE
SHOULDER STRAP
TROUSER BUTTON
TROUSER POCKET

Clothing & Fashion – FASHION DESIGNERS * = company founder

4
DIOR Christian
MUIR Jean
WANG Vera

5
AMIES Sir Hardy
BANKS Jeff
BLOCH Phillip
CLARK Ossie
DOLCE Domenico
GUCCI Guccio*
KARAN Donna
KLEIN Calvin
PATOU Jean
PRADA Miuccia
QUANT Mary
SMITH Sir Paul
ZEGNA Ermenegildo

6
ARMANI Giorgo
CARDIN Pierre
CHANEL Coco
DAVIES George
HERMÈS Thierry*
LAUREN Ralph
MIRMAN Simone

RHODES Zandra
TAKADA Kenzo
UNGARO Emanuel
WALKER Catherine

7
BALMAIN Pierre
BARBOUR John*
BOATENG Oswald
CASSINI Oleg
EMANUEL David,
  Elizabeth
FOURNIÉ Julien
GABBANA Stefano
HECHTER Daniel
LACROIX Christian
MCQUEEN Alexander
RABANNE Paco
SIMMONS Russell
SLIMANE Hedi
VERSACE Donatella,
  Gianni
VUITTON Louis

8
AZZEDINE Alaia
BURBERRY Thomas*
GALLIANO John

GAULTIER Jean-Paul
GIVENCHY Hubert de
HARTNELL Sir Norman
MALHOTRA Manish
MOSCHINO Franco
OLDFIELD Bruce
ROBINSON Antonia
SHILLING David
WESTWOOD Vivienne
YAMAMOTO Yohji

9
COURRÈGES André
LAGERFELD Karl
LOUBOUTIN Christian
MACDONALD Julien
MCCARTNEY Stella
TRUSSARDI Nicola
VALENTINE Anna
VALENTINO Garavani

10
GHESQUIÈRE Nicolas

12
SAINT-LAURENT Yves
SCHIAPARELLI Elsa

Clothing & Fashion – HAIRDRESSING & COSMETICS

3				**4**	
BOB	DYE	NET	TAG	AFRO	BANG
BUN	MAT	PIN	TIE	BALD	CLIP
	MOP	SET	WIG		COMB

CROP
CURL
FUZZ
HAIR
KOHL
LASH
LOCK
MUSK
PACK
PERM
POLL
POUF
PUFF
ROLL
ROOT
SHAG
TAIL
TALC
TINT
TRIM
TUFT
WAVE

5
BEARD
BLUSH
BOTOX
BRAID
BRUSH
CRIMP
CROWN
FRIZZ
HAIRY
HENNA
LINER
PAINT
PATCH
PLAIT

QUEUE
QUIFF
RAZOR
RINSE
ROOTS
ROUGE
SCALP
SCENT
SHAVE
SHOCK
SINGE
SLIDE
SNOOD
STYLE
TRESS

6
BARBER
BAY RUM
CHYPRE
CURLER
FACIAL
FILLET
FRINGE
GOATEE
HAIRDO
LOTION
MAKE-UP
MARCEL
MULLET
PENCIL
PERUKE
POMADE
POWDER
ROLLER
SHAVER
STRAND
TANGLE

TATTOO
THATCH
TOUPEE
WAVING

7
BEEHIVE
BIG HAIR
BLOW-DRY
BLUSHER
BOWL CUT
BRISTLE
CHIGNON
COMBING
COMB-OUT
COMPACT
COWLICK
CREW CUT
CRIMPER
EARLOCK
ESSENCE
EYEBROW
EYELASH
FRIZZLE
HAIRCUT
HAIR DYE
HAIRNET
HAIR OIL
HAIRPIN
HIRSUTE
LACQUER
MASCARA
MOHICAN
MUD PACK
PAGEBOY
PANCAKE
PARTING
PERFUME

PERIWIG
PIGTAIL
RINGLET
SHAMPOO
SHAVING
SHINGLE
STUBBLE
STYLING
STYLIST
TONSURE
TOPKNOT
VANDYKE
WHISKER

8
ATOMISER
BACK-COMB
BALDNESS
BOUFFANT
CLIPPERS
CLIPPING
COIFFURE
COLD PACK
COLD WAVE
COMB-OVER
COSMETIC
DALMAHOY
DANDRUFF
EPILATOR
ETON CROP
EYELINER
FACELIFT
FACE MAST
FACE PACK
FORELOCK
HAIRBAND
HAIRGRIP
HAIRLINE

IMPERIAL
KISS-CURL
LIPGLOSS
LIPSTICK
LOVELOCK
MACASSAR
MANICURE
PEDICURE
PEROXIDE
POMANDER
PONYTAIL
RAT'S TAIL
SCISSORS
SPIT CURL
TRIMMING
TWEEZERS
WARPAINT
WHISKERS

9
BLUE RINSE
BLOW-DRYER
COLD CREAM
CONCEALER
COSMETICS
DEODORANT
DEPILATOR
EPILATION
EYE PENCIL
EYESHADOW
FACE CREAM
HAIRBRUSH
HAIR-DRYER
HAIRINESS
HAIRPIECE
HAIRSPRAY
HAIRSLIDE
HAIRSTYLE

HAND CREAM
MOUSTACHE
PATCHOULI
PERFUMERY
POMPADOUR
ROSE WATER
SCRUNCHIE
SIDEBURNS
SPIRIT GUM
SPLIT ENDS
SUNTAN OIL

10
AFTERSHAVE
BEAUTY SPOT
DEPILATION
DEPILATORY
DREADLOCKS
FACE POWDER
FALSE BEARD
FOUNDATION
MAQUILLAGE
MARCEL WAVE
MUSTACHIOS
NAIL POLISH
POGONOTOMY
POUNCET-BOX
POWDER PUFF
RAZOR BLADE
SHAMPOOING
SIDEBOARDS
SPADE BEARD

TRICHOLOGY
WIDOW'S PEAK

11
BACK-COMBING
CONDITIONER
CURLING IRON
FRENCH BRAID
GREASEPAINT
HAIRDRESSER
HAIR REMOVER
HAIRSTYLIST
MACASSAR OIL
NAIL VARNISH
ORANGE STICK
SAFETY RAZOR
SCENT BOTTLE
SHAVING SOAP

12
BRILLIANTINE
CURLING TONGS
DERMABRASION
EAU DE COLOGNE
ELECTROLYSIS
HAIRDRESSING
HAIR RESTORER
MOUSTACHE CUP
NAIL CLIPPERS
NAIL SCISSORS
SHAVING BRUSH
SHAVING CREAM

SHAVING STICK
SIDE WHISKERS
SUNTAN LOTION
TALCUM POWDER
VANDYKE BEARD

13
EYEBROW PENCIL
LAVENDER WATER
NEWGATE FRINGE
PANCAKE MAKE-UP
PERMANENT WAVE
POWDER COMPACT
SHAMPOO AND SET

14
CUT-THROAT RAZOR
ELECTRIC SHAVER
FALSE EYELASHES
VANISHING CREAM

15
FOUNDATION CREAM
WALRUS MOUSTACHE

17
SHORT BACK AND SIDES

18
HANDLEBAR MOUSTACHE

Clothing & Fashion – JEWELLERY & TRINKETS

3
GEM
ICE
JET
ORB
PIN

4
BEAD
DROP
GOLD
JADE
ONYX
OPAL
PAVÉ
RING
ROCK
ROPE
RUBY
SARD
STUD
TORC
 (or torque)

5
AGATE
AMBER
BERYL
BEZEL
BIJOU
CAMEO
CHAIN
CHARM
CLASP
CORAL
CURIO

FACET
JEWEL
MOTIF
NACRE
PASTE
PEARL
STONE
TOPAZ

6
ALBERT
AMULET
ANKLET
ARMLET
BANGLE
BAUBLE
BROOCH
CHOKER
COLLET
FINERY
GARNET
GEWGAW
HATPIN
IOLITE
JASPER
LOCKET
PRETTY
PYRITE
PYROPE
QUARTZ
ROSARY
SCARAB
SIGNET
SILVER
SPINEL
TIEPIN

TORQUE
 (or torc)
WAMPUM
ZIRCON

7
BIBELOT
CAT'S EYE
CITRINE
CRYSTAL
DIAMOND
EARDROP
EARRING
EMERALD
GIRASOL
JACINTH
KUNZITE
MANILLA
NECKLET
OLIVINE
PARAGON
PENDANT
PERIDOT
REGALIA
RIVIÈRE
SARDIUS
SCEPTRE
SETTING
SLEEPER
SPANGLE
TOE RING
TRINKET
ZOISITE

8
AMETHYST

BAGUETTE
BRACELET
CABOCHON
CUFF-LINK
DIAMANTÉ
FIRE OPAL
FRIPPERY
GEMSTONE
GIMCRACK
HYACINTH
INTAGLIO
MARQUISE
MELANITE
NAVEL BAR
NECKLACE
NEPHRITE
NOSE RING
NOSE STUD
OBSIDIAN
ORNAMENT
PLATINUM
SAPPHIRE
SARDONYX
SPARKLER
SUGILITE
SUNSTONE
TREASURE
TRUMPERY
WRISTLET

9
ALMANDINE
ANDRADITE
BREASTPIN
BRIC-À-BRAC
BRILLIANT

CARBUNCLE
CORNELIAN
DRESS STUD
HAEMATITE
JEWELLERY
JOB'S TEARS
MARCASITE
MOONSTONE
RUBELLITE
SCARF RING
SEED PEARL
SOLITAIRE
TANZANITE
TIGER'S EYE
TRINKETRY
TURQUOISE
UVAROVITE
VALUABLES

10
ANDALUSITE
AQUAMARINE
BIJOUTERIE
BLOODSTONE
CHALCEDONY
CHRYSOLITE
DIAMONIQUE
EYEBROW BAR
KNICK-KNACK
LAVALLIÈRE
RHINESTONE
ROSE QUARTZ
SIGNET RING
SPINEL RUBY
TONGUE STUD
TOPAZOLITE

TOURMALINE	EYEBROW RING	STAR SAPPHIRE	PEARL NECKLACE
WATCH CHAIN	FERRONNIÈRE	WISHBONE RING	PRECIOUS STONE
WORRY BEADS	LAPIS LAZULI		STRING OF BEADS
	ROSE DIAMOND	**13**	
11	WEDDING RING	CHARM BRACELET	**14**
ALEXANDRITE		CUBIC ZIRCONIA	ENGAGEMENT RING
CHRYSOBERYL	**12**	CULTURED PEARL	STRING OF PEARLS
CHRYSOCOLLA	ETERNITY RING	MOTHER OF PEARL	
CROWN JEWELS	MOURNING RING	ORIENTAL TOPAZ	

Clothing & Fashion – MATERIALS

3	HEMP	CLOTH	MOIRE	SURAH	CHINTZ
ABB	HIDE	CONEY	MUNGO	TABBY	CLOQUÉ
FUR	JEAN	(or cony)	NAPPA	TERRY	COTTON
KID	JUTE	CRAPE	NINON	TOILE	CRÉPON
NET	LACE	(or crêpe)	NYLON	TULLE	CREWEL
PVC	LAMÉ	CRASH	ORLON	TWEED	DACRON
REP	LAWN	CRÊPE	PANNE	TWILL	DAMASK
WAX	LENO	(or crape)	PASHM	TWINE	DIMITY
	LINT	DENIM	PIQUÉ	UNION	DOMETT
4	LYNX	DRILL	PLAID	VOILE	DOWLAS
BUFF	MULL	FILET	PLUSH	WIGAN	DRALON
CALF	PELT	FITCH	POULT		DUFFEL
CIRÉ	ROAN	FLOCK	PRINT	**6**	ERMINE
CONY	ROPE	FLOSS	RAYON	ALPACA	FABLON
(or coney)	SILK	GAUZE	SABLE	ANGORA	FABRIC
CORD	VAIR	GENET	SATIN	BARÈGE	FAILLE
CORK	WOOL	GUNNY	SCRIM	BEAVER	FRIEZE
DOWN	YARN	KAPOK	SERGE	BOUCLÉ	GURRAH
DRAB	YUFT	KENTE	SHEER	BURLAP	HODDEN
DUCK		KHAKI	SISAL	BURNET	KERSEY
ECRU	**5**	LINEN	SKUNK	BYSSUS	KEVLAR
FELT	BAIZE	LISLE	STRAW	CALICO	KINCOB
FLAX	BRAID	LUREX	STUFF	CANVAS	LAMPAS
GIMP	CHINO	LYCRA	SUEDE	CATGUT	LUSTRE

MADRAS
MARTEN
MELTON
MERINO
MOHAIR
MOREEN
MOUTON
MUSLIN
NUTRIA
OCELOT
PONGEE
POPLIN
RABBIT
RIBBON
RUBBER
RUSSET
SAMITE
SATEEN
SAXONY
SENDAL
SENNIT
SHODDY
STROUD
TARTAN
THREAD
TISSUE
TRICOT
VELOUR
VELVET
VICUÑA
WINCEY
ZEPHYR

7

ACRILAN
ACRYLIC
BATISTE
BELTING

BROCADE
BUCKRAM
BUNTING
CAMBRIC
CATSKIN
CHALLIS
CHAMOIS
CHEVIOT
CHIFFON
COWHIDE
DELAINE
DOESKIN
DOGSKIN
DORNICK
ELASTIC
FAKE FUR
FISHNET
FLANNEL
FOULARD
FUSTIAN
GALATEA
GINGHAM
GORE-TEX
GROGRAM
GUIPURE
HESSIAN
HOLLAND
HOPSACK
JACONET
KIDSKIN
LEATHER
LEGHORN
MATTING
MECHLIN
MINIVER
MOROCCO
NANKEEN
NETTING

OILSKIN
ORGANZA
OTTOMAN
PADDING
PERCALE
PIGSKIN
PLASTIC
POLYMER
RACCOON
SACKING
SATINET
  (or satinette)
SCHAPPE
SPANDEX
TABARET
TAFFETA
TEXTILE
TICKING
TIFFANY
TORCHON
TUSSORE
VEILING
VIYELLA
WADDING
WEBBING
WORSTED
ZANELLA

8

ARMOZEEN
ASBESTOS
BARATHEA
BEARSKIN
BOBBINET
BUCKSKIN
CALFSKIN
CAPESKIN
CASHMERE

CHENILLE
COONSKIN
CORDOVAN
CORDUROY
CRETONNE
DEERSKIN
DIAMANTÉ
DUCHESSE
DUNGAREE
ELASTANE
ÉOLIENNE
GOATSKIN
GOSSAMER
HOMESPUN
JACQUARD
KOLINSKY
LAMBSKIN
LUSTRINE
  (or lustring)
LUSTRING
  (or lustrine)
MAROCAIN
MATERIAL
MOLESKIN
MOQUETTE
MUSQUASH
NAINSOOK
OILCLOTH
ORGANDIE
OSNABURG
PADUASOY
PRUNELLA
QUILTING
SARSENET
SEALSKIN
SHAGREEN
SHANTUNG
SHEETING

SHIRTING
SHOT SILK
STUFFING
TARLATAN
TERYLENE
WAXCLOTH
WHIPCORD
WHIPPING
WILD SILK
WIRE ROPE
WIRE WOOL
WOLFSKIN

9

ALLIGATOR
ASTRAKHAN
BENGALINE
BOMBAZINE
CALAMANCO
CAMEL HAIR
CARPETING
CHARMEUSE
CRIMPLENE
CRINOLINE
CROCODILE
EIDERDOWN
ELASTOMER
FILOSELLE
FINGERING
FLOSS SILK
FOLKWEAVE
GABARDINE
  (or gaberdine)
GABERDINE
  (or gabardine)
GEORGETTE
GRENADINE
GROSGRAIN

HAIRCLOTH
HORSEHAIR
HUCKABACK
KALAMKARI
LAMBSWOOL
MATELASSÉ
ORGANZINE
PACKCLOTH
PARAMATTA
  (or parramatta)
PETERSHAM
POINT LACE
POLYAMIDE
POLYESTER
POLYTHENE
POLYVINYL
SACKCLOTH
SAILCLOTH
SATINETTE
  (or satinet)
SHAHTOOSH
SHARKSKIN
SHEEPSKIN
SILVER FOX
SNAKESKIN
STOCKINET
  (or stockinette)
SWANSDOWN
TARPAULIN
TOWELLING

VELVETEEN
WIRE GAUZE

10
BALBRIGGAN
BOBBIN LACE
BOOK MUSLIN
BROADCLOTH
CANDLEWICK
CHINCHILLA
COTTON WOOL
EMERY CLOTH
GLASS CLOTH
GRASSCLOTH
IRISH LINEN
KERSEYMERE
MACKINTOSH
MODACRYLIC
MOUSSELINE
NEEDLECORD
PARRAMATTA
  (or paramatta)
PEAU-DE-SOIE
PILOT CLOTH
SEERSUCKER
TATTERSALL
THROWN SILK
TUFTAFFETY
WAXED CLOTH
WINCEYETTE

11
BEDFORD CORD
CHEESECLOTH
DRAP-DE-BERRY
EVERLASTING
FLANNELETTE
HARRIS TWEED
HONITON LACE
KENDAL GREEN
LEATHERETTE
LEOPARD-SKIN
MARQUISETTE
MECHLIN LACE
NEEDLEPOINT
PANNE VELVET
PERSIAN SILK
POULT-DE-SOIE
SHOE LEATHER
SPONGE CLOTH
STOCKINETTE
  (or stockinet)
TOILE DE JOUY
TORCHON LACE
WASH LEATHER
WHITLEATHER

12
BOLTING CLOTH
  (or boulting cloth)
BRUSSELS LACE

BUTTER MUSLIN
CAVALRY TWILL
CIRCASSIENNE
CRÊPE DE CHINE
LEATHER CLOTH
MILANESE SILK
SLIPPER SATIN
VALENCIENNES

13
BOULTING CLOTH
  (or bolting cloth)
CHANTILLY LACE
CHROME LEATHER
CRUSHED VELVET
DUCHESSE SATIN
LEVANT MOROCCO
LINSEY-WOOLSEY
OUTING FLANNEL
PATENT LEATHER
RUSSIA LEATHER

14
CHAMOIS LEATHER
EGYPTIAN COTTON

15
JAPANNED LEATHER
NEEDLEPOINT LACE
TATTERSALL CHECK

Clothing & Fashion – SUPERMODELS

3
ALT Carol
WEK Alek

4
COLE Lily
DAHL Sophie
HALL Bridget,
  Jerry
IMAN
KASS Carmen
KLUM Heidi
LIMA Adrian
MOSS Kate
SIMS Naomi
TREE Penelope
WARD Gemma

5
ADAMS Maud
BALTI Bianca
BANKS Tyra
CASTA Laetitia
COLBY Anita
ELSON Karen
JONES Grace
LE BON Yasmin
LEIGH Dorian
MARKS Heather
MUNOZ Astrid
NORTH Chandra
TIEGS Cheryl

6
ALEXIS Kim
BARROS Ann Beatriz
COOPER Wilhelmina
GHAURI Yasmeen
HADDON Dayle
HARLOW Shalom
HELVIN Marie
HUNTER Rachel
MULDER Karen
PARKER Suzy
RAYDER Frankie
TWIGGY
WASSON Erin

7
BENITEZ Elsa
CARANGA Gia
FONTANA Isabeli
IRELAND Kathy
KURKOVÁ Karolina
NEMCOVÁ Petra
O'CONNOR Erin
PESTOVA Daniela
SEYMOUR Stephanie
TAVARES Fernanda
WARSAME Yasmin
WERBOWY Daria

8
AMBROSIO
  Alessandra

AUERMANN Nadja
BECKFORD Tyson
BRINKLEY Christine
BÜNDCHEN Christine
CAMPBELL Naomi
CRAWFORD Cindy
JOVOVICH Milla
PANTAEVA Irina
SARAHYBA Daniella
SCHIFFER Claudia
TRENTINI Caroline
VALLETTA Amber
VAREKOVA Veronica

9
DICKINSON Janice
HERZIGOVÁ Eva
PORIZKOVA Paulina
SHRIMPTON Jean
VERUSCHKA
VODIANOVA Natalia

10
MACPHERSON Elle
TURLINGTON Christy

11
CHRISTENSEN Helena
EVANGELISTA Linda

12
FONSSAGRIVES Lisa

Crime

Crime – CRIME & PUNISHMENT

3	BOOT	QUOD	CHOKY	NOOSE	BANISH
ABH	BUNG	RACK	(or chokey)	OFLAG	BIGAMY
CAN	CANE	RAID	CLINK	ORDER	BOODLE
CAT	CELL	RAMP	CRIME	PATCH	BURGLE
DAB	CLUE	RAPE	CUFFS	POACH	CANING
GBH	CUFF	SACK	EXILE	SMACK	CHAINS
JOB	E-FIT	SLAP	EXPEL	SPANK	CHISEL
JUG	FINE	SLAY	FILCH	STEAL	CHOKEY
LAW	FLOG	STIR	FIT-UP	STICK	(or choky)
MUG	GAOL	SWAG	FORGE	STRAP	COOLER
PEN	HANG	TIME	FRAUD	TAWSE	DETECT
RAP	HARD	WHIP	GRAFT	THEFT	DUPERY
RIG	JAIL		HEIST	TRACE	DURESS
ROB	KILL	**5**	JOUGS	USURY	EXTORT
ROD	LASH	ALIBI	KNOUT	WHACK	FELONY
SOP	LIFE	ARSON	LIBEL		FETTER
	LOOT	BOBOL	LUCRE	**6**	GIBBET
4	NICK	BOOTY	LYNCH	ABDUCT	HIDING
BEAT	PLOT	BRIBE	MANOR	ARREST	HIJACK

HOLD-UP
INCEST
INFAMY
KIDNAP
LOCK-UP
MURDER
NOYADE
PILFER
PIRACY
POISON
PRISON
PUNISH
RACKET
RAPINE
RAVAGE
RIP-OFF
RUSTLE
SCRUMP
SEARCH
SIMONY
SNATCH
SPOILS
STALAG
STOCKS
SUBORN
THIEVE
THRASH
THWACK
TICKET

7

ANARCHY
ASSAULT
BATTERY
BOOTLEG
BORSTAL
BRIBERY
CORRUPT

CRUELTY
DACOITY
DARBIES
DEFAULT
DEFRAUD
DEICIDE
DESPOIL
DOUCEUR
DUNGEON
FORFEIT
FORGERY
FRAME-UP
GALLOWS
HANGING
HOT SEAT
INQUIRY
KILLING
KNAVERY
KURBASH
LARCENY
LASHING
LECHERY
LEG-IRON
MANACLE
MANTRAP
MISDEED
MOB RULE
MUGGING
MUGSHOT
OFFENCE
OUTRAGE
PENALTY
PENANCE
PERFIDY
PERJURY
PILLAGE
PILLORY
PIMPING

PLUNDER
PONCING
PURLOIN
RAM RAID
RANSACK
RIGGING
ROBBERY
ROGUERY
SACKING
SCOURGE
SHACKLE
SJAMBOK
SLAMMER
SLANDER
SLAYING
SLIPPER
SMUGGLE
STICK-UP
STRETCH
SUICIDE
SWINDLE
TAGGING
TAKE OUT
THUGGEE
TORTURE
TREASONE
TRIGAMY
TURF WAR
WARRANT

8

ADULTERY
ATROCITY
AUTO-DA-FÉ
BIG HOUSE
BULLWHIP
BURGLARY
CHASTISE

CONSPIRE
DEATH ROW
DECIMATE
DISGUISE
EMBEZZLE
ENORMITY
FILCHING
FILICIDE
FLOGGING
FOUL PLAY
GARROTTE
GENOCIDE
GRILLING
HOMICIDE
HOOSEGOW
INIQUITY
LYNCHING
PECULATE
PENALISE
PHOTOFIT
PLOTTING
POACHING
PRECINCT
REGICIDE
ROPE'S END
RUSTLING
SABOTAGE
SCAFFOLD
SEDITION
SENTENCE
SLAPPING
SPANKING
SPEEDING
STEALING
STRANGLE
THE BIRCH
THE CHAIR
THE STAKE

THE WHEEL
THIEVERY
THIEVING
THROTTLE
THUGGERY
TRESPASS
VILLAINY
WAR CRIME
WHACKING
WHIPPING

9

ABDUCTION
BLACKMAIL
BRAINWASH
BRIDEWELL
BRIGANDRY
CALABOOSE
CASTIGATE
CHICANERY
COLLUSION
CRIME RATE
CRIME WAVE
DETECTION
DETENTION
DISHONEST
DUPLICITY
ELIMINATE
EXCLUSION
EXECUTION
EXPULSION
EXTORTION
FOOTPRINT
HANDCUFFS
HORSEWHIP
IDENTIKIT
IMPOSTURE
INDECENCY

JUDGEMENT
LIQUIDATE
LOITERING
MACHINATE
MATRICIDE
PARRICIDE
PATRICIDE
PEDERASTY
PILFERING
POISONING
POLYGRAPH
PYROMANIA
RECEIVING
SACRILEGE
SCRUMPING
SLAUGHTER
SMUGGLING
STATEMENT
STRAPPADO
STRAPPING
SUFFOCATE
SUSPICION
SWEETENER
SWINDLING
TERRORISM
THRASHING
THWACKING
TREACHERY
UXORICIDE
VANDALISE
VANDALISM

10
AID AND ABET
BACKHANDER
BANISHMENT
COMMITMENT
CONSPIRACY

CONSTRAINT
CONTRABAND
CONVICTION
CORRECTION
CORRUPTION
DECIMATION
DISHONESTY
FRATRICIDE
GAS CHAMBER
GUILLOTINE
GUN-RUNNING
HARD LABOUR
ILLEGALITY
IMMORALITY
IMMUREMENT
IMPOSITION
INFRACTION
INTERNMENT
IRON MAIDEN
JUDICATION
KIDNAPPING
MISCONDUCT
NEGLIGENCE
OPEN PRISON
PANOPTICON
PECULATION
PERPETRATE
PERVERSION
PILLIWINKS
PLAGIARISM
PLUNDERING
PRISON YARD
PUNISHMENT
PURLOINING
RACHMANISM
RAVISHMENT
RECIDIVISM
REMAND HOME

SMOTHERING
SORORICIDE
STRANGLING
THROTTLING
TICKING-OFF
UNDERWORLD
WRONGDOING

11
ASSASSINATE
BOOTLEGGING
CASTIGATION
CONFINEMENT
COUNTERPLOT
CRIMINOLOGY
CRUCIFIXION
DEFALCATION
DELINQUENCY
DEPORTATION
DESPOILMENT
ELIMINATION
ENDORSEMENT
FINGERPRINT
FIRE-RAISING
FRAUDULENCE
GALLOWS TREE
GANGSTERISM
HIGH TREASON
HOUSE ARREST
KNEECAPPING
LAW AND ORDER
LAWBREAKING
LESE-MAJESTY
LIE DETECTOR
LIQUIDATION
MACHINATION
MALEFACTION
MALFEASANCE

MALPRACTICE
PAEDOPHILIA
SAFE-BLOWING
SHOPLIFTING
SKULDUGGERY
SPREADEAGLE
SUBORNATION
SUFFOCATION
THIRD DEGREE
THUMBSCREWS
TRAFFICKING
TRESPASSING

12
ARMED ROBBERY
BERTILLONAGE
BRAINWASHING
CHASTISEMENT
CONFISCATION
CUCKING STOOL
DEATH PENALTY
DECAPITATION
DOPE-PEDDLING
DRINK-DRIVING
DUCKING STOOL
EMBEZZLEMENT
EXERCISE YARD
FIRST OFFENCE
GRAND LARCENY
IMPRISONMENT
INCENDIARISM
INFRINGEMENT
KERB-CRAWLING
MALVERSATION
MANSLAUGHTER
MISDEMEANOUR
PENALISATION
PENITENTIARY

PERPETRATION
PETTY LARCENY
PETTY TREASON
PROSTITUTION
RACKETEERING
REFORM SCHOOL
RITUAL MURDER
SAFE-BREAKING
SAFE-CRACKING
STRAIT-JACKET
WHIPPING POST

13
ASSASSINATION
BODY-SNATCHING
CAT-O'-NINE-TAILS
DRUG SMUGGLING
ELECTRIC CHAIR
ELECTROCUTION
FALSIFICATION
HANGING MATTER

HOUSEBREAKING
INCARCERATION
INTERROGATION
INVESTIGATION
MOONLIGHT FLIT
PICKPOCKETING
ROGUES' GALLERY
SEARCH WARRANT
SHEEP-STEALING
STREETWALKING

14
APPROVED SCHOOL
COUNTERFEITING
CRIME PASSIONEL
FINGERPRINTING
GROSS INDECENCY
PENAL SERVITUDE
PURSE-SNATCHING
TRANSPORTATION
WRONGFUL ARREST

15
CARELESS DRIVING
DAYLIGHT ROBBERY
DETENTION CENTRE
MONEY LAUNDERING

16
ACTUAL BODILY HARM
BREACH OF THE PEACE
INDECENT EXPOSURE
MISAPPROPRIATION

17
CAPITAL PUNISHMENT
ELECTRONIC TAGGING

18
CORPORAL PUNISHMENT
GRIEVOUS BODILY HARM

Crime – CRIMINALS (types)

3	**5**	BADDIE	OLD LAG	**7**	MAGSMAN
CON	BRAVO	BANDIT	OUTLAW	ABETTOR	MOBSTER
DIP	CROOK	BRIBER	PIRATE	BRIGAND	PLOTTER
LAG	FAKER	COINER	PUSHER	BURGLAR	POACHER
MOB	FELON	CON MAN	RAIDER	CATERAN	RAVAGER
	FENCE	DACOIT	RAPIST	CONVICT	RUSTLER
4	FRAUD	GUNMAN	ROBBER	CORSAIR	SPEEDER
FAKE	LIFER	HIT MAN	RUNNER	CULPRIT	STEALER
HOOD	THIEF	KILLER	SLAYER	ESCAPEE	SUICIDE
THUG		KLEPHT	TRUSTY	FIREBUG	TRAITOR
	6	LOOTER	USURER	FOOTPAD	VILLAIN
	APACHE	MUGGER	VANDAL	HOODLUM	

8

ABDUCTOR
ARSONIST
ASSASSIN
BIGAMIST
COLLUDER
CRIMINAL
CUTPURSE
FILICIDE
FUGITIVE
GANGSTER
HIJACKER
JAILBIRD
LIBELLER
LYNCH MOB
MARAUDER
MURDERER
OFFENDER
PEDERAST
PERJURER
PETERMAN
PILFERER
PILLAGER
PLUG-UGLY
POISONER
PRISONER
RAPPAREE
RAVISHER
RECEIVER
REGICIDE
SABOTEUR
SIMONIAC
SMUGGLER
SUBORNER
SWINDLER

9

ABSCONDER
ACCESSORY
ADULTERER
ANARCHIST
BANDOLERO
BUCCANEER
CHISELLER
CRACKSMAN
CUT-THROAT
DEFAULTER
DESPOILER
EMBEZZLER
FALSIFIER
FRAUDSTER
GUN-RUNNER
KIDNAPPER
LARCENIST
MATRICIDE
MURDERESS
PARRICIDE
PATRICIDE
PECULATOR
PLUNDERER
PRINCIPAL
PRIVATEER
PURLOINER
RACKETEER
RANSACKER
SLANDERER
SPOLIATOR
STRANGLER
THROTTLER
TRIGAMIST
UXORICIDE
WRONGDOER

10

ACCOMPLICE
ADULTERESS
BOOTLEGGER
CAT BURGLAR
DELINQUENT
DOPE PEDLAR
ELIMINATOR
FIRE-RAISER
FREEBOOTER
HIGHBINDER
HIGHWAYMAN
HORSE THIEF
INCENDIARY
LAWBREAKER
LIQUIDATOR
MOONSHINER
PICKPOCKET
PLAGIARIST
RECIDIVIST
SAFE-BLOWER
SHOPLIFTER
SNEAK THIEF
TERMINATOR
TRAFFICKER
TRESPASSER

11

ARCH-VILLAIN
BLACKMAILER
CONSPIRATOR
DRINK-DRIVER
EXTORTIONER
KERB-CRAWLER

MOSS-TROOPER
PERPETRATOR
PROBATIONER
SAFE-BREAKER
SAFE-CRACKER
SLAUGHTERER

12

BABY-SNATCHER
BODY-SNATCHER
DRUG SMUGGLER
EXTERMINATOR
EXTORTIONIST
HOUSEBREAKER
SHEEP-STEALER

13

CONTRABANDIST
COUNTERFEITER
FIRST OFFENDER
PRIVATEERSMAN

14

BLACK MARKETEER

15

RESURRECTION MAN

Education

Education – EDUCATION TERMS

3	GCSE	CHALK	PAPER	LESSON	ALUMNAE
DON	HALL	CLASS	PRIZE	MASTER	ALUMNUS
FAG	HEAD	COACH	PUPIL	O-LEVEL	BANDING
FEE	MARK	CROSS	RESIT	PERIOD	BURSARY
GYM	MODS	EASEL	STUDY	PRELIM	COLLEGE
LAB	ORAL	ESSAY	TUTOR	PRIMER	CONDUCT
MUG	PASS	EXEAT		RECTOR	CRAMMER
SIT	PREP	EXPEL	**6**	REMOVE	DIPLOMA
	QUAD	FIRST	A-LEVEL	REPORT	DOMINIE
4	ROLL	GAUDY	ALUMNA	REVISE	EDUCATE
COED	ROTE	GRADE	ALUMNI	SCHOOL	EXCLUDE
CRAM	SWOT	GRANT	BURSAR	STREAM	FACULTY
CRIB	TERM	HOUSE	CAMPUS	THESIS	FAGGING
DEAN	TEST	LINES	COURSE	TRIPOS	FRESHER
DESK	TICK	LEARN	CREDIT	TRUANT	HIGHERS
EXAM		LODGE	DEGREE		HONOURS
FAIL	**5**	LYCÉE	HOOKEY	**7**	LEARNER
FORM	BREAK	MOCKS	INTAKE	ABSENCE	LECTURE
GATE	CHAIR	ORACY	LECTOR	ACADEMY	MARKING

MONITOR
PHONICS
PREFECT
PROCTOR
PROJECT
SATCHEL
SCHOLAR
SEMINAR
SESSION
SICK-BAY
STUDENT
SUBJECT
TEACHER
TESTING
TRUANCY
TUITION
VARSITY

8
ACADEMIA
ACADEMIC
ACTIVITY
AEGROTAT
COACHING
ENCAENIA
EXERCISE
FORM ROOM
FRESHMAN
GRADUATE
HALF-TERM
HOMEWORK
KEY STAGE
LAUREATE
LEARNING
LECTURER
LITERACY
MAGISTER
MISTRESS

NUMERACY
PASS MARK
PEDAGOGY
PLAYTIME
REGISTER
REVISION
ROLL-CALL
SEMESTER
SICKROOM
SORORITY
SYLLABUS
TEACHING
TERM-TIME
TEXTBOOK
TRAINING
TUTELAGE
TUTORIAL
TUTORING
VIVA VOCE

9
ALMA MATER
BEHAVIOUR
BENCHMARK
CLASS LIST
CLASSMATE
CLASSROOM
CROCODILE
DAY SCHOOL
DETENTION
DORMITORY
EDUCATION
E-LEARNING
ENROLMENT
EXCLUSION
EXPULSION
GROUNDING
GYMNASIUM

HEURISTIC
HIGH TABLE
INSTITUTE
KNOWLEDGE
PEDAGOGUE
PLAYGROUP
PRACTICAL
PRE-SCHOOL
PROFESSOR
PUPILLAGE
REFECTORY
REFRESHER
RUSTICATE
SCHOOL AGE
SCHOOLBAG
SCHOOLBOY
SCHOOL BUS
SCHOOLING
SOPHOMORE
SPEECH DAY
STAFFROOM
STANDARDS
STREAMING
TEST PAPER
TIMETABLE
TRIMESTER
TUTORSHIP

10
ASSESSMENT
ATTENDANCE
BLACKBOARD
CHALKBOARD
COLLOQUIUM
COMMON ROOM
COURSEWORK
CURRICULUM
DISCIPLINE

ELEVEN-PLUS
EXHIBITION
FRATERNITY
GRADUATION
HEADMASTER
HIGH SCHOOL
IMPOSITION
INSTRUCTOR
INVIGILATE
LABORATORY
PEDAGOGICS
PLAYGROUND
PLAYSCHOOL
PREP SCHOOL
PROSPECTUS
QUADRANGLE
REGISTRARY
SCHOOL BELL
SCHOOLBOOK
SCHOOLDAYS
SCHOOL FEES
SCHOOLGIRL
SCHOOLMARM
SCHOOLMATE
SCHOOLROOM
SCHOOL TERM
SCHOOLWORK
SCHOOL YEAR
UNIVERSITY
VISUAL AIDS
VOCATIONAL
WHITEBOARD

11
CERTIFICATE
CO-EDUCATION
COMPOSITION
DOUBLE FIRST

EXAMINATION
FACILITATOR
HANDWRITING
INSTRUCTION
INVIGILATOR
LECTURESHIP
MATRICULATE
MODERATIONS
NIGHT SCHOOL
PERIPATETIC
POLYTECHNIC
PREPARATION
PRIZE-GIVING
PROCTORSHIP
RUSTICATION
SCHOLARSHIP
SCHOOL BOARD
SCHOOLCHILD
SCHOOLCRAFT
SCHOOLHOUSE
STUDENTSHIP
TOWN AND GOWN

12
ACADEMIC YEAR
CHURCH SCHOOL
COMMENCEMENT
COUNTY SCHOOL
DIRECT METHOD
EXERCISE BOOK

FLANNELBOARD
HEADMISTRESS
INFANT SCHOOL
INVIGILATION
JUNIOR SCHOOL
KINDERGARTEN
MIDDLE SCHOOL
MISBEHAVIOUR
NORMAL SCHOOL
PROFESSORATE
PUBLIC SCHOOL
SCHOOL-LEAVER
SCHOOLMASTER
SENIOR SCHOOL

13
ADVANCED LEVEL
AUTODIDACTISM
BACCALAUREATE
CHARITY SCHOOL
COMPREHENSION
COMPREHENSIVE
GRADUATION DAY
GRAMMAR SCHOOL
MATRICULATION
NON-ATTENDANCE
NURSERY SCHOOL
ORDINARY LEVEL
PRIMARY SCHOOL
PRIVATE SCHOOL

PROFESSORSHIP
RHODES SCHOLAR
QUALIFICATION
SCHOOL-LEAVING
SCHOOL LIBRARY
SCHOOLTEACHER
SCHOOL VOUCHER
SUPPLY TEACHER
UNDERGRADUATE
VOCATIONALISM

14
ACTIVE LEARNING
BOARDING SCHOOL
PROBLEM-SOLVING
RECEPTION CLASS
SCHOOLMISTRESS
SCHOOLTEACHING
TEACHING FELLOW
VISUAL LEARNING

15
HIGHER EDUCATION
REFRESHER COURSE
SCHOOLMASTERING
SECONDARY SCHOOL
TEACHING MACHINE
VOLUNTARY SCHOOL

Education – SUBJECTS & STUDIES

3	**4**	**5**	DRAMA	LATIN	MUSIC
ART	LORE	CRAFT	GAMES	LOGIC	SPORT
LAW		DANCE	GREEK	MATHS	STUDY

6
BOTANY
CIVICS
FRENCH
GERMAN
GREATS
OOLOGY
OPTICS
POETRY
SYNTAX

7
ALGEBRA
ANATOMY
BIOLOGY
BIONICS
COOKERY
ECOLOGY
ENGLISH
GEOLOGY
GRAMMAR
HISTORY
ITALIAN
MYOLOGY
OTOLOGY
PHYSICS
POTTERY
READING
RUSSIAN
SCIENCE
SPANISH
STATICS
UFOLOGY
WRITING
ZOOLOGY

8
AEROLOGY

AGROLOGY
ALGOLOGY
BRYOLOGY
CLASSICS
COMMERCE
CYTOLOGY
DYNAMICS
ETHOLOGY
EUGENICS
FOLKLORE
GENETICS
GEOMETRY
HOROLOGY
KINESICS
KINETICS
MEDICINE
MYCOLOGY
NOSOLOGY
OENOLOGY
ONCOLOGY
ONTOLOGY
PEDOLOGY
PENOLOGY
POLITICS
POSOLOGY
RHEOLOGY
ROBOTICS
ROCKETRY
SEROLOGY
SEXOLOGY
SINOLOGY
SPELLING
TAXONOMY
TECHNICS
THEOLOGY
TOPOLOGY
TYPOLOGY
VIROLOGY

WOODWORK

9
ACOUSTICS
ASTROLOGY
ASTRONOMY
ATHEOLOGY
ATHLETICS
AUDIOLOGY
BIONOMICS
CARPOLOGY
CHEMISTRY
COMPUTING
COSMOLOGY
DIDACTICS
DIETETICS
ECONOMICS
ETHNOLOGY
ETYMOLOGY
FORENSICS
GEMMOLOGY
GENEALOGY
GEOGRAPHY
GEOPONICS
HAGIOLOGY
HIEROLOGY
HISTOLOGY
HYDROLOGY
HYGROLOGY
HYMNOLOGY
ICHNOLOGY
ICONOLOGY
LANGUAGES
LIMNOLOGY
LITHOLOGY
LITURGICS
LOGISTICS
MAGNETICS

MAIEUTICS
MAMMALOGY
MECHANICS
METALWORK
METROLOGY
MNEMONICS
MYTHOLOGY
NEPHOLOGY
NEUROLOGY
OSTEOLOGY
PATHOLOGY
PATRISTICS
PATROLOGY
PETROLOGY
PHENOLOGY
PHILATELY
PHILOLOGY
PHONEMICS
PHONETICS
PHONOLOGY
PHYCOLOGY
RADIOLOGY
RHINOLOGY
RHYTHMICS
SCATOLOGY
SEMANTICS
SEMIOLOGY
SEMIOTICS
SHORTHAND
SOCIOLOGY
SYMBOLOGY
SYNCHRONY
SYNECTICS
TRIBOLOGY

10
ACCOUNTING
ARITHMETIC

ART HISTORY
AUTECOLOGY
BALLISTICS
BIOMETRICS
BIOPHYSICS
CARDIOLOGY
CATOPTRICS
CHROMATICS
CHRONOLOGY
CONCHOLOGY
CRANIOLOGY
CRYOGENICS
CRYPTOLOGY
DELTIOLOGY
DEMOGRAPHY
DEMONOLOGY
DENDROLOGY
DEONTOLOGY
EGYPTOLOGY
EMBRYOLOGY
ENERGETICS
ENTOMOLOGY
ENZYMOLOGY
EPIZOOTICS
ERGONOMICS
ESCAPOLOGY
FLORISTICS
FUTUROLOGY
GASTROLOGY
GEOPHYSICS
GLACIOLOGY
GRAPHEMICS
GRAPHOLOGY
GYMNASTICS
HEPATOLOGY
HUMANITIES
HYDRAULICS
IMMUNOLOGY

KINEMATICS
LEXICOLOGY
LITERATURE
MALACOLOGY
METALLURGY
MINERALOGY
MORPHEMICS
MORPHOLOGY
MUSICOLOGY
NEONTOLOGY
NEPHROLOGY
NUCLEONICS
NUMEROLOGY
OCEANOLOGY
ODONTOLOGY
ONEIROLOGY
ONOMASTICS
ORTHOPTICS
PALYNOLOGY
PAPYROLOGY
PATRISTICS
PHILOSOPHY
PHRENOLOGY
PHYSIOLOGY
PNEUMATICS
POTAMOLOGY
PRAGMATICS
PSEPHOLOGY
PSYCHOLOGY
SEISMOLOGY
SOCIOMETRY
SPELEOLOGY
SPLENOLOGY
STATISTICS
STYLISTICS
SYNECOLOGY
TECHNOLOGY
TERATOLOGY

TOXICOLOGY
TRICHOLOGY

11
AERONAUTICS
AGROBIOLOGY
AGROSTOLOGY
ARACHNOLOGY
ARCHAEOLOGY
ASSYRIOLOGY
BIODYNAMICS
CAMPANOLOGY
CARCINOLOGY
CARTOGRAPHY
CHRISTOLOGY
CLIMATOLOGY
CRIMINOLOGY
CYBERNETICS
DERMATOLOGY
ELECTRONICS
ENGINEERING
EPIGENETICS
ETHNOGRAPHY
FILM STUDIES
GEODYNAMICS
GERONTOLOGY
GYNAECOLOGY
HAEMATOLOGY
HERPETOLOGY
HYDROGRAPHY
HYDROPONICS
HYPERSONICS
ICHTHYOLOGY
KINESIOLOGY
LARYNGOLOGY
LICHENOLOGY
LINGUISTICS
MALARIOLOGY

MARTYROLOGY
MATHEMATICS
METAPHYSICS
METEOROLOGY
METHODOLOGY
MYRMECOLOGY
NATURE STUDY
NUMISMATICS
ORNITHOLOGY
PSYCHOMETRY
PTERIDOLOGY
PURE SCIENCE
SEMASIOLOGY
SOIL SCIENCE
SUPERSONICS
THANATOLOGY
THERMIONICS
ULTRASONICS
VENEREOLOGY
VOLCANOLOGY
  (or vulcanology)
VULCANOLOGY
  (or volcanology)

12
ANTHROPOLOGY
ASTRONAUTICS
ASTROPHYSICS
BACTERIOLOGY
BIOGEOGRAPHY
BIOMECHANICS
CYTOGENETICS
DIALECTOLOGY
ECCLESIOLOGY
ECONOMETRICS
EPIDEMIOLOGY
EPISTEMOLOGY
ETHNOHISTORY

ETHNOSCIENCE
GNOTOBIOTICS
HERMENEUTICS
HUMAN BIOLOGY
HYDROGEOLOGY
LITURGIOLOGY
MACROBIOTICS
MEDIA STUDIES
MICROBIOLOGY
OCEANOGRAPHY
ONOMASIOLOGY
PALAEOBOTANY
PALAEOGRAPHY
PARASITOLOGY
PHARMACOLOGY
PHOTOGEOLOGY
PHYSIOGRAPHY
PNEUMATOLOGY
PROTISTOLOGY
PYROTECHNICS
RHEUMATOLOGY
SELENOGRAPHY
SPECTROSCOPY
TRIGONOMETRY
ZOOGEOGRAPHY

13
ANTHROPOMETRY
CHRONOBIOLOGY
DACTYLOGRAPHY
ELECTRO-OPTICS
GEOCHRONOLOGY
GRAPHIC DESIGN
HELMINTHOLOGY
HOME ECONOMICS
MAGNETO-OPTICS
MNEMOTECHNICS
NUMISMATOLOGY

OPHTHALMOLOGY
PALAEOBIOLOGY
PALAEOECOLOGY
PALAEONTOLOGY
PHARMACEUTICS
PHENOMENOLOGY
PSYCHOMETRICS
PSYCHOPHYSICS
SOCIAL BIOLOGY
SOCIAL SCIENCE
SOIL MECHANICS
TEXTILE DESIGN
WAVE MECHANICS

14
APPLIED SCIENCE
ASTROCHEMISTRY
BIOSYSTEMATICS
ELECTROSTATICS
HISTORIOGRAPHY
HOME MANAGEMENT
METAPSYCHOLOGY

NEUROPATHOLOGY
NUCLEAR PHYSICS
PHYTOGEOGRAPHY
PHYTOPATHOLOGY
PSYCHOGRAPHICS
SYMPTOMATOLOGY
THERMODYNAMICS

15
ANAESTHESIOLOGY
BUSINESS STUDIES
COMBINED SCIENCE
COMPUTER SCIENCE
COMPUTER STUDIES
CRYSTALLOGRAPHY
DERMATOGLYPHICS
DOMESTIC SCIENCE
METALINGUISTICS
MODERN LANGUAGES
MORPHOPHONEMICS
MORPHOPHONOLOGY
NATURAL SCIENCES

PALAEOMAGNETISM
PALAEOPATHOLOGY
PSYCHOACOUSTICS
PSYCHOPATHOLOGY
PURE MATHEMATICS
THERMOCHEMISTRY

16
PHYSICAL SCIENCES
PSYCHOGERIATRICS
PSYCHOPHYSIOLOGY
RELIGIOUS STUDIES
SOCIOLINGUISTICS

17
COMMERCIAL STUDIES
ENGLISH LITERATURE
LITERAE HUMANIORES
PHYSICAL CHEMISTRY
PHYSICAL EDUCATION
PSYCHOLINGUISTICS

Food & Drink

Food & Drink – Food – CELEBRITY CHEFS

3
HOM Ken

4
KERR Graham
KING Simon
ROUX Albert, Michel

5
ALLEN Darina
BLANC Raymond
BOOME Danny
DAVID Elizabeth
FLOYD Keith
LEITH Prue
MYERS David
NAIRN Nick
SMITH Delia
STEIN Rick
WHITE Marco Pierre

6
BEETON Mrs
BOCUSE Paul
BURDEN Ross
HARBEN Philip
LAWSON Nigella
MARTIN James
OLIVER Jamie
PATTEN Marguerite
RAMSAY Gordon
RANKIN Paul
RHODES Gary
SLATER Nigel
TANNER James
TURNER Brian
WATERS Lesley

7
CARRIER Robert
CRADOCK Fanny, Johnnie
DUCASSE Alain

GRANGER Bill
GRIGSON Sophie
JAFFREY Madhur

8
DAY-LEWIS Tamasin
HARRIOTT Ainsley
PATERSON Jennifer
RANHOFER Charles
WOODFORD Kevin

9
ESCOFFIER Auguste

10
BLUMENTHAL Heston
CHRISTOPHE Jean

13
DICKSON-WRIGHT
   Clarissa

15
WORRALL THOMPSON Antony

21
FEARNLEY-WHITTINGSTALL Hugh

Food & Drink – CULINARY TERMS

3	KEEP	CARVE	TANGY	PICKLE	DESSERT
CUT	LARD	CHUCK	TASTE	PICNIC	DHANSAK
FAT	LEAN	COVER	TASTY	PIPING	DOPIAZA
FRY	MEAL	DEVIL	TOAST	RATION	ESSENCE
KAI	MEAT	DOUGH	TWANG	RECIPE	FILLING
MIX	MENU	FEAST	YEAST	RENNET	FLAVOUR
OIL	NOSH	FLOUR		REPAST	FORMULA
PAT	PECK	FRUIT	**6**	SIMMER	GARNISH
SET	PEEL	GRILL	AFTERS	SIPPET	GELATIN
TEA	RIND	GRIST	BAKING	SOLIDS	(or gelatine)
	SIFT	JOINT	BLANCH	SPREAD	HELPING
4	SLAB	KORMA	BRAISE	STAPLE	HIGH TEA
BAKE	SNAP	LUNCH	BROACH	STODGE	KITCHEN
BASE	SPIT	MINCE	BRUNCH	STRAIN	LIQUIDS
BITE	STEW	ROAST	BUFFET	SUPPER	PIQUANT
BOIL	STIR	ROUND	CODDLE	TIFFIN	PORTION
CHOP	SUET	SAUTÉ	COURSE	TITBIT	PROTEIN
COOK	TACK	SCOFF	DAINTY	VIANDS	PUDDING
DICE	TANG	SCRAN	DICING		RATIONS
DIET	TUCK	SERVE	DINNER	**7**	REGIMEN
DISH		SLICE	EDIBLE	BANQUET	SAVOURY
FARE	**5**	SMACK	ENTRÉE	BLOWOUT	SEAFOOD
FAST	BALTI	SMOKE	FARINA	BOILING	SERVICE
FILL	BASTE	SNACK	GALLEY	BRINING	SERVING
FISH	BEANO	SOUSE	HOMINY	CARVING	SETTING
FOOD	BHUNA	SPICE	LARDON	COMMONS	SIFTING
GRUB	BLEND	STEAM	LEAVEN	COOKERY	SLICING
HEEL	BOARD	STEEP	MASALA	COOKING	SMOKING
HERB	BRINE	STOCK	MORSEL	COOKOUT	SOUPÇON
JERK	BROIL	TABLE	PAN FRY	CUISINE	SOUSING

STARTER
STEWING
STIR FRY
TOPPING
VANILLA
VITAMIN

8
ADDITIVE
À LA CARTE
APPETITE
AU POIVRE
BARBECUE
BRAISING
BROILING
BROWNING
BUNFIGHT
CLAMBAKE
CODDLING
CONSERVE
CREAM TEA
DELICACY
DOORSTEP
DRESSING
EN CROUTE
ESCULENT
FAST FOOD
GELATINE
  (or gelatin)
GLUTTONY
GRILLING
JALFREZI
JULIENNE
KICKSHAW
LUNCHEON
MARINATE
MOLASSES
MOUTHFUL

PICKLING
PIQUANCY
POT-ROAST
PRESERVE
ROASTING
ROUGHAGE
SCRAMBLE
SIDE DISH
SPOONFUL
STEAMING
STEEPING
STUFFING
SUPPLIES
TANDOORI
TEA PARTY
TOASTING
TV DINNER
VICTUALS
VINDALOO

9
ALMOND OIL
ANTIPASTO
ANTIPASTI
APPETISER
BEANFEAST
BLANCHING
BREAKFAST
BUTTERFAT
COLOURING
CONDIMENT
ENTREMETS
FOODSTUFF
FOOD VALUE
FORCEMEAT
GROCERIES
ISINGLASS
LEAVENING

LEFT-OVERS
LEMON PEEL
MINCEMEAT
MUSCOVADO
NUTRIMENT
NUTRITION
OLIVE OIL
RÉCHAUFFÉ
REFECTION
SEASONING
SIDE SALAD
STRAINING
TENDERISE
THICKENER
WHOLEFOOD

10
AFTERTASTE
BAKING SODA
BARBECUING
BILL OF FARE
BON APPÉTIT
CONCOCTION
CONFECTION
COOKING FAT
COOKING OIL
DUTCH TREAT
FLAVOURING
FRANGIPANE
GASTRONOMY
INGREDIENT
JARDINIÈRE
MIXED GRILL
ORANGE PEEL
PLAT DU JOUR
PROVISIONS
ROTISSERIE
SCRAMBLING

SPECIALITY
STAPLE DIET
SUSTENANCE
SWEETENING
SWEET TOOTH
TABLE D'HÔTE
TENDERISER
THICKENING
VEGETABLES

11
COMESTIBLES
CONSISTENCY
COVER CHARGE
DEGUSTATION
HORS D'OEUVRE
IRON RATIONS
NOURISHMENT
PREPARATION
REFRESHMENT
REFRIGERANT
SMÖRGÅSBORD
TEASPOONFUL

12
BAKING POWDER
BOUQUET GARNI
CARBOHYDRATE
DAIRY PRODUCE
DAIRY PRODUCT
FINGER BUFFET
HAUTE CUISINE
HORS D'OEUVRES
PRESERVATIVE
REFRESHMENTS
SHORT COMMONS

13
CONFECTIONERY
CUSTARD POWDER
MEALS ON WHEELS
MIDNIGHT FEAST
REFRIGERATION

TABLESPOONFUL

14
RUNNING BANQUET
WHOLEMEAL FLOUR

15
CONVENIENCE FOOD
DESSERTSPOONFUL
LUNCHEON VOUCHER
NOUVELLE CUISINE
PRESSURE COOKING

Food & Drink – Drink – COCKTAILS

5
BRONX
JULEP
YORSH

6
GIBSON
GIMLET
MAI TAI
MIMOSA
MOJITO
ROB ROY
ZOMBIE

7
GIN SOUR
MARTINI
NEGRONI
PINK GIN
SAZERAC
SIDECAR
SLAMMER
STINGER

8
BULLSHOT
COCKTAIL
DAIQUIRI
GEMBILLY
GIN AND IT
SALTY DOG
SANGAREE
SNOWBALL

9
APPLETINI
BUCK'S FIZZ
CUBA LIBRE
FLATLINER
GREYHOUND
MANHATTAN
MARGARITA
MICHELADA
MINT JULEP
RUSTY NAIL
WHITE LADY

10
BLOODY MARY
BLUE BLAZER
CAIPIRINHA
LIME RICKEY
MONTGOMERY
MOSCOW MULE
PIÑA COLADA
TOM COLLINS
VELVET KISS
WHISKY SOUR

11
BOILERMAKER
DEPTH CHARGE
GIN AND TONIC
JOHN COLLINS
MILLIONAIRE
SCREWDRIVER
ZURRACAPOTE

12
BLACK RUSSIAN
BLUE HAWAIIAN
COSMOPOLITAN

FLAMING JESUS
OLD-FASHIONED
VODKA MARTINI
WHITE RUSSIAN

13
BRANDY AND SODA
SEX ON THE BEACH
TINTO DE VERANO
WHISKY AND SODA

14
SINGAPORE SLING
TEQUILA SLAMMER
TEQUILA SUNRISE

15
BRANDY ALEXANDER
FLAMING DR PEPPER

16
HARVEY WALLBANGER

17
LONG ISLAND ICED TEA

Food & Drink – Drink – DRINKS (general)

3
ALE
CHA
  (or char)
DOP
GIN
KIR
NOG
POP
RUM
RYE
TEA

4
BEER
BOCK
BREW
CHAR
  (or cha)
COKE
COLA
FINE
FIZZ
FLIP
GROG
MARC
MATÉ
MEAD
MILD
MILK
OUZO
RAKI
SAKE
SODA
SOMA

5
BOHEA
BOOZE
CIDER
COCOA
CRUSH
CUPPA
DRINK
HOOCH
HYSON
JUICE
JULEP
KUMIS
  (or koumiss)
KVASS
LAGER
LATTE
MIXER
MOCHA
NEGUS
NOYAU
PEKOE
PIMM'S
PUNCH
SHRUB
SLING
STOUT
TAFIA
TODDY
TONIC
VODKA
WATER

6
ARRACK

BISHOP
BITTER
BRANDY
CASSIS
CHASER
CHASSE
CHICHA
COFFEE
COGNAC
EGG-NOG
GENEVA
GRAPPA
KAHLÚA
KIRSCH
KÜMMEL
LIQUOR
MALIBU
MESCAL
METAXA
NECTAR
OOLONG
ORGEAT
PERNOD
PORTER
POSSET
POTEEN
  (or potheen)
PTISAN
PULQUE
ROTGUT
SCOTCH
SHANDY
SPIRIT
SQUASH
STINGO

TIPPLE
WALLOP
WHISKY
ZYTHUM

7
ALCOHOL
AMARULA
AQUAVIT
BACARDI
BAILEY'S
BEEF TEA
BOURBON
BUSH TEA
CAMPARI
CORDIAL
CURAÇAO
DOOLEY'S
EGG-FLIP
GUARANÁ
HERB TEA
ICED TEA
KOUMISS
  (or kumis)
LIMEADE
LIQUEUR
MARTINI
MATÉ TEA
PALE ALE
PILSNER
  (or Pilsener)
POTHEEN
  (or poteen)
RATAFIA
REAL ALE

ROSOLIO
SAMBUCA
SANGRIA
SCRUMPY
SELTZER
SHERBET
SLOE GIN
TEQUILA
WHISKEY

8
ABSINTHE
ADAM'S ALE
ADVOCAAT
AMARETTO
ANISETTE
APERITIF
ARMAGNAC
BEVERAGE
BLACK TEA
BROWN ALE
CALVADOS
CAFÉ NOIR
CHINA TEA
CLUB SODA
DOG'S NOSE
DRAMBUIE
EAU DE VIE
ESPRESSO
GALLIANO
GREEN TEA
HOLLANDS
HOT TODDY
HYDROMEL
ICE WATER

LEMONADE
LIGHT ALE
NEAR BEER
PILSENER
(or Pilsner)
ROOT BEER
SCHNAPPS
SMOOTHIE
SOUCHONG
SOYA MILK
SPRITZER
TAP WATER
TIA MARIA

9
AMERICANO
APPLEJACK
AQUA VITAE
CHERRYADE
CHOCOLATE
COINTREAU
CREAM SODA
DILL WATER
FIREWATER
GINGER ALE
GRENADINE
LAGER BEER
LIME JUICE
MACCHIATO
METHEGLIN
MILK PUNCH

MILKSHAKE
MILK STOUT
MIRABELLE
MOONSHINE
ORANGEADE
PUMP WATER
RICE WATER
RISTRETTO
RYE WHISKY
SLIVOVITZ
SNAKEBITE
SODA WATER
SUNDOWNER

10
APPLE JUICE
BARLEY WINE
BEST BITTER
BUTTERMILK
CAFÉ AU LAIT
CAFFÈ LATTE
CAPPUCCINO
CHARTREUSE
DARJEELING
FRUIT JUICE
GINGER BEER
JAMAICA RUM
LEMON JUICE
LIMONCELLO
MALT WHISKY
MARASCHINO

POUSSE-CAFÉ
RUSSIAN TEA
SPRUCE BEER
TONIC WATER
USQUEBAUGH

11
AGUARDIENTE
BARLEY WATER
BENEDICTINE
BITTER LEMON
BLACK COFFEE
BLACK VELVET
COCONUT MILK
DRAUGHT BEER
IRISH COFFEE
LABRADOR TEA
LEMON SQUASH
MOTHER'S RUIN
MOUNTAIN DEW
ORANGE JUICE
PEACH BRANDY
PISANG AMBON
SKIMMED MILK
SPRING WATER
WATER OF LIFE

12
BITTER ORANGE
CHERRY BRANDY
CRÈME DE CACAO

CRÈME DE NOYAU
DRAUGHT LAGER
FILTER COFFEE
GAELIC COFFEE
GRAND MARNIER
HOT CHOCOLATE
IRISH WHISKEY
KIRSCHWASSER
MINERAL WATER
ORANGE SQUASH
SARSAPARILLA
SCOTCH WHISKY

13
APRICOT BRANDY
CHERRY HEERING
CONDENSED MILK
CRÈME DE BANANE
CRÈME DE CASSIS
CRÈME DE MENTHE
PRAIRIE OYSTER

14
CRANBERRY JUICE
NAPOLEON BRANDY
PINEAPPLE JUICE

15
SEMI-SKIMMED MILK

Food & Drink – Drink – WINES fort = fortified wine

4
CAVA
GAVI
HOCK
PORT fort
SEKT
TENT

5
AIGLE
AIRÉN
BUGEY
CRÉPY
FITOU
KAGOR
GAMAY
MÉDOC
MOSEL (or
  Moselle)
PERLÉ
RIOJA
SOAVE
SYRAH
  (or Shiraz)
TOKAY

6
BAROLO
BARSAC
BEAUNE
CLARET
GRAVES
HUELVA
KERNER
MALBEC
MAVRUD

MELNIK
MERLOT
MORGON
MOULIS
MUSCAT
OSTUNI
SHERRY
  fort
SHIRAZ
  (or Syrah)
VENETO
VOLNAY

7
AMARONE
CATAWBA
CHABLIS
CHIANTI
FRONSAC
LOUPIAC
MACABEO
MADEIRA
  fort
MALMSEY
  fort
MARGAUX
MARSALA
  fort
MOSCATO
MOSELLE
  (or Mosel)
OLOROSO
  fort
ORVIETO
POMEROL
PROSECCO

RETSINA
SETÚBAL
TAURASI
VOUVRAY

8
BERGERAC
BORDEAUX
BROUILLY
BURGUNDY
ERBALUCE
FRASCATI
GIGONDAS
GRENACHE
MUSCADEL
  (or Muscatel)
MUSCADET
MUSCATEL
  (or Muscadel)
NEBBIOLO
PAUILLAC
PINOTAGE
RIESLING
SANCERRE
SANTENAY
SEMILLON
SILVANER
  (or Sylvaner)
ST JULIEN
SYLVANER
  (or Silvaner)
TOURAINE
TRENTINO
VERDELHO
VERMOUTH
  fort

VIOGNIER
ZWEIGELT

9
BARDOLINO
BOURGOGNE
CABRIÈRES
CARMENERE
CHAMPAGNE
HERMITAGE
LAMBRUSCO
MEURSAULT
MINERVOIS
MONT REDON
NYETIMBER
PINOT NOIR
RIDGEVIEW
SAUTERNES
ST ÉMILION
TARRAGONA
  fort
ZINFANDEL

10
BARBARESCO
BEAUJOLAIS
BUTTAFUOCO
CHAMBERTIN
CHARDONNAY
MÂCON
  ROUGE
MANZANILLA
  fort
MATEUS ROSÉ
MAVRODAFNI
MONASTRELL

PIESPORTER
ROSÉ D'ANJOU
TROLLINGER

11
AMONTILLADO
  fort
CHENIN BLANC
NIERSTEINER
PINOT GRIGIO
POUILLY FUMÉ
RÜDESHEIMER
SCUPPERNONG
TEMPRANILLO

12
ASTI SPUMANTE
CÔTES DE BOURG
CÔTES DU RHÔNE
FETEASCĂ ALBĂ
FRANCIACORTE
JOHANNISBERG (or
  Johannisberger)
PEDRO XIMÉNEZ
PINOT MEUNIER
VALPOLICELLA
VOSNE-ROMANÉE

13
AUXEY-DURESSES
ENTRE-DEUX-MERS
LIEBFRAUMILCH
MARTINA FRANCA
MÜLLER THURGAU
PESSAC-LÉOGNAN
POUILLY FUISSÉ

14
CHÂTEAU-GRILLET
GEWÜRZTRAMINER
FETEASCĂ NEAGRĂ
JOHANNISBERGER
(or Johannisberg)

SAUVIGNON BLANC

15
GRÜNER VELTLINER
LACHRYMA CHRISTI

17
CABERNET SAUVIGNON
CHÂTEAUNEUF-DU-PAPE
NUITS-SAINT-GEORGES

Food & Drink – DRINKING & BREWING TERMS

3	LEES	DREGS	TOP-UP	TIDDLY	SHICKER
BAR	LUSH	DRINK	TWIST	TIPPLE	SKINFUL
KEG	MALT	DRUNK	YEAST	ULLAGE	SNIFTER
NIP	MASH	FROTH			SWIZZLE
PEG	MUST	GRAIN	**6**	**7**	TAPROOM
PIN	NOSE	GRAPE	BARREL	ALCOHOL	TASTING
SIP	PINT	GRIST	BENDER	ALEMBIC	TIPPLER
SOT	PONY	OPTIC	BRACER	BAGASSE	TOSSPOT
SUP	PULL	PINTA	BREWER	BOOZE-UP	VINTAGE
TAP	RAPE	PROOF	BREW-UP	BOUQUET	WASSAIL
TOT	SHOT	QUAFF	BUMPER	BREWERY	ZYMURGY
TUN	SLUG	ROUND	CELLAR	BREWING	
	SNUG	SHIVE	CHASER	CAROUSE	**8**
4	SOAK	SHORT	FUDDLE	CORKAGE	BEESWING
BARM	STUM	SNORT	GUZZLE	DRAUGHT	CAROUSAL
BODY	SWIG	SPLIT	JIGGER	DRAYMAN	DRINKING
BREW	TOPE	SPREE	PALATE	DRINKER	DRUNKARD
BUNG	WASH	STAVE	POMACE	FERMENT	FULLNESS
CASK	WINO	STILL	RECIPE	GROUNDS	HAND-PUMP
CORK	WORT	STRAW	REFILL	HEELTAP	HANGOVER
DRAM		SWILL	SALOON	MALTOSE	HIP FLASK
DRAY	**5**	TASTE	SHAKER	MASHING	HOGSHEAD
FOAM	BINGE	TIGHT	SIPHON	MASH TUN	INFUSION
GULP	BOOZE	TIPSY	SPONGE	MEASURE	LANDLADY
HEAD	CUPPA	TOAST	SWIPES	OAK-AGED	LANDLORD
HOPS	DIPSO	TOPER	TEAPOT	SHEBEEN	LICENSEE

LIBATION
NIGHTCAP
PICK-ME-UP
POTATION
PUB CRAWL
QUENCHER
SEDIMENT
SOBRIETY
SWILLING
TEA BREAK
TEA CADDY
TEA PARTY
TEETOTAL
THE USUAL
VENDANGE

9
CAFETIÈRE
CELLARAGE
CELLARMAN
COFFEE POT
DECOCTION
ELEVENSES

INEBRIETY
MALTHOUSE
MOONSHINE
OENOPHILE
PUBLIC BAR
REFRESHER
SALOON BAR
STILL ROOM
TIPSINESS
WASSAILER
YARD OF ALE

10
ABSTINENCE
BARLEYCORN
BAR PARLOUR
CONCOCTION
DIPSOMANIA
DISTILLERY
DISTILLING
INSOBRIETY
INTOXICANT
PERCOLATOR

SHEBEENING
STIRRUP CUP
SODA SIPHON
TEMPERANCE
WASSAILING
WINE CELLAR

11
BACCHANALIA
BARRELHOUSE
CLOSING TIME
DEGUSTATION
DIPSOMANIAC
DRUNKENNESS
INEBRIATION
ON THE RAZZLE
OPENING TIME
PROHIBITION
REFRESHMENT
TEETOTALISM
TEETOTALLER

12
DISTILLATION
DRINKING BOUT
FERMENTATION
INTEMPERANCE
INTOXICATION
KATZENJAMMER
OPENING HOURS
SHORT MEASURE
SWIZZLE STICK

13
BINGE DRINKING
COCKTAIL STICK
DRINKING STRAW

14
COCKTAIL SHAKER
DRINKING-UP TIME
THIRST-QUENCHER

Food & Drink – Food – CHEESES

3	FETA	**5**	LAPPI	**6**	MARIBO
OKA	PIPO	COLBY	QUARK	ACKAWI	OAXACA
	TALA	DERBY	ROULÉ	CHÈVRE	TILSIT
4	YARG	FIGUE	SAMSO	DUNLOP	
BRIE		FYNBO	TAMIE	FONTAL	**7**
EDAM		GOUDA		KASERI	BABYBEL

BALATON
BOURSIN
BROCCIO
CHAUMES
CHEDDAR
FONTINA
GEITOST
GRUYÈRE
GUBBEEN
HAVARTI
IBERICO
KERNHEM
LANGRES
RICOTTA
RUSTINU
SAPSAGO
STILTON
UBRIACO

8
ARDRAHAN
BAVARIAN
BEAUFORT
BEL PAESE
CABRALES

CHESHIRE
EMMENTAL
FRIESIAN
HALLOUMI
PARMESAN
PECORINO
RACLETTE
VALENCAY
VIGNOTTE
ZAMORANO

9
CAMBAZOLA
CAMEMBERT
DEVON BLUE
JARLSBERG
LEICESTER
LIMBURGER
PENCARREG
PORT SALUT
PROVOLONE
ROQUEFORT
SAGE DERBY
SAINT AGUR

10
BLUE CHEESE
BLUE VINNEY
BRESSE BLEU
CAERPHILLY
DANISH BLUE
DOLCELLATE
GLOUCESTER
GORGONZOLA
LANCASHIRE
LEERDAMMER
MASCARPONE
MOZZARELLA
NEUFCHÂTEL
SAINT AUBIN
STRACCHINO

11
COULOMMIERS
CREAM CHEESE
HEREFORD HOP
HUSHALLSOST
PONT L'ÉVÊQUE
SAINT PAULIN
WENSLEYDALE

12
FROMAGE BLANC
FROMAGE FRAIS
MONTEREY JACK
RED LEICESTER
WHITE STILTON

13
BLEU D'AUVERGNE
COTTAGE CHEESE
FOURME D'AMBERT
YORKSHIRE BLUE

14
ABBAYE DE BELLOC
SHROPSHIRE BLUE
STINKING BISHOP
SUSSEX SLIPCOTE

16
DOUBLE GLOUCESTER

Food & Drink – Food – DISHES Also see Pasta

4
DHAL India
FUGU Japan
OLIO Spain/Portugal
SKYR Iceland
TACO Mexico

5
BHAJI India
BIGOS Poland
BÖREK Turkey
CHAMP Ireland
CURRY India
GUMBO West Indies
KISEL Russia

LAKSA Malaysia
PASTA Italy
PILAF (or pilau) Middle East
PILAU (or pilaf) Middle East
PIZZA Italy
RÖSTI Switzerland
SATAY SE Asia
SHCHI Russia

SUSHI Japan
TAPAS Spain
ZRAZY Poland

6

BISQUE France
BORSCH
 (or borscht) Russia
BURGOO USA
DIM SUM China
FLAUTA Mexico
FONDUE Switzerland
GULYAS Hungary
HAGGIS Britain
HARIRA Morocco
KIBBEH Middle East
KIMCHI Korea
KULICH Russia
LOMITO S America
OMELET
 (or omelette) France
PAELLA Spain
PAKORA India
PANADA Spain/Portugal
PASHKA Russia
TAMALE Mexico

7

BAKLAVA Middle East
BARSZCZ Poland
BOBOTIE South Africa
BORSCHT (or borsch)
 Russia
BULGOGI Korea
BURRITO Mexico
CEVICHE Peru
CHOLENT Jewish
CHOWDER USA

FALAFEL Middle East
FATAYER Middle East
FISH PIE Britain
GIUVECH Bulgaria
GNOCCHI Italy
GOULASH Hungary
GRAVLAX (or gravadlax)
 Sweden
MEAT PIE Britain
MEE KROB Thailand
PAD THAI Thailand
PELMENY Russia
RAREBIT Britain
RISOTTO Italy
RUM BABA France
SASHIMI Japan
TARATOR Bulgaria
TEMPURA Japan
TOTOPOS Mexico
TSIMMES (or tzimmes)
 Jewish
TZIMMES (or tsimmes)
 Jewish

8

APPLE PIE various
BANNITSA Bulgaria
BHELPURI India
CALLALOO Latin America
CAPONATA Italy
CHOP SUEY China/USA
CHOW MEIN China/USA
CONSOMMÉ France
COQ AU VIN France
COUSCOUS N Africa
FEIJOADA Brazil
FLUMMERY Britain
FRUMENTY Britain

GADO-GADO Indonesia
GAZPACHO Spain
KEDGEREE Anglo-Indian
LAHMACUN Turkey
MOUSSAKA Greece
OMELETTE
 (or omelet) France
PANDOWDY USA
PASTILLA Morocco
PECAN PIE USA
PLUM DUFF Britain
RACLETTE Switzerland
RED CURRY Thailand
ROLY-POLY Britain
SELYODKA Russia
SHAWARMA Middle
 East
SUKIYAKI Japan
SYLLABUB Britain
TIRAMISU Italy
TZATZIKI Greece
YAKITORI Japan
ZARZUELA Spain

9

CASSOULET France
ČEVAPČIĆI Yugoslavia
CHERRY PIE various
CHURRASCO S America
COLCANNON Ireland/
 Scotland
FRICASSEE French
GALANTINE Britain
GRAVADLAX
 (or gravlax) Sweden
GUACAMOLE Mexico
IRISH STEW Ireland
JAMBALAYA USA

KADIN BUDU Turkey
KAPUŠNIAK Poland
KULEBIAKA Russia
LEBKUCHEN Germany
LOBSCOUSE Britain
MEE GORENG Malaysia
PARILLADA S America
PEPPER POT West
  Indies
ROGAN JOSH India
SAMBOUSEK Middle
  East
SUCCOTASH USA
TABBOULEH Middle
  East
TIDDY OGGY Britain
TIPSY CAKE Britain
WATERZOOI Belgium

10
ALBONDIGAS Spain
BLANQUETTE France
BRIK À L'OEUF Tunisia
COTTAGE PIE Britain
DOBOS TORTE
  Hungary
DONER KEBAB Turkey
FRICANDEAU France
GREEN CURRY Thailand
GULAB JAMUN India
HASH BROWNS USA
KEY LIME PIE USA
NASI GORENG
  Malaysia
PEACH MELBA France
PEKING DUCK China
PEPERONATA Italy
POULE AU POT France

QUESADILLA Spain
RIJSTTAFEL Dutch
SALMAGUNDI Anglo-
  Indian
SAUERKRAUT Germany
SHISH KEBAB Turkey
SKORDHALIA Greece
TARTE TATIN France
TOMATO SOUP various
ZABAGLIONE Italy

11
ALOO GOBI SAG India
BAKED ALASKA USA
ATHOLL BROSE Britain
BANOFFEE PIE Britain
CAESAR SALAD USA
CHICKEN KIEV Ukraine
CLAM CHOWDER USA
CRÈME BRÛLÉE France
CULLEN SKINK Britain
FOUL MEDAMES Egypt
GEFILTE FISH Jewish
HOMINY GRITS USA
IMAM BAYILDI Turkey
JAM ROLY-POLY Britain
JERK CHICKEN
  Caribbean
KADIN GÖBEGI Turkey
MOLE POBLANO
  Mexico
OLLA PODRIDA Spain/
  Portugal
RATATOUILLE France
SACHERTORTE Austria
SALTIMBOCCA Italy
SAUERBRATEN
  Germany

TREACLE TART Britain
VICHYSSOISE France
WELSH RABBIT (or
  Welsh rarebit) Britain

12
APFELSTRUDEL Austria
APPLE CRUMBLE Britain
BEANS ON TOAST
  Britain
BIBER DOLMASI Turkey
BOLLITO MISTO Italy
CHICKEN KORMA India
COCKIELEEKIE Britain
CORNISH PASTY Britain
CRÈME CARAMEL
  France
CRÊPE SUZETTE France
DUBLIN CODDLE
  Ireland
DUBLIN LAWYER
  Ireland
EGG FRIED RICE China
EGGS BENEDICT USA
FISH AND CHIPS Britain
FUSILLI POLLO Italy
LOKSHEN KUGEL
  Jewish
LOX AND BAGELS
  Jewish/USA
MESHANA SKARA
  Bulgaria
MULLIGATAWNY India
MUSHROOM SOUP
  various
PISANG GORENG
  Malaysia
SHEPHERD'S PIE Britain

SHERRY TRIFLE Britain
WALDORF SALAD USA
WELSH RAREBIT (or Welsh rabbit)
  Britain

13

BIRD'S NEST SOUP China
BOUILLABAISSE France
HIMMEL UND ERDE Germany
OEUFS À LA NEIGE France
PATATAS BRAVAS Spain
SHOPSKA SALATA Bulgaria
SOLE VÉRONIQUE France
STRACCIATELLA Italy
TARTE AU CITRON France
TOAD-IN-THE-HOLE Britain
YOGURTLU KEBAB Turkey

14

BANGERS AND MASH Britain
BEEF CARBONNADE Belgium
BEEF STROGANOFF Russia
BEEF WELLINGTON Britain
CANARD À L'ORANGE France
CHARLOTTE RUSSE France
CHICKEN À LA KING USA
CHICKEN MARENGO France
CHICKEN SUPREME USA
CHILES EN NOGADA Mexico
CHILLI CON CARNE USA/Tex-Mex
COCHINITA PIBIL Mexico
LASAGNE AL FORNO Italy
LOBSTER NEWBURG USA
MACARONI CHEESE Italy
QUICHE LORRAINE France
RHUBARB CRUMBLE Britain
SCOTCH WOODCOCK Britain
SOUR CHERRY SOUP Hungary

VITELLO TONNATO Italy

15

ARBROATH SMOKIES Britain
BUBBLE AND SQUEAK Britain
CHICKEN VINDALOO India
CHORIZO AL DIABLO Spain
COCIDO MADRILEÑO Spain
FRENCH ONION SOUP France
LINGUINI AL PESTO Italy
MOULES MARINIÈRE France
PIZZA MARGHERITA Italy
PIZZA NAPOLETANA Italy
POULET BASQUAISE France
QUEEN OF PUDDINGS Britain
ROLY-POLY PUDDING Britain
SPAGHETTI AL RAGÚ Italy
TONNO CON FAGIOLI Italy
WIENER SCHNITZEL Austria

16

BLANQUETTE DE VEAU France
CHRISTMAS PUDDING Britain
FETTUCINE ALFREDO Italy
GRATIN DAUPHINOIS France
LANCASHIRE HOTPOT Britain
LEBERKNÖDELSUPPE Germany
LOBSTER THERMIDOR France
MOROS Y CRISTIANOS Cuba
POTAGE PARMENTIER France
SALTFISH AND ACKEE Caribbean
TOURNEDOS ROSSINI France
YORKSHIRE PUDDING Britain

17

BLACK FOREST GATEAU Germany
CHICKEN CACCIATORE Italy
DEVILS ON HORSEBACK Britain

HUEVOS A LA FLAMENCA Spain
POIRES BELLE HÉLÈNE France
SCALOPPINE MARSALA Italy
SOPA DE HUITLACOCHE Mexico
STEAK AND KIDNEY PIE Britain
STUFFED VINE LEAVES Greece
SUPRÊME DE VOLAILLE France
TORTELLINI IN BRODO Italy

18
CALAMARES EN SU TINTA Spain
CHICKEN TIKKA MASALA Anglo-Indian
QUENELLES DE BROCHET France

SPAGHETTI BOLOGNESE Italy
SPAGHETTI CARBONARA Italy
TRIPE À LA MODE DE CAEN France

19
MELANZANE PARMIGIANA Italy
POLLO ALLA CACCIATORE Italy

20
BEEF IN BLACK-BEAN SAUCE China
MARYLAND FRIED CHICKEN USA
MOZZARELLA IN CARROZZA Italy
SOUTHERN FRIED CHICKEN USA

Food & Drink – Food – FOOD (general)

3	CONE	ROCK	BOMBE	LOLLY	BATTER
BAP	CURD	ROLL	BOXTY	MARGE	BLEWIT
BUN	FARL	RUSK	BREAD	MATZO	BONBON
COB	FLAN	SAGO	BROSE	MEBOS	BURGER
EGG	GHEE	SAMP	BROTH	PASTA	BUTTER
GUM	HASH	SKYR	BUTTY	PASTE	CACHOU
GUR	LOAF	SOUP	CANDY	PASTY	CANAPÉ
ICE	MASH	STEW	CHIPS	PATTY	CEREAL
JAM	MEAL	TART	COUPE	PIZZA	CHEESE
NAN	MUSH	WHEY	CRÊPE	PURÉE	CHILLI
(or naan)	NAAN	WHIP	CRUST	SALAD	COBURG
PAP	(or nan)		CURDS	SALMI	COMFIT
PIE	OATS	**5**	FUDGE	SCONE	COOKIE
PUD	OKRA	ASPIC	GRAIN	SUGAR	CORNET
SOP	PÂTÉ	BAGEL	GRITS	SWEET	CRISPS
	PEEL	BALTI	GRUEL	TOAST	CRUMBS
4	PONE	BLINI	HONEY	WAFER	DRAGÉE
BRAN	PUFF	(or bliny)	JELLY		ECLAIR
CAKE	RICE	BLINY	KEBAB	**6**	FAGGOT
CHIP	RIND	(or blini)	LATKE	BANGER	FONDUE

GATEAU
GROATS
HOT DOG
HOTPOT
HUMBUG
HUMMUS
INJERA
JUJUBE
JUNKET
MEALIE
MOUSSE
MUESLI
MUFFIN
NOUGAT
PARKIN
PASTRY
PINOLE
POTAGE
QUICHE
RAGOUT
RAISIN
SALAMI
SAMOSA
SKILLY
SORBET
SPONGE
SPREAD
SUNDAE
TOFFEE
TRIFLE
WAFFLE
YOGURT
  (or yoghurt)

7
BANNOCK
BATH BUN
BISCUIT
BLINTZE
BLOOMER
BOLOGNA
BOUCHÉE
BOUILLI
BOURBON
BRIOCHE
CARAMEL
CAYENNE
CHICORY
CHOC ICE
CHORIZO
COMPOTE
CRACKER
CROUTON
CRUMPET
CUPCAKE
CUSTARD
FONDANT
FRITTER
GALA PIE
ICED BUN
JAGGERY
JAM PUFF
JAM TART
NOODLES
OATMEAL
PANCAKE
PARFAIT
PIKELET
PLUM JAM
POLENTA
POPADOM
  (or poppadom)
POPCORN
PORK PIE
PRALINE
PRETZEL

PUDDING
RAMEKIN
RATAFIA
RISSOLE
SAUSAGE
SAVELOY
SHERBET
SOUFFLÉ
STRUDEL
SULTANA
SWEETIE
TAPIOCA
TARTLET
TEACAKE
TERRINE
TOSTADA
TRUFFLE
VANILLA
YOGHURT
  (or yogurt)
ZAKUSKA
  (or zakouska)

8
BAGUETTE
BOUILLON
BULLSEYE
CHAPATTI
COLESLAW
COUSCOUS
CRACKNEL
CRUDITÉS
DEMERARA
DOUGHBOY
DOUGHNUT
DRIPPING
DUMPLING
EMPANADA

FISHBALL
FISHCAKE
FLAPJACK
FRIED EGG
GRILLADE
HARD TACK
HOTCHPOT
  (or hotchpotch)
ICE CREAM
ICE LOLLY
KROMESKY
LOLLIPOP
MACAROON
MARINADE
MATELOTE
MEATBALL
MERINGUE
MILK LOAF
MINCE PIE
NAPOLEON
NOISETTE
PASTILLE
PEMMICAN
PEPERONI
  (or pepperoni)
PIECRUST
PLUM CAKE
PLUM DUFF
POPPADOM
  (or popadom)
PORRIDGE
QUENELLE
ROCK CAKE
RYE BREAD
RYE FLOUR
SANDWICH
SEED CAKE
SEMOLINA

SNOWBALL
SOFT ROLL
SQUAB PIE
STUFFING
TANDOORI
TORTILLA
TEA BREAD
TURNOVER
WATER ICE
ZAKOUSKA
 (or zakuska)

9
ACID DROPS
ANGEL CAKE
APPLE TART
BARMBRACK
 (or barnbrack)
BARNBRACK
 (or barmbrack)
BOILED EGG
BREAD ROLL
BROWN RICE
BUBBLE GUM
CANE SUGAR
CARRAGEEN
CASSEROLE
CHIPOLATA
CHOCOLATE
CORNBREAD
CORNFLOUR
CREAM CAKE
CREAM HORN
CROISSANT
CROQUETTE
CROUSTADE
DAMSON JAM
DIGESTIVE

DROP SCONE
EASTER EGG
ENCHILADA
FAIRY CAKE
FISH PASTE
FRUIT CAKE
GARIBALDI
GENOA CAKE
GINGER NUT
HAMBURGER
JELLY BABY
LARDY CAKE
LAVA BREAD
LEMON CURD
LIQUORICE
LOAF SUGAR
LUMP SUGAR
MACÉDOINE
MADELEINE
MARGARINE
MARMALADE
MATZO BALL
MATZO MEAL
MEAT PASTE
MINCEMEAT
NONPAREIL
PEAR DROPS
PEPPERONI
 (or peperoni)
PONE BREAD
POUND CAKE
RABBIT PIE
RICE-PAPER
RUM BUTTER
SALLY LUNN
SCOTCH EGG
SHORTCAKE
SODA BREAD

SOURDOUGH
STICKY BUN
SWEETCORN
SWISS ROLL
VOL-AU-VENT
WHEATGERM
WHOLEMEAL

10
APRICOT JAM
BAKED BEANS
BATH OLIVER
BATTENBERG
BEEFBURGER
BLACK BREAD
BLANCMANGE
BLANQUETTE
BRANDY SNAP
BREADSTICK
BROWN BREAD
BROWN SUGAR
CANDY FLOSS
CARROT CAKE
CELERY SOUP
CHEESECAKE
CHELSEA BUN
CHEWING GUM
COFFEE CAKE
CORNFLAKES
CREAM SLICE
CRUSTY ROLL
CURRANT BUN
CUSTARD PIE
DUNDEE CAKE
ECCLES CAKE
EGG ON TOAST
FISH FINGER
FLORENTINE

FRENCH LOAF
FRIED BREAD
FRUIT SALAD
GINGER CAKE
GINGER SNAP
HOTCHPOTCH
 (or hotchpot)
ICING SUGAR
INDIAN MEAL
JOHNNY CAKE
LEMON DROPS
MINESTRONE
MOUSSELINE
OXTAIL SOUP
PEPPERMINT
PICKLED EGG
POACHED EGG
PUFF PASTRY
RIJSTTAFEL
SEA BISCUIT
SHORTBREAD
SIMNEL CAKE
SPONGE CAKE
SPRING ROLL
SUGAR CANDY
WALNUT WHIP
WHITE BREAD

11
ANISEED BALL
BAKED POTATO
BANANA SPLIT
BANBURY CAKE
BARLEY SUGAR
BOILED SWEET
BREADCRUMBS
CASTER SUGAR
CHEESE STRAW

CHICKEN SOUP
COTTAGE LOAF
CURRANT CAKE
CUSTARD TART
DOUBLE CREAM
FRANKFURTER
FRENCH BREAD
FRENCH FRIES
FRENCH STICK
FRENCH TOAST
FRUIT SUNDAE
GINGERBREAD
HOT CROSS BUN
JAM DOUGHNUT
MADEIRA CAKE
MARSHMALLOW
MILK PUDDING
NICE BISCUIT
PETITS FOURS
PLUM PUDDING
POTATO SALAD
PROFITEROLE
RICE PUDDING
ROAST POTATO
SAUSAGE MEAT
SAUSAGE ROLL
SCOTCH BROTH
SMÖRGÅSBORD
SPOTTED DICK
SUET PUDDING
TOFFEE APPLE
TUTTI-FRUTTI
WEDDING CAKE

12
BAKEWELL TART
BLACK PUDDING
BLOOD PUDDING

BRANDY BUTTER
BUTTERSCOTCH
CHEESEBURGER
CLOTTED CREAM
CLUB SANDWICH
CREAM CRACKER
CUSTARD CREAM
DAMSON CHEESE
DANISH PASTRY
GARLIC BUTTER
HASTY PUDDING
JACKET POTATO
MAID OF HONOUR
MILLEFEUILLE
OPEN SANDWICH
PEANUT BUTTER
PEASE PUDDING
PICKLED ONION
POTATO CRISPS
PRAWN CRACKER
PUMPERNICKEL
QUARTERN LOAF
RAISED PASTRY
RASPBERRY JAM
SCRAMBLED EGG
SHERBET LEMON
SHIP'S BISCUIT
SINGING HINNY
SPONGE FINGER
WATER BISCUIT
WHITE PUDDING

13
APPLE TURNOVER
BANANA FRITTER
DOLLY MIXTURES
FRUIT COCKTAIL
GOOSEBERRY JAM

LEMON MERINGUE
MARRONS GLACÉS
MILK CHOCOLATE
RASPBERRY FOOL
SPONGE PUDDING
STRAWBERRY JAM
SUMMER PUDDING
TREACLE TOFFEE
VIENNESE WHIRL

14
BATTENBERG CAKE
BOLOGNA SAUSAGE
CABINET PUDDING
EGG CUSTARD TART
GINGERBREAD MAN
GOOSEBERRY FOOL
GOOSEBERRY TART
MACARONI CHEESE
MOCK TURTLE SOUP
PAIN AU CHOCOLAT
PÂTÉ DE FOIS GRAS
PICKLED CABBAGE
PLAIN CHOCOLATE
PONTEFRACT CAKE
RICH TEA BISCUIT
THREE BEAN SALAD
TURKISH DELIGHT
WHOLEMEAL BREAD

15
BLACKCURRANT JAM
CHOCOLATE BUTTON
CHOCOLATE MOUSSE
MUSTARD AND CRESS
REDCURRANT JELLY
SHORTENING BREAD

Food & Drink – Food – FRUIT & NUTS

3
COB
COX
FIG
HAW
HIP
NUT

4
AKEE
 (or ackee)
BAEL
CRAB
DATE
GAGE
GALA
GEAN
 (or wild cherry)
KAKI
MAST
PEAR
PEPO
PINE
PLUM
SLOE
SORB
TUNA
UGLI

5
ACKEE
 (or akee)
ACORN
APPLE
ARECA
ARHAT

BERRY
BETEL
DRUPE
FRUIT
GOURD
GRAPE
GUAVA
JAFFA
LEMON
MANGO
MELON
MURTA
MUTSU
NELIS
OLIVE
PAPAW
 (or pawpaw)
PEACH
PECAN
PEQUI
PRUNE
SALAK

6
ACAJOU
ALMOND
BABACO
BANANA
BEURRÉ
BRAZIL
CASHEW
CHERRY
CITRON
COBNUT
COMICE
CONKER

DAMSON
DURIAN
FEIJOA
ILLIPE
JAMBUL
JUJUBE
KARAKA
LANGRA
LICHEE
 (or lychee)
LONGAN
LOQUAT
LYCHEE
 (or lichee)
MAMMEE
MEDLAR
MUSCAT
ORANGE
PAPAYA
PAWPAW
 (or papaw)
PEANUT
PIGNUT
PIPPIN
POMELO
QUINCE
RUSSET
SANTOL
SECKEL
SQUASH
TOMATO
TSAMMA
WALNUT

7
ACEROLA

APRICOT
AVOCADO
BILIMBI
BRINJAL
CATAWBA
COCONUT
CODLING
COSTARD
CUDRANG
CUMQUAT
 (or kumquat)
CURRANT
FILBERT
GENIPAP
 (or genipapo)
GUARANÁ
HAMBURG
HOG PLUM
KEY LIME
KUMQUAT
 (or cumquat)
MORELLO
NAARTJIE
PALMYRA
PINGUIN
PUMPKIN
PUPUNHA
RANGPUR
RHUBARB
RIBSTON
ROSE HIP
SAGUARO
SATSUMA
SHEA NUT
SHIPOVA
SOURSOP

SPARTAN
TANGELO
VALONIA
WILDING
WINESAP
YANGMEI

8
ARECA NUT
BARBERRY
BARTLETT
BAYBERRY
BERGAMOT
BETEL NUT
BILBERRY
BRAEBURN
CALABASH
CAMU CAMU
CANISTEL
CEMPEDAK
CHESTNUT
COWBERRY
DATE PLUM
DEWBERRY
DOGBERRY
EARTHNUT
EGG-PLANT
FENBERRY
GENIPAPO
 (or genipap)
GOOSEGOG
GREENING
HANEPOOT
HAZELNUT
HONEYDEW
IVORY NUT

JONATHAN
MANDARIN
MAY APPLE
MULBERRY
MUSCADEL
  (or muscatel)
MUSCATEL
  (or muscadel)
MUSK PEAR
MUSK PLUM
PEARMAIN
PECAN NUT
PLANTAIN
QUANDONG
QUEENING
RAMBUTAN
SHADDOCK
SWEETING
SWEETSOP

9
ALGARROBA
AUBERGINE
BANEBERRY
  (or herb
  Christopher)
BEARBERRY
BLAEBERRY
BLUEBERRY
BRAZIL NUT
BUTTERNUT
CANDLENUT
CARAMBOLA
CASHEW NUT
CHERIMOYA
COCO DE MER
COLOCYNTH
CRAB APPLE

CRANBERRY
CROWBERRY
GREENGAGE
GROUNDNUT
HACKBERRY
ILLIPE NUT
JACKFRUIT
JUNEBERRY
KIWI FRUIT
LOVE APPLE
MACADAMIA
MANZANITA
MONKEY NUT
MUSK MELON
MYROBALAN
NASEBERRY
  (or sapodilla
  plum)
NECTARINE
NONPAREIL
ORTANIQUE
PERSIMMON
PINEAPPLE
PISTACHIO
RASPBERRY
ROSE APPLE
SAPODILLA
SASKATOON
SNOWBERRY
SOAPBERRY
STAR ANISE
STAR APPLE
TAMARILLO
  (or tree
  tomato)
TANGERINE
WINEBERRY

10
BEEF TOMATO
BLACKBERRY
BLADDER NUT
CANTALOUPE
CHERRY PLUM
CHINQUAPIN
CHOKEBERRY
CLEMENTINE
CLOUDBERRY
CONFERENCE
CORALBERRY
ELDERBERRY
GALIA MELON
GOOSEBERRY
GRANADILLA
  (or grenadilla)
GRENADILLA
  (or granadilla)
GRAPEFRUIT
HONEYBERRY
JABOTICABA
JARGONELLE
LOGANBERRY
MAMONCILLO
MANGOSTEEN
PALMYRA NUT
PIGEON PLUM
PLUM TOMATO
QUARRENDER
REDCURRANT
ROWANBERRY
STONE FRUIT
STRAWBERRY
SUGAR APPLE
TREE TOMATO
  (or tamarillo)
WATERMELON

WILD CHERRY
  (or gean)
YOUNGBERRY

11
BITTER APPLE
BLOOD ORANGE
BOYSENBERRY
CANDLEBERRY
CHOKE CHERRY
CITRUS FRUIT
DRAGONFRUIT
EATING APPLE
GRANNY SMITH
HORNED MELON
HUCKLEBERRY
JAMAICA PLUM
LINGONBERRY
MAMMEE APPLE
NAVEL ORANGE
OSAGE ORANGE
POMEGRANATE
PRICKLY PEAR
QUANDONG NUT
SALMONBERRY
SCUPPERNONG

12
BARTLETT PEAR
BLACKCURRANT
COOKING APPLE
CUSTARD APPLE
GROUND CHERRY
HOTTENTOT FIG
MACADAMIA NUT
MAMMEE SAPOTE
PASSION FRUIT
PISTACHIO NUT

SERVICEBERRY
THIMBLEBERRY
VICTORIA PLUM
WHORTLEBERRY
WINTER CHERRY

13
ALLIGATOR PEAR
BULLOCK'S HEART
CURRANT TOMATO
DOUBLE COCONUT
HONEYDEW MELON
HORSE CHESTNUT

HUBBARD SQUASH
KANGAROO APPLE
QUEENSLAND NUT
RIBSTON PIPPIN
SAPODILLA PLUM
  (or naseberry)
SEVILLE ORANGE
WATER CHESTNUT

14
BARBADOS CHERRY
BERGAMOT ORANGE
BLENHEIM ORANGE

CAPE GOOSEBERRY
MANDARIN ORANGE
PARTRIDGEBERRY

15
BUTTERNUT SQUASH
CANTALOUPE MELON
CORNELIAN CHERRY
GOLDEN DELICIOUS
HERB CHRISTOPHER
  (or baneberry)

Food & Drink – Food – MEAT & FISH

3	HAKE	BELLY	SKIRT	GROUSE	TURKEY
COD	HARE	BRAWN	SNAIL	HASLET	TURTLE
DAB	HOCK	BULLY	SPRAT	(or harslet)	WINKLE
EEL	JERK	CAPON	SQUID	HAUNCH	
HAM	LAMB	FILET	STEAK	KIDNEY	**7**
LEG	LOIN	FLANK	TRIPE	KIPPER	ANCHOVY
RIB	MEAT	GIGOT	TROUT	MUSSEL	BILTONG
ROE	NECK	GOOSE	WHELK	MUTTON	BLOATER
	PORK	HEART		OXTAIL	BRISKET
4	RUMP	JERKY	**6**	OYSTER	BROILER
BARD	SHIN	JOINT	BREAST	PIGEON	BUMMALO
BASS	SIDE	LIVER	CAVIAR	PLAICE	CAVIARE
BEEF	SOLE	MINCE	(or caviare)	RABBIT	(or caviar)
CHOP	SPAM	OFFAL	COCKLE	RASHER	CHICKEN
CRAB	TUNA	PRAWN	COLLAR	SADDLE	HADDOCK
DUCK	VEAL	QUAIL	CUTLET	SALMON	HALIBUT
FISH	WING	ROAST	FILLET	SCAMPI	HARSLET
FOWL		SCRAG	FINNAN	SHRIMP	(or haslet)
FUGU	**5**	SEWIN	FLITCH	TONGUE	HERRING
GAME	BACON	SKATE	GAMMON	TURBOT	KNUCKLE

LOBSTER
OCTOPUS
OX LIVER
POULTRY
RED FISH
RED MEAT
ROLLMOP
ROOSTER
SARDINE
SCALLOP
SEA BASS
SIRLOIN
SNAPPER
TOPSIDE
TROTTER
VENISON
WHITING

8
CHUMP END
CRAYFISH
ESCALOPE
ESCARGOT
FLOUNDER
LAMP CHOP
LEMON DAB
MACKEREL
NOISETTE
OX TONGUE
PHEASANT
PILCHARD
PORK CHOP
POT ROAST
SALT BEEF
SCRAG END
SHOULDER
SPARE RIB
UNDERCUT

9
AITCHBONE
BEEFSTEAK
BULLY BEEF
CHUMP CHOP
CRACKLING
DOVER SOLE
ENTRECÔTE
LEG OF LAMB
LEMON SOLE
MINCEMEAT
PARTRIDGE
PTARMIGAN
ROAST BEEF
ROAST LAMB
ROAST PORK
RUMP STEAK
SCHNITZEL
SHELLFISH
SPARE RIBS
STOCKFISH
TOURNEDOS
WHITEBAIT
WHITE FISH
WHITE MEAT

10
BOMBAY DUCK
BROWN TROUT
CORNED BEEF
FRICANDEAU
JELLIED EEL
JUGGED HARE
LAMB CUTLET
PERIWINKLE
RED HERRING
RED SNAPPER
ROCK SALMON

ROMAN SNAIL
SILVERSIDE
SPATCHCOCK
SPITCHCOCK
SQUETEAGUE
SWEETBREAD
T-BONE STEAK
VEAL CUTLET

11
BARON OF BEEF
FILET MIGNON
FILLET STEAK
MINUTE STEAK
PARSON'S NOSE
PORTERHOUSE

12
LUNCHEON MEAT
RAINBOW TROUT
STREAKY BACON

13
CHÂTEAUBRIAND
FINNAN HADDOCK
POACHED SALMON
SMOKED HADDOCK

14
PICKLED HERRING
SHOULDER OF LAMB

16
PORTERHOUSE STEAK

Food & Drink – Food – PASTA

4
ORZO
ZITI

5
PENNE

7
FUSILLI
LASAGNE
RAVIOLI

8
BUCATINI
FARFALLE
FEDELINI

LINGUINI
MACARONI
RIGATONI

9
AGNOLOTTI
CAVATELLI
FETTUCINE
RADIATORI
SPAGHETTI
TRENNETTE

10
CANNELLONI
TAGLIOLINI
TORTELLINI

TORTELLONI
VERMICELLI

11
CAPPELLETTI
ORECCHIETTE
PAPPARDELLE
TAGLIATELLE

12
CONCHIGLIONI
STROZZAPRETI

13
CONCHIGLIETTE

Food & Drink – Food – SAUCES, TOPPINGS & CONDIMENTS

3
DIP
SOY

4
ROUX
SALT

5
AYVAR
CREAM
GRAVY
ICING
SALSA
SAUCE

SYRUP

6
HOISIN
PEPPER
PICKLE
RELISH

7
CAYENNE
CHUTNEY
HARISSA
KETCHUP
MUSTARD
PIMENTO

(or pimiento)
SOUBISE
TABASCO
TREACLE
VELOUTÉ
VINEGAR

8
BÉCHAMEL
DRESSING
JALAPEÑO
MARZIPAN
OLIVE OIL
PIMIENTO
(or pimento)

PIRIPIRI
SALAD OIL
SOY SAUCE

9
BÉARNAISE
CASSAREEP
FISH SAUCE
MINT SAUCE
SOUR CREAM
VIRGIN OIL

10
APPLE SAUCE
BROWN SAUCE

CAPER SAUCE
MAPLE SYRUP
MAYONNAISE
MOUSSELINE
PICCALILLI
SALAD CREAM
SALSA VERDE

11
BABA GANOUSH
CURRY POWDER
DOUBLE CREAM
GOLDEN SYRUP
HOISIN SAUCE
HORSERADISH

MORNAY SAUCE
OYSTER SAUCE
SINGLE CREAM
TOMATO SAUCE
VINAIGRETTE

12
CLOTTED CREAM
MANGO CHUTNEY
SALSA PICANTE
SOUBISE SAUCE
TABASCO SAUCE
TARAMASALATA

VELOUTÉ SAUCE
WHIPPED CREAM

13
BARBECUE SAUCE
BÉCHAMEL SAUCE
CAYENNE PEPPER
FRENCH MUSTARD
JAMAICA PEPPER
MUSTARD PICKLE
SALAD DRESSING
TOMATO KETCHUP

14
BÉARNAISE SAUCE
CRANBERRY SAUCE
ENGLISH MUSTARD
EXTRA VIRGIN OIL
WORCESTER SAUCE

15
DEVONSHIRE CREAM
MUSTARD AND CRESS

16
HORSERADISH SAUCE

Food & Drink – Food – VEGETABLES

3
CEP
COS
OCA
PEA
YAM

4
BEAN
COLE
DHAL
GUAR
KALE
LEEK
MUNG
NEEP
SOYA
SPUD
TARO

5
CHARD
CHIVE
CIBOL
CRESS
MOREL
ONION
PULSE
SAVOY
SWEDE

6
ADJIGO
BATATA
BLEWIT
CARROT
CELERY
CHIVES
COWPEA
ENDIVE

GARLIC
GREENS
JICAMA
KUMARA
LABLAB
LEGUME
LENTIL
LOVAGE
MARROW
MURPHY
ORACHE
POTATO
PRATIE
RADISH
RAPINI
ROCKET
SORREL
SPROUT
TOMATO
TURNIP

7
BOK CHOY
 (or pak choi)
CABBAGE
CARDOON
CHICORY
COLLARD
FRIJOLE
GHERKIN
GOA BEAN
HARICOT
LETTUCE
PAK CHOI
 (or bok choy)
PARSNIP
RAMPION
SALSIFY
SEA KALE
SHALLOT
SKIRRET

SOYBEAN
 (or soya bean)
SPINACH

8
BEETROOT
BROCCOLI
CASCABEL
CELERIAC
CHICKPEA
CUCUMBER
ESCAROLE
FAVA BEAN
GRASS PEA
KOHLRABI
LIMA BEAN
MUNG BEAN
MUSHROOM
RUTABAGA
SAMPHIRE

SCALLION
SOYA BEAN
 (or soybean)
SPLIT PEA
TUCKAHOE
ZUCCHINI

9
ARTICHOKE
ASPARAGUS
BROAD BEAN
COURGETTE
CURLY KALE
FLAGEOLET
GARDEN PEA
KOMATSUNA
NEW POTATO
RED PEPPER
ROUNCEVAL
SUGAR BEAN
SWEETCORN
VEGETABLE

10
BIRD PEPPER
BUTTER BEAN
CHAMPIGNON
COS LETTUCE
FRENCH BEAN
KIDNEY BEAN

KING EDWARD
LOCUST BEAN
MARIS PIPER
RED CABBAGE
RUNNER BEAN
SCORZONERA
SCOTCH KALE
STRING BEAN
SWISS CHARD
TEPARY BEAN
WATERCRESS
WELSH ONION

11
CAULIFLOWER
CHANTERELLE
CLUSTER BEAN
CURLY ENDIVE
FRENCH ONION
GREEN PEPPER
HARICOT BEAN
SEA LETTUCE
SPRING ONION
SWEET FENNEL
SWEET POTATO
WEBB'S WONDER

12
BLACK-EYED PEA
CHICKLING PEA

CORN ON THE COB
LAMB'S LETTUCE
MARROWFAT PEA
PROCESSED PEA
SAVOY CABBAGE
SPANISH ONION
SPRING GREENS
WATER SPINACH
WHITE CABBAGE
YELLOW PEPPER

13
ASPARAGUS TIPS
BLACK-EYED BEAN
HORSE MUSHROOM
SCARLET RUNNER
SPRING CABBAGE

14
BATAVIAN ENDIVE
BRUSSELS SPROUT
CABBAGE LETTUCE
CHINESE CABBAGE
GLOBE ARTICHOKE
ICEBERG LETTUCE

15
CHINESE BROCCOLI
VEGETABLE MARROW

Food & Drink – HERBS & SPICES med = medicinal

3
BAY
RUE

4
DILL
HOPS
MACE
MATÉ
MINT
SAGE

5
ANISE
BASIL
BUGLE med
CLARY
CLOVE
CUBEB med
CUMIN
CURRY
HENNA
SENNA med
SUMAC
 (or sumach)
TANSY
THYME

6
ARNICA med
BETONY med
BORAGE
CAPERS
CASSIA
CATNIP
CHILLI

CHIVES
CICELY
CLOVES
FENNEL
GARLIC
GINGER
GINKGO med
HYSSOP
LOVAGE
MYRTLE med
NUTMEG
PEPPER
SAVORY
SORREL
STEVIA
SUMACH
 (or sumac)
WASABI

7
ACHIOTE med
ALECOST
ALFALFA
ALLSPICE
ANISEED
BAY LEAF
BEE BALM
BONESET med
BURDOCK med
CARAWAY
CATMINT
CAYENNE
CHERVIL
CHICORY
COMFREY
DAMIANA med

DITTANY med
EPHEDRA med
GENTIAN med
GINSENG
GUARANA med
HENBANE med
JUNIPER
MUGWORT
MUSTARD
NIGELLA med
OREGANO
PAPRIKA
PARSLEY
PIMENTO
ROOIBOS
QUASSIA med
SAFFRON
SUCCORY med
VANILLA
VERVAIN med
ZEDOARY

8
AGRIMONY med
ALLSPICE
ANGELICA
BAYBERRY med
BERGAMOT
BILBERRY med
CAMOMILE
CARDAMOM
CAT'S CLAW med
CILANTRO
CINNAMON
COSTMARY
DONG QUAI

FEVERFEW med
GALANGAL
 (or galingale)
GOAT'S RUE med
HABANERO
 (or Scotch bonnet)
HIBISCUS med
KAVA KAVA med
LAVENDER
LUNGWORT med
MARJORAM
ORIGANUM
ROSEMARY
SKULLCAP med
TAMARIND
TARRAGON
TURMERIC
VALERIAN med
WORMWOOD med

9
ARROWROOT
BUGLEWEED med
COLTSFOOT med
CORIANDER
ECHINACEA med
EYEBRIGHT med
FENUGREEK
GALINGALE
 (or galangal)
GERMANDER med
HOREHOUND med
HORSEMINT
HYPERICUM med
LEMON BALM
LIQUORICE

ORRIS ROOT med
PATCHOULI med
ROCAMBOLE
SAFFLOWER
SPEARMINT
STAR ANISE
SWEET BALM
TONKA BEAN med
TORMENTIL med
WOUNDWORT med
YERBA MATÉ

10
ASAFOETIDA
BLUE COHOSH med
CITRONELLA
DEVIL'S CLAW med
ELDERBERRY
ELECAMPANE
LEMON GRASS
LEMON THYME
MALAGUETTA
MASTERWORT med
MOTHERWORT med

PENNYROYAL med
PEPPERCORN
PEPPERMINT
POPPY SEEDS
PULMONARIA med
SPLEENWORT med
THROATWORT med
YERBA BUENA med

11
BLACK COHOSH med
CELERY SEEDS
CURRY LEAVES
GARAM MASALA
HORSERADISH
MARSH MALLOW
MILK THISTLE med
SESAME SEEDS
SLIPPERY ELM med
ST JOHN'S WORT med
SWEET CICELY

12
BALM OF GILEAD med

CHILLI PEPPER
GINKGO BILOBA med
LEMON VERBENA
SCOTCH BONNET
 (or Habanero)
SOUTHERNWOOD
SUMMER SAVORY
WINTER SAVORY

13
BUTCHER'S BROOM med
CAYENNE PEPPER
HORSE CHESTNUT med
RASPBERRY LEAF med

14
SHEPHERD'S PURSE med

15
EVENING PRIMROSE med
WHITE WILLOW BARK med

16
GRAINS OF PARADISE

Geography

Geography – COUNTRIES * = former country   † = part of United Kingdom

3	5	MALTA	BRAZIL	PERSIA*	BELARUS
UAE	BELAU	NAURU	BRUNEI	POLAND	BELGIUM
USA	(or Palau)	NEPAL	CANADA	RUSSIA	BOLIVIA
	BENIN	NIGER	CEYLON*	RWANDA	BURUNDI
4	BURMA	PALAU (or Belau)	CYPRUS	SERBIA	COMOROS
CHAD	(or Myanmar)	QATAR	FRANCE	SWEDEN	CROATIA
CUBA	CHILE	SAMOA	GAMBIA	TAIWAN	DAHOMEY*
FIJI	CHINA	SPAIN	GREECE	TURKEY	DENMARK
IRAN	CONGO	SUDAN	GUINEA	TUVALU	ECUADOR
IRAQ	EGYPT	SYRIA	GUYANA	UGANDA	ENGLAND†
LAOS	GABON	TIBET*	ISRAEL	ZAMBIA	ERITREA
MALI	GHANA	TONGA	JORDAN		ESTONIA
OMAN	HAITI	WALES†	KUWAIT	**7**	FINLAND
PERU	INDIA	YEMEN	LATVIA	ALBANIA	FORMOSA*
SIAM*	ITALY	ZAIRE*	MALAWI	ALGERIA	GEORGIA
TOGO	JAPAN		MALAYA*	ANDORRA	GERMANY
USSR*	KENYA	**6**	MEXICO	ARMENIA	GRENADA
	KOREA*	ANGOLA	MONACO	AUSTRIA	HOLLAND*
	LIBYA	BELIZE	NORWAY	BAHAMAS	HUNGARY
	MACAO*	BHUTAN	PANAMA	BAHRAIN	ICELAND

JAMAICA
LEBANON
LESOTHO
LIBERIA
MOLDOVA
MOROCCO
MYANMAR (or
  Burma)
NAMIBIA
NIGERIA
PRUSSIA*
ROMANIA
SENEGAL
SOMALIA
ST LUCIA
TUNISIA
UKRAINE
URUGUAY
VANUATU
VATICAN
VIETNAM

8
BARBADOS
BOTSWANA
BULGARIA
CAMBODIA
CAMEROON
COLOMBIA
DJIBOUTI
DOMINICA
ETHIOPIA
HONDURAS
HONG KONG*
KIRIBATI
MALAYSIA
MALDIVES
MONGOLIA

PAKISTAN
PARAGUAY
PORTUGAL
RHODESIA*
SCOTLAND†
SLOVAKIA
SLOVENIA
SRI LANKA
SURINAME
TANZANIA
THAILAND
ZANZIBAR*
ZIMBABWE

9
ABYSSINIA*
ARGENTINA
AUSTRALIA
CAPE VERDE
COSTA RICA
EAST TIMOR
GOLD COAST*
GUATEMALA
INDONESIA
KAMPUCHEA*
LITHUANIA
MACEDONIA
MAURITIUS
NICARAGUA
NYASALAND*
PALESTINE*
SAN MARINO
SINGAPORE
SWAZILAND
VENEZUELA

10
AZERBAIJAN

BANGLADESH
BASUTOLAND*
EL SALVADOR
IVORY COAST (or
  Côte d'Ivoire)
KAZAKHSTAN
KYRGYZSTAN
LUXEMBOURG
MADAGASCAR
MAURITANIA
MONTENEGRO
MOZAMBIQUE
NEW ZEALAND
NORTH KOREA
SEYCHELLES
SOUTH KOREA
TAJIKISTAN
TANGANYIKA*
UPPER VOLTA*
UZBEKISTAN
YUGOSLAVIA*

11
AFGHANISTAN
BURKINA FASO
CÔTE D'IVOIRE
  (or Ivory Coast)
DUTCH GUIANA*
EAST GERMANY*
NETHERLANDS
NEW HEBRIDES*
PHILIPPINES
SAUDI ARABIA
SIERRA LEONE
SOUTH AFRICA
SWITZERLAND
WEST GERMANY*

12
BECHUANALAND*
BELGIAN CONGO*
EAST PAKISTAN*
GUINEA-BISSAU
TURKMENISTAN
WESTERN SAMOA*

13
CZECH REPUBLIC
KHMER REPUBLIC*
LIECHTENSTEIN
UNITED KINGDOM

14
CZECHOSLOVAKIA*
GILBERT ISLANDS*
PAPUA NEW GUINEA
SOLOMON ISLANDS

15
BRITISH HONDURAS*
MARSHALL ISLANDS
NORTHERN IRELAND†
SOUTH WEST AFRICA*
ST KITTS AND NEVIS

16
EQUATORIAL GUINEA

17
ANTIGUA AND BARBUDA
BOSNIA-HERZEGOVINA
DOMINICAN REPUBLIC
REPUBLIC OF IRELAND
TRINIDAD AND TOBAGO

18
SÃO TOMÉ AND PRÍNCIPE
UNITED ARAB EMIRATES

21
UNITED STATES OF AMERICA

22
CENTRAL AFRICAN REPUBLIC

25
DEMOCRATIC REPUBLIC OF CONGO
ST VINCENT AND THE GRENADINES

Geography – DESERTS

3	**6**	KARA-KUM	DZUNGARIA
LUT	BŁĘDÓW	PAINTED	LA GUAJIRA
	GIBSON	SECHURA	
4	MOJAVE	SIMPSON	**10**
GOBI	NUBIAN	SONORAN	BET-PAK-DALA
THAR	SAHARA		CHIHUAHUAN
	SYRIAN	**8**	GREAT BASIN
5	TANAMI	COLORADO	GREAT SANDY
KAVIR	TURFAN	KALAHARI	PATAGONIAN
MARGO	UST-URT	KYZYL-KUM	TAKLAMAKAN
NAMIB		MUYUNKUM	
NEFUD	**7**	TABERNAS	**14**
NEGEV	ALASHAN		BOLSON DE MAPIMI
ORDOS	AL-DAHNA	**9**	
SINAI	ARABIAN	BLACK ROCK	
STURT	ATACAMA	CHOLISTAN	

Geography – EXPLORERS & PIONEERS
ast = astronaut/cosmonaut   m = mountaineer   av = aviation pioneer

4	DIAS	GAMA Vasco da
BEAN Al ast	(or Diaz) Bartolomeu	HUME Hamilton
BYRD Richard av	DIAZ	HUNT Baron John m
CANO Juan	(or Dias) Bartolomeu	MOCK Jerrie L av
CARR Gerald ast	DUKE Charlie ast	MUNK Jens
COOK Captain James	EYRE Edward	PÁEZ Pedro

PARK Mungo
POLO Marco
POST Wiley av
RIDE Sally ast
ROSS Sir James
SOTO Hernando

5

BAKER Sir Samuel
BARTH Heinrich
BOONE Daniel
BRAND Vance ast
BROWN Arthur av,
 Joe m
BRUCE James
BURKE Robert O'Hara
CABOT John, Sebastian
CUNHA Tristão da
DAVIS John
DESIO Ardito m
DRAKE Sir Francis
EVANS Ron ast
FUCHS Sir Vivian
GLENN John ast
HAISE Fred ast
IRWIN Jim ast
KIZIM Leonid ast
LAIRD MacGregor
MEYER Hans m
OATES Lawrence
OJEDA Alonso de
PARRY Sir William
PEARY Robert
POPOV Leonid ast
RAZIN Stepan
REMEK Vladimir ast
ROOSA Stu ast
SCOTT Dave ast,

 Doug m, Sir Robert
 Falcon, Sheila av
SMITH Charles
 Kingsford av
SOLIS Juan Diaz de
SPEKE John Hanning
STURT Charles
TITOV Gherman ast,
 Vladimir ast
WHITE Ed ast
WILLS William
YOUNG John W ast

6

ALCOCK Sir John av
ALDRIN Buzz ast
ANDERS Bill ast
BAFFIN William
BALBOA Vasco
 Nuñez de
BALMAT Jacques m
BERING Vitus
BORMAN Frank ast
BRAZZA Pierre
BURTON Sir Richard
CABRAL Pedro
CARSON Kit
CERNAN Eugene ast
CONRAD Pete ast
COOPER Gordon ast
CORTÉS Hernán
DE WITT Gerrit
EISELE Donn ast
GIBSON Robert L
GORDON Dick ast
HASTON Dougal
HUDSON Henry
IVANOV Leonid ast

JOLIET Louis
LEONOV Alexei ast
LOVELL Jim ast
NANSEN Fridtjof
NOBILE Umberto av
NORGAY Tenzing m
PINZÓN Vicente
RYUMIN Valery ast
SERRÃO Francisco
STUART John
TASMAN Abel
VOLKOV Vladislav ast
WILKES Charles
WORDEN Al ast
WRIGHT Orville av,
 Wilbur av
XAVIER Pierre
YEAGER Chuck av

7

ALVAREZ Alonso
BARENTS William
BLÉRIOT Louis av
CAILLIÉ René-Auguste
CARTIER Jacques
CHAFFEE Roger ast
COLLINS Michael ast
CÓRDOBA Francisco de
COVILHA Pero da
CRIPPEN Robert ast
CROZIER Francis
DAMPIER William
EARHART Amelia av
FAWCETT Captain
 Percy
FIENNES Sir Ranulph
FOSSETT Steve av
FRÉMONT John C

GAGARIN Yuri ast
GILBERT Sir Humphrey
GRECHKO Georgi ast
GRISSOM Gus ast
HAWKINS Sir John
HILLARY Sir Edmund m
HINKLER Bert av
HOUTMAN Frederick de
JOHNSON Amy av
KOMAROV Vladimir ast
KUBASOV Valery ast
LA SALLE Robert
MANAROV Musa ast
MCCLURE Sir Robert
MESSNER Reinhold m
PACCARD Michel m
PAULHAN Louis av
PICCARD Auguste,
    Bertrand av, Jacques,
    Jean av
PIZZARO Francisco
RALEIGH Sir Walter
SCHIRRA Walter ast
SELKIRK Alexander
SHEPARD Alan ast
STANLEY Sir Henry
    Morton
SWIGERT John ast
WEDDELL James
WHYMPER Edward m
WILKINS Sir George
WRANGEL Ferdinand

8
ABALAKOV Vitaly m
ALVARADO Pedro de
AMUNDSEN Roald
CARTERET Philip

COLUMBUS Christopher
COUSTEAU Jacques
ERICSSON Leif
FLINDERS Matthew
FRANKLIN Sir John
HUMBOLDT Baron von
JEFFRIES John av
JOURDAIN John
MAGELLAN Ferdinand
MARCHAND Jean
MCDIVITT Jim ast
MITCHELL Ed ast
MOLLISON Jim av
PALGRAVE William
POPOVICH Pavel ast
SCHOUTEN Willem
SOLOVYOV Anatoly ast
STAFFORD Tom ast
SVERDRUP Harald
VESPUCCI Amerigo
ZEPPELIN Count von av

9
ARMSTRONG Neil ast
BLANCHARD Jean
    Pierre av
BONINGTON Chris m
CASTELNAU Francis de
CHAMPLAIN Samuel de
FROBISHER Sir Martin
HEYERDAHL Thor
IBERVILLE Pierre
LACEDELLI Lino m
LEICHARDT Ludwig
LINDBERGH Charles av
LINDSTROM Per av
MACKENZIE Sir
    Alexander

MACKINDER Halford m
MARQUETTE Jacques
MATTINGLY Ken ast
MIDDLETON Henry
RASMUSSEN Knud
ROMANENKO Yuri ast
VANCOUVER George
VELÁSQUEZ Diego
VERRAZANO
    Giovanni da
YELISEYEV Alexei ast

10
BARRINGTON
    Charles m
CHANCELLOR Richard
COMPAGNONI
    Achille m
CUNNINGHAM Walt
    ast
ERIK THE RED
MCCANDLESS Bruce
    ast
RICHTHOFEN Ferdinand
SAVITSKAYA Svetlana
    ast
SHACKLETON Sir Ernest
TERESHKOVA Valentina
    ast
ZURBRIGGEN
    Matthias m

11
LIVINGSTONE David
MONTGOLFIER Jacques
    av, Joseph av
PONCE DE LÉON Juan
PRZHEVALSKI Nikolai

SCHWEICKART Rusty ast

12
BOUGAINVILLE Louis Antoine de
NORDENSKJÖLD Nils
YOUNGHUSBAND Sir Francis

13
HERRLIGKOFFER Karl m

14
BELLINGSHAUSEN Fabian
DUMONT D'URVILLE Jules
KINGSFORD SMITH Sir Charles av
TEMPLEMAN-ADAMS David

17
HENRY THE NAVIGATOR

Geography – FORESTS (British Isles) In England unless stated

3
NEW
TAY Scotland

4
AFAN Wales
FAWR Wales
KYLE Scotland
LUNE
WARK
WYRE

5
CRAIK Scotland
DALBY

6
ACHRAY Scotland
ARGYLL Scotland
CRERAN Scotland
DAVAGH N Ireland
EPPING
GWYDYR Wales
OGMORE Wales

RADNOR Wales
SALCEY
SLALEY
TORRIE Scotland

7
ASHDOWN
BRECHFA Wales
CARRICK Scotland
CEIRIOG Wales
CHANGUE Scotland
CROPTON
CRYCHAN Wales
DUNWICH
DYFNANT Wales
EREDINE Scotland
ETTRICK Scotland
FIUNARY Scotland
FRISTON
GLENGAP Scotland
GOSFORD N Ireland
HARWOOD
KIDLAND
KIELDER

LOCH ARD Scotland
MILBURN
PEMBREY Wales
SKIDDAW
WAREHAM
WYKEHAM

8
COPELAND
DELAMERE
DUNDEUGH Scotland
GALLOWAY Scotland
GLENMORE Scotland
KEILLOUR Scotland
KERSHOPE
KNAPDALE Scotland
LANGDALE
LEITHOPE Scotland
NATIONAL
NEEDWOOD
PORTUMNA S Ireland
QUANTOCK
RINGWOOD
ROTHBURY

SHERWOOD
THETFORD
TUNSTALL
WAUCHOPE Scotland
WHINFELL
YAIR HILL Scotland

9
BEDGEBURY
BLAIRADAM Scotland
BRACKNELL
CASTLE O'ER Scotland
CHARNWOOD
CLOCAENOG Wales
CORLARACH Scotland
DRUM MANOR
  N Ireland
GARADHBAN Scotland
GLENDUROR Scotland
GLENTRESS Scotland
GLENTROOL Scotland
GRIZEDALE
KILLYKEEN S Ireland
PARKHURST
PITFICHIE Scotland
REDESDALE
SAVERNAKE
STRATHORD Scotland
STRATHYRE Scotland
TENTSMUIR Scotland
TOLLYMORE N Ireland

10
DALBEATTIE Scotland
FOREST OF AE Scotland
GILDERDALE
GLAS FYNYDD Wales
GLENDARUEL Scotland
GLENFESHIE Scotland
HAMSTERLEY
KILMICHAEL Scotland
LAURIESTON Scotland
LOUGH NAVAR N Ireland
NEWBOROUGH Wales
RENDLESHAM
ROCKINGHAM

11
COED Y BRENIN Wales
ESKDALEMUIR Scotland
HALLYBURTON Scotland
INVERLIEVER Scotland
PENNINGHAME
  Scotland
STRATHCONON
  Scotland

12
CARROW VALLEY
  Scotland
FOREST OF DEAN
KIRROUGHTREE Scotland

THORNTHWAITE

13
FOREST OF ARDEN
SLIEVE GULLION
  N Ireland

14
FOREST OF ATHOLL
  Scotland
FOREST OF PENDLE
NORTH PETHERTON

15
FOREST OF BOWLAND
FOREST OF TRAWDEN

16
FOREST OF GLEN
  TANAR Scotland

18
ELIBANK AND
  TRAQUAIR Scotland
FOREST OF
  GLENARTNEY
  Scotland

19
FOREST OF MARSTON
  VALE

Geography – Islands – BRITISH & IRISH ISLANDS
In England unless stated   * = so-called island

3

ELY*
EWE Scotland
HOY Scotland
MAN Isle of Man
MAY Scotland
RAT
RUM Scotland
SOA Scotland

4

ARAN S Ireland
BERE S Ireland
BUTE Scotland
COLL Scotland
DOGS*
EDAY Scotland
EIGG Scotland
HERM Channel Isles
HOLY (or Lindisfarne)
   + Scotland, Wales
IONA Scotland
JURA Scotland
MUCK Scotland
OSEA
ROAN Scotland
RONA Scotland
SARK Channel Isles
SEIL Scotland
SKYE Scotland
SOAY Scotland
TEAN
TORY S Ireland
ULVA Scotland
UNST Scotland

WIAY Scotland
YELL Scotland

5

ANNET
ARRAN Scotland
BARRA Scotland
BARRY Wales
BURGH
CALDY Wales
CANNA Scotland
CLARE S Ireland
CLEAR S Ireland
EAGLE S Ireland
ENSAY Scotland
FIDRA Scotland
FOULA Scotland
FUDAY Scotland
GIGHA Scotland
GRAIN
GREAT S Ireland
HANDA Scotland
HARTY*
HORSE Scotland
ISLAY Scotland
LEWIS Scotland
LUING Scotland
LUNDY
LUNGA Scotland
NEAVE Scotland
PABAY Scotland
READ'S
RONAY Scotland
SANDA Scotland
SHEEP Wales

SHUNA Scotland
SULLY Wales
TAWIN S Ireland
THORN Wales
TIREE Scotland
WIGHT

6

ACHILL S Ireland
ANNAGH S Ireland
BRYHER
BURRAY Scotland
CANVEY
COQUET
DAVARR Scotland
DURSEY S Ireland
ELMLEY*
ERISKA Scotland
FETLAR Scotland
FLOTTA Scotland
HESTAN Scotland
HORSEA
HORSEY
JERSEY Channel Isles
LAMBAY S Ireland
LONGAY Scotland
MERSEA
OLDANY Scotland
PABBAY Scotland
PLADDA Scotland
POTTON
PUFFIN Wales
RAASAY Scotland
RAMSEY Wales
ROUSAY Scotland

SANDAY Scotland
SCARBA Scotland
SKOMER Wales
STAFFA Scotland
STROMA Scotland
THANET*
TORSAY Scotland
TRESCO
WALNEY

7

ARDWALL Scotland
AXHOLME*
BARDSEY Wales
BORERAY Scotland
BRESSAY Scotland
CRAMOND Scotland
ERISKAY Scotland
FLODDAY Scotland
GOMETRA Scotland
GORUMNA S Ireland
GRIMSAY Scotland
HAYLING
HYSKEIR Scotland
KERRERA Scotland
LISMORE Scotland
NORTHEY
ORKNEYS Scotland
ORONSAY Scotland
PORTSEA
PURBECK*
RATHLIN N Ireland
ROCKALL Scotland
RUSHLEY
SANDRAY Scotland
SCALPAY Scotland
SHEPPEY
SHERKIN S Ireland

STAFFIN Scotland
ST AGNES
ST KILDA Scotland
ST MARY'S
THORNEY
TWO TREE
WESTRAY Scotland
WHALSAY Scotland

8

ALDERNEY Channel
   Isles
ANGLESEY Wales
BARLOCCO Scotland
BERNERAY Scotland
BROWNSEA
CARDIGAN Wales
COLONSAY Scotland
FAIR ISLE Scotland
FLAT HOLM Wales
FOULNESS
GATEHOLM Wales
GRUINARD Scotland
GUERNSEY Channel
   Isles
HEBRIDES Scotland
INISHEER S Ireland
MAINLAND Scotland
MINGULAY Scotland
PORTLAND
SCILLIES
SKOKHOLM Wales
STRONSAY Scotland
TARANSAY Scotland
VALENTIA S Ireland
VATERSAY Scotland
WALLASEA

9

BALESHARE Scotland
BENBECULA Scotland
BURNTWICK
CALF OF MAN Isle of
   Man
COPELANDS N Ireland
HAVENGORE
HAVERGATE
INCHKEITH Scotland
INISHMAAN S Ireland
INISHMORE S Ireland
INISHTURK S Ireland
ISLE OF ELY*
ISLE OF EWE Scotland
ISLE OF MAN Isle of
   Man
ISLE OF MAY Scotland
MUCKLE ROE Scotland
NORTH UIST Scotland
SCOLT HEAD
SHAPINSAY Scotland
SHETLANDS Scotland
SOUTH UIST Scotland
STEEP HOLM
ST MARTIN'S
ST TUDWAL'S Wales

10

AILSA CRAIG Scotland
HOLY ISLAND (or
   Lindisfarne),
   + Scotland, Wales
ISLE OF DOGS*
ISLE OF SKYE Scotland
LETTERMORE S Ireland

11

ARAN ISLANDS S Ireland
BARRY ISLAND Wales
GREAT ISLAND S Ireland
INCHMARNOCK Scotland
ISLE OF GRAIN
ISLE OF HARTY*
ISLE OF WIGHT
LINDISFARNE (or Holy Island)
LUNDY ISLAND
PAPA WESTRAY Scotland
READ'S ISLAND
SCILLY ISLES
SHEEP ISLAND Wales
THE MANACLES
THORN ISLAND Wales

12

CANVEY ISLAND
DRAKE'S ISLAND
ELMLEY ISLAND*
FARNE ISLANDS
GREAT BERNERA Scotland
GREAT CUMBRAE Scotland
ISLE OF THANET*
LETTERMULLAN S Ireland
MUCKLE FLUGGA Scotland
PUFFIN ISLAND Wales
SALTY ISLANDS S Ireland
WALNEY ISLAND
WESTERN ISLES Scotland

13

HAYLING ISLAND
HILBRE ISLANDS
INNER HEBRIDES Scotland
ISLE OF AXHOLME*
ISLE OF PURBECK*
ISLE OF SHEPPEY
LITTLE CUMBRAE Scotland
MONACH ISLANDS Scotland
ORKNEY ISLANDS Scotland
OUTER HEBRIDES Scotland
RABBIT ISLANDS Scotland
THORNEY ISLAND
TWO TREE ISLAND

14

BLASKET ISLANDS S Ireland
CARDIGAN ISLAND Wales
CHANNEL ISLANDS Channel Isles
CROWLIN ISLANDS Scotland
FLANNAN ISLANDS Scotland
FOULNESS ISLAND
NORTH RONALDSAY Scotland
PORTLAND ISLAND
SOUTH RONALDSAY Scotland

15

COPELAND ISLANDS N Ireland
LEWIS WITH HARRIS Scotland
SCOLT HEAD ISLAND
SHETLAND ISLANDS Scotland
ST MICHAEL'S MOUNT

The *Puzzler* Crossword Companion

Geography – Islands – CARIBBEAN ISLANDS

4
CUBA
SABA

5
ARUBA
NEVIS
RONDE

6
ANDROS
BEQUIA
INAGUA
RUM CAY
ST JOHN
TOBAGO

7
ACKLINS
ANEGADA
ANTIGUA
BARBUDA
BONAIRE
CANOUAN
CURAÇAO
GRENADA
JAMAICA
MAYREAU
REDONDA

SALT CAY
ST CROIX
ST JOHN'S
ST KITTS
ST LUCIA
TORTOLA
TORTUGA

8
ANGUILLA
BARBADOS
DOMINICA
ELBOW CAY
ISLA AVES
MUSTIQUE
ST MARTIN
  (or St Maarten)
ST THOMAS
TRINIDAD

9
CARRIACOU
CAT ISLAND
ELEUTHERA
GRAND TURK
MARGARITA
MAYAGUANA
ST MAARTEN
  (or St Martin)

ST VINCENT

10
CAYMAN BRAC
EAST CAICOS
GREAT ABACO
GREAT EXUMA
GUADELOUPE
HISPANIOLA
LA DÉSIRADE
LES SAINTES
MAN-O-WAR CAY
MARTINIQUE
MONTSERRAT
PALM ISLAND
PUERTO RICO
WEST CAICOS

11
GRAND BAHAMA
GRAND CAYMAN
JOST VAN DYKE
LITTLE ABACO
NORTH BIMINI
NORTH CAICOS
PETITE NEVIS
SAN SALVADOR
SOUTH BIMINI
SOUTH CAICOS

UNION ISLAND
VIRGIN GORDA

12
KLEIN CURAÇAO
LITTLE CAYMAN
MARIE-GALANTE
MIDDLE CAICOS
NUEVA ESPARTA

13
CROOKED ISLAND
GREAT GUANA CAY
NEW PROVIDENCE

14
GREEN TURTLE CAY
PETIT ST VINCENT
PROVIDENCIALES
SAINT EUSTATIUS

15
SAINT-BARTHÉLEMY

16
ISLA DE LA JUVENTUD
PETITE MARTINIQUE

Geography – Islands – GREEK ISLANDS

3
IOS
KEA
KOS

4
ARKI
HIOS
KYRA
PAXI
SYMI
VOUS

5
ANAFI
CHIOS
CORFU
 (or Kerkyra)
CRETE
 (or Kríti)
DASIA
DELOS
DOKOS
GYALI
HYDRA
KASOS
KEROS
KRÍTI
 (or Crete)
LEROS
LIPSI
 (or Leipsoi)

MAKRI
MILOS
NAXOS
OXEIA
PAROS
PITTA
POROS
PSARA
RODOS
 (or Rhodes)
SAMOS
SARIA
SIROS
THIRA
 (or Santorini)
TILOS
TINOS
ZANTE
 (or Zakynthos)

6
AEGINA
ANDROS
ATOKOS
CHALKI
CHRYSI
EUBOEA
GAVDOS
GIOURA
GYAROS
IKARIA
ITHAKA

KASTOS
LEMNOS
 (or Limnos)
LESBOS
LIMNOS
 (or Lemnos)
PATMOS
PIPERI
RHODES
 (or Rodos)
SIFNOS
SKIROS
VALAXA
ZAFORA

7
AMORGOS
ARKOUDI
KALAMOS
KERKYRA
 (or Corfu)
KIMOLOS
KYTHIRA
KYTHNOS
LAGOUSA
LEFKADA
LEIPSOI
 (or Lipsi)
MYKONOS
NISYROS
OTHONOI
PANAGIA

PETALAS
SALAMIS
SERIFOS
SIKINOS
SPETSES
THASSOS

8
ANTIPAXI
ASTAKIDA
DONOUSSA
IRAKLEIA
KALYMNOS
MATHRAKI
MEGANISI
PONTIKOS
PSERIMOS
SARAKINO
SKIATHOS
SKOPELOS
SKORPIOS
THIRASIA
VROMONAS

9
ALONNISOS
ANTIMILOS
ANTIPAROS
ANTIPSARA
DESPOTIKO
DRAKONERA
KARPATHOS

KEFALONIA
KOUFONISI
OINOUSSES
PERISTERA
POLYAIGOS
PSATHOURA
SANTORINI
 (or Thira)
STROFADES
ZAKYNTHOS
 (or Zante)

10
ASTYPALAIA
EREIKOUSSA
SAMOTHRACE
 (or Samothraki)
SAMOTHRAKI
 (or Samothrace)
SKYROPOULA

11
AGATHONISSI
ANTIKYTHIRA
ELAFONISSOS
FARMAKONISI
FOLEGANDROS
KASTELORIZO
SERIFOPOULA

15
AGIOS EFSTRATIOS

Geography – LAKES (British Isles)
In England unless stated   loch = Scotland   lough = Ireland   llyn = Wales

3
AWE loch
EIL loch
EWE loch
KEN loch
KEY lough, S Ireland
LEE loch
REE lough, S Ireland
TAY loch

4
ALSH loch
BALA (or Tegid)
BUIE loch
CONN lough, S Ireland
DERG lough, S Ireland
DOON loch
EARN loch
ERNE lough, N Ireland
FYNE loch
GARA lough, S Ireland
GARE loch
GORM loch
HOPE loch
INSH loch
LONG loch
LYON loch
MASK lough, S Ireland
MHOR loch
MORE loch
NESS loch
SHIN loch
WAST

5
ALLEN lough, S Ireland
BROOM loch
BRORA loch
CELYN llyn
CONWY llyn
DUICH loch
ETIVE loch
FITTY loch
FLEET loch
FOYLE lough, N Ireland
GARRY loch
GLASS loch
GYNON llyn
HOURN loch
LEANE lough, S Ireland
LEVEN loch
LOCHY loch
LOYAL loch
LOYNE loch
LUSSA loch
MAREE loch
MONAR loch
MORAR loch
MUICK loch
NAVER loch
NEAGH lough, N Ireland
OGWEN llyn
ORRIN loch
QUIEN loch
RYDAL
SHIEL loch
TEGID (or Bala) llyn
TREIG loch
TUATH loch

TULLA loch

6
ARKAIG loch
ASSYNT loch
BRENIG llyn
CALDER loch
CORRIB lough, S Ireland
ERICHT loch
HEILEN loch
LAGGAN loch
LINNHE loch
LOMOND loch
OSSIAN loch
QUOICH loch
RIDDON loch
SUNART loch
SWILLY lough, S Ireland
TUMMEL loch
VYRNWY
  (or Efyrnwy) llyn
WATTEN loch
WILLEN

7
BLAGDON
BRIANNE llyn
CLUANIE loch
CWELLYN llyn
DERWENT
EFYRNWY
  (or Vyrnwy) llyn
EISHORT loch
ERIBOLL loch
FANNICH loch

GRAFHAM
GWYNANT llyn
KATRINE loch
KIELDER
MABERRY loch
MELFORT loch
MOCHRUM loch
RANNOCH loch
RUTLAND
SNIZORT loch
ST MARY'S loch
STRIVEN loch

8
CONISTON
CRUMMOCK
DRAYCOTE
DUNVEGAN loch
GRASMERE
LANGAVAT loch
MENTEITH (only
   Scottish lake)
SCRIDIAN loch
SEAFORTH loch
STENNESS loch
TAL-Y-LLYN llyn
TORRIDON loch
VENACHAR loch

VIRGINIA

9
COLLIFORD
ENNERDALE
ESTHWAITE
HEMPRIGGS loch
KIRBISTER loch
LLANGORSE llyn
OCHILTREE loch
SIBLYBACK
THIRLMERE
ULLSWATER
WAST WATER

10
BROADWATER
BUTTERMERE
CHEW VALLEY
HAWESWATER
LOWESWATER
MALHAM TARN
MULLARDOCH loch
RYDAL WATER
STRANGFORD lough,
   N Ireland
WINDERMERE

11
BROGBOROUGH
GLASCARNOCH loch
HORNSEA MERE
TRAWSFYNYDD llyn

12
AQUALATE MERE
BLATHERWYCKE
DERWENT WATER
GRAFHAM WATER
KIELDER WATER
RUTLAND WATER

13
BASSENTHWAITE
CONISTON WATER
CRUMMOCK WATER
DRAYCOTE WATER
VIRGINIA WATER

14
ENNERDALE WATER

15
CLATTERINGSHAWS loch

Geography – MOUNTAIN RANGES

4
ALPS Europe
JURA France-Switzerland
NAGA India

5
ANDES S America
ATLAS Morocco-Tunisia
GHATS India
URALS Russia-Kazakhstan

6

ALBORZ Armenia-Iran
OCHILS Scotland
PAMIRS Tajikistan-Kyrgyzstan-
  Afghanistan-Pakistan
SUDETY Czech Rep-Poland
TATRAS Poland-Slovakia
VOSGES France

7

BALKANS Bulgaria-Serbia
MENDIPS England
MOURNES N Ireland
ROCKIES USA-Canada
SIDLAWS Scotland

8

AUVERGNE France
CASCADES USA-Canada
CAUCASUS Russia-Georgia
CHEVIOTS England-Scotland
MALVERNS England
PENNINES England
PYRENEES France-Spain
RUAHINES New Zealand
SPERRINS N Ireland
TIAN SHAN Kazakhstan-China

9

APENNINES Italy
BLUE RIDGE USA
CATSKILLS USA
CHILTERNS England
CHIN HILLS Myanmar
COTSWOLDS England
DINARIDES Balkans
DOLOMITES Italy
DRUM HILLS Scotland, Wales

FAUCILLES France
GRAMPIANS Scotland
HIMALAYAS Asia
HINDU KUSH Afghanistan-Pakistan
KARAKORAM Pakistan-China-India
NAGA HILLS India
PENTLANDS Scotland
QUANTOCKS England
SNOWDONIA Wales
TOBO KAKAR Afghanistan-Pakistan

10

CAIRNGORMS Scotland
CARNIC ALPS Austria-Italy
ERZGEBIRGE Czech Rep-Germany
JULIAN ALPS Italy-Slovenia
OCHIL HILLS Scotland
THE GLYDERS Wales

11

ADIRONDACKS USA
BERWYN HILLS Wales
BROOKS RANGE USA
CANTABRIANS Spain
CARPATHIANS Poland-Slovakia-Romania
CLEISH HILLS Scotland
COTTIAN ALPS France-Italy
DINARIC ALPS Balkans
FINTRY HILLS Scotland
LENNOX HILLS Scotland
MENDIP HILLS England
PENNINE ALPS France-Switzerland-Italy
SIDLAW HILLS Scotland
SIERRA MADRE Mexico
SOUTHERN ALPS New Zealand
SWABIAN ALPS Germany

12

APPALACHIANS USA-Canada
BRENDON HILLS England
CASCADE RANGE USA-Canada
CHEVIOT HILLS England-Scotland
CUILLIN HILLS Scotland
DRAKENSBERGS South Africa
ELK MOUNTAINS USA
KILSYTH HILLS Scotland
MALVERN HILLS England
NILGIRI HILLS India
PEAK DISTRICT England
PENNINE HILLS England
PRESELI HILLS Wales
RHAETIAN ALPS Italy-Switzerland-
  Austria
RUAHINE RANGE New Zealand
SIERRA MORENA Spain
SIERRA NEVADA Spain, USA
SIWALIK HILLS Nepal-India-Pakistan
THE CARNEDDAU Wales
VINDHYA RANGE India

13

ARAVALLI RANGE India
BLUE MOUNTAINS Australia, USA
CAHA MOUNTAINS S Ireland
CHILTERN HILLS England
COTSWOLD HILLS England
FLINDERS RANGE Australia
HARZ MOUNTAINS Germany
IRON MOUNTAINS USA
JURA MOUNTAINS France-Switzerland
MASSIF CENTRAL France
MAYA MOUNTAINS Belize
MOORFOOT HILLS Scotland
PENTLAND HILLS Scotland
QUANTOCK HILLS England

RIESENGEBIRGE Czech Rep-Poland
SIERRA MAESTRA Cuba
URAL MOUNTAINS Russia-Kazakhstan

14

ALTAI MOUNTAINS Kazakhstan-
  Mongolia-China
ATLAS MOUNTAINS Morocco-Tunisia
BLACKDOWN HILLS England
BLACK MOUNTAINS USA, Wales
CLEVELAND HILLS England
FICHTELGEBIRGE Germany
GALTY MOUNTAINS S Ireland
GREEN MOUNTAINS USA
GYDAN MOUNTAINS Russia
OZARK MOUNTAINS USA
PAMIR MOUNTAINS Tajikistan-
  Kyrgyzstan-Afghanistan-Pakistan
SHEHY MOUNTAINS S Ireland
SNOWY MOUNTAINS Australia
TATRA MOUNTAINS Poland-Slovakia
WHITE MOUNTAINS USA

15

ANADYR MOUNTAINS Russia
BALKAN MOUNTAINS Bulgaria-Serbia
BERNESE OBERLAND Switzerland
DARTRY MOUNTAINS S Ireland
ELBURZ MOUNTAINS Iran
GALTEE MOUNTAINS S Ireland
HOOSAC MOUNTAINS USA
KILPATRICK HILLS Scotland
KUNLUN MOUNTAINS China
LAMMERMUIR HILLS Scotland
MOURNE MOUNTAINS N Ireland
PARTRY MOUNTAINS S Ireland
PINDUS MOUNTAINS Greece
RODOPI MOUNTAINS Bulgaria-Greece

SIERRA DE CÓRDOBA Argentina
SIERRA DE SAN LUIS Argentina
SUDETY MOUNTAINS Czech Rep-
  Poland
TAUNUS MOUNTAINS Germany
TAURUS MOUNTAINS Turkey
ZAGROS MOUNTAINS Iran-Iraq

16
AHAGGAR MOUNTAINS Algeria
KINGHAN MOUNTAINS China
LEBANON MOUNTAINS Lebanon
SPERRIN MOUNTAINS N Ireland
TORNGAT MOUNTAINS Canada
VIRUNGA MOUNTAINS Rwanda-
  Congo-Uganda
WICKLOW MOUNTAINS S Ireland
YABLONOVY KHERBET Russia

17
CATSKILL MOUNTAINS USA
DOLOMITE MOUNTAINS Italy
GRAMPIAN MOUNTAINS Scotland
KAUMAJET MOUNTAINS Canada

TRANSYLVANIAN ALPS Romania
WRANGELL MOUNTAINS USA

18
BLUE RIDGE MOUNTAINS USA
BLUESTACK MOUNTAINS S Ireland
FAUCILLES MOUNTAINS France
QUEEN MAUD MOUNTAINS Antarctica
TORDRILLO MOUNTAINS USA

19
ADIRONDACK MOUNTAINS USA
CANTABRIAN MOUNTAINS Spain
CARPATHIAN MOUNTAINS Poland-
  Slovakia-Romania
DZHUGDZHUR MOUNTAINS Russia
GREAT SMOKY MOUNTAINS USA
MACGILLYCUDDY'S REEKS S Ireland

20
APPALACHIAN MOUNTAINS USA-
  Canada
DRAKENSBERG MOUNTAINS South
  Africa

Geography – MOUNTAINS

3
APO Philippines
IDA Greece

4
BONA USA
COOK Canada, New Zealand
DANA USA
ETNA Italy
FUJI Japan

HOOD USA
MERU Tanzania
RIGI Switzerland
ROAN USA
TODI Switzerland

5
ADAMS USA
AGUNG Indonesia
ANETO Spain

ASAHI Japan
BAKER USA
BINGA Mozambique-
  Zimbabwe
BORAH USA
DIRAN Pakistan
DJAJA Indonesia
EIGER Switzerland
ELGON Kenya-Uganda
HAYES USA

HEKLA Iceland
HUILA Colombia
KAMET India
KENYA Kenya
KORAB Albania
LOGAN Canada
LYELL USA
MARCY USA
MISTI Peru
PELÉE Martinique
TEIDE Spain
SINAI Egypt
TYREE Antarctica

6

ARARAT Turkey
BAXTER USA
BOGONG Australia
CARMEL Israel
CHO OYU Nepal-China
DAWSON Canada
ELBERT USA
ELBRUS Russia
EREBUS Antarctica
FORBES Canada
HERMON Lebanon-
  Syria
HOTAKA Japan
KAZBEK Georgia
LENNOX USA
LHOTSE Nepal-China
MAKALU Nepal-China
MOROTO Uganda
MUSALA Bulgaria
NOSHAQ Afghanistan-
  Pakistan
ORTLER Italy
  (or Ortles)

ORTLES (or Ortler) Italy
PISSIS Chile
POWELL USA
PUMORI Nepal-China
ROBSON Canada
RUNGWE Tanzania
SAJAMA Bolivia
TAFTAN Iran
TASMAN New Zealand
VIHREN Bulgaria
WILSON USA
ZIRKEL USA

7

BELUCHA Russia
BERNINA Italy
BOLIVAR USA
BROCKEN Germany
CAUBVIK Canada
DAMPIER New Zealand
ELK LICK USA
EVEREST Nepal-China
FITZROY Argentina
HARVARD USA
HOFFMAN USA
ILLAMPU Bolivia
KAILASH China
KERINCI Indonesia
KILAUEA USA
LEMBERG Germany
LUCANIA Canada
MANASLU Nepal
OLYMPUS Greece, USA
PELVOUX France
RAINIER USA
RORAIMA Guyana
SANFORD USA
SCA FELL England

SKIDDAW England
SNOWDON Wales
SRI PADA Sri Lanka
STANLEY Congo-Uganda
ST ELIAS Canada
TORBERT USA
TRIGLAV Slovenia
WHITNEY USA
VENTOUX France

8

ADAMELLO Italy
ANAIMUDI India
BEN NEVIS Scotland
CAMEROON Cameroon
COLUMBIA USA
COTOPAXI Ecuador
DEMAVEND Iran
ILLIMANI Bolivia
JUNGFRAU Switzerland
KINABALU Malaysia
KING PEAK Canada
MAUNA KEA USA
MAUNA LOA USA
MCKINLEY USA
MONT DORE France
MITCHELL USA
MULHACÉN Spain
MURALLÓN Argentina
RAS DEJEN Ethiopia
RUSHMORE USA
SARAMATI India
SMOLIKAS Greece
SNAEFELL Isle of Man
SNÖHETTA Norway
ST HELENS USA
TARAWERA New Zealand
TOWNSEND Australia

VESUVIUS Italy
VICTORIA Australia
WRANGELL USA

9
ACONCAGUA
  Argentina
ANNAPURNA Nepal
AONACH MOR
  Scotland
BEN LAWERS Scotland
BLACKBURN USA
BRAERIACH Scotland
BREITHORN
  Switzerland
BROAD CRAG England
BROAD PEAK China-
  Pakistan
CAIRN GORM Scotland
CAIRN TOUL Scotland
CERRO TORE Argentina
CHURCHILL USA
CROSS FELL England
DACHSTEIN Austria
EMI KOUSSI Chad
GRAN SASSO Italy
GRAY'S PEAK USA
HELVELLYN England
HUASCARÁN Peru
JEFFERSON USA
KARISIMBI Rwanda-
  Congo
KOSCIUSKO Australia
LAFAYETTE USA
LENIN PEAK
  (or Chon-Too Peak)
  Kyrgyzstan
LONG'S PEAK USA

MALADETTA France-
  Spain
MARMOLADA Italy
MONT BLANC France-
  Italy
MONT CENIS France
MONTE ROSA Italy-
  Switzerland
MONT PERDU France-
  Spain
MUZTAGATA China
NANDA DEVI India
PARICUTIN Mexico
PARNASSUS Greece
PIETROSUL Romania
PLYNLIMON Wales
RAKAPOSHI Pakistan
SARAGHRAR Pakistan
STROMBOLI Italy
THE WREKIN England
TIRICH MIR Pakistan
TONGARIRO New
  Zealand
TUPUNGATO Chile-
  Argentina
VANCOUVER Canada
WEISSHORN
  Switzerland
ZUGSPITZE Austria-
  Germany

10
AONACH BEAG
  Scotland
BEN MACDHUI
  Scotland
CADER IDRIS Wales
CASTLE PEAK USA

CATHIN PEAK South
  Africa
CHIMBORAZO Ecuador
DENT DU MIDI
  Switzerland
DHAULAGIRI Nepal
GARNET PEAK USA
GASHERBRUM China-
  Pakistan
GLYDER FAWR Wales
GONGGA SHAN China
GRAND TETON USA
GRASSY KNOB USA
KEBNEKAISE Sweden
MASHERBRUM Pakistan
MATTERHORN
  Switzerland-Italy
MERCEDARIO
  Argentina
MINYA KONKA China
MONTE CINTO Italy
MONTE CORNO Italy
MUZTAGH ATA China
PIZ BERNINA
  Switzerland-Italy
PUNCAK JAYA
  Indonesia
SOMONI PEAK (or
  Communism Peak)
  Tajikistan
SPRUCE KNOB USA
WADDINGTON Canada
WASHINGTON USA
WELLINGTON Australia
  New Zealand
WETTERHORN
  Switzerland
WILDSPITZE Austria

11

ASSINIBOINE USA
CHON-TOO PEAK (or Lenin Peak)
 Kyrgyzstan
CORNO GRANDE Italy
DENT BLANCHE Switzerland
DRACHENFELS Germany
FAIRWEATHER USA
GRAND COMBIN Switzerland
JBEL TOUBKAL Morocco
KILIMANJARO Tanzania
KINDER SCOUT England
KIRKPATRICK Antarctica
LOOLMALASIN Tanzania
MUNKU SARDYK Russia
NAMCHA BARWA China
NANGA PARBAT Pakistan
SCAFELL PIKE England
SCHRECKHORN Switzerland
VATNAJÖKULL Iceland
WHEELER PEAK USA

12

CITLALTEPETL Mexico
GALDHØPIGGEN Norway
GODWIN AUSTEN (or K2) China-
 Pakistan
GRAN PARADISO Italy
HALTITUNTURI Finland
IZTACCIHUATL Mexico
LLULLAILLACO Argentina
MONTE POLLINO Italy
OJOS DEL SALADO Chile
ÖRAEFAJÖKULL Iceland

POPOCATEPETL Mexico
SHISHAPANGMA China
SLIEVE DONARD N Ireland
TINGUIRIRICA Chile
VINSON MASSIF Antarctica

13

CARRANTUOHILL S Ireland
CLINGMAN'S DOME USA
COMMUNISM PEAK
 (or Somoni Peak) Tajikistan
GROSSGLOCKNER Austria
KANGCHENJUNGA Nepal-India
MONT-AUX-SOURCES South Africa
MOUNT OF OLIVES Israel
PICO DA NEBLINA Brazil
PICO DE ORIZABA Mexico
PIDURUTALAGALA Sri Lanka
TABLE MOUNTAIN S Africa

14

FINSTERAARHORN Switzerland
MONCH CHAJRCHAN Mongolia

15

CARNEDD LLEWELYN Wales
GANGKHAR PUENSUM Bhutan

17

SUGAR LOAF MOUNTAIN Brazil

18

KLYUCHEVSKAYA SOPKA Russia

Geography – Physical Geography – COMMUNITIES

3
SPA
WEN

4
BURG
CAMP
CITY
CLAN
DORP
FOLK
PORT
POST
RACE
SLUM
TOWN

5
BORGO
BOURG
BURGH
KRAAL
TRIBE

6
CASBAH
  (or kasbah)
CENTRE
COLONY
FAMILY
GHETTO
HAMLET

KASBAH
  (or casbah)
NATION
PARISH
PEOPLE
PUEBLO
RESORT
RUSTIC
SHTETL
SUBURB
TOWNIE

7
BOROUGH
BURGESS
BURGHER
CAPITAL
CITIZEN
COMMUNE
KAMPONG
KIBBUTZ
MISSION
NEW TOWN
OPPIDUM
OUTPOST
QUARTER
SEAPORT
SOCIETY
SUBURBS
VILLAGE

8
CONURBIA
DISTRICT
FAUBOURG
FREE CITY
FREE PORT
HOME TOWN
POPULACE
POST TOWN
PRESIDIO
RESIDENT
SUBURBIA
TOWNSHIP
TOWNSMAN
URBANITE
VILLAGER

9
BORGHETTO
CHINATOWN
COMMUNITY
GHOST TOWN
HILL TRIBE
INNER CITY
NEIGHBOUR
OUTSKIRTS
OVERSPILL
RANCHERIA

10
CANTONMENT
COSMOPOLIS

COUNTRYMAN
COUNTY TOWN
ENCAMPMENT
GARDEN CITY
MARKET TOWN
METROPOLIS
PIT VILLAGE
POPULATION
SETTLEMENT
SHANTY TOWN
TOWNSWOMAN

11
CAPITAL CITY
CONURBATION
HILL STATION
MEGALOPOLIS
PHALANSTERY
RESERVATION

12
COUNTRYWOMAN
GARRISON TOWN
HEALTH RESORT
LATIN QUARTER
MUNICIPALITY

13
COUNTY BOROUGH
NEIGHBOURHOOD
SATELLITE TOWN

Geography – Physical Geography – GEOGRAPHICAL AREAS

3
BOG
FEN
SEE

4
AREA
BELT
DALE
DELL
DEME
DENE
HOLM
LAND
NOME
PALE
PARK
PUNA
RAND
RIDE
SITE
SOKE
VALE
VEGA
WARD
WOLD
WOOD
ZONE

5
BASIN
BRUSH
CHASE
CLIME
COAST
DOWNS

DUCHY
FLATS
KAROO
LLANO
MANOR
MARCH
MARSH
PATCH
PLAIN
REALM
SHIRE
STATE
TALUK
TRACT
VELDT
VERGE
WEALD
ZILLA

6
BARONY
BORDER
BUSTEE
CANTON
COLONY
COUNTY
DESERT
DOMAIN
EMPIRE
ESTATE
FOREST
INLAND
JUNGLE
LEVANT
LIMITS
OBLAST

OFFING
ORIENT
PAMPAS
PARAMO
POLDER
REGION
RIDING
SANJAK
SECTOR
TEHSIL
THORPE
TUNDRA
UPLAND
VALLEY

7
BARRENS
BOGLAND
BOSCAGE
CIRCUIT
COUNTRY
DIOCESE
DUKEDOM
EARLDOM
EMIRATE
ENCLAVE
EPARCHY
EXCLAVE
EXPANSE
FENLAND
HUNDRED
KHANATE
KINGDOM
LOWLAND
MAREMMA
MIDLAND

PARGANA
PLATEAU
PRAIRIE
PURLIEU
RESERVE
RIVIERA
SATRAPY
SAVANNA
  (or savannah)
SEASIDE
STEPPES
SUBZONE
THE BUSH
THE PALE
TROPICS
VILAYET
WAR ZONE

8
BADLANDS
CAATINGA
DEER PARK
DISTRICT
DIVISION
DOMINION
DUST BOWL
ENVIRONS
FORELAND
FRONTIER
HOMELAND
INTERIOR
LAKESIDE
LOCATION
MAINLAND
MOORLAND
NO-GO AREA

NOMARCHY
OCCIDENT
OILFIELD
PARKLAND
PRESERVE
PROVINCE
REPUBLIC
SAVANNAH
  (or savanna)
SEABOARD
SHEADING
TIME ZONE
WOODLAND

9
ARCHDUCHY
BACKWOODS
BAILIWICK
BISHOPRIC
CALIPHATE
CHAPARRAL
CITY STATE
COALFIELD
CONTINENT
CROWN LAND
DEEP SOUTH
DOCKLANDS
DOWNLANDS
GOLDFIELD
GRASSLAND
GREEN BELT
HEARTLAND
HEATHLAND
MARSHLAND
SCRUBLAND
SHOGUNATE

SHORESIDE
SULTANATE
TABLELAND
TERRITORY
TETRARCHY
UP-COUNTRY
VISCOUNTY
WAPENTAKE
WASTELAND

10
BORDERLAND
DEPARTMENT
 (or département)
DEPENDENCY
EPISCOPATE
FATHERLAND
FRIGID ZONE
GRAND DUCHY

HEMISPHERE
HINTERLAND
MOTHERLAND
OLD COUNTRY
PALATINATE
POSSESSION
PUBLIC LAND
RIVER BASIN
SUPERSTATE
THE OUTBACK
TORRID ZONE
WILDERNESS

11
ARCHDIOCESE
BACK-COUNTRY
BUFFER STATE
BUILT-UP AREA
COUNTRYSIDE

DÉPARTEMENT.
 (or department)
GAME RESERVE
LATIFUNDIUM
SUBDISTRICT

12
CONSTITUENCY
NATIONAL PARK
PRINCIPALITY
PROTECTORATE
SUBCONTINENT
THE PROVINCES

13
ARCHBISHOPRIC
CATCHMENT AREA
DEPRESSED AREA
MOTHER COUNTRY

TEMPERATE ZONE
THE THIRD WORLD

14
ARRONDISSEMENT
BANANA REPUBLIC
BROWNFIELD SITE
COUNTY PALATINE
DISTRESSED AREA
GREENFIELD SITE
RESTRICTED AREA
SATELLITE STATE
TRUST TERRITORY

15
ARCHIEPISCOPATE
DEVELOPMENT AREA
METROPOLITANATE

Geography – Regions – BOROUGHS (London)   * = not a borough

5
BRENT

6
BARNET
BEXLEY
CAMDEN
EALING
HARROW
MERTON
NEWHAM
SUTTON

7
BROMLEY
CROYDON
ENFIELD
HACKNEY
LAMBETH

8
HARINGEY
HAVERING
HOUNSLOW
LEWISHAM
RICHMOND

9
GREENWICH
ISLINGTON
REDBRIDGE
SOUTHWARK

10
HILLINGDON
WANDSWORTH

12
CITY OF LONDON*
TOWER HAMLETS

13
WALTHAM FOREST

17
CITY OF WESTMINSTER

18
BARKING AND DAGENHAM
KINGSTON-UPON-THAMES

20
HAMMERSMITH AND FULHAM
KENSINGTON AND CHELSEA

Geography – Regions – CANTONS (Switzerland)

3
URI
ZUG

4
BERN (or Berne)
JURA
VAUD

5
BERNE (or Bern)

6
AARGAU (or Argovia)
GENEVA (or Genève)
GENÈVE (or Geneva)
GLARUS
OBWALD (or
  Obwalden)
SCHWYZ
ST GALL (or St Gallen)

TICINO
VALAIS
ZURICH

7
ARGOVIA (or Aargau)
GRISONS (or
  Graubünden)
LUCERNE
NIDWALD (or
  Nidwalden)
THURGAU (or
  Thurgovia)

8
FRIBOURG
OBWALDEN
  (or Obwald)
ST GALLEN (or St Gall)

9
NEUCHÂTEL
NIDWALDEN (or Nidwald)
SOLOTHURN
THURGOVIA (or Thurgau)

10
BASEL-STADT
GRAUBÜNDEN (or Grisons)

12
SCHAFFHAUSEN

15
BASEL-LANDSCHAFT

20
APPENZELL INNERRHODEN

21
APPENZELL AUSSERRHODEN

Geography – Regions – COUNTIES (Republic of Ireland) * = province

4
CORK
MAYO

5
CAVAN
CLARE
KERRY
LAOIS

LOUTH
MEATH
SLIGO

6
CARLOW
DUBLIN
GALWAY
OFFALY

ULSTER*

7
DONEGAL
KILDARE
LEITRIM
MUNSTER*
WEXFORD
WICKLOW

8
CONNACHT*
KILKENNY
LEINSTER*
LIMERICK
LONGFORD
MONAGHAN

9
ROSCOMMON
TIPPERARY
WATERFORD
WESTMEATH

Geography – Regions – COUNTIES (UK)
In England unless stated * = former county Also see Unitary Authorities

4
AVON*
BUTE* Scotland
DOWN* N Ireland
FIFE* Scotland
KENT

5
ANGUS* Scotland
CLWYD* Wales
DEVON
DYFED* Wales
ESSEX
FLINT* Wales
GWENT* Wales
MORAY* Scotland
NAIRN* Scotland
POWYS* Wales

6
ANTRIM* N Ireland
ARMAGH* N Ireland
DORSET
DURHAM
ORKNEY* Scotland
SURREY
SUSSEX*
TYRONE* N Ireland

7
BORDERS* Scotland
CENTRAL* Scotland
CUMBRIA
DENBIGH* Wales
GWYNEDD* Wales

LOTHIAN* Scotland
NORFOLK
RUTLAND*
SUFFOLK
TAYSIDE* Scotland

8
ANGLESEY* Wales
AYRSHIRE* Scotland
CHESHIRE
CORNWALL
GRAMPIAN* Scotland
HIGHLAND* Scotland
SHETLAND* Scotland
SOMERSET

9
BERKSHIRE
BRECKNOCK* Wales
CAITHNESS* Scotland
CLEVELAND*
FERMANAGH* N Ireland
GLAMORGAN* Wales
HAMPSHIRE
MERIONETH* Wales
MIDDLESEX*
ROSS-SHIRE*
WILTSHIRE
YORKSHIRE*

10
BANFFSHIRE* Scotland
CUMBERLAND*
DERBYSHIRE
EAST SUSSEX

HUMBERSIDE*
LANCASHIRE
MERSEYSIDE*
MIDLOTHIAN* Scotland
MONTGOMERY* Wales
PERTHSHIRE* Scotland
SHROPSHIRE
SUTHERLAND* Scotland
WEST SUSSEX

11
ARGYLLSHIRE* Scotland
EAST LOTHIAN* Scotland
ISLE OF WIGHT*
LANARKSHIRE* Scotland
LONDONDERRY* N Ireland
OXFORDSHIRE
RADNORSHIRE* Wales
STRATHCLYDE* Scotland
TYNE AND WEAR*
WEST LOTHIAN* Scotland
WESTMORLAND*

12
BEDFORDSHIRE
BERWICKSHIRE* Scotland
KINROSS-SHIRE* Scotland
LINCOLNSHIRE
MID GLAMORGAN* Wales
PEEBLESSHIRE* Scotland
RENFREWSHIRE* Scotland
SELKIRKSHIRE* Scotland
WARWICKSHIRE
WESTERN ISLES* (or Na
    H-Eileanan Siar) Scotland

WEST MIDLANDS*
WIGTOWNSHIRE* Scotland

13
ABERDEENSHIRE* Scotland
CARDIGANSHIRE* Wales
DUMFRIESSHIRE* Scotland
HEREFORDSHIRE*
HERTFORDSHIRE
MONMOUTHSHIRE* Wales
PEMBROKESHIRE* Wales
ROXBURGHSHIRE* Scotland
STAFFORDSHIRE
STIRLINGSHIRE* Scotland
WEST GLAMORGAN* Wales
WEST YORKSHIRE*

14
CAMBRIDGESHIRE
DUNBARTONSHIRE* Scotland
INVERNESS-SHIRE* Scotland

LEICESTERSHIRE
NORTHUMBERLAND
NORTH YORKSHIRE
SOUTH GLAMORGAN* Wales
SOUTH YORKSHIRE*
WORCESTERSHIRE

15
BUCKINGHAMSHIRE
CAERNARVONSHIRE* Wales
CARMARTHENSHIRE* Wales
GLOUCESTERSHIRE
HUNTINGDONSHIRE*
KINCARDINESHIRE* Scotland
NA H-EILEANAN SIAR* (or Western
   Isles) Scotland
NOTTINGHAMSHIRE
ROSS AND CROMARTY* Scotland

16
NORTHAMPTONSHIRE

Geography – Regions – DÉPARTEMENTS (France)

3	JURA	LOIRE	CREUSE	**7**	**8**
AIN	NORD	MARNE	LANDES	ARDÈCHE	ARDENNES
LOT	OISE	MEUSE	LOIRET	AVEYRON	CALVADOS
VAR	ORNE	PARIS	LOZÈRE	BAS-RHIN	CHARENTE
	TARN	RHÔNE	MANCHE	CORRÈZE	DORDOGNE
4		SOMME	NIÈVRE	CÔTE-D'OR	HAUT-RHIN
AUBE	**5**	YONNE	SARTHE	ESSONNE	MORBIHAN
AUDE	AISNE		SAVOIE	GIRONDE	VAL-D'OISE
CHER	DOUBS	**6**	VENDÉE	HÉRAULT	VAUCLUSE
EURE	DRÔME	ALLIER	VIENNE	MAYENNE	YVELINES
GARD	INDRE	ARIÈGE	VOSGES	MOSELLE	
GERS	ISÈRE	CANTAL			

9
FINISTÈRE
PUY-DE-DÔME

10
CORSE-DU-SUD
DEUX-SÈVRES
EURE-ET-LOIR
HAUTE-CORSE
HAUTE-LOIRE
HAUTE-MARNE
HAUTE-SAÔNE
LOIR-ET-CHER
VAL-DE-MARNE

11
CÔTES D'ARMOR
HAUTES-ALPES
HAUTE-SAVOIE
HAUTE-VIENNE
PAS-DE-CALAIS

12
HAUTE-GARONNE
HAUTS-DE-SEINE
INDRE-ET-LOIRE
LOT-ET-GARONNE
MAINE-ET-LOIRE
SAÔNE-ET-LOIRE
SEINE-ET-MARNE

13
ILLE-ET-VILAINE
SEINE-MARITIME
TARN-ET-GARONNE

14
ALPES-MARITIMES
BOUCHES-DU-RHÔNE
HAUTES-PYRÉNÉES

15
LOIRE-ATLANTIQUE
SEINE-SAINT-DENIS

16
CHARENTE-MARITIME

18
MEURTHE-ET-MOSELLE
PYRÉNÉES-ORIENTALES

19
PYRÉNÉES-ATLANTIQUES
TERRITOIRE DE BELFORT

20
ALPES-DE-HAUTE-PROVENCE

Geography – Regions – PROVINCES (Canada) * = territory

5
YUKON*

6
QUEBEC

7
ALBERTA
NUNAVUT*
ONTARIO

8
MANITOBA

10
NOVA SCOTIA

12
NEW BRUNSWICK
NEWFOUNDLAND
SASKATCHEWAN

15
BRITISH COLUMBIA

18
PRINCE EDWARD ISLAND

20
NORTH-WEST TERRITORIES*

Geography – Regions – STATES (Australia)

8
TASMANIA
VICTORIA

10
QUEENSLAND

13
NEW SOUTH WALES

14
SOUTH AUSTRALIA

16
WESTERN AUSTRALIA

17
NORTHERN TERRITORY

26
AUSTRALIAN CAPITAL
  TERRITORY
  (government region)

Geography – Regions – STATES (Germany)

5
HESSE

6
BERLIN
BREMEN
SAXONY

7
BAVARIA
HAMBURG

8
SAARLAND

9
THURINGIA

10
BRANDENBURG

11
LOWER SAXONY

12
SAXONY-ANHALT

16
BADEN-WÜRTTEMBERG

17
SCHLESWIG-HOLSTEIN

19
RHINELAND-PALATINATE

20
NORTH RHINE-WESTPHALIA

27
MECKLENBURG-WESTERN POMERANIA

Geography – Regions – STATES (USA)

4	**5**	**6**		**7**	
IOWA	IDAHO	ALASKA	NEVADA	ALABAMA	GEORGIA
OHIO	MAINE	HAWAII	OREGON	ARIZONA	INDIANA
UTAH	TEXAS	KANSAS		FLORIDA	MONTANA
					NEW YORK

VERMONT
WYOMING

8
ARKANSAS
COLORADO
DELAWARE
ILLINOIS
KENTUCKY
MARYLAND
MICHIGAN
MISSOURI

NEBRASKA
OKLAHOMA
VIRGINIA

9
LOUISIANA
MINNESOTA
NEW JERSEY
NEW MEXICO
TENNESSEE
WISCONSIN

10
CALIFORNIA
WASHINGTON

11
CONNECTICUT
MISSISSIPPI
NORTH DAKOTA
RHODE ISLAND
SOUTH DAKOTA

12
NEW HAMPSHIRE
PENNSYLVANIA
WEST VIRGINIA

13
MASSACHUSETTS
NORTH CAROLINA
SOUTH CAROLINA

18
DISTRICT OF COLUMBIA
(government region)

Geography – Regions – UNITARY AUTHORITIES (UK)
In England unless stated

4
ARDS N Ireland
DOWN N Ireland
FIFE Scotland
HULL
YORK

5
ANGUS Scotland
CONWY Wales
DERBY
DERRY N Ireland
LARNE N Ireland
LUTON
MORAY Scotland
MOYLE N Ireland
OMAGH N Ireland
POOLE
POWYS Wales

6
ANTRIM N Ireland
ARMAGH N Ireland
DUNDEE Scotland
HALTON
MEDWAY
SLOUGH
TORBAY

7
BELFAST N Ireland
BRISTOL
FALKIRK Scotland
GLASGOW Scotland
GWYNEDD Wales
LISBURN N Ireland
READING
RUTLAND
STRABANE N Ireland

SWANSEA Wales
SWINDON
TORFAEN Wales
WREXHAM Wales

8
ABERDEEN Scotland
BRIDGEND Wales
HIGHLAND Scotland
LIMAVADY N Ireland
PLYMOUTH
STIRLING Scotland
THURROCK

9
BALLYMENA N Ireland
BANBRIDGE N Ireland
BLACKBURN
BLACKPOOL

COLERAINE N Ireland
COOKSTOWN N Ireland
CRAIGAVON N Ireland
DUNGANNON N Ireland
EDINBURGH Scotland
FERMANAGH N Ireland
LEICESTER
NORTH DOWN N Ireland
WOKINGHAM

10
BALLYMONEY N Ireland
CAERPHILLY Wales
CEREDIGION Wales
DARLINGTON
EAST RIDING
EILEAN SIAR Scotland
FLINTSHIRE Wales
HARTLEPOOL
INVERCLYDE Scotland
MIDLOTHIAN Scotland
NOTTINGHAM
PORTSMOUTH
WARRINGTON

11
BOURNEMOUTH
CASTLEREAGH N Ireland
EAST LOTHIAN Scotland
ISLE OF WIGHT
MAGHERAFELT N Ireland
SOUTHAMPTON
WEST LOTHIAN Scotland

12
BLAENAU GWENT Wales
DENBIGHSHIRE Wales
EAST AYRSHIRE Scotland

MILTON KEYNES
NEWTOWNABBEY N Ireland
PETERBOROUGH
RENFREWSHIRE Scotland
STOKE-ON-TRENT
WESTERN ISLES (or Na H-Eileanan Siar)
    Scotland

13
ABERDEENSHIRE Scotland
ARGYLL AND BUTE Scotland
CARRICKFERGUS N Ireland
HEREFORDSHIRE
MERTHYR TYDFIL Wales
MIDDLESBROUGH
MONMOUTHSHIRE Wales
NORTH AYRSHIRE Scotland
NORTH SOMERSET
ORKNEY ISLANDS Scotland
PEMBROKESHIRE Wales
SOUTH AYRSHIRE Scotland
SOUTHEND-ON-SEA
WEST BERKSHIRE

14
ISLE OF ANGLESEY Wales
NEWRY AND MOURNE N Ireland
STOCKTON-ON-TEES

15
BRACKNELL FOREST
BRIGHTON AND HOVE
NA H-EILEANAN SIAR (or Western Isles)
    Scotland
NEATH PORT TALBOT Wale
PERTH AND KINROSS Scotland
SCOTTISH BORDERS Scotland
SHETLAND ISLANDS Scotland

VALE OF GLAMORGAN Wales

16
CLACKMANNANSHIRE Scotland
EAST RENFREWSHIRE Scotland
NORTH LANARKSHIRE Scotland
RHONDDA CYNON TAFF Wales
SOUTH LANARKSHIRE Scotland
TELFORD AND WREKIN

17
NORTH LINCOLNSHIRE

18
EAST DUNBARTONSHIRE Scotland

REDCAR AND CLEVELAND
WEST DUNBARTONSHIRE Scotland

19
DUMFRIES AND GALLOWAY Scotland

20
SOUTH GLOUCESTERSHIRE
WINDSOR AND MAIDENHEAD

21
NORTH-EAST LINCOLNSHIRE

24
BATH AND NORTH-EAST SOMERSET

Geography – Rivers – AFRICA

4
BERG
FISH
MARA
NILE
SAVE
TANA
UELE
VAAL

5
BENUE
CONGO
GABON
GROOT
JUBBA

KASAI
KERIO
NIGER
OUEME
SEBOU
SHARI
SHIRE
VOLTA

6
BREEDE
CUANZA
GAMBIA
KUISEB
KUNENE
KWANDA

KWANGO
LOMAMI
MAPUTO
MBOMOU
MOLOPO
NYANGA
OGOOUÉ
ORANGE
RUFIJI
SANAGA
TUGELA
UBANGI

7
ATBARAH
BANDAMA

CUBANGO
 (or Okavango)
LIMPOPO
LUALABA
LUANGWA
OLIFANT
SENEGAL
SHABELE
ZAMBEZI

8
BLUE NILE
MOULOUYA
OKAVANGO
 (or Cubango)

9
BOU REGREG
OUM'ER-RBIA
WHITE NILE

10
BLACK VOLTA
WHITE VOLTA

12
KOUILOU-NIARI
MOUNTAIN NILE

Geography – Rivers – THE AMERICAS In USA unless stated

3
EEL
IÇÁ South America
MAD
NEW

4
BACK Canada
CAMÚ Central America
IOWA
META South America
NAPA
NOYO
OHIO
OTAY
PEEL Canada
YUNA Central America

5
ALAMO
APURE South America
BLACK Central America
CAUTO Central America
JAMES
JURUÁ South America
KOBUK
NANAY South America
NEGRO South America
NEUSE
OBION
PURUS South America
ROGUE
SMITH
TIGRE South America
XINGU South America

YUKON Canada

6
ALBION
AMAZON
    South America
ARAUCA South America
ASHLEY
ATRATO South America
BALSAS Central America
BRANCO South America
BRAZOS
CARONI
    Central America,
    South America
CHOWAN
CHUBUT South America
COOPER
COPPER
EDISTO
FRASER Canada
GARCIA
HUDSON
HUMBER + Canada
JIMANI Central America
MAUMEE
MOBILE
NELSON
OTTAWA Canada
PAJARO
PANUCO
PARANÁ South America
PATUCA Central America
PEE DEE
RIDEAU Canada

SABINE
SANTEE
SENECA
ST JOHN
UMPQUA
YAPURA South America

7
ALABAMA
AUCILLA
GENESEE
HATCHIE
KLAMATH
MADEIRA
    South America
MARAÑÓN
    South America
NAVARRO
NIAGARA + Canada
ORINOCO
    South America
PECONIC
POTOMAC
ROANOKE
SALINAS
SAN JUAN
    Central America
SUSITNA
TAPAJÓS South America
TAUNTON
TIJUANA +
    Central America
TRINITY
TUGALOO
UCAYALI South America

URURGUAY
  South America
VENTURA
YAQUINA

8
ALTAMAHA
AMARGOSA
ARKANSAS
CAPE FEAR
COLORADO
  + South America
COLUMBIA + Canada
COQUILLE
DELAWARE
EXPLOITS Canada
GATINEAU Canada
GUAVIARE
  South America
HUALLAGA
  South America
ILLINOIS
KENNEBEC
MISSOURI
PARAGUAY
  South America
PARNAIBA
  South America
PETALUMA
RED RIVER
RIO NEGRO
  South America
SAGUENAY Canada
SAN DIEGO
SAVANNAH
SUWANNEE

VICTORIA Canada

9
ANACOSTIA
CHURCHILL Canada
DES MOINES
ESSEQUIBO
  South America
GUADALUPE
KALAMAZOO
KUSKOKWIM
MACKENZIE Canada
MAGDALENA
  South America
MERRIMACK
MINNESOTA
RIO GRANDE
  + Central America
SACANDAGA
TENNESSEE
TOCANTINS
  South America
TOMBIGBEE

10
ALMENDARES
  Central America
ARTIBONITE
  Central America
CHOWCHILLA
HOUSATONIC
LOS ANGELES
PASQUOTANK
QUINNIPIAK
SACRAMENTO
SAN JOAQUIN

SAN LUIS REY
SNAKE RIVER
ST LAWRENCE + Canada
USUMACINTA
  Central America

11
ATCHAFALAYA
CONNECTICUT
MISSISSIPPI
SÃO FRANCISCO
  South America
SUSQUEHANNA
YAQUE DEL SUR
  Central America
YELLOWSTONE

12
APALACHICOLA
RAPPAHANNOCK
RIO DE LA PLATA
  South America
SASKATCHEWAN
  Canada

13
CHATTAHOOCHEE
COATZACOALCOS
  Central America
YAQUE DEL NORTE
  Central America

14
SANTA MARGARITA

Geography – Rivers – ASIA

3
FLY
HAI
HAN
ILI
KET
NEN
OKA
TAZ

4
AKSU
AMUR
BEAS
HUAI
LENA
LIAO
RAVI
TAPI
TONE
URAL
YALU
YANA
YUAN

5
ALDAN
IMJIN
INDUS
JUMNA (or
   Yamuna)
KABUL
KARUN
KAYAN
KHETA

KIZIL
KOTUY
LALIN
PERAK
SEPIK
TAPTI
TARIM
TOBOL
TUMEN
XIANG

6
ANGARA
CHENAB
GANGES
IRTYSH
JHELUM
JORDAN
KAPUAS
KAVERI
KHABUR
KOLYMA
LISHUI
MEKONG
RAJANG
SHACHE
SUTLEJ
TIGRIS
USSURI
VAIGAI
YAMUNA
   (or Jumna)

7
CAGAYAN

CAUVERY
CHAMBAL
GHAGGAR
HARI RUD
HELMAND
HOOGHLY
HUANG HE (or
   Hwang Ho,
   Yellow River)
HUANGPU
HWANG HO (or
   Huang He,
   Yellow River)
KOLACHI
KRISHNA
LIJIANG
MURGHAB
ORONTES
SAKARYA
SALWEEN
SELENGA
SHINANO
SONGHUA
SONG-KOI
   (or Red River)
YANGTZE (or
   Chang Jiang)
YENISEI
ZIJIANG

8
AMU DARYA
CHINDWIN
GODAVARI
KHATANGA

MAHANADI
RED RIVER (or Song-Koi)
SEFID RUD
SYR DARYA
TUNGUSKA
ZHUJIANG (or Pearl River)

9
EUPHRATES
INDIGIRKA
IRRAWADDY
SONG-HUONG (or Perfume
   River)
WHITE JADE
ZERAVSHAN

10
AYEYARWADY
CHANG JIANG (or Yangtze)
CHAO PHRAYA
KARNAPHULI
PEARL RIVER (or Zhujiang)

11
BRAHMAPUTRA
SHATT-AL-ARAB
YELLOW RIVER (or Huang He,
   Hwang Ho)

12
PERFUME RIVER (or Song-Huong)

13
BÜYÜK MENDERES
MAHAWELI GANGA

Geography – Rivers – AUSTRALASIA In Australia unless stated

3
ORD

4
AVON
BEGA
COEN
COLO
DART New Zealand
DEUA
HUON
HUTT New Zealand
PEEL
REWA Fiji
SWAN

5
FINKE
GROSE
NAMOI
OPIHI New Zealand
ORARA
ORETI New Zealand
SNOWY
TAMAR
WAIAU New Zealand
WAIPA New Zealand
YARRA

6
ARCHER
BARCOO
BARWON
BULLER New Zealand

CLUTHA New Zealand
DAWSON
GWYDIR
HUNTER
MERSEY
MORUYA
MURRAY
NEPEAN
NERANG
SEVERN
TAIERI New Zealand
TAKAKA New Zealand
TASMAN New Zealand
WAIROA New Zealand

7
AHURIRI New Zealand
APARIMA New Zealand
BURNETT
DARLING
DERWENT
FITZROY
GEORGES
LACHLAN
MACLEAY
MANNING
MATAURA New Zealand
PIONEER
THOMSON
TORRENS
WAIKATO New Zealand
WAIPAOA New Zealand
WAITAKI New Zealand
WARREGO

8
BRISBANE
CALLIOPE
CARDRONA New Zealand
CLARENCE + New Zealand
DUMARESQ
FRANKLIN
GASCOYNE
GOULBURN
HASTINGS
KANGAROO
MAKAREWA New Zealand
MARGARET
MITCHELL
MOLONGLO
NAMBUCCA
SHOTOVER New Zealand
VICTORIA
WANGANUI New Zealand
WORONORA

9
BLACKWOOD
CONDAMINE
CUDGEGONG
EUCUMBENE
GREENOUGH
INANGAHUA New Zealand
MACDONALD
MACQUARIE
MURCHISON
NGARURORO New Zealand
RANGITATA New Zealand

10
DIAMANTINA
HAWKESBURY
KARANGARUA New Zealand
MITTA MITTA
PARRAMATTA
RANGITAIKI New Zealand
SHOALHAVEN

11
ABERCROMBIE

CASTLEREAGH
MARIBYRNONG
ORONGORONGO New Zealand
WOLLONDILLY

12
MURRUMBIDGEE

13
WINGECARRIBEE

Geography – Rivers – BRITISH ISLES In England unless stated

3
ALN
AWE Scotland
AXE
AYR Scotland
BOX
CAM
COE Scotland
CUR Scotland
DEE + Scotland,
  Wales
DON + Scotland
DUN + N Ireland
EAU
ELY Wales
EMS
ESK + Scotland
EWE Scotland
EXE
EYE + Scotland
FAL
HIZ

IRT
LEA
  (or Lee)
LEE (or Lea)
  + Scotland,
  S Ireland
LEW
LUD
LYD
LYN
MOY S Ireland
NAR
NOE
OCK
RAY
RIB
ROE N Ireland
RYE
SOW
TÂF Wales
TAS
TAW

TAY Scotland
TER
UCK
URE
URR Scotland
USK Wales
VER
WEY
WYE + Wales
YAR
YEO
YOX

4
ADUR
AFAN Wales
AIRE
ALAW Wales
ALDE
ALRE
ALUN Wales
ALYN Wales

ARUN
AVON + Scotland
BAIN
BANN N Ireland
BRUE
BURE
BURN
BUSH N Ireland
CALE
CHAR
CHET
CHEW
COLE
COLN
CRAY
CREE Scotland
CULM
DANE
DART
DEEL S Ireland
DERG N Ireland
DIBB

DOON Scotland
DOVE
DYFI (or Dovey)
  Wales
EARN Scotland
EBBW Wales
EDEN + Scotland
EHEN
ELWY Wales
ERCH Wales
ERME
ERNE N Ireland,
  S Ireland
FINN N Ireland
FOSS
GLEN
GOWY
GOYT
HULL
IDLE
INNY S Ireland
ISLA Scotland
ISLE
IVEL
KENN
KENT
LARK
LEAM
LERI Wales
LOOE
LUGG Wales
LUNE
LYME
LYNE
MAUN
MEON
MITE
MOLE

NENE
NESS Scotland
NIDD
NITH Scotland
NORE S Ireland
ONNY
OUSE
PANG
PENK
PINN
PLYM
PONT
POOL
REDE
ROBE S Ireland
RUEL Scotland
SARK Scotland
SEPH
SHIN Scotland
SLEA
SOAR
SOCH Wales
SOWE
SPEY Scotland
SUCK S Ireland
SUIR S Ireland
TAFF Wales
TALE
TALL N Ireland
TAME
TARF Scotland
TAVY
TAWE Wales
TEAM
TEES
TEME
TERN
TEST

THAW Wales
THET
TILL Scotland
TONE
TOVE
TOWY (or Tywi)
  Wales
TYNE + Scotland
TYWI (or Towy)
  Wales
UGIE Scotland
WEAR
WENT
WICK Scotland
WOLF
WYRE + Wales
YARE

5
AERON Wales
ALLAN Scotland
ALLEN
ALWEN Wales
AMBER
ANKER
ANNAN Scotland
ANTON
ARROW
AVICH Scotland
AVOCA S Ireland
BARLE
BEULT
BLYTH
BOVEY
BOYNE S Ireland
BRAIN
BRANT
BREDE

BRENT
BRIDE + S Ireland
BRORA Scotland
CAMEL
CEFNI Wales
CERNE
CHELT
CHESS
CHURN
CLWYD Wales
CLYDE Scotland
CLYST
COLNE
CONON
  Scotland
CONWY Wales
CORFE
COVER
CRANE
DEBEN
DEVER
DOVEY (or Dyfi)
  Wales
DRISH S Ireland
EBBLE
ELLEN
EMBER
ETIVE Scotland
FEALE S Ireland
FORTH Scotland
FOWEY
FOYLE N Ireland
FROME
FRUIN Scotland
GARRY Scotland
GLYME
GREET
GRETA

GWAUN Wales
HAYLE
INVER Scotland
LAGAN N Ireland
LAUNE S Ireland
LEVEN + Scotland
LLEDR Wales
LOCHY Scotland
MAINE N Ireland
MEDEN
MEECE
NAIRN Scotland
NAVER Scotland
NEATH Wales
NEWRY N Ireland
NYFER Wales
OGWEN Wales
ORCHY Scotland
OTTER
OUZEL
OYKEL Scotland
PERRY
RHIEW Wales
ROACH
RODEN
RYTON
SHEAF
SHIEL Scotland
STORT
STOUR
SWALE
TAMAR
TEIFI Wales
TEIGN
TEISE
THAME
THURN
TIDDY

TOLKA S Ireland
TRENT
TRURO
TWEED + Scotland
WAVER
WISKE
WYLYE
YRFON Wales
YTHAN Scotland

6

AILORT Scotland
ALMOND
　Scotland
BANDON
　S Ireland
BARROW
　S Ireland
BEAULY Scotland
BLYTHE
BOLLIN
BORGIE Scotland
BOURNE
BRAINT Wales
BROSNA
　S Ireland
BUTLEY
CALDER
　+ Scotland
CALLAN
　N Ireland
CAMLAD Wales
CARRON
　Scotland
CEIROG Wales
CLOUGH
　+ N Ireland
COCKER

COLHUW Wales
COQUET
CORRIB S Ireland
CREEDY
CROUCH
DARENT
DARGLE S Ireland
DARWEN
DEARNE
DESACH Wales
DODDER
　S Ireland
DUDDON
DWYFOR Wales
DWYRYD Wales
EAMONT
ERRIFF S Ireland
FARSET N Ireland
FESHIE Scotland
GILPIN
GIRVAN Scotland
GLAVEN
GYFFIN Wales
HAFFES Wales
HAMBLE
HEBBLE
HODDER
HUMBER
IRVINE Scotland
IRWELL
ITCHEN
JORDAN
KEEKLE
KELVIN Scotland
KENFIG Wales
KENNET
KENSEY
LAVANT

LEADON
LIFFEY S Ireland
LLIEDI Wales
LLUGWY Wales
LLYFNI Wales
LODDON
LOSSIE Scotland
LOWMAN
LOXLEY
LYDDEN
LYNHER
MACHNO Wales
MAIGUE S Ireland
MARRON
MEDINA
MEDWAY
MERSEY
MIMRAM
MONNOW + Wales
MOURNE
　N Ireland,
　S Ireland
NADDER
NEVERN Wales
OGMORE Wales
ORWELL
OTTERY
PIDDLE
QUAGGY
QUOILE N Ireland
RHONDDA Wales
RHYMNI
　(or Rhymney)
　Wales
RIBBLE
RODING
ROTHER
SEATON

SEIONT Wales
SEVERN + Wales
SKERNE
SLANEY S Ireland
SOLWAY
  + Scotland
SPRINT
STRULE N Ireland
TEVIOT Scotland
THAMES
THURSO Scotland
TUMMEL
  Scotland
VYRNWY Wales
WANDLE
WEAVER
WENSUM
WHARFE
WISSEY
WITHAM
WREAKE
YARROW

7
BATHERM
BRATHAY
CEIDIOG Wales
CHELMER
CLARACH Wales
DERWENT
DEVERON
  Scotland
DOUGLAS
DUDWELL
DWYFACH Wales
DYSYNNI Wales
ENDRICK
  Scotland

EREWASH
GARNOCK
  Scotland
GIPPING
GLASLYN Wales
GWYRFAI Wales
HELFORD
IRTHING
LEANNAN
  S Ireland
LOUGHOR Wales
LUMBURN
MADFORD
MOIDART
  Scotland
PARRETT
POULTER
RAWTHEY
RHEIDOL Wales
RHYMNEY (or
  Rhymni) Wales
RIVELIN
ROUGHTY
  S Ireland
SHANNON
  S Ireland
SOLFACH Wales
TORRENT
  N Ireland
VALENCY
WALKHAM
WAMPOOL
WANTSUM
WAVENEY
WELLAND
WENNING
WHEELER Wales
WINSTER

YSTWYTH Wales

8
ANCHOLME
BADACHRO
  Scotland
BEAULIEU
BLADNOCH
  Scotland
BREAMISH
CHERWELL
CLYWEDOG
  Wales
CUCKMERE
EVENLODE
FINDHORN
  Scotland
GLENELLY
  N Ireland
GRAVENEY
GREAT EAU
HERTFORD
LAMBOURN
LYVENNET
MAWDDACH
  Wales
NORTH ESK
  Scotland
PEMBROKE Wales
SALWARPE
SHERFORD
SKIRFARE
SOUTH ESK
  Scotland
STEEPING
STINCHAR
  Scotland
THRUSHEL

TORRIDGE
TRYSTION Wales
TRYWERYN Wales
ULLAPOOL
WANSBECK
WASHBURN
WHAPLODE
WINDRUSH

9
CARRYDUFF
  N Ireland
GREAT OUSE
GWEEBARRA
  S Ireland
HALLADALE
  Scotland
HARBOURNE
LYMINGTON
MISBOURNE
NORTH TYNE
SOUTH TYNE

10
BLACKADDER
  Scotland
BLACKWATER
  + N Ireland,
  S Ireland
BROADWATER
DAUGLEDDAU
  Wales
GLENWHIRRY
  N Ireland
GREAT STOUR
GWENDRAETH
  Wales
LITTLE OUSE

TILLINGHAM	**11**	LITTLE STOUR
WALLINGTON	COLLYBROOKE	RAVENSBOURNE
WHITEADDER Scotland	INGREBOURNE	WALLABROOKE

Geography – Rivers – EUROPE

3	VIT	KYLL	SADO	BAISE
AAR		LABA	SAJÓ	BEGNA
(or Aare)	**4**	LAHN	SAVA	BESÒS
AHR	AARE	LECH	SAVE	BOSUT
BUG	(or Aar)	LEIE	SIEG	DESNA
DAL	ADDA	(or Lys)	SOČA	DIVES
DON	AGRI	LUGA	SOZH	DOUBS
EMS	ARDA	LULE	SULA	DOURO
ENZ	ARNO	MAAS	SURA	DRAVA
ILL	AUBE	(or Meuse)	SÛRE	(or Drave)
ILM	AUDE	MAIN	(or Sauer)	DRAVE
INN	BÓBR	MIÑO	SVIR	(or Drava)
JIU	BODE	(or Minho)	SYAS	DRINA
LEK	CHER	MIUS	TAJO	DVINA
LOT	DRIN	MURA	TANA	EIDER
LYS	EBRO	NAAB	TARN	ERDRE
(or Leie)	EDER	NAHE	THUR	ETSCH
MUR	ELBE	NEVA	URAL	(or Adige)
OLT	EMME	ODER	VIRE	FULDA
ORB	ENNS	OHRE	WIEN	GAUJA
ROS	EURE	OISE	YBBS	GAULA
RUR	GERS	ORNE		GENIL
SAN	HASE	OSAM	**5**	HAVEL
SIÓ	HRON	OSTE	ADIGE	HUNTE
TER	IPEL'	OTRA	(or Etsch)	ILLER
TÊT	ISAR	PRUT	ADOUR	INDRE
UME	KAMA	PSEL	AISNE	IRPIN
USA	KLAR	(or Psyol)	ALLER	ISÈRE
VÁH	KRKA	RUHR	ÄTRAN	ISKAR
VAR	KUPA	SAAR	AULNE	JAGST

JÚKAR
KOLVA
KUBAN
LEINE
LIPPE
LOIRE
MAINE
MARNE
MESTA
  (or Nestos)
MEUSE
  (or Maas)
MEZEN
MINHO
  (or Miño)
MOSEL
  (or Moselle)
MULDE
MUREŞ
NAREW
NARVA
NEMAN
  (or Niemen)
NOTEĆ
OGLIO
OKHTA
ONEGA
ORKLA
PEENE
PIAVE
PSYOL (or Psel)
RANCE
RAUMA
REGEN
REUSS
RHINE
RHÔNE
RISLE

SAALE
SAÔNE
SAUER (or Sûre)
SEGRE
SEINE
SIRET
SOMME
SPREE
TAGUS
TEREK
TIBER
TIMIŞ
TINTO
TISZA
TORNE
TOSNA
TRAUN
TRAVE
TURIA
VECHT
VEDEA
VENTA
VJOSË
VOLGA
VRBAS
WARTA
WERRA
WESER
YONNE

6
ALLIER
ARGENS
ARIÈGE
BERKEL
BLAVET
BRENTA
CETINA

CHIERS
CREUSE
DANUBE
DONETS
GLOMMA
GUDENÅ
IJSSEL
IZHORA
JARAMA
JIZERA
KINZIG
KOCHER
LAUTER
LEITHA
LIMMAT
LOIRET
MOLDAU (or Vltava)
MORAVA
MOSKVA
MOTALA
NAMSEN
NECKAR
NEISSE
NESTOS (or Mesta)
NIEMEN (or Neman)
NISSAN
OFANTO
OURTHE
PANARO
PILICA
PREGEL (or Pregolya)
SALHIR
SAMARA
SAMBRE
SARTHE
SCARPE
SEGURA
SEMOIS

STRUMA
TÂMEGA
TANARO
TAUBER
TICINO
TRIGNO
VARDAR
VEFSNA
VIENNE
VLTAVA (or Moldau)
VUOKSI
WARNOW
WIEPRZ
YANTRA
ZBRUCH
ZÊZERE

7
ALFEIÓS
ALTMÜHL
ARDÈCHE
BASENTO
CABRIEL
DAUGAVA
DNIEPER
DURANCE
GARONNE
GÖTA ÄLV
HÉRAULT
LIELUPE
MARITSA
MAYENNE
METAURO
MEURTHE
MONDEGO
MOSELLE (or Mosel)
NERETVA
NERVIÓN

NIDELVA
OMBRONE
OREDEZH
PECHORA
PINEIÓS
PRIPYAT
RUBICON
SCHELDE (or Scheldt)
SCHELDT (or Schelde)
SECCHIA
TETERIV
THJÓRSÁ
TOUQUES
TREBBIA
TUNDZHA
UNSTRUT
VILAINE
VISTULA
VOLKHOV
VORSKLA
ZRMANJA

8
ACHELÓOS
ALTAELVA
ANGERMAN
ARMANÇON
AURAJOKI

BEREZINA
CHARENTE
DNIESTER
DORDOGNE
GUADIANA
INHULETS
KALAJOKI
KEMIJOKI
MÅLSELVA
ÖSTERDAL
OULUJOKI
PISUERGA
PREGOLYA (or Pregel)
RECKNITZ
VOLTURNO
VORONEZH

9
GAVE DE PAU
HALIACMON
LLOBREGAT
PAATSJOKI (or Pasvikelva)
VÄSTERDAL

10
BYSTRYTSIA
DORA BÁLTEA
KARASJOHKA

MANZANARES
PASVIKELVA
 (or Paatsjoki)

11
GAVE D'OLORON
GUADALAVIAR

12
BACCHIGLIONE
DRAMMENSELVA
GUADALQUIVIR
KOKEMÄENJOKI
WEISSE ELSTER

13
NUMEDALSLÅGEN
SÈVRE NANTAISE

14
LUSATIAN NEISSE
SCHWARZE ELSTER
SÈVRE NIORTAISE

15
JÖKULSA Á FJÖLLUM

Geography – Towns & Cities – AFRICA

3
FÈS
 (or Fez) Morocco
FEZ
 (or Fès) Morocco

QUS Egypt

4
GHAT Libya
KANO Nigeria

LAMU Kenya
LOMÉ Togo
MERU Kenya
ORAN
 (or Ouahran) Algeria

QENÂ Egypt
SAFI Morocco
SFAX Tunisia
SUEZ Egypt
SURT (or Sirte) Libya

5

ABUJA Nigeria
ACCRA Ghana
ASSAB Eritrea
ASWAN Egypt
ASYÛT Egypt
BATNA Algeria
BEIRA Mozambique
BENHA Egypt
CAIRO Egypt
DAKAR Senegal
DALOA Côte d'Ivoire
DE ARR South Africa
GABÈS Tunisia
GWERU Zimbabwe
HARAR Ethiopia
KAÉDI Mauritania
KIFFA Mauritania
KITWE Zambia
LAGOS Nigeria
LUXOR Egypt
MANSA Zambia
MBEYA TAnzania
OTAVI Namibia
OUJDA Morocco
PAARL South Africa
PRAIA Cape Verde
RABAT Morocco
SIRTE (or Surt) Libya
SOHAG Egypt
TANGA Tanzania
TANTA Egypt

TUNIS Tunisia
WAJIR Kenya
ZOMBA Malawi

6

ABÉCHÉ Chad
AGADIR Morocco
ANNABA Algeria
ARUSHA Tanzania
ASMARA Eritrea
BAMAKO Mali
BANGUI Central African
    Republic
BANJUL Gambia
BENONI South Africa
BISSAU Guinea-Bissau
BOUAKÉ Côte d'Ivoire
DODOMA Tanzania
DOUALA Cameroon
DUMYÂT (or Damietta)
    Egypt
DURBAN South Africa
EL GIZA Egypt
GEORGE South Africa
HARARE Zimbabwe
HUAMBO (or Nova
    Lisboa) Angola
IBADAN Nigeria
KASAMA Zambia
KIGALI Rwanda
KISUMU Kenya
KNYSNA South Africa
KUMASI Ghana
LIKASI Democratic
    Republic of Congo
LUANDA Angola
LUSAKA Zambia
MALABO Equatorial

    Guinea
MAPUTO Mozambique
MARZUQ Libya
MASERU Lesotho
MEKNÈS Morocco
MUTARE Zimbabwe
MWANZA Tanzania
NACALA Mozambique
NAKURU Kenya
NAMIBE
    (or Moçâmedes)
    Angola
NIAMEY Niger
SEROWE Botswana
SKIKDA Algeria
SOUSSE Tunisia
SOWETO South Africa
TABORA Tanzania
TAMALE Ghana
TOBRUK (or Tubruq)
    Libya
TUBRUQ (or Tobruk)
    Libya
UMTATA South Africa
WANKIE Zimbabwe
WELKOM South Africa
ZINDER Niger

7

ABIDJAN Côte d'Ivoire
ALGIERS Algeria
AL-MINYA Egypt
BERBERA Somalia
BIZERTE Tunisia
BRAKPAN South Africa
CHIPATA Zambia
CONAKRY Guinea
CRADOCK South Africa

ELDORET Kenya
EL OBEID Sudan
ENTEBBE Uganda
GOBABIS Namibia
KALEMIE Democratic
  Republic of Congo
KAMPALA Uganda
KANGALA Democratic
  Republic of Congo
KAOLACK Senegal
KENITRA Morocco
LARACHE Morocco
MALINDI Kenya
MARAMBA (or
  Livingstone) Zambia
MASSAWA (or Mits'iwa)
  Eritrea
MBABANE Swaziland
MBARARA Uganda
MITS'IWA (or Massawa)
  Eritrea
MOMBASA Kenya
NAIROBI Kenya
NAMPULA
  Mozambique
ODIENNÉ Côte d'Ivoire
OUAHRAN (or Oran)
  Algeria
SPRINGS South Africa
ST LOUIS Senegal
TANGIER Morocco
TÉTOUAN Morocco
TOLIARY Madagascar
TRIPOLI Libya
YAOUNDÉ Cameroon
ZAGAZIG Egypt

8

AIN SEFRA Algeria
BENGHAZI Libya
BENGUELA Angola
BLANTYRE Malawi
BULAWAYO Zimbabwe
CAPE TOWN South
  Africa
CHINGOLA Zambia
DAMANHÛR Egypt
DAMIETTA (or Dumyât)
  Egypt
DIRE DAWA Ethiopia
DJIBOUTI Djibouti
FREETOWN Sierra
  Leone
GABORONE Botswana
HURGHADA Egypt
ISMAILIA Egypt
KAIROUAN Tunisia
KHARTOUM Sudan
KINSHASA Democratic
  Republic of Congo
LILONGWE Malawi
LÜDERITZ Namibia
MAFEKING South Africa
MONASTIR Tunisia
MONROVIA Liberia
NDJAMENA Chad
OMDURMAN Sudan
PORT SAID Egypt
PRETORIA South Africa
TIMBUKTU Mali
WINDHOEK Namibia
ZANZIBAR Tanzania

9

BUJUMBURA Burundi
EL ALAMEIN Egypt
GERMISTON South
  Africa
GHAZAOUET Algeria
INHAMBANE
  Mozambique
KIMBERLEY South
  Africa
KROONSTAD South
  Africa
LADYSMITH South
  Africa
MARRAKECH Morocco
MBUJI-MAYI
  Democratic Republic
  of Congo
MDANTSANE South
  Africa
MOÇÂMEDES (or
  Namibe) Angola
MOGADISHU Somalia
MOSSEL BAY South
  Africa
PORTO NOVO Benin
PORT SUDAN Sudan
QACENTINA (or
  Constantine) Algeria
QUELIMANE
  Mozambique
SASSANDRA Côte
  d'Ivoire
TOAMASINA
  Madagascar
UITENHAGE South
  Africa
WADI HALFA Sudan

WALVIS BAY Namibia
WORCESTER South Africa

10

ADDIS ABABA Ethiopia
ALEXANDRIA Egypt
CASABLANCA
  (or Dar el Beida) Morocco
DAR EL BEIDA
  (or Casablanca) Morocco
EAST LONDON South Africa
KLERKSDORP South Africa
LIBREVILLE Gabon
LUBUMBASHI Democratic Republic
  of Congo
MALMESBURY South Africa
NOUADHIBOU Mauritania
NOUAKCHOTT Mauritania
NOVA LISBOA
  (or Huambo) Angola
ORANJEMUND Namibia
OUDTSHOORN South Africa
PORT GENTIL Gabon
PORT SAFAGA Egypt
QUEENSTOWN South Africa
WADI MEDANI Sudan
WELLINGTON South Africa

11

ANTSIRANANA Madagascar
BRAZZAVILLE Congo
CONSTANTINE
  (or Qacentina) Algeria
DAR ES SALAAM Tanzania
GRAHAMSTOWN South Africa
KHAYELITSHA South Africa

KRUGERSDORP South Africa
LIVINGSTONE
  (or Maramba) Zambia
OUAGADOUGOU Burkina Faso
PIETERSBURG South Africa
PORT NOLLOTH South Africa
SIDI BARRANI Egypt
VEREENIGING South Africa

12

ANTANANARIVO Madagascar
BEAUFORT WEST South Africa
BLOEMFONTEIN South Africa
FORT BEAUFORT South Africa
GRAAFF REINET South Africa
JOHANNESBURG South Africa
PORT HARCOURT Nigeria
SIDI BEL ABBÈS Algeria
SOMERSET EAST South Africa
SOMERSET WEST South Africa
STELLENBOSCH South Africa
YAMOUSSOUKRO Côte d'Ivoire

13

BOBO DIOULASSA Burkina Faso
PORT ELIZABETH South Africa
POTCHEFSTROOM South Africa
SHARM EL SHEIKH Egypt

15

SEKONDI-TAKORADI Ghana

16

EL MAHALLA EL KUBRA Egypt
PIETERMARITZBURG South Africa

Geography – Towns & Cities – ASIA

3
HUÉ Vietnam
IBB Yemen
QOM
 (or Qum) Iran
QUM
 (or Qom) Iran
SUR Oman

4
ACRE
 (or 'Akko) Israel
ADEN Yemen
AGRA India
'AKKO
 (or Acre) Israel
DAET Philippines
DILI Indonesia
DOHA Qatar
ENDE Indonesia
GIFU Japan
HAMA Syria
KANT Kyrgyzstan
KOBE Japan
MALÉ Maldives
OMSK Russia
ORAL Kazakhstan
ORDU Turkey
ORSK Russia
POSO Indonesia
PUNE India
RABA Indonesia
SIBU Malaysia
TYRE Lebanon
VINH Vietnam

XI'AN China
ZIBO China

5
ADANA Turkey
AHVAZ Iran
AMMAN Jordan
AQABA Jordan
BASRA Iraq
CHITA Russia
DAVAO Philippines
DELHI India
DHAKA Bangladesh
HAIFA Israel
HANOI Vietnam
HERĂT Afghanistan
IZMIR Turkey
JINAN China
KABUL Afghanistan
KANDY Sri Lanka
KOTTE Sri Lanka
KYOTO Japan
LAOAG Philippines
LHASA China
MECCA Saudi Arabia
MEDAN Indonesia
MOSUL Iraq
NUKUS Uzbekistan
OSAKA Japan
PAKSÉ
 (or Pakxe) Laos
PAKXE
 (or Paksé) Laos
PATNA India
PUSAN South Korea

RASHT Iran
ROXAS Philippines
SAÏDA
 (or Sidon) Lebanon
SANA'A Yemen
SEOUL South Korea
SIDON
 (or Saïda) Lebanon
SIMLA India
SURAT India
TAEGU South Korea
TOKYO Japan
TOMSK Russia
WUHAN China

6
ABADAN Iran
ABAKAN Russia
ALEPPO Syria
ALMATY Kazakhstan
ANKARA Turkey
ANSHAN China
AQTÖBE Kazakhstan
ASTANA Kazakhstan
BATUMI Georgia
BEIRUT Lebanon
BHOPAL India
BOMBAY
 (or Mumbai) India
BRATSK Russia
CANTON
 (or Guangzhou) China
DAMMAM Saudi Arabia
DA NANG Vietnam
HARBIN China

HOWRAH India
INCHON South Korea
INDORE India
JAFFNA Sri Lanka
JAIPUR India
JEDDAH (or Jiddah)
  Saudi Arabia
JIDDAH (or Jeddah)
  Saudi Arabia
KAMPOT Cambodia
KANPUR India
LAHORE Pakistan
MADRAS
  (or Chennai) India
MANAMA Bahrain
MANILA Philippines
MATSUE Japan
MEDINA Saudi Arabia
MEERUT India
MERGUI Myanmar
MULTAN Pakistan
MUMBAI
  (or Bombay) India
MUSCAT Oman
MYSORE India
NAGOYA Japan
NAGPUR India
PADANG Indonesia
QUETTA Pakistan
RAIPUR India
RIYADH Saudi Arabia
SAIGON (or Ho Chi-
  Minh City) Vietnam
SENDAI Japan
SUCHOW
  (or Zuzhou) China
TABRIZ Iran
TAIPEI Taiwan

TEHRAN Iran
TYUMEN Russia
ÜRÜMQI China
YANGON Myanmar
ZUZHOU (or Suchow)
  China

7

BAGHDAD Iraq
BANDUNG Indonesia
BANGKOK Thailand
BARNAUL Russia
BEIJING China
BISHKEK Kyrgyzstan
CHENNAI
  (or Madras) India
COLOMBO Sri Lanka
DAGUPAN Philippines
ESFAHAN Iran
FUKUOKA Japan
GANGTOK India
GUIYANG China
GWANGJU South Korea
HSINCHU Taiwan
IRKUTSK Russia
IZHEVSK Russia
JAKARTA Indonesia
JODHPUR India
KARACHI Pakistan
KAYSERI Turkey
KOLKATA
  (or Calcutta) India
KUCHING Malaysia
KUNMING China
LANZHOU China
LATAKIA Syria
LUCKNOW India
MADURAI India

MAGADAN Russia
MASHHAD Iran
MAUMERE Indonesia
NANKING China
NIIGATA Japan
OKHOTSK Russia
SAPPORO Japan
TEL AVIV Israel
THIMPHU Bhutan
TIANJIN China
TRIPOLI Lebanon
ULAN-UDE Russia
USKÜDAR Turkey
YAKUTSK Russia

8

ABU DHABI United
  Arab Emirates
AMRITSAR India
ASHGABAT
  Turkmenistan
CALCUTTA
  (or Kolkata) India
DAMASCUS Syria
DENPASAR Indonesia
DUSHANBE Tajikistan
GUWAHATI India
HAIPHONG Vietnam
HAKODATE Japan
HANGZHOU China
JABALPUR India
JAYAPURA Indonesia
KANDAHAR
  Afghanistan
KUMAMOTO Japan
LIPA CITY Philippines
MANDALAY Myanmar
NAGASAKI Japan

NAZARETH Israel
NEW DELHI India
PESHAWAR India
RAMALLAH West Bank
SANDAKAN Malaysia
SEMARANG Indonesia
SHANGHAI China
SHENYANG China
SHILLONG India
SIEM REAP Cambodia
SRINAGAR India
SURABAYA Indonesia
TASHKENT Uzbekistan
VARANASI India
VICTORIA China
YOKOHAMA Japan

9
AHMEDABAD India
ALLAHABAD India
BANGALORE India
BEERSHEBA Israel
BETHLEHEM West Bank
ÇANAKKALE Turkey
CHANGZHOU China
CHIANG MAI Thailand
CHIANG RAI Thailand
CHUNGKING China
DUBAI CITY United Arab Emirates
GORAKHPUR India
GUANGZHOU
  (or Canton) China
HIROSHIMA Japan
HYDERABAD India, Pakistan
ISLAMABAD Pakistan
JERUSALEM Israel
KAGOSHIMA Japan
KARAGANDA Kazakhstan

KASTAMONU Turkey
KATHMANDU Nepal
KOTA BHARU Malaysia
KUYBYSHEV Russia
MANGALORE India
PALEMBANG Indonesia
PETROPAVL Kazakhstan
PHNOM PENH Cambodia
PHONSAVAN Laos
PYONGYANG North Korea
SAMARKAND Uzbekistan
SINGAPORE Singapore
SINGARAJA Indonesia
ULAN BATOR (or Ulaanbaatar)
  Mongolia
VIENTIANE Laos

10
BALIKPAPAN Indonesia
BANYUWANGI Indonesia
CHITTAGONG Bangladesh
DARJEELING India
FAISALABAD Pakistan
GEORGE TOWN Malaysia
KHABAROVSK Russia
KUWAIT CITY Kuwait
MAWLAMYINE Myanmar
QUEZON CITY Philippines
SVERDLOVSK Russia
YOGYAKARTA Indonesia

11
BANJARMASIN Indonesia
CHELYABINSK Russia
GANDHINAGAR India
KOWLOON CITY China
KRASNOYARSK Russia
KUALA LUMPUR Malaysia

NIZHNY TAGIL Russia
NOVOSIBIRSK Russia
TRINCOMALEE Sri Lanka
ULAANBAATAR (or Ulan Bator) Mongolia
VLADIVOSTOK Russia

12
KOTA KINABALU Malaysia
LUANG PRABANG Laos
MAGNITOGORSK Russia

NOVOKUZNETSK Russia

13
HO CHI-MINH CITY
  (or Saigon) Vietnam
PETROPAVLOVSK Kazakhstan

15
PEMATANGSIANTAR Indonesia
UBON RATCHATHANI Thailand

Geography – Towns & Cities – AUSTRALASIA In Australia unless stated

3
AYR
HAY
4
APIA Samoa
EYRE
GORE New Zealand
NADI Fiji
SALE
SUVA Fiji
YORK

5
BURRA
COLAC
DERBY
DUBBO
JUNEE
KOROR Palau
MOORA
PERTH
QUORN

TULLY
WEWAK Papua New
  Guinea
YAREN Nauru
6
ALBANY
ALBURY
BOURKE
BROOME
CAIRNS
CEDUNA
COLLIE
DARWIN
GAWLER
HOBART
INGHAM
MACKAY
MADANG Papua New
  Guinea
NAPIER New Zealand
NEIAFU Tonga
NELSON New Zealand

OAMARU New Zealand
ONSLOW
ORANGE
PANGAI Tonga
PETONE New Zealand
SYDNEY
TIMARU New Zealand
VAIAKU Tuvalu
WINTON

7
BAIRIKI Kiribati
BENDIGO
BUNBURY
DAMPIER
DENMARK
DUNEDIN New
  Zealand
GEELONG
HONIARA Solomon
  Islands
IPSWICH
LAUTOKA Fiji

LISMORE
LITHGOW
MANUKAU New Zealand
MILDURA
MOTUEKA New Zealand
NORTHAM
PORIRUA New Zealand
ROTORUA New Zealand
TE KUITI New Zealand
WHYALLA
WOOMERA
WYNDHAM

8
ADELAIDE
AUCKLAND New Zealand
BALLARAT
BATHURST
BLENHEIM New Zealand
BRISBANE
CANBERRA
CESSNOCK
COOKTOWN
GISBORNE New Zealand
GOULBURN
HAMILTON New Zealand
HASTINGS New Zealand
INVERELL
MAITLAND
MERREDIN
MOUNT ISA
ONEHUNGA New Zealand
PORT VILA Vanuatu
RANGIORA New Zealand
SOMERSET
TAKAPUNA New Zealand
TAMWORTH
TARCOOLA

TAURANGA New Zealand
WANGANUI New Zealand
WESTPORT New Zealand

9
ALEXANDRA New Zealand
BUNDABERG
CARNARVON
DEVONPORT + New Zealand
ELIZABETH
ESPERANCE
FREMANTLE
GERALDTON
GLADSTONE
GREYMOUTH New Zealand
HUGHENDEN
LIVERPOOL
LONGREACH
LOWER HUTT New Zealand
MASTERTON New Zealand
MELBOURNE
NEWCASTLE
NUKU'ALOFA Tonga
PORT PIRIE
TOOWOOMBA
WENTWORTH
WHAKATANE New Zealand
WHANGAREI New Zealand
WITTENOOM

10
BIRDSVILLE
BROKEN HILL
COOBER PEDY
GOOMALLING
KALGOORLIE
LAUNCESTON
LEIGH CREEK

NEW NORFOLK
PALMERSTON New Zealand
PROSERPINE
QUEENSTOWN New Zealand
SHEPPARTON
TOWNSVILLE
WAGGA WAGGA
WELLINGTON New Zealand
WOLLONGONG

11
BARROW CREEK
CASTLEMAINE
MARYBOROUGH
NEW PLYMOUTH New Zealand
PORT AUGUSTA
PORT LINCOLN
PORT MORESBY Papua New Guinea
ROCKHAMPTON
SOUTH TARAWA Kiribati

WARRNAMBOOL

12
ALICE SPRINGS
CHRISTCHURCH New Zealand
COFF'S HARBOUR
INVERCARGILL New Zealand
MOUNT GAMBIER
PETERBOROUGH

13
PORT MACQUARIE
VICTOR HARBOUR

15
PALMERSTON NORTH New Zealand
SURFERS PARADISE

16
DALAP-ULIGA-DARRIT Marshall Islands

Geography – Towns & Cities – Capitals – CAPITAL CITIES
* = city state   † = joint capital

4
APIA Samoa
BAKU Azerbaijan
BERN (or Berne)
  Switzerland
DILI East Timor
DOHA Qatar
KIEV Ukraine
LIMA Peru
LOMÉ Togo
MALÉ Maldives
OSLO Norway
RIGA Latvia
ROME Italy

SUVA Fiji

5
ABUJA Nigeria
ACCRA Ghana
AMMAN Jordan
BERNE (or Bern)
  Switzerland
CAIRO Egypt
DAKAR Senegal
DHAKA Bangladesh
HANOI Vietnam
KABUL Afghanistan
KOROR Palau

LA PAZ† Bolivia
MINSK Belarus
PARIS France
PRAIA Cape Verde
QUITO Ecuador
RABAT Morocco
SANA'A Yemen
SEOUL South Korea
SOFIA Bulgaria
SUCRE† Bolivia
TOKYO Japan
TUNIS Tunisia
VADUZ Liechtenstein
YAREN Nauru

6

ANKARA Turkey
ASMARA Eritrea
ASTANA Kazakhstan
ATHENS Greece
BAMAKO Mali
BANGUI Central African Republic
BANJUL Gambia
BEIRUT Lebanon
BERLIN Germany
BISSAU Guinea-Bissau
BOGOTÁ Columbia
DODOMA Tanzania
DUBLIN Republic of Ireland
HARARE Zimbabwe
HAVANA Cuba
KIGALI Rwanda
LISBON Portugal
LONDON England/United Kingdom
LUANDA Angola
LUSAKA Zambia
MADRID Spain
MALABO Equatorial Guinea
MANAMA Bahrain
MANILA Philippines
MAPUTO Mozambique
MASERU Lesotho
MONACO* Monaco
MORONI Comoros
MOSCOW Russia
MUSCAT Oman
NASSAU Bahamas
NIAMEY Niger
OTTAWA Canada
PRAGUE Czech Republic
RIYADH Saudi Arabia
ROSEAU Dominica
SKOPJE Macedonia

TAIPEI Taiwan
TEHRAN Iran
TIRANA Albania
VAIAKU Tuvalu
VIENNA Austria
WARSAW Poland
YANGON Myanmar
ZAGREB Croatia

7

ALGIERS Algeria
BAGHDAD Iraq
BAIRIKI Kiribati
BANGKOK Thailand
BEIJING China
BELFAST Northern Ireland
BISHKEK Kyrgyzstan
CARACAS Venezuela
CARDIFF Wales
CETINJE† Montenegro
COLOMBO Sri Lanka
CONAKRY Guinea
HONIARA Solomon Islands
JAKARTA Indonesia
KAMPALA Uganda
MANAGUA Nicaragua
MBABANE Swaziland
NAIROBI Kenya
NICOSIA Cyprus
SAN JOSÉ Costa Rica
SÃO TOMÉ São Tomé and Príncipe
ST JOHN'S Antigua and Barbuda
TALLINN Estonia
TBILISI Georgia
THIMPHU Bhutan
TRIPOLI Libya
VILNIUS Lithuania
YAOUNDÉ Cameroon

YEREVAN Armenia

8

ABU DHABI United Arab Emirates
ASHGABAT Turkmenistan
ASUNCIÓN Paraguay
BELGRADE Serbia
BELMOPAN Belize
BRASILIA Brazil
BRUSSELS Belgium
BUDAPEST Hungary
CANBERRA Australia
CAPE TOWN† South Africa
CASTRIES St Lucia
CHIŞINĂU Moldova
DAMASCUS Syria
DJIBOUTI Djibouti
DUSHANBE Tajikistan
FREETOWN Sierra Leone
GABORONE Botswana
HELSINKI Finland
KHARTOUM Sudan
KINGSTON Jamaica
KINSHASA Democratic Republic of
  Congo
LILONGWE Malawi
MONROVIA Liberia
NDJAMENA Chad
NEW DELHI India
PORT VILA Vanuatu
PRETORIA† South Africa
SANTIAGO Chile
SARAJEVO Bosnia-Herzegovina
TASHKENT Uzbekistan
VALLETTA Malta
VICTORIA Seychelles
WINDHOEK Namibia

9

AMSTERDAM Netherlands
BUCHAREST Romania
BUJUMBURA Burundi
EDINBURGH Scotland
ISLAMABAD Pakistan
JERUSALEM Israel
KATHMANDU Nepal
KINGSTOWN St Vincent and the
  Grenadines
LJUBLJANA Slovenia
MOGADISHU Somalia
NUKU'ALOFA Tonga
PHNOM PENH Cambodia
PODGORICA† Montenegro
PORT LOUIS Mauritius
PORTO NOVO Benin
PYONGYANG North Korea
REYKJAVIK Iceland
SAN MARINO San Marino
SINGAPORE* Singapore
ST GEORGE'S Grenada
STOCKHOLM Sweden
ULAN BATOR (or Ulaanbaatar)
  Mongolia
VIENTIANE Laos

10

ADDIS ABABA Ethiopia
BASSETERRE St Kitts and Nevis
BRATISLAVA Slovakia
BRIDGETOWN Barbados
COPENHAGEN Denmark
GEORGETOWN Guyana
KUWAIT CITY Kuwait
LIBREVILLE Gabon
LUXEMBOURG Luxembourg
MEXICO CITY Mexico

MONTEVIDEO Uruguay
NOUAKCHOTT Mauritania
PANAMA CITY Panama
PARAMARIBO Suriname
WASHINGTON United States of
   America
WELLINGTON New Zealand

11
BRAZZAVILLE Congo
BUENOS AIRES Argentina
KUALA LUMPUR Malaysia
OUAGADOUGOU Burkina Faso
PORT MORESBY Papua New Guinea
PORT-OF-SPAIN Trinidad and Tobago
SAN SALVADOR El Salvador
TEGUCIGALPA Honduras
ULAANBAATAR (or Ulan Bator)
   Mongolia

VATICAN CITY* Vatican

12
ANTANANARIVO Madagascar
PORT-AU-PRINCE Haiti
SANTO DOMINGO Dominican Republic
YAMOUSSOUKRO Côte d'Ivoire

13
GUATEMALA CITY Guatemala

14
ANDORRA LA VELLA Andorra

16
DALAP-ULIGA-DARRIT Marshall Islands

17
BANDAR SERI BEGAWAN Brunei

Geography – Towns & Cities – Capitals – STATE CAPITALS (USA)
* = government region

5
BOISE Idaho
DOVER Delaware
SALEM Oregon

6
ALBANY New York
AUSTIN Texas
BOSTON Massachusetts
DENVER Colorado
HELENA Montana
JUNEAU Alaska
PIERRE South Dakota
ST PAUL Minnesota

TOPEKA Kansas

7
ATLANTA Georgia
AUGUSTA Maine
CONCORD New
   Hampshire
JACKSON Mississippi
LANSING Michigan
LINCOLN Nebraska
MADISON Wisconsin
OLYMPIA Washington
PHOENIX Arizona
RALEIGH North Carolina

SANTA FÉ New Mexico
TRENTON New Jersey

8
BISMARCK North Dakota
CHEYENNE Wyoming
COLUMBIA South Carolina
COLUMBUS Ohio
HARTFORD Connecticut
HONOLULU Hawaii
RICHMOND Virginia

9
ANNAPOLIS Maryland

DES MOINES Iowa
FRANKFORT Kentucky
LITTLE ROCK Arkansas
NASHVILLE Tennessee

10
BATON ROUGE Louisiana
CARSON CITY Nevada
CHARLESTON West Virginia
HARRISBURG Pennsylvania
MONTGOMERY Alabama
MONTPELIER Vermont
PROVIDENCE Rhode Island
SACRAMENTO California

WASHINGTON District of Columbia*

11
SPRINGFIELD Illinois
TALLAHASSEE Florida

12
INDIANAPOLIS Indiana
OKLAHOMA CITY Oklahoma
SALT LAKE CITY Utah

13
JEFFERSON CITY Missouri

Geography – Towns & Cities – CENTRAL AMERICA In Mexico unless stated

4
APAM
LEÓN + Nicaragua
OPAL
RUIZ
TULA

5
AHOME
AMECA
COLÓN Panama
DAVID Panama
EL ORO
LA PAZ
LIMÓN Costa Rica
RIVAS Nicaragua
SILAO
TEPIC
TICUL

6
ALAMOS
ARIZPE
BALBOA Panama
CANCÚN
CELAYA
CHITRÉ Panama
COLIMA
CUMPAS
IGUALA
LA CRUZ
MADERA
MAPIMÍ
MASAYA Nicaragua
MEOQUI
MÉRIDA
NICOYA Costa Rica
PÁNUCO
PUEBLA
SOLOLÁ Guatemala
TOLUCA

TONALÁ
TUXPAN
XALAPA
ZAMORA

7
ALLENDE
ANTIGUA Guatemala
APIZACO
ATLIXCO
CABORCA
CANANEA
CARTAGO Costa Rica
CHOLULA
CÓRDOBA
DURANGO
EL MAYOR
EL SALTO
EL VIEJO Nicaragua
EMPALME
GRANADA Nicaragua

GUAYMAS
HEREDÍA Costa Rica
HUIXTLA
JIMÉNEZ
LA BARCA
LA CEIBA Honduras
LA UNIÓN El Salvador
LINARES
MANAGUA Nicaragua
MORELIA
NAVAJOA
NOGALES
OCOTLÁN
OJINAGA
ORIZABA
PACHUCA
REYNOSA
ROSARIO
SABINAS
SAHUAYO
SAN JOSÉ Costa Rica
SAN LUIS
SONOITA
TAMPICO
TEQUILA
TIJUANA
TIZIMÍN
TORREÓN
ZIMAPÁN

8
ACAJUTLA El Salvador
ACAMBARO
ACAPULCO
ALAJUELA Costa Rica
ALVARADO
BELMOPAN Belize
CAMPECHE

CANATLÁN
CARDENAS
CASTAÑOS
CERRITOS
CHETUMAL
COATEPEC
COMALAPA Guatemala
CULIACÁN
DANGRIGA Belize
EL FUERTE
ENSENADA
ETZATLÁN
IRAPUATO
JINOTEGA Nicaragua
JUCHITÁN
MAZATLÁN
MEXICALI
MONCLOVA
MOROLEÓN
NACOZARI
NAVOLATO
PENONOME Panama
POZA RICA
PROGRESO
RIO ABAJO Panama
ROSARITO
SALTILLO
SANTA ANA + Ecuador
SANTIAGO Panama
SAUCILLO
TEHUACÁN
USULUTÁN El Salvador
VERACRUZ
ZOPILOTE

9
ACAPONETA
CHIHUAHUA

CRISTÓBAL Panama
ESCUINAPA
ESPERANZA
GUADALUPE
LOS MOCHIS
MACUSPANA
MATAGALPA Nicaragua
MATAMOROS
MATEHUALA
MONTERREY
QUERÉTARO
RIO GRANDE
SAHUARIPA
SALAMANCA
SAN MIGUEL
  El Salvador
SONSONATE
  El Salvador
TAPACHULA
TEZIUTLÁN
TURRIALBA Costa Rica
VILA UNIÓN
ZACATECAS
ZITÁCUARO

10
AGUA PRIETA
AHUACHAPÁN
  El Salvador
BELIZE CITY Belize
BLUEFIELDS Nicaragua
BUSTAMANTE
CHINANDEGA
  Nicaragua
CONCEPCIÓN
CUAUHTÉMOC
CUERNAVACA
ECHEVERRÍA

EL DESCANSO
EL PORVENIR
EL PROGRESO Guatemala
HERMOSILLO
IXCATEOPAN
MANZANILLO
MEXICO CITY
MIGUEL AUZA
MINATITLÁN
PANAMA CITY Panama
PUERTO KINO
PUNTARENAS Costa Rica
SOMBRERETE
TULANCINGO
XOCHIMILCO

11

CIUDAD ACUÑA
CIUDAD LERDO
CIUDAD MANTE
GUADALAJARA
MAZATENANGO Guatemala
NUEVA ROSITA
NUEVO LAREDO
OJOCALIENTE
PRINZAPOLCA Nicaragua
SALVATIERRA
SAN SALVADOR El Salvador
TEGUCIGALPA Honduras
TEHUANTEPEC

12

BUENAVENTURA
CIUDAD GUZMÁN
CIUDAD JUÁREZ
CIUDAD MODERO
GÓMEZ PALACIO
HUAUCHINANGO

IXTLÁN DEL RIO
MONTEMORELOS
PUERTO CORTÉS Honduras
SAN PEDRO SULA Honduras
SANTA BARBARA
SANTA ROSALIÁ
TAMAZUNCHALE
TIERRA BLANCA
VILLAHERMOSA
ZACATECOLUCA El Salvador

13

CIUDAD CAMARGO
CIUDAD IXTEPEC
CIUDAD OBREGÓN
COATZACOALCOS
GUATEMALA CITY Guatemala
PIEDRAS NEGRAS
PUERTO BARRIOS Guatemala
PUERTO PANASCO
QUEZALTENANGO Guatemala
SAN LUIS POTOSÍ

14

AGUASCALIENTES
CIUDAD DELICIAS
CIUDAD DE VALLES
CIUDAD VICTORIA
OAXACA DE JUÁREZ
PLAYA DEL CARMEN
SABINAS HIDALGO

15

AUTLÁN DE NAVARRO
CIUDAD DEL CARMEN
HIDALGO DE PARRAL
PUERTO ARMUELLES Panama
TUXTLA GUTIÉRREZ

Geography – Towns & Cities – Europe – BELGIUM

3
ATH
HAL (or Halle)
HUY
MOL
SPA

4
BOOM
BREE
ESCH Luxembourg
GAND (or Ghent)
GENK
LIER (or Lierre)
LUIK (or Liège)
MONS

5
AALST (or Alost)
ALOST (or Aalst)
ARLON
ATTRE
EEKLO
EUPEN
GHENT (or Gand)
GILLY
HALLE (or Hal)
IEPER (or Ypres)
JUMET
LIÈGE (or Luik)
MENEN (or Menin)
MENIN (or Menen)
NAMUR
RONSE (or Renaix)
TIELT

WAVRE
YPRES (or Ieper)
ZEMST

6
ANVERS (or Antwerp, Antwerpen)
BRUGES (or Brugge)
BRUGGE (or Bruges)
DINANT
DUFFEL
FURNES (or Veurne)
LAARNE
LEUVEN (or Louvain)
LIERRE (or Lier)
MODAVE
OSTEND (or Oostende)
REMICH Luxembourg
RENAIX (or Ronse)
VEURNE (or Furnes)

7
ANTWERP (or Antwerpen, Anvers)
DE PANNE
DIXMUDE (or Diksmuide)
HASSELT
HOBOKEN
LOKEREN
LOUVAIN (or Leuven)
MAASEIK
MALINES (or Mechlin)
MALMÉDY
MERKSEM
ROULERS (or Roeselare)

SERAING
ST TROND
   (or St Truiden)
THIENEN (or Tirlemont)
TONGRES (or Tongeren)
TORHOUT
TOURNAI

8
AARSCHOT
BASTOGNE
BRUSSELS (or Bruxelles)
COURTRAI (or Kortrijk)
DIEKIRCH Luxembourg
GRAMMONT
   (or Geraardsbergen)
KORTRIJK (or Courtrai)
MALDEGEM
NIVELLES
OOSTENDE (or Ostend)
TERMONDE
   (or Dendermonde)
TONGEREN (or Tongres)
TURNHOUT
VERVIERS

9
ANTWERPEN
   (or Antwerp, Anvers)
BRUXELLES (or Brussels)
CHARLEROI
DIKSMUIDE
   (or Dixmude)
HERENTALS
POPERINGE

ROESELARE (or Roulers)
ST NICOLAS (or St Niklaas)
ST NIKLAAS (or St Nicolas)
ST TRUIDEN (or St Trond)
TIRLEMONT (or Thienen)

10
LE LOUVIÈRE
LUXEMBOURG Luxembourg
NIEUWPOORT
OUDENAARDE

11
DENDERMONDE (or Termonde)
DIFFERDANGE Luxembourg

KNOCKE-HEIST
NEUFCHÂTEAU

12
BLANKENBERGE
INGELMUNSTER

13
PHILIPPEVILLE

14
GERAARDSBERGEN (or Grammont)

15
MARCHE-EN-FAMENNE

Geography – Towns & Cities – Europe – British Isles – ENGLAND

3	**HOVE**	**5**	**EGTON**	**OADBY**	**6**
ELY	HULL	ACTON	EPSOM	OLNEY	ALFORD
EYE	HYDE	ALTON	ERITH	OTLEY	ALSTON
RYE	IVER	AMBLE	ESHER	POOLE	BARNET
WEM	LEEK	BACUP	EWELL	REETH	BARROW
	LOOE	BLYTH	FILEY	RIPON	BATLEY
4	LYDD	BRIGG	FOWEY	RUGBY	BATTLE
BATH	MERE	CALNE	FROME	SANDY	BAWTRY
BRAY	PEEL	CHARD	GOOLE	SELBY	BEDALE
BUDE	Isle of Man	CHEAM	HAYLE	SOHAM	BELPER
BURY	RYDE	COLNE	HEDON	STOKE	BEXLEY
CLUN	SALE	CORBY	HYTHE	STONE	BODMIN
DEAL	SHAP	COWES	LEEDS	TEBAY	BOGNOR
DISS	STOW	CREWE	LEIGH	THAME	BOLTON
ETON	WARE	CROOK	LEWES	TRING	BOOTLE
HALE	WARK	DERBY	LOUTH	TRURO	BOSTON
HOLT	YARM	DOVER	LUTON	WELLS	BOURNE
HOOK	YORK	EGHAM	MARCH	WIGAN	BRUTON

BUNGAY	LEYTON	RIPLEY	ANDOVER	CHEDDAR
BURTON	LONDON	ROMSEY	APPLEBY	CHESHAM
BUXTON	LOWICK	RYHOPE	ARUNDEL	CHESTER
CANVEY	LUDLOW	SCALBY	ASHFORD	CHOBHAM
CARHAM	LYNTON	SEAHAM	AYLSHAM	CHORLEY
COBHAM	LYTHAM	SEATON	BAGSHOT	CLACTON
CROMER	MALDON	SELSEY	BALDOCK	CLIFTON
CROSBY	MALTON	SETTLE	BAMPTON	CONSETT
CROWLE	MARLOW	SLOUGH	BANBURY	CRAWLEY
DARWEN	MASHAM	SNAITH	BARKING	CROYDON
DAWLEY	MERTON	ST IVES	BECCLES	DATCHET
DIDCOT	MILLOM	STREET	BEDFORD	DAWLISH
DUDLEY	MORLEY	STROOD	BEESTON	DEREHAM
EALING	NASEBY	STROUD	BELFORD	DEVIZES
ECCLES	NELSON	SUTTON	BERWICK	DOCKING
ELSDON	NESTON	THIRSK	BEWDLEY	DORKING
EPPING	NEWARK	THORNE	BEXHILL	DOUGLAS
EXETER	NEWENT	TIPTON	BILSTON	Isle of Man
FELTON	NEWLYN	TOTNES	BINGLEY	DUNSTER
FORMBY	NEWTON	TOW LAW	BIRTLEY	DURSLEY
GORING	NORHAM	WALMER	BOWNESS	EARSDON
HAMBLE	NORTON	WARLEY	BRANDON	ELSTREE
HANLEY	OAKHAM	WATTON	BRISTOL	ENFIELD
HARLOW	OLDHAM	WELWYN	BRIXHAM	EVESHAM
HARROW	ORFORD	WHITBY	BROMLEY	EXMOUTH
HAVANT	OSSETT	WIDNES	BROTTON	EYNSHAM
HEANOR	OTFORD	WIGTON	BURFORD	FAREHAM
HENLEY	OUNDLE	WILTON	BURNHAM	FARNHAM
HESSLE	OXFORD	WITNEY	BURNLEY	FELTHAM
HEXHAM	PENRYN	WOKING	BURSLEM	FLETTON
HORLEY	PEWSEY	WOOLER	BURWELL	FRINTON
HOWDEN	PINNER	WRAGBY	CAISTOR	GLOSSOP
ILFORD	PUDSEY	YEADON	CANNOCK	GOSPORT
ILKLEY	PURLEY	YEOVIL	CARTMEL	GRIMSBY
JARROW	PUTNEY		CATFORD	HALIFAX
KENDAL	RAMSEY	**7**	CHARING	HAMPTON
KIRKBY	Isle of Man	ALLONBY	CHATHAM	HANWELL
KNOWLE	REDCAR	ALNWICK	CHEADLE	HARWICH

HAWORTH
HELSTON
HESWALL
HEYSHAM
HEYWOOD
HINDLEY
HITCHIN
HONITON
HORBURY
HORNSEA
HORSHAM
HORWICH
HOYLAKE
IBSTOCK
IPSWICH
IXWORTH
KESWICK
KINGTON
KIRKHAM
LANCING
LEDBURY
LEISTON
LESBURY
LEYBURN
LEYLAND
LINCOLN
MARGATE
MATLOCK
MORPETH
NEWBURY
NEWPORT
NEWQUAY
NORWICH
OLDBURY
OVERTON
PADSTOW
PENRITH
PRESCOT

PRESTON
PRUDHOE
RAINHAM
READING
REDHILL
REDRUTH
REIGATE
RETFORD
ROMFORD
ROYSTON
RUGELEY
RUISLIP
RUNCORN
RUSHDEN
SALFORD
SALTASH
SANDOWN
SCARTHO
SEAFORD
SHIFNAL
SHILDON
SHIPLEY
SHIPTON
SILLOTH
SILSDEN
SKIPTON
SOUTHAM
SPILSBY
SPITTAL
STAINES
STANLEY
STANWIX
STILTON
ST NEOTS
SUDBURY
SUNBURY
SWANAGE
SWINDON

SWINTON
TAUNTON
TELFORD
TETBURY
THAXTED
TILBURY
TOPSHAM
TORQUAY
TUXFORD
TWYFORD
VENTNOR
WALSALL
WALTHAM
WANTAGE
WAREHAM
WARWICK
WATCHET
WATFORD
WINDSOR
WINSLOW
WINSTER
WISBECH
WORKSOP
YOXFORD

8
ABINGDON
ALCESTER
ALFRETON
ALNMOUTH
AMERSHAM
AMESBURY
AMPTHILL
ASPATRIA
ATHERTON
AXBRIDGE
AYCLIFFE
BAKEWELL

BAMBURGH
BARNSLEY
BASILDON
BEDWORTH
BEVERLEY
BICESTER
BIDDULPH
BIDEFORD
BIRSTALL
BLOXWICH
BOLSOVER
BRACKLEY
BRADFORD
BRAMHALL
BRAMPTON
BRAUNTON
BRIDPORT
BRIGHTON
BROADWAY
BROMYARD
BROSELEY
CALDBECK
CAMBORNE
CARLISLE
CATERHAM
CHERTSEY
CHESHUNT
CLEVEDON
CLOVELLY
CONISTON
CORNHILL
COVENTRY
CREDITON
DARTFORD
DAVENTRY
DEBENHAM
DEPTFORD
DEWSBURY

EAST LOOE
EASTWOOD
EGREMONT
FAIRFORD
FAKENHAM
FALMOUTH
FRODSHAM
GARFORTH
GARSTANG
GOSFORTH
GRANTHAM
GRASMERE
GUISELEY
HADLEIGH
HAILSHAM
HALSTEAD
HASTINGS
HATFIELD
HEDGE END
HELMSLEY
HEREFORD
HERNE BAY
HERTFORD
HINCKLEY
HINDHEAD
HOLBEACH
HORNDEAN
HOUNSLOW
HUCKNALL
HUNMANBY
ILKESTON
INGLETON
KEIGHLEY
KEMPSTON
KEYNSHAM
KEYWORTH
KINGSTON
LAVENHAM

LECHLADE
LEWISHAM
LISKEARD
LONGTOWN
LYNMOUTH
MARYPORT
MELKSHAM
MIDHURST
MINEHEAD
NANTWICH
NEW HAVEN
NEW MILLS
NUNEATON
OLLERTON
ORMSKIRK
OSWESTRY
PAIGNTON
PENZANCE
PERSHORE
PETERLEE
PETWORTH
PEVENSEY
PLYMOUTH
POLPERRO
RADSTOCK
RAMSGATE
RAWMARSH
RAYLEIGH
REDDITCH
RICHMOND
RINGWOOD
ROCHDALE
ROCHFORD
ROTHBURY
ROTHWELL
SALCOMBE
SALTBURN
SANDBACH

SANDGATE
SANDWICH
SEASCALE
SEDBERGH
SHANKLIN
SHEFFORD
SHOREHAM
SIDMOUTH
SKEGNESS
SLEAFORD
SOLIHULL
SOMERTON
SOUTHEND
SPALDING
STAFFORD
STAITHES
ST ALBANS
STAMFORD
STANDISH
STANHOPE
STANWELL
STAVELEY
STEYNING
ST HELENS
ST HELIER
    Channel Islands
STOCKTON
SURBITON
SWAFFHAM
TAMWORTH
THATCHAM
THETFORD
TINTAGEL
TIVERTON
TORPOINT
TUNSTALL
UCKFIELD
UXBRIDGE

WALLASEY
WALLSEND
WANSTEAD
WENDOVER
WESTBURY
WEST LOOE
WETHERAL
WETHERBY
WEYMOUTH
WHITBURN
WICKFORD
WILLITON
WILMSLOW
WINSFORD
WIVENHOE
WOODFORD
WOOLWICH
WORTHING
YARMOUTH

9
ALDEBURGH
ALDERSHOT
AMBLESIDE
ASHBOURNE
ASHBURTON
ASHINGTON
ATHERSTON
AVONMOUTH
AXMINSTER
AYLESBURY
BEBINGTON
BLACKBURN
BLACKHILL
BLACKPOOL
BLANDFORD
BLETCHLEY
BOSCASTLE

BRACKNELL
BRAINTREE
BRENTFORD
BRENTWOOD
BRIGHOUSE
BROUGHTON
CAMBERLEY
CAMBRIDGE
CAMELFORD
CARNFORTH
CATTERICK
CHATTERIS
CHINGFORD
CHUDLEIGH
CLITHEROE
COALVILLE
COLESHILL
CONGLETON
CORBRIDGE
CRANBORNE
CRANBROOK
CREWKERNE
CRICKLADE
CUCKFIELD
DARLASTON
DARTMOUTH
DEVONPORT
DONCASTER
DROITWICH
DRONFIELD
DUNSTABLE
DYMCHURCH
EASTLEIGH
EFFINGHAM
ELLESMERE
FARINGDON
FARNWORTH
FAVERSHAM

FLEETWOOD
GATESHEAD
GODALMING
GORLESTON
GRAVESEND
GREENWICH
GREYSTOKE
GUILDFORD
HALESOWEN
HARPENDEN
HARROGATE
HASLEMERE
HAVERHILL
HAWKSHEAD
HODDESDON
HOLMFIRTH
ILCHESTER
ILMINSTER
IMMINGHAM
KETTERING
KIDSGROVE
KING'S LYNN
KNUTSFORD
LANCASTER
LATCHFORD
LEICESTER
LICHFIELD
LIVERPOOL
LONG EATON
LONGRIDGE
LOWESTOFT
LYME REGIS
LYMINGTON
LYNDHURST
MAIDSTONE
MANSFIELD
MIDDLETON
MORECAMBE

NEWCASTLE
NEWMARKET
NEW ROMNEY
NORMANTON
NORTHWICH
ORPINGTON
OTTERBURN
PENISTONE
PICKERING
RADCLIFFE
ROCHESTER
ROSS-ON-WYE
ROTHERHAM
SALISBURY
SALTFLEET
SEAHOUSES
SEVENOAKS
SHEERNESS
SHEFFIELD
SHERBORNE
SMETHWICK
SOUTHPORT
SOUTHWELL
ST AUSTELL
STEVENAGE
ST HELENS
STOCKPORT
STORUPORT
STRATFORD
STRETFORD
TADCASTER
TARPORLEY
TAVISTOCK
TENTERDEN
THORNBURY
TODMORDEN
TONBRIDGE
TOWCESTER

TYNEMOUTH
ULVERSTON
UPHOLLAND
UPMINSTER
UPPINGHAM
UTTOXETER
WAINFLEET
WAKEFIELD
WARKWORTH
WESTERHAM
WEYBRIDGE
WIMBLEDON
WINCANTON
WOKINGHAM
WOLVERTON
WOODSTOCK
WORCESTER
WYMONDHAM

10

ACCRINGTON
ALTRINCHAM
BARNSTAPLE
BEAMINSTER
BEDLINGTON
BELLINGHAM
BILLERICAY
BILLINGHAM
BIRKENHEAD
BIRMINGHAM
BRIDGEMARY
BRIDGNORTH
BRIDGWATER
BROMSGROVE
BROWNHILLS
BUCKINGHAM
CANTERBURY
CARSHALTON

CASTLE CARY
CASTLEFORD
CASTLETOWN
   Isle of Man
CHELMSFORD
CHELTENHAM
CHICHESTER
CHIPPENHAM
CHULMLEIGH
CINDERFORD
COGGESHALL
COLCHESTER
COTTINGHAM
CULLOMPTON
DARLINGTON
DORCHESTER
DUKINFIELD
EASINGWOLD
EASTBOURNE
ECCLESHALL
EDWINSTOWE
FELIXSTOWE
FOLKESTONE
FRESHWATER
GILLINGHAM
GLOUCESTER
GUNNISLAKE
HALESWORTH
HARTLEPOOL
HASLINGDEN
HEATHFIELD
HIGHBRIDGE
HILLINGDON
HOLSWORTHY
HORNCASTLE
HORNCHURCH
HUNGERFORD
HUNSTANTON

HUNTINGDON
ILFRACOMBE
KENILWORTH
KETTLEWELL
KINGSCLERE
KIRKNEWTON
LAUNCESTON
LEAMINGTON
LEOMINSTER
LETCHWORTH
LIVERSEDGE
LONG SUTTON
MAIDENHEAD
MALMESBURY
MANCHESTER
MEVAGISSEY
MEXBOROUGH
MICKLEOVER
MIDDLEWICH
MILDENHALL
NAILSWORTH
NORTHFLEET
NOTTINGHAM
OAKENGATES
OKEHAMPTON
PEACEHAVEN
PONTEFRACT
PORTISHEAD
PORTSMOUTH
POTTERS BAR
RAMSBOTTOM
RAVENGLASS
SAXMUNDHAM
SCUNTHORPE
SEDGEFIELD
SHEPPERTON
SHERINGHAM
SHREWSBURY

SPENNYMOOR
STALBRIDGE
ST LEONARDS
STOWMARKET
SUNDERLAND
SWANSCOMBE
TEDDINGTON
TEIGNMOUTH
TEWKESBURY
TROWBRIDGE
TWEEDMOUTH
TWICKENHAM
WADEBRIDGE
WALLINGTON
WARMINSTER
WARRINGTON
WASHINGTON
WEDNESBURY
WELLINGTON
WEST MERSEA
WHITCHURCH
WHITEHAVEN
WHITLEY BAY
WHITSTABLE
WHITTLESEY
WILLINGTON
WINCHCOMBE
WINCHELSEA
WINCHESTER
WINDERMERE
WIRKSWORTH
WITHERNDEA
WOLSINGHAM
WOODBRIDGE
WORKINGTON

11
BASINGSTOKE

BERKHAMSTED
BIGGLESWADE
BLITTERLEES
BOGNOR REGIS
BOURNEMOUTH
BOVEY TRACEY
BRIDLINGTON
BROADSTAIRS
BUNTINGFORD
BURGESS HILL
CHORLEYWOOD
CIRENCESTER
CLECKHEATON
CLEETHORPES
COCKERMOUTH
CRAMLINGTON
CROWBOROUGH
FARNBOROUGH
FRAMLINGHAM
GLASTONBURY
GUISBOROUGH
HALTWHISTLE
HATHERLEIGH
HIGH WYCOMBE
KINGSBRIDGE
KNOTTINGLEY
LEATHERHEAD
LOSTWITHIEL
LUTTERWORTH
MABELTHORPE
MANNINGTREE
MARKET RASEN
MARLBOROUGH
MUCH WENLOCK
NEW BRIGHTON
NEWTON ABBOT
NORTHAMPTON
PERRANPORTH

PETERSFIELD
POCKLINGTON
RAWTENSTALL
ROTTINGDEAN
SCARBOROUGH
SEATON CAREW
SHAFTESBURY
SOUTHAMPTON
SOUTH MOLTON
STALYBRIDGE
STAPLEHURST
STOURBRIDGE
ST PETER PORT
Channel Islands
SWADLINCOTE
TATTERSHALL
WALLINGFORD
WALTHAMSTOW
WEST DRAYTON
WOODHALL SPA

12
ATTLEBOROUGH
BARNOLDSWICK
BEACONSFIELD
BRIERLEY HILL
BURNHAM-ON-SEA
CAISTER-ON-SEA
CHESTERFIELD
CHRISTCHURCH
CLACTON-ON-SEA
DROITWICH SPA
FEATHERSTONE
FRINTON-ON-SEA
GAINSBOROUGH
GREAT HARWOOD
GREAT MALVERN
HAYDON BRIDGE

HEBDEN BRIDGE
HECKMONDWIKE
HETTON-LE-HOLE
HOLMES CHAPEL
HUDDERSFIELD
LONGHAUGHTON
LOUGHBOROUGH
MACCLESFIELD
MILTON KEYNES
NEW ALRESFORD
NORTH SHIELDS
NORTH WALSHAM
OTTERY ST MARY
PETERBOROUGH
PORT SUNLIGHT
SHOEBURYNESS
SKELMERSDALE
SOUTH SHIELDS
STOKE-ON-TRENT
TENBURY WELLS
WALTHAM ABBEY
WALTON-LE-DALE
WEST BROMWICH
WIVELISCOMBE

13
ABBOTS BROMLEY
ALLENDALE TOWN
BARNARD CASTLE
BILLINGSHURST
BOROUGHBRIDGE
BRIGHTLINGSEA
BUCKFASTLEIGH
BURNHAM MARKET
BURTON LATIMER
BURY ST EDMUNDS
CASTLE CARROCK
CHANDLERS FORD

DOWNHAM MARKET
EAST GRINSTEAD
EAST WITTERING
ELLESMERE PORT
FORDINGBRIDGE
GODMANCHESTER
GRAYS THURROCK
GREAT YARMOUTH
HAYWARDS HEATH
KIDDERMINSTER
KINGSTEIGNTON
KIRKBY STEPHEN
KNARESBOROUGH
LEAMINGTON SPA
LITTLEBOROUGH
LITTLEHAMPTON
LYTHAM ST ANNE'S
MARKET DEEPING
MARKET DRAYTON
MELTON MOWBRAY
MIDDLESBROUGH
NEWARK-ON-TRENT
NORTHALLERTON
OSWALDTWISTLE
RICKMANSWORTH
ROBIN HOOD'S BAY
SAFFRON WALDEN
SEATON DELAVAL
SHEPTON MALLET
SHOREHAM-BY-SEA
SITTINGBOURNE
SOUTHEND-ON-SEA
SOUTH OCKENDON
SOWERBY BRIDGE
STOW-ON-THE-WOLD
WATERLOOVILLE
WESTGATE-ON-SEA
WEST WITTERING

WOLVERHAMPTON

14
ASHBY-DE-LA-ZOUCH
BISHOP AUCKLAND
BISHOP'S WALTHAM
BLANDFORD FORUM
CHIPPING NORTON
CHURCH STRETTON
GORLESTON-ON-SEA
GREAT DRIFFIELD
GREAT MISSENDEN
HEMEL HEMPSTEAD
HENLEY-ON-THAMES
HURSTPIERPOINT
KIRKBY LONSDALE
KIRKBYMOORSIDE
MARKET WEIGHTON
MIDSOMER NORTON
MORETON-IN-MARSH
NEWPORT PAGNELL
POULTON-LE-FYLDE
STOCKTON-ON-TEES
STONY STRATFORD
THORNABY-ON-TEES
TUNBRIDGE WELLS
WALTON-ON-THAMES
WELLINGBOROUGH
WOOTTON BASSETT

15
ASHTON-UNDER-LYNE
BARROW-IN-FURNESS
BURNHAM-ON-CROUCH
BURTON-UPON-TRENT
CASTLE DONINGTON
CHAPEL-EN-LE-FRITH
CHESTER-LE-STREET

CHIPPING CAMPDEN
CHIPPING SODBURY
DALTON-IN-FURNESS
GRANGE-OVER-SANDS
GREAT TORRINGTON
LEIGHTON BUZZARD
NEWTON-LE-WILLOWS
SHIPSTON-ON-STOUR
SUNBURY-ON-THAMES
SUTTON COLDFIELD
WALTON-ON-THE-NAZE
WELLS-NEXT-THE-SEA

WESTON-SUPER-MARE
WOTTON-UNDER-EDGE

16
BERWICK-UPON-TWEED
BISHOP'S STORTFORD
HOUGHTON-LE-SPRING
KINGSTON-ON-THAMES
MARKET HARBOROUGH
SALTBURN-BY-THE-SEA
SUTTON-IN-ASHFIELD
WELWYN GARDEN CITY

17
BOURTON-ON-THE-WATER
BUDLEIGH SALTERTON
NEWBIGGIN-BY-THE-SEA
NEWCASTLE-UPON-TYNE
PRINCES RISBOROUGH
STOURPORT-ON-SEVERN
STRATFORD-UPON-AVON

18
NEWCASTLE-UNDER-LYME

Geography – Towns & Cities – British Isles – NORTHERN IRELAND

5
DERRY
 (or Londonderry)
KEADY
LARNE
NEWRY
OMAGH

6
ANTRIM
ARMAGH
BANGOR
BELCOO
CLAUDY
CLOUGH
COMBER
KILREA
LURGAN
ROSLEA

7
BELFAST
BELLEEK
CLOGHER
CRUMLIN
DROMARA
DROMORE
DUNDRUM
FINTONA
GARVAGH
GLENARM
KILKEEL
LISBURN
MAGHERA
POMEROY

8
ARDGLASS
DUNGIVEN
HOLYWOOD
LIMAVADY

PORTRUSH
STRABANE

9
BALLYMENA
BANBRIDGE
BUSHMILLS
CARRYDUFF
COLERAINE
COOKSTOWN
CRAIGAVON
CUSHENDUN
DUNGANNON
LISNASKEA
MONEYMORE
NEWCASTLE
PORTADOWN
ROSTREVOR
TANDRAGEE
WHITEHEAD

10
AUGHNACLOY
BALLYCLARE
BALLYMONEY
CASTLEDERG
COALISLAND
CUSHENDALL
DONAGHADEE
KILLYLEAGH
MARKETHILL
PORTAFERRY
STRANGFORD

11
BALLYCASTLE
BALLYGAWLEY
CROSSMAGLEN
DOWNPATRICK
ENNISKILLEN
GREENISLAND

IRVINESTOWN
LONDONDERRY (or Derry)
MAGHERAFELT
NEWTOWNARDS
NUTTS CORNER
PORTGLENONE
PORTSTEWART
RANDALSTOWN

RATHFRILAND
WARRENPOINT

12
BALLYNAHINCH
CASTLEWELLAN
NEWTOWNABBEY

13
CARRICKFERGUS
NEWTOWNBUTLER

14
NEWTOWNSTEWART

Geography – Towns & Cities – Europe – British Isles – REPUBLIC OF IRELAND

4	HOWTH	DUBLIN	DONEGAL	THURLES
BIRR	KELLS	DURROW	DUNDALK	TRAMORE
BRAY	KNOCK	ELPHIN	DUNGLOE	WEXFORD
COBH	LOUTH	FERMOY	DUNLEER	WICKLOW
CORK	LUCAN	FOYNES	DUNMORE	YOUGHAL
GLIN	MOATE	GALWAY	ENFIELD	
GORT	NAVAN	KILKEE	FINGLAS	**8**
INCH	SLANE	MALLOW	FOXFORD	BALLYBAY
NAAS	SLIGO	MOHILL	GRANARD	BALLYGAR
RUSH	TULLA	NENAGH	KANTURK	BANAGHER
TARA	TULSK	NOBBER	KENMARE	BUNCRANA
TRIM		OMEATH	KILDARE	BUNDORAN
TUAM	**6**	ROOSKY	KILRUSH	BUNRATTY
	ACLARE	SWORDS	KINSALE	DROGHEDA
5	ARDARA	TRALEE	LEIXLIP	DUNBOYNE
ARDEE	ARKLOW	TULLOW	LIFFORD	DUNLAVIN
AVOCA	BANDON		LISMORE	GLENTIES
BOYLE	BANTRY	**7**	MACROOM	HEADFORD
CAHIR	BORRIS	ARDMORE	MOVILLE	KILKENNY
CAVAN	CALLAN	ATHENRY	NEWPORT	KILLALOE
CLARA	CARLOW	ATHLONE	NEW ROSS	KILLIMOR
CROOM	CASHEL	BALLINA	PONTOON	KINVARRA
ENNIS	CLONES	BLARNEY	PORTLAW	LIMERICK
FENIT	CLOYNE	CLIFDEN	RATHNEW	LISTOWEL
FERNS	DALKEY	CLOGHAN	ROSCREA	LONGFORD
GOREY	DINGLE	CLONMEL	TARBERT	LOUGHREA

MALAHIDE
MAYNOOTH
MIDLETON
MOLLS GAP
MONAGHAN
PETTIGOE
PORTUMNA
RATHDRUM
ROSSLARE
SKERRIES
SWINFORD
TALLAGHT
VIRGINIA
WESTPORT
WOODFORD

9
ABBEYLEIX
ATHLEAGUE
BALLYDUFF
BALLYMOTE
BELMULLET
BELTURBET
BUTTEVANT
CAPPOQUIN
CASTLEBAR
CASTLERAE
CELBRIDGE
COLLOONEY
COOTEHILL
DUNGARVAN
DUNMANWAY
EDENDERRY
FRESHFORD
GLENBEIGH

GORTAHORK
JOHNSTOWN
KILBEGGAN
KILCORMAC
KILCULLEN
KILLARNEY
KILLYBEGS
MOUNTRATH
MULLINGAR
NEWBRIDGE
NEWMARKET
OLDCASTLE
RATHKEALE
ROSCOMMON
TIPPERARY
TULLAMORE
WATERFORD

10
ABBEYFEALE
BALBRIGGAN
BALLINROBE
BALLYBOFEY
BALLYMAHON
BURTONPORT
CARNDONAGH
CARRICKBOY
CLONAKILTY
CLONDALKIN
CREESLOUGH
CROSSHAVEN
DUNFANAGHY
ENNISTYMON
GLENAMADDY
GREYSTONES

KILLORGLIN
KILMALLOCK
KINGSCOURT
MILLSTREET
OUGHTERARD
PORTLAOISE
RATHMELTON
SHILLELAGH
SKIBBEREEN
STRADBALLY
TEMPLEMORE
THOMASTOWN

11
BALLINASLOE
BALLYBUNION
BALLYCASTLE
BALLYHAUNIS
BALLYRAGGET
BLESSINGTON
CAHIRCIVEEN
CARLINGFORD
CASTLECOMER
CASTLEMAINE
CHARLEVILLE
CLARECASTLE
CLAREMORRIS
ENNISCORTHY
GLENGARRIFF
JULIANSTOWN
LETTERKENNY
STROKESTOWN
TUBBERCURRY

12
BAGENALSTOWN
BALLYSHANNON
BALLYVAUGHAN
 CASTLEISLAND
DÚN LAOGHAIRE
KILLASHANDRA
LISDOONVARNA
MITCHELSTOWN
MONASTEREVIN
MOUNTMELLICK

13
CARRICK-ON-SUIR
CASTLEBLAYNEY
CASTLEPOLLARD
MANORHAMILTON
NEWCASTLE WEST
PORTARLINGTON

14
CARRICKMACROSS
COURTMACSHERRY
EDGEWORTHSTOWN
LEIGHLINBRIDGE
MILLTOWN MALBAY

15
BALLAGHADERREEN
COURTOWN HARBOUR
GRAIGUENAMANAGH

16
CARRICK-ON-SHANNON
CASTLEBELLINGHAM

Geography – Towns & Cities – Europe – British Isles – SCOTLAND

3	KELSO	DYSART	BRODICK	PORTSOY	CROMARTY
AYR	LAIRG	EDZELL	CANTYRE	RENFREW	DALKEITH
UIG	LARGO	FORFAR	CARLUKE	SCOURIE	DALMALLY
	LARGS	FORRES	CUMNOCK	SELKIRK	DINGWALL
4	LEITH	GIRVAN	DORNOCH	STANLEY	DOUNREAY
ALVA	LEVEN	GLAMIS	DOUGLAS	TARBERT	DRUMMORE
DREM	NAIRN	GRETNA	DUNKELD	TAYPORT	DUFFTOWN
DUNS	ONICH	HAWICK	DURNESS	TOMATIN	DUMFRIES
DYCE	PERTH	HUNTLY	FALKIRK	TRANENT	DUNBEATH
ELIE	SALEN	IRVINE	GALSTON	TURRIFF	DUNBLANE
KIRN	SCONE	KILLIN	GLASGOW	TYNDRUM	EYEMOUTH
LUSS	TROON	LAGGAN	GOLSPIE	UNAPOOL	FALKLAND
OBAN		LANARK	GOUROCK	WIGTOWN	FINDHORN
TAIN	**6**	LAUDER	GULLANE		FORTROSE
WICK	ABOYNE	LESLIE	HALKIRK	**8**	GAIRLOCH
	ALNESS	METHIL	KENMORE	ABERDEEN	GLENLUCE
5	ARDLUI	MOFFAT	KILSYTH	ABERLADY	GREENLAW
ALLOA	BARVAS	RENTON	KINROSS	ARBROATH	GREENOCK
ALYTH	BEAULY	ROSYTH	LAMLASH	ARMADALE	HAMILTON
ANNAN	BIGGAR	SHOTTS	LARBERT	ARROCHAR	HOLMHEAD
BANFF	BODDAM	STRUAN	LERWICK	AVIEMORE	INNELLAN
BEITH	BO'NESS	THURSO	LYBSTER	BALLATER	JEDBURGH
BRORA	BUCKIE	TONGUE	MACDUFF	BALMORAL	KINBRACE
CLOVA	CAWDOR	UPHALL	MAIDENS	BANCHORY	KINCRAIG
CRAIL	COMRIE	WATTEN	MALLAIG	BARRHEAD	KINGHORN
CULTS	CRIEFF	WISHAW	MAYBOLE	BARRHILL	KIRKWALL
CUPAR	CURRIE		MELROSE	BATHGATE	KYLEAKIN
DALRY	DARVEL	**7**	METHVEN	BEARSDEN	LANGHOLM
DENNY	DOLLAR	AIRDRIE	MONKTON	BEATTOCK	LATHERON
DOUNE	DRYMEN	ALLOWAY	MUTHILL	BLANTYRE	LEUCHARS
ELGIN	DUNBAR	BALLOCH	NEW DEER	BROXBURN	MILLPORT
ELLON	DUNDEE	BANAVIE	OLD DEER	BURGHEAD	MONIAIVE
FYVIE	DUNLOP	BONHILL	PAISLEY	CARNWATH	MONTROSE
GARVE	DUNNET	BRAEMAR	PEEBLES	CRAWFORD	MUIRKIRK
KEITH	DUNOON	BRECHIN	PORTREE	CREETOWN	NEWBURGH

PENICUIK
ROTHESAY
ROXBURGH
SANQUHAR
STIRLING
STRICHEN
TAYNUILT
TRAQUAIR
ULLAPOOL
WHITHORN

9
ABERFELDY
ABERFOYLE
ABERNETHY
ARDROSSAN
BETTYHILL
BLACKFORD
BROADFORD
BUCHLYVIE
BUCKHAVEN
CALLANDER
CARSTAIRS
CLYDEBANK
DALRYMPLE
DUMBARTON
DUNCANSBY
EDINBURGH
FOCHABERS
GAIRLOCHY
HELMSDALE
INVERARAY
INVERNESS
INVERSHIN
INVERURIE
JOHNSTONE
KILBIRNIE
KILMACOLM

KILMARTIN
KINGUSSIE
KIRKCALDY
LOCHINVER
LOCHMABEN
LOCKERBIE
MILNGAVIE
MONIFIETH
NEW LANARK
OCHILTREE
PETERHEAD
PITLOCHRY
PORT APPIN
PORT ELLEN
PRESTWICK
SALTCOATS
SHIELDAIG
SLAMANNAN
ST ANDREWS
STEWARTON
STORNOWAY
STRANRAER
STRATHYRE
STROMNESS
STRONTIAN
THORNHILL
TOBERMORY
TOMINTOUL
TURNBERRY
WEMYSS BAY

10
ACHNASHEEN
ALEXANDRIA
ALTNAHARRA
ANSTRUTHER
BALLANTRAE
BALLINLUIG

BERRIEDALE
CARNOUSTIE
CARRBRIDGE
CASTLETOWN
COATBRIDGE
COLDSTREAM
CRAIGHOUSE
DALBEATTIE
DALWHINNIE
GALASHIELS
GLENEAGLES
GLENFINNAN
GLENROTHES
HADDINGTON
KILCREGGAN
KILMAINHAM
KILMARNOCK
KILWINNING
KINCARDINE
KINGSBARNS
KINLOCHEWE
KIRKCONNEL
KIRRIEMUIR
LENNOXTOWN
LINLITHGOW
LIVINGSTON
MOTHERWELL
NEW CUMNOCK
NEWTONMORE
OLDMELDRUM
PITTENWEEM
PORT ASKAIG
PORTGORDON
PORTOBELLO
ROSEHEARTY
ROSEMARKIE
RUTHERGLEN
SKELMORLIE

STEVENSTON
STONEHAVEN
STRATHAVEN
WILSONTOWN

11
BALQUHIDDER
BANNOCKBURN
BLAIR ATHOLL
BLAIRGOWRIE
BONAR BRIDGE
BURNTISLAND
CAMPBELTOWN
CLACKMANNAN
COUPAR ANGUS
COWDENBEATH
CUMBERNAULD
DUNFERMLINE
ECCLEFECHAN
FETTERCAIRN
FORT WILLIAM
FRASERBURGH
GRANGEMOUTH
GRETNA GREEN
HELENSBURGH
INVERBERVIE
INVERGORDON
KIRKPATRICK
LOSSIEMOUTH
MAXWELLTOWN
MUSSELBURGH
NETHYBRIDGE
NEW GALLOWAY
PETERCULTER
PORT GLASGOW
PORTPATRICK
PRESTONPANS
STRATHBLANE

12
AUCHTERARDER
BALLACHULISH
BOAT OF GARTEN
CROSSMICHAEL
EAST KILBRIDE
FORT AUGUSTUS
GARELOCHHEAD
INNERLEITHEN
KINLOCHLEVEN
LAURENCEKIRK
LOCHGILPHEAD
MACHRIHANISH
NEWPORT-ON-TAY
NEWTON MEARNS

NORTH BERWICK
PORTNACROISH
STRATHPEFFER
TILLICOULTRY
WEST KILBRIDE

13
AUCHTERMUCHTY
BRIDGE OF ALLAN
BROUGHTY FERRY
CASTLE DOUGLAS
COCKBURNSPATH
DALMELLINGTON
DRUMNADROCHIT
INVERKEITHING

KILLIEKRANKIE
KIRKCUDBRIGHT
KIRKINTILLOCK
NEWTON STEWART
STENHOUSEMUIR

14
GRANTOWN-ON-SPEY
KINLOCH RANNOCH
KYLE OF LOCHALSH

16
GATEHOUSE OF FLEET
NORTH QUEENSFERRY
SOUTH QUEENSFERRY

Geography – Towns & Cities – Europe – British Isles – WALES

3
USK

4
BALA
HOLT
LLAY
MOLD
PYLE
RHYL

5
BARRY
BORTH
BWLCH
CHIRK
CONWY
DINAS

FLINT
MAGOR
NEATH
NEFYN
PORTH
RISCA
TENBY
TOWYN
TYWYN

6
AMLWCH
BANGOR
BEDWAS
BRECON
CORWEN
KILLAY
MARGAM

MATHRY
NELSON
PENNAL
RUABON
RUMNEY
RUTHIN
YSTRAD

7
BLEDDFA
BUCKLEY
CARDIFF
CLYDACH
CWMAFAN
CWMBACH
DENBIGH
DOWLAIS
HARLECH

HIRWAUN
LOUGHOR
MAESTEG
NEWGALE
NEWPORT
NEW QUAY
NEWTOWN
NEYLAND
OVERTON
PENARTH
PENCOED
RHONDDA
ST ASAPH
SWANSEA
TINTERN
WREXHAM

8
ABERAVON
ABERDARE
ABERGELE
BARMOUTH
BENLLECH
BETHESDA
BRIDGEND
BRYNMAWR
CADOXTON
CAERLEON
CALDICOT
CARDIGAN
CHEPSTOW
EBBW VALE
GOODWICK
GRESFORD
HAWARDEN

HAY-ON-WYE
HOLYHEAD
HOLYWELL
KIDWELLY
KNIGHTON
LAMPETER
LLANABER
LLANDAFF
LLANELLI
LLANRWST
MONMOUTH
NARBERTH
PEMBROKE
PENYBONT
PWLLHELI
RHAYADER
RHUDDLAN
ST CLEARS
ST DAVID'S
TALGARTH
TREDEGAR
TREGARON
TREMADOC
WHITLAND

9
ABERAERON
ABERDARON
ABERDOVEY
ABERFFRAW
ABERPORTH
AMMANFORD
BEAUMARIS

BEDWELLTY
BLAENAVON
BURRY PORT
COLWYN BAY
COWBRIDGE
CRICCIETH
DOLGELLAU
FISHGUARD
GORSEINON
GWALCHMAI
LAUGHARNE
LLANBERIS
LLANDEILO
LLANDUDNO
LLANDYSUL
LLANGEFNI
LLANGURIG
MORRISTON
NEW RADNOR
PONTYPOOL
PORT EYNON
PORTHCAWL
PRESTATYN
RHOS-ON-SEA
ST MELLONS
TONYPANDY
TRECASTLE
WELSHPOOL

10
ABERSYCHAN
BEDDGELERT
BETWS-Y-COED

CAERNARFON
CAERPHILLY
CARMARTHEN
CROSS HANDS
FFESTINIOG
LLANDDAROG
LLANDOVERY
LLANDRILLO
LLANFYLLIN
LLANGOLLEN
LLANIDLOES
MONTGOMERY
NEWBOROUGH
PENRHYN BAY
PONTYPRIDD
PORTHMADOG
PORT TALBOT
PRESTEIGNE
THE MUMBLES
WHITCHURCH
YSTALYFERA

11
ABERGAVENNY
ABERTILLERY
ABERYSTWYTH
BRITON FERRY
BUILTH WELLS
CONNAH'S QUAY
CRICKHOWELL
LLANTRISANT
MACHYNLLETH
MENAI BRIDGE

MOUNTAIN ASH
OYSTERMOUTH
PENMAENMAWR
PORTMEIRION
QUEENSFERRY
TRAWSFYNYDD

12
DINAS MAWDDWY
LLANDISSILIO
LLANUWCHLLYN
MILFORD HAVEN
PEMBROKE DOCK
PONTARDULAIS
SAUNDERSFOOT

13
HAVERFORDWEST
LLANTWIT MAJOR
MERTHYR TYDFIL
YSBYTY YSTWYTH
YSTRADGLYNAIS

14
LLANFAIRFECHAN
LLANWRTYD WELLS
NEWCASTLE EMLYN

16
LLANDRINDOD WELLS

17
BLAENAU FFESTINIOG

Geography – Towns & Cities – Europe – CENTRAL EUROPE

4
BAJA Hungary
BRNO (or Brünn)
  Czech Republic
GRAZ Austria
GYÖR Hungary
HALL Austria
IMST Austria
LINZ Austria
ŁÓDŹ Poland
PÉCS Hungary
WELS Austria
WIEN (or Vienna)
  Austria

5
BADEN Austria
BRÜNN (or Brno)
  Czech Republic
CHELM Poland
GMÜND Austria
LIENZ Austria
OPAVA Czech Republic
PLZEŇ (or Pilsen)
  Czech Republic
PRAHA (or Prague)
  Czech Republic
RADOM Poland
STEYR Austria
TORUN Poland

6
CRACÓW (or Kraków)
  Poland
ELBING (or Elblag)
  Poland
ELBLAG (or Elbing)
  Poland
GDANSK Poland
GDYNIA Poland
KALISZ Poland
KIELCE Poland
KOŠICE Slovakia
KRAKÓW (or Craców)
  Poland
LEOBEN Austria
LUBLIN Poland
PILSEN (or Plzeň)
  Czech Republic
POZNAN Poland
PRAGUE (or Praha)
  Czech Republic
PREŠOV Slovakia
RYBNIK Poland
SCHWAZ Austria
SOPRON Hungary
SZEGED Hungary
TARNÓW Poland
UJPEST Hungary
VIENNA (or Wien)
  Austria
WARSAW (or
  Warszawa) Poland
ZWETTL Austria

7
BLUDENZ Austria
BREGENZ Austria
EBENSEE Austria
GLIWICE Poland

GMUNDEN Austria
HALLEIN Austria
JIHLAVA Czech Republic
LANDECK Austria
LEGNICA Poland
LIBEREC Czech
  Republic
MISKOLC Hungary
MÖDLING Austria
OLOMOUC Czech
  Republic
OLSZTYN Poland
OSTRAVA Czech
  Republic
RZESZÓW Poland
VILLACH Austria
WROCLAW Poland
ZELTWEG Austria

8
BAD ISCHL Austria
BUDAPEST Hungary
DEBRECEN Hungary
DORNBIRN Austria
EISENERZ Austria
KATOWICE Poland
KUFSTEIN Austria
LEONDING Austria
PRZEMYŚL Poland
SALZBURG Austria
ST PÖLTEN Austria
SZCZECIN Poland
VESZPRÉM Hungary
WARSZAWA
  (or Warsaw) Poland

9
AMSTETTEN Austria
ANSFELDEN Austria
BIALYSTOK Poland
FELDKIRCH Austria
FOHNSDORF Austria
GRUDZIADZ Poland
INNSBRUCK Austria
JUDENBURG Austria
KECSKEMET Hungary
PARDUBICE Czech Republic
PROSTĚJOV Czech Republic
SOSNOWIEC Poland
TATABÁNYA Hungary
WALBRZYCH Poland
WLOCLAWEK Poland
WOLFSBERG Austria

10
BÉKÉSCSABA Hungary
BRATISLAVA Slovakia
EISENSTADT Austria
KAPFENBERG Austria
KLAGENFURT Austria

11
CZESTOCHOWA Poland
KNITTELFELD Austria
NAGYKANIZSA Hungary
NEUNKIRCHEN Austria

NYÍREGYHÁZA Hungary
SALGÓTARJÁN Hungary
SZOMBATHELY Hungary

12
BIELSKO-BIALA Poland
BRAUNAU AM INN Austria
MÜRZZUSCHLAG Austria
ZALAEGERSZEG Hungary

13
BISCHOFSHOFEN Austria
BRUCK AN DER MUR Austria
HRADEC KRÁLOVÉ Czech Republic

14
KLOSTERNEUBURG Austria
RIED IM INNKREIS Austria
SZÉKESFEHÉRVÁR Hungary
WIENER NEUSTADT Austria

15
ČESKÉ BUDĚJOVICE Czech Republic
KREMS AN DER DONAU Austria

16
SPITTAL AN DER DRAU Austria

19
PIOTRKÓW TRYBUNALSKI Poland

Geography – Towns & Cities – Europe – EASTERN EUROPE

3
KEM European Russia
UFA European Russia

4
BAKU Azerbaijan
KIEV Ukraine

LVIV (or Lvov) Ukraine
LVOV (or Lviv) Ukraine
OREL European Russia

PERM European Russia
RIGA Latvia
TULA European Russia
TVER European Russia

5

BĂLTI Moldova
GOMEL (or Homyel) Belarus
KAZAN European Russia
KIROV (or Vyatka) European Russia
KURSK European Russia
MINSK Belarus
PENZA European Russia
PSKOV European Russia
TARTU Estonia
UKHTA European Russia
YALTA Ukraine

6

BATUMI Georgia
GROZNY European Russia
GYUMRI Armenia
HOMYEL (or Gomel) Belarus
KAUNAS Lithuania
MOSCOW European Russia
ODESSA Ukraine
ROSTOV European Russia
VYATKA (or Kirov) European Russia
VYBORG European Russia

7

DONETSK Ukraine
IVANOVO European Russia
KHARKOV Ukraine
KHERSON Ukraine
KIROVSK European Russia
LUHANSK Ukraine

PODOLSK European Russia
POLTAVA Ukraine
RYBINSK European Russia
SARATOV European Russia
TALLINN Estonia
TBILISI Georgia
VILNIUS Lithuania
VITEBSK Belarus
VOLOGDA European Russia
VORKUTA European Russia
YEREVAN Armenia
ZHDANOV (or Mariupol) Ukraine

8

ÇHISINĂU Moldova
KOSTROMA European Russia
MARIUPOL
  (or Zhdanov) Ukraine
MURMANSK European Russia
NOVGOROD European Russia
ORENBURG European Russia
PECHENGA European Russia
SMOLENSK European Russia
TIRASPOL Moldova
VLADIMIR European Russia
VORONEZH European Russia

9

ARCHANGEL (or Arkhangelsk)
  European Russia
ASTRAKHAN European Russia
CHERNOBYL Ukraine
KRASNODAR European Russia
NARYAN-MAR European Russia
VOLGOGRAD European Russia
YAROSLAVL European Russia

10
CHERNIVTSI Ukraine
DAUGAVPILS Latvia
SEVASTOPOL Ukraine
SVERDLOVSK Ukraine

11
ARKHANGELSK (or Archangel)
   European Russia
KALININGRAD European Russia
KANDALAKSHA European Russia
STERLITAMAK European Russia

12
BORISOGLEBSK European Russia
PETROZAVODSK European Russia
ST PETERSBURG European Russia

14
DNIPROPETROVSK Ukraine
NIZHNY NOVGOROD European
   Russia

15
VELIKIY NOVGOROD European Russia

Geography – Towns & Cities – Europe – FRANCE

3	GIEN	AUTUN	LYONS	TULLE	CALAIS
ARC	LAON	BERCK	MÂCON	USSEL	CANNES
DAX	LENS	BLOIS	MEAUX	VICHY	CARNAC
DIE	LEON	BOURG	MELUN	VITRÉ	CASSEL
DOL	METZ	BREST	MENDE	VITRY	CHAGNY
GAP	NICE	CALVI	NANCY		CHÂLON
GEX	POIX	CORPS	NÎMES	**6**	CHINON
PAU	PONS	COUHÉ	NIORT	ALBERT	CHOLET
VIF	RIOM	CRAON	NOYON	AMIENS	COGNAC
	ROYE	CRÉCY	NUITS	ANGERS	COLMAR
4	SÉES	CREIL	PARIS	ARDRES	DENAIN
AGDE	SENS	DIGNE	REDON	AUMONT	DERVAL
AGEN	SÈTE	DIJON	RODEZ	BASTIA	DIEPPE
AIRE	ST LÔ	DINAN	ROUEN	BAYEUX	DINARD
ALBI	TOUL	DOUAI	ROYAN	BEAUNE	ELBEUF
ALÈS	VIRE	DREUX	SAMER	BELLAC	EMBRUN
AUCH		FEURS	SEDAN	BERNAC	ÉPINAL
BEHN	**5**	GUISE	ST DIE	BOLBEC	EVREUX
CAEN	ARLES	LAVAL	ST POL	BOUCAU	FÉCAMP
DÔLE	ARRAS	LE PUY	TOURS	BRIARE	FIGEAC
FOIX	AURAY	LILLE	TRANS	CAHORS	FRÉJUS

GANNAT
GRASSE
GUÉRET
HIRSON
HYÈRES
ISIGNY
JARNAC
JOIGNY
LAIGLE
LE MANS
LODÈVE
LOUDUN
MAURON
MENTON
MILLAN
MONACO
  Monaco
NANTES
NEVERS
ORANGE
ORTHEZ
POISSY
PRIVAS
RENNES
RETHEL
RHEIMS
ROANNE
SALINS
SAUMUR
SENLIS
SERRES
ST CAST
STENAY
ST MALO
ST OMER
TARBES
THIERS
TOULON

TROYES
UGINES
VAIGES
VANNES
VERDUN
VESOUL
VIENNE
VOIRON
YVETOT

7

AJACCIO
ALENÇON
ANTIBES
ARTENAY
AUBAGNE
AUBIGNY
AUXERRE
AVALLON
AVESNES
AVIGNON
BAYONNE
BELFORT
BELLÊME
BÉZIERS
BOURGES
CAMBRAI
CARMAUX
CASTRES
CHABLIS
CHÂLONS
CORBEIL
DESVRES
DUNKIRK
ÉPERNAY
ÉTAPLES
FALAISE
FIRMINY

LANGRES
LA ROCHE
LAUTREC
LE BLANC
LE HAVRE
LIMOGES
LISIEUX
LORIENT
LOURDES
MAYENNE
MAZAMET
MÉZIDON
MORLAIX
MOULINS
ORLÉANS
PAIMPOL
PAMIERS
PONTIVY
PROVINS
QUILLAN
QUIMPER
ROMILLY
ROSCOFF
ROUBAIX
SAINTES
SALBRIS
ST AMAND
ST DENIS
ST FLOUR
ST JUMEN
ST LOUIS
TRÉLAZÉ
UZERCHE
VALENCE
VENDÔME
VIERZON
VOUVRAY

8

AMBÉRIEU
ARCACHON
ARGENTAN
AUBUSSON
AURILLAC
BAILLEUL
BAR LE DUC
BEAUVAIS
BERGERAC
BESANÇON
BIARRITZ
BORDEAUX
BOULOGNE
BRIANÇON
CARENTAN
CHAMBÉRY
CHARTRES
CHAUMONT
CLERMONT
COUTANCE
FOUGÈRES
GRENOBLE
GUINGAMP
HAGUENAU
HARFLEUR
HONFLEUR
ISSOUDON
LA CIOTAT
LA FLÈCHE
LAMBALLE
LE CATEAU
LE PORTEL
LE VERDON
LIBOURNE
LONGUYON
LOUVIERS
MARMANDE

MARQUISE
MAUBEUGE
MÉZIÈRES
MORTAGNE
MULHOUSE
NARBONNE
POITIERS
PONTOISE
QUIBERON
SÉLESTAT
SOISSONS
SOUILLAC
ST BRIEUC
ST DIZIER
ST MICHEL
ST TROPEZ
ST VALÉRY
TARASCON
TONNERRE
TOULOUSE
VALOGNES
VERNEUIL
VITTEAUX

9

ABBÉVILLE
AGINCOURT
AIGUILLON
AMBRIÈRES
ANGOULÊME
AVRANCHES
BRESSUIRE
BRIGNOGAN
CAVAILLON
CAVALAIRE
CHANTILLY
CHERBOURG
COMPIÈGNE

DEAUVILLE
GRANVILLE
LAPALISSE
L'ARBRESLE
LE CONQUET
LE CREUSOT
LE QUESNOY
LE TOUQUET
LE TRÉPORT
LUNÉVILLE
MIRAMBEAU
MONTARGIS
MONTAUBAN
MONTEREAU
MONTLUÇON
MONTREUIL
OCTEVILLE
PARTHENAY
PÉRIGUEUX
PERPIGNAN
PONT L'ABBÉ
PONT LOUIS
QUIMPERLÉ
ROCHEFORT
ROQUEFORT
ST CHAMOND
ST ÉTIENNE

ST NAZAIRE
ST QUENTIN
ST RAPHAEL
TROUVILLE

10
BAR-SUR-AUBE
CARPENTRAS
CASTELLANE
CHÂTEAULIN
DOUARNENEZ
DRAGUIGNAN
FRONTIGNAN
GRAVELINES
HAZEBROUCK
LA ROCHELLE
MARSEILLES
MONTCORNET
MONTE CARLO
  Monaco
MONTÉLIMAR
NEUFCHÂTEL
PONTARLIER
ROMORANTIN
STRASBOURG
THIONVILLE
VERSAILLES

VILLENEUVE

11
ARMENTIÈRES
ARROMANCHES
CARCASSONNE
CHÂTEAUROUX
DECAZEVILLE
MONTBELIARD
MONTPELLIER
NEUFCHÂTEAU
NOIRMOUTIER
PONT L'EVÊQUE
PORT VENDRES
ST FLORENTIN
ST JEAN DE LUZ
ST POL DE LÉON

12
AIGUES-MORTES
CAYEUX-SUR-MER
MONT DE MARSAN
PORTO VECCHIO
ST PIERRE D'ALB
VALENCIENNES
VILLEFRANCHE
VILLEURBANNE

13
AIX-EN-PROVENCE
ARGÈLES-SUR-MER
CHÂTEAUBRIANT
CHÂTEAU DU LOIR
CHÂTELLERAULT
FONTAINEBLEAU
LONS LE SAUNIER
MEHUN-SUR-YÈVRE
OLORON ST MARIE

14
BEAUVOIR-SUR-MER
CHÂTEAU THIERRY
LA CHAUX DE FONDS
ROMANS-SUR-ISÈRE

15
BLANGY-SUR-BRESLE
CLERMONT FERRAND
LA ROCHEFOUCAULD
ST GERMAIN EN LAYE

16
BRIVE-LA-GAILLARDE

Geography – Towns & Cities – Europe – GERMANY

3	CHAM	KÖLN	UNNA	CELLE	FULDA
HOF	ELZE	(or Cologne)		DÜREN	FÜRTH
ULM	GERA	LEER	**5**	EMDEN	GOTHA
	HAMM	LOHR	AALEN	ENGEN	HAGEN
4	KEHL	PLÖN	BÜNDE	ESSEN	HALLE
BONN	KIEL	PRÜM	BÜSUM	EUTIN	HANAU

The *Puzzler* Crossword Companion

HEIDE	LÜBECK	HANOVER (or	DIEPHOLZ	EBERSBERG
HUSUM	MEPPEN	Hannover)	DORTMUND	EICHSTÄTT
JEVER	MÜNDEN	HARBURG	DUISBURG	ESSLINGEN
KLEVE	MUNICH	HERFORD	ELMSHORN	FLENSBURG
LÜNEN	(or München)	HÜNFELD	ERLANGEN	FRANKFURT
MAINZ	MURNAU	ITZEHOE	FREIBURG	FRIEDBURG
NEUSS	PASING	KEMPTEN	FREISING	GÖPPINGEN
REGEN	PASSAU	KOBLENZ	GLADBECK	GÖTTINGEN
RHEDA	PLAUEN	KORBACH	HANNOVER	HEILBRONN
SOEST	RHEINE	KREFELD	(or Hanover)	KARLSRUHE
TRIER	SEESEN	KRONACH	KONSTANZ	LAUENBURG
WESEL	SIEGEN	LASTRUP	LANDSHUT	LIPPSTADT
WORMS	SINGEN	LEIPZIG	LÖNINGEN	MAGDEBURG
ZEVEN	SOLTAU	LIMBURG	LÜNEBURG	MEMMINGEN
	SPEYER	LÖRRACH	MANNHEIM	MÜNCHBERG
6	UELZEN	MARBURG	MESCHEDE	NUREMBERG
AACHEN	VECHTA	MEISSEN	MÜHLDORF	OBERWESEL
ALTONA	WEIDEN	MÜLHEIM	NIENBURG	OFFENBACH
AMBERG	XANTEN	MÜNCHEN	NORDHORN	OFFENBURG
BASSUM		(or Munich)	RATISBON	OLDENBURG
BERLIN	**7**	MÜNSTER	ROTTWEIL	OSNABRÜCK
BOCHUM	ALSFELD	POTSDAM	SASSNITZ	PADERBORN
BREMEN	ANSBACH	RINTELN	SCHWERIN	PFORZHEIM
COBURG	BAD TÖLZ	ROSTOCK	SOLINGEN	PINNEBERG
DACHAU	BAMBERG	SPANDAU	TÜBINGEN	REMSCHEID
DESSAU	BOCHOLT	SPRINGE	WALDSHUT	ROSENHEIM
DÜLMEN	BOPPARD	WARBURG	WALSRODE	SCHLESWIG
ERFURT	BOTTROP	WETZLAR	WANDSBEK	STRALSUND
FÜSSEN	COLOGNE	ZWICKAU	WEILHEIM	STRAUBING
GOSLAR	(or Köln)	ZWIESEL	WITTLICH	STUTTGART
GRONAU	COTTBUS		WÜNSDORF	WIESBADEN
HÖXTER	DETMOLD	**8**	WÜRZBURG	WUPPERTAL
KASSEL	DRESDEN	AUGSBURG		
KASTEL	EINBECK	BAYREUTH	**9**	**10**
LANDAU	GIESSEN	BIBERACH	BIELEFELD	BAD AIBLING
LEHRTE	GIFHORN	CHEMNITZ	BRUNSWICK	BADEN BADEN
LINDEN	HAMBURG	COESFELD	BUXTEHUDE	BAD PYRMONT
LINGEN	HAMELIN	CUXHAVEN	DARMSTADT	BERNCASTEL

DILLENBURG
DÜSSELDORF
EUSKIRCHEN
HEIDELBERG
HILDESHEIM
IBBENBÜREN
INGOLSTADT
NEUMÜNSTER
OBERHAUSEN
RAVENSBURG
REGENSBURG
REUTLINGEN
SALZGITTER
STADTHAGEN
TRAUNSTEIN
TUTTLINGEN
ÜBERLINGEN
WARNEMÜNDE
WASSERBURG
WEINGARTEN
WITTENBERG

11
BRANDENBURG
BREMERHAVEN
DELMENHORST
LUDWIGSBURG
NEUNKIRCHEN
NEUSTRELITZ
QUAKENBRÜCK
SAARBRÜCHEN
WITTENBERGE
ZWEIBRÜCKEN

12
BAD KREUZNACH
OBERAMMERGAU
SCHWENNINGEN
WILHELMSBURG
WOLFENBÜTTEL

13
ASCHAFFENBURG
BAD LAUTERBERG
BERCHTESGADEN
GELSENKIRCHEN
WILHELMSHAVEN

14
BAD REICHENHALL
KAISERSLAUTEN
NEUBRANDENBURG
RECKLINGHAUSEN

15
FRANKFURT AM MAIN
KARLSTADT AM MAIN
MÖNCHENGLADBACH

16
EISENHÜTTENSTADT

3
BRA

4
ALBA
ASTI
BARI
COMO
FANO
LODI
NOTO
PISA

ROME

5
ANZIO
AVOLA
CUNEO
FERMO
FORLÌ
GAETA
GENOA
IMOLA
IVREA

LECCE
LECCO
LUCCA
MASSA
MILAN
MONZA
OLBIA
OSTIA
PADUA
PALMI
PARMA
PAVIA

PRATO
RIETI
SCHIO
SIENA
TERNI
TURIN
UDINE

6
ANCONA
ANDRIA
AREZZO

CESENA
CHIETI
EMPOLI
FAENZA
FOGGIA
FORMIA
LATINA
MANTUA
MERANO
MESTRE
MODENA
NAPLES

NOVARA
PESARO
RAGUSA
RIMINI
ROVIGO
SAVONA
TIVOLI
TRENTO
URBINO
VARESE
VENICE
VERONA

7
BELLUNO
BERGAMO
BOLOGNA
BOLZANO
BRESCIA
CARRARA
CASERTA
CASSINO
CATANIA
COSENZA
CREMONA
CROTONE
FERRARA
FIDENZA
FIRENZE
 (or Florence)
FOLIGNO
IMPERIA
L'AQUILA
LIVORNO
MARSALA
MESSINA
ORVIETO
PALERMO
PERUGIA
PESCARA
PISTOIA

POTENZA
RAVENNA
ROSSANO
SALERNO
SAN REMO
SASSARI
SONDRIO
SULMONA
TARANTO
TRAPANI
TREVISO
TRIESTE
VICENZA
VITERBO
VOGHERA

8
AVELLINO
BARLETTA
BRINDISI
CAGLIARI
CHIAVARI
CHIOGGIA
FLORENCE
 (or Firenze)
FRASCATI
LA SPEZIA
MOLFETTA

MONOPOLI
PIACENZA
PINEROLA
PIOMBINO
POZZUOLI
ROVERETO
SIRACUSA
 (or Syracuse)
SORRENTO
SYRACUSE
 (or Siracusa)
TAORMINA
VERCELLI

9
AGRIGENTO
BENEVENTO
CATANZARO
CATTOLICA
FROSINONE
GALLIPOLI
PONTEDERA
SAN MARINO
 San Marino
SAN SEVERO
TERRACINA

10
CARAVAGGIO
PORTO TOLLE
SENIGALLIA

11
ALESSANDRIA
CALTAGIRONE
DOMODOSSOLA

12
ASCOLI PICENO
BUSTO ARSIZIO
PORTOFERRAIO

13
CALTANISSETTA
CASTELLAMMARE
CASTROVILLARI
CIVITAVECCHIA
TORRE DEL GRECO

15
TORRE ANNUNZIATA

16
REGGIO DI CALABRIA

Geography – Towns & Cities – Europe – NETHERLANDS

3	**4**	**5**		**6**		**7**
EDE	LEEK	ASSEN	GOUDA	ALMELO	LEIDEN	ALKMAAR
OSS	UDEN	BREDA	HOORN	ARNHEM	VELSEN	DEN HAAG
URK		DELFT	OMMEN	BUSSUM	ZWOLLE	(or 's-Gravenhage,
		EMMEN	VENLO	KAMPEN		The Hague)
			ZEIST			

HAARLEM
HEERLEN
HELMOND
HENGELO
KATWIJK
TILBURG
UTRECHT
ZAANDAM
ZUTPHEN

8
DELFZIJL
DEN BOSCH
  (or Bois-le-Duc,
  's-Hertogenbosch)
DEVENTER
ENSCHEDE
FLUSHING
  (or Vlissingen)
IJMUIDEN
KERKRADE
LELYSTAD
LONNEKER
NIJMEGEN
ROERMOND
SCHIEDAM

THE HAGUE
  (or Den Haag,
  's-Gravenhage)
VOLENDAM

9
AMSTERDAM
APELDOORN
BOIS-LE-DUC
  (or Den Bosch,
  's-Hertogenbosch)
DEN HELDER
DORDRECHT
EINDHOVEN
GORINCHEM
GRONINGEN
HILVERSUM
OLDENZAAL
ROTTERDAM
TERNEUZEN
ZANDVOORT

10
AMERSFOORT
HARDERWIJK
LEEUWARDEN

MAASTRICHT
ROOSENDAAL
VLISSINGEN
  (or Flushing)
WINSCHOTEN
ZOETERMEER

11
'S-GRAVENHAGE
  (or Den Haag,
  The Hague)
VLAARDINGNE
ZWIJNDRECHT

12
BERGEN OP ZOOM

13
HOOK OF HOLLAND
  (or Hoek van Holland)

14
HOEK VAN HOLLAND
  (or Hook of Holland)
'S-HERTOGENBOSCH
  (or Bois-le-Duc, Den Bosch)

Geography – Towns & Cities – Europe – SCANDINAVIA

3
GOL Norway
LIT Sweden
SKI Norway
VIK Iceland,
  Norway

4
ÅNGE Sweden
BODÖ Norway
HÖFN Iceland
KEMI Finland
KØGE Denmark
LUND Sweden

MOSS Norway
OSLO Norway
OULU Finland
PORI Finland
RENA Norway
TANA Norway
TORP Sweden

UMEÅ Sweden
VOSS Norway

5
ÅRHUS Denmark
BODEN Sweden
BORAS Sweden

FALUN Sweden
FLORØ Norway
GÄVLE Sweden
GRENÅ Denmark
HAMAR Norway
HANGÖ Finland
INARI Finland
KOTKA Finland
LAHTI Finland
LULEÅ Sweden
MALMO Sweden
NAMPA Finland
PITEÅ Sweden
RAAHE Finland
SKIEN Norway
SKIVE Denmark
SNÅSA Norway
TURKU Finland
VAASA Finland
VADSÖ Norway
VÄXJÖ Sweden
VEJLE Denmark
VISBY Sweden
YSTAD Sweden

6

ABENRA Denmark
ÅLBORG Denmark
ARVIKA Sweden
ASSENS Denmark
BERGEN Norway
DOMBÅS Norway
EKENÄS Finland
FÅBORG Denmark
HORTEN Norway
KALMAR Sweden
KIRUNA Sweden
KOLARI Finland

KORSØR Denmark
KUOPIO Finland
LARVIK Norway
MANDAL Norway
MOTALA Sweden
MUONIO Finland
NAMSOS Norway
NARVIK Norway
NYBORG Denmark
ODENSE Denmark
OLHAVA Finland
ÖREBRO Sweden
TØNDER Denmark
TORNIO Finland
TROMSÖ Norway
VÄNNÄS Sweden
VIBORG Denmark

7

ÅLESUND Norway
ARENDAL Norway
DRAMMEN Norway
ESBJERG Denmark
HERNING Denmark
HOLBAEK Denmark
HORSENS Denmark
HUSAVIK Iceland
KAJAANI Finland
KARUNKI Finland
KOKKOLA Finland
KOLDING Denmark
LUDVIKA Sweden
NAKSKOV Denmark
NYSÄTRA Sweden
RANDERS Denmark
SALTDAL Norway
SELFOSS Iceland
SOLSTAD Norway

TAMPERE Finland
UPPSALA Sweden
VARBERG Sweden

8

AKUREYRI Iceland
ALINGSÅS Sweden
ARJEPLOG Sweden
BLONDUOS Iceland
BORLÄNGE Sweden
GÖTEBORG
  (or Gothenburg) Sweden
HALMSTAD Sweden
HELSINKI
  (or Helsingfors) Finland
HILLERØD Denmark
HJØRRING Denmark
HÖNEFOSS Norway
JOKKMOKK Sweden
KARLSTAD Sweden
KEFLAVIK Iceland
LYCKSELE Sweden
NAESTVED Denmark
NYKØBING Denmark
NYKÖPING Sweden
RINGSTED Denmark
ROSKILDE Denmark
SLAGELSE Denmark
STENSELE Sweden
TÖNSBERG Norway
VÄSTERÅS Sweden
VATNEYRI Iceland

9

BORGARNES Iceland
ENONTEKIÖ Finland
GÄLLIVARE Sweden
HADERSLEV Denmark

HÄRNÖSAND Sweden
HAUGESUND Norway
HELSINGØR Denmark
JACOBSTAD Finland
JÖNKÖPING Sweden
JYVÄSKYLÄ Finland
KEMIJÄRVI Finland
KØBENHAVN
 (or Copenhagen)
 Denmark
LINKÖPING Sweden
ÖSTERSUND Sweden
REYKJAVIK Iceland
ROVANIEMI Finland
SARPSBORG Norway
SAVUKOSKI Finland
SILKEBORG Denmark
SÖDERHAMN Sweden
STAVANGER Norway
STOCKHOLM Sweden
SUNDSVALL Sweden
SVENDBORG Denmark
TRONDHEIM Norway
UDDEVALLA Sweden
VASTERVIK Sweden

10
BENGTSFORS Sweden
COPENHAGEN
 (or København)
 Denmark
DJÚPIVOGUR Iceland
ESKILSTUNA Sweden
FREDERICIA Denmark
GOTHENBURG
 (or Göteborg) Sweden
HAMMERFEST Norway
KARLSKRONA Sweden
LANDSKRONA Sweden
MIDDLEFART Denmark
NORRKÖPING Sweden
SKELLEFTEÅ Sweden
SØNDERBORG
 Denmark
SUNDBYBERG Sweden
TRELLEBORG Sweden

11
ESKIFJÖRDUR Iceland
FREDRIKSTAD Norway
HÅLSINGBORG Sweden
HELSINGFORS
 (or Helsinki) Finland
LILLEHAMMER Norway

SKANDERBORG
 Denmark
VORDINGBORG
 Denmark

12
KRISTIANSAND Norway
KRISTIANSTAD Sweden
KRISTIANSUND
 Norway
ÖRNSKÖLDSVIK
 Sweden
SANDNESSJÖEN
 Norway
UUSIKAUPUNKI Finland

13
FREDERIKSHAVN
 Denmark
HAFNARFJÖRDUR
 Iceland
SEYDISFJÖRDUR
 Iceland

14
CHARLOTTENBERG
 Sweden

Geography – Towns & Cities – Europe – SOUTH-EAST EUROPE

3
BAR Montenegro
BOR Serbia
NIŠ Serbia
PEĆ Serbia

4
ARAD Romania
BROD Macedonia
CLUJ Romania
FOČA Bosnia-Herzegovina

IASI (or Jassy) Romania
PTUJ Slovenia
PULA Croatia
RUMA Serbia
RUSE Slovenia

5

ARGOS Greece
BACAU Romania
BERAT Albania
BIHAĆ Bosnia-
  Herzegovina
BRČKO Bosnia-
  Herzegovina
BREZA Bosnia-
  Herzegovina
BUDVA Montenegro
CANEA
  (or Khanía) Greece
CELJÉ Slovenia
CHIOS Greece
CORFU
  (or Kérkyra) Greece
ÇORLU European
  Turkey
DOBOJ Bosnia-
  Herzegovina
DRAMA Greece
JASSY
  (or Iasi) Romania
KHIOS Greece
KOPER Slovenia
KORÇÉ Albania
KUKÉS Albania
LAMIA Greece
OHRID Macedonia
PIRAN Slovenia
PIROT Serbia
SIBIU Romania
SISAK Croatia
SOFIA Bulgaria
SPLIT Croatia
TUZLA Bosnia-
  Herzegovina

UŽICE Serbia
VARNA Bulgaria
VIDIN Bulgaria
VLORË Albania
VOLOS Greece
ZADAR Croatia
ZANTE
  (or Zakynthos) Greece

6

ATHENS Greece
BITOLA Macedonia
BRĂILA Romania
BRAŞOV Romania
BURGAS Bulgaria
DELPHI Greece
DURRËS Albania
EDIRNE European
  Turkey
GALAŢI Romania
KAVALA Greece
KHANÍA
  (or Canea) Greece
KOZANI Greece
LINDOS Greece
MOSTAR Bosnia-
  Herzegovina
NIKŠIĆ Montenegro
ORADEA Romania
OSIJEK Croatia
PATRAS Greece
PLEVEN Bulgaria
RHODES Greece
RIJEKA Croatia
ROUSSE Bulgaria
SERRAI Greece
SHUMEN Bulgaria
SKOPJE Macedonia

SLIVEN Bulgaria
SPARTA Greece
TIRANA Albania
TULCEA Romania
VRATSA Bulgaria
XANTHI Greece
ZAGREB Croatia
ZENICA Bosnia-
  Herzegovina

7

CETINJE Montengro
CHALCIS Greece
CORINTH
  (or Kórinthos) Greece
CRAIOVA Romania
FOCŞANI Romania
GIURGIU Romania
GLYFADA Greece
KÉRKYRA
  (or Corfu) Greece
LARISSA Greece
NAUPLIA
  (or Nauplion) Greece
NEGOTIN Serbia
NOVI SAD Serbia
PIRAEUS Greece
PLOVDIV Bulgaria
SHKODËR Albania
SIBENIK Croatia
TRAVNIK Bosnia-
  Herzegovina
TRIPOLI Greece
VALJEVO Serbia
ZAGORJE Slovenia
ZVORNIK Bosnia-
  Herzegovina

8
AGRINION Greece
BELGRADE Serbia
DERVENTA Bosnia-
  Herzegovina
GOSTIVAR Macedonia
IOANNINA Greece
IRÁKLION Greece
ISTANBUL European Turkey
KALAMATA Greece
KARLOVAC Croatia
KASTORIA Greece
KHASKOVO Bulgaria
KOMOTINI Greece
KUMANOVO Macedonia
MYTILENE Greece
NAUPLION
  (or Nauplia) Greece
PLJEVLJA Montenegro
PLOIEŞTI Romania
POSTOJNA Slovenia
PRIJEDOR Bosnia-Herzegovina
PRISTINA Serbia
SARAJEVO Bosnia-Herzegovina
SATU MARE Romania
SUBOTICA Serbia
TEKIRDAĞ European Turkey
TRIKKALA Greece

9
BANJA LUKA Bosnia-
  Herzegovina
BUCHAREST Romania
CONSTANŢA Romania
DUBROVNIK Croatia

GALLIPOLI European Turkey
GEVGELIJA Macedonia
KALAMARIA Greece
KÓRINTHOS
  (or Corinth) Greece
LJUBLJANA Slovenia
NOVO MESTO Slovenia
OBRENOVAC Serbia
PODGORICA Montenegro
SMEDEREVO Serbia
TIMIŞOARA Romania
ZAKYNTHOS
  (or Zante) Greece
ZRENJANIN Serbia

10
KYUSTENDIL Bulgaria
SREBRENICA Bosnia-Herzegovina
TIRGU MURES Romania

11
BIJELO POLJE Montenegro
GJIROKASTËR Albania
NOVA GORICA Slovenia
STARA ZAGORA Bulgaria

12
THESSALONÍKI Greece

13
RÂMNICU VÂLCEA Romania

15
ALEXANDROUPOLIS Greece

Geography – Towns & Cities – Europe – SPAIN & PORTUGAL
In Spain unless stated

3
FOZ
TUI Portugal

4
ADRA
AOIZ
BAZA
BEJA Portugal
FARO Portugal
IRUN
JACA
JAÉN
LEÓN
LOJA
LUGO
MULA
OLOT
OVAR Portugal
REUS
VICH
VIGO

5
AINSA
ALCOY
ALTEA
ATECA
AVILA
BAENA
BÉJAR
BERJA
BRAGA Portugal
CADIZ
CASPE

CEUTA
DENIA
ÉCIJA
ELCHE
ELVAS Portugal
EVORA Portugal
FRAGA
GIJÓN
GRADO
LAGOS Portugal
LALIN
LIRIA
LORCA
LOULÉ Portugal
MAHÓN
MIJAS
MORÓN
MUGIA
NAVIA
NERJA
OLIVA
OSUNA
PALMA
RIAÑO
RONDA
ROSAS
SALOU
SORIA
SUECA
TOMAR Portugal
TREMP
UBEDA
VALLS
VISEU Portugal
YECLA

ZAFRA

6
AGUEDA Portugal
ALCIRA
AVEIRO Portugal
AZUAGA
BARGAS
BILBAO
BLANES
BURGOS
CAMBRE
CUENZA
ESTEPA
GANDÍA
GIRONA
GUADIX
GUARDA Portugal
HELLÍN
HUELVA
HUESCA
JATIVA
LAMEGO Portugal
LAREDO
LEIRIA
LÉRIDA
LISBON Portugal
LLANES
LLORTS Andorra
LUARCA
MADRID
MALAGA
MARTOS
MATARÓ
MÉRIDA

MIERES
MONZÓN
MOTRIL
MURCIA
NAZARÉ Portugal
OLMEDO
OPORTO Portugal
ORENSE
OVIEDO
PINEDA
RIPOLL
SAGRES Portugal
SILVES Portugal
SITGES
SOLDEU Andorra
TAVIRA Portugal
TERUEL
TOLEDO
TOLOSA
TOTANA
TUDELA
UTRERA
VIELLA
VIVERO
ZAMORA

7
AGUILAS
ALCARAZ
ALJEZUR Portugal
ALLARIZ
ALMANSA
ALMERÍA
AMADORA Portugal
AMPOSTA

ANDÚJAR
ARACENA
ARGANDA
ASTORGA
AVEINTA
BADAJOZ
CÁCARES
CAMINHA Portugal
CARMONA
CASCAIS Portugal
CEHEGIN
COIMBRA
CÓRDOBA
COVILHÃ Portugal
CULLERO
DAIMIEL
DURANGO
ESTELLA
ESTORIL Portugal
FUNCHAL Portugal
GRANADA
IRURZUN
JUMILLA
LA LINEA
LA UNIÓN
LINARES
LOGROÑO
MALGRAT
MANRESA
MAYORGA
MÉRTOLA Portugal
MOJÁCAR
MONTORO
NOVELDA
OURENSE
PALAMÓS
PLENCIA
PORT BOU

RIBADEO
SAGUNTO
SANTOÑA
SARRIÓN
SEGOVIA
SETÚBAL Portugal
SEVILLE
TAFALLA
TARRASA
TORTOSA
VINAROZ
VITORIA

8
ABRANTES Portugal
ALBACETE
ALBORAYA
ALENQUER Portugal
ALICANTE
ARANJUEZ
AYAMONTE
BADALONA
BEMBIBRE
BENIDORM
BETANZOS
BRAGANÇA Portugal
CARAVACA
CARBALLO
ESTEPONA
ESTREMOS Portugal
FIGUERAS
GUERNICA
LA CORUÑA
LA GUDIÑA
LAS ROZAS
MARBELLA
MARCHENA
MARQUINA

MAZARRÓN
ORIHUELA
PALENCIA
PAMPLONA
PORTIMÃO Portugal
SABADELL
SAN ROQUE
SANTAREM
TARAZONA
TRUJILLO
VALENCIA
VILALLER
VILA REAL Portugal
VILLALBA
ZARAGOZA

9
ALBUFEIRA Portugal
ALGECIRAS
ANTEQUERA
ASTILLERO
BARAKALDO
BARCELONA
BENAVENTE
BUJARALOZ
CALAHORRA
CALATAYUD
CAÑAVERAL
CARTAGENA
DON BENITO
GIBRALTAR Gibraltar
GUIMARAES Portugal
MARMOLEJO
MORATELLA
PEÑÍSCOLA
PLASENCIA
RIBADAVIA
SALAMANCA

SANTANDER
TARRAGONA
VILLARCAY

10
CARCAGENTE
CARCAVELOS
  Portugal
CIUDAD REAL
FONSAGRADA
FUENGIROLA
LA CAROLINA
MANZANARES
ONTENIENTE
PONFERRADA
PONTEVEDRA
PORTALEGRE Portugal
POZOBLANCO
SANTILLANA
TOSSA DE MAR
VALDEPEÑAS
VALLADOLID
VILLANUEVA

11
FUENLABRADA

GARROVILLAS
GUADALAJARA
LLORET DE MAR
POLA DE SIERO
PUENTE GENIL
PUERTO BANÚS
PUERTOLLANO
RIBADESELLA
SAN FERNANDO
TORDESILLAS
TORREBLANCA
TORRELAVEGA

12
ALCALA LA REAL
HUÉRCAL OVERA
SAN SEBASTIAN
TORREMOLINOS
TORRES VEDRAS
  Portugal
VILLAVICIOSA

13
ARANDA DE DUERO
CASTELO BRANCO
  Portugal

CIUDAD RODRIGO
FIGUERIRA DA FOZ
FUENTEOBEJUNA
ROQUETAS DE MAR
SAMA DE LANGREO
VILLARROBLEDO

14
ANDORRA LA VELLA Andorra
CALDAS DE RAINHA Portugal
MEDINA DEL CAMPO
TORREDONJIMENO
VIANA DO CASTELO Portugal
VILA NOVA DE GAIA Portugal
VITORIA-GASTEIZ

15
ALCALÁ DE HENARES
MEDINA DE RIOSECO
MONFORTE DE LEMOS

17
JERÉZ DE LA FRONTERA

Geography – Towns & Cities – Europe – SWITZERLAND

3	BERN	THUN	BASEL	OUCHY	**6**
BEX	(or Berne)		BERNE	SPIEZ	BRIENZ
WIL	BIEL	**5**	(or Bern)	USTER	GENEVA
ZUG	BRIG	AARAU	BUCHS	VADUZ	GLARUS
	CHUR	AIGLE	DAVOS	Liechtenstein	GOSSAU
4	NYON	ARBON	GLAND	VEVEY	GSTAAD
BAAR	SION	BADEN	OLTEN		HORGEN

LUGANO	VERBIER	ZOFINGEN	WINTERTHUR
SAANEN	ZERMATT		
SCHWYZ		**9**	**11**
SIERRE	**8**	ANDERMATT	GRINDELWALD
THUSIS	BAD RAGAZ	NEUCHÂTEL	
ZERNEZ	BURGDORF	RORSCHACH	**12**
ZÜRICH	DELÉMONT	SOLOTHURN	SCHAFFHAUSEN
	DIETIKON	WÄDENSWIL	
7	FRIBOURG		**14**
ALTDORF	KLOSTERS	**10**	LA CHAUX DE FONDS
HERISAU	LAUSANNE	BELLINZONA	
LIESTAL	MARTIGNY	EINSIEDELN	**15**
LOCARNO	MONTREUX	FRAUENFELD	YVERDON-LES-BAINS
LUCERNE	ST GALLEN	INTERLAKEN	
MONTHEY	ST MORITZ	RAPPERSWIL	

Geography – Towns & Cities – North America – CANADA

4	DAWSON	**7**	SUDBURY	HAMILTON
AJAX	GANDER	BRANDON	TIMMINS	HAY RIVER
HOPE	GILLAM	CALGARY	TISDALE	HAZELTON
HULL	INUVIK	CAMROSE	TORONTO	KAMLOOPS
NAIN	JASPER	CHATHAM	WEYBURN	KINGSTON
WAWA	KENORA	ESTEVAN	WIARTON	MCMURRAY
	LONDON	HALIFAX	WINDSOR	MELVILLE
5	NAKINA	IQALUIT	WYNYARD	MONTREAL
BANFF	NELSON	KELOWNA	YORKTON	MOOSE JAW
GASPÉ	OSHAWA	KITIMAT		MOOSONEE
LEDUC	OTTAWA	LA RONGE	**8**	NORTH BAY
ROUYN	QUEBEC	MELFORT	BATHURST	PEMBROKE
SOREL	REGINA	MONCTON	COCHRANE	RIMOUSKI
TABER	SOURIS	NANAIMO	CORNWALL	ROSETOWN
	SYDNEY	ORILLIA	EDMONTON	SEPT-ÎLES
6	THE PAS	QUESNEL	FLIN FLON	THOMPSON
ARVIDA	WABUSH	RED DEER	GLACE BAY	VICTORIA
BIGGAR		ST JOHN'S	GOOSE BAY	WINNIPEG

9
BRANTFORD
CHURCHILL
DARTMOUTH
FORT CHIMO
JONQUIÈRE
KANGIRSUK
KITCHENER
LUNENBURG
OWEN SOUND
PENTICTON
SAINT JOAN
SASKATOON
VANCOUVER

10
CHICOUTIMI
DRUMHELLER
EDMUNDSTON
FORT GEORGE
FORT NELSON

FORT ST JOHN
GRAND FALLS
LETHBRIDGE
MAPLE CREEK
NEW GLASGOW
PEACE RIVER
PORT ALFRED
PORT RADIUM
SHAWINIGAN
SHERBROOKE
ST BONIFACE
TERRACE BAY
THUNDER BAY
WETASKIWIN
WHITEHORSE

11
CAMPBELLTON
CORNER BROOK
DAWSON CREEK
FORT MACLEOD

FREDERICTON
KAPUSKASING
LAKE HARBOUR
MEDICINE HAT
MISSISSAUGA
NORMAN WELLS
POWELL RIVER
ST HYACINTHE
TUKTOYAKTUK
URANIUM CITY
VALLEYFIELD
YELLOWKNIFE

12
KIRKLAND LAKE
NIAGARA FALLS
PETERBOROUGH
PRINCE ALBERT
PRINCE GEORGE
PRINCE RUPERT
SIOUX LOOKOUT

ST CATHERINE'S
SWIFT CURRENT
WILLIAMS LAKE

13
BATTLE HARBOUR
CHARLOTTETOWN
FORT MCPHERSON
FORT VERMILION
GRANDE PRAIRIE
SAULT STE MARIE
SCHEFFERVILLE
TROIS RIVIÈRES

14
FORT PROVIDENCE
NEW WESTMINSTER
PORT AUX BASQUES

15
NORTH BATTLEFORD

Geography – Towns & Cities – North America – USA

4
ELKO
ERIE
GARY
HILO
LIMA
LYNN
MESA
NOME
RENO
ROME
TROY

WACO
YORK
YUMA

5
AKRON
BAKER
BELEN
BOISE
BUTTE
CRAIG
DOVER

FARGO
FLINT
HAVRE
HURON
MACON
MALTA
MIAMI
MINOT
NEPHI
OGDEN
OMAHA
OZARK

PARIS
PROVO
SALEM
SELMA
SITKA
TAMPA
TULSA
TYLER
UKIAH
UTICA

6
ALBANY
AUBURN
AURORA
AUSTIN
BANGOR
BILOXI
BOSTON
CAMDEN
CANTON
CASPER
DALLAS

DAYTON
DEL RIO
DENTON
DENVER
DULUTH
DURHAM
ELMIRA
EL PASO
EUGENE
EUREKA
FRESNO
HELENA

ITHACA
JOLIET
JOPLIN
JUNEAU
KAILUA
KODIAK
LAREDO
LAWTON
LOWELL
MOBILE
MOLINE
MONROE

NAPLES	CONCORD	ROSWELL	HANNIBAL	WHEELING
NASHUA	CORDOVA	RUTLAND	HARTFORD	
NEWARK	DECATUR	SAGINAW	HONOLULU	**9**
ODESSA	DENISON	SAN JOSÉ	IOWA CITY	ALLENTOWN
ORANGE	DETROIT	SANTA FÉ	IRONWOOD	ANCHORAGE
OSWEGO	DURANGO	SEATTLE	LA CROSSE	ANNAPOLIS
OXFORD	ELK CITY	SPOKANE	LAKELAND	ARLINGTON
OXNARD	EVERETT	ST CLOUD	LAS VEGAS	ASHEVILLE
PAYSON	GADSDEN	ST LOUIS	LAWRENCE	ASHTABULA
PEORIA	HAMMOND	TRENTON	MELBOURNE	BALTIMORE
PIERRE	HAMPTON	VALLEJO	MERIDIAN	BETHLEHEM
PUEBLO	HOUSTON	VENTURA	MISSOULA	BIDDEFORD
QUINCY	JACKSON	WAHIAWA	MONTEREY	BLACKFOOT
RACINE	KEARNEY	WICHITA	MOORHEAD	CAMBRIDGE
SEWARD	KEY WEST	YANKTON	MUSKOGEE	CHAMPAIGN
SPARKS	LANSING	YONKERS	NEW HAVEN	CHARLOTTE
ST PAUL	LARAMIE		NORTHWAY	CLEVELAND
TACOMA	LINCOLN	**8**	OAK RIDGE	DAVENPORT
TELLER	LIVONIA	ABERDEEN	OGALLALA	DES MOINES
TOLEDO	LUBBOCK	AMARILLO	PALO ALTO	DODGE CITY
TOPEKA	MADISON	ANN ARBOR	PASADENA	EAU CLAIRE
TOWSON	MEDFORD	APPLETON	PATERSON	ELIZABETH
TUCSON	MEMPHIS	BEAUMONT	PORTLAND	FAIRBANKS
TUPELO	MIDLAND	BERKELEY	RICHMOND	FALL RIVER
URBANA	MODESTO	BIG DELTA	ROCKFORD	FORT SMITH
WAUSAU	NEWPORT	BILLINGS	SAN DIEGO	FORT WAYNE
WINONA	NEW YORK	BISMARCK	SAN MATEO	FORT WORTH
YAKIMA	NORFOLK	BROCKTON	SANTA ANA	FRANKFORT
	OAKLAND	CHANDLER	SARASOTA	GALVESTON
7	OILDALE	CHEYENNE	SAVANNAH	HENDERSON
ABILENE	OLYMPIA	COLUMBIA	SCRANTON	HOLLYWOOD
ALTOONA	ORLANDO	COLUMBUS	SHERIDAN	JAMESTOWN
ATLANTA	OSHKOSH	DEARHORN	STAMFORD	JOHNSTOWN
AUGUSTA	PHOENIX	FLORENCE	ST JOSEPH	KALAMAZOO
BAY CITY	RALEIGH	GASTONIA	STOCKTON	KNOXVILLE
BOZEMAN	READING	GLENDALE	SUPERIOR	LAFAYETTE
BUFFALO	REDDING	GREEN BAY	SYRACUSE	LANCASTER
CHICAGO	ROANOKE	GULFPORT	WATERLOO	LAS CRUCES

LEXINGTON
LONG BEACH
MILES CITY
MILWAUKEE
NANTUCKET
NASHVILLE
NEW LONDON
OWENSBORO
PALM BEACH
PAWTUCKET
PEARL CITY
PENSACOLA
PINE BLUFF
POCATELLO
PRINCETON
RAPID CITY
RIVERSIDE
ROCHESTER
SAN ANGELO
SANTA ROSA
SIOUX CITY
SOUTH BEND
TEXARKANA
TWIN FALLS
VANCOUVER
WATERBURY
WORCESTER

10

ALEXANDRIA
BATON ROUGE
BELLINGHAM
BIRMINGHAM
BRIDGEPORT
BURLINGTON
CARSON CITY
CEDAR FALLS

CHARLESTON
CHESAPEAKE
CINCINNATI
CUMBERLAND
EVANSVILLE
GRAND FORKS
GRANT'S PASS
GREENSBORO
GREENVILLE
HAGERSTOWN
HARRISBURG
HUNTINGTON
HUNTSVILLE
IDAHO FALLS
JERSEY CITY
KANSAS CITY
LITTLE ROCK
LONG BRANCH
LOS ANGELES
LOUISVILLE
MANCHESTER
MIAMI BEACH
MONTGOMERY
MONTPELIER
NEW BEDFORD
NEW BRITAIN
NEW ORLEANS
OREGON CITY
PETERSBURG
PITTSBURGH
PORT ARTHUR
PORTSMOUTH
PROVIDENCE
ROCK ISLAND
SACRAMENTO
SAN ANTONIO
SANTA MARIA

SHREVEPORT
SIOUX FALLS
TERRE HAUTE
TUSCALOOSA
WASHINGTON
WATERVILLE
WILMINGTON
WOONSOCKET
YOUNGSTOWN

11

ALBUQUERQUE
BAKERSFIELD
BOULDER CITY
BROKEN ARROW
BROWNSVILLE
CEDAR RAPIDS
CHATTANOOGA
EAST ST LOUIS
GRAND RAPIDS
JOHNSON CITY
LAKE CHARLES
MINNEAPOLIS
NEWPORT NEWS
NORTH PLATTE
PALM SPRINGS
REDWOOD CITY
ROCK SPRINGS
SANTA MONICA
SCHENECTADY
SPRINGFIELD
TALLAHASSEE

12

ATLANTIC CITY
DAYTONA BEACH
FAYETTEVILLE

INDEPENDENCE
INDIANAPOLIS
JACKSONVILLE
KLAMATH FALLS
NEW BRUNSWICK
NIAGARA FALLS
OKLAHOMA CITY
PHILADELPHIA
POUGHKEEPSIE
SALT LAKE CITY
SAN FRANCISCO
SANTA BARBARA
ST PETERSBURG
WICHITA FALLS
WINSTON-SALEM

13

CAPE GIRARDEAU
COUNCIL BLUFFS
CORPUS CHRISTI
GRAND JUNCTION
JEFFERSON CITY
SAN BERNARDINO
SAN LUIS OBISPO
VIRGINIA BEACH
WEST PALM BEACH

14

FORT LAUDERDALE

15

COLORADO SPRINGS
FORT WALTON BEACH

Geography – Towns & Cities – SOUTH AMERICA In Brazil unless stated

3
ICA Peru
UBÁ

4
AZUL Argentina
BUGA Colombia
CALI Colombia
CODÓ
CORO Venezuela
GOYA Argentina
LIMA Peru
MELO Uruguay
PUNO Peru

5
ARAXÁ
ARICA Chile
BÁHIA
BAURU
BELÉM
CEARÁ
CUZCO Peru
JUNÍN Argentina
LA PAZ Bolivia
NATAL
ORURO Bolivia
PASTO Colombia
PIURA Peru
QUITO Ecuador
ROCHA Uruguay
SALTA Argentina
SALTO Uruguay
SUCRE Bolivia
TACNA Peru

TALCA Chile
TUNJA Colombia

6
ALAUSI Ecuador
AMBATO Ecuador
BOGOTÁ Colombia
CALLAO Peru
CAMETA
CAMPOS
CANOAS
CÚCUTA Colombia
CUENCA Ecuador
CUIABÁ
CUMANA Venezuela
IBAGUÉ Colombia
IBARRA Ecuador
ILHÉUS
JEQUIE
KOUROU Guyana
MACAPÁ
MACEIÓ
MANAUS
MERIDA Venezuela
OBIDOS
OLINDA
OSORNO Chile
PARANÁ Argentina
POTOSÍ Bolivia
QUIBDÓ Colombia
RECIFE
SANTOS
SOBRAL
TALTAL Chile
TANDIL Argentina

TARIJA Bolivia
TEMUCO Chile
TRELEW Argentina
VALERA Venezuela
VIEDMA Argentina
ZÁRATE Argentina

7
ARACAJU
ARMENIA Colombia
BARINAS Venezuela
CÁCERES
CARACAS Venezuela
CAYENNE Guyana
CHILLAN Chile
CODAJAS
COPIAPÓ Chile
CÓRDOBA Argentina
CORUMBÁ
DOLARES Argentina
GOIÂNIA
GUANARE Venezuela
IQUIQUE Chile
IQUITOS Peru
ITABUNA
LA OROYA Peru
LA PLATA Argentina
LINARES Chile
MACHALA Ecuador
MARACAY Venezuela
MATURIN Venezuela
MENDOZA Argentina
MOSSORÓ
NEUQUÉN Argentina
NITERÓI

PALMIRA Colombia
PELOTAS
PEREIRA Colombia
POPAYAN Colombia
POSADAS Argentina
QUILMES Argentina
QUILPUÉ Chile
ROSARIO Argentina
SANTA FÉ Argentina
SÃO JOSÉ
SÃO LUIS
STANLEY Falkland Islands
SULLANA Peru
UBERABA
VITÓRIA

8
ACARIGUA Venezuela
ALTAMIRA
ANÁPOLIS
AREQUIPA Peru
ASUNCIÓN Paraguay
AYACUCHO Peru
BOA VISTA
BRAGANÇA
BRASILIA
CARÚPANO Venezuela
CASTANHAL
CHICLAYO Peru
CHIMBOTE Peru
COQUIMBO Chile
CURITIBA
DEMERARA Guyana
DOURADOS
FONTE BOA
HUANCAYO Peru
ITAITUBA
JABOATÃO

LA GUAIRA Venezuela
LA SERENA Chile
LINHARES
LONDRINA
MAGANGUE Colombia
MEDELLÍN Colombia
MERCEDES Argentina
MOLLENDO Peru
NOVA LIMA
PAMPLONA Colombia
PARNAIBA
PAYSANDÚ Uruguay
PUCALLPA Peru
RANCAGUA Chile
RIOBAMBA Ecuador
RIOHACHA Colombia
RIO LARGO
RIO TINTO
SALVADOR
SANTAREM
SANTIAGO Chile
SÃO PAULO
SOROCABA
TERESINA
TRUJILLO Peru
UMUARAMA
VALDIVIA Chile
VALENCIA Venezuela

9
ARAÇATUBA
ARAGUAÍNA
ARIQUEMES
BARBACENA
BARCELONA Venezuela
CAJAMARCA Peru
CANELONES Uruguay
CARTAGENA Colombia

CATAMARCA Argentina
CHIVILCOY Argentina
CONCORDIA Argentina
FLORENCIA Colombia
FORTALEZA
GUAYAQUIL Ecuador
LATACUNGA Ecuador
MANIZALES Colombia
MARACAIBO Venezuela
OLAVARRÍA Argentina
PARAGUARI Paraguay
PERGAMINO Argentina
RIO BRANCO
RIO GRANDE
SAN FELIPE Venezuela
SANTA CRUZ Bolivia
SANTA ROSA Argentina
SINCELEJO Colombia
TOCOPILLA Chile

10
COCHABAMBA Bolivia
CONCEPCÍON Chile,
  Paraguay
CORRIENTES Argentina
ESMERALDES Ecuador
FRAY BENTOS Uruguay
GEORGETOWN Guyana
JOÃO PESSOA
JUIZ DE FORA
LAMBAYEQUE Peru
LOS ANGELES Chile
MONTEVIDEO Uruguay
NOVA IGUAÇU
PARAMARIBO Suriname
PERNAMBUCO
PETRÓPOLIS
PORTO VELHO

PORTOVIEJO Ecuador
SAN NICOLÁS Argentina
SANTA MARIA + Colombia
SANTO ANDRÉ
SETE LAGOAS
TALCAHUANO Chile
TRÊS LAGOAS
URUGUAIANA
VALPARAÍSO Chile
VILLA MARIA Argentina
VILLARRICA Paraguay
VIÑA DEL MAR Chile

11
ANTOFAGASTA Chile
BAHÍA BLANCA Argentina
BUCARAMANGA
   Colombia
BUENOS AIRES Argentina
CAMPO GRANDE
GENERAL ROCA Argentina
MAR DEL PLATA Argentina
PONTA GROSSA
PORTO ALEGRE

PUERTO MONTT Chile
PUNTA ARENAS Chile
RIO GALLEGOS
   Argentina
SAN BERNARDO Chile

12
BARQUISIMETO
   Venezuela
BARRANQUILLA
   Colombia
BUENAVENTURA
   Colombia
CERRO DE PASCO Peru
MONTES CLAROS
NEW AMSTERDAM
   Guyana
NOVA FRIBURGO
NOVO HAMBURGO
RIO DE JANEIRO
RONDONÓPOLIS
SAN CRISTÓBAL
   Venezuela
TEÓFILO OTÔNI

VOLTA REDONDA

13
BÉLO HORIZONTE
CAMPINA GRANDE
CIUDAD BOLIVAR
   Venezuela
CIUDAD GUAYANA
   Venezuela
FLORIANÓPOLIS
LOMAS DE ZAMORA
   Argentina
RIBEIRÃO PRÊTO
VILLAVICENCIO
   Colombia

14
FEIRA DE SANTANA
TRENQUE LAUQUEN
   Argentina

15
BAHÍA DE CARÁQUEZ
   Ecuador

History

History – Historical Events – BATTLES

3
ÁCS 1849
DIU 1537, 1545
GOA 1511, 1570
HUÉ 1968
ULM 1805

4
ACRE 1189, 1291
AIZU 1868
ALMA 1854
AONG 1857
BEDR 623
CAEN 1944
CEVA 1796
CYME 474 BC
DEEG 1804
GAZA 1917

GUAM 1944
IRUN 1837
ISLY 1844
IVRY 1590
JENA 1806
KARS 1877
KIEV 1941
KISO 1180
KULM 1813
LADE 494 BC
LAON 1814
LENS 1648
LODI 1796
ŁÓDŹ 1914
LOOS 1915
METZ 1870
MONS 1914
NIVE 1813

NOVI 1799, 1800
OHUD 623
ORAN 1509,
 1940
OREL 1943
POLA 1380
RAAB 1809
RIGA 1621
ROME 387 BC,
 408, 472, 546,
 1527
SCIO 1770
SETA 1183
SOHR 1745,
 1866
ST LÔ 1944
TOBA 1868
TORO 1476

TROY 1184 BC
TRUK 1944
WAWZ 1831
YALU 1894, 1904
ZAMA 202 BC
ZEIM 1877
ZELA 67 BC,
 47 BC

5
ACCRA 1824
ADUWA 1896
AISNE 1914,
 1917, 1918
ALAMO 1836
ALAND 1714
ALLIA 390 BC
ALSEN 1864

AMBUR 1749
ANJOU 1421
ANZIO 1944
ARCOT 1751
ARNEE 1751
ARRAS 1654,
  1917
ARSUF 1191
A SHAU 1966
AURAY 1364
BAHUR 1752
BANDA 1858
BASRA 2003
BEREA 1852
BOSRA 632
BOYNE 1690
BREST 1512
BRILL 1572
BUXAR 1764
CADIZ 1587
CAIRO 1517
CARPI 1701
CESME 1770
CHIOS 357 BC,
  201 BC
CRÉCY 1346
CRETE 1941
CUZCO 1536
DAK TO 1967
DELHI 1297,
  1398, 1803,
  1804
DOURO 1809
DOVER 1652
DREUX 1652
DUNES 1658
ELENA 1877
EL TEB 1884

ENGEN 1800
EYLAU 1807
GENOA 1746,
  1795
GINGI 1689
HANAU 1813
HANGÖ 1714
HERAT 1220
IMOLA 1797
IPSUS 301 BC
ISSUS 333 BC
JASSY 1620
JUNÍN 1824
KABUL 1842
KAGUL 1770
KALPI 1858
KAZAN 1552,
  1774
KOLIN 1757
KURSK 1943
LAGOS 1693,
  1759
LA PAZ 1865
LARGS 1263
LEWES 1264
LEYTE 1944
LIÈGE 1914
LIGNY 1815
LIPAU 1434
LISSA 1866
LUZON 1945
LYONS AD 197
MAIDA 1806
MALTA 1798
MARNE 1914,
  1918
MAXEN 1759
MAYPO 1818

MORAT 1476
MOTYA 398 BC
MUDKI 1845
MUNDA 45 BC
MURET 1213
MYLAE 260 BC
MYLEX 36 BC
NAJAF 2003,
  2004
NARVA 1700
NAXOS 376 BC
NIZIB 1839
ÖLAND 1789
OLPAE 426 BC
OTRAR 1219
PARIS 1814
PARMA 1734
PATAY 1429
PAVIA 568, 1431,
  1525
PERED 1849
PIROT 1885
PODOL 1866
POONA 1802
POSEN 1704
PYDNA 168 BC
RAMLA 1177
REIMS 1814
REVAL 1790
RIETI 1821
SAMOS 1824
SEDAN 1870
SELBY 1644
SEOUL 1950
SESIA 1524
SIRTE 1942
SLUYS 1340
SOMME 1916,

  1918
STOKE 1487
TACNA 1880
TAMAI 1884
TEXEL 1653
TOURS 732
TUNIS 255 BC
UCLES 1109
ULSAN 1904
UTICA 49 BC
VALMY 1792
VARNA 1444
VASAQ 1442
WAVRE 1815
WÖRTH 1817
XERES 711
YPRES 1914, 1915,
  1917, 1918
ZENTA 1697
ZNAIM 1809

6

AACHEN 1944
ABU KRU 1885
ACTIUM 31 BC
ALEPPO 1269,
  1400, 1516
ALFORD 1645
ALIWAL 1846
AL QAIM 2005
AMIENS 1870
ANGORA 1402
ARBELA 331 BC
ARCOLA 1796
ARGAUM 1803
ARKLOW 1798
ARNHEM 1944
ARQUES 1589

ARTOIS 1915
ASHTEE 1818
ASIAGO 1916
ASPERN 1809
ASSAYE 1803
ATBARA 1898
AUNEAU 1587
AUSSIG 1426
AZORES 1591
BAMIAN 1221
BARDIA 1941
BARNET 1471
BAYLEN 1808
BEAUGÉ 1421
BERGEN 1759
BERLIN 1945
BINGEN AD 70
BIRUAN 1221
BOROTA 2006
BOXTEL 1794
BOYACÁ 1819
BUSACO 1810
CABALA 379 BC
CALLAO 1866
CAMDEN 1780
CANDIA 1648
CANNAE 216 BC
CEPEDA 1859
CHANDA 1818
CHIARI 1701
CHILOE 1826
CITATE 1854
CNIDUS 394 BC
CONCON 1891
CUNAXA 401 BC
CYSSUS 191 BC
DANZIG 1627
DARGAI 1897

DELIUM 424 BC
DELPHI 355 BC
DENAIN 1712
DESSAU 1626
DIEPPE 1942
DIPAEA 471 BC
DJERBA 1560
DOLLAR 875
DUNBAR 1296,
 1650
DÜPPEL 1864
EDESSA AD 259
ELINGA 206 BC
EMBATA 356 BC
FAENZA 541
FAMARS 1793
FERKEH 1896
GAZALA 1942
GEBORA 1811
GISORS 1197
GROZNY 1994,
 1995
HALLUE 1870
HARLAW 1411
HASHIN 1885
HATTIN 1187
HAVANA 1748
HEXHAM 1464
HIMERA 480 BC,
 409 BC
HÖCHST 1622
HUESCA 1837
HYSIAE 669 BC
INCHON 1950
INGAVI 1841
INGOGO 1881
ISONZO 1915,
 1916, 1917

JALULA 637
JARNAC 1569
JHANSI 1857
JIJIGA 1977
KALISZ 1706
KAPPEL 1529,
 1531
KHELAT 1839
KIRKEE 1817
KOHIMA 1942
KOKEIN 1824
KOMORN 1849
KONIEH 1831
KRONIA 1738
KURDLA 1795
LANDEN 1693
LANNOY 1567
LARCAY 1829
LAUPEN 1339
LE MANS 1871
LEMNOS 1913
LONATO 1796
LOVCHA 1877
LUNDEN 1676
LUTTER 1626
LÜTZEN 1632,
 1813
MAJUBA 1881
MALAGA 1704
MALAYA 1941
MALDON 991
MANILA 1898
MARGUS AD 285
MEDINA 625
MEDOLA 1796
MEERUT 1398
MÉRIDA 712
MERTON 871

MIDWAY 1942
MINCIO 1796,
 1814
MINDEN 1759
MIRBAT 1972
MOHACS 1526,
 1687
MOSCOW 1941
MUKDEN 1905,
 1948
MULTAN 1848
MUTINA 43 BC
MYCALE 479 BC
MYTTON 1319
NACHOD 1866
NÄFELS 1388
NÁJARA 1367
NANHAN 1904
NARVIK 1940
NASEBY 1645
NOTIUM 407 BC
NOVARA 1513,
 1849
OCKLEY 851
OLMEDO 1467
OPORTO 1809
ORTHEZ 1814
ORTONA 1943
OSWEGO 1756
OTUMBA 1520
PANION 198 BC
PEKING 1214
PINKIE 1547
PLEI ME 1965
PRAGUE 1620, 1757
PUEBLA 1862
QUEBEC 1759
RABAUL 1943

RAPHIA 217 BC
RASZYN 1809
RIVOLI 1797
ROCROI 1643
ROLIÇA 1808
SACILE 1809
SADOWA 1866
SAIGON 1968
SALADO 1340
SANGRO 1943
SEPEIA 494 BC
SESKAR 1790
SHILOH 1862
SIFFIN 657
SILPIA 206 BC
SINOPE 1853
SORATA 1780
SYBOTA 443 BC
TARAWA 1943
TARBES 1814
TAURIS 47 BC
TERTRY 687
THEBES 335 BC
THURII 282 BC
TIFLIS 1386
TOBRUK 1941,
 1942
TOFREK 1885
TORGAU 1760
TOULON 1707,
 1744
TOWTON 1461
TSINAN 1948
TUDELA 1808
ULUNDI 1879
UROSAN 1595
USHANT 1778,
 1794

VARESE 1859
VERDUN 1916
VERONA 312
VIENNA 1683
VYBORG 1918
WAGRAM 1809
WAIZAN 1849
WARSAW 1656,
 1794, 1831,
 1914, 1918,
 1943, 1944
WERBEN 1631
WIAZMA 1812
YARMUK 636
ZALAKA 1086
ZAMORA 901
ZÜRICH 1799

7

ABU KLEA 1885
AGORDAT 1893
ALARCOS 1195
ALBUERA 1811
ALCOLEA 1868
ALIGARH 1803
ALKMAAR 1573,
 1799
ALMANSA 1707
ALNWICK 1093
AMOAFUL 1874
ANTIOCH
 244 BC, 1098
ARAUSIO 105 BC
ASCALON 1099
ASCULUM
 279 BC
ASHDOWN 871
ATHENRY 1316

ATLANTA 1864
AUGHRIM 1691
BADAJOZ 1812
BAGHDAD 1401,
 2003
BAPAUME 1871
BAROSSA 1811
BASSANO 1796
BATOCHE 1885
BAUTZEN 1813
BELMONT 1899
BENBURB 1646
BÉTHUNE 1707
BETIOCA 1813
BEZETHA AD 66
BITONTO 1734
BOKHARA 1220
BRECHIN 1452
BRESLAU 1757
BRIENNE 1814
BULL RUN 1861,
 1862
CADESIA 636
CALAFAT 1854
CARACHA 1813
CARGOUL 1739
CARRHAE 53 BC
CASSANO 1705,
 1799
CASSINO 1944
CHÂLONS 366,
 451
CHETATE 1854
CHOCZIM 1769
CHONG-JU 1904
CIBALIS 315
CLISSAU 1702
COLENSO 1899

COLOMBO 1796
CORINTH
 429 BC,
 394 BC, 1862
CORONEA
 429 BC, 394 BC
CORONEL 1914
CORUNNA 1809
COUTRAS 1587
CRAONNE 1814
CRAVANT 1423
CREFELD 1758
CREMONA
 200 BC, AD 69,
 1702
CRONION
 380 BC
CROTONE 982
CUASPAD 1863
CURICTA 49 BC
CUSTOZA 1866
CYZICUS 410 BC
CZASLAU 1742
DAZAIFU 1281
DEORHAM 577
DODOWAH 1826
DRESDEN 1813
DUNDALK 1318
DUNKELD 1689
DUNKIRK 1666,
 1940
DUPPLIN 1332
DURAZZO 1081
ECKMÜHL 1809
ECNOMUS
 256 BC
EL CANEY 1898
ELK HORN 1862

ENTHOLM 1676
EPHESUS 499 BC,
   262 BC
ESSLING 1809
ÉTAMPES 604
EVESHAM 1265
FALKIRK 1298,
   1746
FERRARA 1815
FLEURUS 1622,
   1690, 1794
FOCŠANI 1789
FORNHAM 1173
FORNOVO 1495
FULFORD 1066
GALICIA 1914
GHERAIN 1763
GORARIA 1857
GRANADA 1319
GRANSON 1476
GRASPAN 1899
GRENADA 1779,
   1983
GROCHÓW 1831
GUJARAT 1849
HASBAIN 1408
HERNANI 1836,
   1837
HERRERA 1837
HWAI-HAI 1948
IDSTÄDT 1850
IWO JIMA 1945
JAMAICA 1655
JAVA SEA 1942
JUTLAND 1916
KALUNGA 1814
KAMBULA 1879
KAPOLNA 1849

KASHGAL 1883
KHARKOV 1942,
   1943
KHE SANH 1968
KILSYTH 1645
KINLOSS 1009
KINSALE 1601
KLISSOW 1702
KOSSOVA 1448
KRASNOI 1812
KROTZKA 1739
LA HOGUE 1692
LARISSA 171 BC
LEGHORN 1653
LEGNANO 1176
LEIPZIG 1813
LEPANTO 1571
LEUCTRA 371 BC
LEUTHEN 1757
LINDLEY 1900
LOC NINH 1967
LUZZARA 1702
MAGENTA 1859
MAGNANO 1799
MAIWAND 1880
MALAKOV 1855
MANSURA 1250
MARENGO 1800
MARGATE 1387
MATCHIN 1791
MEEANEE 1843
MEMPHIS
   459 BC, 638,
   1862
MENTANA 1867
METHVEN 1306
MILAZZO 1860
MINORCA 1756

MÖCKERN 1813
MOGILEV 1812
MONDOVI 1796
MONTIEL 1369
NAISSUS AD 269
NAM DONG
   1964
NANKING 1949
NEUWIED 1797
NEWBURN 1640
NEWBURY 1643,
   1644
NEW ROSS 1798
NINEVEH 627
NIVELLE 1813
OKINAWA 1945
OPEQUON 1864
ORLÉANS 1870
OURIQUE 1139
PAGAHAR 1825
PALERMO 1848
PALMYRA AD 272
PANIPAT 1526,
   1556, 1759
PLASSEY 1757
PLATAEA 479 BC,
   429 BC
PLOVDIV 1878
POLOTSK 1812
POLTAVA 1709
PRESTON 1648,
   1715
PULTUSK 1703,
   1806
PUNNIAR 1843
RASTADT 1796
RAVENNA 729,
   1512

READING 871
REDINHA 1811
REVOLAX 1808
RIO SECO 1808
ROSTOCK 1677
ROUCOUX 1746
RUSPINA 46 BC
SABUGAL 1811
SAGUNTO 1811
SAINTES 1242
SAKARIA 1921
SALAMIS 480 BC,
   307 BC
SALERNO 1943
SAN JUAN 1898
SEGEWÁR 1849
SEMPACH 1386
SENEFFE 1674
SENEKAL 1900
SHARQAT 1918
SINNACA 53 BC
SINUIJU 1951
SKALITZ 1866
SOBRAON 1846
ST DENIS 1567
ST KITTS 1667
ST LUCIA 1794
SVISTOV 1877
TAGINAE 552
TALKHAN 1221
TANAGRA
   457 BC
TARANTO 1501,
   1940
TELAMON 225 BC
TE-LI-SSU 1904
THAPSUS 46 BC
TICINUS 218 BC

TOLBIAC 496
TOURNAI 1581, 1792, 1794
TREBBIA 218 BC, 1799
TRIPOLI 643
TURBIGO 1859
UPPSALA 1520, 1521
VESERIS 339 BC
VIGO BAY 1702
VIMEIRO 1808
VITEBSK 1812
VITORIA 1813
VOUILLÉ 507
WARBURG 1760
WARGAOM 1779
WEPENER 1900
WIMPFEN 1622
WINKOVO 1812
YASHIMA 1184
ZALLACA 1086
ZURAKOW 1676
ZUTPHEN 1586

8

ABERDEEN 1644
ABU HAMED 1897
ACAPULCO 1855
AIX ROADS 1809
AJNADAIN 634
ALICANTE 1706
ALMENARA 1710
AMALINDE 1818
ANAQUITO 1546
ANTIETAM 1862
AQUILEIA 394
ASSUNDUN 1016
AULDEARN 1645
AXARQUIA 1483

AYACUCHO 1824
AZIMGHUR 1858
BAGRADAS 49 BC
BASANTAR 1971
BASSORAH 665
BASTOGNE 1944
BERESINA 1812
BIBRACTE 58 BC
BIR HAKIM 1942
BLENHEIM 1704
BLUEBERG 1806
BORODINO 1812
BOUVINES 1214
BOVIANUM 305 BC
BRIHUEGA 1710
BROOKLYN 1776
BUZENVAL 1871
CALDIERO 1796, 1805
CAPE BONA 468
CARABOBO 1821
CARRICAL 1758
CARTHAGE 152 BC, 533
CASTALLA 1813
CAWNPORE 1857
CHATALJA 1912
CHERITON 1644
CHIPPEWA 1814
CLONTARF 1014
COCHEREL 1364
CORAL SEA 1942
COURTRAI 1302
CRAYFORD 456
CRIMISUS 341 BC
CULLODEN 1746
CUSTOZZA 1848, 1866
DAMASCUS 635, 1401, 1918

DANNOURA 1185
DOMINICA 1782
DREPANUM 249 BC
DROGHEDA 1641
DRUMCLOG 1679
EDGEHILL 1642
EDINGTON 878
ESPINOSA 1808
FAIR OAKS 1862
FALLUJAH 2004
FAVENTIA 82 BC
FLANDERS 1940
FONTENOY 1745
FORMIGNY 1450
FRASTANZ 1499
FREIBURG 1644
FRETEVAL 1194
GADEBESK 1712
GARIBPUR 1971
GAULAULI 1858
GEMBLOUX 1578
GEOK TEPE 1878
GERGOVIA 52 BC
GITSCHIN 1866
GÜNZBURG 1805
HADRANUM 344 BC
HASTINGS 1066
HERACLEA 280 BC
HERDONIA 210 BC
HOMILDON 1402
HONG KONG 1941
INKERMAN 1854
JEMAPPES 1792
JIDBALLI 1904
JOTAPATA AD 67
KANDAHAR 1221, 1648, 1880, 2001
KATZBACH 1813

KIRBEKAN 1885
KLUSHINO 1610
KULEVCHA 1829
KULICOVA 1380
KUMAMOTO 1876
KUMANOVO 1912
LAFFELDT 1747
LANDSHUT 1809
LANGPORT 1645
LANGSIDE 1658
LAUFFELD 1746
LAUTULAE 316 BC
LE CATEAU 1914
LEONTINI 211 BC
LIAOYANG 1904
LIEGNITZ 1760
LOBOSITZ 1756
LUNCARTY 980
MAGNESIA 190 BC
MAHIDPUR 1817
MANDONIA 338 BC
MANTINEA 418 BC,
   362 BC, 295 BC,
   207 BC
MARATHON 490 BC
MEDELLIN 1809
MEDENINE 1943
MELITENE 575
MESSINES 1917
METAURUS 207 BC
MOLLWITZ 1741
MONASTIR 1912
MORTLACK 1010
MOSKIRCH 1800
MÜHLBERG 1547
MÜHLDORF 1322
MUSA BAGH 1858
MYTILENE 406 BC

NANTWICH 1644
NAVARINO 1827
NDJAMENA 2006
NIQUITAS 1813
OBLIGADO 1845
OMDURMAN 1898
OSTROWNO 1812
PALESTRO 1859
PALO ALTO 1846
PANDOSIA 331 BC
PANORMUS 251 BC
PEA RIDGE 1862
PELUSIUM 525 BC,
   321 BC
PESHAWAR 1001
PHILIPPI 42 BC
PIACENZA 1746
PLACILLA 1891
PODHAJCE 1667, 1698
POITIERS 1356
PORTLAND 1653
RATHENOW 1675
RICHMOND 1862
ROSSBACH 1757
ROVEREDO 1796
SAALFELD 1806
SANTAREM 1834
SANTIAGO 1898
SARATOGA 1777
SEMINARA 1495, 1503
SENTINUM 295 BC
SHAH-E-KOT 2002
SHANGHAI 1937
SHOLAPUR 1818
SINSHEIM 1674
SLIVNICA 1885
SMOLENSK 1708,
   1812, 1941

SOISSONS 486
SORAUREN 1813
SPION KOP 1900
ST ALBANS 1455, 1461
ST DIZIER 1814
ST MIHIEL 1918
STRATTON 1643
SYRACUSE 413 BC,
   387 BC
TALAVERA 1809
TALIKOTA 1565
TARAPACA 1879
TEMESVÁR 1849
THE DOWNS 1666
THETFORD 870
TOLOLING 1999
TORA BORA 2001
TOULOUSE 1814
TSUSHIMA 1419, 1905
TURNHOUT 1597
VALLETTA 1798
VALTEZZA 1821
VALUTINO 1812
VERNEUIL 1424
VILLIERS 1870
VOLTURNO 1860
WATERLOO 1815
WIESLOCH 1622
WURSCHEN 1813
YAMAZAKI 1582
YORKTOWN 1781,
   1862
ZENDECAN 1039
ZORNDORF 1758

9
ABENSBERG 1809
AGENDICUM 52 BC
AGINCOURT 1415
AGNADELLO 1509
AHMADABAD 1780
ALCÂNTARA 1580
ALGECIRAS 1801
ALTENDORF 1632
AMSTETTEN 1805
ANGOSTURA 1847
AQUIDABAN 1870
ARGINUSAE 406 BC
ARKINHOLM 1455
ASKULTSIK 1828
ASTRAKHAN 1569
AUERSTÄDT 1806
AYLESFORD 455
BALACLAVA 1854
BALLYMORE 1798
BANGALORE 1791
BARCELONA 1938
BEDRIACUM AD 69
BENEVENTO 1266
BERGENDAL 1900
BHURTPORE 1805
BLACK ROCK 1812
BLUFF COVE 1982
BORGHETTO 1796
BORNHÖVED 1227
BRENTFORD 1642
BRIG OF DEE 1639
BURNS HILL 1847
BYZANTIUM 318 BC
CAMERINUM 298 BC
CAPE HENRY 1781
CAPORETTO 1917
CASILINUM 554

CASTILLON 1453
CERIGNOLA 1503
CERISOLES 1544
CHACABUCO 1817
CHAERONEA 338 BC,
  86 BC
CHALCEDON 74 BC
CHALDIRAN 1514
CHAMPAGNE 1915
CHARASIAB 1879
CHARENTON 1649
CORRICHIE 1652
COULMIERS 1870
CROSSKEYS 1862
CTESIPHON 363
CUDDALORE 1783
CURUPAYTI 1866
CYNOSSEMA 411 BC
DENNEWITZ 1813
DETTINGEN 1743
DEVICOTTA 1749
DORYLAEUM 1097
DUNGENESS 1652
DUNSINANE 1054
EDGEWORTH 1469
EL ALAMEIN 1942
ELCHINGEN 1805
ELLENDUNE 825
ELLEPORUS 389 BC
EMPINGHAM 1470
FISH CREEK 1855
FIVE FORKS 1865
FRIEDLAND 1807
GALLIPOLI 1915
GLADSMUIR 1745
GLEN FRUIN 1603
GLENLIVET 1594
GRANDELLA 1266

GUINEGATE 1513
GUMBINNEN 1914
HALIARTUS 395 BC
HEILSBERG 1807
HEMUSHAGU 1597
HÉRICOURT 1474
HOCHKIRCH 1758
HÖCHSTÄDT 1800
HYDERABAD 1843
JERUSALEM 1187,
  1917, 1948
KARAMURAN 1225
KERESZTES 1596
KISSINGEN 1866
KIZIL-TEPE 1877
LA BICOCCA 1522
LANSDOWNE 1643
LE BOURGET 1870
LEXINGTON 1775,
  1861
LEYTE GULF 1944
LINCELLES 1793
LINKÖPING 1598
LONGEWALA 1971
LOWENBERG 1813
MAKWANPUR 1816
MALAVILLY 1799
MALEGNANO 1859
MANSFIELD 1864
MANZIKERT 1071
MARIAZELL 1805
MARIGNANO 1515,
  1859
MERSEBURG 934
MILLESIMO 1796
MÖESKIRCH 1800
MOGADISHU
  1993, 2006

MONTEREAU 1814
MONTERREY 1846
MONTLHÉRY 1645
MORAZZONE 1848
MORGARTEN 1315
MYONNESUS 190 BC
NAGY-SARLO 1849
NASHVILLE 1864
NASIRAYAH 2003
NAULOCHUS 36 BC
NAUPACTUS 429 BC
NAVARRETE 1367
NEGAPATAM 1746,
1782
NEW MARKET 1864
NICOPOLIS 47 BC,
1396, 1877
NUJUFGHAR 1857
OCEAN POND 1864
OENOPHYTA 457 BC
OLTENITZA 1853
OTTERBURN 1388
OUDENARDE 1708
PELEKANON 1329
PHARSALUS 48 BC
PIRMASENS 1793
PLACENTIA AD 271
PORTO NOVO 1781
PRIMOLANO 1796
PRINCETON 1777
QUISTELLO 1734
RAMILLIES 1706
RAMNUGGUR 1849
RATHMINES 1649
RIACHUELO 1865
ROSEBURGH 1460
RYNEMANTS 1578
SADULAPUR 1848

SALAMANCA 1812
SAMARKAND 1220
SANTA CRUZ 1657,
1797
SANTANDER 1937
SARAGOSSA 1710
SAXA RUBRA 312
SCHLESWIG 1848
SCHWECHAT 1848
SEDGEMOOR 1685
SEVENOAKS 1450
SHEERNESS 1667
SHINOWARA 1183
SHIROYAMA 1877
SIIKAJOKI 1808
SINGAPORE 1942
SOLFERINO 1859
SPICHEREN 1870
STADTLOHN 1623
STAFFARDA 1690
ST ANTOINE 1652
ST CHARLES 1837
STEENKIRK 1692
ST GOTHARD 1664
STORMBERG 1899
ST QUENTIN 1557,
1871
TCHERNAYA 1855
TOLENTINO 1815
TOU MORONG 1966
TOURCOING 1794
TRAFALGAR 1805
TRAUTENAU 1866
TREBIZOND 1461
VAALKRANZ 1900
VARAVILLE 1058
VAUCHAMPS 1814
VERCELLAE 101 BC

VICKSBURG 1862,
1863
VIMY RIDGE 1917
WAKEFIELD 1460
WANDIWASH 1760,
1780
WORCESTER 1642,
1651
WÜRTSBURG 1796
YALU RIVER 1894, 1904
YELLOW SEA 1904
ZUIDER ZEE 1573
ZÜLLICHAU 1759

10
ACULTZINGO 1862
ADRIANOPLE 363, 378,
1205, 1829
ALADJA DAGH 1877
ALEXANDRIA 642,
1801, 1882
ALTOPASCIO 1325
AMPHIPOLIS 422 BC
ANCRUM MOOR 1545
ARGENTARIA 378
ASPROMONTE 1862
AUSTERLITZ 1805
BALL'S BLUFF 1861
BEACHY HEAD 1690
BENEVENTUM 275 BC,
214 BC
BENNINGTON 1777
BLACKWATER 1598
BLORE HEATH 1459
BRANDYWINE 1777
BRIAR CREEK 1779
BRUNANBURH 937
BUENA VISTA 1846

BUNKER HILL 1775
CALATAFIMI 1860
CAMPALDINO 1289
CAMPERDOWN 1797
CAMPO SANTO 1743
CARAGUATAY 1869
CARBISDALE 1650
CEDAR CREEK 1864
CHEVY CHASE 1388
CHINGLEPUT 1752
CHIPPENHAM 878
COLD HARBOR 1864
COPENHAGEN 1801,
  1807
CORUPEDIUM 281 BC
DOGGER BANK 1781,
  1915
ENGLEFIELD 871
FEHRBELLIN 1675
FEROZESHAH 1845
FETHANLEAG 584
FUTTEYPORE 1857
GAINES' MILL 1862
GERMANTOWN 1777
GARIGLIANO 1503
GETTYSBURG 1863
GOOSE GREEN 1982
GORODECZNO 1812
GRANT'S HILL 1758
GRAVELINES 1558
GRAVELOTTE 1870
GUADELOUPE 1794
HARDENBERG 1580
HASTENBECK 1757
HEATHFIELD 633
HEKITAI-KAN 1595
HELIGOLAND 1807
HELIOPOLIS 1800

HELLESPONT 323
HOLLABRUNN 1805
HUMBLEBECK 1700
ICHINOTANI 1189
IMJIN RIVER 1951
INVERLOCHY 1645
JELLALABAD 1842
KALKA RIVER 1224
KEMMENDINE 1824
KHOJAH PASS 1842
KÖNIGGRÄTZ 1866
KRINGELLEN 1612
KUNERSDORF 1759
LAING'S NECK 1881
LAKE GEORGE 1755
LAKE VADIMO 283 BC
LANDSKRONE 1676
LA ROCHELLE 1372
LA ROTHIÈRE 1814
LAS SALINAS 1538
LIPPE RIVER 11 BC
LULE-BURGAS 1912
LUNDY'S LANE 1814
LÜTZELBERG 1758
MAHARAJPUR 1843,
  1857
MALPLAQUET 1709
MARIENDAHL 1645
MARS-LA-TOUR 1870
MARTINESTI 1789
MASERFIELD 642
MELANTHIUS 559
MICHELBERG 1805
MIRAFLORES 1881
MONTEBELLO 1800,
  1859
MONTENOTTE 1796
MONTMIRAIL 1814

MONT THABOR 1799
MORTGARTEN 1315
MURSA MAJOR 351
NAROCH LAKE 1916
NEERWINDEN 1693,
  1793
NESBIT MOOR 1402
NEW ORLEANS 1814,
  1862
NIEUWPOORT 1600
NÖRDLINGEN 1634,
  1645
ORCHOMENUS 85 BC
OSTROLENKA 1831,
  1853
OULART HILL 1798
PAARDEBERG 1900
PALESTRINA 1849
PANDU NADDI 1857
PENSELWOOD 1016
PEREMBACUM 1780
PERRYVILLE 1862
PIAVE RIVER 1918
PONT VALAIN 1370
PORT ARTHUR 1894,
  1904
PORTO-BELLO 1739
QUATRE BRAS 1815
RIVER PLATE 1939
ROMERSWAEL 1574
ROSEBECQUE 1382
RUMERSHEIM 1709
SALANKEMEN 1691
SAN JACINTO 1836
SANNA'S POST 1900
SANTA LUCIA 1842
SEKIGAHARA 1600
SEVASTOPOL 1854

SEVEN PINES 1862
SHREWSBURY 1403
SIDI REZEGH 1941
SOLWAY MOSS 1542
SPHACTERIA 425 BC
STALINGRAD 1942
ST EUSTACHE 1837
STILLWATER 1777
STOLHOFFEN 1707
TALANA HILL 1899
TANNENBERG 1410,
1914
TASHKESSEN 1877
TEL-EL-KEBIR 1882
TETTENHALL 910
TEWKSBURY 1471
TINCHEBRAI 1106
TIPPERMUIR 1644
TRAVANCORE 1789
TUTTLINGEN 1643
UTSONOMIYA 1868
VAL-ES-DUNES 1047
VELESTINOS 1897
WARTEMBERG 1813
WATTIGNIES 1793
ZIEZICKSEE 1302

11
AEGOSPOTAMI 405 BC
ALAM EL HALFA 1942
ALJUBAROTTA 1385
AQUAE SEXTIA 102 BC
BANNOCKBURN 1314
BELLEAU WOOD 1918
BERESTECHKO 1651
BISMARCK SEA 1942
BLADENSBURG 1814
BLANQUEFORT 1450

BRAMHAM MOOR
1408
BREITENFELD 1631,
1642
BRENNEVILLE 1119
CALPULALPAM 1860
CAMELODUNUM
AD 43
CAPE MATAPAN 1941
CAPE PASSARO 1718
CARENAGE BAY 1778
CASTIGLIONE 1706,
1796
CASTILLEJOS 1860
CECRYPHALEA 458 BC
CHAMPAUBERT 1814
CHAPULTEPEC 1847
CHATEAUGUAY 1813
CHATTANOOGA 1863
CHICKAMAUGA 1863
CHILIANWALA 1849
CHRYSOPOLIS 324
CLIFTON MOOR 1745
COLLINE GATE 82 BC
DEUTSCHBROD 1422
DIAMOND HILL 1900
DRIEFONTEIN 1900
DUNGAN'S HILL 1647
DÜRRENSTEIN 1805
DYRRHACHIUM 48 BC
FARRUKHABAD 1804
FERRYBRIDGE 1461
FISHER'S HILL 1864
FORT NIAGARA 1759
FORT ST DAVID 1758
FRAUBRUNNEN 1376
FRAUENSTADT 1706
GIBBEL RUTTS 1798

GORNI-DUBNIK 1877
GROSS-BEEREN 1813
GUADALAJARA 1937
GUADALCANAL 1942
HADRIANOPLE 323
HALIDON HILL 1333
HEAVENFIELD 634
HEILIGERLEE 1568
HELSINGBORG 1710
HENNERSDORF 1745
HOHENLINDEN 1800
HONDSCHOOTE 1793
ISANDHLWANA 1879
KESSELSDORF 1745
KIRK-KILISSE 1912
KLAUSENBURG 1660
LANGENSALZA 1866
LINCOLN FAIR 1217
LOSTWITHIEL 1644
LOUDOUN HILL 1307
MACIEJOWICE 1794
MALVERN HILL 1862
MARSTON MOOR
1644
MASULIPATAM 1759
MEGALOPOLIS 331 BC,
226 BC
MERSA MATRUH 1942
MILETOPOLIS 86 BC
MILL SPRINGS 1862
MODDER RIVER 1899
MONTCONTOUR 1569
MONTE APERTO 1260
MONTMORENCI 1759
MOOKERHEIDE 1574
MORSHEDABAD 1763
MOUNT TIFATA 83 BC
NOISSEVILLE 1870

NORTHAMPTON 1460
PEARL HARBOR 1941
PEIWAR KOTAL 1878
PHILIPHAUGH 1645
PIETER'S HILL 1900
PLATTSBURGH 1814
PONDICHERRY 1778
PRESTONPANS 1745
QUIBERON BAY 1759
RHINEFELDEN 1638
RIETFONTEIN 1899
RORKE'S DRIFT 1879
ROWTON HEATH 1645
SALDANHA BAY 1796
SAUCHIE BURN 1488
SCHIPKA PASS 1877
SHERIFFMUIR 1715
SHIJONAWATE 1339
SIDI BARRÂNI 1940
STAVRICHANI 1739
STONE'S RIVER 1862
STONEY CREEK 1813
TAGLIACOZZO 1268
TAILLEBOURG 1242
THERMOPYLAE 480 BC,
    191 BC
TICONDEROGA 1758
TOBA-FUSHIMI 1868
TRINCOMALEE 1759,
    1782
VILLAFRANCA 1812
VINEGAR HILL 1798
WALTERSDORF 1807
WEDNESFIELD 911
WISSEMBOURG 1870
WHITE PLAINS 1776
WOUNDED KNEE 1890

12
ADWALTON MOOR
    1643
ALGECIRAS BAY 1801
ARCIS-SUR-AUBE 1814
ARGENTORATUM 357
ATHERTON MOOR
    1643
BADLI-KI-SERAI 1857
BARQUISIMETO 1813
BRADDOCK DOWN
    1643
CARBERRY HILL 1567
CHICKAHOMINY 1862
ELANDSLAAGTE 1899
EUTAW SPRINGS 1781
FLODDEN FIELD 1513
FORT DONELSON
    1852
HAMPTON ROADS
    1862
HARPER'S FERRY 1859
HATFIELD CHASE 632
HEDGELEY MOOR
    1464
HOMILDON HILL 1402
ICLISTAVISUS AD 16
KIRCH-DENKERN 1761
KÖNIGSWARTHA 1813
LAKE REGILLUS 497 BC
LYNN HAVEN BAY 1781
MALAKAND PASS 1895
MAZAR-E-SHARIF 2001
MOLINO DEL REY 1808
MONS-EN-PÉVÈLE
    1304
MONTE CASEROS
    1852

MOSTERT'S HOEK
    1900
MÜNCHENGRÄTZ
    1866
MURFREESBORO 1862
NECHTAN'S MERE 685
OONDWA NULLAH
    1763
PENOBSCOT BAY 1779
PETERWARDEIN 1716
PINKIE CLEUGH 1547
PORT REPUBLIC 1862
PRAIRIE GROVE 1862
RADCOT BRIDGE 1387
RICH MOUNTAIN 1861
RONCESVALLES 778,
    1813
ROUNDWAY DOWN
    1643
RULLION GREEN 1666
SERINGAPATAM 1792,
    1799
SOUTHWOLD BAY
    1672
SPOTSYLVANIA 1864
SUNGARI RIVER 1947
TIGRANOCERTA 69 BC
VALENCIENNES 1566,
    1656
VILLAVICIOSA 1710
WILLIAMSBURG 1862
WILSON'S CREEK 1861
WROTHAM HEATH
    1554

13
ADMAGETOBRIGA
    61 BC

AIX-LA-CHAPELLE 1795
BOROUGHBRIDGE 1322
BOSWORTH FIELD 1485
CAPE ST VINCENT 1693, 1780, 1797
CASTELFIDARDO 1860
CASTELNAUDARY 1632
CEDAR MOUNTAIN 1862
CHANDERNAGORE 1757
CHESAPEAKE BAY 1781
CHRISTIANOPLE 1611
CHRYSLER'S FARM 1813
CYNOSCEPHALAE 364 BC, 197 BC
FORT FRONTENAC 1758
FORT SITABALDI 1817
FRANKENHAUSEN 1525
GLENMARRESTON 683
GORLICE-TARNOW 1915
INVERKEITHING 1317
KASSERINE PASS 1943
KILLIEKRANKIE 1689
LITTLE BIG HORN 1876
LOIGNY-POUPREY 1870
MAGERSFONTEIN 1899
MARCIANOPOLIS 376
MASURIAN LAKES 1914, 1915
MEGALETAPHRUS 740 BC
MONS LACTARIUS 553
NEVILLE'S CROSS 1346
NEWTOWNBUTLER 1689
NORTHALLERTON 1138
NORTH FORELAND 1653, 1666
PASSCHENDAELE 1917
PELELIU-ANGAUR 1944
PHILIPPINE SEA 1944
PORTO PRAIA BAY 1781
ROANOKE ISLAND 1862
SIEVERSHAUSEN 1553
SPANISH ARMADA 1588

THE WILDERNESS 1864
WHITE MOUNTAIN 1620
WHITE OAK SWAMP 1862
WIRELESS RIDGE 1982
YOUGHIOGHENNY 1754
ZUSMARSHAUSEN 1647

14

BEAVER DAM CREEK 1862
BERWICK-ON-TWEED 1296
BOTHWELL BRIDGE 1679
BRISTOE STATION 1863
CAMPUS CASTORUM AD 69
CAPE FINISTERRE 1747, 1805
CHALGROVE FIELD 1643
CHÂTEAU THIERRY 1814, 1918
CONSTANTINOPLE 668, 1203, 1261
CROPREDY BRIDGE 1644
DEPTFORD BRIDGE 1497
DRUMOSSIE MOOR 1746
FREDERICKSBURG 1862
FUENTES DE OÑORO 1811
HOHENFRIEDBERG 1745
LA BELLE FAMILLE 1759
MACASSAR STRAIT 1942
MORTIMER'S CROSS 1461
NICHOLSON'S NECK 1899
PASO DE LA PATRIA 1866
PEACHTREE CREEK 1864
PUSAN PERIMETER 1950
ROUVRAY-ST-DENIS 1429
SANTIAGO DE CUBA 1898
SAVAGE'S STATION 1862
SECESSIONVILLE 1862
SINAI PENINSULA 1956
STAMFORD BRIDGE 1066
STIRLING BRIDGE 1297
TONDEMAN'S WOODS 1754

VITTORIO VENETO 1918

15
ALEUTIAN ISLANDS 1943
ALHAMA DE GRANADA 1482
AMATOLA MOUNTAIN 1846
APPOMATTOX RIVER 1865
BATTLE OF BRITAIN 1940
BATTLE OF THE EBRO 1938
BATTLE OF THE NILE 1798
BEAUNE-LA-ROLANDE 1870
FORUM TERBRONII AD 251
GROSS-JÄGERSDORF 1757
HELIGOLAND BIGHT 1914
MALOYAROSLAVETS 1812
MISSIONARY RIDGE 1863
MOUNT TUMBLEDOWN 1982
PLAINS OF ABRAHAM 1759
PUENTE DE LA REYNA 1872
RESACA DE LA PALMA 1846
TEUTOBERGER WALD AD 9

16
BATTLE OF THE BULGE 1944
BRONKHORSTSPRUIT 1880

CHANCELLORSVILLE 1863
FORT WILLIAM HENRY 1757
HASLACH-JUNGINGEN 1805
KENNESAW MOUNTAIN 1864
LAS NAVAS DE TOLOSA 1212
MADONNA DELL'OLENO 1744
MONONGAHELA RIVER 1755
QUEENSTON HEIGHTS 1812
ST JAKOB AN DER BIRS 1444

17
INHLOBANE MOUNTAIN 1879
LA FÈRE-CHAMPENOISE 1814
PITTSBURGH LANDING 1862
VAN TUONG PENINSULA 1965

18
BATTLE OF THE SAINTES 1872
GUILDFORD COURTHOUSE 1781

19
BATTLE OF THE ATLANTIC 1917
BATTLE OF THE PYRAMIDS 1798
CHU PONG-IA DRANG RIVER 1965
GLORIOUS FIRST OF JUNE 1794

History – Historical Events – SIEGES * = police siege

4
ACRE 1799, 1832, 1840
BAZA 1489
BONN 1689, 1703
COMO 1127
CONI 1691, 1744
KARS 1855
KEHL 1796-1797

LOZA 1482
METZ 1552-1553, 1870
MONS 1691, 1709, 1746, 1792
NICE 1705
RIGA 1700, 1710
ROME 1849
SCIO 1822

TYRE 332 BC
VEII 406-396 BC
WACO* 1993
YORK 1644

5
AMIDA 359
ARRAH 1857

ARRAS 1640
BREDA 1625, 1793
CADIZ 1812
CALVI 1794
CAPUA 212 BC, 1501,
   1799
CONDÉ 1676, 1793,
   1794
CORFU 1536, 1716-
   1718
CUMAE 553
DELHI 1857
DOUAI 1710
GAETA 1707, 1734,
   1860-1861
GENOA 1684, 1800
GHENT 1706
GLATZ 1622, 1742,
   1807
HERAT 1837-1838, 1856
KOTAH 1858
LEITH 1560
LIÈGE 1468, 1702
LILLE 1708-1713, 1792
LYONS 1793
MAINZ 1689, 1793
MALTA 1565, 1940-1942
NAMUR 1692, 1695,
   1914
PADUA 1509
PARIS 885-886, 1594,
   1870-1871
PAVIA 1655
PSKOV 1581-1582
ROUEN 1418-1419,
   1449, 1591
THORN 1703
TUNIS 1270, 1535

XERES 1262
YPRES 1648, 1794

6

ALESIA 52 BC
AMIENS 1597
ANCONA 1799
BATAAN 1942
BEIRUT 1982
BERLIN 1948-1949
BILBAO 1835-1836,
   1874, 1937
BURGOS 1812, 1813
CALAIS 1346-1347,
   1558, 1596, 1940
CANDIA 1667-1669
CHALUS 1199
CHUNAR 1538
CRACOW 1702, 1794
DANZIG 1734, 1793,
   1807, 1813-1814
DUBLIN 1170, 1500,
   1649
DUNBAR 1339
EXETER 1136
GERONA 1808-1809
HAVANA 1762
ISMAIL 1770, 1790
JANINA 1913
KONDUZ 2001
LANDAU 1702, 1703,
   1793
LERIDA 1647, 1707,
   1810
LEYDEN 1574
LISBON 1147
MADRID 1936-1939
MALAGA 1487

MANTUA 1796-1797
NAPLES 1495, 1799,
   1806
NICAEA 1097
OLMÜTZ 1741, 1758
OSTEND 1601-1604,
   1706, 1745, 1798
PLEVNA 1877-1878
PRAGUE 1741-1744
RHEIMS 1359
RHODES 1306-1309,
   1480, 1522
TOLEDO 1936
TOULON 1793
VANNES 1342
VENICE 1849
VERDUN 1792
VIENNA 1529, 1848
WARSAW 1939
XATIVA 1246, 1707
ZÜRICH 1544

7

ALGIERS 1682-1683,
   1816, 1830
ALMEIDA 1810
AMORIUM 838
ANTWERP 1584-1585,
   1832, 1914
AVIGNON 1226
BADAJOZ 1385, 1396,
   1542, 1705, 1811
BAGHDAD 1258
BÉTHUNE 1710
BOLOGNA 1506, 1796,
   1799
BRESCIA 1512, 1849
BRESLAU 1807

BRISACH 1638
CHESTER 1643-1646
CHILLON 1536
CHITRAL 1895
CÓRDOBA 1012
CORINTH 1205, 1209
DRESDEN 1756, 1760
DUNKIRK 1646, 1793
ERENKÖY 1964
GRANADA 1491-1492
HAARLEM 1572-1573
HUMAITÁ 1866-1868
KOMÁROM 1849
LA MOTTE 1634
LEIPZIG 1547, 1642
LUCKNOW 1857
MESSINA 1282, 1719,
    1848
MORELLA 1840
NISIBIS 338, 346, 350
ODAWARA 1569, 1590
ORLÉANS 1428-1429,
    1563
QUESNAY 1793-1794
SCUTARI 1474, 1913
SEVILLE 1248
SZIGETH 1566
TANJORE 1758
TERGOES 1572
TORTOSA 1810-1811
TOURNAI 1340, 1513,
    1581, 1667, 1709

8
ASIRGHAR 1819
AVARICUM 53-52 BC
BELGRADE 1456, 1521,
    1717, 1789

BESANÇON 1668, 1674
BORDEAUX 1451, 1453
BOUCHAIN 1711
BOULOGNE 1544
BRUSSELS 1695, 1746
BUDAPEST 1541, 1686,
    1944-1945
CARLISLE 1745
CHARTRES 1568
DROGHEDA 1649
FLUSHING 1809
GERBEROY 1080
HARFLEUR 1415
KANDAHAR 1521,
    1839-1842
KHARTOUM 1884-1885
LIMERICK 1651,
    1690-1691
MAFEKING 1899-1900
MANNHEIM 1793
MAUBEUGE 1914
NUMANTIA 142,
    134-133 BC
OLIVENZA 1811
PAMPLONA 1813
RICHMOND 1864-1865
ROXBURGH 1460
SAGUNTUM 219 BC
SARAJEVO 1992-1996
SMOLENSK 1609-1611
SYRACUSE 213 BC
TEMESVAR 1716
TOULOUSE 848, 1229
TSINGTAO 1914
VALENCIA 1812

9
AIGUILLON 1347

ALGECIRAS 1342-1344
BARCELONA 1471, 1697,
    1705-1706, 1714
BELLE ISLE 1761
BHURTPORE 1827
BOIS-LE-DUC 1601,
    1603, 1794
BOMARSUND 1854
CARTAGENA 1706,
    1873-1874
CHARLEROI 1672, 1690
CHERBOURG 1418,
    1758
COMPIÈGNE 1430
EDINBURGH 1093, 1296
FAMAGUSTA 1570-1571
GIBRALTAR 1333,
    1704-1705, 1779-1783
GÖTTINGEN 1760
GRONINGEN 1594,
    1678
JERUSALEM c1400 BC,
    588 BC, AD 70, 637,
    1099
KIMBERLEY 1899-1900
LADYSMITH 1899-1900
LENINGRAD 1941-1944
MAGDEBURG 1631,
    1806
MANGALORE 1783
MONTARGIS 1427
MONTAUBAN 1621
PERISABOR 363
PERPIGNAN 1473-1474,
    1542, 1642
SARAGOSSA 1808-1809
SILISTRIA 1854
STRALSUND 1628, 1715

TARRAGONA 1811, 1813
WEI-HAI-WEI 1895

10
ADRIANOPLE 1912-1913
CHARLESTON 1780, 1863-1865
CHÂTEAUDUN 1870
COLCHESTER 1648
COPENHAGEN 1658
DONNINGTON 1644
GLOUCESTER 1643
HEIDELBERG 1688
KUT-EL-AMARA 1915
LANDRECIES 1712, 1794
LA ROCHELLE 1573, 1628
LOUISBOURG 1745, 1758
LUXEMBOURG 1795
MAASTRICHT 1579, 1673, 1703,
    1748, 1793-1794
MONTEVIDEO 1807, 1814, 1843,
    1851
PETERSBURG 1864
PHALSBOURG 1814, 1815, 1870
PORT HUDSON 1863
SAVANDROOG 1791
SEVASTOPOL 1854-1855
STALINGRAD 1942-1943
STRASBOURG 1870
THÉROUANNE 1303, 1479, 1513
THIONVILLE 1792

11
BASING HOUSE 1643-1645
DIEN BIEN PHU 1954
ELANDS RIVER 1900
LONDONDERRY 1689
MAOGAMALCHA 363

MISSOLONGHI 1822, 1823, 1825-1826
PONDICHERRY 1748, 1760
SCHWEIDNITZ 1762, 1807
STRANGEWAYS* 1990

12
BERGEN-OP-ZOOM 1588, 1622,
    1747, 1814
BESLAN SCHOOL* 2004
FREDRIKSHALD 1718
PHILLIPSBURG 1644, 1676, 1688,
    1734, 1799-1800
SAN SEBASTIAN 1813, 1836
SIDNEY STREET* 1911
VALENCIENNES 1677, 1793, 1794

13
BELLE-ÎLE-EN-MER 1759
CIUDAD RODRIGO 1810-1812
LIBYAN EMBASSY* 1984
MOSCOW THEATRE* 2002
SPAGHETTI HOUSE* 1975

14
BALCOMBE STREET* 1975
BERWICK-ON-TWEED 1333, 1481
CONSTANTINOPLE 1422, 1453
FORT BEAUSÉJOUR 1755
IRANIAN EMBASSY* 1980
MONTANA FREEMEN* 1996

15
EDINBURGH CASTLE 1571

18
FRANKFURT AN DER ODER 1631

History – Historical Events – WARS

3
COD 1958, 1972-1973,
  1975-1976

4
BOER 1899-1902
COLD 1947-1989
GULF 1980-1988, 1991
IRAQ 2003-
ONIN 1467-1477
ZULU 1879

5
IMJIN 1592-1598
KLANG 1867-1874
OPIUM 1839-1842
PUNIC 264-241, 218-202,
  149-146 BC

6
AFGHAN 1838-1942, 1979-1987
BALKAN 1912, 1913
FULANI 1804-1810
GENPAI 1180-1185
KAFFIR 1846-1852
KARGIL 1999
KOREAN 1950-1953
MALAYA 1948-1960
OGADEN 1977-1978
SIX DAY 1967

7
BOSNIAN 1992-1995
CHECHEN 1994-1996, 1998-
CRIMEAN 1853-1856

HUSSITE 1420-1436
SAMNITE 290 BC
SWABIAN 1499
VIETNAM 1959-1979

8
CHIOGGIA 1378-1381
CRUSADES 1095-1272
IRAN-IRAQ (or Gulf) 1980-1988
SMOLENSK 1632-1634
TEN YEARS 1868-1878
YUGOSLAV 1991-2001

9
ANGLO-SIKH 1845-1848
FALKLANDS 1982
INDO-CHINA 1946-1954
WORLD WAR I 1914-1918
YOM KIPPUR (or Arab-Israeli) 1973

10
ABYSSINIAN 1935-1936
ANGLO-DUTCH 1652-1654,
  1664-1667, 1672-1674
CORINTHIAN 395-387 BC
GREEK CIVIL 1945-1949
IRISH CIVIL 1922-1923
JENKINS' EAR 1739
NAPOLEONIC 1799-1815
PENINSULAR 1808-1814
SEVEN WEEKS (or Austro-Prussian)
  1866
SEVEN YEARS 1756-1763
WORLD WAR II 1939-1945

11
ARAB-ISRAELI 1973
BERKE-HULAGU 1262-1267
FIRST BARONS' 1215-1217
SOMALI CIVIL 1988-
THIRTY YEARS 1618-1648

12
ANGLO-BURMESE 1823-1825,
 1852-1853
CHINESE CIVIL 1927-1937,
 1945-1949
ENGLISH CIVIL 1642-1651
HUNDRED YEARS 1337-1453
INDO-PAKISTAN 1965, 1971
NIGERIAN CIVIL 1967-1970
RUSSO-SWEDISH 1788-1790
RUSSO-TURKISH 1828-1829
RWANDAN CIVIL 1990-1994
SECOND BARONS' 1264-1267
SPANISH CIVIL 1936-1939

13
ALGERIAN CIVIL 1991-2002
AMERICAN CIVIL 1861-1865
LEBANESE CIVIL 1975-1990
GREAT NORTHERN 1700-1721
PELOPONNESIAN 431 BC-404 BC

POLISH-SWEDISH 1600-1611,
 1617-1629
RUSSO-JAPANESE 1904-1905

14
AUSTRO-PRUSSIAN 1866
CAMBODIAN CIVIL 1967-1975
ETHIOPIAN CIVIL 1974-1991
FRANCO-PRUSSIAN 1870-1871
WARS OF THE ROSES 1455-1485

15
DUTCH-PORTUGUESE 1588-1654
MEXICAN-AMERICAN 1846-1848
SPANISH-AMERICAN 1898

17
GREEK INDEPENDENCE 1821-1829
SPANISH SUCCESSION 1701-1713

18
AUSTRIAN SUCCESSION 1740-1748

19
ITALIAN INDEPENDENCE 1859-1870

20
AMERICAN INDEPENDENCE 1775-1783

History – KINGS & QUEENS (Europe) England/Britain unless stated

4
ANNE
EMMA Netherlands
JANE
JOHN + Portugal, Scotland

LUIS Portugal
MARY + Scotland
OLAV Norway
PAUL Greece

5
DAVID Scotland
EDGAR + Scotland
HENRY + France
JAMES + Scotland

LOUIS France
MARIA Portugal
OSCAR Norway;
Sweden
PEDRO Portugal

6
ALBERT Belgium
ALFRED
AMADEO Spain
CANUTE
CARLOS Portugal
DONALD Scotland
DUNCAN Scotland
EADRED
EADWIG
EDMUND
EDWARD
GEORGE + Greece
GUSTAF Sweden
HAAKON Norway
HARALD Norway
HAROLD
INDULF Scotland
MANUEL Portugal
PHILIP Spain

ROBERT Scotland

7
ALFONSO Spain
BEATRIX Netherlands
CHARLES + Belgium,
France, Norway,
Spain, Sweden
FRANCIS France
JULIANA Netherlands
LÉOPOLD Belgium
MACBETH Scotland
MALCOLM Scotland
RICHARD
STEPHEN
UMBERTO Italy
WILLIAM + Netherlands,
Scotland

8
BAUDOUIN Belgium
ETHELRED
FREDERIK Denmark,
Norway
ISABELLA Spain
MARGARET Scotland

VICTORIA

9
ALEXANDER Greece,
Scotland
ATHELSTAN
CHRISTIAN Denmark,
Norway
ELIZABETH
FERDINAND Spain
MARGRETHE Denmark

10
CARL GUSTAF Sweden
JUAN CARLOS Spain
WILHELMINA
Netherlands

11
CONSTANTINE Greece,
Scotland
HARDICANUTE

14
VICTOR EMMANUEL
Italy

History – ROMAN EMPERORS

3	**5**	**6**	PROBUS	GRATIAN	**8**
LEO	CARUS	AVITUS	TRAJAN	HADRIAN	ARCADIUS
	GALBA	DECIUS	VALENS	MARCIAN	AUGUSTUS
4	NERVA	GALLUS		MAXIMUS	AURELIAN
GETA	TITUS	JOVIAN	**7**	TACITUS	BALBINUS
NERO		JULIAN	CARINUS		CALIGULA
OTHO		PHILIP	GORDIAN		CLAUDIUS

COMMODUS
CONSTANS
DOMITIAN
EUGENIUS
HONORIUS
LICINIUS
MACRINUS
MAJORIAN
MAXIMIAN
OLYBRIUS
PERTINAX
POSTUMUS
PUPIENUS
TIBERIUS
VALERIAN
VOLUSIAN

9
ANTHEMIUS
CARACALLA
FLORIANUS
GALLIENUS
GLYCERIUS
JUSTINIAN
MAXENTIUS
MAXIMINUS
VESPASIAN
VITELLIUS

10
AEMILIANUS
DIOCLETIAN
MAGNENTIUS

NUMERIANUS
QUINTILLUS
THEODOSIUS

11
CONSTANTINE
CONSTANTIUS
DIADUMENIAN
HOSTILIANUS
JULIUS NEPOS
LUCIUS VERUS
VALENTINIAN

12
HELIOGABALUS

13
ANTONINUS PIUS
LIBIUS SEVERUS

14
DIDIUS JULIANUS
MARCUS AURELIUS

15
ROMULUS AUGUSTUS
SEPTIMUS SEVERUS

16
ALEXANDER SEVERUS
PETRONIUS MAXIMUS

History – ROMAN PLACE NAMES (British Isles)

4
DEVA Chester
MAIA Bowness
MONA Isle of Anglesey

5
DANUM Doncaster
MAGIS Piercebridge
NAVIO Brough
NIDUM Neath
ONNUM Halton

6
ABONAE Bristol
ALABUM Llandovery
ALAUNA Maryport
ALBION England

ARBEIA South Shields
DUBRIS Dover
GALAVA Ambleside
GLEVUM Gloucester
LINDUM Lincoln
OTHONA Bradwell-on-Sea
OXONIA Oxford
VECTIS Isle of Wight

7
CAMBRIA Wales
CONDATE Northwich
CUNETIO Mildenhall
GALACUM Overborough
LEMANIS Lympne
MONAVIA Isle of Man
OLICANA Ilkley

SALINAE Droitwich
VENONAE High Cross
VINOVIA Binchester

8
ANDERITA Pevensey
CALCARIA Tadcaster
CANONIUM Rivenhall
CORINIUM Cirencester
EBORACUM York
HIBERNIA Ireland
LAVATRAE Bowes
LINDINIS Ilchester
MAMUCIUM
   Manchester
VIGORNIA Worcester

9

BRITANNIA Britain
CALEDONIA Scotland
DERVENTIO Malton
DUNEDINUM Edinburgh
GOBANNIUM Abergavenny
HORTONIUM Halifax
LAGENTIUM Castleford
LONDINIUM London
MORIDUNUM Carmarthen
REGULBIUM Reculver
SEGEDUNUM Wallsend
SEGONTIUM Caernarfon
VINDOMORA Ebchester
VINDOVALA Rudchester

10

AQUAE SULIS Bath
BRANODUNUM Brancaster
BROCOLITIA Carrowburgh
CLAUSENTUM Bitterne
CONCANGIUM Chester-le-Street
DURNOVARIA Dorchester
DUROBRIVAE Rochester
DUROVERNUM Canterbury
HABITANCUM Risingham
LACTODORUM Towcester
LUGUVALIUM Carlisle
MEDIOLANUM Whitchurch
NOVIOMAGUS Chichester
PONS AELIUS Newcastle-upon-Tyne
TRIMONTIUM Newstead
VERULAMIUM St Albans
VINDOLANDA Chesterholme
VIROCONIUM Wroxeter

11

CAMULODUNUM Colchester
CANTABRIGIA Cambridge
CORSTOPITUM Corbridge
GARIANNONUM Burgh Castle
GLANNAVENTA Ravenglass
SORVIODUNUM Old Sarum
VERCOVICIUM Housesteads

12

CAESAROMAGUS Chelmsford
DUROCOBRIVIS Dunstable
ISCA SILURIUM Caerleon
PORTUS ADURNI Portchester
VENTA SILURUM Caerwent

13

BREMETENNACUM Ribchester
CATARACTONIUM Catterick
DUROCORNOVIUM Swindon
VENTA BELGARUM Winchester
VENTA ICENORUM Caister St
    Edmund

15

AQUAE ARNEMETIAE Buxton
ISCA DUMNONIORUM Exeter

16

CALLEVA ATREBATUM Silchester
ISURIUM BRIGANTUM Aldborough
RATAE CORITANORUM Leicester

Household

Household – FITTINGS & APPLIANCES

3	BULB	RACK	ALARM	INGLE	SHEET
BAR	COWL	RAIL	ARRAS	LATCH	SHELF
BIN	DADO	SAFE	BASIN	LEDGE	SHOJI
DVD	DOOR	SASH	BIDET	LIGHT	STACK
FAN	FIRE	SILL	BLIND	MIXER	STAIR
HOB	FLUE	SINK	CLOCK	NEWEL	STAND
JET	FUSE	SLAT	COVER	ORIEL	STOEP
KEY	GATE	STEP	DÉCOR	PANEL	STOVE
MAT	IRON	TANK	DRAIN	PLATE	THROW
PAD	JAMB	TIDY	DRAPE	POINT	TREAD
PEG	KNOB	TILE	DRYER	POKER	U-BEND
POT	LAMP	TRAP	DUVET	POTTY	VIDEO
RUG	LINO	UNIT	GLASS	PRESS	VINYL
TAP	LOCK	VENT	GLOBE	QUILT	
TUB	MAIN	WELL	GRATE	RADIO	6
	OVEN		GRILL	RANGE	AERIAL
4	PIPE	5	HATCH	RISER	AIR BED
BATH	PLUG	AIRER	HINGE	SHADE	ASH PAN

AWNING
BLOWER
BOILER
BUZZER
CANOPY
CARPET
CASTOR
COOKER
COPPER
COVING
DAMPER
DIMMER
DIPPER
DORMER
DOUCHE
DRAPES
FAUCET
FENDER
FRIDGE
FRIEZE
GAS-TAP
GEYSER
GRILLE
GUTTER
HAT-PEG
HEARTH
HEATER
HOT TAP
ICEBOX
JUICER
KETTLE
LOUVRE
MANGLE
MANTEL
MIRROR
PELMET
PILLOW
PIPING

PLAQUE
RUNNER
SCONCE
SCREEN
SHOWER
SOCKET
SOFFIT
SPIGOT
STAIRS
STEREO
SWITCH
TATAMI
TOILET
WICKET
WINDOW

7

ADAPTOR
AERATOR
ANDIRON
ASH TRAY
BATH-TUB
BEDDING
BELLOWS
BLANKET
BLENDER
BOLSTER
BRACKET
CAT FLAP
CISTERN
COLD TAP
CONDUIT
CONSOLE
CURTAIN
CUSHION
DOORMAT
DRAINER
DUSTBIN

DUSTPAN
ELEMENT
FIREDOG
FITMENT
FITTING
FIXTURE
FREEZER
FUSE BOX
GAS FIRE
GAS MAIN
GAS OVEN
GRATING
HAT RACK
HEATING
HIP BATH
JACUZZI
KEYHOLE
KNOCKER
LAGGING
LATTICE
PADLOCK
PARQUET
PICTURE
PLAYPEN
PLUNGER
POSTERN
SHUTTER
SUN LAMP
TOASTER
TRESTLE
VALANCE
WASHTUB

8

BACK DOOR
BACK GATE
BANISTER
BARBECUE

BEDCOVER
BELL PULL
BELL PUSH
BIN-LINER
BOOK-ENDS
BOOK-RACK
CASEMENT
COAT RACK
COVERLET
DOORBELL
DOORKNOB
DOORNAIL
DOORPOST
DOORSTEP
FANLIGHT
FLAT IRON
FLYPAPER
GAS METER
GAS STOVE
GRIDIRON
HALF-DOOR
HANDRAIL
HANGINGS
HEADREST
HOT PLATE
JALOUSIE
LIGHTING
LINOLEUM
MATTRESS
MIXER TAP
OVERFLOW
PEDAL BIN
PEDESTAL
PILOT-JET
PIPE RACK
RADIATOR
SASH-CORD
SHELVING

SIDE DOOR
SINK UNIT
SKIRTING
SKYLIGHT
STAIR ROD
STAIRWAY
STOPCOCK
SUNSHADE
TAPESTRY
TRAPDOOR
TRASH CAN
UNDERLAY
WAINSCOT
WALL UNIT
WIRELESS
YALE LOCK

9

BAY WINDOW
BEDSPREAD
BOOKSHELF
BOW WINDOW
CAT LITTER
CHUBB LOCK
DOORPLATE
DRAINPIPE
DRAPERIES
DUST COVER
DUST SHEET
DUTCH WIFE
DVD PLAYER
EIDERDOWN
EXTRACTOR
FIRE ALARM
FIRE GRATE
FIREGUARD
FIREPLACE
FRONT DOOR

GAS COOKER
GAS MANTLE
GIRANDOLE
GUTTERING
HAIR DRYER
HAND-BASIN
HEARTH RUG
INGLENOOK
LAMPSHADE
LETTER BOX
LIGHT BULB
MICROWAVE
NAMEPLATE
PANELLING
PARTITION
PLATE RACK
RADIOGRAM
SASH-FRAME
SCUNCHEON
SPICE-RACK
SPIN DRYER
STAIRCASE
STAIRWELL
STEAM IRON
SWING DOOR
TELEPHONE
THRESHOLD
TOWEL RACK
TOWEL RAIL
WALL CLOCK
WALLPAPER
WASTE PIPE
WATER BUTT
WATER MAIN
WATER PIPE
WINDOW BOX

10
ALARM CLOCK
BEDCLOTHES
BREADMAKER
CANDELABRA
CHAMBER POT
CHANDELIER
CLOTHES PEG
COAT HANGER
CURTAINING
CURTAIN ROD
DEEP FREEZE
DINNER GONG
DISHWASHER
DOOR HANDLE
DUMB WAITER
FIRE ESCAPE
FIRE SCREEN
GARBAGE CAN
HUMIDIFIER
LAMPHOLDER
LIQUIDISER
LOFT LADDER
NET CURTAIN
NIGHT LIGHT
PHONOGRAPH
PICTURE ROD
PILLOWCASE
PILLOWSLIP
PILOT LIGHT
PLUNGE BATH
POWER POINT
PUSH BUTTON
ROSE WINDOW
ROTISSERIE
SASH WINDOW
SEPTIC TANK
SOLAR PANEL

STRIP LIGHT
TELEVISION
TIME SWITCH
TOILET ROLL
TRAVEL IRON
UPHOLSTERY
WARMING PAN
WINDOW PANE
WINDOW SILL
WINE COOLER

11
BEDSIDE LAMP
CANDLESTICK
CLOTHES LINE
CLOTHES PROP
COUNTERPANE
CURTAIN RING
DOOR KNOCKER
FINGERPLATE
FOLDING DOOR
FURNISHINGS
HEARTHSTONE
JUNCTION BOX
KITCHEN SINK
KITCHEN UNIT
LOUVRE BOARD
MANTELPIECE
MOSQUITO NET
ORIEL WINDOW
PICTURE RAIL
READING LAMP
ROLLER BLIND
ROLLER TOWEL
SLEEPING BAG
SPACE HEATER
STAIR CARPET
TUMBLE DRYER

VIDEO PLAYER
WAINSCOTING
WASHER DRYER
WINDOW FRAME
WIRELESS SET

12
ANTIMACASSAR
BREAKFAST BAR
CANDLE HOLDER
CHEST FREEZER
CLOTHES HORSE
CUSHION COVER
DORMER WINDOW
DEEP FAT FRYER
ELECTRIC FIRE
ELECTRIC OVEN
EXTRACTOR FAN
FESTOON BLIND
INSTALLATION
IRONING BOARD
KITCHEN RANGE
LIGHT FITTING
LOOKING GLASS
LOUVRE WINDOW
MAGAZINE RACK
MASTER SWITCH
PARQUET FLOOR
PICTURE FRAME
RECORD PLAYER
REFRIGERATOR
ROCKER SWITCH
SERVICE HATCH
STANDARD LAMP
STEAM CLEANER
TAPE RECORDER
TROUSER PRESS
VALANCE SHEET

WEATHERSTRIP

13
CANDLE SNUFFER
CARPET SWEEPER
CLOTHES BASKET
DOUBLE ADAPTOR
DOUBLE GLAZING
DRAINING BOARD
EXTENSION LEAD
FOOD PROCESSOR
FRIDGE FREEZER
HALOGEN HEATER
MEDICINE CHEST
MICROWAVE OVEN
PICTURE WINDOW

SEWING MACHINE
SHOWER CURTAIN
SKIRTING BOARD
SMOOTHING IRON
STRIP LIGHTING
TELEVISION SET
VACUUM CLEANER
VENETIAN BLIND
WASH-HAND BASIN

14
ANGLE-POISE LAMP
BATHROOM HEATER
CASEMENT WINDOW
CENTRAL HEATING
ELECTRIC COOKER

HOT-WATER BOTTLE
SPRING MATTRESS
WARM-AIR HEATING
WASHING MACHINE

15
AIR CONDITIONING
ELECTRIC BLANKET
IMMERSION HEATER
SANDWICH TOASTER

16
ANSWERING MACHINE
ELECTRICITY METER
FIRE EXTINGUISHER
WASTE-PAPER BASKET

Household – FURNITURE

3	WING	BUREAU	**7**	LEG REST	DIVAN BED
ARM		CANOPY	ALMIRAH	LOUNGER	DUCHESSE
BED	**5**	CARVER	ARMOIRE	OTTOMAN	FAUTEUIL
COT	BENCH	CRADLE	ARM REST	SEATING	HATSTAND
LEG	CHAIR	DRAWER	BEANBAG	SICK BED	LOO TABLE
PEW	COUCH	LITTER	BEDPOST	SOFA BED	LOVE SEAT
	DIVAN	LOCKER	BUNK BED	TALLBOY	PEDESTAL
4	EASEL	LOWBOY	CABINET	TROLLEY	PLANK BED
BUNK	FUTON	POUFFE	CAMP BED	WHATNOT	PUT-YOU-UP
COSY	STAND	ROCKER	CHARPOY		RECLINER
CRIB	STOOL	SERVER	COMMODE	**8**	SHERATON
DESK	SUITE	SETTEE	CONSOLE	ARMCHAIR	TABLE-LEG
FORM	TABLE	SETTLE	COUNTER	BASSINET	TABLE-TOP
LEAF	TRUNK	TEAPOY	HAMMOCK	BEDSTEAD	TABOURET
POUF		TESTER	HASSOCK	BOOKCASE	TANTALUS
SEAT	**6**	THRONE	HIGHBOY	CHAIR-LEG	TUB CHAIR
SOFA	BUFFET	TOILET	LECTERN	CUPBOARD	TWIN BEDS

VARGUEÑO
WARDROBE
WATER BED

9
BANQUETTE
CANE CHAIR
CARD TABLE
COATSTAND
DAVENPORT
DECKCHAIR
DINING SET
DOUBLE BED
EASY CHAIR
FOOTSTOOL
FURNITURE
HALLSTAND
HALL TABLE
HEADBOARD
HIGH CHAIR
PIER TABLE
SHAKEDOWN
SIDEBOARD
SIDE TABLE
SINGLE BED

TABLE-LEAF
TÊTE-À-TÊTE
WASHSTAND
WORK BENCH

10
CANTERBURY
CHIFFONIER
DUMB WAITER
ESCRITOIRE
FEATHER BED
FOUR-POSTER
MUSIC STOOL
PIANO STOOL
SECRETAIRE
TEA TROLLEY
TOILET SEAT
TRICLINIUM
TRUCKLE BED
TRUNDLE BED
VANITY UNIT
WINDOW SEAT

11
CABRIOLE LEG

CHIPPENDALE
COFFEE TABLE
DINING CHAIR
DINING TABLE
DINNER TABLE
DISPLAY UNIT
HEPPLEWHITE
PERIOD PIECE
READING DESK
ROLL-TOP DESK
STUDIO COUCH
SWIVEL CHAIR
WRITING DESK

12
BEDROOM SUITE
BEDSIDE TABLE
CHAISE LONGUE
CHESTERFIELD
CONSOLE TABLE
GATELEG TABLE
KING-SIZED BED
NEST OF TABLES
ROCKING CHAIR
WINDSOR CHAIR

WRITING TABLE

13
BATHROOM SUITE
BONHEUR-DU-JOUR
CANE FURNITURE
DRAW-LEAF TABLE
DRESSING TABLE
FILING CABINET
FOUR-POSTER BED
PEDESTAL TABLE
PEMBROKE TABLE
PIECRUST TABLE
QUEEN-SIZED BED
UMBRELLA STAND

14
BREAKFAST TABLE
CHEST OF DRAWERS
RECLINING CHAIR

15
DINING-ROOM SUITE
OCCASIONAL TABLE
THREE-PIECE SUITE

Household – KITCHENWARE

3	URN	FORK	DOILY	QUERN	WHISK	GOBLET
CUP	WOK	TRAY	FLUTE	SCOOP		GRATER
JUG			FRYER	SIEVE	**6**	KETTLE
MAT	**4**	**5**	GLASS	SLICE	BOTTLE	MASHER
MUG	BOAT	ASHET	KNIFE	SPOON	CARAFE	NAPKIN
PAN	BOWL	CHINA	LADLE	TAZZA	CARVER	OPENER
POT	COSY	COUPE	PLATE	TIMER	COPITA	PADDLE
TIN	DISH	CRUET	PYREX	TONGS	EGG CUP	PEELER

POPPER
RUMMER
SALVER
SAUCER
SHAKER
SILVER
SKEWER
TEACUP
TEAPOT
TEA SET
TEA URN
TRIVET
TUREEN
TURNER

7

CHARGER
CHIP PAN
CHOPPER
COASTER
COCOTTE
CUTLERY
ÉCUELLE
EGG COSY
EPERGNE
GRIDDLE
MESS TIN
MILK JUG
PAP BOAT
POACHER
PLATTER
RAMEKIN
SAMOVAR
SERVICE
SKILLET
SPATULA
STEWPOT
TEA COSY

TEA TRAY
TERRINE
TOBY JUG
TUMBLER
UTENSIL

8

BAKEWARE
BREAD BIN
COLANDER
CROCKERY
DECANTER
EGG SLICE
EGG SPOON
EGG TIMER
EGG WHISK
JELLY BAG
OVEN TRAY
OVENWARE
SAUCEPAN
SOUP DISH
SQUEEZER
STOCKPOT
STRAINER
TABLE MAT
TEASPOON
TEA TOWEL
TRENCHER

9

BAIN-MARIE
BAKING TIN
CAKE STAND
CAN OPENER
CHINAWARE
COFFEE CUP
COFFEE POT
CORKSCREW

DINNER SET
DISHCLOTH
DUTCH OVEN
EGG BEATER
FISH KNIFE
FISH PLATE
FISH SLICE
FRYING PAN
GLASSWARE
GRAVY BOAT
ICE BUCKET
LOVING CUP
PEPPER POT
PORRINGER
POSSET CUP
PUNCHBOWL
SALT SPOON
SAUCE BOAT
SERVIETTE
SHOT GLASS
SLOP BASIN
SOUP PLATE
SOUP SPOON
SUGAR BOWL
TABLEWARE
TEA THINGS
TIN OPENER
TOAST RACK
WINE GLASS

10

BAKING TRAY
BREADBOARD
BUTTER DISH
CHOPSTICKS
COFFEE MILL
CRUET-STAND
FINGER BOWL

FISH KETTLE
HOLLOW-WARE
JELLY MOULD
KNIFEBOARD
MEAT HAMMER
MUSTARD POT
NAPKIN RING
PERCOLATOR
ROLLING PIN
SALAD PLATE
SALT CELLAR
SUGAR BASIN
SUGAR TONGS
TABLECLOTH
TABLE COVER
TABLE KNIFE
TABLESPOON
TEA SERVICE
TUPPERWARE
WAFFLE IRON
WASSAIL CUP

11

BRANDY GLASS
BUTTER KNIFE
CENTREPIECE
CHAFING DISH
CHEESE KNIFE
EARTHENWARE
HONEY DIPPER
KETTLE CLOTH
KITCHENWARE
NUTCRACKERS
PASTA SERVER
PIZZA SLICER
PLATE WARMER
TABLE NAPKIN
TEA STRAINER

WASSAIL BOWL
WOODEN SPOON

12
APOSTLE SPOON
BALLOON GLASS
BALLOON WHISK
BASTING BRUSH
BOTTLE OPENER
CARVING KNIFE
CHEESE GRATER

DESSERTSPOON
LIQUEUR GLASS
MOUSTACHE CUP
SERVING SPOON
SLOTTED SPOON
SWIZZLE STICK
TOASTING FORK

13
CHOPPING BLOCK
CHOPPING BOARD

COFFEE GRINDER
DINNER SERVICE
GARLIC CRUSHER
LEMON SQUEEZER
PORRIDGE STICK
RUNCIBLE SPOON

14
COCKTAIL SHAKER
ORANGE SQUEEZER
PRESSURE COOKER

Industry & Economy

Industry & Economy – BUSINESS & BANKING

3	4	HYPE	SAVE	BRAND	MERGE	TALLY
AGM	BANK	KITE	SELL	BUYER	OFFER	TERMS
ATM	BEAR	LINE	SIGN	CHAIR	ORDER	TESSA
BID	BILL	LOAN	SNIP	CHECK	OWNER	TRADE
BUY	BOND	LOGO	SPEC	CLAIM	PITCH	TRUST
FEE	BOOM	LOSS	SWAP	CRASH	PRICE	USURY
IOU	BOSS	MAKE	TICK	DEBIT	QUOTA	VALUE
ISA	BULL	NAME	TILL	DRAFT	QUOTE	WAGES
JOB	CASH	NETT	TOLL	DRIVE	RAISE	YIELD
LOT	COST	PAWN	VISA	ENTRY	ROUND	
PAR	DEAL	PERK	WAGE	FLYER	SAVER	6
PAY	DEBT	PLUG	WARE	FLOAT	SCRIP	ADVERT
REP	FILE	PUFF		GILTS	SHARE	AGENCY
RUN	FIRM	PUFF	5	GOODS	SLUMP	AGENDA
TAB	FUND	RENT	AUDIT	GROSS	SPEND	AMOUNT
TAX	GAIN	RING	BOARD	HOUSE	STAFF	ASSETS
VAT	GIRO	RISE	BONUS	ISSUE	STOCK	BANKER
	HIRE	RUIN	BOOKS	LAY-BY	STORE	BARTER
		SALE				

BOURSE	OUTFIT	ANNUITY	PARTNER	(or base rate)
BRANCH	OUTLAY	ARREARS	PAYROLL	BANKROLL
BROKER	OUTPUT	AUCTION	PENSION	BANKRUPT
BUREAU	PAYOLA	AUDITOR	PLACARD	BASE RATE
BUYING	PEDLAR	BACKLOG	PREMIUM	(or bank rate)
CARTEL	POLICY	BAD DEBT	PRODUCT	BILLHEAD
CHARGE	POSTER	BALANCE	PROJECT	BLUE-CHIP
CHEQUE	PROFIT	BANKING	RECEIPT	BRIDGING
COUPON	REFUND	BAR CODE	RECLAIM	BUSINESS
CREDIT	RENTAL	BARGAIN	RESERVE	CAMPAIGN
CUSTOM	RESALE	BULK-BUY	SECONDS	CASHBACK
DEALER	RETAIL	CAPITAL	SELLING	CASH BOOK
EMPLOY	RETURN	CASH COW	SERVICE	CASH CARD
ENGAGE	RIP-OFF	CASHIER	SMALL AD	CASH CROP
EXPORT	SALARY	CHAFFER	SPIN-OFF	CASH FLOW
FILING	SAMPLE	CHARTER	SPONSOR	CHAIRMAN
GROWTH	SAVING	CLOSURE	SQUEEZE	COMMERCE
HAGGLE	SELLER	COMPACT	STORAGE	CONTANGO
HAWKER	SETTLE	COMPANY	SURPLUS	CONTRACT
HIRING	SLOGAN	CONCERN	TAKINGS	DELIVERY
IMPORT	SPIRAL	CONSOLS	TRADE-IN	DIRECTOR
IMPOST	STAPLE	DAYBOOK	TRADING	DISCOUNT
INCOME	STOCKS	DEALING	TRAFFIC	DIVIDEND
INDENT	SUPPLY	DEFICIT	TRANCHE	DRY GOODS
INVEST	TARIFF	DEPOSIT	VENDING	EMPLOYEE
JOBBER	TELLER	ECONOMY	VENTURE	EMPLOYER
JOB LOT	TENDER	EMBARGO	VOUCHER	EQUITIES
LABOUR	TRADER	EXPENSES	WARRANT	ESTIMATE
LAUNCH	TYCOON	FINANCE		EXCHANGE
LEDGER	USANCE	FUTURES	**8**	EXPENSES
MARGIN	USURER	GIMMICK	ACCOUNTS	EXPORTER
MARKET	VENDOR	HAGGLER	AMORTISE	FILE COPY
MERGER	VENDUE	INVOICE	AUDITING	FLAT RATE
METAGE		JOURNAL	BANK BILL	GIVEAWAY
NOTICE	**7**	LIAISON	BANK BOOK	GOODWILL
OFFICE	ACCOUNT	MAGNATE	BANK CARD	HAGGLING
ONCOST	ADVANCE	MANAGER	BANKNOTE	HARD SELL
OPTION	AFFAIRS	MINUTES	BANK RATE	HEADHUNT

HOARDING
IMPORTER
INCREASE
INDUSTRY
INTEREST
INVESTOR
KITEMARK
MERCHANT
MONOPOLY
MORTGAGE
ORDERING
PASSBOOK
PICKINGS
POUNDAGE
PRACTICE
PRICE TAG
PROPOSAL
PURCHASE
RECEIPTS
RECEIVER
RECOURSE
RENT ROLL
RETAILER
SALESMAN
SCHEDULE
SECURITY
SETTLING
SHARE-OUT
SHIPMENT
SHOWCARD
SHUTDOWN
SIDELINE
SOFT SELL
SOLVENCY
SPENDING
STALLAGE
STRADDLE
SWAPPING

TAKEOVER
TURNOVER
UNIT COST
VIREMENT
WARRANTY

9

AGREEMENT
ARBITRAGE
ASSURANCE
 (or insurance)
BANK STOCK
BILLBOARD
BOX NUMBER
BRAND NAME
BROKERAGE
BY-PRODUCT
CASHPOINT
COMMODITY
COST PRICE
DEBENTURE
DEFERMENT
DEFLATION
ENDOWMENT
ESTIMATOR
EXCHEQUER
EXPANSION
EXPORTING
FAIR TRADE
FINANCIAL
FINANCIER
FLOTATION
FRANCHISE
FREE TRADE
GUARANTEE
HALF-SHARE
IMBALANCE
IMPORTING

INCREMENT
INDENTURE
INFLATION
INSURANCE
 (or assurance)
INVENTORY
KEEN PRICE
MAIL ORDER
MARKETING
MORTGAGEE
MORTGAGOR
OLIGOPOLY
ORDER BOOK
ORDER FORM
OUTGOINGS
OVERDRAFT
OVERHEADS
PETTY CASH
PORTFOLIO
PRICE LIST
PRICE RING
PRINCIPAL
PROMOTION
PUBLICITY
QUOTATION
RECESSION
RECKONING
REDUCTION
REFERENCE
REFLATION
SALE PRICE
SIGNBOARD
SOFT GOODS
SPECIALTY
STATEMENT
STOCKLIST
STOCKPILE
STOCKTAKE

TENDERING
TRADEMARK
TRADE NAME
TRUST FUND
UNIT TRUST
UTILITIES
VALUATION
WATERMARK
WHITE SALE
WHOLESALE

10

ACCOUNTANT
ACCOUNTING
AMALGAMATE
AUTOMATION
BANKRUPTCY
BEAR MARKET
BILL OF SALE
BONUS ISSUE
BOOKKEEPER
BULK BUYING
BULL MARKET
CATCHPENNY
CHEQUEBOOK
CHEQUE CARD
 (or banker's card)
COLLATERAL
COMMERCIAL
COMMISSION
CONSORTIUM
CREDIT CARD
CREDIT NOTE
DEPRESSION
EMPLOYMENT
ENGAGEMENT
ENTERPRISE
ESTIMATION

EVALUATION
FISCAL YEAR
FORCED SALE
FORWARDING
FREE SAMPLE
HOME MARKET
INSOLVENCY
INSTALMENT
INVESTMENT
JOINT STOCK
JUMBLE SALE
  (or rummage sale)
KITE-FLYING
LIQUIDATOR
LOSS-LEADER
MAIN CHANCE
MANAGEMENT
MERCANTILE
MORATORIUM
MUTUAL FUND
NON-PAYMENT
OVERCHARGE
PAWNBROKER
PERCENTAGE
PERPETUITY
PRICE POINT
PROPRIETOR
PROSPECTUS
SALES DRIVE
SALESWOMAN
SCRIP ISSUE
SECURITIES
SETTLEMENT
SHOPKEEPER
SPECULATOR
SQUARE DEAL
STOCKTAKER
SUBSIDIARY

TRADE CYCLE
TRADE PRICE
WAGE FREEZE
WHITE GOODS
WHOLESALER
WITHDRAWAL

11
ADVERTISING
APPOINTMENT
ASKING PRICE
BANK BALANCE
BANKER'S CARD
  (or cheque card)
BANK MANAGER
BIG BUSINESS
BLACK MARKET
BLANK CHEQUE
BOOKKEEPING
CASH PAYMENT
CONSIGNMENT
COUNTERFOIL
COUNTERMARK
DEVALUATION
DIRECT DEBIT
DOUBLE-ENTRY
DOWN PAYMENT
ENDORSEMENT
EXPENDITURE
EXPORTATION
FLUCTUATION
FIXED ASSETS
FIXED CHARGE
IMPORTATION
KEY INDUSTRY
LIQUIDATION
MARKET PRICE
MARKET VALUE

MERCHANDISE
MONEY-LENDER
MONEY MARKET
OVERPAYMENT
PACKAGE DEAL
PART-PAYMENT
PARTNERSHIP
PAWNBROKING
PILOT SCHEME
PROPOSITION
REPEAT ORDER
REQUISITION
RISK CAPITAL
  (or venture capital)
RUMMAGE SALE
  (or jumble sale)
SALES LEDGER
SHAREHOLDER
SINGLE-ENTRY
SINKING FUND
SPECULATION
SPONSORSHIP
STOCKBROKER
STOCKJOBBER
STOCK MARKET
STOCKPILING
STOCKTAKING
SUBCONTRACT
TESTIMONIAL
TRADE SECRET
TRANSACTION
UNDERCHARGE
UNDERWRITER
WAREHOUSING

12
AMALGAMATION
AMORTISATION

APPRECIATION
BALANCE SHEET
BANKER'S DRAFT
BOARD MEETING
BOUGHT LEDGER
BRAND LOYALTY
BRIDGING LOAN
BUYERS' MARKET
CAPITAL GAINS
CAPITAL GOODS
CAR INSURANCE
CHARTER PARTY
CLEARING BANK
CONGLOMERATE
COST ANALYSIS
CREDIT RATING
DEPRECIATION
DISBURSEMENT
DISCOUNT RATE
DUTCH AUCTION
ENTREPRENEUR
EXPORT MARKET
FIXED CAPITAL
GOING CONCERN
GROUP PENSION
HIRE PURCHASE
  (or the never-never)
HORSE-TRADING
JOINT ACCOUNT
LOSS ADJUSTER
MERCANTILISM
MONEY-LENDING
MONEY-SPINNER
MORTGAGE RATE
ORGANISATION
PASSING TRADE
PRICE CONTROL
PRICE-CUTTING

PROFIT MARGIN
REINVESTMENT
RESERVE PRICE
SALESMANSHIP
SELLING PRICE
SHARE CAPITAL
SHELL COMPANY
SPECIAL OFFER
STOCKBROKING
STOCK-IN-TRADE
STOCKJOBBING
TRADING STAMP
UNDERWRITING

13
ADVERTISEMENT
APPROPRIATION
BACKWARDATION
BUSINESS CYCLE
CHARGE ACCOUNT
CLEARING HOUSE
CONSUMER GOODS
DOUBLE-DEALING
ESTABLISHMENT
FINANCIAL YEAR
FIRE INSURANCE
FRINGE BENEFIT
HEAVY INDUSTRY
INDUSTRIALISM
LIFE INSURANCE
LIGHT INDUSTRY
MARKETABILITY
ORDINARY SHARE
OVERVALUATION
PARENT COMPANY
PUBLIC COMPANY
SANDWICH BOARD
SELLERS' MARKET

SHARP PRACTICE
STANDING ORDER
STOCK EXCHANGE
SWITCH SELLING
THE NEVER-NEVER
  (or hire purchase)
VICIOUS SPIRAL

14
BALANCE OF TRADE
BILL OF EXCHANGE
BUREAU DE CHANGE
COMPANY PENSION
CORPORATION TAX
COST ACCOUNTANT
COST ACCOUNTING
CURRENT ACCOUNT
DEFERRED SHARES
DEPOSIT ACCOUNT
EXPENSE ACCOUNT
FLOATING CHARGE
FREE ENTERPRISE
GROUP INSURANCE
HOLDING COMPANY
HOUSE INSURANCE
INERTIA SELLING
INSURANCE AGENT
INSURANCE CLAIM
INVISIBLE TRADE
LETTER OF CREDIT
LIMITED COMPANY
MARKET RESEARCH
OVERPRODUCTION
PRIVATE COMPANY
PROMISSORY NOTE
PUBLICITY STUNT
PYRAMID SELLING
REORGANISATION

UNDERVALUATION
VENTURE CAPITAL
 (or risk capital)
VESTED INTEREST
VISIBLE EXPORTS
VISIBLE IMPORTS

15
BUILDING SOCIETY
BUSINESS MEETING
CAPITAL GAINS TAX
DEFERRED ANNUITY
DIVIDEND WARRANT
ENDOWMENT POLICY

ESCALATOR CLAUSE
FLOATING CAPITAL
GOLDEN HANDCUFFS
GOLDEN HANDSHAKE
INSURANCE BROKER
INVESTMENT TRUST
MARINE INSURANCE
PERSONAL PENSION
PREFERENCE SHARE
PREFERENCE STOCK
SLEEPING PARTNER
SUPPLY AND DEMAND
SUSPENSE ACCOUNT
UNDERPRODUCTION

16
BUY ONE GET ONE FREE
INVISIBLE EXPORTS
INVISIBLE IMPORTS
OFFICIAL RECEIVER
TRAVELLER'S CHEQUE

17
ENDOWMENT MORTGAGE
REPAYMENT MORTGAGE
VENTURE CAPITALIST

Industry & Economy – Engineering – INSTRUMENTS & GAUGES

4	ETALON	SOUNDER	RHEOSTAT	ENDOSCOPE
RULE	FINDER	SUNDIAL	SPYGLASS	ERGOMETER
	LOGGER	SYRINGE		FLOWMETER
5	SCALER	T-SQUARE	**9**	GRADUATOR
BEVEL	SCALES	VERNIER	AEROMETER	GYROSCOPE
CLOCK	SQUARE		ALTIMETER	HAEMOSTAT
GAUGE	STROBE	**8**	ASPIRATOR	HELIOSTAT
GLASS		CALIPERS	ASTROLABE	HODOSCOPE
LEVEL	**7**	DETECTOR	BAROGRAPH	HOURGLASS
METER	ALIDADE	DIPSTICK	BAROMETER	HYDROSTAT
NORMA	AMMETER	DIVIDERS	BOLOMETER	INDICATOR
PLUMB	ANEROID	GAS METER	CAPACITOR	KONIMETER
RULER	BALANCE	MYOGRAPH	CLEPSYDRA	KYMOGRAPH
SCALE	COHERER	ODOMETER	COELOSTAT	MACHMETER
SIZER	COMPASS	OHMMETER	COMPASSES	MANOMETER
WATCH	MEASURE	OTOSCOPE	CRYOMETER	METRONOME
	MONITOR	OXIMETER	DOSIMETER	NAVIGATOR
6	PELORUS	QUADRANT	DUROMETER	OPTOMETER
ABACUS	SEXTANT	RESISTOR	ECHOGRAPH	OSMOMETER

PEDOMETER
PERIMETER
PERISCOPE
PILOT TUBE
PLUMB LINE
PLUMB RULE
POLYGRAPH
  (or lie detector)
PYROMETER
RAIN GAUGE
  (or pluviometer)
REFLECTOR
REFRACTOR
SANDGLASS
SET SQUARE
SLIDE RULE
STOPWATCH
TAXIMETER
TELEMETER
TELESCOPE
TILTMETER
TONOMETER
VOLTMETER
WATTMETER
WIND GAUGE
  (or anemometer)

10
ACIDIMETER
ALTAZIMUTH
ANEMOGRAPH
ANEMOMETER
  (or wind gauge)
AUDIOMETER
BATHYMETER
BINOCULARS
CLINOMETER
COLLIMATOR

COMPARATOR
CYCLOMETER
CYSTOSCOPE
DENSIMETER
DUMPY LEVEL
EUDIOMETER
FATHOMETER
GONIOMETER
GRAVIMETER
HELIOGRAPH
HELIOMETER
HYDROMETER
HYGROMETER
HYGROSCOPE
HYPSOMETER
INSTRUMENT
INTEGRATOR
MICROMETER
MICROSCOPE
OPISOMETER
PANTOGRAPH
PELVIMETER
PHOTOMETER
PIEZOMETER
PLANE TABLE
PLANIMETER
PLANOMETER
PROTRACTOR
PULSOMETER
PYCNOMETER
RADIOMETER
RHINOSCOPE
SIDEROSTAT
SPIROGRAPH
SPIROMETER
STABILISER
STATOSCOPE
STEAM GAUGE

STORM GLASS
TACHOGRAPH
TACHOMETER
TACHYMETER
THEODOLITE
THERMISTOR
THERMOSTAT
TRIBOMETER
VARIOMETER
VISCOMETER
  (or viscosimeter)
WATER GLASS
WATER LEVEL
WATER METER

11
ACTINOMETER
ATOMIC CLOCK
AUSCULTATOR
BEVEL SQUARE
CALIPER RULE
CALORIMETER
CARDIOGRAPH
CHRONOGRAPH
CHRONOMETER
COLORIMETER
DIVINING ROD
DYNAMOMETER
ECHO SOUNDER
FEELER GAUGE
FLUOROSCOPE
GRADIOMETER
GYROCOMPASS
INTOXIMETER
JACOB'S STAFF
KERATOSCOPE
LIE DETECTOR
  (or polygraph)

PLUVIOMETER
  (or rain gauge)
POLARIMETER
  (or polariscope)
POLARISCOPE
  (or polarimeter)
RANGEFINDER
SALINOMETER
SEISMOGRAPH
  (or seismometer)
SEISMOMETER
  (or seismograph)
SPEEDOMETER
SPIRIT LEVEL
STEREOMETER
STETHOSCOPE
STROBOSCOPE
SWINGOMETER
THERMOGRAPH
THERMOMETER
VAPORIMETER

12
BOW COMPASSES
BREATHALYSER
BRONCHOSCOPE
CATHETOMETER
DECLINOMETER
DE PRONY BRAKE
ELECTROMETER
ELECTROSCOPE
EXTENSOMETER
FIELD GLASSES
GALVANOMETER
GALVANOSCOPE
GUNTER'S CHAIN
GUNTER'S SCALE
INCLINOMETER

KATHAROMETER
LARYNGOSCOPE
MAGNETOGRAPH
MAGNETOMETER
MEASURING ROD
METEOROGRAPH
MICROBALANCE
MYRINGOSCOPE
NEPHELOMETER
OSCILLOSCOPE
PSYCHROMETER
RADIO COMPASS
SCINTILLATOR
SENSITOMETER
SLIDING SCALE
SPECTROGRAPH
SPECTROMETER
SPECTROSCOPE
SPHYGMOGRAPH
SPHYGMOMETER
STRAIGHT EDGE
VERNIER SCALE
VISCOSIMETER
  (or viscometer)
WEATHER GLASS
WEATHER HOUSE

13
ACCELEROMETER
ALCOHOLOMETER
COUNTING FRAME
GEIGER COUNTER
METAL DETECTOR
PARALLEL RULER
POTENTIOMETER
PRESSURE GAUGE
REFRACTOMETER
SACCHAROMETER
SMOKE DETECTOR
SPRING BALANCE
TACHISTOSCOPE
TRANSIT CIRCLE
  (or meridian circle)

14
ABSORPTIOMETER
DIFFRACTOMETER
ENCEPHALOGRAPH
ENGINEER'S SCALE
INTERFEROMETER
LASER LINE LEVEL
MERIDIAN CIRCLE
  (or transit circle)

OPHTHALMOSCOPE
RADIO TELESCOPE
SPINTHARISCOPE
TORSION BALANCE
WEIGHING SCALES

15
ARCHITECT'S SCALE
ELECTROMYOGRAPH
MAGNIFYING GLASS
PHASE MICROSCOPE
RADIO-GONIOMETER
ULTRAMICROSCOPE

16
ELECTRICITY METER
LASER RANGEFINDER
MASS SPECTROMETER
WHEATSTONE BRIDGE

17
NICHOLS RADIOMETER
TYRE-PRESSURE GAUGE

18
ELECTRON MICROSCOPE

Industry & Economy – Engineering – WEIGHTS & MEASURES

3	CUP	MHO	OKA	TON	BUTT	FEET
AMP	DAY	(now	PIN	TUN	BYTE	FOOT
ARE	ELL	siemens)	RAD		CORD	GILL
BAR	ERG	MIL	REM	**4**	CRAN	GRAM
BEL	HIN	NIP	ROD	ACRE	DRAM	(or gramme)
BIT	LUX	OHM	TOG	BARN	DYNE	HAND

HOUR	COUNT	WIDTH	SQUARE	QUINTAL	SHORT TON
INCH	CUBIT		STOKES	RÖNTGEN	SPOONFUL
KILO	CURIE	**6**	TALENT	SCRUPLE	WATT-HOUR
KNOT	CUSEC	AMOUNT	TIERCE	SEA MILE	
LINK	DEBYE	AMPERE	WEIGHT	SIEMENS	**9**
MILE	DEPTH	BARREL		STADIUM	BOARD FOOT
MOLE	FARAD	BUNDLE	**7**	TONNAGE	CENTIGRAM
NAIL	FERMI	BUSHEL	ACREAGE	VOLTAGE	CUBIC FOOT
PECK	GAUGE	CANDLE	AIR MILE	WATTAGE	CUBIC INCH
PHON	GAUSS	(now	BREADTH	YARDAGE	CUBIC YARD
PHOT	GIRTH	candela)	CALIBRE		DECALITRE
PINT	GRAIN	CUPFUL	CALORIE	**8**	DECAMETRE
PIPE	HENRY	DECADE	CANDELA	AMPERAGE	DECILITRE
POLE	HERTZ	DEGREE	CENTURY	ÅNGSTRÖM	DECIMETRE
REAM	JOULE	DENIER	COULOMB	CAPACITY	FOOT-POUND
ROOD	LITRE	DRACHM	CUP SIZE	CENTIARE	FREQUENCY
SEER	LUMEN	FATHOM	DECIARE	CUBIC TON	HALF-OUNCE
SHOT	METRE	FIRKIN	DECIBEL	DECAGRAM	HALF-POUND
SIZE	MINIM	GALLON	DIOPTRE	DECIGRAM	HECTOGRAM
SONE	MONTH	GRAMME	FARADAY	DISTANCE	KILDERKIN
SPAN	NEPER	(or gram)	FOOTAGE	GROSS TON	KILOCYCLE
TAEL	OUNCE	HEIGHT	FURLONG	HALF-INCH	KILOHERTZ
TORR	PERCH	JIGGER	HECTARE	HALF-PINT	KILOLITRE
TROY	PINCH	KELVIN	KILOBAR	HOGSHEAD	KILOMETRE
UNIT	POINT	LEAGUE	KILOTON	JEROBOAM	LIGHT YEAR
VOLT	POISE	LENGTH	LAMBERT	KILOGRAM	MEGACYCLE
WATT	POUND	MAGNUM	(now	KILOWATT	MEGAFARAD
WEEK	QUART	MEGOHM	candela)	LEAP YEAR	MEGAHERTZ
YARD	QUIRE	MICRON	LONG TON	MEGAVOLT	METRIC TON
YEAR	STERE	MINUTE	LUSTRUM	MEGAWATT	MICROGRAM
	STILB	MORGEN	MAXWELL	MICROBAR	MICROWATT
5	STONE	NEWTON	MEASURE	MICROLUX	MILLIGRAM
ANGLE	TESLA	NOGGIN	MEGATON	MILLIARE	NANOMETRE
BIGHA	THERM	PARSEC	MICROHM	MILLIBAR	SCANTLING
BUNCH	TONNE	PASCAL	MILEAGE	MUTCHKIN	STERADIAN
CABLE	TRUSS	RADIAN	OERSTED	POUNDAGE	TRAIN MILE
CARAT	VERST	SECOND	POUNDAL	QUANTITY	WHEELBASE
CHAIN	WEBER	SI UNIT	QUARTER	REHOBOAM	

10
BARLEYCORN
CENTILITRE
CENTIMETRE
CUBIC METRE
DRY MEASURE
FLUID OUNCE
FREIGHT TON
HECTOLITRE
HECTOMETRE
HORSEPOWER
LEAP SECOND
MEGANEWTON
MICROFARAD
MICROHENRY
MILLENNIUM

MILLILITRE
MILLIMETRE
NANOSECOND
SQUARE FOOT
SQUARE INCH
SQUARE MILE
SQUARE YARD
TROY WEIGHT

11
AVOIRDUPOIS
CANDLEPOWER
KILOCALORIE
LONG MEASURE
MEASUREMENT
MICROAMPERE

MICROSECOND
MILLIAMPERE
PENNYWEIGHT
SQUARE METRE
TEASPOONFUL
THERMAL UNIT

12
CUBIC MEASURE
ELECTRON VOLT
KILOWATT-HOUR
METRIC SYSTEM
NAUTICAL MILE

13
CUBIC CAPACITY

DECIMAL SYSTEM
HUNDREDWEIGHT
LIQUID MEASURE
SQUARE MEASURE
TABLESPOONFUL

14
CYCLE PER SECOND
  (now hertz)
IMPERIAL WEIGHT

15
BRAKE HORSEPOWER
CUBIC CENTIMETRE
DESSERTSPOONFUL
IMPERIAL MEASURE

Industry & Economy – FARMING & GARDENING

3
BED
CRU
CUT
DIG
DIP
FAN
FOG
HAY
HOE
LEA
LEY
MOW
PEN
PIT
POT
RUN

RUT
SET
SOD
SOW
STY
TED

4
BALE
BARN
BYRE
CART
COOP
CRIB
CROP
DUNG
DYKE

FARM
FEED
FOLD
GATE
GROW
HA-HA
HAND
HERD
KERF
LAND
LAWN
LOAM
LOFT
MARL
OATS
OXER
PALE

PATH
PEON
PEST
PLOT
POST
RAKE
REAP
RICK
SEED
SILO
SOIL
SPIT
TILL
TURF
WAIN
YARD
YOKE

5
BAULK
BOWER
BRAND
BREED
CLAMP
CROFT
CRUSH
DAIRY
DITCH
DRAIN
EARTH
FENCE
FIELD
FLAIL
FRAME
GLEAN

GRAFT
GRASS
GUANO
HEDGE
HUMUS
HUTCH
LEVEL
MOULD
MOWER
MULCH
NURSE
OASIS
PADDY
PATIO
PLANT
POUND
PRUNE

RANCH
RANGE
REPOT
RIDGE
ROGUE
ROOST
SHARE
SHEAF
SHOCK
SPADE
STACK
STALL
STILE
STOCK
STOOK
STORE
STRAW

SWARD
SWILL
TILTH
TRUSS
YIELD

6
ANNUAL
APIARY
ARBOUR
BINDER
BLIGHT
BORDER
CLOCHE
CORRAL
CRATCH
DERRIS
DIBBER
DIBBLE
DROVER
EDGING
FALLOW
FANNER
FARMER
FODDER
FORAGE
FURROW
GARDEN
GARNER
GROUND
GROWTH
HARROW
HAYING
HAYMOW
HEN RUN
HERDER
HOPPER
HOTBED

HUSKER
HYBRID
KHARIF
LISTER
LITTER
MANGER
MANURE
MARKET
MEADOW
MOWING
PALING
PAVING
PIGMAN
PIG PEN
PIG STY
PLOUGH
RATOON
REAPER
RENNET
RIDDLE
ROLLER
SCREEN
SCYTHE
SEEDER
SHEARS
SICKLE
SILAGE
SLURRY
SOWING
STABLE
TEDDER
THRESH
TRENCH
TROUGH
TROWEL
VINERY
WEEDER
WINNOW

7
BATTERY
BEDDING
BEEHIVE
BREEDER
CHANNEL
COMBINE
COMPOST
COPPICE
COULTER
COWBELL
COWSHED
CROPPER
CUTTING
DECKING
DIGGING
FARMING
FEEDLOT
FENCING
GRANARY
GRAZING
HARVEST
HAYCOCK
HAYLAGE
HAYLOFT
HAYRICK
HAYSEED
HEDGING
HEN COOP
HOLDING
HOPPING
KIBBUTZ
KOLKHOZ
LINDANE
MILKING
MOWINGS
NETTING
NITRATE

NURSERY
ORCHARD
OX-FENCE
PADDOCK
PASTURE
PEONAGE
PERGOLA
PIGGERY
PINETUM
PLANTER
PRODUCE
PRUNING
REAPING
ROCKERY
SEEDBED
SEEDBOX
SPRAYER
STADDLE
STUBBLE
SUBSOIL
TILLAGE
TILLING
TOPIARY
TOPSOIL
TRACTOR
TRAILER
TRELLIS
TURFING
VINTAGE
WEEDING
WINDROW

8
AGRARIAN
AGRONOMY
APHICIDE
BARN DOOR
BARNYARD

BEANPOLE
BIANNUAL
BIENNIAL
BIRDBATH
BONEMEAL
BREEDING
COMPOUND
COWHOUSE
CROFTING
CROPPING
CROSSING
CRUSH-PEN
DEADHEAD
DRAINAGE
DOVECOTE
DUNGHEAP
DUNGHILL
DUTCH HOE
ELEVATOR
ENSILAGE
ESPALIER
ESTANCIA
FARMHAND
FARMYARD
FATSTOCK
FISH POND
GARDENER
GLEANING
GOATHERD
GRAFTING
GRASSBOX
HATCHERY
HAYMAKER
HAYSTACK
HEDGEROW
HENHOUSE
HOME FARM
HOSEPIPE

HOSEREEL
HOTHOUSE
IRRIGATE
LOOSE BOX
NOSE RING
ORANGERY
OUTFIELD
PALISADE
PARAQUAT
PARTERRE
PEDIGREE
PLANTING
PLANT POT
POMOLOGY
POT PLANT
PRICK OUT
RANCHING
ROOT CROP
ROSARIUM
ROTATION
ROTENONE
SEEDSMAN
SHEARING
SHEEP DIP
SHEEP RUN
SPRAY GUN
SPRAYING
SPREADER
STABLING
STAMPEDE
STEADING
STOCKADE
THRESHER
VENDANGE
VIGNERON
VINEYARD
VINTAGER
WINDFALL

9
AFTERMATH
ALLOTMENT
ARBORETUM
BARLEYMOW
BEESTINGS
BELL GLASS
BIRD TABLE
BROADCAST
COLD FRAME
CORNFIELD
COVER CROP
CULTIVATE
DEER FENCE
DUTCH BARN
ENCLOSURE
FLOWER BED
FLOWERPOT
FUNGICIDE
GARDENING
HARVESTER
HERBARIUM
HERBICIDE
HOP GARDEN
HUSBANDRY
INCUBATOR
INTERCROP
IRRIGATOR
LAWNMOWER
LEAF MOULD
LIVESTOCK
PASTURAGE
PERENNIAL
PERPETUAL
PESTICIDE
PHOSPHATE
PIG FARMER
PITCHFORK

PROPAGATE
REPOTTING
RICEFIELD
RING FENCE
SCARECROW
SECATEURS
SEED DRILL
SHEEPFOLD
SHEEP WALK
SHRUBBERY
SPRINKLER
STACKYARD
STOCK WHIP
STOCKYARD
SUBSOILER
TEA GARDEN
THRESHING
TROUT FARM
UNDERSOIL
VITICETUM
WEEDICIDE
WHIP GRAFT
WINDOW BOX
WINNOWING

10
APICULTURE
BACK GARDEN
BARBED WIRE
CATTLE GRID
CHICKEN RUN
CULTIVATOR
DEEP LITTER
DISC HARROW
DRY FARMING
FERTILISER
GARDEN PATH
GARDEN WALL

GREENHOUSE
HERB GARDEN
HILL FARMER
INCUBATION
IRRIGATION
MEADOWLAND
MUCK-RAKING
MUTUAL WALL
NESTING BOX
PADDY FIELD
PARIS GREEN
PIGEON LOFT
PLANTATION
PLOUGHLAND
PRODUCTION
PROPAGATOR
ROCK GARDEN
ROOF GARDEN
ROSE GARDEN
SEWAGE FARM
SUBSOILING
TOPSOILING
WEEDKILLER
WHEATFIELD

11
AGRICULTURE
AGROBIOLOGY
CHAIN HARROW
COMPOST HEAP
CRAZY PAVING
CROP DUSTING
CULTIVATION
FACTORY FARM
FLOWER CLOCK
FRONT GARDEN
GARDEN GNOME
GREEN MANURE

HARDY ANNUAL
HARVEST HOME
HEAVY ROLLER
HILL FARMING
HYDROPONICS
INSECTICIDE
LINSEED CAKE
MONOCULTURE
ORCHID HOUSE
OSTRICH FARM
PASTEURISER
PASTURELAND
PICKET FENCE
PLOUGHSHARE
POMICULTURE
POULTRY FARM
PRODUCE SHOW
PROPAGATION
PRUNING HOOK
RABBIT HUTCH
SALMON FARM
SERICULTURE
SHEEP FARMER
SWINGLETREE
TANK-FARMING
TOP DRESSING
VERMICULITE
VINICULTURE
VITICULTURE
WATERING CAN
WHEELBARROW
WIRE NETTING
ZERO-GRAZING

12
AGRICULTURAL
CONSERVATORY
CROP ROTATION

CROP SPRAYING
FLORICULTURE
FORCING HOUSE
GREEN FINGERS
HEAD GARDENER
HORTICULTURE
HUMIFICATION
MARKET GARDEN
MILKING STOOL
PISCICULTURE
PRUNING KNIFE
SHEEP FARMING
SHEEP SHEARER
SMALLHOLDING
STOCKBREEDER
STUBBLE FIELD
TRANSHUMANCE
WINNOWING FAN

13
ARBORICULTURE
CROSSBREEDING
ELECTRIC FENCE
ITALIAN GARDEN
KITCHEN GARDEN
LAWN SPRINKLER
MUCK-SPREADING
PRUNING SHEARS
SHEEP SHEARING
STOCKBREEDING
TEA PLANTATION

14
COLLECTIVE FARM
DRY-LAND FARMING
FACTORY FARMING
HARDY PERENNIAL

JAPANESE GARDEN
MARKET GARDENER
MILKING PARLOUR
PASTEURISATION
SUPERPHOSPHATE
THRESHING FLOOR

15
BORDEAUX MIXTURE
GARDENING GLOVES
HARVEST FESTIVAL
WINDOW GARDENING

16
COMBINE HARVESTER
CONTOUR PLOUGHING
FISH, BLOOD AND BONE
THRESHING MACHINE

Industry & Economy – Finance – CURRENCIES

3
KIP Laos
LAT Latvia
LEK Albania
LEU Moldova, Romania
LEV Bulgaria
SOL Peru
SOM Kyrgyzstan,
 Uzbekistan
WON North Korea,
 South Korea
YEN Japan

4
BAHT Thailand

BIRR Ethiopia
CEDI Ghana
DONG Vietnam
DRAM Armenia
EURO Andorra,
 Austria, Belgium,
 Finland, France,
 Germany, Greece,
 Republic of Ireland,
 Italy, Luxembourg,
 Monaco, Montenegro,
 Netherlands, Portugal,
 San Marino, Slovenia,
 Spain, Vatican
KINA Papua New Guinea

KUNA Croatia
KYAT Myanmar
LARI Georgia
LIRA Malta, Turkey
LOTI Lesotho
MARK Bosnia-
 Herzegovina
PESO Argentina, Chile,
 Colombia, Cuba,
 Dominican Republic,
 Mexico, Philippines,
 Uruguay
PULA Botswana
RAND South Africa
REAL Brazil

RIAL Iran, Oman
RIEL Cambodia
TAKA Bangladesh
TALA Samoa
VATU Vanuatu
YUAN China

5

COLÓN Costa Rica
DENAR Macedonia
DINAR Algeria, Bahrain, Iraq, Jordan, Kuwait, Libya, Serbia, Sudan, Tunisia
DOBRA São Tomé and Príncipe
FRANC Benin, Burkina Faso, Burundi, Central African Republic, Cameroon, Chad, Comoros, Congo, Côte d'Ivoire, Democratic Republic of Congo, Djibouti, Equatorial Guinea, Gabon, Guinea, Guinea-Bissau, Liechtenstein, Mali, Niger, Rwanda, Senegal, Switzerland, Togo
KRONA Iceland, Sweden
KRONE Denmark, Norway
KROON Estonia
LEONE Sierra Leone
LITAS Lithuania
MANAT Azerbaijan, Turkmenistan
NAIRA Nigeria

NAKFA Eritrea
POUND Cyprus, Egypt, Lebanon, Syria, United Kingdom
RIYAL Qatar, Saudi Arabia, Yemen
RUPEE India, Mauritius, Nepal, Pakistan, Seychelles, Sri Lanka
SUCRE Ecuador
TENGE Kazakhstan
ZLOTY Poland

6

ARIARY Madagascar
BALBOA Panama
DALASI Gambia
DIRHAM Morocco, United Arab Emirates
DOLLAR Antigua and Barbuda, Australia, Bahamas, Barbados, Belize, Brunei, Canada, Dominica, El Salvador, Fiji, Grenada, Guyana, Jamaica, Kiribati, Liberia, Marshall Islands, Namibia, Nauru, New Zealand, Palau, St Kitts and Nevis, St Lucia, St Vincent and the Grenadines, Singapore, Solomon Islands, Suriname, Taiwan, Trinidad and Tobago, Tuvalu, United States, Zimbabwe

ESCUDO Cape Verde
FORINT Hungary
GOURDE Haiti
KORUNA Czech Republic, Slovakia
KWACHA Malawi, Zambia
KWANZA Angola
PA'ANGA Tonga
ROUBLE Belarus, Russia
RUPIAH Indonesia
SHEKEL Israel
SOMONI Tajikistan
TUGRIK Mongolia

7

AFGHANI Afghanistan
BOLIVAR Venezuela
CÓRDOBA Nicaragua
GUARANI Paraguay
HRYVNIA Ukraine
LEMPIRA Honduras
METICAL Mozambique
OUGUIYA Mauritania
QUETZAL Guatemala
RINGGIT Malaysia
RUFIYAA Maldives

8

NGULTRUM Bhutan
SHILLING Kenya, Somalia, Tanzania, Uganda

9

BOLIVIANO Bolivia
LILANGENI Swaziland

Industry & Economy – Finance – MONETARY TERMS

3
APR
ATM
BET
DUD
FEE
IOU
LET
OOF
PAY
POT
PYX
SOP
SUB
SUM
TAX
TIN
TIP
VAT
WAD

4
BANK
BILL
BUCK
BUNG
CASH
COIN
COST
DISC
DOLE
DUES
DUTY
FARE
FINE
FUND

GOLD
HIRE
LEVY
LOAN
LOOT
MILL
MINT
NETT
NOTE
PAYE
PELF
PILE
PONY
QUID
RATE
RENT
RISE
SCOT
STUB
SUBS
TOLL
WAGE

5
BANCO
BRASS
BREAD
BRIBE
DEBIT
DOUGH
DOWRY
FIVER
FLOAT
GRAND
GRANT
HEADS

INGOT
KITTY
LOLLY
LUCRE
MEANS
MONEY
ONCER
ORDER
PIECE
PRICE
RAISE
RATES
REMIT
RHINO
SCREW
STACK
STAGE
SUGAR
TAILS
TITHE
TOKEN
TRONC
USURY
VALUE
WAGER
WAGES
WORTH

6
BOODLE
CHANGE
CHEQUE
COPPER
CREDIT
EXCISE
FISCAL

FLIMSY
GAMBLE
INCOME
MAZUMA
MONKEY
MOOLAH
PAY-OFF
PAYOLA
RANSOM
REBATE
REFUND
RENTAL
RIP-OFF
SALARY
SILVER
SPECIE
STUMER
SURTAX
TAXING
TENNER
VALUTA
WAMPUM

7
ACCOUNT
ALIMONY
BACK-PAY
BENEFIT
BULLION
CAPITAL
COINAGE
CUSTOMS
DEPOSIT
EXERGUE
FINANCE
GARNISH

HALF-PAY
HAULAGE
IMPREST
INVOICE
JACKPOT
LAND TAX
LENDING
LOTTERY
MILLING
MINTAGE
MOORAGE
OBVERSE
PACKAGE
PAYMENT
PENSION
POLL TAX
PORTAGE
POSTAGE
RAKE-OFF
READIES
REVENUE
REVERSE
ROULEAU
SAVINGS
STIPEND
SUBSIDY
SURPLUS
TRIBUTE
WARRANT

8
BANKNOTE
BANK RATE
BANKROLL
BANKRUPT
CURRENCY

DONATION
DRAWDOWN
EARNINGS
ENTRY FEE
EUROLAND
EXCHANGE
GRATUITY
HARD CASH
HOT MONEY
INTEREST
KEY MONEY
KICKBACK
MINT MARK
MONETARY
MORTGAGE
PIN MONEY
PITTANCE
PLANCHET
POUNDAGE
PROCEEDS
RACK RENT
RESERVES
RETAINER
SALES TAX
SHARE-OUT
STERLING
SUPERTAX
TAXATION
WHARFAGE
WINDFALL

9
BAKSHEESH
BEER MONEY
DEATH DUTY
DEFLATION

DIRECT TAX
EASY MONEY
EMOLUMENT
ENDOWMENT
EXCHEQUER
FACE VALUE
FACTORAGE
FINANCIAL
GATE MONEY
GREENBACK
GROUNDAGE
HALF-PRICE
INCOME TAX
INFLATION
LAGNIAPPE
OVERISSUE
PAY PACKET
PETTY CASH
PORTERAGE
PRINCIPAL
READY CASH
REFLATION
RESOURCES
RISK MONEY
STAMP DUTY
STATEMENT
STOPPAGES
SURCHARGE
WATERMARK
WHIP-ROUND

10
CAPITATION
COLLECTION
COUNCIL TAX
CREDIT CARD
CREDIT NOTE

DIRTY MONEY
FREIGHTAGE
GRANT-IN-AID
GROUND RENT
HONORARIUM
LIVING WAGE
MONETARISM
MONEY ORDER
PAPER MONEY
PREPAYMENT
PRIZE MONEY
READY MONEY
RECOMPENSE
REMITTANCE
SCHOOL FEES
SECURITIES
SETTLEMENT
SHELL MONEY
SHOESTRING
SMART MONEY
STAKE MONEY
SUBVENTION
TABLE MONEY
TOKEN MONEY
WAR PENSION

11
BANK ACCOUNT
CIRCULATION
COUNTERFEIT
COUNTERFOIL
DANGER MONEY
DEVALUATION
DOWN PAYMENT
ENTRANCE FEE
GRESHAM'S LAW
HIGH FINANCE

INDIRECT TAX
LEGAL TENDER
MAUNDY MONEY
MINIMUM WAGE
NUMISMATICS
OVERPAYMENT
POCKET MONEY
POSTAL ORDER
PROPERTY TAX
REVALUATION
RISK CAPITAL
SPONDULICKS
TAKE-HOME PAY
TURNOVER TAX
WINDFALL TAX

12
DISBURSEMENT
EXCHANGE RATE
GOLD STANDARD
HARD CURRENCY
PAY AS YOU EARN
REMUNERATION
RETAINING FEE
SEVERANCE PAY
SHARE CAPITAL
SOFT CURRENCY
STATE PENSION
STERLING AREA
SUBSCRIPTION
TREASURY NOTE
UNDERPAYMENT

13
CONSIDERATION
DILAPIDATIONS
EXCHEQUER BILL

INLAND REVENUE
MEMBERSHIP FEE
OLD AGE PENSION
REIMBURSEMENT
SPENDING MONEY
TRIAL OF THE PYX
VALUE ADDED TAX

14
BUREAU DE CHANGE
CURRENT ACCOUNT
DIRECT TAXATION
DEPOSIT ACCOUNT
HIDDEN RESERVES
INHERITANCE TAX
PEPPERCORN RENT
PROMISSORY NOTE
SAVINGS ACCOUNT
SUPERANNUATION
SURRENDER VALUE
THE WHEREWITHAL
UNEARNED INCOME
VENTURE CAPITAL

15
CAPITAL GAINS TAX
EXCHANGE CONTROL
GOLDEN HANDSHAKE
PROTECTION MONEY
PURCHASING POWER
REDUNDANCY MONEY
SUBSCRIPTION FEE

16
INDIRECT TAXATION

Industry & Economy – TOOLS & EQUIPMENT

3	GLUE	5	PANGA	6	PULLEY	CALIPERS
AWL	GRIP	ANVIL	PASTE	BEETLE	PUTLOG	CHOPPER
AXE	HAFT	AUGER	PLANE	BODKIN	REAMER	CLEAVER
BIT	HASP	BESOM	POKER	BOW SAW	RIBBON	CLOBBER
DIE	HAWK	BLADE	PUNCH	BROACH	RIDDLE	CROWBAR
DOG	HOOK	BORER	PUTTY	CHISEL	RIPPER	FLESHER
GIN	HOSE	BRACE	RIVET	COTTER	RIPSAW	FRETSAW
GUM	IRON	BRAND	RULER	CRADLE	ROLLER	GIN TRAP
GUN	JACK	BROOM	SCOOP	DIBBER	SANDER	GRAPNEL
HOD	LAST	BRUSH	SCORP	DIBBLE	SAW SET	GRAPPLE
HOE	MAUL	BURIN	SCREW	ENAMEL	SCREEN	GRIPPER
JIG	NAIL	CABLE	SHAFT	GADGET	SCRIBE	GRUBBER
KEY	PALM	CHICK	SHANK	GIMLET	SCYTHE	HACKSAW
KIT	PEEL	CLAMP	SHARE	GRAVER	SHEARS	HANDSAW
NUT	PICK	CLASP	SIEVE	HAMMER	SHOVEL	HATCHET
PEG	PLUG	CLEAT	SNARE	HANDLE	SICKLE	HOBNAIL
PIN	PROD	CLOUT	SNIPS	JIGSAW	SIFTER	JIM CROW
RAM	PUMP	CORER	SPADE	JUMPER	SIZING	JOINTER
SAW	RAKE	DOWEL	SPIKE	LADDER	SKEWER	LACQUER
SAX	RASP	DRILL	SPRIG	MALLET	SLEDGE	MANDREL
SET	ROLL	EDGER	STAKE	MARKER	SPACER	MATTOCK
TAP	ROSE	EMERY	STAMP	MASTIC	SQUARE	MORDANT
TAR	RULE	FLOAT	STEEL	MORTAR	STAPLE	NAIL GUN
VAN	SHIM	GAVEL	STEPS	MULLER	TACKLE	NIPPERS
	SIZE	GIZMO	STROP	NEEDLE	TAMPER	PICKAXE
4	SLEY	GOOSE	SWAGE	PADDLE	TINGLE	PINCERS
ADZE	SPUD	GOUGE	TONGS	PALLET	TROWEL	PLANTER
BOLT	STAY	GROUT	TURPS	PEAVEY	WASHER	PLUNGER
BRAD	STUD	HELVE	U-BOLT	PESTLE	WRENCH	POINTER
BURR	TACK	HINGE	VALVE	PIT SAW		POLEAXE
CARD	TANG	JAPAN	WEDGE	PLIERS	7	RAG BOLT
FILE	TAPE	JEMMY	WINCH	PLOUGH	AIR PUMP	RIFFLER
FLEX	TOOL	KNIFE	WREST	POMMEL	BANDSAW	SCAUPER
FORK	TRAP	LEVER		PONTIL	BRADAWL	SCORPER
GEAR	VICE	PAINT		PRIMER	BUZZ SAW	SCRIBER

SHACKLE
SKIMMER
SOLVENT
SPANNER
SPRAYER
SPRINGE
STAPLER
STAY BAR
STAY ROD
SWINGLE
THINNER
TIN-TACK
TOOL KIT
TOOL SET
TRAMMEL
TRENAIL
TRIMMER
T-SQUARE
UPRIGHT
UTENSIL
VARNISH
WHIPSAW

8

ABRASIVE
ADHESIVE
AIRBRUSH
ALLEN KEY
BILLHOOK
BLOWLAMP
CHAINSAW
CLIPPERS
CORUNDUM
CREOSOTE
CROWN SAW
DOORNAIL
DOWEL PIN
DRIFT PIN

DUTCH HOE
EDGE TOOL
EMULSION
FIRE HOSE
FIREPLUG
FOOT-PUMP
FRAME SAW
GROUTING
HAND-PUMP
HARDENER
HOLDFAST
LAPSTONE
LIMEWASH
MEAT HOOK
OILSTONE
PALSTAVE
PANEL PIN
PENKNIFE
PICKLOCK
POWER SAW
PUNCHEON
RAWLPLUG
RING-BOLT
ROCK WOOL
ROULETTE
SAW FRAME
SAWHORSE
SCISSORS
SCREW EYE
SCREW TAP
SET SCREW
SHOEHORN
SHOE TREE
SNAP-HOOK
SNAP-LOCK
SNUFFERS
SPARABLE
SPRAY GUN

STILETTO
STONE AXE
STRICKLE
STRIPPER
STUD BOLT
SURFACER
TABLE SAW
TENON SAW
THINNERS
TOMMY BAR
VIBRATOR
WINDLASS
WIRE WOOL

9

APPARATUS
APPLIANCE
BURNISHER
CAN OPENER
CENTRE BIT
CLOUT NAIL
COMPASSES
COPING SAW
CORKSCREW
COTTER PIN
DISTEMPER
DRAW-KNIFE
EQUIPMENT
FORCE PUMP
GOOSENECK
GLASS WOOL
GREASE GUN
HANDSPIKE
HOLE PUNCH
HOT-AIR GUN
IMPLEMENT
JACK-KNIFE
JACK PLANE

LAZY TONGS
LEAD PAINT
MOUSETRAP
NAIL PUNCH
PITCHFORK
PLANISHER
POOP SCOOP
REED KNIFE
ROCK DRILL
SANDPAPER
SCARIFIER
SCREW HOOK
SCREW JACK
SCRIBE AWL
SCROLL SAW
SECATEURS
SEED DRILL
SET SQUARE
SHARPENER
SLEEVE NUT
STAPLE GUN
STEEL WOOL
STRETCHER
SUBSOILER
SUPERGLUE
TIN OPENER
TWO-MAN SAW
UNDERCOAT
WHETSTONE
WHITEWASH
WOOD SCREW

10

BOX SPANNER
CLAW HAMMER
COLD CHISEL
COMPASS SAW
EMERY BOARD

EMERY CLOTH
EMERY PAPER
EPOXY RESIN
FIBREGLASS
GLASS FIBRE
GLASSPAPER
GLOSS PAINT
GRINDSTONE
GUILLOTINE
INSTRUMENT
LACQUERING
LOFT LADDER
LUMP HAMMER
MARINE GLUE
PAINTBRUSH
PAPER KNIFE
PERFORATOR
PROTRACTOR
PUTTY KNIFE
ROPE LADDER
SCOTCH GLUE
SCOTCH TAPE
SCREW VALVE
SHACKLE PIN
SPOKESHAVE
SPRAY PAINT
STEPLADDER
TENTERHOOK
TRIP HAMMER
TUNING FORK
TURF-CUTTER
TURNBUCKLE

TURNING SAW
TURPENTINE
WOOL SHEARS

11
BASTARD FILE
BOTTLE BRUSH
BRACE AND BIT
BREAST DRILL
CALIPER RULE
CARBORUNDUM
CENTRE PUNCH
CIRCULAR SAW
CROSS-CUT SAW
FEELER GAUGE
FRENCH CHALK
GARDEN SPADE
GLASS-CUTTER
HARDY CHISEL
JAPANESE SAW
MARLINSPIKE
MASKING TAPE
OVERGRAINER
PAINT-ROLLER
PAPER-CUTTER
PLOUGHSHARE
POCKET KNIFE
PRUNING HOOK
REAPING HOOK
REBATE PLANE
RING SPANNER
ROTTENSTONE

SCREWDRIVER
SHACKLE BOLT
SHEATH KNIFE
SLEEVE VALVE
STOVE-ENAMEL
STRAW-CUTTER
TICKET PUNCH
TURFING IRON
WHITE SPIRIT
WOODRUFF KEY

12
BRANDING IRON
BUTTERFLY NUT
CAULKING IRON
CRIMPING IRON
CURLING TONGS
DIAMOND DRILL
ENDLESS SCREW
HEDGE TRIMMER
MONKEY WRENCH
NAIL CLIPPERS
POTTER'S WHEEL
PRUNING KNIFE
RUBBER MALLET
SELF-TAP SCREW
SLEDGEHAMMER
SNARLING IRON
TORQUE WRENCH

13
CHOPPING BLOCK
DENTIST'S DRILL
ELECTRIC DRILL
EMULSION PAINT
EXPLOSIVE BOLT
EXTENSION LEAD
FRAMING HAMMER
GRAPPLING HOOK
GRAPPLING IRON
LUMINOUS PAINT
PAINT STRIPPER
PHILLIPS SCREW
PINKING SHEARS
POMPIER LADDER
PRUNING SHEARS
SCALING LADDER
SMOOTHING IRON
SOLDERING IRON

14
BALL-PEEN HAMMER
BLOCK AND TACKLE
BUTTERFLY SCREW
EXPLOSIVE RIVET
FLOORING CHISEL
INSULATION TAPE
SMOOTHING PLANE

15
PESTLE AND MORTAR
WHEEL-NUT SPANNER

Language

Language – LANGUAGES
* = dead/moribund language   † = artificial language   †† = language group

3	4	GE'EZ*	PALI*	BALTI	GREEK
ASI	ACEH	(or Ethiopic)	SHAN	BANTU††	GUSII
EWE	AFAR	IBAN	SIKA	BASAA	HAKKA
FON	AINU*	IGBO	SORA	BEMBA	HAUSA
FUR	AKAN	(or Ibo)	SUSU	BERTA	HINDI
GEN	(or Twi)	ISAN	THAI	BHILI	HMONG
IBO	AVAR	KAWI*	TULU	BIKOL	INUIT
(or Igbo)	BEJA	KOMI	URDU	CARIB	IRAQI
IDO†	BÉTÉ	LAPP	VÕRO	CZECH	IRISH
LAO	CREE	LOZI	ZULU	DINKA	JARAI
LAZ	CROW	LURI		DOGRI	KAREN
MAM	DIDA	MANX*	5	DUTCH	KHASI
MON	ERSE	MARI	ABAZA	EKOTI	KHMER
TAT	(or Gaelic)	MONO	ALTAY	ERZYA	KOINE*
TIV	FANG	NAMA	ARYAN*	FARSI	KONGO
TWI	FULA	NORN*	ATESO	(or Persian)	KUMYK
(or Akan)	GAYO	PÁEZ	AZTEC*	GONDI	LATIN*

LEZGI
LOTHA
MAKUA
MALAY
(or Malayan)
MALVI
MANDE††
(or Mandingo)
MAORI
MARIA
MEHRI
NOGAI
NORSE*
ORIYA
OROMO
OSCAN*
PUNIC*
SAKHA
(or Yakut)
SALAR
SANGO
SCOTS
(or Scottish)
SHONA
SILT'E
SIOUX
(or Dakota)
SODDO
SWATI
TAJIK
TAMIL
TATAR
TETUM
THARU
TIGRE
TONGA
TUVAN
UZBEK

VENDA
WELSH
(or Cymric)
WOLOF
XHOSA
XIANG
YAKUT
(or Sakha)
YUPIK
ZOQUE

6

ABKHAZ
ADYGHE
ANGIKA
APACHE*
ARABIC
AWADHI
AYMARA
BADAGA
BASQUE
BERBER
BRAHUI
BRETON
BUKUSU
BULGAR*
BURYAT
CELTIC††
CREOLE††
COPTIC*
CYMRIC
(or Welsh)
DAKOTA
(or Sioux)
DANISH
DARGIN
DHATKI
DIOULA

DUNGAN
EVENKI
FIJIAN
FRENCH
GAELIC
(or Erse)
GAGAUZ
GERMAN
GILEKI
GOTHIC*
GULLAH
HEBREW
HERERO
IBANAG
IBIBIO
INGUSH
KABYLE
KALAMI
KALMYK
(or Kalmuck)
KAONDE
KAZAKH
KHAKAS
KHALAJ
KHOWAR
KIKUYU
KOREAN
KYRGYZ
LADINO
LINCOS†
LOGLAN†
LOJBAN†
LUSOGA
LYDIAN*
MAGYAR
(or Hungarian)
MANCHU
MASABA

MEITEI
MICMAC
MOHAWK
MONGOL
(or Mongolian)
MOKSHA
NAVAJO
NDONGA
NEPALI
NGUMBA
NOVIAL†
ONEIDA*
PASHTO
(or Pushtu)
PIDGIN
(or Tok Pisin)
POLISH
PUSHTU
(or Pashto)
ROMAND
(or Arpitan)
ROMAIC
ROMANY
SAMOAN
SHELTA*
SHUGNI
SIDAMO
SINDHI
SLOVAK
(or Slavonic)
SOMALI
SYRIAC
TALYSH
TAUSUG
TELUGU
TONGAN
TSONGA
TSWANA

TUAREG††
TUROYO
TUSCAN
UDMURT
UYGHUR
YORUBA
ZAZAKI
ZHUANG

7

AKLANON
AMHARIC
ARAMAIC
ARAPAHO*
ARPITAN
(or Romand)
BALOCHI
BAMBARA
BASHKIR
BENGALI
BOSNIAN
BURMESE
CATALAN
CATAWBA*
CEBUANO
CHAOUIA
CHECHEN
CHINESE
CHINOOK*
CHOCTAW*
CORNISH*
CUMBRIC*
CUYONON
DHIVEHI
ENGLISH
FAROESE
(or Faeroese)
FINNISH

FLEMISH
FRISIAN
GAULISH*
GUARANÍ
HITTITE*
ILOKANO
ITALIAN
KALMUCK
 (or Kalmyk)
KANNADA
 (or Kanarese)
KIROMBO
KIRUNDI
KIVUNJO
KONKANI
KUMAONI
KURDISH
LADAKHI
LATVIAN
LINGALA
LUGANDA
MAGADHI
MALAYAN
 (or Malay)
MALTESE
MARANAO
MARATHI
MUNDARI
NAHUATL
NDEBELE
NYNORSK
 (or Landsmål)
OCCITAN
 (or Langue d'oc)
OSSETIC
PAHLAVI*
PERSIAN (or Farsi)
PICTISH*

PRAKRIT*
PUNJABI
QASHQAI
QUECHUA
ROMANCE††
ROMANSH
 (or Romansch)
RUSSIAN
SAMOYED
SEMITIC††
SERBIAN
SESOTHO
SINHALA
 (or Sinhalese)
SIRAIKI
SOQOTRI
SORBIAN
 (or Wendish)
SPANISH
SUPYIRE
SWAHILI
SWEDISH
TAGALOG
TARIFIT
TIBETAN
TLINGIT*
TRUKESE
 (or Chuukese)
TUMBUKA
TURKISH
TURKMEN
UMBRIAN*
VOLAPÜK†
WALLOON
WENDISH
 (or Sorbian)
WINARAY
 (or Waray-waray)

YAEYAMA
YIDDISH
ZAPOTEK

8
ALBANIAN
ARMENIAN
ASSAMESE
ASSYRIAN*
ASTURIAN
BALINESE
BAVARIAN
BHOJPURI
BUGINESE
CHALDEAN*
CHAMORRO
CHERKESS
 (or Circassian)
CHEROKEE
CHEYENNE*
CHICHEWA
CHUUKESE
 (or Trukese)
COMANCHE*
COMORIAN
CORSICAN
CROATIAN
DZONGKHA
EGYPTIAN*
ESTONIAN
ETHIOPIC*
 (or Ge'ez)
ETRUSCAN*
FAEROESE
 (or Faroese)
FILIPINO
FRIULIAN
GALICIAN

GEORGIAN
GUJARATI
HAWAIIAN
IKALANGA
ILLINOIS*
JAKALTEK
JAPANESE
JAVANESE
KANARESE
 (or Kannada)
KARELIAN
KASHMIRI
KINARAY-A
KWANYAMA
LANDSMÅL
 (or Nynorsk)
LEPONTIC*
LOW LATIN*
MAITHILI
MALAGASY
MANDAEAN
MANDARIN
MANDINGO††
 (or Mande)
MANDINKA
MENTAWAI
NAFAANRA
PHRYGIAN*
ROMANIAN
ROMANSCH
 (or Romansh)
SANSKRIT*
SCOTTISH
 (or Scots)
SEMINOLE
SHIMAORE
SHOSHONE
SILESIAN

SLAVONIC
  (or Slovak)
TAHITIAN
TEUTONIC*
THRACIAN*
TIGRINYA
TOK PISIN
  (or Pidgin)
TSHILUBA

9
AFRIKAANS
BATAK TOBA
BLACKFOOT
BULGARIAN
CANTONESE
CASTILIAN
CHAVACANO
CHICKASAW*
DALMATIAN*
DONGXIANG
DRAVIDIAN††
ESPERANTO†
HUNGARIAN
  (or Magyar)
ICELANDIC
INUKTITUT
KABARDIAN
KASHUBIAN
LANGUE D'OC
  (or Occitan)
LOW GERMAN
  (or Plattdeutsch)
MALAYALAM

MEÄNKIELI
MEGRELIAN
MENOMINEE*
MONGOLIAN
  (or Mongol)
NORWEGIAN
PENOBSCOT*
POTHOHARI
PROVENÇAL
SAMARITAN*
SARDINIAN
SINHALESE
  (or Sinhala)
SLOVENIAN
SUNDANESE
TABASARAN
UKRAINIAN

10
ANDALUSIAN
ANGLO-SAXON*
  (or Old English)
BANYUMASAN
BELARUSIAN
  (or Belorussian)
CIRCASSIAN
  (or Cherkess)
GILBERTESE
HILIGAYNON
HINDUSTANI††
INDONESIAN
KARAKALPAK
KIMATUUMBI
LANGUE D'OÏL*

LITHUANIAN
MACEDONIAN
MAPUDUNGUN
MASBATENYO
MELANESIAN††
NEAPOLITAN
NEPAL BHASA
OLD ENGLISH*
  (or Anglo-Saxon)
PANGASINAN
PAPIAMENTO
PHOENICIAN*
PORTUGUESE
POTAWATOMI*
RAJASTHANI
SERBO-CROAT
  (or Serbo-
  Croatian)
TASHELHIYT
VIETNAMESE
WARAY-WARAY
  (or Winaray)

11
ANISHINAABE
AZERBAIJANI
BELORUSSIAN
  (or Belarusian)
INTERLINGUA†
KALAALLISUT
KAPAMPANGAN
KINYARWANDA
KOYRA CHIINI
MAGUINDANAO

MARSHALLESE
MAZANDARANI
MINANGKABAU
MONTENEGRIN
ROMBLOMANON
YUKATEK MAYA

12
CHITTAGONIAN
LINGUA FRANCA
PLATTDEUTSCH
  (or Low German)

13
CHHATTISGARHI
HAITIAN CREOLE
LUXEMBOURGISH
MAKHUWA-MEETTO
MIDDLE ENGLISH*
RHAETO-ROMANIC††
SERBO-CROATIAN
  (or Serbo-Croat)

14
KARACHAY-BALKAR

15
AMERICAN ENGLISH

17
PENNSYLVANIA DUTCH

Language – LANGUAGE TERMS

3
DOT
MOT
PUN

4
BURR
CASE
DASH
FORM
MODE
MOOD
MUTE
NOUN
OGAM
  (or ogham)
PAST
ROOT
RUNE
SIGN
STEM
STOP
SURD
TERM
VERB
WORD

5
ADAGE
BLANK
COLON
COMMA
ELIDE
ENTRY
GLIDE
IMAGE
INFIX
IRONY
MAXIM
NASAL
NONCE
OGHAM
  (or ogam)
PARSE
POINT
QUOTE
SCHWA
SLASH
SPELL
TENSE
THEME
TILDE
TROPE
VELAR
VOCAL
VOICE
VOWEL

6
ABLAUT
  (or vowel
  gradation)
ACCENT
ACTIVE
ADVERB
AORIST
ASPECT
BROGUE
CLAUSE
CLICHÉ
CLIMAX
COPULA
CRASIS
DATIVE
ENDING
EPONYM
ETYMON
FUTURE
GENDER
GERUND
HIATUS
HYBRID
HYPHEN
LABIAL
LENGTH
LETTER
MACRON
MEMBER
NEUTER
NUMBER
OBJECT
PENULT
PERIOD
PERSON
PHRASE
PLURAL
PREFIX
SAYING
SIMILE
SPEECH
STRESS
STROKE
SUFFIX
SUPINE
SYNTAX
TMESIS
TONEME
TONGUE
UMLAUT
ZEUGMA

7
ACRONYM
ADJUNCT
ANAGRAM
ANALOGY
ANTONYM
APHESIS
APOCOPE
CADENCE
CEDILLA
DECLINE
DICTION
DIGRAPH
ELISION
EPIGRAM
EPITHET
FORMANT
FUTHARK
  (or futhork)
FUTHORK
  (or futhark)
GRAMMAR
HOMONYM
IMAGERY
INITIAL
JUSSIVE
LINGUAL
LITOTES
  (or meiosis)
MEANING
MEIOSIS
  (or litotes)
METONYM
NEOLOGY
OXYTONE
PARADOX
PARONYM
PARSING
PASSIVE
PERFECT
PHONEME
PRESENT
PRONOUN
SPIRANT
SUBJECT
SYNONYM
VIRGULE
VOCABLE
WORDING

8
ABLATIVE
ABSOLUTE
ALPHABET
ANAPHORA
APHORISM
APODOSIS
ASPIRATE
BILABIAL
CHIASMUS
COMPOUND
DEPONENT
ELLIPSIS
EMPHASIS

ENCLITIC
FEMININE
FULL STOP
FUNCTION
GENITIVE
GRAPHEME
GUTTURAL
IDEOGRAM
LANGUAGE
LOCATIVE
METAPHOR
METONYMY
MISSPELL
MODIFIER
MORPHEME
MUTATION
NEGATIVE
OPTATIVE
OXYMORON
PARADIGM
PARONYMY
PARTICLE
PHONETIC
PHRASING
PLEONASM
POLYSEME
POLYSEMY
POSITIVE
PROTASIS
QUANTITY
RELATIVE
RHETORIC
SEMANTIC
SENTENCE
SIBILANT
SINGULAR
SOLECISM
SPELLING

SYLLABLE
TRIGRAPH
UNIVOCAL
VOCALISM
VOCATIVE

9

ADJECTIVE
AFFRICATE
ALLOMORPH
ALLOPHONE
ANAPTYXIS
APHERESIS
ASSONANCE
ASYNDETON
ATTRIBUTE
AUXILIARY
BILINGUAL
CAUSATIVE
CONDITION
CONJUGATE
CONSONANT
DIAERESIS
DIPHTHONG
DOWNDRIFT
 (or declination)
EQUIVOQUE
ETYMOLOGY
EUPHEMISM
EXPLETIVE
EXPLOSIVE
FORMATIVE
FORM CLASS
FRICATIVE
GERUNDIVE
GRIMM'S LAW
HAPLOLOGY
HENDIADYS

HETERONYM
HOMOGRAPH
HOMOPHONE
HYPALLAGE
HYPERBOLE
HYPOTAXIS
IMPERFECT
IMPLOSIVE
INCEPTIVE
INFLEXION
INTENSIVE
INVERSION
MASCULINE
NEOLOGISM
NONCE WORD
OBJECTIVE
OBSTRUENT
PARAGRAPH
PARATAXIS
PARTITIVE
PAST TENSE
PHILOLOGY
PHONETICS
PREDICATE
PRETERITE
PRIMITIVE
PRIVATIVE
PROCLITIC
PROLEPSIS
REFLEXIVE
SEMANTEME
SEMANTICS
SEMICOLON
SEMIVOWEL
SIBILANCE
SYLLABARY
SYLLEPSIS
TAUTOLOGY

VERBALISE
VERBALISM

10

ACCUSATIVE
ANASTROPHE
ANTECEDENT
ANTEPENULT
ANTITHESIS
APOPHTHEGM
APOSTROPHE
APPOSITION
ASPIRATION
ASSIBILATE
CIRCUMFLEX
COMMON NOUN
COMPARISON
COMPLEMENT
COPULATIVE
DECLENSION
DEFINITION
DERIVATION
DERIVATIVE
DIMINUTIVE
DISYLLABLE
EPENTHESIS
EPEXEGESIS
EPISTROPHE
EXPRESSION
FINITE VERB
GOVERNMENT
HIEROGLYPH
HOLOPHRASE
HYPERBATON
IMPERATIVE
INCHOATIVE
INDICATIVE
INFINITIVE

INFLECTIVE
INTONATION
LEXICOLOGY
LINGUISTRY
METAPHRASE
METATHESIS
NOMINATIVE
NOUN CLAUSE
PARAPHRASE
PAROXYTONE
PARTICIPLE
PEJORATIVE
PLUPERFECT
 (or past perfect)
POSSESSIVE
PROPER NOUN
RHETORICAL
SOUND SHIFT
SPOONERISM
SUBJECTIVE
SYNECDOCHE
TRIPHTHONG
VERBAL NOUN
VERNER'S LAW
VOCABULARY
VOWEL POINT

11
ACTIVE VOICE
ACUTE ACCENT
AMPHIBOLOGY
ANACOLUTHON
ANTONOMASIA
APOSIOPESIS
CATACHRESIS
COMPARATIVE
CONJUGATION
CONJUNCTION

CONNOTATION
CONTRACTION
DECLINATION
 (or downdrift)
DISJUNCTIVE
FIRST PERSON
FUTURE TENSE
GLOTTAL STOP
GRAMMATICAL
GRAVE ACCENT
HETEROCLITE
HOLOPHRASIS
HYPERBOLISM
HYPHENATION
LINGUISTICS
MALAPROPISM
MISSPELLING
MONOPHTHONG
PARENTHESIS
PARANOMASIA
PAST PERFECT
 (or pluperfect)
PERIPHRASIS
PHONETICISM
PHRASEOLOGY
PREDICATION
PREPOSITION
PRETERITION
PUNCTUATION
REDUPLICATE
REGULAR VERB
SUBJUNCTIVE
SUBSTANTIVE
SUPERLATIVE
TAUTOLOGISM
TERMINOLOGY
THIRD PERSON
TRISYLLABLE

12
ABBREVIATION
ABSTRACT NOUN
ALLITERATION
ASSIBILATION
CONCRETE NOUN
CONSTRUCTION
DENTILINGUAL
DEPONENT VERB
DIRECT OBJECT
DIRECT SPEECH
DISTRIBUTIVE
HIEROGLYPHIC
INTERJECTION
LEXICOGRAPHY
MONOSYLLABIC
MONOSYLLABLE
MULTILINGUAL
ONOMATOPOEIA
PART OF SPEECH
PASSIVE VOICE
PERFECT TENSE
POLYSYLLABLE
QUESTION MARK
SECOND PERSON
SIGN LANGUAGE
VOCALISATION

13
AUXILIARY VERB
BACK-FORMATION
CAUSATIVE VERB
COGNATE OBJECT
ETHICAL DATIVE
FOLK ETYMOLOGY
FREQUENTATIVE
FUTURE PERFECT
HIEROGLYPHICS

INTERROGATIVE
IRREGULAR VERB
MIXED METAPHOR
MORPHOPHONEME
OVERSTATEMENT
PARASYNTHESIS
POLYSYNTHESIS
POLYSYNTHETIC
PRONUNCIATION
REDUPLICATION
REFLEXIVE VERB
RHOTACISATION
TETRASYLLABLE
VERBALISATION

14

CLOSED SYLLABLE
DOUBLE ENTENDRE
FIGURE OF SPEECH
FINGER ALPHABET
  (or manual alphabet)
HAPAX LEGOMENON

IMPERATIVE MOOD
IMPERFECT TENSE
INDICATIVE MOOD
INDIRECT OBJECT
INDIRECT SPEECH
INVERTED COMMAS
LEXICAL MEANING
MANUAL ALPHABET
  (or finger alphabet)
PAST PARTICIPLE
POSSESSIVE CASE
QUOTATION MARKS
REPORTED SPEECH
SIMPLE SENTENCE
TRANSITIVE VERB
UNDERSTATEMENT
VOWEL GRADATION
  (or ablaut)

15

COMPLEX SENTENCE
CONJUNCTIVE MOOD

DEFINITE ARTICLE
DIACRITICAL MARK
ETHICAL GENITIVE
EXCLAMATION MARK
HISTORIC PRESENT
PERSONIFICATION
PLUPERFECT TENSE
  (or past perfect tense)
PORTMANTEAU WORD
PUNCTUATION MARK
RELATIVE PRONOUN
SPLIT INFINITIVE
SUBJUNCTIVE MOOD
SYLLABIFICATION

16

INTRANSITIVE VERB
PAST PERFECT TENSE
  (or pluperfect tense)

17

INDEFINITE ARTICLE

Military

Military – AIR FORCE TERMS Also see Ranks, Air & Space Transport

3	DECK	SLEW	CHORD	STAGE	GASBAG	THRUST
ACE	DIVE	SOAR	DITCH	STALL	GEORGE	VECTOR
ERK	DRAG	SPAN	DRIFT	STICK	GLITCH	VOYAGE
BAY	FLAP	SPAT	FLAPS	STRUT	HANGAR	YAWING
FIN	FLIP	TAIL	FLARE	SURGE	JET LAG	
FIX	GATE	TAXI	FLY-BY	WHEEL	JOIN UP	7
FLY	HOLD	TRIM	FLYER	WINGS	MID-AIR	AILERON
HOP	JATO	VTOL	LORAN		MODULE	AIRBASE
PAD	LIFT	WING	NAAFI	6	PARADE	AIR CREW
RAF	LOOP	ZOOM	ORDER	AIRWAY	RADOME	AIR DROP
RIB	MACH		PILOT	BASKET	REHEAT	AIR LANE
VOR	NOSE	5	PRANG	BEACON	ROCKET	AIRLIFT
VTO	PACK	APRON	PROBE	DROGUE	RUDDER	AIRLINE
YAW	PORT	BLITZ	RADAR	ELEVON	RUNWAY	AIRLOCK
	PROP	BRAKE	RANGE	ENLIST	SLEEVE	AIRMAIL
4	RAID	CABIN	RECCE	FAN-JET	SORTIE	AIR MILE
BANK	RANK	CADET	ROTOR	FLIGHT	STRIKE	AIR MISS
BODY	ROOF	CARGO	SPACE	FLOATS	TARGET	AIRPORT
COWL	SKID	CHOCK	STACK	FLYING	TARMAC	AIR RAID

AIR SHOW
AIRSIDE
ARRIVAL
AVIATOR
BALLAST
BALLOON
BANKING
BOOSTER
CAPSULE
CEILING
CHASSIS
CHECK-IN
COCKPIT
COMMAND
CONSOLE
CONTROL
CO-PILOT
COWLING
FAIRING
FLYOVER
FLY-PAST
GONDOLA
GREMLIN
HELIPAD
JET PIPE
LANDING
LIFT-OFF
MILK RUN
MISSION
NACELLE
PANCAKE
PAYLOAD
PONTOON
RE-ENTRY
REGULAR
RIGGING
RIPCORD
SOARING

SPONSON
STEWARD
SURGING
TAKE-OFF
TAXIING
WING-TIP
ZOOMING

8

AEROFOIL
AIR BRAKE
AIR COVER
AIRFIELD
AIR FORCE
AIR POWER
AIRSCREW
AIRSPACE
AIR SPEED
AIRSTRIP
ALTITUDE
APPROACH
ARRESTER
ATTITUDE
AVIATION
AVIATRIX
AVIONICS
BLACK BOX
BRIEFING
BURBLING
CAROUSEL
CONTRAIL
DIVE-BOMB
DOGFIGHT
EJECTION
ELEVATOR
ENVELOPE
FREE FALL
FUSELAGE

GROUNDED
HEADWIND
HELIPORT
JOYSTICK
LONGERON
MOONSHOT
NOSE-CONE
NOSE-DIVE
PILOTAGE
PILOTING
SCRAMBLE
SEAT BELT
SIDE-SLIP
SNAP ROLL
SPACEMAN
SQUADRON
STACKING
STALLING
STRINGER
TAIL BOOM
TAIL SKID
TAILSPIN
TAILWIND
TURBO-FAN
TURBO-JET
VOLPLANE
WINDSOCK
WING-FLAP
WING-SPAN
ZERO HOUR

9

AERODROME
AEROSHELL
AEROSPACE
AIR BRIDGE
AIR POCKET
AIR STRIKE

AIRWORTHY
ASTRODOME
ASTRONAUT
AUTOFLARE
BUFFETING
CABIN CREW
CLEARANCE
COSMONAUT
COUNTDOWN
CRASH-DIVE
CRASH-LAND
DASHBOARD
DEPARTURE
EMPENNAGE
FLARE PATH
FLY-BY-WIRE
FOOTPRINT
FORMATION
GLIDE PATH
JET ENGINE
JET STREAM
LAUNCH PAD
MONOCOQUE
NAVIGATOR
OVERSHOOT
PARACHUTE
PASSENGER
PERIMETER
POWER DIVE
PROPELLER
SONIC BOOM
STARBOARD
TEST PILOT
THRESHOLD
TOUCHDOWN

10

AEROBATICS
AIR CUSHION
AIRMANSHIP
AIR SUPPORT
AIR TRAFFIC
BALLOONIST
BLITZKRIEG
ENLISTMENT
FIRST CLASS
FLIGHT CREW
FLIGHT DECK
FLIGHT PATH
FLIGHT PLAN
GROUND CREW
HEAT SHIELD
MACH NUMBER
NAVIGATION
PATHFINDER
ROTOR BLADE
SHOCK STALL
SPACE PROBE
SPACEWOMAN
SPLASHDOWN
STABILISER
STATIC LINE
STEWARDESS
TEST FLIGHT
TURBULENCE
UNDERSHOOT
WIND TUNNEL

11

AERONAUTICS
AIR CORRIDOR
AIR TERMINAL
COMPRESSION
DIVE-BOMBING

EJECTOR SEAT
GROUND SPEED
HEAT BARRIER
LANDING GEAR
LEADING EDGE
NIGHT-FLYING
RECONNOITRE
RETRO-ROCKET
ROCKET MOTOR
SMOKE TUNNEL
STAGING POST
TALK-YOU-DOWN
VAPOUR TRAIL

12
AERODYNAMICS
AIR-SEA RESCUE
ASTRONAUTICS
BELLY LANDING
BOARDING PASS
CONTROL TOWER
COURT MARTIAL
CRASH-LANDING
ECONOMY CLASS
HEDGE-HOPPING
LANDING FIELD

LANDING SPEED
LANDING STRIP
LAUNCHING PAD
PILOT BALLOON
SOUND BARRIER
SPACE STATION
TRAILING EDGE

13
AIRWORTHINESS
APPROACH SPEED
BURBLING POINT
BUSINESS CLASS
CARPET-BOMBING
CHARTER FLIGHT
CONTACT FLIGHT
FLIGHT CONTROL
FORCED LANDING
GROUND CONTROL
IMMELMANN TURN
JET PROPULSION
LANDING LIGHTS
ROYAL AIR FORCE
SPACE PLATFORM
UNDERCARRIAGE

14
AUTOMATIC PILOT
FLIGHT ENGINEER
FLIGHT ENVELOPE
FLIGHT RECORDER
PROPELLER-BLADE
PROPELLER-SHAFT
RECONNAISSANCE
WEIGHTLESSNESS

15
DEPARTURE LOUNGE
FLIGHT ATTENDANT
FLIGHT SIMULATOR
NATIONAL SERVICE
SCHEDULED FLIGHT
THRESHOLD LIGHTS
VERTICAL TAKE-OFF

16
PRESSURISED CABIN

17
AIR TRAFFIC CONTROL

Military – ARMY TERMS Also see Ranks

3	POW	AWOL	FIRE	PARA	ROLL	**5**
BAR	SAP	AXIS	FLAG	PLAN	ROUT	BADGE
BAY	WAR	BASE	HALT	POST	STAR	BATON
FOE		CAMP	LINE	PUSH	TAPS	CACHE
KIT	**4**	DUMP	LIST	RAID	TRAP	CADET
MEN	ALLY	DUTY	MESS	RANK	UNIT	CADRE
PIP	ARMY	FILE	MINE	REAR	YOMP	CLASP

CORPS	STORM	LIMBER	**7**	REVERSE	FIELD DAY
COVER	SWOOP	MANUAL	ARMOURY	SANDBAG	FIGHTING
CREST	TOMMY	MORALE	ARSENAL	SECTION	FURLOUGH
CROSS	TRAIN	MUSTER	BAGGAGE	SERVICE	GARRISON
DECOY	TROOP	MUTINY	BARRAGE	SNIPING	INFANTRY
DEMOB	TRUCE	ONRUSH	BATTERY	SOLDIER	INSIGNIA
DEPOT	WEDGE	ORDERS	BIVOUAC	SUPPORT	INVASION
DRAFT		PARADE	BLIGHTY	TACTICS	LAST POST
DRILL	**6**	PARLEY	BRIGADE	THEATRE	LOCKSTEP
ENEMY	ACTION	PATROL	CANTEEN	TROOPER	MAGAZINE
FIELD	AFFAIR	PICKET	CASHIER	VETERAN	MARCHING
FIGHT	AMBUSH	RANKER	CAVALRY	VICTORY	MESSMATE
FLANK	ATTACK	RATION	CHEVRON	WARFARE	MILITARY
FLARE	BANNER	REDCAP	COLOURS	WARRIOR	MUSKETRY
FLASH	BATMAN	RELIEF	COMMAND	YOMPING	ON PARADE
FORAY	BATTLE	RESCUE	COMPANY		ORDNANCE
GUARD	BEACON	REVIEW	DEFENCE	**8**	PALISADE
ISSUE	BILLET	RIBBON	DRAFTEE	ALL-CLEAR	PASSWORD
LEAVE	BREVET	ROOKIE	DRAGOON	ALLIANCE	QUARTERS
LINES	CALL-UP	ROSTER	ECHELON	ARMY LIST	REGIMENT
MARCH	CHARGE	SALUTE	FALL OUT	ASSEMBLY	RESERVES
MEDAL	COHORT	SAPPER	FOXHOLE	BARRACKS	REVEILLE
MÊLÉE	COLUMN	SCREEN	JANKERS	BLOCKADE	ROLL CALL
NAAFI	COMBAT	SECTOR	LANDING	BRIEFING	SALUTING
ONSET	DEFEAT	SENTRY	LATRINE	CAMPAIGN	SENTRY-GO
ORDER	DEPLOY	SIGNAL	MANIPLE	CASUALTY	SHELLING
PARTY	DETAIL	SNIPER	MILITIA	CITATION	SHOOTING
PEACE	DOUBLE	SORTIE	MISSION	CIVIL WAR	SKIRMISH
RADAR	EMBLEM	SQUARE	ORDERLY	COLLAPSE	SOLDIERY
RANGE	ENLIST	STORES	OUTFALL	COMMANDO	SQUADDIE
RECCE	ENSIGN	STRAFE	OUTPOST	CONQUEST	STANDARD
ROUTE	FORCES	STRIPE	PHALANX	DAD'S ARMY	STOCKADE
SALLY	GROUND	TARGET	PLATOON	DISPATCH	STORMING
SIEGE	GUARDS	TATTOO	RATIONS	DIVISION	STRATEGY
SNIPE	GURKHA	TRENCH	RECRUIT	ENFILADE	STRENGTH
SQUAD	JOIN UP	TROOPS	REGULAR	ENGINEER	SUPPLIES
STAND	KIT-BAG	VOLLEY	REPULSE	ESCALADE	THE FRONT
STONK	LEGION	WAR CRY	RETREAT	FATIGUES	TOP BRASS

TRAINING
UMBRELLA
ZERO HOUR

9
ABOUT-FACE
ABOUT-TURN
AMBUSCADE
ARTIFICER
ARMISTICE
ARMY ISSUE
ARTILLERY
ATTENTION
BATTALION
BEACHHEAD
BILLETING
BLOODSHED
BUGLE CALL
CANNONADE
CEASEFIRE
CHALLENGE
COMBATANT
CONSCRIPT
CROSSFIRE
DESERTION
DISCHARGE
EPAULETTE
EQUIPMENT
FIREPOWER
FIRST POST
FORMATION
FUSILLADE
GOOSE-STEP
GUARDROOM
GUERRILLA
HOME GUARD
INCURSION
INSURGENT

IRON CROSS
IRREGULAR
LIGHTS OUT
MANOEUVRE
MARCH PAST
MILITARIA
MINEFIELD
MUNITIONS
OBJECTIVE
OFFENSIVE
ONSLAUGHT
OPEN ORDER
OPERATION
PACK DRILL
SAND TABLE
SENTRY BOX
SHELLFIRE
SLOW MARCH
SPEARHEAD
STRATAGEM
SURRENDER
SWORD KNOT
WHITE FLAG

10
ACTIVE DUTY
ACTIVE LIST
APPROACHES
BOMB CRATER
BRIDGEHEAD
CAMOUFLAGE
CASHIERING
CASUS BELLI
COMMISSION
DECAMPMENT
DECORATION
DEPLOYMENT
DISCIPLINE

DISPATCHES
ENCAMPMENT
ENGAGEMENT
ENLISTMENT
EVACUATION
EXPEDITION
FIRING LINE
GLASSHOUSE
GUARDHOUSE
INDIAN FILE
INSPECTION
INSURGENCY
INVESTMENT
MANOEUVRES
MILITARISM
MUSTER ROLL
NO MAN'S LAND
NUCLEAR WAR
OCCUPATION
PATROLLING
PICKET DUTY
QUICK MARCH
RIFLE RANGE
RIGHT-ABOUT
ROUTE MARCH
SECONDMENT
SENTRY DUTY
SERVICEMAN
SHELLSHOCK
SIEGE TRAIN
SIGNALLING
SOLDIERING
TOUR OF DUTY

11
AIGUILLETTE
ARMY SURPLUS
BATTLEFIELD

BESIEGEMENT
BOMBARDMENT
DEMARCATION
DISARMAMENT
EMBARKATION
ENTRAINMENT
FIRING SQUAD
FLAG OF TRUCE
FORCED MARCH
GEORGE MEDAL
GERM WARFARE
INFANTRYMAN
ORDERLY BOOK
ORDERLY ROOM
PARATROOPER
PURPLE HEART
RECONNOITRE
REQUISITION
SEARCHLIGHT
SKIRMISHING
SMOKESCREEN
STAGING AREA
TOMMY ATKINS

12
ARTILLERYMAN
BASE HOSPITAL
CANNON FODDER
CAPITULATION
CHURCH PARADE
CIVIL DEFENCE
CONSCRIPTION
COUNTERMARCH
COURT MARTIAL
COVERING FIRE
FIELD BATTERY
FRIENDLY FIRE
GENERAL STAFF

HEADQUARTERS
HORS DE COMBAT
INDIRECT FIRE
INTELLIGENCE
LINE OF BATTLE
MALTESE CROSS
MOBILISATION
NON-COMBATANT
OFFICERS' MESS
ON MANOEUVRES
PARADE GROUND
RE-ENGAGEMENT
RETRENCHMENT
SEALED ORDERS
SERVICEWOMAN
SIEGE TACTICS
SIEGE WARFARE
SURVEILLANCE

13

ACTIVE SERVICE
ASSAULT COURSE
BARRACK SQUARE
BATTLE FATIGUE
BELEAGUERMENT

COUNTER-ATTACK
CROIX DE GUERRE
DISENGAGEMENT
FIELD HOSPITAL
KIT INSPECTION
LISTENING POST
MILITARY CROSS
MILITARY MEDAL
ORDER OF BATTLE
PITCHED BATTLE
PRISONER OF WAR
SABRE-RATTLING
SPIT AND POLISH
SQUARE-BASHING
TRENCH WARFARE
VICTORIA CROSS

14

ACTION STATIONS
BALANCE OF POWER
BALLOON BARRAGE
DEMOBILISATION
DISEMBARKATION
FIELD ARTILLERY
LEGION D'HONNEUR

MARCHING ORDERS
NUCLEAR WARFARE
OPERATIONS ROOM
PINCER MOVEMENT
PYRRHIC VICTORY
RECONNAISSANCE
REINFORCEMENTS
RIGHT ABOUT-FACE
STANDING ORDERS
WINTER QUARTERS

15

CHEMICAL WARFARE
DIRECTION-FINDER
DISCHARGE PAPERS
DRESSING STATION
INSUBORDINATION
MARRIED QUARTERS
NATIONAL SERVICE
OBSERVATION POST

16

COLLATERAL DAMAGE
GUERRILLA WARFARE
PRECISION BOMBING

Military – NAVAL TERMS Also see Ranks

3	LEE	SOS	BANK	BULK	DOCK	HARD
AFT	LOG	TAR	BARB	BUNK	FLAG	HEAD
BOW	OAR	TOP	BASE	BUOY	FLAT	HELM
COT	RAM	TOW	BEAM	CLEW	FLOW	HOLD
EBB	RIB	YAW	BELL	CORD	FOAM	HULL
FID	RIG		BEND	CREW	FORE	KEEL
GUY	RIP	**4**	BOOM	DECK	GAFF	KITE
JIB	SEA	BACK	BOWS	DIVE	GYBE	KNOT

LEAD	TILT	FLARE	SHOAL	CAREEN	ROLLER	BUNTING
LEAK	TRIM	FLEET	SONAR	COMBER	ROPING	BUOYAGE
LINE	VANG	FLOAT	SPOON	CONVOY	RUDDER	CAPSIZE
LIST	VEER	FLUKE	SPRAY	COURSE	SAILOR	CAPSTAN
LOOM	WAKE	GENOA	SPRIT	CRUISE	SALUTE	CATHEAD
LUFF	WALE	HATCH	STACK	DODGER	SCREEN	CHANNEL
MAIN	WAVE	HAVEN	STERN	DROGUE	SEA BED	COCKPIT
MARK	WELL	HAWSE	STOCK	ENSIGN	SEAWAY	COMMAND
MAST	WIND	HITCH	SURGE	FATHOM	SHEETS	COMPASS
MESS	YARD	HOIST	SWEEP	FENDER	SIGNAL	CORDAGE
MOOR		JETTY	SWELL	FIDDLE	SORTIE	CORSAIR
NAVY	**5**	KEDGE	THOLE	FO'C'S'LE	SPARKS	CRINGLE
OARS	ASDIC	LEECH	TRICK	FUNNEL	STEEVE	CURRENT
PACK	BERTH	LIGHT	TRUSS	GALLEY	STORES	DOCKAGE
PIER	BILGE	LORAN	WAIST	GRIPES	STRAKE	DOCKING
PIPE	BITTS	LURCH	WATCH	GROUND	TACKLE	DRAUGHT
POOP	BLOCK	NAAFI	WHARF	GUNNEL	THROAT	DRY DOCK
PORT	BOARD	NAVAL	WHEEL	HAMPER	THWART	DRY LAND
PROW	BOWER	OAKUM	WRECK	HAWSER	TILLER	EBB TIDE
QUAY	BRINE	OCEAN		JETSAM	TIMBER	EMBARGO
RAID	CABIN	ORDER	**6**	JIGGER	TROUGH	FAIRWAY
RAIL	CABLE	ORLOP	ABOARD	LADING	ULLAGE	FISHERY
RAKE	CADET	PERCH	ADRIFT	LASCAR	VOLLEY	FLOTSAM
RANK	CARGO	PITCH	ANCHOR	LATEEN	VOYAGE	FOG BANK
REAR	CAULK	PLUMB	ARMADA	LAUNCH		FOGHORN
REEF	CHAIN	RADAR	ASTERN	LEEWAY	**7**	FORETOP
ROLL	CHART	RANGE	BATTEN	MARINA	AGROUND	FOUNDER
ROPE	CHIME	REACH	BATTLE	MARINE	AIRLOCK	FREIGHT
SAIL	CHIPS	REFIT	BEACON	MARKER	ARRIVAL	FUTTOCK
SINK	CLEAT	RHUMB	BECKET	MAYDAY	BALLAST	GANGWAY
SPAR	CLEWS	ROACH	BILLOW	MIZZEN	BEAM SEA	GRAPNEL
STAY	CLOTH	ROADS	BOTTOM	MUTINY	BEARING	GUN DECK
STEM	CREST	ROPES	BRACES	PADDLE	BOBSTAY	GUN PORT
STOW	CUDDY	ROYAL	BRAILS	PARADE	BOLLARD	GUNWALE
SURF	DAVIT	SALVO	BRIDGE	PIRATE	BOOT TOP	GUY ROPE
SWAB	DEPTH	SCREW	BUFFER	PURSER	BOWLINE	HALYARD
TACK	DRIFT	SCULL	BURDEN	RATING	BREAKER	HAMMOCK
TIDE	FLAKE	SHEET	CANVAS	REVIEW	BULWARK	HARBOUR

HEAD SEA
HORIZON
INBOARD
JACK TAR
JIB BOOM
JIB STAY
KEELSON
KILLICK
LANDING
LANYARD
LEE GAGE
LEE HELM
LEE SIDE
LEE TIDE
LEEWARD
LISTING
LOADING
LOGBOOK
LOG LINE
LOW TIDE
LUFFING
LUGSAIL
MAINTOP
MARINER
MARLINE
MATELOT
MOORAGE
MOORING
NUN BUOY
ON BOARD
ONSHORE
OPEN SEA
OUTFLOW
OUTHAUL
OUTPORT
PAINTER
PASSAGE
PENNANT

PLUMMET
REEFING
REGULAR
RIGGING
RIP TIDE
ROLLING
ROWLOCK
RUMMAGE
SAILING
SALVAGE
SCUPPER
SCUTTLE
SEACOCK
SEA LANE
SEA LEGS
SEA MARK
SEAPORT
SEA ROOM
SEASICK
SEAWARD
SEXTANT
SHIPLAP
SHIPWAY
SICK BAY
SINKING
SKIPPER
SKYSAIL
SLIPWAY
SNOTTER
SPANKER
SPENCER
SPONSON
STATION
STOPPER
STOWAGE
STOWING
SURGING
TACKING

THE DEEP
TIDE RIP
TILTING
TONNAGE
TOP DECK
TOPMAST
TOPSAIL
TOWLINE
TOWROPE
TRANSOM
TRYSAIL
VEERING
VICTORY
WET DOCK
WHISTLE
YARD-ARM

8

APPROACH
ARRESTER
BACKSTAY
BACKWASH
BEAM ENDS
BEARINGS
BELL BUOY
BINNACLE
BLOCKADE
BOARDING
BOAT DECK
BOATHOOK
BOATLOAD
BOLT ROPE
BOWSPRIT
BRIEFING
BULKHEAD
BULWARKS
BUNTLINE
CATAPULT

CAULKING
CHANDLER
COAMINGS
COASTING
CROSSING
CRUISING
CUTWATER
DECKHAND
DOCKSIDE
DOCKYARD
DOG WATCH
DOLDRUMS
DOWNHAUL
DRIFTING
FLAG RANK
FLOTILLA
FOOT ROPE
FOREDECK
FOREFOOT
FOREMAST
FOREPEAK
FORESAIL
FORESTAY
FREE PORT
GANTLINE
GARBOARD
GRIDIRON
GUNWALES
HANDRAIL
HATCHWAY
HEADRAIL
HEADWIND
HEAVY SEA
HIGH SEAS
HIGH TIDE
HORNPIPE
JACKSTAY
JETTISON

JIB SHEET
JURY MAST
LAZY JACK
LEEBOARD
LEE SHORE
LIFEBELT
LIFEBUOY
LIFELINE
LOAD LINE
LOW WATER
MAINMAST
MAINSAIL
MAINSTAY
MAL DE MER
MANIFEST
MAROONED
MASTHEAD
MESS DECK
MOORINGS
NAUTICAL
NAVY LIST
NAVY YARD
NEAP TIDE
OFFSHORE
OUTBOARD
OVERHAUL
OVERSEAS
POOP DECK
PORTHOLE
QUAYSIDE
RATLINES
REEF KNOT
SAIL PLAN
SCUPPERS
SEABOARD
SEAFARER
SEA POWER
SHALLOWS

SHIPLOAD
SHIPMATE
SHIPMENT
SHIPPING
SHIPYARD
SNUBBING
SONOBUOY
SOUNDING
SPAR BUOY
SPAR DECK
STAYSAIL
STEERAGE
STEERING
STERNWAY
STORM JIB
STRINGER
SUBMERGE
TAFFRAIL
THE BRINY
THE DRINK
THOLE PIN
TRIMMING
UNDERTOW
WALE KNOT
WARDROOM
WATERWAY
WELL DECK
WHARFAGE
WINDLASS
WINDWARD
WRECKAGE

9

AFTERDECK
AMIDSHIPS
ANCHORAGE
ANCHORING
BILGE KEEL

BLUE PETER
BLUE WATER
BROADSIDE
BUCCANEER
BUNKERING
CAREENAGE
CHANDLERY
CHARTROOM
COMPANION
CORPOSANT
CROW'S NEST
DECKHOUSE
DEMURRAGE
DEPARTURE
DOGSHORES
DRIFTWOOD
EYE SPLICE
FLOOD TIDE
FLYBRIDGE
FORECABIN
FORESHORE
FOUR BELLS
GANGPLANK
HALF-HITCH
HAWSEPIPE
HIGH WATER
HOLYSTONE
HOUSE FLAG
ICE ANCHOR
JACKSTAFF
LAUNCHING
LAZARETTE
LOWER DECK
LOXODROME
MAINBRACE
MAINSHEET
MANOEUVRE
MONOCOQUE

MOONRAKER
NAVIGATOR
OUTRIGGER
OVERBOARD
PERISCOPE
PREVENTER
PRIVATEER
PROPELLER
RED DUSTER
RED ENSIGN
REEFPOINT
REFITMENT
RHUMB LINE
ROADSTEAD
ROYAL MAST
ROYAL NAVY
ROYAL SAIL
SAILCLOTH
SAILORING
SALT WATER
SCRIMSHAW
SEA ANCHOR
SEA BATTLE
SEAFARING
SEAWORTHY
SEMAPHORE
SHIPBOARD
SHIPWRECK
SOUNDINGS
SPINDRIFT
SPINNAKER
SPRITSAIL
STARBOARD
STATEROOM
STERNPOST
STOKEHOLD
STORM CONE
STORM SAIL

TARPAULIN
TIDE TABLE
TIDEWATER
TIMENOGUY
TOP HAMPER
UPPER DECK
VERY LIGHT
WASHBOARD
WATERLINE
WHALEBACK

10

AIR STATION
BELOW DECKS
BILGE WATER
BLUE ENSIGN
BOTTOM DECK
CHAINPLATE
CLOVE HITCH
COMMISSION
CROSSTREES
ENGAGEMENT
ENGINE ROOM
ENLISTMENT
FIDDLEHEAD
FIGUREHEAD
FIRST CLASS
FIRST WATCH
FLIGHT DECK
FORE AND AFT
FORECASTLE
FREEBOOTER
FREIGHTAGE
HARBOURAGE
JOLLY ROGER
LANDLUBBER
LATEEN SAIL
LIFE JACKET

LIGHTERAGE
LIGHTHOUSE
LUBBER LINE
MAIN COURSE
MARKER BUOY
MIZZEN MAST
MIZZEN SAIL
MUSTER ROLL
NAVIGATING
NAVIGATION
PILOT HOUSE
PORT OF CALL
QUARANTINE
ROPE LADDER
ROUNDHOUSE
SALOON DECK
SAMSON POST
SEAMANSHIP
SHEEPSHANK
SHORE LEAVE
SIGNALLING
SMOKESTACK
SPRING TIDE
SQUARE KNOT
SQUARE SAIL
STABILISER
STATE CABIN
SUBMERSION
SUPERCARGO
TABERNACLE
TOPGALLANT
WATER LEVEL
WATERPLANE
WHARFINGER
WHEELHOUSE

11
BELAYING PIN

BOWER ANCHOR
BOWLINE KNOT
CARRICK BEND
CENTREBOARD
CHAFING GEAR
COMPASS CARD
COMPASS ROSE
DRIFT ANCHOR
ECHO SOUNDER
EMBARKATION
ESCAPE HATCH
FORETOPMAST
FORETOPSAIL
GRAVING DOCK
GROUNDSWELL
GYROCOMPASS
HARBOUR DUES
LANDING DECK
MAINTOPMAST
MAINTOPSAIL
MIDDLE WATCH
MOORING FEES
NAVAL STORES
PADDLE WHEEL
PLANING HULL
PORT OF ENTRY
QUARTERDECK
RECONNOITRE
RECRUITMENT
RIDING LIGHT
RUNNING KNOT
SEASICKNESS
SHEET ANCHOR
SMOKESCREEN
SOUNDING ROD
STEERAGE WAY
ST ELMO'S FIRE
STERN SHEETS

STORM SIGNAL
TORPEDO TUBE
WEATHER GAGE
WEATHER HELM
WHITE ENSIGN

12
AIR-SEA RESCUE
BETWEEN-DECKS
BILL OF HEALTH
BILL OF LADING
BREECHES BUOY
CLINKER-BUILT
COMPANIONWAY
CONNING TOWER
COURT MARTIAL
DISPLACEMENT
ECHO SOUNDING
FLOATING DOCK
FLYING BRIDGE
FORETRIANGLE
GROUND TACKLE
JACOB'S LADDER
LANDING STAGE
MAIDEN VOYAGE
MARINE STORES
MERCHANT NAVY
MINESWEEPING
MORNING WATCH
NAUTICAL MILE
NAVIGABILITY
PLIMSOLL LINE
PLIMSOLL MARK
PRIVATEERING
RECOMMISSION
SHIPBUILDING
SHIPPING LANE
SHIPPING LINE

SHIP'S COMPANY
SHIP'S HUSBAND
SOUNDING LINE
STUDDING SAIL
TOURIST CLASS
UNDERCURRENT
WEATHERBOARD

13
BRIDGE OF BOATS
DEAD RECKONING
FIDDLER'S GREEN
FORENOON WATCH
HARBOUR LIGHTS
HARBOUR MASTER
HIGH-WATER MARK
HURRICANE DECK
LIFE PRESERVER
ORDER OF BATTLE
PROMENADE DECK
RUBBING STRAKE
RUNNING LIGHTS
SAILING ORDERS
SEAWORTHINESS
TRANS-SHIPMENT
TRANS-SHIPPING

14
AFTERNOON WATCH
COMPASS BEARING
COUNTERCURRENT
COURSE-PLOTTING
DISEMBARKATION
DISTRESS SIGNAL
FORE-AND-AFT SAIL
GARBOARD STRAKE
GYROSTABILISER
LETTER OF MARQUE

PROPELLER BLADE
PROPELLER SHAFT
RECONNAISSANCE
RUNNING RIGGING
SCREW PROPELLER
SUPERSTRUCTURE
TOPGALLANT MAST

15
BOATSWAIN'S CHAIR
COMPANION LADDER
MARINE INSURANCE
NATIONAL SERVICE
NAUTICAL ALMANAC
STANDING RIGGING

VICTUALLING YARD

16
DAVY JONES'S LOCKER

18
SPLICE THE MAINBRACE

Military – RANKS

3
NCO

4
MATE

5
BOSUN
 (or boatswain)
MAJOR

6
AIRMAN
CORNET
ENSIGN
GUNNER
MARINE
MASTER
SEAMAN

7
ADMIRAL
CAPTAIN
COLONEL
GENERAL
MARSHAL

OFFICER
PRIVATE

8
ADJUTANT
AIRWOMAN
CORPORAL
COXSWAIN
SERGEANT

9
BOATSWAIN
 (or bosun)
BRIGADIER
COMMANDER
FIRST MATE
PIPE MAJOR
SUBALTERN

10
ABLE SEAMAN
AIDE-DE-CAMP
AIR MARSHAL
BOMBARDIER
COMMANDANT
LIEUTENANT

MIDSHIPMAN
SECOND MATE

11
FIELD CORNET
REAR-ADMIRAL
VICE-ADMIRAL

12
AIR COMMODORE
AIRCRAFTSMAN
FIELD MARSHAL
FLEET ADMIRAL
GROUP CAPTAIN
MAJOR-GENERAL
PETTY OFFICER
PILOT OFFICER

13
FLYING OFFICER
LANCE CORPORAL
LEADING SEAMAN
SECOND OFFICER
SERGEANT MAJOR
SUB-LIEUTENANT
WING COMMANDER

14
AIR VICE-MARSHAL
COLONEL-IN-CHIEF
COLOUR SERGEANT
FLAG LIEUTENANT
ORDINARY SEAMAN
SQUADRON LEADER
WARRANT OFFICER

15
ADJUTANT GENERAL
AIR CHIEF MARSHAL
FIRST LIEUTENANT
LANCE BOMBARDIER
MARSHAL OF THE RAF

16
BRIGADIER GENERAL
FLIGHT LIEUTENANT
GENERAL OF THE ARMY
SECOND LIEUTENANT

17
ADMIRAL OF THE FLEET
CHIEF PETTY OFFICER
LIEUTENANT-COLONEL
LIEUTENANT-GENERAL

19
LIEUTENANT-COMMANDER

20
GENERAL OF THE AIR FORCE

Military – WEAPONRY

3	BOMB	MACE	FLAIL	SABRE	CANNON	POM-POM
ARM	BORE	MERE	FORTE	SALVO	CHARGE	POPGUN
AXE	BREN	MINE	FUSIL	SARIN	CUDGEL	POWDER
BAT	BUTT	PIKE	GRAPE	SHAFT	CUPOLA	PRIMER
BOW	CANE	SHOT	GUARD	SHELL	DAGGER	PURDEY
CAT	CLUB	SILO	H-BOMB	SKEAN	DUMDUM	QUIVER
DUD	COCK	SLUG	KNIFE	SLING	FIRING	RAMROD
GAT	COLT	STEN	KNOUT	SPEAR	HAMMER	RAPIER
GUN	COSH	UMBO	KUKRI	STICK	HANDLE	RECOIL
RAM	DART	WHIP	KYLIE	STOCK	LARIAT	ROCKET
ROD	DIRK		LANCE	SWORD	LIMBER	SEMTEX
TNT	ÉPÉE	**5**	LASSO	TRAIL	MAUSER	SHEATH
UZI	FIRE	A-BOMB	LUGER	WADDY	MORTAR	SHIELD
	FLAK	ARROW	MAXIM		MUSKET	SIGHTS
4	FOIL	BILBO	PANGA	**6**	MUZZLE	SIX-GUN
AMMO	FROG	BIZON	PELTA	ACK-ACK	NAPALM	TRACER
ARMS	FUSE	BLADE	PIECE	AIR GUN	PARANG	VOLLEY
BALL	HILT	BLANK	QUOIN	BARREL	PELLET	WEAPON
BEAD	KICK	BLAST	RICIN	BOFORS	PETARD	WEBLEY
BILL	KRIS	BOLUS	RIFLE	BREECH	PISTOL	
BOLT	LOCK	CS GAS	ROUND	BULLET	POMMEL	

7

ARMOURY
ARSENAL
ASSEGAI
BATTERY
BAYONEY
BAZOOKA
BLOWGUN
BOMBARD
BREN GUN
BUCKLER
CALIBRE
CALTROP
CARBINE
CHAMBER
CURTANA
CUTLASS
FIREARM
GRENADE
GUNFIRE
GUNSHOT
HALBERD
HANDGUN
HARPOON
HATCHET
HOLSTER
JAVELIN
LOADING
LONGBOW
LONG TOM
MACHETE
MARTINI
MEGATON
MISFIRE
MISSILE
PAYLOAD
POLARIS
POLEAXE

PONIARD
POT-SHOT
PRIMING
PUMP GUN
QUARREL
RELEASE
RIFLING
SHOOTER
SHOTGUN
SIDEARM
STEN GUN
TAMPION
  (or tompion)
TEAR GAS
TESTUDO
TOMPION
  (or tampion)
TORPEDO
TRIDENT
TRIGGER
TUMBLER
TWIBILL
WARHEAD
WINDAGE

8

ARBALEST
ARMAMENT
ARQUEBUS
  (or harquebus)
ATOM BOMB
BALLISTA
BLOWPIPE
BLUDGEON
BRICKBAT
BROWNING
BUCKSHOT
CANISTER

CARRIAGE
CASE-SHOT
CATAPULT
CLAYMORE
CROSSBOW
CULVERIN
DRUMFIRE
DUST SHOT
DYNAMITE
FALCHION
FIELD GUN
FIREBALL
FIRELOCK
FOUGASSE
GUNSIGHT
GUNSTOCK
HALF-COCK
HIELAMAN
HOWITZER
LAND MINE
LEWIS GUN
LEWISITE
LINSTOCK
MAGAZINE
MANGONEL
MAXIM GUN
MUNITION
MUSKETRY
NAIL BOMB
NERVE GAS
OERLIKON
OMPHALOS
ORDNANCE
PARAVANE
PETRONEL
PHOSGENE
PLATFORM
PORTFIRE

REPEATER
REVOLVER
RICOCHET
SCABBARD
SCIMITAR
SHRAPNEL
SIEGE GUN
SILENCER
SKEAN-DHU
SLOW FUSE
STILETTO
TIME BOMB
TIME FUSE
TOMAHAWK
TOMMY GUN
TRIP-WIRE
VAMPLATE
WEAPONRY
YATAGHAN

9

ARMAMENTS
ARROWHEAD
ARTILLERY
BACKSIGHT
BACKSWORD
BANDOLEER
  (or bandolier)
BANDOLIER
  (or bandoleer)
BATTLEAXE
BIG BERTHA
BLACKJACK
BOFORS GUN
BOMBSHELL
BOOBY TRAP
BOOMERANG
BROADSIDE

CANNELURE
CARRONADE
CARTRIDGE
CHAIN SHOT
COLD STEEL
DERRINGER
DETERRENT
DETONATOR
DIRTY BOMB
DISCHARGE
DOODLEBUG
EXPLOSION
EXPLOSIVE
FIRING PIN
FLINTLOCK
FORESIGHT
GELIGNITE
GRAPESHOT
GREEK FIRE
GUN BARREL
GUNCOTTON
GUNPOWDER
GUN TURRET
HARQUEBUS
  (or arquebus)
HORSEWHIP
LIVE SHELL
MATCHLOCK
MILLS BOMB
MINUTEMAN
MUNITIONS
PEEP SIGHT
PIKESTAFF
PINEAPPLE
POISON GAS
RIFLE SHOT
SAFETY PIN
SLINGSHOT

SLOW MATCH
SMALL ARMS
SMALL-BORE
SMOKE BALL
SMOKE BOMB
SPEARHEAD
STAR SHELL
STINK BOMB
SWORD BELT
TOUCH HOLE
TREBUCHET
TRUNCHEON
TURRET GUN
WHEEL LOCK
ZUMBOORUK

10
AMMUNITION
BOWIE KNIFE
BROADSWORD
CANNONBALL
CLASP KNIFE
CROSS GUARD
DETONATION
DISCHARGER
FLICK KNIFE
FLYING BOMB
FUSION BOMB
GATLING GUN
HARPOON GUN
INCENDIARY
KNOBKERRIE
LEE-ENFIELD
LETTER BOMB
MACHINE GUN
MISERICORD
MUSTARD GAS
NAPALM BOMB

NERVE AGENT
NIGHTSTICK
NULLA-NULLA
PISTOL SHOT
POWDER HORN
PROJECTILE
PROPELLANT
RIFLESCOPE
RIOT SHIELD
SAFETY FUSE
SAFETY LOCK
SCATTER GUN
SERPENTINE
SHILLELAGH
SIX-SHOOTER
SMOOTH-BORE
SWORDSTICK
WINCHESTER

11
AGENT ORANGE
ANTI-TANK GUN
BLOCKBUSTER
BLUNDERBUSS
BOW AND ARROW
CALIBRATION
DEPTH CHARGE
EMPLACEMENT
FISSION BOMB
GARAND RIFLE
GUN CARRIAGE
GUN PLATFORM
HAIR TRIGGER
HAND GRENADE
HORSE PISTOL
KALASHNIKOV
MARLINSPIKE
MORNING STAR

NEUTRON BOMB
NUCLEAR BOMB
PEPPER SPRAY
PLASTIC BOMB
POCKET KNIFE
POWDER FLASK
RANGEFINDER
SAFETY CATCH
SIEGE ENGINE
SINGLE STICK
THOMPSON GUN
TORPEDO TUBE
WATER CANNON

12
BATTERING RAM
BREECH-LOADER
DUMDUM BULLET
EXPRESS RIFLE
FLAME-THROWER
FOWLING PIECE
HUNTING KNIFE
HYDROGEN BOMB
MAGNETIC MINE
MARTINI-HENRY
MUZZLE-LOADER
QUARTERSTAFF
ROCKET MORTAR
SHOOTING IRON
SIGHTING SHOT
TRACER BULLET
TRENCH MORTAR

13
CARTRIDGE BELT
CAT-O'-NINE-TAILS
DAMASCUS STEEL
GUIDED MISSILE

HIGH EXPLOSIVE
KNUCKLEDUSTER
LIFE PRESERVER
LIVE CARTRIDGE
NUCLEAR WEAPON
PERCUSSION CAP
PLASTIC BULLET
POISONED ARROW
PROXIMITY FUSE
SUB-MACHINE GUN

14
AMMUNITION BELT

BLANK CARTRIDGE
GUN EMPLACEMENT
INCENDIARY BOMB
NUCLEAR MISSILE
PERCUSSION LOCK
POWDER MAGAZINE
SAWN-OFF SHOTGUN
SMITH AND WESSON
WEBLEY REVOLVER

15
ANTI-AIRCRAFT GUN
LEE-ENFIELD RIFLE

MOLOTOV COCKTAIL
OFFENSIVE WEAPON
SHOULDER-HOLSTER
SOFT-NOSED BULLET
TELESCOPIC SIGHT
WINCHESTER RIFLE

16
BALLISTIC MISSILE

17
BROWNING AUTOMATIC

Mythology

Mythology – EGYPTIAN MYTHOLOGY

* = location   † = creature All characters unless stated.

3
BES
GEB
MIN
MUT
NUN*
NUT
SET
  (or Seth)
SHU

4
AMON
  (or Amun)
AMUN
  (or Amon)
APIS†
ATUM
BAST

BUTO
EDFU*
HAPI
ISIS
MAAT
MONT
NILE river
PHRA
PTAH
SATI
SETH
  (or Set)

5
ANHUR
BENNU†
HEKET
HORUS
KHNUM

KHONS
NEITH
NUBIA*
SEBEK
SEKER
THOTH

6
ANUBIS
ANUKET
AVARIS*
BUCHIS†
BYBLOS*
HATHOR
KHEPRI
MNEVIS†
OSIRIS
RENPET
SCARAB†

SELKET
SESHAT
SUTEKH
TEFNUT
UPUAUT

7
ANDJETI
BEHDETY
BUSIRIS*
KEBEHUT
ONUPHIS†
RENENET
SEKHMET
TAUERET

8
DUAMUTEF
HAROERIS

MESHKENT
NEFERTUM
NEKHEBET
NEPHTHYS

9
AKHENATON
AMENHOTEP
HARSAPHES
MALCANDRE
MERTSEGER
NEFERTITI

10
HATSHEPSUT
PETESUCHOS†

The *Puzzler* Crossword Companion

Mythology – GREEK MYTHOLOGY
* = location   † = creature(s) All characters unless stated.

3
DIA
EOS
IDA mount
INO
ION
PAN

4
ABAS
ACIS
AJAX
ARES
ARGO ship
AUGE
BIAS
CETO
CIOS*
CLIO Muse
ECHO
ELIS*
ERIS
EROS
ERYX mount
ETNA mount
GAEA
HEBE
HERA
HERO
ILUS
IOLE
IRIS
ISSA
ITYS
LEDA

LETO
NIKE
NYSA mount
OLEN
OSSA mount
OTUS
RHEA
STYX river
TROS
TROY*
  (or Ilium)
TYRO
ZEUS

5
AEAEA*
AEDON
AESON
AËTES
ALEUS
ARGOS*
ARGUS
ARION†
ATLAS
ATTIS
AULIS*
BELUS
BITON
CHAOS*
CHILO
CHIOS*
CIRCE
COEUS
CREON
CRETE*

DANAË
DELOS*
DIONE
DOLON
DORUS
DRYAD
ERATO Muse
EURUS
FATES
GYGES†
HADES*
HELEN
HELLE
HETIS
HORAE
HYDRA†
HYLAS
HYMEN
IDAEA
ILIUM*
  (or Troy)
IRENE
IXION
JASON
LADON†
LAIUS
LAMIA
LAMUS
LERNA*
LETHE river
LEUCE
LINUS
LYDIA*
MAERA†
MANTO

MEDEA
MEDUS
METIS
MIDAS
MINOS
MYSIA*
NAIAD
NAXOS*
NIOBE
NISUS
NOTUS
ORION
PARIS
PERSE
PLUTO
PRIAM
PYLUS*
RHODE
SATYR
SIBYL
SINIS
SINON
SOLON
TALOS
TEGEA*
TEMPE*
TENES
THEBE
THOAS
THYIA
TITAN
TROAS*
TYCHE
ZETES

6
ACAMAS
ADONIS
AEACUS
AEGEUS
AEGINA*
AENEAS
AEOLUS
AEROPE
AETHRA
AGENOR
AGLAIA Grace
ALCYON*
ALECTO Fury
ALIPES sandals
AMAZON
AMYCUS
APHAIA
APOLLO
ASOPUS
ATHENA
  (or Athene)
ATHENE
  (or Athena)
ATHENS*
ATREUS
ATTICA*
AUGIAS
BALIAS†
BAUCIS
BOREAS
CADMUS
CALAIS
CANACE
CASTOR

CELEUS
CHARON
CHIONE
CLAROS*
CLOTHO Fate
COTTUS†
CREUSA
CRONUS
  (or Kronos)
CYBELE
CYNCUS
CYRENE
DANAID
DANAUS
DAPHNE
DELPHI*
DICTYS
DIDYMA*
DODONA*
DRYADS
DRYOPE
DRYOPS
ECHION
ELATUS
EPEIUS
EREBUS
EUBOEA*
EUROPA
EVADNE
FURIES
  (or Eumenides)
GRACES
GRAEAE
HAEMON
HECATE
HECTOR
HECUBA
HELIOS

HELLEN
HERMES
HESTIA
HYADES
HYGEIA
HYLLUS
HYPNOS
IASION
ICARUS
IOLCUS*
ISMENE
ITHACA*
KRONOS
  (or Cronus)
LEMNOS*
LESBOS*
LICHAS
LYCAON
MAERAE
MEDUSA
  Gorgon
MEGARA
MEMNON
MENTOR
MEROPE Pleiad
MINYAE
MOPSUS
NAIADS
NELEUS
NEREID
NEREUS
NESTOR
OENEUS
OENONE
OGYGIA*
OILEUS
OTONIA
OTRERE

PALLAS
PAPHOS*
PELEUS
PELIAS
PELION mount
PELOPS
PENEUS
PERDIX
PERSES
PHAROS*
PHOCIS*
PHOCUS
PHOEBE
PHOLUS†
POLLUX
PONTUS
PROCNE
PSYCHE
PYTHIA
PYTHON†
RHESUS
RHODES*
SATYRS
SCIRON
SCYLLA†
SCYROS*
SELENE
SESTOS*
SICILY*
SIGEUM*
SPARTA*
SPARTI
SPHINX†
STHENO Gorgon
SYRINX
TALAUS
TEREUS
TETHYS

THALES
THALIA Muse
THEBES*
THEMIS
THETIS
THRACE*
TIRYNS*
TITANS
TITYUS
TMOLUS mount
TRITON lake
TYDEUS
TYPHON†
UDAEUS
URANIA Muse
URANUS
XUTHUS
ZEPHYR
  (or Zephyrus)

7

ABDERUS
ACASTUS
ACHAEUS
ACHERON river
ACTAEON
ADMETUS
AETOLIA*
ALCAEUS
ALCMENE
ALCYONE Pleiad
ALTHAEA
AMAZONS
AMPHION
AMYCLAE*
AMYMONE*
ANTAEUS
ANTENOR

ANTEROS
ANTIOPE
ARACHNE
ARCADIA*
ARGOLIS*
ARIADNE
ARTEMIS
ASTYNAX
ATHAMAS
ATROPOS Fate
AVERNUS lake
BOEOTIA*
BRAURON*
BRISEIS
BRONTES
BROTEAS
CAENEUS
CALCHAS
CALYDON*
CALYPSO
CECROPS
CELOENO Pleiad
CENTAUR†
CEPHEUS
CERCYON
CHEIRON
CISSEUS
CLEOBIS
CLYMENE
COCALUS
COCYTUS river
COLCHIS*
CORINTH*
CORONIS
CROESUS
CURETES
CYCLOPS
CYLLENE mount

CYTHERA*
DACTYLI
DANAIDS
DEIPYLE
DEMETER
DINDYMA mount
ECHEMUS
ECHIDNE†
ELECTRA
ELECTRA Pleiad
ELEUSIS*
ELPENOR
ELYSIUM*
EMPUSAE
ENIPEUS
EPAPHUS
EPHESUS*
EPIGONI
ERGINUS
ERIGONE
ERYTHIA*
EUMAEUS
EURYALE Gorgon
EURYTUS
EUTERPE Muse
GALATEA
GLAUCUS
GORDIUS
GORGONS
HARPIES
HELENUS
HELICON mount
HESIONE
HYPENOR
IAPETUS
ICARIUS
ILYTHIA
INACHUS

IOBATES
IPHITUS
JOCASTA
LACONIA*
LAERTES
LAOCOÖN
LAODICE
LARISSA*
LEANDER
LYDIANS
LYNCEUS
LYSIPPE
MACARIA
MAENADS
MAGAERA Fury
MARSYAS
MEANDER river
MEGAEIA
MILETUS
MISENUS
MUSAEUS
MYCENAE*
NEMESIS
NEPHELE
NEREIDS
NICIPPE
OCEANUS
OEAGRUS
OEDIPUS
OLYMPIA*
OLYMPUS mount
ORESTES
ORPHEUS
ORTHRUS†
ORTYGIA*
PANDION
PANDORA
PEGASUS†

PELORUS
PERSEUS
PETASUS hat
PHAEDRA
PHAETON
PHINEUS
PHOENIX†
PHORCUS
PHRIXUS
PLEIONE
POLITES
POLYBUS
PRIAPUS
PROCRIS
PROETUS
PROTEUS
PYLADES
PYRRHUS
  (or Neoptolemus)
SALMONE*
SCHERIA*
SILENUS
SIPYLUS mount
STENTOR
STEROPE Pleiad
STRYMON river
STRYMOR
TAYGETE Pleiad
TELAMON
TENEDOS*
THEBANS
THESEUS
THYADES
THYRSUS wand
TROJANS
XANTHUS†
ZAGREUS

8

ACHELOUS
ACHILLES
ACRISIUS
ADRASTUS
AEACIDES
AGAMEDES
AGANIPPE*
ALCESTIS
ALCINOUS
ALCMAEON
AMALTHEA†
AMYTHAON
ANCHISES
ANTIGONE
APSYRTUS
ARETHUSA
ARIMASPI
ASCANIUS
ASTRAEUS
ASTYANAX
ATALANTA
ATLANTIS*
BEBRYCES
BEBRYCOS*
BRIAREUS
CADUCEUS staff
CALLIOPE Muse
CALLISTO
CAPANEUS
CASTALIA
CAUCASUS*
CENTAURS†
CEPHALUS
CERBERUS†
CHIMAERA†
CHRYSAOR
CHRYSEIS

CRETHEUS
CYCLOPES
DAEDALUS
DAMOCLES
DANAIDES
DARDANUS
DEIDAMIA
DEMOPHON
DESPOENA
DIOMEDES
DIOSCURI
ENDYMION
ERIDANUS river
ERIPHYLE
ETEOCLES
EUMOLPUS
EURIDYCE
EURYNOME
EURYTION
GANYMEDE
GIGANTES
HARMONIA
HELLENES
HEMITHEA
HERACLES
HERMIONE
HESPERUS
HYPERION
ILIONEUS
ILITHYIA
IPHICLES
LABDACUS
LACHESIS Fate
LAODAMIA
LAOMEDON
LAPITHAE
LYCURGUS
LYSANDER

MACAREUS
MARPESSA
MELAMPUS
MELEAGER
MENELAUS
MILANION
MINOTAUR†
MOLOSSUS
MORPHEUS
MYRTILUS
NAUPLIUS
NAUSICCA
NYCTINUS
ODYSSEUS
OECHALIA*
OENOMAUS
OENOPION
PACTOLUS river
PALAEMON
PANDARUS
PANOPEUS
PASIPHAË
PENELOPE
PENTHEUS
PHILEMON
PHLEGYAS
PITTACUS
PLEIADES
POLYXENA
POSEIDON
PSAMATHE
SARPEDON
SISYPHUS
SPARTANS
TANTALUS
TARTARUS*
TELEPHUS
TEUTHRAS

THANATOS
THESPIUS
THESSALY*
THYESTES
TITANESS
TITHONUS
ZEPHYRUS
 (or Zephyr)

9

ACROPOLIS*
AEGISTHUS
AGAMEMNON
ALCYONEUS
AMPHIARUS
ANDROMEDA
APHRODITE
APOLLONIA*
AREOPAGUS*
ARGONAUTS
ARISTAEUS
ASCLEPIUS
ASIA MINOR*
AUTOLYCUS
BASSAREUS
CALLIRHOË
CASSANDRA
CHARYBDIS†
CITHAERON mount
DEIPHOBUS
DEUCALION
ELECTRYON
ENCELADUS
EPHIALTES
EPIDAURUS*
EUMENIDES
 (or Furies)
EUPHORBUS

HAMADRYAD
HARPALYCE
HIPPOCOÖN
HIPPOLYTA
IDOMENEUS
IPHIGENIA
LEUCIPPUS
LOTOPHAGI
  (or Lotus Eaters)
LYCOMEDES
LYRNESSUS*
MELPOMENE Muse
MENOECEUS
METANEIRA
MNEMOSYNE
MYRMIDONS
NARCISSUS
OCEANIDES
OREITHYIA
PALAMEDES
PALLADIUM statue
PARNASSUS mount
PATROCLUS
PAUSANIUS
PERIANDER
PIRITHOUS
POLYDORUS
POLYNICES
PYGMALION
SALMONEUS
SCAMANDER
STHENELUS
TEIRESIAS
TELCHINES
THERSITES
TISIPHONE Fury
TYNDAREUS

10
AMPHITRITE
AMPHITRYON
ANDROMACHE
ANTILOCHUS
BACCHANTES
CASSIOPEIA
CIMMERIANS
CORNUCOPIA horn
CORYBANTES
CRETAN BULL†
EPIMETHEUS
ERECHTHEUS
EUPHROSYNE Grace
HAMADRYADS
HELLESPONT*
HEPHAESTUS
HESPERIDES
HIPPOCRENE*
HIPPODAMIA
HIPPOLYTUS
HYACINTHUS
IPHIANASSA
MENESTHEUS
NEMEAN LION†
ORCHOMENUS
PALINAURUS
PERIPHETES
PERSEPHONE
PHLEGETHON river
POLYHYMNIA Muse
POLYMESTER
POLYPHEMUS
PORPHYRION
PROCRUSTES
PROMETHEUS
SCAEAN GATE*
STYMPHALUS lake

TELEMACHUS
TELEPHASSA
TITANESSES
TROPHONIUS

11
AGATHYRSANS
BELLEROPHON
BRITOMARTIS
CRESPHONTES
ERYSICHTHON
GOLDEN BOUGH
GORDIAN KNOT
LOTUS EATERS
  (or Lotophagi)
NEOPTOLEMUS
  (or Pyrrhus)
PALLANTIDES
PENTHESILEA
PHILOCTETES
TERPSICHORE Muse
TROJAN HORSE

12
CLYTEMNESTRA
DICTAEAN CAVE*
ERICHTHONIUS
GOLDEN APPLES
GOLDEN FLEECE
HYPERBOREANS
LAESTRYGONES
PELEPONNESUS*
PERICLYMENUS
RHADAMANTHUS
TARPEIAN ROCK*

13
AUGEAN STABLES*

CERYNEIAN HIND†
HALIRRHOTHIUS
PARTHENOPAEUS
PONTUS EUXINUS*
SOW OF CROMMYUM†
THE UNDERWORLD*

14
APPLE OF DISCORD
CALYDONIAN BEAR†
CATTLE OF GERYON†
HECATONCHEIRES
HERMAPHRODITUS

15
CASTALIAN SPRING*
MARES OF DIOMEDES†
SWORD OF DAMOCLES

Mythology – HINDU MYTHOLOGY
* = avatar of Vishnu   † = Aditya All characters unless stated.

3
UMA

4
AGNI
ANSA†
DEVI (or Shakti)
RAMA* prince, then
   king
RAVI
SOMA
VAYU (or Pavana)
YAMA

5
BHAGA†
DURGA
DYAUS
ESWAR
INDRA
KALKI* eternity
KURMA* tortoise
MITRA†
RUDRA
SHIVA
SURYA (or Savitr)

6
BRAHMA
DAKSHA†
GANESH
KUBERA
MATSYA* fish
NARADA
PAVANA
   (or Vayu)
SAVITR
   (or Surya)
SHAKTI
   (or Devi)
VAMANA* dwarf
VARAHA* boar
VARUNA†
VISHNU

7
ADITYAS
ARYAMAN†
ASPARAS
HANUMAN
KRISHNA* supreme
   being
LAKSHMI

MURUGAN
PARVATI
PRITHVI

8
BALARAMA* strong
   Rama

9
KARMADEVA
NARASIMHA*
   man-lion
PRAJAPATI
SARASWATI

10
BRIHASPATI
GANDHARVAS

11
PARASHURAMA*
   Rama with an axe

Mythology – ROMAN MYTHOLOGY
* = location All characters unless stated.

3
DIS*
OPS
PAX
SOL

4
CACA
DIDO
JUNO
LARA
LUNA
MARS
MORS
NEMI lake
NUMA
RHEA
 (or Rhea Silvia)
ROME*

5
ARDEA*
CACUS
CERES
CUPID
DIANA
FLORA
JANUS
LARES
MANES
MANIA
ORCUS
PALES
PICUS
REMUS

TIBER river
VENUS
VESTA

6
AQUILO
ARICIA*
AURORA
AUSTER
CHARIS
CONSUS
EGERIA
FAUNUS
HEBRUS river
LATIUM*
LATONA
PARCAE
POMONA
RAMNES
SATURN
TELLUS
TITIES
TURNUS
VACUNA
VULCAN

7
ACESTES
BACCHUS
BELLONA
BONA DEA
CAELIAN
 Rome hill
CHLORIS
CLOELIA

CURATII
ETRURIA*
EVANDER
FEBRUUS
FORTUNA
GRACCHI
HORATII
JUPITER
JUTURNA
LATINUS
LEMURES
LUCERES
MERCURY
MINERVA
NEPTUNE
NUMITOR
OMPHALE
PENATES
ROMULUS
SABINUS
TARCHON
TARPEIA
ULYSSES
VIMINAL
 Rome hill

8
ANGERONA
AVENTINE
 Rome hill
CHALYBES
COECULUS
CLOACINA
CORNELIA
DIS PATER

FAVONIUS
HERCULES
HORATIUS
JUVENTAS
LAVINIUM*
LIBITINA
NUMICIUS river
PALATINE
 Rome hill
PILUMNUS
PORTUNUS
QUIRINAL
 Rome hill
QUIRINUS
SILVANUS
TARENTUM*
TARPEIUS
VICTORIA

9
ALBA LONGA*
CONSUALIA
ESQUILINE
 Rome hill
ETRUSCANS
FAUSTULUS
PRAENESTE*
TIBERINUS
VERTUMNUS

10
BACCHANTES
CAPITOLINE
 Rome hill
GAETULIANS

LIBER PATER
PHALANTHUS
PROSERPINA
RHEA SILVIA (or Rhea)
TARQUINIUS

11
AESCULAPIUS
SABINE WOMEN

TELLUS MATER

12
ACCA LARENTIA
ANCUS MARTIUS

13
NUMA POMPILIUS
VESTAL VIRGINS

14
GATE OF CARMENTA*
SERVIUS TULLIUS

15
TULLUS HOSTILIUS

Mythology – SCANDINAVIAN MYTHOLOGY

* = location   † = creature All characters unless stated.

3
ASK
BOR
HEL
SIF
TIW
ULL

4
FREY
HRYM
HUGI
IDUN
LOKI
MODI
ODIN
 (or Woden)
SIGI
SURT
THOR
VILI
YMIR

5
AESIR
BRAGI
EMBLA
GERDA
GJÖLL river
FREYA
 (or Frigga)
HYMIR
LODUR
MAGNI
MIMIR
NJÖRD
NORNS
RERIR
TROLL†
VANIR
VIDAR
WODEN
 (or Odin)

6
ASGARD*
BALDER

FENRIR†
FRIGGA (or Freya)
FREYJA
HERMOD
HOENIR
SIGURD
THJAZI
TROLLS†

7
AUDUMLA†
BIFRÖST bridge
GUNGNIR spear
MIDGARD*
MJOLNIR hammer
NIDHÖGG†
ODRERIR cauldron
SIGMUND
SKRYMIR
SUTTUNG
THJALFI
VOLSUNG

8
DRAUPNIR ring
HEIMDALL
HRUNGNIR
NILFHEIM*
RATATOSK†
SLEIPNIR†
VALHALLA*
VIDOFNIR†

9
JOTUNHEIM*
THRUDVANG*
VALKYRIES
YGGDRASIL tree

10
HVERGELMIR roaring
 kettle

11
SKIDBLADNIR ship
URDARBRUNNR well
 of fate

Names

Names – BOYS' NAMES

3	DEN	JAN	LEX	ROG	WAT	ASIF	CHAN
ABE	DES	JAY	LOU	RON	WES	AXEL	CHAS
ABI	DEV	JED	MAX	ROY	WYN	BART	CHAY
ALF	DOM	JEM	MEL	SAM	ZAK	BEAU	CHIP
ALI	DON	JIM	NAT	SEB		BERT	CURT
ANT	ELI	JOB	NED	SID	4	BILL	CLAY
ART	ERN	JOE	NYE	SLY	ABEL	BING	CLEM
ASA	GAY	JON	ODO	STU	ADAM	BOYD	DALE
BAS	GIL	KAI	PAT	SYD	ALAN	BRAD	DANA
BAZ	GUS	KEN	PER	TAM	ALDO	BRAM	DAVE
BEN	GUY	KEV	PIP	TED	ALEC	BRET	DAVY
BOB	HAL	KIM	RAB	TEX	ALED	BRYN	DEAN
BUD	HAM	KIT	RAY	TIM	ALEX	BUCK	DICK
COL	HEW	LEE	RED	TOM	ALGY	BURT	DINO
DAI	HUW	LEN	REG	URI	ALUN	CAIN	DIRK
DAN	IAN	LEO	REX	VAL	ALVA	CARL	DION
DEC	IKE	LES	RIO	VAN	ALYN	CARY	DOUG
DEE	IRA	LEV	ROB	VIC	AMOS	CERI	DREW
DEL	IVO	LEW	ROD	VIV	ANDY	CHAD	DUFF

DUKE	JAKE	MICK	SETH	ALVAR	CARLO	DWANE	GERRY
EARL	JEAN	MIKE	SHAW	ALVIN	CAROL	DYLAN	GILES
EDDY	JEFF	MILO	SHEM	ALWIN	CASEY	EAMON	GLENN
EGON	JESS	MORT	STAN	ALWYN	CECIL	EARLE	GRANT
EHUD	JIMI	MOSS	SVEN	AMAND	CÉSAR	EDDIE	GRIFF
EMIL	JOCK	MUIR	THEO	AMYAS	CHICO	EDGAR	GUIDO
ERIC	JODY	NEIL	THOR	ANDRÉ	CHRIS	EDWIN	GYLES
ERIK	JOEL	NERO	TOBY	ANGEL	CHUCK	ELDON	HAGAR
ERLE	JOEY	NICK	TODD	ANGUS	CLARK	ELIAS	HAKIM
ERYL	JOHN	NIKI	TONY	ANTON	CLAUD	ELLIS	HARDY
ESAU	JOSÉ	NOAH	TREV	ARCHY	CLAUS	ELMER	HARRY
EUAN	JOSH	NOËL	TROY	ARTIE	CLIFF	ELTON	HEINZ
EVAN	JUAN	ODIE	VERE	AUBYN	CLINT	ELVIS	HENRI
EWAN	JUDE	OLAF	WALT	AVERY	CLIVE	ELWYN	HENRY
EZRA	KANE	OLAV	WARD	BARRY	CLYDE	EMERY	HIRAM
FAHD	KARL	OLEG	WILF	BASIL	COLIN	ÉMILE	HOMER
FATS	KEIR	OMAR	WILL	BENNY	CONAN	EMLYN	HORST
FINN	KENT	OTIS	WYNN	BERRY	COREY	EMRYS	HUMPH
FRED	KIAN	OTTO	YURI	BEVIS	COSMO	ENOCH	HYRAM
FULK	KING	OWEN	YVES	BILLY	CRAIG	ERNIE	HYWEL
GARY	KIRK	OZZY	ZANE	BJORN	CYRIL	ERNST	IANNI
GENE	KRIS	PAUL	ZEKE	BLAKE	CYRUS	ERROL	INIGO
GLEN	KURT	PEPE	ZENO	BOBBY	DACRE	ETHAN	INNES
GLYN	KYLE	PETE		BONAR	DAMON	EWART	IRVIN
GREG	LARS	PHIL	**5**	BOOTH	DANNY	FELIX	IRWIN
HANK	LEIF	PIUS	AARON	BORIS	DARCY	FERDY	ISAAC
HANS	LEON	RAVI	ABDUL	BRENT	DARYL	FIDEL	IZAAK
HOPE	LEVI	RENÉ	ABNER	BRETT	DAVID	FLANN	JABEZ
HUEY	LIAM	RHYS	ABRAM	BRIAN	DAVIE	FLOYD	JACKY
HUGH	LOYD	RICK	ADOLF	BRUCE	DENIS	FRANK	JACOB
HUGO	LUCA	ROLF	AIDAN	BRUNO	DENNY	FRANS	JAIME
IAGO	LUDO	RORY	AIREY	BRYAN	DENYS	FRANZ	JAMES
IAIN	LUKE	ROSS	ALAIN	BUDDY	DEREK	FRITZ	JAMIE
IGOR	LYLE	RUDI	ALBAN	BUNNY	DICKY	FULKE	JARED
ILIE	MARC	RUSS	ALFIE	BUSBY	DIEGO	GARRY	JASON
IVAN	MARK	RYAN	ALICK	CAIUS	DIGBY	GARTH	JAVED
IVOR	MATT	SAUL	ALLAN	CALEB	DONAL	GAVIN	JERRY
JACK	MERV	SEAN	ALLEN	CAREW	DUANE	GEOFF	JESSE

JÉSUS
JIMMY
JONAH
JONAS
JOOLS
JULES
KAROL
KEITH
KELLY
KENNY
KEVIN
LANCE
LARRY
LEIGH
LENNY
LEROY
LEWIN
LEWIS
LINUS
LLOYD
LORNE
LOUIE
LOUIS
LUCAS
LUIGI
MAJOR
MANNY
MARCO
MARIO
MARTY
MASON
MICAH
MICKY
MILES
MITCH
MONTY
MOSES
MUNGO

MURDO
NAHUM
NEDDY
NEVIL
NIALL
NICKY
NICOL
NIELS
NIGEL
NOLAN
OGDEN
OLLIE
OSCAR
OSKAR
OSMAN
OSRIC
OSSIE
OSWIN
PABLO
PADDY
PAOLO
PAVEL
PEDRO
PERCY
PERRY
PETER
PHILL
PIERS
PIRAN
RALPH
RAMON
RANDY
RAOUL
REECE
RHETT
RICKY
RIDER
RINGO

ROALD
ROBIN
ROCKY
RODDY
ROGER
ROLLO
ROMEO
ROWAN
RUBIN
RUFUS
SACHA
SAMMY
SANDY
SASHA
SCOTT
SELBY
SERGE
SHANE
SILAS
SIMON
SOLLY
SONNY
SPIKE
SPIRO
STEVE
SUNIL
TAFFY
TEDDY
TERRY
TIBOR
TIGER
TIMMY
TITUS
TOMMY
TORIN
TRENT
TUDOR
TYLER

ULICK
ULRIC
ULTAN
UPTON
URBAN
URIAH
VASCO
VINCE
VITUS
WAHAB
WALDO
WALLY
WAYNE
WILLY
WOLFE
WOODY
WYATT
YANNI
ZAFIR
ZUBIN

6

ADOLPH
ADONIS
ADRIAN
AENEAS
ALARIC
ALBERT
ALDOUS
ALDRED
ALEXEI
ALEXIS
ALFRED
ALONSO
ANDREW
ANGELO
ANSELM
ANTONY

ARCHIE
ARMAND
ARNOLD
ARTHUR
ASHLEY
ASHOKA
AUBREY
AUGUST
AUSTIN
AYLMER
AYLWIN
BAMBER
BARNEY
BENITO
BENJIE
BENNIE
BENOIT
BERNIE
BERTIE
BLAISE
BOGDAN
BRUTUS
BUSTER
CAESAR
CALLUM
CALVIN
CARLOS
CASPAR
CEDRIC
CLAUDE
COLLEY
CONNOR
CONRAD
CUDDIE
CURTIS
DAFYDD
DAMIAN
DAMIEN

DANIEL
DARIUS
DARREL
DARREN
DARRYL
DECLAN
DELROY
DENNIS
DENZEL
DENZIL
DERMOT
DERYCK
DÉSIRÉ
DEXTER
DICKIE
DIDIER
DMITRI
DONALD
DONNIE
DORIAN
DOUGAL
DUARTE
DUGALD
DUGGIE
DUNCAN
DUNDAS
DUSTIN
DWIGHT
EAMONN
EDMOND
EDMUND
ÉDUARD
EDVARD
EDWARD
EGBERT
ELDRED
ELIJAH
ELLIOT

EMILIO
ERNEST
ESMOND
EUGENE
EVELYN
FABIAN
FELIPE
FERGUS
FINLAY
FORBES
FRANCO
FRASER
FYODOR
GARETH
GASPAR
GASTON
GAWAIN
GEORGE
GERALD
GERARD
GIDEON
GODWIN
GORDON
GRAEME
GRAHAM
GREGOR
GROGAN
GROVER
GUNTER
GUSTAV
GWILYM
HAMISH
HAMLET
HANSEL
HAROLD
HARRIS
HARVEY
HAYDEN

HAYDON	JUSTIN	MODEST	REGGIE	SYDNEY	ALISTER	CLEMENT
HECTOR	JUSTUS	MORGAN	RETIEF	TALBOT	ALMERIC	CLINTON
HEDLEY	KELVIN	MORRIS	REUBEN	THOMAS	AMADEUS	COMPTON
HELMUT	KIERAN	MOSTYN	RHODES	TOBIAS	AMBROSE	CONNELL
HERMAN	KONRAD	MURPHY	RICHIE	TRAVIS	ANATOLE	CRISPIN
HILARY	LAUREN	MURRAY	ROBBIE	TREVOR	ANATOLY	CYPRIAN
HILTON	LAURIE	NATHAN	ROBERT	TYBALT	ANDREAS	DELBERT
HORACE	LAWRIE	NEDDIE	RODGER	TYRONE	ANEURIN	DENHOLM
HOWARD	LEMUEL	NELSON	RODNEY	ULRICH	ANTHONY	DERRICK
HOWELL	LENNIE	NICHOL	ROLAND	VÁCLAV	ANTOINE	DESMOND
HUBERT	LEONID	NICOLO	RONALD	VALERY	ANTONIN	DIGGORY
HUGHIE	LESLIE	NIKITA	ROWLEY	VASILY	ANTONIO	DOMINIC
HUNTER	LESTER	NINIAN	RUDOLF	VASLAV	ARTEMUS	DONOVAN
IANNIS	LIONEL	NORMAN	RUPERT	VERNON	ATTICUS	DOUGLAS
IGNACE	LONNIE	NORRIS	SABINE	VICTOR	AUBERON	DUNSTAN
INGRAM	LORCAN	OBERON	SAMSON	VIRGIL	AUGUSTE	ÉDOUARD
IRVINE	LORENZ	OLIVER	SAMUEL	VITALY	BALDWIN	ELEAZAR
ISAIAH	LOVELL	ONSLOW	SANCHO	VIVIAN	BARCLAY	ELLIOTT
ISODOR	LUCIEN	OSBERT	SANJAY	VYVIAN	BARNABY	ENRIQUÉ
ISRAEL	LUCIUS	OSMOND	SEAMAS	WALLIS	BENTLEY	EPHRAIM
JACKIE	LUDWIG	OSMUND	SEAMUS	WALTER	BERNARD	ERASMUS
JACOPO	LUTHER	OSWALD	SEFTON	WARNER	BERTRAM	EUSTACE
JARROD	MAGNUS	PASCAL	SELWYN	WARREN	BOTOLPH	EVERARD
JARVIS	MANLEY	PASCOE	SERGEI	WESLEY	BRADLEY	EZEKIEL
JASPER	MANUEL	PAULUS	SERGIO	WILBUR	BRANDON	FEARGAL
JEREMY	MARCEL	PEARCE	SEXTON	WILLEM	BRENDAN	FINDLAY
JEROME	MARCUS	PELHAM	SIDNEY	WILLIE	BRIGHAM	FLORIAN
JERVIS	MARIUS	PERKIN	SILVIO	XAVIER	BRYNMOR	FRANCIS
JETHRO	MARTIN	PHILIP	SIMEON	YANNIS	CAMERON	FRANKIE
JOHANN	MARTYN	PIERCE	SIMKIN	YEHUDI	CARADOC	FREDDIE
JOHNNY	MELVIN	PIERRE	SIXTUS		CARLTON	GABRIEL
JOLYON	MELVYN	RABBIE	SOAMES	**7**	CASIMIR	GAYLORD
JORDAN	MERLIN	RAFAEL	STEFAN	ABELARD	CHARLES	GEORGES
JOSEPH	MERVYN	RAMSAY	STEPAN	ABRAHAM	CHARLEY	GEORGIE
JOSHUA	MICHEL	RAMSEY	STEVEN	ABSALOM	CHARLIE	GERAINT
JOSIAH	MICKIE	RANDAL	STEVIE	AINSLEY	CHESTER	GERALDO
JULIAN	MIGUEL	RASTUS	ST JOHN	ALFONSO	CHRISTY	GERVAIS
JULIUS	MILTON	RAYNER	STUART	ALFREDO	CLAYTON	GERVASE

GIACOMO	LINDSAY	REDVERS	WILFRED	BROOKLYN	HERCULES
GILBERT	LORENZO	REYNARD	WILFRID	CAMPBELL	HEREWARD
GLOSTER	LUDOVIC	REYNOLD	WILHELM	CHRISTIE	HERNANDO
GODFREY	MALACHI	RICARDO	WILLARD	CLARENCE	HEZEKIAH
GREGORY	MALCOLM	RICHARD	WILLIAM	CLAUDIUS	HORATIUS
GUSTAVE	MANFRED	RINALDO	WINSTON	CLIFFORD	HUMPHREY
HADRIAN	MATTHEW	ROYSTON	WOODROW	CONSTANT	IGNATIUS
HALBERT	MAURICE	RUDOLPH	WYNDHAM	COURTNEY	IMMANUEL
HAMMOND	MAXWELL	RUDYARD	WYNFORD	CRAWFORD	INNOCENT
HARTLEY	MAYNARD	RUSSELL	ZACHARY	CRISPIAN	JEDEDIAH
HERCULE	MERRICK	SAMPSON	ZEBEDEE	CUTHBERT	JEREMAIH
HERBERT	MICHAEL	SANJEEV		DIARMUID	JERMAINE
HERMANN	MIKHAIL	SEYMOUR	**8**	DINSDALE	JOHANNES
HILAIRE	MILBURN	SHELDON	ABDULLAH	DOMINICK	JONATHAN
HORATIO	MONTAGU	SHELLEY	ACHILLES	EBENEZER	KIMBERLY
HUMBERT	MYRDDIN	SIGMUND	ADOLPHUS	EMMANUEL	KINGSLEY
HUMPHRY	NEVILLE	SOLOMON	AGAPETUS	ETHELRED	LANCELOT
HUSSEIN	NICOLAS	SPENCER	ALASDAIR	EUGENIUS	LAURENCE
ICHABOD	NORBERT	STANLEY	ALASTAIR	EUSEBIUS	LAWRENCE
INGLEBY	OBADIAH	STAVROS	ALGERNON	FARQUHAR	LEIGHTON
ISHMAEL	OCTAVUS	STEPHEN	ALISTAIR	FERNANDO	LEONARDO
ISIDORE	ORLANDO	STEWART	ALOYSIUS	FRANCHOT	LEONIDAS
JACKSON	ORPHEUS	TANCRED	ALPHONSE	FRANÇOIS	LLEWELYN
JACQUES	ORVILLE	TARQUIN	ALPHONSO	FRANKLIN	LUDOVICK
JAPHETH	OSBORNE	TERENCE	ANTONIUS	FREDERIC	LUTWIDGE
JEFFREY	PADRAIG	THESEUS	AUGUSTUS	GARFIELD	MATTHIAS
JOACHIM	PATRICK	THIERRY	AURELIUS	GEOFFREY	MEREDITH
JOCELYN	PERSEUS	TIMOTHY	BARDOLPH	GERVAISE	MITCHELL
JOHNNIE	PHILEAS	TOMASSO	BARNABAS	GIOVANNI	MOHAMMED
KENNETH	PHINEAS	TORQUIL	BENEDICK	GIUSEPPE	MONTAGUE
KENRICK	PRESTON	TRISTAN	BENEDICT	GREVILLE	MORDECAI
KIMBALL	QUENTIN	UCHTRED	BENJAMIN	GRIFFITH	MORTIMER
LACHLAN	QUINTIN	ULYSSES	BERKELEY	GUSTAVUS	MUHAMMAD
LAMBERT	RANDALL	UMBERTO	BERNARDO	HAMILTON	NAPOLEON
LAZARUS	RANULPH	VAUGHAN	BERTHOLD	HANNIBAL	NEHEMIAH
LEANDER	RAPHAEL	VINCENT	BERTRAND	HARRISON	NICHOLAS
LEONARD	RAYMOND	WALLACE	BEVERLEY	HAVELOCK	OCTAVIUS
LEOPOLD	RAYMUND	WENDELL	BONIFACE	HEINRICH	OLIPHANT

OUGHTRED	THEODORE	DIONYSIUS	NATHANIEL	CHRISTOPHE
PAULINUS	THORNTON	ENGELBERT	NICODEMUS	DESIDERIUS
PERCEVAL	TRISTRAM	ETHELBERT	PEREGRINE	HIERONYMUS
PERCIVAL	VINCENZO	FERDINAND	RUPPRECHT	HILDEBRAND
PETERKIN	VLADIMIR	FRANCESCO	SALVATORE	HIPPOLYTUS
PHILEMON	WOLFGANG	FREDERICK	SEBASTIAN	MAXIMILIAN
RANDOLPH	ZEDEKIAH	GERONTIUS	SIEGFRIED	MONTGOMERY
REGINALD		GILLESPIE	SIGISMUND	PIERREPONT
ROBINSON	**9**	GLADSTONE	STANISLAS	STANISLAUS
RODERICK	ALEXANDER	GRANVILLE	STRATFORD	THEODOSIUS
RUAIRIDH	ALPHONSUS	GRENVILLE	SYLVESTER	THEOPHILUS
SALVADOR	ARCHIBALD	GUGLIELMO	THADDAEUS	WASHINGTON
SECUNDUS	ARISTOTLE	GUILLAUME	THEODORIC	WILLOUGHBY
SEPTIMUS	ATHELSTAN	JEFFERSON	VALENTINE	
SHERIDAN	AUGUSTINE	JUSTINIAN	ZACHARIAH	**11**
SHERLOCK	BALTHAZAR	KIMBERLEY	ZACHARIAS	BARTHOLOMEW
SIEGMUND	BARTIMEUS	LAUNCELOT	ZECHARIAH	CHRISTOPHER
SINCLAIR	BRODERICK	LLEWELLYN		CONSTANTINE
STAFFORD	CELESTINE	LUCRETIUS	**10**	DESIDERATUS
STIRLING	CHRISTIAN	MACKENZIE	ANASTASIUS	GILLEASBUIG
SYLVANUS	CHRISTOPH	MARCELLUS	ATHANASIUS	SACHEVERELL
THADDEUS	CORNELIUS	MARMADUKE	BARRINGTON	
THEOBALD	DEMETRIUS	NATHANAEL	CARACTACUS	

Names – GIRLS' NAMES

3	CAT	FLO	KIM	MEL	PIA	TIB	**4**	ANNE
ABI	CIS	GAY	KIT	MEG	RAE	SUE	ABBY	ANYA
ADA	CYD	IDA	LEA	MIA	RAY	UNA	ADDY	AVIS
AMY	DEB	INA	LEE	MIN	RIA	UTA	AGGY	BABS
ANN	DEE	ISA	LIL	NAN	RIO	VAL	AIMI	BEBE
AVA	DOT	IVY	LIZ	NAT	ROS	VIV	ALEX	BELL
BEA	ENA	JAN	LOU	PAM	SAL	WIN	ALLY	BESS
BEE	EVA	JEN	LYN	PAT	SAM	ZIA	ALMA	BETH
BEL	EVE	JOY	MAI	PEG	SIB	ZOË	ALVA	CARA
BET	FAY	KAY	MAY	PEN	TIA		ANNA	CASS

CATH	GLAD	LISA	ROSA	ALEXA	CELIA	ETHEL	JENNI
CERI	GWEN	LITA	ROSE	ALICE	CHLOË	EVITA	JENNY
CHER	HANA	LIZA	RUBY	ALINA	CHRIS	FAITH	JILLY
CLEO	HEBE	LOIS	RUTH	ALINE	CILLA	FANNY	JODIE
CORA	HEDY	LOLA	SARA	ALLIE	CINDY	FIONA	JOSIE
DALE	HOPE	LORI	SIAN	AMBER	CIRCE	FLEUR	JOYCE
DANA	IMAN	LUCE	SINE	ANAÏS	CISSY	FLORA	JULIA
DAWN	INES	LUCY	SUKY	ANGEL	CLAIR	FLYNN	JULIE
DEMI	INEZ	LULU	SUSY	ANGIE	CLARA	FREDA	KAREN
DIDO	INGA	LYNN	SUZE	ANITA	CLARE	FREYA	KATIE
DOLL	INGE	MARY	SUZI	ANNIE	CORAL	GABBY	KEIRA
DORA	IONA	MAUD	SUZI	ANONA	DAISY	GAYLE	KELLY
EDIE	IRIS	META	TARA	APHRA	DEBBY	GEMMA	KERRY
EDNA	IRMA	MIMA	TERI	APRIL	DEBRA	GERDA	KETTY
ELLA	ISLA	MIMI	TESS	AUDRA	DELIA	GILDA	KITTY
ELSA	JADE	MINA	THEA	AVICE	DELLA	GILLY	KYLIE
ELSE	JANE	MOLL	TINA	AVRIL	DIANA	GINNY	LAILA
EMMA	JEAN	MONA	TONI	BEATA	DIANE	GRACE	LAURA
ENID	JESS	MYRA	TRIX	BECKY	DILYS	GREER	LAYLA
ERIN	JILL	NANA	VERA	BELLA	DINAH	GRETA	LEIGH
ESMA	JOAN	NELL	VIDA	BELLE	DOLLY	GUSSY	LEILA
ESME	JODI	NEVA	VIKI	BERRY	DONNA	HALEY	LETTY
ETTA	JODY	NINA	VITA	BERYL	DORIS	HALLE	LIANA
ETTY	JONI	NITA	ZARA	BESSY	EBONY	HAZEL	LIBBY
EVIE	JUDY	NOËL	ZENA	BETSY	EDITH	HEIDI	LILLY
FAYE	JUNE	NOLA	ZOLA	BETTE	EFFIE	HELEN	LINDA
FERN	KATE	NONA		BETTY	ELENA	HELGA	LINDY
FIFI	KATH	NORA	**5**	BIDDY	ELISA	HILDA	LORNA
FRAN	KATY	OLGA	ABBIE	BRIDE	ELISE	HOLLY	LOTTY
GABY	KIKI	OONA	ADDIE	BUNNY	ELIZA	HONOR	LUCIA
GAIL	LALA	ORLA	ADELA	BUNTY	ELLEN	HYLDA	LUCIE
GAYE	LANA	ORLA	ADÈLE	CANDY	ELLIE	ILANA	LYDIA
GENE	LARA	POLL	ADINA	CARLA	ELSIE	IRENE	LYNDA
GERT	LAYA	PRUE	AGGIE	CARLY	EMILY	JANET	LYNNE
GIGI	LEAH	RENA	AGNES	CAROL	EPPIE	JANIE	MABEL
GILL	LENA	RHEA	AILIE	CARYL	ERICA	JANIS	MADDY
GINA	LEXI	RITA	AILSA	CASEY	ERIKA	JAYNE	MADGE
GITA	LILY	ROMA	AIMÉE	CATHY	ESSIE	JAYNE	MAEVE
		RONA	ALANA			JENNA	

MAGDA	NORAH	SIBYL	ZELMA	BESSIE	DENISE	GRACIE
MAGGY	NORMA	SINDY		BETHAN	DERVLA	GRETEL
MAMIE	NORNA	SISSY	**6**	BETSEY	DIANNE	GUDRUN
MANDY	NYREE	SONIA	AGATHA	BEULAH	DIONNE	GUSSIE
MARIA	OLIVE	SONJA	AGNETA	BIANCA	DIVINA	GWENDA
MARIE	OLWEN	SONYA	AILEEN	BILLIE	DIVINE	HANNAH
MARTI	OLWIN	STACY	AILITH	BLANCH	DORCAS	HATTIE
MATTY	PADDY	SUKEY	ALEXIA	BOBBIE	DOREEN	HAYLEY
MAUDE	PAIGE	SUSAN	ALEXIS	BONITA	DORITA	HEDWIG
MAVIS	PANSY	SUSIE	ALICIA	BONNIE	DULCIE	HELENA
MEAVE	PARIS	SYBIL	ALISHA	BRANDY	EDWINA	HELENE
MEERA	PATSY	TAMMY	ALISON	BRENDA	EILEEN	HERMIA
MEGAN	PATTY	TANIA	ALTHEA	BRIDIE	ELAINE	HESTER
MARCY	PAULA	TANYA	ALYSSA	BRIGID	ELINOR	HILARY
MERLE	PEARL	TEGAN	AMANDA	BRIONY	ELOÏSA	HONORA
MERRY	PEGGY	TERRY	AMELIA	BROOKE	ELOÏSE	IANTHE
MERYL	PENNY	TESSA	AMINTA	BRYONY	ELUNED	IMELDA
MILLY	PIPPA	TESSY	ANDREA	CARMEL	ELVIRA	IMOGEN
MINNA	POLLY	THORA	ANGELA	CARMEN	EMILIA	INGRID
MITZI	POPPY	TILLY	ANNEKA	CAROLE	ESTHER	ISABEL
MOIRA	RAISA	TOYAH	ANTHEA	CARRIE	EUNICE	ISOBEL
MOLLY	REINE	TRACY	ARETHA	CECILE	EVADNE	ISOLDA
MORAG	RENÉE	TRINA	ARIANE	CECILY	EVELYN	ISOLDE
MOYNA	RHIAN	TRISH	ARLEEN	CHARIS	FATIMA	JACKIE
MOYRA	RHODA	TRIXY	ARLENE	CHERIE	FELICE	JACOBA
NADIA	RHONA	TRUDY	ASTRID	CHERRY	FINOLA	JANICE
NANCE	RIKKI	UNITY	ATHENA	CHERYL	FLAVIA	JEMIMA
NANCY	ROBIN	VANDA	ATHENE	CICELY	FRIEDA	JENNIE
NAOMI	ROBYN	VENUS	AUDREY	CISSIE	FRIGGA	JESSIE
NELLY	ROSIE	VESTA	AURIEL	CLAIRE	GAYNOR	JOANNA
NERYS	RUPAL	VICKY	AURORA	CONNIE	GERTIE	JOANNE
NESSA	SADIE	VIOLA	AVERIL	DAGMAR	GINGER	JOLEEN
NESTA	SALLY	WANDA	AYESHA	DAPHNE	GLADYS	JOLENE
NETTA	SAMMY	WENDY	BARBIE	DAVINA	GLENDA	JUDITH
NIAMH	SANDI	WILLA	BARBRA	DEANNA	GLENYS	JULIET
NIKKI	SANDY	WILMA	BEATTY	DEANNE	GLORIA	KEELEY
NIOBE	SARAH	XENIA	BENITA	DEBBIE	GLYNIS	KIRSTY
NOËLE	SHONA	ZELDA	BERTHA	DELYTH	GOLDIE	LALAGE

LALLIE	MOLLIE	SABINE	URSULA	BELINDA	DEBORAH
LAUREN	MONICA	SALOME	VALERY	BENAZIR	DEIRDRE
LEANNE	MORGAN	SANDIE	VALMAI	BERNICE	DELILAH
LEONIE	MORWEN	SANDRA	VANORA	BETHANY	DEMELZA
LESLEY	MURIEL	SAPPHO	VERENA	BETTINA	DÉSIRÉE
LETTIE	MYRTLE	SELINA	VERITY	BLANCHE	DESTINY
LILIAN	NADINE	SERENA	VIOLET	BLODWEN	DOLORES
LILITH	NELLIE	SHANIA	VIVIEN	BLOSSOM	DORINDA
LILLIE	NESSIE	SHARON	VYVIEN	BRIDGET	DOROTHY
LINSAY	NETTIE	SHEENA	WALLIS	BRONWEN	DYMPHNA
LINSEY	NICOLA	SHEILA	WINNIE	BRONWYN	ELEANOR
LIZZIE	NICOLE	SHERRY	YASMIN	CAITLIN	ELFREDA
LOLITA	NOREEN	SIGRID	YVETTE	CAMILLA	ELSPETH
LOTTIE	ODETTE	SILVIA	YVONNE	CAMILLE	ESTELLA
LOUISA	OLIVIA	SIMONE	ZILLAH	CANDICE	ESTELLE
LOUISE	OONAGH	SINEAD	ZINNIA	CANDIDA	EUGÉNIA
LYNSEY	OTILIE	SOPHIA		CAPRICE	EUGÉNIE
MADDIE	PAMELA	SOPHIE	**7**	CARMELA	EULALIA
MADHUR	PARNEL	SORCHA	ABIGAIL	CAROLYN	EVELINA
MAGGIE	PATTIE	STEFFI	ADELINA	CECILIA	EVELINE
MAISIE	PERNEL	STELLA	ADELINE	CELESTE	FELICIA
MARCIA	PERSIS	STEVIE	ADRIANA	CHANTEL	FENELLA
MARCIE	PETULA	SUMMER	ALBERTA	CHARITY	FIDELIA
MARGIE	PHOEBE	SYLVIA	ALFREDA	CHARLEY	FLOELLA
MARGOT	PORTIA	SYLVIE	ALOYSIA	CHARLIE	FLORRIE
MARIAN	PSYCHE	TAMARA	ANNABEL	CHELSEA	FLOSSIE
MARINA	PURDIE	TAMSIN	ANNETTE	CHLORIS	FRANCES
MARION	QUEENY	TERESA	ANTOINE	CLARICE	GEORGIA
MARNIE	RACHEL	TESSIE	ANTONIA	CLARRIE	GILLIAN
MARSHA	RAMONA	THALIA	ARIADNE	CLAUDIA	GISELLE
MARTHA	REGINA	THECLA	ARLETTE	CLODAGH	GWENNIE
MATTIE	RENATA	THELMA	ATHENIA	COLETTE	GWYNETH
MAXINE	RHONDA	TOMINA	AUGUSTA	CORALIE	HARRIET
MELODY	ROBINA	TRACEY	AURELIA	CORINNE	HEATHER
MHAIRI	ROSINA	TRINNY	AVELINE	CORINNA	HELOÏSE
MILLIE	ROWENA	TRIXIE	BABETTE	CRYSTAL	HILLARY
MINNIE	RUTHIE	ULRICA	BARBARA	CYNTHIA	HORATIA
MIRIAM	SABINA	ULRIKA	BEATRIX	DAVINIA	HYPATIA

ISADORA	LUCILLA	PASCALE	VALERIA	CONCHITA	JEANETTE
ISIDORA	LUCILLE	PAULINA	VALERIE	CONSUELA	JENNIFER
JACINTA	LUCINDA	PAULINE	VANESSA	CORDELIA	JOCELINE
JACQUIE	LUCRECE	PERDITA	VENETIA	CORNELIA	JULIETTA
JANETTA	LYNETTE	PHYLLIS	YOLANDA	COURTNEY	JULIETTE
JANETTE	MADISON	QUEENIE	YOLANDE	DANIELLA	KATARINA
JASMINE	MADONNA	RAELENE	ZENOBIA	DANIELLE	KATERINA
JEANNIE	MARGERY	REBECCA	ZULEIKA	DIONYSIA	KATHLEEN
JESSICA	MARILYN	RICARDA		DOROTHEA	KAYLEIGH
JILLIAN	MARJORY	RICHMAL	**8**	DRUSILLA	KIMBERLY
JOCASTA	MARLENA	ROBERTA	ADELAIDE	DULCINEA	KIRSTEEN
JOCELYN	MARLENE	ROSALIA	ADRIANNE	ELEANORE	LAETITIA
JOHANNA	MARTINA	ROSALIE	ADRIENNE	EMMELINE	LAURETTA
JOSEPHA	MATILDA	ROSANNA	ANGELICA	ETHELIND	LAURINDA
JONQUIL	MAUREEN	ROSETTA	ANGELINA	EUPHEMIA	LAVENDER
JUANITA	MELANIE	ROSHEEN	ANGHARAD	EUSTACIA	LORRAINE
JULIANA	MELISSA	ROXANNA	ANNALISA	FAUSTINA	LUCRETIA
JUSTINA	MICHELE	ROXANNE	ARABELLA	FELICITY	LUDMILLA
JUSTINE	MILDRED	SABRINA	ATALANTA	FLORENCE	MADELINE
KATHRYN	MINERVA	SEONAID	BASHEERA	FLORINDA	MAGDALEN
KATRINE	MIRABEL	SHAMEEM	BEATRICE	FRANCINE	MARCELLE
KATRINA	MIRANDA	SHANNON	BERENICE	GEORGINA	MARGARET
KIRSTEN	MODESTY	SHELAGH	BEVERLEY	GERMAINE	MARIANNE
KRISTIN	MONIQUE	SHELLEY	BIRGITTA	GERTRUDE	MARIELLA
LAVERNE	MORGANA	SHIRLEY	BRIGITTE	GRETCHEN	MARIETTA
LAVINIA	MORWENA	SIDONIA	CALLISTA	GRISELDA	MARIGOLD
LEONORA	MYFANWY	SIDONIE	CARLOTTA	GRIZELDA	MARJORIE
LETITIA	NATALIA	SIOBHAN	CAROLINA	GWYNNETH	MATHILDA
LETTICE	NATALIE	SUSANNA	CAROLINE	HERMIONE	MERCEDES
LILLIAN	NATASHA	SUSANNE	CATRIONA	HORTENSE	MICHAELA
LILLIAS	NIGELLA	SUZANNE	CHARLENE	HYACINTH	MICHELLE
LINDSAY	NINETTE	SYBILLA	CHARMIAN	INGEBORG	MIREILLE
LISBETH	NOËLEEN	TABITHA	CHRISSIE	IOLANTHE	MORWENNA
LISETTE	OCTAVIA	TATIANA	CLARINDA	ISABELLA	MYRTILLA
LIZBETH	OLYMPIA	TATYANA	CLARISSA	ISABELLE	NATHALIE
LORELEI	OPHELIA	THERESA	CLEMENCY	JACINTHA	PATIENCE
LORETTA	OTTILIA	THERESE	CLOTILDA	JACOBINA	PATRICIA
LORINDA	PANDORA	TIFFANY	CLOTILDE	JAMESINA	PENELOPE

PHILIPPA	VIOLETTA	CLAUDETTE	IPHIGENIA	ANTOINETTE
PHILLIDA	VIRGINIA	CLEOPATRA	JACQUELYN	BERENGARIA
PHYLLIDA	VIVIENNE	CLOTHILDA	JACQUETTA	BERNADETTE
PRIMROSE	WILFREDA	CLOTHILDE	JESSAMINE	CHRISTABEL
PRUDENCE	WILFRIDA	COLUMBINE	JOSEPHINE	CHRISTIANA
PRUNELLA	WINIFRED	CONSTANCE	KATHARINE	CINDERELLA
RHIANNON		DESDEMONA	KATHERINE	CLEMENTINA
ROSALIND	**9**	DOMINIQUE	KIMBERLEY	CLEMENTINE
ROSALINE	ALBERTINA	ELISABETH	MADELEINE	DESIDERATA
ROSAMOND	ALBERTINE	ELIZABETH	MAGDALENA	ERMINTRUDE
ROSAMUND	ALEXANDRA	ERNESTINE	MAGDALENE	EVANGELINA
ROSEANNA	ANASTASIA	ESMERELDA	MARGARITA	EVANGELINE
ROSEANNE	ANGELIQUE	FRANCESCA	MEHITABEL	GWENDOLINE
ROSEMARY	ANNABELLA	FRANÇOISE	MILLICENT	HILDEGARDE
SAMANTHA	ANNABELLE	FREDERICA	PHILOMENA	IRMENTRUDE
SANGEETA	APHRODITE	GABRIELLA	POLLYANNA	JACQUELINE
SAPPHIRE	BATHSHEBA	GABRIELLE	PRISCILLA	MARGHERITA
SCARLETT	BENEDICTA	GENEVIEVE	ROSABELLA	MARGUERITE
SHEELAGH	BRUNHILDE	GEORGETTE	SOPHRONIA	PETRONELLA
STEFANIE	CASSANDRA	GEORGIANA	STEPHANIE	PETRONILLA
STEPHANA	CATHARINE	GERALDINE	THEODOSIA	PHILIPPINA
SUSANNAH	CATHERINE	GHISLAINE	THOMASINA	WILHELMINA
SVETLANA	CELESTINE	GUINEVERE	VALENTINA	
TALLULAH	CHARLOTTE	GWENDOLEN	VALENTINE	**11**
THEODORA	CHARMAINE	HENRIETTA	VÉRONIQUE	ALEXANDRINA
TRYPHENA	CHRISTIAN	HEPHZIBAH		CHRISTIANIA
VERONICA	CHRISTINA	HILDEGARD	**10**	CONDOLEEZZA
VICTORIA	CHRISTINE	HORTENSIA	ALESSANDRA	

Politics

Politics – PARLIAMENTARY TERMS

3	RULE	POWER	LABOUR	TICKET	HANSARD
ACT	SEAT	RÉGIE	LEAGUE	TREATY	HECKLER
AID	VETO	SPLIT	MOTION	VOTING	LIBERAL
AYE	VOTE	STATE	OFFICE		MANDATE
LAW	WHIP	UKASE	POLICY	**7**	MARXISM
MEP		UNION	QUORUM	ADDRESS	MEASURE
NAY	**5**		RECALL	BOROUGH	MISRULE
	CABAL	**6**	RECESS	CABINET	MISSION
4	COUNT	BALLOT	RED BOX	CHAMBER	NEUTRAL
ASBO	DRAFT	BUDGET	REFORM	CHAPTER	ORATION
AXIS	EDICT	CARTEL	REGIME	CHARTER	PAIRING
BILL	FLOOR	CAUCUS	RENVOI	CLOSURE	PASSAGE
COUP	HOUSE	CENSUS	REPORT	COUNCIL	POLLING
DIET	JUNTA	CLAUSE	RESULT	DÉTENTE	PREMIER
MOOT	LOBBY	COLONY	RETURN	DIARCHY	PRIMARY
PACT	ORDER	DEBATE	RULING	EMBARGO	READING
PAIR	PAPER	DECREE	SENATE	ENCLAVE	RECOUNT
PINK	PARTY	DIKTAT	SPEECH	FACTION	RED BOOK
POLL	PLANK	GOVERN	SUMMIT	GALLERY	REDRAFT

RED TAPE
REVENUE
SESSION
SPEAKER
SITTING
SOAPBOX
STATUTE
SUBSIDY
THE LEFT

8
ALLIANCE
ASSEMBLY
AUTARCHY
AUTONOMY
BLACK ROD
BLUE BOOK
CARD VOTE
CHARTISM
CLAWBACK
CONGRESS
DÉMARCHE
DISPATCH
DIVISION
DOMINION
ELECTION
FREE VOTE
GYNARCHY
HECKLING
HEGEMONY
HOME RULE
HUSTINGS
LOBBYIST
MAJORITY
MINISTER
MINISTRY
MINORITY
MODERATE

MONARCHY
MORI POLL
OLD GUARD
PETITION
PLATFORM
POLITICS
PROTOCOL
QUESTION
REPUBLIC
REVANCHE
SAFE SEAT
SANCTION
SCHEDULE
SCRUTINY
SUFFRAGE
THE RIGHT
THE STATE
TREASURY
WOOLSACK

9
ADMIRALTY
AMENDMENT
AUTOCRACY
BACKBENCH
BALLOT BOX
BICAMERAL
BLOCK VOTE
CAMARILLA
CHIEF WHIP
CITY STATE
CIVIL LIST
COALITION
COBDENISM
COMMITTEE
COUP D'ÉTAT
DEMOCRACY
DESPOTISM

DIPLOMACY
ENACTMENT
EXCHEQUER
EXECUTIVE
EXEQUATUR
EXPANSION
FRANCHISE
HEPTARCHY
HIERARCHY
INTERDICT
MANIFESTO
MOBOCRACY
MONOCRACY
OLIGARCHY
ORDER BOOK
PARTITION
PARTY LINE
PENTARCHY
PLURALITY
PORTFOLIO
PRESIDENT
PRESIDIUM
PRIVILEGE
PROCEDURE
RULE OF LAW
SET SPEECH
SLUSH FUND
SOCIALISM
SPLIT VOTE
STATESMAN
STRAW POLL
TERRITORY
THE CENTRE
THEOCRACY
TIMOCRACY
VOX POPULI
WITCH-HUNT

10
BY-ELECTION
CAPITALISM
COMMISSION
CONFERENCE
CONVENTION
CROSSBENCH
DELEGATION
DEPARTMENT
DEPENDENCY
DEPUTATION
DEVOLUTION
DISPATCHES
DUUMVIRATE
FEDERATION
FILIBUSTER
FRONT BENCH
FUNDED DEBT
GALLUP POLL
GOVERNANCE
GOVERNMENT
GREEN PAPER
GUILLOTINE
HAGIOCRACY
HIEROCRACY
HOME OFFICE
LIBERALISM
LOG-ROLLING
LOWER HOUSE
MARTIAL LAW
MATRIARCHY
MEMORANDUM
MODERATISM
MONARCHISM
MONETARISM
NEUTRALISM
NEUTRALITY
NOMINATION

OCHLOCRACY
OPPOSITION
ORDER PAPER
PARLIAMENT
PATRIARCHY
PATRIOTISM
PEACE PARTY
PLEBISCITE
PLUTOCRACY
POLITICIAN
POSTAL VOTE
PRESIDENCY
PRIVY PURSE
PSEPHOLOGY
RADICALISM
RE-ELECTION
REFERENDUM
REFORM BILL
REGULATION
RESOLUTION
REVANCHISM
SATYAGRAHA
SEPARATISM
SETTLEMENT
STATECRAFT
STATE HOUSE
STATUTE LAW
SUPERPOWER
UPPER HOUSE
WHITE PAPER
WORLD POWER

11
ADJOURNMENT
APPEASEMENT
ARISTOCRACY
BACKBENCHER
BACKBENCHES

BALLOT PAPER
BUFFER STATE
BUREAUCRACY
CASTING VOTE
CONDOMINIUM
CROWN COLONY
DEVOLVEMENT
DIRECTORATE
DISPATCH BOX
DISSOLUTION
DREAM TICKET
ENABLING ACT
EXTRADITION
GEOPOLITICS
GERRYMANDER
IMPEACHMENT
KING'S SPEECH
LEGISLATION
LEGISLATIVE
LEGISLATURE
MEMBER STATE
MERITOCRACY
NATIONALISM
NEGOTIATION
OBSTRUCTION
POLICE STATE
POLITICKING
PREMIERSHIP
PRIVATE BILL
PROROGATION
PUBLIC FUNDS
PUBLIC PURSE
REPORT STAGE
ROYAL ASSENT
SECRETARIAT
SENATE HOUSE
SOVEREIGNTY
STATUTE BOOK

TRIUMVIRATE

12
BILL OF RIGHTS
CIVIL SERVICE
COLLECTIVISM
COLONISATION
COMMAND PAPER
COMMONWEALTH
CONSERVATISM
CONSTITUENCY
CONSTITUTION
DICTATORSHIP
DIVISION BELL
ENABLING BILL
FAMILY CREDIT
FIRST READING
FLOATING DEBT
GERONTOCRACY
HOUSE OF LORDS
INDEPENDENCY
INTERDICTION
ISOLATIONISM
LAISSEZ-FAIRE
LAW OF THE LAND
LOWER CHAMBER
MACHTPOLITIK
MAIDEN SPEECH
MARGINAL SEAT
NATIONAL DEBT
NON-ALIGNMENT
POINT OF ORDER
POLLING BOOTH
PRESS GALLERY
PROCLAMATION
PROTECTORATE
QUEEN'S SPEECH
RATIFICATION

SECOND BALLOT
SUBCOMMITTEE
THIRD READING
TREASURY BILL
TRIPARTITION
UPPER CHAMBER
WELFARE STATE

13
CABINET OFFICE
CONFEDERATION
COUNTY COUNCIL
FOREIGN OFFICE
FRANCHISEMENT
HOME SECRETARY
INLAND REVENUE
MISGOVERNMENT
ORDER OF THE DAY
PARTY POLITICS
PLENARY POWERS
POCKET BOROUGH
POWER POLITICS
PRIME MINISTER
PRIVATISATION
QUADRUMVIRATE
RAPPROCHEMENT
REPUBLICANISM
ROTTEN BOROUGH
SECOND CHAMBER
SECOND READING
SHADOW CABINET
STANDING RULES
STATESMANSHIP
STRAIGHT FIGHT
TEN MINUTE RULE
THE OTHER PLACE
THREE-LINE WHIP
TREASURY BENCH

UNICAMERALISM
VOTE OF CENSURE
VOTING MACHINE

14
ADMINISTRATION
BLOCKING MOTION
CABINET COUNCIL
CABINET MEETING
CENTRALISATION
COLONIAL OFFICE
COMMITTEE STAGE
DISTRICT COUNCIL
EARLY DAY MOTION
ELECTIONEERING
EXCLUSION ORDER
GERRYMANDERING
GOVERNMENT WHIP
HOUSE OF COMMONS

INTERPELLATION
LOCAL AUTHORITY
ORDER IN COUNCIL
POLLING STATION
RECONSTITUTION
SELF-GOVERNMENT
SOCIAL CONTRACT
SOCIAL SECURITY
STANDING ORDERS
STRAIGHT TICKET
TWO-PARTY SYSTEM
VICE-PRESIDENCY

15
ACT OF PARLIAMENT
ALTERNATIVE VOTE
ENFRANCHISEMENT
ENTENTE CORDIALE
FAMILY ALLOWANCE

GENERAL ELECTION
LOCAL GOVERNMENT
NATIONALISATION
PARLIAMENTARISM
PETITION OF RIGHT
PUBLIC OWNERSHIP
ROYAL COMMISSION
SELECT COMMITTEE
SOCIAL DEMOCRACY
STATE DEPARTMENT
TOTALITARIANISM
WHISTLE-STOP TOUR
WORKING MAJORITY

16
CUMULATIVE VOTING
FOREIGN SECRETARY
LEADER OF THE HOUSE
UNITARY AUTHORITY

Politics – PARLIAMENTS * = legislative assemblies

4
DUMA* Russia
SEJM* Poland

6
CORTES Spain
GUKHOE South Korea
MAJLIS various Islamic
  countries
SAEIMA Latvia
SANSAD India, Nepal
SEIMAS Lithuania
SENATE* various
  countries

7
ALTHING Iceland
KNESSET Israel
LANDTAG Liechtenstein
QUOC HOI Vietnam
RIKSDAG Sweden
TYNWALD Isle of Man

8
CONGRESS various
  countries
LOK SABHA* India
SOBRANIE Macedonia
STORTING Norway

9
BARLAMENE Mauritania
BUNDESRAT* Austria,
  Germany
BUNDESTAG Germany
EDUSKUNTA Finland
FOLKETING Denmark
RIIGIKOGU Estonia
SKUPŠTINA
  Montenegro, Serbia

10
OIREACHTAS Republic
  of Ireland

RAJYA SABHA* India
RATHASAPHA Thailand

11
DÁIL ÉIREANN* Republic of Ireland
DEWAN RAKYAT* Malaysia
DEWAN NEGARA* Malaysia
EERSTE KAMER* Netherlands
HOUSE OF KEYS* Isle of Man
MILLI MACLIS Azerbaijan
NATIONALRAT* Austria, Switzerland
TWEEDE KAMER* Netherlands

12
HOUSE OF LORDS* United Kingdom
MAJLIS AL-UMMA Kuwait
ORSZÁGGYÜLÉS Hungary

13
HRVATSKI SABOR Croatia

MAJLIS-E-SHOORA Pakistan
MILLET MECLISI Turkey
SEANAD EIREANN* Republic of Ireland
STATES-GENERAL Netherlands
VERKHOVNA RADA Ukraine

14
HOUSE OF COMMONS* United
  Kingdom
RASHTRIYA SABHA* Nepal

15
PRATINIDHI SABHA* Nepal
VOULI TON ELLINON Greece

16
NATIONAL ASSEMBLY various
  countries
NATIONAL CONGRESS various
  countries

Politics – Political Leaders – PRESIDENTS (USA)

4
BUSH George, George W
FORD Gerald R
POLK James K
TAFT William H

5
ADAMS John, John
  Quincy
GRANT Ulysses S
HAYES Rutherford B
NIXON Richard M
TYLER John

6
ARTHUR Chester A
CARTER Jimmy
HOOVER Herbert C
MONROE James
PIERCE Franklin
REAGAN Ronald
TAYLOR Zachary
TRUMAN Harry S
WILSON Woodrow

7
CLINTON Bill

HARDING Warren G
JACKSON Andrew
JOHNSON Andrew,
  Lyndon B
KENNEDY John F
LINCOLN Abraham
MADISON James

8
BUCHANAN James
COOLIDGE Calvin
FILLMORE Millard
GARFIELD James A

HARRISON Benjamin, William H
MCKINLEY William
VAN BUREN Martin

9
CLEVELAND Grover

JEFFERSON Thomas
ROOSEVELT Franklin D, Theodore

10
EISENHOWER Dwight D
WASHINGTON George

Politics – Political Leaders – PRIME MINISTERS (British)

4
EDEN Sir Anthony – Earl
  of Avon
GREY Earl Charles
LAMB Henry – Viscount
  Melbourne
PEEL Sir Robert
PITT William – the Elder,
  Earl of Chatham
PITT William – the
  Younger

5
BLAIR Tony
BROWN Gordon
CECIL Robert – Marquis
  of Salisbury
HEATH Sir Edward
MAJOR Sir John
NORTH Lord Frederick
  – Earl of Guildford
PETTY William – Earl of
  Shelburne

6
ATTLEE Clement – Earl
  Attlee of Walthamstow

GORDON George – Earl
  of Aberdeen
PELHAM Henry
STUART John – Earl of
  Bute
TEMPLE Henry –
  Viscount Palmerston
WILSON Harold – Lord
  Wilson of Rievaulx

7
ASQUITH Herbert
BALDWIN Stanley – Earl
  Baldwin of Bewdley
BALFOUR Arthur
CANNING George
COMPTON Sir Spencer
  – Earl of Wilmington
FITZROY Duke of Grafton
RUSSELL Earl John
STANLEY Edward – Earl
  of Derby
WALPOLE Sir Robert
  – Earl of Orford

8
BONAR LAW Andrew

DISRAELI Benjamin
  – Earl of Beaconsfield
PERCEVAL Spencer
PRIMROSE Archibald
  – Earl of Rosebery
ROBINSON Frederick
  – Viscount Goderich
THATCHER Margaret
  – Baroness Thatcher
  of Kesteven

9
ADDINGTON Henry
  – Viscount Sidmouth
CALLAGHAN James
  – Lord Callaghan of
  Cardiff
CAVENDISH William
  – Duke of Devonshire
CHURCHILL Sir Winston
GLADSTONE William
  Ewart
GRENVILLE George,
  Lord William
JENKINSON Robert
  – Earl of Liverpool
MACDONALD Ramsay

MACMILLAN Harold
 – Earl of Stockton
WELLESLEY Arthur
 – Duke of Wellington
WENTWORTH Charles
 – Marquis of
 Rockingham

11
CHAMBERLAIN Neville
DOUGLAS-HOME Sir
 Alec – Earl Home of
 the Hirsel
LLOYD GEORGE David
 – Earl of Dwyfor

12
PELHAM-HOLLES Thomas
 – Duke of Newcastle

17
CAMPBELL-BANNERMAN
 Sir Henry
CAVENDISH-BENTINCK
 William – Duke of Portland

Religion & Philosophy

Religion & Philosophy – BELIEFS & PHILOSOPHIES

3
ZEN

5
ISLAM

6
BABISM
PAPISM
SHINTO
SUFISM
TAOISM
VEDISM
VOODOO

7
ATHEISM
BAHA'ISM

JAINISM
JUDAISM
LAMAISM
MAHDISM
SIKHISM

8
BUDDHISM
DRUIDISM
ESSENISM
FATALISM
HINDUISM
HUMANISM
PUSEYISM
STOICISM

9
CALVINISM
DARWINISM
JESUITISM
METHODISM
MITHRAISM
MORMONISM
MYSTICISM
QUAKERISM
SHAKERISM
WAHHABISM

10
ANABAPTISM
ASCETICISM
BENTHAMISM
GNOSTICISM
KANTIANISM

LOLLARDISM
PURITANISM
SCEPTICISM

11
AGNOSTICISM
ANGLICANISM
CATHOLICISM
DETERMINISM
LUTHERANISM
SCIENTOLOGY
WESLEYANISM
ZEN BUDDHISM

12
CHRISTIANITY
CONFUCIANISM
EPICUREANISM

SPIRITUALISM
UNITARIANISM

13
PROTESTANTISM
SCHOLASTICISM

14
ALBIGENSIANISM
EXISTENTIALISM
NIETZSCHEANISM
RASTAFARIANISM
ZOROASTRIANISM

15
PRESBYTERIANISM
TOTALITARIANISM

Religion & Philosophy – Bible – BOOKS Old Testament unless stated

3
JOB

4
ACTS NT
AMOS
EZRA
JOEL
JOHN NT
JUDE NT
LUKE NT
MARK NT
RUTH

5
HOSEA
JAMES NT
JOHN I NT
JONAH
MICAH
NAHUM
TITUS NT

6
DANIEL
ESTHER
EXODUS
HAGGAI
ISAIAH
JOHN II NT
JOSHUA
JUDGES
KINGS I
PETER I NT
PSALMS
ROMANS NT

7
EZEKIEL
GENESIS
HEBREWS NT
JOHN III NT
KINGS II
MALACHI
MATTHEW NT
NUMBERS

OBADIAH
PETER II NT
SAMUEL I

8
HABAKKUK
JEREMIAH
NEHEMIAH
PHILEMON NT
PROVERBS
SAMUEL II
TIMOTHY I NT

9
EPHESIANS NT
GALATIANS NT
LEVITICUS
TIMOTHY II NT
ZECHARIAH
ZEPHANIAH

10
COLOSSIANS NT
REVELATION NT

11
CHRONICLES I
DEUTERONOMY
PHILIPPIANS NT

12
CHRONICLES II
CORINTHIANS I NT
ECCLESIASTES
LAMENTATIONS

13
CORINTHIANS II NT
SONG OF SOLOMON

14
THESSALONIANS I NT

15
THESSALONIANS II NT

Religion & Philosophy – Bible – CHARACTERS

3	GOG	ZUR	AHAZ	CUSH	HELI	JOHN	MARK	OREB
ASA	HAM		AMOK	DOEG	HIEL	JUDE	MARY	OZEM
DAN	HUR	**4**	AMON	EHUD	JAEL	KISH	MICA	OZNI
ELI	JOB	ABEL	AMOS	ELON	JEHU	LEAH	MOAB	PAUL
EVE	LOT	ADAH	ARAM	ENOS	JOAB	LEVI	OBED	REBA
GAD	NUN	ADAM	BOAZ	ESAU	JODA	LOIS	ODED	RUTH
GOD	TOI	AHAB	CAIN	EZRA	JOEL	LUKE	OMRI	SARA

SAUL	HAMOR	MOSES	ZERAH	HANNAH	NEREUS	ZETHAR
SEBA	HANUN	NABAL	ZIMRI	HASHUM	NIMROD	ZIBIAH
SETH	HARAN	NADAB	ZOHAR	HAZAEL	NIMSHI	ZILLAH
SHEM	HEROD	NAHOR		HOPHNI	OPHRAH	ZILPAH
TEMA	HIRAM	NAHUM	**6**	HOSHEA	PHILIP	ZIPPOR
TOLA	HOBAB	NAOMI	ABIJAH	HULDAH	PHOEBE	ZOPHAR
ZIBA	HOHAM	NOGAH	ACHISH	ISAIAH	PILATE	
ZUPH	HORAM	ORPAH	AGABUS	ISRAEL	RACHEL	**7**
	HOSEA	PEKAH	AHIJAH	JABESH	RADDAI	ABIGAIL
5	IBZAN	PETER	ANDREW	JAIRUS	RECHAB	ABINOAM
AARON	ISAAC	RAHAB	AQUILA	JASHUB	REUBEN	ABISHAI
ABIHU	JABAL	RAPHA	BAANAH	JEMIMA	RIMMON	ABRAHAM
ABNER	JABIN	REKEM	BAASHA	JETHER	RIZPAH	ABSALOM
AMASA	JACOB	REZIN	BALAAM	JETHRO	SALMON	AHAZIAH
AMNON	JAMES	REZON	BARUCH	JOANNA	SALOME	AHINOAM
AMRAM	JASON	RHODA	BILDAD	JOSEPH	SAMSON	AMARIAH
ANNAS	JAZIZ	RUFUS	CAESAR	JOSHUA	SAMUEL	AMAZIAH
ASHER	JESSE	SARAH	CANAAN	JOSIAH	SARGON	AMITTAI
BALAK	JESUS	SATAN	CARPUS	JOTHAM	SHAAPH	ANANIAS
BARAK	JOASH	SCEVA	CHRIST	JULIUS	SHELAH	ANTIPAS
CALEB	JOBAB	SERAH	DANIEL	KOHATH	SHEMER	APOLLOS
CHLOË	JONAH	SHAUL	DARIUS	LAMECH	SHOBAB	ARAUNAH
CYRUS	JORAM	SIHON	DATHAN	LUCIUS	SIMEON	ARTEMAS
DAVID	JOSES	SILAS	DORCAS	MAACAH	SISERA	AZARIAH
DEMAS	JUBAL	SIMON	ELIJAH	MAHLON	SYMEON	BENAIAH
DINAH	JUDAH	TAMAR	ELISHA	MANOAH	TABEAL	BERNICE
EGLON	JUDAS	TERAH	ELOHIM	MARTHA	TALMAI	BEZALEL
ELDAD	KENAN	TIMON	ELYMAS	MERARI	TERESH	CANDACE
ELIAB	KORAH	TITUS	ESTHER	MICHAL	THOMAS	CLAUDIA
ELIAS	LABAN	URIAH	EUNICE	MIDIAN	URIJAH	CLEMENT
ELIHU	LAHMI	ZABAD	FESTUS	MILCAH	UZZIAH	CLEOPAS
ENOCH	LINUS	ZABDI	GALLIO	MIRIAM	VASHNI	CRISPUS
FELIX	LYDIA	ZABUD	GASPAR	MNASON	VASHTI	DEBORAH
GAIUS	MAGOG	ZADOK	GEHAZI	NAAMAH	XERXES	DELILAH
GOMER	MERAB	ZAHAM	GIDEON	NAAMAN	ZEBOIM	DIDYMUS
HADAD	MEROZ	ZEBAH	GILEAD	NABOTH	ZERESH	ELEAZAR
HAGAR	MESHA	ZEBUL	HAGGAI	NAHASH	ZERUAH	ELHANAN
HAMAN	MICAH	ZENAS	HAMATH	NATHAN	ZERUIA	ELIPHAZ

ELKANAH
EPHRAIM
ERASTUS
EUBULUS
EZEKIEL
GERSHOM
GOLIATH
HAMUTAL
HAVILAH
HILKIAH
ICHABOD
ISHMAEL
JAPHETH
JEHOASH
JEHORAM
JEHOVAH
JETHETH
JEZEBEL
JOHANAN
JONADAB
KETURAH
LAZARUS
MAGADAN
MALACHI
MALCHUS
MATTHEW
MENAHEM
MESHACH
MICAIAH
MICHAEL
NAHSHON
NICANOR
NYMPHAS
OBADIAH
OLYMPAS
OTHNIEL
PUBLIUS
QUARTUS

RAMESES
REBECCA
REBEKAH
SERAIAH
SHALLUM
SHAMGAR
SHAMMAH
SHAMMUA
SHAPHAN
SHAPHAT
SHEBUEL
SHELEPH
SHIMEAH
SHIMRON
SOLOMON
SOPATER
STEPHEN
SUSANNA
TAPHATH
TERTIUS
TIMAEUS
TIMOTHY
URBANUS
ZEBEDEE
ZEBIDAH
ZEBULUN

8

ABEDNEGO
ABIATHAR
ABINADAB
ADONIJAH
ALPHAEUS
AMRAPHEL
APPELLES
ATHALIAH
BARABBAS
BARNABAS

BEN HADAD
BENJAMIN
CAIAPHAS
CRESCENS
DRUSILLA
EMMANUEL
EPAPHRAS
EUTHCYUS
GAMALIEL
GEMARIAH
HABAKKUK
HERODIAS
HERODION
HEZEKIAH
IMMANUEL
ISSACHAR
JEHOAHAZ
JEPHTHAH
JEREMIAH
JEROBOAM
JOCHEBED
JONATHAN
LOT'S WIFE
MAHALATH
MANASSEH
MATTATHA
MATTHIAS
MELCHIOR
MERAIOTH
MORDECAI
NAPHTALI
NEHEMIAH
NETHANEL
ONESIMUS
OSNAPPAR
PARMENAS
PEKAHIAH
PHILEMON

PHILETUS
PHINEHAS
POTIPHAR
REHOBOAM
SAPPHIRA
SECUNDUS
SELEUCUS
SHADRACH
SHAREZER
SHEMAIAH
SHIMSHAI
SIBBECAI
SYNTICHE
TAHPENES
TATTENAI
THADDEUS
TIBERIUS
TIRHAKAH
TYCHICUS
TYRANNUS
ZARETHAN
ZEBADIAH
ZEDEKIAH
ZERAHIAH
ZIPPORAH

9

ABIMELECH
AHASUERUS
AHIMELECH
ALEXANDER
ANTIOCHUS
ARCHELAUS
ARCHIPPUS
BALTHAZAR
BARSABBAS
BARZILLAI
BASHEMATH

BATHSHEBA
CORNELIUS
DEMETRIUS
DIONYSIUS
ELIMELECH
ELISABETH
EPAENETUS
HADADEZER
HAMMURABI
HYMENAEUS
JASHOBEAM
LAPPIDOTH
MESHULLAM
NATHANAEL
NICODEMUS
PROCHORUS
QUIRINIUS
SANBALLAT
SHEALTIEL
SHELEMIAH
SOSTHENES
STEPHANAS
TERTULLUS
THADDAEUS
TIMOTHEUS
TROPHIMUS
ZACCHAEUS
ZACHARIAH
ZALMUNNAH
ZECHARIAH
ZEPHANIAH

10

AHITHOPHEL
ANDRONICUS
ARTAXERXES
BARTIMAEUS
BELSHAZZAR

DIOTREPHES	ZELOPHEHAD	**12**	PONTIUS PILATE
EBEDMELECH	ZERUBBABEL	CHEDOR-LAOMER	SHETHARBOZNAI
ESARHADDON		EPAPHRODITUS	
FORTUNATUS	**11**	EVIL MERODACH	**14**
HERMOGENES	ARISTARCHUS	HEROD AGRIPPA	CLAUDIUS LYSIAS
ISHBOSHETH	ARISTOBULUS	HEROD ANTIPAS	GOOD SAMARITAN
JEHOIACHIN	BARTHOLOMEW	MEPHIBOSHETH	HEROD ARCHELAUS
MALCHI-SHUA	JEHOSHAPHAT	QUEEN OF SHEBA	JOHN THE BAPTIST
MATTANAIAH	JESUS CHRIST	SAUL OF TARSUS	NEBUCHADNEZZAR
METHUSELAH	MELCHIZEDEK		SIMON THE ZEALOT
MITHREDATH	NEBUZARADAN	**13**	TIGLATH PILESER
OHOLIBAMAH	ONESIPHORUS	FELIX ANTONIUS	
SIMON MAGUS	SENNACHERIB	JOHN THE DIVINE	**15**
SIMON PETER	SHALMANESER	JUDAS ISCARIOT	MERODACH BALADAN
THEOPHILUS	SHESH BAZZAR	MARY MAGDALENE	
VIRGIN MARY		PAULUS SERGIUS	

Religion & Philosophy – FESTIVALS

3	RAKHI	**7**	**8**	SETSUBUN
EID	VASSA	ARBA'EEN	DUSSEHRA	SHAVUOTH
URS	VESAK	HOLY DAY	(or	(or Pentecost[2])
		KATHINA	Vijayadashami)	UPOSATHA
4	**6**	LADY DAY	EPIPHANY	YULETIDE
HOLI	ADVENT	(or The	FEAST DAY	ZADUSZKI
LENT	DASARA	Annunciation)	FESTIVAL	
OBON	(or Navratri)	RAMADAN	HANUKKAH	**9**
ONAM	DIWALI	SABBATH	HOGMANAY	CANDLEMAS
XMAS	EASTER	(or Lord's Day)	HOLY WEEK	CHRISTMAS
YULE	FALLES	SHAWWAL	LORD'S DAY	DOLAYATRA
	LAMMAS	SUKKOTH	(or Sabbath)	EASTER DAY
5	MAWLID	(or Feast of	MUHARRAM	(or Easter
PURIM	PONGAL	Tabernacles)	NAVRATRI	Sunday)
(or Feast	SUKKOT	WHITSUN	(or Dasara)	EID UL-ADHA
of Lots)	YOM TOV		PASSOVER	EID UL-FITR
RAJAB			PAVARANA	EMBER DAYS

HALLOWEEN
LOW SUNDAY
MARTINMAS
OSHOGATSU
PENTECOST[1]
(or Whit Sunday)
PENTECOST[2]
(or Shavuoth)
RADONISTA
SAINT'S DAY
YOM KIPPUR
(or Day of Atonement)

10
ALL HALLOWS
(or All Saints' Day)
AMBARVALIA
ASALHA PUJA
ASSUMPTION
CHILDERMAS
EASTERTIDE
GOOD FRIDAY
LAMMASTIDE
LUPERCALIA
MICHAELMAS
PALM SUNDAY
RATHAYATRA
SATURNALIA
SEXAGESIMA
WHIT MONDAY
WHIT SUNDAY
(or Pentecost[1])

11
ALL SOULS' DAY

BACCHANALIA
DAY OF ASHURA
FEAST OF LOTS
(or Purim)
HOLYROOD DAY
NEW YEAR'S DAY
NEW YEAR'S EVE
PASSIONTIDE
THE NATIVITY
WHITSUNTIDE

12
ALL SAINTS' DAY
(or All Hallows)
ASCENSION DAY
ASH WEDNESDAY
CHRISTMAS DAY
EASTER MONDAY
EASTER SUNDAY
(or Easter Day)
HOLY THURSDAY
(or Maundy Thursday)
INNOCENTS' DAY
(or Holy Innocents'
Day)
JANAMASHTAMI
LESSER BAIRAM
MOVABLE FEAST
ROGATION DAYS
ROSH HASHANAH
SEPTUAGESIMA
THANKSGIVING

13
CHRISTMASTIDE

CORPUS CHRISTI
GREATER BAIRAM
PASSION SUNDAY
QUINQUAGESIMA
SHROVE TUESDAY
TRINITY SUNDAY
VIJAYADASHAMI
(or Dussehra)

14
CHINESE NEW YEAR
DAY OF ATONEMENT
(or Yom Kippur)
EASTER SATURDAY
MAUNDY THURSDAY
(or Holy Thursday)
ROGATION SUNDAY

15
GANESH CHATURTHI
HARVEST FESTIVAL
SHEMINI ATZERET
THANKSGIVING DAY
THE ANNUNCIATION
(or Lady Day)

16
HOLY INNOCENTS' DAY
(or Innocents' Day)

18
FEAST OF TABERNACLES
(or Sukkoth)
THE TRANSFIGURATION

Religion & Philosophy – PHILOSOPHERS

4
AYER AJ
HUME David
KANT Immanuel
KUHN TS
MILL John Stuart
RAND Ayn
RYLE Gilbert
VICO Giambattista
WEIL Simone

5
BACON Sir Francis,
  Roger
BRUNO Giordano
BUBER Martin
BURGE Tyler
BURKE Edmund
COMTE Auguste
DEWEY John
HAACK Susan
HEGEL Georg
IQBAL Sir Muhammad
LOCKE John
NAGEL Ernest
PAINE Thomas
PLATO
PRICE Richard
QUINE Willard
SMITH Adam
TAINE Hippolyte

6
ADORNO Theodor
AGNESI Maria

ANSELM
BERLIN Isaiah
BUTLER Joseph
CARNAP Rudolf
CICERO
EUCKEN Rudolf
HOBBES Thomas
LAO-TZU
MACKIE JL
PEIRCE Charles
POPPER Karl
SARTRE Jean-Paul
STILPO
TARSKI Alfred
THALES

7
ABELARD Peter
AQUINAS Thomas
BARTHES Roland
BENTHAM Jeremy
BURIDAN Jean
DIDEROT Denis
EMERSON Ralph Waldo
ERASMUS Desiderius
GENTILE Giovanni
HYPATIA
LEIBNIZ Gottfried
NEURATH Otto
RICARDO David
RUSSELL Earl Bertrand
SPENCER Herbert
SPINOZA Baruch

8
AVERROËS
AVICENNA
BERKELEY George
BRENTANO Franz
COCKBURN Catharine
DIOGENES
EPICURUS
FOUCAULT Michel
PLOTINUS
ROUSSEAU Jean-Jacques
SOCRATES
VOLTAIRE
XENOPHON

9
ARISTOTLE
CONFUCIUS
D'ALEMBERT Jean
DESCARTES René
DIADOCHUS
EPICTETUS
HEIDEGGER Martin
HÉLVETIUS Claude-Adrien
HUTCHESON Francis
NIETZSCHE Friedrich
RENOUVIER Charles

10
ANAXAGORAS
CHRYSIPPUS
DEMOCRITUS
DUNS SCOTUS John
HERACLITUS
PHYROGENAS

PROTAGORAS
PYTHAGORAS
SWEDENBORG
  Emanuel
XENOPHANES
ZENO OF ELEA

11
KIERKEGAARD Søren
MACHIAVELLI Niccolo

REICHENBACH Hans
ZENO OF SIDON

12
PYRRHO OF ELIS
THEOPHRASTUS
WITTGENSTEIN Ludwig
ZENO OF CITIUM

14
ALBERTUS MAGNUS
MARCUS AURELIUS

15
WILLIAM OF OCKHAM

16
AUGUSTINE OF HIPPO
PARMINEDES OF ELEA

Religion & Philosophy – POPES Number of each name in brackets

3
LEO (13)

4
JOHN (23)
MARK (1)
PAUL (6)
PIUS (12)

5
CONON (1)
DONUS (1)
FELIX (5)
GAIUS (1)
LANDO (1)
LINUS (1)
PETER (1)
SOTER (1)
URBAN (8)

6
ADRIAN (6)
AGATHO (1)

ALERIC (1)
FABIAN (1)
HILARY (1)
JULIUS (3)
LUCIUS (3)
MARTIN (3)
PHILIP (1)
SIXTUS (5)
VICTOR (5)

7
ANTERUS (1)
CLEMENT (14)
DAMASUS (2)
GREGORY (16)
HYGINUS (1)
MARINUS (2)
PASCHAL (4)
PONTIAN (1)
ROMANUS (1)
SERGIUS (4)
STEPHEN (10)
URSINUS (1)

ZOSIMUS (1)

8
AGAPETUS (2)
ANICETUS (1)
BENEDICT (16)
BONIFACE (9)
CALIXTUS (3)
EUGENIUS (4)
EULALIUS (1)
EUSEBIUS (1)
FORMOSUS (1)
GELASIUS (2)
HONORIUS (4)
INNOCENT (13)
JOHN PAUL (2)
LIBERIUS (1)
NICHOLAS (6)
NOVATIAN (1)
PELAGIUS (2)
SABINIAN (1)
SIRICIUS (1)
THEODORE (3)

VIGILIUS (1)
VITALIAN (1)

9
ADEODATUS (1)
ALEXANDER (8)
ANACLETUS (2)
CELESTINE (5)
CORNELIUS (1)
DEUSDEDIT (1)
DIONYSIUS (1)
DIOSCORUS (1)
EUTYCHIAN (1)
EVARISTUS (1)
HORMISDAS (1)
MARCELLUS (2)
MILTIADES (1)
SEVERINUS (1)
SILVERIUS (1)
SISSINIUS (1)
SYLVESTER (4)
SYMMACHUS (1)
THEODORIC (1)

VALENTINE (1)
ZACHARIAS (1)

SIMPLICIUS (1)
ZEPHYRINUS (1)

ELEUTHERIUS (1)
MARCELLINUS (1)
TELESPHORUS (1)

10
ANASTASIUS (4)
LAURENTIUS (1)

11
CHRISTOPHER (1)
CONSTANTINE (2)

Religion & Philosophy – RELIGIOUS PEOPLE

3	**5**	BISHOP	MULLAH	VESTAL
DOM	ABBOT	CANTOR	MUSLIM	VOTARY
FRA	AMISH	(or hazzan)	(or Moslem)	
JEW	BAHA'I	CLERGY	MYSTIC	**7**
NUN	BONZE	CLERIC	NOVICE	ACOLYTE
	CANON	CULDEE	PALMER	APOSTLE
4	CHELA	CURATE	PAPIST	ASCETIC
ABBA	CLERK	DEACON	PARSEE	BAPTIST
ABBÉ	DEIST	DIVINE	(or Zoroastrian)	BÉGUINE
BABI	DRUID	DOCTOR	PARSON	BRAHMAN
COPT	ELDER	DOPPER	PASTOR	BROTHER
CURÉ	FAKIR	ESSENE	PRIEST	CLUNIAC
DEAN	FRIAR	EXARCH	PRIMUS	CONVERT
GURU	HINDU	FATHER	QUAKER	DERVISH
HAJI	MAGUS	HAZZAN	RANTER	DOMINEE
IMAM	MUFTI	(or cantor)	READER	DOMINIE
JAIN	PADRE	HERMIT	RECTOR	GENERAL
LAMA	PRIOR	JESUIT	SABIAN	HOLY JOE
MAGE	RABBI	LAYMAN	SCRIBE	HUSSITE
MONK	SADHU	LECTOR	SERVER	JACOBIN
PAPA	SAIVA	LEVITE	SEXTON	JUDAIST
POPE	SOFTA	MARIST	SHAKER	LAMAIST
SHIA	SUNNI	MARTYR	SHIITE	LOLLARD
(or Shiite)	SWAMI	MOONIE	(or Shia)	MAHDIST
SIKH	VICAR	MORMON	SISTER	MUEZZIN
SUFI		MOSLEM	TAOIST	ORDINEE
YOGI	**6**	(or Muslim)	THEIST	PILGRIM
	ABBESS	MOTHER	VERGER	PONTIFF

PRELATE
PRIMATE
PROPHET
PROVOST
PURITAN
REGULAR
SECULAR
SERVITE
STYLITE
TEMPLAR
WAHHABI
WEE FREE

8
ANGLICAN
ANTIPOPE
BACCHANT
BASILIAN
BELIEVER
BRETHREN
BUDDHIST
CANONESS
CAPUCHIN
CARDINAL
CATHOLIC
CHAPLAIN
CORYBANT
CRUCIFER
DIOCESAN
DISCIPLE
DITHEIST
DRUIDESS
EXORCIST
HUGUENOT
INITIATE
LUTHERAN
MAN OF GOD
MARABOUT

MINISTER
MINORITE
MONASTIC
NAZARENE
NEOPHYTE
ORDAINER
ORDINAND
ORDINARY
PENITENT
PHARISEE
PONTIFEX
PREACHER
PRIORESS
PROVISOR
PUSEYITE
REVEREND
SADDUCEE
SALESIAN
SIDESMAN
SKY PILOT
SUPERIOR
TALAPOIN
TERTIARY
THE CLOTH
THURIFER
TRAPPIST
URSULINE
WESLEYAN

9
ADVENTIST
ANCHORITE
ASHKENAZI
AUGUSTINE
 (or Augustinian,
 Austin Friar)
AYATOLLAH
BACCHANTE

BLACK MONK
 (or Benedictine)
CALVINIST
CARMELITE
 (or White Friar)
CATECHIST
CELEBRANT
CELESTINE
CHRISTIAN
CHURCHMAN
CLERGYMAN
COENOBITE
CONFESSOR
CORDELIER
DALAI LAMA
DOMINICAN
 (or Black Friar)
GOSPELLER
GREY FRIAR
 (or Franciscan)
INCUMBENT
IRVINGITE
JANSENIST
LAYPERSON
LAY READER
LAY SISTER
MENDICANT
MENNONITE
METHODIST
MISSIONER
MONSIGNOR
NOVITIATE
OBSERVANT
OFFICIANT
PATRIARCH
POSTULANT
PRECENTOR
PREDICANT

PRESBYTER
PRIESTESS
PROSELYTE
RECHABITE
RELIGIEUX
RELIGIOUS
RURAL DEAN
SACRISTAN
SHINTOIST
SUBDEACON
SUCCENTOR
UNITARIAN
VAISHNAVA
VESTRYMAN
ZWINGLIAN

10
ANABAPTIST
ARCHBISHOP
ARCHDEACON
ARCHPRIEST
BLACK FRIAR
 (or Dominican)
CARTHUSIAN
CATHOLICOS
CHURCH-GOER
CISTERCIAN
EVANGELIST
FRANCISCAN
 (or Grey Friar)
HIEROPHANT
HIGH PRIEST
ILLUMINATI
LAY BROTHER
LICENTIATE
MESSIANIST
MINOR CANON
MISSIONARY

MONOTHEIST
MYSTAGOGUE
NORBERTINE
POLYTHEIST
PREBENDARY
PROLOCUTOR
PROTESTANT
REVIVALIST
RUSSELLITE
 (or Jehovah's Witness)
SANCTIFIER
SCHOLASTIC
SEMINARIST
SERMONISER
THEOLOGIAN
THEOLOGIST
THE PRELACY
WHITE FRIAR
 (or Carmelite)
WORSHIPPER

11
ARCHPRELATE
AUGUSTINIAN
 (or Augustine, Austin Friar)
AUSTIN FRIAR
 (or Augustine, Augustinian)
BENEDICTINE
 (or Black Monk)
CAMALDOLITE
CHURCHWOMAN
CLERGYWOMAN
CONSECRATOR
CREATIONIST
ECCLESIARCH
HIS EMINENCE

HIS HOLINESS
INTERCESSOR
LAY PREACHER
MONSEIGNEUR
OBEDIENTARY
ORTHODOX JEW
PANCHEN LAMA
PARISHIONER
RASTAFARIAN
RELIGIONIST
ROSICRUCIAN
SABBATARIAN
SCEUOPHYLAX
WHITE FATHER
ZEN BUDDHIST
ZOROASTRIAN
 (or Parsee)

12
CANON REGULAR
CHURCHWARDEN
ECCLESIASTIC
HAPPY CLAPPER
HOT GOSPELLER
LOW CHURCHMAN
METROPOLITAN
PARISH PRIEST
PENITENTIARY
PRESBYTERIAN
RESIDENTIARY
SALVATIONIST
SPIRITUALIST
THE PRELATURE
VESTAL VIRGIN
VICAR GENERAL

13
ANGLO-CATHOLIC
ARCHIMANDRITE
CRUTCHED FRIAR
FIELD PREACHER
HIGH CHURCHMAN
HIGH PRIESTESS
KNIGHT TEMPLAR
LOCAL PREACHER
REDEMPTIONIST
ROMAN CATHOLIC
SISTER OF MERCY
TITULAR BISHOP

14
CHURCH MILITANT
FUNDAMENTALIST
LORDS SPIRITUAL
MILLENARIANIST
MOTHER SUPERIOR
 (or Reverend Mother)
REVEREND MOTHER
 (or Mother Superior)
VICAR APOSTOLIC

15
CHRISTADELPHIAN
JEHOVAH'S WITNESS
 (or Russellite)
PONTIFEX MAXIMUS
SUFFRAGAN BISHOP
WHIRLING DERVISH

16
PLYMOUTH BRETHREN

Science

Science – ANATOMY (Human)

3	4	CYST	LOBE	SOLE	CHEEK	GROIN
ARM	ANUS	DISC	LOIN	TEAT	CHEST	GYRUS
EAR	ARCH	DUCT	LUNG	ULNA	CHOPS	HEART
EYE	AXIS	FACE	NAIL	UVEA	COLON	HELIX
GUM	AXON	FIST	NAPE	VEIN	CROWN	HILUS
GUT	(or nerve	FOOT	NECK	WOMB	CUTIS	HYMEN
HAM	fibre)	GLIA (or	NOSE		(or dermis)	HYOID
HIP	BACK	neuroglia)	PALM	5	DIGIT	ILEUM
JAW	BODY	GUTS	PATE	ANKLE	ELBOW	ILIUM
LAP	BONE	HAIR	PONS	ANVIL	FEMUR	INCUS
LEG	BROW	HAND	PORE	(or incus)	(or thigh	(or anvil)
LIP	BULB	HEAD	PULP	AORTA	bone)	INION
ORB	BUST	HEEL	RETE	ATLAS	FLESH	JOINT
PIA	CALF	IRIS	ROOT	BELLY	FOSSA	LABIA
RIB	CAUL	JOWL	RUMP	BLOOD	FOVEA	LIVER
ROD	CHIN	KNEE	SEAT	BOSOM	FRAME	MALAR
SAC	CONE	LENS	SHIN	BOWEL	FRONT	MEDIA
TOE	COXA	LIMB	SIDE	BRAIN	GLAND	MOLAR
VAS	CUSP	LIPS	SKIN	CANAL	GLANS	MOUTH

NATES
(or buttocks)
NAVEL
(or umbilicus)
NERVE
ORBIT
ORGAN
OVARY
PENIS
PINNA
PSOAS
PUBES
PUBIS
PUPIL
QUICK
RAMUS
SCALP
SINEW
SINUS
SKULL
SPINE
TALUS
(or astragalus)
THIGH
THUMB
TIBIA
(or shin bone)
TOOTH
TORSO
TRUNK
UVULA
VAGUS
VALVE
VELUM
(or soft palate)
VOMER
VULVA
WAIST

WRIST

6
AIR SAC
AMNION
ANTRUM
AREOLA
ARMPIT
(or axilla)
ARTERY
AXILLA
(or armpit)
BEHIND
BICEPS
BIG TOE
(or hallux)
BOTTOM
BOWELS
BREAST
BRIDGE
CAECUM
(or blind gut)
CANINE
CARPAL
CARPUS
CAVITY
CERVIX
COCCYX
CONCHA
CORNEA
CORTEX
CROTCH
CUSPID
DERMIS
(or cutis)
EYELID
FAUCES
FIBULA

FINGER
FLEXOR
FORNIX
FRENUM
(or frenulum)
FUNDUS
GIRDLE
GULLET
HALLUX
(or big toe)
HAMMER
(or malleus)
HAUNCH
INSTEP
INSULA
KIDNEY
LAMBDA
LARYNX
(or voice box)
LUNULA
MARROW
MEATUS
MIDGUT
MUSCLE
NEURON
(or nerve cell)
NIPPLE
(or mamilla)
PALATE
PAUNCH
PELVIS
PLEURA
PLEXUS
RADIUS
RECTUM
RECTUS
RETINA
SACRUM

SCLERA
SCRUFF
SEPTUM
SEROSA
SOCKET
SOLEUS
SPLEEN
STAPES
(or stirrup)
SULCUS
TARSAL
TARSUS
TEMPLE
TENDON
TENSOR
TESTIS
(or testicle)
THORAX
THROAT
THYMUS
TISSUE
TONGUE
TONSIL
TRAGUS
URETER
UTERUS
VAGINA
VENULE
VERMIS
VERTEX
VESSEL
VILLUS
ZYGOMA
(or
zygomatic
arch)

7
ABDOMEN
AURICLE
BLADDER
BUTTOCK
CANTHUS
CENTRUM
CHOROID
COCHLEA
CONDYLE
CRANIUM
CRICOID
CUTICLE
DECIDUA
DILATOR
EARDRUM
(or myringa)
EARHOLE
ERECTOR
ETHMOID
EYEBALL
EYEBROW
EYELASH
FISSURE
FORAMEN
FOREARM
GLOTTIS
GLUTEUS
GRISTLE
HIP BONE
HUMERUS
HUNKERS
(or haunches)
INCISOR
ISCHIUM
JAWBONE
JEJUNUM
JUGULAR

KNEECAP
(or patella)
KNUCKLE
LEVATOR
MALLEUS
(or hammer)
MAMILLA
(or nipple)
MASTOID
MAXILLA
MEDULLA
MIDRIFF
MYRINGA
(or eardrum)
NOSTRIL
OCCIPUT
ORIFICE
OSSICLE
OVIDUCT
PAPILLA
PAROTID
PATELLA
(or kneecap)
PHALANX
(or phalange)
PHARYNX
PREPUCE
(or foreskin)
PUDENDA
PUNCTUM
PUTAMEN
PYLORUS
SACCULE
SCAPULA (or
shoulder blade)
SCROTUM
STERNUM
(or breastbone)

STIRRUP
(or stapes)
STOMACH
STYLOID
SYNAPSE
THYROID
TOENAIL
TONSILS
TRACHEA
(or windpipe)
TRICEPS
TRUE RIB
URETHRA
UTRICLE
(or utriculus)
VESICLE
VISCERA

8
ABDUCTOR
ADENOIDS
ALVEOLUS
AMYGDALA
APPENDIX
BACKBONE
BACKSIDE
BICUSPID
BILE DUCT
BLIND GUT
(or caecum)
BRAINPAN
BRONCHUS
BUTTOCKS
(or nates)
CEREBRUM
CLAVICLE
(or collar bone)
CLITORIS

CORACOID
DUODENUM
ELEVATOR
END ORGAN
(or target organ)
EXTENSOR
EYE TOOTH
FALSE RIB
(or floating rib)
FENESTRA
FOREHEAD
FORESKIN
(or prepuce)
FRENULUM
(or frenum)
GALL DUCT
GANGLION
(or nerve centre)
GENITALS
GLABELLA
HAIRLINE
HAUNCHES
(or hunkers)
HIP JOINT
INNER EAR
LACTEALS
LIGAMENT
LOWER LIP
MANDIBLE
MASSETER
MEMBRANE
MENINGES
MENISCUS
MIDBRAIN
(or mesencephalon)
MODIOLUS
NERVE-END
PALATINE

PANCREAS
PERINEUM
PETROSAL
PHALANGE
(or phalanx)
PIA MATER
PISIFORM
PLACENTA
PLATYSMA
PREMOLAR
PRONATOR
PROSTATE
PUDENDUM
SACCULUS
SESAMOID
SHIN BONE
(or tibia)
SHOULDER
SINCIPUT
SKELETON
SKULLCAP
SPHENOID
SPLENIUM
SPLENIUS
STRIATUM
TEAR DUCT
TESTICLE
(or testis)
THALAMUS
TYMPANUM
UPPER LIP
VENA CAVA
VERTEBRA
VINCULUM
VOICE BOX
(or larynx)
WINDPIPE
(or trachea)

9

ARTERIOLE
ARYTENOID
BLIND SPOT
CALCANEUS
CAPILLARY
CARTILAGE
CHEEKBONE
CORPUSCLE
DEPRESSOR
DIAPHRAGM
DIAPHYSIS
DURA MATER
EPIDERMIS
EPIPHYSIS
　(or pineal gland)
FINGERTIP
FLOCCULUS
FOREBRAIN
　(or prosencephalon)
FUNDAMENT
FUNICULUS
FUNNY BONE
GENITALIA
HAMSTRING
HINDBRAIN
　(or rhombo-
　encephalon)
HYOID BONE
INTESTINE
INVOLUCRE
LABYRINTH
MALAR BONE (or
　zygomatic bone)
MALLEOLUS
MANUBRIUM
MESENTERY
MIDDLE EAR

MILK TOOTH
NAVICULAR
NERVE CELL
　(or neuron)
NEUROGLIA
　(or glia)
OBTURATOR
OLECRANON
OPTIC LOBE
POSTERIOR
QUADRATUS
SARTORIUS
SPHINCTER
SUPINATOR
TASTE BUDS
TENTORIUM
THIGH BONE
　(or femur)
THUMBNAIL
TRABECULA
TRAPEZIUM
TRAPEZOID
TURBINALS
UMBILICUS
　(or navel)
UTRICULUS
　(or utricle)
VENTRICLE
VESTIBULE

10

ACETABULUM
ADAM'S APPLE
　(or thyroid
　cartilage)
AORTIC ARCH
ASTRAGALUS
　(or talus)

BONE MARROW
BREASTBONE
　(or sternum)
BUCCINATOR
CEREBELLUM
COLLAR BONE
　(or clavicle)
ENCEPHALON
EPIGLOTTIS
EPISTERNUM
EPITHELIUM
FINGERNAIL
FONTANELLE
FOREFINGER
　(or index finger)
FOURCHETTE
GREY MATTER
HEMISPHERE
HYPODERMIS
INTESTINES
METACARPAL
METACARPUS
METATARSAL
METATARSUS
MYOCARDIUM
NERVE FIBRE
　(or axon)
NEURAL ARCH
OESOPHAGUS
OPTIC NERVE
PELVIC ARCH
PERIOSTEUM
PERITONEUM
PORTAL VEIN
PROMONTORY
PSOAS MAJOR
PULP CAVITY
QUADRICEPS

SACROILIAC
SCALA MEDIA
SENSE ORGAN
SOFT PALATE
　(or velum)
SPINAL CORD
TRIQUETRAL
TROCHANTER
VOCAL CORDS
YELLOW SPOT
　(or macula lutea)

11

APONEUROSIS
BLOOD VESSEL
CANINE TOOTH
CONJUNCTIVA
CONSTRICTOR
ENARTHROSIS
ENDOCARDIUM
ENDOMETRIUM
EPIGASTRIUM
ETHMOID BONE
FLOATING RIB
　(or false rib)
GALL BLADDER
HIPPOCAMPUS
INDEX FINGER
　(or forefinger)
JUGULAR VEIN
KNUCKLE BONE
MACULA LUTEA
　(or yellow spot)
MEDIASTINUM
MITRAL VALVE
NASAL CAVITY
NERVE CENTRE
　(or ganglion)

NERVE-ENDING
PARATHYROID
PERICARDIUM
PERICRANIUM
PERINEURIUM
PINEAL GLAND
  (or epiphysis)
PONS VAROLII
RADIAL NERVE
SOLAR PLEXUS
SPINAL CANAL
TARGET ORGAN
  (or end organ)
VAS DEFERENS
WHITE MATTER
WISDOM TOOTH

12
ALVEOLAR ARCH
DIVERTICULUM
ELASTIC FIBRE
ENDOSKELETON
GLENOID FOSSA
HYPOGASTRIUM
HYPOTHALAMUS
MAMMARY GLAND
OPTIC CHIASMA
PARIETAL BONE
PAROTID GLAND
PELVIC GIRDLE
PORTAL SYSTEM
RADIAL ARTERY
SPHENOID BONE
SPINAL COLUMN
  (or vertebral
  column)
TEMPORAL BONE
THORACIC DUCT

THYROID GLAND
TYMPANIC BONE
XIPHISTERNUM

13
ADIPOSE TISSUE
ADRENAL CORTEX
ADRENAL GLANDS
CAROTID ARTERY
DELTOID MUSCLE
DILATOR MUSCLE
FALLOPIAN TUBE
FEMORAL ARTERY
FORAMEN MAGNUM
GASTROCNEMIUS
GLENOID CAVITY
MESENCEPHALON
  (or midbrain)
NAVICULAR BONE
NERVOUS SYSTEM
OCCIPITAL BONE
PERICHONDRIUM
PROSTATE GLAND
RED CORPUSCLES
SHOULDER BLADE
  (or scapula)
SHOULDER JOINT
SPERMATIC CORD
UMBILICAL CORD
ZYGOMATIC ARCH
  (or zygoma)
ZYGOMATIC BONE
  (or malar bone)

14
ACHILLES TENDON
BRACHIAL ARTERY
CEREBRAL CORTEX

CORONARY ARTERY
CORPUS STRIATUM
DIGESTIVE TRACT
DUCTLESS GLANDS
EUSTACHIAN TUBE
FALLOPIAN TUBES
FENESTRA OVALIS
GLUTEUS MAXIMUS
INNOMINATE BONE
INNOMINATE VEIN
LARGE INTESTINE
MASTOID PROCESS
MUCOUS MEMBRANE
PECTORAL GIRDLE
PERMANENT TOOTH
PITUITARY GLAND
PROSENCEPHALON
  (or forebrain)
SCALA VESTIBULI
SEROUS MEMBRANE
SMALL INTESTINE
STYLOID PROCESS
SYLVIAN FISSURE
TRIFACIAL NERVE
  (or trigeminal nerve)
TROCHLEAR NERVE
XIPHIHUMERALIS

15
ABDOMINAL CAVITY
ALIMENTARY CANAL
CORACOID PROCESS
CRYSTALLINE LENS
DIGESTIVE SYSTEM
EUSTACHIAN VALVE
FENESTRA ROTUNDA
MEDULLARY SHEATH
OCCIPITAL ARTERY

PULMONARY ARTERY
RECTUS ABDOMINIS
RHOMBENCEPHALON
 (or hindbrain)
TRIGEMINAL NERVE
 (or trifacial nerve)
VERTEBRAL COLUMN
 (or spinal column)

WHITE CORPUSCLES

16
CRICOID CARTILAGE
INNOMINATE ARTERY
MEDULLA OBLONGATA
PREFRONTAL CORTEX
PTERYGOID PROCESS

THYROID CARTILAGE
 (or Adam's apple)
ZYGOMATIC PROCESS

Science – Archaeology – ARCHAEOLOGICAL SITES (UK)
Also see Ancient Stone Monuments

6
BIGNOR
JORVIK

7
FLAG FEN
TRELECH

8
CAERLEON
DANEBURY
MAES HOWE
MINE HOWE
SEAHENGE

STAR CARR
WROXETER

9
FAIRY TOOT
SKARA BRAE
SUTTON HOO
WOODHENGE
YEAVERING

10
CHYSAUSTER
EMAIN MACHA
FISHBOURNE

GOUGH'S CAVE
IRONBRIDGE
TRIMONTIUM
VERULAMIUM
VINDOLANDA

11
HOUSESTEADS
SILBURY HILL
STANTON DREW

12
ANTONINE WALL
DUGGLEBY HOWE

GRIMES GRAVES
HADRIAN'S WALL
LULLINGSTONE
WINDMILL HILL

13
CASTLE HENLLYS

14
KIRKSTALL ABBEY
LITTLE WOODBURY

Science – Archaeology – ARCHAEOLOGICAL TERMS

3	**4**	OVEN	**5**	HENGE	QUOIT	**6**	DOLMEN
DIG	CAMP	RATH	AMBER	HOARD	RELIC	BARROW	DROMOS
HUT	CAVE	RUNE	BROCH	INCAN	ROMAN	CASTRO	EOLITH
PIT	DYKE	TELL	CAIRN	MAYAN	SHARD	CIRCLE	FOSSIL
	KILN	TOMB	FLAKE	MOUND	SPOIL	CURSUS	ICE AGE
	KIVA	WELL	GRAVE	MUMMY	STELA	DATING	IN SITU

KURGAN
MENHIR
MINOAN
NAVETA
SERIES
SURVEY
SYRINX
THOLOS
VELLUM

7
ANTIQUE
BONE BED
CHAMBER
CHULLPA
DEMOTIC
DIGGING
HISTORY
IRON AGE
MEGARON
NEOLITH
PAPYRUS
PYRAMID
SCRAPER
STRATUM
TALAIOT
TRILITH
TUMULUS
ZOOLITH

8
AMMONITE
ARTEFACT
BONE CAVE
CALAMITE
CAMBRIAN
CROMLECH
EXCAVATE

GRATTOIR
HIERATIC
HILL FORT
JURASSIC
MEDIEVAL
MEGALITH
OSTRACON
POTSHERD
STONE AGE
TERTIARY
TRIASSIC
TROCHITE
URNFIELD

9
ALIGNMENT
ANTIQUITY
BONE BLACK
BRACTEATE
BRONZE AGE
CARTOUCHE
CATALOGUE
COPPER AGE
   (or Chalcolithic)
CUNEIFORM
FOSSILISE
GONIATITE
HOARSTONE
HUT CIRCLE
MICROLITH
MUMMY CASE
NEOLITHIC
PARCHMENT
PICTOGRAM
SERPULITE
TERRAMARE
TRILITHON
TRILOBITE

10
BELL BARROW
CARTONNAGE
CHRONOLOGY
COURT CAIRN
   (or horned cairn)
CUP-AND-RING
DISC BARROW
EGYPTOLOGY
EXCAVATION
HIEROGLYPH
MESOLITHIC
OVAL BARROW
PALAEOLITH
PALIMPSEST
PETROGLYPH
PICTOGRAPH
POND BARROW
PREHISTORY
SHOVEL TEST
WHEELHOUSE

11
ARCHAEOLOGY
ASSYRIOLOGY
BONE BRECCIA
BURIAL MOUND
CHAMBER TOMB
CONTOUR FORT
CYPRO-MINOAN
HELLENISTIC
HIEROGLYPHS
HORNED CAIRN
   (or court cairn)
ICHTHYOLITE
PERISTALITH
PRECAMBRIAN
RADIOCARBON

REINDEER AGE
ROUND BARROW
SARCOPHAGUS
TENTACULITE
TRACE FOSSIL
VARVE DATING

12
ANTHROPOLOGY
CARBON DATING
CHALCOLITHIC
   (or Copper Age)
CIVILISATION
CYLINDER SEAL
FLUORINE TEST
GALLERY GRAVE
HIEROGLYPHIC
LAKE DWELLING
MOABITE STONE
OPISTHOGRAPH
PALAEOGRAPHY
PALAEOLITHIC
PASSAGE GRAVE
PROTOHISTORY
ROSETTA STONE
STRATIGRAPHY
STROMATOLITE

13
FOSSILISATION
GEOCHRONOLOGY
GLACIAL PERIOD
HIEROGLYPHICS
METAL DETECTOR
OPISTHOGRAPHY
PALAEONTOLOGY
STANDING STONE

14	PICTURE-WRITING	EPIPALAEOLITHIC
ANCIENT HISTORY		OCCUPATION LEVEL
COLLECTIVE TOMB	**15**	
EXTENDED BURIAL	ANCIENT MONUMENT	**17**
OBSIDIAN DATING	DRUIDICAL CIRCLE	RADIOCARBON DATING

Science – Astronomy – ASTEROIDS & COMETS Asteroids unless stated

3	**6**	**7**	**9**
IDA	ADONIS	ANTIOPE	HERCULINA
	AUSTIN comet	ASTRAEA	HYAKUTAKE comet
4	CYBELE	CAMILLA	IKEYA-SEKI comet
EMMA	DAVIDA	EUGENIA	PATROCLUS
EROS	DONATI comet	EUNOMIA	
FAYE comet	EGERIA	EUTERPE	**10**
JUNO	FINLAY comet	FORTUNA	AMPHITRITE
WEST comet	HALLEY comet	HIDALGO	EUPHROSYNE
WOLF comet	HEKTOR	PULCOVA	INTERAMNIA
	HYGIEA	WHIPPLE comet	
5	OLBERS comet		**11**
BIELA comet	PALLAS	**8**	AREND-ROLAND comet
BERNA	PROKNE	BAMBERGA	SWIFT-TUTTLE comet
DANAË	PSYCHE	HALE-BOPP comet	
ENCKE comet	SAPPHO	HERMIONE	**12**
FLORA	SYLVIA	KOHOUTEK comet	PONS-WINNECKE comet
JUEWA	THALIA	MASSALIA	
VESTA	THEMIS		**13**
	UNDINA		SHOEMAKER-LEVY comet

Science – Astronomy – **ASTRONOMERS** * = Astronomer Royal

4
AIRY* Sir George
BODE Johann
BOND William
GOLD Thomas
HALE George
LEVY David H
OORT Jan
POND* John
PONS Jean-Louis
REES* Lord Martin
RYLE* Sir Martin
WEST Richard

5
ADAMS John Couch
AMICI Giovanni
AREND Sylvain
BAILY Francis
BLISS* Nathaniel
BRAHE Tycho
DYSON* Sir Frank
ENCKE Johann
GALLE Johann
HOOKE Robert
HOYLE Sir Fred
JEANS Sir James
JONES* Sir Harold
KOWAL Charles T
MOORE Sir Patrick
REBER Grote
ROSSE Earl William
SAGAN Carl
TULLY R Brent

6
ALCOCK George
DONATI Giambattista
DREYER John
GUNTER Edmund
HALLEY* Edmond
HUBBLE Edwin
KEPLER Johannes
LOVELL Sir Bernard
LOWELL Percival
NEWTON Sir Isaac
SPÖRER Gustav
THALES

7
BRADLEY* James
CASSINI Giovanni,
  Jacques
CELSIUS Anders
GALILEO
  (or Galileo Galilei)
HUGGINS Sir William
HUYGENS Christiaan
JANSSEN Pierre
KOZYREV Nikolai
LALANDE Jérôme
LAMBERT Johann
LANGLEY Samuel
LAPLACE Pierre
LEAVITT Henrietta Swan
LOCKYER Sir Norman
MESSIER Charles
PTOLEMY
SANDAGE Allan Rex

SCHMIDT Maarten
SHAPLEY Harlow
WOOLLEY* Sir Richard
ZÖLLNER Johann

8
ALBITZKY Vladimir
ARZACHEL
BAILLAUD Benjamin
CHARLIER Carl
CHRISTIE* William
HERSCHEL Caroline,
  Sir John, Sir William
LEMAÎTRE Georges
REINMUTH Karl
RHETICUS
TOMBAUGH Clyde
VAN ALLEN James
WINNECKE Friedrich

9
AL-BATTANI
ALBUMAZAR
AL-BUZJANI
EDDINGTON Sir Arthur
FABRICIUS David,
  Johannes
FLAMSTEED* John
LE VERRIER Urbain
MASKELYNE* Nevil
PICKERING Edward,
  William
SHOEMAKER Carolyn
VYSSOTSKY Emma

10
COPERNICUS Nicolaus
HIPPARCHUS
NASIR AL-DIN
OSTERBROCK Donald
WOLFENDALE* Sir Arnold

11
AL-KHWARIZMI
ARISTARCHUS
GRAHAM-SMITH* Sir Francis
HERTZSPRUNG Ejnar
OMAR KHAYYÁM

SCHLESINGER Frank

12
AMBARTSUMIAN Viktor
ERATOSTHENES
SCHIAPARELLI Giovanni

13
CHANDRASEKHAR Subrahmanyan
REGIOMONTANUS

14
GALILEO GALILEI or Galileo

Science – Astronomy – ASTRONOMICAL TERMS

3	WANE	**6**	ZENITH	TRANSIT
SKY		APOGEE		TWINKLE
SUN	**5**	BOLIDE	**7**	
WAX	APSIS	COLURE	ANOMALY	**8**
	COMET	CORONA	AUREOLE	ACHROMAT
4	CYCLE	COSMOS	AZIMUTH	AEROLITE
COMA	EPACT	CRATER	ECLIPSE	APHELION
CUSP	EPOCH	FACULA	EQUATOR	APOAPSIS
DISC	LUNAR	GALAXY	EQUINOX	ASTEROID
HALO	NADIR	METEOR	GRAVITY	CRESCENT
HORN	ORBIT	NEBULA	HEAVENS	ECLIPTIC
MARE	PHASE	ORRERY	MOCK SUN	EMERSION
MOON	PLAGE	PARSEC	NEW MOON	EVECTION
NODE	PLAGE	PLANET	NUCLEUS	FILAMENT
NOVA	PULSE	PULSAR	PERIGEE	FIREBALL
PATH	SAROS	QUASAR	PRIMARY	FULL MOON
POLE	SOLAR	SPHERE	RADIANT	HALF-MOON
RING	SPACE	SUN DOG	STARLET	LUNAR DAY
STAR	TRINE	SYSTEM	STAR MAP	LUNATION
VOID	UMBRA	SYZYGY	SUNSPOT	MERIDIAN
	WORLD			

MOCK MOON
NUTATION
PENUMBRA
RED DWARF
RED GIANT
RED SHIFT
SOLAR DAY
SOLSTICE
TWINKLER
UNIVERSE

9
ASTRONOMY
BLACK HOLE
EPHEMERIS
EXOSPHERE
FIRMAMENT
FIXED STAR
FLOCCULUS
IMMERSION
LIGHT YEAR
LUNAR NODE
LUNAR YEAR
MACROCOSM
MAGNITUDE
METEORITE
METEOROID
MID-HEAVEN
MOONSCAPE
PARHELION
PLANETOID
RADIO STAR
REFRACTOR
SATELLITE
SOLAR MASS
SOLAR WIND
SOLAR YEAR
STAR CLOUD

SUPERNOVA
TELESCOPE
WHITE HOLE

10
ABERRATION
BINARY STAR
EARTHSHINE
ELONGATION
KUIPER BELT
LUNAR CYCLE
LUNAR MONTH
OPPOSITION
OUTER SPACE
PARASELENE
PERIASTRON
PERIHELION
PRECESSION
QUADRATURE
SELENOLOGY
SIDEROSTAT
SOLAR FLARE
STARGAZING
TERMINATOR
WHITE DWARF

11
BAILY'S BEADS
CONJUNCTION
DECLINATION
FALLING STAR
GIBBOUS MOON
GRANULATION
GRAVITATION
HARVEST MOON
HUNTER'S MOON
KEPLER'S LAWS
MINOR PLANET

NEUTRON STAR
OBSERVATORY
OCCULTATION
PHOTOSPHERE
PLANISPHERE
SIDEREAL DAY
SOLAR SYSTEM
STAR CLUSTER

12
ASTROPHYSICS
BINARY SYSTEM
CHROMOSPHERE
CRESCENT MOON
HEAVENLY BODY
LUNAR ECLIPSE
MEAN SOLAR DAY
METEOR CRATER
MULTIPLE STAR
PERTURBATION
PLANETESIMAL
PROPER MOTION
RADIANT POINT
SELENOGRAPHY
SHEPHERD MOON
SHOOTING STAR
SIDEREAL TIME
SIDEREAL YEAR
SOLAR ECLIPSE
TOTAL ECLIPSE
VARIABLE STAR

13
ASCENDING NODE
BIG BANG THEORY
COMPANION STAR
CONSTELLATION
EPHEMERIS TIME

LUNAR DISTANCE
MEAN SOLAR TIME
METEOR SHOWER
OPTICAL BINARY
PRIMARY PLANET
RETROGRESSION
SIDEREAL CLOCK
SIDEREAL MONTH

14
ANNULAR ECLIPSE
DESCENDING NODE
EQUATION OF TIME
HELIACAL RISING
INFERIOR PLANET

MERIDIAN CIRCLE
PARTIAL ECLIPSE
RADIO ASTRONOMY
RADIO TELESCOPE
RETROGRADATION
RIGHT ASCENSION
SUPERIOR PLANET

15
ANGULAR DIAMETER
ANOMALISTIC YEAR
ARMILLARY SPHERE
CELESTIAL EQUATOR
CHANDLER'S WOBBLE
HELIACAL SETTING

HUBBLE'S CONSTANT
PTOLEMAIC SYSTEM

16
COPERNICAN SYSTEM

17
ABSOLUTE MAGNITUDE
CELESTIAL LATITUDE
STEADY STATE THEORY

18
CELESTIAL LONGITUDE

Science – Astronomy – PLANETS & SATELLITES
Satellites (with their named planets) unless stated

3
MAB Uranus
PAN Saturn

4
ERIS dwarf planet
KALE Jupiter
LEDA Jupiter
MARS planet
MOON Earth
PUCK Uranus
RHEA Saturn
YMIR Saturn

5
AITNE Jupiter
AOEDE Jupiter

ARCHE Jupiter
ARIEL Uranus
ATLAS Saturn
CARME Jupiter
CARPO Jupiter
CERES dwarf planet
CUPID Uranus
DIONE Saturn
EARTH planet
ELARA Jupiter
JANUS Saturn
METIS Jupiter
MIMAS Saturn
MNEME Jupiter
NAIAD Neptune
NARVI Saturn
PLUTO dwarf planet

THEBE Jupiter
TITAN Saturn
VENUS planet

6
ANANKE Jupiter
BIANCA Uranus
CHARON Pluto
DEIMOS Mars
EUROPA Jupiter
HELENE Saturn
HELIKE Jupiter
IJIRAQ Saturn
ISONOE Jupiter
JULIET Uranus
KALYKE Jupiter
KIVIUQ Saturn

NEREID Neptune
OBERON Uranus
PHOEBE Saturn
PHOBOS Mars
PORTIA Uranus
SATURN planet
SINOPE Jupiter
SKATHI Saturn
SPONDE Jupiter
TARVOS Saturn
TETHYS Saturn
THRYMR Saturn
THYONE Jupiter
TRITON Neptune
URANUS planet

7

AUTONOE Jupiter
BELINDA Uranus
CALIBAN Uranus
CALYPSO Saturn
CYLLENE Jupiter
DAPHNIS Saturn
DESPINA Neptune
ERINOME Jupiter
ERRIAPO Saturn
EUANTHE Jupiter
EUPORIE Jupiter
GALATEA Neptune
HIMALIA Jupiter
IAPETUS Saturn
IOCASTE Jupiter
JUPITER planet
LARISSA Neptune
MERCURY planet
METHONE Saturn
MIRANDA Uranus
NEPTUNE planet
OPHELIA Uranus
PAALIAQ Saturn
PALLENE Saturn
PANDORA Saturn
PERDITA Uranus

PROTEUS Neptune
SETEBOS Uranus
SIARNAQ Saturn
SYCORAX Uranus
TAYGETE Jupiter
TELESTO Saturn
TITANIA Uranus
UMBRIEL Uranus

8

ADRASTEA Jupiter
ALBIORIX Saturn
AMALTHEA Jupiter
CALLISTO Jupiter
CHALDENE Jupiter
CORDELIA Uranus
CRESSIDA Uranus
EUKELADE Jupiter
EURYDOME Jupiter
GANYMEDE Jupiter
HEGEMONE Jupiter
HERMIPPE Jupiter
HYPERION Saturn
LYSITHEA Jupiter
MARGARET Uranus
ORTHOSIE Jupiter
PASIPHAË Jupiter

PASITHEE Jupiter
PROSPERO Uranus
PSAMATHE Neptune
ROSALIND Uranus
STEPHANO Uranus
SUTTUNGR Saturn
THALASSA Neptune
THEMISTO Jupiter
TRINCULO Uranus

9

DESDEMONA Uranus
ENCELADUS Saturn
FERDINAND Uranus
FRANCISCO Uranus
HARPALYKE Jupiter
MEGACLITE Jupiter
PRAXIDIKE Jupiter
THELXINOE Jupiter

10

CALLIRRHOE Jupiter
EPIMETHEUS Saturn
KALLICHORE Jupiter
MUNDILFARI Saturn
POLYDEUCES Saturn
PROMETHEUS Saturn

Science – Astronomy – STARS & CONSTELLATIONS
Star unless stated   con = constellation

3

ARA (or The Altar) con
LEO (or The Lion) con
SUN

4

ALYA
CAPH
CRUX (or The Southern
    Cross) con

ENIF
GRUS (or The
    Crane) con
IZAR
LYNX con

LYRA (or The Lyre)
  con
MAIA
MIRA
NAOS
PAVO (or The
  Peacock) con
SADR
SKAT
VEGA
VELA (or The Sails)
  con

5
ACRUX
ALCOR
ALGOL
ARIES (or The Ram)
  con
ARNEB
ATLAS
CETUS (or The
  Whale) con
CURSA
DABIH
DENEB
DRACO (or The
  Dragon) con
DUBHE
ER RAI
GEMMA (or
  Alphecca)
HADAR
HAMAL
HARIS
HOMAM
HYDRA (or The Water
  Snake) con

INDUS (or The Indian)
  con
LEPUS (or The Hare)
  con
LIBRA (or The Scales)
  con
LUPUS (or The Wolf)
  con
MATAR
MENSA (or The Table
  Mountain) con
MERAK
MIZAR
MUSCA (or The Fly)
  con
NORMA (or The Level)
  con
NUNKI
ORION (or The Hunter)
  con
PYXIS (or The
  Compass) con
RIGEL
SABIK
SAIPH
SPICA
VIRGO (or The Virgin)
  con
WEZEN
ZOSMA

6
ACAMAR
ADHARA
ALAMAK
ALBALI
ALFIRK
ALGEDI

ALIOTH
ALNAIR
AL NASL
ALTAIR
ALUDRA
ANTLIA (or The Air
  Pump) con
AQUILA (or The Eagle)
  con
AURIGA (or The
  Charioteer) con
BOÖTES (or The
  Herdsman) con
CAELUM (or The
  Chisel) con
CANCER (or The Crab)
  con
CARINA (or The Keel)
  con
CASTOR
CORVUS (or The Crow)
  con
CRATER (or The Cup)
  con
CYGNUS (or The Swan)
  con
DIADEM
DORADO (or The
  Goldfish) con
EL NATH
FORNAX (or The
  Furnace) con
GEMINI (or The Twins)
  con
GIENAH
HYDRUS (or The Lesser
  Water Snake) con
MARKAB

MEGREZ
MENKAR
MEROPE
MIMOSA
MIRACH
MIRZAM
NEKKAR
OCTANS (or The
 Octant) con
PHECDA
PICTOR (or The Painter's
 Easel) con
PISCES (or The Fishes)
 con
POLLUX
PUPPIS (or The Stern)
 con
RUKBAT
SCHEAT
SCUTUM (or The Shield)
 con
SIRIUS (or Dog Star)
TAURUS (or The Bull)
 con
THE CUP (or Crater)
 con
THE FLY (or Musca) con
THE FOX (or Vulpecula)
 con
THE NET (or Reticulum)
 con
THE RAM (or Aries) con
THUBAN
TUCANA (or The
 Toucan) con
VOLANS (or The Flying
 Fish) con

7
ACUBENS
ALBIREO
AL CHIBA
ALCYONE
ALGENIB
ALGIEBA
ALNILAM
ALNITAK
ALPHARD
ALSHAIN
ANTARES
ARRAKIS
CANOPUS
CAPELLA
CELEANO
CEPHEUS con
COLUMBA (or The
 Dove) con
DOG STAR (or Sirius)
ELECTRA
ELTANIN
GOMEISA
LACERTA (or The
 Lizard) con
MINTAKA
NASHIRA
PEGASUS (or The
 Winged Horse) con
PERSEUS con
PHERCAD
PHOENIX con
PLEIONE
POLARIS (or Pole
 Star)
PORRIMA
PROCYON
REGULUS

ROTANEV
SAGITTA (or The Arrow)
 con
SCHEDAR
SERPENS (or The
 Serpent) con
SEXTANS (or The
 Sextant) con
SHELIAK
TARAZED
TAYGETA
THE BULL (or Taurus)
 con
THE CRAB (or Cancer)
 con
THE CROW (or Corvus)
 con
THE HARE (or Lepus)
 con
THE KEEL (or Carina)
 con
THE LYRE (or Lyra) con
THE DOVE (or Columba)
 con
THE LION (or Leo) con
THE SWAN (or Cygnus)
 con
THE WOLF (or Lupus)
 con

8
ACHERNAR
ALPHECCA (or Gemma)
AL RISCHA
AQUARIUS (or The Water
 Carrier) con
ARCTURUS
ASTEROPE

CIRCINUS (or The
  Compasses) con
DENEBOLA
DSCHUBBA
EQUULEUS (or The Little
  Horse) con
ERIDANUS (or The River)
  con
GRAFFIAS
HERCULES con
KITALPHA
LEO MINOR (or The Lesser
  Lion) con
POLE STAR (or Polaris)
RASTABAN
SCORPIUS (or The
  Scorpion) con
SCULPTOR con
SHERATAN
SUALOCIN
THE ALTAR (or Ara) con
THE ARROW (or Sagitta)
  con
THE CRANE (or Grus) con
THE EAGLE (or Aquila)
  con
THE LEVEL (or Norma)
  con
THE RIVER (or Eridanus)
  con
THE SAILS (or Vela) con
THE STERN (or Puppis)
  con
THE TWINS (or Gemini)
  con
THE WHALE (or Cetus)
  con
YED PRIOR

9
ALDEBARAN
ALDERAMIN
ALPHERATZ
ANDROMEDA con
BELLATRIX
CENTAURUS (or The
  Centaur) con
COR CAROLI
DELPHINUS (or The
  Dolphin) con
FOMALHAUT
MESARTHIM
MONOCEROS (or The
  Unicorn) con
OPHIUCHUS (or The
  Serpent Holder)
  con
RETICULUM (or The
  Net) con
SADACHBIA
SADALSUUD
THE ARCHER (or
  Sagittarius) con
THE CHISEL (or
  Caelum) con
THE DRAGON (or
  Draco) con
THE FISHES (or Pisces)
  con
THE HUNTER (or
  Orion) con
THE INDIAN (or
  Indus) con
THE LIZARD (or
  Lacerta) con
THE OCTANT (or
  Octans) con

THE SCALES (or Libra)
  con
THE SHIELD (or
  Scutum) con
THE TOUCAN (or
  Tucana) con
THE VIRGIN (or Virgo)
  con
UNUKALHAI
URSA MAJOR (or The
  Great Bear) con
URSA MINOR (or The
  Little Bear) con
VULPECULA (or The
  Fox) con

10
ALKALUROPS
ARKAB PRIOR
BENTNASCH
BETELGEUSE
CANIS MAJOR (or The
  Greater Dog) con
CANIS MINOR (or The
  Lesser Dog) con
CASSIOPEIA con
CHAMAELEON (or The
  Chameleon) con
HOROLOGIUM (or The
  Pendulum Clock) con
MENKALINAN
RAS ALGETHI
RAS ALHAGUE
SADALMELIK
THE AIR PUMP (or
  Antlia) con
THE CENTAUR (or
  Centaurus) con

THE COMPASS (or Pyxis) con
THE DOLPHIN (or Delphinus) con
THE FURNACE (or Fornax) con
THE GIRAFFE (or Camelopardalis)
con
THE PEACOCK (or Pavo) con
THE SEA GOAT (or Capricornus) con
THE SERPENT (or Serpens) con
THE SEXTANT (or Sextans) con
THE UNICORN (or Monoceros) con
TRIANGULUM (or The Triangle) con

11

CAPRICORNUS (or The Sea Goat)
con
DENEB KAITOS
MIAPLACIDUS
SAGITTARIUS (or The Archer) con
TELESCOPIUM (or The Telescope)
con
THE GOLDFISH (or Dorado) con
THE HERDSMAN (or Boötes) con
THE SCORPION (or Scorpius) con
THE TRIANGLE (or Triangulum) con

12

BARNARD'S STAR
DELTA PAVONIS
DENEB ALGIEDI
KAPTEYN'S STAR
MICROSCOPIUM (or The
Microscope) con
THE CHAMELEON (or Chamaeleon)
con
THE COMPASSES (or Circinus) con
THE GREAT BEAR (or Ursa Major) con
THE LESSER DOG (or Canis Minor)
con

THE TELESCOPE (or Telescopium) con
VINDEMIATRIX
YED POSTERIOR
ZUBENELAKRAB

13

ALPHA CENTAURI
BERENICE'S HAIR (or Coma Berenices)
con
CANES VENATICI (or The Hunting
Dogs) con
COMA BERENICES (or Berenice's Hair)
con
KAFFALJIDHMAH
THE CHARIOTEER (or Auriga) con
THE FLYING FISH (or Volans) con
THE GREATER DOG (or Canis Major)
con
THE LESSER LION (or Leo Minor) con
THE MICROSCOPE (or Microscopium)
con
THE LITTLE BEAR (or Ursa Minor) con
THE WATER SNAKE (or Hydra) con
ZUBENELGENUBI

14

ARKAB POSTERIOR
CAMELOPARDALIS (or The Giraffe)
con
CORONA BOREALIS (or The Northern
Crown) con
RIGIL KENTAURUS
THE HUNTING DOGS (or Canes
Venatici) con
THE LITTLE HORSE (or Equuleus) con
THE WINGED HORSE (or Pegasus)
con
ZUBENESCHAMALI

15

CORONA AUSTRALIS (or The Southern Crown) con
PISCIS AUSTRINUS (or The Southern Fish) con
THE SOUTHERN FISH (or Piscis Austrinus) con
THE WATER CARRIER (or Aquarius) con

16

THE NORTHERN CROWN (or Corona Borealis) con
THE PAINTER'S EASEL (or Pictor) con
THE PENDULUM CLOCK (or Horologium) con
THE SERPENT HOLDER (or Ophiuchus) con
THE SOUTHERN CROSS (or Crux) con

THE SOUTHERN CROWN (or Corona Australis) con
THE TABLE MOUNTAIN (or Mensa) con

17

THE BIRD OF PARADISE (or Apus) con

18

TRIANGULUM AUSTRALE (or The Southern Triangle) con

19

THE LESSER WATER SNAKE (or Hydrus) con
THE SOUTHERN TRIANGLE (or Triangulum Australe) con

Science – Botany – BOTANICAL TERMS

3	4	CLAW	HUSK	SCAR	5	FLESH	HUMUS
AWN	ARIL	CONE	KNOT	SEED	BEARD	FLORA	HYPHA
BUD	AXIL	CORK	LEAF	SKIN	BERRY	FROND	JUICE
EAR	AXIS	CORM	LIMB	SPUR	BLADE	FRUIT	LAYER
KEY	BARK	CULM	LOBE	STEM	BLOOM	FUNGI	MOULD
LIP	BEAN	CYME	NODE	TREE	BOUGH	GENUS	ORDER
NUT	BOLE	FALL	PEEL	TRUE	BRACT	GLUME	OVARY
PIP	BOLT	FERN	PITH	TUFT	CALYX	GNARL	OVULE
PIT	BULB	GALL	POME	TWIG	CLASS	GRAFT	PETAL
POD	BURR	HEAD	PULP	VEIN	CLONE	GRASS	PINNA
SAP	BUSH	HEEL	RIND	WEED	CROWN	HABIT	PLANT
	CANE	HERB	RING	WILT	DRUPE	HAULM	PULSE
	CELL	HULL	ROOT		DWARF	HEART	SCALE

SCAPE	AREOLE	POLLEN	FOLIAGE	**8**	OFFSHOOT
SCION	BLIGHT	RACEME	FUNICLE	ALLIANCE	OPPOSITE
SCRUB	BOTANY	RACHIS	GLOCHID	ALLOGAMY	PEDUNCLE
SEPAL	BRANCH	RUNNER	HERBAGE	BIENNIAL	PERIANTH
SHELL	BULBIL	SECUND	LATERAL	BRYOLOGY	PERICARP
SHOOT	CANKER	SERIES	LEAFLET	CAT'S TAIL	PERIDERM
SHRUB	CARPEL	SHEATH	NECTARY	CICATRIX	PERIDIUM
SPEAR	CATKIN	SIMPLE	NERVURE	COMPOUND	PETALOID
SPIKE	CAUDEX	SPADIX	PALMATE	CULTIVAR	PHYLLODE
SPINE	CEREAL	SPATHE	PANICLE	CYATHIUM	PLACENTA
SPORE	CORONA	SPROUT	PAPILLA	DIVISION	PLANTLET
SPORT	CORTEX	STAMEN	PEDICEL	DOMINANT	POLARITY
SPRAY	CORYMB	STIGMA	PELTATE	DRUPELET	PROLIFIC
SPRIG	DRUPEL	STOLON	PETIOLE	ENDOCARP	PULVINUS
STALK	EMBRYO	SUCKER	PINNATE	ENDOGAMY	PYXIDIUM
STICK	ENTIRE	TEGMEN	PINNULE	EPIPHYTE	QUICKSET
STING	FAMILY	TILLER	PLUMULE	FILAMENT	RACEMOSE
STOCK	FARINA	TURION	PRICKLE	FLOWERER	RAY PETAL
STOMA	FLORET	VESSEL	RADICLE	FOLLICLE	RECURVED
STONE	FLOWER		RHIZOME	FRUITING	REFLEXED
STUMP	FUNGUS	**7**	ROSETTE	GLABROUS	REGROWTH
STYLE	GROWTH	AURICLE	SEGMENT	GRAFTING	RIPENESS
TEPAL	HISPID	BLOOMER	SESSILE	GREENERY	ROOT HAIR
THORN	HYBRID	BLOSSOM	SOROSIS	HOMOGAMY	ROOT-KNOT
TOOTH	KERNEL	BULBLET	SPECIES	HONEYDEW	SCANDENT
TRUNK	LEADER	CAMBIUM	STERILE	HYMENIUM	SCARRING
TRUSS	LEGUME	CAPSULE	STIPULE	LABELLUM	SEED COAT
TUBER	LINEAR	CLADODE	TAPROOT	LAYERING	SEED HEAD
UMBEL	LOMENT	CLIMBER	TENDRIL	LEAF CURL	SEED LEAF
VALVE	MIDRIB	CLUSTER	THALLUS	LEAF-FALL	SEEDLING
WHORL	MILDEW	COROLLA	TRAILER	LENTICEL	SELF-SEED
XYLEM	NECTAR	CREEPER	TREETOP	MARGINAL	SKELETON
	NEEDLE	CUTICLE	TREFOIL	MATURITY	SPIKELET
6	OFFSET	CUTTING	TRUMPET	MERISTEM	STANDARD
ACHENE	PAPPUS	DENIZEN	UPRIGHT	MUCILAGE	SUBSHRUB
ALPINE	PHLOEM	DENTATE	VARIETY	MYCELIUM	SYCONIUM
ANNUAL	PILEUS	DIEBACK	YELLOWS	NUTATION	TOMENTUM
ANTHER	PISTIL	EPICARP		NUTSHELL	TRICHOME

TUBERCLE
TUBEROUS
VASCULAR
VERDANCY
VERJUICE
XENOGAMY
ZONATION

9
ALTERNATE
BRANCHLET
BRYOPHYTE
CAPITULUM
CARPOLOGY
CARYOPSIS
CHLOROSIS
COLUMELLA
COMPOSITE
COTYLEDON
CROWN GALL
DECIDUOUS
DECUMBENT
DICHASIUM
DICHOGAMY
DIOECIOUS
EMERGENCE
ENDOSPERM
EVERGREEN
FAIRY RING
FLOWER BUD
FOLIATION
FOOTSTALK
GEMMATION
GERM LAYER
GUTTATION
HALOPHYTE
HEARTWOOD
HERBARIUM

HETEROSIS
HYDATHODE
HYPOCOTYL
INVOLUCRE
ISOTROPIC
LEAF STALK
LEAF TRACE
MESOPHYTE
MICROPYLE
NERVATION
PERENNIAL
POLLINIUM
RAY FLORET
REMONTANT
ROCK PLANT
ROOTSTOCK
SCALE LEAF
SCUTELLUM
SIDE SHOOT
STAMINODE
STROBILUS
SUBSTRATE
SUCCULENT
SYMBIOSIS
SYMPODIUM
TREE TRUNK
UNDERWOOD
VALLECULA
VEGETABLE
VERNATION
WATERWEED
XENOGRAFT
XEROPHILY
XEROPHYTE

10
ABSCISSION
ACOTYLEDON

AERENCHYMA
AERIAL ROOT
ANDROECIUM
ANEMOPHILY
ANGIOSPERM
ANISOTROPY
ANNUAL RING
APPOSITION
CARPOPHORE
COLEORHIZA
DAMPING OFF
DEHISCENCE
DENDROLOGY
DISC FLORET
ETIOLATION
FALSE FRUIT
FASCIATION
FLOWER HEAD
GEOTROPISM
GRAFT UNION
GYMNOSPERM
HERBACEOUS
HETEROGAMY
HONEYGUIDE
HYDROPHILY
HYDROPHYTE
HYGROPHYTE
HYPANTHIUM
INNOVATION
INTEGUMENT
ISOTROPISM
LITHOPHYTE
MATURATION
MONOCARPIC
MONOPODIUM
NYCTINASTY
PARAPHYSIS
PARASTICHY

PARENCHYMA
PERIGYNOUS
PERSISTENT
POLLEN TUBE
POLYGAMOUS
POPULATION
PROCUMBENT
PSEUDOBULB
PSEUDOCARP
PUBESCENCE
RECEPTACLE
RESUPINATE
ROOT SYSTEM
SAPROPHYTE
SCHIZOCARP
SCLEROTIUM
SEED VESSEL
SHADE PLANT
SILVER LEAF
SPORANGIUM
SPOROPHORE
SPOROPHYTE
TRIFOLIATE
UNDERBRUSH
VEGETATION
VIVIPAROUS
WATER PLANT
ZYGOMORPHY

11
AESTIVATION
AIR LAYERING
ANTHERIDIUM
ANTHEROZOID
ARCHEGONIUM
BIFURCATION
CHLOROPHYLL
CLEISTOGAMY

COLLENCHYMA
CORK CAMBIUM
DEFOLIATION
DOCOTYLEDON
DISSEMINULE
DISSEPIMENT
ENGRAFTMENT
ENTOMOPHILY
EXFOLIATION
FLORESCENCE
FOLIAGE LEAF
GEITONOGAMY
GERMINATION
GRAFT HYBRID
GROUND COVER
HARDY ANNUAL
HESPERIDIUM
HETEROSTYLY
HYDROPONICS
INDEHISCENT
LACINIATION
MONOCHASIUM
ORTHOSTICHY
PERITHECIUM
PHOTOPERIOD
PHYLLOCLADE
PHYLLOTAXIS
POLLEN GRAIN
POLLINATION
PROPAGATION
PROTANDROUS
PROTOGYNOUS
PULLULATION
ROOT CLIMBER
SCLEROPHYLL
SOFT-STEMMED
SPOROGENOUS

SPORULATION
STEM SEGMENT
TERRICOLOUS
THALLOPHYTE
UNDERGROWTH
VARIEGATION
XANTHOPHYLL
XEROPHILOUS

12

ADVENTITIOUS
ANEMOPHILOUS
ARBORESCENCE
COMPOUND LEAF
CONSOCIATION
DORSIVENTRAL
GROWING POINT
HELIOTROPISM
HYBRID VIGOUR
HYDROPHILOUS
NATURAL ORDER
ORTHOTROPISM
PALAEOBOTANY
PHOTOTROPISM
PHREATOPHYTE
PHYTOGENESIS
PTERIDOPHYTE
SHY FLOWERING
SPOROGENESIS
TRIFURCATION
TROPHIC LEVEL
TUBEROUS ROOT
WITCHES' BROOM
WOODY-STEMMED

13

EFFLORESCENCE
ENTOMOPHILOUS
HERMAPHRODITE
INFLORESCENCE
INSECTIVOROUS
MONOCOTYLEDON
MULTIPLE FRUIT
NITROGEN CYCLE
PARTHENOCARPY
PHYTOPLANKTON
PNEUMATOPHORE
PROLIFERATION
PROLIFICATION
SPERMATOPHYTE
THERMOTROPISM
TRANSPIRATION
VASCULAR PLANT

14

APHELIOTROPISM
EUTROPHICATION
FRUCTIFICATION
LINNAEAN SYSTEM
NATURAL HISTORY
NATURALISATION
PHOTOPERIODISM
PHOTOSYNTHESIS
SPORANGIOPHORE
VASCULAR BUNDLE

15

COLLECTIVE FRUIT
MEDULLARY SHEATH
PERIANTH SEGMENT
PLANT SUCCESSION
SELF-POLLINATION

Science – Botany – CEREALS & GRASSES

3
RYE

SPELT
WHEAT

RYE GRASS
WILD OATS
WILD RICE

11
CANARY GRASS
KIKUYU GRASS
MEADOW GRASS

4
BENT
CORN
OATS
RAGI
 (or finger millet)
RICE
TEFF

6
BAMBOO
BARLEY
CEREAL
DARNEL
FESCUE
KAÑIWA
KIKUYU
MARRAM
MELICK
MILLET
QUINOA
QUITCH
 (or couch)

9
BENT GRASS
BLUEGRASS
 (or meadow
 grass)
BUCKWHEAT
COCKSFOOT
CORD GRASS
HAIR GRASS
SOUR GRASS
TRITICALE
WATER RICE
WIRE GRASS

 (or bluegrass)
MELICK GRASS
MILLET GRASS
PAMPAS GRASS
PEARL BARLEY
PEARL MILLET
 (or bajra)
QUITCH GRASS
 (or couch grass)
VERNAL GRASS

5
BAJRA
 (or pearl millet)
BROME
COUCH
 (or quitch)
DURRA
 (or Indian millet,
 jowar)
DURUM
EMMER
FONIO
GRASS
JOWAR
 (or durra, Indian
 millet)
MAIZE
 (or Indian corn)
PANIC

7
ESPARTO
FOXTAIL
PAPYRUS
SORGHUM
TIMOTHY

8
COW WHEAT
DOGSTAIL
KAOLIANG
OAT GRASS
PASPALUM

10
BUNCH GRASS
CITRONELLA
COUCH GRASS
 (or quitch grass)
INDIAN CORN
 (or maize)
LEMON GRASS
PANIC GRASS
SPEAR GRASS
SUDAN GRASS

12
BUFFALO GRASS
COMMON MILLET
FINGER MILLET
 (or ragi)
INDIAN MILLET
 (or durra, jowar)
QUAKING GRASS
SHEEP'S FESCUE
SQUIRREL-TAIL
TIMOTHY GRASS
TUSSOCK GRASS

13
ELEPHANT GRASS
KANGAROO GRASS

Science – Botany – FLOWERS & PLANTS

3
BAY
HOP
IVY
MAY
OCA
RUE
TEA

4
ACER
ALGA
ALOE
ARUM
BEET
COCA
DOCK
FERN
FLAG
FLAX
GUAR
HEBE
HEMP
IRIS
JUTE
KAVA
KELP
LILY
LING
MATÉ
  (or yerba)
MINT
MOSS
OMBU
PINK

POKE
RAPE
REED
ROSE
RUSH
SAGE
SOLA
TANG
  (or tangle)
TARE
TULE
TUNA
TUTU
VINE
WELD
  (or dyer's
  rocket)
WHIN
WOAD

5
ABACA
AGAVE
ANISE
ASTER
BABUL
BRAKE
BRIAR
  (or brier)
BRIER
  (or briar)
BROOM
BUGLE
CALLA
CAMAS

(or camass)
CANNA
DAGGA
DAISY
DRYAS
  (or mountain
  avens)
DULSE
DWALE
ERICA
FURZE
GORSE
GOWAN
HENNA
HOLLY
HOSTA
KUDZU
LAVER
LIANA
LILAC
LOTUS
LUPIN
MULGA
MYRRH
  (or sweet
  cicely)
NOPAL
OX-EYE
OXLIP
PANSY
PEONY
PHLOX
POPPY
RAMIE
SALAL

SALLY
  (or sallee)
SAVIN
SEDGE
SEDUM
STOCK
TANSY
TULIP
VETCH
VIOLA
WRACK
YERBA
  (or maté)
YUCCA
  (or Adam's
  needle)
YULAN

6
ABELIA
ACACIA
AGARIC
ALSIKE
ARABIS
  (or rock cress)
AZALEA
BALSAM
BETONY
BLINKS
BORAGE
BRYONY
BURNET
CACTUS
CAMASS
  (or camas)

CASSIA
CATNIP
  (or catmint)
CICELY
CLOVER
CORNEL
COROZO
COTTON
CROCUS
CROTAL
  (or crottle)
CROTON
DAHLIA
DAPHNE
DATURA
DESMID
DODDER
ERYNGO
HENBIT
INDIGO
JUJUBE
KIEKIE
KNAWEL
LABLAB
LAUREL
LICHEN
MADDER
MAGUEY
MALLOW
MEDICK
MIMOSA
MOUTAN
MYRTLE
NETTLE
OLD MAN

(or southernwood)
ORACHE
ORCHIL
ORCHID
ORPINE
PRIVET
PROTEA
QUINOA
RATTAN
SALLEE
(or sally)
SALVIA
SESAME
SPURGE
SQUILL
SUNDEW
TANGLE
(or tang)
TEASEL
THRIFT
(or sea pink)
TUTSAN
VIOLET
WATTLE
YAUPON
YARROW
(or milfoil)
ZINNIA

7
ABSINTH
(or wormwood)
ACONITE
ALFALFA
(or lucerne)
ALKANET
ALLHEAL
ALLSEED

ALYSSUM
ANEMONE
(or windflower)
ARBUTUS
BANKSIA
BEGONIA
BISTORT
BOG ARUM
BOGBEAN
(or buckbean)
BOG MOSS
(or peat moss)
BONESET
BRACKEN
BRAMBLE
BUGBANE
BUGLOSS
BULLACE
BULRUSH
BURDOCK
BUR-REED
CALAMUS
(or sweet flag)
CALTROP
CAMPION
CARAWAY
CARDOON
CARLINE
CATMINT
(or catnip)
CAT'S EAR
CHAMISE
CHICORY
CLARKIA
CLOTBUR
COMFREY
COWBANE
COWSLIP

CROTTLE
(or crotal)
CUDWEED
DAY LILY
DITTANY
(or gas plant)
DOG ROSE
DOGWOOD
(or dogberry)
FELWORT
FIGWORT
FREESIA
FROGBIT
FUCHSIA
GENISTA
GENTIAN
GINGILI
GINSENG
GLADDON
GODETIA
GUAYULE
GUNNERA
HAWKBIT
HEATHER
HEMLOCK
HENBANE
HOGWEED
(or cow parsnip)
HONESTY
JASMINE
(or jessamine)
JEW'S EAR
JONQUIL
JUNIPER
KINGCUP
(or marsh
marigold)
LOBELIA

LUCERNE
(or alfalfa)
MANGOLD
(or mangel-wurzel)
MAYWEED
MERCURY
MILFOIL
(or yarrow)
MUDWORT
MUGWORT
MULLEIN
NEMESIA
NIGELLA
NONSUCH
(or nonesuch)
OAK FERN
OARWEED
OPUNTIA
PETUNIA
PICOTEE
PIGWEED
PRIMULA
PUCCOON
RAGWEED
RAGWORT
RAMPION
RAMSONS
RHATANY
RHODORA
RIBWORT
ROSEBAY
SAFFRON
SAGUARO
SANICLE
SAW-WORT
SEA KALE
SEA LILY
SEA PINK

(or thrift)
SEAWEED
SKIRRET
SPIGNEL
 (or baldmoney)
SYRINGA
TAGETES
TARWEED
TEA ROSE
THISTLE
TOBACCO
TREFOIL
TRUFFLE
VANILLA
VERBENA
VERVAIN
WALL RUE
WARATAH
WITLOOF
WOURALI
ZEDOARY

8
ACANTHUS
AGRIMONY
ALUM ROOT
 (or heuchera)
AMARANTH
ARUM LILY
ASPHODEL
AUBRETIA
 (or aubrietia)
AURICULA
 (or bear's ear)
BAYBERRY
 (or wax myrtle)
BEAR'S EAR
 (or auricula)

BEDSTRAW
BERBERIS
BINDWEED
BIRD'S EYE
BLUEBELL
 (or wood hyacinth)
BUCKBEAN
 (or bogbean)
BUDDLEIA
CALAMINT
CAMELLIA
CAMOMILE
 (or chamomile)
CANNABIS
 (or marijuana)
CAPSICUM
CATCHFLY
CAT'S FOOT
CENTAURY
CHARLOCK
 (or wild mustard)
CLEAVERS
 (or goosegrass)
CLEMATIS
CLUB MOSS
CLUBRUSH
COSTMARY
CROWFOOT
CRUCIFER
CYCLAMEN
DAFFODIL
DEATH CAP
DIANTHUS
DOGBERRY
 (or dogwood)
DROPWORT
DUCKWEED
DUMB CANE

EELGRASS
FIREWEED
FLAX LILY
 (or New
 Zealand flax)
FLEABANE
FLIXWEED
FLUELLEN
FOXGLOVE
FUMITORY
GARDENIA
GAS PLANT
 (or dittany)
GERANIUM
 (or pelargonium)
GLORY PEA
 (or clianthus,
 kaka-beak)
GLOXINIA
GOAT'S RUE
GOUTWEED
GROMWELL
GULFWEED
 (or sargassum)
HARD FERN
HAREBELL
HAWKWEED
HAWTHORN
 (or quickthorn,
 whitethorn)
HENEQUEN
HEUCHERA
 (or alum root)
HIBISCUS
HORNWORT
HYACINTH
ICE PLANT
JAPONICA

KAKA-BEAK
 (or clianthus,
 glory pea)
KNAPWEED
KNOTWEED
LADY FERN
LARKSPUR
LAVENDER
LENT LILY
LIVELONG
LOCOWEED
LUNGWORT
MAGNOLIA
MALE FERN
MANDRAKE
MARIGOLD
MESQUITE
MEZEREON
MILKWEED
MILKWORT
MOONSEED
MOONWORT
MOUSE-EAR
MUSK ROSE
MYOSOTIS
 (or forget-me-not)
NEPENTHE
NONESUCH
 (or nonsuch)
OLEANDER
 (or rosebay laurel)
OPOPANAX
OX-TONGUE
PATIENCE
PEAT MOSS
 (or bog moss)
PILEWORT (or
 lesser celandine)

PILLWORT
PIPEWORT
PLANTAIN
PLUMBAGO
POKEWEED
POLYPODY
PONDWEED
PRIMROSE
PRUNELLA
PUFFBALL
PURSLANE
ROCK ROSE
ROSEROOT
SAINFOIN
SALTBUSH
SALTWORT
SAMPHIRE
SANDWORT
SCABIOUS
SCAMMONY
SEAGRASS
SEA HEATH
SEA HOLLY
SELF-HEAL
SHADBUSH
SHAMROCK
SKULLCAP
SNOWDROP
SOAPWORT
SOWBREAD
SPEKBOOM
SPHAGNUM
STAPELIA
  (or carrion
  flower)
STARWORT
SUNDROPS
SWEET BAY

SWEET PEA
TAMARISK
TEA PLANT
TOADFLAX
TREE FERN
TUBEROSE
TURK'S CAP
TURNSOLE
VALERIAN
VERONICA
WISTARIA
  (or wisteria)
WISTERIA
  (or wistaria)
WOODBINE
WOODRUFF
WOODRUSH
WOOD SAGE
WORMWOOD
  (or absinth)
ZINGIBER

9
AARON'S ROD
ADDERWORT
AMARYLLIS
ARROWHEAD
ARROWROOT
ARTEMISIA
AUBRIETIA
  (or aubretia)
BALDMONEY
  (or spignel)
BEAR'S FOOT
BEECH FERN
BEE ORCHID
BIRD'S FOOT
BIRTHWORT

BLOODROOT
BOG MYRTLE
  (or sweet gale)
BRAKE FERN
BROMELIAD
BROOKLIME
BROOKWEED
BROOMRAPE
BUCKTHORN
BUTTERBUR
BUTTERCUP
CALENDULA
CALLA LILY
CANDYTUFT
CANNA LILY
CARNATION
CELANDINE
CERASTIUM
CHAMOMILE
  (or camomile)
CHICKWEED
CINERARIA
CLIANTHUS
  (or glory pea,
  kaka-beak)
CLOVE PINK
COCKLEBUR
COCKSCOMB
COLOCYNTH
COLTSFOOT
COLUMBINE
CORALLINE
CORALROOT
CROSSWORT
CUP LICHEN
DANDELION
DEVIL'S BIT
DOG VIOLET

EARTHSTAR
EDELWEISS
EGLANTINE
EUPHORBIA
EUPHRASIA
FIRETHORN
  (or pyracantha)
FLY AGARIC
FLY ORCHID
FORSYTHIA
GALINGALE
GLADIOLUS
GLASSWORT
GOLDEN ROD
GOOSEFOOT
GRAPEVINE
GROUND IVY
GROUNDSEL
GYPSYWORT
HARE'S FOOT
HELLEBORE
HERB PARIS
HOLLY FERN
HOLLYHOCK
HORSETAIL
HOUSELEEK
HYDRANGEA
JESSAMINE
  (or jasmine)
KNOTGRASS
LIVERWORT
LOUSEWORT
MAN ORCHID
MARE'S TAIL
MARIJUANA
  (or cannabis)
MARSH FERN
MARSHWORT

MAYFLOWER
  (or trailing arbutus)
MEADOW RUE
MILK VETCH
MISTLETOE
MONEYWORT
  (or creeping Jenny)
MONKSHOOD
MOSCHATEL
NARCISSUS
NAVELWORT
  (or pennywort)
NICOTIANA
  (or tobacco plant)
PATCHOULI
PEARLWORT
PELLITORY
PENNYWORT
  (or navelwort)
PETTY WHIN
PIGEON PEA
PIMPERNEL
POISON IVY
POISON OAK
PYRETHRUM
QUILLWORT
RED RATTLE
ROCK CRESS
  (or arabis)
ROYAL FERN
RUDBECKIA
SAFFLOWER
SAGEBRUSH
SARGASSUM
  (or gulfweed)
SAXIFRAGE
SHEEP'S BIT
SHOREWEED

SMARTWEED
SMOKE BUSH
SNAKEROOT
SNOWFLAKE
SPEARWORT
SPEEDWELL
SPICE BUSH
SPIKE MOSS
SPIKENARD
STINKHORN
STONECROP
STONEWORT
SUGAR BEET
SUNFLOWER
SWEET FLAG
  (or calamus)
SWEET GALE
  (or bog myrtle)
TAPE-GRASS
  (or ribbon-grass)
TIGER LILY
TOADSTOOL
TOOTHWORT
TWAYBLADE
VETCHLING
WAKE-ROBIN
  (or cuckoo pint)
WATER FERN
WATERLEAF
WATER LILY
WAX FLOWER
WAX MYRTLE
  (or bayberry)
WINEBERRY
WOLFSBANE
WOOD AVENS
  (or herb
  bennet)

10
ALEXANDERS
ARROWGRASS
ASARABACCA
ASPIDISTRA
BARRENWORT
BELLADONNA
  (or deadly
  nightshade)
BELLFLOWER
BLACKTHORN
BLUEBOTTLE
BURNET ROSE
BUSY LIZZIE
BUTTERWORT
BUTTONBUSH
CAMEL THORN
CHASTE TREE
CHINA ASTER
CINQUEFOIL
CORNCOCKLE
CORNFLOWER
COTTONWEED
COW PARSLEY
COW PARSNIP
  (or hogweed)
CRANESBILL
CUCKOO PINT
  (or wake-robin)
CURRY PLANT
DAMASK ROSE
DELPHINIUM
DRAGON ARUM
EASTER LILY
ELECAMPANE
FLEUR-DE-LIS
FOUR O'CLOCK
  (or marvel of

Peru)
FRANGIPANI
FRITILLARY
GOAT'S BEARD
GOLDEN SEAL
GOLDILOCKS
GOLD THREAD
GOOSEGRASS
  (or cleavers)
GREASEWOOD
GROUND PINE
GYPSOPHILA
HAWKSBEARD
HEART'S-EASE
  (or love-in-
  idleness)
HELIANTHUS
HELIOTROPE
HEMP-NETTLE
HERB BENNET
  (or wood avens)
HERB ROBERT
HOBBLEBUSH
IMMORTELLE
  (or everlasting)
INDIAN PIPE
INDIAN POKE
JIMSON WEED
  (or thorn apple)
JUJUBE BUSH
KAFFIR LILY
LADY'S SMOCK
  (or cuckoo flower)
MAIDENHAIR
MARGUERITE
  (or ox-eye daisy)
MASTERWORT
MIGNONETTE

MOCK ORANGE
MONKEY ROPE
MONTBRETIA
MOONFLOWER
NASTURTIUM
NIGHTSHADE
NIPPLEWORT
OX-EYE DAISY
 (or marguerite)
PENNYCRESS
PEPPERMINT
PEPPERWORT
PERIWINKLE
POINSETTIA
POLYANTHUS
POTENTILLA
PULMONARIA
PYRACANTHA
 (or firethorn)
QUICKTHORN
 (or hawthorn,
 whitethorn)
RANUNCULUS
RESTHARROW
ROSE MALLOW
SARRACENIA
SCORZONERA
 (or viper's grass)
SHIELD FERN
SILVERWEED
SNAPDRAGON
 (or antirrhinum)
SNEEZEWEED
SNEEZEWORT
SOW THISTLE
SPIDERWORT
STAVESACRE
STITCHWORT

STORKSBILL
SUPPLEJACK
SWEET BRIAR
THALE CRESS
THORN APPLE
 (or jimson weed)
TOUCH-ME-NOT
 (or noli me
 tangere)
TREE MALLOW
TROPAEOLUM
TUMBLEWEED
VELVETLEAF
VENUS'S COMB
 (or shepherd's
 needle)
WALLFLOWER
WALL PEPPER
WALL ROCKET
WELSH POPPY
WHITETHORN
 (or hawthorn,
 quickthorn)
WILD GINGER
WILLOW HERB
WINDFLOWER
 (or anemone)
WITCH HAZEL
WOOD SORREL
YELLOW-WORT

11
AARON'S BEARD
 (or Rose of
 Sharon)
ADAM'S NEEDLE
 (or yucca)
ANTIRRHINUM

(or snapdragon)
BALLOON VINE
BEAR'S BREECH
BITTERCRESS
BITTERSWEET
 (or woody
 nightshade)
BLADDERWORT
BOG ASPHODEL
BOTTLEBRUSH
BRISTLE FERN
BUR-MARIGOLD
BURNING BUSH
CABBAGE PALM
CABBAGE ROSE
CAPE JASMINE
CAPER SPURGE
CONVOLVULUS
COTONEASTER
COTTON GRASS
COTTON PLANT
DOG'S MERCURY
DUSTY MILLER
DYER'S ROCKET
 (or weld)
ELEPHANT EAR
EVERLASTING
 (or immortelle)
FORGET-ME-NOT
 (or myosotis)
GILLYFLOWER
GLOBEFLOWER
GREEN DRAGON
GUELDER ROSE
HART'S TONGUE
HEDGE GARLIC
 (or Jack-by-the-
 hedge)

HELLEBORINE
HONEYSUCKLE
HORNED POPPY
ICELAND MOSS
IPECACUANHA
KIDNEY VETCH
 (or lady's finger)
LABRADOR TEA
LADY'S FINGER
 (or kidney vetch)
LADY'S MANTLE
LAURUSTINUS
LONDON PRIDE
 (or none-so-
 pretty)
LOOSESTRIFE
LOVE-IN-A-MIST
MADONNA LILY
MARSH MALLOW
MEADOWSWEET
MILK THISTLE
MOUTAN PEONY
MUSK THISTLE
NAKED LADIES
 (or meadow
 saffron)
PARMA VIOLET
PARROT TULIP
PELARGONIUM
 (or geranium)
RAGGED ROBIN
RED-HOT POKER
RIBBON-GRASS
 (or tape-grass)
RUPTUREWORT
SAINTPAULIA
 (or African violet)
SCURVY GRASS

SEA LAVENDER
SEA PURSLANE
SILVERBERRY
SPANISH MOSS
SPINACH BEET
STAR THISTLE
STEPHANOTIS
SULPHUR TUFT
SWALLOW-WORT
SWEET CICELY
  (or myrrh)
SWEET ROCKET
SWEET SULTAN
SWEET VIOLET
TRUMPET VINE
VIPER'S GRASS
  (or scorzonera)
WATER PEPPER
WATER VIOLET
WILD MUSTARD
  (or charlock)
WINTERBERRY
WINTER CRESS
WINTERGREEN
  (or checkerberry)
WOOD ANEMONE

12
ADDER'S TONGUE
AMERICAN ALOE
  (or century plant)
BLADDER SENNA
BLADDERWRACK
BUFFALO THORN
CENTURY PLANT
  (or American aloe)
CHECKERBERRY
  (or wintergreen)

CHERRY LAUREL
CHRIST'S THORN
CORN MARIGOLD
CREOSOTE BUSH
CUCKOO FLOWER
  (or lady's smock)
EASTER CACTUS
FOOL'S PARSLEY
GLOBE THISTLE
GOLDEN WATTLE
GROUND CHERRY
HEMP AGRIMONY
HOTTENTOT FIG
HOUND'S TONGUE
ICELAND POPPY
JACOB'S LADDER
LADY'S SLIPPER
LEOPARD'S BANE
MANGEL-WURZEL
  (or mangold)
MARTAGON LILY
MARVEL OF PERU
  (or four o'clock)
MONKEY FLOWER
MORNING GLORY
MULBERRY BUSH
NONE-SO-PRETTY
  (or London pride)
OLD MAN'S BEARD
  (or traveller's joy)
PARSLEY PIERT
PASQUE FLOWER
PHEASANT'S EYE
PICKERELWEED
PINK PURSLANE
PITCHER PLANT
REINDEER MOSS
RHODODENDRON

ROSE OF SHARON
  (or Aaron's beard)
SALPIGLOSSIS
SEA BUCKTHORN
SHEEP'S SORREL
SHIRLEY POPPY
SKUNK CABBAGE
SNOWBALL BUSH
SNOW-IN-SUMMER
SOLOMON'S SEAL
SOUTHERNWOOD
  (or old man)
SPANISH BROOM
SPRING BEAUTY
SPURGE LAUREL
STAGHORN FERN
SWEET WILLIAM
TOBACCO PLANT
  (or nicotiana)
TRADESCANTIA
VENUS FLYTRAP
VIRGIN'S BOWER
WANDERING JEW
WATER HEMLOCK
WATER MILFOIL
WATER PARSNIP
WATER SOLDIER
WHITLOW-GRASS
WINTER CHERRY
WOOD HYACINTH
  (or bluebell)
YELLOW RATTLE
YORKSHIRE FOG

13
AFRICAN VIOLET
  (or saintpaulia)
BLEEDING HEART

BOUGAINVILLEA
BUTCHER'S BROOM
BUTTERFLY WEED
CANADA THISTLE
CANARY CREEPER
CARRION FLOWER
  (or stapelia)
CHRISTMAS ROSE
CHRYSANTHEMUM
CRANBERRY TREE
CREEPING JENNY
  (or moneywort)
CROWN IMPERIAL
DUTCHMAN'S PIPE
FLANDERS POPPY
FLOWERING RUSH
GOOD KING HENRY
GRAPE HYACINTH
JERUSALEM SAGE
MARSH MARIGOLD
  (or kingcup)
MEADOW SAFFRON
  (or naked ladies)
MOUNTAIN AVENS
  (or dryas)
NOLI ME TANGERE
  (or touch-me-not)
PASSION FLOWER
PINEAPPLE WEED
ROSEBAY LAUREL
  (or oleander)
ROSE OF JERICHO
SCORPION SENNA
TRAVELLER'S JOY
  (or old man's beard)
VIPER'S BUGLOSS

VIRGINIA STOCK
WATER DROPWORT
WATER HAWTHORN
WATER PLANTAIN
WATER PURSLANE
WATER STARWORT
WAYFARING TREE
WINTER JASMINE
WITCHES' BUTTER
YELLOW JASMINE

14

ALDER BUCKTHORN
BELLADONNA LILY
CANTERBURY BELL
CARDINAL FLOWER
CHINCHERINCHEE
DYER'S GREENWEED
FRENCH MARIGOLD
GOLD OF PLEASURE
JACK-BY-THE-HEDGE
  (or hedge garlic)
JERUSALEM THORN
LOVE-IN-IDLENESS
  (or heart's-ease)
MAIDENHAIR FERN
MOUNTAIN LAUREL
NEW ZEALAND FLAX
  (or flax lily)
PRINCE'S FEATHER
SHEPHERD'S PURSE
SPANISH BAYONET
SPANISH NEEDLES
STINGING NETTLE
TELEGRAPH PLANT
YELLOW CENTAURY

15

BLACK NIGHTSHADE
BURNET SAXIFRAGE
BUTTERFLY ORCHID
CHRISTMAS CACTUS
CORNELIAN CHERRY
DOG'S TOOTH VIOLET
GOLDEN SAXIFRAGE
JACK-IN-THE-PULPIT
LESSER CELANDINE
  (or pilewort)
LILY OF THE VALLEY
MICHAELMAS DAISY
SHEPHERD'S NEEDLE
  (or Venus's comb)
STAR OF BETHLEHEM
TRAILING ARBUTUS
  (or mayflower)
VIRGINIA CREEPER
WOODY NIGHTSHADE
  (or bittersweet)

16

DEADLY NIGHTSHADE
  (or belladonna)
DEVIL'S PAINTBRUSH
FALSE HELLEBORINE
JAPANESE KNOTWEED
LOVE-LIES-BLEEDING
STURT'S DESERT ROSE

17

DUTCHMAN'S BREECHES

Science – Botany – TREES

3
ASH
BAY
BOX
ELM
FIG
FIR
GUM
KOA
OAK
SAL
ULE
YEW

4
AKEE
 (or ackee)
BAEL
BALM
BITO
DHAK
DIKA
ILEX
 (or holly oak,
 holm oak)
JACK
LIME
 (or linden)
NIPA
PALM
PEAR
PINE
PIPI
PLUM
POON

RATA
SAGO
SHEA
 (or karité)
TEAK
UPAS

5
ABELE
 (or white
 poplar)
ACKEE
 (or akee)
ALDER
ARGAN
ASPEN
 (or trembling
 poplar)
ASSAI
BALSA
BEECH
BIRCH
BOREE
BUNYA
 (or bunya
 bunya)
CACAO
CAROB
CEDAR
EBONY
ELDER
GUAVA
HAZEL
JAMBU
JARUL

KARRI
KAURI
KOKKO
 (or lebbek)
KOKUM
LARCH
LEMON
LILAC
MAHUA
MANGO
MAPLE
MVULE
MYALL
NGAIO
OLIVE
OSIER
PALAS
PAPAW
 (or papaya,
 pawpaw)
PIÑON
PIPAL
 (or peepul)
PLANE
ROBLE
ROWAN
 (or mountain
 ash)
SAPAN
SENNA
 (or cassia)
SITKA
SUMAC
 (or sumach)
TUART

WAHOO

6
ACAJOU
 (or cashew)
ALERCE
ALMOND
ANGICO
AROLLA
BANANA
BANYAN
 (or Indian fig)
BAOBAB
BOG OAK
BONSAI
BO TREE
BRAZIL
BURITI
CASHEW
 (or acajou)
CASSIA
 (or senna)
CHENAR
CHERRY
CITRON
CITRUS
COHUNE
CORDON
DEODAR
DURIAN
FUSTIC
GINKGO
 (or maidenhair
 tree)
GOMUTI

GRUGRU
GURJUN
IDIGBO
ILLIPE
JARRAH
JUPATI
KAMAHI
KAMALA
KARAKA
KARITÉ
 (or shea)
KITTUL
KOWHAI
LAUREL
LEBBEK
 (or kokko)
LICHEE
 (or lychee)
LINDEN
 (or lime)
LONGAN
LYCHEE
 (or lichee)
MALLEE
MAMMEE
MANUKA
MASTIC
 (or lentisc)
MEDLAR
MIRITI
OBECHE
ORANGE
PAPAYA
 (or papaw,
 pawpaw)

PAWPAW
  (or papaw,
  papaya)
PEEPUL (or pipal)
POMELO
POPLAR
RAFFIA
RED-BUD
RED GUM
SALLOW
SANDAL
SAPELE
SAPPAN
SAXAUL
SOUARI
SPRUCE
SUMACH
  (or sumac)
TAMANU
TARATA
  (or lemonwood)
TITOKI
TUPELO
WALNUT
WILLOW

7
AMBATCH
APRICOT
BABASSU
BAY TREE
BEBEERU
BILIMBI
  (or cucumber
  tree)
BOX TREE
BUCKEYE
CAMWOOD

CHAMPAK
COCONUT
CONIFER
COQUITO
CORK OAK
COW TREE
CYPRESS
DOGWOOD
ELM TREE
FAN PALM
FIG TREE
FIR TREE
GEEBUNG
GUM TREE
HICKORY
HOG PLUM
HOLM OAK
  (or holly oak,
  ilex)
HOOP ASH
KERUING
LENTISC
  (or mastic)
LIVE OAK
LUMBANG
MADROÑO
MARGOSA
NUT TREE
OAKLING
OAK TREE
OIL PALM
PALMYRA
PAXIUBA
POLLARD
QUASSIA
REDWOOD
SAPLING
SEQUOIA

  (or California
  redwood)
SERVICE
SHITTAH
SOURSOP
TALIPOT
WALLABA
WAX PALM
WAX TREE
WYCH ELM
YEW TREE

8
BASSWOOD
BEEFWOOD
BLACKBOY
  (or grass tree)
CALABASH
CARNAUBA
CHESTNUT
CINCHONA
CINNAMON
COOLABAH
  (or coolibah)
COOLIBAH
  (or coolabah)
CORKWOOD
CRAB TREE
DATE PALM
DOUM PALM
EUCALYPT
  (or eucalyptus)
GENIPAPO
GUAIACUM
  (or lignum vitae)
HARDWOOD
HOLLY OAK
  (or holm oak,

  ilex)
HORNBEAM
HUON PINE
IRONBARK
IRONWOOD
JACK PINE
JACK TREE
JELUTONG
LABURNUM
LACEBARK
LIME TREE
  (or linden tree)
LOBLOLLY
MAHOGANY
MANNA ASH
MESQUITE
  (or algarroba)
MULBERRY
NAPA PALM
OPOPANAX
  (or sponge tree)
PALMETTO
PALM TREE
PANDANUS
  (or screw pine)
PEAR TREE
PINASTER
PINE TREE
PLUM TREE
QUANDONG
RAIN TREE
RAMBUTAN
RED CEDAR
ROSEWOOD
SAGO PALM
SEA GRAPE
SHEA TREE
SILKY OAK

SOFTWOOD
SUGAR GUM
SYCAMORE
TAMARACK
TAMARIND
UPAS TREE
WHITE ASH

9
AILANTHUS
ALGARROBA
(or mesquite)
APPLE TREE
BALSAM FIR
BLACKWOOD
BLOODWOOD
BREAD PALM
(or bread tree)
BREAD TREE
(or bread palm)
CANDLENUT
CARAMBOLA
CAROB TREE
CASUARINA
CHILE PINE
(or monkey
puzzle tree)
CORAL TREE
COURBARIL
DECIDUOUS
EVERGREEN
FLAME TREE
FRUIT TREE
GRASS TREE
(or blackboy)
HACKBERRY
INDIAN FIG
(or banyan)

IVORY PALM
JACARANDA
JUDAS TREE
KERMES OAK
KURRAJONG
LANCEWOOD
LEMONWOOD
(or tarata)
LEMON TREE
MACADAMIA
MYROBALAN
NUX VOMICA
PEACH TREE
PERSIMMON
PITCH PINE
PLANE TREE
POINCIANA
QUEBRACHO
ROSE APPLE
ROYAL PALM
SACRED FIG
SAPODILLA
SASSAFRAS
SATINWOOD
SCOTS PINE
SCREW PINE
(or pandanus)
SILVER FIR
SMOKE TREE
SNAKEWOOD
SOAPBERRY
STAR ANISE
STINKWOOD
STONE PINE
(or umbrella
pine)
TACAMAHAC
(or balsam

poplar)
TEREBINTH
TULIP TREE
TURKEY OAK
WHITEBEAM
WHITEWOOD
ZEBRAWOOD

10
AFRORMOSIA
ALMOND TREE
AROLLA PINE
BANANA TREE
BIRD CHERRY
BOTTLE TREE
BUNYA BUNYA
(or bunya)
BUTTONWOOD
(or buttonball
tree)
CALAMANDER
(or coromandel)
CHERRY TREE
CHINQUAPIN
COROMANDEL
(or calamander)
COTTONWOOD
CURTAIN FIG
DOUGLAS FIR
DRAGON TREE
DURMAST OAK
(or sessile oak)
EUCALYPTUS
(or eucalypt)
FLAMBOYANT
FOREST TREE
GOAT WILLOW
(or pussy willow)

GREENHEART
HACKMATACK
HEMLOCK FIR
LINDEN TREE
(or lime tree)
MANCHINEEL
MANGOSTEEN
MANNA LARCH
NETTLE TREE
ORANGE TREE
PAPER BIRCH
PRICKLY ASH
PUPUNHEIRA
RUBBER TREE
SANDALWOOD
SAND CHERRY
SESSILE OAK
(or durmast
oak)
SILVER TREE
SPONGE TREE
(or opopanax)
SUGAR MAPLE
TALLOW TREE
WEEPING ASH
WEEPING ELM
YELLOW-WOOD
YLANG-YLANG

11
AMBOYNA TREE
CABBAGE PALM
CABBAGE TREE
CAMPHOR TREE
CHAULMOOGRA
CLUSTER PINE
(or maritime
pine)

COCONUT PALM
COPPER BEECH
CRYPTOMERIA
(or Japanese
cedar)
DAWN REDWOOD
FALSE ACACIA
FEATHER PALM
HONEY LOCUST
LACQUER TREE
LIGNUM VITAE
(or guaiacum)
LOBLOLLY BAY
MAMMEE APPLE
MOUNTAIN ASH
(or rowan)
MULBERRY FIG
NORWAY MAPLE
OSAGE ORANGE
POMEGRANATE
PURPLE HEART
PUSSY WILLOW
(or goat willow)
SAUSAGE TREE
SERVICE TREE
SILVER BIRCH
SITKA SPRUCE
SLIPPERY ELM
STRINGY-BARK
TRUMPET TREE
WHITE POPLAR
(or abele)

12
ANGELICA TREE
BALSAM POPLAR
(or tacamahac)
BLUE QUANDONG
CALABASH TREE
CHERRY LAUREL
CHESTNUT TREE
CHIQUICHIQUI
CUCUMBER TREE
(or bilimbi)
GIANT REDWOOD
HERCULES' CLUB
LOBLOLLY PINE
MAMMEE SAPOTE
MARITIME PINE
(or cluster pine)
MASSARANDUBA
MONKEY PUZZLE
(or Chile pine)
NORWAY SPRUCE
SNOWDROP TREE
SWAMP CYPRESS
TREE OF HEAVEN
UMBRELLA PINE
(or stone pine)
WEEPING BIRCH

13
BRAZIL-NUT TREE
CAMPHOR LAUREL
CHRISTMAS TREE
HORSE CHESTNUT
JAPANESE CEDAR
(or cryptomeria)

MARMALADE TREE
PAPER MULBERRY
RED SANDALWOOD
SWAMP MAHOGANY
WEEPING CHERRY
WEEPING WILLOW

14
BUTTONBALL TREE
(or buttonwood)
CANNONBALL TREE
CEDAR OF LEBANON
JAPANESE MEDLAR
LOMBARDY POPLAR
MAIDENHAIR TREE
(or ginkgo)
STRAWBERRY TREE
TURPENTINE TREE

15
EMBLIC MYROBALAN
SHAGBARK HICKORY
TREMBLING POPLAR
(or aspen)
WESTERN RED CEDAR
WHITE SANDALWOOD

16
MONKEY PUZZLE TREE
(or Chile pine)

17
CALIFORNIA REDWOOD
(or sequoia)

Science – CHEMICAL ELEMENTS followed by their symbols

3
TIN Sn

4
GOLD Au
IRON Fe
LEAD Pb
NEON Ne
ZINC Zn

5
ARGON Ar
BORON B
RADON Rn
XENON Xe

6
BARIUM Ba
CARBON C
CERIUM Ce
COBALT Co
COPPER Cu
CURIUM Cm
ERBIUM Er
HELIUM He
INDIUM In
IODINE I
NICKEL Ni
OSMIUM Os
OXYGEN O
RADIUM Ra
SILVER Ag
SODIUM Na

7
ARSENIC As
BISMUTH Bi
BOHRIUM Bh
BROMINE Br
CADMIUM Cd
CAESIUM Cs
CALCIUM Ca
DUBNIUM Db
FERMIUM Fm
GALLIUM Ga
HAFNIUM Hf
HASSIUM Hs
HOLMIUM Ho
IRIDIUM Ir
KRYPTON Kr
LITHIUM Li
MERCURY Hg
NIOBIUM Nb
RHENIUM Re
RHODIUM Rh
SILICON Si
SULPHUR S
TERBIUM Tb
THORIUM Th
THULIUM Tm
URANIUM U
WOLFRAM (now
    tungsten)
YTTRIUM Y

8
ACTINIUM Ac

ANTIMONY Sb
ASTATINE At
CHLORINE Cl
CHROMIUM Cr
EUROPIUM Eu
FLUORINE F
FRANCIUM Fr
HALOGENS (group)
HYDROGEN H
LUTETIUM Lu
NITROGEN N
NOBELIUM No
PLATINUM Pt
POLONIUM Po
RUBIDIUM Rb
SAMARIUM Sm
SCANDIUM Sc
SELENIUM Se
TANTALUM Ta
THALLIUM Tl
TITANIUM Ti
TUNGSTEN W
UNUNBIUM Uub
VANADIUM V

9
ACTINIDES (group)
ALUMINIUM Al
AMERICIUM Am
BERKELIUM Bk
BERYLLIUM Be
BRIMSTONE (now
    Sulphur)

GERMANIUM Ge
LANTHANUM La
MAGNESIUM Mg
MANGANESE Mn
NEODYMIUM Nd
NEPTUNIUM Np
NON-METALS (group)
PALLADIUM Pd
PLUTONIUM Pu
POTASSIUM K
RUTHENIUM Ru
STRONTIUM Sr
TELLURIUM Te
UNUNTRIUM Uut
YTTERBIUM Yb
ZIRCONIUM Zr

10
DYSPROSIUM Dy
GADOLINIUM Gd
LAWRENCIUM Lr
MEITNERIUM Mt
METALLOIDS (group)
MOLYBDENUM Mo
NOBLE GASES (group)
PHOSPHORUS P
POOR METALS (group)
PROMETHIUM Pm
SEABORGIUM Sg
TECHNETIUM Tc
UNUNHEXIUM Uuh
UNUNOCTIUM Uuo

11
CALIFORNIUM Cf
EINSTEINIUM Es
LANTHANIDES (group)
MENDELEVIUM Md
QUICKSILVER
(now mercury)
ROENTGENIUM Rg
UNUNPENTIUM Uup

UNUNQUADIUM Uuq
UNUNSEPTIUM Uus

12
ALKALI METALS (group)
DARMSTADTIUM Ds
PRASEODYMIUM Pr
PROTACTINIUM Pa

13
RUTHERFORDIUM Rf

16
TRANSITION METALS (group)

19
ALKALINE EARTH METALS
(group)

Science – INVENTORS

3
GED William –
stereotyping
KAY John – flying shuttle
LEE William – knitting
machine
SAX Adolphe
– saxophone

4
BAER Ralph H – video
game console
BELL Alexander Graham
– loudspeaker,
telephone
BENZ Karl – 2-stroke car
engine
BIRÓ László – ballpoint
pen
BOYS CV – radio
micrometer
COLT Samuel – revolver
DAVY Sir Humphry
– miner's safety lamp

DREW Richard – Scotch
tape
FICK Adolf Eugen
– contact lenses
HUNT Walter – lock-
stitch sewing machine,
safety pin
IVES Frederic – halftone
engraving
KLIC Karl – rotogravure
LAKE Simon – periscope
LAND Edwin – Polaroid
camera
MOOG Dr Robert
– Moog synthesizer
OTIS Elisha – safety
elevator
OTTO Nikolaus –
4-stroke car engine
SHAW Percy – Catseye
SWAN Sir Joseph
– bromide paper,
electric light-bulb
TULL Jethro – seed drill

VERY EW – flare signal
WATT James
– condensing steam
engine
WOOD Dr Alexander
– hypodermic needle
YALE Linus – cylinder
lock
ZUSE Konrad
– programmable
computer

5
AIKEN Howard – digital
computer
BACON Roger
– magnifying glass
BAIRD John Logie
– mechanical television
BÁNKI Donát
– carburettor, co-
inventor with Csonka
BAUMÉ Antoine – scale
hydrometer

BOOTH H Cecil
– vacuum cleaner
BRAUN Karl – cathode
ray tube
BUTTS Alfred – Scrabble
CARRÉ Ferdinand
– refrigerator
CHANG MC –
contraceptive pill, co-
inventor with Pincus
DEWAR Sir James
– vacuum flask
DIEHL Philip – electric
ceiling fan
DYSON Sir James
– bagless vacuum
cleaner
FABRE Henri – seaplane
FARIA James – AstroTurf,
co-inventor with
Wright
GABOR Dennis
– holography
GARNS Howard
– sudoku
GOULD Gordon – laser
GREEN George – electric
dental drill
GREGG David Paul
– laser disc
GROVE William – fuel
cell
HOPPS John – cardiac
pacemaker
JACOB Mary Phelps
– brassiere
KILBY Jack – integrated
circuit

KOLFF Willem – kidney
dialysis machine
MAGEE Carl – parking
meter
MAXIM Sir Hiram – self-
powered machine gun
MOORE Hiram
– combine harvester
MORSE Samuel
– telegraph
NOBEL Alfred
– dynamite
PAPIN Denis – pressure
cooker
PASCH Gustaf – safety
match
PERKY Henry – shredded
wheat
RITTY James – cash
register
RUBIK Ernö – Rubik's
cube
SMITH Francis – ship's
propeller
STONE Marvin
– drinking straw
TESLA Nikola
– induction motor,
Tesla coil
VOLTA Alessandro
– electric battery
WYNNE Arthur
– crossword puzzle

6
ARGAND Aimé – Argand
lamp
ASPDIN William

– Portland cement
BAYLIS Trevor
– clockwork radio
BOHLIN Nils – 3-point
safety belt
BRAMAH Joseph – beer
pump, hydraulic press
BUNSEN Robert
– Bunsen burner, co-
inventor with Desaga
CAYLEY George – glider
CHAPIN Daryl – solar
cell, co-inventor with
Fuller & Pearson
CLAUDE Georges
– neon lamp
CSONKA János
– carburettor, co-
inventor with Bánki
CUGNOT Nikolas-
Joseph – steam wagon
DARROW Charles
– Monopoly
DESAGA Peter – Bunsen
burner, co-inventor
with Bunsen
DIESEL Rudolf – diesel
engine
DONATI Giuseppe
– ocarina
DUNLOP John Boyd
– pneumatic tyre
ECKERT J Presper
– electronic computer,
co-inventor with
Mauchly
EDISON Thomas
– incandescent light-

bulb, kinetoscope, phonograph

FERRIS George W – Ferris wheel

FULLER Calvin – solar cell, co-inventor with Chapin & Pearson

FULLER R Buckminster – geodesic dome

FULTON Robert – steam-powered ship

GAGNAN Emile – aqualung, co-inventor with Cousteau

GALTON Francis – fingerprinting

GEIGER Hans – Geiger counter

GUNTER Edmund – Gunter's chain

HADLEY John – sextant

HORNBY Frank – Meccano

HUGHES David Edward – carbon microphone

JUDSON Whitcomb – zip fastener

KALMUS Dr Herbert – Technicolor

LARSEN Norm – WD-40

LARSON John – lie detector

LENOIR Jean – internal combustion engine

MCADAM John – macadamised road surface

MILLER John A – roller-coaster

MORGAN William – volleyball

MÜLLER Willy – automatic answering machine

NIEPCE Nicéphore – permanent photograph

NISSEN George – trampoline

NISSEN Peter – Nissen hut

NYBERG Carl – blowtorch

PARKES Alexander – celluloid

PETERS Dr Arno – equal area map projection

PINCUS Gregory – contraceptive pill, co-inventor with Chang

PUSKÁS Tivadar – telephone exchange

POLHEM Christopher – padlock

SAVERY Thomas – steam pump

SCHICK Jacob – electric razor

SINGER Isaac – practical sewing machine

SPERRY Elmer – gyrocompass

TALBOT William Fox – calotype

TEETOR Ralph – cruise control

TELLER Edward – hydrogen bomb

TOWNES Charles – maser

TUPPER Earl – Tupperware

WALKER Craven – lava lamp

WALKER John – friction match

WALLIS Sir Barnes – bouncing bomb

WALTON Frederick – linoleum

WRIGHT Orville & Wilbur – aeroplane

WRIGHT Robert – AstroTurf, co-inventor with Faria

7

ALBERTI Leon – anemometer

BARDEEN John – transistor, co-inventor with Brattain & Shockley

BISSELL Melville – carpet sweeper

BRADHAM Caleb – Pepsi Cola

BRAILLE Louis – 'reading' system for the blind

BUDDING Edwin – lawnmower

CARLSON Chester F

– photocopier
CARRIER Willis – air conditioning
COCHRAN Josephine – dishwasher
CURTISS Glenn – aileron
DAIMLER Gottlieb – petrol engine, co-inventor with Maybach
DICKSON James – terylene, co-inventor with John Whinfield
EASTMAN George – roll film
FARADAY Michael – electromagnetic generator
FOGARTY Thomas – balloon catheter
GATLING Richard – rapid fire gun
GLIDDEN Carlos – practical typewriter, co-inventor with Scholes
GLIDDEN Joseph H – barbed wire
GREGORY James – reflecting telescope
HANDLER Ruth – Barbie doll
LAENNEC René – stethoscope
LANSTON Tolbert – monotype
LUMIÈRE Auguste &

Louis – ciné camera
MARCONI Guglielmo – wireless
MAUCHLY John – electronic computer, co-inventor with Eckert
MAYBACH Wilhelm – petrol engine, co-inventor with Daimler
MESTRAL George de – Velcro
MURDOCK William – gas lighting
NEILSON James – hot blast furnace
PARSONS Sir Charles – turbine steamship
PEARSON Gerald – solar cell, co-inventor with Chapin & Fuller
POENARU Petrache – fountain pen
POULSEN Valdemar – tape recorder
RÖNTGEN Wilhelm – X-ray machine
RUSSELL James – compact disc
SCHOLES Christopher – practical typewriter, co-inventor with Glidden
SEGALAS Pierre – endoscope
SOBRERO Ascanio – nitroglycerine

STANLEY William – electric transformer
WHEELER Dr Schuyler – electric fan
WHITNEY Eli – cotton gin
WHITTLE Sir Frank – jet engine

8

AYSCOUGH James – sunglasses
BEAUFORT Sir Francis – wind scale
BERLINER Emile – gramophone
BESSEMER Henry – steel converter
BIRDSEYE Clarence – frozen food process
BLODGETT Katherine – non-reflective glass
BRATTAIN Walter – transistor, co-inventor with Bardeen & Shockley
BREWSTER Sir David – kaleidoscope
BROWNING John – automatic rifle
BUSHNELL David – 'Turtle' or combat submarine
CHRISTIE Samuel Hunter – Wheatstone bridge
COUSTEAU Jacques – aqualung, co-inventor

with Gagnan
CROMPTON Samuel
– spinning mule
DAGUERRE Louis
– Daguerreotype
EVINRUDE Oli
– outboard motor
FOUCAULT Léon
– gyroscope
FRANKLIN Benjamin
– bifocals, lightning
rod, odometer
GILLETTE King C
– safety razor
GOLDMARK Peter
– long-playing record
GOODYEAR Charles
– vulcanised rubber
HANCHETT Waldo
– dentist's chair
HARRISON John
– chronometer
JACOBSEN Clayton
– jet ski
JACQUARD Joseph
– Jacquard loom
JEFFREYS Sir Alec – DNA
fingerprinting
MERCATOR Gerardus
– cylindrical map
projection
MICHELIN Édouard
– inflatable car tyre
NAISMITH James
– basketball
NEWCOMEN Thomas
– steam engine
OUGHTRED William

– slide rule
PHILLIPS Henry
– Phillips head screw
PLANTSON Anthony
– dental plate
PLUNKETT Roy – Teflon
SHOCKLEY William
– transistor, co-
inventor with Bardeen
& Brattain
SHRAPNEL Henry
– shrapnel shell
SIKORSKY Igor
– helicopter
STURGEON William
– electromagnet
TILGHMAN Benjamin
– sandblasting
WINCHELL Paul
– artificial heart
ZEPPELIN Count
Ferdinand von – rigid
airship
ZWORYKIN Vladimir
– practical television

9
ARKWRIGHT Richard
– spinning frame
ARMSTRONG Sir
William – hydraulic
crane
ATANASOFF John
– programmable
computer
BAEKELAND Leo
– Bakelite,
photographic paper

BLANCHARD Jean-
Pierre – parachute
BURROUGHS William
– commercial adding
machine
CAILLETET Louis
– altimeter
CAROTHERS Wallace
– neoprene, nylon
COCKERELL Sir
Christopher
– hovercraft
ENGELBART Dr Douglas
– computer mouse
FESSENDEN Reginald
– radio telephone
GASCOIGNE William
– micrometer
GUILLOTIN Dr Joseph
– guillotine
GUTENBERG Johannes
– printing press
LAUTERBUR Paul – MRI
scanner, co-inventor
with Mansfield
MACINTOSH Charles
– waterproof fabrics
MACMILLAN
Kirkpatrick – practical
bicycle
MANSFIELD Sir Peter
– MRI scanner,
co-inventor with
Lauterbur
MCCORMICK Cyrus
– mechanical reaper
PEMBERTON Dr John
– Coca Cola

PONIATOFF Alexander
– videotape recorder
SPILSBURY John
– jigsaw puzzle
STEVENSON Thomas
– lighthouse lighting
system
WHINFIELD John –
terylene, co-inventor
with Dickson
WHITEHEAD Robert
– self-propelled
torpedo
WHITWORTH Sir
Joseph – screw thread
standardisation

10

BERNERS-LEE Sir Tim
– world wide web
BOMBARDIER
Joseph-Armand
– snowmobile
CARTWRIGHT Edmund
– power loom
CRISTOFORI
Bartolomeo

– pianoforte
DE LA CIERVA Juan
– autogyro
FAHNESTOCK Samuel
– soda fountain
FAHRENHEIT Gabriel –
mercury thermometer
FARNSWORTH Philo
– electronic television
HARGREAVES James
– spinning jenny
HARRINGTON Sir John
– water closet
LANCHESTER Frederick
– disc brake
LIPPERSHEY Hans
– telescope
SENEFELDER Alois
– lithography
STEPHENSON George
– practical steam
locomotive
TORRICELLI Evangelista
– barometer
TREVITHICK Richard
– steam locomotive
WATSON-WATT Sir

Robert – radar
WHEATSTONE Charles
– concertina,
stereoscope

11

BASKERVILLE John
– advanced printing
fonts
MÈGE-MOURIÉS
Hippolyte – margarine
MONTGOLFIER Jacques
& Joseph – hot-air
balloon

12

FRIESE-GREENE William
– cinematography
MERGENTHALER
Ottmar – linotype
WESTINGHOUSE
George – air brake

13

BRANDENBERGER
Jacques – cellophane

Science – Mathematics – MATHEMATICAL TERMS

3	MAT	TOT	BASE	DUAD	LINE	OVAL	ROOT
ADD	ODD		CONE	DUAL	LOCI	PLUS	SIDE
ARC	RAY	**4**	COSH	DYAD	LUNE	POLE	SIGN
COS	SET	APEX	COTH	EDGE	MEAN	RANK	SINE
COT	SUM	AREA	CUBE	EVEN	MODE	RATE	SINH
LOG	TAN	AXIS	CUSP	FACE	NODE	RING	STAR

SURD
TANH
TERM
TRIG
UNIT

5
ACUTE
ANGLE
ARRAY
AXIOM
CHART
CHORD
CONIC
COSEC
COSET
COTAN
COUNT
CURVE
DECAD
DEPTH
DIGIT
FIELD
FOCUS
GRAPH
GROUP
HELIX
HEXAD
IMAGE
INDEX
LEMMA
LIMIT
LOCUS
LOGIC
MATHS
MINUS
OCTAD
ORDER

OVOID
PLANE
POINT
POWER
PRIME
PRISM
PROOF
RADII
RADIX
RANGE
RATIO
RHOMB
SCALE
SHAPE
SLOPE
SOLID
TABLE
TALLY
TORUS
TOTAL
TRIAD
UNITY
VALUE
WHOLE
WIDTH

6
ABACUS
AFFINE
AMOUNT
BINARY
BISECT
CENTRE
CIPHER
CIRCLE
COLUMN
CONICS
CONOID

CONVEX
CORNER
COSINE
CUBAGE
CUBING
CUBOID
DEGREE
DENARY
DIVIDE
DOMAIN
ENNEAD
FACTOR
FAMILY
FIGURE
GNOMON
HEIGHT
HEPTAD
LENGTH
LINEAR
LOG-LOG
MATRIX
MEDIAN
METRIC
MODULO
MOMENT
NORMAL
NUMBER
OBLATE
OBLONG
OBTUSE
OCTANT
ORIGIN
PENCIL
PENTAD
PERIOD
RADIAL
RADIAN
RADIUS

RECKON
SECANT
SECTOR
SERIES
SPHERE
SPIRAL
SQUARE
SUBSET
SYMBOL
TENSOR
TETRAD
VECTOR
VERTEX
VOLUME

7
ALGEBRA
ALIQUOT
ANNULUS
ANTILOG
APOTHEM
ASTROID
AVERAGE
BALANCE
BREADTH
CONCAVE
CYCLOID
DECAGON
DECIMAL
DIAGRAM
DIAMOND
DIVISOR
ELLIPSE
EVOLUTE
EXAMPLE
FLUXION
FORMULA
FRACTAL

FRUSTUM
HEXAGON
INDICES
INTEGER
INVERSE
LOGICAL
LOZENGE
MAPPING
MAXIMUM
MINIMUM
MINUEND
MODULUS
NETWORK
NONAGON
NUMERAL
OBLIQUE
OCTAGON
OPERAND
ORDINAL
PER CENT
POLYGON
PROBLEM
PRODUCT
PROLATE
PYRAMID
QUANTIC
QUARTIC
RADICAL
RHOMBUS
SECTION
SEGMENT
SUMMAND
SURFACE
TANGENT
TERNARY
THEOREM
TRISECT
UNKNOWN

VARIATE

8
ABSCISSA
ADDITION
ANALYSIS
ARGUMENT
BAR CHART
BAR GRAPH
BINOMIAL
BISECTOR
CALCULUS
CAPACITY
CARDINAL
CARDIOID
CATENARY
CENTROID
CIRCULAR
CONCHOID
CONSTANT
CONVERSE
COSECANT
COUNTING
CRESCENT
CUBATURE
CUBE ROOT
CYLINDER
DIAGONAL
DIAMETER
DIHEDRAL
DISTANCE
DIVIDEND
DIVISION
EPICYCLE
EQUALITY
EQUATION
EVALUATE
EXPONENT

FRACTION	RATIONAL	COTANGENT	NUMERICAL	DUODECIMAL
FUNCTION	REPETEND	CURVATURE	PARAMETER	EIGENVALUE
GEODESIC	RHOMBOID	DATUM LINE	PENTAGRAM	ELLIPTICAL
GEOMETRY	ROTATION	DEDUCTION	PERIMETER	EPICYCLOID
GRADIENT	SEQUENCE	DIMENSION	POSTULATE	EQUALS SIGN
HARMONIC	SINE WAVE	DIRECTRIX	QUADRATIC	EQUIVALENT
HEPTAGON	SINUSOID	DODECAGON	RECKONING	EVALUATION
HEXAGRAM	SOLUTION	ECCENTRIC	RECTANGLE	EXPRESSION
INCENTRE	SPHEROID	ELEVATION	REDUCTION	GENERATRIX
INFINITE	SPHERULE	ELLIPSOID	RE-ENTRANT	GOLDEN MEAN
INFINITY	SQUARING	ENNEAGRAM	REMAINDER	GRAND TOTAL
INSCRIBE	SUBTENSE	ENUMERATE	SET THEORY	HEMISPHERE
INTEGRAL	SUBTRACT	EVOLUTION	SINE CURVE	HENDECAGON
INVOLUTE	SUM TOTAL	FACTORIAL	SPHERICAL	HEXAHEDRON
LOGISTIC	SYMMETRY	FACTORISE	STATISTIC	HORIZONTAL
MANIFOLD	TABULATE	FLOW CHART	STERADIAN	HYPOTENUSE
MANTISSA	TANGENCY	GENERATOR	SUBDIVIDE	INEQUALITY
MATRICES	TETRAGON	GEOMETRIC	SUMMATION	INVOLUTION
MONOMIAL	TOPOLOGY	HAVERSINE	TETRAGRAM	IRRATIONAL
MULTIPLE	TRACTRIX	HEMICYCLE	TRAPEZIUM	MULTIPLIER
MULTIPLY	TRIANGLE	HISTOGRAM	TRAPEZOID	NUMERATION
NEGATIVE	TROCHOID	HODOGRAPH	TRINOMIAL	OCTAHEDRON
NOMOGRAM	TRUNCATE	HYPERBOLA	TRISECTOR	PARABALOID
NOTATION	VARIABLE	INCREMENT		PERCENTAGE
NUMERATE	VARIANCE	INTEGRAND	**10**	PERCENTILE
OPERATOR	VERTICAL	INTEGRATE	ACUTE ANGLE	POLYHEDRON
ORDINATE	VINCULUM	INTERCEPT	ANTECEDENT	POLYNOMIAL
PARABOLA		INTERSECT	ARITHMETIC	PROJECTION
PARALLEL	**9**	INVARIANT	CALCULATOR	PROPORTION
PENTAGON	AGGREGATE	INVERSION	COMPLEMENT	QUADRANGLE
PIE CHART	ALGORITHM	LINEARITY	CONCENTRIC	QUADRATURE
PLUS SIGN	AMPLITUDE	LOGARITHM	CONCURRENT	QUATERNION
POSITIVE	ASYMPTOTE	MAJOR AXIS	CONVERGENT	RECIPROCAL
PRISMOID	BILATERAL	MINOR AXIS	CO-ORDINATE	REGRESSION
QUADRANT	BISECTION	MINUS SIGN	DECAHEDRON	RIGHT ANGLE
QUANTITY	CONFIGURE	NOMOGRAPH	DERIVATIVE	SEMICIRCLE
QUARTILE	CONGRUENT	NUMBERING	DIFFERENCE	SOLID ANGLE
QUOTIENT	COROLLARY	NUMERATOR	DISPERSION	SQUARE ROOT

STATISTICS
SUBTRAHEND
SUPPLEMENT
TABULATION
TANGENTIAL
TESSELLATE
TRIANGULAR
TRILATERAL
TRISECTION
TRUNCATION
TRUTH TABLE

11
ASSES' BRIDGE
  (or pons
  asinorum)
BINARY DIGIT
CALCULATION
COEFFICIENT
COMBINATION
CONCURRENCE
CONVERGENCE
CONVOLUTION
CO-ORDINATES
CURVILINEAR
DENOMINATOR
DETERMINANT
ELLIPTICITY
ENUMERATION
EQUIANGULAR
EXTRAPOLATE
FACTORISING
GEOMETRICAL
GREAT CIRCLE
HEXADECIMAL
HYPERBOLOID
HYPOCYCLOID
ICOSAHEDRON

INCONGRUENT
INDEX NUMBER
INDIVISIBLE
INTEGRATION
INTERPOLATE
KLEIN BOTTLE
LOGARITHMIC
MAGIC NUMBER
MAGIC SQUARE
MATHEMATICS
MENSURATION
METRICATION
MÖBIUS STRIP
NAPIER'S RODS
OBTUSE ANGLE
PERMUTATION
PRIME NUMBER
PROBABILITY
PROGRESSION
PROPOSITION
RECTANGULAR
RECTILINEAR
REFLEX ANGLE
RULE OF THREE
SEMI-ELLIPSE
SEXAGESIMAL
SMALL CIRCLE
SUBDIVISION
SUBMULTIPLE
SUBTRACTION
TETRAHEDRON
TRANSLATION
TRANSVERSAL
VENN DIAGRAM
WHOLE NUMBER

12
ARITHMETICAL

BINARY SYSTEM
CIRCUMCIRCLE
CIRCUMSCRIBE
CONIC SECTION
DECIMAL PLACE
DECIMAL POINT
DIFFERENTIAL
DISCRIMINANT
DIVISIBILITY
DIVISION SIGN
DODECAHEDRON
ECCENTRICITY
EQUIDISTANCE
EVOLUTE CURVE
GEODESIC LINE
HARMONIC MEAN
HEMISPHEROID
INVERSE RATIO
LONG DIVISION
MATHEMATICAL
MULTIPLICAND
NAPIER'S BONES
NEGATIVE SIGN
NUMBER THEORY
PONS ASINORUM
  (or asses' bridge)
POSITIVE SIGN
PROPORTIONAL
QUADRINOMIAL
RADIUS VECTOR
RANDOM NUMBER
REGULAR SOLID
RHOMBOHEDRON
SEMI-CIRCULAR
SEMI-CYLINDER
SEMI-DIAMETER
SLIDING SCALE
STRAIGHT LINE

TESSELLATION
TRIGONOMETRY
UNIVERSAL SET

13
ANTILOGARITHM
APPROXIMATION
ARABIC NUMERAL
CIRCUMFERENCE
COMPLEX NUMBER
CONCENTRICITY
CONFIGURATION
DIFFERENTIATE
EXTERIOR ANGLE
EXTRAPOLATION
FACTORISATION
GEOMETRIC MEAN
GOLDEN SECTION
IMAGINARY LINE
INFINITESIMAL
INTERIOR ANGLE
INTERQUARTILE
INTERPOLATION
MANDELBROT SET
NATURAL NUMBER
NEGATIVE ANGLE
NEIGHBOURHOOD
ORDINAL NUMBER
PARALLEL LINES
PARALLELOGRAM
PERFECT NUMBER
PERFECT SQUARE
PERPENDICULAR
PLATONIC SOLID
POLAR DISTANCE
POSITIVE ANGLE
QUADRATIC MEAN
QUADRILATERAL

SEMI-ELLIPTICAL
SHORT DIVISION
STANDARD ERROR
STRAIGHT ANGLE
TRAPEZIUM RULE
TRAPEZOHEDRON
TRIANGULARITY
TRIANGULATION
TROCHOID CURVE
VERTICLE ANGLE

14
ARITHMETIC MEAN
BOOLEAN ALGEBRA
CARDINAL NUMBER
CHARACTERISTIC
COMMON FRACTION
COMMON MULTIPLE
DECIMALISATION
DIAGONAL MATRIX
DIFFERENTIATOR
HYPERBOLIC SINE
IDENTITY MATRIX

IMAGINARY POINT
INDIVISIBILITY
MISCALCULATION
MULTIPLICATION
OBLATE SPHEROID
PARALLELEPIPED
PROBLEM-SOLVING
PROPER FACTION
RATIONAL NUMBER
RIEMANN SURFACE
TANGENTIAL LINE
TRANSFORMATION
TRANSVERSALITY
VULGAR FRACTION

15
BINOMIAL THEOREM
DIFFERENTIATION
FIBONACCI SERIES
GOLDEN RECTANGLE
LISSAJOUS FIGURE
NUMBER CRUNCHING
PROLATE SPHEROID

PURE MATHEMATICS
RIEMANNIAN SPACE
TRANSVERSAL LINE
TRIANGULAR PRISM
UNKNOWN QUANTITY

16
COMPLEX CONJUGATE
FIBONACCI NUMBERS
POLAR CO-ORDINATES

17
EQUIANGULAR SPIRAL
EUCLIDEAN GEOMETRY
GEOMETRICAL SERIES
HYPERBOLIC TANGENT
PYTHAGORAS' THEOREM
RIEMANN HYPOTHESIS

18
MULTIPLICATION SIGN
RIEMANNIAN GEOMETRY

Science – Mathematics – **MATHEMATICIANS**

4
ABEL Niels
VENN John
ZENO

5
BOOLE George
DIRAC Paul
EULER Leonhard
FREGE Gottlob

GAUSS Johann
GÖDEL Kurt
HARDY GH
JEANS James
KLEIN Felix
MONGE Gaspard
RADAU Rodolphe
SEGAL Irvine
WOODS Mary Lee

6
AGNESI Maria
BARROW Isaac
BOLYAI János
BRIGGS Henry
BUFFON George, Comte de
CANTOR Georg
CAUCHY Augustin
CAYLEY Arthur
CONWAY John Horton

CRAMER Gabriel
EUCLID
FERMAT Pierre
GALOIS Évariste
GUNTER Edmund
JACOBI Carl
JORDAN Camille
KEPLER Johannes
LOOMIS Elisha S
MARKOV Andrei
MÖBIUS August F
NAPIER John
NEWTON Sir Isaac
PAPPUS
PASCAL Blaise
PEIRCE Benjamin
RAMSEY Frank P
STEVIN Simon
STIFEL Michael
STOKES Sir George
TAYLOR Richard
THALES
TURING Alan
WESSEL Caspar
WIENER Norbert

7

BABBAGE Charles
CARDANO Girolamo
EUDOXUS
FOURIER Joseph
GALILEO
(or Galileo Galilei)
HERMITE Charles
HILBERT David
HUYGENS Christiaan
LAMBERT Johann
LAPLACE Pierre Simon

LEIBNIZ Gottfried
MAXWELL James
NEUMANN John van
POISSON Siméon-Denis
PTOLEMY
RIEMANN Bernhard
RUSSELL Earl Bertrand

8

DEDEKIND Richard
DE MOIVRE Abraham
DE MORGAN Augustus
EINSTEIN Albert
HAMILTON Sir William
LAGRANGE Joseph-Louis
LEGENDRE Adrien-Marie
LEONARDO
(or Leonardo da Vinci)
MERSENNE Marin
POINCARÉ Henri
PONCELET Jean-Victor
RHETICUS Georg
STIRLING James

9

AL-BUZJANI
BERNOULLI Johann
BRONOWSKI Jacob
CONDORCET Marquis
Marie
D'ALEMBERT Jean
DESARGUES Gérard
DESCARTES René
EDDINGTON Arthur
FIBONACCI Leonardo
KRONECKER Leopold
MACLAURIN Colin
RAMANUJAN Srinivasa

SYLVESTER James
WHITEHEAD Alfred North

10

ANAXAGORAS
ARCHIMEDES
COPERNICUS Nicolaus
DIOPHANTUS
HIPPARCHUS
KOLMOGOROV Andrei
MANDELBROT Benoit
NICOMACHUS
PYTHAGORAS
WHITEHOUSE John

11

AL-KHWARIZMI
ARISTARCHUS
LOBACHEVSKY Nikolai
OMAR KHAYYÁM
WEIERSTRASS Karl

12

ERATOSTHENES

13

REGIOMONTANUS

14

GALILEO GALILEI
(or Galileo)

15

LEONARDO DA VINCI
(or Leonardo)

16

LEJEUNE DIRICHLET Johann

Science – Mathematics – NUMBERS & FRACTIONS

3
NIL
ONE
SIX
TEN
TWO

4
FIVE
FOUR
HALF
NINE
ZERO

5
DOZEN
EIGHT
FIFTH
FIFTY
FORTY
GROSS
NINTH
SCORE
SEVEN
SIXTH
SIXTY
TENTH
THIRD
THREE

6
CIPHER
EIGHTH
EIGHTY
ELEVEN

FOURTH
GOOGOL
MYRIAD
NINETY
NOUGHT
THIRTY
TWELVE
TWENTY

7
BILLION
FIFTEEN
HUNDRED
MILLION
QUARTER
SEVENTH
SEVENTY
SIXTEEN
TWELFTH
UMPTEEN

8
EIGHTEEN
ELEVENTH
FIFTIETH
FIFTY-ONE
FIFTY-SIX
FIFTY-TWO
FORTIETH
FORTY-ONE
FORTY-SIX
FORTY-TWO
FOURTEEN
MILLIARD
NINETEEN

SIXTIETH
SIXTY-ONE
SIXTY-SIX
SIXTY-TWO
THIRTEEN
THOUSAND
TRILLION

9
BILLIONTH
EIGHTIETH
EIGHTY-ONE
EIGHTY-SIX
EIGHTY-TWO
FIFTEENTH
FIFTY-FIVE
FIFTY-FOUR
FIFTY-NINE
FORTY-FIVE
FORTY-FOUR
FORTY-NINE
FOURSCORE
HALF-DOZEN
HUNDREDTH
LONG DOZEN
MILLIONTH
NINETIETH
NINETY-ONE
NINETY-SIX
NINETY-TWO
SEVENTEEN
SIXTEENTH
SIXTY-FIVE
SIXTY-FOUR
SIXTY-NINE

SQUILLION
THIRTIETH
THIRTY-ONE
THIRTY-SIX
THIRTY-TWO
TWENTIETH
TWENTY-ONE
TWENTY-SIX
TWENTY-TWO
TWO FIFTHS
TWO THIRDS

10
EIGHTEENTH
EIGHTY-FIVE
EIGHTY-FOUR
EIGHTY-NINE
FIFTY-EIGHT
FIFTY-SEVEN
FIFTY-THREE
FIVE SIXTHS
FORTY-EIGHT
FORTY-SEVEN
FORTY-THREE
FOUR FIFTHS
FOURTEENTH
HALF A DOZEN
NINETEENTH
NINETY-FIVE
NINETY-FOUR
NINETY-NINE
SEVENTIETH
SEVENTY-ONE
SEVENTY-SIX
SEVENTY-TWO

SIX HUNDRED
SIXTY-EIGHT
SIXTY-SEVEN
SIXTY-THREE
THIRTEENTH
THIRTY-FIVE
THIRTY-FOUR
THIRTY-NINE
THOUSANDTH
THREESCORE
TRILLIONTH
TWENTY-FIVE
TWENTY-FOUR
TWENTY-NINE
TWO HUNDRED

11
BAKER'S DOZEN
EIGHTY-EIGHT
EIGHTY-SEVEN
EIGHTY-THREE
FIVE EIGHTHS
FIVE HUNDRED
FOUR HUNDRED
NINE HUNDRED
NINETY-EIGHT
NINETY-SEVEN
NINETY-THREE
SEVENTEENTH
SEVENTY-FIVE
SEVENTY-FOUR
SEVENTY-NINE
SIX SEVENTHS
TEN THOUSAND
THIRTY-EIGHT

THIRTY-SEVEN
THIRTY-THREE
THREE FIFTHS
TWENTY-EIGHT
TWENTY-SEVEN
TWENTY-THREE
TWO SEVENTHS

12
EIGHT HUNDRED
FIVE SEVENTHS
FOUR SEVENTHS
SEVEN EIGHTHS
SEVEN HUNDRED
SEVENTY-EIGHT
SEVENTY-SEVEN
SEVENTY-THREE

THREE EIGHTHS
THREE HUNDRED

13
THREE QUARTERS
THREE SEVENTHS

15
HUNDRED THOUSAND

Science – Meteorology – METEOROLOGICAL SEA AREAS   * = former area

4
SOLE
TYNE

5
DOVER
FORTH
LUNDY
MALIN
WIGHT

6
BAILEY

BISCAY
DOGGER
FISHER
HUMBER
THAMES
VIKING

7
FAEROES
FASTNET
FITZROY
FORTIES
ROCKALL

SHANNON

8
CROMARTY
FAIR ISLE
HEBRIDES
IRISH SEA
PLYMOUTH
PORTLAND

9
TRAFALGAR

10
FINISTERRE*
(now Fitzroy)
HELIGOLAND*
(now German Bight)

11
GERMAN BIGHT
NORTH UTSIRE
SOUTH UTSIRE

16
SOUTH-EAST ICELAND

Science – Meteorology – METEOROLOGICAL TERMS

3	EYE	SKY	BISE wind	COOL	FRET	HEAT
AIR	FOG	SUN	BLOW	CONE	GALE	HIGH
COL	HOT	WET	BORA wind	DAMP	GUST	HOAR
DEW	ICE		BORE	FLAW	HAAR	LULL
DRY	ICY	**4**	CALM	FLOW	HAIL	MELT
EBB	LOW	BANK	COLD	FÖHN wind	HAZE	MIST

PELT
POUR
RAIN
RIME
SCUD
SMOG
SNOW
SPIT
TEEM
THAW
TIDE
VANE
VEER
WIND

5
ALIZÉ wind
BLAST
BRUME
BURAN
CHILL
CLOUD
CLOSE
DRIFT
EAGRE
ETHER
FLOOD
FOGGY
FRONT
FROST
HALNY wind
MARIN wind
NOSER
QUAKE
RAINS
RAINY
SLEET
SLUSH

SONDE
SPATE
SPOUT
STORM
VIRGA
WATER
WINDY
ZONDA wind

6
AURORA
BAGUIO
BAYAMO wind
BREATH
BREEZE
CIRRUS cloud
CLOUDY
CORONA
DELUGE
FLURRY
FOGBOW
FREEZE
FROZEN
HABOOB wind
ICICLE
ISOBAR
ISOHEL
KHAZRI wind
KOSAVA wind
METEOR
MIZZLE
NIMBUS cloud
PILEUS cloud
SEICHE
SEREIN
SHOWER
SIMOOM wind
SOLANO wind

SQUALL
SULTRY
TEBBAD
TORRID
TRADES wind
TREMOR
TROUGH
VORTEX

7
AUREOLE
BACKING
BLUSTER
CELSIUS
CHINOOK wind
CLEMENT
CLIMATE
CUMULUS cloud
CYCLONE
DEWFALL
DRAUGHT
DRIZZLE
DROUGHT
EBB TIDE
ETESIAN wind
FOG BANK
GREGALE wind
ISOHYET
KHAMSIN wind
MELTING
MISTRAL wind
MONSOON wind
NORTHER wind
PAMPERO wind
PELTING
RAINBOW
SEA FRET
SEISMIC

SHAITAN
SIROCCO wind
SIZZLER
SOUTHER wind
SPATTER
STRATUS cloud
SUMATRA
TEEMING
TEMPEST
THAWING
THERMAL
THUNDER
TORNADO
TSUNAMI
TYPHOON
VEERING
WEATHER

8
ABLATION
AERONOMY
BLACK ICE
BLIZZARD
COLD SNAP
CYCLONIC
DEW POINT
DOWNPOUR
ELEMENTS
FIREBALL
FLOODING
FOGBOUND
HEADWIND
HEAT HAZE
HEATWAVE
HUMIDITY
ISOBRONT
ISOCHASM
ISOCHEIM

ISOCRYME
ISOPLETH
ISOTHERE
ISOTHERM
KUROSHIO
LEVANTER wind
LIBECCIO wind
LIGHT AIR
MILLIBAR
MOISTURE
NEAP TIDE
RAINDROP
RAINFALL
SCORCHER
SCUDDING
SEAQUAKE
SIDEWIND
SNOWFALL
SPLATTER
SUNBURST
SUNSHINE
TAILWIND
VENDAVEL wind
WHITE-OUT
WIND ROSE

9
AFTERGLOW
ANTHELION
BAROMETER
BAROMETRY
BOURASQUE
CLOUD BASE
COLD FRONT
CROSSWIND
DUST DEVIL
DUST STORM
EPICENTRE

FRESH GALE
HAILSTONE
HARMATTAN wind
HOAR FROST
HURRICANE
INCLEMENT
ISALLOBAR
LAPSE RATE
LIGHTNING
MAELSTROM
MELTWATER
MESSENGER
NOR'EASTER wind
OCCLUSION
PEA-SOUPER
RAIN CLOUD
RAIN GAUGE
RAINSTORM
RAINSWEPT
RAINWATER
SANDSTORM
SEA BREEZE
SNOWBOUND
SNOWDRIFT
SNOWFLAKE
SNOWSTORM
SOU-WESTER wind
TIDAL BORE
TIDAL WAVE
UPDRAUGHT
VARIABLES wind
WARM FRONT
WHIRLPOOL
WHIRLWIND
WHOLE GALE
WIND CHILL
WIND GAUGE

10
ANEMOGRAPH
ANEMOMETER
ANEMOMETRY
ANTITRADES wind
ATMOSPHERE
BLACK FROST
CAPE DOCTOR wind
CENTIGRADE
CLOUDBURST
CLOUDINESS
DEPRESSION
EARTHQUAKE
FAHRENHEIT
FLOODWATER
HYGROMETER
HYGROMETRY
HYGROSCOPE
INUNDATION
IONOSPHERE
ISOSEISMAL
ISOSEISMIC
ISOTHERMAL
LAND BREEZE
LINE SQUALL
MARE'S TAILS
MICROSEISM
RADIOSONDE
RAIN SHADOW
SCOTCH MIST
SEISMOGRAM
SPRING TIDE
STORM CLOUD
STORM SURGE
STORM WATER
STRONG GALE
THERMOGRAM
TRADE WINDS

TRAMONTANA wind
TURBULENCE
VISIBILITY
WATER-SPOUT
WEATHER EYE
WEATHER MAP

11
AIR PRESSURE
ALTOCUMULUS cloud
ALTOSTRATUS cloud
ANTICYCLONE
DOWNDRAUGHT
EARTH TREMOR
GROUND FROST
GROUNDSWELL
HYDROMETEOR
LIGHT BREEZE
LOW PRESSURE
MACKEREL SKY
METEOROLOGY
NORTH-EASTER wind
NORTH-WESTER wind
PERTH DOCTOR wind
PLUVIOMETER
PRECIPITATE
PYROCUMULUS cloud
SEISMOGRAPH
SOUTH-EASTER wind
SOUTH-WESTER wind
TEMPERATURE
THERMOGRAPH

THERMOMETER
THERMOMETRY
THUNDERBOLT
THUNDERCLAP
THUNDERHEAD
TOURBILLION
TROPOSPHERE
WEATHERCOCK
WEATHERVANE

12
CIRROCUMULUS cloud
CIRROSTRATUS cloud
CONDENSATION
CUMULONIMBUS cloud
GENTLE BREEZE
HIGH PRESSURE
INDIAN SUMMER
JAPAN CURRENT
MICROCLIMATE
MODERATE GALE
NIMBOSTRATUS cloud
RICHTER SCALE
STRATOSPHERE
STRONG BREEZE
THERMOGRAPHY
THUNDER CLOUD
THUNDERSTORM
WEATHER GLASS

13
BALL LIGHTNING

BEAUFORT SCALE
CIRRUS UNCINUS cloud
ELECTRIC STORM
FORK LIGHTNING
MAGNETIC STORM
OCCLUDED FRONT
PRECIPITATION
STRATOCUMULUS cloud
VARIABLE WINDS
WEATHER REPORT

14
ANTITRADE WINDS
AURORA BOREALIS
CHAIN LIGHTNING
CUMULUS HUMILIS cloud
MODERATE BREEZE
NORTHERN LIGHTS
SHEET LIGHTNING
SOUTHERN LIGHTS
WEATHER STATION

15
AURORA AUSTRALIS
SOUTHERLY BUSTER wind
WEATHER FORECAST
WIND CHILL FACTOR

16
CUMULUS CONGESTUS
    cloud

Sports & Games

Sports & Games – Games – BOARD GAMES

3
HEX

4
LUDO
RISK

5
CHESS
HALMA
GOOSE
LASCA
L-GAME
NYOUT
SCOOP
SENET
SHOGI
SORRY

TABOO
TWIXT

6
ALASKA
BOGGLE
CLUEDO
MERILS
PAY DAY
RAKADO

7
ABALONE
CAREERS
CHAUPAR
ENTROPY
MAH-JONG
 (or mah-jongg)

MANCALA
OTHELLO
 (or reversi)
PACHISI
RAT RACE
REVERSI
 (or Othello)
UPWORDS

8
CHECKERS
 (or draughts)
DRAUGHTS
 (or checkers)
ESCALADO
L'ATTAQUE
MAH-JONGG
 (or mah-jong)

MONOPOLY
OUTBURST
SCRABBLE
TOTOPOLY

9
ALQUERQUE
BUCCANEER
DIPLOMACY
LABYRINTH
OPERATION
SOLITAIRE

10
ARTICULATE
BACKGAMMON
KENSINGTON
PICTIONARY

11
BATTLESHIPS
CONNECTIONS
DOVER PATROL
FOX AND GEESE

13
THE GAME OF LIFE

14
NINE MEN'S MORRIS
TRIVIAL PURSUIT

15
CHINESE CHECKERS
HARE AND TORTOISE

16
SNAKES AND LADDERS

17
NOUGHTS AND CROSSES

18
DUNGEONS AND DRAGONS

Sports & Games – Games – CARD GAMES

3
GIN
LOO
NAP
  (or Napoleon)
PIT
UNO

4
BRAG
CRIB
  (or cribbage)
FARO
GOAL!
HOKM
POKE
ROOK
SKAT
SNAP
SOLO
TONK
VINT
WHOT?

5
BARBU
CHEAT
DURAK
NODDY
OMBRE
PAIRS
  (or concentration)
PASUR
PEDRO
PITCH
POKER
RUMMY
SCOPA
SHOOT
SUECA
TAROT
TICHU
WHIST

6
BANKER
BOURRÉ
BRIDGE
CHEMMY

  (or chemin de fer)
DONKEY
ÉCARTÉ
EUCHRE
FAN-TAN
GO FISH
HEARTS
OH HELL
PIQUET
SEVENS
SPADES
TRUMPS
  (or knockout
  whist)
WIZARD

7
BEZIQUE
CANASTA
CASSINO
CHICAGO
COONCAN
ELEUSIS
LEXICON
OLD MAID

PENALTY
POKÉMON
PONTOON
RAINBOW
TIEN LEN

8
BACCARAT
CRIBBAGE
  (or crib)
CUARENTA
DESMOCHE
KLONDIKE
NAPOLEON
  (or nap)
PATIENCE
PINOCHLE
POPE JOAN
ZWICKERN

9
BLACKJACK
LONG WHIST
NEWMARKET
QUADRILLE

SOLO WHIST
STUD POKER
TOP TRUMPS
VINGT-ET-UN

10
BLACK MARIA
CONTRABAND
LANSQUENET
SHEEPSHEAD
SHORT WHIST
STRIP POKER

11
BLIND HOOKEY
CATCH THE TEN
 (or Scotch whist)
CHASE THE ACE

CHEMIN DE FER
 (or chemmy)
CRAZY EIGHTS
FIND THE LADY
 (or three-card monte)
KLABBERJASS
SCOTCH WHIST
 (or catch the ten)

12
FIVE-CARD STUD
NINE-CARD BRAG
PARTNER WHIST

13
AUCTION BRIDGE
CONCENTRATION
 (or pairs)

HAPPY FAMILIES
KNOCKOUT WHIST
 (or trumps)
THREE-CARD BRAG

14
CONTRACT BRIDGE
MINNESOTA WHIST
SNIP-SNAP-SNORUM
THREE-CARD MONTE
 (or find the lady)

15
CALIFORNIA SPEED
DUPLICATE BRIDGE

17
BEGGAR-MY-NEIGHBOUR

Sports & Games – Games – PARTY GAMES

4
I SPY
QUIZ
WINK

5
BINGO
LIMBO
LOTTO
SPOOF

6
BEETLE
CLUMPS
CRAMBO

I NEVER
MURDER
WHO AM I?

7
BUFFALO
HAND PAT
ORANGES
TOY WALK
TWISTER

8
CHARADES
FORFEITS
KIM'S GAME

LUCKY DIP
PEEKABOO
SARDINES
STATIONS

9
CELEBRITY
LOOKABOUT
SIMON SAYS

10
DUCKY DUCKY
DUMB CRAMBO
HANDY-DANDY
PASS THE KEY

SPILLIKINS
SPOON RELAY

11
HIDE-AND-SEEK
PARLOUR GAME
SPELLING BEE
TRUTH OR DARE

12
APPLE-BOBBING
CONSEQUENCES
TREASURE HUNT

13
BLIND MAN'S BUFF
CROSS PURPOSES
EASTER EGG HUNT
KISS-IN-THE-RING
MUSICAL CHAIRS
PASS THE PARCEL
POSTMAN'S KNOCK
SLEEPING LIONS
SPIN THE BOTTLE

14
BRITISH BULLDOG
CAPTURE THE FLAG
FOLLOW-MY-LEADER
HUNT THE SLIPPER
HUNT THE THIMBLE
MUSICAL STATUES
SLEEPING PIRATE

15
CHINESE WHISPERS
PUSS IN THE CORNER

THE MINISTER'S CAT
TWENTY QUESTIONS

17
SQUEAK PIGGY SQUEAK

18
THE FARMER'S IN HIS DEN

21
PIN THE TAIL ON THE
DONKEY

Sports & Games – Sport – Racehorses – EQUESTRIAN

5
CHAKA
PIAFF
PSALM
TIGRE

6
APOLLO
BIG BEN
GAMMON
JAYBEE
PHILCO
ROCKET

7
DEISTER
DOUBLET
HOUDINI
KILBALA
LINCOLN

RAFFLES
TOYTOWN

8
BLUEBIRD
CHARISMA
COLUMBUS
FLANAGAN
KILLAIRE
LAW COURT
MON SANTA
RYAN'S SON
STROLLER
SUNSALVE

9
BEETHOVEN
BOOMERANG
BUDDY BUNN
EAGLE LION

FIRECREST
FOXHUNTER
MOONFLEET
PRICELESS
SIR WATTIE
TAMARILLO

10
CUSTOM MADE
MIDDLE ROAD
MY MESSIEUR
READY TEDDY
REGAL REALM
STAR APPEAL

11
BALLINCOOLA
BERTIE BLUNT
HIGHLAND LAD
HORTON POINT

KIBAH TIC TOC
KING WILLIAM
SUPREME ROCK

12
MISTER SOFTEE

13
A TOUCH OF CLASS

14
MERELY A MONARCH
PRIMMORE'S PRIDE

15
MASTER CRAFTSMAN

17
HEADLEY BRITANNIA

Sports & Games – Sport – Racehorses – FLAT RACING

4
MELD
OATH
TROY

5
DANTE
LADAS
PINZA
RELKO
RIBOT
TRIGO
UNITE

6
ALIYSA
DAHLIA
DARIUS
DIOMED
EMPREY
ERHAAB
GRUNDY
HENBIT
KAZZIA
MY LOVE
NIMBUS
RIBERO
SAGACE
TULYAR
VIRAGO

7
ALLEGED
BUSTINO
ECLIPSE

ESWARAH
GALILEO
IMAGINE
KAHYASI
KRIS KIN
MAHMOUD
MORSTON
NASHWAN
PARTHIA
PHAR LAP
PSIDIUM
RAMRUMA
RIBOCCO
ROBERTO
SECRETO
SHAAMIT
SHADEED
SHERGAR
SINNDAR
SIR IVOR
ST PADDY
TEENOSO

8
AFFIRMED
BLAKENEY
CREPELLO
GALCADOR
GENEROUS
HIGH RISE
HYPERION
LARKSPUR
LAVANDIN
MAN OF WAR
MILL REEF

NIJINSKY
NONOALCO
SALSABIL
SIR PERCY

9
DR DEVIOUS
HIGHCLERE
LADY CARLA
LAMMTARRA
MOONSHELL
MOTIVATOR
OH SO SHARP
PERSIMMON
PHIL DRAKE
RHINEGOLD
SHAHTOUSH
SNOW BRIDE
TAP ON WOOD

10
BALANCHINE
BELLA PAOLA
CASUAL LOOK
DIMINUENDO
HARD RIDDEN
JET SKI LADY
LOVE DIVINE
MIDWAY LADY
NORTH LIGHT
OUIJA BOARD
PEARL DIVER
POCAHONTAS
SANGLAMORE
SANTA CLAUS

SLIP ANCHOR
SNOW KNIGHT
WINDSOR LAD

11
ALEXANDROVA
ALLEZ FRANCE
BENNY THE DIP
CHARLOTTOWN
CIRCUS PLUME
DUNFERMLINE
EL GRAN SEÑOR
HERRINGBONE
INTREPIDITY
MOON MADNESS
NEVER SAY DIE
ROYAL PALACE
SECRETARIAT
SHAHRASTANI
SUN PRINCESS
THE MINSTREL

12
ARCTIC PRINCE
COMMANCHE RUN
DANCING BRAVE
DON'T FORGET ME
GOLDEN FLEECE
ÎLE DE BOURBON
NATIVE DANCER
PETITE ETOILE
QUEST FOR FAME
RAINBOW QUEST
REAMS OF VERSE
STRAIGHT DEAL

USER FRIENDLY

13
CAPTAIN CUTTLE
EXHIBITIONIST
HIGH CHAPARRAL
TUDOR MINSTREL

14
DIAMOND JUBILEE
NORTHERN DANCER
REFERENCE POINT
SHIRLEY HEIGHTS

15
BRIGADIER GERARD
PRIVY COUNCILLOR

16
COMMANDER-IN-CHIEF

Sports & Games – Sport – Racehorses – NATIONAL HUNT

3
ESB
OXO

4
BULA
CROW
TEAL

5
ANGLO
ARKLE
AYALA

6
JODAMI
LUCIUS
MR WHAT
RED RUM
SIR KEN
SUNDEW

7
BOBBYJO
CAUGHOO
DAWN RUN

ECLIPSE
GAY TRIP
GRITTAR
KILMORE
MR FRISK
RUBSTIC
SEAGRAM
SPECIFY
WEST TIP

8
ALDANITI
BEN NEVIS
BEST MATE
BINDAREE
COOL DAWN
CORBIÈRE
FOINAVON
JAY TRUMP
PAPILLON
RAG TRADE
WELL TO DO

9
EARLY MIST
LANZAROTE

L'ESCARGOT
MANIFESTO
MINNEHOMA
MILL HOUSE
SEA PIGEON
THE FELLOW
WHAT A MYTH

10
COOL GROUND
FREEBOOTER
HALLO DANDY
MASTER OATS
MONKSFIELD
MONTY'S PASS
NICKEL COIN
NIGHT NURSE
PERSIAN WAR
QUARE TIMES
ROUGH QUEST
SEE YOU THEN
TEAM SPIRIT
THE THINKER

11
COTTAGE RAKE

EARTH SUMMIT
HEDGEHUNTER
KICKING KING
LAST SUSPECT
LORD GYLLENE
NORTON'S COIN
RED MARAUDER
RUSSIAN HERO

12
CHARTER PARTY
DESERT ORCHID
GOLDEN MILLER
IMPERIAL CALL
MAORI VENTURE
RED ALLIGATOR
REYNOLDSTOWN
RHYME 'N' REASON
ROYAL ATHLETE

13
LITTLE POLVEIR
LOVELY COTTAGE
PARTY POLITICS

14
CAPTAIN CHRISTY
COMEDY OF ERRORS
FORGIVE 'N' FORGET
MISTER MULLIGAN
NICOLAUS SILVER

SHEILA'S COTTAGE
WAR OF ATTRITION

15
AMBERLEIGH HOUSE
BURROUGH HILL LAD

HIGHLAND WEDDING
SEE MORE BUSINESS

16
GARRISON SAVANNAH
LOOKS LIKE TROUBLE

Sports & Games – Sport – SPORT EQUIPMENT

3	BUCK	ROPE	STOOL	STUMPS	**8**
BAR	(or	SHOT	STUMP	TACKLE	AQUALUNG
BAT	vaulting	SLED	SWORD	TARGET	BIRD CALL
BOW	horse)	WHIP	WEDGE	TENPIN	CROSSBAR
BOX	CARD	WOOD		WICKET	DUMB-BELL
CUE	CLUB		**6**		FOOTBALL
FLY	DART	**5**	BASKET	**7**	GOALPOST
GUN	ÉPÉE	ALLEY	BULLET	ARMBAND	GOLF BALL
KIT	FLAG	ARROW	CHEESE	BARBELL	GOLF CLUB
MAT	FOIL	BAILS	DISCUS	BRASSIE	LEG GUARD
NET	HOOK	BANDY	DRIVER	CRAMPON	OBSTACLE
OAR	HOOP	BLADE	HURDLE	CUE BALL	PLASTRON
PAD	IRON	CABER	ICE AXE	FLIPPER	PUNCHBAG
PEG	JACK	CHALK	MALIBU	GOLF BAG	SAND IRON
PIN	JUMP	CLEEK	MALLET	JAVELIN	(or sand wedge)
ROD	LUGE	DECOY	MARKER	NET CORD	TOBOGGAN
SKI	LURE	FLOAT	PADDLE	NETTING	WALL BARS
TEE	NETS	FRAME	PIOLET	NINEPIN	WATER SKI
TIP	OCHE	HORSE	POCKET	SHIN PAD	
	PADS	PITON	PUTTER	SHUTTLE	**9**
4	PILL	RIFLE	QUIVER	SKI POLE	APPARATUS
BAIL	POLE	RINGS	RACKET	SKITTLE	AQUAPLANE
BAIT	POOL	SABRE	RAPIER	SNORKEL	BOBSLEIGH
BALL	POST	SCUBA	SLEDGE	UPRIGHT	BOWSTRING
BARB	PUCK	SCULL	SLEIGH	WHISTLE	DARTBOARD
BEAM	RACK	SKATE	SPIDER		FACE GUARD
BOWL	REST	STICK	STICKS		KARABINER

POOL TABLE
PUNCHBALL
RUGBY BALL
SAILBOARD
SAND WEDGE
  (or sand iron)
SCOREBOOK
SCORECARD
STOPWATCH
STRETCHER
SURFBOARD
SWEATBAND

10
BANDERILLA
CLAY PIGEON
CORNER FLAG
CRICKET BAG
CRICKET BAT

FISHING ROD
HOCKEY BALL
SCOREBOARD
SCORESHEET
SKATEBOARD
SQUASH BALL
TENNIS BALL
TRAMPOLINE
WATER WINGS

11
BASEBALL BAT
BOXING GLOVE
CRICKET BALL
DIVING BOARD
FRENCH CHALK
HOCKEY STICK
HUNTING CROP
MALIBU BOARD

ROLLER SKATE
SHINTY STICK
SHUTTLECOCK
SIGHT SCREEN
SNOOKER BALL
WINNING POST

12
BILLIARD BALL
CUE EXTENSION
CURLING STONE
ELECTRIC HARE
MEDICINE BALL
PARALLEL BARS
SQUASH RACKET
TENNIS RACKET

13
BILLIARD TABLE

CHEQUERED FLAG
FINISHING POST
FISHING TACKLE
ISOMETRIC BARS
LACROSSE STICK
STARTING BLOCK
VAULTING HORSE
  (or buck)

14
ASYMMETRIC BARS
COCONUT MATTING
STARTING BLOCKS
STARTING PISTOL
TABLE-TENNIS BAT

15
BADMINTON RACKET
TABLE-TENNIS BALL

Sports & Games – Sport – SPORTING TERMS

3	NIL	BASE	DUCK	JUMP	PACE	SWIM	BADGE
BYE	OFF	BITE	FACE	KICK	PASS	TAPE	BASHO
CUP	PAR	BOUT	FOUL	KISS	PITS	TEST	BAULK
CUT	RUN	BOWL	GAME	LIFT	PLAY	TOSS	BLOCK
END	SET	BULL	GOAL	LINE	PLOY	TOTE	BOGEY
HIT	TIE	BUNG	HALF	LOSS	PUNT	TRAP	BREAK
JAB	TON	BUTT	HEAT	LOVE	PUTT	WALL	CAROM
LAP	TOP	CAST	HOLD	LUTZ	RACE	WIDE	CARRY
LAW	TRY	CERT	HOLE	MARK	RING		CATCH
LBW	VAN	CHIP	HOME	MOVE	RUCK	**5**	CHASE
LEG	WIN	CHOP	HOOK	NICK	SAVE	ALLEY	CRAWL
LET		DIVE	HUNT	NOCK	SHOT	ANGLE	CROSS
LIE	**4**	DRAG	JERK	ODDS	SPIN	ARENA	DERBY
LOB	AXEL	DRAW	JINK	OVER	SPOT	AWARD	DOLLY

DRIVE	STEAL	LENGTH	VOLLEY	PLAYING
DUMMY	SWEEP	MAIDEN	WARM-UP	PLAY-OFF
EAGLE	SWING	MISCUE	WEIGHT	POTTING
EVENT	THROW	MISHIT	WICKET	PURSUIT
EXTRA	TOUCH	NO-BALL	YORKER	QUARTER
FAULT	VAULT	NELSON		REGATTA
FEINT		NO SIDE	**7**	RIPOSTE
FIELD	**6**	ONSIDE	AVERAGE	RIVALRY
FIGHT	APPEAL	PERIOD	BATTING	ROUNDER
FINAL	ATTACK	PLUNGE	BEATING	RUNNING
FLUFF	BEAMER	RACING	BENEFIT	SCORING
FLUKE	BIRDIE	RECORD	BOUNCER	SCRATCH
FRAME	BORROW	REPLAY	BOWLING	SERVICE
HOMER	BOUNCE	RESULT	CENTURY	STADIUM
IN-OFF	BUMPER	RETURN	CHICANE	STAMINA
LINKS	BUNKER	ROQUET	CIRCUIT	STRETCH
MASSÉ	CANNON	RUBBER	CONTEST	TACTICS
MATCH	CHUKKA	RUN-OFF	CORRIDA	THE TURF
PARRY	CLINCH	RUN-OUT	DECIDER	THROW-IN
PISTE	CORNER	SAFETY	DEFENCE	TOP SPIN
PITCH	COURSE	SERIES	DOUBLES	TOURNEY
PRIZE	CREASE	SINGLE	FAIRWAY	UPSWING
PURSE	CUP TIE	SITTER	GOLFING	VICTORY
RALLY	DEFEAT	SLALOM	HOME RUN	WEIGH-IN
RANGE	DOG-LEG	SPRINT	INFIELD	WINNING
REACH	DOUBLE	SQUARE	INNINGS	WORK-OUT
RELAY	DUGOUT	STAKES	JUMP-OFF	WRESTLE
ROUGH	FINISH	STRIKE	KICK-OFF	WRONG 'UN
ROUND	FOOZLE	STROKE	KNOCK-ON	(or googly)
SCORE	GLANCE	STYMIE	KNOCK-UP	
SCRUM	GOOGLY	SWERVE	LINE-OUT	**8**
SERVE	(or wrong	TACKLE	MAXIMUM	APRÈS-SKI
SLICE	'un)	TACTIC	MEETING	AQUACADE
SNICK	HAZARD	TICKET	NET PLAY	AQUATICS
SPARE	HEADER	TIMING	OFFSIDE	AVERAGES
SPOOR	INJURY	TOUCHÉ	OPENING	BACKHAND
SPORT	LEAGUE	TREBLE	PENALTY	BACK-HEEL
STAND	LEG BYE	TROPHY	PIT STOP	BACK PASS

BALL GAME
BASELINE
BOAT RACE
BONSPIEL
BOUNDARY
BULLRING
BULLSEYE
BULLY-OFF
CHEATING
CHINAMAN
CHIP SHOT
CLINCHER
CUP FINAL
CUP MATCH
DEAD HEAT
DELIVERY
DIVISION
DRAG RACE
DRAG SHOT
DROP GOAL
DROP KICK
DROP SHOT
FAIR PLAY
FIELDING
FLAT RACE
FOLLOW-ON
FOOT RACE
FOOTWORK
FOREHAND
FOUL PLAY
FREE BALL
FREE KICK
FREE SHOT
FULL TIME
FULL TOSS
GLASS JAW
GOAL AREA
GOAL KICK

GOAL LINE
GRIDIRON
GYMKHANA
HALF-TIME
HAND BALL
HANDICAP
HAT TRICK
HAYMAKER
HEADLOCK
HURDLING
KNOCKOUT
LEFT HOOK
LEFT WING
LEG BREAK
LEG GUARD
LEG SWEEP
LONG SHOT
LONG ODDS
LOVE GAME
MIDFIELD
MISMATCH
MULLIGAN
NOBLE ART
OFF BREAK
OFF DRIVE
OLYMPIAD
OLYMPICS
OUTFIELD
OUTSWING
POSITION
PRACTICE
PUSH SHOT
RACECARD
RINGSIDE
SAND TRAP
SCRAMBLE
SET POINT
SHOOTING

SPARRING
STRAIGHT
STRIKING
STUMPING
STUN SHOT
TEAMWORK
TELEMARK
TERRACES
THE COUNT
THE FANCY
THROWING
TRANSFER
VAULTING
WALKOVER
WEIGH-OUT

9

ALL-TICKET
ADVANTAGE
BACKSWING
BAULK LINE
BELLYFLOP
BLEACHERS
BULLFIGHT
BUTTERFLY
CHALLENGE
DISMISSAL
DRIBBLING
EQUALISER
EXTRA TIME
FAVOURITE
FOOTFAULT
FREESTYLE
FULL PITCH
GATE MONEY
GLASS CHIN
GOLD MEDAL
GOLF LINKS

GRAND PRIX
GRAND SLAM
HORSE RACE
INSWINGER
LEG BEFORE
LOB VOLLEY
MATCH PLAY
MEDAL PLAY
MIDWICKET
NINE HOLES
OBJECTION
OVERTHROW
PLACE KICK
PRIZE RING
PROGRAMME
PROMOTION
RACEGOING
RAIN CHECK
REPÊCHAGE
RIGHT HOOK
RIGHT WING
ROCK CLIMB
SCREW SHOT
SCRUMMAGE
SELECTION
SEMI-FINAL
SHADOW-BOX
SHORT ODDS
SPRINTING
SWORDPLAY
TERRACING
TEST MATCH
TOTALISER
TOUCHDOWN
TOUCHLINE
TOXOPHILY
TRAMLINES
VELODROME

WHITEWASH

10

ATTENDANCE
BACKSTROKE
BLOOD SPORT
BOOBY PRIZE
BOXING RING
CENTRE SPOT
COMMENTARY
CROWN GREEN
ELIMINATOR
EQUITATION
ESKIMO ROLL
FIELD EVENT
FIELD SPORT
FLAT RACING
FLYING MARE
FORMULA ONE
FORMULA TWO
FULL NELSON
GOLDEN GOAL
GOLF COURSE
GRANDSTAND
HALF NELSON
HALF-VOLLEY
HAMMERLOCK
HURDLE RACE
INJURY TIME
INSIDE EDGE
INSIDE LANE
KARATE CHOP
MAIDEN OVER
MATCH POINT
OUTSWINGER
POT-HUNTING
PRIZE FIGHT
PUSH STROKE

RACECOURSE
REFEREEING
RELEGATION
RUGBY MATCH
RUGBY PITCH
SAFETY PLAY
SAFETY SHOT
SIDESTROKE
STABLEFORD
STROKE PLAY
SUSPENSION
TARGET AREA
TEAM SPIRIT
TITLE FIGHT
TOURNAMENT
TRACK EVENT
WATER SPORT

11

ATHLETICISM
BRONZE MEDAL
CLASSIC RACE
CLOSE SEASON
COMPETITION
COUNTY MATCH
DAISY-CUTTER
DECLARATION
DOUBLE FAULT
FAST BOWLING
FLYING START
FOSBURY FLOP
HOCKEY MATCH
HOCKEY PITCH
INSIDE TRACK
LAP OF HONOUR
LEAGUE MATCH
NET PRACTICE
OBSTRUCTION

OUTSIDE EDGE
OUTSIDE LANE
PENALTY AREA
PENALTY GOAL
PENALTY KICK
PENALTY SPOT
PHOTO FINISH
PREMIERSHIP
RABBIT PUNCH
RACE MEETING
RETURN MATCH
ROUND OF GOLF
SEAM BOWLING
SELLING RACE
SERVICE LINE
SILVER MEDAL
SKATING RINK
SLOW BOWLING
SPIN BOWLING
SQUASH COURT
SUDDEN DEATH
TENNIS COURT
TENNIS MATCH
TEST CRICKET
TOTALISATOR
TRACK RECORD
WESTERN ROLL
WOODEN SPOON
WORLD RECORD

12

APPROACH SHOT
BASEBALL GAME
BOWLING ALLEY
BOWLING GREEN
BREASTSTROKE
CENTRE CIRCLE
CHAMPIONSHIP

CRASH BARRIER
CRICKET MATCH
CRICKET PITCH
GAMESMANSHIP
GROUND STROKE
HOME STRAIGHT
HORSEMANSHIP
INFRINGEMENT
MAIDEN STAKES
MARATHON RACE
MIXED DOUBLES
NETBALL MATCH
NURSERY SLOPE
OBSTACLE RACE
OLYMPIC GAMES
OUTSIDE TRACK
PERSONAL BEST
PLAYING FIELD
POINT-TO-POINT
POLE POSITION
POSTPONEMENT
PUTTING GREEN
QUARTER-FINAL
RETURN CREASE
RINGSIDE SEAT
RUNNING TRACK
SERVICE COURT
SHADOW-BOXING
SHAMATEURISM
SKITTLE ALLEY
SPORTS CENTRE
STARTING GATE
STARTING POST
STAYING POWER
STICKY WICKET
STONEWALLING
SUBSTITUTION
SWIMMING GALA

SWIMMING POOL
WINTER SPORTS

13
BOWLING CREASE
COUNTER-ATTACK
COUNTY CRICKET
EIGHTEEN HOLES
EQUESTRIANISM
FOLLOW-THROUGH
FOOTBALL MATCH
FOOTBALL PITCH
INNINGS DEFEAT
INTERNATIONAL
NURSERY CANNON
ONE-DAY CRICKET

PITCH INVASION
POPPING CREASE
QUALIFICATION
SHOOTING RANGE
SPORTSMANSHIP
SPORTS STADIUM
STARTING PRICE
STARTING STALL
SWORDSMANSHIP
WRESTLING RING

14
BADMINTON COURT
CAULIFLOWER EAR
FOOTBALL GROUND
LEAGUE FOOTBALL

NINETEENTH HOLE
SHEEPDOG TRIALS
SPORTING CHANCE
STEEPLECHASING
TRANSFER WINDOW
WEIGHT TRAINING

15
BODYLINE BOWLING
CONSOLATION PRIZE
FOOTBALL STADIUM
LEG BEFORE WICKET
PENALTY SHOOT-OUT
PROFESSIONALISM
THREE-LEGGED RACE

Sports & Games – Sport – SPORT PLAYERS

3	SIDE	LOSER	ARCHER	GOALIE	MARKER
ACE	SKIP	MID-ON	ATTACK	HAND-IN	MID-OFF
COX	SLIP	MILER	BATTER	HAWKER	OPENER
OAR	TAIL	PACER	BEATER	HITTER	PLAYER
PRO	TEAM	POINT	BOBBER	HOLDER	PUNTER
SUB		RACER	BOWLER	HOOKER	PUTTER
	5	RIDER	BOWMAN	HUDDLE	RABBIT
4	BOXER	RIVAL	CADDIE	HUNTER	RUNNER
BACK	CHAMP	ROVER	CENTRE	HURLER	SCORER
BLUE	CHEAT	ROWER	CUEIST	JOCKEY	SEAMER
COLT	COACH	SKIER	CURLER	JOGGER	SECOND
CREW	COVER	SLIPS	DRY BOB	JUMPER	SERVER
LOCK	DIVER	SQUAD	ELEVEN	JUNIOR	SKATER
PACK	EIGHT		FENCER	KEEPER	STROKE
PROP	GUARD	**6**	GILLIE	KICKER	SURFER
SEED	GULLY	ANCHOR	(or ghillie)	LINE-UP	SURFIE
SHOT	JUDGE	ANGLER	GLIDER	LONG ON	TORERO

UMPIRE
VICTOR
WET BOB
WINGER
WINNER

7
ALSO-RAN
AMATEUR
ATHLETE
BACK ROW
BASEMAN
BATSMAN
BEAGLER
BRUISER
CAPTAIN
CATCHER
CLIMBER
COURSER
CYCLIST
DEFENCE
FIELDER
FIGHTER
FINE LEG
FLY HALF
FORWARD
GHILLIE
 (or gillie)
GYMNAST
HAND-OUT
HARRIER
HURDLER
INFIELD
JOUSTER
LEG SLIP
LINEMAN
LONG LEG
LONG OFF

MARSHAL
MATADOR
OARSMAN
PARTNER
PICADOR
PITCHER
QUICKIE
REFEREE
RESERVE
SHIKARI
SHOOTER
SKIPPER
SLOGGER
SPINNER
STALKER
STARTER
STEWARD
STOPPER
STRIKER
STUMPER
SWEEPER
SWIMMER
TACKLER
TRAINER
VAULTER
VICTRIX
YACHTIE

8
ABSEILER
AQUANAUT
ATTACKER
CANOEIST
CHAMPION
COXSWAIN
CRAGSMAN
DEFENDER
DRIBBLER

FALCONER
FINALIST
FRONT ROW
FULL BACK
HALF-BACK
HALF-BLUE
HORSEMAN
HUNTRESS
HUNTSMAN
LEFT BACK
LEFT HALF
LINESMAN
LONG STOP
MARKSMAN
OFFICIAL
OLYMPIAN
OPPONENT
OUTFIELD
OUTSIDER
POSSIBLE
POTHOLER
PROBABLE
PUGILIST
RALLYIST
RECEIVER
RUNNER-UP
SELECTOR
SHORT LEG
SKYDIVER
SOUTHPAW
SPRINTER
STAND-OFF
TEAM-MATE
THIRD MAN
TOREADOR
UNDERDOG
VOLLEYER
WATERMAN

WING BACK
WING HALF
WRESTLER

9
ANCHORMAN
BLACK BELT
BROWN BELT
COMBATANT
CONTENDER
CRICKETER
DRAG RACER
FAVOURITE
FIELDSMAN
FIRST SLIP
FISHERMAN
FLY-FISHER
FLYWEIGHT
FOX-HUNTER
GLADIATOR
HOT-RODDER
ICE SKATER
INFIELDER
LINE JUDGE
NET PLAYER
NOSE GUARD
OARSWOMAN
PACEMAKER
POT-HUNTER
QUALIFIER
RELAY TEAM
RETIARIUS
RETRIEVER
SCRUM HALF
SEA ANGLER
SHAMATEUR
SHORT STOP
SKIN-DIVER

SPORTSMAN
SQUARE LEG
STROKE OAR
SWORDSMAN
TACTICIAN
TAIL-ENDER
THIRD SLIP
WHIPPER-IN
WHITE BELT
YACHTSMAN

10
ALL-ROUNDER
AQUAPLANER
BACK-MARKER
BALLOONIST
CENTRE BACK
CENTRE HALF
CHALLENGER
COMPETITOR
CONTESTANT
CORNERBACK
COVER POINT
DART-PLAYER
DECATHLETE
EQUESTRIAN
EXTRA COVER
FAST BOWLER
FOOTBALLER
GOALKEEPER
GOAL-KICKER
GROUNDSMAN
HANG-GLIDER
HIGH JUMPER
HORSEWOMAN
INSIDE LEFT
LEFT-HANDER
LEFT-WINGER

LONG JUMPER
MARKSWOMAN
MIDFIELDER
OPPOSITION
OUTFIELDER
PACE-SETTER
POLO PLAYER
POOL PLAYER
SCRIMMAGER
SCRUMMAGER
SCUBA DIVER
SEAM BOWLER
SECOND SLIP
SHOWJUMPER
SHOT-PUTTER
SILLY MID-ON
SILLY POINT
SLOW BOWLER
SPIN BOWLER
SUBSTITUTE
THE BATTERY
TOBOGGANER
TOUCH JUDGE
TWELFTH MAN
WATER SKIER
WINDSURFER

11
ADJUDICATOR
BULLFIGHTER
DEERSTALKER
FRONT RUNNER
GROUND STAFF
HEAVYWEIGHT
INSIDE RIGHT
LIGHTWEIGHT
LOCK FORWARD
MOUNTAINEER

OUTSIDE LEFT
PARACHUTIST
PARTICIPANT
PENTATHLETE
PINCH-HITTER
PLACE-KICKER
POLE VAULTER
PROP FORWARD
QUARTERBACK
RALLY DRIVER
ROCK CLIMBER
RUGBY PLAYER
SAILBOARDER
SILLY MID-OFF
SLIP FIELDER
SPORTSWOMAN
STONEWALLER
STRAW-WEIGHT
THIRD UMPIRE
TOBOGGANIST
TOXOPHILITE
VICE CAPTAIN

12
BANDERILLERO
BANTAMWEIGHT
CLOSE CATCHER
CLOSE FIELDER
EQUESTRIENNE
FIGURE SKATER
MIDDLEWEIGHT
NET-CORD JUDGE
OUTSIDE RIGHT
PENALTY TAKER
PRIZE-FIGHTER
PROFESSIONAL
RACING DRIVER
ROLLER SKATER

SEMI-FINALIST
SHARPSHOOTER
SKATEBOARDER
STAND-OFF HALF
TENNIS PLAYER
THREE-QUARTER
TRAMPOLINIST
TRIPLE JUMPER
WEIGHTLIFTER
WELTERWEIGHT
WICKETKEEPER

13
BIG GAME HUNTER
BUTTERFINGERS
CENTRE FORWARD
CORNER MARSHAL
CRUISERWEIGHT
DISCUS THROWER
FEATHERWEIGHT
INSIDE FORWARD
INTERNATIONAL
LIGHT FLYWEIGHT
NIGHT-WATCHMAN
RECORD-BREAKER
SNOOKER PLAYER
SPEEDWAY RIDER
STEEPLECHASER

14
BASEBALL PLAYER
BASELINE PLAYER
BILLIARD PLAYER
FOURTH OFFICIAL
MARATHON RUNNER
MASTER OF HOUNDS
OUTSIDE FORWARD
SIDE MIDFIELDER

15
JAVELIN THROWER
SPARRING PARTNER
SQUARE LEG UMPIRE

16
BACKWARD SHORT LEG
CENTRE MIDFIELDER

LIGHT HEAVYWEIGHT
SUPER LIGHTWEIGHT

17
LIGHT BANTAMWEIGHT
SUPER MIDDLEWEIGHT
SUPER WELTERWEIGHT

18
LIGHT FEATHERWEIGHT
SUPER FEATHERWEIGHT

19
ATTACKING MIDFIELDER
DEFENSIVE MIDFIELDER

Sports & Games – Sport – SPORTS * = event

4
GOLF
JUDO
LUGE
POLO
POOL
SUMO

5
BANDY
BOCCE
BOWLS
DARTS
FIVES
FOOTY
KENDO
RUGBY
SKEET

6
AIKIDO
BOULES
 (or pétanque)
BOXING
DISCUS*

DIVING
FOOTER
HAMMER*
HOCKEY
KARATE
KUNG FU
PELOTA
RACING
RIDING
ROWING
RUGGER
SEVENS
SHINTY
SKIING
SOCCER
SQUASH
TENNIS

7
ANGLING
ARCHERY
BOWLING
CRICKET
CROQUET
CURLING

CYCLING
FENCING
FISHING
GLIDING
HUNTING
HURLING
JAI ALAI
JAVELIN*
JU-JITSU
KAATSEN
KABADDI
NETBALL
RACKETS
RUNNING
SAILING
SHOT-PUT*
SKATING
SNOOKER
SURFING
THE DOGS
 (or dog racing,
 greyhound racing)

8
BASEBALL

BIATHLON*
CANOEING
CLIMBING
COURSING
DRESSAGE*
EVENTING*
FOOTBALL
HANDBALL
HIGH JUMP*
HURDLING
JOUSTING
KAYAKING
KORFBALL
LACROSSE
LANGLAUF
LONG JUMP*
MARATHON*
MUAY THAI
 (or kick-boxing)
PÉTANQUE
 (or boules)
PING-PONG
 (or table tennis)
RALLYING
ROUNDERS

SCULLING
SHOOTING
SLEDGING
SOFTBALL
SPEEDWAY
SWIMMING
TRAPBALL
TROTTING
TROUTING
TUG OF WAR
WALL GAME
  (or Eton wall game)
YACHTING

9
ABSEILING
AIR RACING
ATHLETICS
AUTOCROSS
BADMINTON
BILLIARDS
DECATHLON*
DOG RACING
  (or greyhound
  racing, the dogs)
DRY SKIING
FIVE-A-SIDE
GO-KARTING
ICE HOCKEY
MOTOCROSS
PAINTBALL
POLE VAULT*
POTHOLING
SKIJÖRING
SKI-FLYING
SKYDIVING
STOOLBALL
TAEKWONDO

TRIATHLON*
WATER POLO
WRESTLING

10
BALLOONING
BASKETBALL
CYCLOCROSS
DRAG RACING
FLY-FISHING
FOX-HUNTING
GYMNASTICS
HEPTATHLON*
ICE SKATING
KICK-BOXING
  (or muay Thai)
LAWN TENNIS
PENTATHLON*
REAL TENNIS
  (or royal tennis)
RUGBY UNION
SCRAMBLING
SEA FISHING
SKI-BOBBING
SKI-JUMPING
SKIN DIVING
TRIPLE JUMP*
VOLLEYBALL

11
CAMEL RACING
FIELD HOCKEY
HANG-GLIDING
HORSE RACING
MOTOR RACING
PARAGLIDING
PIG-STICKING
ROYAL TENNIS

  (or real tennis)
RUGBY LEAGUE
SCUBA DIVING
SHORT TENNIS
SHOWJUMPING*
TABLE TENNIS
  (or ping-pong)
TOBOGGANING
WATER SKIING
WINDSURFING

12
BOBSLEIGHING
BULLFIGHTING
CROSS-COUNTRY
ETON WALL GAME
  (or wall game)
INLINE HOCKEY
KNUR AND SPELL
MOTORCYCLING
ORIENTEERING
PADDLE TENNIS
PARASCENDING
PONY-TREKKING
ROCK CLIMBING
ROLLER HOCKEY
SAILBOARDING
SPEED SKATING
STEEPLECHASE*
TRAMPOLINING

13
COARSE FISHING
EQUESTRIANISM
ROLLER SKATING
RUGBY FOOTBALL
SKATEBOARDING
SQUASH RACKETS

TENPIN BOWLING
WEIGHTLIFTING

14
GAELIC FOOTBALL
GROUSE SHOOTING
MOUNTAINEERING

STOCK-CAR RACING

15
AUSTRALIAN RULES
CROWN GREEN BOWLS
GREYHOUND RACING
(or dog racing, the dogs)

POWERBOAT RACING
TOSSING THE CABER*

16
AMERICAN FOOTBALL
MODERN PENTATHLON*

Sports & Games – Sport – Sportspeople – CRICKETERS
England players unless stated

3
FRY CB
MAY Peter
OLD Chris

4
AMES Leslie
BEDI Bishen – India
BELL Ian
BOON David – Aus
COOK Alastair, Nick
CORK Dominic
HALL Wes – WI
HICK Graeme
LAMB Allan
LARA Brian – WI
LOCK Tony
MEAD CP
NASH Malcolm
REID John – NZ
RICE Clive – SA
ROSE Brian
SNOW John
TATE Maurice
VOCE Bill

WOOD Barry,
    Graham – Aus

5
ADAMS Jimmy – WI
AGNEW Jonathan
ALLEN Gubby
AMISS Dennis
ATHEY Bill
BROAD Chris
CAPEL David
CLOSE Brian
CROWE Jeff – NZ,
    Martin – NZ
DUJON Jeff – WI
EVANS Godfrey
GAYLE Chris – WI
GIBBS Herschelle
    – SA, Lance – WI
GILES Ashley
GOMES Larry – WI
GOOCH Graham
GOUGH Darren
GOWER David
GRACE WG

GREIG Tony
GROUT Wally – Aus
HIGGS Ken
HOBBS Jack
JESTY Trevor
JONES Dean – Aus, Simon
KNOTT Alan
LAKER Jim
LAWRY Bill – Aus
LEVER John
LEWIS Chris, Tony
LLOYD Clive – WI
LOGIE Gus – WI
LYNCH Monte – WI
MARKS Vic
MARSH Graham, Rodney
    – Aus
MOXON Martin
NURSE Seymour – WI
PARKS Jim
ROOPE Graham
SLACK Wilf
SMALL Gladstone
SMITH Graeme – SA,
    Mike, Robin

TYSON Frank
WALSH Courtney – WI
WARNE Shane – Aus
WAUGH Mark – Aus,
  Steve – Aus

6

ALLOTT Paul
ARNOLD Geoff
BAILEY Trevor
BASHAR Habibul
  – Bangladesh
BEDSER Alec, Eric
BENAUD Richie – Aus
BISHOP Ian – WI
BORDER Allan – Aus
BOTHAM Ian
CONNOR Cardigan – WI
COWANS Norman
CRONJE Hansie – SA
DANIEL Wayne – WI
DEXTER Ted
DILLEY Graham
DILLON Mervyn – WI
DONALD Allan – SA
DRAVID Rahul – India
EDRICH Bill, John
FENDER Percy
FLOWER Andy – Zim
FOSTER Neil
FOWLER Graeme
FRASER Angus
GARNER Joel – WI
HADLEE Sir Richard
  – NZ
HARVEY Neil – Aus
HAYDEN Matthew – Aus
HAYNES Desmond – WI

HOOPER Carl – WI
HUDSON Andrew – SA
HUGHES Merv – Aus
HUTTON Sir Len
INSOLE Doug
KALLIS Jacques – SA
KANHAI Rohan – WI
KATICH Simon – Aus
KUMBLE Anil – India
LANGER Justin – Aus
LAWSON Geoff – Aus
LILLIE Dennis – Aus
LOADER Peter
MASHUD Khaled
  – Bangladesh
MENDIS Duleep – Sri
  Lanka
MILLER Keith – Aus
OLONGA Henry – Zim
ONTONG Rodney – SA
PARKER Paul
PATHAN Irfan – India
PULLAR Geoff
RADLEY Clive – NZ
RAHMAN Naimur
  – Bangladesh
RHODES Wilfred
SARWAN Ramnaresh
  – WI
SEHWAG Virender
  – India
SELVEY Mike
SHARMA Chetan – India
SOBERS Sir Garfield – WI
STREAK Heath – Zim
TAVARE Chris
TAYLOR Bob
TITMUS Fred

TURNER Glenn – NZ
VERITY Hedley
WARNER Pelham
WEEKES Everton – WI
WILLEY Peter
WILLIS Bob

7

AMBROSE Curtly – WI
BARNETT Kim
BOYCOTT Geoff
BRADMAN Sir Don
  – Aus
BURGESS Mark – NZ
BUTCHER Roland
CADDICK Andrew
COMPTON Denis
CONGDON Bev – NZ
COWDREY Baron Colin
DENNESS Mike
DE SILVA Aravinda – Sri
  Lanka
DOWLING Graham – NZ
DOWNTON Paul
EDMONDS Phil
ELLISON Richard
EMBUREY John
ENGINEER Farouk
  – India
FLEMING Stephen – NZ
GANGULY Saurav
  – India
GATTING Mike
GIFFORD Norman
HAMMOND Wally
HENDREN Patsy
HOGGARD Matthew
HOLDING Michael – WI

HOWARTH Geoff – NZ
HUSSAIN Nasser
JACKMAN Robin
JARDINE Douglas
LARKINS Wayne
LARWOOD Harold
MALCOLM Devon
MCGRATH Glenn – Aus
MILBURN Colin
MORTAZA Mashrafe
   – Bangladesh
NEWPORT Phil
PANESAR Monty
PARFITT Peter
POLLOCK Shaun – SA
PONTING Ricky – Aus
PRINGLE Derek
PROCTER Mike – SA
RANDALL Derek
ROBERTS Andy – WI
ROEBUCK Peter
RUSSELL Jack
SHASTRI Ravi – India
STATHAM Brian
STEWART Alec
STRAUSS Andrew
THOMSON Jeff – Aus
TRUEMAN Fred
VAUGHAN Michael
WALCOTT Clive – WI
WESSELS Kepler – Aus
WOOLLEY Frank
WOOLMER Bob
WORRELL Frank – WI
YARDLEY Norman

8
ALDERMAN Terry – Aus

AMARNATH Mohinder
   – India
ATAPATTU Marvan – Sri
   Lanka
ATHERTON Mike
BAIRSTOW David
BAPTISTE Eldine – WI
BENJAMIN Winston – WI
BREARLEY Mike
CHAPPELL Greg – Aus,
   Ian – Aus
ENGINEER Farouk – India
FLETCHER Keith
FLINTOFF Andrew
GAVASKAR Sunil – India
GRAVENEY David, Tom
HARMISON Steve
KAPIL DEV India
KLUSENER Lance – SA
LINDWALL Ray – Aus
MADAN LAL India
MARSHALL Malcolm
   – WI
MOIN KHAN Pakistan
MULLALLY Alan – SA
PONSFORD William
   – Aus
RICHARDS Barry – SA,
   Jack, Sir Viv – WI
ROBINSON Tim
SHEPHERD John
SHEPPARD David
SUBBA ROW Raman
   – India
SURRIDGE Stuart

9
APPLEYARD Bob

D'OLIVEIRA Basil
GILCHRIST Adam – Aus
GILLESPIE Jason – Aus
GREENIDGE Gordon
   – WI
IMRAN KHAN Pakistan
LUCKHURST Brian
PATTERSON Patrick
   – WI
PIETERSEN Kevin
RANATUNGA Arjuna
   – Sri Lanka
SAINSBURY Peter
SRIKKANTH Kris – India
SUTCLIFFE Herbert
TENDULKAR Sachin
   – India
UNDERWOOD Derek
VISWANATH Gundappa
   – India

10
ABDUL QADIR Pakistan
AZHARUDDIN
   Mohammad – India
BARRINGTON Ken
GREATBATCH Mark
   – NZ
JAYASURIYA Sanath
   – Sri Lanka
KASPROWICZ Michael
   – Aus
RAMEEZ RAJA Pakistan
RAMPRAKASH Mark
RICHARDSON Richie
   – WI
RUTHERFORD Ken – NZ
SAEED ANWAR Pakistan

SHACKLETON Derek
VENGSARKAR Dilip
  – India
WASIM AKRAM Pakistan
YOUNIS KHAN Pakistan

11
CHANDERPAUL
  Shivnarine – WI
COLLINGWOOD Paul
CONSTANTINE Baron
  Learie – WI

FAIRBROTHER Neil
ILLINGWORTH Ray
RASHID LATIF Pakistan
TRESCOTHICK Marcus
WAQAR YOUNIS
  Pakistan

12
INTIKHAB ALAM
  Pakistan
INZAMAM-UL-HAQ
  Pakistan

JAVED MIANDAD
  Pakistan
KALLICHARRAN Alvin
  – WI
MURALITHARAN
  Muttiah – Sri Lanka

13
CHANDRASEKHAR
  Bhagwat – India

Sports & Games – Sport – Sportspeople – FOOTBALLERS

3
LAW Denis – Scotland
LEE Francis, Sammy
REP Johnny –
  Netherlands
SIX Didier – France
URE Ian – Scotland

4
BALL Alan
BELL Colin
BEST George
  – N Ireland
BOYD Tom – Scotland
BUTT Nicky
COLE Ashley, Joe
DEAN Dixie
DIDI Brazil
FIGO Luis – Portugal
GOOR Bart – Belgium
GRAY Eddie – Scotland

HILL Jimmy
HOWE Don
HUNT Roger
JACK David
KAKÁ Brazil
KOPA Raymond
  – France
KUYT Dirk –
  Netherlands
LATO Grzegorz
  – Poland
NEAL Phil
OWEN Michael
PAGE Robert – Wales
PELÉ Brazil
RAÚL Spain
REID Peter
RICE Pat – N Ireland
RIVA Gigi – Italy, Luigi
  – Italy
RUSH Ian – Wales

SONG Rigobert
  – Cameroon
STAM Jaap – Netherlands
SWAN Peter
TODD Colin
VAVÁ Brazil
WARK John – Scotland
WEBB Neil
WEIR David – Scotland
ZOFF Dino – Italy

5
ADAMS Tony
ALLEN Clive, Ronnie
ASTLE Jeff
BAKER Joe
BANKS Gordon
BONDS Billy
BRADY Liam – S Ireland
BURNS Kenny – Scotland
BYRNE Roger

COHEN George
COSTA Rui – Portugal
DIXON Kerry, Lee
DOWIE Iain – N Ireland
DRAKE Ted
ELDER Alex – N Ireland
GIGGS Ryan – Wales
GILES Johnny – S Ireland
GOUGH Richard
– Scotland
GREGG Harry
– N Ireland
HEALY David – N Ireland
HENRY Thierry – France
HURST Sir Geoff
JAMES Alex – Scotland,
Leighton – Wales
JONES Cliff, Paul,
Vinnie – Wales
KEANE Robbie
– S Ireland, Roy
– S Ireland
LÚCIO Brazil
MAIER Sepp – Germany
MARSH Rodney
MILLS Mick
MOORE Bobby
NEILL Terry – N Ireland
NESTA Alessandro
– Italy
NURSE Mel – Wales
PAINE Terry
PAPIN Jean-Pierre
– France
PETIT Emmanuel
– France
PIRÈS Robert – France
PLATT David

QUINN Jimmy
– N Ireland, Niall
– S Ireland
REGIS Cyrille
REINA Pepe – Spain
REVIE Don
RIOCH Bruce – Scotland
SMITH Bobby, Tommy
SORIN Juan Pablo
– Argentina
SWIFT Frank
TERRY John
VILLA Ricardo
– Argentina
VOGTS Berti – Germany
WHITE John – Scotland
WOODS Chris
YOUNG George
– Scotland

6
A'COURT Alan
ALBERT Flórián
– Hungary
ALONSO Xabi – Spain
BAGGIO Roberto – Italy
BARESI Franco – Italy
BARNES John
BASTIN Cliff
BAXTER Jim – Scotland
BONIEK Zbigniew
– Poland
BOZSIK József
– Hungary
BOWLES Stan
BUCHAN Charlie,
Martin – Scotland
CARTER Raich

CLARKE Allan
CLOUGH Brian, Nigel
CROOKS Garth
CROUCH Peter
CRUYFF Johan
– Netherlands
CULLIS Stan
CURRIE Tony
DAILLY Christian
– Scotland
DOUGAN Derek
– N Ireland
DROGBA Didier – Côte
d'Ivoire
FINNEY Sir Tom
GEORGE Charlie
GINOLA David – France
GULLIT Ruud
– Netherlands
HANSEN Alan
– Scotland
HARRIS Ron
HAYNES Johnny
HODDLE Glenn
HUGHES Aaron
– N Ireland, Emlyn,
Mark – Wales,
Michael – N Ireland
HUNTER Norman
JORDAN Joe – Scotland
KEEGAN Kevin
KELSEY Jack – Wales
LABONE Brian
LAWTON Tommy
LENNON Aaron
MACARI Lou – Scotland
MACKAY Dave
– Scotland

MARTIN Alvin
MCSTAY Paul – Scotland
MEAZZA Giuseppe
  – Italy
MEDWIN Terry – Wales
MERCER Joe
MILLER Kenny
  – Scotland, Willie
  – Scotland
MÜLLER Gerd
  – Germany
NETZER Günter
  – Germany
NORMAN Maurice
O'LEARY David
  – S Ireland
O'NEILL Martin
  – N Ireland
ONOPKO Viktor – Russia
OSGOOD Peter
PARKES Phil
PEARCE Stuart
PETERS Martin
PUSKÁS Ferenc
  – Hungary
RAMSEY Sir Alf
RATTÍN Antonio
  – Argentina
RIVERA Gianni – Italy
ROBSON Sir Bobby,
  Bryan
ROONEY Wayne
SANSOM Kenny
SEAMAN David
SEELER Uwe – Germany
SPRAKE Gary – Wales
STILES Nobby
ST JOHN Ian – Scotland

SUÁREZ Luis – Spain
TAYLOR Maik –
  N Ireland, Tommy
VIEIRA Patrick – France
VÖLLER Rudi – Germany
WADDLE Chris
WATSON Dave
WILSON Bob
  – Scotland, Ray
WRIGHT Billy, Ian
YASHIN Lev – Russia
YORATH Terry – Wales
ZIDANE Zinédine
  – France

7
ADAMSON Jimmy
ARDILES Osvaldo
  – Argentina
BALLACK Michael
  – Germany
BARTHEZ Fabien
  – France
BARTRAM Sam
BECKHAM David
BELLAMY Craig – Wales
BENTLEY Roy
BINGHAM Billy
  – N Ireland
BLOKHIN Oleg – Russia
BONETTI Peter
BREMNER Billy
  – Scotland
BUTCHER Terry
CANTONA Éric – France
CHANNON Mick
CHARLES John – Wales,
  Mel – Wales

CHIVERS Martin
COPPELL Steve
DOUGLAS Bryan
EASTHAM George
EDWARDS Duncan
ENGLAND Mike – Wales
EUSÉBIO Portugal
FASHANU John, Justin
FLOWERS Ron
FRANCIS Gerry, Trevor
GEMMILL Archie
  – Scotland
GENTILE Claudio – Italy
GERRARD Steven
GREAVES Jimmy
HAPGOOD Eddie
HARTSON John – Wales
HATELEY Mark, Tony
JEZZARD Bedford
KNOWLES Cyril
LAMPARD Frank
LAUDRUP Brian, Michael
  – Denmark
LEHMANN Jens
  – Germany
LIDDELL Billy – Scotland
LINEKER Gary
LORIMER Peter
  – Scotland
MABBUTT Gary
MALDINI Paolo – Italy
MARINER Paul
MANNION Wilf
MCCOIST Ally
  – Scotland
MCGRAIN Danny
  – Scotland
MCILROY Jimmy

– N Ireland, Sammy
– N Ireland
MCLEISH Alex
– Scotland
MERRICK Gil
MILBURN Jackie
MULLERY Alan
NEVILLE Gary
NICHOLL Chris
– N Ireland
PAULETA Portugal
PLATINI Michel – France
QUIXALL Albert
RADFORD John
RIVALDO Brazil
RONALDO Brazil
SALENKO Oleg – Russia
SCHOLES Paul
SCOULAR Jimmy
– Scotland
SHANKLY Bill – Scotland
SHEARER Alan
SHILTON Peter
SOUNESS Graeme
– Scotland
TOSHACK John – Wales
WILKINS Ray

8
ANDERSON Viv
ARMFIELD Jimmy
BERGKAMP Dennis
– Netherlands
BROOKING Sir Trevor
CAMPBELL Sol
CANTWELL Noel
– S Ireland
CHARLTON Sir Bobby,

Jack
CLEMENCE Ray
DALGLISH Kenny
– Scotland
DEL PIERO Alessandro
– Italy
FERGUSON Barry
– Scotland
GAVRILOV Yuri – Russia
HARTFORD Asa
– Scotland
JENNINGS Pat
– N Ireland
JOHNSTON Mo
– Scotland
KLUIVERT Patrick
– Netherlands
LEIGHTON Jim
– Scotland
LUBAŃSKI Włodzimierz
– Poland
MAKÉLÉLÉ Claude
– France
MARADONA Diego
– Argentina
MATTHÄUS Lothar
– Germany
MATTHEWS Sir Stanley
MCFADDEN James
– Scotland
MEREDITH Billy – Wales
NICHOLAS Charlie
– Scotland, Peter
– Wales
OVERMARS Marc
– Netherlands
PERRYMAN Steve
RIVELINO Brazil

ROBINSON Paul
SAUNDERS Dean
– Wales
SIMONSEN Allan
– Denmark
SOUTHALL Neville
– Wales
STRACHAN Gordon
– Scotland
THOMPSON Phil
VAN HIMST Paul
– Belgium
VENABLES Terry
WOODCOCK Tony

9
ALLCHURCH Ivor – Wales
BATISTUTA Gabriel
– Argentina
BEARDSLEY Peter
BROADBENT Peter
CALLAGHAN Ian
CANNAVARO Fabio
– Italy
CEULEMANS Jan
– Belgium
DICKINSON Jimmy
DI STÉFANO Alfredo
– Argentina/Spain
DITCHBURN Ted
FERDINAND Les, Rio
GARRINCHA Brazil
GASCOIGNE Paul
GILLESPIE Keith
– N Ireland
HUTCHISON Tommy
– Scotland
JAIRZINHO Brazil

JOHNSTONE Willie
– Scotland
KLINSMANN Jürgen
– Germany
LAWRENSON Mark
– S Ireland
LOFTHOUSE Nat
MACDONALD Malcolm
MCDERMOTT Terry
MCFARLAND Roy
MCLINTOCK Frank
– Scotland
MCMANAMAN Steve
MORTENSEN Stan
RAVANELLI Fabrizio
– Italy
SCHNEIDER Bernd
– Germany
SOUTHGATE Gareth
SPRINGETT Ron

STAPLETON Frank
– S Ireland
SUMMERBEE Mike
VAN BASTEN Marco
– Netherlands
VAN DER SAR Edwin
– Netherlands
WHITESIDE Norman
– N Ireland
ZAGORAKIS Theodoros
– Greece

10
GROBBELAAR Bruce
– Zimbabwe
HARGREAVES Owen
MCALLISTER Gary
– Scotland
RONALDINHO Brazil
RUMMENIGGE Karl-

Heinz – Germany
SCHMEICHEL Peter
– Denmark
SHACKLETON Len

11
BECKENBAUER Franz
– Germany
WORTHINGTON Nigel
– N Ireland
ZUBIZARRETA Andoni
– Spain

12
BLANCHFLOWER Danny
– N Ireland

14
WRIGHT-PHILLIPS Shaun

Sports & Games – Sport – Sportspeople – GOLFERS
American unless stated

3
ELS Ernie – South Africa
WAY Paul – England
WIE Michelle

4
AOKI Isao – Japan
BEAN Andy
BECK Chip
DALY John
FUNK Fred
HUNT Bernard
– England

KITE Tom
LEMA Tony
LOVE Davis
LYLE Sandy – Scotland
MIZE Larry
OWEN Greg – England
PATE Jerry
REES Dai – Wales
ROSE Justin – England
TWAY Bob
WOOD Craig

5
AARON Tommy
BJØRN Thomas
– Denmark
BRAID James – Scotland
BRAND Gordon
– Scotland
BROWN David
– Scotland, Ken
– Scotland
CLARK Clive – England,
Howard – England
COLES Neil – England

DARCY Eamonn
 – S Ireland
DUVAL David
FALDO Nick – England
FAXON Brad
FLOYD Ray
FURYK Jim
GRADY Wayne
 – Australia
GREEN Hubert
HAGEN Walter
HOGAN Ben
IRWIN Hale
JAMES Mark – England
JONES Bobby
LEVET Thomas
 – France
LOCKE Bobby
LOPEZ Nancy
MARSH Graham
 – Australia
NAGLE Kel – Australia
NORTH Andy
OCHOA Lorena
 – Mexico
PRICE Nick –
 Zimbabwe
ROCCA Constantino
 – Italy
SINGH Vijay – Fiji
SMYTH Des –
 S Ireland
SNEAD Sam
WOODS Tiger

6
ALLISS Peter – England
ARMOUR Tommy

BARNES Brian
 – Scotland
BREWER Gay
CASPER Billy
CLARKE Darren
 – N Ireland
COTTON Henry
 – England
CURTIS Ben
DAVIES Laura
 – England
DONALD Luke
 – England
GARCÍA Sergio
 – Spain
GOOSEN Retief
 – South Africa
GRAHAM David
 – Australia
HORTON Tommy
 – England
JACOBS John
 – England, John
LANGER Bernhard
 – Germany
LAWRIE Paul
 – Scotland
LEHMAN Tom
MILLER Johnny
MORRIS Tom
 – Scotland
NELSON Byron, Larry
NORMAN Greg
 – Australia
O'MEARA Mark
PALMER Arnold
PIÑERO Manuel
 –Spain

PLAYER Gary – South
 Africa
ROGERS Bill
SUTTON Hal
TAYLOR JH – England
VARDON Harry
 – England
WATSON Tom

7
AZINGER Paul
CABRERA Angel
 – Argentina
CHARLES Bob – New
 Zealand
COUPLES Fred
FEHERTY David
 – N Ireland
GARRIDO Antonio
 – Spain
HUGGETT Brian – Wales
INKSTER Juli
JACKLIN Tony – England
LEONARD Justin
LITTLER Gene
MCNULTY Mark
 – Zimbabwe/S Ireland
O'CONNOR Christy
 – S Ireland
SANDERS Doug
SARAZEN Gene
STADLER Craig, Kevin
STEWART Payne
STRANGE Curtis
THOMSON Peter
 – Australia
TREVINO Lee
WADKINS Lanny

WOOSNAM Ian
– Wales
ZOELLER Fuzzy

8
BAIOCCHI Hugh
– South Africa
CRENSHAW Ben
FAULKNER Max
– England
HAMILTON Todd
LONGMUIR Bill
– Scotland
NAKAJIMA Tommy
– Japan
NICKLAUS Jack
OLAZÁBAL José Maria
– Spain
PARNEVIK Jesper
– Sweden
RAFFERTY Ronan
– N Ireland

STUPPLES Karen
– England
TORRANCE Sam
– Scotland
WEISKOPF Tom
WESTWOOD Lee
– England
WETHERED Joyce
– England

9
BEMBRIDGE Maurice
– England
BONALLACK Michael
– England
BROADHURST Paul
– England
CAÑIZARES José Maria
– Spain
GALLAGHER Bernard
– Scotland
MICKELSON Phil

SÖRENSTAM Annika
– Sweden

10
BAKER-FINCH Ian
– Australia
HARRINGTON Pádraig
– S Ireland
OOSTERHUIS Peter
– England

11
BALLESTEROS Severiano
– Spain
MONTGOMERIE Colin
– Scotland

12
CALCAVECCHIA Mark

3
DAY Pat
FOX Freddie

4
CARR Harry
DURR Frankie
HEAD Freddy
HIDE Eddie
REID John

SWAN* Charlie
WYER* Lorcan

5
BARRY* Ron
DWYER Mark*,
    Martin
GUEST* Richard
HILLS Michael,
    Richard

LEWIS Geoff
MCCOY* Tony
MOORE Ryan
QUINN
    Richard
ROUSE Brian
SMITH Doug
STACK*
    Tommy
WRAGG Harry

6
ARCHER Fred
BAILEY Jerry
CARSON Willie
DARLEY Kevin
DAVIES* Bob
EDDERY Pat, Paul
FALLON Kieren
HUGHES Richard
JARNET Thierry

KINANE Michael,
  Tommy*
KNIGHT* Stephen
MELLOR* Stan
MERCER Joe
MURRAY Tony
NEWNES Billy
O'NEILL* Jonjo
PINCAY Laffit
PITMAN* Richard
RIMELL* Fred
SMIRKE Charlie
TAAFFE* Pat
TAYLOR Brian
UTTLEY* Jimmy
WINTER* Fred

7

BARCLAY Sandy
CAUTHEN Steve
CULLOTY* Jim
DETTORI Frankie
FENWICK* Charlie
FRANCIS* Dick

GIFFORD* Josh
JOHNSON Ernie, Richard*
MAGUIRE* Adrian
MURTAGH Johnny
LINDLEY Jimmy
PESLIER Olivier
PIGGOTT Lester
RAYMOND Bruce
STARKEY Greville
THORNER* Graham
TINKLER Kim

8

ASMUSSEN Cash
BRABAZON* Aubrey
BREASLEY Scobie
CARBERRY* Paul, Tommy
CHAMPION* Bob
COCHRANE Ray
DONOGHUE Steve
DUFFIELD George
DUNWOODY* Richard
FLETCHER* Brian
FRANCOME* John

KELLEWAY* Paul
MCCARRON Chris
PASQUIER Stéphane
RICHARDS Sir Gordon
ROBINSON* Willie
SAUNDERS* Dick
SWINBURN Walter

9

BRODERICK* Paddy
BROOKSHAW* Tim
POINCELET Roger
SCUDAMORE* Peter
SHOEMAKER Willie

10

HUTCHINSON Ron
WILLIAMSON Bill

11

BIDDLECOMBE* Terry
SAINT-MARTIN Yves
SMITH-ECCLES* Steve

Sports & Games – Sport – Sportspeople – RACING DRIVERS
* = rally driver

4

AMON Chris
BELL Derek
HILL Damon,
  Graham, Phil
HUNT James
ICKX Jacky

LOEB*
  Sébastien
MASS Jochen
MOSS Sir
  Stirling
PACE Carlos

5

ALESI Jean
BEHRA Jean
CLARK Jim, Roger*
HULME Denny
JONES Alan
LAUDA Niki

MASSA Felipe
PANIS Olivier
PROST Alain
RINDT Jochen
ROHRL* Walter
SAINZ* Carlos
SENNA Ayrton

6

ALONSO Fernando
ARNOUX René
ASCARI Alberto
AURIOL* Didier
BERGER Gerhard
BROOKS Tony
BUTTON Jenson
CHIRON* Louis
EKLUND* Per
ELFORD* Vic
FANGIO Juan Manuel
FARINA Nino
GURNEY Dan
IRVINE Eddie
MUNARI* Sandro
PIQUET Nelson
PIRONI Didier
TAMBAY Patrick
TRULLI Jarno
WATSON John

7

BANDINI Lorenzo
BIASION* Miki
BONNIER Jo
BOUTSEN Thierry
BRABHAM Sir Jack
BRUNDLE Martin
CHEEVER Eddie
COLLINS Peter

FAGIOLI Luigi
GINTHER Richie
HERBERT Johnny
HOPKIRK* Paddy
IRELAND Innes
LAFITTE Jacques
MÄKINEN* Timo, Tommi
MANSELL Nigel
MCLAREN Bruce
MIKKOLA* Hannu
MONTOYA Juan Pablo
NILSSON Gunnar
PARNELL Reg
PATRESE Riccardo
ROSBERG Keke
SIFFERT Jo
STEWART Sir Jackie
SURTEES John
VATANEN* Ari
WARWICK Derek

8

AALTONEN* Rauno
ALBORETO Michele
ANDRETTI Mario
BELTOISE Jean-Pierre
BLUNDELL Mark
CARLSSON* Erik
DE LA ROSA Pedro
HÄKKINEN Mika
HAMILTON Lewis

HAWTHORN Mike
NUVOLARI Tazio
PETERSON Ronnie
VON TRIPS Wolfgang

9

AIRIKKALA* Pentti
BLOMQVIST* Stig
COULTHARD David
DE ANGELIS Elio
DE CESARIS Andrea
KANKKUNEN* Juha
RÄIKKÖNEN Kimi
REGAZZONI Clay
REUTEMANN Carlos
RODRIGUEZ Pedro
SALVADORI Roy
SCHECKTER Jody
WALDEGÅRD* Björn

10

FISICHELLA Giancarlo
FITTIPALDI Emerson
SCHUMACHER
   Michael, Ralf

VILLENEUVE Gilles,
   Jacques

11

BARRICHELLO Rubens

Sports & Games – Sport – Sportspeople – Rugby Players – RUGBY LEAGUE
England unless stated * = also rugby union

3
FOX Neil

4
TAIT* Alan – Scotland

5
ASTON Mark
CRAIG Andy – Scotland
HORNE Willie
JONES Lewis – Wales
LYDON Joe

6
BISHOP Tommy
BOSTON Billy – Wales
CARNEY Brian – Ireland

DAVIES* Jonathan
  – Wales
FOSTER Trevor – Wales
HANLEY Ellery
HARRIS Tommy – Wales
MURPHY Alex
NORTON Steve
OFFIAH Martin
REILLY Martin
RISMAN Gus – Wales

7
BRISCOE Shaun
EDWARDS Shaun
FARRELL Andrew
GREGORY Andy
TOPLISS Dave

WATKINS* David
  – Wales

8
KARALIUS Vince
MILLWARD Roger
ROBINSON Jason
THOMPSON Cec
WAGSTAFF Harold

9
CANTILLON Phil
  – Ireland
MCDERMOTT Barry
  – Ireland
SCHOFIELD Garry

Sports & Games – Sport – Sportspeople – Rugby Players – RUGBY UNION
* = also rugby league

3
FOX Grant – New
  Zealand
OTI Chris – England

4
ELLA Mark – Australia
GRAY Ken – New
  Zealand
HARE Dusty – England
JOHN Barry – Wales
KEFU Toutai – Australia

KYLE Jack – Ireland
LOMU Jonah – New
  Zealand
MASO Jo –France
PRAT Jean – France
ROFF Joe – Australia
TAIT* Alan – Scotland
WEIR Doddie – Scotland
WOOD Keith – Ireland

5
BOTHA Naas – S Africa

BROWN Gordon
  – Scotland
BURKE Matt – Australia
CHAMP Eric – France
COHEN Ben – England
DEANS Colin – Scotland
EALES John – Australia
ELLIS Jan – S Africa
GOING Sid – New
  Zealand
HADEN Andy – New
  Zealand

HORAN Tim – Australia
JAMES Carwyn – Wales
JEEPS Dickie – England
JONES Ken – Wales,
   Michael – New
   Zealand
LOGAN Kenny
   – Scotland
MEADS Colin – New
   Zealand
MOORE Brian – England
PORTA Hugo
   – Argentina
PRICE Graham – Wales
RIVES Jean-Pierre
   – France
SELLA Philippe – France
SHARP Richard
   – England
SMITH Arthur
   – Scotland
UMAGA Tana – New
   Zealand
WHITE Jason – Scotland
YOUNG David, Jeff
   – Wales

6
ANDREW Rob – England
BETSEN Serge – France
BLANCO Serge – France
CALDER Finlay
   – Scotland
CLARKE Don – New
   Zealand
COTTON Fran
   – England
CRAVEN Danie – S Africa

DAVIES Gerald,
   Jonathan*, Mervyn
   – Wales
DOOLEY Wade
   – England
GIBSON Mike – Gibson
GREGAN George
   – Australia
HENSON Gavin – Wales
IRVINE Andy – Scotland
KIRWAN John – New
   Zealand
LATHAM Chris
   – Australia
LYNAGH Michael
   – Australia
MARTIN Ronaldo
   – Argentina
MILLAR Syd – Ireland
MORGAN Cliff – Wales
MOTOKI Yukio – Japan
MULLER Hennie
   – S Africa
MULLIN Brendan
   – Ireland
NATHAN Waka – New
   Zealand
PAULSE Breyton
   – S Africa
PROBYN Jeff – England
SEREVI Waisale – Fiji
STOICA Cristian – Italy
TEAGUE Mike – England
THORNE Reuben – New
   Zealand
UTTLEY Roger – England
WILSON Stu – New
   Zealand

7
BENNETT Phil – Wales
BROUZET Olivier
   – France
CAMPESE David
   – Australia
CARLING Will – England
DUCKHAM David
   – England
DU PREEZ Frik – S Africa
EDWARDS Gareth
   – Wales
FLATLEY Elton
   – Australia
FOUROUX Jacques
   – France
GALTHIÉ Fabien
   – France
GUSCOTT Jeremy
   – England
JACKSON Peter
   – England
JEFFREY John – Scotland
JOHNSON Martin
   – England
LACROIX Thierry
   – France
LARKHAM Stephen
   – Australia
LENIHAN Donal
   – Ireland
LEONARD Jason
   – England
LOCHORE Brian – New
   Zealand
MCBRIDE Willie John
   – Ireland
O'REILLY Tony – Ireland

PIENAAR François
– S Africa
PROSSER Ray – Wales
TREMAIN Kel – New
Zealand
TRONCON Alessandro
– Italy
WATKINS* David – Wales
WHEELER Peter
– England

8
ALBANESE Diego
– Argentina
BEAUMONT Bill
– England
HASTINGS Gavin, Scott
– Scotland
MOSCARDI Alessandro
– Italy
POIDEVIN Simon
– Australia
QUINNELL Derek
– Wales

SHELFORD Wayne
– New Zealand
SLATTERY Fergus
– Ireland
STRANSKY Joel – S Africa
WHINERAY Sir Wilson
– New Zealand
WILLIAMS JJ, JPR – Wales

9
ARMSTRONG Gary
– Scotland
CATCHPOLE Ken
– Australia
DALLAGLIO Lawrence
– England
DU PLESSIS Morne
– S Africa
FARR-JONES Nick
– Australia
GREENWOOD Dick, Will
– England
HUMPHREYS David
– Ireland

LOVERIDGE Dave – New
Zealand
O'DRISCOLL Brian
– Ireland
SPANGHERO Walter
– France
UNDERWOOD Rory,
Tony – England
WILKINSON Jonny
– England

10
MCLOUGHLIN Ray
– Ireland
VILLEPREUX Pierre
– France

11
BUTTERFIELD Jeff
– England
FITZPATRICK Sean
– New Zealand
KIRKPATRICK Ian – New
Zealand

Sports & Games – Sport – Sportspeople – SNOOKER PLAYERS
* = billiard player

3
LEE Stephen,
Sydney
MEO Tony
RAE Jackie

4
BOND Nigel
DING Junhui
DOTT Graeme
HANN
Quinten
MANS Perrie

5
DAVIS Fred,
Joe, Steve
DRAGO Tony
EBDON Peter
MILES Graham
SELBY Vera

SETHI* Geet
SWAIL Joe
VIRGO John
WHITE Jimmy

6
DAGLEY* Norman

FISHER Allison, Kelly
FOULDS Neal
HENDRY Stephen
HUNTER Paul
NEWMAN* Tom
O'BRIEN Fergal
PULMAN John
TAYLOR Dennis
THORNE Willie
WILSON Cliff

7

DOHERTY Ken
HIGGINS Alex, John

JOHNSON Joe
KARNEHM* Jack
KNOWLES Tony
LINDRUM Horace,
 Walter*
MAGUIRE Stephen
MCMANUS Alan
PARROTT John
REARDON Ray
RUSSELL* Mike
SPENCER John
STEVENS Kirk,
 Matthew
WATTANA James

8

CHARLTON Eddie
MOUNTJOY Doug
THORBURN Cliff
WILLIAMS Mark, Rex*

9

DONALDSON Walter
FRANCISCO Silvino
GRIFFITHS Terry
ROBERTSON Neil
O'SULLIVAN Ronnie
WERBENIUK Bill

Sports & Games – Sport – Sportspeople – TENNIS PLAYERS
USA tennis players unless stated

4

ASHE Arthur
CASH Pat – Australia
BORG Björn – Sweden
GRAF Steffi – Germany
HART Doris
HOAD Lew – Australia
KING Billie Jean
WADE Virginia
 – Britain

5

BUENO Maria – Brazil
BUDGE Don
CHANG Michael
COURT Margaret
 – Australia

EVERT Chris
JANES see Truman
JONES Ann – Britain
KODES Jan – Czech
 Republic
LAVER Rod – Australia
LENDL Ivan – Czech
 Republic
MOODY Helen Wills
NADAL Rafael – Spain
PERRY Fred – Britain
RIGGS Bobby
ROCHE Tony
 – Australia
SAFIN Marat – Russia
SELES Monica – Serbia/
 USA

SMITH Stan
STICH Michael – Germany
VILAS Guillermo
 – Argentina
VINES Ellsworth

6

AGASSI André
AUSTIN Tracy
BARKER Sue – Britain
BECKER Boris – Germany
CAWLEY see Goolagong
COCHET Henri – France
EDBERG Stefan – Sweden
GIBSON Althea
HENMAN Tim – Britain
HEWITT Lleyton – Australia

HINGIS Martina
– Switzerland
KRAMER Jack
MURRAY Andy
– Britain
PIERCE Mary – France
RAFTER Pat – Australia
SEGURA Pancho
– Ecuador/USA
TANNER Roscoe
TAYLOR Roger
– Britain
TILDEN Bill
TRUMAN Christine
– Britain

7

BOROTRA Jean
– France
CONNORS Jimmy
COURIER Jim
EMERSON Roy
– Australia
FEDERER Roger
– Switzerland
KUERTEN Gustavo
– Brazil
LACOSTE René
– France
LENGLEN Suzanne
– France

MCENROE John
NASTASE Ilie
– Romania
NOVOTNA Jana
– Czech Republic
RODDICK Andy
SAMPRAS Pete
SEDGMAN Frank
– Australia

8

AMRITRAJ Vijay – India
CAPRIATI Jennifer
CONNOLLY Maureen
GONZALES Pancho
KRAJICEK Richard
– Netherlands
MARTINEZ Conchita
– Spain
MAURESMO Amélie
– France
MORTIMER Angela
– Britain
NEWCOMBE John
– Australia
ROSEWALL Ken
– Australia
RUSEDSKI Greg
– Britain
WILANDER Mats
– Sweden

WILLIAMS Serena,
Venus

9

CLIJSTERS Kim
– Belgium
DAVENPORT Lindsay
GOOLAGONG Evonne
– Australia
SHARAPOVA Maria
– Russia

10

IVANIŠEVIC Goran
– Croatia
KAFELNIKOV Yevgeny
– Russia
MANDLIKOVÁ Hana
– Czech Republic
SRICHAPHAN Paradorn
– Thailand

11

NAVRATILOVA Martina
– Czech Republic/USA

13

HENIN-HARDENNE
Justine – Belgium
PHILIPPOUSSIS Mark
– Australia

Sports & Games – Sport – Teams – CRICKET

* = national team

4
KENT

5
ESSEX
INDIA*
6
DURHAM
SURREY
SUSSEX

7
ENGLAND*

8
PAKISTAN*
SOMERSET
SRI LANKA*
ZIMBABWE*

9
AUSTRALIA*
GLAMORGAN
HAMPSHIRE

MIDDLESEX
YORKSHIRE

10
BANGLADESH*
DERBYSHIRE
LANCASHIRE
NEW ZEALAND*
WEST INDIES*

11
SOUTH AFRICA*

12
WARWICKSHIRE

14
LEICESTERSHIRE
WORCESTERSHIRE

15
GLOUCESTERSHIRE
NOTTINGHAMSHIRE

16
NORTHAMPTONSHIRE

Sports & Games – Sport – Teams – FOOTBALL (Europe)

4
AJAX Netherlands
LYON France
NICE France

5
BETIS Spain
LAZIO Italy
LILLE France
MALMO Sweden
PARMA Italy
PORTO Portugal
SIENA Italy

6
AS ROMA Italy
HONVÉD Hungary
MONACO Monaco

NANTES France
NAPOLI Italy
RENNES France
SPARTA Netherlands
TORINO Italy
ÚJPEST Hungary

7
AC MILAN Italy
AUXERRE France
BENFICA Portugal
OSASUNA Spain
SEVILLA Spain
SOCHAUX France

8
BEIRA-MAR Portugal
BOAVISTA Portugal

BORDEAUX France
ESPANYOL Spain
JUVENTUS Italy
MALLORCA Spain
VALENCIA Spain
ZARAGOZA Spain

9
BARCELONA Spain
EINTRACHT Germany
FEYENOORD
 Netherlands
MARSEILLE France
SAMPDORIA Italy
ST ÉTIENNE France
STUTTGART Germany

10
ANDERLECHT Belgium
CLUB BRUGGE Belgium
DYNAMO KIEV Ukraine
FIORENTINA Italy
INTER MILAN Italy
OLYMPIAKOS Greece
REAL MADRID Spain

11
FERENCVÁROS Hungary
HAMBURGER SV Germany
IFK GÖTEBORG Sweden

12
CERCLE BRUGGE Belgium
DYNAMO MOSCOW Russia
GRASSHOPPERS Switzerland
PSV EINDHOVEN Netherlands
REAL SOCIEDAD Spain
SPARTA PRAGUE Czech Republic
WERDER BREMEN German

13
BAYERN MÜNCHEN Germany
PANATHANAIKOS Greece
SPARTAK MOSCOW Russia
STANDARD LIÈGE Belgium
UDINESE CALCIO Italy

14
ATLÉTICO BILBAO Spain
ATLÉTICO MADRID Spain
BAYER LEVERKUSEN Germany
PARIS ST GERMAIN France

15
RED STAR BELGRADE Serbia

16
BORUSSIA DORTMUND Germany

17
DEPORTIVO LA CORUÑA Spain

23
BORUSSIA MÖNCHENGLADBACH
   Germany

Sports & Games – Sport – Teams – FOOTBALL (UK)
All English unless stated

4
BURY

5
CLYDE Scotland

6
BARNET

CELTIC Scotland
DUNDEE Scotland
FULHAM
GRETNA Scotland

7
ARSENAL
BURNLEY

CHELSEA
EVERTON
FALKIRK Scotland
RANGERS Scotland
READING
WALSALL
WATFORD
WREXHAM Wales

8
ABERDEEN Scotland
ARBROATH Scotland
BARNSLEY
EAST FIFE Scotland
HULL CITY
MILLWALL
MONTROSE Scotland
PORT VALE
ROCHDALE
ST MIRREN Scotland

9
AYR UNITED Scotland
BLACKPOOL
BRENTFORD
DUMBARTON Scotland
ELGIN CITY Scotland
HIBERNIAN Scotland
LIVERPOOL
LUTON TOWN
PETERHEAD Scotland
STOKE CITY
STRANRAER Scotland

10
ASTON VILLA
DARLINGTON
GILLINGHAM
KILMARNOCK Scotland
LIVINGSTON Scotland
MOTHERWELL Scotland
PORTSMOUTH
QUEENS PARK Scotland
ROSS COUNTY Scotland
SUNDERLAND
YEOVIL TOWN

11
BOURNEMOUTH
BRECHIN CITY Scotland
BRISTOL CITY
CARDIFF CITY Wales
CHESTER CITY
COWDENBEATH
    Scotland
DERBY COUNTY
GRIMSBY TOWN
IPSWICH TOWN
LEEDS UNITED
LINCOLN CITY
NORWICH CITY
NOTTS COUNTY
RAITH ROVERS Scotland
SOUTHAMPTON
ST JOHNSTONE Scotland
SWANSEA CITY
SWINDON TOWN

12
ALBION ROVERS
    Scotland
BOSTON UNITED
BRADFORD CITY
CHESTERFIELD
COVENTRY CITY
DUNDEE UNITED
    Scotland
LEYTON ORIENT

13
AIRDRIE UNITED
    Scotland
ALLOA ATHLETIC
    Scotland

BRISTOL ROVERS
CRYSTAL PALACE
LEICESTER CITY
MANSFIELD TOWN
MIDDLESBROUGH
STENHOUSEMUIR
    Scotland
TORQUAY UNITED
WEST HAM UNITED
WIGAN ATHLETIC

14
BERWICK RANGERS
BIRMINGHAM CITY
CARLISLE UNITED
CHELTENHAM TOWN
CREWE ALEXANDRA
FORFAR ATHLETIC
    Scotland
GREENOCK MORTON
    Scotland
HEREFORD UNITED
MANCHESTER CITY
OLDHAM ATHLETIC
PARTICK THISTLE
    Scotland
PLYMOUTH ARGYLE
SHREWSBURY TOWN
SOUTHEND UNITED
STIRLING ALBION
    Scotland
TRANMERE ROVERS

15
BLACKBURN ROVERS
BOLTON WANDERERS
DONCASTER ROVERS

NEWCASTLE UNITED
NORTHAMPTON TOWN
PRESTON NORTH END
QUEEN OF THE SOUTH Scotland
ROTHERHAM UNITED
SHEFFIELD UNITED
STOCKPORT COUNTY

16
CHARLTON ATHLETIC
COLCHESTER UNITED
HARTLEPOOL UNITED
HUDDERSFIELD TOWN
MACCLESFIELD TOWN
MANCHESTER UNITED
MILTON KEYNES DONS
NOTTINGHAM FOREST
SCUNTHORPE UNITED
TOTTENHAM HOTSPUR
WYCOMBE WANDERERS

17
ACCRINGTON STANLEY

EAST STIRLINGSHIRE Scotland
HEART OF MIDLOTHIAN Scotland
QUEENS PARK RANGERS

18
HAMILTON ACADEMICAL Scotland
PETERBOROUGH UNITED
SHEFFIELD WEDNESDAY
WEST BROMWICH ALBION

19
DUNFERMLINE ATHLETIC Scotland

21
BRIGHTON AND HOVE ALBION

22
WOLVERHAMPTON WANDERERS

26
INVERNESS CALEDONIAN THISTLE
  Scotland

**Sports & Games – Sport – Teams – North American Sport –
AMERICAN FOOTBALL**

4
JETS New York
RAMS St Louis

5
BEARS Chicago
BILLS Buffalo
COLTS Indianapolis
LIONS Detroit

6
BROWNS Cleveland
CHIEFS Kansas City
EAGLES Philadelphia
GIANTS New York
RAVENS Baltimore
SAINTS New Orleans
TEXANS Houston
TITANS Tennessee

7
BENGALS Cincinnati
BRONCOS Denver
COWBOYS Dallas
FALCONS Atlanta
JAGUARS Jacksonville
PACKERS Green Bay
RAIDERS Oakland
VIKINGS Minnesota

8
CHARGERS San Diego
DOLPHINS Miami
PANTHERS Carolina
PATRIOTS New England

REDSKINS Washington
SEAHAWKS Seattle
STEELERS Pittsburgh

9
CARDINALS Arizona

10
BUCCANEERS Tampa Bay

Sports & Games – Sport – Teams – North American Sport – BASEBALL

4
CUBS Chicago
METS New York
REDS Cincinnati

5
TWINS Minnesota

6
ASTROS Houston
BRAVES Atlanta
GIANTS San Francisco
MARLINS Florida
PADRES San Diego
RED SOX Boston
ROYALS Kansas City

TIGERS Detroit

7
BREWERS Milwaukee
DODGERS Los Angeles
INDIANS Cleveland
ORIOLES Baltimore
PHILLIES Philadelphia
PIRATES Pittsburgh
RANGERS Texas
ROCKIES Colorado
YANKEES New York

8
BLUE JAYS Toronto
MARINERS Seattle

WHITE SOX Chicago

9
ATHLETICS Oakland
CARDINALS St Louis
DEVIL RAYS Tampa Bay
NATIONALS Washington

12
DIAMONDBACKS Arizona

15
ANGELS OF ANAHEIM
    Los Angeles

Sports & Games – Sport – Teams – North American Sport – ICE HOCKEY

4
WILD Minnesota

5
BLUES St Louis
DUCKS Anaheim
KINGS Los Angeles

STARS Dallas

6
BRUINS Boston
DEVILS New Jersey
FLAMES Calgary
FLYERS Philadelphia

OILERS Edmonton
SABRES Buffalo
SHARKS San José

7
CANUCKS Vancouver
COYOTES Phoenix

RANGERS New York

8
CAPITALS Washington
PANTHERS Florida
PENGUINS Pittsburgh
RED WINGS Detroit
SENATORS Ottawa

9
AVALANCHE Colorado
CANADIENS Montreal
ISLANDERS New York
LIGHTNING Tampa Bay
PREDATORS Nashville
THRASHERS Atlanta

10
BLACKHAWKS Chicago
HURRICANES Carolina
MAPLE LEAFS Toronto

11
BLUE JACKETS Columbus

Sports & Games – Sport – Teams – RUGBY LEAGUE

4
HULL

7
HALIFAX

8
ST HELENS

10
HEMEL STAGS
WHITEHAVEN

11
LEEDS RHINOS

12
DEWSBURY RAMS
HARLEQUINS RL
HUNSLET HAWKS
SWINTON LIONS

13
BARROW RAIDERS
BRADFORD BULLS
LONDON SKOLARS
WIDNES VIKINGS
WIGAN WARRIORS

14
BATLEY BULLDOGS
DEWSBURY CELTIC
WORKINGTON TOWN

15
CELTIC CRUSADERS Wales
DONCASTER LAKERS
KEIGHLEY COUGARS
LEIGH CENTURIONS
OLDHAM ROUGHYEDS
ROCHDALE HORNETS
SALFORD CITY REDS
SHEFFIELD EAGLES

YORK CITY KNIGHTS

16
BRADLEY BUFFALOES
CASTLEFORD TIGERS
GATESHEAD THUNDER
WARRINGTON WOLVES

17
BLACKPOOL PANTHERS
WARRINGTON WIZARDS

18
BRADFORD DUDLEY HILL
FEATHERSTONE ROVERS
HUDDERSFIELD GIANTS
HULL KINGSTON ROVERS
ST ALBANS CENTURIONS

24
WAKEFIELD TRINITY WILDCATS

Sports & Games – Sport – Teams – RUGBY UNION
* = national nickname

3
AYR Scotland

4
BATH
BEES

5
KIWIS* New Zealand
LIONS* Britain
NEATH Wales
OTLEY
PUMAS* Argentina
WASPS

6
BEDWAS Wales
CURRIE Scotland
DUNDEE Scotland
HAWICK Scotland
ULSTER N Ireland

7
BRISTOL
CARDIFF Wales
HERIOTS Scotland
MAESTEG Wales
MELROSE Scotland
MOSELEY
MUNSTER S Ireland
NEWBURY
NEWPORT Wales
OSPREYS Wales
SWANSEA Wales

8
ABERAVON Wales
ABERDEEN Scotland
CONNACHT S Ireland
COVENTRY
LEINSTER S Ireland
LLANELLI Wales
NUNEATON
SARACENS
WATERLOO

9
CAMBRIDGE
DONCASTER
GLOUCESTER
PONTYPOOL Wales
WALLABIES* Australia

10
BLACKHEATH
CARMARTHEN Wales
HARLEQUINS
LEEDS TYKES
NOTTINGHAM
PONTYPRIDD Wales
SALE SHARKS
SPRINGBOKS* South
    Africa
WATSONIANS Scotland

11
BOROUGHMUIR
    Scotland
EARTH TITANS
LONDON IRISH

LONDON WELSH
SEDGLEY PARK
STOURBRIDGE

12
BEDFORD BLUES
CARDIFF BLUES Wales
EXETER CHIEFS

13
BORDER REIVERS Scotland

14
BRIDGEND ROVERS Wales
CORNISH PIRATES
PLYMOUTH ALBION

15
GLASGOW WARRIORS
    Scotland
LEICESTER TIGERS

16
EDINBURGH GUNNERS
    Scotland
LLANELLI SCARLETS Wales
NEWCASTLE FALCONS

17
NORTHAMPTON SAINTS
WORCESTER WARRIORS

19
NEWPORT GWENT DRAGONS
    Wales

Sports & Games – Sport – Venues – CRICKET GROUNDS (UK)
* = Test ground

5
LORD'S* Middlesex

7
NEW ROAD Worcestershire
THE OVAL* Surrey

8
EDGBASTON* Warwickshire

9
EATON ROAD Sussex
GRACE ROAD Leicestershire
NEVIL ROAD Gloucestershire
RIVERSIDE* Durham

10
HEADINGLEY* Yorkshire

11
OLD TRAFFORD* Lancashire
THE ROSE BOWL Hampshire
TRENT BRIDGE* Nottinghamshire
WANTAGE ROAD Northamptonshire

12
OLD DOVER ROAD Kent

13
SOPHIA GARDENS Glamorgan

14
NOTTINGHAM ROAD Derbyshire
ST JAMES'S STREET Somerset

16
NEW WRITTLE STREET Essex

Sports & Games – Sport – Venues – FOOTBALL GROUNDS
* = national stadium

5
IBROX Rangers

6
AZTECA* Mexico
BESCOT Walsall
NEW DEN Millwall

7
ANFIELD Liverpool

BALMOOR Peterhead
BAYVIEW East Fife
DENS PARK Dundee
FIRHILL Partick Thistle
FIR PARK Motherwell
NOU CAMP Barcelona
OAKWELL Barnsley
RÅSUNDA Sweden
SAN SIRO AC Milan,
  Inter Milan

ST MARY'S
  Southampton
WEMBLEY* England

8
BERNABÉU Real Madrid
DEEPDALE Preston
  North End
FIRS PARK East
  Stirlingshire

GIGG LANE Bury
HOME PARK Plymouth
 Argyle
LUZHNIKI* Russia
MARACANÃ* Brazil
MILLMOOR
 Rotherham United
MOLINEUX
 Wolverhampton
 Wanderers
MOSS ROSE
 Macclesfield Town
SPOTLAND Rochdale
TURF MOOR Burnley
ULLEVAAL* Norway
VALE PARK Port Vale
WITHDEAN Brighton &
 Hove Albion

9
BROADWOOD Clyde
DEAN COURT
 Bournemouth
EWOOD PARK
 Blackburn Rovers
FIELD MILL Mansfield
 Town
FORTHBANK Stirling
 Albion
GAY MEADOW
 Shrewsbury Town
GLEBE PARK
 Brechin City
HUISH PARK Yeovil
 Town
JJB STADIUM Wigan
 Athletic
KC STADIUM Hull City

LAYER ROAD
 Colchester United
LINKS PARK Montrose
PITTODRIE Aberdeen
PLAINMOOR
 Torquay United
PRIDE PARK Derby
 County
ROOTS HALL
 Southend United
RUGBY PARK Kilmarnock
STAIR PARK Stranraer
ST ANDREWS
 Birmingham City
THE VALLEY Charlton
 Athletic
UNDERHILL Barnet
VILLA PARK Aston Villa

10
ALMONDVALE
 Livingston
ASHTON GATE
 Bristol City
CARROW ROAD
 Norwich City
CELTIC PARK Celtic
EASTER ROAD Hibernian
ELLAND ROAD
 Leeds United
GRESTY ROAD Crewe
 Alexandra
LOFTUS ROAD Queens
 Park Rangers
LONDON ROAD
 Peterborough United
MEADOW LANE Notts
 County

NINIAN PARK
 Cardiff City
RICOH ARENA
 Coventry City
SINCIL BANK
 Lincoln City
STARK'S PARK Raith
 Rovers
TYNECASTLE Hearts
YORK STREET
 Boston United

11
BRAMALL LANE
 Sheffield United
BRUNTON PARK
 Carlisle United
CENTRAL PARK
 Cowdenbeath
CLIFTONHILL Albion
 Rovers
CROWN GROUND
 Accrington Stanley
DEVA STADIUM
 Chester City
EARTH STADIUM
 Doncaster Rovers
EAST END PARK
 Dunfermline Athletic
EDGAR STREET
 Hereford United
EDGELEY PARK
 Stockport County
ERNST HAPPEL* Austria
FRATTON PARK
 Portsmouth
GRIFFIN PARK Brentford
HAMPDEN PARK*

Scotland, Queens Park
KARAISKÁKIS* Greece
OLD TRAFFORD
   Manchester United
PORTMAN ROAD
   Ipswich Town
PRENTON PARK
   Tranmere Rovers
RAYDALE PARK Gretna
STATION PARK Forfar
   Athletic
ST JAMES' PARK
   Newcastle United
WHADDON ROAD
   Cheltenham Town
WINDSOR PARK*
   Northern Ireland

12
BLUNDELL PARK
   Grimsby Town
BOLEYN GROUND
   West Ham United
BOUNDARY PARK
   Oldham Athletic
CITY GROUND
   Nottingham Forest
COUNTY GROUND
   Swindon Town
EL MONUMENTAL*
   Argentina
GAYFIELD PARK
   Arbroath
GLANFORD PARK
   Scunthorpe United
GOODISON PARK
   Everton
HILLSBOROUGH

Sheffield Wednesday
SELHURST PARK
   Crystal Palace
SOMERSET PARK
   Ayr United
ST MIRREN PARK St
   Mirren
THE HAWTHORNS
   West Bromwich
   Albion
VALLEY PARADE
   Bradford City
VICARAGE ROAD
   Watford
VICTORIA PARK Ross
   County

13
BOROUGH BRIGGS
   Elgin City
CAPPIELOW PARK
   Greenock Morton
CRAVEN COTTAGE
   Fulham
LANSDOWNE ROAD*
   Republic of Ireland
MCDIARMID PARK
   St Johnstone
OCHILVIEW PARK
   Stenhousemuir
REEBOK STADIUM
   Bolton Wanderers
STADE DE FRANCE*
   France
TANNADICE PARK
   Dundee United
WHITE HART LANE
   Tottenham Hotspur

14
BLOOMFIELD ROAD
   Blackpool
BROOMFIELD PARK
   Airdrie United
ESTÁDIO DO JAMOR*
   Portugal
FALKIRK STADIUM
   Falkirk
KENILWORTH ROAD
   Luton Town
LIBERTY STADIUM
   Swansea City
MADEJSKI STADIUM
   Reading
NEW DOUGLAS PARK
   Hamilton Academical
OLYMPIASTADION*
   Germany
PALMERSTON PARK
   Queen of the South
RECREATION PARK Alloa
   Athletic
SHIELFIELD PARK
   Berwick Rangers
STADIO FLAMINIO* Italy
STADIUM OF LIGHT
   Sunderland
STAMFORD BRIDGE
   Chelsea
VICTORIA GROUND
   Hartlepool United
WALKERS STADIUM
   Leicester City

15
CAUSEWAY STADIUM
   Wycombe Wanderers

DARLINGTON ARENA Darlington
EMIRATES STADIUM Arsenal
GALPHARM STADIUM Huddersfield
  Town
MEMORIAL STADIUM Bristol Rovers

16
BRITANNIA STADIUM Stoke City
MATCHROOM STADIUM Leyton
  Orient
RACECOURSE GROUND Wrexham
RECREATION GROUND Chesterfield
RIVERSIDE STADIUM Middlesbrough
SIXFIELDS STADIUM Northampton
  Town

17
CALEDONIAN STADIUM Inverness
  Caledonian Thistle

ESTÁDIO CENTENARIO* Uruguay
MILLENNIUM STADIUM* Wales

18
PRIESTFIELD STADIUM Gillingham

19
KING BAUDOUIN STADIUM* Belgium

21
NATIONAL HOCKEY STADIUM Milton
  Keynes Dons

23
CITY OF MANCHESTER STADIUM
  Manchester City
STRATHCLYDE HOMES STADIUM
  Dumbarton

Sports & Games – Sport – Venues – GOLF COURSES
In England unless stated

5
TROON Scotland

6
WOBURN

7
AUGUSTA USA
HOYLAKE
  (or Royal Liverpool)
OAKMONT USA

8
DALMAHOY Scotland
PORTRUSH N Ireland
ST PIERRE Wales
THE K CLUB S Ireland
VALHALLA USA

9
ABERDOVEY Wales
BALTUSROL USA
HAZELTINE USA
MUIRFIELD Scotland
PINEHURST USA

ST ANDREWS Scotland
ST MELLION
THE BELFRY
TURNBERRY Scotland
WENTWORTH

10
CARNOUSTIE Scotland
COUNTY DOWN
  N Ireland
DRUID'S GLEN
  S Ireland
GLENEAGLES Scotland

WINGED FOOT USA

11
BALLYBUNION S Ireland
CELTIC MANOR Wales
MOUNT JULIET S Ireland
PEBBLE BEACH USA
PORTMARNOCK S Ireland
SUNNINGDALE
WALTON HEATH
WOODHALL SPA

12
HANBURY MANOR
MISSION HILLS USA

13
FOREST OF ARDEN

ROYAL BIRKDALE
SOUTHERN HILLS USA

14
ROYAL LIVERPOOL
  (or Hoylake)
ROYAL ST GEORGE'S

15
SHINNECOCK HILLS USA

18
EAST SUSSEX NATIONAL

21
ROYAL LYTHAM AND ST ANNES

Sports & Games – Sport – Venues – RACECOURSES
In England unless stated

3
AYR Scotland

4
BATH
CORK S Ireland
EVRY France
NAAS S Ireland
YORK

5
ASCOT
EPSOM
KELSO Scotland

NAVAN S Ireland
PERTH Scotland
RIPON
SLIGO S Ireland

6
EXETER
GALWAY S Ireland
HEXHAM
LUDLOW
REDCAR
SHA TIN Hong Kong, China
THIRSK
TRALEE S Ireland

7
AINTREE
AUTEUIL France
CARTMEL
CHESTER
CLONMEL S Ireland
DUNDALK S Ireland
LAYTOWN S Ireland
NEWBURY
PIMLICO USA
TAUNTON
THURLES S Ireland
TRAMORE S Ireland
WARWICK

WEXFORD S Ireland
WINDSOR

8
BEVERLEY
BRIGHTON
CARLISLE
CHEPSTOW Wales
FAKENHAM
GOODWOOD
HEREFORD
LIMERICK S Ireland
LISTOWEL S Ireland
PLUMPTON
WETHERBY

9
CATTERICK
CHANTILLY France
DEAUVILLE France
DONCASTER
DOWN ROYAL N Ireland
KILBEGGAN S Ireland
KILLARNEY S Ireland
LEICESTER
LONGCHAMP France
NEWCASTLE
NEWMARKET
ROSCOMMON
  S Ireland

SALISBURY
SOUTHWELL
TIPPERARY S Ireland
TOWCESTER
UTTOXETER
VINCENNES France
WINCANTON
WORCESTER

10
BALLINROBE S Ireland
CHELTENHAM
FAIRYHOUSE S Ireland
FLEMINGTON Australia
FOLKESTONE
GOWRAN PARK
  S Ireland
HUNTINGDON
NOTTINGHAM
PONTEFRACT
SEDGEFIELD
THE CURRAGH S Ireland

11
BANGOR-ON-DEE Wales
BELLEWSTOWN
  S Ireland
BELMONT PARK USA
DOWNPATRICK
  N Ireland

HAPPY VALLEY Hong
  Kong, China
HAYDOCK PARK
KEMPTON PARK
MARKET RASEN
MUSSELBURGH Scotland
NEWTON ABBOT
PUNCHESTOWN
  S Ireland
SANDOWN PARK

12
FONTWELL PARK
HAMILTON PARK
  Scotland
LEOPARDSTOWN
  S Ireland

13
ARLINGTON PARK USA
GREAT YARMOUTH
LINGFIELD PARK
WOLVERHAMPTON

14
CHURCHILL DOWNS USA

15
STRATFORD-ON-AVON

Transport

Transport – Air – AIR & SPACE TRANSPORT

3
JET
UFO

4
KITE

5
BLIMP
CRATE
DRONE
PLANE
PROBE
SCOUT

6
BOMBER
FAN-JET

GLIDER
RAIDER
ROCKET
TANKER

7
AIRSHIP
BALLOON
BIPLANE
CAPSULE
CHOPPER
FIGHTER
JUMP JET
PROP JET
SHUTTLE
SPUTNIK
TRAINER

8
AEROSTAT
AIRCRAFT
AIRLINER
AIRPLANE
AUTOGYRO
JETLINER
JET PLANE
JUMBO JET
SEAPLANE
TRIPLANE
TURBO-FAN
TURBO-JET
ZEPPELIN

9
AEROPLANE
DELTA-WING

DIRIGIBLE
EGG BEATER
GYROPLANE
HELIPLANE
LANDPLANE
MONOPLANE
MOON BUGGY
PARACHUTE
SAILPLANE
SATELLITE
SPACESHIP
SWING-WING
TURBO-PROP
TWO-SEATER

10
CARGO PLANE
DIVE-BOMBER

FLOATPLANE
FLYING BOAT
FLYING WING
GYROCOPTER
HANG-GLIDER
HELICOPTER
JET FIGHTER
MICROLIGHT
MOTHER SHIP
PARAGLIDER
ROTORCRAFT
SPACECRAFT
SPACE PROBE
WHIRLYBIRD

11
INTERCEPTOR
LUNAR MODULE

ORNITHOPTER	FLYING SAUCER	SPACE SHUTTLE	HOT-AIR BALLOON
SPACE ROCKET	LUNAR ORBITER	TROOP CARRIER	STEALTH BOMBER
	NIGHT FIGHTER		
12	SINGLE-SEATER	**13**	**14**
AIR AMBULANCE	SPACE CAPSULE	FLYING MACHINE	PASSENGER PLANE

Transport – Air – AIRLINES * = low-cost airline

3
BMI UK
EVA Taiwan
JAL Japan
LAN Chile
LAP Paraguay
LOT Poland
MAS Malaysia
MAT Macedonia
PIA Pakistan
SAA South Africa
SAS Norway-Sweden
SIA Singapore
TAM Brazil
TAP Portugal
THY Turkey

4
ALIA Jordan
EL AL Israel
MIAT Mongolia
NICA Nicaragua
NIKI* Austria
TAAG Angola

5
ADRIA Slovenia
DELTA USA

FLYBE* UK
FLYME* Sweden
LACSA Costa Rica
MALÉV Hungary
PLUNA Uruguay
TAROM Romania
VARIG Brazil

6
ARIANA Afghanistan
CONDOR* Germany
CUBANA Cuba
GARUDA Indonesia
IBERIA Spain
LUXAIR Luxembourg
QANTAS Australia
SAUDIA Saudi Arabia
VIRGIN UK

7
AVIANCA Colombia
BELAVIA Belarus
DRUK AIR Bhutan
EASYJET* UK
FIJI AIR Fiji
FINNAIR Finland
GULF AIR Bahrain-Oman
IRAN AIR Iran

MONARCH UK
OLYMPIC Greece
RYANAIR* Republic of
  Ireland
WIZZ AIR* Hungary

8
AEROFLOT Russia
AIR CHINA China
AIR INDIA India
AIR LUXOR* Portugal
ALITALIA Italy
CENTAVIA* Serbia
CONVIASA Venezuela
EGYPTAIR Egypt
EMIRATES United Arab
  Emirates
STERLING* Denmark
TUNISAIR Tunisia

9
AER LINGUS Republic of
  Ireland
AIR ASTANA Kazakhstan
AIR BALTIC Latvia
AIR CANADA Canada
KOREAN AIR South Korea
LUFTHANSA Germany

TRANSAVIA* Netherlands

10
AEROMÉXICO Mexico
AIR JAMAICA Jamaica
AIR NIUGINI Papua New Guinea
BLU-EXPRESS* Italy
ICELANDAIR Iceland
SMART WINGS* Czech Republic

11
AIR BOTSWANA Botswana
AIR CARAÏBES Guadeloupe-Martinique
THAI AIRWAYS Thailand

12
AIR FRANCE-KLM France-Netherlands
KENYA AIRWAYS Kenya

13
AIR NEW ZEALAND New Zealand
CATHAY PACIFIC Hong Kong
KUWAIT AIRWAYS Kuwait
ROYAL AIR MAROC Morocco
VIRGIN EXPRESS* Belgium

14
BRITISH AIRWAYS UK
ICELAND EXPRESS* Iceland
UNITED AIRLINES USA

16
AMERICAN AIRLINES USA

18
MIDDLE EAST AIRLINES Lebanon

Transport – Air – AIRPORTS

3
JFK New York
  (or John F
  Kennedy)
MOI Mombasa
SAL Espargos,
  Cape Verde
ZIA Dhaka

4
CORK
DYCE Aberdeen
FARO
MALÉ
ORLY Paris

OULU
OVDA Negev
RIGA

5
BRNIK Ljubljana
CAIRO
DUBAI
ITAMI Osaka
KABUL
KIMPO Seoul
KNOCK
LOGAN Boston
LUNGI
  Freetown

LUTON
LUXOR
MACAU
MAHON
  Menorca
MALTA
MIAMI
O'HARE
  Chicago
PERTH
RINAS Tirana
SUNAN
  Pyongyang
TEGEL Berlin
VARNA

6
ATHENS
BANGOR
CAIRNS
CANCÚN
CHANGI
  Singapore
CHANIA Crete
DENVER
DEURNE Antwerp
DUBLIN
DULLES
  Washington DC
DUM DUM
  Kolkata

DURBAN
EL PRAT Barcelona
EXETER
EZEIZE Buenos Aires
FINDEL Luxembourg
GALEÃO Rio de Janeiro
GANDER
HANEDA Tokyo
JINNAH Karachi
JUNEAU
KLOTEN Zürich
MALAGA
MOSTAR
NAPLES
NARITA Tokyo
NEWARK New York
NOI BAI Hanoi
PAPHOS
PUDONG Shanghai
RUZYNĚ Prague
SEA-TAC Seattle-
  Tacoma
SKOPJE
STURUP Malmo
VANTAA Helsinki
VC BIRD St John's
VIENNA
ZAGREB

7

ANTALYA
ARLANDA Stockholm
ATATÜRK Istanbul
BAGHDAD
BAHRAIN
BARAJAS Madrid
BELFAST
BLAGNAC Toulouse

CARDIFF
CATANIA
CAUMONT Avignon
FUNCHAL Madeira
GATWICK London
GLASGOW
HAMBURG
HOPKINS Cleveland
KASTRUP Copenhagen
KERKYRA Corfu
LAMBERT St Louis
LARNACA
MIRABEL Montreal
NICOSIA
NORWICH
NYERERE Dar es
  Salaam
ORLANDO
PEARSON Toronto
PORTELA Lisbon
PULKOVO
  St Petersburg
TAOYUAN Taiwan
TBILISI
VNUKOVO Moscow

8

ABU DHABI
ADELAIDE
ALICANTE
ARRECIFE Lanzarote
AUCKLAND
BEGUMPET Hyderabad
BORYSPIL Kiev
CANBERRA
CAPE TOWN
COINTRIN Geneva
DAMASCUS

DEBRECEN
DIAGORAS Rhodes
ENTZHEIM Strasbourg
ESENBOGA Ankara
FERIHEGY Budapest
FLESLAND Bergen
HEATHROW London
HONOLULU
KANDAHAR
KING FAHD Dammam
LA AURORA Guatemala
  City
MALPENSA Milan
MCCARRAN Las Vegas
PORTLAND
SANGSTER Montego
  Bay
SARAFOVO Burgas
SCHIPHOL Amsterdam
STANSTED Bishop's
  Stortford
ÜLEMISTE Tallinn
WINNIPEG
ZAVENTEM Brussels

9

BANGALORE
BEN GURION Tel Aviv
CÔTE D'AZUR Nice
DON MUEANG
  Bangkok
EDINBURGH
FAIRBANKS
FIUMICINO Rome
  (or Leonardo de Vinci)
FRANKFURT
GUANGZHOU
GUARULHOS São Paulo

HEWANORRA St Lucia
ISLAMABAD
JOSÉ MARTI Havana
LAGUARDIA New York
LAS PALMAS Gran
  Canaria
LOS RODEOS Tenerife
MARCO POLO Venice
MELBOURNE
NEWCASTLE
NGURAH RAI Bali
PODGORICA
PRESTWICK Glasgow
REYKJAVIK
SKY HARBOR Phoenix
VANCOUVER

10
BIRMINGHAM
CHEK LAP KOK Hong
  Kong
DOMODEDEVO
  Moscow
DÜSSELDORF
GARDERMOEN Oslo
GEORGE BUSH Houston
GUARARAPES Recife
JEAN LESAGE Quebec
JOHN LENNON
  Liverpool
JOHN PAUL II Kraków
KING KHALID Riyadh
LANDVETTER Göteborg
LOS ANGELES
MAHOVLJANI Banja
  Luka
MANCHESTER
MEXICO CITY

MINGALODON Yangon
REINA SOFIA Tenerife
SHAH AMANAT
  Chittagong
SCHÖNEFELD Berlin
TAN SON NHAT Ho
  Chi-Minh City
VRAZHDEBNA Sofia
WELLINGTON
WILL ROGERS
  Oklahoma City

11
ALLAMA IQBAL Lahore
HENRI COANDĂ
  Bucharest
JORGE CHÁVEZ Lima
KUALA LUMPUR
NIKOLA TESLA
  Belgrade
NINOY AQUINO
  Manila
SOUTHAMPTON
VLADIVOSTOK

12
CHRISTCHURCH
EAST MIDLANDS Castle
  Donington
IMAM KHOMEINI
  Tehran
INDIRA GANDHI New
  Delhi
JOHANNESBURG
JOHN F KENNEDY (or
  JFK) New York
JOMO KENYATTA
  Nairobi

LAS AMÉRICAS Santo
  Domingo
MELVILLE HALL Marigot,
  Dominica
METROPOLITAN
  Detroit
MILAS-BODRUM
NORMAN MANLEY
  Kingston
PHILADELPHIA
RONALD REAGAN
  Washington DC
SAINT-EXUPÉRY Lyon
SALT LAKE CITY
SAN FRANCISCO
SHEREMETYEVO
  Moscow
SUVAR NABHUMI
  Bangkok
THESSALONIKI

13
LEEDS BRADFORD
MILAN ŠTEFÁNIK
  Bratislava
NNAMDI AZIKIWI Abuja
SOEKARNO-HATTA
  Jakarta
TUNIS-CARTHAGE

14
BEIJING CAPITAL
FRÉDÉRIC CHOPIN
  Warsaw
JUAN SANTAMARIA San
  José
KINGSFORD SMITH
  Sydney

LOUIS ARMSTRONG New Orleans
LUIS MAÑOZ MARÍN San Juan
PROVIDENCIALES Turks & Caicos

15

CHARLES DE GAULLE Paris
DALLAS-FORT WORTH
GENERAL MITCHELL Milwaukee
LEONARDO DE VINCI (or Fiumicino)
    Rome
MONTRÉAL-TRUDEAU
MURTALA MOHAMMED Lagos
PALMA DE MALLORCA
PHILIP SW GOLDSON Belize City
SIR SERETSE KHAMA Gaborone
TOULOUSE BLAGNAC

16

MACDONALD-CARTIER Ottawa
NANTES ATLANTIQUE Bouguenais

17

FRANZ JOSEF STRAUSS Munich
HARTSFIELD-JACKSON Atlanta
MINNEAPOLIS-ST PAUL

18

CHHATRAPATI SHIVAJI Mumbai

19

TOUSSAINT LOUVERTURE Port-au-
    Prince

Transport – Land – Cars – CAR MAKES
* former car maker

3	FORD	HONDA	AUSTIN*	LIGIER*	BRISTOL
BMC*	LADA	ISUZU	DAEWOO	MORGAN	BUGATTI*
BMW	OPEL	LOTUS	DATSUN*	MORRIS*	CITROËN
FSO*	SAAB	MAZDA	(now	NISSAN	DAIMLER
GAZ	SEAT	RILEY*	Nissan)	PROTON	FERRARI
KIA	YUGO*	ROVER*	DELAGE*	SATURN	HILLMAN*
NSU*	(now	SIMCA*	DESOTO*	SINGER*	HYUNDAI
TVR	Zastava)	SKODA	HOLDEN	SUBARU	INVICTA*
ZIL		SMART	HUDSON*	SUZUKI	LAGONDA*
	5	VOLVO	HUMBER*	TALBOT*	LINCOLN
4	ALVIS*		JAGUAR	TOYOTA	MAYBACH
AUDI	BUICK	**6**	JENSEN*		MERCURY
BOND*	DACIA	ALBION*	JOWETT*	**7**	OAKLAND*
FIAT	DODGE	ALLARD*	LANCIA	BENTLEY	PACKARD*

PANTHER*
PEUGEOT
PONTIAC
PORSCHE
RELIANT*
RENAULT
SUNBEAM*
TRIUMPH*
ZASTAVA

8
CADILLAC
CHRYSLER
DAIHATSU

DELAHAYE*
DE LOREAN*
MASERATI
PLYMOUTH*
STANDARD*
VAUXHALL
WOLSELEY*

9
ALFA ROMEO
AUTO UNION*
CHEVROLET
HOTCHKISS*
LAND-ROVER

10
FRAZER-NASH*
LANCHESTER*
MITSUBISHI
OLDSMOBILE*
ROLLS ROYCE
STUDEBAKER*
VOLKSWAGEN

11
ASTON MARTIN
LAMBORGHINI

12
AUSTIN-HEALEY*
DE DION-BOUTON*
HISPANO-SUIZA*
MERCEDES-BENZ

14
BRITISH LEYLAND*

15
PANHARD-LEVASSOR*

17
ARMSTRONG SIDDELEY*

Transport – Land – Cars – CAR MODELS

3
ACE AC
AMI Citroën
ELF Riley
FOX Reliant,
   Volkswagen
IMP Hillman
MGA MG
MGB MG
MGC MG
OKA Lada
REX Subaru
TEN Standard
UNO Fiat

4
ALTO Suzuki
ARNA Alfa Romeo
ASKA Isuzu

AURA Saturn
AXEL Citroën
BAJA Subaru
BÉBÉ Peugeot
BETA Lancia
BORA Maserati
CIMA Nissan
CITY Honda
CLIO Renault
COLT Mitsubishi
DART Daimler,
   Dodge
DINO Ferrari, Fiat
ELAN Lotus
FURY Plymouth
GOLF Volkswagen
HAWK Humber,
   Studebaker
INDY Maserati

ISIS Morris
ITAL Morris
JAZZ Honda
LARK Studebaker
LEÓN Seat
LOGO Honda
LUCE Mazda
LYNX Mercury
MAXI Austin
MINI Austin,
   BMW, Morris
MINX Hillman
MUSA Lancia
NEON Chrysler,
   Dodge
NIVA Lada
NOVA Chevrolet,
   Vauxhall
OMNI Dodge

POLO
   Volkswagen
PONY Hyundai
RENO Daewoo
RIVA Lada
SANA Yugo
SAXO Citroën
S-MAX Ford
STAG Triumph
TIPO Fiat
VEGA Chevrolet
VIVA Vauxhall
WASP Hudson,
   Wolseley

5
ACECA AC
AGILA Vauxhall
ALPHA Lancia

APPIA Lancia
ALTEA Seat
ARDEA Lancia
ARIES Dodge
ARROW Plymouth
ASPEN Chrysler, Dodge
ASTRA Vauxhall
ASTRE Pontiac
AVANT Audi, Citroën
AXIOM Isuzu
AZURE Bentley
BRERA Alfa Romeo
CADET Vauxhall
CAMRY Toyota
CAPRI Ford
CAROL Mazda
CIVIC Honda
COBRA AC
COMET Mercury
COPEN Daihatsu
CORSA Vauxhall
COSMO Mazda
CROMA Fiat
CROWN Toyota
C-TYPE Jaguar
DAVOS Daimler
DEDRA Lancia
DELTA Lancia,
  Oldsmobile
DENEM Dacia
DERBY Volkswagen
DEVON Austin
D-TYPE Jaguar
DYANE Citroën
ECLAT Lotus
EDSEL Ford
EIGHT Morris, Standard
ELISE Lotus

ELITE Lotus
ESSEX Hudson
E-TYPE Jaguar
EXCEL Lotus
FABIA Skoda
FOCUS Ford
FUEGO Renault
GAMMA Lancia
HUSKY Hillman
IBIZA Seat
IGNIS Subaru
JALPA Lamborghini
JETTA Volkswagen
JIMNY Suzuki
JUSTY Subaru
KALOS Daewoo
KAPPA Lancia
KARIF Maserati
KORAL Zastava
LASER Chrysler, Ford
LEONE Subaru
LEXUS Toyota
MAGNA MG
MANTA Opel
MAREA Fiat
MARK X Jaguar
MERAK Maserati
METRO Austin
MICRA Nissan
MINOR Morris
MIURA Lamborghini
MODUS Renault
MONZA Chevrolet,
  Opel
NOMAD Chevrolet
NUOVA Fiat
OMEGA Oldsmobile,
  Vauxhall

ORION Ford
PALIO Fiat
PANDA Fiat
PILOT Ford, Rover
PINTO Ford
PRINZ NSU
PRIUS Toyota
PUNTO Fiat
RAPID Skoda
REBEL Reliant
REGAL Buick
RELAY Saturn
ROBIN Reliant
RODEO Isuzu
SABLE Mercury
SABRE Reliant
SAMBA Talbot
SEVEN Austin, Lotus
SIGMA Mitsubishi
SKALA Zastava
S-TYPE Jaguar
SUNNY Datsun
SWIFT Suzuki
TAHOE Chevrolet
TAMAR TVR
TEMPO Ford
THEMA Lancia
TIGER Sunbeam
TIGRA Vauxhall
TODAY Honda
TOPAZ Mercury
TREVI Lancia
VELOX Vauxhall
VERSO Toyota
VOGUE Singer
VOLGA GAZ
XSARA Citroën
X-TYPE Jaguar

YARIS Toyota

6
ACCORD Honda
ALMERA Nissan
ALPINE Renault,
   Sunbeam, Talbot
ALTIMA Nissan
AMAZON Volvo
ANGLIA Ford
ARIANE Simca
ARMADA Nissan
ARNAGE Bentley
ARONDE Simca
ARTENA Lancia
ASCONA Opel
ASTURA Lancia
AVANTI Studebaker
BEETLE Volkswagen
BEL AIR Chevrolet
BIG SIX Studebaker,
   Vauxhall
BOBCAT Mercury
CALAIS Oldsmobile
CAMARO Chevrolet
CARINA Toyota
CAYMAN Porsche
CEDRIC Nissan
CELICA Toyota
CHERRY Nissan
CIRRUS Chrysler
COBALT Chevrolet
CONSUL Ford
CORDIA Mitsubishi
CORONA Toyota
COUGAR Ford,
   Mercury
COWLEY Morris

CRESTA Vauxhall
CUSTOM Dodge, Ford
DIABLO Lamborghini
DOMINO Daihatsu
DORSET Austin
ENSIGN Standard
ESCORT Ford
ESPACE Renault
ESPADA Lamborghini
ESPRIT Lotus
EUROPA Ferrari, Lotus
FALCON Ford
FARINA Austin
FIESTA Ford
FLAVIA Lancia
FULVIA Lancia
FUTURA Ford
GALANT Mitsubishi
GALAXY Ford
GENTRA Daewoo
GHIBLI Maserati
GIULIA Alfa Romeo
GLORIA Nissan
HERALD Triumph
HUNTER Hillman,
   Singer
HORNET Wolseley
IMPALA Chevrolet
JARAMA Lamborghini
KADETT Opel
KALINA Lada
KANGOO Renault
KITTEN Reliant
LAGUNA Renault
LAMBDA Lancia
LANCER Mitsubishi
LAUREL Nissan
LEGACY Subaru

LEGEND Honda
LE MANS Pontiac,
   Singer
LUMINA Chevrolet
MAGNUM Vauxhall
MAGNUS Daewoo
MALAGA Seat
MALIBU Chevrolet
MARINA Morris
MATRIX Toyota
MAXIMA Nissan
MÉGANE Renault
MERKUR Mercury
METEOR Mercury,
   Rover
MIDGET MG
MINICA Mitsubishi
MIRADA Dodge
MIRAGE Mitsubishi
MODEL T Ford
MONACO Dodge, Riley
MONDEO Ford
OXFORD Morris
PASSAT Volkswagen
PHEDRA Lancia
PIAZZA Holden
POLARA Dodge
PREVIA Toyota
PRISMA Toyota
RAPIER Sunbeam
RED RAM Dodge
REGATA Fiat
REGENT Opel
REKORD Opel
RENOWN Triumph
RIALTO Reliant
ROYALE Vauxhall
SAMARA Lada

SCÉNIC Renault
SCOUPE Hyundai
SENTRA Nissan
SEPHIA Kia
SHADOW Dodge
SHARAN Volkswagen
SHELBY Dodge
SIERRA Ford
SIGNUM Opel
SILVIA Nissan
SIRION Daihatsu
SOARER Toyota
SOLARA Toyota
SONATA Hyundai
SONETT Saab
SPIANO Mazda
SPIRIT Nissan
SPIDER Alfa Romeo
SPRINT Chevrolet
SPRITE Austin-Healey
SPYDER Maserati
SQUIRE Ford
STANZA Nissan
STRADA Fiat
SUPERB Skoda
SYRENA FSO
TALBOT Sunbeam
TAUNUS Ford
TAURUS Ford
TEMPRA Fiat
TERCEL Toyota
THESIS Lancia
TOLEDO Seat, Triumph
TORINO Ford
TOURAN Volkswagen
TRAFIC Renault
TREDIA Mitsubishi
TROFEO Oldsmobile

TUSCAN TVR
TWINGO Renault
VECTRA Vauxhall
VEYRON Bugatti
VICTOR Vauxhall
VIOLET Nissan
VIRAGE Aston Martin
VITARA Suzuki
VOLARE Plymouth
WIZARD Isuzu
WYVERN Vauxhall
ZAFIRA Vauxhall
ZAGATO Aston Martin
ZEPHYR Ford
ZODIAC Ford

7

ACCLAIM Triumph
ADELPHI Riley
ADMIRAL Opel
ALFASUD Alfa Romeo
ALFETTA Alfa Romeo
ALLANTE Cadillac
ALLEGRO Austin
AMERICA Ferrari
APRILIA Lancia
ARGENTA Fiat
AURELIA Lancia
AVENGER Chrysler,
   Hillman, Talbot
AVENSIS Toyota
BALILLA Fiat
BALLADE Honda
BELLETT Isuzu
BELMONT Vauxhall
BERETTA Chevrolet
BITURBO Maserati
BOXSTER Porsche

BRIGAND Bristol
CALIBRA Vauxhall
CAPELLA Mazda
CARIOCA Volvo
CARLTON Vauxhall
CARRERA Porsche
CAYENNE Porsche
CELESTE Mitsubishi
CENTURY Buick, Toyota
CERBERA TVR
CHAMADE Renault
CHARADE Daihatsu
CHARGER Dodge
CLASSIC Ford
CONCORD Kia
CÓRDOBA Chrysler,
   Seat
COROLLA Toyota
CORONET Dodge
CORRADO Volkswagen
CORSAIR Ford
CORSICA Chevrolet
CORTINA Ford
CORVAIR Chevrolet
CRICKET Plymouth
CRUISER Chrysler
CUTLASS Oldsmobile
DAYTONA Dodge,
   Ferrari
DELMONT Oldsmobile
DEVILLE Cadillac
DE VILLE Panther
DIALPHA Lancia
ELECTRA Buick
EQUINOX Chevrolet
ESTELLE Skoda
FAMILIA Mazda
FAVORIT Skoda

The *Puzzler* Crossword Companion

FELICIA Skoda
FIRENZA Oldsmobile, Vauxhall
FLORIDA Zastava
FLORIDE Renault
FORENZA Daewoo
FRÉGATE Renault
GALAXIE Ford
GAZELLE Singer
GRANADA Ford
HORIZON Chrysler, Plymouth, Talbot
IMPREZA Subaru
IMPULSE Isuzu
INTEGRA Honda
JAVELIN Jowett
JETFIRE Oldsmobile
JUPITER Jowett
KAPITAN Opel
KESTREL Riley
KHAMSIN Maserati
KYALAMI Maserati
LAGONDA Aston Martin
LEBARON Chrysler
LEOPARD Nissan
LESABRE Buick
MAESTRO Austin
MARQUIS Mercury
MISTRAL Maserati
MONARCH Mercury
MONDIAL Ferrari
MONTEGO Austin
MUSTANG Ford
NEWPORT Chrysler
OCTAVIA Skoda
OLYMPIA Opel
PENNANT Standard

PHANTOM Rolls Royce
PHOENIX Pontiac
POLONEZ FSO
POPULAR Ford
PRAIRIE Nissan
PREFECT Ford
PRELUDE Honda
PRIMERA Nissan
PROWLER Plymouth
PUBLICA Toyota
PULLMAN Humber
QUATTRO Audi
QUINTET Honda
REGENCY Daimler
RIVIERA Buick
SAGARIS TVR
SANTANA Suzuki, Volkswagen
SAPPORO Mitsubishi
SAVANNA Renault
SCEPTRE Humber
SCORPIO Ford
SENATOR Opel, Vauxhall
SEBRING Chrysler
SEVILLE Cadillac
SKYHAWK Buick
SKYLARK Buick
SKYLINE Nissan
SPECIAL Buick
STARION Mitsubishi
STARLET Toyota
STELLAR Hyundai
STRATOS Lancia
STRATUS Dodge, GAZ
ST REGIS Dodge
SUNBIRD Pontiac
TEMPEST Pontiac

TORPEDO Pontiac
TOWN CAR Lincoln
TRIBECA Subaru
TROOPER Isuzu
VALIANT Plymouth
VANTAGE Aston Martin
VENTORA Vauxhall
VENTURA Pontiac
VENTURE Chevrolet
VICEROY Vauxhall
VITESSE Rover, Triumph
VOLANTE Aston Martin
WILDCAT Buick
WINDSOR Chrysler
YPSILON Lancia

8

ALHAMBRA Seat
APPLAUSE Daihatsu
ASCENDER Isuzu
ATLANTIC Austin
BISCAYNE Chevrolet
BLUEBIRD Datsun
BREVETTI Fiat
CAMARGUE Rolls Royce
CATALINA Pontiac
CAVALIER Chevrolet, Vauxhall
CHAMPION Studebaker
CHARMANT Daihatsu
CHEVELLE Chevrolet
CHEVETTE Chevrolet, Vauxhall
CHIMAERA TVR
CIMARRON Cadillac
CITATION Chevrolet
CONCERTO Honda
CONCORDE Chrysler

CONQUEST Daimler
CONSORTE Daihatsu
CORNICHE Bentley,
  Rolls Royce
CORVETTE Chevrolet
COUNTACH
  Lamborghini
CRESSIDA Toyota
DAUPHINE Renault
DEBONAIR Mitsubishi
DEFENDER Land-Rover
DICTATOR Studebaker
DILAMBDA Lancia
DIPLOMAT Dodge,
  Opel
DOLOMITE Triumph
EL CAMINO Chevrolet
ELDORADO Cadillac
FAIRLADY Nissan
FAIRLANE Ford
FAIRMONT Ford
FIREBIRD Pontiac
FLAMINIA Lancia
FOUR-FOUR Morgan
FRONTERA Vauxhall
GALLARDO
  Lamborghini
GRAN FURY Plymouth
GRANTURA TVR
GREY LADY Alvis
GRIFFITH TVR
HEREFORD Austin
IMPERIAL Chrysler
KALLISTA Panther
LIGHT SIX Vauxhall
MAGNETTE MG
MAJESTIC Daimler
MARBELLA Seat

MAVERICK Ford
MILLENIA Mazda
MINI MOKE Austin
MONTEREY Mercury
MONTREAL Alfa Romeo
MONTROSE Mazda
MULSANNE Bentley
PACIFICA Chrysler
PARK LANE Mercury
PLUS FOUR Morgan
PRESTIGE Citroën
PRINCESS Austin
ROADSTER Triumph
ROOMSTER Skoda
SAPPHIRE Armstrong
  Siddeley
SARATOGA Chrysler
SCIMITAR Reliant
SCIROCCO Volkswagen
SEICENTO Fiat
SOMERSET Austin,
  Buick
SPECTRUM Chevrolet
SPITFIRE Triumph
SPRINTER Toyota
STERLING Rover
STILETTO Sunbeam
SUNDANCE Plymouth
TOPOLINO Fiat
TORONADO
  Oldsmobile
TOWNSMAN Chevrolet
TRIKAPPA Lancia
UPLANDER Chevrolet
VANGUARD Standard
VANQUISH Aston
  Martin
VEL SATIS Renault

VISCOUNT Vauxhall
WARSZAWA FSO
WAYFARER Dodge

9
BABY GRAND Chevrolet
BARRACUDA Plymouth
BELVEDERE Plymouth
BRITANNIA Bristol
BROOKWOOD
  Chevrolet
CAMBRIDGE Austin
CARAVELLE Plymouth,
  Renault
CELEBRITY Chevrolet
CHIEFTAIN Pontiac
COMMODORE Opel
CROSSFIRE Chrysler
DISCOVERY Land-Rover
DOUBLE SIX Daimler
FLEETWOOD Cadillac
GIULIETTA Alfa Romeo
GRAND PRIX Pontiac
HAMPSHIRE Austin
HURRICANE Armstrong
  Siddeley
INTEGRALE Lancia
KINGSWOOD
  Chevrolet
LITTLE SIX Chevrolet
MARANELLO Ferrari
MARQUETTE Buick
MAYFLOWER Triumph
MIRAFIORI Fiat
MONTCLAIR Mercury
MURCIÉLAGO
  Lamborghini
NEW YORKER Chrysler

PRESIDENT Nissan,
Studebaker
ROADPACER Mazda
SHEERLINE Austin
SOVEREIGN Daimler,
Jaguar
STAR CHIEF Pontiac
SUPERFAST Ferrari
TRAVELLER Morris
WAGONAIRE
Studebaker

10
AMBASSADOR Austin
BERLINETTA Ferrari
BONNEVILLE Pontiac
FOUR-NINETY Chevrolet
FREELANDER Land-
Rover
GOLDEN HAWK
Studebaker
JUVAQUATRE Renault
LAUBFROSCH Opel
LITTLE FOUR Chevrolet
MINI COOPER Austin,
BMW, Morris
MONTE CARLO
Chevrolet, Lancia
PARISIENNE Pontiac
PATHFINDER Riley
RANGEROVER Land-
Rover
ROADMASTER Buick
ROAD RUNNER
Plymouth
SCAGLIETTI Ferrari
SILVER DAWN Rolls
Royce

SILVER HAWK Studebaker
SILVER SPUR Rolls Royce
SUPER SNIPE Humber
TERRAPLANE Hudson
TESTAROSSA Ferrari
VERSAILLES Lincoln

11
BEAUFIGHTER Bristol
CALIFORNIAN Hillman
CINQUECENTO Fiat
CONTINENTAL Bentley,
Lincoln
EAGLE VISION Chrysler
FIFTH AVENUE Chrysler
FLIGHT SWEEP Chrysler
INTERCEPTOR Jensen
KARMANN GHIA
Volkswagen
MEADOWBROOK Dodge
NINETY-EIGHT
Oldsmobile
QUADRILETTE Peugeot
REINASTELLA Renault
SILVER CLOUD Rolls
Royce
SILVER GHOST Rolls
Royce
STREAMLINER Pontiac
TARGA FLORIO Frazer-
Nash
THUNDERBIRD Ford
TRAILBLAZER Chevrolet
WESTMINSTER Austin

12
COMET CYCLONE
Mercury

COSMOPOLITAN Lincoln
CUTLASS CIERA
Oldsmobile
GRAND MARQUIS
Mercury
GRAND VOYAGER
Chrysler
LOTUS CORTINA Ford
METROPOLITAN Austin
QUATTROPORTE
Maserati
SILVER SERAPH Rolls
Royce
SILVER SHADOW Rolls
Royce
SILVER SPIRIT Rolls Royce
SILVER STREAK Pontiac
SILVER WRAITH Rolls
Royce
SUPERAMERICA Ferrari

13
CROWN VICTORIA Ford
MAJESTIC MAJOR
Daimler

14
CUTLASS SUPREME
Oldsmobile
SIERRA COSWORTH Ford
SIERRA SAPPHIRE Ford
SUPERMIRAFIORI Fiat

15
DAUPHINE GORDINI
Renault

Transport – Land – LAND TRANSPORT

3
BOB
BUS
CAB
CAR
CAT
FLY
GIG
VAN

4
AUTO
BIKE
CART
DRAY
EKKA
HEAP
JEEP
KART
LIMO
LOCO
LUGE
PRAM
SLED
SOLO
TANK
TAXI
TRAM
TRAP
WAIN

5
ARTIC
BRAKE
BUGGY

COACH
COUPÉ
CRATE
CROCK
CYCLE
FLOAT
HOBBY
LORRY
MOPED
MOTOR
RACER
SEDAN
STAGE
SULKY
TONGA
TRAIN
TRIKE
TRUCK
WAGON

6
BANGER
BARROW
BOWSER
CALASH
  (or caleche)
CAMPER
CHAISE
DOOLIE
ENGINE
FIACRE
GHARRY
GO-KART
HANSOM
HEARSE

HOT ROD
JALOPY
JITNEY
KIT CAR
LANDAU
LITTER
OX CART
PICK-UP
PUFFER
SALOON
SKI-BOB
SLEDGE
SLEIGH
SURREY
TANDEM
TANKER
TIPPER
TOURER
TRICAR
TROIKA
TUK-TUK
WHISKY

7
AMTRAC
AUTOCAR
BICYCLE
BOBSLED
BRITZKA
CALECHE
  (or calash)
CARAVAN
CHARIOT
CRAWLER
DOG CART

DROSHKY
EXPRESS
FLIVVER
FRITTER
GROWLER
HACKNEY
HANDCAR
HIRE CAR
KIBITKA
KOMATIK
MAIL VAN
MINIBUS
MINICAB
OMNIBUS
PEDICAB
PHAETON
SCOOTER
SIDECAR
SOFT TOP
SPECIAL
TALLY-HO
TAXICAB
TILBURY
TRACTOR
TRAILER
TRAMCAR
TRAVOIS
TRISHAW
TROLLEY
TUMBREL
  (or tumbril)
TUMBRIL
  (or tumbrel)
VEHICLE
WRECKER

8
BAROUCHE
BROUGHAM
CABLE CAR
CARRIAGE
CARRIOLE
CARRYALL
CLARENCE
CURRICLE
DRAGSTER
DROPHEAD
DUSTCART
HANDCART
HORSEBOX
MAIL CART
MOTOR BUS
MOTOR CAR
ORDINARY
PANDA CAR
PUSHBIKE
PUSHCART
QUAD BIKE
RICKSHAW
ROADSTER
RUNABOUT
SCOUT CAR
STAFF CAR
STANHOPE
STOCK CAR
TOBOGGAN
TRICYCLE
UNICYCLE
VICTORIA

9
AMBULANCE
AMPHIBIAN
APPLE CART
BABY BUGGY
BANDWAGON
BATH CHAIR
BATTLE BUS
BILLYCART
BOAT TRAIN
BOBSLEIGH
BUBBLE CAR
BULLDOZER
CABRIOLET
CAMPER VAN
CHAIRLIFT
CHARABANC
DILIGENCE
DORMOBILE
ESTATE CAR
EXCAVATOR
HANSOM CAB
HATCHBACK
IRON HORSE
LANDAULET
LAND YACHT
LIMOUSINE
LOW-LOADER
MAIL TRAIN
MILK FLOAT
MOTORBIKE
PALANQUIN
PATROL CAR
PUSHCHAIR
RACING CAR
RENTAL CAR
SALOON CAR
SAND YACHT

SPORTS CAR
STREETCAR
STRETCHER
TARANTASS
TUBE TRAIN
TWO-SEATER
TWO-STROKE
WAGONETTE
WINNEBAGO

10
AUTOMOBILE
BLACK MARIA
BONESHAKER
CHUCK WAGON
CONVEYANCE
FIRE ENGINE
FOUR-IN-HAND
FOUR-SEATER
GOODS TRAIN
HACKNEY CAB
HOVERTRAIN
JINRICKSHA
JUGGERNAUT
LOCOMOTIVE
MOBILE HOME
MOTOR COACH
MOTORCYCLE
NIGHT TRAIN
PEDAL CYCLE
POST-CHAISE
REMOVAL VAN
SEDAN CHAIR
SKATEBOARD
SNOWMOBILE
SNOWPLOUGH
STAGECOACH
STATE COACH

TIP-UP TRUCK
TOURING CAR
TROLLEY BUS
TROLLEY CAR
TWO-WHEELER
VELOCIPEDE
VETERAN CAR
VINTAGE CAR
WHEELCHAIR

11
ARMOURED CAR
CARAVANETTE
CATERPILLAR
CATTLE TRUCK
COMBINATION
CONVERTIBLE
CRASH TENDER
ELECTRIC CAR
FOUR-WHEELER
GUN CARRIAGE
JAUNTING CAR
PICK-UP TRUCK
SECURITY VAN
STEAMROLLER
STRETCH LIMO
TRANSPORTER
WHEELBARROW

12
BABY CARRIAGE
COACH-AND-FOUR
COACH-AND-PAIR
COVERED WAGON
DOUBLE-DECKER
EXPRESS TRAIN
FREIGHT TRAIN
FURNITURE VAN

HORSE AND CART
MOTOR SCOOTER
MOTOR VEHICLE
PANTECHNICON
PERAMBULATOR
RAILWAY TRAIN
SINGLE-DECKER
SINGLE-SEATER
STATION WAGON
THREE-WHEELER

13
CORRIDOR TRAIN
FIRE APPLIANCE
FORK-LIFT TRUCK
HORSE AND BUGGY
PENNY-FARTHING
PEOPLE CARRIER
SLAM-DOOR TRAIN
SHOOTING BRAKE
STOPPING TRAIN

14
CAR TRANSPORTER
CONTAINER LORRY
FIELD AMBULANCE
PASSENGER TRAIN
TRACTION ENGINE

15
BICYCLE RICKSHAW
CARRIAGE AND PAIR
HACKNEY CARRIAGE
PRAIRIE SCHOONER
SHOPPING TROLLEY

Transport – Land – LONDON TUBE STATIONS

4
BANK
OVAL

5
ANGEL
UPNEY

6
BALHAM
CYPRUS
DEBDEN
EPPING
EUSTON
KENTON
LEYTON
MORDEN
PINNER
POPLAR
TEMPLE

7
ALDGATE
ARCHWAY
ARSENAL
BARKING
BECKTON
BOROUGH
BOW ROAD
BRIXTON
CHESHAM
CROXLEY
EAST HAM
EDGWARE
ELM PARK

FAIRLOP
HOLBORN
KILBURN
MILE END
NEASDEN
OAKWOOD
OLYMPIA
PIMLICO
RUISLIP
ST PAUL'S
WAPPING
WATFORD
WEST HAM

8
ALPERTON
AMERSHAM
BARBICAN
BURNT OAK
CHIGWELL
EASTCOTE
HAINUALT
HIGHGATE
ICKENHAM
LEWISHAM
LOUGHTON
MONUMENT
MOORGATE
MOOR PARK
MUDCHUTE
NEW CROSS
NORTHOLT
OSTERLEY
PERIVALE
PLAISTOW

RICHMOND
ROYAL OAK
SHADWELL
STANMORE
UXBRIDGE
VAUXHALL
VICTORIA
WANSTEAD
WATERLOO
WOODFORD

9
ACTON TOWN
ALL SAINTS
BAYSWATER
BECONTREE
BLACKWALL
BOW CHURCH
CHALK FARM
COLINDALE
CUTTY SARK
EAST ACTON
EAST INDIA
GANTS HILL
GREENFORD
GREEN PARK
GREENWICH
HAMPSTEAD
HARLESDEN
KINGSBURY
LIMEHOUSE
MAIDA VALE
NORTHWOOD
OLD STREET
PARK ROYAL

QUEENSWAY
REDBRIDGE
SOUTHGATE
SOUTH QUAY
SOUTHWARK
STOCKWELL
STRATFORD
TOWER HILL
UPMINSTER
UPTON PARK
WEST ACTON
WEST FERRY
WHITE CITY
WIMBLEDON
WOOD GREEN

10
ARNOS GROVE
BERMONDSEY
BOND STREET
BRENT CROSS
CAMDEN TOWN
CANONS PARK
DEVONS ROAD
DOLLIS HILL
EARL'S COURT
EAST PUTNEY
EMBANKMENT
FARRINGDON
GRANGE HILL
HANGER LANE
HERON QUAYS
HIGH BARNET
HILLINGDON
HORNCHURCH

KENNINGTON
KENSINGTON
KEW GARDENS
MANOR HOUSE
MARBLE ARCH
MARYLEBONE
NORTH ACTON
PADDINGTON
QUEENSBURY
QUEEN'S PARK
TOOTING BEC
WEST HARROW

11

ALDGATE EAST
BAKER STREET
BARKINGSIDE
BARONS COURT
BECKTON PARK
BELSIZE PARK
BLACKFRIARS
BOSTON MANOR
BOUNDS GREEN
CANADA WATER
CANARY WHARF
CANNING TOWN
CHORLEYWOOD
COCKFOSTERS
CUSTOM HOUSE
EDGWARE ROAD
GUNNERSBURY
HAMMERSMITH
HATTON CROSS
HOLLAND PARK
KENSAL GREEN
KENTISH TOWN
KILBURY PARK
KING GEORGE V

LATIMER ROAD
LEYTONSTONE
NEWBURY PARK
NORTH EALING
NORTHFIELDS
NORTH HARROW
PONTOON DOCK
PRESTON ROAD
RAYNERS LANE
REGENT'S PARK
ROTHERHITHE
ROYAL ALBERT
SNARESBROOK
SOUTH EALING
SOUTHFIELDS
SOUTH KENTON
SOUTH HARROW
ST JOHN'S WOOD
SUDBURY HILL
SUDBURY TOWN
SURREY QUAYS
THEYDON BOIS
TUFNELL PARK
WEMBLEY PARK
WESTMINSTER
WEST RUISLIP
WHITECHAPEL

12

BETHNAL GREEN
BROMLEY-BY-BOW
CANNON STREET
CHANCERY LANE
CHARING CROSS
CHISWICK PARK
CLAPHAM NORTH
CLAPHAM SOUTH
COLLIERS WOOD

COVENT GARDEN
CROSSHARBOUR
DAGENHAM EAST
EALING COMMON
EAST FINCHLEY
ELVERSON ROAD
EUSTON SQUARE
FINCHLEY ROAD
FINSBURY PARK
GOLDERS GREEN
GOLDHAWK ROAD
GOODGE STREET
HOLLOWAY ROAD
HOUNSLOW EAST
HOUNSLOW WEST
LAMBETH NORTH
LONDON BRIDGE
MANSION HOUSE
MILL HILL EAST
NEW CROSS GATE
NORTH WEMBLEY
OXFORD CIRCUS
PARSONS GREEN
PRINCE REGENT
PUTNEY BRIDGE
RODING VALLEY
RUISLIP MANOR
SEVEN SISTERS
SLOANE SQUARE
SOUTH RUISLIP
STEPNEY GREEN
ST JAMES'S PARK
SWISS COTTAGE
TURNHAM GREEN
TURNPIKE LANE
WARREN STREET
WEST BROMPTON
WEST FINCHLEY

WOODSIDE PARK

13
BUCKHURST HILL
CLAPHAM COMMON
GALLIONS REACH
HENDON CENTRAL
ISLAND GARDENS
KNIGHTSBRIDGE
LADBROKE GROVE
LANCASTER GATE
NORTHWICK PARK
RICKMANSWORTH
ROYAL VICTORIA
RUSSELL SQUARE
SHEPHERD'S BUSH
SOUTH WOODFORD
STAMFORD BROOK
TOTTENHAM HALE
TOWER GATEWAY
WARWICK AVENUE
WEST HAMPSTEAD
WEST INDIA QUAY
WIMBLEDON PARK

14
BLACKHORSE ROAD
CALEDONIAN ROAD

DEPTFORD BRIDGE
EALING BROADWAY
FULHAM BROADWAY
GLOUCESTER ROAD
HYDE PARK CORNER
NORTH GREENWICH
NORTHWOOD HILLS
RUISLIP GARDENS
SOUTH WIMBLEDON
WEMBLEY CENTRAL
WESTBOURNE PARK
WEST KENSINGTON
WILLESDEN GREEN

15
FINCHLEY CENTRAL
HARROW-ON-THE-HILL
HEATHROW CENTRAL
HOUNSLOW CENTRAL
LEICESTER SQUARE
LIVERPOOL STREET
NOTTING HILL GATE
PUDDING MILL LANE
RAVENSCOURT PARK
SOUTH KENSINGTON
STONEBRIDGE PARK
TOOTING BROADWAY
UPMINSTER BRIDGE

16
DAGENHAM HEATHWAY
PICCADILLY CIRCUS

17
ELEPHANT AND CASTLE
LONDON CITY AIRPORT
WILLESDEN JUNCTION

18
CHALFONT AND LATIMER
MORNINGTON CRESCENT
TOTTENHAM COURT ROAD
WALTHAMSTOW CENTRAL

19
GREAT PORTLAND STREET
HARROW AND WEALDSTONE
KING'S CROSS-ST PANCRAS

20
HIGHBURY AND ISLINGTON
HIGH STREET KENSINGTON

22
TOTTERIDGE AND WHETSTONE

Transport – Water – SEACRAFT (notable)

3	**4**		
REX liner	AJAX various RN vessels	DRUM yacht	– Amundsen, Nansen
		– Le Bon	GJØA sloop –
	CUBA steamship	ELLA steamship	Amundsen
		FRAM schooner	HOOD battle-cruiser

IOWA battleship
NIÑA caravel
TAKU submarine
VEGA yacht
– Greenpeace

5
BRAER tanker
EMDEN cruiser
EVOHE exploration
vessel
JUNYO aircraft carrier
MAINE battleship
PASHA sailing ship
– Drake
PINTA caravel
STARK frigate
TYGER sailing ship
– Block

6
AFFRAY submarine
ARDENT frigate
BARHAM battleship
BEAGLE brig – Darwin
BOUNTY sailing ship
– Bligh
BREMEN liner
ENIGMA yacht
– Barclay
EREBUS exploration
vessel – Franklin,
Ross
EUROPA liner
EXETER destroyer
FRANCE – see Norway
GLOIRE battleship
HERMES aircraft carrier

HUNLEY submarine
JUDITH sailing ship
– Drake
MEDUSA frigate
MIKASA battleship
NIMITZ supercarrier
NIMROD exploration
vessel – Shackleton
NORWAY liner
ONEIDA yacht
– Hearst
ORIANA liner
PUEBLO research ship
RENOWN submarine
SCHEER – see Admiral
Scheer
STRUMA refugee ship
TERROR bomb ship
– Franklin
THERON exploration
vessel – Fuchs
THETIS submarine
TIGRIS reed boat
– Heyerdahl
TRITON submarine
VIKING converted
whaler – Nansen
WAWONA schooner
YAMATO battleship

7
ALINGHI yacht
ALTMARK supply ship
AMERICA yacht
ARIZONA battleship
ATHENIA liner
AUSTRIA steamship
BELFAST cruiser

BRISTOL destroyer
CALYPSO expedition
vessel – Cousteau
COSSACK destroyer
DUNEDIN cruiser
FREEDOM yacht
FURIOUS cruiser
GABRIEL barque
– Frobisher
KON-TIKI raft
– Heyerdahl
LETITIA liner
LIBERTY yacht
– Pulitzer
MATTHEW sailing ship
– Cabot
MONITOR warship
NOMADIC liner
NORFOLK sloop
– Flinders
OLYMPIC liner
PELICAN – see Golden
Hind
PELORUS yacht
– Abramovich
REPULSE submarine
REVENGE submarine
ROSARIO galleon
SHANNON frigate
SHEMARA yacht
– Docker
SUHAILI yacht – Knox-
Johnston
SULTANA riverboat
TATOOSH yacht
– Allen
TIRPITZ battleship
TITANIC liner

VALIANT battleship
VICTORY warship
– Nelson
WARRIOR battleship

8

ACHILLES various RN
vessels
AMETHYST sloop
ANTELOPE frigate
ARK ROYAL aircraft
carrier
BELGRANO see
General Belgrano
BISMARCK battleship
BLUEBIRD speedboat
– Campbell
BLUENOSE schooner
CANBERRA liner
COVENTRY destroyer
DAUPHINE sailing
ship – Verrazano
FEARLESS various RN
vessels
GOOD HOPE cruiser
GRAF SPEE see
Admiral Graf Spee
HOPEWELL barque
– Hudson
INTREPID warship
IRON DUKE battleship
KALAKALA ferry
MARY ROSE carrack
MISSOURI battleship
MONMOUTH warship
MONTROSE liner
NAUTILUS submarine
ROYAL OAK warship

SARATOGA aircraft
carrier
SAVANNAH steamship
SCORPION submarine
SHAMROCK yacht
– Lipton
SOBERTON
minesweeper
SPLENDID submarine
SQUIRREL frigate
– Gilbert
THRESHER submarine
UPHOLDER submarine
VANGUARD warship
– Nelson
VICTORIA sailing ship
– Magellan
VIRGINIA warship
YORKTOWN aircraft
carrier

9

ADVENTURE barque
– Cook
AQUITANIA liner
BRITANNIA yacht
– Royal Family
BRITANNIC liner
CARPATHIA liner
CHRISTINA yacht
– Onassis
CHURCHILL submarine
CUTTY SARK tea
clipper
DISCOVERY barque
– Scott, sailing ship
– Hudson
EDINBURGH cruiser

ENDEAVOUR sailing
ship – Cook
ENDURANCE
barquentine
– Shackleton
GNEISENAU battle-
cruiser
GULLIVER G yacht
– Francis
HAMPSHIRE cruiser
ITALY MARU freighter
JERVIS BAY converted
liner
LUSITANIA liner
MAYFLOWER sailing
ship – Pilgrim Fathers
MERRIMACK frigate
NEW JERSEY battleship
NORMANDIE liner
QUEEN MARY liner
RAMILLIES battleship
SHEFFIELD destroyer
STOCKHOLM liner
TÉMÉRAIRE warship
TERRA NOVA converted
whaler – Scott
TRUCULENT submarine

10

AMOCO CADIZ tanker
BIRKENHEAD
troopship
BIRMINGHAM cruiser
BLACK MAGIC yacht
BUCENTAURE
battleship
CUMBERLAND various
RN vessels

DEVONSHIRE cruiser
ENTERPRISE aircraft
  carrier
FORMIDABLE tall ship
GOLDEN HIND
  galleon – Drake
INVINCIBLE aircraft
  carrier
LADY NELSON
  exploration vessel
LISBON MARU
  troopship
LIVELY LADY yacht
  – Rose
MANCHESTER
  destroyer
MAURETANIA liner
PRINZ EUGEN cruiser
REDOUTABLE warship
  – Villeneuve
RESOLUTION sloop
  – Cook
SANTA MARIA carrack
  – Columbus
SIR GALAHAD landing
  ship
VINDICTIVE aircraft
  carrier

11
ANDREA DORIA liner
AUSTRALIA II yacht
BELLEROPHON
  warship
DORSETSHIRE cruiser
DREADNOUGHT
  battleship
EXXON VALDEZ tanker

FLYING CLOUD
  clipper
FORFARSHIRE paddle
  steamer
GIPSY MOTH IV
  yacht – Chichester
ILLUSTRIOUS aircraft
  carrier
MARY CELESTE
  brigantine
QUEEN MARY II liner
ROYAL GEORGE
  warship
SCHARNHORST
  battleship
SIR TRISTRAM
  landing ship
SOUTHAMPTON
  various RN vessels
THERMOPYLAE
  clipper

12
ACHILLE LAURO liner
ARANDORA STAR
  liner
BRITISH STEEL yacht
  – Blyth
CONSTITUTION
  frigate
GRAF ZEPPELIN
  aircraft carrier
GREAT BRITAIN
  steamship
GREAT EASTERN
  steamship
GREAT WESTERN
  steamship

INVESTIGATOR
  converted collier
  – Flinders
MARIE CELESTE – see
  Mary Celeste
MORNING CLOUD
  yacht – Heath
SEAWISE GIANT tanker
TORREY CANYON
  tanker
UNITED STATES liner

13
ADMIRAL SCHEER
  battleship
CHRISTOS BITAS
  tanker
GENERAL SLOCUM
  steamship
KOWLOON BRIDGE
  tanker
LADY GHISLAINE
  yacht – Maxwell
MISS ENGLAND II
  speedboat – Don,
  Segrave
PRINCE OF WALES
  transport ship
PRINCESS ALICE
  steamship
WHITE CRUSADER
  yacht

14
GREAT BRITAIN II
  yacht – Blyth
QUEEN ELIZABETH
  liner

RAINBOW WARRIOR converted trawler
  – Greenpeace
VITTORIO VENETO cruiser

15
ADMIRAL GRAF SPEE battleship
BONHOMME RICHARD frigate
CHARLOTTE DUNDAS paddle steamer
EXPRESS CRUSADER yacht – James
GENERAL BELGRANO cruiser

ROBERTSON'S GOLLY yacht
  – Francis
STARS AND STRIPES yacht
WILHELM GUSTLOFF liner

16
EDMUND FITZGERALD cargo ship
FREEDOM OF THE SEAS liner
QUEEN ELIZABETH II liner

Transport – Water – WATER TRANSPORT

3	PUNT	SCOUT	DINGHY	WHERRY	GONDOLA
ARK	RAFT	SCULL	DOGGER		GUNBOAT
CAT	SCOW	SHELL	DUGOUT	**7**	ICEBOAT
COG	SHIP	SKIFF	GALLEY	BIRLINN	JETFOIL
GIG	YAWL	SLOOP	HOOKER	BUMBOAT	LIGHTER
HOY		SMACK	HOPPER	CARAVEL	MONITOR
SUB	**5**	TRAMP	LAUNCH	CARRACK	PEARLER
TUB	BARGE	U-BOAT	LUGGER	CARRIER	PINNACE
TUG	BUTTY	UMIAK	MALIBU	CATBOAT	PIROGUE
	CANOE	WRECK	PACKET	CLIPPER	PONTOON
4	COBLE	XEBEC	PEDALO	COASTER	ROWBOAT
BOAT	CRAFT	YACHT	PUFFER	COLLIER	SCOOTER
BRIG	E-BOAT		RIGGER	CORACLE	SCULLER
DHOW	EIGHT	**6**	SAILER	CRUISER	SEA BOAT
DORY	FERRY	ARGOSY	SAMPAN	CURRACH	SHALLOP
FOUR	FLEET	ARMADA	SLAVER	DREDGER	STEAMER
HULK	JOLLY	BARQUE	TANKER	DRIFTER	TRAWLER
JUNK	KAYAK	BATEAU	TARTAN	DROMOND	TRIREME
KEEL	KETCH	BAWLEY	TENDER	FELUCCA	TUGBOAT
PINK	LAKER	BIREME	TRADER	FRIGATE	VEDETTE
PRAM	LINER	CAIQUE	VESSEL	GALLEON	WARSHIP
PROA	OILER	CUTTER	WHALER	GALLIOT	

8
BOMB SHIP
BUDGEROW
CAR FERRY
COCKBOAT
CORVETTE
FIRESHIP
FLAG BOAT
FLAGSHIP
FLOTILLA
GALLIASS
ICE YACHT
INDIAMAN
IRONCLAD
KEELBOAT
LIFEBOAT
LONGBOAT
LONGSHIP
MAIL BOAT
MAN-OF-WAR
MONOHULL
SAILBOAT
SCHOONER
SHOWBOAT
TALL SHIP
TRIMARAN

9
AMPHIBIAN
BLOCKSHIP
BUTTY BOAT
CANAL BOAT
CARGO SHIP
CATAMARAN
DESTROYER
FERRY BOAT
FREIGHTER
HERRINGER

HOUSEBOAT
HYDROFOIL
JOLLY BOAT
LAPSTRAKE
LIGHTSHIP
MINELAYER
MOTOR BOAT
MULTIHULL
OIL TANKER
OUTRIGGER
POWERBOAT
PRIVATEER
RIVERBOAT
SAILBOARD
SLAVE SHIP
SPEEDBOAT
STEAMBOAT
STEAMSHIP
SUBMARINE
SURFBOARD
TROOPSHIP
VAPORETTO
WATER TAXI
WHALEBOAT

10
BANANA BOAT
BATTLESHIP
BRIGANTINE
DAHABEEYAH
DIVING BELL
HOVERCRAFT
HYDROPLANE
ICE-BREAKER
KNOCKABOUT
MOTHER SHIP
MOTOR YACHT
NARROWBOAT

OCEAN LINER
PACKET BOAT
PADDLE BOAT
PATROL BOAT
PIRATE SHIP
QUADRIREME
ROWING BOAT
SCHOOL SHIP
SLOOP-OF-WAR
SUPPLY SHIP
SURVEY SHIP
TEA CLIPPER
TRAIN FERRY
WATERCRAFT
WINDJAMMER

11
BARQUENTINE
BATHYSCAPHE
BATHYSPHERE
BULK CARRIER
CAPITAL SHIP
CARLEY FLOAT
COCKLESHELL
DREADNOUGHT
DUGOUT CANOE
FACTORY SHIP
FISHING BOAT
LIBERTY BOAT
MALIBU BOARD
MERCHANTMAN
MINESWEEPER
MOTOR LAUNCH
QUINQUEREME
SAILING BOAT
SAILING SHIP
STEAM PACKET
SUBMERSIBLE

SUPERTANKER
TORPEDO BOAT
WEATHER SHIP

12
CABIN CRUISER
EAST INDIAMAN
HEAVY CRUISER
HOSPITAL SHIP
LANDING CRAFT
LONGTAIL BOAT
MERCHANT SHIP
PLEASURE BOAT
POLICE LAUNCH
RUBBER DINGHY
SQUARE-RIGGER
STERN-WHEELER
SUPERCARRIER
TRAINING SHIP
TRAMP STEAMER

13
BATTLE-CRUISER
CENTREBOARDER
CONTAINER SHIP
FLOATING LIGHT
PADDLE STEAMER
PASSENGER SHIP
SHIP OF THE LINE

15
AIRCRAFT CARRIER

16
NUCLEAR SUBMARINE

Index

The *Puzzler* Crossword Companion